KU-397-244

CENTRAL LIBRARY

24 HOUR RENEWALS HOTLINE
TEL: 01902 552500

Please return/renew this item by the last date shown
Thank you for using your library

Wolverhampton Libraries

LS 1636a 6.11

X400 000018 5593

ENCYCLOPEDIA OF

VOLUME 3

CHRISTIAN THEOLOGY

ENCYCLOPEDIA OF

VOLUME 3

CHRISTIAN THEOLOGY

JEAN-YVES LACOSTE

EDITOR

P-Z

ROUTLEDGE

New York • London

Published in 2005 by
Routledge
270 Madison Avenue
New York, NY 10016

Published in Great Britain by
Routledge
2 Park Square
Milton Park, Abingdon
Oxon, OX14 4RN

Originally published as *Dictionnaire critique de théologie (Nouvelle Edition),* edited by Jean-Yves Lacoste (Paris: Presses Universitaires de France, 1999), ISBN 2–13–048825–0
©Presses Universitaires de France, 1998 and 1999

Published with the participation of the *Ministère français chargé de la Culture–Centre National du Livre* (French Ministry of Culture–National Book Center)

All rights reserved. No part of this book may be reprinted or reproduced or utilized in any form or by any electronic, mechanical, or other means, now known or hereafter invented, including photocopying and recording, or in any information storage or retrieval system, without permission in writing from the publisher.

10 9 8 7 6 5 4 3 2 1

Library of Congress Cataloging-in-Publication Data

Dictionnaire critique de théologie. English.
  Encyclopedia of Christian theology / Jean-Yves Lacoste, editor.
    p. cm.
  Includes bibliographical references and index.
    ISBN 1–57958–250–8 (set: alk. paper)—ISBN 1–57958–236–2 (v. 1: alk. paper)—ISBN 1–57958–239–7 (v. 2: alk. paper)—ISBN 1–57958–332–6 (v. 3: alk. paper) 1. Theology—Encyclopedias. I. Lacoste, Jean-Yves. II. Title.
BR95.D5313 2004
230'.03—dc22
2004004150

Printed in the United States of America on acid-free paper.

WOLVERHAMPTON LIBRARIES	
H J	249268
230.03 ENC	£245.00
CR	1 b i ᴌᴅ 2005 ✓

Contents

Foreword

A reader about to venture into a thick reference work (especially one dealing with theology) has the right to ask for additional mercy from its editor: that is, that the editor specifies the aim and use of the work. A few glosses about the title will answer this request. First and foremost, this is an encyclopedia of theology, meaning, in a restrictive sense that is also a precise sense, the massive amount of discourse and doctrines that Christianity has assembled about God and its experience of God. There are other discourses on God, and theology was often the first to champion their rationality. By selecting one term to refer to one practice (historically circumscribed) of the logos and one call (historically circumscribed) in the name of God, we do not pretend to deny the existence or the rationality of other practices or calls—we are only offering to make use of *theological* to name the fruits of a kind of covenant between the Greek logos and the Christian restructuring of the Jewish experience. When the philosopher discusses God, it rarely appears that his interest is theological, in the fixed sense of the term. Because Judaism was able to tie in the richest things it had to say without pillaging the theoretical legacy of classical antiquity, it is also unlikely that *theological* needs to be applied to its doctrines. Likewise, because the Islamic Kalam itself follows some rather original structuration rules, it is inadequate to baptize it "Islamic theology," unless one accepts a certain vagueness. As for the rigorous comparative study of all the discourses in which the signifier *God* (whether its intervention be that of name, concept, or other) appears, it is still in its infancy.

Second, this is an encyclopedia, by which we mean an academic tool serving knowledge. It is one thing to produce knowledge and another to transmit it. Thus, we will not expect from this collegiate effort, which the present foreword concludes, that it was a work of creation. In the organized disorder presided over by the alphabetical order of the entries, its ambition was modest: to provide readers with a starting point for the main theological objects. Events, doctrines, contributors, theories and metatheories, over five hundred objects are to be found within the pages of this encyclopedia. The reader who wants to browse through the pages following a question will always find stand-alone entries and the point about the question. The reader who prefers long explorations can rely on the navigational tools provided to learn, one entry after another, for example, about Biblical theology in general or about medieval theology or about Lutheran theology or more. For want of a consensus among scholars, which cannot be found anywhere, this work is expected to keep the promises inherent to its scientific genre: legibility, intellectual honesty, and historical precision.

Last, this intends to be a critical work, which doesn't bound its fate to some deconstructing temerity but rather emphasizes the native condition of any academic endeavor at the service of truth. The first task of critical reasoning is to criticize itself. Although it was critical of the objects it inherited from tradition, the reason of the Enlightenment was less critical of itself, its powers, duties, and agents. One demand remains, which we owe and of which we should not be afraid: we will expect from the "critical" history of the doctrines or from the "critical" presentation of the theological traditions that they wanted to identify their own objects so that they appear as they are, in all their diachronic or synchronic complexity, sometimes in all indecision. Theology concerns itself mostly with phenomena that never demand intellection without also demanding adhesion, and the historical work of discernment that the encyclopedia undertook will not deprive anybody of the necessity to forge a personal opinion. One never believes, however, without knowing slightly. If one wants to forge a straight opinion, then it is best to know critically rather than precritically.

The editor has one pleasant remaining task: that of giving thanks. Firstly, he wishes to thank the 250 contributors, from about one hundred institutions and representing about fifteen nationalities. They made this encyclopedia and accepted the many constraints imposed by such an exercise. All graciously complied with the editorial goal of global cohesiveness, and their good will allowed the work to be more than a collection of stand-alone entries. All used their own voice, however, and this allows the work to let its authors speak with the accents peculiar to their cultural and scientific traditions.

Secondly, the editor wishes to thank all colleagues and friends who, flying to the rescue at the last minute, helped fill gaps, update bibliographies, refine translations, and verify thousands of references. I thus burn the incense of my gratitude to Daniel Bourgeois, Rémi Brague, Michel Cagin, Olivier de Champris, Michel Corbin, Michel Gitton, Jérôme de Gramont, Yves-Jean Harder, Max Huot de Longchamp, Goulven Madec, Thaddée Matura, Cyrille Michon, Bruno Neveu, Jacqueline de Proyart, and Daniel de Reynal. The members of the editorial board know how dear their collaboration was to me as well as the pleasure I had working with them. It is fair that the reader should know about them, too. My thanks turn superlative for Marie-Béatrice Mesnet, who bore the final responsibility of the French manuscript, from disks to proofs, including the organization of the bibliographies, cross-references, and abbreviations: I fear to think what we would have published without her help. As for Jacqueline Champris, she allowed for this work to be published while its editor was alive, or that its editor would not die in the process: each reader will judge its merit.

Our first French edition owed its index to Georges Leblanc, and we kindly remember Edith Migo providing us with secretarial help early on. The logistical support from Franços de Vorges and Didier Le Riche greatly eased the work of the editorial board. Françoise Muckensturm and Renza Arrighi also provided their biblical knowledge. The published work bore the mark of their labors.

Some members of the editorial board and the like spent more time than others in compiling the second French edition: my hat off thus to Paul Beauchamp, Olivier Boulnois, Vincent Carraud, Irène Fernandez, Marie-Béatrice Mesnet, Oliver O'Donovan, and Françoise Vinel as well as to the knowledgeable and devoted editor of the encyclopedia. As with the first, the second edition also had many benefactors who wrote entries in a few days, suggested useful amendments, and published encouraging notices. I cannot name them all, but I do want to name Cyrille Michon, Hervé Barreau, Rémi Brague, Claude Bressolette, Yves Delorme, Henri de L'Éprevier, Bernard de Guibert, Dominique Le Tourneau, Roger Pouivet, Émile Poulat, Michel Sales, Yves Tourenne, and Claude Villemot. The first French edition was honored by the Académie des Sciences Morales et Politiques, which awarded it the Chanoine Delpeuch Prize. As for Tabatha, finally, she knows what we owe her: a lot.

Jean-Yves Lacoste

Introduction

The *Dictionnaire critique de théologie* was first published in French in 1998. When in 1999 work began on an anglophone presentation, the U.S. publishers had at their disposal the French additions and modifications to the original text undertaken with a view to its second edition. The present work is a translation of the second edition of the French original.

Users of the *Encyclopedia of Christian Theology,* whether chiefly interested in consulting it for specific information or in browsing more widely, may well wish to begin with the index. The French editorial committee and the editorial director have achieved the not inconsiderable feat of containing very nearly all the material falling within the ambit of a critical work of theology, as those terms are defined in the foreword, within some five hundred entries.

Theology remains the rationally structured discussion of the Christianized experience of Hebrew monotheism, as it was originally elaborated with the help of Greek philosophical categories and considerations familiar to the early Christian Greek-speaking world and subsequently developed during two millennia of Christian thought.

This has meant paying little more than passing attention to other important aspects of Christian life as it developed. Its liturgies, its widely diverging spiritualities, its administrative hierarchy, and its noncore teaching even about important moral and social issues occurring in response to the often political constraints that arose in the course of history are not central to its theology as here understood. Attention is concentrated on such matters as Trinitarian theology, Christology, the Incarnation, the Redemption, revelation, ecclesiology, and the understanding of the workings of the divine plan for humanity. The definition also excludes formal consideration of eastern religions and even of Islam, immensely powerful in its own right and also the vehicle for carrying the thought of Aristotle, heavily contaminated by Neoplatonism, to the Christian scholastic theologians of the High Middle Ages.

Philosophy itself, as an intellectual discipline, does not fall within the ambit of the reference function of the *Encyclopedia,* but its exclusion poses more difficult problems. As the editor of the French original, Jean-Yves Lacoste, points out in his own entry on philosophy, it is still possible in the twentieth century with Barth or Heidegger to conduct philosophical discussion without reference to any theological position. In fact, however, the possibility of the autonomous conduct of philosophical investigation, although it is not discussed in the *Encyclopedia,* looks today increasingly fragile.

Christian theology as a discipline, particularly on account of the Greco-Roman legacy still woven into it, is much more difficult to insulate from its philosophical substructure. In many of its entries, the *Encyclopedia,* having expounded the theology with which they are concerned, concludes them with philosophical considerations. Philosophically speaking, Christian theology has for centuries relied on a *philosophia perennis,* drawing its categories and premises largely from Aristotelian and Platonist traditions.

Certain aspects of that traditional substructure, notably its anthropology, its epistemology, and its ontology, are no longer generally considered useful and at least in non-English-speaking Europe have been replaced by a newer tradition. In the *Encyclopedia,* no attempt has been made to diminish the reliance on philosophical reflections developed from the mainstream European, mostly German-language tradition as it has emerged from Kant and the German idealists and subsequently been developed by Hegel, Husserl, and Heidegger, and from more recent variations of an essentially phenomenological approach to the subject such as appear also in the work of some modern theologians like Karl Rahner.

The content of the work, as indicated in the foreword, is laid out alphabetically, and anglophone readers will have no difficulty finding the keyword for many of the most important themes, events, people, and topics discussed. There is an elaborate system of cross-referencing, but, as the relative length of the entries and the bibliographies makes clear, a format of relatively long entries and essays, still within the scope of what is known as a *dictionnaire* in French, has been chosen rather than that of a high number of short entries generally denoted by the word *dictionary* in English.

Some of the new entries, like that for Moses, fill lacunae in the original text, and very few important topics will be found to have been altogether neglected, although to locate the several treatments of such themes as transsubstantiation or of theologians as important as Melanchthon, it is necessary to refer first to the index. It is even possible that certain readers will feel that occasionally, like the original eighteenth-century French *Encyclopédie,* this *Encyclopedia* advances views or developments that it purports merely to transmit or that it gives an acceptably ecumenical doctrinal spin to the historical record by omitting to dwell on or even to note some of the harsher reactions perceivable in the decrees of the council of Trent or of Vatican I or in the decisions of the Pontifical Biblical Commission. Theologians of the last fifty years are not unreasonably accorded a prominence that implies a value judgment about their work, which is inevitably less certain to endure than judgments made about theologians from centuries earlier than the twentieth whose historical contribution to the development of today's theology cannot be challenged.

It will not be difficult for users to identify the corporate viewpoint of the editorial committee of the *Encyclopedia.* It is, however, as the third paragraph of the foreword makes clear, important to preserve the work's intellectual integrity. That means identifying and acknowledging what its point of view is, especially on account of the probability that here and there the more speculative essays may seem to be urging Catholic theology to develop in a particular direction and the further probability that any such direction will be one with which the original French readership may feel more at ease than theologians brought up in some of the traditions at present current in different degrees in the various anglophone regions of the globe.

The university level that determines the amount and type of information contained in the *Encyclopedia* requires its content to be not only historically accurate, deep enough for university-level reflection, and well enough written to be readily intelligible but also useful in a university context, that is, one in which reasonably ample library resources are available. Users wishing to follow up references to patristic works, the scholastics, or modern books and articles will often require the bibliographic resources normally found only in theological colleges or in large, general academic institutions.

Because the *Encyclopedia* is intended also to serve outside a formal university context as an initial guide to the state of theological discussion on all major topics covered by its definition of theology, the references to reviews, editions, and relatively small-circulation journals are included simply for the convenience of those who wish to pursue further research. Further investigation into most of the topics covered is likely to require access to good editions of the Fathers of the Church and, where there are any, of the scholastics, as well as to more recent theologians from the nineteenth and twentieth centuries. The entries are written with a view to being easily intelligible even where there is no immediate access to the cited sources.

Some topics, like the Dead Sea Scrolls, have primarily been discussed only in languages other than English and chiefly in specialist journals. In such instances, the *Encyclopedia* attempts primarily to do service as a handbook or guide to the present state of discussion, giving only pointers in its references to places or sources where the discussion has been further developed or on which advocates of different views have relied. In all cases, and in spite of its inevitable point of view, the *Encyclopedia* attempts an objective exposition of the facts and arguments, without bias, prejudice, or any viewpoint that could be interpreted as sectarian.

The *Encyclopedia* does not aspire to be historical in that it does not undertake to cover the history of the theology of the topics that it includes except incidentally, in order to explain and contextualize them, and except insofar as the sources for contemporary theological views are necessarily grounded in the historic sources of the Christian revelation. The method adopted is, however, critical. At every point it goes out of its way to confront doctrines and views with the sources and traditions on which they rely, and it is relentless in its pursuit of theological truth as warranted by the sources and the historical facts. This criticism is not destructive of anything but falsehood, although when applied as rigorously as it is here to the legitimacy of some of the emphases of medieval theology, it produces results that are likely to surprise many brought up on a precritical tradition. The critical account of the tradition reveals, for instance, that the notion of an individual judgment at the moment of death appeared only relatively late in eastern theology and shows that the virginity of Mary has a less strong scriptural basis than is often assumed.

Without a doubt, the critical expertise of the theologians on whom the editorial committee has drawn for the entries is where this work's serious theological interest primarily lies. Whatever services may be rendered by the utility of its reference function, the most significant achievement of the entries in the work consists overwhelmingly in the critical acumen applied by its authors to their subject matter, invariably through a rigorous treatment of the sources and tradition underlying the historical and contemporary theological discussion of all theology's major issues. To this critical treatment of the tradition is often appended a more speculative section, as in the entry on being, pointing to tasks remaining to be accomplished and to directions in which theological discussion appears to be moving.

The critical method used is essentially based on a balanced appraisal of the theological sources that time, tradition, and individual religious spiritualities, such as those developed within the great religious orders or outside them by popular devotion, have inevitably tended to obscure. By confronting patterns of Christian religious belief and behavior with the sources of the Christian revelation and with the major developments in theological tradition, the *Encyclopedia* no doubt implicitly calls for a reevaluation of some views and attitudes that may at different periods have been too uncritically, and perhaps wrongly, assumed to have been dictated by fundamental theological dogma. The critical function of the *Encyclopedia* lies not in criticizing them but in confronting them with a more authentic understanding of the Christian revelation, leaving it to individuals to mold the moral and religious commitments that best both fulfil their own spiritual needs and accord with the revelation. Insofar as the *Encyclopedia* fulfils the task it has taken on itself, it must promote a pluralism of religious attitudes, both moral and devotional, capable of fulfilling the individual hunger for spiritual nourishment on the basis of a critical understanding of genuine theological truth.

It is difficult to think of any earlier attempt to produce a comprehensive critical theological handbook in the sense in which the *Encyclopedia* defines theology. There are no doubt historical reasons why this should be so, and the appearance of the *Encyclopedia* marks an important stage in the diminution of sectarian slants on theological discussion as well as a hope that a point has been reached when all those whose experience is enhanced by a spirituality situated within the Judeo-Christian religious tradition can look forward to agreeing on the theology that lies at its center. The *Encyclopedia,* in giving, however succinctly, a fully critical account of that tradition, is a product of progress already made as well as a pointer to what questions still urgently await their resolution and an indicator of the most promising paths to be followed. It summarizes the present state of theological discussion without dwelling on what has recently been achieved or laying down firm paths for the future. It may well constitute a milestone in the progress toward a truly critical theology and therefore also toward promoting a religious awareness and providing the basis for an intelligently reflective religious commitment without laying down new orthodoxies. Its task is to present the critical summary of Judeo-Christian theology necessary to further the personal and corporate attitudes of those who seek to live by the norms it promotes.

Anthony Levi

Alphabetical List of Entries

Abbreviations

A. Usual Abbreviations

a.	articulus
ACFEB	Association catholique française pour l'étude de la Bible
adv.	adversus
anath.	anathema
anon.	anonymous
Apos. Const.	Apostolic Constitution
ap.	*apud* (according to)
ARCIC	Anglican-Roman Catholic International Commission
arg.	argumentum
art.	article
BHK	Biblia Hebraica, ed. Kittel
BHS	Biblia Hebraica Stuttgartensia
bibl.	includes a bibliography
c.	circa
CADIR	Centre pour l'analyse du discours religieux, Lyon
can.	canon
CEPOA	Centre d'étude du Proche-Orient ancien, Louvain
ch(ap).	chapter
COE	Conseil œcuménique des Églises (see WWC)
col.	column
coll.	collection
comm.	*Commentum,* commentary
concl.	conclusio
d.	distinctio
Decr.	Decretal
diss.	dissertatio
dub.	dubium
ed.	edidit, editio
ed.	editor
ep.	epistula(e), letters
f	next verse (biblical citations)
ff	two following verses (biblical citations)
FS	Festschrift
GA	Gesamtausgabe
gr.	Greek
GS	Gesammelte Schriften
GW	Gesammelte Werke
hb, hebr.	Hebrew
hom.	homily
l.	*liber*
lat.	latin
lect.	*lectio*
MA	Middle Ages
ms.	manuscript
mss	manuscripts
n.	note/*numerus*
NT	New Testament
O.P.	Order of Preachers (Dominicans)
O.S.B.	Order of Saint Benedict (Benedictines)
OC	Œuvres complètes; Complete Works
Op.	*Opera* (Works)
OT	Old Testament
par.	parallel passages (in synoptic gospels)
Ps.-	Pseudo-
q.	quaestio
qla	quaestiuncula
quod.	quodlibet
quod sic	videtur quod sic
resp.	responsio, solutio
sess.	session
SIDC	Société internationale de droit canonique
S.J.	*Societatis Jesu* (Jesuits)
Sq	*sequen(te)s,* and following
SW	Sämtliche Werke
syr.	syriac
tract.	tractatus
v.	verse
Vulg.	Vulgate, Latin version latine of the Bible, by Jerome
vv.	verses
WWC	World Council of Churches
WW	Werke
Ia Iiae	Thomas Aquina, Summa Theologiae,

	prima secundae, first part of the second part
IIa Iiae	*Ibid., secunda secundae,* second part of the second part
LXX	Septuagint, Greek version of the Hebrew Bible

B. Biblical Texts

The Hebrew and Greek transcription of biblical texts come from the *Concordance de la Traduction œcuménique de la Bible.*

Biblical References

Colon(:) between chapter and verse. For example, Dt 24:17 refers to Deuteronomy, chapter 24:verse 17.

Hyphen: indicates the verses. For example, Dt 24:17–22 (from v. 17 to 22).

The letter *f* next to a verse refers to this verse and the following one. For example, Dt 24:17f (chapter 24:verses 17 and 18).

The letters *ff* refers to the verse and the following two. For example, Dt 24:17ff (chapter 24:verses 17, 18, and 19).

Acts	Acts of the Apostles		Jl	Joel
Am	Amos		Jn	John
Bar	Baruch		Jon	Jonah
1 Chr	1 Chronicles		Jos	Joshua
2 Chr	2 Chronicles		1 Jn	1 John
Col	Colossians		2 Jn	2 John
1 Cor	1 Corinthians		3 Jn	3 John
2 Cor	2 Corinthians		Jude	Jude
Dn	Daniel		1 Kgs	1 Kings
Dt	Deuteronomy		2 Kgs	2 Kings
Eccl	Ecclesiastes		Lam	Lamentations
Eph	Ephesians		Lk	Luke
Est	Esther		Lv	Leviticus
Ex	Exodus		1 Macc	1 Maccabees
Ez	Ezekiel		2 Macc	2 Maccabees
Ezr	Ezra		Mal	Malachi
Gal	Galatians		Mi	Micah
Gn	Genesis		Mk	Mark
Hb	Habakkuk		Mt	Matthew
Heb	Hebrews		Na	Nahum
Hg	Haggai		Neh	Nehemiah
Hos	Hosea		Nm	Numbers
Is	Isaiah		Ob	Obadiah
Jas	James		Phil	Philippians
Jb	Job		Phlm	Philemon
Jdt	Judith		Prv	Proverbs
Jer	Jeremiah		Ps	Psalms
Jgs	Judges		1 Pt	1 Peter
			2 Pt	2 Peter
			Rev	Revelation
			Rom	Romans
			Ru	Ruth
			Sg	Song of Songs
			Sir	Sirach
			1 Sm	1 Samuel
			2 Sm	2 Samuel
			Tb	Tobit
			1 Thes	1 Thessalonians
			2 Thes	2 Thessalonians
			Ti	Titus
			1 Tm	1 Timothy
			2 Tm	2 Timothy
			Wis	Wisdom
			Zep	Zepaniah

C. Writings from Ancient Judaism

a) Qumran Writings

11QT	The Temple Scroll
1QH	Hodayot, Hymns
1Qisa	Great Isaiah Scroll (Is 1–66)
1Qisb	Qumran Scroll of Isaiah
1QM	Serekh ha-Milhamah, The War Rule

1QpHab	Pesher on Habakkuk (Commentary)
1QS	Serek ha-Yachad, the Rule of the Community
1Qsa	The Rule of the Congregation
4QapMess	Messianic Apocrypha (= 4Q521)
4QDeutero-Ez	Deutero-Ezekiel (= 4Q385)
4Qenastr	Astronomical fragment from the Book of Enoch
4Qflor	Pesharim, 4Qflorilegium (= 4Q174)
4QMMT	Miqsat ma'ase ha-torah (= 4Q394–399)
4Qps-Danc	Pseudo-Daniel, ms c (= 4Q245)
4QtestQah	Testament of Qahat
4QtgJob	Targum de Job
4QviscAmrf	Visions of Amram
CD	Ciaro Damascus Document

(The numeral preceding the letter "Q" indicates the Grotto number)

b) Other Writings

Ant	Antiquitates judaicae (Flavius Josephus)
Ap	Contra Apionem (Id.)
2 Ba	Syriac Apocalypse of Baruch
Bell	De bello judaico (Flavius Josephus)
3 Esd/4 Esd	3rd/4th book of Esdras
Hen	Henoch
Lib Ant	*Biblical Antiquities* (Pseudo-Philo)
Or Sib	*Sibylline Oracles*
Ps Sal	*Psalm of Solomon*
T	Targum
TB	Talmud of Babylon
TJ	Talmud of Jerusalem
Test	Testament
Test XII	*Testaments of the Twelve Patriarchs*
Test Zab	*Testament of Zebulon*
Vita	Vita Josephi (Flavius Josephus)

D. Documents from the Second Vatican Ecumenical Council

AA	*Apostolicam Actuositatem,* decree on the apostolate of the laity, November 18, 1965
AG	*Ad Gentes,* decree on the mission activity of the Church, December 7, 1965
CD	*Christus Dominus,* decree concerning the pastoral office of bishops in the Church, October 28, 1965
DH	*Dignitatis Humanae,* declaration on religious freedom, December 7, 1965
DV	*Dei Verbum,* dogmatic constitution on divine revelation, November 18, 1965
GE	*Gravissimum Educationis,* declaration on Christian education, October 28, 1965

GS	*Gaudium et Spes*, pastoral constitution on the Church in the modern world, December 7, 1965
IM	*Inter Mirifica,* decree on the media of social communication, December 4, 1963
LG	*Lumen Gentium,* dogmatic constitution on the Church, November 21, 1964
NA	*Nostra Aetate,* declaration on the relation of the Church to non-Christian religions, October 28, 1965
OE	*Orientalium Ecclesiarum,* decree on the Catholic Churches of the Eastern rite, November 21, 1964
OT	*Optatam Totius,* decree on priestly training, October 28, 1965
PC	*Perfectae Caritatis,* decree on the adaptation and renewal of religious life, October 28, 1965
PO	*Presbyterorum Ordinis,* decree on the ministry and life of priests, December 7, 1965
SC	*Sacrosanctum Concilium,* constitution on the sacred liturgy, December 4, 1963
UR	*Unitatis Redintegratio,* decree on ecumenism, November 21, 1964

E. Editions, Collections, and Classic Works

The journal and collections abbreviations are from *Abkürzungsverzeichnis* from the *TRE* (rev. ed. 1994).

AA	Kant, Akademie Ausgabe
AAS	Acta apostolicae sedis, *Vatican City, 1909 (ASS, 1865–1908)*
AAWLM	Abhandlungen der Akademie der Wissenschaften und der Literatur in Mainz, Mainz
AAWLM.G	—Geistes- und Sozialwissenschaftliche Klasse, 1950–
ABAW	Abhandlungen der (k.) bayerischen Akademie der Wissenschaften, Munich
ABAW. PH	—Philosophisch-historische Abteilung, NS, 1929–
ABAW. PPH	—Philosophisch-philologische und historische Klasse, 1909–1928
ABC	Archivum bibliographicum carmelitanum, Rome, 1956–1982
ABG	*Archiv für Begriffsgeschichte,* Bonn, 1955–
ACan	*L'Année canonique,* Paris, 1952–
ACar	Analecta Cartusiana, Berlin, etc., 1970–1988; NS, 1989–
ACHS	American Church History Series, New York, 1893–1897
Aci	*Analecta Cisterciensa,* Rome, 1965–

ACO	*Acta conciliorum œcumenicorum,* Berlin, 1914–
Adv. Haer.	Irenaeus, *Adversus Haereses* (Against Heresies)
AF	*Archivio di filosofia,* Rome, 1931–
AFH	*Archivum Fransciscanum historicum,* Florence, 1908–
AFP	*Archivum Fratrum Praedicatorum,* Rome, 1930–
AGJU	Arbeiten zur Geschichte des antiken Judentums und des Urchristentums, Leiden, 8, 1970–15, 1978
AGPh	*Archiv für Geschichte der Philosophie und Soziologie,* Berlin, 1888–
AHC	*Annuarium historiae conciliorum,* Amsterdam, etc., 1969–
AHDL	*Archives d'histoire doctrinale et littéraire du Moyen Age,* Paris, 1926/1927–
AHP	*Archivum historiae pontificiae,* Rome, 1963–
AISP	*Archivio italiano per la storia della pietà,* Rome, 1951–
AkuG	*Archiv für Kulturgeschichte,* Berlin, 1903–
ALKGMA	Archiv für Literatur- und Kirchengeschichte des Mittelalters, Berlin, etc., 1885–1900
Aloi.	Aloisiana, Naples, 1960–
ALW	*Archiv für Liturgiewissenschaft,* Ratisbonne, 1950–
AmA	*American Anthropologist,* Menasha, Wis., 1888–1898; NS, 1899–
AnBib	Analecta biblica, Rome, 1952–
AncBD	*Anchor Bible Dictionary,* New York: Doubleday, 1992
AnCl	*Antiquité classique,* Bruxelles, 1932–
Ang.	Angelicum, Rome, 1925–
AnGr	Analecta Gregoriana, Rome, 1930–
ANRW	*Aufstieg und Niedergang des römischen Welt,* Berlin, 1972–
Anton.	Antonianum, Rome, 1926–
AphC	*Annales de philosophie chrétienne,* Paris, 1830–1913
Apol.	Luther, *Apologia confessionis Augustanae* (Apology of the Augsburg Confession)
Aquinas	*Aquinas. Revista internazionale de filosofia,* Rome, 1958–
ARMo	*L'actualité religieuse dans le monde,* Paris, 1983–
ArPh	*Archives de philosophie,* Paris, 1923–
AsbTJ	*The Asbury Theological Journal,* Wilmore, Ky, 1986–
ASCOV	*Acta synodalia sacrosancti Concilii Œcumenici Vaticani II,* Vatican City, 1970–1983
ASEs	*Annali di storia dell'esegesi,* Bologna, 1984–
ASI	*Archivio storico italiano,* Florence, 1852–
ASOC	*Analecta Sacri Ordinis Cisterciensis,* Rome, 1945–1964 (= *ACi,* 1965–)
ASS	*Acta sanctae sedis,* Rome, 1865–1908
ASSR	*Archives de sciences sociales des religions,* Paris, 1973–
A-T	Descartes, *Œuvres* (Works), eds. C. Adam and P. Tannery
ATA	Alttestamentliche Abhandlungen, Munich, 1908–1940
Ath	*L'année théologique,* Paris, 1940–1951
AthA	*Année théologique augustinienne,* Paris, 1951–1954 (= *REAug,* 1955–)
AThANT	Abhandlungen zur Theologie des Alten und Neuen Testaments, Zurich, 1944–
Aug.	*Augustinianum,* Rome, 1961–
Aug(L)	*Augustiniana,* Louvain, 1951–
AUGL	*Augustinus-Lexicon,* edited by C. Mayer, Basel, etc., 1986–
AugM	*Augustinus Magister,* Année théologique. Supplement, 3 vols., Paris: Études augustiniennes, 1954–1955
BAug	Bibliothèque augustinienne, Paris, 1936–
BBB	Bonner biblische Beiträge, Bonn, 1950–
BBKL	Biographish-bibliographisches Kirchenlexicon, edited by F. W. Bautz, Hamm, 1970–
BCG	Buchreihe der Cusanus-Gesellschaft, Münster, 1964–
BCNH	Bibliothèque copte de Nag Hammadi, Quebec.
BCPE	*Bulletin du Centre protestant d'études,* Geneva, 1949–
BEAT	Beiträge zur Erforschung des Alten Testaments und des antiken Judentums, Frankfurt, 1984–
BEL.S	Bibliotheca (Ephemerides Liturgicae), Subsidia, Rome 1975–
BEM	COE, Foi et Constitution, *Baptême, eucharistie, ministère. Convergence de la foi* (Lima, January 1982), Paris, 1982

BEThL	Bibliotheca ephemeridum theologicarum Lovaniensium, Louvain, 1947–
BevTh	Beiträge zur evangelischen Theologie, Munich, 1940–
BGLRK	Beiträge zur Geschichte und Lehre der reformierten Kirche, Neukirchen, 1937–
BGPhMA	Beiträge zur Geschichte der Philosophie (1928) und Theologie des Mittelalters, Münster, 1891–
BHK	Biblia Hebraica, ed. R. Kittel. Stuttgart, 1905/1906; 16th ed., 1973
BHS	Biblia Hebraica Stuttgartensia, Stuttgart, 1969–1975; 2nd ed., 1984
BHSA	*Bulletin historique et scientifique de l'Auvergne.* Clermont-Ferrand, 1881–
BHTh	Beiträge zur historischen Theologie, Tübingen, 1929–
Bib	*Biblica.* Commentarii periodici ad rem biblicam scientifice investigandam, Rome, 1920–
BICP	*Bulletin de l'Institut catholique de Paris,* Paris, 2nd ser., 1910–
Bidi	Bibliotheca dissidentium, Baden-Baden, 1980–
BIHBR	*Bulletin de l'Institut historique belge de Rome,* Rome, etc., 1919–
Bijdr	*Bijdragen.* Tijdschrift voor philosophie en theologie, Nimègue, etc., 1953–
BIRHT	*Bulletin de l'Institut de recherche et d'histoire des textes,* Paris, 1964–1968 (= RHT, 1971–)
BJ	*La Bible de Jérusalem* (Jerusalem Bible)
BJRL	*Bulletin of the John Rylands Library,* Manchester, 1903–
BLE	*Bulletin de littérature ecclésiastique,* Toulouse, 1899–
BN	Catalogue général des livres imprimés de la bibliothèque nationale, Paris, 1897 (General catalog of printed works from the Bibliothèque Nationale in Paris)
BN	*Biblische Notizen. Beiträge zur exegetischen Diskussion,* Bamberg, 1976–
BPhM	*Bulletin de philosophie médiévale,* Louvain, 1964–
Br	Pascal, Blaise. *Pensées.* Brunschvig.
BS	*Bibliotheca sacra,* London, 1843 (= *BSTR,* Andower, Mass.; 1844–1851 = *BSABR*; 1851–1863 = BS, Dallas, etc. 1864–)

BSFP	*Bulletin de la Société française de philosophie,* Paris, 1901–
BSGR	*Bibliothek der Symbole und Glaubensregeln der Alten Kirche,* edited by A. and C. L. Hahn, Breslau, 1842; reprinted 1962, Hildesheim
BSHPF	*Bulletin de la Société d'histoire du protestantisme français.* Paris, 1852–
BSKORK	*Bekenntnisschriften und Kirchenordnungen der nach Gottes Wort reformierten Kirche,* edited by W. Niesel, Zollikon, etc., 1937–1938; 2nd ed., 1938 (etc.) (*CCFR,* Geneva, 1986)
BSLK	*Bekenntnisschriften der evangelisch-lutherischen Kirche,* Göttingen, 1930; 10th ed., 1986; 11th ed., 1992 (FEL, Paris-Geneva, 1991)
BSS	*Bulletin de Saint-Sulpice.* Revue internationale de la Compagnie des prêtres de Saint-Sulpice, Paris, 1975–
BSSV	*Bollettino della Società di studi Valdesi,* Torre Pellice, 1934–
BSt	Biblische Studien. Neukirchen, 1951–
BT.B	Bibliothèque de théologie. 3rd ser. Théologie biblique, Paris, 1954–
BTB	*Biblical Theology Bulletin,* New York, 1971–
BTB(F)	—French ed.
BThom	*Bulletin thomiste,* Étiolles, etc., 1924–1965
BThW	*Bibeltheologisches Wörterbuch,* Graz, etc., 1–2, 19673 (Eng. Ed. *EBT*)
BTT	Bible de tous les temps, Paris, 8 vol., 1984–1989
BullFr	*Bullarium Franciscanum,* Rome, etc., 1929–1949
BWANT	Beiträge zum Wissenschaft vom Alten und Neuen Testament, Stuttgart, 1926 (= BWAT, 1908–1926)
BWAT	*Beiträge zum Wissenschaft vom Alten Testament,* Stuttgart, 1908–1926
Byz	*Byzantion,* Bruxelles, 1924–
BZ	*Biblische Zeitschrift,* Paderborn, etc., 1903–1938; NF 1957–
BZAW	Beihefte zur Zeitschrift für die alttestamentliche Wissenschaft, Berlin, 1896–
BZNW	Beihefte zur Zeitschrift für die neutestamentliche Wisssenschaft, Berlin, etc., 1923–
BZRGG	Beihefte der Zeitschrift für Religions- und Geistesgeschichte, Leyden, 1953–
CA	*Confession of Augsburg*

CAG	Commentaria in Aristotelem Graeca, Berlin, 1883	*ChPR*	*Chroniques de Port-Royal,* Paris, 1950–
CAR	Cahiers de l'actualité religieuse, Tournai, 1954–1969 [Continued after 1969 as *Cahiers pour croire aujourd'hui*]	*CIC*	*Codex iuris canonici,* Rome, 1917 and Rome, 1983
CAT	Commentaire de l'Ancien Testament, Neuchatel, 1963	*CIC(B).C*	*Corpus iuris civilis,* ed. P. Krueger, T. Mommsen, Berlin, -2. *Codex Iustianus,* 1874–1877; 2nd ed., 1880, etc.
Cath (M)	*Catholica. Jahrbuch für Kontroverstheologie,* Munster, etc. 1932–39, 1952/53–	*CIC(L)*	*Corpus iuris canonici,* ed. E. Friedberg, Leipzig, 1837–1839; Graz, 1955 (reprint)
Cath	*Catholicisme. Hier, aujourd'hui, demain,* Paris, 1948–	CILL	Cahiers de l'Institut de linguistique de Louvain, Louvain, 1972–
CBFV	Cahiers bibliques de *Foi et Vie,* Paris, 1936–	*Cîteaux*	*Cîteaux: commentarii cistercienses,* Westmalle, 1959–
CBiPA	Cahiers de Biblia Patristica, Strasbourg, 1987–	Citeaux, SD	—*Studia et documenta,* 1971–
CBQ	*Catholic Biblical Quarterly,* Washington, DC, 1939–	*COD*	*Conciliorum oecumenicorum Decreta,* eds. Albergio and Jedin, Bologna, 3rd ed., 1973 (*DCO,* 1994)
CCEO	*Codex Canonum ecclesiarum orientalium.* Rome, 1990	*Com(F)*	*Communio. Revue catholique internationale,* Paris, 1975/76–
CCFR	Confessions et catéchismes de la foi reformée, ed., Oliver Fatio, Geneva, 1986 (*BSKORK,* Zollikon)	*Com(US)*	*Communio. International Catholic Review,* Spokane, Wash., 1974–
CCG	Codices Chrysostomi Graeci, Paris, 1968–	*Con*	*Contemporain,* Paris, 1866–
CCChr	Corpus Christianorum, Turnhout	*Conc(D)*	*Concilium. Internazionale Zeitschrift für Theologie,* Einsiedeln, 1965–
CChr.CM	—Continuatio mediaevalis, 1966	*Conc(F)*	*Concilium. Revue internationale de théologie,* Paris, 1965–
CChr.SA	—Series Apocryphorum, 1983–		
CChr.SG	—Series Graeca, 1977	*Conc(US)*	*Concilium. Theology in the Age of Renewal,* New York, 1965–
CChr.SL	—Series Latina, 1953		
CCist	*Collecteana Cisterciensia,* Westmalle, Forges, etc. 1934–	*ConscLib*	*Conscience et Liberté,* Paris, 1971–
CCMéd	*Cahiers de civilisation médiévale. X^e–XIIe siecles,* Poitiers, 1958–	*Corp IC*	see *CIL (L)*
		CPG	Clavis Patrum Graecorum, Turnhout, 1974– (= CChr.SG)
CDTor	*Collationes Diocesis Tornacensis,* Tournai, 1853–	*CPIUI*	*Communio. Pontificium Institutum Utriusque Juris,* Rome, 1957–
CEC	*Catéchisme de l'Eglise catholique (Catechism of the Catholic Church),* Paris, 1992 (Typical Latin text, Vatican City, 1992; rev. ed., 1997.	CPPJ	Cahiers de philosophie politique et juridique, Caen, 1982–
		CR	Corpus reformatorum, Berlin, 1834–
CEv	Cahiers évangile, Paris, 1972–	CRB	Cahiers de la *Revue Biblique,* Paris, etc., 1964–
CFan	Cahiers de Fangeaux, Fanjeaux, etc., 1966–	*CrSt*	*Cristianesimo nella storia,* Bologna, 1980–
CFi	Cogitatio fidei, Paris, 1961		
CFr	Collecteana franciscana, Rome, etc.,1931–	CR.Th.Ph	*Cahiers de la Revue de théologie et de philosophie,* Geneva, 1977–
CG	*Summa Contra Gentiles*	CSCO	Corpus scriptorum Christianorum orientalum, Rome, etc., 1903–
CGG	*Christlicher Glaube in moderner Gesellschaft,* Fribourg, 1981–1984	CSEL	Corpus scriptorum ecclesiasticorum Latinorum, Vienna, 1866–
CHFMA	Classiques de l'histoire de France au Moyen Age, Paris, 1923–	*CT*	*Concilium Tridentinum. Diarium, actorum, epistularum, tractatum nova collectio,* Fribourg, 1901–1981
ChGimG	see *CGG*		
ChH	*Church History,* Chicago: American Society of Church History, 1932–	CTh	Cahiers théologiques, Neuchâtel, etc., 27, 1949– (= CthAP, 1923–1949)
		CTh.HS	—*Hors série,* 1945– (Special edition)

CTJ	*Calvin Theological Journal,* Grand Rapids, Mich, 1966–
CUFr	Collection des Universités de France (Les Belle Lettres), Paris, 1920–
DA	*Deutsches Archiv für Erforschung des Mittelalters,* Marburg, etc., 1937–
DACL	*Dictionnaire d' archéologie chrétienne et de liturgie,* Paris, 1924–53
DAFC	*Dictionnaire apologétique de la foi catholique,* Paris, 1889; 4th ed., 1909–1931
DB	*Dictionnaire de la Bible,* Paris, 1895–1928
DBS	*Dictionnaire de la Bible. Supplément,* Paris, 1928–
DBW	*Dietrich Bonhoeffer, Werke,* ed. E. Bethge *et al.,* Munich, 1986–
DC	*Documentation Catholique,* Paris: 1919–
DCO	*Conciliorum oecumenicorum Decreta; Les Conciles Oecuméniques,* II, 1 and 2. *Les Décrets.* ed. Albergio, Paris, 1994 (trans. of *COD*)
DCTh	*Dictionnaire critique de théologie.* ed. Jean-Yves Lacoste, Paris, 1998; 2nd revised ed., 1999
DDC	*Dictionnaire de droit canonique,* Paris, 1924–1965
DEB	*Dictionnaire encyclopédique de la Bible,* Turnhout, 2 vols., 1956–1987
DECA	*Dictionnaire encyclopédique du christianisme ancien.* ed. A. di Bernardino, Paris, 2 vols., 1990. (Trans. of *DPAC*)
DEPhM	*Dictionnaire d' éthique et de philosophie morale,* edited by M. Canto Sperber, Paris, 1996
DH	*Enchiridion Symbolorum.* Eds. H. Denzinger and P. Hunerman, Fribourg, 37th ed., 1991
DHGE	*Dictionnaire d' histoire et de géographie ecclésiastiques.* Paris, 1912–
DHOP	Dissertationes historicae. Institutum historicum FF. Praedicatorum, Rome, etc., 1931–
DJD	*Discoveries in the Judean Desert,* Oxford, 1955–
DK	*Die Fragmente der Vorsokratiker,* eds. H. Diels and W. Kranz, Berlin, 1903; 13th ed., 1972 (= *FVS*)
DMA	*Dictionary of the Middle Ages,* ed. R. Strayer, New York, 1982–
DoC	*Doctor Communis,* Rome, 1948–
Doc.-épisc.	*Documents-épiscopat,* Bulletin du secrétariat de la Conférence des évêques de France, Paris, 1965–
DOP	*Dumbarton Oaks Papers,* Cambridge, Mass., 1941–
DOPol	*Dictionnaire des oeuvres politiques,* Paris, 1986
DPAC	*Dizionario patristico e di antichità cristiane,* edited by A. di Berardino, Casale Monferrato, 1–3, 1983–1988 (French trans. *DECA*)
DPhP	*Dictionnaire de philosophie politique,* eds. Ph. Raynaud and St. Rials, Paris, 1997
DR	*Downside Review,* Bath, 1880–
DS	*Enchiridion Symbolorum,* eds. H. Denzinger and A. Schönmetzer, Freiburg, 36th ed., 1976
DSp	*Dictionnaire de spiritualité ascétique et mystique,* Paris, 1932–1995
DT	*Divus Thomas. Jahrbuch für Philosophie und spekulative Theologie,* Fribourg, 1914–1953
DT(P)	*Divus Thomas. Commentarium de philosophia et theologia,* Plaisance, 1880–
DTF	*Dizionario di Teologia Fondamentale,* eds. R. Latourelle et R. Fisichella, Assisi, 1990. (*Dictionnaire de Théologie Fondamentale,* Paris, 1992)
DThC	*Dictionnaire de Théologie Catholique,* Paris, 1–15, 1903–1950 + tables 1–3, 1951–1972
Dumeige	*La Foi Catholique,* G. Dumeige, Paris, 1975
DViv	*Dieu Vivant,* Paris, 1945–1955
EAug	Études augustiniennes, Paris, 1954– (Studies on Augustine)
EBT	*Encyclopedia of Biblical Theology,* London, 1970, etc. (Eng. ed. of *BThW*)
ECQ	*Eastern Churches Quarterly,* Ramsgate, 1936–1964 (= *OiC,* 1965–)
ECR	*Eastern Churches Review,* Oxford, 1966–1978
EdF	Erträge der Forschung, Darmstadt, 1970–
EE	Estudios ecclesiásticos, Madrid, 1922–
EeT	*Église et théologie,* Paris, 1958–1962 (= *BFLTP,* 1934–1958)
EETS	Early English Text Society, London, 1864–
EFV	*Enchiridion fontium valdensium,* Torre Pelice, 1958

EI(F)	*Encyclopedia of Islam,* French ed, Leyden. 1913–1936; new ed. 1954–
EJ	*Encyclopaedia Judaica,* Jerusalem 1–16, 1971; 17, 1982–
EKK	Evangelisch-katholischer Kommentar zum Neuen Testament, Neukirchen, 1975–
EKL	*Evangelisches Kirchenlexikon,* Göttingen, 1956–1961; 2nd ed., 1961–1962; 3rd ed., 1986–1997
EN	*Ethica nicomachea* Aristotle
En. Ps.	*Enarrationes in Psalmos,* Augustine
EnchB	*Enchiridion Biblicum,* Rome, 1927; 4th ed., 1961
EnchP	*Enchiridion patristicum,* M.J. Rouët de Journel, Fribourg, 1911; 25th ed., 1981
EncProt	*Encyclopédie du Protestantisme,* edited by P. Gisel, Paris-Geneva, 1995
EncRel(E)	*The Encyclopedia of Religion,* edited by M. Eliade, New York, 1–16, 1987
EncRel(I)	*Enciclopedia delle religioni,* edited by M. Gozzini, Florence, 1970–1976
Enn.	*Enneads,* Plotinus
EO	*Ecclesia orans.* Periodica de scientiis liturgicis, Rome, 1984–
EOr	*Échos d' Orient,* Bucharest, 1897/1898–1942/1943 (= *EtByz,* 1943–1946; *REByz,* 1946–)
Eos	Eos. Commentarii societatis philologae Polonorum, Wroclaw, etc., 1894–
Eph	*Études philosophiques,* Paris, 1927–
EPRO	Études préliminaires aux religions orientales dans l'Empire romain, Leyden, 1961–
ER	*Ecumenical Review,* Lausanne, 1948–
ErIs	*Eretz Israel,* Jerusalem, 1951–
EstB	*Estudios biblicos,* Madrid, 1929–
EStL	*Evangelisches Staatslexikon,* Stuttgart, 3rd ed., 1987
EstLul	*Estudios lulianos,* Palma de Mallorca, 1957–
EtB	Études bibliques, Paris, 1903–
EtCarm	*Études carmélitaines,* Paris, 1911–1964
Eth. à Nic.	*Ethica nicomachea,* Aristotle (Éthique à Nicomaque; Nichomachean Ethics)
Éthique	*Éthique. La vie en question,* Paris, 1991–1996 (22 issues)
EthL	*Ephemerides theologicae Lovanienses,* Louvain, etc., 1924–
EtMar	*Études mariales,* Paris, 1947–
ETR	*Études théologiques et religieuses,* Montpellier, 1926–
EU	*Encyclopaedia Universalis,* Paris, 1968–1986, 1985–1988
EvTh	*Evangelische Theologie,* Munich, 1934–1938; NS, 1946/1947–
EWNT	*Exegetisches Wörterbuch zum Neuen Testament,* Stuttgart, etc., 1–3, 1980–1983
FEL	La foi des Églises luthériennes: confessions et catéchismes, eds. A. Birmele and M. Lienhard, Paris-Geneva, 1991 (*BSLK* Göttingen)
FOP	Faith and Order Paper(s), World Council of Churches, Geneva, NS, 1949–
FKTh	*Forum katholische Theologie,* Aschaffenburg, 1985–
FRLANT	Forschungen zur Religion und Literatur des Alten und Neuen Testaments, Göttingen, 1903–
FrSA	*Fransciscan Studies Annual,* St. Bonaventure, NY, 1963– (= *FrS,* 1924–1962)
FS	Franziskanische Studien, Münster, etc., 1914–
FS.B	—Beiheft, 1915–
FSÖTh	Forschungen zur systematischen und ökumenischen Theologie, Göttingen, 1962–
FThSt	Freiburger theologische Studien, Fribourg, 1910–
FTS	Frankfurter theologische Studien, Frankfurt, 1969–
FV	*Foi et Vie,* Paris, 1898–
FVS	*Die Fragmente der Vorsokratiker,* eds. H. Diels and W. Kranz, Berlin, 1903; 13th ed., 1972 (= *DK*)
FZPhTh	*Freiburger Zeitschrift für Philosophie und Theologie,* Freiburg (Switzerland), 1954–
GCFI	*Giornale critico della filosofia italiana,* Florence, etc., 1920–
GCS	Die griechischen christlichen Schriftsteller der ersten drei Jahrhunderte, Berlin, 1897–
GNO	*Gregorii Nysseni Opera,* ed. Werner Jaeger, Berlin then Leiden (= Jaeger), 1921
GOTR	*Greek Orthodox Theological Review,* Brookline (Mass.), 1954–
Gr	*Gregorianum,* Rome, 1920–
GRBS	Greek, Roman and Byzantine Studies, Cambridge, Mass., 1958–

Grundfr. syst. Th.	*Grundfragen systematischer Theologie,* W. Pannenberg, Göttingen, 1967, vol 2, 1980
GS	Germanische Studien, Berlin, etc., 1919–
GuV	*Glauben und Verstehen, Gesammelte Aufsätze,* R. Bultmann, 4 vol., Tübingen, 1933–1965
GVEDL	Die geltenden Verfassungsgesetze der evangelisch-deutschen Landeskirchen, edited by Emil Friedberg, Fribourg, 1885 and suppl. 1–4, 1888–1904
IIadSt	*Haddock Studies,* Moulinsart, 1953–
Hahn	see *BSGR*
HBT	*Horizons in Biblical Theology,* Pittsburg, Pa, 1979–
HCO	*Histoire des conciles œcuméniques,* ed. G. Dumeige, Paris, 1962–
HDG	*Handbuch der Dogmengeschichte,* edited by M. Schmaus, A. Grillmeier, *et al.,* Fribourg, etc., 1951–
HDThG	*Handbuch der Dogmen- und Theologiegeschichte,* edited by C. Andresen, Göttingen, 1982–1984
HE	*Historia ecclesiastica.* Eusebius
Hermes	*Hermes. Zeitschrift für klassische Philologie,* Wiesbaden, 1866–1944, 1952–
HeyJ	*Heythrop Journal,* Oxford then London, 1960–
HFTh	*Handbuch der Fundamentaltheologie,* edited by W. Kern *et al.,* 4 vol., Fribourg, 1985–1988
Hier. eccl.	*Hiérarchie ecclésiastique (Ecclesiastica hierarchia)*
HistDog	*Histoire des dogmes,* Paris, 1953–1971 (unfinished trans. by *HDG*)
HJ	*Historisches Jahrbuch der Görresgesellschaft,* Munich, etc., 1880–
HKG(J)	*Handbuch der Kirchengeschichte,* edited by H. Jedin, Fribourg, etc., 1962–1979
HMO	*Handbook of Metaphysics and Ontology,* eds. H. Burkhardt and B. Smith, Munich-Philadelphia-Vienna, 1991
HST	*Handbuch systematischer Theologie,* Gütersloh, 1979–
HThK	Herders theologisches Kommentar zum Neuen Testament, Fribourg, 1953–
HThR	*Harvard Theological Review,* Cambridge, Mass., 1908–
HThS	Harvard Theological Studies, Cambridge, Mass., 1916–
HTTL	*Herders theologisches Taschenlexikon,* edited by K. Rahner, 8 vol., Fribourg, 1972–1973
HUCA	*Hebrew Union College Annual,* Cincinnati, Ohio, 1924–
HWP	*Historisches Wörterbuch der Philosophie,* Basel-Stuttgart, 1971–
HZ	*Historische Zeitschrift,* Munich, etc., 1859–
IDB	*The Interpreter's Dictionary of the Bible,* New York, 1/4, 1962 +suppl., 1976
IkaZ	*Internationale katholische Zeitschrift Communio,* Frankfurt, 1972–
IKZ	*Internationale kirchliche Zeitschrift. Revue Internationale ecclésiastique. International Church Review,* Berne, 1911–
In Sent.	*Commentary on the Sentences*
Inst.	*Institutes of the Christian Religion,* Calvin
Irén	Irénikon, Chèvetogne, etc., 1926–
Ist	*Istina,* Boulogne-sur-Seine, etc., 1954–
JAAR	*Journal of the American Academy of Religion,* Boston, Mass., etc., 1967–
JAC	*Jahrbuch für Antike und Christentum,* Münster, 1958–
JAC.E	*—Ergänzungsband,* 1964–
Jaeger	*Gregorii Nysseni Opera,* ed. W. Jaeger, Berlin then Leyden (= *GNO*), 1921–
JBL	*Journal of Biblical Literature,* Philadelphia, Pa., 1890–
JCSW	*Jahrbuch für christliche Sozialwissenschaften,* Münster, 1968–
JEH	*Journal of Ecclesiastical History,* London, etc., 1950–
JES	*Journal of Ecumenical Studies,* Philadelphia, etc., 1964–
JHI	*Journal of the History of Ideas,* New York, etc., 1940–
JJS	*Journal of Jewish Studies,* London, 1948–
JLW	*Jahrbuch für Liturgiewissenschaft,* Münster, 1921–1941
JÖBG	*Jahrbuch der österreichischen byzantinischen Gesellschaft,* Vienna, etc., 1951–1968 (= *JÖB,* 1969–)
JRE	*Journal of Religious Ethics,* Waterloo, Ont., etc., 1973–
JSNTSS	*Journal for the Study of the New Testament,* Supplement series, Sheffield, 1980–

JSOT	*Journal for the Study of the Old Testament,* Sheffield, 1976–
JSOT.S	—Supplements Series, 1976–
JSPE.*S*	Journal for the Study of the Pseudepigrapha. Supplement series, Sheffield, 1987–
JThS	*Journal of Theological Studies,* Oxford, etc., 1899–1949; NS, 1950–
KD	*Die Kirchliche dogmatik,* K. Barth, Zollikon-Zurich, vol. I to IV, 1932–1967 + Index, 1970 (*Dogmatique,* 26 vol., Geneva, 1953–1974, + Index, 1980)
KiKonf	Kirche und Konfession, Göttingen, 1962–
Kirch	*Enchiridion fontium historiae ecclesiasticae,* ed. C. Kirch, Freibourg, 1910; 6th ed., 1947
KKD	*Kleine Katholische Dogmatik,* edited by J. Auer and J. Ratzinger, Ratisbonne, 1978–1988
KJ	*Kirchliches Jahrbuch für die Evangelische Kirche in Deutschland,* Gütersloh, 1900– (= *ThJb,* 1873–1899)
KL	*Kirchenlexicon oder Encyklopädie der katholischen Theologie und ihrer Hilfswissenschaften,* edited by H. J. Wetzer and B. Welte, Fribourg, 1847–1860; 2nd ed., 1882–1903
Kotter	*Die Schriften des Johannes von Damaskus,* ed. B. Kotter, Berlin, 1969–
KrV	*Kritik der reinenVErnunft,* Kant
KSA	*Kritische Studienausgabe,* Nietzsche; edited by Colli and Montinari, ed. minor
KuD	*Kerygma und Dogma,* Göttingen, 1955–
Lat	Lateranum, Rome, NS, 1935–
LCL	Loeb Classical Library, London, 1912–
LeDiv	Lectio divina, Paris, 1946–
Leit	*Leiturgia. Handbuch des evangelischen Gottesdienstes,* Kassel, 1952–1970
Liddell-Scott	*A Greek-English Lexicon,* Liddell-Scott-Jones, Oxford
LJ	*Liturgisches Jahrbuch,* Münster, 1951–
LNPh	*Les notions philosophiques,* edited by S. Auroux, vol. II of the *Encyclopédie philosophique universelle,* edited by A. Jacob, Paris, 2 vol., 1990
LO	Lex orandi, Paris, 1944–
LouvSt	*Louvain Studies,* Louvain, 1966/1967–
LR	*Lutherische Rundschau,* Stuttgart, etc., 1951–1977
LSEO	Libri symbolici Ecclesiae orientalis, ed. E. J. Kimmel, Iéna, 1843; 2nd ed., 1850
LThK	*Lexikon für Theologie und Kirche,* Fribourg-Basel-Vienna, 1930–1938; 2nd ed., 1957–1967; 3rd ed., 1993
LTP	*Laval théologique et philosophique,* Quebec, 1944/1945–
LuJ	*Luther-Jahrbuch,* Leipzig, etc., 1919–
LV(L)	*Lumière et vie,* Lyon, 1951–
LWF.R	*Lutheran World Federation Report,* 1978–
Mansi	*Sacrorum conciliorum nova et amplissima collectio,* edited by J. D. Mansi, Florence, 1759–1827; Paris-Leipzig, 1901–1927
Mar.	*Marianum. Ephemerides Mariologiae,* Rome, 1939–
Maria	*Maria. Études sur la Sainte Vierge,* edited by H. du Manoir, 8 vol., Paris, 1949–1971
MCS	Monumenta christiana selecta, Tournai, etc., 1954–
MD	*La Maison-Dieu. Revue de pastorale liturgique,* Paris, 1945–
MDom	*Memorie Domenicane,* Florence, etc., NS, 1970–
MethH	*Methodist History,* Lake Junaluska, NC, 1962–
MF	*Miscellanea francescana,* Rome, etc., 1936– (= *MFS,* 1886–1935)
MFEO	Monumenta fidei Ecclesiae orientalis, ed. H. J. C. Weissenborn, Iéna, 1850
MFCG	Mitteilungen und Forschungsbeiträge der Cusanus-Gesellschaft, Mainz, 1961–
MGH	Monumenta Germaniae historica inde ab a. C. 500 usque ad a. 1500, Hanover, etc.
MGH.Conc	—Concilia, 1893–
MGH.Ep	—Epistolae, 1887–
MGH.L	—Leges, 1835–1889
MHP	*Miscellanea historiae pontificae,* Rome, 1939–
MHSJ	Monumenta historica Societatis Jesu, Rome, etc., 1894–
MiHiEc	*Miscellanea historiae ecclesiasticae,* Congrès…de Louvain, 1960–
ML.T	Museum Lessianum. Theological section, Bruxelles, 1922–

MM	Miscellanea mediaevalia, Berlin, etc., 1962–		1957; 2nd ed., 1974 (F. L. Cross and E. A. Livingstone); 3rd ed. rev. and augm., 1997 (by E. A. Livingstone)
MS	*Mediaeval Studies,* Toronto, 1939–	*OED*	*The Oxford English Dictionary*
MSR	*Mélanges de science religieuse,* Lille, 1944–	*OGE*	*Ons geestelijk erf,* Anvers, etc., 1927–
MSSNTS	Monograph Series. Society for New Testament Studies, Cambridge, 1965–	*OiC*	*One in Christ,* London, 1965–
MThZ	*Münchener theologische Zeitschrift,* Munich, etc., 1950–1984	*OR*	*L'Osservatore romano,* Vatican City, 1849–
MySal	*Mysterium Salutis,* Grundriß heils-geschichtlicher Dogmatik, vol. I to V, edited by J. Feiner and M. Löhrer, Einsiedeln, etc., 1965–1976 + supplements, 1981, etc. (*Dogmatique de l'histoire du salut,* vol. I–III/2 and IV/1 (p. 457–599), 14 vol., 1969–1975)	*ÖR*	*Ökumenische Rundschau,* Stuttgart, 1952–
		Or.	*Orientalia,* Rome, 1920–
		OrChr	*Oriens Christianus,* Rome, 1901–
		OrChrA	see OCA
		OrChrP	see *OCP*
		OS	Ostkirchliche Studien, Würzburg, 1952–
NBL	*Neues Bibel-Lexikon,* Zurich, 1991	*OstKSt*	*Ostkirchliche Studien,* Würzburg, 1952–
NCE	*New Catholic Encyclopaedia,* New York, 1967–1979	ÖTh	Ökumenische Theologie, Zurich, etc., 1978–
NHThG	*Neues Handbuch Theologischer Grundbegriffe,* edited by P. Eicher, 2nd ed. augm., Freibourg-Basel-Vienna, 1991	OTS	Oudtestamentische Studien, Leyden, etc., 1942–
Not	*Notitiae. Commentarii ad nuntia et studia de re liturgica,* Vatican City, 1975–	Par.	Paradosis. Études de littérature et de théologie ancienne, Fribourg (Switzerland), 1947–
NRTh	*Nouvelle revue théologique,* Louvain, 1869–1940; 1945–	*PAS*	*Proceedings of the Aristotelian Society,* London, 1887; NS, 1900/1901–
NSchol	*New Scholasticism,* Washington D.C., 1927–	PatSor	Patristica Sorbonensia, Paris, 1957–
NStB	Neukirchener Studienbücher, Neukirchen, 1962–	PG	Patrologia Graeca, ed. J.-P. Migne, Paris, 1857–1866
NT	*Novum Testamentum,* Leyden, 1956–	*PGL*	*Patristic Greek Lexicon,* ed. G. W. H. Lampe, Oxford, 1961–1968
NTA	Neutestamentliche Abhandlungen, Münster, 1908–	*Ph*	*Philologus. Zeitschrift für das klassische Altertum,* Wiesbaden, etc., 1846–
NTS	*New Testament Studies,* Cambridge, 1954–	*Phil.*	*Philosophy,* London, 1916–
NTTS	New Testament Tools and Studies, Leyden, 1960–	*PhJ*	*Philosophisches Jahrbuch der Görres-Gesellschaft,* Fulda, etc., 1888–
Numen	*Numen. International Review for the History of Religions,* Leyden, 1954–	PiLi	Pietas liturgica. Studia, St. Ottilien, 1983–
NV	*Nova et vetera,* Geneva, 1926–	PL	Patrologia Latina, ed. J.-P. Migne, Paris, 1841–1864
OBO	Orbis biblicus et orientalis, Fribourg (Switzerland), 1973–	PLS	Patrologiae Latinae supplementum, Paris, 1958–1970
OCA	Orientalia christiana analecta, Rome, 1935–	PO	Patrologia Orientalis, Paris, etc., 1907–
OCP	*Orientalia christiana periodica,* Rome, 1935–	*POC*	*Proche-Orient chrétien,* Jerusalem, 1951–
Oec.	*Œcumenica. Jahrbuch für ökumenische Forschung,* Gütersloh, etc., 1966–1971/1972	*PosLuth*	*Positions luthériennes,* Paris, 1953–
		PoTh	Point théologique, Institut catholique de Paris, 1971–
ODCC	*Oxford Dictionary of the Christian Church,* edited by F. L. Cross, London,	*PPR*	*Philosophy and Phenomenological Research,* Buffalo, NY, 1940/1941–
		PRMCL	*Periodica de re morali,* canonica, liturgica, Rome, 1907–

PuN	*Pietismus und Neuzeit*, Göttingen, 1974–
PTS	Patristische Texte und Studien, Berlin, 1964–
QD	Quaestiones Disputatae, Fribourg-Basel-Vienna, 1958–
QFRG	*Quellen und Forschungen zur Reformationsgeschichte*, Gütersloh 1921–, includes *QGT*
QGT	*Quellen zur Geschichte der Taüfer*, Gütersloh 1951–
QRT	*Quaker religious Thought*, New Haven, Conn., 1959–
Qschr	*Quartalschrift*, Milwaukee, Wis., 1947–
QuLi	*Questions liturgiques*, Louvain, 1910–
RAC	*Reallexikon für Antike und Christentum*, Stuttgart, 1950–
RAM	*Revue d'ascétique et de mystique*, Toulouse, 1920–1971
RB	*Revue biblique*, Paris, 1892–1894; NS, 1915–
RBen	*Revue bénédictine de critique, d'histoire et de littérature religieuses*, Maredsous, 1890–
RDC	*Revue de droit canonique*, Strasbourg, 1951–
RDCCIF	Recherches et débats du Centre catholique des intellectuels français, Paris, 1948–1952; NS, 1952–1980
RdQ	*Revue de Qumrân*, Paris, 1958–
RE	*Realencyklopädie für protestantische Theologie und Kirche*, Gotha, 3rd ed., 1896–1913
REAug	*Revue des études augustiniennes*, Paris, 1955– (= *AThA*, 1951–1954)
REByz	*Revue des études byzantines*, Paris, 1946–
RECA	*Real-Encyclopädie der classischen Altertumswissenschaft*, edited by A. Pauly, Stuttgart, 1839–1852
RechAug	*Recherches augustinien*nes, Paris, 1958–
RechBib	Recherches bibliques, Bruges, etc., 1954–
RecL	*Revue ecclésiastique de Liège*, Liège, 1905–1967
REG	*Revue des études grecques*, Paris, 1888–
REL	*Revue des études latines*, Paris, 1923–
RelSt	*Religious Studies*, London, etc., 1965/1966–
RET	*Revista española de teología*, Madrid, 1940–
RevBib	*Revista biblica*, Buenos Aires, 1939–
RevPhil	*Revue de philosophie*, Paris, 1900–1940
RevSR	*Revue des sciences religieuses*, Strasbourg, 1921–
RFNS	*Rivista di filosofia neoscolastica*, Milan, 1909–
RGG	*Die Religion in Geschichte und Gegenwart*, Tübingen, 1909–1913; 2nd ed., 1927–1932; 3rd ed., 1956–1965
RH	*Revue historique*, Paris, 1876–
RHDF	*Revue historique de droit français et étranger*, Paris, 1855–1869; 1922–
RHE	*Revue d'histoire ecclésiastique*, Louvain, 1900–
RHEF	*Revue de l'histoire de l'Église de France*, Paris, 1910–
RHMo	*Revue d'histoire moderne*, Paris, 1926–1940 (= 1899–1914, 1954–, *RHMC*)
RHMC	*Revue d'histoire moderne et contemporaine*, Paris, 1899–1914, 1954– (= 1926–1940, *RHMo*)
RHPhR	*Revue d'histoire et de philosophie religieuses*, Strasbourg, etc., 1921–
RHR	*Revue de l'histoire des religions*, Paris, 1880
RHSp	*Revue d'histoire de la spiritualité*, Paris, 1972–1977
RHT	*Revue d'histoire des textes*, Paris, 1971– (= *BIRHT*)
RICP	*Revue de l'Institut catholique de Paris*, Paris, 1896–1910 (= *BICP*, 1910–)
RIPh	*Revue Internationale de Philosophie*, Bruxelles, 1938–
RITh	*Revue internationale de théologie*, Berne, 1893–1910
RivBib	*Rivista biblica*, Rome, 1953–
RLT	*Rassegna di letteratura tomistica*, Naples, 1966–
RMAL	*Revue du Moyen Age latin*, Paris, etc., 1945–
RMM	*Revue de métaphysique et de morale*, Paris, 1893–
ROC	*Revue de l'Orient chrétien*, Paris, 1896–1936
RPFE	*Revue Philosophique de la France et de l'étranger*, Paris, 1876–
RPL	*Revue philosophique de Louvain*, Louvain, etc., 1946–
RSF	*Rivista di storia della filosofia*, Rome, 1946; NS, 1984–

RSHum	*Revue des sciences humaines,* Lille, NS, 45, 1947–
RSLR	*Rivista di storia e letteratura religiosa,* Florence, 1965–
RSPhTh	*Revue des sciences philosophiques et théologiques,* Paris, 1907–
RSR	*Recherches de science religieuse,* Paris, 1910–
RThAM	*Recherches de théologie ancienne et médiévale,* Louvain, 1929–
RThom	*Revue thomiste,* Bruges, etc., Toulouse, 1893–
RThPh	*Revue de théologie et de philosophie,* Lausanne, 1868–1911; 3rd ser., 1951–
RTL	*Revue théologique de Louvain,* Louvain, 1970–
RTLu	*Revue théologique de Lugano,* Facoltà di teologia di Lugano, 1996–
Sal	*Salesianum,* Turin, 1939
SBAB	Stuttgarter biblische Aufsatzbände, Stuttgart, 1988–
SBi	Sources Bibliques, Paris, 1963–
SBS	Stuttgarter Bibelstudien, Stuttgart, 1965–
SC	Sources Chrétiennes, Paris, 1941–
ScC	*Scuola Cattolica,* Milan, 1873, 6th ser., 1923–
SCA	Studies in Christian Antiquity, Washington, D.C., 1941–
SCE	*Studies in Christian Ethics,* Edinburgh, 1988–
ScEc	*Sciences écclesiastiques: Revue philosophique et théologique,* Bruges, 1948–1967 (= *ScEs,* 1968–)
ScEs	*Science et esprit,* Bruges, 1968–
SCH(L)	Studies in Church History, London, 1964–
Schol.	*Scholastik. Vierteljahresschrift für Theologie und Philosophie.* Fribourg, 1926–1965 (= *ThPh,* 1966–)
Schr.zur Th.	*Schriften zur Theologie,* K. Rahner. Einsiedeln-Zürich-Cologne, 1954–1983
SE	*Sacris erudiri,* Steenbrugge, etc., 1948–
SecCent	*The Second Century.* Abilene, Tex., 1981
SémBib	*Sémiotique et Bible,* Lyon, 1975–
Semeia	*Semeia.* An Experimental Journal for Biblical Criticism. Atlanta, Ga, 1974–
SemSup	Semeia Supplements. Philadelphia, Pa., etc., 1975–
Sent.	*Sententiarum Libri IV,* Peter Lombard
SESJ	Suomen Eksegeettisen Seuran julkaisuja. Helsinki, 1966–
SHCSR	*Spicilegium historicum Congregationis SSmi Redemptoris.* Rome, 1953–
SHCT	Studies in the History of Christian Thought. Leyden, 1966–
SJP	*Salzburger Jahrbuch für Philosophie und Psychologie,* Salzburg, 1957–
SJTh	*Scottish Journal of Theology.* Edinburgh, 1948–
SKG	Schriften der Königsberger Gelehrten Gesellschaft. Halle
SKG.G	—Geisteswissenschaftliche Klasse, 1924–1944
SM (D)	*Sacramentum Mundi. Theologisches Lexikon für die Praxis.* ed. K. Rahner. Fribourg, 1967–1969
SM (E)	*Sacramentum Mundi. An Encyclopedia of Theology.* New York, 1968–1970
SO	Symbolae Osloenses. Oslo, 1923–
Sob	*Sobornost.* London, 1979–
Sommervogel	Bibliothèque de la Compagnie de Jésus, new edition by C. Sommervogel, Bruxelles, 1890–1930; 3rd ed., 1960–1963
SOr	Sources orientales. Paris, 1959–
SPAMP	Studien zur Problemgeschichte der antiken und mittelalterlichen Philosophie, Leyden, 1966–
SpOr	Spiritualité orientale, Bégrolles-en-Mauges, 1966–
SSL	Spicilegium sacrum Lovaniense, Louvain, 1922–
SST	*Studies in Sacred Theology.* Washington, D.C., 1895–1947; 2nd ser. 1947–
ST	*Summa Theologica,* Thomas Aquinas
StA	*Werke in Auswahl (Studien Ausgabe),* P. Melanchthon, edited by R. Stupperich, Gütersloh, 1951–1955
StAns	Studia Anselmiana. Rome, 1933–
StANT	Studien zum Alten und Neuen Testament. Munich, 1960–1975
StCan	*Studia Canonica,* Ottawa, 1967–
StEv	Studia Evangelica, Berlin, 1959–1982 (= TU 73, etc.)
StGen	*Studium Generale,* Berlin, 1947–1971
STGMA	Studien und Texte zur Geistesgeschichte des Mittelalters, Leyden, 1950–
StMed	*Studi medievali,* Turin, etc.; NS, 1960–
StMiss	*Studia missionalia.* Rome, 1943
StMor	*Studia moralia,* Rome, 1963–

STMP	Studia theologiae moralis et pastoralis, Salzburg, 1956–
StPatr	Studia patristica, Berlin, 1957–
StPh	*Studia philosophica,* Basel, 1946–
STPIMS	Studies and texts, Pontifical Institute of Mediaeval Studies, Toronto, 1955–
Strom.	*Stromata,* Clement of Alexandria
StSS	Studia scholastico-scotistica. Rome, 1968–
StT	Studi e testi, Biblioteca Apostolica Vaticana, Vatican City, 1900–
StTom	Studi tomistici, Vatican City, 1974–MMMM
StZ	*Stimmen der Zeit,* Fribourg, 1914–
SVF	*Stoicorum Veterum Fragmenta,* ed. J. von Arnim, Stuttgart. 3 vol. + index, 1903–1924, etc.
SVTQ	*St. Vladimir's Theological Quarterly,* New York, 1969–
Symb. Ath.	Symbol of Athanasius
TAPhS	*Transactions of the American Philosophical Society,* Philadelphia, Pa, 1769–1809; NS, 1818–
TDNT	*Theological Dictionary of the New Testament,* Grand Rapids, Mich., 1964–1977 (trans. of *ThWNT*)
TEH	Theologische Existenz heute, edited by K. Barth *et al.,* Munich, 1933–1941; NS, 1946–
TFil	*Tijdschrift voor filosofie.* Louvain, 1962– (= *TPh,* 1939–1961)
THAT	*Theologisches Handwörterbuch zum Alten Testament,* ed. E. Jenni and C. Westermann, Munich, 1971–1976
Theos. H.	*Theosophical History.* A Quarterly Journal of Research, London, 1985–1989; Fullerton, Calif., 1990–
ThGl	*Theologie und Glaube,* Paderborn, 1909–
ThH	Théologie historique, Paris, 1963–
ThJb	*Theologisches Jahrbuch,* Gütersloh, 1873–1899 (= *KJ,* 1900–)
ThJb(L)	*Theologisches Jahrbuch.* Leipzig, 1957–
ThLZ	*Theologische Literaturzeitung,* Leipzig, 1876–
Thom	*Thomist,* Washington, D.C., 1939–
ThPh	*Theologie und Philosophie,* Fribourg, 1966–
THPQ	*Theologisch-praktische Quartalschrift,* Linz, 1848–
ThQ	*Theologische Quartalschrift,* Tübingen, etc., 1819– (1960–1968 = *TThQ*)
ThR	*Theologische Rundschau.* Tübingen, 1897–1917; NF 1929–
ThSt(B)	Theologische Studien, edited by K. Barth *et al.,* Zurich, 1938–
ThTo	*Theology Today.* Princeton, N.J., etc., 1944/1945–
ThW	*Theologische Wissenschaft,* Stuttgart, etc., 1972–
ThWA	*Theorie Werkausgabe,* Hegel, Frankfurt, 1970, 20 vols.
ThWAT	*Theologisches Wörterbuch zum Alten Testament,* edited by G. J. Botterweck and H. Ringgren, Stuttgart, etc., 1973–
ThWNT	*Theologisches Wörterbuch zum Neuen Testament,* edited by G. Kittel, Stuttgart, 1933–1979
ThZ	*Theologische Zeitschrift,* Basel, 1945–
TKTG	Texte zur Kirchen und Theologiegeschichte, Gütersloh, 1966–
TOB	Traduction oecuménique de la Bible
TPh	*Tijdschrift voor philosophie,* Louvain, 1939–1961 (= *Tfil,* 1962–)
Tr	Traditio. Studies in Ancient and Medieval History, Thought and Religion, New York, etc., 1943–
TRE	*Theologische Realenzyklopädie,* edited by G. Krause and G. Muller, Berlin, 1976–
Trin	*De Trinitate,* Augustine
TS	*Theological Studies,* Woodstock, Md., etc., 1940–
TSTP	Tubinger Studien zur Theologie und Philosophie, Mainz, 1991–
TTh	*Tijdschrift voor theologie,* Nimègue, 1961–
TThQ	*Tübinger theologische Quartalschrift,* Stuttgart, 1960–1968 (= ThQ)
TThZ	*Trierer Theologische Zeitschrift,* Trier, 1947–
TTS	Tübinger theologische Studien, Mainz, 1973–1990
TU	Texte und Untersuchungen zur Geschichte der altchrislichen Literatur, Berlin, 1882–
TuG	Theologie und Gemeinde, Munich, 1958–
UB	Urban-Bücher, Stuttgart, 1953–
UnSa	Unam Sanctam, Paris, 1937–
VC	*Verbum Caro. Revue théologique et ecclésiastique œcuménique,* Taizé, etc., 1947–1969
VerLex	*Deutsche Literatur des Mittelalters. Verfasserlexikon,* Berlin, etc, 1933–1955; 2nd ed., 1978–

VetChr	*Vetera Christianorum*, Bari, 1964–
VieCon	*Vie consacrée*, Bruxellcs, 1966–
VigChr	*Vigiliae Christianae*, Amsterdam, 1947–
VS	*Vie spirituelle*, Paris, 1946–
VT	*Vetus Testamentum*, Leyden, 1951–
VT.S	—Suppl., 1953–
VThB	*Vocabulaire de théologie biblique*, edited by X. Léon-Dufour, Paris, 1962; 2nd ed., 1970
WA	*Werke. Kristiche Gesamtausgabe*, Luther (Weimarer Ausgabe), 1883–
WA.B	*—Briefwechsel*, 1930–
WA.DB	*—Deutsche Bibel*, 1906–
WA.TR	*—Tischreden*, 1912–
WBS	Wiener byzantinistische Studien, Graz, etc., 1964–
WdF	Wege der Forschung, Darmstadt, 1956–
Weischedel	*Werkausgabe*, Kant, edited by W. Weischedel, Frankfurt, 1958–1964
WMANT	Wissenschaftliche Monographien zum Alten und Neuen Testament, Neukirchen, 1960–
WSAMA.T	Walberger Studien der Albertus-Magnus-Akademie, Mainz, Theologische Reihe, 1964–
WUNT	Wissenschaftliche Untersuchungen zum Neuen Testament, Tübingen, 1950–
WuW	*Wort und Wahrheit*, Vienna, etc., 1946–1973

ZAW	*Zeitschrift für die alttestamentliche Wissenschaft und die Kunde des nach-biblischen Judentums*, Berlin, 1881–
ZDP	*Zeitschrift für deutsche Philologie*, Berlin, etc., 1869–
ZDPV	*Zeitschrift des deutschen Palästina-Vereins*, Wiesbaden, 1978–
ZevKR	*Zeitschrift für evangelisches Kirchen-recht*, Tübingen, 1951–
ZKG	*Zeitschrift für Kirchengeschichte*, Stuttgart, 1877–
ZKTh	*Zeitschrift für katholische Theologie*, Vienna, etc., 1877–
ZNW	*Zeitschrift für die neutestamentliche Wissenschaft und die Kunde der äl-teren Kirche*, Berlin, etc., 1900–
ZSRG.K	*Zeitschrift der Savigny-Stiftung für Rechtsgeschichte. Kanonistische Abteilung*, Weimar, 1911–
ZPE	*Zeitschrift für Papyrologie und Epigraphik*, Bonn, 1967–
ZThK	Zeitschrift für Theologie und Kirche, Tübingen, 1891–

Frankfurt = Frankfurt am Main
Fribourg = Fribourg-en-Brisgau
Fribourg-Paris = Fribourg (Switzerland)—Paris
A hyphenated date (1963–) means that the publishing is not complete or that the collection or journal is still ongoing.

P

Paganism

A. Biblical Theology

The adjective "pagan" comes from the Latin *paganus,* which means "country-dweller," often with a negative connotation. Its meaning as "non-Christian," idolater, appeared in the third century in the context of a Christianity that was primarily urban. Previously, in biblical history*, other oppositions had been presented: Israel* confronts foreign "nations" or *gôyim*. The Greek Bible translates this Hebrew word with the plural *ethnè*. The New Testament adds (five times) the adjective *ethnikos* (belonging to the nations), and the Latin versions translate these two terms respectively by *gentes* (the Gentiles) and *gentilis.*

a) Old Testament. Choice*, consecration to the holy God (Lv 19:2), implies a radical separation from all ritual and moral impurity. The *gôyim* are impure (Lv 20:26); they are deprived of circumcision, the sign of the covenant* (Gn 17:11). The prophets (prophet* and prophecy) of the exile excluded these "uncircumcised" from the Holy Land and from the temple* to come (Is 52:1; Ez 44:4). The concern with purity* affects everyday relations. Although dietary rules (Lv 11) do not forbid sharing a table with *gôyim*, they make it complicated (e. g., Jdt 10:5, 12:1–4, 17ff.). The Israelites forbid lending at interest among themselves, but they practice it with pagans (Dt 23:21); they even give pagans meat of dubious cleanness (Dt 14:21). Marriages are made with *gôyim* (*see* R. de Vaux, *Institutions de l'Ancien Testament,* 1957). But Deuteronomy 7:1–4 prohibits these marriages, which lead the Israelites to

"to serve other gods." Thus, Israel fears the seduction of idolatry* and relies on war* to destroy the cults that threaten the Yahwist faith* (Dt 7:5f.).

Attitudes vary according to situation. Priestly circles favor the assimilation of foreigners, particularly through circumcision (Ex 12:44), when Israel finds itself too much of a minority in its own land (Grelot *VT* 6, 1956). On the other hand, in the late fifth century, Nehemiah and Ezra were concerned about the dilution of Jewish identity in the midst of non-Jews, and demanded "separation" from foreign women (Ezr 10; Neh 13; *see* Dion 1975).

Political history influenced the judgment* of the chosen people* on their Canaanite neighbors and on the traditional oppressors (Assyria, Babylon, Egypt). While Canaan symbolizes the idolatry that is to be destroyed, the name of Sodom sums up pagan immorality (Is 1:9) and the name of Babel (Babylon) evokes the arrogance of the rivals of YHWH (Is 47; Ps 137). In this context the prophets composed "oracles against the nations." According to them, God would carry out his eschatological vengeance*, in just compensation, by subjecting to Israel the *gôyim* who had enslaved it (Is 45:14–17, 60:1ff.). But he would also restore his honor, which had been tarnished by the sins* of Israel (Ez 36:23f.). As early as the seventh century Amos included Judah/Israel among the peoples subject to judgment (Am 1:3–2:16). In fact, God evaluates the conduct of all nations according to the same rules of morality (e.g., the relations between Tyre and Edom,

Am 1:9f.), and chosenness is not a privilege without obligation (Am 9:7).

The complaints of the small nation against the powerful *gôyim* can be understood in the light of history. But other elements in the Old Testament point in different directions. For example, the *gôyim* are not circumcised, but Israel confesses itself uncircumcised in its heart, unfaithful to the Lord (Dt 10:16; Jer 9:24). The Canaanites are delivered by God to the conquering army of Israel; but, because of her faith, Rahab the Canaanite is accepted among the chosen people (Jos 2:1–21, 6:22–25). The burden of old conflicts prohibits the acceptance of Moabites and Ammonites (Dt 23:4–9), but Ruth the Moabite becomes the ancestor of David (Ru 4:13ff.); *see also* the case of Achior the Ammonite in Judith 5:5–6A:21; 13:5–10 (Dion 1975). The genealogy of Jesus* includes Rahab and Ruth (Mt 1:5). This remission of punishment, which sees in certain *gôyim* an exemplary faith and discovers within Israel the impiety for which other nations are reproached, fosters the universalism* of the Old Testament.

b) From the Old Testament to the New Testament. By foretelling an unavoidable cosmic judgment (*see* Dn 7), the apocalyptic prophets hardened the antagonism toward pagans; but they also altered its borders, since the camp of darkness now also included impious Jews.

Around 174 B.C., a faction of the leaders of Jerusalem* opted for a Hellenization*, which threatened the religion of Israel (1 Macc 1:10–15, 41–64). It was then that the word "Judaism*" appeared (struggle for Jewish values 2 Macc 2:21, 8:1, 14:38), in opposition to "Hellenism" (2 Macc 4:13).

According to the apocalypses of Enoch, the *gôyim* will not suffer an unbending judgment, since they know a pre-Mosaic law* demanding respect for the cosmic order (1 Enoch 82:1ff.) and for social justice* (1 Enoch 94–100). Although the prolific literature of the Jewish diaspora emphasizes the analogy between the revelation* of Israel and Hellenistic values (Conzelmann 1981), it also stigmatizes the immorality of the pagans and their difficulty in recognizing the Creator (Wis 13–14; *see* Sibylline Oracles III. 29–45). Romans 1:18–32 was to repeat this assessment in order to establish universal salvation on the single justice of God (Cerfaux 1954). Jesus knew the opposition between Israel and the *gôyim,* but he defined a new and more decisive border between those who accepted his message and those who rejected it. Thus the impenitent cities of Lake Tiberias are guiltier than ancient Sodom (Mt 11:20–24; *see* 10:15); and chosenness is not a safe-conduct for a final salvation that will include many pagans (Lk 13: 28ff. and parallel passages; Jeremias 1956).

In the Judeo-Christian circle that is reflected in Matthew, the *ethnikos,* along with the publican, remains the natural type of the sinner (Mt 18:17; *see* 5:47, 6:7). According to this circle, mission* should be confined, in imitation of Jesus, "to the lost sheep of the house of Israel" (Mt 10:5f., 23, 15:24); only after that, by its example, will the Jewish community restored in Christ draw the rest of humanity to salvation (Mt 13–16f.). Matthew notes this position with respect. But, for him, Jesus has completed his mission as Messiah* of Israel and, through his Resurrection*, has received a universal power. Mission must therefore now open itself to all the *gôyim,* without discrimination (Mt 28:16–20).

● G. Bertram, K.L. Schmidt (1935), "*Ethnos," ThWNT* 2, 362–70.
L. Cerfaux (1954), "Le monde païen vu par saint Paul," in *Recueil L. Cerfaux,* Gembloux, vol. II, 415–23.
J. Jeremias (1956), *Jesu Verheißung,* Stuttgart.
H.D. Preuss (1971), *Verspottung fremder Religionen im AT,* Stuttgart.
P.E. Dion (1975), *Dieu universel et peuple élu,* LeDiv 84.
H. Conzelmann (1981), *Heiden, Juden, Christen,* Tübingen.

CLAUDE TASSIN

See also **Choice; Idolatry; Israel; Kingdom of God; Mission/Evangelization; Purity/Impurity; Universalism; War**

B. Historical Theology

In its threefold reality—social, intellectual, and religious—it was the Roman Empire that embodied the biblical reality of paganism for the Christianity of the early centuries; and it was in thinking concretely about the relationship between Christianity and Classical Antiquity that the earliest Christian theologies (theology*) established their relations with nonbelievers, more precisely with those among them who did not belong to the people of Israel*. As a nonbeliever the pagan was defined in negative terms; he was primarily the idolater, the member of a social body whose cohesion was guaranteed by false gods. But because Christianity understood itself from the very beginning as being charged with a universal mission, pagans were also an intended audience for the gospel. Furthermore, by virtue of a consistently developed doctrine of creation* and of providence*, patristic thought, in a movement that began with Justin and culminated with Eusebius of Caesarea, came to interpret pagan experience as a certain *expectation* of the gospel and a *preparation* for it.

Between the Peace* of the Church* and the end of the patristic age, paganism ceased to possess a social and religious reality within the confines of the Roman world. Since Theodosius, the Eastern Church existed on the lands of an empire of which Christianity was the official religion, and on the lands of the Eastern Empire, the Church had to deal with Arian heretics more than with pagans. In the same period, paganism had ceased to represent an intellectual entity in relation to which Christianity would have to take a position. The Empire still contained pagan intellectuals, but the Church now occupied the position of transmitter of the classical legacy. Outside cities the *paganus* had probably not disappeared, and the underlying presence of pre-Christian observances was to be a perpetual problem for a "multitudinist" Church whose task was now to proclaim the gospel within itself just as much as to the outside world. In any case, from then on the pagan no longer had the qualities of the Greek or the Roman in whom the quest for wisdom* fostered objections to Christianity.

The nominal Christian became an "internal" pagan who later became the target for actual missions (mission*/evangelization). The pagan on the fringes of the Church would be the Muslim, who demanded from Christianity (particularly Byzantine Christianity) a vigorous reaffirmation of its monotheism*, but never appeared as the representative of a culture awaiting evangelization—the relationship of medieval Christianity to Islam was in fact modeled on its relationship to heresies (heresy*). Finally, the "external" pagan would come to be represented by any member of those societies that had newly appeared in Christian consciousness as a result of the conquest of new worlds. The *conquista* again raised theoretical problems of evangelization in an acute form and a new Christian evaluation of non-Christian religious experiences became an urgent necessity. To attitudes of violent negation, for which the paganism of the "Indian" was merely barbarism, were opposed methods of evangelization respectful of the new recipients of the gospel (B. de Las Casas, the Jesuit missions of Paraguay, among others),

or even reaffirmations of patristic themes (e.g., Luther* defined the theological status of the Indians as a situation of "waiting," a definition taken up and extended by the Pietist theologian Zinzendorf).

It should also no doubt be noted that the Renaissance experienced a revival of the cultural ideals of classical antiquity (already at work, in fact, since the Averroist Aristotelianism of the faculties of arts in the 13th century had brought about the rebirth of a strictly Hellenic ideal of the philosophical life), which was in part accompanied by the reappearance of a pagan quasi-religiosity. Christianity entered into modernity by learning that it was no longer the only guardian of ancient *paideia,* that the *philosophia Christi* was no longer universally considered as the paradigm of the life worth living, and that the evangelization of the intelligence was a task to be undertaken rather than one already accomplished.

An intense missionary life (from the 16th to the late 19th century), then the conclusion (often critical) of centuries of mission by a genuine flowering of the theology of missions has led recent theology to adopt a new branch, the "theology of religions" (religions*, theology of). To this is owed simultaneously a new awareness of major theological problems—"salvation* of unbelievers," "evangelization and inculturation*," and so forth—the vigorous reaffirmation of patristic solutions, and, in some cases, innovative theories. An ecclesiology* wishing to reach its maximum dimensions was thus able to investigate the theme of the Church descended from Abel, *Ecclesia ab Abel* (Y. Congar). In a theology concerned with establishing a "transcendental" bond between God* and humanity, the non-Christian might then appear in the guise of the "anonymous Christian" (K. Rahner*). A renewed hermeneutics* of non-Christian religions has been able to draw attention to the "unknown Christ* of Hinduism" (R. Pannikar), or to the pre-comprehensions of the Christian experience* provided by the *vodun* of Bénin (B. Adoukonou). As a conclusion as well as an encouragement, the declaration *Nostra aetate* and the decree *Ad gentes* of Vatican* II, which were not addressed only to Catholics, finally set out the guidelines for a missionary praxis and theory conceived of on the privileged model of a "dialogue" with non-Christian religions, and which accepted as a first recommendation the need to "uncover with joy and respect the seeds of the Word*" hidden in non-Christian experiences (*AG* 11; *see* Dournes 1963). The term *paganism* itself has disappeared, except in a passage of *AG* 9, where its meaning is not negative.

These theological discourses have, however, been produced in a period in which the Christianity of the West, in the name of "secularization*," is experiencing a phenomenon that cannot be interpreted solely in terms of the erosion of traditional religious meanings, because it is also accompanied by a certain anarchic reappropriation of a totally non-Christian form of religion, frequently called post-Christian. Nietzsche* is no doubt the intellectual source of this phenomenon, not content to proclaim the "death" of God, but also embracing the cause of Dionysus against that of the Crucified One. The question of paganism can thus be raised again; and since a "neo-paganism" has appeared that bears no relation, beyond an occasional borrowing, to traditional religions, it has to be posed in new terms. It will perhaps be the role of a theological hermeneutics of the end of modernity to ask whether pagan experience (whatever the variety of styles it may adopt) is not dialectically linked to an atheism* that was initially considered as the sole spring of secularization—in short, whether in the world* reduced to its "world-being," it is not the same thing to live "without God" (Eph 2:12) as to live under the anonymous protection of numinous beliefs. And to this end, it will always be necessary that the highly differentiated work of the theology of religions also set aside a place for the theology of religion itself.

● E. Peterson (1933), "Die Kirche aus Juden und Heiden," in *Theologische Traktate, Ausgewählte Schriften* 1, Würzburg, 1994, 141–74.

G. Fessard (1960), *De l'actualité historique,* vol. 1, Paris.
J. Dournes (1963), *Dieu aime les païens: Une mission de l'Église sur les plateaux du Viet-Nam,* Paris.
L. Debruyne (1971), *Le Païen? Le Salut? Questions posées au décret* Ad Gentes, *aux théologiens, aux missionnaires,* Louvain.
R.P.C. Hanson (1972), "The Christian Attitude to Pagan Religions up to the Time of Constantine the Great," *ANRW* II, 23/2, 910–73.
P. Damboriena (1973), *La salvación en las religiones no cristianas,* Madrid.
R. Bastide (1975), *Le sacré sauvage,* Paris.
Cl. Bruaire (1976), "Le nouveau défi du p.," *Com(F)* I/1, 28–33.
H.U. von Balthasar (1978), *Theodramatik* II/2, *Die Personen in Christus* 331–410, "Die Kirche aus Juden und Heiden," Einsiedeln (*Dramatique divine* II/2, 1988, 288–366).
A. Dumas (1982), "Renaissance des paganismes," *LV(L)* 31, 7–18.
C.S. Song (1982), *The Compassionate God: An Exercise in the Theology of Transposition,* London, not. 41–64, 127–41, and 145–260.
A. Dumas (1985), "La séduction nouvelle du néo-paganisme," *Conc(F)* 197, 99–108.
H.-G. Gensichen (1985), "Heidentum I," *TRE* 14, 590–601.
H.J. Klauck (1995), *Die religiöse Umwelt des Urchristentums,* vol. 1, Stuttgart.

JEAN-YVES LACOSTE

See also **Hellenization of Christianity; Inculturation; Mission/Evangelization; Philosophy; Religion, Theology of**

Pagans

The theology* of pagans as individuals or groups should be distinguished both from believers and from heretics who have lapsed from belief. The theology of pagans is particularly important because, historically, it created complications for generations of Christians, particularly but not only in the late Middle Ages, and while unevangelized continents were being discovered during the Renaissance*.

If the pagans could be saved without evangelization, what necessary role, if any, did the Church* play in the mediation of salvation to the individual, whether pagan *or* Christian? If the pagans could not be admitted to the beatifying vision* of God, was God not creating rational beings who were ineluctably destined to have the final satisfaction demanded by their nature

thwarted through no fault of their own? Was it possible so to construe the theology of the creation* and fall that human nature was not itself inscribed with an aspiration to a supernatural destiny, but might find the only satisfaction it was owed by its creator in a purely natural felicity? Would such a solution also dispose of difficulties about those dying before the birth of Jesus*, or unbaptized as infants?

The intensity of debate occasioned by these questions for 1,500 years necessarily affected the development of doctrine in western Christendom. It explains the strength of current movements in theological thinking, like salvation history, which make such Scholastic questions otiose by by-passing the whole Augustinian understanding of original sin*, grace*, and individual salvation* and the Neoplatonist (Neoplatonism*) gradations of being on which they are predicated.

It was with Augustine* that the debate became acute, although it was dominated by the ancient Greek assumption, taken for granted by Aquinas and systematized by such Renaissance authors as Pico della Mirandola and Marsilio Ficino, that being itself admits of discrete degrees. In the formal exposition given to it during the Renaissance, an exposition derived by Ficino from Plotinus and no doubt from the various hierarchies of the Dionysian corpus, the theory was modified to place humanity mid point in the order of things, with God alone having the plenitude of being, and after him coming the angels* as pure spirits, humanity as body-soul, the animals*, and then the inanimate creation.

The assumption that there was a hierarchy* of being created a host of problems for the Scholastics, including their theology of beatitude*, which required "uncreated" grace or participation in the divine being itself. But what principally concerns us here is that, on the assumption of any such hierarchy, aspiration and fulfillment do not cross from one order to another. Flowers do not aspire to bark. Human nature cannot itself aspire to, accept, or be fulfilled by a supernatural* satisfaction. It is true that human nature could have been considered to have been retrospectively endowed with an aspiration to supernatural fulfillment by virtue of the redemption, but that solution carried the heretical implication that the unevangelized pagans, too, would have shared that aspiration.

God would manifestly have been unjust in creating human beings destined to be deprived of the beatitude, which alone could fulfill their aspirations, or salvation would not have depended, as it was defined to depend, on orthodoxy* of belief. The moral theologians of the later Middle Ages struggled for centuries to define the minimum creedal content of the faith* without which there could be no justification*. Invariably they insisted at least on an acknowledgement of the existence of a God who remunerated after death, and even as late as the second half of the 20th century, Catholic theological textbooks normally insisted on belief in God's triune form as absolutely necessary for salvation.

From Augustine in the fifth century to Aquinas in the 13th, there was no doubt that human nature aspired to a fulfillment that was supernatural. It was not until the publication of Henri de Lubac*'s 1946 *Surnaturel*, which had to be withdrawn, and the refinement of de Lubac's view by Karl Rahner*, that a theologically acceptable explanation was elaborated for the aspirations of redeemed humanity to supernatural fulfillment, and with it the conceptual explanation of the implied act of faith necessary for salvation.

There was now no need to suppose that non-believers innocent of personal sin and capable of virtual or implied acts of faith were bound, along with unbaptized babies, to inhabit forever the *limbo* in which the saints of the Old Testament had waited for admission to heaven until its portals were opened by the risen Christ*. The act of faith implicit in all moral activity could be seen as depending on justifying grace whose availability became, by virtue of the redemption, an inviolable human right. Personal moral self-determination, involving the acceptance of sanctifying grace, could be asserted without Pelagian implications, and implicit acts of faith with no creedal content could be considered to create an invisible affiliation to the perhaps unknown or even repudiated Church, normally identified with the visible hierarchical institution. It was essentially the need to account for the fate of virtuous pagans that drove theology forward toward this solution, while discussion of the destiny of unbaptized babies forced the formal abandonment of the assumption that there were grades of being. Their redeemed human nature demanded that their ultimate felicity be in the supernatural order.

What de Lubac, Rahner, their precursors and followers, had achieved naturally meant a breakdown of the fundamental metaphysical assumption that there were orders of being. This, and not Pelagianism*, was the real flaw in Molina's theology, and its rectification was at the root of the theology of Michel de Bey (Baius) and of its defense by Cornelius Jansen, both of whom were forced into the alternative heresy of refusing any power of autonomous self-determination—"free will"—to rational human adults. If human nature was elevated to supernatural status in Adam*, then after the fall it retained that aspiration, and human beings could do nothing at all to avoid damnation. Salvation depended on an inevitably arbitrary selection by God of individuals from among the *massa damnata* on whom irresistible efficacious grace was to be bestowed.

The Scholastic dilemma about pagan salvation therefore concerned matters of fundamental importance to all Christian theology, from the nature and purpose of the Church to the modality of salvation within it, and even, as Hebrews xi makes clear, outside it. The question, much discussed in the first four centuries while Christian theology was still in its formative stage, became acute during the high Middle Ages. The canonical work on its history is still Louis Capéran's 1912 *Le Problème du salut des infidèles. Essai historique*, and it confirms that the problem was indeed by and large limited to Latin, that is essentially Augustinian, Christendom. For the Greeks, Christ's "descent into hell" offered pagans a chance of posthumous conversion*.

The intolerance of the western Church was beginning to increase from perhaps the 12th century, when the first public lynchings for heterodoxy are recorded. Gratian, although himself hostile to the death penalty for heresy, drew attention to its possible justification in terms of the Roman law *Quisquis,* which transformed the crime of injuring the *maiestas* of the Roman people into that of injuring the *maiestas* of the emperor, and carried the sentence of death, the confiscation of goods, posthumous dishonor, and the exclusion of heirs from office.

This was easily extended to cover counterfeiting, since the emperor's image appeared on the coinage, and in the Middle Ages came to be used for any sort of treason, and in particular to the offense to God included in the crime of disbelief in his revelation. The death penalty for heresy* was introduced into legislation in Aragon by 1197, into France under Louis VIII and Louis IX, and into the empire between 1234 and 1238. Innocent IV extended it to the whole of western Christendom in 1252. In his bull *Unam sanctam* of 1302 Boniface VIII laid down formally that there could be no salvation outside the Church, itself conceived essentially as the communion of believers. That doctrine was reiterated in the 1564 profession of faith of the Council of Trent*, and was not withdrawn in any document of the magisterium until the bull *Cum occasione* of 1653, which condemned the view attributed to Jansen that it was heretical to hold that Christ had died for all humanity.

The formal teaching of the Church, no doubt not universally enforced, precluded the salvation of pagans for a good three and a half centuries, during which the unevangelized continents were discovered. The result, naturally, was the huge and hugely dangerous missionary endeavor of the newly founded missionary orders, and the administrative modifications needed to deal with the missions. In 1622 Gregory XV established the Sacred Congregation for the Propagation of the Faith.

A century earlier, encouraged by the abbot Trithemius and developing the idea of mitigated punishment after death for the unevangelized, Claude Seyssel had had recourse to the state of natural felicity without either the beatific vision or any pain of loss and the state of limbo, a solution that worked only on the hypothesis that human beings did not in fact have supernatural aspirations. Luther and Melanchthon on the other hand had no doubt that God had his faithful among the unevangelized, and therefore saw less urgency in missionary activity in the New World. Nevertheless, the majority of 16th-century theologians on both sides of the schisms believed in the damnation of the pagans, or retreated between such hypotheses as that of Zwingli*, that the apostles had actually themselves evangelized most of the globe. Erasmus had come very near to stating openly that Cicero had been saved.

As the theology needed to solve the problem of the non-evangelized was forced into a more liberal stance, theologians like Suarez* began to speak of faith *in voto,* that is, by desire. It meant a religious attitude that would have been Christian had its holder known the gospel message. Finally, of course, it was the problem of morally upright and religious unbelievers, "pagans," that forced the rethinking of the Church's nature and function in the history of salvation that has taken place with growing intensity since the Second World War, having barely been adumbrated much before it.

• Louis Capéran, *Le Problème du salut des indifèles. Essai historique,* Paris 1912.
Heiko Augustinus Oberman, *The Harvest of Medieval Theology,* Cambridge, Mass., 1963.

ANTHONY LEVI

See also **Paganism**

Pantheism

"Pantheist," coined by John Toland (*Socinianism Truly Stated,* 1705), joins two Greek words: *pan* (all) and *theos* (god). The noun "pantheism" spread rapidly. A good deal of confusion was created by the practice, soon adopted, of applying the term retrospectively to earlier metaphysical or theological doctrines and of considering pantheism, as deism* had been in the past, as a disguised atheism*. For example, the label was applied to any metaphysical or religious doctrine that, denying the idea of a transcendent creator god, identified God* and the world*, whether the world was seen as an emanation of God (following a Neoplatonic model); or even as the body of which God was the soul; or whether God was considered as the principle and unified totality of everything that is. "'Pantheism' means both that everything is God and that it is the totality that is God" (Alain, *Définitions*). However, the doctrine does not have the same meaning if God is identified with the whole or with nature as it does if the totality of existents is related to God, in whom all things, according to Paul (Acts 17:28), are said to have "*life, movement, and being.*" C. Krause (1781–1832) coined *panentheism* to designate the doctrine that everything is in God without implying that everything is God. In fact, when it comes to philosophies (philosophy*) such as that of Spinoza, this term is more suitable than *pantheism,* which is primarily a polemical term.

The basic ontological presupposition is that of the singleness of being*. By means of a monist argument (or even the idea of a singleness of substance), which implies the immanence of God in everything that is, minds as well as bodies (soul*-heart-body), pantheism carries to its logical conclusion the idea of a substantial unity of all things. In this sense, a physical monism such as that of the Stoics (for whom every mind was a body, a warm breath, and even God a body made of pure fire) may be considered a form of pantheism. For its advocates, pantheism had as consequences the perfect intelligibility of all reality, a thoroughgoing necessitarianism (hence the impossibility of miracles [miracle*]), divine omnipresence*, and the ascent of all things to God: in short, a mysticism* without mystery*. But its adversaries saw other consequences: 1) the confusion of all things and the loss of individuality, a fortiori of all personality, both for God and for individual minds; 2) indifference in morality because of the lack of discrimination between all values: good* and evil*, the true and the false, freedom and necessity; 3) the equivalence of all beliefs and all religions and, in the end, the death of religion, morality, and politics.

a) History of Doctrines. Spinoza is generally considered as the archetype of the pantheist system and the model of all those that followed, because of the monism of substance and the modal status of finite individuals, in particular of man. An orthodox theologian would accept without difficulty the proposition that "nothing can either be or be conceived without God," but not what immediately precedes it: "Whatever is, is in God" (*Ethics* I, Prop. XV). Spinozism is, however, rather a panentheism than pantheism, for if everything is in God, God is neither identical with the world nor with the totality of its modes. Indeed,

Spinoza maintains the distinction, of Scholastic* origin, between *natura naturans* (God as the principle of being and life irreducible to any particular living being) and *natura naturata,* the totality of infinite and finite modes. Since God is made up of an infinity of infinite attributes*, only two of which we possess—namely, thought and extension—Spinozistic metaphysics can be interpreted neither as a materialist pantheism nor as a spiritualist pantheism, because God is said to be both *res extensa* and *res cogitans.*

Since the refutation of the Abbot Maret, the term *pantheism* has been applied to henologist metaphysics, pre-Socratic (Xenophanes), and Neoplatonic (Plotinus, Proclus) metaphysics. But if the Principle or the First is indeed the source from which freely and necessarily proceeds everything that is, the One, which is "beyond being and essence," as it is beyond any determination and thus any thing, can never be identified with the totality of beings of the second rank (the One that exists or the intellect, the soul of the world, individual souls, and bodies) that derive from it (procession) and reascend to it (conversion) following an eternal and infinite movement.

Just as questionable is the description as pantheist of religious doctrines with no personal divinity, such as Indian Brahmanism or Buddhism. When John the Scot Eriugena (c. 800–877) attempted in the *De divisione naturae* to transpose Neoplatonic arguments into the framework of Christian thought and vocabulary, he arrived at ambiguous formulations (created things, creative and not creative, come from God and return to God in accordance with an eternal process) and was condemned by Pope Honorius III in 1225. Another modality of pantheism appeared in Germany in the late 18th century and served to reconcile the ancient veneration of nature, the aspiration to a mystical fusion with God, and the Christian concept of salvation*. This is found in Goethe, as well as in the English poet, Byron.

b) Disputes of Pantheism. The question of pantheism became particularly acute with the dispute that arose in Germany out of Jacobi's disclosure of a concealed pantheism (or more precisely a Spinozism) in Lessing. A correspondence followed with Mendelssohn (who defended a rationalist theism* opposed to Jacobi's religion of feeling). This dispute, into which all German philosophers were drawn, played a decisive role in the genesis of German idealism. For example, it was by challenging the presumed necessary link between pantheism and fatalism that Schelling* made pantheism into the precondition for a "system of freedom." The debate once again raised the questions of the reality of the external world, of the nature of existence, of the understanding of identity, and of the status of the absolute.

A second dispute arose in France around 1840. This concerned the spiritualism of the school of Victor Cousin (1792–1867) and the defense of an impersonal divine reason* (Francisque Bouillier 1813–99). "There is no possible middle term between Catholicism* and pantheism," according to the Abbot Maret, who set out in his *Essai sur le panthéisme des sociétés modernes* what became the common form of the accusation, in Catholic terms: the refutation of a pantheism inherent in rationalist philosophies, which denied revelation* and necessarily led to fatalism, "to the cult of the senses, to the adoration of matter identified with spirit" (I. Goschler). This dispute explains the reaction among Cousin's disciples (such as Jules Simon, 1814–96), who were concerned to distance themselves from Spinoza's pantheism.

c)   The theological condemnation comes from the fact that pantheism, by making everything that is into a necessary emanation of God, denies in principle creation* *ex nihilo* (the world or reality is eternal), the Incarnation*, the spirituality of God, and the distinction between nature and the supernatural*. What has been considered retrospectively as the earliest condemnations of pantheism concern in fact theological formulations attempting to express the relationship of man to God or the paths to salvation in a Neoplatonic language, as in John the Scot Eriugena (the translator of Proclus, among others).This is the case, for example, for the proposition that through his creatures, as so many theophanies (theophany*), God creates himself as God, that is, moves from ineffability to intelligibility (Amaury de Bène, condemned by the Council of Paris in 1210). It is also true for certain formulations of Meister Eckhart. The formal condemnation of pantheism by the Catholic Church* dates from the *Syllabus* (§1, *DS* 2901) of 1864, which condemns the identification of God and nature and the substantial identity of God with beings, from which follows the confusion of all values and all orders. The First Vatican* Council (*De fide catholica* [April 24, 1870], ch. 1: *De Deo omnium creatore, DS* 3023–25) declared that God is distinct from the world in reality and by his essence. And in canons 3 to 5 it anathematized a certain number of propositions considered to be pantheist, such as the substantial unity of God and things, emanationism and the denial of creation *ex nihilo,* and the universal and indefinite character of a God who constitutes the totality of things in determining himself. Having ceased to be a theological position in the 20th century, pantheism is no longer the object of specific condemnation, except if we discern an implicit condemnation in the suspicion provoked by the thought of Teilhard of Chardin (1881–1955), sometimes considered as a resurgence of pantheism, even though he wrote in *Le phénomène humain* (1955): "…differentiated union. The parts perfect themselves and complete themselves in any organized totality. It is because they neglected this universal rule that so many pantheisms have led us astray into the cult of a great whole in which individuals were supposed to lose themselves like drops of water, to dissolve like grains of salt in the sea." This is proof that pantheism has remained a polemical and reductive label in relation to the monist doctrines to which it should be applied.

● John the Scot Eriugena (864–66). *De divisione naturae.*
Spinoza (1677), *Ethica.*
J. Toland (1720), *Pantheisticon.*
F. H. Jacobi (1785), "Über die Lehre des Spinoza," in *Briefen an den Hernn Moses Mendelssohn,* Breslau.
M. Mendelssohn (1785), *Morgenstunden oder über das Daseyn Gottes,* Berlin.
M. Mendelssohn (1786), *An die Freunde Lessings,* Berlin.
F. W. J. Schelling (1809), *Philosophische Untersuchungen über das Wesen der menschlischer Freiheit.*
C. Krause (1828), *System der Philosophie,* Göttingen.
H. Ritter (1829), *Die Halbkantianer und der Pantheismus,* Berlin.
I. Goschler (1832), *Du panthéisme,* Strasbourg.
G. W. F. Hegel (1832), *Vorlesungen über die Philosophie der Religion,* Berlin.
Abbé H. Maret (1835), *Essai sur le panthéisme dans les sociétés modernes,* Paris.
F. Bouillier (1844), *Théorie de la raison impersonnelle,* Paris.
J. Simon (1856), *La religion naturelle,* Paris.
Aug. Valensin (1925), *A travers la métaphysique,* Paris.
W. Schröder (1989), "Pantheismus," *HWP* 7, 59–63.
H. L. Nouty (1990), "Le panthéisme dans les lettres françaises au XVIIIe siècle," *RSHum,* 435 Sq.

JACQUELINE LAGRÉE

See also **Atheism; Deism and Theism; Omnipresence, Divine; Platonism, Christian; Vatican I, Council of**

Pantocrator. *See* **Omnipotence, Divine**

Papias of Hierapolis. *See* **Apostolic Fathers**

Parable

---

1. A Method of Literary and Theological Expression of the Historic Jesus

a) Sources. As a teller of parables Jesus* joined the long Jewish Old Testament Tradition* of the *mashal.* In the Old Testament the *mashal* is a statement in the form of a comparison. The parable is a particular type of *mashal.* It aims to reveal the meaning of a person, object, or event by linking the subject—by means of a developed comparison—to another sphere of reality. The Old Testament includes five real parables: the one about the poor man's ewe that Nathan relays to David (2 Sm 12:1–7), Tekoa's parable (2 Sm 14:1–20), the parable of one of the Sons of the Prophets (1 Kgs 20:39–43), the Song of the Vineyard (Is 5:1–7), and the Parable of the Farmer (Is 28:23–29).

In the Jewish tradition, the *mashal* (*matla* in Aramaic) is a general term, used for any of a number of different types of figurative discourse, including simple comparison, developed example, parable, fable, allegory, symbol, saying, and maxim. Most of the rabbinic parables are authentic parables, to which should be added many allegories. Parables belong to the Haggada. "From a literary viewpoint, it is a form of the midrash, its *Sitz im Leben* [placement in social life] is the rabbinic homily, its aim is pedagogic" (Dietrich 1958). It borrows its wealth of imagery from everyday life. Thanks to the parable "one grasps the words of the Torah as a king finds a lost pearl in a palace thanks to the flame of a lamp " (*Midrash Genèse Rabbah* I, 8). *Parabolè* is the usual term in the New Testament (it is used 50 times); but John chooses the term *paroimia* (which he uses five times).

b) Attribution. In the unanimous opinion of the critics, parables are one of the most characteristic expressions of the historic Jesus' preaching*. The synoptic tradition (the Gospels* of Matthew, Mark, and Luke)

has preserved about 40 of them. This important collection makes it possible to discover Jesus' language, his pragmatic aims, and the theological heart of his message. However, only a critical analysis makes it possible to reconstitute the original form of Jesus' words, for Jesus himself wrote nothing down and the only documentation available today consists of the Greek translations of the parables preserved in the first three Gospels in the second half of the first century (*see also* the Gnostic *Gospel According to Thomas* 9, 64, 65, 107, etc.).

2. Forms of the Parable

Among the extant parables, the history of biblical forms, or genres, distinguishes the following categories: 1) The *word-image* is a rhetorical device in which the thing mentioned and the image are juxtaposed, without a particle of comparison, as in Mark 2:21–22. 2) The *metaphor* is an abridged comparison without a particle of comparison; the image is substituted for the thing meant, as in Matthew 5:13. 3) The *simile* is a comparison in which the thing meant and the image are ordered correctly in relation to each other by the particle of comparison *as* or *like*—for example, Matthew 24:27. 4) The *hyperbole* is an exaggeration of the image, as in Matthew 10:30. 5) The *similitude,* in the strict sense of *Gleichnis,* is a word-image or a developed comparison that brings to the language a typical scene of everyday life. Its persuasive powers come from the evocation of what is commonly accepted. What is not very clear or disputed is thus elucidated analogically by what is well known—for example, Luke 15:4–7. 6) The true *parable* (*Parabolè*) seems like the narration of a particular interesting event involving one or several people. It makes no appeal to common sense but gets its suggestive powers from the extraordinary episode that it evokes, as in Luke 15:3–7, the Parable of the Lost

Sheep. 7) The *exemplary narrative** is similar to the parable because of its narrative character, but it differs from it by its lack of a metaphoric dimension. It offers an example of behavior that calls for imitation, without any other transposition—for example, Luke 10:30–36. 8) The *Allegory* is "a developed metaphor in which each trait has its own meaning" (X. Léon-Dufour, *Dictionnaire du Nouveau Testament*), as in Mark 4:13–20.

3. From Comparison to Metaphor

Among the forms listed above, two of them, similitude and the parable proper, attract particular attention. The controversy centers on the way in which they should be interpreted. Recent research, enriched by work on the metaphor (*see* Jüngel, Ricoeur, and Wilder) has proposed a new reading of the parables (*see* J. D. Crossan, Funk, Harnisch, and Weder) without, at the same time, totally abandoning the classical approach proposed by A. Jülicher. The question of the historicity of the opening formula: "the Kingdom* of God is like…" is a possible starting point (but not the only one!), which might lead to the discovery of the solution to the discussion. If this formula goes back to the historic Jesus, the parables should be read as similes. If this introductory phrase is a later addition, then another method is required. Both types of images appear, in fact, in the most ancient examples of the tradition.

a) Analogy. In at least five cases the introductory formula seems to go back to the historic Jesus (Mk 4:26 and 4:30–31 and Mt 13:33 and 13:44). If that is so, the image (*Bildhälfte*) set in motion by the parable—an image that consists either of an everyday scene or of a particular instance—is at the service of the theme (*Sachhälfte*). In this hypothesis (*see* Jülicher) the parable aims at cognitive enhancement. Based on the principle of analogy*, it invites the reader to make a transfer of judgment. The concept discovered at the level of the image (*Bildhälfte*) should be carried over to the initial theme (*Sachhälfte*). From the moment that the addressee has discovered the *tertium comparationis,* which links the theme and the image, he is empowered to solve the problem the parable wanted to deal with, and he can do that by applying to the set problem the solution induced by the image. The parable thus functions as a transfer of judgment by analogy, it has a rhetorical function.

One should beware of all simplifications. The appeal to common sense, which characterizes the parable constructed on the model of a simile, can also appear in parables lacking an introductory formula (*see*, for instance, Lk 11:5–8 and 15:3–10). Only the analysis of the logical functioning of the parable makes it possible to class it as a rhetorical parable-argument or as a parable-metaphor.

b) Change. However, it so happens that in their original phrasing the majority of the parables lack an introductory formula. How should these little fictional narratives be read then? Here the theory of metaphor is brought into play. The parable aims to be read as an expanded metaphor. What does that mean? In the poetic, the metaphor's distinctive feature is the tension established between the word and the heterogeneous semantic field into which it is introduced. From the dissonance thus created flows a wealth of unexpected meaning. When the metaphor is got up as a narrative, the tension is embedded in the organization of the plot. This tension results from the collision of two conceptions of reality—that is, when an initial conception, derived from the ordinary and everyday, clashes with an extraordinary conception. This irruption of the extraordinary, although it may sometimes have dramatic reasons, responds, in fact, to deeper necessities. It is a matter of disconcerting the reader, of unsettling his image of the world, and of making him discover new existential possibilities. The parable then becomes a language of change.

c) Performativity. The above shows that Jesus' parables are not in the first place a teaching about the reign/kingdom of God, but that the very enunciation by Jesus of a parable makes the reign/kingdom of God happen as an event in the present. This performative character of the parable signals at the same time that the identity of the speaker takes on a decisive significance. Only the one who claims to be the eschatological envoy of God* can create from the enunciation of a parable the space in which the reign/kingdom of God can become an event.

4. Message of the Parables

Jesus' eschatological preaching, that is, the announcement of the fact that the kingdom of God is near, constitutes the central theme developed in the parables. This theme is approached from the following angle. What happens when God establishes his reign? How does this reign reveal itself in the midst of the world of men? How are human reality and existence affected by it?

According to Jesus' parables, God enters the everyday in a hidden and unexpected way. He challenges reality as it is experienced; he transforms it and opens it onto a completely new and surprising future. For the listeners, this future comes to pass at the very moment when the parable is told by Jesus. A fragment of the eschatological kingdom, this future that bursts into the present, transforms it into a place of happiness and promise*. It bears witness to the immeasurable love of God for all his creatures and to his gift to mankind of incomprehensible liberty*. The God who suddenly appears in the parables frees men from their problematic past, from their alienating attachments; he begins a new history* with them. According to Crossan's beautiful expression, the parables are "the house of God" in the midst of the history of man. If that is so, the parable is not simply a pedagogical tool that Jesus used to expound in a figurative way a theological theme and that could, when necessary, be dispensed with; it is only as a parable and in the shape of a parable that the reign of God can enter into language and appear before Jesus' listener.

The reign of God that comes as Jesus tells a parable, constitutes a call to conversion*. The required change is adhesion to Jesus in whose person the Kingdom is near and divine love is offered to all, particularly to the excluded. But if the parables are an appeal to change, they simultaneously make change possible. The Jesus of the parables gives what he demands.

5. Reception of the Parables in the Gospels

The transmission of the parables during the first Christian generations led to their being put into writing. This transfer to written form was a major event, for the parables thus became texts open to interpretation. The act of putting the parables into a narrative form, the developments and modifications they underwent, the commentaries to which they gave rise are so many traces of this interpretative work. The history of the reception of the parables in the Gospels raises the following question: Are we dealing with a history of textual corruption marked by the distortion of the parabolic tradition or are we faced with a story in which the true tradition of Jesus has been preserved? It does not seem wise to make a unilateral decision on this alternative, because consistent arguments can be marshaled for both theses. It can be said at the onset that, during the course of their transmission, the original form of Jesus' words has undeniably been modified.

Joachim Jeremias, in his influential book on the parables, brought up four characteristic elements of this process: 1) the putting into narrative form of the synoptic parables in the Gospels involved a transfer of communication—a change of the speaker and of the listener; 2) the parables were often slanted in an ethical sense; 3) the time of the Church* from Easter to the Parousia*,

with all its specific problems, was often inserted into the plot of the parables; 4) many parables were subjected to the process of allegorization. But, on the other hand, it should be noted that the history of the parable's reception is not necessarily the reflection of textual corruption; we should not exclude the idea that the processes of modification were induced by the parables themselves. Thus, the frequently observed secondary adjunction "the kingdom of God is like..." does no more than bring into the language the original theme of the parables—that is, the advent of God's reign.

Finally, the progressive Christologization of the parables (the inclusion of the parables in the evangelical narrative and the introduction of the person* of Jesus into the parable's narrative itself) does no more than assert in a pertinent way that the evangelical parables are inseparable from their original hearer. In the end, in order to evaluate in a relevant way whether the reception of the parables is marked with the seal of fidelity or of distortion, one should ask oneself, in each individual case, whether the parable has remained "that fictional narrative which makes the nearness of the *basileia* [Kingdom] happen as an event of which Christ* is an integral part" (Marguerat 1989).

- A. Jülicher (1910), *Die Gleichnisreden Jesu,* 2nd Ed., Tübingen (repr. Darmstadt, 1976).
- C.H. Dodd (1935), *The Parables of the Kingdom,* London (2nd Ed. 1941).
- J. Jeremias (1947), *Die Gleichnisse Jesu,* Göttingen (2nd Ed. 1970).
- R. Bultmann (1957), *Die Geschichte der synoptischen Tradition,* 6th Ed., Göttingen.
- E.L. Dietrich (1958), "Gleichnis und Parabel," *RGG3* 2, 1616–17.
- W. Harnisch (Ed.) (1982 a), *Die Gleichnisse Jesu: Positionen der Auslegung von Adoph Jülicher bis zur Formgeschichte,* Darmstadt; id. (1982 b), *Die neutestamentliche Gleichnisforschung im Horizont von Hermeneutik und Literaturwissenschaft,* Darmstadt.
- H. Weder (1984), *Die Gleichnisse Jesu als Metaphern,* 5th Ed., Göttingen.
- H.J. Klaus (1986), *Allegorie v. Allegorese in synoptischen Gleichnistexten,* 2nd Ed., Münster.
- J. Delorme (Ed.) (1989), *Les paraboles évangéliques: Perspectives nouvelles,* Paris.
- D. Marguerat (1989), "La parabole, de Jésus aux Évangiles; une histoire de réception," in J. Delorme (Ed.) 1989, 61–88.

JEAN ZUMSTEIN

See also **Hermeneutics; Jesus, Historical; Kingdom of God; Literary Genres in Scripture; Mystery; Narrative; Prophet and Prophecy; Wisdom**

Paraclete. *See* **Holy Spirit**

Paradise. *See* **Life, Eternal; Vision, Beatific**

Parish. *See* **Local Church; Pastor**

Parousia

The Greek work *parousia* simply means "presence." In Hellenistic usage, however, it was often used in a technical sense for the visit of a ruler or the manifestation of a god. The visit of an imperial ruler to a provincial city was a momentous occasion. Diodore of Sicily (4, 3, 3) tells of the cultic parousia of Dionysus in the Theban mysteries, and the parousia of a god could also be experienced in dreams.

In the New Testament, *parousia* is a technical term for the manifestation of Christ* in glory*. It occurs six times in the Thessalonian correspondence (1 Thes 2:19, 3:13, 4:15, 5:23; 2 Thes 2:1, 2:8), and once in Corinthians 15:23. In the synoptics, it is found only in Matthew, who uses it four times (24:3, 27, 37, 39) in his apocalyptic discourse. It also occurs in 1 John 2:28; 2 Peter 1:16, 3:4, and 3:12; and James 5:7f. The synoptic parallels to Matthew 24 point the way to Parousia in a Jewish context. Where Matthew speaks of the Parousia, Luke refers to the "Son of Man in his day" (Lk 17:24) or to the "days of the Son of Man" (17:26). It seems, therefore, that the term *parousia* is used primarily in Hellenistic contexts to refer to the coming of the Lord. The more traditional Jewish expressions are "the day of the Lord" and the coming of the Son of Man. *Parousia* does not occur in Revelation, the New Testament work that is most preoccupied with the coming of the Lord.

The Christian expectation of the Parousia of Christ must be seen against the background of Israelite and Jewish traditions. The oldest traditions concern the manifestation of YHWH as a warrior who leads his people from the southern mountains to the promised land (Dt. 33:2–3; Jgs 5:4–5). The Psalms* reflect the expectation that God* will come to judge the Earth (Ps 98:9). The prophet* Amos, however, turns this expectation against the people of Israel*. For him, the day of the Lord will be a day of darkness and not light (Am 5:18). Thereafter, the prophets associate the day of the Lord with the terrible judgment* of God (e.g., Zep 1:14–15 and 2:2; Jl 1:15 and 2:1). In the Book of Daniel, however, the emphasis is once again on the deliverance of Israel. Daniel's vision of "one like a son of man" who comes on the clouds and receives a kingdom from the Ancient of Days (Dn 7) had enormous importance for early Christianity. The "one like a son of man" is clearly distinguished from YHWH, yet he rides on the clouds like a divine figure. From a very early time, this figure was identified as the Messiah*, even though he has a heavenly character (1 Enoch 37–71; 4 Ezr 13). We continue to find references to the coming of God in the Pseudepigrapha (e.g., 1 Enoch 1: 3–9; Assumption of Moses 10:3–7), but the advent of a messianic figure of God's agent is more directly relevant to the Christian expectation of the Parousia of Christ.

In the New Testament, *Parousia* always refers to the coming of Christ in glory. This expectation must have arisen in the earliest stage of the Christian movement, after Easter. There can be little doubt that the formulation of this expectation in terms of the coming of the Son of Man originated in the Aramaic-speaking environment of Palestine. The use of the term *Parousia* in Paul's letters is already a secondary development, which reformulates the expectation in Greek terminology for a Diaspora setting.

Matthew 24 provides the most complete description of the anticipated Parousia (compare the apocalyptic discourses in Mark 13 and Luke 26, where the term is not used). It will be preceded by various signs, but it will come "as lightning comes from the East and flashes as far as the West" (Mt 24:27). It will be accompanied by cosmic disturbances (the sun will be darkened, etc.) and then the Son of man will gather the elect with the blast of a trumpet (24:31). The trumpet blast is also mentioned in 1 Thessalonians 4:16. In this passage, Paul makes it clear that he expects the Parousia within the lifetimes of his generation. The sense of anticipation and vigilance required by the imminence of the Parousia is vividly seen in Matthew's parable* of the 10 bridesmaids (Mt 25:1–13): "Keep awake, therefore, for you know not the day nor the hour." Where Matthew urges wakefulness, James calls for patience (Jas 5:7–8). Paul finds in the imminence of the Parousia a source of encouragement.

Parousia is never used in the New Testament with reference to the earthly life of Jesus. There is only one Parousia and it is not properly a "return." It is the first coming of Christ in glory. Only later, in the early church*, do we find the idea of two Parousias (e.g., Justin, *Apologia* 52, 3; *Dialogus cum Tryphone* 14, 8; 49, 2 and 7; 53,1; 54,1). By then, the expectation of a glorious Parousia had receded into the future.

● A. Oepke (1967), "*Parousia, pareimi,*" *ThWNT* 5, 856–69.
C. Perrot (1983), *La venue du Seigneur: Le retour du Christ*, Brussels.
R. Jewett (1986), *The Thessalonian Correspondence*, Philadelphia.
C. Rowland (1992), "Parousia," *AncBD* 5, 166–70.

JOHN J. COLLINS

See also **Apocalyptic Literature; Eschatology; Intertestament; Judgment; Messianism/Messiah; Son of Man**

Participation. *See* **Analogy; Being**

Pascal, Blaise

1623–1662

In Pascal's complete works the word "theology*" occurs very seldom and it is doubtful whether the idea it represents would in itself have interested him. The famous §65 of his *Pensées* mentions it only as a representative example of "diversity": "Theology is a science, but at the same time how many sciences are there?" No doubt Pascal would only have drafted a truly theological discourse at the close of his *Apologie de la religion chrétienne.* Several concepts or doctrines, however, can be defined as representing an undeniable theological endeavor on Pascal's part.

a) Christology: Jesus Christ the Mediator. Despite his family's (second) conversion under the influence of a disciple of Saint-Cyran in 1646, and despite his friendships at Port-Royal, Pascal would be known solely as a precocious scientific genius if he had not become aware of one certainty: nothing can separate us from the love* of God* that is in Jesus* Christ, according to Romans 8, 38 *et seq.* Apamphlet, called by its editors *Le Mémorial,* and dated 23 November 1654, attests to that awareness. Both existential and theoretical, this fundamental text unfolds the problematics of access to God: it is in Jesus Christ alone that God consents to manifest himself; God is "the God of Jesus Christ," "not the God of the philosophers and scholars." Access to God occurs within a struggle between separation, which is sin, and non-separation, which is acquired by conversion: "Jesus Christ, I separated myself from him: I fled from him, renounced him, crucified him. May I never be separated from him." Pascal's singularity consists in his simultaneous imagining of absolute separation, and even "the unconquerable difference between God and us" (§378; §418; *see also Le Mystère de Jésus,* §919), and conversion. The latter option is no longer understood as a *metanoia* or an *épistrophè* that would cause one to turn toward the being of which one is the image (Pascal never quotes Genesis 1, 26). Instead, conversion "consists of annihilating oneself" (§378), because it is Christ* himself who annihilates himself in one (Galatians 2:19 *Sq;* §919). The fact that Christ is the unique mediator means therefore that he is himself the disunion, the disproportion between God and man, the infinite* and the finite, holiness and sin: "In Jesus Christ all contradictions are brought into harmony" (§257), that is, not resolved but preserved and accepted. Conversely, God himself "regards men only through the mediator Jesus Christ" (*Lettre sur la mort de son père,* 1651).

b) Quarrels about Grace and the Morality of the Casuists. From the year 1655 onward, Pascal devoted the greater part of his energies to serving Port-Royal, firstly with his *Ecrits sur la grâce* (1655–56), and then, in the polemic against the Jesuits, by composing under a pseudonym the *Lettres écrites par Louis de Montalte à un provincial…* (1656–57), better known as *The Provincial Letters.* The first four deal with the question of grace*. The remainder attack the Jesuits on the grounds of their moral theology. They are called "the new casuists," and accused of having the "intention" of "corrupting morals" by means of their two highly effective weapons: the "doctrine of probabilism" and the "method of directing the intention." In the *Provinciales* it is difficult to to make a precise distinction between Pascal's work, and that of Arnauld and Nicole, who prepared most of the documentation for him. Be that as it may, although *Les Provinciales* express a strictly Jansenist theology and morality, and although they became unprecedented bestsellers by using the clandestine press to carry into the public arena debates hitherto reserved for specialists, they are not totally exempt from a charge of unfairness in their treatment of the quotations borrowed from their Casuist adversaries. The magisterium* found the Jansenists in error regarding the question of grace: on the other hand it took its lead from the *Provinciales* as well as the *Ecrits des Curés de Paris* (the production of which Pascal had been involved in) by condemning laxism (1665–66). But the final failure of the *Provinciales* (Pascal put an end to their campaign with the 18th *Letter,* dated 24 March 1657, after the Bull *Ad sacram*'s condemnation of the "Five Propositions of Jansenism") led Pascal to turn toward an ambitious project, his *Apologie de la religion.*

c) Apologetics: The Greatness and Wretchedness of Man. The *Conférence à Port-Royal* (probably 1657) laid out the traditional bipartite anthropology* of man's greatness (*dignitas*) and wretchedness (*miseria*), which had already provided the organizing principle of the *Entretien avec M. de Sacy.* The *Conférence* used the idea of a "twofold state of the nature*" of humankind (§131), incomprehensible to philosophy*, in order to undertake to show, by following the Augustinian model of apologetics in his *De vera religione,* that there exists a true religion that alone can explain the "astonishing contradictions" of/in man (§149). For wretchedness and greatness should be attributed to different *objects,* to nature and to grace respectively, of which man is a synthesis just as Christ is a union of two natures. Man is undecipherable without the key to the two *states:* the state that he had at the creation* and the one in which he found himself after the Fall (Magnard 1975). In the prosopoeia of §149, Wisdom* tells men: "You are not in the state of your creation…Look at yourselves and see whether you do not find in yourselves the living characteristics of those two natures." His ahistorical use of the concept of state is seemingly an original point among Pascal's resumption of classical themes; even more original appears to be his fixing of man's state between two extremes, called "the two infinities," a theme that *Disproportion de l'homme* (§199) elaborates.

Other reflections and other documents (probably conceived earlier) and that make up the collection that is known today by the title *Pensées* later joined the fundamental structure of Pascal's projected *Apologie,* based on that bipartite anthropology. Two of them should be mentioned. Firstly, the material about miracles (miracle*) as proof of the truth* of the Christian religion, a reflection provoked by the miracle of the Holy Thorn. This occurred a year before the last Provincial Letter, on 24 March 1656, at Port-Royal in Paris, and cured Marguerite Périer, Pascal's niece, of a weeping fistula (the ecclesiological and apologetic issues arising from miracles of the Holy Thorn would remain very important throughout the 17th century). Secondly, the concept of figurative structures, which orders all the proofs drawn from the Bible* ("That the law* was a figure," §245—Pascal's interpretation of the Scriptures is always basically figurative, which is remarkable for the 17th century). Pascal accomplished groundbreaking work in this area: because, although his God is a hidden God, *Deus absconditus* (Is 45:15), it would be a matter of *seeing* him, something of which the Eucharist is the paradigm: "This sacrament contains at the same time both Jesus Christ's presence and his image" (§733).

d) Ecclesiology: The Limbs of Thought. Pascal's last reflection abandons apologetics to meditate on Paul's doctrine of the mystical body by setting out the broad lines of a "Christian morality, that is, by developing the passage about the "the reflections of the limbs." Pascal used the model of the relation between the body's limbs (soul*-heart-body) (Rom 12 and 1 Cor 12) in order to solve the problem of justified self-love*, according to the Cartesian definition of love (*Passions de l'âme,* art. 80): "In order to regulate the love one feels for oneself, one must imagine a body composed of thinking members, for we are members of the whole, and then we must see how each member ought to love itself" (§368).

The I loves itself legitimately only by loving the whole, that is by loving itself as the whole loves it: the legitimate love of oneself consists therefore in internalizing a difference: the I should love itself in the way that another—Christ—loves it. This is how Pascal understood 1 John 4, 19 ("We love because he first loved us"). Thereafter, Descartes* supplied the conceptual tools for thinking about Christ's body, since it is love that creates the whole. There followed a new reading of 1 Corinthians 12, 14ff. followed, which differs from its mystical interpretation: "By loving the body, it [the limb] loves itself, because it has no being except in the body, through the body, and for the body. '*Qui adhaeret Deo, unus spiritus est*' [He who cleaves to God is a single spirit]" (§372). The Trinity*, very rarely evoked by Pascal, forms its model: "We love ourselves because we are members of Jesus Christ; we love Jesus Christ because he is the body of which we are members. All is one, one is in the other, like the Three Persons [person*]" (§372).

The surprising metaphor according to which Christ is the body (and not the body's head) to which one belongs as a limb, and that the Port-Royal edition corrected, finds a parallel in the *Prière pour demander à Dieu le bon usage des maladies* (whose "thinking limbs" resemble his theological borrowing) that, after having addressed the Father, addresses the Son: "Your passion*, which you accomplish in your members, as far as the your body's perfect consummation." This original, somewhat Johannine-Cartesian doctrine of Christ's body, therefore constitutes a discourse on freedom of consent (§370), or on the identification of love and will. It is undoubtedly here that Pascal, making his final escape from the "narrow confines of Port-Royal" (Balthasar*), anticipates Rousseau by imagining a concrete figure of the will. Pascal's apologetics end with an "ecclesiological synthesis" (Martineau 1994), a synthesis accepted from the moment when "unity *in* love" forced Pascal to conceive "love *as* a unity."

● *Works,* Ed. L. Lafuma, Paris, 1963.
Oeuvres Complètes, Ed. Jean Mesnard, 4 vols. published, Paris, 1964–92.
About *Pensées*: *Pensées de M. Pascal sur la religion, et sur quelques autres sujets* (Ed. of Port-Royal), Paris, 1670 (repr. Saint-Étienne, 1971); *Pensées…,* Ed. L. Lafuma, 3 vols., Paris, 1951; *Discours sur la religion et sur quelques autres sujets,* Ed. E. Martineau, Paris, 1992; our citations follow the Lafuma numbering.
About *Provinciales*: Ed. L. Cognet, Paris, 1965.
♦ H. Bremond (1920), *Histoire littéraire du sentiment religieux…,* vol. 4, Paris.
J. Lhermet (1931), *P. et la Bible,* Paris.
R. Guardini (1935), *Christliches Bewußtsein: Versuche über P.,* Leipzig.
J. Russier (1949), *La foi selon Pascal,* Paris.
J. Laporte (1950), *Le cœur et la raison selon Pascal,* Paris.
H.-U. von Balthasar (1962), *Herrlichkeit* II/2, Einsiedeln, 537–600.
G. Rodis-Lewis (1963), "Les trois concupiscences," *ChPR* 11–14 (and in coll., *Pascal. Textes du Tricentenaire,* Paris, 1963).
H. Gouhier (1966), *Blaise Pascal Commentaires,* Paris.
P. Sellier (1966), *Pascal et la liturgie,* Paris.
A. Gounelle (1970), *La Bible selon Pascal,* Paris.
J. Miel (1970), *Pascal and Theology,* London-Baltimore.
P. Sellier (1970), *Pascal et saint Augustin,* Paris.
J. Orcibal (1972), "La signification du miracle et sa place dans l'ecclésiologie pascalienne," *ChPR* 20–21, 83–95.
H. Gouhier (1974), *Pascal et les humanistes chrétiens: L'affaire Saint-Ange,* Paris.
P. Magnard (1975), *Nature et histoire dans l'apologétique de Pascal,* Paris.
J. Mesnard (1976), *Les Pensées de Pascal,* Paris.
A. Feuillet (1977), *L'agonie de Gethsémani,* Paris.
T. Shiokawa (1977), *Pascal et les miracles,* Paris.

J. Mesnard (1983), "Pascal," *DSp* 12, 279–91.

H. Gouhier (1986), *Blaise P. Conversion et apologétique,* Paris.

J.-L. Marion (1986), *Sur le prisme métaphysique de Descartes,* ch. V, Paris.

P. Force (1989), *Le problème herméneutique chez Pascal,* Paris.

V. Carraud (1992), *Pascal et la philosophie,* Paris.

J. Mesnard (1992), *La culture du XVIIe siècle,* Paris, 305–484.

V. Carraud (1994), "Les deux infinis moraux et le bon usage des passions: Pascal et les *Passions de l'âme,*" XVIIe siècle 46, 4, 669–94.

E. Martineau (1994), "Deux clés de la chronologie des discours pascaliens," ibid., 695–729.

D. Leduc-Fayette (1996), *Pascal et le mystère du mal,* Paris.

V. Carraud (1997), "Des concupiscences aux ordres de choses," *RMM* 102, 41–66.

VINCENT CARRAUD

See also **Anthropology; Apologists; Augustine of Hippo; Bañezianism-Molinism-Baianism; Casuistry; Christ and Christology; Conversion; Descartes, René; Ecclesiology; Jansenism; Love**

Paschal Mystery. *See* **Passover**

Paschasius Radbert. *See* **Eucharist**

Passion

A. Biblical Theology

Passio in Latin and *pathèma* in Greek mean "what one experiences," in feeling or suffering. The last meaning survives in English only for the passion of Christ*, the sum of his suffering, from his agony in Gethsemane (Mt 26: 36–46 and parallels) to his death on the cross and burial (Mt 27:50–61 and parallels). The expression "passion of Christ" is found nowhere in the New Testament, and the noun is used only in the plural *pathèmata*. The Gospels* do not use the substantive but the verb form, notably in foretelling the passion: "And he

began to teach them that the Son of man must suffer *(pathein)* many things, and be rejected…and be killed" (Mk 8:31 and parallels). The verb is also used without an object (without naming the types of sufferings) in Luke, Acts, and Hebrews, and in 1 Peter 2:21: "Christ also suffered *(epathen)* for you."

It is noteworthy that the Easter proclamation of Jesus'* resurrection* did not have the consequence of causing his passion to be understood as an unfortunate interlude that was soon remedied. On the contrary, believers were led to remember it all the better. Being the very fruit of his passion, the glory* of the Risen One revealed the value of his sufferings, which were understood as the source of "a newness of life" (Rom 6:4) and as providing "an example" to be followed (1 Pt 2:21).

a) Predictions. The narrative of the passion takes up a large part of the Gospels and forms a coherent whole. In the synoptics its importance is emphasized in advance by three predictions, which provide a structure for the second half of those Gospels (Mk 8:31–33, 9:31, 10:32–34 and parallels). The literary nature of this presentation should not lead us to doubt its historical basis. Jesus was aware that his words and actions were provoking growing hostility (*see* Mk 2:8, 3:5, and 3:22–23). Determined not to "resist one who is evil" (Mt 5:39), he foresaw the consequence and recognized in it an aspect of God*'s plan as revealed in the Scriptures, a plan that would find fulfillment in divine victory (*see* Mt 21:38–42 and parallels; Gn 37:20, 45:17, and 50:20; and Is 52:13–53:12). We see the same thing in the Fourth Gospel, where Jesus' trial is anticipated in the course of his public life (Jn 5:16–45, 8:12–59, and 10:24–39). Jesus shows himself to be aware that he is threatened with death (Jn 7:1, 7:19, 8:37, and 8:40). There are attempts to arrest Jesus (Jn 7:30, 7:44, and 10:39) and to stone him (Jn 8:59 and 10:31), though these do not meet with success, "because his hour had not yet come" (Jn 7:30 and 8:20).

b) Principal Facts. The passion narratives are not historical reconstructions but religious narratives* intended for use in preaching* and meditation. The passion is presented as a mysterious and very disconcerting event, even though it was predicted by Scripture (Mk 14:49 and parallels). The narratives show human sin*, as well as the divine manner of confronting that sin by bearing its terrible consequences. Written with surprising restraint, the narratives do not express pity at Jesus' suffering. His agony, however, shows him afflicted with deathly sorrow (Mt 26:38 and parallels; Ps 42:6), which he overcomes by praying intensely (Mt 26:39–44 and parallels). Then comes the arrest on the Mount of Olives, brought about through Judas' betrayal of his master (Mt 26:47–50 and parallels); Jesus forbids his disciples to offer any armed resistance (Mt 26:51–54 and parallels). Taken before the high priest, he is questioned and accused; it is decided that he should be put to death (Mt 26:57–66 and parallels). Peter*, who has come as far as the courtyard, loses courage and denies his master (Mt 26:69–75 and parallels). In the course of the night Jesus is subjected to harsh treatment (Mt 26:67–68 and parallels). In the

morning the Sanhedrin turns him over to the Roman authorities (Mt 27:2 and parallels). Pilate questions him (Mt 27:11–14 and parallel s), then makes an offer to the crowd either to release Jesus or a rebel called Barabbas (Mt 27:15–23 and parallels). Mocked by Roman soldiers, who crown him with thorns (Mt 27:27–31 and parallels), Jesus is whipped (Mt 27:26 and parallels), and taken to Calvary, where he is crucified between two thieves (Mt 27:31–38 and parallels). He dies on the cross, giving a loud cry (Mt 27:50 and parallels). A rich man takes care of his burial (Mt 27:57–61 and parallels). At more than one point, variations among the narratives and other considerations pose problems in establishing historical accuracy in the modern sense.

c) Spiritual Meaning. The beginnings of the synoptic narratives show that the passion is a part of God's plan (Mt 26:42 and parallels) and was necessary for the fulfillment of Scripture* (26:54, 56 and parallels). The "must" of the passion predictions (Mk 8:31 and parallels) had already suggested this perspective. The narratives provide no other explanation as they unfold. The deeper sense of the events is never explained. It is in earlier portions of the Gospels that light is cast on the passion, as, for example, by Jesus' words when he declares that he has come "to give his life as a ransom for many" (Mt 20:28 and parallels; *see also* Jn 6:51), and particularly by what he does during the Last Supper (Eucharist*). There he presents in advance his body and the blood he will shed, and he transforms these into a gift of himself to his disciples (Mt 26:26–28 and parallels). In this way he accomplishes a complete reversal of the meaning of the event: the execution of a condemned man, a radical break, is transformed into the foundation of a perfect covenant* (*see* 1 Cor 1:18–25). The Fourth Gospel provides the key to this accomplishment: The passion is a work of love*. The love given by God (Jn 3:16 and 15:9) has led Jesus to be "the good shepherd," who "lays down his life for the sheep" (Jn 10:11). "Greater love has no man than this, that a man lay down his life for his friends" (15:13; *see* 13:1; 19:30). The apostle Paul sees the passion in the same light (Rom 5:6–8, Gal 2:20, and Eph 5:2 and 25–27). Understood in this way, the cross of Christ, instead of seeming absurd and scandalous, is recognized as "the power of God and the wisdom of God" (1 Cor 1:24), for it is an instrument of redemption, of reconciliation, and of the covenant. According to Hebrews the passion is a new type of priestly sacrifice, which makes of Christ a perfect "mediator of a new covenant" (Heb 9:15). On the one hand, he is fully accepted by God, whose salvific will he has generously fulfilled (Heb 5:8–10 and 10:5–10). On the other hand, he is closely united with the people, "his brethren," whose suffering he has taken on himself (Heb 2:17–18).

d) Participation.

To "share Christ's sufferings" (1 Pt 4:13) is thus a grace* at the same time as a duty of love. One cannot be a disciple of Christ without bearing the cross after him (Mt 16:24 and parallels). Peter explains that it is a matter of "doing right" (1 Pt 2:15), even and especially when "you do right and suffer for it" (1 Pt 2:20). John declares: "we ought to lay down our lives for the brethren" (1 Jn 3:16). Paul insists on the necessity of participating in the passion in order to be united with Christ (Rom 8:17 and Phil 3:10). He calls his tribulations as an apostle* a sharing in "Christ's sufferings" (2 Cor 1:5); they bring him comfort and great joy (2 Cor 7:4–7) and they are fruitful for the Church* (2 Cor 4:8–12 and Col 1:24).

e) Narrative Perspectives.

While generally in agreement, each gospel narrative of the passion has its own perspective.

Writing with his customary spontaneity, Mark allows us to experience the shock of events, the disconcerting fulfillment of God's plan. He bluntly describes Jesus' fate as anguished, betrayed, denied, falsely accused, condemned, and crucified. To those who know how to read him, however, Mark shows light through the darkness. The passion, in his understanding, reveals the identity of Jesus, the "Son of God" (Mk 15:39; see also 14:61–62), as well as his work, which is that of putting an end to the old cult* and of building a new, immaterial, temple* so that human beings may meet God (Mk 14:58).

More ecclesial and doctrinal, Matthew sheds light on events by using Jesus' own words (Mt 26:52–54) and by allusions to the Old Testament (Mt 26:38, 26:56, 27:9, 27:35, 27:43, and 27:46). The episode of the "blood money" (Mt 27:3–10) clearly establishes responsibility. Whereas a Gentile woman intervenes on the side of Jesus (Mt 27:19), his own people condemn him (Mt 27:25). Accompanied by an eschatological upheaval (Mt 27:51ff.; see also Mt 28:2–4), the death of Jesus provokes a collective confession of faith* (Mt 27:54).

Sometimes considered more of an historian, Luke moves the interrogation that Mark places at night to the morning (Lk 22:66–71) and adds an appearance before Herod (Lk 23:6–12). His narrative especially demonstrates the personal attachment of the disciple, seen in repeated affirmations of Jesus' innocence (Lk 23:4, 23:14–15, 23:22, and 23:41), insistent exhortations (Lk 22:40, 22:46, 23:28–31, and 23:40), and the omission of offensive and cruel details, including accounts of hostile witnesses, condemnation, and harsh treatment. The cross produces conversion* (23:47–48) and salvation* (23:42f.).

Very different from the others, John presents a glorifying passion (see Jn 12:27–28 and 17:1). Against their intention, Jesus' enemies contribute to the manifestation of his glory as sovereign (Jn 18:6–9), royal (Jn 18:33–37, 19:2–5, and 19:22), and filial (Jn 19:7–11). The passion is a "lifting up" (Jn 3:14, 8:28, 12:32–33). The episode of the piercing of Jesus' side demonstrates the fruitfulness of the passion and calls on us to contemplate the Crucified One (Jn 19:31–37).

The writings of the New Testament are unanimous in presenting the passion as the decisive victory of Christ and of God over evil* for the good of humanity. "By his blood" the sacrificial Lamb* has redeemed us and made of us "a kingdom and priests" (Rev 5:10), able to conquer by his blood (Rev 12:11).

- M. Dibelius (1943), "La signification religieuse des récits évangéliques de la passion," RHPhR 13, 30–45.
- K. H. Schelkle (1949), Die P. Jesu in der Verkündigung des Neuen Testaments, Heidelberg.
- X. Léon-Dufour (1960), "Passion (Récits de la)," DBS 6, 1419–92.
- J. Blinzler (1969), Der Prozeß Jesu, 4th Ed., Regensburg.
- P. Benoit (1966), Passion et résurrection du Seigneur, Paris.
- A. Vanhoye (1967), "Structure et théologie des récits de la passion dans les évangiles synoptiques," NRTh 89, 135–63.
- La mort du Christ (1971), LV(L) 20, 2–121.
- L. Marin (1971), Sémiotique de la passion, Paris.
- H. Cohn (1972), The Trial and Death of Jesus, London.
- G. S. Sloyan (1973), Jesus on Trial, Philadelphia.
- F. Bovon (1974), Les derniers jours de Jésus, Neuchâtel.
- H. Cousin (1976), Le prophète assassiné, Paris.
- M. Hengel (1976), "Mors Turpissima Crucis: Die Kreuzigung in der antiken Welt und die 'Torheit' des 'Wortes vom Kreuz,'" in Rechtfertigung. Festschrift für E. Käsemann, 125–84, Tübingen.
- X. Léon-Dufour (1979), Face à la mort, Jésus et Paul, Paris.
- M. Hengel (1981), La crucifixion dans l'Antiquité et la folie du message de la croix (trans. of Mors Turpissima... and other texts), Paris.
- M. Limbeck (Ed.) (1981), Redaktion und Theologie des Passionsberichtes nach den Synoptikern, WdF 481.
- Coll. (1985), Narrativité et théologie dans les récits de la passion, RSR 73, 6–244.
- I. de la Potterie (1986), La passion de Jésus selon l'Évangile de Jean, Paris.
- M. Gourgues (1989), Le Crucifié, Montréal.
- K. Kertelge (Ed.) (1989), Der Prozeß gegen Jesus, Freiberg.
- R. Meynet (1993), Passion de Notre Seigneur Jésus-Christ, Paris.
- R. Brown (1994), The Death of the Messiah, New York.
- S. Légasse (1994), Le procès de Jésus, Paris.

ALBERT VANHOYE

See also **Death; Eucharist; Expiation; Gospels; Jesus, Historical; Lamb of God/Paschal Lamb; Passover; Sacrifice; Salvation; Scripture, Fulfillment of; Servant of YHWH; Violence**

B. Systematic Theology

If the term *the passion of Christ* designates the totality of Jesus' suffering, from his agony in the garden to his death and burial, as stated above, it also refers to an essential aspect of the mystery* of Jesus Christ and his Easter experience; the aspect that precedes and conditions the resurrection* and that could also be designated by the word *cross*. The New Testament clearly shows the prominent place that Christian faith*, from its very beginning, accorded to the passion and the cross of Christ as it was understood. Neither the great patristic tradition* nor contemporary theology* lags behind in this respect. For clarity, it is useful to distinguish and to bring together four aspects: historical, eschatological, soteriological, and theological.

1) Historical Event

There is no doubt that Jesus* died on the cross after a hurried trial and after having experienced a harsh night of anguish. Jesus suffered various kinds of ill treatment, was abandoned by his disciples, and was mocked by the soldiers who had come to seize him, as well as by the curious mob that had followed him. Not only cruel but dishonorable, the torture of the cross, as practiced by the Romans, was used particularly against slaves and against conquered enemies whom they wished to deride (Tacitus, *Hist.* IV. 11). This element alone is enough to indicate that the execution of Jesus had a political character, as indicated moreover by the inscription on the cross stating, "This is Jesus the King of the Jews" (Mt 27:37). However, Jesus was handed over to Pilate, representing Roman authority, by the Sanhedrin, the religious ruling body of the Jewish people, which was determined to bring him down with the accusation of blasphemy (Mt 26:57–66). Jesus had in fact claimed "I am able to destroy the temple of God, and to build it in three days" (Mt 26:61). He had thereby—as with his behavior in general toward the sabbath*, sin*, and God* himself—undermined the principles and foundations of the Jewish religion and identified his person* with the fulfillment of the messianic hope* of his people*. Such blasphemy could only deserve death*.

But the passion and crucifixion of Jesus did not result only from the condemnation of human powers in opportunistic complicity with one another. These events were also, and even primarily, situated not only by a very conscious determination on the part of Jesus himself, but also—the first disciples soon discovered it—in the perspective of the fulfillment of a paradoxical divine intention. Just as much as it is intent on emphasizing the historicity of the passion, so is Christian faith intent on making it known that the passion enacted a drama that goes far beyond history*: In and through the passion of Jesus, God himself was "involved" (Balthasar*). The simple fact that the different New Testament traditions do not agree on the moment of the crucifixion shows that the evangelists wish to make their readers attentive to a meaning that goes beyond pure and simple historical fact. Whereas the synoptics present the Last Supper of Jesus as the new Passover, John by contrast places Jesus' death on the day of preparation for the Jewish Passover (John 19:14) in order to make Jesus appear as the true paschal lamb (John 19:36). In either case, the same historical reality is in question; the same event is being described. Contemporary scholarship tends to judge that John's version is more accurate; with the help of astronomical calculations, it has even specified that Jesus probably died on 7 April of the year 30.

2) Eschatological Dimension

The very motives that led Jesus to his passion and cross give the facts of the events a genuinely eschatological import. The accusation of blasphemy is revealing in this respect. In his attitude toward the temple, as in his public behavior as a whole, Jesus had expressed a veritable "demand for transcendence," a real "claim" (W. Pannenberg): a claim to echo in his speech (in the antitheses of the Sermon on the Mount, and in the invocation of God as "Abba") the very "authority" of God; a claim to set forth in his action (the miracles* and exorcisms*, the meals with sinners, and the forgiveness of sins) the signs of the coming of the kingdom of God, only hoped for until then. With his coming and his public ministry, in his personal fate, and finally in his very being, the eschatological times were beginning. What until then had been only promised and expected, or only present "figuratively," was now beginning to be fulfilled "in actions and in truth*." The end of time had arrived, salvation* had been definitively offered, and the "new and eternal covenant*" according to God's plan had been established.

This was the reading that the disciples of Jesus thought they should make of his life, and of his passion and death, after they had been led to experience and confess his resurrection. But this post-Easter reading of the passion and the cross was nonetheless in direct consonance with what had gradually and with increasing clarity entered into Jesus' own consciousness throughout his public ministry, as he confronted the re-actions he provoked. Even if their formulation reflects in part a *vaticinia ex eventu*, there can be no doubt that the three foreshadowings of the passion (Mk 8:31, 9:31, and 10:33–34 and parallels) refer to the word and hence the consciousness of Jesus himself; the parable* of the wicked tenants (Mk 12:1–12) is sufficient evidence. The accounts of the Last Supper confirm it. Very probably authentic, the statement: "Truly, I say to you, I shall not drink again of the fruit of the vine until that day when I drink it new in the kingdom of God" (Mark 14:25), clearly shows that Jesus was convinced of two things. While, on the one hand, the passion and death toward which he was moving, and that he anticipated with the signs of bread and wine, seemed directly related to the eschatological character of his mission, they also seemed to him to make up both the culminating point and the basis for interpretation of that mission.

3) Soteriological Effect

Recognizing that the historical reality of the passion-cross-death sequence has an eschatological dimension implies the simultaneous recognition of its soteriological effect. According to Christian faith this sequence occupies an essential place in the revelatory and salvific plan of God. Why and how? An answer to these questions requires the development of a theology of salvation* and an understanding of how to interpret the cross and the death of Jesus as sacrifice*. However, it is appropriate first to specify the basis on which this confession of faith was developed. The essential point lies in the fact that, on the part of Jesus, the passion does not appear as something merely undergone, but rather clearly foreseen and formally accepted, in obedience to the mysterious and yet entirely loving will of the Father*. Indeed, this is the meaning Jesus' words one two occasions. The first are spoken in prayer during his agony in Gethsemane: "My Father, if it be possible, let this cup pass from me; nevertheless, not as I will, but as thou wilt' (Mt 26:39 and parallels; Mk 14:36 adds the Hebrew *Abba*). Jesus makes the second utterance just before his death on the cross: "My God, my God, why hast thou forsaken me?" (Mk 15:34 and Mt 27:46), for this final expression is not only a cry of distress but also an invocation addressed to the Father in total surrender "into thy hands I commit my spirit" (*see* Lk 23:46).

In relation to the will of Jesus fulfilling the will of the Father, the passion seems to be set under the sign of a radical "for us" outside of which it would be only a nonsense and a scandal. Having come "for us and for our salvation," Jesus went to his death and gave himself up to it—during the Last Supper Jesus offered the gift of his life "for many" (Mk 14:24). This was to show how far the sin of human beings would go, for they would turn out to be capable of putting to death the "Holy and Righteous One" of God (Acts 3:14). It would also reveal to them that not only were they not rejected, but that God's forgiveness was mercifully offered to them and that they continued to be loved by him despite all their sins, which they could now repent. All faith in salvation as the redemption brought by Christ originates there.

This point is all the more important because it merely brings to fulfillment—"to the end" (Jn 13:1)—what was characteristic of the teaching, the activity, and the existence of Jesus, because "the Son of man also came not to be served but to serve, and to give his life as a ransom for many" (Mk 10:45). Similarly, according to his explicit teaching, believing in him, following in his footsteps, and being able to benefit from the salvation that he brings means that his disciples are also called upon to make themselves "the last of all and servant of all" (Mk 9:35 and parallels). Each believer in Christ must in turn "take up his cross" (Mk 8:34). Through the ordeals of the apostolic ministry*, the apostle* is led to supplement "what is lacking in Christ's afflictions for the sake of his body, that is, the church" (Col 1:24). We know the position held by the cross in the great Christian spiritual and mystical tradition (mysticism* of the passion or of the cross).

4) Theological Meaning

The fact remains, however, that the passion of Jesus could have that eschatological dimension and soteriological effect only to the degree that God himself was able to act through it and even truly engage himself in it. How can such a thing be accepted? How is it possible to reconcile weakness and suffering, abandonment, and even ignominy on the one hand, and sovereignty, lordship, and omnipotence—in other words, divinity—on the other?

a) The Scripture is clear: the hymn of Philippians 2:6–11 celebrates the *kenosis* * of the one "who though he was in the form of God...emptied himself, taking the form of a servant...and being found in human form he humbled himself and became obedient unto death, even death on a cross" But taking on the *condition* of servant did not bring about the loss of the divine *condition.* Christian faith asserts that it was as a man, and according to the common human condition—apart from sin, but including suffering and death—that Christ was incarnated, as God-the-Son in humanity.

The patristic tradition strove to hold the two aspects of the mystery together: the reality of the incarnation* of the Word (thus including vulnerability to suffering and death) and the truth of the Word's divinity (despite the undermining of the immutability* and hence the impassibility that Greek philosophy* in general and Neoplatonic philosophy in particular considered characteristic of the divine). Ignatius of Antioch is a good example of this when he speaks of "the Timeless, the Unseen, the One who became visible for our sakes, who was beyond touch and passion, yet who for our sakes became subject to suffering and endured everything for us" (*To Polycarp* III. 2; *see also* Irenaeus*, *Adversus haereses* IV. 20. 4 and Tertullian*, *De Carne Christi* V. 4). There were many debates, from the Trinitarian controversies of the second half of the third century, those surrounding monarchianism and modalism* and Sabellianism, with the Patripassianism that they implied (Noetus in Smyrna and Praxeas in Carthage, attacked by Tertullian in Carthage and Hippolytus in Rome*), down to the Theopaschite dispute of the sixth century involving Scythian monks and their formulation: "The one of the Trinity* was crucified." But the aspect of the "communication of idioms*" that was at issue was finally understood by the Alexandrians as well as the Antiochenes and the Latins in the orthodox sense of the doctrine of Ephesus on the *Theotokos* (*DS* 263).

Several Fathers* of the Church, however, expressed original views, which contemporary theology will have occasion to reconsider. Origen* (*De Principiis* IV.2.4) pointed out that it would be less surprising that the Son was able to share our misery—and the Father himself experience something of human suffering—if it were seen that the entire "economy " is governed by divine compassion and mercy*. Hilary* (*De Trinitate.* VIII.45), Gregory* of Nyssa (*Cathechetical Orations*), and others suggested that this be seen not as the indication of a limit but as a sign of sovereign power and freedom. Maximus* the Confessor, arguing against monophysitism* and its monothelite revival, explained (Constantinople* III) that the existence in Christ of a complete human nature that remained distinct from divine nature—within the very union according to the single person of the Word*—permitted a true theology of the agony of Gethsemane.

b) Strongly shaped by the metaphysical approach, Scholastic* theology was on this point strongly challenged by the *theologia crucis* of Luther*. But although the theory of the "communication of idioms*" that Luther advocated clearly articulated the elements of the problem, it did not resolve it, as was shown by the development of the dispute over *kenosis* through the 16th and 17th centuries (schools of Giessen and Tübingen). German idealist philosophy—Hegel*, of course, above all—and the so-called *kenotic* theology derived from it in the 19th and 20th centuries in Germany, England,

and Russia, further sharpened awareness of the importance of what was at stake: If the Absolute must necessarily "externalize" itself, does it remain the Absolute? If it cannot, can Christ continue to be considered God? If it does, to what extent can we recognize a true humanity in Jesus in whom it is supposed to reveal itself?

c) All contemporary theologies, from that of "the death of God" and "*process* theology" to the dialectical theology of Karl Barth* and the existential theology of Rudolf Bultmann*, and even "liberation* theology," have dealt more or less systematically with these questions, in confrontation with the "hard word" characteristic of modernity: "God is dead." All modern theologians recognize that they still have to confront this assertion. At least three of them—J. Moltmann and E. Jüngel on the one hand, and Hans Urs von Balthasar* on the other—have fostered significant advances in thinking, which we will describe briefly in concluding.

Among their propositions, the following elements are especially important: 1) The coming of the Son of God into humanity (incarnation) quite logically entailed that he had to experience passion and death, and even "descent* into Hell." 2) This represents neither an "alienation" nor a de-divinization of God, nor the manifestation in him of a limit, a lack, or a necessity, but the sovereignty free expression of a radical movement that can only be designated by the word "love*." 3) As a consequence, far from opposing to what indeed presents itself as a *kenosis* an objection derived from a preconceived idea of "God," we should make an effort to decipher his "essence" by starting with what he himself revealed of it in coming himself to open the way of Salvation to "what is not himself." 4) Beginning with that, we should learn to recognize that the divine power (omnipotence*, divine) is of the order of a love that is "communication," and a total "surrender" of the self. Such a love certainly entails and brings about some "effects of vulnerability," but that does not prevent him from being *all*-powerful. 5) In order to be effective in history, the self-communication of God must, however, already be verified from all eternity in the divine immanence itself. "The eternal intra-divine distinction between the Father and the Son is the theological-transcendental condition for the possibility of the self-alienation of God in the incarnation and on the cross (W. Kasper). As a consequence, it is the condition of his self-revelation*.

● *See* bibliography for Christ and Christology.
P. Henry (1957), "Kénose," *DBS* 5, 7–161.
J. Blinzler (1960), *Der prozess Jesu.*
X. Léon-Dufour (1960), "Passion (récits de la)," *DBS* 6, 1419–92; id. (1963), *Les Évangiles et l'histoire de Jésus,* Paris.

Th. Ogletree (1966), *The Death of God Controversy,* Nashville-New York.

H. U. von Balthasar (1969), "Mysterium Paschale," *MySal,* III/2, Einsiedeln (*Mysterium Salutis,* vol. 12, 1972).

H. Schürmann (1975), *Jesu ureigener Tod,* Leipzig.

E. Brito (1978), *Hegel et la tâche actuelle de la christologie,* Paris-Namur.

X. Léon-Dufour (1979), *Face à la mort: Jésus et Paul,* Paris; id. (1982), *Le partage du pain eucharistique selon le Nouveau Testament,* Paris.

F.-M. Léthel (1979), *Théologie de l'Agonie du Christ,* Paris.

C. Perrot (1979), *Jésus et l'histoire,* Paris.

A. Gounelle (1981), *Le dynamisme créateur de Dieu: Essai sur la théologie du Process,* Montpellier (*ETR* special issue).

M. Hengel (1981), *La crucifixion dans l'Antiquité et la folie du message de la Croix* (original French ed.), Paris.

W. Kasper (1982), *Der Gott Jesu Christi,* Mayence.

B. Sesboüé (1982), *Jésus-Christ dans la tradition de l'Église,* Paris; id. (1988, 1991), *Jésus-Christ, l'unique Médiateur,* vols. I and II, Paris.

M. Lienhard (1991), *Au cœur de la foi de Luther: Jésus-Christ,* Paris.

S. Légasse (1994–95), *Le procès de Jésus,* vols. I and II, Paris.

O. González de Cardedal (1997), *La entraña del cristianismo,* Salamanca, 523–618, "La muerte de Jesús: símbolo, crimen, misterio."

U. Köpf (1997), "Passionsfrömmigkeit," *TRE,* 27, 722–64.

JOSEPH DORÉ

See also **Balthasar, Hans Urs von; Christ and Christology; Constantinople III, Council of; Descent into Hell; Ephesus, Council of; Jesus, Historical; Kenosis; Monophysitism; Monothelitism/Monoenergism; Resurrection of Christ; Salvation; Trinity**

Passions

a) *Hellenistic Background.* For the Greeks, the problem of the passions revolved around two notions: self-rule *(autarkeia)* and self-control *(egkrateia).* Reason endows whoever possesses it with a measure of self-sufficiency and free choice. By contrast, the passions are involuntary perturbations of the soul* that threaten and sometimes eclipse reason. The question is the extent to which *egkrateia* can achieve and preserve *autarkeia* by repressing the passions or making them serve rational ends.

Both Plato and Aristotle insisted that virtue* involves subordinating the passions to reason: the morally imperfect life is the fruit of ignorance and passions. According to Plato, the passions are diseases, engendered by a principle of covetousness *(to epithumetikon)* and a principle of anger *(to thumikon),* both opposed to the principle of reason *(to logistikon)* (*Rep.* IV, 439 *d*–41 *c*). It should be noted, however, that the principle of anger is also the principle of a virtue, that is, the principle of courage. Aristotle takes a different line. Because the order of the passions is that of motions imposed upon us, passions do not make human beings either good or bad (*EN* II, 1105 *b* 29–06 *a* 2). The order of the virtues and vices is not that of motion, but of disposition; yet Aristotle certainly draws a contrast between "living in accordance with passions" and the rational life (I, 1095 *a* 8–10; IX, 1169 *a* 1–5). Stoicism goes further. Identifying the rational and happy life with *apatheia,* the absence of feeling, and with *ataraxia,* the absence of internal disturbance, Stoicism in fact entailed identifying the passions with vices. Alongside *patheia,* passions that, as such, were seen as being contrary to nature, the Stoics also identified some *eupatheia,* "good" passions, such as joy, circumspection *(eulabeia),* and will; but such observations did not detract from their generally hostile attitude.

b) *Early Christian Discussions.* To begin with, these discussions do not stand out against the intellectual background of late antiquity. In the apostolic and suba-postolic literature, the passions as such are neither affirmed nor rejected. Attention to the passions is generally limited to warnings against anger and "carnal lusts" (Jas 4:1, 1 Pt 2:11; *Didache* 1, 4; *2 Clem.* 10). However, the literature of early Christian asceticism* is at times contemptuous of the passions, while the more urbane attitude of a moralist such as Clement of Alexandria seems thoroughly stoical: "the sacrifice that is acceptable to God is unswerving abstraction from the body and its passions" (*Stromata* 5, 11, 67). As late as the fourth century, even the most orthodox christological reflections display a certain reluctance to associate the passions with the perfect human nature of Jesus*.

Autarkeia is not an ultimate value in the New Testament, where the term appears only in 2 Corinthians 9:8 and 1 Timothy 6:6, in addition to *autarkes* in Philippians 4:11, and all three occurrences are unemphatic. Reason and liberty* are fulfilled in desire for God, and hence in the surrender of autonomy. It is this surrender that true *egkrateia* both assists in and reflects (Hermas, *Shepherd* 2, 1–5). This relativization of *autarkeia* goes hand in hand with Christian affirmation of the body and its passibility. These developments positively affected Christian attitudes to the passions in three ways. First, the integration of passivity into the notion of human reason enabled theology* to distinguish less sharply between the realm of reason and the realm of the passions. Second, the new dignity attached both to the body and to its suffering was reflected in the dignity accorded to the passions themselves. Finally, increasing respect for the body, in the light of the incarnation* of the Word* and the resurrection* of the flesh* yielded a corresponding respect for the passions, inasmuch as these demonstrate the close connection between body and soul. The improved moral status of the passions is illustrated early on in the Epistles of Ignatius of Antioch, who comes close to equating the emotional passion of the Christian in his life of prayer*, the physical passion of Christian martyrdom, and the spiritual passion of the rational soul as it yields itself in faith to the divine initiative (e.g., *Ad Romanos* 6). In all three senses, passion rivals *autarkeia* as a mark of moral action* and spiritual attainment. Another positive conception of the passions was provided by Lactantius († c. 325–30), for whom, by contrast to both Aristotelianism and Stoicism, *affectus* ("passion") "is like a natural fecundity of souls" (CSEL 19, 337). However, ethical condemnation of the passions continued within Monachism: thus, Evagrius, with his teaching of *praktike* (monastic asceticism), reprises the theme of *apatheia*, making it into "the flower of practice" (SC 171, 670).

c) Augustine and Later Christian Thought.

The Christian reversal of values achieved its clearest articulation in Augustine*. For him, sin* lies not in the unruly passions but in the rational will that refuses to be moved by God, and so becomes enslaved by passion for created things. However, true love* of God is itself a kind of passion, and it brings virtuous passions in its train. Far from standing in opposition to the rational will, the passions, whether virtuous or vicious, reveal the will's true inclinations. The healthy soul will experience healthy passions, including grief and anger, and

Augustine is loath to deny that the saints in heaven will experience at least the passions of joy and holy fear.

The exception to Augustine's general account of the passions is his treatment of sexual desire, which can be rightly used but never innocently felt. It is notoriously easy to misread Augustine on this point. Despite his emphasis on the involuntary character of *libido,* Augustine's negativity about sex is not a return to the glorification of *autarkeia.* On the contrary, Augustine insists that the involuntary character of sexual passion is the punishment inflicted on prideful reason, which has placed a higher value on self-rule than on submission to being ruled by God. It is not because sexual desire is a passion that Augustine condemns it, but because it is the otherwise unnecessary sign of spiritual perversity (*Civ. Dei* 14, 15). Whatever else we may say about Augustine's view of sex, it does not constitute a rejection of the passions as such.

Thomas* Aquinas also locates sin in reason than in the passions, and provides an analysis of the connection between the passions, embodiment, and rational desire (*STh* Ia IIae, q. 22–48). Nevertheless, Aquinas's subordination of will to intellect leads him to deemphasize the intentional character of reason, thus opening a conceptual gap between desire and reason, and laying the groundwork for the problematizing of the notion of rational desire.

d) Modern and Contemporary Discussions.

In the early modern period, a few theologians—notably Jonathan Edwards*—testified to continuing interest in the passions as indicators of the soul's love for God, or lack thereof. Mostly, however, the early moderns betray two contradictory tendencies: either identifying reason with cognition only (e.g., Descartes, in an era marked, in France, by a renewal of interest in the Stoic theory of the passions); or unmasking reason as a function of "mere" passions and drives (e.g., David Hume [1711–76], *Treatise on Human Nature* 2, 2, 3). The second tendency has proved to be the more common one. Freud* asserts (with Augustine) that human reason is a dynamic of desire, but also claims (unlike Augustine) that reason is the expression of unconscious drives. Thus, the intentionality of reason reveals the irrationality of reason, and this irrational reason is in the service of passions whose object is only survival or pleasure.

Kant*'s moral project attempts once again to ground the rational will in the idea of a transcendent moral law*. Kant's project may be understood largely as the recovery of Augustine's understanding of reason, but this recovery is not possible without paying a high price: reason loses its passivity before God. Kant rehabilitates practical reason by defending it from any imputation of passivity: the "good will" is an autonomous legislator, free from the constraint or impulsion of any inclination, passion or divine command.

Recent theological discussion of the passions has been allied to an attempt to develop an understanding of rational desire that avoids the voluntarist and "decisionist" tendencies of Kantian ethics*, as well as the determinist presuppositions of Freudian psychology (McClendon 1986). This project involves attention to the human body, understood as the irreducible datum of selfhood (Ricoeur 1950, Wyschogrod 1990); reinterpretation of reason as a bodily and passionate faculty (Henry 1965); consideration of the moral status of human suffering (Porée 1993); and meditation upon the resurrection as it relates to Christian attitudes to embodiment (Bruaire 1968). At stake is the coherence of a Christian notion of freedom that also insists on human passivity in relation to the pure agency of God. At stake, also, is the making of passion into virtue.

THOMAS E. BREIDENTHAL

● J. Edwards (1746), *A Treatise Concerning Religious Affections*, repr. Grand Rapids, Mich., 1982.
K. Kirk (1931), *The Vision of God*, London, 312–19.
P. Ricœur (1950), *Le volontaire et l'involontaire*, Paris.
J. N. D. Kelly (1958), *Early Christian Doctrines*, London (2nd Ed. 1977), 280–309.
S. Pfürtner (1958), *Triebleben und sittliche Vollendung*, Fribourg (Switzerland).
M. Henry (1965), *Philosophie et phénoménologie du corps*, Paris.
C. Bruaire (1968), *Philosophie du corps*, Paris.
J. Lanz (1971), "Affekte," *HWP* 1, 89–100.
M. Miles (1979), *Augustine on the Body*, Missoula, Mont.
A. Solignac (1984), "Passions et vie spirituelle," *DSp* 12/1, 339–57.
J. McClendon (1986), *Ethics*, Nashville, Tenn., 79–155.
P. Brown (1988), *The Body and Society: Men, Women and Sexual Renunciation in Early Christianity*, London.
E. Wyschogrod (1990), *Saints and Postmodernism*, Chicago.
G. C. Harak (1993), *Virtuous Passions*, New York.
J. Porée (1993), *La philosophie à l'épreuve du mal: Pour une phénoménologie de la souffrance*, Paris.
D. Kambouchner (1996), "Passions," *DEPhM*, 1081–87.

See also **Ethics; Ethics, Autonomy of; Ethics, Sexual; Voluntarism**

Passover

A. Biblical Theology

a) Origin of the Passover and Ritual.   Originally, the Passover was a celebration for shepherds, whose flocks were their most important and most precious resource. This origin explains why the Passover was distinct from the other feasts of Israel*, in particular from the three pilgrimage* celebrations that are mentioned in the oldest liturgical calendars (Ex 23:14–17, 34:18–23) and that are indicative of a sedentary society (feast of unleavened bread, feast of weeks, feast of booth). The Passover is a spring festival; the celebration takes place at night, during the full moon; it brings together the whole family*. With the sacrifice of a year-old animal*, which is either a lamb or a kid, the head of the family fulfilled the ritual of the blood, and then he presided over a meal for which the flesh of the victim had been roasted. The ritual of the blood and the Passover supper are the most characteristic elements of the ancient Arabic sacrifice* and of the Israelites' Passover (J. Henninger).

The ritual of the blood consisted in anointing the poles of the tent with the blood of the paschal victim; it was an apotropaic ritual, with magical properties, intended to avert hostile powers and to protect the dwelling as well as those who live in it. Was it also aimed at protecting the cattle? This is possible, but the signs of such a practice in Pre-Islamic Arabia are extremely rare. In any case, the ritual was intended to ward off some beings outside the dwelling, since the anointing of blood was done only on the poles and on the lintel of the entrance (Ex 12:23). The blood ritual was to be associated with the ritual of the supper, which complemented it by representing communion* with the deity who dispenses rain and bestows fecundity on the flock. The Passover required neither sanctuary nor priest; it was a nocturnal celebration by the family.

According to Exodus 12:21ff., which is probably the oldest written account of the Passover, there is a relation between the ritual and YHWH's action that strikes Egypt and spares the homes of the Israelites. Next to God*, the written account presents another character, also capable of striking: he is the "destroying angel," whose identity is unclear. In this written account, he is a personal being (Ex 12:23), whereas another written account (Ex 12:13) transforms him into an impersonal power, in order to ensure the preeminence of the God of Israel. This destroying angel has been identified as the god of the plague in 2 Samuel 24, but the identification is far from certain. The destroying angel's presence is an element of the original Passover, but in the biblical account he is placed in a relationship of dependence with YHWH. He may have the power to strike, but he cannot do it against the Israelites. Although the account given in Exodus 12, 21 *Sq* does not mention the ritual of the supper, it must indeed have been real, but the Passover commemorates first of all the divine protection granted to the people of Israel.

b) Reform of the Passover. The oldest among the liturgical calendars (Ex 23:14–17, 34:18–23) do not mention the Passover, but Deuteronomy places it at the top of the calendar: "Observe the month of Abib and keep the Passover to the Lord your God, for in the month of Abib the Lord your God brought you out of Egypt by night" (Dt 16:1). The Passover is a nocturnal celebration related to the Exodus from Egypt. The main ritual, the sacrifice of the paschal victim, must take place in ""the evening at sunset" (Dt 16:6). This indication is reinforced by the order to go back home in the morning (16:7). The celebration lasts from evening to morning, but that was possible only at the time when the Passover was not yet linked to the feast of the unleavened bread, which lasts seven days. This link was definitively established at the time of the postexilic calendars (Lv 23:5–8; Nb 28:16ff., 25), but was already present in Deuteronomy 16:3–8, in which the seven-day duration necessarily included the feast of the unleavened bread.

The ritual, in Deuteronomy 16, is not greatly developed. The emphasis is on the place where the victim is sacrificed: ""in the place that the Lord your God will choose" (16:5ff.). From then on the Passover becomes an official sacrifice celebrated in the central sanctuary. Furthermore, the animal that is being sacrificed may be taken from among the bigger cattle, which is a new feature; but this is easily understandable in a farming economy based in part on cattle-rearing. The victim must be cooked and not roasted, as was the case in the older ritual. Deuteronomy 16 tells of a paschal ritual in the local sanctuaries at a time prior to the end of the eighth century B.C.

Originally a family rite, in Deuteronomy the Passover becomes an action that all the Israelites celebrate when they come to Jerusalem*; it is the action that reunites the people* in order that they may proclaim their faith* to the God who made possible their Exodus from Egypt. The Passover is thus a national celebration that contributes to unity among people, but it seems that such a significance was attributed to the celebration before the reign of Josias (*see* 2 Kgs 23:21ff.). The allusions to the Passover in the book of Is (30:29, 31:5: *psch*) date back to the reign of that king.

c) Passover According to Exodus 12:3–14. The most precise text regarding the Passover and its ritual is still Exodus 12:3–14. In it, the Passover is carefully dissociated, in the way it unfolds, from the celebration of the unleavened bread (Ex 12:15–21). The Passover must be celebrated in the first month of the year (12:2), in a calendar that starts in the spring, another departure from the preexilic custom that placed the start of the year in the autumn. The victim must be obtained on the tenth day of the first month and kept apart until the 14th, which is to become the date of the Passover (Lv 23:5); the throat of the victim is slit between the two evenings (Ex 12:16) and the Passover meal should take place at night (12:8). The ritual is described in great detail, including the description of the clothes that the participants must wear. In contrast to what is recorded in Deuteronomy, the ritual goes back to ancient customs; the ritual of the blood has its place, as in the original Passover; the victim is taken from among the smaller animals, lamb or kid; it is roasted on the fire. The celebration does not take place in the sanctuary; the meal is taken at home (12:43–46); the blood must be used to anoint the poles and the lintels of the houses (12:7, 13). The vocabulary of sacrifice does not appear in this written account; likewise, there is no mention of an altar. The motive of the celebration remains, however, the same: it is to celebrate the fact that YHWH punished the Egyptians and spared the Israelites as they were coming out of Egypt. The Passover must serve as a memorial for the people of Israel (12:14).

This text from Exodus 12:3–14 takes up an ancient ritual. But why the concern to be absolutely precise? The text may have helped the people to observe the Passover during their exile, when, deprived of a sanctuary, they found themselves no longer capable of celebrating the pilgrimage feasts. It is also understandable why all these precise instructions were placed in the book of Exodus before the episode on Sinai, during which God gave Moses his instructions concerning the way to organize the ritual of worship.

It should be mentioned, however, that the celebration of the Passover and that of the unleavened bread are connected to the Exodus from Egypt and are linked to the law* concerning the firstborn (Ex 13:1f.; 11–16). This link finds its explanation in the account of the 10th plague (Ex 11), which befalls the firstborn of Egypt, a scourge that the Israelites are spared thanks to the paschal victim's blood (Ex 12:13). For this reason, Exodus 13:15 declares that all the firstborn of man must be "redeemed." This does not mean, however, that the Passover is transformed into a ritual of offering concerning the firstborn of the flock.

d) Judaism and the New Testament. In early Judaism* the paschal celebration gave rise to the development of a genuine theology*. Thus, the Targum interpretive tradition* links the Passover with the episode of Genesis 22 on the binding *(aquedah)* of Isaac, as expressed in the poem of the "four nights" (Le Déaut 1963). The night of the Passover, memorial of salvation* for Israel, is also a reminder of God's covenant* with Abraham (*see* Gn 15:13f.), and also signals a future liberation (according to Wis 18:6).

In the New Testament, the Passover occupies a decisive place on two accounts. On the one hand, the death* of Jesus* takes place in the context of the Passover. Thus, in the Gospel* of John there is a recurrent mention of the Passover (Jn 2:13, 6:4, 11:55; *see* 5:1), but above all Jesus died on the day of the Passover, as Jerusalem was experiencing the influx of a crowd of pilgrims for the feast. On the other hand, the meaning of Jesus' death is enhanced by the paschal symbolism. Jesus is the true paschal lamb* (Jn 1:29, 36, *see* Rev 5:6, 12); he was immolated at the time when the lambs intended for the paschal supper were being sacrificed in the Temple* (Jn 18:28, 19:36 quoting Ex 12:46 and Ps 34:21). Paschal symbolism can also be found in the synoptic Gospels, where the Last Supper (Eucharist*) has the characteristics of a paschal meal (Mt 26:26–29; Mk 14:22–25; Lk 22:14–20); and also in Paul (1 Cor 11:23). In the parable of the ten virgins (Mt 25:6), the arrival of the spouse in the middle of the night is a reminder of the messianic expectation linked to the paschal night.

- R. de Vaux (1960), *Les institutions de l'Ancien Testament,* vol. II, Paris, 383–94.
  R. Le Déaut (1963), *La nuit pascale,* AnBib 22.
  R. Martin-Achard (1974), *Essai biblique sur les fêtes d'Israël,* Geneva, 29–51.
  J. Henninger (1975), *Les fêtes de printemps chez les Sémites et la Pâque israélite,* Paris.
  S. Ros Garmendia (1978), *La Pascua en el Antiguo Testamento,* 3rd Ed., Vitoria.

JACQUES BRIEND

See also **Book; Eucharist; Liturgy; Passion; Pilgrimage; Sacrifice; Scapegoat; Temple**

B. Paschal Mystery in the Liturgy

From a historical point of view the expression "paschal mystery" designates the event of the death* and of the resurrection* of Christ*; from a liturgical point of view it indicates the sum of rituals that celebrate that event, every year at Eastertide, and every day in the Eucharist*.

a) From the Origins to the Fourth Century. The expression "mystery of the Passover" *(to tou paskha mustèrion),* which first came into use in the second century (SC 123, 94; 27, 125) as an equivalent of the Pauline formula "mystery of Christ" (Col 4:3; Eph 3:4), designates the whole of God*'s saving plan, announced in the Old Testament and realized in Christ. In earlier times, when the notion of the Passover particularly evoked the Passion*, it referred mainly to the immolation of Christ (1 Cor 5:7) but also to the tension between death and resurrection, between abasement and exaltation, since the death of Christ is celebrated, in direct accordance with Johannine* theology, as the time of his glorification and as "the death out of which comes life."

The expression "paschal mystery" takes on a fairly different significance among those who, following Origen*, interpret the Passover as a rite of passage, in the allegorical sense that Philo of Alexandria had already attributed to it. In this context the expression designates what is deepest in the historical facts and in the accounts (narrative*) that concern the Passover; it designates their mystical (mysticism*) meaning: the flesh of the paschal lamb* represents the Scriptures, with which we must sustain ourselves (GCS 7, 218).

Augustine* gives the paschal mystery its definitive formulation by making a double synthesis between Passion and passage, and between the passage of Christ and the passage of man: "With his Passion, the

Lord passed from death to life, and thus he opened the way for us who believe in his Resurrection also to pass from death to life" (CChr.SL 40, 1791).

Augustine distinguishes the Passover, celebrated "as a mystery" *(in sacramento),* from Christmas, and from all the other feasts that are celebrated as commemorations. By celebrating the Passover as a mystery, Christians not only recall an event whose anniversary is upon them, but they also understand and greet with their faith* the meaning that this event has "for them" (CSEL 34, 2, 170).

b) From Paschal Mystery to Liturgical Year. The notion of paschal mystery went through a profound change toward the end of the fourth century. A *synthetic celebration* included until then all the events of the Passover in one unique dialectic of death and life, like a unique mystery actualizing all the history* of salvation*, from the Exodus to the Parousia*. From then onwards, with the growing importance granted to other feasts such as Christmas, and under the influence of the rituals being followed in Jerusalem*, an *analytical celebration* started to make its appearance; this distinguished the different events from one another and commemorated each one on its anniversary day. Consideration for the unity of the mystery yielded priority to a historical concern for distribution over time*. We go from a unique celebration of the Passover to the paschal cycle, and then to the liturgical* year. For Leo the Great, the central importance of the paschal mystery resided uniquely in the fact that it offered in one single event, and more richly, what the various mysteries celebrated throughout the year in a partial manner (PL 54, 301).

In short, the name of the Passover became synonymous with "the Sunday of the Resurrection*," and, save for very rare exceptions (e.g., Rupert de Deutz, CChr.CM 7, 207), this has remained so up to the present; it lost its organic link with the Passion of Christ, which tended, for its part, to move from the domain of mystery to that of piety. The Resurrection itself came to be considered from an apologetic angle, as an argument in favor of Christ and of the Church*, rather than for its significance as a mystery.

c) Rediscovery of the Paschal Mystery. In more recent times the reform of the paschal rituals under Pius XII, preceded by the liturgical movement and by the *Mysterienlehre* (Mystery) (Casel, L. Bouyer), brought about a revival of interest in the paschal mystery. The original unity of death and resurrection has been reaffirmed, as well as the saving characteristic that they possess by rights (F.-X. Durrwell). The expression "paschal mystery" is sometimes employed to designate the whole process of redemption (Balthasar*), and we are also seeing an attempt to refound on the paschal mystery—and on the cross in particular—everything up to the theology* of the Trinity* (J. Moltmann).

Having rediscovered within the paschal mystery the unity of death and resurrection, theology is applying itself nowadays to shedding light on the close unity between the Incarnation* and the paschal mystery, and, as a consequence of this, to uniting the Greek soteriology of deification (holiness*) with the Latin soteriology of atonement and of redemption (J.-P. Jossua, Balthasar). What remains to be achieved is a deeper understanding of Pentecost, as the coming of the Holy* Spirit, in relation to the Incarnation and the paschal mystery.

● O. Casel (1934), "Art und Sinn der ältesten christlichen Osterfeier," *JLW* 14, 1–78.
L. Bouyer (1945), *Le mystère pascal,* Paris.
Fr.-X. Durrwell (1950), *La résurrection de Jésus, mystère de salut,* Le Puy-Paris.
J. A. Pascual (1964), "El misterio pascual segùn san Leon Magno," *RET* 24, 299–319.
J.-P. Jossua (1968), *Le salut: Incarnation ou mystère pascal,* Paris.
H. U. von Balthasar (1969), "Mysterium paschale," *MySal* III/2, 133–392.
J. Moltmann (1972), *Der gekreuzigte Gott,* Munich.
R. Cantalamessa (1978), *La pasqua nella Chiesa antica,* Turin; id. (1985), *Il misterio pasquale,* Milan (3rd Ed. 1999).

RANIERO CANTALAMESSA

See also **Cult; Liturgy; Scripture, Senses of**

Pastor

From the Latin *pastor*, "shepherd," the pastor is the head of a local* church. He is also called *parochus*, in charge of a parish (Latin *parochia*, from the Greek *paroikia*). *Pastor* is the usual Protestant term used to designate the minister of the local community. It is through him that Christ* brings together and builds the flock (the *congregatio*). The Second Vatican* Council gave new currency to the term within Catholicism* and speaks of the bishop* as a pastor.

a) Biblical Elements. In the Old Testament the common notions of shepherd and flock are applied to the relations between Israel* and its leaders: the king is charged by God* to be a shepherd for the people. The function is often badly performed, and we frequently hear the lament of a flock without a shepherd (1 Kgs 22:17; Zec 10:2; and so on), or whose bad shepherds (Jer 23:1–2 and Ez 34:2–4) will feel the judgment of God come down on them (Jer 23:34 and Zec 11:3 and 11:17). The prophets (prophet* and prophecy) foretell new and good shepherds ("shepherds after my own heart" in Jer 3:15, Cyrus in Is 44:28, and a new David in Ez 34:23–24), in the service of God, the supreme shepherd of his people (Ps 23, 80:2; Is 40:11; Jer 31:10; and Ez 34:11–13).

In the New Testament, Christ is the good shepherd (Jn 10:2, 10:11, 10:14–16, 10:27–28), just as he is the Lamb* of God who gives his life for his own (Jn 10:11 and 10:15 and Reve 7:17; *see also* Lk 15:3–5). He will exercise his pastoral function at the Last Judgment (1 Pt 5:4; *see also* Mt 25:32–33). It is to this pastor that we must turn in order to be saved (1 Pt 2:25 and Heb 13:20). He sends his disciples to the lost sheep of the house of Israel (Mt 10:5–7; *see also* Mt 9:36–38), then to all nations (Mt 28:18–20; *see also* Acts 10). Peter* (Jn 21:15–17; *see also* Mt 16:17–19) occupies a privileged place in this pastoral mission that he transmits to the elders (1 Pt 5:1–3), as does Paul, who institutes presbyters (presbyter*/priest) to watch over the flock (Acts 20:17, 28–30). In order to maintain his Church*, God gives it prophets and evangelists, pastors and teachers (Eph 4:11; in this connection, *also see* the Pastoral Epistles, 1 and 2 Tm and Ti).

b) Ancient and Medieval Church. A common theme of early Christian art, the figure of the Good Shepherd was used by the Fathers* of the Church to evoke Christ and the "pastoral" function of bishops and priests (priesthood*). It was linked particularly to their teaching responsibility: "He who is *pastor* should also be *magister;* no one in the Church can take the name of pastor if he cannot be the teacher of those for whom he is the pastor," wrote Jerome (about 347–419; *Comm. Eph.*, 4, 11). Gregory* the Great was the author of a pastoral *(Liber Regulae Pastoralis)*. Pastoral responsibility was exercised in relation with the patriarchs, and, for the Latin Church, particularly with the bishop of Rome*. It was centered on the "cure of souls," *cura animarum,* the spiritual support of souls (soul*-heart-body). According to Thomas* Aquinas, the pastoral charge included *auctoritas* and *caritas.* In the Middle Ages, "pastoral" defined both the ministry* of the diocesan bishop and that of the parish priest.

c) Reformation Churches. The Lutheran Reformation introduced a new emphasis by focusing on the tasks of preaching* and catechesis*. In the local community, the pastor played the role of a bishop. He guarded its unity and acted as minister of the Word* and of the sacraments* (see *Augsburg Confession,* art. 5, 7, 14, and 28). In principle, by virtue of the universal priesthood*, every believer participated in the cure of souls, the *mutuum colloquium et consolatio fratrum (Articles of Smalcald,* art. 4); but this collective exercise of the pastoral ministry supplemented the particular ministry of the pastor without replacing it. In Calvinism*, the pastoral charge was the responsibility of four *offices* (pastor, elder, teacher, and deacon). In fulfilling his duty, the pastor would visit the faithful, lead the parish with the presbyters or elders (who were of the laity [lay*/laity]), and with them carry out church discipline (ecclesiastical* discipline). Pastors met frequently for sharing and spiritual development based on the study of the Holy* Scriptures. Pastor and presbyters led the consistory, which brought together several parishes, and they formed the synodal structure of a regional or national church. The deacons provided service for the poor and the ill; the teachers were responsible for schools and teaching (see *Ecclesiastical Ordinances from the Church of Geneva,* 1561). All churches derived from the Reformation generally adopted this conception, which required from the pastor a high level of competence (note, e.g., the pastoral robe, an indication of his university training). A particular place was reserved for the pastoral family, the *Protestant presbytery.* Since Luther*, pastors have generally been married and assisted in their duties by their spouses. The pastoral ministry today is no longer confined to men; women are often pastors.

d) Contemporary Catholicism. Vatican II, following in the footsteps of Vatican* I, "Teaches and declares with it that Jesus Christ, the eternal pastor, has built holy Church by sending his apostles (apostle*), as he himself had been sent by the Father* (*see* Jn 20:21); he wanted their successors, that is, the bishops, to be pastors in his Church until the end of time" (*LG* 18). The unity of pastors is derived from the pastoral ministry of the successor of Peter (*see* the constitution *Pastor Aeternus* of Vatican I). Vatican II has confirmed his primacy of the pope and his infallible magisterium*. It emphasizes the teaching duty of the bishops, inseparable from their priestly duty and their ministry of church government* (*LG* 20:24–27). Priests participate in the pastoral ministry of the bishop; they are ministers of the Word* and of the sacraments (sacrament*), and in the first place of the Eucharist*. They are assisted by deacons "in the 'deaconship' of the liturgy*, of the Word, and of charity" (*LG* 20, 28, and 29).

e) Current Problems. In the contemporary context, the pastoral ministry is confronted with a number of challenges. The proclamation of the Word, the celebration of the sacraments, the cure of souls, the concern for the unity and the government of the community all remain central. The many expectations of the parish and of society*, however, often make the pastor a "representative of the Church" who must provide for almost everything; and these demands, which presuppose an extraordinary availability may go beyond the human capacities of the pastor. His or her ministry also requires a high level of qualification (including in the areas of communication, pedagogy, and psychology), which gives rise to a tension between professionalism and vocation, and, in the highly institutionalized majority Churches, even a certain "bureaucratization" of the ministry. All confessional families have to meet these challenges.

- J.J. von Allmen (1956), *La vie pastorale,* Neuchâtel; id. (1964), *Le saint ministère selon la conviction et la volonté des réformés du XVIe siècle,* Neuchâtel.
- O. Semmelroth (1958), *Das geistliche Amt,* Frankfurt.
- N. Jossutis (1982), *Der Pfarrer ist anders: Aspekte einer zeitgenössischen Pastoraltheologie,* Munich.
- P. Barrau (1984), "Pastorale," *DSp* 12/1, 376–87.
- M. Greiffenhagen (Ed.) (1984), *Das evangelische Pfarrhaus,* Stuttgart.
- J.-M. Chappuis (1985), *La figure du Pasteur: Dimensions théologiques et composantes culturelles,* Geneva.
- J.-P. Willaime (1986), *Profession Pasteur: Sociologie de la condition du clerc à la fin du XXe siècle,* Geneva.
- P.-L. Dubied (1990), *Le pasteur, un interprète: Essai de théologie pastorale,* Geneva.
- G. Siegwalt (1992), *Dogmatique pour la catholicité évangélique* II/2, Paris-Geneva, 300–321, 354–76.

GÉRARD SIEGWALT

See also **Apostolic Succession; Bishop; Deacon; Local Church; Ministry; Ordination/Order; Presbyter/Priest**

Patriarchate

The title of patriarch was first used after the Council of Chalcedon*. It was long reserved for the most important sees, as determined by age, establishment by the apostles, and eminence of their position in the empire: Rome*, Constantinople (a "new Rome" after Constantinople* I)—Alexandria, Antioch, and Jerusalem*—under the jurisdiction of Caesarea in Palestine until Chalcedon assigned it the fifth place in order of precedence at the session of 26 October 451 (*see* G. Alberigo et al., *The Oecumeniques Councils* 1, History). These five patriarchates, which the imperial *novelles* (or constitutions) called the five senses of the empire, made up what was called the "pentarchy." This was the group of influential bishoprics that divided up the "inhabited world" (or the known world), the *oikumenè,* into spheres of influence in which each patriarch presided over the election of metropolitans and diocesan bishops (bishop*) and heard appeals. (For Rome, Alexandria, and Antioch, *see* Nicaea* I, can. 6.) Each of these patriarchates was an "autocephalous" church (one that chose its own primate, as distinguished from an "autonomous" church, the primate of which was chosen with the participation of the primate of an autocephalous church). Not included in the pentarchy was the Church of Cyprus, which had been made autocephalous by the Council of Ephesus* ("Vote," *DCO,* 160–61), and whose primate was an archbishop not a patriarch. Thus a patriarchate was a group of metropolises, capitals of provinces, presided over by a patriarch, generally corresponding, especially since the beginning of the Constantine period, to administrative divisions of the empire. A metropolis, presided over by a metropolitan or a metropolite, grouped together a certain number of dioceses (a diocese being a city with an Episcopal see, together with its dependent territory). These dioceses and metropolises met periodically, under the presidency of the patriarch, in a synod* or local council*. This practice is still followed in most Eastern, particularly Orthodox, churches, as well as in many Western churches (conferences of bishops, synods of Anglican provinces, and of Lutheran and Reformed Churches).

It should be noted that the patriarch, while playing the role of president within a patriarchate, was a bishop like other bishops, with no Episcopal power higher than that of the others. All bishops were equal, all participated in the same apostolic* succession, and all were similarly called upon to be guarantors of the true faith*. However, although the Episcopal power of a patriarch (or of a metropolitan) was the same as that of any other bishop and his title as primate essentially honorific, his role as president conferred on him a certain moral authority. For example, it devolved on him to approve elections of bishops for the provinces and metropolises in his jurisdiction; to preside over the election of metropolitans; and to call the synods or local councils (the Greek word *sunodos* means "council").

The pentarchy, as defined above, existed—with some tensions between Rome and Constantinople, which assumed the title of ecumenical patriarchate in 588, while still recognizing the traditional privileges of ancient Rome—until the gradual separation between the Catholic and Orthodox Churches. When communion* with Rome was broken, it was quite natural that Constantinople, second in the order of precedence, would become the see of the primate of the Orthodox Church. It has remained so until now (and will until communion with Rome is restored).

With the development of the Church of Russia and the transfer in the 14th century of the primate's see from Kiev to the new capital of Moscow, the autocephalous status of that church was solemnly recognized in 1589, when the ecumenical patriarch Jeremiah II came to consecrate the first patriarch of Moscow "and of all the Russias," Job. The pentarchy was thus restored for a short time, with Moscow assuming the fifth place previously held by Jerusalem.

Later developments were increasingly related to the rise of nationalism, particularly in the 19th century. Autocephalous churches appeared (or reappeared) in significant numbers. These churches increasingly identified themselves with the territories of sovereign states and thus tended to become "national" and not simply local churches (the Church of Antioch remains an example of a truly territorial church: its primatial see is in Damascus and its territory covers Syria and Lebanon). As a result, patriarchates proliferated, and the title of patriarch, formerly reserved, as we have seen, for bishops occupying prestigious sees, became widespread. The Orthodox world now includes eight churches headed by patriarchs, and, in all, sixteen autocephalous or "autonomous" churches.

The title patriarch has no specifically theological meaning. It has the same ecclesiastical significance as those of other primates (archbishop, metropolitan, catholicos, the title varying from one church to the next). In the Orthodox Church the primate presides over a local church as *primus inter pares* and in communion with all the other primates. One of these primates is endowed with a universal presidency under the same conditions: it is, actually, the patriarch of Constantinople.

Finally, it should be noted that some patriarchates, such as Antioch, Alexandria, and Jerusalem, now have several patriarchs: one Orthodox, one Catholic, one pre-Chalcedonian, which is contrary to the most ancient canon* law.

● J. Meyendorff (1960), *L'Église orthodoxe hier et aujourd'hui,* Paris (new rev. Ed., J. Meyendorff and N. Lossky, 1995).

T. Ware (Bishop Kallistos of Diokleia) (1963), *The Orthodox Church,* 4th Ed., London (New Ed. 1993).

J.-M. R. Tillard (1995), *L'Église locale: Ecclésiologie de communion et catholicité,* CFi 191, 241–99, 431–52, and passim.

Nicolas Lossky

See also **Government, Church; Hierarchy; Infallibility; Irenaeus of Lyons; Lay/Laity; Magisterium; Ministry; Ordination/Order; Pastor; Pope; Priesthood**

Patripassianism. *See* **Modalism**

Paul of Tarsus. *See* **Pauline Theology**

Pauline Theology

The Pauline letters can be classified in three groups, from earliest to latest: 1) the letters known as ministry and recognized as authentic (1 Thes, 1 and 2 Cor, Gal, and Rom); 2) the prison letters, Philippians and Philemon, also authentic; Colossians and Ephesians, whose authenticity is questioned (as 2 Thes), considered by some as Deutero-Pauline; and 3) the Pastoral letters, 1 and 2 Timothy and Titus, attributed by most exegetes to disciples of Paul (Bible*).

Paul's letters are not systematic, exhaustive expositions but circumstantial texts addressed to problems that arose in the first communities. However, they contain a number of constants that do not derive from circumstances or from the religious milieu (Jewish and/or Greek), but from Paul himself. This applies particularly to a generalized christologization of theological discourse.

I. A Christologized Theology

1. The Gospel That Is Christ
Paul was sent (1 Cor 1:17a) to preach the gospel that is Christ* (1 Thes 3:2; 1 Cor 9:12, 2:2; 2 Cor 1:19, 2:12, 4:4f., 9:13, 10:14; Gal 1:7; Rom 1:1ff., 15:19, 16:25; Phil 1:12–18, 27; Col 1:27; etc.), a gospel that is also "of God*" (1 Thes 2:2, 8f.; 2 Cor 11:7; Rom 15:16) because it fully and paradoxically manifests his impenetrable ways (Rom 11:33). Why must the apostle*'s proclamation be essentially christological? The answer

is suggested at the end of the hymn in Philippians 2 (vv. 9ff.); if God glorified Jesus* and made him Lord so that all creation without exception recognizes him as such, how could one be excused for keeping silent about that lordship—and about all that preceded it. Accepting the gospel means believing in Jesus Christ. This is clearly illustrated in Romans 9:30–10, 21; the only reproach leveled against Israel* is that it refused the gospel, in other words Jesus Christ, in the name of fidelity to the Torah. To proclaim that divine justice* was fully and definitively manifest in Jesus Christ comes down to describing Christ's course, presenting him crucified, dead, and raised to life for our salvation*.

Paul could not accept that anyone should preach or believe in "another Jesus" than the one he preaches (2 Cor 11:4), meaning a Jesus whose scandalous death is hidden, or a Jesus who came to put us back under the yoke of the law*. It is Christ's death on the cross that determines the components of the evangelical message, and leads Paul to declare that circumcision (*see* Gal 5:11) cannot be an integral part of the gospel.

2. Christ and Salvation for All
Paul's discourse on salvation is also fundamentally christologized. In it are recounted two complementary forms of salvific intervention that have taken place in the past: by God, who wished to show his justice and mercy* in sending Christ for our redemption or libera-

tion (*see,* among others, 2 Cor 5:18f., 5:21; Gal 4:4ff.; Rom 3:21–26, 5:8, 8:3f.; Col 1:22, 2:13; Eph 2:4f.), and by Christ (1 Thes 5:9f.; 1 Cor 8:11, 15:3; 2 Cor 5:14f., 8:9; Gal 1:4, 2:20, 3:13; Rom 5:6, 5:8, 5:12–19, 14:15; Pho; 2:7f.; Col 2:14f.; Eph 2:13–17, 5:2, 5:23, 5:25). Depending on the thrust of his argument, Paul drew on different semantic fields to express the interventions of God and Christ: love*, grace*, redemption, liberation (from the law, from sin*, from death*), justification*, forgiveness, reconciliation, solidarity, obedience and humiliation, expiation* (or propitiation), sacrifice*, creation*, life, salvation. He also insisted on the efficacy and the universal scope of Christ's redemptive work.

Christ's salvific mediation is still exercised today because, being risen, he reigns over the living and the dead (1 Cor 15:23–28; Rom 14:9; Phil 2:10f.). Believers have died with him to the Law and to sin, and have been buried with him so as to live with him (Rom 6:1–11, 8:17; Col 2:11; Eph 2:4) and "for him" (2 Cor 5:15; Rom 14:7f.), to know him (Phil 3:8, 10; Col 2:2; Eph 3:19, 4:13), and even to live through him, because he lives, lives in them (Gal 2:20; Eph 3:17), his life (as Resuscitated) is manifest, shines in their mortal existence (2 Cor 3:18, 4:8, 4:11; Rom 8:29), they belong to him (1 Cor 3:23) and for them living is Christ (Phil 1:21; Col 3:4). Christ's mediation also continues in the relation of believers to God, because he protects them from the wrath to come (1 Thes 1:10) and intercedes for them (Rom 8:34). Christ never abandons those he restored to God's friendship.

Paul's interpretation of the role of Mosaic law is determined by the effects of Christ's mediation in his own life and the lives of other believers. Good and holy as it may be, Mosaic law remains in the service of sin, because it makes us know sin but cannot deliver us from it (Rom 7:7–25). Moreover, it was and remains the identifying feature of the people of the covenant*, protecting them and separating them from all other nations. By highlighting the saving universality of Christ's death on the cross and of his resurrection*, Paul sets forth the common vocation of all mankind.

Admittedly, Paul's vocabulary does not seem to be directly christological when he expresses the identity and dignity of the faithful. He says that they have become children of God (filiation*) (*see* 2 Cor 6:18; Gal 3:26, 4:5f.; Rom 8:15ff., 8:19, 8:21, 8:23, 9:26; Phil 2:15; Eph 1:5). But Christ does not stand outside the relation established between God and mankind, because "God has sent the Spirit of his Son into our hearts" (Gal 4:4): Christ lives in us, loves in us; we are sons/daughters with and in him. This is why the baptized can say "*Abba!* Father*!" to God who desires to seem them reproduce the image of his Son (1 Cor 15:49; 2 Cor 3:18, 4:6; Rom 8:29). The mediator carries them into his own relationship with his Father, so that their being-as-son becomes inseparable from his itinerary.

3. Christ and Awaiting the End of Time

a) Christological or Apocalyptic? Paul expresses his hope* primarily in christological terms. But do the death and resurrection of Jesus have decisive meaning and scope if separated from the apocalyptic interpretation of the imminent, final victory of God over evil*, the ultimate manifestation of his justice? Paul sees the resurrection of Jesus as the event that calls forth the final resurrection. He prefers to focus on the modalities or ways by which divine justice and mercy have already been revealed, because the real question is the "how" of that manifestation, meaning the death on the cross. This is why the apocalyptic framework is less important than has been thought in the structure of the Pauline eschatology*. The apostle was hardly interested in the final divine vengeance* or victory. Not that he denied them (*see* 1 Thes 4:6, 5:3, 5:9; 2 Thes 2:12; Gal 5:21; 1 Cor 6f.; Rom 1:32, 2:5–10, 2:16, 3:5f.; Eph 5:5) (violence*), but all his preaching* bears on the mercy granted to our humanity by the Son's death on the cross, when the majesty of God had never been more triumphant! The apocalyptic scenarios in 1 Thessalonians 4, 15ff.; 1 Corinthians 15:23–28 and 1 Corinthians 15:52f. are important only for the coming of Christ; this alone gives all its weight to the events of the last days, because it allows the faithful, living and dead, to be forever with him in his glory*. The only true misfortune would be to not be with him forever.

The christologization of Pauline eschatology has an even more decisive function: eternal life* means not only being with Christ but inheriting his own risen life resuscitated. Resurrection (resurrection* of the dead) for punishment or destruction is totally excluded (*see* 1 Cor 15:35–49); the worst that can happen is to not be raised, not to share in the glory of Christ. Pauline eschatology is thus steeped in Christology (Christ* and Christology), and it is from this that it draws its finality, its content, and its scope.

b) Transformations of Eschatology. Did this insistence on the present and future relation of Christ with believers displace Pauline eschatology to a position where the final resurrection of believers (in 1 Thes 1; 2 Cor; Gal; Rom; Phil) was replaced by a resurrection and salvation that had already occurred (Col 2:12, 3:1; Eph 2:5f., 2:8)? In fact the tension between the "already occurred" and the "not yet" is not dissipated by Colossians and Ephesians because these letters do say that believers already have a glorious body (soul*-heart-body). Proclaiming that the faithful are raised to life with their Lord does not remove them from history*. Rather, it highlights the Christologization of their existence in all its dimensions—personal, ecclesial, and social.

4. Christ and the Discourse on God

a) Christ and His Relation to God.   Paul places Jesus Christ next to God; this could be described as a progressive theologization of his Christology. From the first to the last letters, one or another divine title is attributed to Christ. He is declared "Lord" (*kurios,* e.g., 1 Cor 2:8, 8:5f.; 2 Cor 3:14–17; Rom 10: 6–13; Phil 2:9ff.) by his resurrection. This term may certainly be used of other figures, but applied to Christ it assumes a particularly strong connotation (*see* 1 Cor 8:5; Col 3:22, 4:1; Eph 6:5, 6:9). In fact Paul takes several biblical passages where *kurios* manifestly designates God, translating *hb Adonaï* or even YHWH, and applies them to Jesus (*see* Jl 3:5 in Rom 10:13; Is 45:23 in Phil 2:10f.) (name*). Other titles, such as *sôtèr* ("savior"), which appear only in the prison and pastoral letters, are applied equally to God (1 Tm 1:1, 2:3; Ti 1:3, 2:10, 3:4) and to Christ (Phil 3:20; Eph 5:23; 1 Tm 4:10; 2 Tm 1:10; Ti 1:4, 2:13, 3:6).

b) Christologization of Theology.   Concomitantly, Paul christologizes his theology*. He never mentions God's redemptive work without mentioning Christ, thus making of him the proof par excellence of divine love and mercy (Gal 2:20f.; Rom 5:8, 8:39; Eph 2:4f., 4:32, 5:1f.; 2 Thes 2:16). And from then on God is "the Father of Our Lord Jesus Christ" (*see* 2 Cor 1:3, 11:31; Rom 15:6; Col 1:3; Eph 1:3). Paul sees this paternity as the definition of God himself. In the Bible God is already called the Father of the poor and the orphaned, the Father of Israel (Ps 68:6f., 103:13f., etc.). But in the Pauline letters this relation of God to human beings is understood only as a function of the father's relation to his son Jesus Christ; their filial adoption (*huiothesia*) is connected to the filiation of Jesus (Gal 4:4ff.). Further, it is the paths taken by the Son that reveal the extraordinariness of the paternity of God.

c) The Spirit of Christ.   Paul underscores the connection between the sending of the Son and the reception of the filial Spirit (Gal 4:4ff.). And he refuses any separation of the Spirit (*pneuma*) from Christ, Lord and Spirit of God. His pneumatology depends on his Christology and theology (1 Cor 12:4ff.; Rom 8:9, 14ff.) and is connected to his discourse on the Church* (1 Cor 12:12–30). The gift of the filial Spirit, the Spirit of the promise*, was made in connection with Jesus' death/resurrection. Paul's belief that Christ inaugurated the era of the *pneuma* and is himself "a life-giving spirit" (1 Cor 15:45) clearly indicates that all life comes through him.

The connection Christ/Spirit is also decisive for the opening of Scripture. According to what Paul himself says in 2 Co 3, it is by the Spirit that we can understand how Scripture itself, designated here as "the Old Testament" (2 Cor 3:14), takes meaning with reference to Christ, because all of Scripture speaks of him.

5. Christ and the Discourse on the Church

Pauline ecclesiology is not exclusively christological. When the term *Church* is used in the letters, it is followed by diverse noun complements (Church "of God," "of the Thessalonians," etc.) but is never designated as the Church of Christ. Furthermore, Paul does not limit himself to christological expressions to describe the community of the faithful in its unity and growth; for example, they form the temple* of God, an abode of the Spirit, or a single new man (1 Cor 3:9, 16f.; Eph 2:15, 2:21f.). Nevertheless the multiform presentation of being—in—the—Church is not separated from Christology, because Christ is the foundation (1 Cor 3) or the cornerstone (Eph 2) of the temple constituted by the Church.

a) Church as the Body of Christ.   Numerous expressions show clearly that the Church was described by the Paul primarily in christological terms. First, the repetition of the syntagm "in Christ." Second, the fact that, with the exception of two biblical citations (Rom 9:25f.; 2 Cor 6:16), the baptized are not called "people of God." This term is reserved for Israel, including Jews who believe in Jesus Christ and those who reject him in the name of fidelity to the Mosaic law. The thematic of the people is too particular to designate God's project for the whole human race; Paul prefers a familial vocabulary that makes the community of believers "the family*" of God. But it is a vocabulary of the body that allows him to signify the privileged relation between the Church and Christ. There were numerous reasons why this vocabulary was attractive, including its connotations of growth, of unity in diversity, and of the complementarity of members, but the christological determination is fundamental. The faithful do not form a social body but the body of Christ; of which they are the limbs (1 Cor 1:13, 6:15, 12:12–27; Rom 12:5; Col 1:18, 22; Eph 1:23, 4:12f., 4:25, 5:23, 5:30). Because this relation constitutes the Church as an eschatological entity, it is not counted with others of this world, such as the social, the political, or the religious. For that reason it is not a substitute for the people of Israel.

1 Corinthians 1–4 is a thorough demonstration of Paul's use of Christology to formulate intra-ecclesial relations. The first section, which is christological, gives the values that generate the physiognomy of the ecclesial group and its true hierarchy (the ministers being in the service of the Church and not vice versa). In its fundamental dependence the Church must testify to the Son's unique lordship over it. In Colossians 1:18a the vocabulary is the same as in the preceding letters (*see* Rom 12:4f.; 1 Cor 10:16f., 12:12f.) but the emphasis is different. What matters here is not the Church in its organic reality, forming a unity in the multiplicity and complementarity of its members, but its dependence with respect to the Son and the unicity of this relation (the Church alone is his body). He goes even further in Ephesians: because the Church is closely united to its Lord and vivified by him, it becomes the privileged sign of the grace of God offered to all humankind. Moreover, it becomes responsible for manifesting the totally gratuitous, reconciling love of Christ for all, and the new humanity should be traced in the Church, which is the body of Christ in growth.

Aside from the head/body relation used to describe the unique, privileged bond between Christ and his Church, a husband/wife type of relation figures in 2 Cor 11:2; this is articulated with the corporeal relation and treated at greater length in Ephesians 5:26f. (couple*).

b) Sacraments of Christ. The Church remains indefectibly united to its Lord by the baptism* received in Christ, with Christ or in his name (*see*, e.g., 1 Cor 1:13; Gal 3:27; Rom 6:3f.; Col 2:12) and by the Lord's, where the community also receives its unity (1 Cor 10:16f.) (Eucharist*).

Baptism determines the true dignity (Christly and spiritual) of believers, and it is on this basis that Paul is able to combat all kinds of false intra-ecclesial hierarchization. Though some ministries or charisms may be superior to others (1 Cor 12:27–31), they must not determine a difference in status (*see* 1 Cor 3).

c) Christ and the Ministries. Paul also connected to Christ the apostolic ministry and the proclamation of the gospel: he introduces almost all his letters by presenting himself as apostle, minister (*diakonos*), or servant "of Christ" The purpose of the ministry is also to make Christ known, make the faithful increase, etc. Paul does everything so that Christ will be formed in his converts (Gal 4:19); he is like a father who keeps his daughter pure and a virgin so as to present her to

her husband, the Christ (2 Cor 11:2). When the finality is theological, it is associated with a christological determination ("in Christ" or an equivalent) as in 1 Corinthians 3. The true apostle can be recognized by the way he suffers and endures for the gospel, reproducing in his flesh the itinerary of Christ for his Church (*see* 1 Cor 4 and 9; 2 Cor 6:4–10, 11:23–12:10; Phil 3; Col 1:24; 2 Tm 1:12). And in Ephesians 4:7–12 the ministries are completely christologized; it is Christ who distributes them to his Church, thus ensuring its growth. This does not mean that Christ substitutes himself for God but that God himself, by giving Christ to the Church and making him its head, wished to give his all to the Church (Eph 1:20–23).

6. Christologization of Ethics and Anthropology

a) Christological Motives. Clearly Pauline morality does not draw on the the Mosaic Torah for its major justification, despite the Jewish background of several directives, in particular the commandment to love one's fellow human being (Lv 19:18; Gal 5:14; Rom 13:9). Christ does have a decisive function because Paul's exhortations are made in reference to him (1 Thes 4:1; Rom 14:14; 15:30; Phil 2:5) or in his name (1 Thes 4:2; 1 Cor 7:10f.). He cites Christ's liberality and humility, his love for all, especially for the humble, and invites his readers to imitate him in that (1 Cor 11:1; 2 Cor 8:9; Rom 15:7; Phil 2:5–11; Col 3:13; Eph 5:2, 5:25–30). Along with God the Father, Christ is an ethical model to follow. This is why Paul does not entertain the question of the priority of the Torah over Christ. Granting that the requisite "Love your neighbor as yourself" is more appropriate in his day than ever, Paul does not attribute this to its origin as an order in the Torah, which undoubtedly expresses the divine will, but to the fact that the baptized have experienced the extent of the love of God and of Christ. Christ remains the ultimate recipient of ethical action and indication of its consequences (1 Cor 8:12f.). The dignity of the believer, which is derived from the love Christ has shown for him (in dying for him) and from his union with Christ, perhaps finds its most notable consequence here. Elsewhere Christ's being and action served as a more elaborate principle of argumentation (1 Cor 5:6ff., 6:13 and 15, 8:11; Rom 6, 14:15; 1 Cor 11:4; Col 3:1; Eph 5:23). In more formal terms, the christological justifications pertain to what is commonly called "the indicative," to which the "ethical" imperative is attached. Paul exhorts his readers in the name of their being-in-Christ (or with Christ), in virtue of what they themselves have perceived and received of the love of God in Jesus Christ.

In Colossians and Ephesians christological motivations are extended to every aspect of the life of the ecclesial group, especially relations between husband and wife, parents and children, masters, and servants. Does this mean that Christology validates society's assignment of statutory inferiority to wives, or its demand for the unconditional obedience of slaves? In reality such directives should not be interpreted as the ingenuous "baptism" of these culturally imposed social structures but a wish to humanize and transform them, to show how they can and must open themselves to the gospel. Far from bending the gospel to worldly values, these prison letters make of it an instrument for the conversion* of all codes, moral and otherwise.

b) New Humanity in Christ. Pauline anthropology* is also christologized. Christ is the last Adam* and the eschatological man bears his features (*see* 1 Cor 15:44b–49). It is because of the unity and dignity of our humanity in Christ that Paul is able to outline the kinds of worldly discrimination that are to be excluded from the Church (whether it be dsicrimation based on religion (Jew, Greek; circumcised or not), sex (man, woman*) or class (free man, slave; *see* Gal 3:28; Col 3:11). And again, on the basis of redemption in Christ he describes, in Romans 7:7–25, the enslavement of man as subject of the Law and still subject to the flesh* *(sarx);* and it is always in terms of Christ that he develops, in Colossians and Ephesians, the beginnings of a concept of a "new man," as opposed to the "old" one who is prisoner of sin and death (Col 3:9 ff.; Eph 4:22–25). But it is first and foremost in the Son that our humanity discovers the dimensions of its filial dignity, and at the same time the exigency of fraternity, of loving attention, so as to truly form the family of God (1 Thes 4:9; Rom 8:29, 12:9f.). As for Paul's preference for celibacy, that too is determined by christological reasons—the proclamation of the Gospel (1 Cor 7:29–35).

Thus the figure of Christ structures the various fields of Pauline theology. But this is more a christologization than a systematic reflection on the status and being of Christ. The importance of Christology in Paul's letters is measured more by its role and dissemination than its internal development.

II. A Paradoxical Theology

1. A Paradoxical Formulation of the Itinerary of Christ and the Baptized

a) Folly of the Death on the Cross. Although Jesus Christ is the primary subject of Paul's gospel, he retains little more than the death on the cross (1 Cor 1:18–25; Gal 3:1). Not that he had a predilection for this type of death—quite the contrary, he considered God's instrument as an abasement. But this unbearable event became the site of his absolute consolation. This does not mean that he sought to minimize the scandal*, in the sense that its soteriological purpose (a death on the cross for all) would reduce the enigma. Even though, following the apostolic tradition*, he reinterpreted and re-read the event in the light of Scripture (*see* 1 Cor 15:3f.), and even though he overcame his rejection and acknowledged the coherence of such a death, he always expressed it in paradoxical terms, in abrupt phrases meant to awaken his readers to the extremity of divine ways. God "gave up" his Son (Rom 8:32): could a father worthy of the name deliver his beloved son to such a death, even for the most worthy reasons? Then would he hesitate to give up all of humanity? There are other, stronger statements: "Fdor our sake, he made him to be sin who knew no sin, so that in him we might become the righteousness of God" (2 Cor 5:21; a similar formulation in Rom 8:3f.). This gesture of God's is inseparable from that of his Son who so loved mankind that he gave up himself for its sake (Gal 1:4, 2:20), and became a curse so that in him the blessing of Abraham is extended to all people (Gal 3:13f.). There is nothing ornamental about this rhetoric—especially the two metonymies, sin and curse—it simply serves to mark the stupefaction of one who could not see the event of the cross as anything but a folly (1 Cor 1:21ff.) to which God resorted in order to save the world. Paul not only retained the excess of an ignominious death, he also underscored the extraordinariness and the extension of its effects for anyone who accepts to believe—filial adoption, Spirit received, etc. Again, it is the means taken by Christ to return us to divine friendship that are highlighted in 2 Corinthians 8:9, when he says that Jesus, rich though he was, became poor for our sake so that "you by his poverty might become rich."

Paul's paradoxical affirmations not only upset worldly wisdom*, they also indicate the orientation of Christian discourse. The apostle recognized that the extremity of divine ways could be recognized in the itinerary of Christ, and meditating on Jesus' death on the cross takes us into the mystery* of the fatherhood of God. Undoubtedly the best description of the importance of Christ's death on the cross for announcing the gospel is in the passage 1 Corinthians 1–2. Paul denies himself brilliant discourse so as not to reduce it to nothingness. In opting for a rhetoric of humility and simplicity, Paul definitively eschewed the seduction of the word. But Christ's death on the cross does much more than change the rules of the rhetorical game. It determines the message itself, because it indicates definitively God's wretched choice: that "unto" the death on the cross reveals a divine folly wiser than human wisdom, a poverty more powerful than anything. The cross changes how one views the world and its values: " But far be it from me to boast except in the cross of our Lord Jesus Christ, by which the world has been crucified to me, and I to the world" (Gal 6:14). Paul can only proclaim the death of Jesus on the cross as the supreme, definitive subversion of worldly values.

This importance of the "extreme" also explains why Paul says almost nothing about the life of Jesus except that he was born to a woman, was Jewish and subject to the Law (Gal 4:4), and descended from David (Rom 1:3). This does not mean that the apostle did not know more, or found nothing else worthy of mention; he summarized his argument in a single expression, "being born in the likeness of men" (Phil 2: 7), precisely obeying the dynamics of humbling. Certainly, the climax of humiliation and kenosis* is not the end of the journey, and the Pauline gospel also includes the element of the "resurrection" without which his preaching would be false Good News and our faith* vain and empty (1 Cor 15:17). But this element should not make us forget the first, because that is the source of the indispensable condition: the exaltation of a crucified, humiliated man who is the Son of God.

b) Paradoxical Condition of the Baptized. Several passages unequivocally indicate the connection between the Lord's itinerary and that of the baptized (1 Cor 1:26–31; Rom 6; Phil 3:2–11), expressed no less paradoxically. Henceforth, the baptized are dead and their life is hidden with Christ in God (Col 3:3); liberated from sin they have become slaves of justice (Rom 6:18). Although they should not become slaves of men (1 Cor 7:23), they must "serve" (*douleuete*) one another (Gal 5:13), just as Paul, free with respect to everyone, made himself slave of all in order to win the greatest number (1 Cor 9:19). He goes so far as to praise—without masochism or complacency—his weakness (2 Cor 11:30), because in that weakness the strength of God can work (2 Cor 12:10). Does God need our chronic weakness so as to manifest in and by us his strength? In reality, he himself followed this path in his Son (Phil 2:6ff.). On this point Paul's affirmations are comparable to those of Jesus—he who humbles himself will be raised up, the greatest will be in the service of all, etc. But Paul must turn to the rhetoric of excess (*auxèsis*) to formulate such reversals, especially with regard to the beautiful religious privilege granted to the Israelite he was and still is (Rom 11:1), now voluntarily turned into sweepings, filth, by love of Christ (Phil 3:8).

The event of the death of the Son on the cross and the life of the baptized are caught up in the broader logic of redemption in an even more paradoxical formulation in the *Epistle to the Romans* that seems to make God the first agent of our rejection (*see* Rom 5:20, 11:32). Paul does not forget human resistance but he sees it ordained and adopted by an unfathomable divine wisdom, just when it lets itself be recognized (Rom 11:33–36) (knowledge* of God).

2. A Paradoxical Description of Israel and the Torah

a) Destiny of Israel. Paul believed that the present and future situation of Israel was integral to the logic of salvation. Israel remained the people of God, even if most of its members rejected the gospel of Christ in the name of fidelity to Mosaic law. Their zeal for God paradoxically distanced them from his justice (Rom 10:1ff.) (hardening*), but this distance, which is not permanent, comes from God himself, who hardened them so that non-Jews could receive the gospel (Rom 11:25–32). How can God behave this way toward the people he loves? Paul can align these paradoxes by virtue of his own experience; he himself had fought against the gospel out of zeal (Gal 1:13f.), and if God had made him the instrument of the evangelization of the nations, is this to show in advance the future role of his people, a role now passive, but a people that retain a decisive eschatological vocation. Paul never calls Israel "people of the ancient covenant" because the reality of Israel cannot be exclusively or adequately defined by Mosaic law (for a Jew faithful to the Torah this idea was quite monstrous). And so it is the few Jews who have accepted the Gospel and proclaimed it to the nations—the remnants (Rom 11:5)—who bear the future deliverance of the whole people, and testify to God's unfailing love for his chosen people (Rom 11).

b) Mosaic Law. It is true that Pauldoes call the books (book*) of the Mosaic law "Old Testament" (*palaia diathèkè*–the second word, meaning "disposition," may designate an ordinance, testament, or covenant) (2 Cor 3:14f.). Does he mean this to indicate their age, or the fact that they have been supplanted? He does consider them prophetic books that announce not only the evangelical times (such as Dt 30:12ff. in Rom 10:6–10), but God's impartial justice (Dt 10:17; *see* Gal 2:6; Rom 2:11) and justification by faith alone (Gn 15:6; *see* Gal 3:6; Rom 4). As for the ethical prescriptions, especially the Decalogue* (Rom 13:9), completely recapitulated in Leviticus 19:18 (Gal 5:14; Rom 13:9), the baptized are not dispensed from respecting them. Paul does not ignore the morality of the Pentateuch, but he is against imposing rites of circumcision and dietary purification (Col 2:20f.) on the non-

Jewish baptized (Gal 5:2; Phil 3:3). Although he seems to pick and choose among prescriptions of the Torah, he never says that they are to take and leave; the Law is one, and its subjects should obey in all (Gal 5:3). Though not subject to the letter of the Law, the baptized should nevertheless respect and manifest its Spirit, by reciprocal love.

Paul did not deny the role of the Torah in the past (Gal 3:24) but his unconditional attachment to Christ—who had become his law—showed him that the Mosaic regime had to be regarded as culture-specific, not universal (1 Cor 9:20–23; Phil 3:7–11), and that the gospel could be practiced within any type of cultural system. Paul did not seek the abolition of Mosaic law as such, in its holiness* and finality. He did not want to impose a lawless regime in which the baptized would be free of all systems of ethical and religious values; but he did refuse subjection to this law as a condition of entry into the friendship of God and hope for salvation. Reduction of the soteriological extension of the Mosaic regime went along with a shift in Paul's language; the term *people* almost disappeared, replaced by frequent use of the vocabulary of family (father, children, husband, wife). Paradoxically, however, this refusal to confine the faithful within a single code is what led the Pauline gospel to adopt a standardizing universal quality.

3. Reading of the Biblical Past

The Pauline letters do not have the same perspective as the gospel narratives (narrative*) (Gospels*), where typology is omnipresent and often determines the choice of episodes. Not that the letters ignore typological exegeses (exegesis*) (*see*, among others, 1 Cor 10; 2 Cor 3; Rom 5:12–19), but Paul's positions on justification by faith alone (independent of Mosaic law) demanded a reading that underscored the coherence of the divine plan of salvation and verified the convergence of divine declarations according to prevailing rules of the times. This undoubtedly explains why the apostle's theology becomes more exegetical in Galatians and Romans.

Although Paul believes that faith in Christ lifts the veil that obscured the understanding of Scripture, he never claims that events of the past were nothing but shadows; the reality was already given to be experienced by the Fathers. The rock in the desert was Christ (1 Cor 10:4), the manna was really spiritual nourishment (1 Cor 10:3) and, well before the episodes in the desert, divine action had already signified its orientation because it justified by faith alone (Rom 4; *see* Gn 15:6). This explains why Rm presents the gospel not as something new but as the ultimate manifestation of divine justice, the confirmation of what God had said

and done ever since the first patriarch (*see* Rom 3:21f.). So it is no surprise that scriptural argumentation such as found in Romans 4 is not christological. As object—whether ultimate or absolute—of the promise and faith of Abraham, Christ does not have to be mentioned; what matters is the "when" (before the Mosaic law) and the "how" (without the good works* required by that law) of the act of believing and the justification. What should be underscored is Paul's extraordinarily audacious reading of the story of Abraham against the interpretation of his Jewish contemporaries, found partially in James 2:14–26.

III. Influence of Pauline Theology

The pastoral letters—perhaps as early as Colossians and Ephesians—show that Paul's successors adapted Pauline themes and ideas for the post-apostolic period. There is a continuity of the desire to make the gospel live without compromise but with an open attitude based on the discernment that was demanded in a constantly changing world. The narrative in Acts presents the figure of the Paul more than the components of his theology. The narrator does not mention the existence of the letters, but he makes Paul the perfect representative of the Nazarene "sect" (*see* Acts 24:5, 14) that remained faithful to the promises, and in whom the promises were fulfilled (Acts 26:2–29). Even if it is not out of the question that the author of Acts wanted to present the Christian movement *ad extra*, his account is also a plea in favor of the Pauline position within the Church (the refusal to impose Mosaic law on converts from paganism*), to counterbalance the aggressive reactions of some Christian groups of Jewish origin. And in fact the influence of Pauline theology increased proportionately as the Church moved away from its Jewish birthplace, even if some interpretations of his theology, such as that of Marcion (Marcionism*) in the second century, did him more harm than good.

● A. Schweitzer (1930), *Die Mystik des Apostels Paulus,* Tübingen.
L. Cerfaux (1942), *La théologie de l'Église suivant saint Paul,* Paris; id. (1951), *Le Christ dans la théologie de saint Paul,* Paris.
J. Bonsirven (1948), *L'Évangile de Paul,* Paris.
P. Benoit et al. (1966), "Paul (Épîtres attribuées à saint)," *DBS* 7, 155–279.
J. A. Fitzmyer (1967), *Paul and His Theology: A Brief Sketch,* Englewood Cliffs, N.J (2nd Ed. 1989).
E. Käsemann (1969), *Paulinische Perspektiven,* Tübingen.
J. Murphy-O'Connor (1974), *L'existence chrétienne selon saint Paul,* Paris.
W. Klaiber (1982), *Rechtfertigung und Gemeinde: Eine Untersuchung zum paulinischen Kirchenverständnis,* Göttingen.
G. Lüdemann (1983), *Paulus, der Heidenapostel,* t. 2: *Antipaulinismus im frühen Christentum,* Göttingen.

E. P. Sanders (1983), *Paul, the Law and the Jewish People*, Philadelphia.

A. J. M. Wedderburn (1987), *Baptism and Resurrection: Studies in Pauline Theology against Its Greco-Roman Background*, Tübingen.

M. C. de Boer (1988), *Defeat of Death: Apocalyptic Eschatology in 1 Corinthians 15 and Romans 5*, Sheffield.

S. Westerholm (1988), *Israel's Law and the Church's Faith: Paul and His Recent Interpreters*, Grand Rapids, Mich.

J. Becker (1989), *Paulus, der Apostel der Völker*, Tübingen.

W. S. Babcock (Ed.) (1990), *Paul and the Legacies of Paul*, Dallas.

M.-A. Chevallier (1990), *Souffle de Dieu: Le Saint-Esprit dans le Nouveau Testament*, vol. II: *L'apôtre Paul: L'héritage paulinien*, Paris.

R. O'Toole (1990), *Who Is A Christian? A Study in Pauline Ethics*, Collegeville, Minn.

H. Hübner (1993), *Biblische Theologie des Neuen Testaments*, vol. 2: *Die Theologie des Paulus*, Göttingen.

J.-N. Aletti (1994), *Jésus-Christ fait-il l'unité du Nouveau Testament?*, Paris, 29–117.

Y. Redalié (1994), *Paul après Paul: Le temps, le salut, la morale selon les épîtres à Timothée et à Tite*, Geneva.

J. D. G. Dunn (1998), *The Theology of Paul the Apostle*, Edinburgh (reported in JSNTSS 72, 67–112, author's response, ibid., 113–20).

JEAN-NOËL ALETTI

See also **Adam; Anthropology; Apocalyptic Literature; Apostle; Barth, Karl; Bible; Christ and Christology; Church; Eschatology; Ethics; Faith; Filiation; Gospels; Grace; Hardening; Holy Spirit; Inculturation; Israel; Justification; Kenosis; Lawand Christianity; Liberty; Luther, Martin; Scripture, Fulfillment of; Soul-Heart-Body; Universalism; Violence; Wisdom**

Peace

Peace, in Christian thought, is not mere absence of conflict or the end of a state of war*. On the contrary, peace is an inclusive concept, encompassing the manifold reality—spiritual, interpersonal, social, international, and even ecological—of an order and a harmony that harken back to the creation* even as they prefigure the eschatological recapitulation of all things.

a) *Biblical Theology.* In the Old Testament, "peace" (shalom) has two meanings, one ontological and the other eschatological. The ontological sense of peace is based upon the essential goodness of the world, affirmed by the very word* of its Creator (Gn 1:21, 25, and 31). It is eschatological because true peace cannot be truly realized within the time-frame of history*, or can only be realized therein through an anticipatory mode. Certainly, the historical relationship between God and human beings opens up a realm of peace, as in the "covenant of peace" with Israel* (Ez 37:26); and peace, frequently associated with justice*, is God's gift and blessing* truly provided to the righteous (Ps 85:10–11; Is 32:16–18). However, since human sinfulness (sin*) prohibits God's peace to reign (Jer 6:13–14), the promises (promise*) of peace go beyond

any present experience of peace. Peace is linked to salvation*, to which the historical Israel has already borne witness, but the full realization of which is the object of eschatological hope* (Is 57:19–21).

In the New Testament, peace *(eirene)* appears predominantly as a personal gift from Jesus*. The word is used conventionally as a salutation (Mk 5:34; Jn 14:27 and 20:19, 20:21, 20:26). "Peacemakers" are mentioned as the subject of one of the Beatitudes (Beatitude*) (Mt 5:9), and the declaration of the Kingdom begins with an invocation of peace (Lk 10:5f.). The commandments not to resist evil* with evil (Mt 5:39), to love one's enemies (Mt 5:43–47), and to do unto others as you would have them do unto you (Mt 7:12) are also related to the preaching* of peace and peacemaking. Nevertheless, it is in the epistles of Paul that peace gains crucial importance. For Paul, peace means salvation realized, the reconciliation with God that results here and now from justification* by faith* (Rom 5:1); Jesus is thus, in the present, "our peace" (Eph 2:14–18). Used also as a formula of greeting to the churches, peace symbolizes the unity* of the church* in Christ*, as a community of the peace of God (Rom 14:17–19). The peacemaking duties of the faithful follow from the actualized reality of peace: in order to bear witness to Christ's work, Christians are called upon to live in peace with the whole world, and not only with other Christians (Rom 12:18).

b) Augustine. The biblical concept of peace was significantly developed by Augustine*, who defines peace on three levels. Ontologically and protologically, peace is a vestige of creational goodness in human nature. Christologically, it is a gift from Christ for a humanity that lost original peace after original sin*. Eschatologically, it is a reality that is hoped for but cannot be fully accommodated within earthly time*. Peace thus defined—with a sharp distinction between "perfect" and "imperfect peace"—should reign in all realms, from bodily to spiritual, from individual to social, from earthly to heavenly. Envisaging earthly peace as the proper but not wholly realizable goal of political activities, Augustine recognizes it as a value in itself, and urges Christians to "make use of…the temporal peace of the meantime, common to good and bad alike" (*Civ. Dei* 19, 26, BAug 37). However, he recommends that they labor for earthly peace without "taking pleasure in it," that is, without treating it as an end in itself. We also owe to Augustine one of the first theological clarifications of the conditions for a just war: it must be part of coercive justice, waged in search of peace (*Ep.* 189, 6, CSEL 47) and in the spirit of love (*Ep.* 138, 13, CSEL 44), and ordered by a legitimate authority* (*Contra Faustum* 22, 75, PL 42, 448), for legitimate reasons (*Civ. Dei* 4, 15, BAug 33).

c) Modern Times. The Augustinian concept was dominant until the beginning of the modern era, when a less pessimistic view of human nature and of reason* appeared. According to Erasmus*, for example, peace is a divine imperative transmitted, of course, by Christ, but also by the rationality of human nature; and peace is guaranteed more by "a heartfelt desire for peace" than by "treaties and alliances" (/*QP* LB638, 636/ > /*Querela pacis, Opera omnia* IV/2 [1977], 59–100/).

An optimistic faith in reason is indeed the main characteristic in the works of Hobbes (1588–1679. The state of nature is assuredly a state of war ("the war of all against all"), but peace may be fully instituted in the "artificial person" of the social body established by the social contract (*Leviathan,* chs. 16–17), through a rational calculation that aims to protect natural rights, without, however, dealing directly with the individual's moral or religious dispositions.

It was probably in the work of Kant* (*Zum ewigen Frieden,* Weischedel 7) that the modern political concept of peace found its fullest programmatic form. Perpetual peace, the ultimate goal of the historical progress of humanity, guided and guaranteed by "Na-

ture," is "the end of all hostilities" under a threefold rule of law: 1) in a state with a "republican" constitution based on social contract; 2) by a treaty to create a "confederation" of autonomous states; and 3) by the mutual recognition of "universal human rights." The state of peace is therefore a legal condition in which the autonomy of a person* or a state is secured both individually and universally according to the dictates of practical reason.

d) Pacifism. The most widely debated problem in recent theology* is that of pacifism. Historically, pacifism has grown out of a strand of Christianity that has taken opposition to violence* to its logical conclusion and refused to participate in war. Theologically, pacifism is clearly based on the Gospels: pacifists literally interpret the commandment "thou shall not kill," which they consider to be one of the fundamental implications of the divine commandment to love that was transmitted by Christ. There is also an eschatological element at stake: since Christians define themselves as having already begun a new life in the Kingdom, they can and must allow peace to reign already in this world. Pacifists are also cautious, and even suspicious, of political authority: its peacemaking methods, such as punishment and war, are inherently coercive and external.

The pacifist attitude was prevalent among Christians in the first three centuries, who were predominantly concerned with whether they could serve in a pagan emperor's army. "No," says Tertullian*, not only for fear of idolatry*, but because killing is incompatible with the new law of love* proclaimed by Christ: "the Lord unbelted every soldier when he disarmed Peter" (*De Idol.* 19, CChr.SL II, 1120). While insisting that it is "more lawful" for Christians "to be slain than to slay" (*Apol.* 37, CChr.SL I, 148), Tertullian nonetheless sanctions a possibly coercive maintenance of order by political authority, which is not bound by the new law.

There was a minority of Christian pacifists in the Middle Ages, such as the Waldensians (Waldensian*), but a more systematic form of pacifism emerged out of the Reformation, advocated primarily by churches of Anabaptist* origin, like the Mennonites, and by the Society of Friends (Quakers). These advocates of strict nonviolence and antimilitarism all agree that peacemaking is the crux of the Christian life. For some (Anabaptists and Mennonites), however, Christian pacifism is a nonpolitical principle held only by believers, while others (Quakers) think it is a principle universally applicable to all peoples and nations. Tolstoy (1828–1910) represents a remarkable and yet controversial offshoot of this Christian pacifism. His renunciation of violence and war proceeded by a radically simplified Christianity, one reduced to a way of "life" based on the Sermon on the Mount and combined with his almost anarchistic rejection of the state. He proclaimed that "Christianity in its true sense puts an end to government" (*The Kingdom of God Is Within You*, 1893).

Contemporary pacifism embraces a wide range of approaches, such as "vocational" pacifism, which is in line with the traditional view, and which treats the duty of peacemaking as a special calling for the most virtuous Christians; "humanistic" pacifism, widely shared both within and outside Christianity (e.g., *Pacem in terris,* 1963); "technological" pacifism, based upon scientific rationalism* (nuclear deterrence); and "just war" pacifism, which is concerned with, in principle, defining the limits of warfare. Consequently, there are numerous pacifist attitudes, ranging from nonresistance to nonviolent resistance, from total condemnation of war to selective limitation and justification of war. Moreover, pacifism must engage with new critiques. To the extent that pacifism defines peace in a negative way, as absence of open strife, it faces a challenge from a theology (or philosophy) of liberation* that reflects on structural violence and the justified use of force to put an end to it. To the extent that the classic problematic of pacifism leaves aside everything that is not involved in human relations, it must also respond to environmentalists who suggest that it should take the destruction of ecological balances into consideration and come to a theological understanding of peace between human beings and nature.

SHINJI KAYAMA

e) Systematic Theology. Theological discussion of peace stands at the crossroads of three problematics. The first is that of spiritual anthropology*. Because peace reigns between God and humanity, it may also reign between human beings and themselves. The spiritual traditions of East and West have thought of this pacification or unification of the self in terms of various concepts—*quies, hesukhia*—and have seen them as ways of being that anticipate the *eschaton.*

The second problematic arises from the fact that

such a pacification cannot yield all its meaning except within the communion* of a church that has an obligation to be present within history as a pacified community. The idea of an ontology of communion (e.g., in the writings of J.D. Zizioulas) will always be liable to the objection that what it speaks of has only a limited descriptive force. On the other hand, its prescriptive force is very great: as the only association that believes in the possibility of an existence that is faithful to the Beatitudes, the church should seek to embody, as concretely as possible, the peace that it proclaims, signifies liturgically, and confers sacramentally.

The third and final problematic concerns the fact that the church is not the only space in which the blessing of the peacemakers is audible. Peace should reign in the city*, and Christians are citizens. Undoubtedly, they can only make a credible contribution to political life, in which they have only a limited power, if they have first given an evangelical visage to those communities in which their power is much greater. In any case, ecclesiastical responsibilities cannot be separated from political responsibilities. It is necessary to seek to make "all things new" (Rev 21:5).

THE EDITORS

● R.H. Bainton (1960), *Christian Attitudes toward War and Peace,* Nashville, Tenn.
J.M. Hornus (1960), *Évangile et Labarum,* Geneva.
Jean XXIII (1963), *Pacem in terris,* AAS 55, 257–304.
P. Ramsey (1968), *The Just War,* New York.
J.H. Yoder (1971), *Nevertheless: The Varieties of Religious Pacifism,* Scottdale, Pa.; id. (1972), *The Politics of Jesus,* Grand Rapids, Mich.
J. Ellul (1972), *Contre les violents,* Paris.
W.B. Gallie (1978), *Philosophers of Peace and War: Kant, Clausewitz, Marx/Engels and Tolstoy,* Cambridge.
S. Hauerwas (1983), *The Peaceable Kingdom,* Notre Dame, Ind.
J.H. Yoder (1984), *The Priestly Kingdom,* Notre Dame, Ind.
D. Brown (1986), *Biblical Pacifism: A Peace Church Perspective,* Elgin, Ill.
J. Finnis, J.M. Boyle, G. Grisez (1987), *Nuclear Deterrence, Morality and Realism,* Oxford.
O. O'Donovan (1988), *Peace and Certainty: A Theological Essay on Deterrence,* Oxford.

See also **Anabaptists; Ecology; Eschatology; Legitimate Defense; Violence; War**

Pelagianism

Understood for a long time solely in terms of its refutation by Augustine*, Pelagianism has today been restored to its context. Its fundamental characteristics—the orientation toward asceticism*, the rejection of original sin* and of traducianism*, and the emphasis on liberty*—now appear to have been distilled from various currents of thought belonging to the first decades of the fifth century.

a) Representative Figures. The best-known representative of the movement is Pelagius. Little is known about his background, other than that he was given the epithet "Britannicus" in reference to his country of origin. He lived in Rome*, where he was baptized in around 380. He then sought to uncover the roots of the gospel, possibly became a monk, and had some influence in the Christian community of the city. In 410, when Rome was conquered by Alaric, Pelagius departed to Africa and then went to Palestine. He explained in various writings that human beings are free, that they participate as created beings in the grace* of the Creator, and that they can become true images of God* by their own efforts alone. He also stated that some people could be without sin and that some had been liberated from sin before they died. He rejected the idea of original sin and proposed the abandonment of infant baptism* (which he accepted as a custom) in favor of a return to adult baptism. Above all, he desired a "Church of the pure," a Church* of perfect Christians, and his ideal found an echo among aristocrats.

Celestius, a lawyer and an ascetic who became a disciple of Pelagius in around 390, made himself the spokesperson for Pelagius's ideas and may even have become the first member of the Pelagian group. He took Pelagius's ideas further, giving them a more rational and organized form, as set out in the *Definitiones,* which Celestius may have written.

Bishop Julian of Eclanum, born around 380–86, joined the Pelagians after refusing to sign Pope Zosimus's *Tractoria* (418), a condemnation of Pelagius and Celestius. Julian had a reputation as an exegete and translator, notably of works by Theodore of Mopsuestia, but he brought few new ideas into the group. The second stage of the Pelagian controversy may be said to have begun with him.

b) Crisis of Pelagianism. It is in fact possible to distinguish three stages in the controversy: the first, which was relatively serene, up to 411; the second, which was more problematic, between 411 and 418; and the last, after 418, which then gave rise to what was later labeled "semi-Pelagianism."

Up to 411 Pelagius was developing his ideas, which found expression in a treatise that has been attributed to him, *God's Hardening of Pharaoh's Heart.* He opposed the doctrine of predestination taught by Manicheanism* and made himself the theologian of the notion of a salvation* that one comes to deserve through the exercise of one's liberty. He even enjoyed a degree of approval from Augustine, with whom he had a brief meeting in Carthage.

Between 411 and 418, tensions culminated in crisis. In 412 Celestius, who refused to conduct infant baptisms—a practice cherished in the African church—was condemned by the Council of Carthage. After the Council of Diospolis, which reexamined the question of Pelagianism in a relatively favorable way, Augustine studied Pelagius's teachings as set out in *De natura,* a treatise that presents an optimistic vision of humanity and its natural liberty. It was in response to this treatise that Augustine wrote his *De gestis Pelagii.* In 416 the African bishops asked Pope Innocent I to condemn Pelagius and Celestius: he did so in 417. This was the first occasion on which Pelagius was condemned. In order to justify himself, he wrote a *Libellus Fidei* and a treatise *On Free Will.* After the death of Innocent I, his successor, Zosimus, went back on the condemnation of Pelagius and suspended it. The African bishops* protested, while the Pelagians stirred up trouble. Pope Zosimus was compelled to reopen the question. In 418 he published a statement about the controversy, the *Tractoria* mentioned above, and renewed the excommunication of Pelagius and Celestius. As we have seen, Julian of Eclanum's opposition to this document led him into the ranks of the Pelagians.

The controversy took a new turn after 418. While Augustine continued his polemic with Julian of Eclanum, the monastic theologians of Hadrumetum and Provence (Jean Cassien, Faustus of Riez, and Vincent of Lérins) developed a theology in which liberty played a larger role than it did in Augustine's, although there is no evidence that Pelagius influenced them. Augustine responded calmly in four treatises: *De gratia et libero arbitrio, De correptione et gratia, De praedestinatione sanctorum,* and *De dono perseverantia.* There can be no doubt that these polemics led Augustine to take a harder line on his doctrine of grace and free will. After what had become one of the major theological debates of the fifth century, Augustine's disciples, among whom Prosper of Aquitaine was the most influential, put forward the version of Augustinianism* that was given official sanction by the Western Church at the Council of Orange in 529. Meanwhile, Pelagianism, as represented by Celestius, had been condemned as heretical by the Council of Ephesus*. These polemics made no impact on the development of doctrine in Eastern Christianity, and the theological refinements that they supported were never accepted within Greek theology—which, we should perhaps conclude, never had any need to accept them.

● BAug 21–24, Augustin et la crise pélagienne.
Julien d'Éclane, CChr.SL 88.
Pelagius, PLS 1, 1101–560.
◆ G. de Plinval (1943), *Pélage, ses écrits, sa vie et sa réforme: Étude d'histoire littéraire et religieuse,* Lausanne; id.

(1967), "Vue d'ensemble sur la littérature pélagienne," *REL* 29, 284–94.
T. Bohlin (1957), *Die Theologie des Pelagius,* Uppsala.
H.-I. Marrou, J.R. Palanque (1967), *Prosopographie pélagienne,* Paris.
P. Brown (1968), "Pelagius and His Supporters. Aims and Environment," *JThS,* NS 19, 93–114.
G. Bonner (1972), *Augustine and Modern Research on Pelagianism,* Villanova.
G. Greshake (1972), *Gnade als konkrete Freiheit: Eine Untersuchung des Pelagius,* Mayence.
O. Wermelinger (1975), *Rom und Pelagius: Die theologische Position der römischen Bischöfe im pelagianischen Streit in den Jahren 411–432,* Stuttgart; id. (1979) *Das Pelagiusdossier,* Stuttgart.
F.G. Nuovolone, A. Solignac (1986), "Pélage et le pélagianisme," *DSp* 12, 2889–942.
C. Pietri (1995), "Les difficultés du nouveau système (395–431): La première hérésie d'Occident: Pélage et le refus rigoriste," in C. (†) and L. Pietri (Ed.), *Histoire du christianisme,* vol. 2: *Naissance de la chrétienté (250–430),* 453–79, Paris.
J.M. Salamito (1997), "Excellence chrétienne et valeurs aristocratiques: la morale de Pélage dans son contexte ecclésial et social," in G. Freyburger, L. Pernot (Eds.), *Du héros païen au saint chrétien,* Paris, p. 139–57.

MARIE-ANNE VANNIER

See also **Asceticism; Augustine of Hippo; Manicheanism; Predestination**

Penance

1. Baptism, the First Sacrament of the Forgiveness of Sins

At Pentecost, Peter preached "Repent, and be baptized every one of you in the name of Jesus Christ for the forgiveness of your sins; and you shall receive the gift of the Holy Spirit" (Acts 2:38). "I acknowledge one baptism for the forgiveness of sins," says the creed of Constantinople* (381). In Christian antiquity, baptism was often called "remission of sins" (e.g., Tertullian* in *De bapt.* 18. 5). Until the late second century baptism was in fact the only penitential practice, and for the first four or five centuries Christians who were faithful to their baptism knew no other "sacrament*" of forgiveness. Minor sins (later often called *peccata mi-nuta*) committed after baptism were remitted by God* because of inner regret (conversion*) and its expression in outward "works" of penance, among which the triad of almsgiving, fasting, and prayer* held a privileged position. The first of these, because of its importance in the Bible (Tb 4:10 and 12:9, Sir 3:30; and Mt 6:2–4; and the theme of *koinônia* through sharing: Acts 2:44–45 and Heb 13:16), was often preeminent: "Almsgiving is excellent penance for sin; fasting is better than prayer, but almsgiving is better than either" (2 Clement 16:4, about 150). Thus all of Christian life is a baptismal existence, which is nothing but the daily exercise of conversion *(metanoia)* and its outward expression in penitential behavior. Well before becoming the object of what was later called a "sacrament," penance was a fundamental attitude (a "virtue*") of the Christian. With few exceptions, the Fathers* of the Church spoke much more of this daily penance than of the disciplinary form of it that was reserved for serious sins.

When it came into existence, the practice of post-baptismal penance was understood and experienced as a kind of copy of baptism ("second baptism," "laborious baptism," "baptism of tears," says Tertullian). In any event, in the third and fourth centuries there was a generally parallel development in length (several years) and severity (harsh prohibitions) of catechumenical practice in preparation for baptism, and in the practice of penance for the forgiveness of serious sins committed after baptism. Similarly, when the catechumenate was reduced to the period of Lent in the seventh century, there was a parallel reduction in the period of penance (*Old Gelasian Sacramentary* I. 15–16 and 38). Moreover, catechumens and penitents each formed a group apart, and being considered only peripheral members of the Church*, were dismissed on Sunday* after the homily, that is, before the offering of the Eucharist*.

2. Origin and Development

a) Ecclesiastical Post-Baptismal Penance Appears. Until the second half of the second century, each local* church treated instances of unfaithfulness to baptism on a case by case basis, as Paul had done with the fornicators of Corinth (1 Cor 5). As long as Christian communities were small and found themselves in a precarious situation (harassed and threatened with persecution), and were moreover characterized by a vivid expectation of the coming Parousia* of the Lord Jesus*, the "sacrament-oath" of baptism was experienced as a veritable pact between God and the Christian. It marked a definitive passage from the kingdom of Satan to the kingdom of Christ*, from the "old nature" to the "new nature" (*see* Col 3:9–11), and there is a good deal of evidence to suggest that this passage had a psychological effect as powerful perhaps as that of the vows taken today by monks and nuns. It is understandable, in these circumstances, that cases of serious unfaithfulness were relatively rare.

Those cases became much more frequent when Christians began to find themselves in a Church that was growing in numbers ("multitudinism"), with the relative decline in fervor such a sociological situation involved (in contrast to that of a "sect"), and when they were less inspired by the "enthusiastic" expectation of an imminent Parousia. And it was in order to provide a remedy for the increase in cases of unfaithfulness to the "pact" and the sanctity of baptism that a penitential practice other than baptism came into being. It was a difficult birth. If we are to believe *The Shepherd* of Hermas (Rome*, mid-second century), many Christian "doctors" rejected the reintegration of serious sinners into the community. Against these rigorists who left no hope of salvation* to those who had betrayed their baptism, Hermas took a position, expressed in the course of a vision, that guaranteed a second chance—but in order to bar the door to laxity, this would be the last chance (*Pastor[or Shepherd],* Mandate IV. 29. 8). A few decades later, Tertullian attested to the existence of this penitential practice, which historians usually call "canonical" (*De. paen.*; SC 316).

b) System of Canonical Penance. The canonical system governed the penitential discipline of the Church until the seventh century. It was reserved for sins that were considered very serious, those that, like the triad of apostasy, adultery, and murder, constituted a break with baptism. Everyday sins were remitted by God through the practice of daily penance. Fully developed in the fourth century, canonical penance had two major characteristics. First it was an entirely ecclesiastical process, which meant not only that it was public (only the confession of serious sins to the bishop* himself was not, even though some people refused to confess until the bishop, knowing their sins, obliged them to), but also that its public nature, through association with the *ordo poenitentium* and the various forms of asceticism* that were connected to it in matters of dress, food, and sexual conduct, was not primarily intended to humiliate the penitent, but to call on the Christian community to support him with its prayer of intercession and by its example. Second, this process was unrepeatable: The second chance for salvation "after the shipwreck" (Tertullian), it was also the last, or else it would have "seemed [they were] opening a new path for sin" (*DE paen.* VII. 2). This second principle constituted a kind of practical dogma*. For example, speaking of "penance carried out publicly," Ambrose* writes: "Just as there is only one baptism, so there is only one penance." (*De paen.* II. 95; SC 179). Of course, many bishops, including some of the most eminent, demonstrated a certain pastoral flexibility, but these exceptions confirmed a rule that was considered inviolable.

However, although this long and severe system was able to function relatively well in the framework of "confessing" communities, its limits soon became apparent. This is attested to by many patristic sources from the second half of the fourth century. Many of the baptized who were guilty of serious sins constantly delayed their request to enter into penance because they were discouraged in advance by the rigors of the ordeal. As for those who had made the request, few carried out their penance "as they should" (Ambrose, ibid., II. 96). The situation even reached the point that, in order to avoid relapses that would now be irremediable, and in order not to create an aberrant ecclesiology* (Christian communities would have ended by being made up of a mass of penitents much more numerous than those faithful to baptism), several synods (synod*) in the fifth and sixth centuries took the step of prohibiting the entry into penance "to people who are still young...because of the weakness of their age" (synod of Agde, 506) and to married people insufficiently "advanced in age" (synod of Orléans, 538). The bishops themselves thereby officially recognized the failure of the canonical system. However, they did not replace it with any other institutional form; there was indeed no question of challenging the singleness of penance. For example, in the sixth century, Caesar of Arles took note of the fact that nearly all sinners who were seriously guilty would ask for and be given penance only toward the end of their lives or even on their deathbeds. But he warned them that a penance of this kind may well be ineffective if it is not prepared for by a truly penitential life (*Serm.* 60. 3–4; SC 330). This was perhaps an appropriate pastoral solution, but it made even more apparent the impasse at which the sacramental institution had arrived. In any event, the canonical system had become distorted. From a demanding remedy reserved for a few serious sinners so that they might experience a true conversion with the support of the community, it had now become a means of salvation demanded by everyone on their deathbeds.

c) System of Tariffs and Repeatable Penance. Given this impasse, it is easy to understand the rapid success achieved by the practice of establishing tariffs for repeatable penance that the Irish monks of Saint Columbanus introduced on the continent in the seventh century. Of course, there were protests, such as that of the synod of Toledo (589), scandalized by the "atrocious audacity" of those who allowed the faithful not to do penance "according to the canonical manner" and offered them reconciliation "each time they sinned"; there were similar objections from the synods of Chalon-sur Saône (813) and Paris (829) (Vogel 1969). But to no avail; social and cultural developments and the dominant position of the Church in society* had made it impossible to return to the old system, despite all the "authorities" with which it was crowned.

The new system remained in competition with other penitential practices, from entry into a monastery, considered the most efficacious penitential rite, to direct confession to God (Council of Chalon-sur-Saône [813], can. 33; Vogel 1969), and including pilgrimages (pilgrimage*) imposed by confessors and almsgiving. The new practice had three principal characteristics. The most important was the fact that Christians could now have access to "sacramental" penance as often as they wished. The second is related to the ritual process: Confession was most often made on the basis of a series of questions that the confessor would put to the penitent following the book known as a "penitential"

that he had at hand. The confessor would then add up the tariffs corresponding to each sin, which often amounted to several months or years of fasting, or the recitation of a certain number of complete psalteries, or, from the Carolingian period and for particularly serious sins, a pilgrimage. The penitent would normally return after completing his penance to receive "absolution" from the priest (the term began to replace the former vocabulary of *reconciliation*). We may note in passing that oral confession, which was required only in the case of serious sins, was no longer merely a prerequisite for penance; it took on an entirely different significance, because it was now the means of establishing the expiatory punishment, which remained the most important element in the process, because, as Paschasius Radbert wrote in the ninth century, that was "what obtained the remission of sins" (*In Mt.*, about 155). However, and this was the third characteristic, the length of penances imposed after confession was so great that a system of redemption or compensation had to be established: you could have a certain number of masses said, or recite a certain number of psalms*, or perform a certain number of genuflections, or give specific amounts of money in alms, these amounts redeeming a specific number of days, months, or even years of penance. As a consequence, this system too eventually became corrupt, since the better off could afford to have many masses said or even pay someone to fast in their place.

d) "Modern" System of Penance. After the first two "revolutions" represented by the institutionalization of a post-baptismal penance and then the possibility of repeated penance, there came a third. This has come to be called "modern," for want of a better term, and made its first appearance in the 12th century. From that time onward, absolution preceded the penance that was to be carried out. In practice this had begun with the introduction of the system of tariffs. Many penitents, because of distance or misunderstanding, did not return to ask for absolution after completing their expiation*. But the practice was now justified theoretically, for, as was stated in the celebrated letter *De vera et falsa paenitentia* (11th century, although it was at the time attributed to the authority of Augustine*): "the shame inherent in confession itself accomplishes a large part of the remission" as well as "a large part of the expiation" (no. 10). In any event, in the late 12th century Pierre le Chantre stated what would soon become a commonplace: "Oral confession makes up the largest part of satisfaction" (PL 205, 342). This theory obviously presupposed that particular importance was now given to confession, in some ways more than to expiation, at a time, moreover, when the latter was becoming simultaneously less severe and more inward. In fact, in order to justify its expiatory import, confession, which was now expected to be precise and detailed (see the 16 conditions given in the *Supplement* to the *Summa Theologica* of Thomas* Aquinas, q. 9. a.4), became more humiliating; and this situation was aggravated by the fact that many priests (priesthood*) were ignorant and lacked the necessary discernment, as Thomas noted with sadness in the 13th century (*Suppl.* q. 8. a. 4. ad 6) and Johann Eck in the 16th (Duval 1974 [1985]). This shift in emphasis in the 12th century went along with the abandonment of the penitentials, which were out of tune with the new culture, and their replacement by the "confessors' manuals," which made their appearance in the 13th century. Even more significant was the fact that, in line with Thomas, confession was now considered as being, along with contrition and satisfaction on the one hand, and absolution by the priest on the other, one of the "integral parts" of the sacrament, which existed only when all four elements were present (*ST* IIIa. q. 90). As a consequence, the confession of each and every serious sin was no longer a mere prerequisite for the penitential process as in antiquity, nor a mere ritual device necessary for the establishment of the tariff as in the early Middle Ages. It had become a constituent element of the sacrament itself. It is also clear that the Church found in confession an effective tool for social control, both for detecting heretics (*Suppl.* q. 6. a. 3) and for inculcating the people with a Christian ethos.

In 1215, canon 21 of the Fourth Lateran* Council made it an obligation of every Christian to confess at least once a year to his own priest (but not to receive absolution, which had only ever been required by the Church for mortal sins) (*DS* 812). At the time, only a handful of *perfectissimi,* like Saint Louis, confessed weekly or more often; the majority of Christians confessed very infrequently (N. Bériou, in Groupe de la Bussière 1983): "It is usually thought that if annual confession gradually became customary, this was as much because of social constraint as because of the persuasive power of preachers." The pastoral theory and practice that came out of the Counter Reformation succeeded in inculcating in a large segment of the population the practice of three or four confessions a year, whereas an elite frequented the confessional (due to Carlo Borromeo after Trent) every week or even more often. This practice of "devotional" confession, with the many debates to which it gave rise on attrition and contrition, on delays in absolution, on moral dilemmas, and on "probable" and "more probable" opinions (*see* Delumeau 1990), obviously derived from a conception of the sacrament different from the one that prevailed in the early Church. It is to

be associated more with the monastic practice of therapeutic confession or the practice of spiritual* direction. In any event, it was grafted onto ecclesiastical penance for the forgiveness of serious sins—the definition of which, it is true, varied from period to period—and the sacrament of penance in its modern form was thus a blend of two different kinds of practice and of theory: sacramental penance for the reconciliation of Christians who have broken faith with their baptism, and spiritual companionship on the path to evangelical perfection (at the risk of making both lose their relevance).

e) Reformation and the Council of Trent.   The leaders of the 16th-century Reformation recognized only two sacraments attested in the Scriptures: baptism and holy communion. However, in 1520 (*WA* 6. 501, 543, 572), 1522 (10/3. 395), and 1545 (54. 427), Luther* had been hesitant about confession, whose benefits he personally appreciated. As for Melanchthon, he had explicitly recognized penance as a "sacrament properly speaking" in the *Apology of the Augsburg Confession* (*BSLK* 259, 292). In addition, they all attached great importance to the confession of sins, whether in a general form by the community at the beginning of the service (e.g., Calvin* in *The Form of Prayers and Ecclesiastical Chants* of 1542, *CR* 34. 172–83), or privately, "to a brother," even if he was not a priest. In that case, wrote Luther, "I do not doubt that absolution of his hidden sins will be granted to whoever asks forgiveness and reforms in the presence of a brother alone" (*De capt. bab.*, *WA* 6. 547).

In 1551 the Council of Trent* (*DS* 1667–1715) opposed the Reformation on three points. First, it affirmed the sacramental status of penance; second, it required the confession of all sins (still with the meaning of "mortal sins") and reserved to priests the power to absolve in the name of God; finally, absolution was defined "as a judicial act," which meant that, like a legal decision, it accomplished what it said. It had a "performative" and not merely a declarative effect (*see* Duval 1985).

f) Ritual of Vatican II.   The *ordo paenitentiae* promulgated in 1973 was an innovation in the existing situation, in particular because it suggested several forms for the celebration of the sacrament: individual reconciliation of the penitents (numbers 41–47); reconciliation of several penitents with individual confession and absolution (numbers 48–59); reconciliation of penitents with collective confession and absolution (numbers 60–66), the latter possibility being reserved for exceptional circumstances. This pluralism has not stemmed a noticeable decline in the participation by

Catholics in the sacrament, and the link between confession and communion* that was still so strong in the 1950s has very substantially loosened. In three decades (1952–83) the percentage of the French population that identifies itself as Catholic and going to confession "at least once a month" has fallen from 15 to 1 percent, and those going "at least once a year" from 51 to 14 percent (J. Potel, *MD* 167). A decline of this order is obviously linked to the cultural transformations of late modernity: displacement of the feeling of guilt, currently weak impact of the sacrament on the social fabric, loss of influence of the institution of the Church, emphasis on the individual ability to choose, and the like. But it is not out of the question that such social and cultural changes will gradually lead to a transformation of the current practice—despite its "modernization," still very much bound up with the Tridentine spirit—into a new penitential system.

3. Some Particular Points

a) Each Penitential System is the Reflection of a Historical Period. The appearance of *canonical* penance corresponded to a necessity, that of struggling against a relative decline in fervor in a period in which Christian communities were becoming more numerous. However, because of its demands, the system could function well only in "confessing" communities; it thus proved inadequate when the Church became "multitudinist" and it became socially advantageous to be a Christian: "I have had less trouble meeting people who have preserved their baptismal innocence than people who have done penance as they should," Ambrose noted bitterly (*De paen.* II. 96). And Augustine complained that "what should be a place of humility has become a place of iniquity" (*Serm.* 232. 7, 8). We have seen how the synods of Gaul declared that canonical penance was a failure. As for the system of tariffs, which came from outside the hierarchy*, it was fairly well adapted to a Church that wanted to convert the "barbarian" invaders. In a world marked by Germanic feudal law, in which any disorder, by an offense or the shedding of blood, was subject to carefully calculated compensation, the application of penitential tariffs was not at all surprising. And as for the *modern* system, with its insistence on the detailed confession of every sin and the evaluation of its gravity as a function of its subjective aspects, particularly in relation to intentions and circumstances, that itself seems to have corresponded to the new Scholastic culture that emerged in the 12th century. Hence, each penitential system was to some extent a reflection of the social and cultural situation of the Church, and that extended to the hierarchy of sins that it established and its emphasis on one kind of sin or another: sins, too, have their history. And it is no doubt the search for an new coherence of penance with contemporary culture that has given rise to current perplexities in this area.

b) Each System Emphasized a Different Point. Whatever the penitential system of the period, the Church never forgot the primordial role of inner repentance, or contrition, in the reconciliation of the sinner with God; it can even be said that the primary focus has always been placed on this conversion of the heart. The external manifestation of this inner movement has, however, been subject to different emphases. In antiquity the emphasis was on the effective conversion of the sinner throughout the penitential process, and not primarily on the rite of reconciliation by the bishop. The rite was certainly not without importance, but it was understood rather differently from the way the Scholastics were to understand it. First, it was related to the prayer for intercession by the entire community. The *Didascalia* (II. 12) says: "Bishop…lay your hand on the sinner while the entire assembly prays for him, and then allow him to go into the church and receive him into your community." The exhortation that "all the brothers" join in the prayer of the penitent (Tertullian, *De paen.* IX. 4) and that the sinner ask God's forgiveness "through the prayers of all the Christian people" (Ambrose, *De paen.* I. 89) was so insistent that Caesar of Arles had to warn penitents against the temptation of resting too comfortably on "the intercession of the whole community" (*Serm.* 67. 3). This intercession took place not only in the course of the period of penance, but in the course of the reconciliation itself. Was it not, according to Augustine, the whole Church (which required the bishop and his indispensable role of presiding), represented by the "confessing" Peter* in Matthew 16:16–19 or by the apostles in John 20:21–23, that remitted or retained sins (*De bapt.* XVIII. 23, BAug 29)? In any event, the bishop of Hippo had no hesitation in declaring to his entire community: "You also bind and you also loosen" (*Serm. Guelf.* 16. 2, SC 116. 41), clearly implying that this action of the Church in prayer during the celebration for the reconciliation of penitents shortly before Easter (Holy Thursday in Rome and Milan) achieved decisive efficacy only in its relation to the sacramental action of the bishop. This action demonstrated in particular that full reconciliation with God could not take place unless it was linked to a reconciliation with the Church (release from excommunication, understood in the form of an exclusion from Eucharistic communion, hence reintegration into the "peace" of the Church), which played the role of the "first effect of the sacrament," *res et sacramentum* in Scholastic language (Rahner* 1955).

In the second place, the rite of reconciliation by the bishop was understood as putting a seal on a reconciliation with God that God himself, and he alone—for "who can forgive sins but God alone?" (Mk 2:7)—had accomplished as the sinner gradually returned to him. The last point is in agreement with two gospel pericopes that the Fathers of the Church commented on most frequently with reference to ecclesial penance: the healing* of the ten lepers (Lk 17:11–19) and the resurrection of Lazarus (Jn 11). God alone can heal or give life; the role of the Church is to officially recognize this or to "unbind" (Jn 11:44) the one who has recovered life to allow him to enjoy it. Most of the Fathers of the Church would probably have adopted the formulation of Gregory* the Great (†604) commenting on the resurrection of Lazarus: "We must absolve through our pastoral authority* those of whom we know that they have already been given life by grace*" (*Homilies on the Gospels* 26. 6; Vogel 1969).

In penance by tariff the emphasis was still placed on the conversion of the sinner and its link to expiation. Expiation, however, had particular weight, as indicated by the use of the word "satisfaction" to denote it at that time. It is probable that the greater part of the theologians of the early Middle Ages could have adopted the formulation of one of them, the ninth-century Paschasius Radbert: "Confession indicates repentance, repentance brings about satisfaction, and satisfaction brings about the remission of sins" (in Mt., about 154). Absolution is not even mentioned. But we know that it existed, although the only role that it played, as Anselm* (†1109) said, was that through it, sinners "are shown (*ostenduntur*) pure before men" (*Homily on Luke,* 13; PL 158. 662). The emphasis was thus placed on the penitential works through which the sinner "repaired" the disorder introduced into the world by his sins and thereby "satisfied" God.

In "modern" penance, on the other hand, the emphasis was rather placed on confession itself and on the shame that it provoked. We have earlier seen the principal reasons for this and their coherence with the new culture of the 12th and 13th centuries. The importance of confession became so great, as indicated by the expression "go to confession," still in common use only a few decades ago, that a part was taken for the whole. We may wonder whether today, as shown by the success of community celebrations of reconciliation, the emphasis has not been displaced onto absolution itself.

c) What Is the Efficacy of the Sacrament? The first effect of absolution, reconciliation of the penitent with the Church, has always been clear as far back as the penance of antiquity; but it tended to be forgotten as the sacrament became more private and was associated

almost exclusively with "venial" sins, particularly in devotional confession. The second effect, on the other hand, reconciliation with God, did not clearly appear until the 13th century, as indicated by the formulations of Gregory the Great, Paschasius Radbert, and Anselm of Canterbury, quoted earlier. Like the latter, all the theologians of the 12th century, beginning with Peter Lombard, considered that the power of binding and loosing granted to priests by God meant the power "to show that men are bound or loosed" ("...*id est ostendendi homines ligatos vel solutos,*" *Sent.* IV. d. 18; PL 192. 887). But that meant that the sinner was generally forgiven by God before the sacrament. This was true during the first millennium to the extent that his conversion was accomplished through a sincere expiation; it was true in modern penance through his contrition (his *paenitentia interior,* in which Lombard saw the *res et sacramentum* of penance): "However small it may be [referring the amount of pain or distress felt], contrition erases all sin," wrote Thomas Aquinas (*Suppl.* q. 5. a. 3), because it proceeds from a true love* of God (unlike attrition, which is closer to "servile fear" and remorse). Thomas, however, opposed those of his predecessors and contemporaries who, like Bonaventure*, reduced absolution of the sin (*culpa*) to a simple manifestation of what God had already done (according to Bonaventure, "*absolvit solum ostendendo, scil. demonstrando absolutum*" [*In IV Sent.* d. 18. p. 1. a. 2. q. 2]). Of course, God does remit the sin when the sinner sincerely repents for it, but this repentance is authentic contrition only if, by virtue of the theory of the "integral parts" of penance, it implies the intent (*votum*) to submit to the "keys" of the Church. This is the usual case. However, Thomas explains, "nothing prevents that sometimes (*aliquando*) a person at confession receives grace and the forgiveness of the guilt of sin by the power of the keys at the very instant of absolution [and not before that moment]," just as this also "sometimes" happens to the catechumen at the time of his baptism (*CG* IV, c. 72).

In this respect, later doctrine effected a significant reversal, indicated by the Council of Trent itself. The adverb *aliquando* is indeed found in chapter four of its "doctrine on the sacrament of penance," but it is used there to make an assertion in opposition to theologians of the 13th century: it is "sometimes" that a sinner may be justified by God before the sacrament, to the extent that he has "perfect contrition," which includes the desire for the sacrament (*DS* 1677). But the notion of "perfect contrition" was set so high that it could clearly be reserved only for a small elite (*see* the *Catechism* of Trent, ch. XXIII. 2). The council thus closed the door on the presumptuous who would claim to have been forgiven before the sacrament. What was considered the rule three centuries earlier had become the exception, and this point manifests in pure form the difficulties that theology* has encountered in the articulation of a theory of penance and reconciliation. It was probably inevitable; it has always been difficult to find a balance between the subjective aspect of the sacrament, connected to the personal elements of guilt, sin, and contrition of the heart, and its objective aspect, connected to the Church as an institution. And it is not surprising that there has been a similar problem in the case of marriage*. As soon as the "matter" or rather the "quasi-matter" of a sacrament is no longer an objective reality such as water, bread and wine, or oil, but a reality dependent on human subjects (which is true for penance and marriage), sacramental theology comes up against its most troubling problems.

d) In the East. Since the Second Council of Lyon (1274, *DS* 860), "Greek theologians have expressly emphasized the sacramental character of penance" (Vorgrimler 1978). Important differences from the Latin Church nevertheless remained, particularly with respect to the meaning of confession and the role of the minister. 1) In the East, confession at first had a purpose that was more therapeutic than sacramental, and so the confessor had a role that was more medicinal than judicial. The latter aspect was not of course denied, but it "played no part" (ibid.).Therefore: "It has been emphasized since Basil* that not every ordained priest is qualified to receive the confession of sins, while conversely, for centuries, it was not required of the *patèr pneumatikos* that he be an ordained priest." In any event, "from the eighth century...confessors were almost exclusively monks" (ibid.), and most monks were not priests. 2) The East, then, officially recognized that each monk had a role as spiritual therapist through confession and penance, so that the status of a monk who is not a priest cannot, contrary to the Western practice, be assimilated to that of a member of the laity* (Taft 1987). 3) In the third place, absolution is given in the East in deprecative (exhortatory), not declarative, form, as was true for the West until the 13th century, the period when Thomas Aquinas evidences the shift from "May God forgive you" to "I forgive you in the name of..." (*De forma absol.*, c. 5); forgiveness by means of prayer sits easily with the status of monk. 4) Finally, we must take into account the more vivid awareness in the East than in the West of the Eucharist as a sacrament of the "blood

shed for the remission of sins." The requests for forgiveness in Eastern anaphorae, as well as communion itself, seem to hold not only for forgiveness of minor sins, but also for those that could be called "serious" though not "mortal," absolution of the latter being reserved to priests (Taft 1987; Ligier 1963). On this point as on many others, the East shows a sensibility different from that of the Latin Church.

● C. Vogel (1966, 1969), *Le pécheur et la pén*, I: *Dans l'Église ancienne*, II: *Au Moyen Age*, Paris.

H. Karpp (1970), *La penitence: Textes et commentaires des origines de l'ordre pénitentiel dans l'Église ancienne (Ier-IIIe s.)*, Neuchâtel.

◆ B. Xiberta (1922), *Clavis ecclesiae*, Rome, Barcelona (2nd Ed. 1973).

K. Rahner (1955), "Vergessene Wahrheiten über das Bußsakrament," *Schr. zur Th.* 2, Einsiedeln-Zürich-Köln, 143–83.

I.-H. Dalmais (1958), "Le sacrement de pénitence n. chez les Orientaux," *MD* 56, 22–29.

L. Ligier (1963), "Pénitence et eucharistie en Orient," *OCP* 29, 5–78.

L. Braeckmans (1971), *Confession et communion au Moyen Age et au concile de Trente*, Gembloux.

K. Rahner (1973), "Frühe Bußgeschichte," *Schr. zur Th.* 11, Einsiedeln-Zürich-Köln.

M.-F. Berrouard (1974), "La pénitence publique durant les six premiers siècles: Histoire et sociologie," *MD* 118, 92–130.

A. Duval (1974), "Le concile de Trente et la confession," *MD* 118, 131–80.

P.-M. Gy (1974), "Les bases de la pénitence moderne", *MD* 117, 63–85; id. (1984), "La pénitence et la reconciliation," in A.-G. Martimort (Ed.), *L'Église en prière*, vol. 3, 115–31.

H. Vorgrimler (1978), *Buße und Krankensalbung*, HDG IV/3 (reference work).

P. Adnès (1981), *La penitencia*, Madrid.

H. P. Arendt (1981), *Bußsakrament und Einzelbeichte*, FThSt.

P. De Clerck (1982), "Célébrer la pénitence ou la réconciliation? Essai de discernement théologique à propos du nouveau rituel," *RTL* 13, 387–424.

Groupe de la Bussière (1983), *Pratiques de la confession, des Pères du désert à Vatican II: quinze études d'histoire*, Paris.

R. Marlé (1983), "Crise du sacrement de pénitence," *Études*, 701–14.

P. Rouillard (1985), "Sacrement de pénitence," *Cath* 10, 1135–61.

R. Taft (1987), "La pénitence aujourd'hui: État de la recherche," *MD* 171, 7–35.

J. Delumeau (1990), *L'aveu et le pardon: Les difficultés de la confession: XIIIe-XVIIIe siècle*, Paris.

L.-M. Chauvet, P. De Clerck (Eds.) (1993), *Le sacrement du pardon entre hier et demain*, Paris.

LOUIS-MARIE CHAUVET

See also **Anointing of the Sick; Baptism; Confirmation; Eucharist; Marriage; Ordination/Order; Punishment; Sacrament**

Pentecostalism

1. Classical Pentecostalism

Pentecostalism is a revival movement dating from 1906. It is centered on the experience* of "baptism* in the Holy* Spirit, and its "first sign" is glossolalia or "speaking in tongues" (prayers in unknown or angelic languages: 1 Cor 13:1 and Acts 2:6), in accordance with Scripture (*see* Mk 1:8 and parallel passages; Lk 24:49; Acts 1:5, 2:4). Pentecostalism is today the largest of the Protestant churches (church).

a) History. Pentecostalism had precursors in the 19th century, but it really came into existence in 1906 in Los Angeles, in a chapel on Azuza Street whose pastor, W. Seymour, was the son of former slaves. At that time, there was a "new Pentecost," with baptism in the Holy Spirit and charismatic manifestations (glossolalia, prophecy*, healing*). From 1910 to 1939 the movement spread throughout the world, particularly among the working classes. Other churches did not recognize Pentecostalism, which rejected them in turn as untrue to apostolic faith* and experience, although it too had internal tensions and divisions. The first world Pentecostal congress took place in Zurich in 1947, an expression of the desire for unity. Pentecostalism has continued to grow since the 1950s, but in spite of greater ecumenical openness (e.g., a dialogue with the Catholic Church begun in 1971), few Pentecostal churches have joined the Ecumenical Council of Churches, for fear of inopportune alliances and doctrinal compromises.

b) Doctrine. Most Pentecostals are doctrinally orthodox. They particularly emphasize salvation* by the blood of Christ*, charismatic gifts, and the return of Christ. According to them: 1) Any Christian at any time can have access to baptism in the Holy Spirit and to charismatic gifts (Acts 2:37–38). Baptism in the Holy Spirit has a dual purpose: to provide greater sanctity and a spiritual power for proclaiming the gospel. 2) The essential elements of salvation are repentance, conversion*, justification*, new birth, and personal relationship with Jesus* Christ. 3) Baptism by water, preferably by immersion, is associated with conversion. Baptism in the Holy Spirit may precede it, particularly for the newly converted, but it generally comes afterward for regenerated Christians. 4) For some Pentecostals, sanctification is an instantaneous experience, for others it is a process lasting an entire lifetime. It is difficult to reconcile the doctrines of justification and sanctification. 5) Emphasis is placed on eschatology* and on a Parousia* of a premillenarian kind; before his reign of a thousand years on earth, Jesus Christ prepares a people by baptizing it in the Holy Spirit, hence the importance of 6) the proclamation of the gospel. 7) The Bible* is the word* of God, inspired and inerrant. 8) Theology* is not very important, nor is direct change in political and social structures. 9) Pentecostal morality is rigid and aims for personal sanctity. 10) Pentecostal ecclesiology deals primarily with the local, autonomous assembly of the "born-again saints," which is where the Holy Spirit manifests itself and makes visible the Church of Jesus Christ. But the existence of Pentecostal churches throughout the world, as well as the ecumenical experience, have obliged Pentecostalism to think more systematically in this area. 11) The organization of Pentecostal Churches has very varied forms. Pastors (pastor*) are in principle men, but women have played a major role in Pentecostalism, through the exercise of spiritual gifts and ministries (ministry*) (particularly in the proclamation of the gospel). 12) Charismatic manifestations, prayer* (sometimes spontaneous), and preaching* are the rule in Pentecostal services, where it is in fact difficult to reconcile liturgy* and free expression in the Holy Spirit. Communion is understood in the manner of Zwingli*, with no doctrinal insistence, but as the object of great fervor.

2. Charismatic Renewal

Charismatic Renewal, whose roots are Pentecostal, also attaches great importance to baptism in the Holy Spirit and to spiritual gifts, but it does not make glossolalia the "first sign" of that experience. Baptism in the Holy Spirit is a vital link between Pentecostalism and Charismatic Renewal, but the two movements are independent. Charismatic Renewal originated in the United States in the 1960s, first in Protestant churches, then in 1967 in the Catholic Church, among student groups who saw in baptism in the Holy Spirit a divine response to the initiatives of Vatican* II. Since then it has penetrated all Christian churches, including the Orthodox Church. It was established in France in the

1970s. Jews have also been influenced, and there are "messianic" communities, particularly in the United States and Israel. It has been estimated that in 2000, about a third of those who profess the Christian faith have had the experience of baptism in the Holy Spirit.

Charismatic Renewal, ecumenical in essence, has done a good deal for ecumenism. Officially accepted in the Catholic Church by Pope Paul VI in 1975, and in the Anglican Church by the archbishop of Canterbury, Donald Coggan, in 1978, it seeks to revitalize the whole body of Christ in every confessional family and to establish cooperation among churches for the spread of the gospel.

Charismatic Renewal has been able to adapt to different circumstances. Structured communities are frequent among Catholics, particularly in France (e.g., le Chemin neuf, L'Emmanuel, les Béatitudes); renewed parishes and groups are characteristic among Anglicans and Protestants. Small prayer groups can be found everywhere. Charismatic Renewal takes more interest than Pentecostalism in life in society*, but it does not give priority to political action. The essential thing is to be fully Christian, in the power of the Holy Spirit, and to seek to put into practice the ethics* of the kingdom* of God.

- L. Christenson (1963), *Speaking in Tongues: A Gift for the Body of Christ,* London.
- D. DuPlessis (1963), *The Spirit Bade Me Go,* Oakland, Calif.
- D. Wilkerson (1963), *The Cross and the Switchblade,* New York.
- M. Harper (1964), *Power for the Body of Christ,* London.
- M. Harper (1965 a), *The Third Force in the Body of Christ,* London; id. (1965 b), *As at the Beginning: The Twentieth Century Pentecostal Revival,* London.
- J. Sherrill (1965), *They Speak with Other Tongues,* Westwood, N.J.
- A. Bittlinger (1967), *Gifts and Graces, A Commentary on I. Corinthians 12: 12–14,* London.
- D. Gee (1967), *Wind and Flame,* Croydon.
- D. Bennett (1969), *Nine O'Clock in the Morning,* Plainfield, N.J.
- W. Hollenweger (1969), *Enthusiastisches Christentum: die Pfingstbewegung in Geschichte u. Gegenwart,* Zürich-Wuppertal.
- K. and D. Ranaghan (1969), *The Return of the Spirit,* New York.
- D. Gelpi (1971), *Pentecostalism: A Theological Viewpoint,* London.
- V. Synan (1971), *The Holiness-Pentecostal Movement in the United States,* Grand Rapids, Mich.
- A. Bittlinger, K. McDonnell (1972), *The Baptism in the Spirit as an Ecumenical Problem,* Notre Dame, Ind.
- M. Carothers (1972), *Prison to Praise,* Plainfield, N.J.
- W. Pulkingham (1972), *Gathered for Power,* New York.
- S. Tugwell (1972), *Did You Receive the Spirit?,* London.
- H. Mühlen (1974), *Die Erneuerung des christlichen Glaubens,* Munich.
- E. O'Connor (Ed.) (1975), *Charismatic Renewal,* Notre Dame, Ind.
- K. McDonnell (1976), *Charismatic Renewal and the Churches,* New York.
- A. Bittlinger (1978), *Papst u. Pfingstler,* Frankfurt-Bern-Las Vegas.
- K. McDonnell (Ed.) (1980), *Presence, Power, Praise: Documents on the Charismatic Renewal,* 3 vols., Collegeville, Minn.
- A. Bittlinger (Ed.) (1981), *The Church Is Charismatic,* Geneva.
- G. Stotts (1981), *Le pentecôtisme au pays de Voltaire,* Grézieu-la-Varenne.
- D. Dayton (1987), *Theological Roots of Pentecostalism,* Metuchen, N.J.
- P. Hollenweger (1988), *Geist u. Materie,* Munich.
- S. Burgess, G. McGee (Ed.) (1990), *Dictionary of Pentecostal and Charismatic Movements,* Grand Rapids, Mich.
- K. McDonnell, G. Montague (1991), *Christian Initiation and Baptism in the Spirit: Evidence from the First Eight Centuries,* Collegeville, Minn.
- *Tychique,* Lyon, vol. 93 (1991), *20 ans de Renouveau charismatique en France;* vol. 95 (1992), *Brighton 91;* vol. 99 (1992), *Les 25 ans du Renouveau charismatique catholique;* vol. 101 (1993), *La prière.*
- T. Smail, A. Walker, N. Wright (1993), *Charismatic Renewal: The Search for a Theology,* London.

GEORGE HOBSON

See also **Ecumenism; Holy Spirit; Methodism; Millenarianism; Pietism; Protestantism; Scripture, Fulfillment of**

People of God

1. Terminology

Two terms constantly interact in biblical Hebrew: *'am* and *gôy,* translated respectively as "people" and "nation." A third term, *le' ôm,* belongs to poetic language (psalms*).

'Am is the most frequently used (1,826 times), with

the following characteristics: most often in the singular, often followed by a possessive or a noun phrase, as in "my people" (Hos 1:9) and "the people of the Lord" (Ez 36:20). It may also become a proper noun (Ex 6:23; Nm 13:12). The word refers to a particular human community based on familial or political covenant relations. The expression 'am ha' ârèç, "people of the land," designates a local population (Gn 23:12) or an assembly of the people distinguished from its leaders (Jer 1:18 and 2 Kgs 11:14).

Gôy is less frequent (561 times); in the plural (the majority of cases) it is used to designate the many "nations" scattered over the earth (Gn 10:32). The construction "nation of" followed by "YHWH" or another god does not occur. The "nations" are the other peoples in relation to a community of reference, 'am.

Israel is thus normally designated by 'am. But it may also be called gôy when its behavior makes it resemble other "nations." The fact of having a king is a form of assimilation to the "nations" (1 Sm 8:20). It is possible to maintain both that Israel is a "nation" out of which God* makes a "people" (Ex 33:13) and that the descendants of Abraham will be a great "nation" (Gn 12:2).

The Greek of the Septuagint and of the New Testament generally respects the Hebrew distinction by using laos for 'am and ethnos for gôy. But the tendency is to strengthen the identification of laos with the people of God—Israel in the Septuagint; sometimes for Luke the Gentile Christians (Acts 15:14) or the Jewish Christians (Acts 18:10).

2. Old Testament

a) Structures and Developments. The people does not originate from the coming together of subjects or citizens around the authority* of a king or a law*. It seems rather to be built up out of the alliance of human groups ("clans" and "tribes") whose forms and places of residence are shifting (Gn 34:16) and on the basis of the recognition of belonging to a "God of the father" who gradually becomes the God of a people that is in making (Gn 49:24). The hypothesis that there was a stable organization, such as a "league" of tribes or a central cult* (in Gilgal?), at the time the Israelites conquered Canaan and defended themselves against the Philistines is not very likely; these events took place in a disorganized manner (Judges) rather than the contrary (Joshua). It was the need for a political and military order "like the other nations" that gave Israel the form of a monarchy. The people were then organized on a territorial and administrative basis that consolidated the settlement in the land of Canaan. The king made a covenant in the presence of YHWH (2 Sm

5:1–3) with the "twelve tribes of Israel" mentioned in Genesis 49:28. The king, a "son" of God (*see* Ps 2:7: "You are my son") represented the unity of the people before the God of Israel. His greatness or his faults gave rise to the admiration of the wise (Sir 47) or the harsh criticism of the prophets (prophet* and prophecy) (Jer 36). What the prophets said in the presence of the people often represented a challenge to royal government. But the end of political monarchy with the exile could not bring about the end of God's covenant with the people of Israel (Jer 31:31), nor of the dynastic promise made to David (Jer 33:14–15). The life of Israel was subsequently organized around the priestly class. The insurrection of the Maccabees (begun in 167 B.C.) succeeded in restoring independence to the people, though this was lost again with the arrival of the Romans (63 B.C.).

b) Ritual Signs and Election. It is thus over the course of a long historical development that we can distinguish two characteristic traits of this people at once so close to and so different from all others. Israel was a people called on to gather together around the major events of its history*, with commemorative rituals sometimes retrospectively introduced into the narrative* of the events themselves (Passover, Sinai, the crossing of the Jordan). The capacity to come together was expressed in the notion of *qâhâl,* as it appears for example in Exodus 12:6 (Passover). It was rooted in places and times (sanctuaries and feasts), but also required signs differentiating the people of Israel from other peoples. *Qâhâl* is thus in part a ritual notion requiring specific conditions such as circumcision (Gn 17:9–14 and Ex 12:44 and 12:48), and imposing criteria of genealogy (Dt 23:3) or purity* (Nm 19:20). A necessity for the life of the people, the assembly was embodied in the temple liturgy*, the pilgrimage* festivals, and the hearing and teaching of the law (Neh 8). God has even planned to call an assembly of all the nations on the holy mountain of Zion (Is 60:3 and 66:18).

The people of Israel is the object of a special choice, something commonly referred to by the term *election.* This confers on it the status of a consecrated people, "a kingdom of priests and a holy nation *(gôy)*" (Ex 19:6). This is a free act of God (Dt 7:6–8), who has conferred on one people among all the others the sanctity of his name. This status of being chosen can be called into question by this "stiff-necked" people (Ex 32:9), but it can never be erased for good. At the worst moments of history the prophets developed a theology* of a "remnant" of Israel from which a new people would be born: the survivors of the punitive catastrophe (Is 4:2) or the "Servant" chosen from among the people (Is 42:6 and 53:11) to bear its sins (sin*) and its suffering.

The permanence of the status as chosen people echoes the promises made to Abraham (Gn 12) and to David (2 Sm 7).

c) *Symbols.* Two varieties may be noted. One, along *familial* lines, in which YHWH governs all relations in the manner of a father. For example, the people is given the name of "son" (Dt 14:1) and, as chosen people, "first-born son" (Ex 4:22). But it is also an heir and identified with the "heritage" of YHWH (Ps 33:12). Another common image is that of the human couple*, with the man making an unfaithful wife return to him (Hos 2:16–25; Jer 2).

The other variety of symbol is that of the rootedness of the people in the *earth* that God has created, a part of which he has given them. Use is also made of the image of clay shaped by the hand of the potter, who is free to make and remake what he creates (Jer 18:5–6). But it is especially the image of the vine planted with love* (Is 5:1–7) or transplanted from Egypt (Ps 80:8–16), and the image of the flock led by a trustworthy and benevolent shepherd (Is 40:11 and Ps 77:20; and 95:7), that express the emotional bonds between God and his people. It represents the mercy* of the Lord and the call to the people to return to the God who has chosen them.

3. New Testament

a) *Jesus and His People.* Jesus* belonged to his people as an inhabitant of Galilee in a period when it and Judea were under Roman authority. He was born in the tribe of Judah (Bethlehem), "born under the law" (Gal 4:4), and circumcised (Lk 2:21). He came among a very divided people. The unity of the people, in whose name Caiaphas declared that the death of Jesus was necessary "that the whole nation shall not perish" (Jn 11:50), could not be constructed around the authority of the chief priests, which was more apparent than real. In this troubled context several "parties" proposed solutions with a political (Saducees, Zealots) or religious (Pharisees, Essenes) emphasis. Part of the teaching of Jesus was aimed at bringing together the dispersed people that he considered deprived of a shepherd (Mt 15:24 and 23:37). His mission was limited to them (Mt 10:7 and 15:24; *see also* Rom 15:8). He particularly called on all those "who labor and are heavy laden" (Mt 11:28). Some wanted to make him "king" (Jn 6:15). By virtue of the particular offense of which his judges convicted him, as well as by virtue of his crucifixion (a "curse", according to Dt 21:22–23.; *see also* Gal 3:13), in terms of the law, Jesus was cut off from the people.

b) *Universality.* After Easter the Spirit of God brought into being among the disciples a new people that maintained the characteristics of assembly (*ekklèsia* is a translation of *qâhâl*) and of being chosen. The Christian tradition* proclaims the fulfillment in Jesus Christ of the covenant formula: "And I will walk among you, and will be your God, and you shall be my people (Lv 26:12; *see also* Jer 31:33, 2 Cor 6:16, and Heb 8:10). Baptism* brings together in a single rite all the conditions required for belonging to the people of God (Acts 2:38).

From the moment of Christ's resurrection, this people becomes a new people through the welcome it offers to the "nations", who are thus called to share the same heritage: "by abolishing in his flesh the law of commandments and ordinances, that he might create in himself one new man in place of the two" (Eph 2:14), for the blood of Christ saved and consecrated an immense people "from every tribe and tongue and people and nation" (Rev 5:9).

In this way the people of God becomes a basic image of the reality of the Church* by opening up for it a historical and eschatological perspective: throughout history, this people is on its way toward a new world*. It is first of all a people of the baptized, endlessly sent out and brought together in order to exist before God. Entrusted to human "pastors" or "shepherds" who watch over the transmission of the gospel*, it proclaims to all people that they are called to come together under the sign of the kingdom* of God. In Christian language, "people" manifests the dynamism of the whole Church, whereas the "body of Christ" expresses a more organic, functional, and mystical dimension.

● H. Strathmann (1942), "Laos," *ThWNT* 4, 29–57.
E. A. Speiser (1960), "'People' and 'Nation' of Israël," *JBL* 79, 157–63.
A. Cody (1964), "When Is the Chosen People Called a *gôy*?," *VT* 14, 1–6.
E. Jacob (1968), *Théologie de l'Ancien Testament*, Geneva.
P. Grelot (1970), "Peuple," *VThB2*, 979–91.
S. Pancaro (1970), "People of God in St John's Gospel," *NTS* 16, 114–29.
A. George (1972), "Le peuple de Dieu dans la pensée de Jésus," *Masses ouvrières* 291, 3–49.
H. Cazelles (1982), *Histoire politique d'Israël*, Paris.
J. Dupont (1985), "Un peuple d'entre les nations, Ac 15, 14," *NTS* 31, 321–35.
H. Cazelles (1993), "Clans, État monarchique et tribus," in *Essays in Honour of G. W. Anderson*, Sheffield, 77–92.

XAVIER DURAND

See also **Choice; Church; Church and State; City; Covenant; Israel; Jerusalem; Jesus, Historical; Kingdom of God; Pagans; Political Theology; Secularization; Universalism**

Perichoresis. *See* Circumincession

Perseitas. *See* Aseitas

Person

Developed in the fourth and fifth centuries with the debates that elaborated the dogma* of the Trinity*, the concept of "person" would become a keyword in anthropology*, both philosophical and theological, to the point of obscuring its meaning as determined by the Councils of Nicaea* and Chalcedon*. The theoretical context in which the term *person* was used solely to speak of God* was replaced in modern times by a different context, in which the term seems to have no other use than to speak of human beings. Although no name* can refer to both God and humanity, analogic language must however remain a possibility, and a major theologoumen* (the creation* of man "in the image" of God) will always lead theologians to link what it says of God with what it says of human beings, even though the dissimilarity is greater than any resemblance, which preserves divine transcendence within the analogic relationship (analogy*). However, if it was to be possible to "offer the concept of 'person' to history" (Zizioulas 1981), the initial requirement was that the Greek Fathers* break with Hellenism, first by distinguishing God from the world as its *free* creator, then by making the Father the *free* source of divinity and, therefore, "the ultimate reason of being" (ibid.).

1. Origins: Antiquity

a) Rome.   The Etruscan cult of the goddess, P(h)ersephone, involved rites in which a mask, *phersu,* was worn. The Romans adopted the word and called *persona* (from *per-sonare,* "to speak through") the mask ordinarily worn by actors and, thereby, the role being played. In the third century B.C.E., grammarians used *persona* to indicate the first, second, and third persons. Then the legal sense of a person subject to law* emerged. In the first century before Christ, the same man could exercise numerous roles, or *personae,* within the social and legal fabric. Personhood was fluid, not fundamental.

b) Greece.   The Greek word *prosopon* means "face," and also came to designate the theatrical mask, but within a context in which the philosophical implications of this usage were clearer. Greek thought, in its spontaneous trends, has always tended to unite God and the world* so as they make a harmonious whole. In this whole, man owns nothing unique or lasting: at the time of death* the soul* either unites with another body (Plato), or disappears (Aristotle). There is no room for liberty*, and if theatre allows to dream of liberty and if it stages the revolt of human beings against necessity, such revolt always ends tragically, as the order of the cosmos* is reasserted.

2. Origins: Christianity

In antiquity, one common narrative procedure consisted in creating roles and assigning dialogue to significant characters. Ancient scholars used "prosopographic" exegesis* to interpret this technique. Early Christian theologians (e.g., Justin) found many scriptural instances in which God leads a self-dialogue (e.g., Gen 1:26; 3:22). They did not interpret them as they would literary fiction but as to means to show true differences. Thus, Tertullian* spoke of God in terms of one substance and three persons (PL 2, 167–68) and, to unite the divine and the human within Christ*, he spoke of Jesus* as one person, both God and man (PL 2, 191), thereby giving to the word *person (persona)* its full weight for the first time. Hippolytus (c. 170–c. 236) was the first to apply *prosôpon* to speak about the Trinity (PG 10, 821 A).

3. Greek Fathers

a) Athanasius. The first major theorizations of "person" arose with the fight against Arianism*, starting with Athanasius*. Arianism was countered by teaching that the Son belonged to the substance of God while the world came out of the will of God: the Son was not part of the created order. This new formulation departed from Greek thought in two ways. First, Athanasius denied any kinship (*suggeneia*) between God and the world: the world was a product of freedom, not an eternal given. Second, although he continued to consider substance as primordial, he recognized that the Son was other from the Father within the being *(ousia)* or substance *(hupostasis)* of God (PG 26, 53 B).

To name the deity*, Athanasius used *hupostasis* and *ousia* interchangeably, as did the Fathers that preceded him. *Hupostasis* is the literally equivalent of "substance" (*see* Heb 1:1), even though in the fourth century it could also refer to a real individual. Thus Arius maintained that there were three *hupostaseis* in God; meaning three substances (PG 26, 709 B). The Synod* of Sardica (342) responded to Arius by declaring that there was only one *hupostasis* of the Father, the Son, and the Holy Spirit (PG 82, 1012 C). To avoid the hint of heresy* that accompanied the term, Athanasius never applied *hupostasis* to the three persons of the Trinity.

b) Cappadocians. The theological contribution of the Cappadocian Fathers Basil*, Gregory* of Nyssa, and Gregory* of Nazianzus resulted from their struggle against Sabellianism—a modalism* that reduced the divine persons to the level of divine ways of being. They had to assert that each of the divine persons was a true being, against the view that Father, Son, and Spirit are simply roles assumed by one divine monad. Since the term *prosopon (persona)* recalled the idea of a theatrical role, the Cappadocians tried to give it ontological weight by identifying it with *hupostasis,* in the

sense of a concrete being, and by forbidding the assimilation of *hupostasis* with *ousia.* Basil warned (PG 32, 884 C): "Those who say that *ousia* and *hupostasis* are the same are compelled to confess only different *prosopa,* and by the use of the words *treis hupostaseis* (three *hupostaseis*) do not succeed in escaping the Sabellian evil." However, the *hupostasis* did not cease to possess divine *ousia:* a divine person is "neither an individual of the species 'Divinity' nor an individual substance of divine nature" (Lossky 1967) but rather the full reality of the divine nature.

When applied to man, the distinction between "nature" and "person" allows to set a limit: with man, nature precedes the person, so that no one can carries the totality of human nature with himself and therefore the death of one does not entail the death of all. In God, however, no limitation of person by nature is conceivable: nature and persons, the one and the many, coincide in him, and each person is unthinkable without the others. Nature is defined by the three persons, and their relationship is of the essence of the deity, so much so that Basil equaled divine nature and the communion* of the divine persons: "in the divine and incomposite nature, in the communion of the Deity, is the union" (PG 32, 149 C).

The communion of the divine persons has an intrinsic structure. God does not have a source *(arkhe),* but the person of the Father is, in God, both origin and cause *(aition)* (Gregory of Nyssa, PG 45, 133 B and 180 C). "It is as Father, and not as 'substance,' and from the fact that he perpetually 'is', that God confirms his free will to exist. His existence as a Trinity constitutes precisely this confirmation" (Zizioulas 1981). The Cappadocians thus identified, at the origin of being*, the person of the Father, characterized by absolute freedom in communion with the Son and the Spirit. This is the pattern of true personhood; and, in so far as humanity is made in the image of God, this pattern also has relevance for anthropology (PG 45, 24 C–D).

c) Chalcedon. The identity of being and of being in communion is not inscribed in the nature of humanity. According to Gregory of Nyssa (PG 44, 701 D–704 A), however, freedom is precisely what gives human beings the possibility of overcoming the given character of his nature to obtain a personal existence. Christology* provides the necessary notions to help conceive how this possibility becomes reality. Between the Councils of Ephesus* and Chalcedon, and in the wake of Chalcedonian theology, the problem was to conceive the union "according to hypostasis," *kath'hupostasin,* confessed at Ephesus so that the humanity of Christ would not be blended with his divinity. The Chalcedon council confirmed the duality of natures after the union, while stating that the natures are united in a single person ("*prosopon* and *hupostasis*" in Greek, "*persona* and *subsistentia*" in Latin), namely, that of the "only-begotten Son" (*DS* 302). The main consequence was that the human nature of Christ had to be conceived as devoid of human hypostasis. This consequence led to a great paradox: the very nature in which the fulfillment of humanity is perceived is a nonpersonal nature, which exists without hypostasis (anhypostasy*), and is hypostasized in the hypostasis of the Word* of God. The neo-Chalcedonian theologians of the sixth century would make this paradox their key theoretical interest.

On the other hand, a hypothesis can be made: if Jesus' existence without a hypostasis is not simply an absolute *hapax legomenon,* and if it suggests that human nature is not defined in essence by the need for a human "hypostasis," then the Christian experience may be perceived as one of "Christification," in which human beings receive new modes of being that fundamentally constitute their persons more than they add to them. Access to existence as a person thus comes into question in the adoptive filiation* conferred in baptism*, in the life lived in the communion of the church*, and, above all, in the celebration of the Eucharist*.

4. The West and Augustine

With the Trinitarian theology and Christology, the Greek patristics was led to define the person as a being in communion, and this could be applied to the divine persons and to the human person. It can be said of the Latin tradition that its theology of the Trinity led it to illustrate another Christian notion, that of the individual as created, known, and loved personally by God (Mt 10:29ff.). Latin theology thinks of the human person in terms of its uniqueness. Consequently, interpersonality and communion became secondary and sometimes even disappeared.

a) Augustine. For Augustine*, person means—in God—"relation." The divine persons "are nothing but the act of relativity toward each other" (Ratzinger 1973), a statement that can easily rely on John's Gospel* (5:19, 10:30). John extends this relational model of persons to humanity (15:5, 17:11); Augustine may be said to have made (Ratzinger 1973) "a crucial mistake" by seeking an analog for the divine persons, not in the relations between human beings but in a triad of mental processes—memory, intelligence, and will, which he relates to being, knowledge, and love*, and constitute the image of the Trinity in human beings (PL 42, 982–84). One may then be misled to imagine

God as one person possessing these three faculties. Augustine may think of divine life as a logic of the lover, loved one, and love (PL 42, 960), this theology provides no basis for the idea of human personhood fed by interpersonal relations.

b) Boethius. What Augustine does not allow for will be made almost impossible after Boethius* had defined the person as "an individual substance of a rational nature" (*naturae rationalis individua substantia,* PL 64, 1343). It is true that the human person has a substantial existence, that it exists in itself and to itself; it is also true that rationality is essential to humanity. However, this definition can not be used in Trinitarian theology because it puts the emphasis on the being in itself and not interrelatedness ("being toward," *esse ad*); nor can it be used in Christology, because it does not allow us to think of the being-in-another that would be proper to the human nature of Christ. It was therefore destined to dominate anthropology, but also to legitimize an anthropology that, on one crucial point, the status of the relation, cuts humanity off from God.

c) Richard of Saint Victor. Richard witnesses this cut: the necessities of Trinitarian theology would lead him to amend Boethius's definition, although he would consider it valid in his anthropology. Richard defines the divine person as "an incommunicable existence of the divine nature" (*divinae naturae incommunicabilis existentia,* PL 196, 945), which does not really reflect the going out of one's self that characterizes the persons in God—this going out of one's self is barely hinted at by the notion of existence. Richard resorted to the psychology of human love to develop a model analogic to the Trinity as "lover-loved one-mutually loved (*condilectus*)" (PL 196, 922–27). This allowed him to compensate for the relative scantiness of his definition. He did not, however, really draw the consequences on the human person out of his construct: he used the grammar of human love to speak of the love of the Trinity, without having it affect the definition of the former.

d) Thomas Aquinas. Unlike Richard, Thomas* Aquinas regards Boethius's definition as applicable to divine as well as human persons, providing that "rational" is understood as "intellectual" and "individual" as "incommunicable" (*ST* Ia, q. 29, a. 3, ad 4). This could not, of course, be the last word on the subject. Aquinas states that "person" is used for God "in a higher sense" than it is used of creatures (Ia, q. 29, a. 3 resp.); "distinction in God only comes from original relations," so that "divine person" means "subsisting relation"

(I, q. 29, a. 4 resp.); and God is distinguished from human beings to the extent that the *esse ad* is primary in him. Therefore, relation enters into the definition only of *divine* persons. As a result, God's relatedness is a "theological exception" to the philosophical definition of the person, instead of being the new norm for philosophy* itself (Ratzinger). Generally, Thomas finds it sufficient, to speak of the one God or of human persons, to use a nonrelational definition of "person" as "a *hupostasis* distinguished by dignity," God's dignity surpassing all dignities (Ia, q. 29, a. 3, ad 2). "Dignity" here resides in the freedom of persons to determine their own actions (q. 29, a. 1 resp.).

e) Luther.   One of the great merits of Luther*, who said that faith* makes the person (*fides facit personam, WA* 39, I, 283 A/B), is to have conceived a completely theological anthropology in which human beings accede to themselves only within and through their justifying and liberating relationship with God (but in which the interpersonal relationship of the self and the other is not significant for the advent of the person). It is facing God, the "*coram* relationship" (G. Ebeling) that is key. Luther certainly does not deny the reality of autonomy, but he thinks of it in terms of the interpretation of the sinful condition, and uses the image of humanity "folded over itself" (*incurvatus in se*).]

5. Modern Times and the Contemporary Era

a) Back to the Self.   The theological anthropology of medieval western Europe was characterized by a certain neglect of the ontological issues of the relational being. Modernity is also "Roman" by virtue of a similar neglect. With Descartes, for example, the quest for the basis of knowledge leads to make subjectivity the key part of the person. Locke offers a new and modern definition of the person: the person is "a thinking, intelligent Being, endowed with reason and thought, aware of his identity and of his permanence in time and space." (*Essay* II, 27, 9). Both anchor the person in its vertical relationship with God; but neither they nor their contemporaries gave any importance to interpersonality in the constitution of the self. The self they describe is the one that would be claimed by the liberalism of the 18th century: humanity consists of fundamentally independent individuals.

From the Cartesian ego to Kant*'s notion of self and the German idealism and beyond, the variety of discourses and their oppositions presupposed a tacit agreement about the possession of the self by the self. For Kant, the other is the object of unconditional respect due to what cannot be transformed into a means, and ethics* can even lead to the elaboration of a transcendental ecclesiology*; but there is no authentic communion present at the birth of the "kingdom of ends." For Fichte, the self tends to absorb into itself everything that has precisely the status of non-self. Hegel* was a thinker concerned with going outside the self, and he was not capable of conceiving of a humanity that is abstractly equal to itself; but, while relations enter into the genesis of the person, its destiny is to go back to itself and to be satisfied with itself. Kierkegaard* thought only of "Christian becoming" and provided a spectacular development of Luther's intuitions; but, the human being who happens into a relationship of faith with God is a "unique one" or an "individual" (*det Enkelte),* who expects everything from God and nothing from other human beings. When Marx* developed the first systematic criticism of subjectivity, the result was certainly to make the person the product of relationships, but also to dissolve any consciousness into relationships that its only role (a final form of *persona*) is to represent.

b) Personalist Philosophy.   The emergence of philosophies in which communion is part of the genesis of the self is characteristic of the 20th century. Perhaps started by Max Scheler (1874–1928), such a philosophy was to be found amongst many authors, who often shared the same theism: Ferdinand Ebner (1882–1931) and Martin Buber (1878–1965) in Germany, Emmanuel Mounier (1905–50) and Maurice Nédoncelle (1905–76) in France, and so on. Their personalism, which is "philosophical" in the conventional definition of the term, seeks in various ways to base interpersonality, understood as *communio personarum* ("communion of persons"), in the relationship between the human person and a personal God. Still, the notion that the deity might live by itself a relational existence, which could analogically rule the relations between "I," "you," and "we," is missing from their work.

c) From Theology to Ontology.   In spite of the personalist protest, the definition of the person provided by Locke is still dominant, if not in philosophy then at least in mentalities. In the list of ideas inherited from the classical age, the person is a center of self-consciousness, an individual atom that freely determines its activity and its relations with others, including its relations with God. One can see why several contemporary Trinitarian theologies have suggested that the term *person* could no longer be used for theological purposes. Indeed, if the term has to be understood in this way, references to the three persons of God may be misunderstood for a confession of tritheism*. Because of this blurring of meanings, Rahner* recommended to use a different terminology: one would thus say that in God there are "three distinct ways of subsisting "*Subsistenzweisen*" (*MySal* II, pp. 389–93). Barth* had previously proposed an overhaul of theological discourse and had suggested to substitute "modes of being" (*Seinsweisen, KD* I/1, pp. 379–80) to "persons," which he thought as having been unclear from its earliest use. Rahner's proposed term is closer to Thomas Aquinas; as for Barth's term, it simply translated the Cappadocians' *tropos huparxeos.*

In opposition to proposals that continue to legitimize the strict separation of the theology of the Trinity from philosophical and theological anthropology, there has been a return in recent theology to a theocentric perspective on anthropology. For Henri Sonier de Lubac*, the theology of the supernatural* is directly correlated to a rejection of any monadic conception of the self: "possession is ecstasy" (1946). At the same time, an ecclesiology drawn from patristic sources allows one to overcome pietistic individualism ("the detestable self", 1938, 7th Ed., 1983); and the Holy Spirit intervenes as the creator of a profound communication between the soul and God, and between Christians in the sacrament of the Church. The Spirit is the one of whom it can be said that "he personalizes and he unifies" (ibid.). The person is thus "a centrifugal center" (ibid.). In the Trinitarian meditation of J. Monchanin (1895–1957), the circumincession* of the divine persons is also the last mystery of humanity. For J.D. Zizioulas, the search for an ontology of communion leads beyond a personalism based upon the requests and results of intersubjectivity to link personal existence with "ecclesial being." Because communion has a cause among human beings as well as within God, it is the Christian community gathered around the bishop* that is the image of the Son and the Spirit together with the Father. "In the Eucharist, the church becomes the reflection of the eschatological community of Christ,…an image of God's life as Trinity" (Zizioulas 1981). This view is also found in the *Catechism of the Catholic Church,* as well as in the first agreed statement of the Catholic-Orthodox theological dialogue: "The eucharistic celebration…makes present the Trinitarian mystery of the church" (1982). It offers the benefits of reuniting what the history of theology had set apart, and it reappears with other questions, under other names (Trinitarian ontology, eschatological ontology, and so on), as a contemporary task. To think of a being in the Trinitarian image of God, and of the humanity of human beings in this same image, to state the conditions under which humanity lives by vocation *(see Catechism of the Catholic Church)* what God is by nature, is certainly not a new endeavor, but it is not either anything that what recent research would have accomplished.

● A. Michel (1922), "Hypostase," *DThC* 7, 369–437.

M. Buber (1923), *Ich und Du,* Munich.

K. Barth (1932), *KD* I/1, Munich (*Dogmatique,* Geneva, 1953).

H. de Lubac (1938), *Catholicisme,* Paris (7th Ed. 1983); id. (1946), *Surnaturel,* Paris.

M. Nédoncelle (1948), "*Prosopon* et *persona* dans l'Antiquité classique," *RevSR* 22, 277–99.

B. Casper (1967), *Das dialogische Denken: Eine Untersuchung der religionsphilosophischen Bedeutung Franz Rosenzweigs, Ferdinand Ebners und Martin Bubers,* Freiberg.

Vl. Lossky (1967), *A l'image et à la ressemblance de Dieu,* Paris.

K. Rahner (1967), "Der dreifaltige Gott als transzendenter Urgrund der Heilsgeschichte," *MySal* II, 317–97.

J. Ratzinger (1973), "Zum Personverständnis in der Theologie," in *Dogma und Verkündigung,* Munich, 205–23.

P.H. Nidditch (Ed.) (1975), *J. Locke: Essay Concerning Human Understanding (1690),* Oxford.

J. Zizioulas (1975), "Human Capacity and Human Incapacity: A Theological Exploration of Personhood," *SJTh* 28, 401–48; id. (1981), *L'être ecclésial,* Geneva (*Being as Communion: Studies in Personhood and the Church,* Crestwood, N.Y, 1985).

J. Auer (1979), *Person: Ein Schlüssel zum christlichen Mysterium,* Regensburg.

L.B. Poerter (1980), "On Keeping 'Persons' in the Trinity: A Linguistic Approach to Trinitarian Thought," *TS* 41, 530–48.

Commission mixte internationale de dialogue théologique entre l'Église catholique romaine et l'Église orthodoxe (1982), "Le mystère de l'Église et de l'eucharistie à la lumière du mystère de la Sainte Trinité," *Irén* 55, 350–62.

K.L. Schmitz (1986), "The Geography of the Human Person," *Com(US)* 13, 27–48.

M. Fuhrmann et al. (1989), "Person," *HWP* 7, 269–338.

C. Schwöbel, C.E. Gunton (Eds.) (1991), *Persons, Divine and Human,* Edinburgh.

P. McPartlan (1993), *The Eucharist Makes the Church: Henri de Lubac and John Zizioulas in Dialogue,* Edinburgh.

J.S. Grabowski (1995), "Person: Substance and Relation," *Com(US)* 22, 139–63.

A.J. Torrance (1996), *Persons in Communion: Trinitarian Description and Human Participation,* Edinburgh.

PAUL McPARTLAN

See also **Anhypostasy; Christ and Christology; Circumincession; Consubstantial; Holiness; Hypostatic Union; Trinity**

Peshitta. *See* **Translations of the Bible, Ancient**

Peter

a) Until Easter.   A native of Bethsaida (Jn 1:44), Simon, son of John (Jn 1:42, 21:15ff.), *bar Iôna* in Mt 16:17, was a fisherman from Capernaum, where he had a house and family* (Mk 1:29f.; *see* 1 Cor 9:5). His brother Andrew, a former disciple of John the Baptist, already knew Jesus (Jn 1:40ff.). But it was at the beginning of the latter's ministry that Peter decided to follow him and become a "fisher of men" (Mk 1:16ff.; Mt 4:18ff.; *see* Lk 5:1–11).

The synoptic Gospels make Peter a special witness of the preaching of the Nazarene. Set at the head (Mt 10:2: "the first") of the list of the Twelve, who are the cornerstones of the new Israel* (Rev 21:14), Jesus gives him the Aramaic name *Képha,* "the Rock," in Greek *Kephas* and *Petros.* This name reveals as much the communitarian project of the Master as the role assigned by him to his disciple. Elsewhere it is family relationship that is emphasized (James and the brothers of Jesus) or a personal charism (Paul). It was their presence beside Jesus during his ministry that gave Peter and the Twelve their authority over subsequent Christian communities, including those who were not of the same persuasion.

Peter's authority is again underlined by his attitude during the "Galilean crisis." At that point he becomes the spokesperson of the faithful disciples. Here we touch on the historical basis of the "confessions of Caesarea" (*see* Mt 16:13–20) (confessions* of faith), of which John himself kept the memory alive for us (Jn 6:68f.). Until recently the exegetical debate on Mt 16:17ff was dominated by the question of authenticity. Today, many discern in this a creation of the community of Antioch , inserted here by Matthew (Refoulé, *RB* 99, 261–90); others see it as a creation of the community of Jerusalem (Grappe 1992). We might also consider that Matthew found verse 18 in a previous version of the pericope, distinct from Mark's. In the latter case, reinterpreting the name of Peter would serve to express the faith* of a community that was

certainly Galilean. This group was then waiting for the imminent coming of the "Son of the living God" (filiation*), who was to build ("I will build") his eschatological union himself. Caesarea Philippi, the site of the "confession," located at the foot of Mount Hermon, was considered one of the favored places of revelations* (Nickelsburg, *JBL* 101, 575–600).

However, differences did remain between Jesus and Peter. The cry, "Get behind me, Satan!" in Mark 8:33/Matthew 16:23 is the best example. Jesus firmly reminds Peter, who is strongly opposed to going up to Jerusalem* because he thinks it dangerous, of his disciple status: "behind the master." Accurately foretold (Mk 14:29ff.), Peter's denial (Mk 14:66–72) sanctions his human faults. At the same time, behind the reinterpretations developed by Luke, the demand made on Peter—"when you have turned again, strengthen your brothers" (Lk 22:31) clearly shows the theological dimension of Jesus' confidence that his work will survive his death ("I have prayed for you," Lk 22:32).

Luke 24:12 and John 20:2–10 point to Peter's confusion before the empty tomb; 1 Corinthians 15:5 and Luke 24:34 make him the first to see the Risen One. Most commentators are ready to explain by this experience the "principal role played by Peter in the early Church*" (Brown-Donfried-Reumann, 1974). We do not, however, have any account of the event and this raises questions. For this reason, we can assume that, in its first version, the 1 Corinthians 15:5 passage referred to the time when Jesus had followers while on earth, a time that is seen as a founding period. Furthermore, the manifestation to Cephas (and then to the Eleven) serves as a guarantee of the validity of the passages concerning Christ's redeeming death and Resurrection*. Moreover, in Luke 24:34 it has a ratifying function. This function of primary guarantor of community faith, already attested to by Matthew 16:18, is undoubtedly the oldest attributed to Peter.

b) Until Martyrdom. Acts presents Peter as the head of the church of Jerusalem. A spokesman for the apostles (apostle*) (Acts 2:14, 3:12, 4:8, 5:29), often accompanied by John (Acts 1:13, 3:1, 3:4, 3:11, etc.), he performs miracles (miracle*) "in the name of Jesus" (Acts 3:1–10, 5:15, 9:32–43); he presides over a gathering (Acts 1:15–26, 5:1–11), is sent to Samaria (Acts 8:14–25), baptizes the first uncircumcised male (Acts 10:1–48). In the end comes arrest and marvelous liberation (Acts 1:1–19); Peter then hands responsibility over to James (Cullmann 1952). These facts, to which Grappe (1992) assigns great importance, partly rest on ancient traditions. But in order to appreciate them correctly, Luke's literary and theological agenda also needs to be taken into account. For Luke, Peter is primarily an ideal figure of the past, the connection that guarantees continuity between Jesus' ministry on earth and what communities experience today, despite the ruptures caused by Jesus' death (Lk 22:31f., 24:3) and by pagan integration (Acts 10:1–11; 10:28) (universalism*). Given the brevity of Luke 24:6 on the post-Resurrection meeting in Galilee (Mk 16:7/Mt 28:7, 28:10), one can see in Peter's Jerusalem ministry a largely editorial construction on the part of Luke. We can draw this conclusion particularly from Acts 12:17, where Luke's intention is to show that James did not hold the chief position in Jerusalem outside the authority of Peter (Dupont 1984), but that James himself was, from the beginning, the "head" of the Jerusalem church (Gal 2:9; Acts 15:13; 21:18; *see* Jn 7:3; Eusebius, *HE,* II, 1, 2–4). Peter's own area of ecclesial jurisdiction was Capernaum and Galilee, as Mark and Matthew give us to understand, and as is supported by archeology (Claudel, *CrSt* 1993, *Sq; Bib* 74, 105).

Paul speaks of Cephas in Galatians and 1 Corinthians. In Galatians, and in the face of a challenge to his authority, Paul defends the legitimacy of "his gospel," by going so far as to recall an altercation with Peter in Antioch (Gal 2:11–14): therefore, Peter should not be pitted against him. The mention of Cephas in 1 Corinthians does not prove that he stayed for a long time with the addressees (Pesch 1980). But it is evident that here too, Paul sees in Cephas as the ultimate reference that is overly promoted around him (see the ancestral list in 1 Cor 1:12: Paul, Apollos, Cephas, Christ*). Although in 1 Corinthians 15:3b–5 Paul revives a tradition, received from Peter, which grants priority to the latter as the guardian of the kerygma, he takes care to extend this tradition in the ensuing verses (vv. 6–11) in order to legitimize his own role as apostle.

We meet a similar reserve in John. Certainly there is the confession of faith in Jn 6:68f, but in Jn 18:15f.; 20:2–10 the evangelist introduces the figure of that other disciple whose positive characteristics are highlighted by Peter's deficiencies. The "beloved disciple" is introduced in John 13:23f. (*see* 19:25ff., 21:7, 21:20–24). To Peter belongs the care of the flock and the witness of martyrdom; and to the beloved disciple belongs the privilege of "remaining" through the written account of his gospel.

c) More Recent Traditions. The question of the authenticity of Peter's first epistle remains the subject of great debate: certainly it would be better to speak of it as a production of "Petrine" circles. Whatever the case may be, according to 1 P 5:15 the apostle writes from Rome (in 96), the city named by Clement of Rome as the place of Peter's suffering (see *1 Clement* 5, 4 *Sq*; see Gaius's account around 200, in Eusebius, *HE* II, 25, 7)—a detail confirmed by archeologists. 1 Peter 5:12 also specifies that the writer of the letter is a certain Silvanus, identified by many as Silas, the companion of Paul and co-author of the epistles to the Thessalonians (1 Thes 1:1; 2 Thes 1:1). Mark, another old companion of Paul (Col 4:10; 2 Tm 2:11; Phlm 24), is also mentioned as being with Peter. These are the premises of the tradition* that regards Mark as Peter's interpreter (Papias; Eusebius, *HE* III, 39, 15). These are the first literary signs of the relationship, in Rome, between the figures of Peter and Paul. The reference to the letters of Paul in 2 Peter 3:15 ("our beloved brother") reflects the same trend. In this pseudo-epigraphic epistle, Peter also appears in the role of the guardian of orthodoxy* (Brown-Donfried-Reumann 1974; Grappe 1995). Gradually, along with other discourses, there emerges a discourse that will admit the "magisterium* of Peter."

● O. Cullmann (1952), *Petrus. Jünger, Apostel, Märtyrer,* Zurich.
R. E. Brown, K. P. Donfried, J. Reumann (1973), *Peter in the New Testament,* Minneapolis-New York.
R. Pesch (1980), *Simon-Petrus,* Stuttgart.
J. Dupont (1984), *Nouvelles études sur les Actes,* Paris.
G. Claudel (1988), *La Confession de Pierre,* Paris.
Ch. Grappe (1992), *D'un Temple à l'autre,* Paris; id. (1995), *Images de Pierre aux deux premiers siècles,* Paris.
R. Minnerath (1994), *De Jérusalem à Rome,* Paris.

GÉRARD CLAUDEL

See also **Apostle; Apostolic Succession; Authority; Church; Jerusalem; Jesus, Historical; Johannine Theology; Magisterium; Martyrdom; Mission/Evangelization; Pauline Theology; Pope; Rome; Tradition**

Philocalia. *See* **Hesychasm; Orthodoxy, Modern and Contemporary**

Philoponus, John. *See* **Aristotelianism, Christian; Tritheism**

Philosophy

1. The Logos and the Cross

It was in the general context of a confrontation between Christianity and classical antiquity that philosophy acquired the status of a theological object. This confrontation began in the Pauline corpus, where it took the form of an exclusion: while paganism* was defined by a search for wisdom*, *sophia,* Christianity's understanding of itself was characterized in contrast by a divine "folly," the folly of the cross (1 Cor 1:23). Just as much as it violated the principles of Judaism, the *logos* peculiar to Christianity thus appeared at once as contradicting the whole apparatus of pagan rationality (1 Cor 3:19). God*'s cause was that of Christ crucified, and the promise of the cross (1 Cor 1:18) was a thing that nothing in the *epistemè* of classical antiquity could in any way comprehend or accept. Athens had nothing in common with Jerusalem* (Tertullian*, also Tatian, *Oratorio ad Graecos,* etc.).

The words *philosophia* and *philosophos* appear only twice in the New Testament. In Colossians 2, 8 the distinctive characteristic of philosophy is its deceptiveness, inasmuch as it is connected to the "elemental spirits of the world*" *(stoikheia tou kosmou),* in other words the mythological and possibly demonic forces at work in paganism (*see* E. Lohse, HThK XI/1 ad. loc.). In Acts 17:18 the philosophers—"Epicurean and Stoic"—appear on the scene and provoke Paul's apologetic speech, only to end by mocking him: Athens does not wish to have anything in common with Jerusalem. It is notable, by the by, that Paul had some knowledge of popular Hellenistic philosophy: for example, he knew the Skeptic paradox of the liar (Ti 1:12).

2. Christianity as a Philosophy

The mutual exclusion of theology and philosophy could not, however, be the last word. Because the Christian discourse aspired to be accepted by pagans, just as it set out to be accepted by Israel*, the question of rationality and in turn of credibility* could not be dealt with by a simple, even simplistic, recourse to contradictions. Like any words, the words that it was Christianity's vocation to transmit could not be transmitted without the existence of a common vocabulary shared by Christian and pagan; it is therefore unsurprising that a large part of the theological efforts of the patristic age, from the time of the apologists*, should have taken the form of producing an interpretation of philosophy that would endow the evangelization of the Greco-Roman world with an adequate theoretical basis. Philosophical authority acquired a theological relevance in two ways:

1) Because classical antiquity, as theology attempted to interest it in certain events that had occurred in Palestine, revealed that its intellectual history was not just one of idolatry*, but also of a genuine desire for God, it became vital

that its principles should be in some way preordained to the gospel (that there should be a "preparation for the gospel"). And since a single God was Father* and Creator of everything, the hypothesis that there was some truth* ("seeds of truth," e.g. Justin, I *Apol.* 44, 16, II *Apol.* 8, 13 and 13, 5; Clement of Alexandria, *Strom.* VI, 68, 2, VII, 74, 7, etc. [apologists]) to be found in the pagan searches for wisdom could readily be based on that common origin of all humankind—if philosophy was able to speak the truth, this was because God had granted it a partial unveiling of his mystery*. Perhaps philosophical wisdom was in fact rooted in a *prisca philosophia* or a *sapientia antiqua,* in an ancient (and vanished) heritage common to both pagan and biblical expression. Clement of Alexandria did not hesitate to accord Greek philosophy the theological status of a *covenant* (*Strom* VI, 8, 67).

2) There was one fact that could not remain unnoticed for long. Theology did not have a vocabulary that belonged to it alone, and it was forever borrowing words and sometimes even principles from philosophy, both popular and learned. The same theologians who borrowed concepts of established philosophical origin were, however, careful to insist that they meant to speak "in the manner of the Fisherman and not in the manner of Aristotle", *alieutikôs, ouk aristotelikôs* (*see ACO* II 5, 84, 2–3). The decision, taken at the First Council of Nicaea*, to introduce the non-biblical concept of *homoousia* into the confession of faith* was, however, never called into question. Origen* had been the first to justify it: Christianity was entitled to plunder the philosophical reserves of the pagan world, just as the Hebrews, on the day of the Exodus, were authorized to seize "spoils from the Egyptians" (*Ep. Greg. Thaum.* 1–2, SC 148 186–191; *see* Augustine, *De doctrina christiana* II, 40). Pious fables reinforced the theological arguments: Greek wisdom was in fact a mere offshoot of biblical wisdom; not only was the wisdom of Moses older than that of Homer (*see* J. Pépin, *RevSR* 29, 1955), but Greece had even borrowed from Israel—instances were the borrowings from Solomon (Origen, GCS 8, 75, l. 23), the thefts of the Pythagoreans (Origen, *Against Celsus* I, 15), Plato's debts to a Judaism that he had encountered in Egypt (ibid., VI, 19). At any event, one point acquired the strength of an axiom: not only was dialogue possible between the philosopher and the theologian, on a basis of common rationality, but theology defined itself in terms of its

greater wisdom and no longer by a subversion of wisdom.

It was thus possible to turn the tables and claim for Christianity the status of genuine wisdom and genuine philosophy, while accusing classical antiquity of irrationality. The mere title of Theodoret of Cyrrhus's (c. 393–c. 466) *Cure for the Ills of the Greeks* is enough to show that over the course of four centuries theology had ceased to see itself as a form of unreason with divine support, and desired henceforth to be the guardian and arbiter of all rationality. It is therefore unsurprising that Christianity now presented itself as the representative of the true philosophy, understood as an existence in keeping with the nature of things, as a choosing of the good life. So Evagrius begins his *Ascetic Discourse* with the assertion that "numerous Greeks, and just as many Jews, have attempted to philosophize, but [...] only the disciples of Christ* have desired true wisdom" (*Philocalia,* ed. Astir, v. 1, 190). John Chrysostom* appears to have been the first to speak of "Christian philosophy" (PG 48, 956). A few years later Synesius, on being appointed as a bishop*, could declare that his transition to Christianity "is not an abandonment of philosophy, but an ascent towards it." During the same period, Christian monasticism* presented itself as an embodiment of the true philosophical life (*see,* e.g., Cassian, *Collatio* 4, PL 49, 583 C; Gennadius of Marseilles, PL 58, 1074 B). When in 529 Justinian closed the philosophical school at Athens, it must have seemed as though philosophy had in any case deserted it. Within the topology of the Christian experience* (i.e., within the recasting in terms of Christian "contemplation*" of the whole theoretical and religious complex that made up the pagan *theôria*), the monk, who led the life most worthy of being lived, became heir to the philosopher. Not only did Christianity speak the truth, and absorb into its pronouncements all the truths that paganism had had the grace to perceive, but the Christian ascetic, moreover, lived the true life, the wisdom or *hèsychia* that justified in existential terms the outcome of the philosophical experience . "Our philosophy" (e.g., Tatian, *Or. ad Graecos,* PG 6, 868 C), "the philosophy of the Christians" (e.g., Evagrius, PG 32, 248 A), "inspired philosophy" (e.g., Eusebius, *HE* VI, 19, 10, SC 41, 116), "philosophy drawn from divine Scripture" (e.g., Clement of Alexandria, *Strom.* VI, 17, 149)—such expressions, among others, became current as soon as Christianity began to dispute with classical antiquity. This was initially a matter of expressing the truth of an experience rather than of a theory. The shift in meaning that "philosophy" underwent in late antiquity, as is well illustrated by Christian usage, did not, however, give rise to any ambiguity: Christianity was certainly also indicating by such terms its participation in philosophical rationality, and in the end its out-and-out appropriation of it. Nobody can lead the true life without possessing the knowledge that gives access to that life.

3. Philosophy in the Service of Theology

Philosophy taken in its existential sense was to remain Christian, in the monastic environment, for a large part of the Middle Ages. This was true both in the East (Dölger 1953) and in the West, where the monastery was a "school of Christian philosophy" (Guerric of Igny, PL 185, 101 B), the monk a "true philosopher of Christ" (Peter Damian, PL 145, 251 C), the monastic experience "true philosophy" (Bernard* of Clairvaux, PL 183, 206; Peter of Celle, PL 202, 605 A, etc.), where Mary* herself became a "philosophical" figure (Leclercq 1956) and where finally "Christ is philosophy itself," *ipsa philosophia Christus* (Rochais 1951). These themes were to recur within Christian humanism*, and are central to the work of Erasmus*, who also recognized a "Christian philosophy," a philosophy, "doctrine," or "wisdom" of Christ (by which he meant not the experience of a particular group of believers but rather a characteristic of the Christian experience itself). Nonetheless, they were overshadowed during the Middle Ages by a more spectacular phenomenon: the strict dissociation of philosophy and theology, as enshrined in the organization of university work. The very period during which theology began to exist under the name of *theologia*—and began to regard itself as a science—saw the establishment of a strict division of intellectual work in which philosophy gradually lost the all-encompassing and existential sense that it had formerly had and came to be seen as a mere theoretical task. In the 12th-century schools* it was still possible to regard Moses as "the most intelligent of the philosophers" (Thierry of Chartres*). From the 11th century, however, the argument between the "dialecticians" and "anti-dialecticians" had clearly shown that philosophy was now seen—and practiced—more and more as a technique unconnected to Christian experience, whether this technique was seen as the prelude to a higher knowledge or as a "carnal," "worldly," "secular," and "vain" exercise (Peter Damian, Otloh of St-Emmeram, etc.).

The distinctions would become clearer once theology acquired the strictly "scientific" conception of itself that appeared in the work of William of Auxerre, which made it possible to develop an equally "scientific" conception of philosophy. An already ancient phrase, "philosophia ancilla theologiae" (*see* Baudoux 1937; the theory was prefigured as early as Origen; *see* Crouzel 1962), thereby acquired a new significance:

philosophy could bear fruit through its integration into a scientific progression culminating in the teaching of theology. On the one hand, philosophical reason was a profane form of reason, strictly ignorant of the mysteries of faith. On the other hand, it was not in its own right that it was interesting, but rather for its usefulness in the understanding of faith: if the love of Scripture can go hand in hand with a love of philosophy, Bonaventure says, it is because the latter can "confirm" faith (Quaracchi, 9, 63 A). Of course, admits Thomas Aquinas, "the study of philosophy in itself is permissible and praiseworthy, by virtue of the truth which the philosophers have grasped" (*ST* IIa IIae, q. 167, a. 1, ad 3). It was not for its own sake, however, that the theologian had recourse to philosophy; and the existence of a relationship of subordination enabled theology to "give orders" to philosophy and to use its contents (Thomas, *In Sent.* I, d. 1, q. 1, a. 1) to provide more evidence for its own sequences of reasoning (*ST* Ia, q. 1, a. 5, ad 2). Differences of emphasis can certainly be discerned, resulting from different conceptions of theology. These differences, however, are comprehensible only within a single framework of theoretical work and its relationship with truth. Philosophy had the status of a theological object in the Scholastic* scheme for two main reasons: it was a repository of conceptual tools, and it was a discipline bordering on theology. On the one hand, the theologian could define the limits of his domain only by locating the border between theology and philosophy; on the other hand, he could not inhabit his domain effectively without employing the conceptual techniques offered him by the philosophers. Any problems of coexistence were therefore a matter between the Faculty of Arts and the Faculty of Theology—but with the reservation that philosophy agreed to represent a body of knowledge less rich than theology, since it was a priori unaware of everything that is known in the element of faith and was thus incapable of pronouncing the last word.

However, neither the instrumentalization of Aristotelianism*, on which the theologians embarked with gusto, nor the status of a subordinate discipline accorded to philosophy by the theologians, could prevent the development of a purely philosophical Aristotelianism among the masters of arts at the University of Paris, in the hands of a Siger of Brabant (1240–84) or a Boethius of Dacia (?—c. 1270). This was a complex phenomenon. Some have seen in the work of the "*artiens*" a claim for the legitimate independence of secular reason* (Dante* was to place Siger alongside Thomas* Aquinas in his *Paradiso*). But even if the originator of the 1277 condemnations, Étienne Tempier, was paradoxically also the true author of the "theory of two truths," the Aristotelianism of the Parisian philosophers, influenced by Averroes, already contained in embryo (and perhaps more than that) the foundations of a rejection of theological reason and a reduction of the truly rational to the philosophical (*see* Bianchi 1990 and naturalism*).

It is not insignificant, moreover, that a secular ideal of "philosophical life" was experiencing a resurgence at this time; that this led to a degree of identification between beatitude* and the philosophical experience (or at least to the development of a concept of philosophical "bliss" that pushed theological beatitude into the background); and that it transferred the most significant characteristics of religious life to philosophy (*see* Siger, *Quaest. Mor.*, Boethius of Dacia, *De summo bono*). The monk had been considered as the true philosopher, but now the philosopher in the classical sense reappeared on the scene, investing his experience with the prestige that the monk and friar had enjoyed before him.

4. Philosophy Separated

The balance desired by high Scholasticism was unstable, or appeared stable only by virtue of the hegemony enjoyed by the faculties of theology. Henry of Ghent expressed the epistemological wishes of 13th-century theologians when he asserted that philosophy and theology share one single object that each approaches in a different way: the philosopher's path proceeds from created things to the knowledge* of God, while the theologian's leads from God to created things; the philosopher considers God by way of the general definitions through which God reveals himself in created things, while the theologian considers him in terms of the properties of the divine persons (person*) (*Summae quest. ordin.* a. 7, q. 1, fol. 48E). Such a harmony of philosophical practice and theological practice was no longer possible, however, once philosophy refused to exist simply in order cheerfully to play the part assigned to it by theology, and instead established itself as an autonomous branch of learning, a process that included several remarkable trends and episodes.

a) Nominalism and the Organization of Knowledge. Unsurprisingly, opinions differ regarding the nominalist influences that bore on theology from the 14th century to the time of the Reformation. The intellectual history of these two centuries can be interpreted in two ways: either as the tragic disintegration of a happy synthesis, or as the gradual putting into place of the elements for a fruitful reconstruction (the gradual disappearance of the Aristotelian cosmos* and its final causes, the progressive erosion of the theological primacy of the concept of cause, etc.). In any event, two

things are clear: on the one hand the Faculty of Philosophy's internal debates (between *reales* and *nominales*) took center stage; and on the other hand an ever-widening gulf opened up between the two orders of reason, theological and philosophical, which Thomas Aquinas's synthesis had distinguished while at the same time considering them to be extremely close. Admittedly, theology did not hesitate to use and apply the conceptual tools forged by terminist philosophies (and logics): the appeal to God's "absolute power" (omnipotence*, divine) and a religious epistemology in which God's authority* did not find its authorized image in human reason. The impact of the new philosophers was almost as widespread as Aristotle's had been; but the theologians were unable to take the liberties with these new philosophers that their predecessors had taken with Aristotle.

b) Humanism and Philosophy. Between the (original) Scholasticism and that known as the "second" or "baroque" Scholasticism, the 15th century and the Renaissance saw another gap open up between the faculties of theology and the places where philosophical texts were produced. The humanist philosophers were sometimes academics—like Erasmus, who was at one time Lady Margaret Professor at Cambridge, or the Aristotelians of Padua—but most were not. The medieval masters of arts shared a language—Scholastic Latin—with the theologians, but the humanist thinkers wrote in another kind of Latin, or even in the vernacular. Their literary forms themselves gave rise to a sense of distance: whether taking the form of private correspondence, free "essays" (Montaigne), or learned satire (Erasmus, *Praise of Folly*), any work worthy of being regarded as "philosophical" sought to prove at every opportunity that it was not the work of a professor of philosophy. It was thus a period of twofold emancipation, from both official theology and official philosophy. In the universities the theoretical difficulties created by the Paris and Oxford condemnations had not disappeared, and in 1515 they gave rise to the Catholic magisterium*'s first formal intervention into philosophical affairs: the condemnation of Pomponazzi at the Fifth Lateran* Council. While censuring Averroism, the Church* pleaded eloquently for the unity of truth and for the former distribution of theoretical responsibilities (*COD* 605–606). Certainly, it had to be conceded that the principle of contradiction could not be put into parenthesis when comparing theological and philosophical utterances (no logic could deny bivalence!). But the second point was no more than a pious hope. The philosophical text—most often written from the Renaissance onward by intellectuals unconnected to the schools where theology continued to defend its status as queen of the sciences (Marsilio Ficino, Pico della Mirandola, Descartes, etc.)—was henceforth a "separate" text. Such a text could be strongly religious: Ficino, for example, writes that "the philosopher [...] lifts us up to the contemplation of God [and] fires us with love* for the divine goodness" (ed. Kristeller, I, 854), and Descartes uses the language of adoration in the conclusion of his third *Méditation*. Rather than leading on to theology, however, these philosophical texts actually took the place of theological texts: in the case of Erasmus, Descartes, and later Leibniz*, the philosopher assumed strictly theological responsibilities, doubtless because he judged professional theologians incapable of using the new conceptual tools that he himself had made.

c) Official Philosophies and New Influences. Nevertheless, at the end of the Middle Ages the philosophers did not cease to endow their work with a "scholarly," academic finish and finality, nor did the churches cease inviting them to do so. Despite Luther*'s hostility toward philosophy, we need wait no longer than the second generation of reformers—that of Melanchthon—for the first attempts to circumvent the prohibition that hung over natural* theology. It was at this point that the logic of Ramus (Pierre de La Ramée, 1515–1572) served to assemble the first philosophy intended for theologians ("Philippo-Ramism", *see HWP* 7, [1989], 671 *Sq*). More remarkably, 17th-century Lutheran orthodoxy forgot Luther's pronouncements against Aristotle (e.g., the *Disputatio contra scholasticam theologiam* of 1517, prop. 43) to the extent that its schools offered apprentice theologians a neo-Aristotelian philosophical training. Even more strikingly, the philosophical treatise that was to serve as the basis of teaching in Catholic countries until the start of the 20th century, Suarez*'s *Disputationes Metaphysicae,* also held a preeminent place in the Germanic Protestant world (*see* Petersen 1921, Wundt 1939) and even within Russian Orthodoxy. Through the 17th century and the Enlightenment, the schools of theological thought continued to extend their hospitality to the dominant philosophies of the moment. A large proportion of 18th-century theology, especially in the Protestant sphere ("physico-theology," "neology," *see* "rationalism*"), followed Wolff. Cartesianism exerted a powerful influence, in Louis XIV's France and elsewhere; and the new physics propounded by Descartes seemed to demand a reorganization of the central concepts of theology (such as the eucharistic* theology of Dom R. Desgabets, *see* Armogathe, 1976). Malebranche, Spinoza, Leibniz, Hobbes, Locke, Hume, all the major thinkers of the period took a position on theological topics—grace* (Malebranche, Leibniz),

political* theology (Spinoza, Hobbes), belief (Locke, Hume), miracles (miracle*) (Hume)—and did so with enough force and relevance that the theologians thought it best to give them not merely a reply, but a reception. Whether in Catholicism* or Protestantism*, theology thus acquired its modern face as a result of a deficiency—after Suarez, the company of theologians no longer counted a powerful philosophical head among its number—for which it attempted to compensate by a perpetual openness to the dominant philosophical thinking, or even to merely fashionable philosophies.

Within the Protestant intellectual world, fidelity to the scriptural principle (*sola scriptura*) and an anti-philosophical stance strictly faithful to Luther (Barth*—Calvin offers no orthodoxy on this point, notwithstanding the triumphant tone of the "Calvinist theory of knowledge," Reformed epistemology, which spread through the English-speaking cultural sphere at the end of the 20th century, chiefly under the influence of Alvin Plantinga [*see* Plantinga 1983 and the criticisms of D.Z. Phillips, *Faith after Foundationalism,* London/New York 1988]) at no point prevented the interplay of influences. Thus the 19th and 20th centuries saw theologies adopting Schleiermacher*'s religious philosophy (which does not imply the adoption of all his theological ideas), theologies that remained faithful to an "enlightened" conception of rationality ("liberal Protestantism," *see* liberalism*), theologies inspired by Hegel (e.g., the "evangelical school of Tübingen*" or W. Pannenberg in the 20th century), by Kierkegaard ("dialectical theology"), or by Heidegger* (e.g., Bultmann*, E. Fuchs, E. Jüngel), theologies inspired too by the humanist Marxism of E. Bloch (J. Moltmann), by contemporary English-speaking philosophy in general (I.U. Dalferth, D. Ritschl), or by Wittgenstein* in particular (G. Lindbeck, P. Holmer, O. Bouwsma, R. Bell), by post-structuralist critiques of modernity (the "radical orthodoxy" of the younger Cambridge school [J. Milbank, G. Ward, C. Pickstock]), and others besides. (*See* Dalferth 1988 on Protestant models of the relationship between theological and philosophical reason.) However, post-Enlightenment philosophy gave rise to a redefinition of the terms of the problem, and 19th-century Catholicism also saw the appearance of a new philosophical and theological program, calling for a return to the "good old days." The understanding of that redefinition and that program holds the key to the interpretation of present-day difficulties and challenges.

5. Restorations and Redistributions

The Enlightenment had its theological side, and its influence brushed aside denominational barriers, which in any case were tending to become incomprehensible to the religious ecumenism of the time. The 18th century, moreover, came to a violent conclusion whose principles, causes, and ideologies were associated with the Enlightenment: the French Revolution, the fall of the "old regimes," the Napoleonic Wars, all represented a kind of culmination of the effects exerted on the social body by a particular group of doctrines. Consequently, the political restorations and reconstitutions of the period after Waterloo could not fail to arouse among the intelligentsia a desire for a critique of enlightened reason, often linked to programs of intellectual "restoration:" henceforth, the history of the debates between theology and philosophy alternated between criticism and restoration.

a) The first major event was a reversal, which is clearly to be seen in Hegel*'s work and in the late philosophy of Schelling*, and then appears in Kierkegaard's writing in a way that owes little to "German idealism"—in short, among thinkers who all accepted that theological principles could be at work in texts produced outside the theology faculties. In Hegel's *Logic* the fundamental mechanism is christological and Trinitarian. In Schelling's essays on the *Philosophy of Revelation,* the a priori evaluation of "anything subject to revelation" (which was Kant*'s objective as well as that of the young Fichte) disappears in favor of a form of thought referred to as "positive," based on divine self-manifestation as a first principle. Kierkegaard's *Philosophical Fragments* form a christological sketch, and his *Concept of Anxiety* is presented as a contribution to the doctrine of original sin*. While they deal with theological subjects, however, these works are marginal, and it has been questioned whether they have the slightest theological authority. Even though they received their initial training in the Lutheran seminary at Tübingen, the *Stift,* Schelling and Hegel were professors of philosophy. The latter was considered enough of a practising Lutheran to be entrusted with the commemorative address for the *Augsburg Confession* in 1830, but his relations with the Berlin theology faculty were notoriously frosty. Kierkegaard, meanwhile, was a Danish Lutheran who ultimately broke with the established Church. The objection has conventionally been leveled against Schelling and particularly against Hegel that their project assumed a Gnostic character: the use within philosophy of Christian theologoumena or conceptual schemes did not make philosophy Christian but rather mythological (a criticism that goes back as far as F.C. Baur's *Christliche Gnosis* [1835])...As for Kierkegaard, only the good fortune not to have been read before the 20th century can have saved him

from being considered as a heresiarch, a status that his fideism*, his extreme voluntarism, and his "noncognitivist" conception of the Christian experience* would certainly have earned him. However, it remains clear, supported by the conclusions of several generations of historians, that these works are not *primarily* important because of the conceptual tools that they put at the disposal of the theologian, but rather because a strictly theological task is carried out in them. Consequently, the response to these authors by the theology faculties could not fail to break with the typical pattern illustrated by the Scholastic reception of the Philosopher *par excellence,* Aristotle. Theology, and in a sense the most powerful theology, here lies outside the official theology of the churches. Indeed the history of ecclesiastical theology from the Romantic period (e.g. the Catholic school of Tübingen) to the end of the 20th century (e.g., the Catholic Hegelianism of G. Fessard or A. Chapelle) could be written as the history of a sustained effort by theology faculties determined to produce orthodox versions of inspired philosophical/theological constructions not distinguished by their great concern for literal orthodoxy.

b) The second major event—though one that was confined to Catholicism—was the development of a persistent myth whose best and most typical expression is provided by two works by J. Kleutgen S.J. (1811–83), one of the influential experts at the First Vatican* Council, the *Theologie der Vorzeit vertheidigt* (1853–1870, Münster, 4 vols.) and the *Philosophie der Vorzeit vertheidigt* (1860–1863, Münster, 2 vols.). A concordance of the Fathers* with one another, and a concordance of the medieval Doctors (Doctor* of the Church) with the Fathers and with each other, Kleutgen's synthesis is guided by hermeneutic principles that make it the perfect manifesto of Neoscholasticism and enable him to describe an idyllic past (*Vorzeit,* "good old days") that is lost but recoverable. Modernity could be understood as the dramatic story of this loss, for which J. Maritain would later (in his 1925 pamphlet *Les trois réformateurs*) chiefly blame Luther, Descartes, and Rousseau. To escape the perplexities of modernity (subjectivism, idealism, laicism, irreligiousness, secularization*, etc.), Neoscholastic discourse offered a step backward toward the Middle Ages, associated with a vision of the Middle Ages in which Christian rationality culminated with Thomas Aquinas in a harmonious synthesis of philosophical reason (with Aristotle becoming the Philosopher once again) and Christian doctrine. Because the founding texts—those of the Fathers and the Doctors—not only had to be reissued for the benefit of a modern audience but also interpreted, the Neoscholastics combined successes with failures: the most brilliant historical work (Gilson was an important figure, but not the only one) appeared alongside "Thomist" and "Aristotelio-Thomist" ramblings entirely alien to the genuine Thomist tradition, starting with an astonishing confusion among the teaching institutions of the Society of Jesus between the ontology of Thomas and that of Suarez.

c)   Interpreting the Eden of Scholasticism as exemplifying the model that should govern relations between philosophy and theology, and believing itself capable of identifying a specifically Thomist philosophy, Neoscholasticism in effect created its own model: a theory of knowledge on two levels—a philosophical level (the realm of nature*) and a theological level (the realm of grace or "supernature")—which was supposed to reproduce the medieval universities' division of intellectual work, and to reproduce it moreover without the risk of a "battle of the faculties." Nobody until H. de Lubac* dared suggest that the theological basis of this model was a theology of the supernatural* that was both decadent and inexact. It was not until a new historical approach to the classical period arose (J.-L. Marion, J.-F. Courtine, V. Carraud et al., most of them influenced by Heidegger) that Suarez's true role— much more of a founder than a follower—could be assessed, along with the part really played by Baroque Scholasticism in the birth of a secularized mode of thought (see M. Buckley, At the Origins of Modern Atheism, New Haven and London, 1987, about Lessius). And it was not until the encyclical Fides et ratio, published by Pope John Paul II at the very end of the 20th century, that the Catholic Church—more than a century after Leo XIII's encyclical that recommended Catholics to philosophize "in the spirit of Saint Thomas" (Aeterni Patris, 1879) without explaining exactly what this mens was—renounced the idea of official philosophy, albeit in a context marked by the return to influence of the Neoscholastic program.

d)   In the meantime the world of philosophy had been stirred up by a classic quarrel regarding "Christian philosophy." According to E. Bréhier, whose pronouncements incited the debate, Christianity is essentially the mysterious story of God's relations with mankind, a mysterious story that can only be revealed, while the substance of philosophy is rationalism, in other words the clear and distinct consciousness of the reason that exists in things and in the universe" (BSFP, v. XXXI, 1931, 49–52). Maritain's reply (or that of P. Mandonnet O.P. [1856–1936], who had not specialized in Siger in vain) retained the strict distinction between the two authorities: on the one hand, the philosopher's Christian faith* might make his work easier, but it left the pure rationality of philosophy intact; infringing upon the autonomy of the philosophical, on the other hand, would simply lead to an intellectual regression. For Blondel*, however, philosophy was a priori open to the light of the theological: the task was to show "how reason, far from stabilizing everything into closed concepts, discovers in itself needs that nature does not satisfy, something incomplete, forever unable to be completed by natural means yet irrepressibly eager to be fulfilled" (Le problème de la philosophie catholique, Paris, 1932). Gilson steered the debate into historical territory when he emphasized the existence of "philosophemes" of theological, and sometimes Christian, origin: the idea of the person, or the idea of creation. (There was, however, one concept whose origins Gilson attributed to Christianity in general, and to Thomas Aquinas in particular—the identification of God with the action of pure being—which now seems to have been more than sketched out in a text attributed to Porphyry: see P. Hadot, "God as Act of Being," in coll. Étienne Gilson et nous, Paris, 1980.) During the same period, Heidegger contended that the idea of Christian philosophy was that of a "circle squared" (GA 40, p. 9; 48, p. 163; see J. Baufret, "Christian philosophy," in Dialogue avec Heidegger, Paris, 1973). Also at the same period, Barth expressed his doubts regarding this same idea: "If it [is] philosophy, it [can]not be Christian; if it [is] Christian, it [is] therefore not philosophy" (KD I/1 p. 4).

6. Tasks and Prospects

Composed as it is of old questions as much as new ones, the problem may at least stand forth in all its complexity after this historical outline. Any attempt to define the relative status of philosophy and theology must fulfil several requirements:

a)   The first is to have some kind of theory of truth*—more essential even, perhaps, than at the time of Parisian, Oxonian, or Paduan Averroism. On the one hand, in what way does theology claim to be true? On the other hand, in what way does it put its trust in philosophical claims to truth? To answer these questions one must be able to form a metadiscourse powerful enough to illuminate the logic of theology (T. F. Torrance: a "philosophy of theology"), and that of philosophy, in a way that respects similarities and differences, intentions and realizations, objects and domains. Theology and philosophy are human artifacts: and therefore the idea of a common measure, or a common submission to the logos, to the elementary rules that govern any production of a genuine discourse, and so on, may be no more than common sense—but is certainly no less than that.

b) In addition, history reminds us that theology and philosophy are not merely theories, but also ways of living (Wittgenstein: "forms of life"). The philosophical discourse refers to the ("existential") project of the *vita philosophica,* the theological discourse claims to be born of a new experience that reorganizes what can be thought, or what is thought, only by reorganizing man's whole relationship to things and their origin. Just as one may master several languages, so one may make several forms of life one's own. However, while philosophy and the *vita philosophica* are put forward, in their Greek origins, as *arche*-language and *arche*-experience, theology's first response to them is to deny them this status. From here on, the problem of "Christian philosophy" is practical rather than theoretical: it is a matter of knowing how Christians may make the philosophical project their own, and how they redefine it if they do succeed in making it their own.

c) If philosophy and theology conceive or reconceive of themselves as forms of life or as paths to wisdom, they cannot therefore appear as two scientific disciplines that may be practised at the same time (as one may practise two disciplines with a common boundary, e.g., logic and mathematics), nor indeed as two paths that may be followed either simultaneously or in turn. While it is not certain, *pace* Heidegger, that the Christian faith removes the believer's ability to ask certain questions, this is perhaps for the reasons put forward by H.U. von Balthasar* ("Vermächtnis und christlicher Auftrag," in *Herrlichkeit* III/1, 943–982): in a time of enormous philosophical uncertainty—in the age of nihilism—the Christian's destiny is also that of a "guardian of metaphysics," and the task of a Christian utterance is also to show concern for what are vaguely known as "values," or what is equally vaguely called the "sense of being*;" to utter, above and beyond the gospel, a certain number of words (not from the gospel) that are necessary for any acceptance of that gospel. It does not, however, follow, from the fact that the theologian may use the language of the philosopher, that he should live the philosophical life: what he desires, after all, is a wisdom experienced in the shadow of the cross (*see,* e.g., Breton 1981). The Christian may put all his love into a fruitful philosophical labor (love of truth, and love for a neighbor to whom the truth must be spoken), but he cannot put into it either his faith or his hope*; philosophy is not (or is no longer, in spite of Clement of Alexandria) a path to salvation*.

d) Another requirement is a response to Heidegger's central pronouncements on what he calls "metaphysics," on the "end of philosophy and the task of thinking." Should Christianity's Christian identity be classically expressed with the "help" of terminology that is now obsolescent? And if philosophy has uttered its final word, should not wisdom urge theology to think and speak for itself, without calling on the services of an authority that may no longer exist? Before this question can be answered, there is a necessary preliminary that has not yet been satisfied, which is to verify or disprove Heidegger's hypotheses in detail. Leaving aside the closure and destiny of metaphysics, however, one fact at least is clear: no healthy theology can throw in its lot with a particular philosophy and/or a culture (*see* Hellenization* of Christianity and inculturation*).

e) Beyond any clear-cut distinction (natural/supernatural, historical/metaphysical), it remains to consider the discourses, put forward by various authors (Hegel, Schelling, Kierkegaard), which display "philosophical" characteristics but are shaped from within by allegedly "theological" principles. Abandoning the desire to mark out a line of demarcation would lead to the admission that there was an area of overlap. Such a region is by definition a vague object, whose existence we can be aware of without knowing where it begins or ends. There are exclusively philosophical questions—for example, that of the ontological status of mathematical entities; and there are exclusively theological questions—for example, that of the internal coherence of the seven sacraments or that of the connection between the ministry* of the Church and the apostolic* succession. There are also realities that one may consider as a philosopher or equally as a theologian, though the shared subject does not lead to a common discourse. But there are also (especially in this case), as it were as a counterpart to Meinong's "stateless" subjects, subjects that seem able to enjoy dual nationality. "Trinitarian ontology" (*see* being), "philosophical Christology" (X. Tilliette)—discourses with names such as these immediately admit that they decline to make a clear choice between philosophical and theological ambition; and they should probably be forced to admit their secret, which is of course that they are the cartographers of a frontier region.

- P. Petersen (1921), *Geschichte der aristotelischen Ph. im protestantischen Deutschland,* Leipzig (2nd Ed. 1964, Stuttgart-Bad Cannstatt).
B. Baudoux (1937), "Philosophia ancilla theologiae," *Anton.* 12, 293–326.
M.-D. Chenu (1937), "Les "philosophes" dans la ph. chrétienne médiévale," *RSPhTh* 26, 27–40.
J. Leclercq (1939), "La th. comme science d'après la littérature quodlibétique," *RThAM* 11, 351–74.
M. Wundt (1939), *Die deutsche Schulmetaphysik des 17. Jahrhunderts,* Heidelberg.

G. Bardy (1949), "'Philosophie' et 'philosophe' dans le vocabulaire chrétien des premiers siècles," *RAM* 25, 97–108.

H. Rochais (1951), "Ipsa philosophia Christus," *MS* 13, 244–47.

J. Leclercq (1952), "Pour l'histoire de l'expression 'philosophie chrétienne," *MSR* 9, 221–26; id. (1956), "Maria christianorum philosophia," *MSR* 103–6.

F. Dölger (1953), "Zur Bedeutung von *Philosophos* und *Philosophia* in der byzantinischer Zeit," in *Byzanz und die europäische Staatenwelt,* Ettal, 197–208.

H. Blumenberg (1959), "Kritik und Rezeption antiker Ph. in der Patristik," *StGen* 12, 485–97.

W. Pannenberg (1959), "Die Aufnahme des philosophischen Gottesbegriffs als dogmatisches Problem der frühchristlichen Theologie," in *Grundfr. syst. Th.,* Göttingen, 296–346; id. (1996), *Theologie und Ph.,* Göttingen.

É. Gilson (1960), *Le philosophe et la théologie,* Paris.

J. Daniélou (1961), *Message évangélique et culture hellénistique aux IIe et IIIe siècles,* Paris-Tournai, 11–128.

È. Gilson (1961), "Autour de Pomponazzi: Problématique de l'immortalité de l'âme en Italie au début du XVIe s.," *AHDL* 28, 163–279.

A.-M. Malingrey (1961), "*Philosophia,*" *Étude d'un groupe de mots dans la littérature grecque...,* Paris, 119 *Sq,* 137 *Sq,* 148 *Sq.*

H. U. von Balthasar (1961), "Ph., Christentum, Mönchtum," in *Sponsa Verbi,* Einsiedeln, 349–87.

H. Crouzel (1962), *Origène et la ph.,* Paris.

B. Welte (1965), "Die Ph. in der Theologie," in *Auf der Spur des Ewigen,* Fribourg-Bâle-Vienne, 366–79.

H. Chadwick (1966), *Early Christian Thought and the Classical Tradition,* Oxford.

A. Henrichs (1968), "Philosophy the Handmaiden of Theology," GRBS 9, 437–50.

L. Malevez (1968), "Le croyant et le philosophe," in *Pour une théologie de la foi,* Paris-Bruges, 9–44.

B. J. F. Lonergan (1970), "Philosophy and Theology," in *A Second Collection,* Toronto, (2nd Ed. 1996), 193–208.

R. Paqué (1970), *Das Pariser Nominalistenstatut,* Berlin.

O. Michel (1973), "Philosophia," "Philosophos," *ThWNT* 9, 169–85.

G. Podskalsky (1977), *Theologie und Ph. in Byzanz,* Munich.

S. Breton (1981), *Le Verbe et la croix,* Paris.

A. Plantinga (1983), "Reason and Belief in God," in A. Plantinga, N. Wolterstorff (Ed.), *Faith and Rationality,* Notre Dame and London, 16–83.

H. M. Schmidinger (1987), "Zur Geschichte des Begriffs 'christliche Ph.,'" in E. Coreth et al. (Ed.), *Christliche Ph. im katholischen Denken des 19. und 20. Jahrhunderte,* vol. 1, Graz-Vienna, 29–45.

I. U. Dalferth (1988), *Theology and Philosophy,* Oxford.

H. M. Schmidinger (1989), "Ph., christliche," *HWP* 7, 886–98.

L. Bianchi (1990), *Il vescovo e i filosofi: La condanna parigina del 1277 e l'evoluzione dell'aristotelismo scolastico,* Bergame.

J.-F. Courtine (1990), *Suarez et le système de la métaphysique,* Paris, 9–99.

X. Tilliette (1990), *Le Christ de la philosophie,* CFi 155, 17–136.

A. de Libera (1991), *Penser au Moyen Age,* Paris.

J. Pieper (1995), *Schriften zum Philosophiebegriff,* WW, vol. 3, Hamburg.

M. Henry (1996), *C'est moi la vérité: Pour une philosophie du christianisme,* Paris.

JEAN-YVES LACOSTE

See also **Being; God; Reason; Theology; Truth**

Physical Premotion. *See* Bañezianism-Molinism-Baianism

Pietism

Pietism was the most important movement of Protestant religious revival after the Reformation. In the first instance a theological phenomenon, its major figures have also left a significant impression on all aspects of German culture up to the present time.

a) Pietism emerged in reaction to Protestant orthodoxy; it wanted to recapture the momentum of early Christianity, as well as the initial impetus of the Reformation. It also presented itself as a decisive return to the Bible*, for the purposes of meditation and mutual edification, as well as for science and knowledge. Lastly, it wanted to promote individuality and personal faith*—or that of a small group of believers—in the face of church* hierarchies (hierarchy*). Besides an easily identifiable theology*, its language, its music*, and its ethics*, even its policies, were easily recognizable, particularly in certain regions such as Prussia and Wurtemberg.

Pietism put its faith in the gap between doctrine, as expressed in the public confessional theology of the churches, and private faith. According to the title of a work by Pierre Poiret (1646–1719), which would be taken up by Zinzendorf, Pietism wanted to represent a *theology of the heart* (1690), indifferent to doctrinally specific features, and whose fundamental criterion was authenticity (implying a re-appropriation, against the official churches, of John 4:23, of worship "in spirit and in truth"). Its theoretical work was therefore, in the first instance, that of an "affective transposition of Christian doctrine" (Pelikan 1989), of which Zinzendorf's *Ein und zwanzig Discurse über die Augspurgische Confession* (1747–48) were the best example. Anxious to get back to the central role of religious "practice", this transposition was necessarily inseparable from morality, which Kant* would theorize as "the moral law* within my own self" (*Critique of Practical Reason,* 1788). Whether the matter at issue is prayer*, faith, knowledge, practice, etc., insistence on the singularity of the self is one of the prominent features of Pietism.

The coordination of doctrine and life, meaning the requirement for conversion* that is typical of Pietism, is made very clear in the long conflict on *theologia irregenitorum,* the theology of the non-regenerated. Is it essential for whoever studies theology to possess the knowledge and experience* of those who have been genuinely converted to God (Francke, *Methodus studii theologici,* 1723)? *Essential,* here, does not only mean essential for salvation*, according to an opinion commonly accepted, but also essential for a correct understanding of the Holy* Scriptures and of Christian doctrine. A sound understanding of the Scriptures actually commits the whole person*, and not only the intellect. Conversely, one may be a "false master" and teach an orthodox doctrine. But "what I deny," wrote Joachim Lange, "is that a bad and non-regenerated master can teach the word* of God…soundly and without corruption" (*Antibarbarus…,* 1709). This insistence on the "illumination" of the exponent of the Scriptures, inasmuch as it confuses the theologian as a subjective individual with his objective ecclesiastical task, has been seen as Donatist. And in a more general way, the subjectivism of Pietism, founded, as it is, on the knowledge one has of one's own conversion, even

of one's salvation, constituted a real peril for Protestant orthodoxy, by emphasizing a subjective definition of faith as *assurance,* a definition that could sap the objective foundations of the doctrine of justification (Pelikan 1989).

b)   There is general agreement Pietism began with Philipp Jakob Spener (1635–1705), who was born at Rappoltsweiler in Alsace, and died in Berlin. He studied in Strasbourg, Basel and Geneva, and he translated into German (1667) *La pratique de l'oraison et méditation chrétienne* (1660) by Jean de Labadie. While he was a minister* at Frankfurt am Main he created the *collegia pietatis,* which explains the name given to Pietism; the function of the *collegia* was the reading of the Scriptures and mutual edification. With that institution, Pietism had its own home; with the *Pia desideria,* it got its own charter. Published in 1675, that charter was a full-fledged program that vehemently criticized the state of the churches, and proposed remedies like the greater public and private use of the Bible, a genuinely universal priesthood involving the laity, small groups for prayer and Bible study, and reform in the education of ministers. Pietism subsequently spread like wildfire in a Germany that was recovering with great difficulty from the Thirty Years' War. In 1686 Spener was in Dresden, and in 1691 in Berlin, where his influence grew considerably. Prussia quickly became fertile territory for this spirituality and its activities.

August Hermann Francke (1663–1727) strongly emphasized certain points of Spener's program. He had met Spener in 1687, and he implanted Pietism in Prussia-Brandenburg: it became a real political* theology there, during the first half of the 18th century. In 1686, after his studies at Kiel, Hamburg and Leipzig, Francke founded a *collegium philobiblicum* in this latter city. There, every Sunday*, a passage from the Bible was read in its original language, and explained, with approximately ten persons in attendance. While remaining technical, the exegesis* gradually became existential as well, and all the more so as Francke, on Spener's advice, translated the *Guida spirituale* of Miguel de Molinos from Italian into Latin (Quietism*). In 1687 Francke had a mystical experience, "Bekehrungserlebnis," a crisis of faith followed by a regeneration that refocused his life. Such an experience was to give rise to a literary genre that would achieve a considerable vogue in this type of Pietism, from Hamann to Jung-Stilling. In 1689 a real "Kulturkampf" descended on Leipzig: so divided was the city that meetings were forbidden in public places in 1690. Having moved to Erfurt, where he had previously spent time, Francke had to leave that city again in 1691. The following year he was appointed to Glaucha, in the nearby suburbs of Halle; and that city remained for 35 years the European center of Pietism. Francke helped found the University (1694), which became a bastion of the movement: he preached, taught, developed Orientalism, and above all, in a series of "Foundations," the famous "Franckesche Stiftungen", brought the Pietist message into the social, economic, and political reality, by means of charitable institutions with pedagogical intentions: an orphanage, German and Latin schools, a *pædagogium regium,* a *seminarium præceptorum,* a bookstore, a publisher, a Bible bookstore, and even a pharmacy. The young pupils, the students and the teachers were, as a whole, efficient intermediaries in all strata of society*. The activity that was most visible and most famous was the founding, with Carl Hildebrand von Canstein, of the "Cansteinsche Anstalt," a printing house that published several million Bibles during the 18th century, in all kinds of formats, and in the most exotic languages. Thus, ministers and missionaries were able to spread the message everywhere, but they also reported regularly to Halle on their intense activities. In the unconditional support of Frederick William I, who reigned from 1713 to 1740, Pietism found a precious ally and was able to unify a little the two societies of Prussia and Brandenburg.

Today it is in Wurtemberg that Pietism remains very much alive. It is also the only place where, from 1743 onwards, it was enshrined in the country's clergy constitution. Thanks to Johann Albrecht Bengel (1687–1752), biblical science still appears here to be the movement's great strength; this shows moreover that a critical method, far from taking faith away, can actually fortify it. On this particular point, therefore, there is no opposition between Pietism and the Enlightenment. Following his studies at the Stift, Bengel spent his whole career within the ecclesiastical hierarchy working at solidly establishing the textual criticism of the New Testament. He produced a new edition of the New Testament in Greek (1734), commented on it (*Gnomon Novi Testamenti,* 1742) and translated it (published posthumously, 1753). Above all he was interested in John's gospel and in Revelation, and he predicted for 1836 the beginning of the thousand year reign of Christ (Rev 20:1f.). He corrected and kept in perspective a millenarianism* that was widespread in Pietism. With Friedrich Christoph Oetinger (1702–82), Pietism also produced a much more speculative version of itself, one that would influence the great thinkers of German idealism. Metaphysics, the Kabbala, everything was of use to Oetinger in his pursuit of a sacred philosophy*. A Professor at the Stift of Tübingen, he too, however, pursued a church career outside the University.

Beside contributing numerous translations of the Scriptures to establish in the daily life of their believers, as well as the numerous hymns that gave rhythm to their lives, Pietism also wanted to promote a new attitude regarding Jews and Judaism*. The major figures of Pietism were all very good scholars of Hebrew. It may be an exaggeration to claim, as some have done in the past, that Pietism was a precursor of the emancipation of the Jews. It remains the case, however, that Pietism resolutely moved away from the Judeo-phobia of the Lutherans, rejecting compulsory sermons and forced baptisms (baptism*), and striving to present a more positive image of the Jews.

Pietism also saw a very original development with the community of the Moravian Brethren, reorganized by Count Nikolaus Ludwig von Zinzendorf (1700–1760), a development that continued into the 20th century. Zinzendorf had a Lutheran background, suffused with the spirit of Johann Arndt's *True Christianity* (*Vom wahren Christentum,* 1609), but he was raised in an atmosphere of affective piety, and he was much influenced by Francke. On his Saxony estates (called Herrhut) he gave hospitality to the Moravian Brethren, spiritual descendants of the Hussites (their leader, in the 17th century, had been the Czech philosopher Comenius, 1592–1670), who believed that total moral perfection was accessible on this earth and who lived in a sort of utopian community. They were at some point later expelled (other communities would be established as a consequence, such as the one in Georgia, in the United States) then rehabilitated. When the English Parliament, in 1749, recognized the Moravian Church under the name of *Unitas fratrum,* Zinzendorf, who had finally fallen out with the Pietists, decided to take up residence in London. The fact remains that the search for evangelical perfection is indeed one of the stable and permanent features of Pietism.

Often endangered by all kinds of separatism and by chiliasm, and driven by original personalities, Pietism took up many Lutheran themes but also irrigated the Reformed lands themselves. It constituted an essential moment in the history of German theology, and most probably a kind of cultural revolution*.

● P. J. Spener, new edition of the works and correspondence (1979–), Hildesheim.

A. H. Francke, *Werke in Auswahl,* Ed. E. Peschke (1969), Berlin.

N. L. von Zinzendorf, new Ed.: works (1962–63), correspondence and documents (1962–82), Hildesheim.

♦ H. M. Rotermund (1959), *Orthodoxie und Pietismus,* Berlin.

E. Beyreuther (1962), *Studien zur Theologie Zinzendorfs,* Neukirchen.

E. Peschke (1964–66), *Studien zur Theologie August Hermann Frankes,* 2 vols., Berlin.

L. Bouyer (1965), *La spiritualité orthodoxe et la spiritualité protestante et anglicane,* Paris.

P. Deghay (1969), *La doctrine ésotérique de Zinzendorf,* Paris.

K. Aland (1970) (Ed.), *Pietismus und Bibel,* Witten.

G. Mälzer (1970), *Johann Albrecht Bengel: Leben und Werk,* Stuttgart.

J. Wallmann (1970), *Philipp Jakob Spener und die Anfänge des Pietismus,* Tübingen (2nd Ed. 1986).

PuN (1974–).

H. Leube (1975), *Orthodoxie und Pietismus: Gesammelte Studien,* Bielefeld.

E. Beyreuther (1978), *Geschichte des Pietismus,* Stuttgart.

S. Grossmann (1979), *Friedrich Christoph Œtingers Gottesvorstellung,* Göttingen.

M. Schmidt (1984), *Der Pietismus als theologische Erscheinung,* Göttingen.

Y. Belaval, D. Bourel (1986) (Eds.), *Le siècle des Lumières et la Bible,* Paris.

J. Pelikan (1989), *The Christian Tradition,* vol. 5, in part. chap. 3, 118–73, Chicago.

J. Wallmann (1990), *Der Pietismus,* Göttingen.

M. Chevallier (1994), *Pierre Poiret, 1646–1719: Du protestantisme à la mystique,* Geneva.

M.C. Pitassi (Ed.) (1994), *Le Christ entre orthodoxie et Lumières,* Geneva.

DOMINIQUE BOUREL

See also **Conversion; Exegesis; Kant, Immanuel; Luther, Martin; Methodism; Predestination; Protestantism**

Pilgrimage

---

1. History

Pilgrimage, that is to say travel for religious purposes—be it wandering undertaken for its own sake, or travel to a place held to be holy, and visited and venerated for that reason—was hardly a feature of Christianity before the fourth century. Ascetic wandering, of which numerous examples are to be found from this time on (*see* Guillaumont 1979), soon aroused the suspicion of the ecclesiastical and civil authorities, but was to give rise to a long, if limited, tradition within Christianity (*see* the 19th-century *Stories of a Russian Pilgrim*). It was, above all, pilgrimage to holy places, carried on outside the ordinary framework of religious practice, which was to spread and become a common practice of the Christian people.

a) First Centuries. The earliest recorded pilgrimage to Palestine was that of the Empress Helena, Constantine's mother, and such journeys were facilitated by the Peace of the Church. Following Helena, a woman named Egeria, who probably came from southern Gaul, the Bordeaux Pilgrim, and many others travelled to Jerusalem, and their narratives furnish valuable information about Christian liturgy* and architecture* (Maraval 1996). The first holy places promoted by Christians, from the fourth century, were the locations of the events in the history of salvation* recorded in the Bible*. Places relating to the New Testament included, in Jerusalem* and throughout Palestine, the locations of the Nativity, the Passion*, the Resurrec-

tion*, the Ascension, and other events in the lives of Christ* and his apostles (apostle*). Old Testament locations in Palestine and the Sinai, and even in Egypt and Mesopotamia, were linked to the memory of the patriarchs or the prophets (prophet* and prophecy). All these places, and the relics* they might contain, were gradually inventoried and provided with churches, monasteries, and hostels; and the faithful thronged to them from every region of the Christian world. The tombs of martyrs also became holy places and gave rise to the construction of buildings and to pilgrimages. At this time they were numerous in the East (*see* Maraval 1985)—for example, those of Saint Menas in Egypt and Saint John at Ephesus. But some were also established in the West, the most famous being those of Saints Peter* and Paul at Rome*. Pilgrimage also encompassed visits to those living saints who were the monks—or at least some of them (such as the two Syrian stylites called Simeon).

b) Middle Ages. In the East, pilgrimages continued after the Arab conquest, particularly to Palestine, even though the Muslim occupation on several occasions made them more difficult and even prevented them. Serious Muslim resistance included the destruction of the Holy Sepulchre by Hakim in 1008 and various acts of harassment committed against pilgrims. This situation was among the motives for the First Crusade. Pope Urban II called for the deliverance of the Holy Land, and in particular Christ's tomb, from the Infidel yoke. The Crusades, for all their loss of direction, can thus in a sense be seen as a huge collective pilgrimage.

In the West, Rome remained the most frequent place of pilgrimage during the high Middle Ages, though there was a decline between the 11th and 13th centuries for essentially political reasons. On the other hand, it was at this time that the pilgrimage to Compostela developed, to the presumed tomb of the apostle James (the Great). For Western Europe as a whole, this was the commonest pilgrimage during the 12th century; and the famous routes of St James appeared at this time. After Mount Gargano during the high Middle Ages, Mont-Saint-Michel also acquired an international reputation. Marian pilgrimages developed too, the most important in the 12th century being that of Rocamadour. At the close of the Middle Ages, pilgrimage was an established practice and Rome regained its power of attraction in the field. However, the concomitant abuses were beginning to provoke widespread criticism, particularly in the milieu of the *devotio* moderna.

c) Modern and Contemporary Periods. This criticism grew louder with the Renaissance. The Christian humanists, led by Erasmus*, viewed pilgrimage unfavorably, but it was above all the reformers who denounced it and attacked the "false piety" that characterized it to their eyes. Many pilgrim shrines consequently fell victim to the iconoclastic zeal of the supporters of the Reformation. The Catholic Renaissance re-emphasized the practice of pilgrimage. The pilgrimage to St. Peter's in Rome regained its popularity, and a number of Marian sanctuaries drew large crowds (the most renowned at the time being the House of the Virgin at Loreto, to which Descartes* went on a pilgrimage). During the 18th century, on the other hand, the practice of pilgrimage declined, being criticized by many clerics (cleric*) and forbidden or restricted by rulers touched by the spirit of the Enlightenment. Once-famous shrines saw their visitors dry up—in France, for example, Mont-Saint-Michel. But many local pilgrimages continued to be frequented.

In the first half of the 19th century, pilgrimages slowly returned to popularity. They saw their greatest development during the pontificate of Pius IX (1846–78), which was the time of the first railways. There were Marian pilgrimages to La Salette (from 1846) and to Lourdes (from 1864), pilgrimages to shrines dedicated to Christ and his saints (Paray-le-Monial, Sainte-Anne-d'Auray, Ars, etc.), the pilgrimage to Rome (from 1870), and the pilgrimage to the Holy Land, for which the Assumptionists assumed responsibility in 1882. Recent times have witnessed a proliferation of pilgrimages. Every country has its own local pilgrimages (including many Marian shrines) and new ones regularly appear. A few attract pilgrims from all around the world. Jerusalem, Rome, and Lourdes are undoubtedly the most visited holy places.

2. Spirituality

What exactly is a "holy place," then? The concept appeared within Christianity in the fourth century, applied to places that had witnessed theophanies (theophany*) or events in the history of salvation, but also to places were the relics of a holy person were kept. The motivations of the faithful who visit these places have always been very varied. There has always been a wandering spirituality, linked to the theme of the Christian as a "stranger in this world," certain elements of which are no doubt to be found in the spirituality of travel that has developed in the modern period. The visiting and veneration of holy places has other aims, however. In Palestine, particularly, the desire to *see* the holy places is related to their symbolic function. They are signs that enable the pilgrim to commemorate, as he or she calls them to mind, the events of salvation that occurred there or the figures venerated there. This goes hand in hand with the desire to *touch* these places, or the material relics to be found there, and is sometimes even confused with it. Many pilgrims are driven by the desire to touch what is sacred in order to partake in its virtues. Hence the appearance, at a very early date, of healing shrines where the believer came in search of a cure.

To material healing* was added spiritual healing. The penitential pilgrimage appeared from the sixth century, and became very popular during the Middle Ages, as did pilgrimages undertaken for the salvation of one's soul (soul*-heart-body). So, at the end of the Middle Ages, pilgrimages became an opportunity to seek indulgences*. The pastoral theology of pilgrimage has in every age sought to spiritualize a practice that can easily tend toward a certain materialism.

● *Récits des premiers pèlerins chrétiens au Proche-Orient*, French trans. P. Maraval, 1996, Paris.
♦ P. Sigal (1974), *Les marcheurs de Dieu: Pèl. et pèlerins au Moyen Age*, Paris.
A. Guillaumont (1979), "Le dépaysement comme forme d'ascèse dans le monachisme ancien," in *Aux origines du monachisme chrétien*, SpOr 30, 89–116.
J. Chélini, H. Branthomme (Eds.) (1982), *Les chemins de Dieu: Histoire des pèlerins chrétiens des origines à nos jours*, Paris.
P. Maraval (1985), *Lieux saints et pèlerins d'Orient: Histoire et géographie des origines à la conquête arabe*, Paris.
A. Dupront (1987), *Du sacré. Croisades et pèl: Images et langages*, Paris.

PIERRE MARAVAL

See also **Asceticism; Conversion; Cult of Saints; Mary; Monasticism; Penance**

Platonism, Christian

1. Plato and the Platonic Tradition

a) Christian Platonism resulted from the reciprocal influence of two evolving traditions. Plato (427–347 B.C.E.) was influenced by Socrates's effort to clarify those moral concepts, such as justice, that could be applied in a large number of cases. In addition, under the influence of others, still largely unknown to us, Plato arrived at a "theory of Ideas" that offers explanations of mathematical terms and natural beings alike. Each set of cases is designated by a name that refers to an ideal, objective, unchangeable Form, to which each case is an approximation. Plato hoped to achieve explanations of every class of objects by ranging them in a hierarchy dominated by the Idea of the Good*. According to his theory, the ordered interrelations of things is the best possible: evil* exists only when things are separated from their Form.

Plato's works have had a very great influence on Christian theology*. Attacked by some, passed over in silence by others, they had a presence in each of the great Christian traditions, and many educated Christians, such as Augustine*, regarded them as a good preparation for becoming a Christian. However, selections were made among them. Clement of Alexandria, for example, called himself a Platonist, and quotes more than 24 passages from *The Republic,* almost 40 shorter passages from *Phaedrus* and *Phaedo,* and almost 30 from *Timaeus;* yet, despite its philosophical importance, he quotes only once from *Parmenides.* More generally, *Phaedo* was appreciated for its passages expressing approval of asceticism* and its arguments in favor of the survival of the soul*, *Timaeus* for its references to a divine creation* of the world*, *Phaedrus* and *The Symposium* for their eulogies of love* as a guide toward the divine, and Book X of *The Laws* for its natural* theology. There was some ambivalence about *The Republic,* although certain passages were held in high regard, including the description of the ascent from the perceptible world to the intelligible world in Book VII, and the doctrine of the sensual, aggressive and intellectual "parts" of the soul, which offsets the excessively simple contrast in *Phaedo* between an idealized intellectual soul and a coarsely material body. Certain short passages or aphorisms were taken in isolation and cited time and again, including the text of *Theaetetus,* in which Plato affirms the inevitability of evil and exhorts his readers to become more like God* (176 *a–c*).

b) Christians came under the influence, not of Plato alone, but of a whole series of Platonists. Xenocrates (396–14 B.C.E.) had attempted to unify Plato's hypotheses, which in many cases are incompatible with each other, into a dogmatic system. Aristotle (384–22 B.C.E.) broke away from Plato and vastly enlarged the domain of philosophy*, but this did not prevent him from being treated as Plato's "valet" *(pedisequus)* by later authors who failed to take account of his criticisms of the theory of Ideas. The element of scepticism in Socrates's thought eventually became dominant within Plato's school, the Academy, which, under Arcesilaus (c. 316–c. 242 B.C.E.) and Carneades (c. 214–c. 129 B.C.E.), rejected the stoic idea that infallible knowledge is possible, holding that reasonable certainty is all that can be attained. Cicero (106–43 C.E.) took the same view. Meanwhile, however, there had been a revival of dogmatism under Antiochus (c. 130–c. 68 B.C.E.), who claimed to have reconciled Platonism and stoicism. This dogmatic turn made relatively little impact, although it did influence Philo of Alexandria, whose Platonic idealism incorporates the materialist pantheism* of the stoics. According to Philo, the divine Logos is physically extended in the world (*see,* e.g., *Quis rerum divinarum heres… §217*), but it is also the transcendent architect of the world, the "separator" (*tomeus,* ibid., §130), dividing pure being* into however many classes God wishes to create. It was Philo, along with other apologists from the Hellenistic Jewish milieu, who inspired Christians to make use of Greek philosophy. This use is already perceptible in the Pauline* corpus (e.g., Rom 1:20; *see* Acts 17:22ff.) and, it has been argued (by C.H. Dodd), in John's Gospel* (as well as in Sg). For several centuries, Christians called on the resources of Platonism within this framework, while exerting little influence on Platonism itself.

The mainstream Platonism of the period from around 50 B.C.E. to 200 C.E. has been labeled "middle Platonism" (Dillon 1977): its best known representative is Plutarch. Numenius (probably around 150 C.E.), who argued for a trinity of divine principles, won the respect of Plotinus, the greatest pagan philosopher of late antiquity, who is generally regarded as the founder of neo-Platonism. Plotinus accepts Aristotle's conception of knowledge as the identity of mind and object (*Soul* 3. 5, 430 *a* 20; *Metaphysics* 11, 1072 *b* 22; see *Enneads* VI . 5 . 7), and argues that the whole of knowable reality is, in a certain sense, intelligent. Everything proceeds, outside time, from an ultimate principle that is perfectly simple, unchangeable, and unknowable—and, indeed, unknowing, since knowledge implies multiplicity. This ultimate principle, the One, engenders two other principles in succession—Intelligence, and then the Soul, which is extended in creative activity. There is no principle of evil; matter, which is in fact merely the most distant point reached by intelligent life, comes closest to it. Each level of being displays a tendency to return to its transcendent source.

Plotinus's basic ideas reappear in the writings of his disciple and biographer, Porphyry (c. 232–305), although he reduces the distinctions among the three primary principles by making them into three hypostases. Porphyry was to have his greatest influence through his defense of Aristotle's logic, which he considered to be the best guide to the study of natural phenomena and methods of reasoning. Like his successors Iamblichus (c. 250–c. 325) and Proclus (c. 412–485), Porphyry was fiercely opposed to Christianity. Proclus was the dominant figure in the school of Athens when an ever more complex hierarchy of transcendent principles, grouped into triads, was being elaborated there. In Alexandria, another, less remarkable school displayed greater tolerance of Christianity. Its members included Alexander of Lycopolis (perhaps c. 280), Theo, Theo's daughter Hypatia (who was murdered by Christians in 415), and Synesios, who was both an ardent Platonist and an unwilling bishop (c. 370–413).

In fact, the influence of Plotinus and Porphyry over Christian thought began with Augustine (Rist 1981), who was very impressed by the conversion* to Christianity of the eminent neo-Platonist Marius Victorinus. Marius. He himself wrote several treatises on elementary logic; after his time, commentaries on Plato and Aristotle continued to be produced up to the end of antiquity, including those by Boethius* in the West and John Philoponus in the East. The tradition was then taken up within Islam and survived in the Christian East, for example in the work of Michael of Ephesus (who was active between around 1118 and 1138). By contrast, Platonism was practically forgotten in the West: all that was known of it was a Latin translation of *Timaeus* and the writings of Boethius. Its gradual reappearance began with John the Scot Eriugena (c. 810–c. 877), who translated the works of Pseudo-Dionysius* into Latin.

2. Understanding of Platonism among Christians

a) Philosophy was not to the taste of every Christian. Many contented themselves with echoing Colossians 2:8, and stereotypical images of philosophers arguing can be found in the writings even of highly educated authors, who occasionally quote the sceptics in favor of their point of view. However, Platonism soon came to enjoy relative tolerance to the extent that it seemed to confirm several points of Christian doctrine. Some scholars who had access to good libraries were able to transcribe the texts of Plato and his commentators, and others probably made use of anthologies of well-known passages, but transmission was frequently indirect. Thus, Justin, who once taught philosophy, has left us a description of his contacts with various schools (*Dial.* 2), in which he expresses his appreciation the attention that Platonism gives to transcendent realities and its confirmation of a theistic vision of the world. An attentive reader of this description could draw a notion of Plato's teachings from it, along with a number of imprecise quotations. On the other hand, Athenagoras and Theophilus provide fairly precise quotations and summaries of the whole of Platonism.

b) The writings of Clement of Alexandria (c. 150–c. 215) show that he had authentic knowledge of Plato and the Platonists; his interest in Plato's epistemology, as well as in his metaphysics and ethics*, is exceptional. Origen* was a great speculative thinker who mixed Platonism with stoicism, although the Bible*, freely interpreted, was always his ultimate authority. Origen's influence was pervasive for 50 years after his death in 254, although it met with some resistance. Eusebius of Caesarea (c. 260–c. 340) was not an original thinker, but he was an industrious scholar, and he quotes Plato and Plato's successors—not without mentioning his reservations—in his *Preparation for the Gospel* (13. 14–16). Eusebius was the first Christian writer to quote Plotinus, but not in Porphyry's edition. With this one exception, Plotinus was practically unknown among, Christians before Augustine. The Cappadocian Fathers relied mainly on earlier Platonists, who also influenced Augustine.

c) Augustine himself owed much to Plotinus and Porphyry, but, being a Christian, he could not accept a number of their basic ideas, such as their principle of the eternity of the world and of the creative process, their definition of God as situated "above the mind" and therefore unknowing, their trinity* of unequal hypostases, or their non-moral explanation of evil. Platonism led Augustine to envisage an intuitive knowledge of transcendent realities, such as love, and to give an important role to memory, for the alternative was to go back to Plato's original doctrine of reminiscence, the idea that intuitive knowledge is a memory of what was learned in a previous life. It appears that certain Platonists were still teaching skepticism in Augustine's time: his *Contra Academicos* is intended as a refutation of their ideas.

Augustine was a first-rate theologian, but in erudition and logic he was inferior to Boethius, who translated and commented on Aristotle, and wrote tractates on the Trinity and Christology (Christ* and Christology), as well as *De Consolatione Philosophiae* (*The Consolation of Philosophy*). A little later after Boethius's time, the Emperor Justinian closed the pagan school of Athens and the Christians rapidly came to enjoy a monopoly in the teaching of Platonism within the empire. The most remarkable of the Christian Platonists of late antiquity was Dionysius (c. 500), known as "the Areopagite" by confusion with the Dionysius in Acts 17:34. His writings on the *Divine Names,* angels, the sacraments (sacrament*), and the ascent of the soul toward God were freely inspired by Proclus, whose works he had read.

3. Influence of Platonism on Christian Doctrine

a) During the second century, apologists* who were adherents of a somewhat stoicized Platonism adapted its conceptions of the Father* and the Logos, but tended to neglect the Holy* Spirit, for whom they had to rely on the tradition* of the church. Irenaeus* and Tertullian* were among those who objected to this neglect. As for the Logos, which had already been subjected to diverse interpretations up to and including Philo's, it eventually took at least three forms: as the equivalent of the mind of God; as the Word sent out by God, a distinct being that organizes the created world; or as the immanent master of this world, comparable to the soul of the world. For many Christians, who took no account of the distinctions among them, the Logos was all of these at once; according to some Christians, such as Tertullian or, later, Marcellus of Ancyra, the Logos could pass from one condition to another. Only those who took this view may be appropriately regarded as advocating a theory of the Logos in two or three forms.

During this period, pagan Platonists such as Moderatus or Numenius worked out "triadic" theologies in which three principles were ranged in order of decreasing status. Such theories attracted Origen, Eusebius, and other Christian authors, who accepted a trinity of distinct and unequal powers. The Council of Nicaea* put an end to this rapprochement, yet at a much later date Augustine was still capable of praising neo-Platonism for confirming, even if imperfectly, the Nicene faith. What is astonishing is that it was Porphyry, an enemy of Christianity, who came closest.

b) Christian authors were consistently opposed to the Platonic doctrines of the eternity of the world and the existence of uncreated matter, but they took over the concept of an intelligible world that contains the prototypes of both earthly species and immaterial intelligences: the latter were assimilated to the angels mentioned in the Bible, or to the souls of the elect. Origen's adoption of the theory of transmigration of souls, giving rise to successive lives before and after the death of the individual, was much more controversial. Origen's intention was an excellent one: to use transmigration to explain disconcertingly unequal endowments of characteristics and opportunities, and to avoid the brutal notion of instant damnation. Around 400, however, this theory was replaced by the idea that God creates each soul uniquely and gives it a single life on Earth (although other views were still being discussed as late as Augustine's time).

The Old Testament presents death as a total annihilation, followed by universal bodily resurrection* and judgment*. This tradition survives in the ancient Latin Creed: (*hujus*) *carnis resurrectionem.* Nevertheless, Plato's arguments for survival did not lack support, although most Platonists thought that the body is nothing but a burden and that the soul alone survives. It was possible to adopt a halfway position, based on 1 Corinthians 15:35ff., by postulating a "heavenly body," but whether it resembles or differs from the earthly body was the subject of extensive debate. Paul, moreover, thought that the resurrection would take place in the near future; as this horizon receded, many Christians interpreted the immediate destiny of the soul in Platonic terms (*see* Lk 23:43), while expecting a general resurrection in which the soul would be raised through the gift of a glorified body.

Plato's contrasts between soul and body, and between the intellect and other elements of the soul, also influenced Christian spirituality. For most educated Christians, it went without saying that the first step on the road of moral progress consisted in ignoring or repressing bodily incitements and concentrating on higher realities, while conscientiously performing material works* of charity in the name of a passionless duty. The nascent monastic movement largely reversed this Platonizing tendency by glorifying simplicity in life and thought alike. Even before that, the importance attached by most Christians to faith* and good works had already modified the Platonic idealization of the intellect.

4. Rediscovery of Platonism

Plato's writings were lost to the medieval West, apart from a Latin translation of part of *Timaeus,* and even when Greek texts were available hardly anyone was capable of reading them before the Renaissance. Nevertheless, both Augustine and Pseudo-Dionysius retained their influence throughout this period. Plato became directly influential once again through the work of Nicholas* of Cusa and Marsilio Ficino, even though they interpreted him largely by way of Plotinus. The study of Plato's writings became important in England in the 16th century—Thomas More's *Utopia,* for example, recalls *The Republic*—as well as among the Cambridge Platonists of the 17th century. Schleiermacher* introduced a new way of approaching Plato by deciding to interpret the dialogues in their original context and to reject later additions. This approach has become the standard one, so much so that today only a minority of Plato specialists take an interest in Christian theology, and vice versa. Nevertheless, in recent years there has been a renewal of attention to the "unwritten" doctrines of Plato, which Aristotle mentions briefly, to certain early Christian writers who have been neglected, to "middle Platonism," and to the later commentators on Aristotle, all of which allows us to hope that there will be a degree of rapprochement among them.

● O. Bigg (1886), *The Christian Platonists of Alexandria,* Oxford (2nd Ed. 1913).
É. Bréhier (1908), *Les idées philosophiques et religieuses de Philon d'Alexandrie,* Paris (3rd Ed. 1950).
A. E. Taylor (1926), *Plato, the Man and his Work,* London (5th Ed. 1948).
L. Robin (1938), *Platon,* Paris (rev. Ed. 1968).
R. Klibanski (1939), *The Continuity of the Platonic Tradition during the Middle-Ages,* London.
F. Solmsen (1942), *Plato's Theology,* New York.
W. D. Ross (1951), *Plato's Theory of Ideas,* Oxford.
E. Cassirer (1953), *The Platonic Renaissance in England,* Edinburgh.
J. K. Feibleman (1959), *Religious Platonism,* London.
E. von Ivánka (1964), *Plato Christianus,* Einsiedeln.
A. H. Armstrong (Ed.) (1967), *The Cambridge History of Later Greek and Early Medieval Philosophy,* Cambridge.
J. Moreau (1967), *Le sens du platonisme,* Paris.
J. M. Rist (1967), *Plotinus, the Road to Reality,* Cambridge.
S. R. C. Lilla (1971), *Clement of Alexandria,* Oxford.
R. T. Wallis (1972), *Neoplatonism,* London.
E. N. Tigerstedt (1974), *The Decline and Fall of the Neoplatonic Interpretation of Plato,* Helsinki.
P. Courcelle (1974–75), *Connais-toi toi-même, de Socrate à saint Bernard,* 3 vols., Paris.
J. Dillon (1977), *The Middle Platonists,* London.
J. M. Rist (1981), "Basil's 'Neoplatonism'; Its Background and Nature," in P. J. Fedwick (Ed.), *Basil of Caesarea, Christian, Humanist, Ascetic,* Toronto, vol. 1, 137–220.
H. D. Saffrey (1987), *Recherches sur la tradition platonique au Moyen Age et à la Renaissance,* Paris.
C. B. Schmitt et al. (1988) (Ed.), *The Cambridge History of Renaissance Platonism,* Cambridge.
J. Hankins (1990), *Plato in the Italian Renaissance,* Leyden.
R. Kraut (1992), *The Cambridge Companion to Plato,* Cambridge (bibl.).
C. G. Stead (1994), *Philosophy in Christian Antiquity,* Cambridge.

CHRISTOPHER STEAD

See also **Aristotelianism, Christian; Basil (the Great) of Caesarea; Gregory of Nazianzus; Gregory of Nyssa; Skepticism, Christian; Spiritual Theology; Stoicism, Christian**

Pluralism. *See* **Theological Schools**

Pneumatology. *See* **Holy Spirit**

Political Theology

The phrase "political theology" belongs to the 20th century. Its use is to be contrasted with the term, *civil theology*, which, since Varron (116–27 B.C.E.), has referred to a theology* embodied in the laws* and cults* of the city*. In the 20th century, the question of political theology has been invoked in three contexts: in the debate between Erik Peterson (1890–1960) and Carl Schmitt (1888–1985); in the German "political theology" of the 1960s; and in relation to the question of "political Augustinianism*."

1. Schmitt-Peterson Debate

a) Carl Schmitt. Schmitt (1888–1985) was a German conservative political philosopher who, at first, criticized Nazism but later "pedagogically" supported it. In his view, the social structure of an epoch is isomorphic with its metaphysical world picture, no order of casual priority being assigned: that is why he believed there was a "political theology." Indeed, in Schmitt's eyes, the most rigorous concepts of political philosophy*, especially those derived from Bodin (c. 1529–96) or Hobbes (1588–1679), are secularized theological concepts. Less realistic political theories (Kant*, Rousseau [1712–78]) call upon notions of universal norms and general consent, correlated with a vague deism*. The more strictly scientific theories deriving from Hobbes assert, by contrast, the priority of the *exception* in politics, the emergency situation that justifies extraordinary measures, and correlate this idea with that of an unfathomable, voluntaristic deity* who can suspend every natural law.

b) Erik Peterson. Against Schmitt, the German theologian Erik Peterson (1890–1960) contended that "political monotheism*," in the sense of sacralization of an imperial power, and more generally of a sovereign power, did not originate in Christianity. This sacralization was derived from a fusion, cemented by Philo (13 B.C.E.–54 C.E.), between the cosmic monotheism of late antiquity (a single divine power reigning over the cosmos*) with Jewish monotheism. This fusion then had influence on Arian and semi-Arian Christian theologians (Arianism*), in particular Eusebius of Caesarea (c. 260–c. 340), all the more that they were witnessing the unity of the

Roman Empire and thought that *Pax Augustana* had providentially allowed the spread of the gospel. While, according to Peterson, it is true that all Christian theologians associated monotheism with both cosmic and political *monarchia,* theologians of a more orthodox Trinitarian bent saw the latter notion more as a unity *of principle* and *in mutual agreement,* rather than the exercise of a single will. This is very clear in, for example, the writings of Gregory* of Nazianzus. These theologians did not spell out the political consequences that could be drawn from these positions; it is nonetheless striking, according to Peterson, that a hierarchical and theocratic view of imperial power was associated with the semi-Arian outlook.

c) Yves Congar. Up to a point, Yves Congar (1904–95) concurred with Peterson. In their view, Christian political thought had been dominated all too often by a "paternalism" or "patriarchalism" that ignored the fact that God* is only Father* in relation to a Son to whom he gives all, and with whom he therefore also has a fraternal relationship. For this reason, we have access to Father and Son only through their bond of fraternal love, the Spirit. If one ignores the Holy* Spirit, one will arrive at a entirely paternal notion of royal authority* that excludes any fraternity, reducing subjects to a condition of permanent infancy (Bossuet [1627–1704], *Politique tirée de l'Écriture sainte;* Louis-Gabriel-Ambroise de Bonald [1754–1840]).

Congar confirms Peterson's line of argument, pointing out the significance of the fact that the orthodox theologians thought of the Trinity with the aid of physical, cosmic or psychological analogies (analogy*), rather than political ones. One may add that, according to the Arian Eunomios, for example, the divine *dynamis* may be exercised or not at will, like an imperial fiat, while according to Gregory* of Nyssa it is an inevitably self-communicating power (omnipotence*, divine), like fire (M. Barnes 1991). It can also be pointed out that Hobbes, who seeks to invest all religious as well as secular power in the sovereign, specifically reverts to an Arian Christology* (*Leviathan* II, 41).

2. Political Theology in Germany

The work of Erik Peterson was one ingredient in the emergence of a left-oriented political theology in Germany in 1960s. The Lutheran theologian J. Moltmann stressed (citing Peterson) that the identification of the second person* of the Trinity with a man crucified by the state points to a theology permanently critical of every political regime, and not one inclined to sacralize the social order.

Both Moltmann and the Catholic theologian J.-B. Metz combined Peterson's perspectives with those of the Frankfurt School. In the latter's wake, they sought to reinvoke the Kantian concept of ethical liberty* against a rationalism* that tends to degenerate into mere instrumental control of both humanity and nature. In Metz's early work especially (1968), he accepted, as did Friedrich Gogarten (1887–1967), the Christian character of secularization*, which releases humanity into adult responsibility. At the same time, Metz insisted, along with Karl Rahner*, on the a priori impulse in every human person to self-transcendence toward *esse* or toward God. All these ingredients permitted Metz to conclude that, through a gradual progress toward Habermas's "ideal speech situation," in which there are no constraints on free communication, we realize the divine will for humanity.

3. Problem of Political Augustinianism

a) Maurras. In France, Charles Maurras (1868–1952) and *Action Française* came from the same reactionary tradition (traditionalism*) that inspired Schmitt's thinking in Germany. Their opposition involved the question of political theology. The problem brought by Maurras was that he combined positivism with theocracy. On the one hand, he thought that agreement about facts and consent to formal procedures for securing civil peace* are sufficient for securing social cohesion. On the other hand, he argued that the church*, even though its domain is purely spiritual and apolitical, can arrive at a dominant political position by manipulating social mechanisms. Hence, opponents of Maurras had to refuse at once both the political role of religion *and* his rigid dualism of natural and supernatural. This gave rise to problems that are perhaps still not resolved.

b) Criticism of Maurras. At first, the Maurrasian mixture of "science" and "religion" appeared congenial to some Catholics, but it was eventually rejected by Jacques Maritain (1882–1973) and Maurice Blondel* (Virgoulay 1980) in France, and by Luigi Sturzo (1871–1959) in Italy. All three rejected theocracy as temporal power of the church, as well as positivism, insisting on the "integral" unity of grace* and nature* in human affairs, under the "primacy of the spiritual." They therefore called for a Christian influence to pervade social and political life. This perspective has been well summed up by Henri Sonier de Lubac (1984a): "As the supernatural is not separated from nature, and the spiritual is everywhere mixed with the temporal, the church eminently has…authority over all, without having to depart from its role. Otherwise, it would be necessary to admit that the church has no authority in practice over anything and can never speak except in the abstract." This position was prevalent in the 1930s, when it was associated with the idea of renewed Christendom. (It also existed among "High Church" Anglicans in England [Anglicanism*], such as V. A. Demant [1893–1983] or T.S. Eliot [1888–1965]).

Fascism and Nazism had the effect not only of discrediting Maurras, and any idea of church authority in politics, but also of encouraging a more enthusiastic embrace of liberal democracy* as a bulwark against totalitarianism, leading to the disappearance of the theme of "Christendom." (This applies, for example, to Maritain's postwar work in this area.) In the 1950s, Congar spoke of a "distinction of planes" to argue that politics is the concern of the state and not of the church, of the laity* and not of the priesthood*. Later, Gustavo Gutierrez retorted (1971) that this position is not entirely in agreement with the theological "integralism" regarding grace and nature still espoused by Congar. In fact, in his critique of Maurrasianism, Congar passes a more severe verdict on theocracy than on positivism (secular autonomy).

One could say the same of Lubac's rebuttal of Arquillière's thesis (1955) on political Augustinianism. Thus, Lubac argues that Augustine*'s distinction between the "two cities" is an essentially spiritual distinction between the elect and the reprobate. He therefore denies that Augustine offers any "political theology" (this term is used); and insists that Augustine and his legitimate heirs (e.g., Charlemagne's court theologians, such as Jonas d'Orléans [c. 780–842/3], *Le métier de roi*, SC 407) considered all pagan states to have the same legitimacy, conferred by the binding of a people* around a common good* (*Civ. Dei* 19, 21). Finally, he adds that for Augustine there can be adequate *political* justice* under natural law, and that the fulfillment of true justice by true worship is a requirement of the *spiritual* life.

Apart from the fact that Lubac here appears to interpose a dualism of grace and nature, which he otherwise refuses, one might think that he has not read Augustine with all his customary rigor. The "two cities" are undoubtedly mystical, but for Augustine they are also historical bodies modeled on Israel* and Babylon. When Augustine criticizes pagan virtue*, including Roman civic virtue and imperial practice, as merely *limiting* violence* or unruly passion*, he is elaborating a political theology. Augustine's criterion is ironic: a society* that is undeniably a polity may therefore be oriented to injustice. Augustine explicitly denies that Rome* was just *as a polity,* since it lacked true worship and therefore made a temporary city falsely absolute. It is true that Augustine does not deny Rome's legitimacy according to natural law, but this is a second-best, postlapsarian natural law, which justifies any regular order as better than mere anarchy. For Augustine, as for Paul, political power is at once a punishment for sin* and a way of limiting its effects (Carraud 1984). Genuine social and political justice requires obeisance to the true God, which is possible only through Christ* (Williams 1987; Milbank 1990). One can add that Arquillière was partly justified in interpreting the Carolingian theologians as more theocratic than Augustine. For the latter, the "good prince" is certainly within the church in so far as he exercises justice informed by charity, but princely power (*regnum*) is not identical to priestly power (*sacerdotium*), for the prince must do what is necessary to quell anarchy, and the coercive methods that he uses therefore make him belong to "the city of this world." The later theologians seem to see fewer difficulties in the wielding of the sword by a "pastor."

In short, the systematic refusal of a political theology that fuses theocracy with positivism has criticized the former more than the latter aspect, and thereby minimized the possibility of a theological interpretation of the social and political as such. (A start was made by Maritain and Sturzo, but their reflections were insufficiently theological.) The problem that may then be posed is that of the hypostasization of the "political." It is assumed as self-evident that politics has a "realm." Yet Schmitt himself saw the difficulty of determining "where" politics is, among civil association, education, learning, trade, family*, and so forth. Hence, there is no purely political sphere over against the church, the still imperfect presence of the Kingdom*. Regrettably, 20th-century political theology has not grasped that ecclesiology, if it is not to be lost in abstraction, must take the whole of society into account.

- C. Schmitt (1935), *Politische Theologie: Vier Kapitel zur Lehre der Souveranität,* Munich.

J. Maritain (1936), *Humanisme integral: Problèmes temporels et spirituels d'une nouvelle chrétienté,* Paris.

H. de Lubac (1938), *Catholicisme: Les aspects sociaux du dogme,* Paris; id. (1984 *a*), "L'autorité de l'Église en matière temporelle," in *Théologies d'occasion,* Paris, 217–40; id. (1984 *b*), "Augustinisme politique?," ibid., 255–308.

L. Sturzo (1947), *La vera vita: Sociologia del Soprannaturale,* Rome.

E. Peterson (1951), "Der Monotheismus als Politisches Problem," in *Theologische Traktate,* Munich, 45–147.

Y. Congar (1954), *Jalons pour une théologie du laïcat,* Paris.

H. X. Arquillière (1955), *L'augustinisme politique,* Paris.

H. Arendt (1958), *The Human Condition,* Chicago; id. (1961), *Between Past and Future,* New York; id. (1962), *Origins of Totalitarianism,* Cleveland, Ohio.

J. B. Metz (1968), *Zur Theologie der Welt,* Mainz; id. (1977), *Glaube in Geschichte und Gesellschaft,* Mainz.

C. Schmitt (1970), *Politische Theologie II: Die Legende von der Erledigung jeder Politischen Theologie,* Berlin.

M. Theunissen (1970), *Hegel's Lehre vom Absoluten Geist als Theologisch-Politischer Traktat,* Berlin; id. (1991), *Negative Theologie der Zeit,* Frankfurt.

G. Gutierrez (1971), *Teologia de la Liberación,* Lima.

H. Muhlen (1972), *Entsakralisierung: Ein Epocheres Schlagwort in seiner Bedeutung für die Zukunft der Christlichen Kirchen,* Paderborn.

M. Xhaufflaire (1972), *La théologie politique: Introduction à la théologie politique de J.-B. Metz,* vol. I., Paris.

J. Moltmann (1973), *Der gekreuzigte Gott: das Kreuz Christi als Grund und Kritik christlicher Theologie,* Munich.

H. Peukert (1976), *Wissenschaftstheorie—Handlungstheorie—fundamentale Theologie: Analysen zu Ansatz und Status theologischer Theoriebildung,* Dusseldorf.

R. Virgoulay (1980), *Blondel et le modernisme: La philosophie de l'action et les sciences religieuses (1896–1913),* Paris.

Y. Congar (1981), "Le monothéisme politique et le Dieu Trinité," *NRTh* 103, 3–17.

S. Hauerwas (1983), *The Peaceable Kingdom,* London.

V. Carraud (1984), "La généalogie de la politique—Pascal," *Com(F)* IX/3, 26–37.

R. Williams (1987), "Politics and the Soul: A Reading of the City of God," in *Milltown Studies* 19/20, 55–72.

J. Milbank (1990), *Theology and Social Theory,* Oxford.

M. Barnes (1991), *The Power of God: The Significance of Dynamis in the Development of Gregory of Nyssa's Polemic against Eunomios of Cyzicus,* Toronto, unpublished thesis.

S. Hauerwas (1991), *After Christendom?,* London.

J. Taubes (1993), *Die Politische Theologie des Paulus,* Munich.

O. O'Donovan (1996), *The Desire of the Nations,* Cambridge.

JOHN MILBANK

See also **Authority; Church and State; Democracy; Ecclesiology**

Polycarpus of Smyrna. *See* Apostolic Fathers

Polygenesis. *See* Monogenesis/Polygenesis

Pomponazzi, Pietro. *See* Naturalism; Philosophy; Truth

Pope

The history* of the Church* is much more complex than that of the Christian faith*'s tradition*; likewise, the historical reality of the papacy, "the most famous institution of the whole Western world" (Toynbee) goes beyond expressing only the theological essence of Peter*'s ministry*. In relation to his own expressions in the New Testament, Peter has been going through considerable developments (I), which acquired dogmatic strength only recently (II). When freed from its past interpretations, which crystallized in a very obvious fashion the division among Christians, Peter's ministry is seen by contemporary popes as helping to serve the unity* of all Christians (III).

I. Developments Leading to the Primacy of the Pope

The New Testament does give evidence of Peter's primacy among the Twelve and among the early Churches; he also holds authority* in the domain of faith. However, no guiding statements are provided regarding his succession.

The link between Peter's ministry and the Church of Rome* began to be established at the time of his martyrdom* (with Paul in 64) in that city. The Church of Rome was thus going to enjoy great prestige, a development also due to the following facts: it was located in the capital of the Empire, it was sharing generously its resources and it was taking care of the orthodoxy of

the faith, since Peter had established the seat of his authority in the city. From the middle of the third century, Matthew 16:18–19 started being interpreted as the founding primacy of the Church of Rome (thus Stephen in his controversy with Cyprianus [Cyprian*] and Firmilianus of Caesarea). The evolution toward the present status of the papacy was going to be, however, a slow and dramatic process.

From the edict of Milan to the fall of the Empire, the authority of the bishop* of Rome grew mainly on account of his being a qualified witness of faith, but this did not imply any jurisdiction* over the Churches that were not part of an immediate dependency (thus, canon 28 of Carthage in 419 [CChr.SL 149, 109–111] excommunicated those who appealed to Rome). During all of the first millennium, Rome had as partners the patriarchal primacies (at least Constantinople, after the Arabic invasions), the ecumenical councils (council*) and the Emperor. On the other hand, except at Sardica (343), the East and the West never gave the same interpretation regarding the Roman primacy. A breaking off followed: the *Dictatus Papae* (Fliche and Martin 8, 79–80) of Gregory VII, who was asking for full powers, in 1075, during his conflict with the Germanic emperor, illustrated well the reasons behind his perseverance.

In 10 of these 27 propositions regarding the power of the pope, the term *solus* keeps on coming back and its extension is described thus: "No synod* can be labeled "general " without his order" (16); "No canonical text can exist outside his authority" (17); "A sentence passed by him cannot be modified by anybody, and he alone can change the sentences passed by everybody else" (18); "He must not be judged by anybody else" (19).

As an echo, Nicetas of Nicomedia said to Anselm of Havelberg: "the authority of the Roman bishop, according to your words, is well above all; let him then be the only bishop, the only doctor, the only educator, let him alone be above everything that has been entrusted to him alone [...]. But if in the Vineyard of the Lord, he wishes to have collaborators [...], let him not despise his brothers that the truth* of Christ* has brought into the world, not for slavery, but for freedom in the heart of the Mother Church" (Dialogues [1136], PL 188, 1218–1219).

This potential rise of pontifical power (which ended up relying on the *False Decretals;* see *Pseudo-Isidorian, DHGE* XXV, 1995, 222–224) went through some tendencies that, if not theocratic, were at least hierocratic; they increased in the 13th century; and then the rise of pontifical power sustained two grave failures. In the name of the superiority of the general council over the pope, in 1415 the Council of Constance* deposed the three competing popes (*COD* 409) and attempted to establish a conciliar regime (Decr. *Frequens,* 1417, *COD* 438 *Sq*);—the attempt did not succeed, in particular because the Greeks favored dealing with their union to Florence (1439), with the pope rather than with the members of the Basel* council. And at the time of the Reformation, the popes were unable to understand the matters to be dealt with and they did not know how to reform the Church at the right time; as a result, the Catholic Church was reduced practically to the Mediterranean area. The papacy reached its doctrinal zenith at the end of the 19th century.

II. Definitions of the First Vatican Council and the Usual Titles of the Pope

1. Definitions of Vatican I

Vatican* I (*Pastor aeternus,* 1870) defined the universal jurisdiction of the pope and the infallibility* of his *ex cathedra* teaching, using a technical language that requires an exegesis: it is possible to borrow from the exegesis that was provided to the Fathers, in the council, by the spokesman, prior to the votes.

a) Primacy of Jurisdiction. It is defined as being immediate, ordinary, really Episcopal, plenary and supreme; of all these terms, only the first one has here its usual meaning: *immediate* indicates that such a power "can be exercised without having to go necessarily through an intermediary" (Mansi 52, 1105). *Ordinary* is the opposite of "*delegated*": the *ordinary* power is one that belongs to someone because of his functions, whereas a *delegated* power is exercised in the name of another person for whom it is *ordinary*" (ibid.). Thus, it is not taught that the powers of the pope must be exercised daily or even usually, but it means that they do not arise out of a process of *delegation. Really Episcopal* is a misleading expression, because it does not mean that the pope is the bishop of the entire Church, but it means, rather, that his power "is of the same nature as that of the bishops: it is a manner of designating an aspect of jurisdiction exercised by the pope and the bishops" (ibid., 1104). This designation is secondary anyway, since it is not even mentioned in the final canon and its anathema. *Plenary and supreme:* this plenitude is such "that no superior human power whatsoever could restrict it; only natural and divine law could" (ibid., 1108–9). Is the pope, then, some kind of absolute monarch, in the Church, by divine right? A great many people interpreted it this way, and not only non-Catholics. The texts actually say something else: "the power of the sovereign pontiff is not an obstacle to the power of Episcopal jurisdiction; the bishops, established by the Holy* Spirit (Acts 20:28), are the successors of the apostles (apostle*); they do have Episcopal jurisdiction, *ordinary* and *immediate,* and each of them guides as a real pastor* the flock entrusted to him. Thus, the pope is not an obstacle to Episcopal jurisdiction; on the contrary, Episcopal power is confirmed, strengthened and defended by the supreme and universal pastor" (*DS* 3061).

The power of the bishops being conferred by divine right as much as that of the pope, the finality of his plenary jurisdiction is that "the episcopate be one and undivided" (*DS* 3051). Finally, according to Vatican I, the definition as a whole must be understood in "the light of the ancient and constant faith of the universal Church" (*DS* 3052); it should be expressed in the language of the "acts of the ecumenical councils and of the holy canons" (*DS* 3059); it should be experienced in accordance with "the perpetual customs in use in the Churches", and it found its expression above all "in those councils where the East met with the West in the unity of faith and charity" (*DS* 3065). Pius IX himself confirmed, "with the plenitude of his apostolic authority", the explanations given to Bismarck by the German episcopate (*DS* 3112–3116): this jurisdiction does not make the pope the exclusive trustee of the full and entire Episcopal power. The dogma* of 1870 does not, therefore, legitimize a Roman centralization; it does not act as a basis for the present appointment of almost all the bishops directly by the pope, nor is it the basis for the responsibilities that come within the remit of the Roman Curia and for the power of the nuncios.

b) Solemn Magisterium of the Pope and His Infallibility. The text that defines infallibility is clearer than the text that writes about jurisdiction; it says the following: "When the pope speaks *ex cathedra,* i.e. when he performs his duties of doctor and pastor of all the Christians, he defines in fact, in his capacity as incumbent of the supreme apostolic authority, a doctrine on faith or moral standards that must be held by the entire Church"; he thus "has, thanks to the divine assistance promised to him in his capacity as Saint-Peter's successor, the privilege of infallibility; this is a privilege that the divine Redeemer wished the Church to have for its work regarding the establishment of a doctrine on faith and morals. As a consequence, the way the Church defined that doctrine is unchallengeable, *per se,* and not by virtue of Church's consent" (*DS* 3074). It is, therefore, only the *solemn* magisterium of the pope that is declared infallible; the pope is infallible merely in the act of defining and not in a habitual manner—the medieval canonical tradition that considered the possibility of finding heresy* in a pope's conduct ("nisi forte a fide devius"), for instance for a private interpretation of doctrine, is therefore not revoked. Furthermore, infallibility does not guarantee that the teaching is formulated in the best possible manner (even if it becomes unchallengeable), or that it is promulgated at the most opportune time; it only guarantees that the teaching is exempt of error. As for the unchallengeable nature of infallibility *ex sese,* it is stated for the purpose of excluding the necessity of a previous consent legally verified, even if—this is a further detail supplied by the spokesman—"the consensus regarding the teaching of all the present magisterium* of the Church, united with its leader, is a rule of faith for the definitions given by the pope" (Mansi 52, 1216).

It is clear, as well, that infallibility does not cover the disciplinary acts or the acts of government coming from the pope (approval of the execution of heretics and witches); it does not cover either his political decisions (condemnation of constitutions that guaranteed religious freedom) or scientific decisions (the Galileo affair). Pius XII is the only pope, since then, to have made use of the prerogative of infallibility (definition of the Assumption of Mary*).

2. Usual Titles of the Pope

a) Bishop of Rome. When he is elected, the pope becomes the successor of Peter, as well as bishop of Rome: Vatican I (*DS* 3057) re-stated that very point, which the East proclaims as well, and that title has an ecumenical pertinence that the title "leader of the college of bishops" cannot have. Paul VI signed the Acts of Vatican* II in his capacity as "bishop of the Catholic Church": by using that title, which dates back to the fourth century, he did not aspire to universal episcopate, but he was adopting a formula that designates him as bishop of the Catholic Church of the city of Rome (H. Marot [1964], *Irén.* 37, 221–26).

b) Patriarch of the West. This title, always in use, is of great ecumenical importance; it clarifies the fact that "Rome has no other rights than those of the other patriarchates [patriarchate*], which means that its primacy for the whole Church does not include central administration" (J. Ratzinger, *Le nouveau peuple de Dieu,* Paris, 1971).

c) Leader of the Church. This expression, restricted by a medieval elaboration that made everything stem from the pope, is used only once by Vatican II (*LG* 18), accompanied by the adjective "visible."

d) Sovereign Pontiff. This frequently used title *(summus pontifex),* is often wrongly confused with the pagan dignity of *pontifex maximus,* as if the popes had actually wished to be the successors of that dignity. This title started being used during the Renaissance under the humanistic influence (R. Schieffer [1971], "Der Papst als pontifex maximus", *ZSRG.K* 57, 300–309). It is unintelligible to the non-Catholics and cannot be translated, for example, in Greek.

e) Vicar of Christ. This title was conferred to all the Western bishops until the 12th century; later, it started to be reserved only for the popes in order to characterize the plenitude of their power (Innocent IV even assumed the title of "vicar of God"). Vatican II marginalized that title significantly by conferring it only twice to the pope (*LG* 18 and 22; *OT* 9 is edifying) and especially by giving it again to each bishop (*LG* 27).

The International Theological Commission making representations to the pope recommended that the latter three titles be given up (Congar 1975).

f) Sovereign of the State of Vatican City. This title of sovereignty, even though very modest materially (44 ha), symbolizes, in the eyes of the Orthodox and the Protestants, the temporal power of the popes from the eighth century to 1870, and the present disparity between them and the Holy See in the matter of diplomatic representation in the world (165 States were represented at the Holy See in 1995) and in international organizations.

III. Toward Ecumenical Discussions on the Ministry of Peter as Unity Ministry

The ecclesiological orientations of Vatican II have allowed the pope and the principal representatives of the other Churches to meet: in the past thirty years; personal dialogue has been rekindled among all of them. The international bilateral commissions for theological dialogue have not, however, put Peter's ministry on their agenda. Only some national commissions have done so (for instance Catholics and Lutherans in the United States: *Papal primacy and the Universal Church,* Minneapolis, 1974; *Groupe des Dombes* (France): *The ministry of communion in the universal Church, DC* 83, 1986, 1112–42). In 1995, John-Paul II expressed the wish "to search, of course together, the forms according to which Peter's ministry might produce this work of love*, recognized by all [. . .]. It is a huge task [. . .] that I can't carry to fruition by myself" (*Ut unum sint,* #95–96). The conditions of that endeavor will depend on who the partners are.

The Catholics and the Orthodox recognize, moreover, that they have to resolve a problem that they have in common, which is how to articulate the communion* between local* and regional Churches in a Church that is *one.*

J. Meyendorff wrote the following as early as 1960: "The Orthodox will have to think more seriously than they have so far about the role that the common testimony of the local Churches could or should have, and more precisely about the role that the *primus inter pares* has in this testimony" (*L'Église orthodoxe,* Paris, 184). Later, in 1981, he was even more explicit: "The Orthodox are obviously not entitled to object to Roman primacy by simply basing their objection on the ethnic provincialism of their national and autocephalous Churches [. . .]; these are undoubtedly excuses for separatism [. . .]. If a council for union ever gets assembled, it will have to put on its agenda the matter of the autocephalous characteristic [. . .] and also, naturally, the matter of Roman primacy" (*Les Églises après Vatican II,* ThH 61, Paris, 344).

As for the Catholic side, it will have a key to solve the problem if a way is found to make a much clearer distinction between the pope's primacy and his patriarchal functions.

Thus, Monsignor Damaskinos, secretary of the future Orthodox council, wrote the following: "Regarding the power and the functions of the pope, it is clear that the Eastern tradition acknowledges that the bishop of Rome has a special authority within the Church [. . .]. That authority differs from the actual patriarchal authority of the pope in the Western world, and it is out of the question that acknowledging the authority of the bishop of. Rome may signify at all that the Orthodox Church is acquiescing to the pope's patriarchal authority" (*Irén* 47, 1975, 221).

Catholic ecclesiology* may express itself as follows: "The unitarian ecclesial law*, the unitarian liturgy*, one single procedure for the appointment of bishops by Rome, from the center, all these things are not necessarily part of primacy *per se,* but can be verified only when the two ministries (pope and patriarch) become one. As a consequence, consideration ought to be given, in the future, to distinguish more clearly the actual function of Peter's successor from the patriarchal function" (J. Ratzinger, *Le nouveau peuple de Dieu,* 142).

That would require from Catholic theology* a better explanation of primacy and collegiality*, a more precise definition of the status of local and particular Churches within the communion and a simultaneous renewal of conciliarity.

The declaration of Balamand (International Catholic-Orthodox Commission) opens the doctrinal road to this common examination; it states the following: "The Catholic Church and the Orthodox Church acknowledge each other as Sister-Churches, with the common responsibility of maintaining the Church of God in a state of faithfulness to the divine design, specially in regards to unity" (n. 14; *DC* 90, 1993, 712). Usually, the non-Chalcedonian Churches have the same attitude as the Orthodox Church toward the ministry of the pope, which they know through the Churches of their own rite united to Rome.

The dialogue with the Reformed Churches will be more complex, not only for the reason the polemic was more violent (Luther* and most of the Reformers after him identified the pope with the Antichrist), but for ecclesiological reasons. The Protestant tradition shows in fact little homogeneity in its views regarding the *episkopè*/episcopate as an instrument of communion among the Churches. As a matter of fact, the Petrine responsibility means that bishops observe a ministry of communion that requires serving in unity with the colleagues in the episcopate. Furthermore, acceptance of the papal magisterium will be even more difficult, because for the members of the Reformed Churches no magisterial decision can be protected from questioning, whereas the ministry of the pope is meant, in certain circumstances, to leave absolutely no option to the faithful: an obligation for which the John Paul II's motu proprio (1998) provides disciplinary sanction.

In Catholic theology, a rigorous exegesis of the definitions provided by Vatican I will prove insufficient as long as the other Churches strongly perceive the Catholic Church as the pope's Church, or as the Church of Rome (*Dict. of the Ecum. Mov.* [1991], 877). Furthermore, the ministry of Peter will convince the other Churches only to the extent that they will see it as serving the legitimate plurality of Churches expressing itself in a vigorous synodal and conciliar fashion.

- M. Maccarone (1952), Vicarius Christi: *Storia del titolo papale,* Rome.
Y. Congar (1970), *L'Église, de saint Augustin à l'époque moderne* (*HistDog* 20), Paris.
W. de Vries (1974), *Orient et Occident: Les structures ecclésiales vues dans l'histoire des sept premiers conciles,* Paris.
Y. Congar (1975), "Titres donnés au pape," *Conc(F)* 108, 55–64.
H. Legrand (1975), "Ministère romain et ministère universel du pape," *Conc(F)* 108, 43–54.
J.-M.R. Tillard (1982), *L'évêque de Rome,* Paris.
F. Frost (1987), "Primauté," *Cath* 11, 986–1027.
W. Klausnitzer (1987), *Das Papstamt in Disput zw. Lutheranern u. Katholiken,* Innsbruck-Vienna.
K. Schatz (1990), *Der päpstliche Primat: Seine Geschichte von den Ursprüngen bis zur Gegenwart,* Würzburg.
Comité mixte catholique orthodoxe en France (1991), *La primauté romaine dans la communion des Églises,* Paris.
R. Leuze (1992), "Papst (systematisch-ökumenisch)," *EKL* 8, 1027–33.
H. Legrand (1993), "Les ministères dans l'Église locale," in B. Lauret and F. Refoulé (Ed.), *Initiation à la pratique de la théologie,* 2nd Ed., vol. 3, 275–329, Paris.
S. Vacca (1993), Prima sedes a nemine iudicatur. *Genesi e sviluppo dell'assioma fino al Decreto di Graziano,* MHP 61.
H. Leipold (1995), "Papsttum II, Die neuere ökumenische Diskussion," *TRE* 25, 676–95 (bibl.).

HERVÉ LEGRAND

See also **Collegiality; Council; Dogma; Ecumenism; Infallibility; Jurisdiction; Ministry; Patriarchate; Structures, Ecclesial; Vatican I, Council of; Vatican II, Council of**

Porete, Marguerite. *See* **Beguines; Vienna, Council of**

Positive Theology

Contrary to common belief, the notion of "positive theology" is not in opposition to "negative theology," but to "speculative" or "Scholastic theology." However, this is not enough to define the content of a term whose meanings are almost as numerous as the texts in which it has appeared. It was not until the 19th century that the usage prevailing down to the present was established. Since then, positive theology has designated the branch of theology that examines the historical sources of theological statements in order to bring out the normative contents provided by Holy* Scripture and the tradition* of the Church*. Thereafter, speculative work is grafted onto this foundation. It seeks to throw the light of reason* on the meaning of the material collected and thereby make it accessible to different eras. But this now common meaning is not the one the term had originally and that long remained in use. The older meaning can be brought to light by a fragmentary sketch of the concept's history.

a) First Approaches. The first known occurrence of the term is in a Catalan work of Ramon Lulle (Raymond Lully) dating from the late 13th century: "Positive theology is a product of the will, demonstrative theology a product of the understanding" (*Proverbis de Ramon,* c. 276, 2: 209f.; Garcías-Palou 1958).

This usage probably shows the trace of Arabic influences (Lohr 1973), but certainly also represents the articulation of a legal perspective (adopting the Greek opposition between what exists "by nature" and what is "established by man" (*phusei/thèsei*)), which since the early 12th century had distinguished between positive law* and natural law (Kuttner 1936). This distinction was explicitly adopted by Lully, who also connected it to the grammatical theory of degrees of comparison (positive-comparative-superlative) (*Ars brevis de inventione iuris*, CChr. CM 38. 296, 321). Hence, positive theology represents an elementary level of theological thinking, which consists of recognizing the evidence of authority*, whereas demonstrative theology brings all beings endowed with reason to a necessary understanding of the truths of faith*. The Latin translation of Lully's proverbs by J. Lefèvre d'Étaples (Rogent-Duràn 1927) seems to have had a wide influence, and most particularly on the Scottish theologian Johannes Maior (John Major). Major was indeed the first known writer to adopt the concept of positive theology, which he introduced in the fourth edition of his *Commentary on the Fourth Book of Sentences* (1515, fol. i, v), published in the same year as the translation by Lefèvre d'Étaples. The meaning that Maior gave to the term is not clear from the context, but this is the first appearance of the terminological distinction between positive theology and Scholastic theology.

b) Transformations of the Concept by Jesuit Writers. The next significant stage in the history of the concept is represented by the *Spiritual Exercises* of Ignatius of Loyola. Perhaps influenced by the tradition derived from Raymond Lully, he distinguishes between positive teaching and Scholastic teaching, as well as between the teachers of each discipline (MHSJ 100. 410ff.). Whereas the former act primarily on people's affective capacities, the latter address themselves principally to their cognitive faculties. Among the positive teachers he names the church fathers* Augustine*, Jerome, and Gregory, and among the Scholastic teachers the major medieval theologians Peter Lombard, Thomas* Aquinas, and Bonaventure*.

In its program of studies the Society of Jesus founded by Ignatius of Loyola reinterpreted this distinction (*Ratio studiorum* 1586: MHSJ 129. 85; P. Ximénez, *De cursu triennali theologiae positivae* 1608; MHSJ 141. 653), giving the name "positive theology" to the courses for candidates preparing for a simple ministry* of preaching* and spiritual* direction, whereas "Scholastic theology" designated the course of study reserved for future university theologians. The former consisted principally in the study of Scripture, a source for preaching; in the analysis of questions of conscience with which future confessors

would inevitably be confronted (casuistry*); and—but only for students from European countries north of the Alps—in the acquisition of knowledge needed in that region to argue against non-Catholic doctrines. During the same period, however, there was a Jesuit theologian who defined positive theology in an entirely different way, coming close to the sense in which the term was used later: "Theology is called positive to the extent that it is principally devoted to explaining the senses of Scripture* by various means, primarily by the authority of the holy Fathers. It thereby establishes the solid principles from which other theological conclusions may be drawn" (Gregory of Valencia 1591, I. 7ff.). This writer was perhaps adopting a terminological tradition current at the University of Salamanca, where he had been a student.

c) Development of the Concept after the 17th Century. The later development of the concept goes beyond the framework established by these definitions. Protestant theologians either adopted the principles of the Jesuit curriculum, distinguishing between positive or church theology that was obligatory for all candidates for the pastorate and an academic theology reserved for those who were interested in a more scientific approach to theology (Calixt 1628–56), or they identified the former with what was later called dogmatics (dogmatic* theology) (Calov 1682). Catholic theologians such as Mabillon and Du Pin also offered divergent definitions of positive theology.

Both certainly agreed in seeing positive theology and Scholastic theology as disciplines that, far from being in opposition, overlapped to a great degree; and both interpreted Scripture by means of the testimony of the tradition. But whereas Mabillon recognized the specific character of Scholastic theology in the implementation of a philosophical argument (1692), Du Pin ascribed that character solely to the systematic organization of subject matters, which became themselves an object of study (1716).

In the history of theology of the French classical era, these two writers were the principal representatives of a tendency later generally identified with positive theology. They undertook philological and historical research aimed at restoring the letter and the spirit of the evidence of tradition, and they considered that this would enable them to help to resolve the major theological and ecclesiastical questions of their time, more than would the subtlety of a style of argument that they called "Scholastic." Both invoked the Catholic tradition of *loci* * *theologici*.

In addition to the theologians already mentioned and their immediate associates, this current mainly included writers attempting to relate the themes of dogmatic theology to the evidence of the tradition (e.g., Petau and Thomassin). The strength and concomitant difficulty of this kind of positive theology lay in the fact that the neutral tool of philological and historical knowledge was placed at the service of an ecclesial theology that had necessarily predetermined its chosen sources and its results. This association made it a "mixed genre" of a special kind (Neveu 1994). Therefore, it was not long before the magisterium* of the Church began to evince a marked skepticism about the results and about the increasing influence of this positive theology, in which it discerned a tendency to introduce autonomous criteria into the Church, a tendency associated with an "objective or documentary notion of tradition" (Congar 1960).

Added to the internal difficulties already mentioned, these external problems accompanied the entire development of positive theology from the Augustinian theologians of the 16th and 17th centuries (Augustinianism*, Jansenism*) to 20th-century writers subject to ecclesiastical* discipline, such as P. Battifol and H. de Lubac*. The Neoscholastic tendency that appeared in the 19th century, and was favored by the Roman magisterium, attempted by contrast to integrate positive theology in such a way that the evidence of Scripture and of tradition would no longer function as probative elements (*dicta probantia*) confirming contents of faith already formulated and set in normative terms (theological notes*).

d) Positivity as an Element of Any Theology. After the controversies with the philosophy* of the Enlightenment, which had led to the propounding of a purely "natural" religion (Lagrée 1991) and had given a pejorative meaning to the notion of "positive theology" or "positive religion," some philosophers and theologians of the 19th century endeavored to understand theology as necessarily "positive," because it was irremediably linked to revelation*, and to its historical testimonies and its current manifestations in the Church (Schelling* 1803, Lectures 8 and 9; Schleiermacher* 1811; Drey 1819). They thereby made it into a science in its own right, as opposed to a purely philosophical or purely historical approach to religion (*see* more recently Heidegger* 1970; Seckler 1977).

Although the term *positive theology* has largely been erased from current theological vocabulary, the problems linked with the notion and with its history nevertheless remain, particularly with respect to the relationship of dogmatic theology to its sources, and with respect to the "theological qualification" of biblical and historical disciplines within theology (exegesis*, history* of the Church).

● J. Maior (1516), *In IV sententiarum,* 4th Ed., Paris.
G. de Valentia (1591), *Commentarii theologici,* Ingolstadt.
G. Calixt (1628–56), *Apparatus sive introductio in studium et disciplinam sanctae theologiae,* in *Werke in Auswahl,* vol. I, Ed. I. Mager, Göttingen, 1978, 48–364.
A. Calov (1682), *Theologia positiva,* Wittenberg.
J. Mabillon (1692), *Traité des études monastiques,* 2nd Ed., Paris.
L. E. Du Pin (1716), *Méthode pour étudier la théologie,* Ed. J.-P. Migne, *Theologiae cursus completus,* vol. 26, Paris, 1842, 1194–296.
F. W. J. Schelling (1803), *Vorlesungen über die Methode des academischen Studiums,* Tübingen.
F. D. E. Schleiermacher (1811), *Kurze Darstellung des theologischen Studiums,* Berlin.
J. S. Drey (1819), *Kurze Einleitung in das Studium der Theologie,* Tübingen.
E. Rogent, E. Duràn (1927), *Bibliografía de les impressions lullianes,* Barcelona.
St. Kuttner (1936), "Sur les origines du terme 'droit positif,'" *RHDF* 15, 728–40.
S. Garcías-Palou (1958), "¿Fué Ramón Llull el primero en usar las expresiones "teología positiva" y 'teologo positivo'?" *EstLul* 2, 187–96.
Y. Congar (1960), *La Tradition et les traditions,* vol. 1, Paris.
P. Clair (1964), *Louis Thomassin,* Paris.
Th. Tshibangu (1965), *Théologie positive et théologie spéculative,* Louvain.
M. Heidegger (1970), *Phänomenologie und Theologie,* Frankfurt.
L. Karrer (1970), *Die historisch-positive Methode des Theologen Dionysius Petavius,* Munich.
Ch. Lohr (1973), "Lección inaugural," *EstLul* 17, 114–23.
M. Hofmann (1976), *Theologie, Dogma und Dogmenentwicklung im theologischen Werk Denis Petaus,* Munich.
M. Seckler (1977), "Theologie-Religionsphilosophie-Religionswissenschaft," *ThQ* 157, 163–76.
J. Gres-Gayer (1986), "Un théologien gallican, témoin de son temps: Louis Ellies Du Pin," *RHEF* 72, 67–121.
Y. Chaussy (1989–91), *Les bénédictins de Saint-Maur,* 2 vols., Paris.
J. Lagrée (1991), *La religion naturelle,* Paris.
B. Neveu (1994), *Érudition et religion aux XVIIe et XVIIIe siècles,* Paris.

LEONHARD HELL

See also **History of the Church; Loci theologici; Notes, Theological**

Postmodernism

a) History of the Term. Following certain sporadic occurrences, the history of the term *postmodernism* began with the borrowing of the term from Arnold Toynbee (1889–1975) by American "new critics" in the late 1960s (S. Maier 1989). They employed it in a derogatory sense, to denote a falling away from the rigors of high modernism. In short order, however, postmodernism was given a positive meaning by Leslie A. Fiedler and Susan Sontag, who were attracted by the fusion of modernism with populism that they found in certain literary works.

The term was then extended to other arts, especially architecture*. The American Charles Jencks emerged in the 1970s and 1980s as the most notable protagonist of a "postmodern" architecture that marries gratuitous ornament to modernist functionalism, and uses earlier styles with an ironic lack of commitment to their original cultural or religious intent. I. Hassan applied the term to the culture in general: in his view, ideas that were once avant-garde have today been recuperated by a society dominated by advertising and mass media, and in which indeterminacy and transgression are becoming common (*see also* Guardini 1950).

Lyotard (1979) also gives the term a very broad meaning. He identifies three phases of modernity: the age of the Enlightenment, when belief in objective truth* was expressed by the "great narratives" of the simultaneous historical liberation of both liberty* and reason; the modern age, dating from 19th-century positivism, when truth was defined as pragmatic success; and, finally, the "postmodern" age, when the truth acquires a plural status because of the different plays on language. For Lyotard, postmodernism tends toward nihilism, holding that there is no longer any objective truth or coherent subjectivity.

The Anglophone world, however, finds in postmodernism a rediscovery of certain aspects of premodernity as in the case of Jencks's neoclassicism or the notions of virtue* and norms of truth advocated by A. MacIntyre, C. Taylor or M. Sandel. Such authors are indeed postmodern, to the extent that they reject the taste for foundations ("foundationalism") that characterized the modern era, and insist that objective truth is available only via insertion in a narrative tradition*. Likewise, in Germany, P. Koslowski has advocated a "substantial" postmodern that, following the ideas of

R. Spaemann, fuses Aristotelian essentialism with modern liberty.

b) Fluidity of the Concept. If—despite its ambiguity—the term *postmodernism* is at all useful, it is to denote three recent phenomena. The first is the switch in the arts from abstraction and representation of subjective truth to ironic use of earlier narrative and mimetic modes. The second is the merging of avant-garde devices with commercial manipulation of images. The third is the switch in philosophy from a theory of knowledge, which assumes that there are recognizable subjects and objects, to a philosophy* of "the event," which embraces both the subjective and the objective realms. Only the second of these developments can be dated at all precisely. As for the arts, their history has long contained "postmodern" characteristics, as in 19th-century symbolism and 20th-century modernism (e.g., Conrad). In the philosophical realm, "postmodern" questioning is traceable as far back as Renaissance philosophy and Spinoza (1633–77), and was reinstated at the outset of the 20th century with Bergson (1859–1941), Whitehead (1861–1947), and Heidegger*. Nevertheless, its development has been radically accentuated since the 1960s.

c) Theology and Postmodernism. Four currents can be identified. 1) The term *postmodern* has been used by Marc C. Taylor (1984) to describe his reworking of an atheistic "death of God" theology* in more explicitly nihilistic terms, under the influence of Derrida. 2) Certain Anglophone theologians (K. Hart [1989], G. Ward [1995]) have sought to render Derrida's theory of *différance* ("difference") consistent with orthodox [theology] and Christology (Christ* and Christology). 3) Several French phenomenologists (J.-L. Marion, J.-L. Chrétien, P. Ricoeur, M. Henry) have accepted the "end of metaphysics" proclaimed by Heidegger, while elaborating a theological critique of Heidegger's theory of being* and therefore, explicitly or by implication, of Derrida's thought. However, their way of refusing the nihilism of difference by appealing to a phenomenological analysis of experience appears foundationalist and therefore "modern" to British or American readers. 4) Several Anglophone theologians, often informed by Wittgenstein, exhibit affinities with the "substantive postmodernism" of a MacIntyre or a Spaemann. "The Yale School" (H. Frei, G. Lindbeck, B. Marshall) defines itself as "postliberal", and the "Cambridge School" (R. Williams, N. Lash, J. Milbank, G. Loughlin, G. Ward) integrates themes borrowed from French nihilists as well as from philosophers in the third group.

● A. Toynbee (1947), *A Study of History,* vols. I–VI (abridged), London.

R. Guardini (1950), *Das Ende der Neuzeit: Ein Versuch zur Orientierung,* Basel.

H. Levin (1966), *Refractions,* New York.

I. Howe (1971), *Decline of the New,* London.

H. Frei (1974), *The Eclipse of Biblical Narrative,* New Haven, Conn.

J.-L. Marion (1977), *L'idole et la distance,* Paris.

J.-F. Lyotard (1979), *La condition postmoderne: Rapport sur le savoir,* Paris.

I. Hassan (1980), "The Question of Postmodernism,", in H. Garvin (Ed.), *Romanticism, Modernism, Postmodernism,* Toronto, 117–26.

J.-L. Marion (1982), *Dieu sans l'être,* Paris.

M.J. Sandel (1982), *Liberalism and the Limits of Justice,* Cambridge.

G. Lindbeck (1984), *The Nature of Doctrine: Religion and Theology in a Postliberal Age,* Philadelphia.

G. Rose (1984), *Dialectic of Nihilism: Poststructuralism and Law,* Oxford.

M.C. Taylor (1984), *Erring: A Postmodern A/Theology,* Chicago.

C. Jencks (1986), *What Is Postmodernism?,* London.

P. Koslowski, R. Spaemann, R. Löw (1986), *Moderne oder Postmoderne?,* Stuttgart.

J.-F. Lyotard (1986), *Le postmoderne expliqué aux enfants: Correspondance, 1982–1985,* Paris; id. (1989), "Defining the Postmodern," "Complexity and the Sublime," "Response to Kenneth Frampton, 'Brief Reflections on Popular Culture,'" in L. Appignanese (Ed.), *Postmodernism: ICA Documents,* London.

L.A. Fiedler (1987), "Cross the Border, Close that Gap: Postmodernism," in M. Cunliffe (Ed.), *American Literature Since 1900,* London, 329–51.

N. Lash (1988), *Easter in Ordinary,* London.

K. Hart (1989), *The Trespass of the Sign,* Cambridge.

S. Maier (1989), "Postmoderne," *HWP* 7, 1141–45.

J. Milbank (1990), *Theology and Social Theory,* Oxford.

G. Rose (1992), *The Broken Middle,* Oxford.

J.-Y. Lacoste (1994), *Expérience et absolu,* Paris.

G. Ward (1995), *Barth, Derrida and the Language of Theology,* Cambridge.

R. Williams (1995), "Between Politics and Metaphysics: Reflections in the Wake of Gillian Rose," in L.G. Jones and S.E. Fowl (Eds.), *Rethinking Metaphysics,* Oxford, 3–22.

C. Strube, D. Brown, B. Beuscher (1997), "Postmoderne," *TRE* 27, 82–95.

LEONHARD HELL

See also **Atheism; Freud, Sigmund; Heidegger, Martin; Language, Theological; Marx, Karl; Nietzsche, Friedrich Wilhem; Nothingness**

Potentia Absoluta. *See* **Nominalism; Omnipotence, Divine**

Potentia Ordinata. *See* **Nominalism; Omnipotence, Divine**

Poverty. *See* **Bonaventure; Property; Spirituality, Franciscan**

Power. *See* Authority

Power, Divine. *See* Omnipotence, Divine

Power, Ecclesiastical. *See* Canon Law; Ecclesiastical Discipline; Jurisdiction

Power, Obediential. *See* Supernatural

Praise

Addressing praise to God* means recognizing his grandeur and the magnificence of his gifts, rendering him homage, and glorifying him. Praise is the most perfect form of prayer*, for it consists entirely of attention to God in a willing transcendence of particular interests. The article "Psalms*" sets forth the principal aspects of praise in the Old Testament. We will describe here the place this theme occupies in the writings of the New Testament and that given it by Jesus Christ, in whom the praise of the prayers of the Old Testament is brought to perfection.

a) *Vocabulary of Praise.* Praise is expressed in the New Testament by means of the verb *aineô* and the corresponding noun *ainos*. In the Greek of the Septuagint, *aineô* is most frequently a translation of the Hebrew *hâlal,* "to praise," two thirds of whose appearances are in the Psalms. The other Hebrew equivalents of *aineô* are enlightening. We find *bârak,* "to bless," *yâdâh,* "to praise," "to celebrate," "to confess," *rû',* "to cry out," a term evoking a war* cry, but one that might also be a cry of joy or triumph, *shûr,* "to sing," *shâbach,* "to praise," "to celebrate," with the reflexive sense of "to glorify oneself." Another root, *hâdar,* adds the ideas of splendor, beauty*, and honor.

The terms connected to *aineô* in the New Testament generally coincide with these shadings in meaning, although they add some original touches. The verb most

often used is *doksazô,* "to glorify," "to render glory*."
We also find *megalunô,* "to magnify," "to exalt." In
this context are set *eulogeô,* "to bless," *eksomologeo-
mai,* "to confess," "to celebrate." Song is also a part of
praise with the verbs *adô,* "to sing," *humneô,* "to sing a
hymn or a psalm." In them are celebrated the glory of
God, *doksa,* his honor, *timè,* his strength and his power
(omnipotence*, divine), *kratos.*

The compound verb *epaineô* translates both *hâlal*
and *shâbach.* It is the verb used to compliment a human being, whereas *aineô* is reserved for God.

b) Praise of God in the New Testament.   Luke is the
evangelist of praise, which he presents at decisive moments in his work, from the praise of the heaven host
and the shepherds at the Nativity (Lk 2:13, 20) to the
praise of the disciples after the departure of Jesus* (Lk
24:53). Of the first Christian community, he notes that
it praised God (Acts 2:47). It is always God who is the
object of praise. It springs from the miracles (mira-
cle*) performed by Jesus (Lk 19:37) or by his disciples
in his name* (Acts 3:8f.). The converted Gentiles celebrate the grandeur of God (Acts 10:46) and glorify him
(Acts 13:48). Praise is not reduced to sentimental ardor. Intimately linked to listening to the Word* and to
faith*, it expresses the deepest admiration (Lk 2:18ff.).
In the gospel* narrative of the childhood of Jesus,
Luke presents three remarkable canticles (Lk 1:46–55,
68–79; 2:28–32).

The major epistles of Paul contain strong expressions of praise, as in the conclusions to the principal
sections of Romans (Rom 11:33–36; 16:25f.). The
Second Epistle to the Corinthians begins with a formula of blessing* (2 Cor 1:3). Praise is even more
prominent in the epistles of captivity. Ephesians opens
with a great blessing (Eph 1:3–14), punctuated by the
repetition of the formula "to the praise of his glory,"
and the first part of the letter ends with a doxology
(Eph 3: 20f.). The liturgical language of these passages
is particularly well adapted to the expression of praise.
The hymns of Philippians 2:6–11 and Colossians
1:15–20 should also be noted. Studded with many
liturgical fragments, the pastoral epistles express the
praise of God throughout (*see* 1 Tm 1:17, 6:15f.).

The presence of so many canticles is one of the
characteristics that gives Revelation its originality
(Rev 1:4–8, 11:16ff., 14:1–5, 15:3f.). Praise is an integral part of the book. The canticle of the marriage of
the Lamb* (Rev 19:1–8) echoes the Psalms in some of
its references and its four Alleluias.

c) Praise of God in Jesus Christ.   Closely related to
thanksgiving, praise is rooted in an admiring knowl-
edge* of God. It assumes an openness to hearing the
word of God and a capacity to discern him in his actions and his works. It is expressed in joy and in faith. It
is a confession that proclaims the love* of God, a blessing that sends back up to him the good that he has done,
the glorification of a God who has manifested his glory.

The pinnacle of prayer, praise is the unparalleled
place in which God is recognized as God and in which
man is situated in the truth* of his being in the face of
God. In it, God is celebrated with ardor for his qualities and his attributes*, for his work in creation*, for
his marvelous actions in the history* of salvation*.
Man, the principal subject of praise, realizes his vocation to the extent of his ability to celebrate the power
and the love of the God who freely calls him to union
with himself. Mans acts of praise are intended to become an integral part of a life that is entirely praise of
the glory of the Father.

As the only mediator, Jesus is in the strongest sense
both the subject and the object of praise. He causes the
believer to enter into his own prayer of praise and
thanksgiving (Matthew 11:25–27), because he is the
immolated Lamb worthy of receiving power, wealth,
wisdom*, strength, honor, glory, and praise (Revelation 5:12). Bringing to an end the sacrifices (sacrifice*)
of the old covenant*, he is the one through whom we
offer unceasingly to God a sacrifice of praise (Heb
13:15; *see* Lv 7:11–15). The life of man united to the
offering of Jesus becomes praise.

● H. Schlier (1933), "*Aineô, ainos,*" *ThWNT* 1, 176–77.
J. Gaillard (1976), "Louange," *DSp* 9, 1020–34 (esp. 1020–24).
H. Balz (1980), "*Aineô, ainesis, ainos,*" *EWNT* 1, 94–95.

JOSEPH AUNEAU

See also **Cult; Liturgy; Prayer; Psalms**

Prayer

I. Definitions

Prayer is perhaps the fundamental religious activity; as such, it is elusive of definition, being implied in diverse activities and taking various forms. One may, however, distinguish two basic aspects of prayer. The first is generally implied in the word used in most languages (*prière,* "prayer," *Gebet, proseukhe,* etc.): the notion of asking or request, primarily addressed to God*. The second aspect appears as human beings reflect on what is involved in the possibility of communication with God: prayer is communion* or even union with God. This link between what is passing—the human—and what is ultimate—the divine—is open to philosophical questions that the Christian tradition* has often approached from a Platonic perspective (Christian Platonism*). The two aspects of prayer are summed up in the definition often quoted from John Damascene: "prayer is the soul's ascent to God or requesting from God what is necessary" (*Expositio fidei* 68).

II. Prayer in the Scriptures and the Early Church

In the Scriptures, *petition* is a basic aspect of prayer. Prayer is an acknowledgment of frailty and dependence, and of the need for God's help or grace*. Prayer thus implies *repentance* and *confession of sin** (with a petition for forgiveness), as well as *thanksgiving, praise,* and *adoration.* Prayer is thus far from consisting only of petition, for oneself and for others. The Psalms* have traditionally formed the bedrock of Jewish and Christian prayer, but the whole Bible* also illuminates what makes prayer possible—what can be called its foundations—and gives examples of prayer, in particular, the example of the prayer of Christ*.

1. Grounds of Prayer

a) Creation of Human Beings in the Image of God. According to Genesis, human beings were created "in our [God's] image, after our likeness" (Gn 1:26). Although the Bible rarely recalls this, the notion of human beings as being in God's image very quickly came to dominate Christian thought. If the idea is true, then it is natural to communicate or commune with God in prayer. This notion of man is also central to the Christian conception of original sin*: it is the image of God in man that has been damaged as a result of the Fall, thus making difficult a relationship with God in prayer that should be entirely natural. One can therefore understand why to pray is to follow a difficult path, but also how it resembles a return to oneself. It is especially in the Greek Fathers* that we find an understanding of prayer rooted in the notion of man in the image of God; for them, the goal of prayer is to attain a growing transparency to God, or transfiguration in God, which they call "deification" *(theosis).*

b) The Covenant. The idea of the covenant* between God and human beings is central to the Old Testament. After the Flood, the rainbow is the sign of the covenant established between God and Noah (the "Noachic covenant"), and of the promise* never to destroy Noah's descendants in a new flood (Gn 9:12f.). Circumcision is the sign of the covenant between God and Abraham, and of the promise that the posterity of Abraham will be blessed (Gn 17:9–14). A covenant is established between God and Jacob (or Israel*) in the episode of Jacob's dream (Gn 28:11–15). The law* given to Moses is the sign of the covenant between God and the chosen people* (Ex 19:4ff.). Through the covenant, the chosen people become God's own people (*see* Dt 7:6–11). Its continuance is conditional on the people's fulfilling moral and ceremonial obligations, and the prophets (prophet* and prophecy) warned that it would be abrogated (*see* Am 7–9) if they did not fulfil these obligations. Prayer is implicit in the covenant: in prayer, the people acknowledge that they depend on God, that they need his grace, and that they celebrate his wonders and his glory* (*see* 1 Chr 6:14–42). In this context, prayer is primarily communal: it is the prayer of the people, celebrated in the cult* of the tabernacle (and, after the settlement in the promised land, in the cult of the Temple*); individual prayer is secondary. The prayer of an individual can, however, assume huge importance, especially in the person of a prophet, whose vocation is to call the people back to faithfulness to the covenant, and part of whose role is to be an intercessor for the people. Those whose prayer remains faithful constitute the "remnant."

c) *Existence in Christ.* In the New Testament, prayer is the activity par excellence of the Church*, the community of those who are "in Christ" as a result of baptism*. In Christ, we are present with the Father*, who hears and grants our prayers. This is one of the recurrent themes in the last "discourses" in the fourth Gospel (Jn. 14–17). We are "sons and daughters" in the Son: we take part in his communion with the Father and in the bond of love* that binds them together, which is the basis of the confidence (*parresia*) that we have in the effectiveness of our prayer (Jn. 16: 23–27).

d) *Prayer as the Inner Working of the Spirit.* With their understanding of the Holy* Spirit, the Johannine* and Pauline* traditions give a still greater depth to this theme. In John's Gospel, we find the notion of the *Paracletos,* the advocate or comforter who is "with you" and brings us to the divine presence (Jn 14:25–26, 15:26–27, 16:7–15). In Paul's letter to the Romans, we find the idea of the Spirit working within us, interceding for us "in inexpressible lamentations," and enabling us to enter into intimacy with the Father by saying "Abba," as Jesus* himself did (Rom 8:14–23; *see* Gal 4:6 and Mk 14:36).

2. Examples of Prayer

a) *Old Testament.* Most of the significant figures in the Bible are presented as exemplars of prayer. It is, as we have already noticed, one of the roles of the prophet to be a man of prayer, an intercessor for the people. Several exemplars are worth dwelling on: first of all, the psalmist, conventionally identified with David. The Psalms are a collection of prayers, many of which have their origin in the worship of the Temple. They lay bare a relationship with God that is anything but conventional. We find praise, thanksgiving, repentance, and petition in them, but they also express questioning, anger, and depression, as well as joy or hope*. It is a form of prayer characterized by what the later ascetic tradition called *parresia,* an openness before God, a confidence in him in which absolutely nothing is held back or concealed. Abraham's prayer for Sodom (Gn 18:22–33), Jacob's dream (Gn 28:11–17), and as his wrestling with the angel* (Gn 32:24–30) are examples that are often recalled. Moses's ascent of Sinai is interpreted by Philo as a type of the soul's ascent to God, and many Christian authors follow Philo in this (e.g., Clement of Alexandria and Gregory* of Nyssa). Elijah is another exemplar, especially in his experience on Horeb (1 Kgs 19:9–13), in which God is revealed not in his power but in a "low whisper." Elijah's austere life made him a popular model within the Christian ascetic movement.

b) *New Testament.* John the Baptist is explicitly compared to Elijah (Mt 17:13), principally in his prophetic role. In the apostolic church, prayer is prominent. All the letters ascribed to Paul or Peter* include prayer, while the letter to the Hebrews and the letter of James both contain teaching on prayer. The community at Jerusalem* after Pentecost is characterized by "teaching and fellowship, the breaking of bread, and prayers" (Acts 2:42).

c) *Jesus.* All the Evangelists, but especially Luke, portray Jesus as one who spent considerable periods of time in prayer (*see* Lk. 5:16 and 6:12). According to Luke, it was while Jesus was praying on Tabor that he was transfigured before his disciples (Lk. 9:29). John develops this theme by seeing the whole of Christ's earthly life as transfiguration, and the communion between the Father and Son, expressed in prayer, as a mutual glorification, culminating in the raising up onto the cross. This is also expressed by the other evangelists in their account of Jesus' prayer to his Father in the garden of Gethsemane. As well as being an exemplar of prayer, or because of that fact, Jesus teaches his disciples to pray, by giving them the pattern prayer, the Paternoster ("Our Father") (Mt 6:9–13; Lk 11:1–4: note that Luke states that John the Baptist had also taught his disciples to pray). This prayer, which moves from adoration to petition, has been endlessly commented on. However, there is further dominical teaching on prayer. It should not be a matter of display, but done in secret, behind a shut door, "to your Father who is in secret" (Mt 6:6). It should not consist of long, empty phrases (Mt 6:7). We should add two parables (parable*) from Luke, the parable of the importunate widow, and the parable of the Pharisee and the publican, with their respective emphases on perseverance and humility in prayer (Lk 18:1–14).

3. Early Church

a) *Paternoster.* The fullest early Christian reflection on prayer is in fact commentary on *the* prayer: there have come down to us from the pre-Nicene Church (Nicaea*) commentaries by Tertullian*, Origen*, and Cyprian*. There is much that is common to all three. All speak of prayer as something that is secret and inward, and yet they insist that it is communal: Christians pray to "*our* Father." As a corollary, they also stress the importance of prayer for forgiveness, and the consequent requirement to forgive each other. Without excluding an interpretation of the petition for our "daily bread" as a prayer for the necessities of life (out of which Gregory of Nyssa later drew a demand for social justice*: "you are master of your prayer...if no one is hungry or distressed because you are fully satisfied," *De orat. dom.* 4), they all interpret this petition with reference to the Eucharist*. The idea of the Eucharist as the Christian prayer *par excellence* is one that had already established itself in Christian consciousness. Polycarp prepares for martyrdom* in a prayer, summing up his whole life, that is clearly modeled on the eucharistic prayer (*Mart. Pol.* 14); for Irenaeus*, the Eucharist, as sacrifice* and sacrament*, expresses the fullness of the proper Christian attitude to God (*Adv. Haer.* IV, 18, 4–6).

b) *Place of the Body in Prayer.* Another dominant feature of this early Christian teaching is the importance attached to the place of the body (soul*-heart-body) in prayer. Christians are to pray standing up (Tertullian, *De orat.* 23; Origen, *De orat.* 31, 2; Cyprian, *De orat.* 31), holding their arms up (or, according to Tertullian, holding them out in cross-fashion, *De orat.* 14), and facing East (*see* Origen, *De orat.* 32). Kneeling is not a normal position for praying, although it is appropriate for prayers of penitence* (Tertullian, *De orat.* 23; Origen, *De orat.* 31, 3). The ban on praying kneeling on Sundays* and during Pentecost was reiterated at the First Council of Nicaea in 325 (canon 20). Praying toward the East, the direction from which Christ was expected to come at the moment of the Parousia*, or the direction in which the earthly Paradise was believed to be situated (Gen. 2:8), long remained a Christian custom, and is reflected in the orientation of churches (architecture*). Such a concern for the direction in which prayer is offered is also found among Jews, who pray facing Jerusalem, and Moslems, who pray facing Mecca; in all cases, it reflects an awareness of the cosmic significance of prayer. However, alongside this consciousness of the importance of the external conditions of prayer, there is found an emphasis, already mentioned, on prayer as an inward, even secret activity, addressed to "the Father who sees in secret."

III. Liturgical Prayer and Private Prayer

Reflection on Christian prayer often focuses on the polarities in prayer, already apparent, between the individual and the liturgical, the vocal and the silent. In fact, they clearly overlap. While liturgical prayer is not necessarily vocal (liturgical movements can be silent, and the significance of the liturgy* is not necessarily brought out by anything uttered), the liturgical and the vocal tend to belong together, as do the individual and interior. Yet there can be communal experiences of interiority, as was the case for Augustine* and his mother at Ostia (*Confessions* IX, 10, 23–25), or communication

by glance and gesture, as described by William of St Thierry (*De natura et dignitate amoris* 13).

1. Liturgical Prayer

a) *Origins.* Christian liturgical prayer eventually developed into an elaborate "consecration of time" through the cycle of short services celebrated throughout the day—the "hours," or the "divine office." This rhythm of prayer existed in the early third century: both Tertullian and Cyprian speak of prayer at the third, sixth, and ninth hours, as well as morning and evening prayer, and prayer during the night, and Cyprian develops Tertullian's suggestion of these hours as commemorative. The third hour commemorates the coming of the Holy Spirit, the sixth the crucifixion, and the ninth Christ's death* (*see* Tertullian, *De orat.* 25; Cyprian, *De orat.* 34–36). These writings give the impression of individual prayer at these hours, although there is nothing in them to contradict the idea that there were sometimes collective celebrations. From the fourth century onward, the monastic office gradually eclipsed the "cathedral" office (morning and evening prayer in the main churches of the cities), and the familiar structure was put in place: matins (in the East, *orthros*, "dawn office," preceded by the midnight office); lauds ("praises," from Ps 147–50, an invariable part of this service); offices for the first, third, sixth, and ninth hours; vespers; and the final service before the night (*apodeipnon*, "after supper," in the East; compline, "completion," in the West). There was a development of set forms for these services, with prayers and hymns appropriate to each one of them, but they were all based on the recitation of psalms. Eventually, the weekly recitation of the whole psalter was incorporated into the offices in the West as in the East, where the psalter was divided into 20 groups of Psalms, the *kathismata*.

b) *Office as a Public Form of Prayer?* The cycle of liturgical prayer—the divine office and the celebration of the Eucharist—formed the backbone not only of monastic life but also, in principle, of the life of the cities of medieval Europe. It is, however, by no means clear what happened in reality. The development of the parish system in the West perhaps encouraged a development of this sort, but what evidence there is of the Byzantine world suggests that this was not the case in the East: it was, rather, processions, which took place with relative frequency, that represented public prayer for the ordinary citizen. It seems that processions also played an important role of this type in the West in the later Middle Ages, where there were processions in honor of saints and, especially, of Christ's body.

c) Interpretations of the Liturgical Cycle. The daily cycle can, however, take various forms. The basic form, as we have seen, regards the liturgical cycle as a sanctification of time. In the West, the daily cycle is understood primarily to sanctify the day, even though the eschatological meaning of nocturnal prayer is included within it: the cycle begins shortly before daybreak and punctuates the hours of the day with regular times of prayer until sunset. In the East, especially as celebrated in monasteries nowadays, night is evidently the time of prayer. The liturgical day begins with the ninth hour and vespers (at sunset); there is a brief period of sleep after compline, and then matins, lauds, the day hours, and the celebration of the Eucharist usher in the new day. During daylight, there are no formal services. Making night a time for prayer as watching (on great feasts, there is a "vigil," and the offices last throughout the night) underlines the eschatological nature of prayer as praying and waiting for the second coming of Christ, a nature enshrined in the Paternoster, with its petition for the coming of the Kingdom*.

A different interpretation of the liturgical cycle emerged in the Middle Ages, when the recitation of the divine office became an obligation laid on the individual monk or priest. This typically western form of discipline was bound up with the development of the mendicant orders in the 13th century. It went hand in hand with a dispersed community, in which individuals and small groups moved about preaching, and led to the development of a condensed form of the divine office, the breviary, with abridged readings that could be contained in one volume: in the end, there were four of them, one for each season. This was one of the signs of the growing individualism that marked late medieval devotion in the West.

2. Personal Prayer

To begin with, there was no contrast between personal prayer and liturgical prayer: we have seen that the times fixed for prayer were originally times for individual prayer, and almost certainly involved no set form. Gradually, perhaps under the influence of the Platonic sense that the immaterial is higher than the material, there developed a tendency to consider personal and inward prayer as the real thing. Christ's emphasis on "prayer in secret" also encouraged this tendency, but it was slow to develop. Even in a document as late as the *Rule* of St. Benedict (mid-sixth century) there is nothing specific about any other form of prayer than the communal prayer of the divine office, which Benedict calls the "work of God," *opus dei,* over which nothing is to take precedence (*Rule* 43).

3. Ceaseless Prayer

The tendency to privilege personal prayer was favored by the idea that prayer should not only take place at set times, but should be continual (*see* what Paul says:"pray without ceasing," 1 Thess. 5:17). The divine office itself, with its ceaseless cycle of prayer, was already an attempt to obey this injunction. At various times, individual monasteries have sought to be places where prayer never ceases, the earliest example being the monastery of the *Akoimetai,* "the sleepless ones," in fifth-century Constantinople. The perpetual light—in Greek, the "sleepless" light—that has burned in church buildings from at least the fifth century is a symbol of this ideal. However, the best way of making ceaseless prayer a practical ideal is to define prayer, not as an action*, mental or otherwise, but as a state. Probably the first to do this was the great theorist of the early monasticism* of the Fathers of the desert, Evagrius (346–99).

IV. Prayer as a State

1. East

Despite the repeated condemnations of Evagrius, his conception of prayer became fundamental in the eastern Church. For Evagrius, prayer is a state in which the intellect, left in peace* by the lower, irrational part of the soul, is able to contemplate God (*De orat.* 53). It is the natural state of the intellect (*Prak.* 49): inability to attain this state is a result of the disordered, unnatural state in which humanity has been ever since the Fall. Prayer thus understood is contemplation*. (The understanding of contemplation as the true state of the intellect had a long history behind it, especially in Platonic philosophy: *see* Aristotle, *Nicomachean Ethics* 10.) From this point of view, teaching on prayer becomes an exploration of ways of fostering contemplation. For Evagrius, this teaching has two parts. The purpose of the first is the attainment of *apatheia,* the state of freedom from passions* or disturbing movements in the lower, irrational part of the soul. The purpose of the second part is the accustoming of the soul, once it has attained such serenity, to the practice of contemplation, initially of the divinely given meaning of the created cosmos, and then of the divine nature itself. Evagrius devotes much time and care to the first stage, and displays great psychological insight. In particular, one should note his analysis of the kinds of passions (asceticism*), an analysis summed up in his teaching on the eight *logismoi,* or obsessive thoughts inspired by one or other of the passions (see *Prak.* 6–33; these eight *logismoi* reappear as the seven deadly sins). Such passions prevent contemplation by imposing upon the intellect images (whether visual or entering by other senses) that distract it from its goal or make it incapable of attaining it. For Evagrius, the presence of images in prayer is evidence of attachment to the world of the senses from which the imagination draws them. They arouse this attachment through the objects that they evoke. An important stage in attaining pure prayer is, therefore, to be able to form thoughts that are free from any attachment to the world of the senses, which Evagrius calls "mere thoughts" (*psila noemata*). The second stage is essentially the passage from contemplation of these "mere thoughts" to contemplation of God: it is a simplification of one's attention, which passes from what still partakes of multiplicity to the simplicity* of the divine essence. Such an understanding of imageless prayer correlates profoundly with a theology in which God is beyond any image or concept (negative* theology). Many aspects of Evagrius's teaching were modified later (especially by Maximus* the Confessor), but his conception became the dominant one in Orthodox monastic spirituality.

2. West

(a) Cassian and Early Monastic Writers. A similar understanding of prayer as contemplation that, in principle, is uninterrupted is to be found in the West. It is already present in the writings of Evagrius's disciple John Cassian, who speaks of "a loftier state," formed by "contemplation of God alone and the ardor of love" (*Conference* 9,18). Cassian represents this form of prayer as something that comes upon someone who is ready for it, rather than an attainment that one can aim at, for the state of perfect purity*, without which such prayer is impossible, is a grace (*Conf.* 9, 26). Similar ideas are found in the writings of Gregory* the Great, notably in his life of St. Benedict (*Dialogues* II, 2, especially). However, the dominant strand of reflection on prayer grew out of the Benedictine tradition, even though, as we have seen, there is nothing on prayer other than liturgical prayer in St. Benedict's *Rule*. Nevertheless, Benedict does make provision for *lectio divina,* sacred reading, which is to occupy the monk when he is not engaged in the offices or in manual work* (*Rule* 48). *Lectio divina* meant primarily reading of Scripture, but also the reading of the works of the Fathers. It is necessary to read and to meditate (*legere, meditare,* ibid.). This developed in monastic circles in the form of a triad of reading, meditation, and prayer (*lectio, meditatio, oratio*), for the purpose of reading was not to acquire information, but to allow the meaning of what was read to move the heart and mind toward God, in other words to prayer.

(b) Meditation and Contemplation. This triad of reading, meditating and praying has been given several formulations, and in one of them Cassian's term for the "loftier state" of prayer replaces simple "praying": one then has reading, meditating, and contemplating. On the basis of this formula, meditation was more and more clearly distinguished from contemplation, and this was to have a profound impact on late medieval and modern Catholicism*. The distinction between these two forms of prayer came to be articulated in two different ways. On the one hand, the distinction was made between meditation, which uses imagination and reason*, and contemplation, which dispenses with these and attains a state of simple attention. On the other hand, meditation was seen as a mode of prayer related to human activity, and contemplation was seen as a state in which the human being is passive and God alone is active. This second distinction was the fruit of a fundamentally Augustinian understanding of grace developed during the western Middle Ages, where the gratuity of grace demands human passivity. This was why there developed, at the close of the Middle Ages, a widespread notion that contemplative prayer is a special grace that cannot be sought, only prepared and waited for. It is to be attained by submitting to a divine call, which prevents you from praying as you once did, so that you feel abandoned by God at the very moment when he makes a special sign to you. The most thorough analysis of this understanding of prayer is found in the writings of Teresa of Avila and John* of the Cross. Both present contemplation as, at least initially, a bewildering, disorientating experience, which John describes with the image of the "dark night of the soul." This is only one metaphor (although it has attained commanding significance) for a state that others call "indifference"—the Jesuits (Ignatian spirituality*), François de Sales (Salesian spirituality*)—or "abandonment to divine providence" (Caussade).

V. Specific Forms of Prayer

1. West

The divine office required literacy and a knowledge of either Latin, in the West, or literary Greek, in the East. Monasteries therefore became centers of culture. In the West, however, the growth of the Cistercian order led to the creation of a group of religious, the lay brothers, who were to be the servants of the community and who were denied access to education and, with it, the possibility of participating fully in the divine office. For them, a substitute form of the office was provided in which, in particular, recitation of repeated *Ave Marias* was substituted for recitation of the Psalms. Out of this developed the *rosary,* a string of 150 beads (the same number as the Psalms), for each of which an *Ave Maria* was recited. This came to be supplemented by larger beads representing the Paternoster, which separated the smaller beads into strings of 10: at the end of each "decade" of *Ave Marias* the *Gloria Patri* was recited. The rosary developed into a popular form of devotion, promoted especially by the Dominicans. Recitation of a decade accompanied meditation on a "mystery*" associated with the life of Jesus or that of Mary*. These mysteries eventually formed three groups: the Joyful, the Sorrowful, and the Glorious Mysteries. The events of these mysteries, such as the birth of Christ or his scourging, were often depicted in iconography, and this form of devotion eventually provided rich spiritual nourishment, especially for those whose level of literacy denied them full participation in the Latin liturgy.

2. East

The history of popular devotion in the eastern Christian world is much less clearly understood. Liturgical prayer remained more accessible in the Orthodox world. Although the Greek of the liturgy was in a literary form, much of it remained comprehensible to those whose mother tongue was Greek; and, when Orthodoxy was brought to the Slav nations, an alphabet was created by the Greek missionaries Cyril and Methodius, and the liturgy was translated into Slavonic. The reflection on Scripture and the mysteries of the faith* that was called "meditation" in the West was never isolated as a specific form of prayer in the East, and it seems that its role was fulfilled by the repetition of the prayers and hymns of the liturgy.

a) Icons. We should also note the important role of images* or icons in the eastern Church from the sixth century onward. After the decisive rejection of iconoclasm (the "triumph of Orthodoxy") in the mid-ninth century, icons became an essential part of the devotion and liturgical practice of Orthodox Christianity. Icons are more than illustrations: they are mediators of the presence of what is depicted, and thus they are themselves objects of devotion on behalf of those depicted. Defenders of the icons argue that the imagination plays a positive role in the ascent of the soul, and comes into play in the veneration of icons, which are "doors" that open onto the realm of God and his saints. The presence of icons in churches, and their use in personal prayer, bring those who pray into the communion of saints and the presence of God.

b) "Jesus Prayer." The use in prayer of some formula addressed to and naming Jesus can be traced back at least to the fifth century, although its general use in Orthodox circles is much later, and was associated with the growth of hesychasm* in the 13th and 14th centuries. Hesychasm was a monastic movement, associated especially with Mount Athos, that laid stress on the inward search for an experience* of union with God. The method comprises long periods of contemplative prayer, assisted by repetition of the Jesus prayer, and, in some cases, by the control of breathing and adoption of a crouching posture. The normal form of the Jesus prayer is: "Lord Jesus Christ, Son of God, have mercy on me, a sinner." This is repeated slowly as one prays and forms a focus for the attention, enabling the intellect to be free of images and receptive to the divine presence. The experience of union with God is often described as an experience of vision of the uncreated light of the Godhead (deity*). It is common when praying the Jesus prayer to use a knotted rope with, usually, 100 knots, not primarily to count the number of times it is repeated, but rather as an aid to concentration and the establishment of a regular rhythm. This practice is seen as a way of attaining inner stillness and of finding the heart, the center of being, the organ of prayer. It was originally a monastic practice. The 18th-century hesychast anthology, the *Philokalia,* made it more widely available, especially through the Old Slavonic translation by Païssy Velichkovsky. A notable example of the use of the prayer by someone who seems to have had a peasant background, and who remained a layman, can be found in the 19th-century *Otkrovennye rasskazy strannika duhovnomu svoemu otcu* (Narratives of a Russian Pilgrim). In the 20th century, the Jesus prayer has become very widespread, even among non-Orthodox.

- Anon., *Otkrovennye rasskazy strannika duhovnomu svoemu otcu,* Kazan, 1884 (*Récits d'un pèlerin russe,* Neuchâtel, 1943).
  Anon., *Martyre de Polycarpe,* in F. X. Funk, K. Bihlmeyer, W. Schneemelcher (Ed.), *Die apostolischen Väter,* Tübingen, 3rd Ed. 1970.
  Augustine, *Confessions,* BAug 13–14.
  Rule of St. Benedict, SC 181–86.
  Cassien, *Conférences,* SC 42, 54, 64.
  Chariton de Valamo, *Umnoe delanie: O molitve Iisusovoj,* Valamo, 1936.
  Cyprian, *De oratione dominica,* CSEL 3, 1, 265–94.
  Evagrius, *Practical Treatise,* SC 170 and 171; *De oratione,* in Nicodème l'Hagiorite (Ed.), *Philokalia* I, 176–89; *see infra* (French trans. and commentary by I. Hausherr, *Les leçons d'un contemplatif. Le traité de l'oraison d'Évagre le Pontique,* 1960).
  Gregory the Great, *Dialogues,* SC 251, 260, 265.
  Gregory of Nyssa, *De oratione dominica,* Leyden-New York, 1992.
  William of Saint-Thierry, *De natura et dignitate amoris,* PL 184, 379–407.
  Irenaeus, *Adversus haereses,* SC 100, 152–53, 210, 263, 293–94.
  John of Damascus, *Expositio fidei,* PTS 12.
  Nicodème l'Hagiorite (and Macaire de Corinthe) (Ed.),

Philokalia tôn hierôn nèptikôn, 5 vols., Athens, 3rd Ed. 1957–63.

Origen, *De oratione,* GCS 3, 297–403.

Tertullian, *De oratione,* CChr.SL 1, 257–74.

♦ F. Heiler (1918), *Das Gebet: Eine religionsgeschichtliche und religionspsychologische Untersuchung,* Munich.

O. Wyon (1943), *The School for Prayer,* London.

S. Weil (1950), *Attente de Dieu,* Paris.

H. U. von Balthasar (1957), *Das betrachtrende Gebet,* Einsiedeln.

I. Hausherr (1960), *Noms du Christ et voies d'oraison,* Rome.

M. Nédoncelle (1962), *Prière humaine, prière divine,* Paris.

D. Z. Phillips (1965), *The Concept of Prayer,* London.

J. N. Ward (1967), *The Use of Praying,* London.

P. Evdokimov (1968), *La connaissance de Dieu selon la tradition orientale,* Lyon (on icons *see* 107–25).

T. Merton (1968), *The Climate of Monastic Prayer,* Kalamazoo.

E. Wilkins (1969), *The Rose-Garden Game: The Symbolic Background to the European Prayer-Beads,* London.

A. Bloom (1970), *School for Prayer,* London.

Un moine de l'Église d'Orient (1974), *La prière de Jésus,* Paris.

R. Burrows (1976), *Guidelines for Mystical Prayer,* London.

H. U. von Balthasar (1977), *Der dreifache Kranz: Das Heil der Welt im Mariengebet,* Einsiedeln.

L. Ouspensky (1980), *La théologie de l'icône,* Paris.

W. Brümmer (1984), *What Are We Doing When We Pray?,* London.

S. Tugwell (1984), *Ways of Imperfection,* London.

K. Ware (1986), *The Power of the Name: The Jesus Prayer in Orthodox Spirituality,* Oxford.

M. Rubin (1991), Corpus Christi. *The Eucharist in Late Medieval Culture,* Cambridge.

ANDREW LOUTH

See also **Asceticism; Contemplation; Life, Spiritual; Mystery; Spiritual Theology**

Preaching

a) Definition. In the broad sense the Christian tradition* understands by preaching any activity that aims, in various forms, to announce and proclaim the Good News, the gospel*. "Preaching" is thus a synonym of "proclamation." Activity of this kind is already evident in the New Testament (the preaching of Jesus* and of the early communities) and is rooted in the Old Testament (notably in the "preaching" of the prophets [prophet* and prophecy]). In the narrow sense the term *preaching* designates the discourse, usually restricted to ordained ministers of the Church*, which, within the framework of worship, proposes a present-day interpretation of a passage of the Bible* (in this context we can also speak of sermon or homily). To the extent that this preaching brings forth for today the Word* of God that inhabits Scripture, it is itself the word of God.

b) Some Elements of History. The New Testament provides some indirect traces of preaching in the narrow sense (some of the speeches in Acts; some epistles—especially Hebrews—may have first existed in the form of sermons). The linking of preaching to the interpretation of a passage of the Bible appeared very early as a particularity of Christian religious discourse. From the early Church, preaching made up a fixed element in liturgical worship. Its purpose was to recall the dogmatic foundations of faith*, but also to exhort believers (parenesis) and to reply to objections (the apologetic function). It also had a strongly catechistic purpose. Toward the end of classical antiquity, there was in the East a perceptible influence of rhetoric on preaching, which sometimes turned it into a discourse for the cultivated; whereas the West more frequently placed the emphasis on a requirement for simplicity and intelligibility (the *sermo humilis* of Augustine*). The history of preaching in the Middle Ages witnessed the juxtaposition of moments of extreme impoverishment and moments of renewal. On the one hand there was a loss of hermeneutic* force and theological sophistication, a lack of passion, and a homiletic "routine" (collections of constantly reused homilies); on the other hand we find exceptionally creative preaching in mendicant orders, in schools of mystics, and elsewhere.

The Protestant Reformation produced a renaissance in preaching, emphatically conceived as the central element of worship. The pastor* was primarily a preacher; as an interpreter of the gospel he repeated in human language the word of God that gave life to human beings. This homiletic effort grew more prominent in modern times and has constantly attempted to respond to all the challenges of modern culture. This characteristic is all the more striking given that the Catholic tradition continues to privilege ritual language, especially in the celebration of the Eucharist* (although Vatican* II reasserted the value of preaching). The same is true in the Orthodox tradition, where preaching has been losing ground to the performance of a liturgy* celebrated in communion* with the heavenly liturgy.

c) Theological Stakes. Preaching is at the service of the dynamics of the word of God. The fact that it is anchored in the gospel links it directly with the New Testament dimension of the kerygma: its reading of the text is aimed at bringing to life the gospel contained in Scripture, so that it is, in effect, a constantly renewed repetition, in new contexts, of the word of God made flesh in Jesus Christ. This aspect was emphasized in the Reformation, which used the vocabulary of the promise* (*promissio*) in this connection. As such, preaching calls its listeners to faith. But this fortunate effect does not depend on the preacher; only the Holy* Spirit can give effectiveness to the word of the preacher, by working for his inspiration and for the receptivity of his listeners.

There are many interfaith debates bearing on the relationship between preaching and the sacraments (sacrament*) in the overall economy of worship. The Catholic tradition gives pride of place to the sacrament, because it alone truly enables participation in divine grace*. The Reformation tradition places great value on preaching because it is, also and above all, a genuine gift of the word of God. That word, however, is given in both forms, so that the Church is in fact made up of two proclamations:

The Church is the congregation of saints, in which the Gospel is rightly taught and the Sacraments are rightly administered (*Augsburg Confession,* Art. VII). Giving liturgical expression to and renewing that twofold reality remains a task to be accomplished.

● D. Bonhoeffer (1935–36), *Finkenwalder Homiletik, DBW* 14, 478–529.
V. Vajta (1952), *Die Theologie des Gottesdienstes bei Luther,* Göttingen (3rd Ed. 1959).
A. Niebergall et al. (1961), "Predigt," *RGG3* 5, 516–39.
G. Ebeling (1975), "Fundamentaltheologische Erwägungen zur Predigt," in *Wort und Glaube* 3, Tübingen, 554–73.
F. Craddock (1985), *Preaching,* Abington, Mass.
A. Gounelle (1990), "Protestantisme et prédication," *LV(L)* 199, 35–43.
G. Theissen et al. (1994), *Le défi homilétique,* Geneva.
H.-J. Klimkeit et al. (1997), "Predigt," *TRE* 27, 225–330.

PIERRE BÜHLER

See also **Bible; Cult; Exegesis; Gospels; Hermeneutics; Holy Scripture;**

Precepts

"I have set before you life and death, blessing and curse. Therefore choose life" (Dt 30:19): thus God* spoke to Israel*. Jesus* said to his disciples: "Enter by the narrow gate. For the gate is wide and the way is easy that leads to destruction, and those who enter by it are many. For the gate is narrow and the way is hard that leads to life, and those who find it are few" (Mt 7:13–14). The oldest Christian texts likewise warn believers that they must walk along the "way of life" and not the "way of death" (*Didache* 1, SC 248, *Epistle of Barnabas* 18–20, SC 172). Clearly, it was always a matter of imperatives: it is salvation* that is at stake. Here, precept is fundamental. Paul, however, speaks on behalf of virginity, celibacy, and widowhood, not as obligations but as recommendations (1 Cor 7), and thus introduces the idea of counsel. Yet the very fact that he calls them elective shows the predominance of obligation.

The early Christians ran the risk of martyrdom*. One should not provoke it, but it was necessary to die rather than apostatize. Sometimes, even the avoidance of martyrdom was judged to be a sin*. Thus, Cyprian*, who went into hiding during one of the persecutions, was criticized for the safety he enjoyed while others were dying, so he came back and died as a martyr. There was no question, in this case, of shirking his duty any longer.

After the Peace* of the Church*, when there was no longer any danger in being a Christian, the fear of halfheartedness and conformism peopled the desert with hermits. They did not, however, choose this life as if it was a question of one option among others: they were penitents struggling to be saved, whether it be Anthony (c. 251–356) and his fellow anchorites (solitary hermits), or Pachomius (c. 290–346) and his cenobites. The cenobitic (communal) life was also considered to be more severe than the life of hermits, because of the obedience that was necessary to it. Yet, in all these cases, the monks thought that they were doing no more than their duty and saw themselves as "unworthy servants" (Lk 17:10).

The movement became more strictly communal under the *Rules* of St. Basil* (358–64) and St. Benedict (c. 540), which structured monastic life in the East and in the West. Here, too, men and women accepted these rules, not as counsels, but as "precepts of the Master" and as means of being "partakers of his kingdom" (Prologue to the *Rule* of St. Benedict, SC 181).

However, when attention was turned to Christians in general, their duties were presented quite differently. Ambrose*, for example, borrowed from Cicero *(De officiis)* the Stoic distinction between "perfect" *(perfectum, primum, rectum, absolutum)* and "moderate" *(medium, commune)* duty *(officium)* and used this distinction to interpret the Gospels *(De officiis ministrorum/*CUFr 1, 11, 36–39; 3, 2, 10), for example, the episode of the rich young man (Mt 19:16–22). The youth had kept the commandments, only to be told by Jesus that in order to obtain eternal life*—to be "perfect"—he must abandon his wealth and follow Jesus. Ambrose flinches from this boundless duty, interpreting "If you would be perfect" to mean: "If you wish to exceed what is required by the law." In Ambrose's view, this youth was already a "moderate" (yet adequate) disciple. If he was to do more than that, by loving his enemies, praying for his detractors, and so on, then he could become a "perfect" disciple. Accordingly, for God there are two weights and two measures.

The vocabulary developed after Ambrose, but one still finds the same idea in the contrast between precept and counsel. The precept is an explicit obligation (often a prohibition) prescribing what is necessary for salvation; the counsel is the elective choice of the most expeditious means of attaining it. In practice, precepts indicated all that is required for peaceable living in this world, and counsels were identified with the vows of religious orders (poverty, chastity, and obedience) (*see* Thomas* Aquinas, *ST* Ia IIae, q. 108, a. 4). Moral instruction was thus divided into exhortations to follow counsel, on the one hand, and closely defined precepts on the other. Some Scholastics (Scholasticism*), such as Alexander of Hales (c. 1186–1245), Bonaventure*, and Aquinas, even accepted the idea that "works of supererogation"—a term derived from Luke 10:35 in the text of the Vulgate—yields for the church a surplus of merit from which Christians of mediocre zeal could benefit (indulgences*).

This weakening of the gospel scandalized more fervent Christians, such as those in Franciscan circles, who expressed doubts about the existence of a moral double standard. John Wyclif (c. 1330–84) thought that poverty was a condition to which the church as a whole was called, and that, for priests (priesthood*) at least, a counsel must have the force of a precept; the church could not be involved with property without compromise with sinful structures (*De civili dominio* III, 14). Luther*, for personal reasons, rejected the tradition of "counsels of perfection," and, for theological reasons, inveighed against the very notion of counsel, which seemed to him to imply a choice that took something away from the primacy of the will and commands of God. Every individual Christian, he argues, is obliged to obey all the requirements of the Sermon on the Mount (*WA* 32, 299–301). This position was echoed by Thomas Cranmer (1489–1556), who derided the idea that one could do more for God's sake than one is obliged to by him (*42 Articles* 13, "Articles of Religion," in E.C.S. Gibson, *The 39 Articles of the Church of England,* London 1896). From the 13th century onward, there was a continual dispute between those for whom everything had to be a precept, and those who maintained the distinction between precept and counsel: Waldensians (Waldensian*) versus Franciscans, the Synod of Pistoia (1786) versus the Council of Trent*, Jansenists versus Jesuits, Bossuet (1627–1704) versus Fénelon (1651–1715).

Within Catholicism*, the distinction between what is imperative and what is counseled has nourished the moral double standard identified with religious orders and lay life. Within Protestantism*, the affirmation of a single morality tended in practice to mute or marginalize the stronger forms of witness. By presenting some moral maxims as advisory, the Catholic tradition* encouraged the laity* to be spiritually content with little. By making all maxims into commands, the Protestant tradition unwittingly opened the door to a liberalism that considers them all choices. Thus, casuistry* and antinomiansim are the twin children of this debate.

Nevertheless, some Doctors (Doctors* of the Church), such as Aquinas (*ST* IIa IIae, q. 184, a. 3; q. 186, a. 2) or François de Sales (*Traité de l'amour de Dieu* 8, 5–9, in *Oeuvres,* Pléiade collection; Salesian spirituality*), while accepting Ambrose's interpretation of the theme of the rich young man, add that there is not all that much difference between fidelity in marriage* and monastic fidelity. "Perfection consists essentially in precepts" (*ST* IIa IIae, q. 184, a. 3), since love* is the greatest precept (ibid.).

• K.E. Kirk (1930), *The Vision of God,* London.
B. Häring (1954), *Das Gesetz Christi,* Freiberg.
L. Bouyer (1960), *La spiritualité du Nouveau Testament et des Pères,* Paris.
J.O. Urmson (1969), "Saints and Heroes," in J. Feinberg (Ed.), *Moral Concepts,* Oxford, 60–73.
D. Little (1992), "The Law of Supererogation," in E. Santurri and W. Werperhowski (Ed.), *The Love Commandments,* Washington, D.C, 157–81.

JAMES TUNSTEAD BURTCHAELL

See also **Asceticism; Ethics; Holiness; Imitation of Christ; Jansenism; Lay/Laity; Monasticism; Religious Life; Works**

Predestination

Although it is a doctrine that, when understood in terms of the eternal gratuity of divine grace*, does not lack a biblical foundation, in the history of Western theology* the notion of predestination has been very much linked to the personal and radical interpretation proposed by Augustine*. A rereading of the biblical texts and of the Greek Fathers* will enable us to distinguish between Christian faith* and the teaching of a doctor of the Church.

a) Scripture. In order to describe the abundance of God*'s gifts to us and the response that we ought to have, Scripture uses a variety of themes among which predestination represents only one element. It should never be isolated as though it were the only word capable of giving an account of the totality of the mystery* of God and of the initiatives of his love*.

The substance of the Bible*'s testimony about Israel* is that this people* exists and wishes to exist in history* only by reason of being freely chosen by God (Ex 3:7–10). This choice is independent of any merit. (Dt 26:5–10). It is irrevocable (Is 41:14–16). Sin* confirms its gratuitous character (Hos 2:16–20; 11:8–10), and the certainty of this surprising choice penetrates and soothes the heart of every believer (Ps 16:8–11). Understood in this way, the choice always presupposes human liberty*, for human beings must ratify it (Dt 30:15–20) and respond to it with a permanent conversion* (Jer 4:1; 15:19), which in turn brings forth the promise* of a new covenant* (Ez 36:23–33).

The New Testament fully enters into this inherited perspective. Opening his mouth to "utter what has been hidden since the foundation of the world" (Mt 13:35), Christ* announces the coming of the kingdom* of God, to be made known to "all nations" (Mt 28:19) and to all creation* (Mk 16:15). The Kingdom is indeed "the gospel of grace" (Acts 20:24), the grace of God "who desires all people to be saved and to come to the knowledge of the truth*" (1 Tm 2:4).

In both Old and New Testaments the full and irreplaceable forethought of God is affirmed simultaneously with the total responsibility of the human individual. A synthesis of the two is never presented, nor could it be considered as a kind of compromise. God's initiative and the free response of human beings always go together; neither of the two terms can be sacrificed to the other, for they are not of the same order, although they remain rigorously inseparable.

This is the paradox that we need to appropriate if we wish to understand that God "chose us in him [Christ] before the foundation of the world, that we should be holy and blameless before him" (Eph 1:4).

b) Greek Fathers. Whereas in their understanding of faith the Greek Fathers considered principally the person* of Christ and its Trinitarian implications, they were not subject to the obsession with predestination that was to dominate Latin theology, particularly from Augustine onward. They had no hesitation in accepting divine foreknowledge, which for them as for Scripture was derived from the creative transcendence of God. But they were fiercely determined to understand it in a manner that would not contradict human freedom.

Arguing against the Gnostics, who denied free will, Irenaeus* reminded them that God "made [man] free, possessing from the beginning his own ability to choose, and his own soul*, to take the advice of God voluntarily and without constraint. Indeed, violence* is not associated with God (*Bia gar theô ou prosestin*), but good advice always attends Him." (*Adv. Haer.* IV. 37. 1). Five centuries later, it was just as unthinkable for John of Damascus that God could "assault virtue*" (*oude biazetai tèn aretèn*; *De fide orthodoxa* II, PG 94. 972 A). It was no less unthinkable for the Greek Fathers, as Basil* of Caesarea stated in the homily *Quod Deus non est auctor malorum* (PG 31. 329–53), that despite his omnipotence* God was the author of evil*. Moreover, because they saw evil primarily as privation, its existence in sin did not imply any positive action by God; it was due only to the fault of human beings (315 A). Origen* could thus take literally the words of Matthew 7:23, and say of the wicked that "I [the Lord] never knew you," because knowing them in these circumstances would mean not disavowing what they did (*Comm. in epistulam ad Rom.* VII, PG 14. 1125 b-c). As a consequence, he could not "predestine" them, in the ambiguous sense of the word, a sense against which the Greek Fathers guarded themselves when they found the term in Scripture. On the other hand, John* Chrysostom was not afraid to warn that, if "God has made us holy, it is up to us to stay holy" (*epoièsen hèmas autos hagious, alla dei meinai hagious* [*In epistulam ad Eph.* Hom II. 2, PG 62. 17–22]).

This approach suggests that the doctrine of Pelagius (Pelagianism*) posed no problems for the Greek Fathers. On the other hand, they were troubled by everything that might produce an erroneus identification of Christian predestination with Manichean fate. This is why, according to John of Damascus, who crystallizes the thinking of the Greek Fathers, "it is important to know that God has foreknowledge of all but he does not predestine all" (*pant men proginôskei, ou panta de proorizei* [969 b–972A]); "He knows in advance what is in our power but he does not predestine it" (*proginôskei gar ta eph'hèmin, ou proorizei de auta* [972 A]).

c) Augustine and Latin Theology. A remarkable teacher in his reflections on the gratuitous nature of grace, Augustine enters the realm of the ambiguous when he turns to predestination. In this area he bears responsibility for the ambiguities that were to weigh so heavily on the West. From as early as his question LXVIII on Romans 9:20 (*De diversis quaestionibus LXXXIII*), Augustine takes the view that everything depends on the evident fact that the totality of mankind became in Adam* a *massa damnata*, deprived thereby of any right to salvation* (*see* e.g., *Enchiridion* VIII. 23–30; *De civitate Dei* XX. 1). Over this *massa damnata* reigns predestination, which is in fact only a narrow predestination. Indeed, predestination "is nothing but the foreknowledge and anticipation of the benefits of God through which those who are delivered are infallibly delivered" (*De praedestinatione sanctorum* 35). This formula is clearly limited because according to Augustine not all members of the *massa damnata* are predestined to salvation, nor even capable of being so. It is in fact necessary that a certain number not be saved, in order for those who are saved to know that they are saved. "It is a well established conclusion," he writes, that God does not give his grace according to the merits of those who receive it, but according to the free disposition of his will, in order that the person who is glorified be in no way glorified in himself but in the Lord (*De dono perseverantiae* XII. 28).

Who would wish to call into question the gratuitous nature of grace? But in order to recognize it, is it necessary to say that the grace of salvation will not be granted to all? Yes, answers Augustine: "By giving it to certain ones and regardless of any merit, God shows his intention that it be gratuitous and thereby justify its name of grace...*Good,* in the benefit granted to some, God is *just* in the punishment inflicted on others; even more, he is good toward everyone, because favor does not injure anyone's rights." (ibid.) In other words, the grace whose absolutely gratuitous nature Augustine has admirably established with respect to the individual would require, with reference to humanity as a whole, a predestination necessarily restricted in its distribution.

Understanding Paul to have said that "in Adam [*epi* interpreted as meaning *in*] all have sinned" (Rom 5:12), Augustine sees them as inexorably damned. In fact, Paul teaches the opposite: "For God has consigned all to disobedience, *that* (*hina*) he may have mercy on all" (Rom 11:32). In omitting this statement by Paul in favor of the preconceived idea that he has of restricted predestination, Augustine, despite his usually scrupulous respect for Scripture, is forced to correct 1 Timothy 2:4. He proposes to replace "all" by a "many" of his own invention (*Contra Julianum pelagianum* IV. viii. 44). Even if he accepts the reading, "God wishes to save all," this is, he says, "so that we might understand by that all the predestined, for the whole human race is in them" (*De correptione et gratia* XIV. 44). As early as the *Enchiridion,* Augustine had confined himself within the tautology according to which "none is saved other than those whom God wished to save" (XXVIII. 103), and Augustine finds it necessary to think that God did not wish to save all in order that salvation might remain truly gratuitous for those who are saved.

On this point Thomas* Aquinas did not deviate from Augustine's thinking. Indeed, for him, God's salvific will remains limited by predestination (*ST* Ia. q. 23). Prevailing over the authority* of Scripture, Augustine was therefore invoked to support a kind of predestinarianism that creates despair among human beings and is unworthy of God, such as we find in Gottschalk in the ninth century, Calvin* in the 16th, and Jansenism* in the 17th.

In order to counter this position, the magisterium* rejected, in the name of Scripture, any divine predestination to evil (*DS* 621ff. and 625ff.); it maintained the existence of free will for all human beings (*DS* 622), the will toward universal salvation in God according to 1 Timothy 2:4 (*DS* 623), and the death of Christ on the cross for all people (*DS* 2005). A truly scriptural interpretation of predestination was thereby left open.

d) Return to Scripture. Because the mystery of predestination is bound up with the depths of the God of revelation* (Rom 11:33–36), it is necessary to go beyond any thinking based on the divine attributes*, however essential they may be (goodness, justice*, mercy), that would fail to see these attributes as the outpouring of the Trinitarian love of God, who has given us so much in giving us his Son (*see* Rom 8:32) and in destining us to be conformed to his image (*see* Rom 8:28ff.).

In this light the mystery of predestination is first and foremost the mystery of our eternal election in Jesus Christ, "to the praise* of his glorious grace*, with which he has blessed us in the Beloved" (Eph 1:6). It goes without saying that a love of this kind cannot fail to imply on God's part an infinite respect for the freedom of its beneficiaries. "He predestined us for adoption through Jesus Christ, according to the purpose of his will" (Eph 1:5), this is by reason of our radical difference from his Son and from him, a difference that he intended to respect while at the same time he "has blessed us in Christ with every spiritual blessing in the heavenly places" (Eph 1:3).

Sin, which dramatically confirms the difference, is, however, not the cause of election, because that election is nothing but God's intention "before the foundation of the world" (Eph 1:4), hence before any consideration of our responsibility, good or evil, in history. This election nevertheless takes place through our redemption in "the blood of Christ" (Eph 1:7). In him, forgiveness is given to us unstintingly by God, because "where sin increased, grace abounded all the more" (Rom 5:20). This forgiveness, like our election in Jesus Christ, is rooted in the eternity* of the love of God (*see* 1 Pt 1:20).

It follows from this that predestination cannot possibly restrict the scope of redemption. Through the intention for universal salvation (1 Tm 2:4) that characterizes it, redemption corresponds in history to the "mystery of his will, according to his purpose, which he set forth in Christ as a plan for the fullness of time, to unite all things in him" (Eph 1:9f.), a purpose that is itself without limits.

As a consequence, the scriptural passages (notably Rom 9) that seem to exclude from election and salvation some rather than others must be understood in relation to the economy of history (grace *gratis data*) and not to the eschatology* of salvation (grace *gratum faciens*).

This is why "nor height nor depth" of Romans 8:39, so dear to Augustine, designates the infinity of God's love for the world, and in no way a presumed partiality for its realization in history. God's conduct is as free and as gratuitous when addressed to *all* as though it applied only to *some*. It does not have to be restricted to *some* in order to be gratuitous for *all*. It does not depend on the limited number of its beneficiaries, but on the free purpose of love given unstintingly to all. There is thus a concord between the reservations of the Greek Fathers concerning a predestination contrary to human freedom and Augustine's legitimate concern to preserve the gratuitous character of predestination, without compromising its complete universality; Only such a universality is worthy of a God who reveals himself as love itself and who can only be love in all truth.

- M. Jacquin (1904), "La question de la prédestination aux Ve et VIe s.", *RHE* 5, 265–283, 725–754.
M. Jacquin (1906), "Saint Prosper d'Aquitaine, Vincent de Lérins, Cassien," *RHE* 7, 269–300.
E. Portalié (1923), "La prédestination augustinienne," in "Augustin," *DThC* 1, 2398–408.
J. Saint-Martin (1930), *La pensée de saint Augustin sur la prédestination gratuite et infaillible des élus à la gloire, d'après ses derniers écrits* (426–30), Paris.
J. Guitton (1933), *Le temps et l'éternité chez Plotin et saint Augustin,* Paris (4th Ed. 1971).
E. Przywara (1934), *Augustinus: Die Gestalt als Gefüge.*
B. Lavaud (1935), "La controverse sur la prédestination au IXe siècle," ibid., 2901–35.
J. Saint-Martin (1935), "La prédestination d'après les Pères latins, particulièrement d'après saint Augustin," ibid., 2832–96.
H.D. Simonin (1935), "La prédestination d'après les Pères grecs," in "Prédestination," *DThC* 12, 2815–32.
G. Pelland (1936), *S. Prosperi Aquitani doctrina de praedestinatione et voluntate Dei salvifica,* Montréal.
K. Barth (1942), *KD* II/2 (*Dogmatique,* Geneva, 1958, 1–96; on Barth's Christocentric position, 97–150).
O. Rottmaner (1944), "L' 'augustinisme': Étude d'histoire doctrinale," *MSR 6,* 29–48.
G. de Plinval (1954), *La pensée de saint Augustin,* Paris, 204–14.
H.-I. Marrou (1955), *Saint Augustin et l'augustinisme,* Paris; id. (1958), *Saint Augustin et la fin de la culture antique,* Paris.
G. Nygren (1956), *Das Prädestinationsproblem in der Theologie Augustins,* Göttingen.
E. Dinkler (1957), "Prädestination bei Paulus," *FS für G. Dehn,* Neukirchen, 81–102.
J. Chêne (1961), *La théologie de saint Augustin: Grâce et prédestination,* Le Puy-Lyon.
S. Lyonnet (1962), *Quaestiones in epistulam ad Romanos, se-*

ries altera: De praedestinatione Israël et theologia historiae, Pontificio Istituto Biblico, Rome.

K. Rahner (1963), "Prädestination," LThK2 8, 661–70.

H. Rondet (1964), Essai sur la théologie de la grâce, Paris, 201–43.

R. Bernard (1965), "La prédestination du Christ total selon saint Augustin," RechAug 3, 1–58.

F. Ferrier (1988), "La prédestination," Cath 11, 764–81.

O. H. Pesch (1988), Thomas von Aquin: Grenze und Grösse mittelalterlicher Theologie: Eine Einführung, Mayence.

A. Birmelé, M. Lienhard (Ed.) (1991), FEL, §922–26, 1098–126.

Ch. Reynier (1996), "La bénédiction en Ép 1, 3–14. Élection, filiation, rédemption," NRTh 118, 182–99.

P. Gerlitz et al. (1997), "Prädestination," TRE 27, 98–160.

GUSTAVE MARTELET

See also **Augustine of Hippo; Eschatology; Gnosis; Grace; Hell; Judgement; Manicheanism; Pelagianism; Purgatory**

Presbyter/Priest

1. New Testament

a) Vocabulary. In the New Testament there are twelve occurrences of *presbuteros,* eight of which refer to the ministry* typical of the Church* of Jerusalem*, probably inspired by the Jewish council of elders. These presbyters are associated with the apostles (apostle*) or with James (Acts 11:30, 15:2, 15:4, 15:6, 15:22, 15:23, 16:4, 21:18). They appear in the margins of Paul's activity (Acts 14:23, 20:17) and are already clearly described in 1 Timothy 5:17 and Titus 1:5; they are also mentioned in James 5:14 and 1 Peter 5:1.

b) Functions. In Jerusalem the presbyters participated actively in the administration of the Church; elsewhere, they were identified with the *episcopes* (bishop*) and were required to have the same qualifications.

2. History

a) Early Church. After the generalization of the monoepiscopate, completed around 170, the institution of the presbyter, subordinate to the bishop, maintained a collegial form. With the arrival of parishes, presbyters preached as of right and exercised a priestly ministry. They were trained by the bishop or by experienced presbyters. By the fourth century they were part of a hierarchical clergy. A system of major and minor orders* became general; presbyters occupied a rank superior to deacons (deacon*); they had to observe ritual continence. This development led to a certain religious disqualification of the laity (lay*/laity), something that was aggravated by the general condition of illiteracy that prevailed after the fall of the Roman Empire.

b) Medieval Church. In the 12th and 13th centuries the connection was loosened between the office of presbyter and pastoral charge, and the ministry of the presbyter was interpreted primarily in sacerdotal terms. The marriage* of priests was rendered invalid (can. 7 of Lateran* II, 1139, *COD* 198). At the urging of the mendicants, absolute ordination* (with no pastoral duties) became frequent. The system of benefices was set up; an economic title could now replace the ecclesiological title of ordination; there grew up a proletariat of untrained "altarists," assigned to the celebration of basic masses. Of them it was "asked only to consecrate; all they need is the knowledge required for the observation of the rite of the performance of the sacrament*" (Thomas* Aquinas, *ST suppl.* q. 36. a. 2. ad 1), whereas holders of wealthy benefices evaded their pastoral duties.

A parallel doctrinal development occurred, in which the notion of sacramental character played a significant role. It appeared with Peter of Corbeil, who described it as the character of baptism* (c. 1160) and was later developed by William of Auvergne and Alexander of Hales. Thomas Aquinas conceived of sacramental character essentially as a deputation to worship (*ST* IIIa. q. 63. a. 6). The consecration of the eucharistic body thus became the principal function of priests, and the care of the mystical body of Christ* a secondary function, entrusted to only some among them. This concentration on eucharistic power (in a context in which the mass had already been largely privatized) ultimately produced a series of dissociations: The ministry of the word and the care of souls became secondary constituents of the office of presbyter, the common priesthood* of the baptized fell into near oblivion, the three-part division of the ordained ministry was organized around the priesthood, with the episcopacy distinguished from it only by a higher jurisdiction* (a position already held by Peter Lombard), and the diaconate reduced to a stage in a career path, because neither bishop nor deacon had any specific power in the celebration of the Eucharist*.

c) Reformation and the Counter Reformation. The reform of the clergy's morals was not the principal purpose of the Reformation, but because it wished to return to the Scriptures it applied a doctrinal program that emphasized the singleness of the pastoral ministry (abolition of minor orders and the diaconate; a single ordination even in circumstances in which the *épiskopè* was preserved), a minimization of its priestly character (the pastor* was a preacher within a priestly people), and the end of clerical characteristics (abolition of monasticism*, of the celibacy of the clergy, and of jurisdictional privileges the clergy immunity from civil processes; and a loss of interest in the theory of the indelible character of ordination).

The disciplinary decrees of the Council of Trent* brought about a moral and spiritual reform of priests— for example, giving rise to seminaries—and also compelled priests to deliver homilies and to catechize (sess. 24, can. 4; *COD* 763). At the doctrinal level, however, the Council merely reiterated the medieval conception that the Reformation had challenged, anathematizing the following propositions in session 23: "There is no visible and external priesthood in the New Covenant... [nor] a power to consecrate the true body of Christ and the true blood of Christ...those who do not preach are not priests" (can. 1, *COD* 743); "outside the priesthood, there are no other major and minor orders" (can. 2, ibid.); "ordination is not a sacrament truly and properly instituted by Christ the Lord" (can. 3, ibid.); "in the Catholic Church there is no hierarchy* instituted by divine will" (can. 6, *COD* 744).

Post-Tridentine language about priests was characterized by a few doctrinal additions. For example, the *Roman Catechism for Priests* (1566), known as the catechism "of the Council of Trent," teaches that "they are rightfully called not only angels* but even gods because they represent among us the power (omnipotence*, divine) and majesty of the immortal God*" (ch. 26, §1; *see also* the *Traité des Saints Ordres* by J.-J. Olier, as revised by Tronson [1676]). Influenced by the regular clergy* (including the Jesuits) and by the French school of spirituality (in which the Sulpicians played an important role), the post-Tridentine clergy was characterized by a solid piety and a serious pastoral concern, following a model that was perpetuated up to Vatican* II.

3. Contribution of Vatican II

The most productive ideas concerning priests did not come from *PO,* a decree focused more on spirituality than on dogma*, and one that juxtaposed without critical analysis some rather heterogeneous theological elements (Cordes 1972). For example, ordination is conceived of principally as a consecration for mission*. The concept of the office of presbyter, which was intentionally given prominence in the final drafts of the document, is poorly linked with the concept of priesthood, because a choice was made to designate by this term priests and bishops together, and also because the priestly ministry in the precise sense is not clearly related to the two other functions that devolve on priests, the ministry of the word and the governance of the people of God. Priests are also charged with the representation of Christ the Head (*PO* 2. 6. 12), a new idea, and one that Vatican II never extended to bishops; and it is not clear whether this representation of Christ is permanent in their persons or in the exercise of their ministry. This Christocentric emphasis pushes the pneumatological dimension of their ministry into the background, which handicaps the necessary collaboration between the community of faithful and individuals in the local* church. In fact, the relation of priests to the universal Church seems to precede their bonds with the diocesan church (*PO* 2. 10).

New impetus in this area comes from an understanding of the Church as a communion*, as expressed in chapters 2 and 3 of *LG,* which locates ministers—in respective order—in the people of God, in the designation of priests as "presbyters" *presbyteri,* in the final title of *PO* (previously entitled *de Clericis* and then *de Sacerdotibus*), and in the religious requalification of the laity, who participate in the threefold royal, priestly, and prophetic role of Christ (*LG* 10, 11, 12, 34, 35, 36), with baptism establishing the equal dignity and common responsibility of all in the Church (*LG* 32). These shifts have begun to find expression (not only theological but institutional) in the increased value placed on local Churches: the institution of diocesan synods (synod*), in which the laity are in the majority, and especially the flourishing of pastoral councils at various levels of the life of the Church augur well for a desirable collaboration between individuals and the community of faithful at a time when priests are becoming rare in the West.

In thirty years the number of priests has declined by half in France: from 40,000 (1965) to 21,000 (1995).

The stable average of 108 ordinations per year (for 94 dioceses) between 1981 and 1995 indicates the structural character of a pastoral question that is as theological as it is spiritual. A well thought out theology* of the vocation for the ordained ministries and the relation between the person of the minister and the purpose of the ministry is a priority.

4. Ecumenical Convergences

Catholicism* has a merely disciplinary dispute with the Orthodox Church, in reference to married priests. As for the Reformation churches engaged in bilateral dialogues with the Catholic Church, they are troubled by the ordination of men alone (Apostolic Letter *Ordinatio Sacerdotalis* [1994]), by the insistence on celibacy (encyclical *Sacerdotalis Caelibatus* [1967]), and by some particularities of the teaching of the popes (pope*), for example, the apostolic exhortation *Pastores dabo vobis* (1992), in which John Paul II asserts insistently that the character of the order configures the priest to Christ in a manner distinct from baptism, and in which he uses the term *priest* three times more often than the term *presbyter*. The bilateral commissions for theological dialogue nevertheless consider that the remaining differences are not doctrinally divisive (e.g., the International Anglican-Catholic Commission, *Ministry and Ordination* [1973]; the International Lutheran-Catholic Commission, *The Ministry in the Church* [1981], and on the national level, in Germany, *Are the Anathemas of the Sixteenth Century Still Relevant?* [1987]).

● A. Duval (1957–62), *Des sacrements au concile de Trente*, new Ed., Paris, 1985, 327–404.
P. J. Cordes (1972), *Sendung zum Dienst* (comm. of *Presbyterorum Ordinis*), Frankfurt.
C. Vogel (1978), *Ordinations inconsistantes et caractère inamissible*, Turin.
Coll. (1982), *Prêtres, pasteurs et rabbins dans la société contemporaine*, Paris.
G. Greshake (1981–84), *Priestersein: Zur Theologie und Spiritualität des priesterlichen Amtes*, 4th Ed., Freiburg-Basel-Vienna.
W. Klein et al. (1997), "Priester/Priestertum," *TRE* 27, 379–434.

HERVÉ LEGRAND

See also **Bishop; Deacon; Ministry; Priesthood; Vatican II, Council of**

Presbyterianism. *See* **Congregationalism; Puritanism**

Prescience, Divine. *See* **Knowledge, Divine**

Prescriptivism. *See* **Ethics, Autonomy of**

Priest. *See* Presbyter/Priest

Priesthood

A. Biblical Theology

1. Old Testament

a) Vocabulary. In Hebrew, "priest" is *kohen* (about 750 times; etymology unclear) in relation to the cult* of the God* of Israel*, and occasionally also to that of other gods; *komer* (3 times only) is used solely in relation to the latter (2 Kgs 23:5, Hos 10:5, Sg 1:4). The expression for "high priest," *ha-kohen ha-gadol* (without addition), does not appear until after the Exile. The "Levite" or *lewi* (345 times; etymology: dedicated, or rather "attached" [to God]; *see* de Vaux), is a religious official, a priest, or sometimes, an auxiliary to the priesthood. In the Septuagint, *kohen* is translated as *hiereus,* which in Latin becomes *sacerdos* or, occasionally, *pontifex* (Ex 28:38, 1 Chr 9:10; translations* of the Bible).

b) Functions. Priests delivered oracles: when consulted, they requested a response from God. They gave blessings (blessing*) (Nm 6:22–27, Sir 50:20f.). They gave instruction and made decisions in matters of law* (Dt 18:10f. and 24:8; Hos 4:6; Jer 18:18; Ez 22:26). Once the sanctuary at Jerusalem* had eclipsed the others, priests gradually took responsibility for rendering sacrifice* at the altar.

Accordingly, priestly functions took on a variety of forms during the history* of Israel. However, this set of functions (Dt 33:8–11) may be unified by a single characteristic: that of mediator. Priests were priests "by status" (de Vaux 1960) and hereditary right. In various ways, they assured the permanence of order in the cosmos* for the sake of life in society*.

c) History. The priesthood was always connected with the sanctuaries at Dan (Jgs 17–18 is an archaic narrative of the installation of a Levite), Bethel (Am

7:10–17), and elsewhere. Shiloh was destroyed (Jer 7:12–14 and 26:6; Ps 78:60) and its priests were deposed (1 Sm 2:27–36), but one of their descendants, the Levite Abiatar, coexisted at Jerusalem (2 Sm 15:24–29, 17:15, 19:12) with Zadok (of local pre-Israelite stock?), whose lineage became dominant after the death of David and up to the Exile. In the last days of the monarchy, the Levites were compelled to abandon their sanctuary for the one authorized temple*, at Jerusalem. After the Exile, the priests of the reconstructed Temple were divided into Zadokites and Aaronites. These latter probably represented a resurgence of the lineage of Abiatar, but they linked that lineage to the brother of Moses and to the priestly traditions that made him a priest (a notion that is absent from Ex 32, Nm 12, etc.). Early in the second century B.C.E., the high priests were subjected to the domination of Hellenizers, until the revolt of the Maccabees, which was led by a priest (in 167 B.C.E.:1 Macc 2); he then founded a new priestly lineage, the Asmoneans. The high priest was gradually confirmed as a substitute for the king, and received that title in 104–103 B.C.E. With this title, the priestly function lost all independence, until it disappeared along with the Temple. Nevertheless, its central place and its majesty have always remained in the memory of Israel.

d) Theological Themes. The various aspects of the priesthood reflect differences among periods, places, and schools of thought.

The uprooted Levites are praised for their zeal, but condemned for their violence* (Gn 34:25–31 and 49:5ff.); they are also compared to the poor and to foreigners (Dt 12:12, 12:18f., 14:27, 14:29, 26:11ff.), and given much the same status. Ezekiel denigrates the Levites (44:6–31), but the writer of the Chronicles makes a more positive judgment (2 Chr 29:34; see 30:3 and 30:22), linking them to the hymnal activity of David. The Psalms* show the influence of the Levites, whose special offering was music* and song.

Melchizedek, King and Priest of Canaan, symbolizes the recognition of a pre-Israelite priesthood in the traditions of Jerusalem. His title, "priest of God Most High" (Gn 14:18), and his God "possessor of heaven and earth" (14:19), introduce the tension between Jewish priesthood and pagan priesthood that was to be fertile for both (paganism*). Abraham receives the blessing of the Canaanite (Gn 12:3; universalism*).

Those texts in the Pentateuch that originate from the priestly caste (Bible*) trace the divine plan for the whole world (Gn 1:1–2 and 4a; 9:9–17). In the Mesopotamian myth* of the *Enuma Elish,* the creation* had already been presented as the victory of the hero Marduk over the monster Tiamat, immediately followed by the making of the heavens into a replica of the dwelling of the higher gods (col. IV, 135–45). The destiny of the priesthood is to take an interest in the whole of existence, in order to locate the steps that lead on to holiness*, the fundamental category of its activities.

Israel may have been the "kingdom of priests" (Ex 19:6)—composed of priests, or for the sake of a priesthood benefiting all the nations?—or it may have been a "realm of priests"—a nation governed by priests, as was the case (*see* Ps 110:4) after the Exile (Cazelles). In any case, the context is a universal one:"all the earth is mine" (Ex 19:5b).

To this period of prosperity for the priesthood, thus understood, (before the reign of Antiochus Epiphanes) there corresponds the enthusiastic portrayal of a high priest by Ben Sirach. In Ecclesiasticus 50, the high priest, when officiating, is compared to the morning star, the Moon, the Sun, flowers, stones, and trees. According to Ecclesiasticus 24 (the praise of Wisdom*), he fulfils the duties of a steward of creation on behalf of all.

A person who offers and, normally, immolates a sacrificial victim hands that victim to the priest so that it may be presented to God in accordance with the rituals of sacrifice. This crucial function reached its apogee when the high priest, who had already received anointment as a king after the Exile (*see* Ps 110:4, Dn 9:25f., 2 Macc 1:10), celebrated the ritual of the Day of Atonement (Lv 16).

2. New Testament

The Epistle to the Hebrews adopts the perspective of the whole of the Old Testament by situating the activity of Jesus* in relation to the actions of the high priest on the Day of Atonement (Heb 2, 17; expiation*), but the other books of the New Testament do not make such an explicit reference to the priesthood of Christ*. Nevertheless, we should not conclude that their authors were capable of disengaging themselves from such an essential aspect of the religion of Israel.

Luke's Gospel* begins with a family of priests in the Temple: this was the start of a long transition. It continued after Jesus had departed: the apostles (apostle*) worshipped regularly at the Temple (Lk 24:53, Acts 3:1, 5:12, 5:42) and some of the priests were converted (Acts 6:7). Paul's expulsion (Acts 21:30) marked the end of this process. Luke tries to show that, despite the ruptures in the tradition, if there had no longer been any priesthood, then the priest Zacharias and Aaron's descendant Elizabeth would not have been the first to welcome the Messiah*.

Nevertheless, in the Gospels the Greek word *hiereus* (11:3) is almost always replaced by *archiereus,* "high priest" (25:3) or *archiereis,* "high priests" (58:3), who are presented as the principal agents in the death* of Jesus. As for Jesus, he neither attributes the title of "priest" to himself, nor receives that title from others: he does nothing that has any connection with the institution of the priesthood, nor does he make any link between it and his disciples (ministry*). In its own way, the Epistle to the Hebrews emphasizes the distance: "Now if he were on earth, he would not be a priest at all" (Heb. 8:4), since he was not a Levite (7:13f.). Indeed, Jesus becomes the one and only high priest solely by virtue of his passion*, through which he offers up the only true sacrifice. This suggests that we should identify his priesthood first and foremost by reference to its effects.

According to Matthew 28:19f., Jesus invested the 11 disciples with a duty to instruct that has more in common with priesthood than with prophecy. Christians form a *basileion hierateuma,* a "royal priesthood" (1 Pt 2:9; Rev 1:6, 5:10, 20:6; *see* Ex 9:6). Those who are in Christ are capable of forming the temple of God (1 Cor 3:16f.; Eph 2:21f.) solely by way of the priesthood of Christ. Jesus takes up his role not just in relation to the Temple, but within the Temple (Lk 19:47, 21:37; Jn 18:20), for the sake of a teaching that is to replace the priestly Torah.

One could therefore propose that in this way the priestly aspect of Jesus pervades the whole of the gospel tradition* (even though this position is hardly represented at all in contemporary exegesis* of the New Testament). Like priestly wisdom in Ecclesiasticus 24 (Sir 50), or cosmic wisdom in Sg 18:24, Christ, as the Son (filiation*) and Logos (Word*), is mediator for the whole of the universe. It is this idea that is expressed in John 17, a passage that Cyril* of Alexandria (PG 74, 505) calls "the prayer of the high priest."

● G. Schrenk (1938), *"hieros…hiereus, archiereus," ThWNT* 3, 220–84.

R. de Vaux (1960), *Les Institutions de l'Ancien Testament,* Paris, t. II.

A. George (1970), "Sacerdoce," *VThB*2 (7th Ed. 1991), 1153–63.

A. Vanhoye (1980), *Prêtres anciens, prêtre nouveau selon le Nouveau Testament,* Paris.

J. Auneau, P.-M. Beaude (1985), "Sacerdoce," *DBS* 10, 1170–342.

H. Cazelles (1987), "Royaume de prêtres et Nation consacrée" (Ex 19, 6), in *Autour de l'Exode (Études),* Paris, 289–94.

Y. Simoens (1990), "La création selon l'Écriture. Commencement, milieu et fin du dessein unique de Dieu," *Christus* 147, 290–303.

M. D. Rehm (1992), "Levites and Priests," *AncBD,* 297–310.

YVES SIMOENS

See also **Cosmos; Creation; Cult; Expiation; Law and Christianity; Ministry; People of God; Sacrifice; Society; Temple; Wisdom**

B. Universal Priesthood

a) Definition. "Universal priesthood" refers to the priesthood shared in by all Christians by virtue of their participation in the priesthood of Christ*. Other terms are sometimes used to express similar ideas: the *priesthood of all believers* or the *common priesthood.* While Protestants have most often emphasized universal priesthood, all Christian traditions affirm a "universal priesthood" of some sort.

b) New Testament. Several Old Testament texts state that Israel* will be not just a people with priests (priesthood*), but a priestly kingdom (Ex 19:6; Is 61:6). Various New Testament texts apply these statements to the church*, in particular 1 Peter 2:9: "You are a chosen race, a royal priesthood." Here, the people as a whole are spoken of as a "priesthood" (*hierateuma*). Similarly, Revelation 1:6 states that Christ has "made us to be a kingdom, priests serving his God and Father" (*see also* Rev 5:10 and 20:6). The linking of priest and kingdom, as in 1 Peter, echoes Exodus 19:6. Here, however, not just the entire people, but individual Christians are spoken of as "priests" (*hiereis*). The claim that the church constitutes a priestly people is an aspect of the claim that the promises (promise*) made to Israel are fulfilled in the church. For 1 Peter, this royal priesthood exists in order "that you might proclaim the mighty acts of him who called you into his marvelous light." Revelation speaks only of serving God as priests, without further specification. Any relation between this priesthood and the priesthood of Christ (itself extensively discussed in the New Testament only in the Epistle to the Hebrews) is not developed.

Christians are not called priests elsewhere in the New Testament, either individually or as a group. Paul does not use priestly language in urging the Roman Christians to present their bodies as a living and holy sacrifice* to God (Rom 12:1), but a clear idea of Christians as priests cannot be found in his writings.

c) Patristic Period and Middle Ages. Statements similar to those in 1 Peter and Revelation about Christians as priests can be found in authors of the second century: sometimes the entire body of Christians is spoken of (Justin, *Dial.* 116), sometimes each Christian (Irenaeus, *Con. Haer.*, 4, 8, 3; 5, 34, 3). In this period, such references to universal priesthood were still made as part of an argument about the relation of the church to Israel or about the distinctive character of Christians as offering right worship to God. Only Tertullian*, during his Montanist period (*Ex. Cas.* 7) seems to have argued from the priestly status of all Christians to the capacity of all Christians to carry out what were coming to be seen as tasks reserved for an ordained priesthood.

Changes in the fourth and fifth centuries, especially the growing identification of priestly standing with the ordained priesthood, led to a qualification of the idea of universal priesthood. Augustine* is typical of this development: commenting on Revelation 20:6, he states that, while every Christian is a priest as a member of Christ, the one true priest, only bishops (bishop*) and presbyters are properly (*proprie*) called priests (*Civ. Dei,* 20:10). For Augustine and the medieval tradition, universal priesthood centered on the self-offering of every Christian to God. It did not find its center in a particular relation to the Eucharist* (*see* Congar). This priestly status was particularly connected with the anointing that occurs in relation to baptism* (*Enar. Ps.* 26, 2, 2; *Quaest. Ev.* 2, 40).

Thomas* Aquinas restates this Augustinian position.

The sacramental character bestowed in baptism and confirmation* involves a participation in the priesthood of Christ (*ST* III, q. 63. a.3). This priesthood, however, does not relate to a sacramental power to consecrate the Eucharist, but to the offering of spiritual sacrifices, as Paul states in Romans 12:1 (*ST* IIIa, q. 82, a. 1., ad. 2). Peter Lombard's definition of ordination* as granting a "spiritual power" (*Sent.* 4, 24, 13) gave a basis for more precisely distinguishing the ordained priesthood from the universal priesthood. While Augustine still stated that the church offers the Eucharist (*Civ. Dei* 10, 6), Gabriel Biel (c. 1420–95) states that, strictly speaking, the priest offers immediately and the people offer only mediately and spiritually, through the priest (*Canonis missae exposito*, Lec. 22a, 29a).

d) Reformation. The concept of universal priesthood was central to Luther*'s polemical writings of the early 1520s, especially in his pamphlet *The Babylonian Captivity of the Church* and in his appeal *To the German Nobility.* Luther repeats the earlier assertion that all Christians are priests by virtue of their baptism and their participation in Christ through faith* (*WA* 6, 407), but adds that all Christians are *equally* priests (*WA* 6, 564). Whatever ordination does, it does not confer a distinct priestly status or power. Baptism makes every Christian priest, bishop, and pope* (*WA* 6, 408). Universal priesthood thus includes the power (even if not the authorization) to carry out all priestly activities. Echoing 1 Peter, Luther stresses that, as a royal priest, every Christian is empowered to take part in judging doctrine (*WA* 11, 41ff.). Taken together, these assertions undermined the power of the clergy over the laity*. Ordained ministry, while divinely instituted, possesses no unique powers and requires the consent of the priestly people (*WA* 6, 564).

Combined with this polemical use of the concept of universal priesthood is the positive assertion that, as priests, all Christians are called to witness to the gospel and, even more, to intercede before God for others (*WA* 7, 57). While Luther speaks of universal priesthood in relation to individuals and not in relation to the entire church, he does so as part of an understanding of the church as a community of priestly self-offering of each for others.

Luther's thinking about universal priesthood, especially in its relation to ordained ministry, has been interpreted in all sorts of ways, and it remains a subject of controversy among Lutherans. Luther himself never rejected the basic principle of universal priesthood asserted in the early 1520s, but the concept of universal priesthood clearly recedes in his later writings as greater stress falls on the authoritative role of ordained ministry. Melanchthon was very cautious in speaking about universal priesthood and the concept is not explicitly addressed in the Lutheran confessions of faith. Within the pietist movement, Philipp Jakob Spener (1635–1705), for example, argued for certain forms of lay witness as an expression of their "spiritual priesthood." Discussion of universal priesthood again became lively among Lutheran theologians in the 19th and 20th centuries in debates about ministry and about authority* in the church after the end of princely rule in the churches.

Calvin mentions, but does not emphasize, the concept of universal priesthood (*Inst.* II.15. 6; IV, 18.17, 19.28), as do various Reformed confessions (e.g., *Second Helvetian Confession,* Ch. 18). Under the term *priesthood of all believers,* universal priesthood became an unquestioned but not widely discussed part of the Calvinist tradition.

The concept of universal priesthood has played a surprisingly small role in the reassertion of the laity within the Protestant churches in the 20th century. Kraemer (1958) argues that the concept of universal priesthood as it has developed in Protestantism* is too individualistic and too tied to anti-Catholic arguments to be useful. Use is rather made of concepts such as "the ministry of the laity," similar to universal priesthood but not burdened with a particular history.

e) Catholicism After the Reformation. The Council of Trent* did not address universal priesthood, except to reject Protestant denials of the special character of ordained priesthood, or the assertion that all Christians are equally priests (*DS* 1768). The *Catechism of the Council of Trent* (1566) essentially repeats the medieval understanding of universal priesthood. A new Catholic emphasis on universal priesthood and the role of the laity began with such 19th-century theologians as Möhler (schools of Tübingen*) and Newman*, and, in the 20th century, papal statements (e.g., *Mediator Dei,* 1947, *DS* 3851).

Vatican* II gave a new emphasis to universal priesthood. In addition to the decree on the lay apostolate, *Apostolicam actuositatem,* the constitution on the church, *Lumen gentium* (*LG*), not only contains a chapter on the laity, but sets a chapter on the people of God before its chapters on the hierarchy* and the laity. Instead of universal priesthood, these texts usually speak of "common priesthood." This common priesthood derives, as before, from the participation of all the baptized in Christ's priesthood (*LG* 10). More than in earlier texts, however, consequences are drawn from common priesthood for the life of the church, including, for example, the right of the laity to "full, conscious, and active participation" in the liturgy* (*SC* 14). While universal priesthood is mentioned in the decree on the lay apostolate (2, 10), it plays no important role there. The *Catechism of the Catholic Church* (1993) returns to the traditional division among Christ as priest, church as priestly people, and laity and priests as participating in Christ's priesthood in distinct ways (1546). The ministerial priesthood is said to serve the common priesthood (1547).

f) Ecumenical Problems.　While ecumenical discussions have begun with an appeal to "the vocation of the whole people of God" as the context for addressing difficult issues related to ministry (*see,* e.g., *Baptism, Eucharist, Ministry,* M, 1), universal priesthood has not played a significant role in these discussions. The "Ministry" section of *Baptism, Eucharist, Ministry* makes no mention of universal priesthood in its opening chapter, where it is merely implicit in its definition of ministerial priesthood (M 17, with commentary). Some Protestant churches (e.g., the National Alliance of Lutheran Churches of France) were critical of *Bap-*

tism, Eucharist, Ministry because of this. Most ecumenical dialogues have agreed on the concept of universal priesthood as distinct from ministerial priesthood, and have agreed that ordained ministry is not a direct expression of universal priesthood. Disagreement continues on the precise relation between universal priesthood and ordained ministry.

● P. Dabin (1950), *Le sacerdoce royal des fidèles dans la tradition ancienne et moderne,* Paris.
H. Kraemer (1958), *A Theology of the Laity,* London.
C. Eastwood (1963), *The Royal Priesthood of the Faithful,* London.
Y. Congar (1964), *Jalons pour une théologie du laïcat,* 3rd Ed., Paris.
COE (1982), *BEM,* Paris.
H-M. Barth (1990), *Einander Priester sein: Allgemeines Priestertum in ökumenischer Perspektive,* Göttingen.

MICHAEL ROOT

See also **Baptism; Ministry**

C. Ministerial Priesthood

From the middle of the second century onward, the main Christian ministries constituted a strong triad of bishops (bishop*), priests, and deacons (deacon*). Starting in the third century, bishops were known, uncontroversially, as *sacerdotes,* "priests," more because of the influence of Old Testament typology than through any relation to the priesthood of Christ*. From the late fourth century, in the East as in the West, the same term was extended to priests, although not so frequently. Later, a sacral sense of mediation was attached to the ordained priesthood, partly under the influence of the two *Hierarchies* of Pseudo-Dionysius*, which were widely read in the West as well as in Byzantium during the Middle Ages. Finally, the three great movements of reform within the Catholic Church (Carolingian, Gregorian, Tridentine) enhanced still further the understanding of the ordained priesthood in terms of its function in the eucharistic sacrifice*. The Reformation challenged this development. It was only in the 20th century that Catholic theologians once again took up this complex problem, making use both of the New Testament and of new systematic structures of interpretation.

1. The Sacerdotalization of the Ministry: Development and Debates

In the New Testament, the uniqueness of Christ's priesthood is presented as a truism: "he holds his priesthood permanently, because he continues forever" (Heb. 7:24); "Consequently he is able to save to the uttermost those who draw near to God through him, since he always lives to make intercession for them" (Heb. 7:25); "He has no need, like those high priests, to offer sacrifices daily... since he did this once for all when he offered up himself" (7:27); "There is one mediator between God and men, the man Christ Jesus" (1 Tim. 2:5).

In addition, the people as a whole are priestly through the offering of their lives in righteousness and holiness*. They form "a holy priesthood [*hierateuma*] to offer spiritual sacrifices acceptable to God through Jesus Christ" (1 Pet. 2:5 and 2:9). Revelation (1:6, 5:10, 20:6) gives this priesthood a more liturgical tone: without being ministers individually, each Christian has unmediated access to God. There was, therefore, linguistic innovation when bishops, and then priests, began to be known as *sacerdotes.*

According to Hippolytus, bishops are like high priests (*TA* 3, 8, 34); for Tertullian*, they *are* high priests (*De Bapt.* 17, 1; *Pud.* 21, 17); and Cyprian* extensively refers to them as priests in his correspondence. Optatus of Mileva was the first (360) to apply the term to presbyters (presbyter*/priest), coining the phrase *secundi sacerdotii,* "secondary priests" (PL 11, 911); afterwards, others also spoke of *secundi meriti* or *ordinis,* "those with secondary merit or ordination." However, these terms did not become common currency until the second millennium. Deacons were never called priests, but continued to be treated as in *TA* 18: "He is ordained, not to the priesthood, but to the service of the bishop" (reprised in *LG* 29).

Nevertheless, the priesthood remained a corporate body, functioning within a congregation through the act of epiclesis*. Indeed, congregations offered only those sacrifices that their presiding officers made; yet, because Christ offered the sacrifice, each member of his "body" also made it (*see* Guerric of Igny, late 12th century: "The priest neither consecrates alone nor sacrifices alone, for the whole congregation of believers consecrates and sacrifices with him," PL 185, 87). Accordingly, as Thomas* Aquinas puts it (*ST* IIIa, q. 64, a. 1), the role of the priest is solely to act as instrument, *in persona Christi:* "There are two ways of realizing an effect: as principal agent, or as instrumental agent. In the first case, it is God alone who realizes the *internal* effect of the sacrament. It belongs to God alone to produce grace...In the second case, minister and instrument have the same definition: the action of both is exercised *externally,* and results in an internal effect through the motion of the principal agent."

The opposition of the reformers, and particularly of Luther*, to the use of the concept of priesthood arose, first of all, from the overestimation of this concept at the expense of the ministry of the word*: "The apostolic, episcopal or clerical order has been given no other ministry than that of the word" (*WA* 6, 51). In addition, their opposition was a protest against the existence of a clerical estate as the foundation of "the detestable tyranny of the clergy over the laity" (*WA* 6, 563). It was in order to reestablish Christian fraternity that Luther insisted on the priesthood of all believers and on the functional nature of ministry (*WA* 6, 407–08): Some have supposed that priests and people in cloisters should be called the ecclesiastical estate, while all the lords, laborers, and peasants form the lay estate...This is a fine invention and conspiracy...In truth, all Christians form the ecclesiastical estate, and there is no difference among them, other than difference of function...All who have received baptism are capable of being glorified for having received the con-

secration necessary to become a priest, a bishop, or a pope, even though it is not appropriate that each and every one of them should exercise such functions."

The Council of Trent* concluded that this dispute was based on a misunderstanding, at least in terms of the Bible, since the priesthood never appears in the New Testament as a foundation for ministry. Yet the Council was not at liberty to undertake a fundamental reexamination of the question of ministry, for the popes, anxious about their jurisdiction* over the bishops, opposed any such undertaking (H. Jedin [1965], *Crise et dénouement du concile de Trente,* Ch. 5). The Council therefore revived the concept of priesthood. At the same time, common priesthood continued to be minimized, even to the point of being denied (see *KL,* 1884², 3, 546).

2. Systematic Treatments

Like other modern languages, French has just one word—*prêtre,* "priest"—with which to translate both *presbuteros* ("elder," without a priestly connotation) and *hiereus* (a priestly figure offering a sacrifice that reconciles God and humanity). References to priests as holders of a priestly status thus carry the risk of obscuring perception of the uniqueness of Christ's priestly status, in relation to which priests and bishops have no more than a "ministerial priesthood." This expression appears only once in the documents of Vatican* II, in *LG* 10, and there it forms part of a quotation—"*sacerdotium hierarchicum seu ministeriale*" ("hierarchical or ministerial priesthood") from Pius XII's address *Magnificate Dominum* (*AAS* 46 [1954], 669).

a) Existence of a Priestly Ministry as Part of Christian Faith.   All are priests before God and all have direct access to him. In addition, all are priests before human beings, through the spiritual sacrifice of their lives, led in righteousness and holiness. However, within the domain of salvation*, all have need for a priestly ministry. Even on the human plane, people are not the authors of their own birth, and no one can find by his or her own efforts the righteousness that has been lost. The same is true within the order of salvation: people cannot baptize themselves, for they cannot be the authors of their own rebirth; nor can anyone absolve himself of his own sins. The priestly ministry stands witness to these truths and operates ministerially through its visible integration into the community of salvation (the communion* of believers). To make use of the priestly ministry is thus to confess salvation through faith. Constituted as an office, the priestly ministry is entrusted to pastors (pastor*), for it is logical that those who preside over the church* as a communion of salvation should preside at the celebration of the sacraments of salvation. According to the Council of Trent (*COD* 743, 30; see *LG* 10), this is the significance of the external and visible priestly ministry, which cannot be reduced to the priesthood of the baptized.

b) Reception of the Priestly Ministry by Pastors and Its Exercise within the Church. Since it juxtaposes common priesthood and ministerial priesthood, *Lumen gentium* 10 could be understood as affirming the existence of two priesthoods: "Although the common priesthood of the faithful differs from the ministerial or hierarchical priesthood in essence, and not only by degree, they are both ordained nonetheless." In reality, however, it is the same, unique priesthood of Christ that is thus made operative through two modalities: the priesthood exercised by all (that of the holy life and of access to God in prayer), and the priestly ministry of certain persons, entrusted to pastors (and therefore described as "hierarchical"). The fact that it is a matter of modalities is shown by the linguistic corrections of Pius XII's address in *LG* 10, where the ministerial priesthood is deprived of the qualifying phrase "priesthood properly so called" and the common priesthood loses the quotation marks that weakened its effect in the original text. Thus, the ministerial priesthood is presented as being fundamentally different from the common priesthood, and the text emphasizes that these two institutions are different and distinct from one another. This also confirms the ecclesiology of the Reformation churches, which do not accept that any ministry can be attributed to a Christian solely on the basis of his baptismal priesthood.

Protestant theologians generally state that Catholic theology makes a distinction of essence or being as between priests and laity (e.g., Ratschow, *TRE* 2 [1978], p. 611, with reference to *LG* 10; Dubied, *Encyclopédie du protestantisme* [1995], with reference to Vatican II; Willaime, ibid. entry "ontologique" ["ontological"], without references). By doing so, these authors transpose the essential difference between priesthood and ministry onto the persons who perform these functions, which is something that Vatican II never does. Teheir approach may perhaps be justified by their reading of the communications submitted to the Council before the final vote on that *LG* 10—the *Nota explicativa praevia,* which form part of the acts of the Council but are not among the texts that were submitted to votes. Indeed, in relation to the ordination of bishops these notes state that "an *ontological* participation in sacred functions is conferred in the consecration..." It must be emphasized, however, that in the very same notes it is the pastoral office, not the person of the bishop, that is thus characterized as being "ontologically sacramental." In any case, it should be possible to avoid such perpetually revived misunderstandings about terminology if one notes that "ontological" here means "real." If reality is attributed to anything, there is an ontology—an ordered inventory of what is thought, said, and believed to be real—in which this reality is given a place. Accordingly, no reification is implied, nor does philosophy intrude into theology: in this case, the intention is to state that the priestly content of baptism, and ordination to the ministry, are not simply rational constructs.

It is certainly Catholic doctrine that, if necessary, laypeople can exercise the ministerial priesthood of Christ. Every Christian man or woman can perform baptism (*CIC* can. 861, §2). From the 11th century onward, spouses were considered by the Roman tradition to be ministers of the sacrament of marriage*, the priest being no more than a witness. For centuries, laypeople customarily administered the sacrament to the sick (A. Chavasse [1942], *Étude sur l'onction des infirmes dans l'Église latine du IIIe au XIe s.,* Lyon). Even confession to a layperson, if necessary, was long held to be sacramental (A. Teetaert [1926], *La confession aux laïcs dans l'Église latine depuis le VIIIe jusqu'au XVe s.,* Paris), and it was practiced up to the Reformation (e.g., by Bayard at Pavia, or by Ignatius Loyola at Pamplona). After the Council of Trent, however, laypeople were no longer recognized as capable of administering the sacrament to the sick or hearing confession.

c) Priestly Ministry as a Dimension of the Pastoral Ministry of Which It Forms a Part. Vatican II generally uses the expression "priestly ministry," which is more appropriate in terms of dogma than the *hapax legomenon* (unique occurrence) "ministerial priesthood" (*LG* 10), for here "priestly" is an attribute of ministry, since it is no more than an instrumental activity referring to Christ the only priest (*see* quotation from Aquinas above). Nevertheless, "priestly ministry" in turn is not as appropriate as "pastoral ministry" (of priests and bishops), or "presbyterial ministry," for it does not encompass all three of the ministerial tasks listed by Calvin (*Inst.,* Ch. 2, 5): teaching, sanctifying, and governing. In exceptional cases, laypeople can exercise it, but it seems that they do not have the same authority* as the bishops in relation to governing the church in communion or officially defining its faith.

In Catholic theology*, therefore, the most inclusive concept is that of the pastoral ministry of presidency. The Catholic ritual for the ordination* of priests is entitled the *ordinatio presbyterorum* ("ordination of presbyters"). It is through being ordained to preside over the church that one receives the ministry of the sacraments that construct the church, in particular the presidency of the Eucharist*, which is a sacrament of the church for the Orthodox as it is for Catholics (see *ASCOV* III, I, 57 [twice]: *presbyteri ut rectores ecclesiae sunt rectores eucharistiae,* "the presbyters, as rectors of the church, are the rectors of the Eucharist"). The priest or bishop acts *in persona Christi* because he acts *in persona ecclesiae*. However, the faithful do not offer the Eucharist "only through the hands of the priest, but also together with him" (*SC* 48).

d) Toward a Clarification of Vocabulary. Recent systematic theology has confirmed the legitimacy of, and the necessity for, a ministerial and priestly vocabulary with which to express the gratuitous nature of salvation based on the uniqueness of Christ's priesthood. It has also shown, however, that this vocabulary has only a limited relevance when it comes to describing the general ministry of bishops and priests, which also includes the ministry of the word (and "faithfully overseeing the Catholic faith received from the Apostles") and the ministry of government (presiding in the church and in communion between churches). The expressions "presbyterial ministry" and "episcopal ministry" are required for these cases. These terms also allow us to articulate the services and ministry of all and of some more easily than the terms *common priesthood* and *ministerial priesthood*. Finally, these terms are less likely to cause confusion in ecumenical dialogue.

● P.M. Gy (1957), "Remarques sur le vocabulaire antique du sacerdoce Chrétien," in Coll., *Études sur le sacrement de l'ordre*, LO 22, 125–45.

J.-M.R. Tillard (1973), "La 'qualité sacerdotale' du ministère chrétien," *NRTh* 95, 481–514.

H. Legrand (1977), "La présidence de l'eucharistie selon la tradition ancienne," *Spiritus* 18, 409–31.

B.-D. Marliangeas (1978), *Clés pour une théologie du ministère: In persona Christi: In persona ecclesiae*, ThH 51.

A. de Halleux (1987), "Ministère et sacerdoce," *RTL* 18, 289–316, 425–53.

W. Pannenberg (Ed.) (1990), *Lehrverurteilungen-Kirchentrennend?*, vol. 3, *Materialien zur Lehre von den Sakramenten und vom kirchlichen Amt*, Freiberg-Göttingen.

HERVÉ LEGRAND

See also **Calvin, John; Ecumenism; Luther, Martin; Ministry; Presbyter/Priest; Sacrifice; Trent, Council of; Vatican II, Council of**

Probabiliorism. *See* Alphonsus Liguori; Casuistry

Probabilism. *See* Alphonsus Liguori; Casuistry

Process Theology

a) Notion of Process. It means that reality is not made up of pieces with their own substance, but of events and movements. This statement has two consequences: 1) Every being* is born of an interconnection of encounters and relationships. There are not in the first place objects and persons (person*) that subsequently enter into contact with one another, but rather a network of conjunctions that give rise to persons and objects. The theory of Process thus opposes analytical procedures that distinguish, isolate, and attempt to understand relationships by starting from individuals. 2) Reality is constantly developing and changing; stability, inertia, and fixity are illusions. The world* and every being constitute a flux, a continuous movement that changes ceaselessly. This approach rejects substantialist conceptions that make becoming an accident of being, and not its very nature.

b) Process Philosophy. A mathematician turned philosopher, Alfred North Whitehead (1861–1947), established its foundations in several works, most notably *Process and Reality.* Rooted in the English philosophical tradition, and also close to Henri Bergson (1859–1941), he is unlike the existentialists in that he does not separate human beings from other beings in the world and because he works out a cosmology. A nonconformist Christian, he suggests some religious consequences of his thinking.

Charles Hartshorne, an American philosopher, develops the theological dimensions of this philosophy*. He argues for the total relativity (i.e., the "relationality") of God*. He criticizes the notions of divine perfection and omnipotence and refutes what he calls "classical theism." He proposes a "natural* theology" which, adopting in a nonsubstantialist perspective the proofs of the existence* of God, attempts to show that the universe is unintelligible without the divine energy that gives it life.

c) Process Theology. Process theology uses the conceptual system set forth by Whitehead and Hartshorne to develop an original and innovative interpretation of Christian faith*. Its best known representatives are the Methodist John Cobb, Schubert Ogden (a theologian also influenced by Bultmann*), David Griffin (who is engaged in a complex debate with postmodern

thinkers), Norman Pittinger, Lewis Ford, and Marjorie Suchocki. They make up a dynamic current of thought that has a certain audience in the United States, particularly among Protestants (although it is challenged by more classical theologies and by fundamentalists).

d) Themes of Process Theology. 1) Process theology rejects the notion of divine omnipotence*. God carries on an action in the world through his capacity to persuade beings (human and non-human) to listen to him and to respond to his promptings. It is not possible for him to obligate them, and he depends in part on their responses and reactions. He has real force, but does not exercise absolute power. The world resists him and sometimes stymies him. There is exchange and interaction in both directions: God influences the world; what happens in the world affects the being of God. 2) The activity of God brings forth newness. He instills his dynamism into the universe, makes unprecedented possibilities available to it, and urges it to move forward. He creates constantly, not beginning from nothing (process theology rejects the theme of creation* *ex nihilo,* pointing out that it is not biblical), but from what exists, using the "given." Process theology therefore rejects the positions of revolutionaries, because God creates out of the past, which provides him with the materials he needs; and the positions of conservatives, because God is not hostile to change. Faith implies indestructible hope*: God always opens up a future. Easter shows that he is even able to reverse so apparently irremediable a disaster as Golgotha. 3) Christ* is God's power of creative transformation. Because Jesus* brought about and continues to bring about changes and because he mobilizes us for God's plan, he is the supreme Christ. But other people endowed with analogous powers and other Christ-like actions manifest themselves in the world, in particular (but not exclusively) in the several different religions. It is therefore important to promote interfaith dialogue. 4) Very sensitive to relationships and conjunctions, process theology also deals with ecological questions and is concerned with social and political matters (e.g., in dialogue with liberation* theology). Finally, it is open to feminism (woman*); against the masculine representation of the dominating God, it proposes the image (considered more feminine) of a God who listens, inspires, understands, helps, and often suffers.

● A. N. Whitehead (1929), *Process and Reality,* Cambridge-New York.
C. Hartshorne (1941), *Man's Vision of God and the Problem of Theism,* Chicago; id. (1948), *The Divine Relativity,* New Haven, Conn.
J. B. Cobb (1966), *A Christian Natural Theology, Based on the Thought of A. N. Whitehead,* London.
S. L. Ogden (1966), *The Reality of God and Other Essays,* New York.
W. P. Pittenger (1968), *Process-Thought and Christian Faith,* New York.
D. D. Williams (1968), *The Spirit and the Forms of Love,* New York.
J. B. Cobb, D. Griffin (1976), *Process Theology: An Introductory Exposition,* Philadelphia.
♦ A. Parmentier (1968), *La philosophie de Whitehead et le problème de Dieu,* Paris.
D. Brown (Ed.) (1971), *Process Philosophy and Christian Thought,* Indianapolis.

H. J. Cargas, B. Lee (1976), *Religious Experience and P.T.,* New York.
D. R. Griffin, T. J. J. Altizer (Ed.) (1977), *John Cobb's Theology in Process,* Philadelphia.
A. Gounelle (1980), *Le dynamisme créateur de Dieu,* Montpellier.
M. H. Suchocki (1982), *God-Christ-Church: A Practical Guide to P.T.,* New York.
J. B. Cobb, F. I. Gamwell (Ed.) (1985), *Existence and Actuality: Conversation with C. Hartshorne,* Chicago.
S. Sia (Ed.) (1985), *Charles Hartshorne's Concept of God: Philosophical and Theological Responses,* The Hague.
M. Welker (1988), *Universalität Gottes und Relativität der Welt,* 2nd Ed., Neukirchen.
I. U. Dalferth (1989), "Prozeßtheologie," *HWP* 7, 1562–65.
A. Gounelle (1990), *Le Christ et Jésus,* Tournai.
M. Welker (1997), "Prozeßtheologie/Prozeßphilosophie,"*TRE* 27, 597–604.

ANDRÉ GOUNELLE

See also **Creation; Evolution; Omnipotence, Divine; World**

Procreation

The Christian tradition* sees procreation as one of the purposes of marriage* and as one of the criteria permitting the attribution of moral legitimacy to sexual activity. This tradition, which went uncontested from the Old Testament until the early modern era, must doubtless be reconsidered in order to respond to theoretical and practical objections, which have been amplified by the progress of biotechnology and by planetary demographic problems.

a) Bible. The biblical tradition envisages procreation within a double perspective. In terms of a theology* of creation*, fertility fulfils a blessing addressed to man and woman* at the first moments of humanity, at its creation: "Be fruitful and multiply" (Gen 1:28). However, because sin* has marred the creation, the human couple*, as such, experiences a punishment that makes the inequality of the sexes obvious. The woman is therefore to suffer pain in order to bring her children into the world, and is to be subject to her husband (Gen 3:16; *see* 1 Tm 2:15). The stories of the patriarchs thus reflect a system of family relations in which privileges were granted to male heirs; in which the existence of women found meaning from the sons that they gave to their spouses (Gen 16–17); in which sterility was a curse (1 Sm 1); and in which virginity seems never to have been recognized as valuable (Jgs 11:37, BJ note c, TOB note g).

These a priori assumptions undergo significant modification in the New Testament. On the one hand, the disciple is called to follow Christ* by virtue of a personal commitment that has nothing to do with membership of a family. On the other hand, the eschatological hope* of the earliest communities included the expectation of an imminent Parousia*, which did not fail to reduce the significance of family responsibilities and loyalties (Mt 10:37 and 12:46–50; Mk 3:31–35 and 10:29f.; Lk 8:19f. and 14:26), and de-emphasized procreation. In the longest discussion on sexuality and marriage in the New Testament (1 Cor 7:2–40), Paul does not mention the command given in Genesis 1:28, although he does mention the "holiness" of the children of Christians (7:14). He may be condemning abortifacient drugs when he speaks of *pharmakeia* in Galatians 5:20.

b) Tradition. As was already the case in the Pauline corpus, patristic theology preferred virginity to mar-

1289

riage, a position that is still held in the Catholic tradition (see *Catechism of the Catholic Church,* 1619–20). In their treatment of marriage, the Fathers* took inspiration from the Greek (and especially Stoic) view that the passions* must be subject to reason*, and thus they saw procreation as a purpose of marriage that allows the disciplining of sexual desire (Clement of Alexandria, *Strom.* II, 23, SC 38). In western Christianity, the most important approach was, as in many other cases, that of Augustine*. Where Tertullian* and Jerome (c. 342–420) praised virginity almost to the point of condemning marriage, Augustine set himself to defend marriage (*De bono conjugali,* BAug 2; see *Ep.* 188, CSEL 57). He says that there is a good* in marriage, which indeed is necessary for Augustine in refuting dualistic views, such as those of the Manicheans, who exacerbated the Greek idea of the body as a prison or tomb of the soul*, and attributed to sexuality no more than the negative meaning attached to all that was of the flesh. Like Clement before him, Augustine makes procreation the divinely ordained end of sexual intercourse. Although mutual faithfulness (*fides*) and the indissoluble bond that constitutes the couple (*sacramentum*) are joined with it as goods of marriage, procreation alone gives order to sexual activity, which is taken to be (venially) sinful when undertaken for other reasons. It was therefore very logical for Augustine to share the special admiration of his contemporaries for couples who had decided to live as brother and sister.

Augustine's idea of the three ends of marriage was adopted by the Scholastics (Scholasticism*), including Thomas* Aquinas (*Suppl.* q. 49; see *ST* IIIa, q. 29, a. 2), and then by the Reformers, including Luther* and Calvin*. It remained central to Christian teaching until the 20th century. Yet a richer theory, in which three goods of conjugal intimacy correspond to the three ends of marriage, appeared in the Middle Ages (*see* school of Saint* Victor, *De sacramentis christianae fidei,* PL 176, 174–613; II, 11, on marriage), and became established in the 16th century. Aquinas's conception of marriage as a specific form of friendship also broadened the range of possible changes; and when the Reformers suggested that the only restraints appropriate to marital intercourse were those required by charity and mutual consideration, they too were heading in the direction of a reconstruction of the theory.

A certain approach to education went together with this procreation-oriented sexual ethics*. It consisted in a Christianization of the Greek *paideia,* understood as the art of training children for their responsibilities as adults. Methods included exhortation, encouragement, praise and blame, fear* of the Lord, and frequent beatings. According to John Chrysostom (*On vanity and the education of children* SC 188) and Jerome (*Ep.* 107, CSEL 55, 290–305), the duties of education are to protect children from bad influences, to instruct them in the biblical narratives (narrative*), and to give them a Christian morality. They were provided with the model of the martyrs and holy persons, many of them women, who had abandoned their families (family*) to accept death*, go on pilgrimage*, or enter a convent or monastery (e.g., the first-century martyr Perpetua, the fifth-century matron Melania the Younger, or Paula, friend of Jerome). Certain children themselves were admired for their spiritual precocity: Jerome tells of Eupraxia, for example, who dedicated herself to Christ at the age of seven (*Ep.* 24 CSEL 54, 214–17).

Children were not infrequently given over to convents or monasteries for their education. The duty to provide a solid education for these children pertained largely sons, but monasteries and convents also allowed girls to acquire an education. The custom of "offering" one's child, that is, dedicating him or her to the monastic life, was strong from the patristic era to the late Middle Ages; it was one means of securing the future of children who could not be married off without dividing the family inheritance. However, this practice was already beginning to arouse some reservations in the 12th century, a period that saw the appearance of a new perception of individual liberty*.

In the writings of Luther and Calvin, marriage, procreation, and the education of children all represent a natural form of life (a reality of the created order) capable of being transformed and sanctified by the practice of the Christian virtues*. Puritanism* brought to bear a very specific emphasis on the role as educators that was entrusted to parents: because, according to Puritan theology, God's covenant* with believers was extended through baptism* to their children, it was a strict duty to raise them in the ways of the Lord, using harsh measures if necessary, in view of the salutary effects of such an upbringing on their everlasting destiny. Children were often sent to reside with other Puritan families, as apprentices or domestic servants, in order to ensure that their Christian education would not be hindered by parental leniency.

After the Reformation and the age of the Enlightenment, various factors led to changes in received ideas. The emphasis was placed on liberty and equality, personal fulfillment came to be valued, and the idea of happiness appeared, effacing Christian conceptions of beatitude*. Childhood began to be considered as a phase of life with its own needs, and the good of children was therefore defined from the vantage point of their own experience. At the same time, there appeared a form of economic organization that was less dependent on the existence of large families; it was discovered that in human beings, unlike other mammals, the sex drive is not limited to periods of female fertility; and, finally, reliable contraception appeared, and roles for women became more varied. For all these reasons, the couple has gradually ceased to be defined as a relationship of communal living ordained for procreation.

c) Recent Debates. Having long opposed all these changes, the Lambeth Conference, the supreme body of the Anglican Communion, took note of them and authorized contraception in 1930. Other Protestant and Orthodox churches (church*) were soon to follow suit. In the Catholic Church, an official position was defined, after much debate, in Paul VI's encyclical *Humanae vitae* (1968, *AAS* 60, 481–503). The text reprises the statements of Vatican* II (*GS,* §47–51), which addressed the question in terms of two purposes of sexuality, love* and procreation, without making a hierarchy of them. The encyclical mentions a duty of "responsible parenthood," which requires that couples avoid having more children than they can nurture. It gives up one of Augustine's ideas, stating that procreation need no longer be intended, or even physically possible, for sexual relations to be morally good. However, the Pope* rejects all contraceptive methods, with the exception of so-called "natural means," based on women's infertile cycles. This text has not ceased to arouse controversy on this last point.

Two recent phenomena oblige us to consider the question of the moral and Christian meaning of procreation as being still open: medically assisted procreation, and the population crisis. 1) The Catholic Church was the first church to make a pronouncement on *in vitro* fertilization and related techniques. In 1987, it condemned (*Donum vitae, AAS* 80, 70–102) all reproductive technologies, because they endanger embryos, which are recognized as having the ontological status of persons (person*); because they permit procreation that is not the result of sexual relations; and because they introduce third parties into the couple, in such a way that a child can have more than two "parents." Protestant churches have rarely put forward definitive judgments on the morality of the new methods, and they generally allow a larger role for individual decisions taken within the limits of what is authorized by law. 2) The contrast between the high-technology remedies for the sterility of couples in the developed world, for whom procreation seems to be a right, and the large families of the Third World, in whose case one might wonder whether numerous children are a blessing, may suggest that the moral problem of procreation can also be posed in terms of economic justice*. Indeed, it is clear that the question of the overpopulation of the globe cannot be resolved by appealing merely to individual freedom, nor to the deeper nature of marriage and sexuality, unless one takes the social and economic determinants of the problem into consideration. When voluntary sterilization, or even abortion*, are advocated as means to reduce population growth, two errors are committed. First, one underestimates the cultural value of family in many parts of the world. Second, one fails to perceive that an improvement in social conditions is necessary in order to ensure that children are no longer the only form of wealth for some people—it is well-known that fertility rates fall when standards of living rise.

A stocktaking of Christian moral concepts would provide several ways of thinking afresh about the link between marriage and procreation.

● P. Ariès (1960), *L'enfant et la vie familiale sous l'Ancien Régime,* Paris.
É. Fuchs (1979), *Le désir et la tendresse: Sources et histoire d'une éthique chrétienne de la sexualité et du marriage,* Geneva.
J. Noonan (1986, rev. Ed.), *Contraception: A History of Its Treatment by the Catholic Theologians and Canonists,* Cambridge, Mass., and London.
J.-L. Bruguès (1989), *La fécondation artificielle au crible de l'éthique chrétienne,* Paris.
G. Moore (1992), *The Body in Context: Sex and Catholicism,* London.
D. Wood (Ed.) (1994), *The Church and Childhood,* Oxford and Cambridge, Mass.

LISA SOWLE CAHILL

See also **Couple; Ethics, Sexual; Family; Manicheanism; Marriage**

Proexistence

Term coined by the exegete Heinz Schürman (1913–99) and used to describe the experience of Jesus as an "existence *for*" others: a life turned toward the Father and other people and lived for them. Recent Christology and salvation theology have made extensive use of this term. It is also used in the ecclesiological context of the "diaspora" of Christian communities living within de-Christianized or non-Christian societies.

JEAN-YVES LACOSTE

See also **Christ and Christology; Salvation**

Promise

"Promise, " in Greek, is generally expressed by the verb *epaggellô* and its substantive *epaggelia,* but there is no specific term for promise in Hebrew. A promise is a commitment to give something at a later date. An oracle of good fortune is not in itself a promise, nor is a benediction. However, when words (word*) that concern the future come from God*, they are necessarily a commitment, and even more so if they are accompanied by an oath. Thus, many promises are formulated with the simple verb *dâvar* (intensive, "to say"; nouns: '*émèr* and *dâvâr*) or *shâva'* ("to swear"; nouns: *shevoû'âh,* '*âlâh*). Similarly, when God concludes (*kârat*) an unconditional covenant*, this is a promise.

a) Old Testament. The divine word opens the history* of Israel* with the double promise made to Abraham, of a land (Gn 12:1) and descendants (Gn 12:2). The series continues from one patriarch to the other: Gn 15, 17, 18:18f., 22:16ff., 26:3f., 26:24, 35:11f., 48:3. The promise includes the benevolence of other groups (Gn 12:2f.) or supremacy over them (22:17, 32:29).

This triple schema was carried over to the benediction of the first human couple in Genesis 1:28 (fecundity, possession of the land, supremacy). It is transformed but recognizable in Genesis 3:15ff.: descendants and the fruits of the land will be obtained by suffering. According to the traditional reading, supremacy over the serpent is later granted to the woman* by way of her posterity (collective in Hebrew, masculine individual in the *Septuagint,* feminine in the *Vulgate*). Revelation 12:13–16 would seem to recall what was named the "first Gospel" (proto-Gospel), but there it is an angel* who is victorious. Other readings of Genesis 3:15ff. see only the announcement of endless combat.

The series is crowned, before the conquest of Canaan, by the oracle (benediction and promise) of Balaam (Nm 24:9 carried over from Gn 12:3). In the current book* the promises of Genesis appear as a progressive reorientation toward the original gift: recall of Genesis 3:17f in Genesis 5:29, renunciation of the deluge in Genesis 9:5–17.

It is with the book of Deuteronomy that the concept of promise takes on a particular coloration. Very often related to the memory of the Fathers* (the patriarchs in 1:8, 9:27, 34:4, etc., but more often to the generation of the Exodus), the promise, which doubles the benediction itself (Dt 1:11), applies to the nation or the land (1:21, 6:3, 6:18), descendants (Dt 13:18 and passim), and victory (Dt 7:16, 15:6, 28:7, 28:12 b). It is most often connected with the divine oath (19 times with respect to the land), confirmed by Joshua 1:3: [. . .] "*As I said it to Moses.*" Posterior to the fulfillment of the promise, testament to the prophetic preaching* that marked it as it marked the ultimate composition of certain collections of the prophets (prophet* and prophecy), Deuteronomy, "seeking origins" (Römer

1992), makes a new start toward the future. Not unrelated to the covenant promise in Jeremiah 31:31ff.; it joins the present state of life, guarantee a future (*see* Dt 4:40), and a past of election (Dt 7:7–16).

The promise, which initially concerns David's line (2 Sm 7:5–16), is renewed in the prophetic context of the imminence of chastisement (e.g. Is 7:10–17, 8:21f.), and organized toward a restoration that gradually takes an eschatological form (*see* Is 11:1–16). Finally, a manifestation of celestial or divine order will be awaited in an apocalyptic context (Zec 3:8ff.; Dn 7:11–14: line 14 b amplifies 2 Sm 7:16; *see* Lk 1:32f.), at the same time as the promise of the effusion of the Spirit confirms the radical renewal of the people* (Jl 3:1–5).

b) New Testament. The Old Testament as a whole has been read in terms of "promise/fulfillment," with this pairing representing a key to true interpretation. The New Testament retains as "promises" essentially those proclaimed in the ancient Scriptures. Undoubtedly the concept of promise flows back into the New Testament with Paul, notably in Galatians and Romans, and with the Epistle to the Hebrews, following the heritage of the Old Testament and acquiring a new use of meaning. Neither should we neglect to mention the Gospel* of John and its promise of the Spirit. The recall of the promise in Abraham (Rom 4:20; Heb 6:13ff.), Isaac, and Jacob (Heb 11:9) and its consistently maintained validity in the destiny of Israel (Rom 9:4, 9:8f.) does not detract from the newness of the promises of which Christ*'s disciples will be both the beneficiaries and the sign. These are the promises of a reception of the Spirit (Lk 24: 49; Acts 1:4; 2:33, 2:39; Gal 3:14; Eph 1:13; *see* Jn 16:7–15), in an unconditional gift whose gratuitousness would be obliterated by a return to the regime of the law* (Gal 3:17–29). This is a promise of the life that is in Jesus* Christ (2 Tm 1:1), blessed holder of the promises (Heb 7:6), while Christians, subject to the test of the times (time*), await according to the promise (2 Pt 3:13; *see* 1 Jn 2:25). In conclusion, it could be said that the gospel is *"The Evangelism of the accomplished promise made to our fathers"* (Acts 13:32f.; *see* Eph 1:2).

● A. G. Hebert (1941), *The Throne of David: A Study of the Fulfilment of the Old Testament in Jesus-Christ and his Church,* London.

W. Zimmerli (1952, 1953), "Verkeißung und Erfüllung," *EvTh* 12, 34–59.

G. von Rad (1965), *Theologie des Alten Testaments,* 4th Ed., vol. 1, 370–401.

P. Grelot (1962), *Sens chrétien de l'Ancien Testament. Esquisse d'un traité dogmatique,* Tournai, 328–45, 388–404.

A. de Pury (1975), *Promesse divine et légende cultuelle dans le cycle de Jacob,* Paris.

Ch. Levin (1985), *Die Verheißung des neuen Bundes in ihrem theologiegeschichtlichen Zusammenhang ausgelegt,* Göttingen.

R. Rendtorff (1977), *Das überlieferungsgeschichtliche Problem des Pentateuch,* Berlin (*The Problem of the Process of the Transmission in the Pentateuch,* Sheffield, 1990).

Th. Römer (1990), *Israels Väter: Untersuchungen zur Väterthematik im Deuteronomium und in der deuteronomistischen Tradition,* Göttingen; id. (1992), "Le Deutéronome à la recherche des origines," in P. Haudebert (Ed.) (ACFEB), *Le Pentateuque. Débats et recherches,* Paris, 65–100.

PIERRE GIBERT

See also **Adam; Blessing; Covenant; Eschatology; Father; Good; Gospels; Hope**

Property

The word *property* is descended from Latin *proprietas,* formed from the adjective *proprius,* meaning "one's own, "special," "particular," "proper." Retaining these nuances, *proprietas* has the twofold meaning of a peculiarity, particular nature or quality of something, and right of possession of something. Property in the latter sense refers to the complex of rights and liabilities that governs the relationship between persons (natural or juristic) and objects (material or immaterial).

Property, in the classical sense of the term, is the right to be in secure possession of an object, to use and manage it, to enjoy financial benefit from it, to consume, waste, alienate or bequeath it. However, the characteristics of property rights vary widely according to the sorts of objects owned and the legal category to which they belong, for example, movable or immovable, personal or real property, items of production or consumption. Likewise, the restrictions and liabilities attached to property vary widely, depending largely on the extent to which third parties are potentially affected. Thus, the disposition and use of property in land is generally subject to stricter limitations than personal property is, with the exception of inherently dangerous possessions such as firearms and automobiles.

The creation and determination of property by conventions and statutes, and its enforcement by public authority*, indicate its thoroughly social, political, moral and hence, philosophical and theological character. In the western Christian political/legal tradition, property has undergone significant changes, notably concerning the breadth of its definition, the various types of property recognized, its teleological and etiological justifications, its moral standing, and the scope of its conditions (limitations). We shall examine the biblical foundations of property and then retrace its evolution in patristic, medieval, early modern and modern thought.

First, we must outline two partially intersecting distinctions concerning property: between individual and collective property, on the one hand, and between private and public property on the other. Property rights may be held by natural individuals or by collectivities construed in law* as artificial persons. Collective property is *common* in the sense that every member of the group has some claim in what is owned, for example, to use and enjoy it. Private property is the *exclusive* right of individual or collective owners to goods, which right is defensible against all other persons. Public property refers to the *inclusive* right held by members of comprehensive collectivities, such as the modern civil polity or the medieval ecclesiastical polity. Public property is *common* in a more universal sense than the property of less comprehensive, more particular "private" collectivities.

a) Biblical Foundations. The theological backdrop of property is the biblical account (Gn 1:28–30, 2:15, 2:19f.) of the establishment of Adam* as master over the nonhuman creation*; he is called to fill and subdue the Earth, to cultivate it, and to use its fruits to sustain human life. The Fall (original sin*) then introduces elements of struggle, anxiety, and domination into "dominion," focused in the theme of painful toiling, the price that humanity must henceforth pay in order to meet physical necessities. The idea of property is brought to the fore in the covenant* by which God* elects Israel* as his special possession (Ex 19:5f.) and promises that the 12 tribes will, in their obedience to his covenant, occupy by conquest and settle the land of Canaan. Israel's possession of the land is both collective and distributive: every family is allotted an equal

portion in the nation's patrimony (Nm 26:52–56). The permanent inalienability of the familial holdings, evidenced by the institution of the Jubilee Year (Lv 25:8–13), and the obligation to redeem all land ceded in the interim (Lv 25:25–28), point not only to the origin of Israel's "inheritance" as a divine gift, but also to the continuing proprietary right of the divine giver (Lv 25:23). As sovereign proprietor, God limits Israel's rights of possession by requiring provision for the poor from gleanings (Lv 19:9f. and 23:22; Dt 24:19ff.) and tithes (Dt 14:28f. and 26:12); concession to the hungry wayfarer (Dt 23:25f.); annual tithes to God himself (Lv 27:30ff.); and respect for the sabbatical rest for the land (Lv 25:2–7). The example of the Levites, who are excluded from the tribal land distribution and rely solely on tithes for sustenance, also reminds us that Israel not only has a vocation as proprietor, but is also called to serve God directly in the practice of worship (Nm 18:21–24; Dt 8:1f.). The falling away of God's people* from the covenantal terms of property toward the unscrupulous accumulation of land and wealth (1 Kgs 21:1ff.; Is 5:8; Mi 2:1f.), and the neglect and oppression of the vulnerable poor (Is 3:14f., 58:6–7; Am 8:4–14), are common targets of condemnation by the prophets (prophet* and prophecy). According to the prophetic literature, it is because of this infidelity that the Israelites must be collectively and individually dispossessed of their land.

The Gospels* depict Jesus proclaiming an eschatological Jubilee, wedded to his own character as Messiah* (Lk 4:16ff.), and announcing a new covenant in which earthly property plays hardly any role. On the contrary, Luke's account of the Sermon on the Mount stresses that the Kingdom* of God is the inheritance of those who are spiritually and physically dispossessed (Lk 6:20f. and 24f.). Jesus censures the service of "unrighteous wealth" as an idolatrous pursuit of false security, and exhorts those who wish to follow him to part with their possessions and their proprietary rights, in fulfillment of their true obligations to love God and their neighbors (Mt 5:42, 6:24–34, 19:16–26; Mk 10:17–31, 12:41–44; Lk 6:32–35, 12:13–31, 18:18–30, 21:1–4). In sending out the 12 and the 70 on missions (mission*/evangelization), Jesus permits them only the barest necessities and daily sustenance freely provided by others (Mt 10:5–14; Mk 6:8–11; Lk 9:3–5 and 10:3–9), in imitation of the "Son of Man" (Lk 9:58). He promises to all who renounce earthly possessions in his name their recovery in eschatological and spiritual abundance (Mt 19:29; Mk 10:29f.; Lk 18:29f.).

According to Luke's narrative* in Acts, under the leadership of the apostles (apostle*) the post-resurrection gatherings of believers in Jerusalem held all things in common, each surrendering his property to supply his brother's need, so manifesting their communion* in faith* and love* (Acts 2:44–47 and 4:32f.). Paul, who himself loosely practiced the missionary discipline of poverty, exhorts the Corinthian faithful to emulate the churches (church*) of Macedonia, which, out of "their abundance of joy and their extreme poverty," gave liberally for the relief of the impoverished church in Jerusalem; Christ*, though rich, became poor (kenosis*) so that they might become rich (Rom 15:26ff.; 1 Cor 16:1–4; 2 Cor 8:1–9). Some subsequent New Testament writings, echoing Greco-Roman philosophical themes, sustain the antithesis between spiritual and material riches (Heb 10:34; Rev 2:9 and 3:17f.), and between the vice of avarice and the godly virtue* of temperance (1 Tm 6:6–10; Heb 13:5), while not debarring the materially wealthy from embracing the riches of faith and righteous works (1 Tm 6:17ff.).

b) Subapostolic and Patristic Periods. For subapostolic authors, the *koinonia* ("sharing," "community," "communion") in both "immortal" ("incorruptible") and "mortal" ("corruptible") goods enjoyed by the Jerusalem church remained a dominant theme in their exhortations to unreserved sharing of one's possessions with the needy (*Didache* IV, 5–8; *Epistle of Barnabas* XIX, 8, PG 2, 777–78). Also prominent was the idea that superfluous property entraps its possessors in the present order, sapping their understanding and will, rendering them too feeble to stand fast in God's order under persecution (*Hermas, Sim.* I, 1–7, PG 2, 951–52). The Pseudoclementine Homilies, carrying to Gnostic extremes the dualism of the two kingdoms, repudiate all property, beyond the bare necessities, as belonging to the "foreign king" of the evil earthly city* (PG 2, 359–62).

From the later second century onward, Christian considerations of property demonstrated, on the one hand, a more conscious antagonism to the Roman law concept of *dominium (proprietas)* as a relatively unrestricted individual power over possessions, and, on the other, a more explicit appropriation of Stoic ideas about human nature and society*. In the wake of Irenaeus* of Lyon, who sets up a bold contrast between the *inherently* unrighteous acquisition of property and its righteous use in generous almsgiving (PG 7, 1064–65), Clement of Alexandria describes the righteous use of property as a restoration of the original *koinonia* of created humanity called to share all things, beginning with "God's own word" (PG 8, 541–44). Some subsequent Greek and Latin Fathers* presented Christian communion in the use of earthly goods as a reflection of both the Adamic community, drawing collectively on God's gifts for sustenance (the Stoic state

of nature), and the universal bounty of the divine giver (Basil* the Great PG 31, 275–78, 299–302; Cyprian*, CSEL 3, 232; Zeno of Verona, PL 11, 287; Ambrose*, PL 14, 263f., 731, 734, 747; PL 16, 61f.; PL 17, 313f.; John Chrysostom*, PG 62, 562ff.). Conversely, they portrayed the refusal of proprietors to share possessions with the needy as a form of theft, because it contravenes divinely ordained equality in the use of necessities, and moreover, is a sort of idolatry*, because it repudiates the true owner of the Earth's bounty (Basil, PG 31, 261–64, 276f.; Ambrose, PL 14, 734, 747; PL 15, 1303f.; PL 17, 434f.; John Chrysostom, PG 48, 986–88; PG 57, 706f.; PG 62, 562ff.; Augustine*, PL 33, 665; PL 38, 326). Some denied that even patrimonial concerns could lessen the individual's obligation to generous giving (Cyprian, CSEL 3, 387f.; Augustine, PL 38, 89f.).

Many third- and fourth-century Fathers came close to endorsing Seneca's interpretation of the institution of private property as originating in human avarice and yet performing a divinely ordained remedial service, coterminous with political authority and law (the most notable exception being Lactantius, *Inst. div.* 3. 21f.). However, it is Augustine who formulates most explicitly the dependence of property on the *imperium,* and its social benefit of rendering the abuse of wealth "less injurious" (PL 33, 665; PL 35, 1437). At the same time, he distinguishes sharply between human property right and the divine right of possession, according to which "all things belong to the just"—to those whose use of things conforms to the love of Christ and of neighbor (PL 34, 20f.)—and he concludes that the infidel lacks just (divine) title to his possessions (PL 33, 665).

c) Middle Ages. Medieval thought about property was dominated by two somewhat antithetical developments of the patristic (primarily Augustinian) inheritance—the Franciscan and the papalist—in relation to which divergence the ideas of Thomas* Aquinas approach a middle position. Before the growth of the mendicant orders, ecclesiastical property formed a seamless garment uniting the secular clergy and the monastic orders, based, in theory, on the harmonious application of the New Testament models furnished by Christ, his apostles, and the Jerusalem church. The Franciscan theology of "evangelical perfection," definitively set forth in Bonaventure*'s *Apologia pauperum* (c. 1269), rent the garment by distinguishing the collective property of the larger church from the Minorites' absolute renunciation of all property (private and common). Within Bonaventure's Augustinian ethics* of ordered love, the "simple" (nonproprietary) use of goods owned and conceded by others represents a "higher" participation in Christ's selfless obedience, a more efficacious overcoming of avarice, and a recovery of humankind's just possession of the creation.

As a result of rancorous disputes over "absolute poverty" among the friars, the papacy gradually discerned the threat posed by their doctrine to the church, which over several centuries had been canonistically expounded as a mystical and political body with wide-ranging proprietary rights. Toward the close of the 13th century, Franciscan rigorism was polarized against a high papalist ecclesiology* that had converted the church's common property over goods entrusted to it into the pope*'s supreme and unlimited property (both enforcible jurisdiction* and right of use) over all the church's temporal possessions. Papal publicists deployed the Augustinian concept of just possession to assert that only proprietors judged worthy by the Roman church possessed their goods justly, and therefore that all unworthy proprietors—heretics, excommunicates, and infidels—lacking divine right, were liable to just deprivation of their property by the church (Giles of Rome, 1302; James of Viterbo, 1301–02). In his systematic repudiation of Franciscan poverty, Pope John XXII (1316–34) made property intrinsic to evangelical perfection, attributing it to Christ and to Adamic *dominium* from the beginning (BF, 5, 408–49). Fifty years later, in the footsteps of Richard FitzRalph, John Wyclif produced a late and unsurpassed flowering of the Franciscan theology of poverty, elaborating the concept of natural and Christological nonproprietary community within a neo-Platonic framework of participatory realism. He used this concept, in the manner of Marsilius of Padua, to justify the expropriation of the English church by the secular authorities.

On the question of whether property is natural, Thomas Aquinas attempted to harmonize patristic statements with contemporary Aristotelian arguments. He therefore presents property as the optimum mode of possessing material things, the best way in which humankind exercises its natural dominion of use over the rest of the creation. To the patristic mainstream, he concedes that private property belongs not to natural law but to human agreement and legislation (*ST* IIa IIae, q. 66, a. 2, ad 1). At the same time, however, he argues, somewhat against the spirit of the Fathers, that the introduction of property was a rational addition to natural law, a complement that, far from derogating from it, fulfills its requirements most efficiently. Man's natural dominion includes not only the common use of material resources, but also their care and distribution, and these latter are best accomplished by private property for the reasons that Aristotle gives (*ST* IIa IIae, q. 66, a. 2, 1–2). As these reasons have chiefly to do

with individual self-interest, Aquinas shows his distance from the Augustinian, Franciscan, and Wycliffite vision of a participatory community capable of going back to conditions before the Fall.

Going beyond the Middle Ages, Aquinas's conception of property was in tune with canonist theory, which, although it perpetuated the classical debates over the naturalness of property, was increasingly guided by the *ius gentium* and Roman civil law, mainly on account of the legal exigencies created by the growth of industry, trade, and commerce. In addressing the emerging capitalist economy, and its legal devices of production and exchange (limited liability partnerships, insurance, banking, bills of exchange, letters of credit, and so on), the canonists introduced novel ethical distinctions that mitigated older biases against such forms of property acquisition as *negotiatio* (buying and selling for profit), trade, productive investment, and commercial loans (Gilchrist 1969; Berman 1983). Moreover, like Aquinas, they relaxed earlier admonitions, for example by defining "necessary" or "sufficient" wealth that the owner was not obliged to part with charitably as that required to sustain him decently in his social position. They extolled the virtue of liberality in a manner that was more Aristotelian than Christian (Tierney 1959; *ST* IIa IIae, q. 32, a. 5, ad 3, a. 6; q. 134, a. 2–3).

d) Early Modern Period. From the 15th to the 17th centuries, the concept of property acquired a controlling position in western political thought, in which it became a natural (subjective) human right, or *the* paradigmatic natural right. In the footsteps of William of Ockham, the Parisian nominalist Jean Gerson (1363–1429) defined man's natural *dominium* over the nonhuman creation as a God-given *ius,* that is, as a "dispositional *facultas* or power to dispose of" things and to use them for his own preservation, and he included liberty* in this natural *dominium,* drawing a parallel between man's original power over exterior things and his power of using himself, his body, and his actions (action*) (Tuck 1979). Under the influence of Gerson's followers, especially John Mair and Jacques Almain, certain Neoscholastic thinkers of the 16th and 17th centuries (Fernando Vazquez y Menchaca, Luis de Molina, Suarez*, and others) cast natural dominion as property right and natural freedom as personal property that could be alienated by contract, in part or in whole, to the point of individual or collective enslavement (Molina 1614; F. Suarez [1612] 1944; Tuck 1979). In his attempt to extract natural property right from the absolutist and statist theories of his day, Locke conceived property in external things to be the outcome and expression—and not merely the condition (as in Aristotle)—of creative freedom of action. Individuals, the sole masters of their own productive capacities, are also the sole proprietors of the product of their work*, in the image of the exclusive proprietary right that God exercises over his creatures (*Second Treatise on Government* 5). The theory that man, the worker, is naturally led to transform the common resources of the Earth into private possessions was therefore born here, and from this move flowed several key theorems of liberal capitalism: wage-labor as voluntary alienation of a personal property, one's labor power; the private character of producing and consuming activities; the moral acceptability of the unlimited accumulation of wealth in a money economy; and the inevitable benefit that the collectivity derives from it. Already, in the writings of Hobbes, the idea of the natural proprietorship of individuals in their productive capacities, wedded to their constant need for self-enhancement, had issued in a liberal and utilitarian conception of property; it achieved its most complete expression in the economistic theory of morality and jurisprudence developed by Jeremy Bentham (1748–1832).

By comparison with the more radical natural right theorists, the magisterial Reformers remained closer to the patristic and medieval traditions, but with some shifts of perspective. Luther* and Calvin* concurred, against the Anabaptists*, in defending the indispensability of property; without property, the Christian could not serve God and neighbor within the social order. Luther's view resulted from a complex ethical application of his doctrine of "two reigns." Property and its derivative economic transactions are certainly intrinsic to every ordered community; they are necessary, first of all, for the satisfaction of human material needs and for the performance of divinely ordained temporal offices (*WA* 32, 307; 39/2, 39), and they are conformable to the practice of love* and equity (*WA* 15, 294, 296, 303; *WA. B*, 485f.; 6, 466; 32, 395). This practice also leads to an understanding of the injunction to eschatological detachment from all property, because property in the last instance is to be given away (*WA* 6, 3, 36; 10/3, 227, 275; 15, 300, 302; 19, 231, 561; 39/2, 40). In Calvin's writings, two theological norms govern the problem of property: the duty of stewardship of the gifts of creation, and the duty to see to the common good of the church. The right modes of acquisition and use of property are revealed in God's law. The individual can freely dispose of property in a virtuous manner (*Inst.* II.8. 47–48; III.7.5).

e) Modern Period. The primary distinctive trait of this period is the abandonment of Locke's model of property based on creative activity—and of the utilitarian pleasure/pain calculus closely associated with it—which have revealed themselves to be ill-adapted to the most modern forms of wealth production (e.g., investment, interest, and speculation). Supporters of unlimited private acquisition have recourse to the more open theory provided by Kant* and Hegel* (*Grundlinien der Philosophie des Rechts*): property *as such* (no matter how abstract or removed from the subject it may be) is an embodiment of personal freedom, an objectification of the private will. This theory had its advantages: it permitted, as easily as was possible, the assertion that the inequalities that arise from the relentless pursuit of self-interest in a market economy are "efficient," necessary, and of eventual benefit to the poorest in society. However, most serious analyses of capitalist property in the last two centuries have required major modifications of all panegyrics of individual enrichment.

Of the socialist critiques that proliferated from the early 19th century onward—whether utopian, romantic, Hegelian, anarchist or Christian—the most theologically interesting is that of Karl Marx*, because, even more than his influential contemporary Pierre-Joseph Proudhon, he revived the primacy of communal participation over economic distribution. He thus rediscovered the idea of common possession and nonproprietary community that had characterized Christian Platonism* up to the Anabaptist sects of the Reformation period. Shedding the doctrinal, theological, mystical, and contemplative elements of the tradition, Marx saw the collective ownership of the means of production as the fairest relationship of producing humanity to nonhuman nature, and common work as the fairest means for its appropriation of earthly goods, and thus of acceding to its own essence, which is creative freedom. Marx, however, is not a critic of all forms of property, but only of one specific form of property, property organized as *capital.* It is in this form, and in this form only, that the question of property becomes a factor in alienation, dispossessing human beings of the conditions, products, activities, and moral relations of work, and consequently dispossessing them of their humanity (*Ökonomisch-philosophische Manuskripte,* 1844; *Das Kapital Capital,* 1867).

From Leo XIII's encyclical *Rerum novarum* (1891) onward, Catholic teaching on property has consistently offered a synthetic and coherent exegesis of the theological tradition* in an attempt at a response to the realities of technological liberalism, whether capitalist, communist, or socialist. The doctrinal strategy that has been followed is reasonably clear: to synthesize biblical, patristic and (chiefly) Thomist treatments of property with modern liberal ideas and aspirations. On the side of tradition, the Roman *magisterium* has retained above all the idea of a common teleology of earthly goods, divinely given for the use of all persons: justice and charity dictate that all superfluous wealth should be used to serve the needs of the poor (on a national and international scale) (*Rerum novarum RN* 19; *Quadragesimo anno QA* 56ff.; *Gaudium et spes* 69; *Populorum progressio PP* 22ff.; *Sollicitudo rei socialis SRS* 39; *Centesimus annus CA* 30–31). Faithful to the Thomist conception of the "common good," the Popes have also defined the role that public authorities should play in relation to regulating the conditions for the enjoyment of private property, overseeing the just distribution of goods and services, establishing public property in common resources, and protecting universal access to them (*RN* 25ff.; *QA* 49, 74–75, 132; *Mater et Magistra MM* 77, 79, 88, 116–17, 127–40, 150–52; *Pacem in Terris PT* 46–69, 132–45; *PP* 23–24, 33–35, 51–53; *SRS* 42–43; *CA* 44–49). Less central but still emphatic has been their condemnation of avarice and their upholding of the subordination of material riches to spiritual and eschatological riches (*RN* 18f.; *QA* 132, 136; *MM* 245–51; *PP* 19; *SRS* 28). One may also note some concessions to technological liberalism: defense of private property as a (paradigmatic) natural right of persons and families (*RN* 4–10; *QA* 44–45; *MM* 109–12; *PT* 21; *SRS* 42; *CA* 30); ratification of the Lockean theory that property in things is acquired through productive labor, and of the correlative understanding of individuals as proprietors of their own productive capacities (*RN* 34; *QA* 52; *MM* 112; *CA* 31); a conception of property as the indispensable condition and pivotal expression (via work) of the freedom, responsibility, subjectivity, and creativity of rights-bearing individuals made in the image of God—and thus a conception in which property seems, purely and simply, intrinsic to human perfection (*RN* 8; *QA* 49; *MM* 109–12; *PT* 8–27, 80, 86, 139; *PP* 15–16, 27–28; *Gaudium et spes* 71; *Laborem exercens* 4, 7, 10, 15; *CA* 13, 42–43).

The theoretical accomplishment of the Roman synthesis is incontestable. One may nonetheless fear that what has been lost here (excepting the encouraging intimations of John Paul II, e.g., *SRS* 28–29) is a vision of humanity that is less volitional and more contemplative, and that would permit a clearer perception of the flaws intrinsic to every theory of property—as well the brand of sin on every use of property.

● F. Suarez (1612), *Tractatus de legibus ac Deo legislatore,* Ed. L. Peréna, V. Abril, P. Suñer, 8 vols., Madrid, 1971–81.

L. de Molina (1614), *De iustitia et iure,* Köln.

L. Duguit (1912), *Les transformations générales du droit privé,* Paris.

J. B. Kraus (1930), *Scholastik, Puritanismus und Kapitalismus,* Munich-Leipzig.

J. Ellul (1946), *Le fondement théologique du droit,* Neuchâtel-Paris.

H. Borge (1951), *Luther und der Frühkapitalismus,* Gütersloh.

R. Schlatter (1951), *Private Property in Modern Christian Thought,* Urbana, Ill.

B. Tierney (1959), *Medieval Poor Law: A Sketch of Canonical Theory and Its Application in England,* Berkeley, Calif.

C. B. Macpherson (1962), *The Political Theory of Possessive Individualism,* Oxford.

P. Althaus (1965), *Die Ethik Martin Luthers,* Gütersloh.

J. Gilchrist (1969), *The Church and Economic Activity in the Middle Ages,* London.

C. B. MacPherson (Ed.) (1978), *Property: Mainstream and Critical Positions,* Toronto.

R. Tuck (1979), *Natural Rights Theories: Their Origin and Development,* Cambridge.

C. Avil (Ed.) (1983), *Ownership: Early Christian Teaching,* London.

H. J. Berman (1983), *Law and Revolution: The Formation of the Western Legal Tradition,* Cambridge, Mass.

J. L. González (1990), *Faith and Wealth: A History of Early Christian Ideas on the Origin, Significance and Use of Money,* San Francisco.

JOAN L. O'DONOVAN

See also **Authority; Creation; Decalogue; Law and Legislation; Marx, Karl; Utilitarianism; Work**

Prophet and Prophecy

1. Old Testament

In the Delphic oracle, the Pythia's incoherent words had to be translated into intelligible speech and the *prophetès* performed this function. The words

"prophet" and "prophecy" derive from this Greek term. From an anthropological viewpoint, prophetism falls into the sphere of man's desire to lose his uncertainty about the future and of his conviction that the gods—or God*—are willing to reveal their knowledge about it. In this sense, prophecy is closely related to divination. Although similar traits could also be found in Mari and in Greece, biblical prophecy's peculiarity was that God did not restrict himself to answering self-interested requests, but that he required a prescribed behavior. On the other hand, the gods were not in the habit of revealing their will directly themselves, but through go-betweens. In the biblical context, the first mediators were the priests (priesthood*) and the prophets. In early times, the priests played an important oracular role (Jgs 18:5–6 and 1 Sm 14:36–37, 22:10–18, 23:9–12, and 30:7–8). However, the chief mediators for gaining knowledge of God's will were the prophets. They were the only ones to be accepted by the Deuteronomic Code (Dt 18:14–18).

a) Terminology. We use a single word, *prophet,* to refer to people to whom the Bible* gives very different titles: seer *(rô'èh),* visionary *(chôzèh),* man of God *('ish hâ'èlôhîm)* and prophet *(nâvî').* The first two terms (reported, respectively, 11 and 16 times) show that the prophet was always considered to be a person capable of "seeing" what the vast majority could not see. The title man of God (used 76 times) was applied in particular to people such as Elijah, Elisha, Moses, and Samuel, who transmitted God's word* but who were chiefly miracle workers. The most commonly used term is *nâvî'* (used 315 times).

The title *nâvî'* does not imply a high regard for an individual so named; it was also applied to the prophets of Baal and to the false prophets of YHWH. During the course of history the *nâvî'*'s meaning and function has varied, but its chief characteristic is the transmission of another person's—especially God's—words (of YHWH or Baal). The *nâvî'* operated either independently or in a group, but the most ancient information shows him in a group. In this corporative tradition, the prophets of the kingdom of the North are seen gathered about the king, while in the South the center of attention is the Temple of Jerusalem*, which suggests a close relationship with the priests. The phenomenon that the *nâvî'* represents is not homogeneous either in its message or in its manifestations, giving rise to the great quarrels among the prophets. Women could be prophets, and even prophets of great prestige—a very important fact, given that in Israel* women were barred from the priesthood. In certain prophetic movements, as in those of Isaiah or Micah, the term *nâvî'* was not held in great favor; it was more common to speak of "contemplating" *(hâzâh)* rather than of "prophesying."

b) Revelation and Prophecy. The prophetic mediators claimed to know what the average mortal did not know, thanks to God's transmitting to them visions and auditory messages. The prophet did not speak in his own name, but began and ended his speech with expressions such as "oracle of the Lord," "word of the Lord," "thus says the Lord," and "this is what the Lord allowed me to see." These turns of phrase were commonly employed by the prophets throughout the whole of the Ancient East. But the prophet's chief source of knowledge was life itself. When he denounced an evil*, the prophet knew what his contemporaries knew: Naboth's murder (1 Kgs 21) was iniquitous; a military alliance with Egypt was being prepared; stripped of their land, small farmers were reduced to selling themselves into slavery; and people committed injustices and at the same time they visited sanctuaries. The revelation* from God consisted in making visible and audible to the prophet what was voluntarily overlooked, to make him feel how much such acts contravened his will.

In the same way, when the prophets announced a peaceful and hopeful future, there is no reason to conclude that it was a special revelation. In principle, whoever put his faith* in the God who would not abandon his people*, even the sinner, would reach the same certainty. This certainty was not taken for granted however, not even by religious men.

c) Prophet and Society. The prophets had to suffer at the hands of all levels of society*. However, the prophet also found, at least in certain groups, the support that made his mission* possible. Society provided him with a stock of truths* and values: faith in YHWH, this God who was not the prophet's own discovery but inherited from earlier generations; the election of Israel as God's people; the criteria of social justice that made the prophets famous, but which their ancestors had, in large part, bequeathed to them through the cult*, popular wisdom*, the laws (law*). No doubt the prophetic attitude toward the traditions was not simply one of acceptance, as its critical aspect is known. But whether the prophets praised it or condemned it, tradition* was indispensable for understanding their message. The support given to the prophet was sometimes posthumous, in the form of a wreath laid on his tomb, but the fact that prophets existed proves that at least a part of society accepted them. This is evident in the cases of Hosea, Amos, Isaiah, and Jeremiah. However, the clearest testimony to the support that society gave the prophet is seen in the existence of their books (book*), the fruit of patient work* by their disciples and compilers.

Despite the above, in very many instances the prophet challenged various sectors of society. Relations with the kings were always the subject of a power struggle. Samuel consecrated Saul as king (1 Sm 9:1–10:6), but he also deposed him (1 Sm 15). Nathan did not spare David (2 Sm 12). The condemnations brought against the dynasties of the North follow each other from Ahijah of Siloh, through Jehu, Elijah, Micah, Elisha, Hosea, and Amos. In the South, Isaiah harshly opposed the court (Is 3:12–15) and various kings (Is 7 and 39). Jeremiah publicly accused Shallum of being a thief and an assassin (Jer 22:13–19). Ezekiel condemned Zedekiah (Ez 17).

The same conflict raged between the prophets and the priests. Pronouncing God's sentence on Eli (1 Sm 3), Samuel heralded what the conflict between Amos and Amaziah would later become (Am 7:1–17). The conflict raged between Hosea and the priests of his time, whom this prophet accused of rejecting knowledge* of God (Hos 4:4) and of being assassins (Hos 6:9). It also raged between Micah and his contemporaries, whom he denounced for their ambition (Micah 3, 11), and between Jeremiah and Pashhur and the other priests in whom the prophet from Anathoth saw nothing but disinterest in God, abuse of power, fraud, impiety (Jer 2:8, 5:31, 6:13, and 23:11). Even Isaiah, a friend of the priest Zachariah, did not neglect to describe priests as drunkards who had turned their faces from God's will (Is 28:7–13). Zephaniah accused them of profaning the sacred and of violating the law (Zep 3:4), a theme that would reappear literally in Ezekiel (Ez 22:26). To end the history of prophetism, Malachi seems to have adopted Hosea's thinking when he accused the priests of leading the people astray (Malachi 2:8–9).

The other groups who held some form or other of political, economic, or social power were also the victims of the prophets' attacks. But the conflict with the false prophets was even more violent. This group included not only the prophets of Baal, but also, and foremost, those who spoke in the name of YHWH without him having spoken to them and without him having sent them (see 1 Kgs 22, Jer 6:13–15, 14:13–16, 23:9–32, Ez 13:1–23, 22:28–31, and Mi 3:5–11).

d) History of the Prophetic Movement. The phenomenon of prophetism is clearly attested in Mesopotamia (especially in the town of Mari) and in Canaan. It is probable that the first prophets of Israel were inspired by these individuals. Although the title was later applied to Moses and Abraham, the Israelite prophetic movement must have emerged with Samuel in the eleventh century B.C. During the ninth century, Elijah and Elisha, as well as a group of anonymous prophets, played a primary role. However, the golden age of prophecy was the eighth century with Amos, Hosea,

Isaiah, and Micah. Their activities extended to all domains, including denunciation of idolatry* and of the false cult of YHWH, orientation of domestic and foreign policies, and exhortations to practice social justice. After a period of silence, prophecy sprang vigorously to life again at the end of the seventh century, and at the beginning of the sixth century, when the kingdom of Judah was moving toward catastrophe. It was at this time that Zephaniah, Habakkuk, Jeremiah, and Ezekiel appeared. The end of what are generally seen as prophecies of doom or condemnation came with the exile to Babylon. Such a negative view of these prophecies calls for reservations, but it is clear that the prophets before the exile were concerned, above all, with denouncing and condemning the many faults they found in the society of their times and of pointing out the consequences of continuing in these faults.

With the exile to Babylon there began what can be called the prophecy of salvation. The old threats had been realized, and God was announcing forgiveness. Jeremiah's words "There is hope for your future" (Jer 31:17) could sum up the prophets' message after the exile. During the years of exile (586–538 B.C.), Ezekiel and the Deutero-Isaiah encouraged their contemporaries with promises (promise*) of a return to their country, of the reconstruction of the ruined towns (especially of Jerusalem), and of a life of peace* and freedom* under the authority of a descendent of David (a new David sometimes portrayed in an ideal light). Later prophets—Haggai, Zechariah, and Trito-Isaiah—adopted these themes, sometimes accompanied by a serious call to practice love* and justice—caring for those in need is the the fast that is "acceptable to the Lord" (Is 58:1–12). Sometimes there was a subtle criticism against the reigning xenophobia (the case of Jonah), but a message of hope was paramount.

From the fifth century onward prophecy lost its impetus, then vanished completely. Several explanations for this have been suggested. Some think that prophecy had evolved toward the apocalyptic. Others base their theories on sociology: the role of prophecy might have reached the point of losing the people's acceptance. According to D. S. Russel (1964), the most important causes of the decline of prophecy were: 1) the canonization of the law (Pentateuch), which gave the word of God clearly, dispensing with the need for prophets; 2) the impoverishment of prophetic themes, which were often too centered on a distant future and almost incapable of speaking of the present in the ancient prophets' incisive way; 3) the growing swarm of religions featuring salvation, with their wise men and soothsayers, whom the people often equated with prophets.

In any event, prophecy continued to enjoy great prestige in Israel, but with an important difference. The esteem was limited to past and future prophets. The Israelites held the prophets of earlier times in high esteem and they expected a great prophet in the future (1 Macc 4:46 and 14:41). According to an early trend, it would be a prophet like Moses (Dt 18:18); another wave expected Elijah's return (Mal 4:5). For the Christians these hopes would be realized with the advent of John the Baptist and Jesus*.

2. New Testament

The Christian message based itself firmly on the prophets of the Old Testament, mentioned abundantly as a single block turned toward the New Testament (Lk 24:25–27, Acts 3:18–24, Rom 1:2, 1 Pt 1:10, 2 Pt 1:19f, etc.). The most frequent quotations are those from the prophets or the Psalms*—for David was a prophet (Acts 2:29–30). The Jewish authorities and the people wondered whether the "prophet like me" announced by Moses (Dt 18:15) was John the Baptist (Jn 1:21) or Jesus (Jn 6:14), as a sermon by Peter* suggests (Acts 3:22–26) The coming of John the Baptist was regarded as the high point of the whole line of prophets (Mt 11:13). Jesus' deeds were reminiscent of Elijah and Elisha, his words and the effect they produced brought to mind the prophets of the past (Lk 24:19). Jesus himself even compared himself to them (Mt 13:57, and parallels, and Lk 13:33). But there was a radical difference: Jesus did not preface his teachings with "oracle of YHWH" or "thus says the Lord," but *"I say to you."* He issued an invitation to follow him *(akolouthein)* and to believe in him, which was unprecedented.

The Sermon on the Mount included all the disciples among the heirs of the prophets (Mt 5:11). The attribution of the title varies. On the Pentecost after Jesus' resurrection, the Holy* Spirit bestowed the gift of prophecy (Acts 2:17–18; *see also* 19:6) on the whole community, which was made up of the symbolic number of 120 people (Acts 1:15). According to Ephesians 2:20 and 3:5, apostles (apostle*) and prophets were the foundations. But the list of gifts in Romans 12:6 and in 1 Corinthians 14:1 places the prophets in first place; 1 Corinthians 12:28 and Ephesians 4:11 put them immediately after the apostles, and specify their role, distinguishing them from the thaumaturges and those who spoke in tongues. Acts mentions several prophets (Acts 11:27–28, 13:1–2, 15:32, and 19:6). There were also prophetesses, including the aged Anne, who resides in the Temple (Lk 2:36), the four daughters of Philip the evangelist (Acts 21:9), and others (Acts 2:17–18 and 1 Cor 11:5). That there were false prophets even in Christianity seems to have been part of their contemporary experience* (Mt 7:15, 7:22–23, 24:11, and 24:24; Lk 6:26; and 1 Jn 4:1). The false prophets from the whole span of history* are gathered together in a symbolic image in Revelation 16:13, 19: 20, and 21:10.

- A. Guillaume (1938), *Prophecy and Divination among the Hebrews and Other Semites,* London.
- A. Neher (1955), *L'essence du prophétisme,* Paris.
- O. Cullmann (1958), *Christologie du Nouveau Testament,* 18–47.
- G. Friedrich (1959), "*Prophêtês.* Neues Testament,"*ThWNT* 6, 829–63.
- A.J. Heschel (1962), *The Prophets,* London.
- J. Lindblom (1962), *Prophecy in Ancient Israel,* Oxford.
- D.S. Russell (1964), *The Method and Message of Jewish Apocalyptic,* Philadelphia.
- S. Herrmann (1965), *Die prophetische Heilserwartungen im Alten Testament,* Stuttgart.
- G. von Rad (1967), *Die Botschaft der Propheten,* Munich.
- L. Monloubou (1968), *Prophète qui es-tu? Le prophétisme avant les prophètes,* Paris.
- C. Westermann (1971), *Grundformen prophetischer Rede,* Munich.
- L. Ramlot (1972), "Prophétisme," *DBS* 8, 811–1222.
- J. Delorme (Ed.) (1974), *Le ministère et les ministères selon le Nouveau Testament,* Paris.
- P. Beauchamp (1976), *L'Un et l'Autre Testament: Essai de lecture,* Paris, 74–105; 214–18.
- J. Bright (1977), *Covenant and Promise: The Future in the Preaching of the Pre-exilic Prophets,* London.
- W. Brueggemann (1978), *The Prophetic Imagination,* Philadelphia.
- R.R. Wilson (1980), *Prophecy and Society in Ancient Israel,* Philadelphia.
- C. Tresmontant (1982), *Le prophétisme hébreu,* Paris.
- T.W. Overholt (1986), *Prophecy in Cross-Cultural Perspective,* Atlanta.
- C. Westermann (1987), *Prophetische Heilsworte im Alten Testament,* Göttingen.
- J.L. Sicre (1992), *Profetismo en Israel,* Estella.
- W. Klein et al. (1997), "Propheten/Prophetie," *TRE* 27, 473–517.

JOSÉ LUIS SICRE

See also **Apostle; City; Eschatology; Ethics; Hardening; Holy Spirit; Judgment; Justice; Law and Christianity; Messianism/Messiah; Ministry; Parousia; People of God; Promise; Revelations, Individual; Scripture, Fulfillment of; Word**

Proportionalism

Proportionalism, a term used in Catholic moral theology*, designates a theory of the concrete, material norms for human action*. Its proponents seek a more satisfactory basis for moral judgment* than that given in manuals of theology, which, in their view, relies on an unduly physical interpretation of human action and natural law. P. Knauer proposed the initial idea in 1965. J. Fuchs, L. Janssens, R. A. McCormick, B. Schüller, and many others developed the notion, gaining it wide influence, especially in Germany and in English-speaking countries. Proportionalism is more than a revision, it is a revolution within moral theology, because it denies that certain acts are intrinsically evil. Not surprisingly, therefore, it has many critics (e.g., S. Pinckaers, M. Rhonheimer, J. Finnis).

Despite differences among proponents of proportionalism, there are some points on which they generally agree. For them, a conception of the person*, understood in all its dimensions, is the fundamental norm. Thus, actions are morally good if they contribute to the good* of persons; actions that undermine the good of persons are morally wrong. One is obligated to avoid moral evil*—for example, inducing another to violate his or her conscience*—but there is also an obligation to avoid causing evils such as poverty, illness or death*. As evils like these may be the effects of human action, or since their existence may push us to act to rectify them, they are morally relevant, although they do not constitute moral evil. Proportionalism refers to such evils as "premoral" or "ontic."

According to a more traditional view, the analysis of an act must be made from the perspective of the person choosing. Thus, the object of the act must be considered as being related to free choice, and therefore belonging to the moral order. Such a view has no place for the notion of the "premoral." A distinction, however, is made between morally significant acts and others that are morally neutral. The perspective of proportionalism is different. Here, an observer seeks to evaluate an act that has been or could have been performed in certain circumstances. One may identify an evil (e.g., a death). This is not morally neutral, but, at this point of the analysis, it is not known whether a moral evil is entailed or not, because all the circumstances have not yet been considered.

For proportionalism, causing premoral evil may be justified for "proportionate" reasons. Moral evil arises when a premoral evil is permitted or caused without a proportionate reason.

Proportionalism also adopts the distinction between "goodness" and "rectitude." "Goodness" refers to the sincere striving of the subject to do good, "rectitude" to those actions that are proportioned to this end. A person may be good, and yet, through error or incapacity, perform an act that is not right. It is goodness that is moral. However, one is obligated to strive toward rightness; it must therefore be considered as moral in a derived or analogous sense, and not as merely premoral.

The term *proportion* is taken from the "principle of double effect" (intention*), according to which an act that produces both good and bad effects can be justified under certain conditions. One of these conditions is that there should be "proportion" between the act and its end, for example, between an act of violence* and legitimate defense, or between its good and bad effects. Proportionalism makes everything depend on this notion alone, without taking into account the other conditions.

According to traditional Catholic theology, certain actions are intrinsically evil by reason of their object, independently of circumstances, consequences, or the intention of the person who acts. For proportionalism, however, it is impossible to designate an action as intrinsically evil in the abstract. Only after one has considered all aspects, especially the consequences and the intention, can one make such a judgment. Proportionalism accepts that there are acts that are wrong by reason of their object, for example, murder or stealing, but it requires that this object be determined teleologically. Thus, not every killing is murder, since for there to be a murder it is necessary that the action is chosen without a proportionate reason like self-defense. Some evils are such that it is impossible to conceive of a proportionate reason that could justify them, and they are thus prohibited "with no exception."

Traditionally, certain actions are wrong because they are contrary to the natural law, infringe on the divine dominion over life, or cause harmful consequences. For proportionalism, it is the last consideration that ultimately counts: it is in the consequences of the act that one must seek criteria of judgment. Proportionalism is therefore classed with consequentialism and utilitarianism* as a "teleological" theory. However, a moral judgment may not be based on consequences only; it must equally include consideration of the intention and the way in which the act is carried out. Hence, proportionalism is sometimes referred to as "mixed consequentialism." Further, while proportionalism agrees with utilitarianism that values are to be maximized, for proportionalism these are objective values, founded in the nature of the person, and not merely preferences or interests. Nevertheless, some see in the requirement to maximize or "produce" results a form of "technical" or instrumental reason* that is typical of utilitarianism.

Some claim that, according to proportionalism, good intentions can make a morally wrong act right. Proponents of proportionalism reject this charge, and insist that they are not defending relativism*. They hold that an act that is morally wrong (in their terms, because it brings about premoral evil without a proportionate reason) cannot be transformed into a good act by intention.

A major objection brought against proportionalism is that it does not offer any means of evaluating proportion. To establish a proportion, one must measure goods and evils in relation to each other; but these are often incommensurable. Proportionalism replies that proportion does not require measuring, but interpreting the relation of the act to the value sought. Proportion is absent if the act contradicts or undermines that value in the long term. However, the long-term effects of our actions depend on unpredictable factors, such as what others may or may not choose to do, and they therefore elude the assessment that is needed to establish proportion. Contemporary moral theology, while not ignoring the question of norms, is more concerned with developing an ethics* of virtues*.

John Paul II's 1993 encyclical, *Veritatis Splendor,* rejects proportionalism, which it identifies with consequentialism. Proportionalism is held to be without basis in the Catholic tradition (§75–83).

●P. Knauer (1965), "La détermination du bien et du mal moral par le principe du double effet," *NRTh* 87, 356–76.
B. Schüller (1970), "Zur Problematik allgemein verbindlicher ethischer Grundsätze," *ThPh* 45, 1–23.
J. Fuchs (1971), "The Absoluteness of Moral Terms," *Gr* 52, 415–58.
L. Janssens (1972), "Ontic Evil and Moral Evil," *LouvSt* 4, 115–56.
R. A. McCormick, P. Ramsey (1978), *Doing Evil to Achieve Good*: *Moral Choice in Conflict Situations,* Chicago.
♦S. Pinckaers (1982), "La question des actes intrinsèquement mauvais et le 'proportionnalisme,'" *RThom* 82, 181–212.
B. Hoose (1987), *Proportionalism*: *The American Debate and Its European Roots,* Washington.
M. Rhonheimer (1987), *Natur als Grundlage der Moral*: *Eine Auseinandersetzung mit autonomer und teleologischer Ethik,* Innsbrück.
J. Finnis (1991), *Moral Absolutes*: *Tradition, Revision, and Truth,* Washington.

BRIAN JOHNSTONE

See also **Decalogue; Ethics; Good; Prudence; Utilitarianism**

Protestantism

a) "Protestantism" generally covers the range of Christian churches (church*) that owe their origins, directly or indirectly, to the Reformation of the 16th century. At the second Diet of Speyer (1529) the representatives of the Reformers "protested" in favor of the liberty* of individuals to choose their own religion according to their conscience. Their opponents described them as "Protestants," while they preferred to call themselves "evangelicals." In France the 16th article of an edict issued on 14 May 1576 compelled the use of the term *la religion prétendue réformée* ("the so-called reformed religion") in all official statements and acts. Such official labels were used alongside alternatives, such as "the Protestant religion" or "the Protestant Church," from the 17th century onward; the term *Protestantism* came into widespread use in the 19th century.

Protestantism is not a church, and the various churches that are covered by the term—whether Lutheran, Calvinist, Methodist, Anabaptist*, Baptist*,

Pentecostalist, or other—are not all in communion* with each other. Nor does Protestantism have precisely drawn frontiers: for example, there is controversy within Anglicanism* as to whether it belongs within the Protestant fold. Protestantism has generally been held to exclude such diverse sects as the Jehovah's Witnesses, the Plymouth Brethren, the New Apostolic Church, or the Mormons.

b) Despite its numerous components, and its pluralism, Protestantism may be characterized by reference to certain widely shared convictions. Priority is given to salvation*, and to justification* by faith* alone. Believers are justified before God* not by their works* or their merit, but by grace* alone. The Bible* provides the exclusive standard for the Christian life, and derives its meaning from its central figure, Jesus* Christ, the sole mediator between God and human beings. Faith consists, not in acceptance of a doctrine, but in a living and personal relationship with God. The Church is a community of believers who have committed themselves to listening to the word* of God and to celebrating the sacraments (sacrament*) together. Only baptism* and the Lord's Supper (the Eucharist*) are recognized as sacraments, since they were instituted by Jesus Christ himself.

Protestants are convinced that unceasing reform of the Church is required, but they have some distrust with regard to the institutional dimensions of the Church. A Protestant Church may be governed by synods or other collegiate bodies, or by bishops (bishop*) or other types of officials, and the decisions of these authorities are imposed on all believers, but they can and should be continuously revised in the light of the biblical message. While Protestantism does not reject the need for a ministry* of universal unity, from the very beginning it has opposed the way in which this ministry has been exercised by the popes (pope*). The Catholic redefinition of the papacy at Vatican* I (1870) only intensified the Protestant rejection of all claims that the Catholic magisterium* is endowed with either infallibility* or primacy of jurisdiction*. Protestantism insists on the priesthood* of all baptized believers, although it does not question the need for specific forms of ministry. Nevertheless, the Church and its ministers always remain secondary to the message of salvation, the sole criterion of the authenticity of any Christian and ecclesial life.

The Protestant emphasis on grace has as its ethical corollary (ethics*) a strong commitment to witness and service in this world. Ethical choices are not defined once and for all, but result from constant attention, both individual and communal, to the word of God in concrete situations. The Church is not to extend its authority over society*: rather, the Church is at the service of a world that has its own raison d'être.

c) The study of Protestantism as a social phenomenon made its appearance during the 18th century. Johann Gottfried von Herder (1744–1803) considered freedom of conscience to be the fundamental principle of Protestantism, while Hegel* singled out individual freedom. Ernst Troeltsch (1865–1923) argued that Protestantism had made a decisive contribution to the formulation of the democratic ideals of the modern world. According to Troeltsch, the roots of "neo-Protestantism" were not limited to the ideals of the Reformation, but also included the heritage of the Enlightenment and the French Revolution. In *Die protestantische Ethik und der Geist des Kapitalismus (The Protestant Ethic and the Spirit of Capitalism)*, Max Weber (1864–1920) developed the controversial view that there was a particular affinity between the ascetic ethics of Calvinist Protestantism and the mentality of capitalist entrepreneurs. He also argued that, by desacralizing the priesthood and every other ecclesial institution, Protestantism had played an important role in the modern "disenchantment" of the world. Paul Tillich* interpreted Protestantism as a prophetic critique of every structure of power, whether religious or secular: Protestantism, which advocated every secularized form of grace, had been betrayed, in part, by those who claimed to represent it but were incapable of being satisfied with its institutional and dogmatic "weakness."

d) Precisely because of its sheer multitude of forms and the many divisions within it, which primarily concern questions of ecclesiology*, Protestantism has always been confronted with the problem of *ecumenism**. Ever since the Reformation there has been a desire for the assembling of a universal council*, and both the modern ecumenical movement and the establishment of the World Council of Churches originated within Protestantism. Protestantism seeks a reconciliation of the churches through respect for their legitimate and desirable diversity; its concern is not merely with church unity* but with the unity and reconciliation of the whole of humanity. However, there is fierce controversy within Protestantism itself over the ways in which this goal might be achieved. The permanent role of Protestantism remains: to act as vigilant critic of the whole of life, in society and in the Church, in the light of the gospel of Jesus Christ alone.

● P. Tillich (1950), *Der Protestantismus: Prinzip und Wirklichkeit*, Stuttgart.

E. G. Léonard (1961–64), *Histoire générale du protestantisme*, Paris.

J. Baubérot, J.-P. Willaime (1990), *ABC du protestantisme*, Geneva.

R. Mehl (1991), "Protestantism," in N. Lossky et al. (Ed.), *Dictionary of the Ecumenical Movement*, Geneva, 830–38.

J.-P. Willaime (1992), *La précarité protestante: Sociologie du protestantisme contemporain*, Geneva.

P. Gisel (1995) (Ed.), *Encyclopédie du protestantisme*, Geneva-Paris.

H. Fisher, F. W. Graf (1997), "Protestantismus," *TRE* 27, 542–80.

L. Gagnebin (1997), *Le protestantisme*, Paris.

T. Wanegffelen (1998), *Ni Rome ni Genève: Des fidèles entre deux chaires en France au XVIe siècle*, Paris.

ANDRÉ BIRMELÉ

See also **Anabaptists; Anglicanism; Baptists; Calvinism; Catholicism; Ecumenism; Family, Confessional; Lutheranism; Methodism; Orthodoxy; Pentecostalism; World Council of Churches**

Protocatholicism

1. History of Research

The question of protocatholicism, or *Frühkatholizmus,* is principally a matter of concern for German Protestant exegesis*. It emerged with the *Aufklärung* (Enlightenment), was developed by the liberal tradition (Troeltsch, Harnack), and then taken up by Bultmann* and his students (in particular Käsemann). Protocatholicism should be understood as denoting theological tendencies emerging in the last quarter of the first century, "tendencies which are perceptible in almost all the ecclesiastical writings of the second century, and which were essential components of later Catholicism" (Luz 1974).

2. Sources and Chronology

Protocatholicism is known through New Testament writings (except for Paul's Epistles), the apostolic* Fathers, and the oldest apocryphal* Gospels*. The historical delimitation of the phenomenon is a matter of controversy. The protocatholic period begins with the disappearance of the first Christian generation (fall of Jerusalem*; death of Paul and Peter*) and concludes in the late second century with the establishment of the canon.

3. Criteria

a) Reference to the Apostolic Tradition. Because the apostolic age was retrospectively considered as the founding past of the faith*, the tradition* of the apostles (apostle*) thereafter took on a normative function. Whoever claimed adherence to them and their message and took his place in their succession had authority* in the Church*. Among the consequences of this were the development of the literary genre of the apostolic letter as expression of the truth* (*see* the deutero-Pauline and Catholic letters) and the creation of the canon.

b) Distinction between Orthodoxy and Heresy. Whereas in its earliest formulations, primitive Christianity was multifarious, protocatholicism was characterized by the concern to distinguish between true and false teaching; the criterion of truth* then became conformity to the apostolic tradition.

c) Emphasis on Ethics. Parenesis (moral exhortation) occupies a central place in protocatholic writings; it is aimed at a better integration of Christians in the world. It tends to become an autonomous discourse containing its own basis: the dialectics of the indicative and the imperative (e.g., "you are light in the Lord. Walk as children of light" [Ephesians 5:8]) loses its force.

d) Development of Institutional Ecclesiology. It became more important to think about the visible organization of the Church. This development was particularly perceptible at the level of ordained ministries (ministry*) and their hierarchical organization. Having begun as regulatory, the legal order became foundational.

e) Delay in the Parousia. The expectation of the imminent return of Christ faded, although the apocalyptic framework was formally maintained. The relationship to the world* and to history* was thereby changed.

f) Theological Significance. This is a matter of controversy (Küng 1962). Three aspects deserve mention: 1) Protocatholicism is an indisputable fact of the post-apostolic age, although not its exclusive characteristic (Hahn 1978). 2) It is not a deviation from primitive Christianity, because it is already evident in the New Testament (see in particular the writings of Luke, the pastoral and Catholic Epistles, but also Paul [Käsemann 1965]). 3) Protocatholicism in this sense constitutes a possible form of the reception of nascent Christianity.

• R. Bultmann (1958), *Theologie des Neuen Testaments,* Tübingen, 446–587.
E. Käsemann (1960), "Eine Apologie der urchristlichen Eschatologie," *Exegetische Versuche und Besinnungen,* Göttingen, vol. 1, 135–57; id. (1965), "Paulus und der Frühkatholizismus," ibid., vol. 2, 239–52.
H. Küng (1962), "Der Frühkatholizismus im Neuen Testament als kontroverstheologisches Problem," *ThQ* 142, 385–424.
U. Luz (1974), "Erwägungen zur Entstehung des Frühkatholizismus: Eine Skizze," *ZNW* 65, 88–111.
F. Hahn (1978), "Das Problem des Frühkatholizismus," *EvTh* 38, 340–57.
R. E. Brown (1984), *The Church the Apostles Left Behind,* New York.
K. Kertelge (1995), "Frühkatholizismus," *LThK3* 4, 201–4.

JEAN ZUMSTEIN

See also **Apostolic Fathers; Apostolic Succession; Authority; Catholicism; Ecclesiology; Eschatology; Gospels; Hierarchy; Ministry; Parousia; Tradition**

Providence

The word *providence* designates the way in which God* rules the world according to his purposes. In the broad sense, providence concerns all of creation*; more narrowly, humanity; and still more specifically, the direction of history*. Anthropocentrism has been an essential characteristic of the concept of providence from the beginning, but the idea of a general design of providence in and through history dates from the 18th century.

1. Antiquity

a) Greek World. The concept of providence is traditionally traced back to Anaxagoras. However, although for him mind (*noûs*) has full knowledge of everything" and "orders all things" (*fr.* 12), purpose plays no role. So much so, indeed, that in his *Phaedo* Plato has Socrates say that Anaxagoras "made no use of mind and assigned to it no causality for the order of the world, but adduced causes like air and æther and water and many other absurdities" (*Phaedo* 98 b-c; see *Laws* 896 e-907b-c).

Although the earliest mentions of providence are in Plato, the concept of *pronoia* occurs explicitly in the Stoics, particularly from time of Chrysippus (third century B.C.) and Xeno (third and second centuries B.C.). According to Cicero (*On the Nature of the Gods* II. 14. 37, *SVF* II. 332), Chrysippus, the proponent of a resolute anthropomorphism (Isnardi Parente 1993), argued that everything has a cause, and that vegetables exist for animals* and animals for man (*see also* ibid.).

According to Diodorus (Theiler 1982), the Stoic Posidonius (135–51 B.C.) stated that "by virtue of the relations among human families, it happens that distant peoples unknown to one another aspire to the same political system, making themselves into instruments and concomitant causes of the providential government of the cosmos*" (*see* Isnardi Parente 1993).

Cicero, who had heard Posidonius in 78 BC, expresses the idea that the world "is created and directed by divine providence" (*On the Nature of the Gods* III. 92, *SVF* II. 322) and that "it must therefore be governed by their [the gods'] will and their providence" (II. 80., *SVF* II. 327; see II. 154, *SVF* II. 328). Cicero also sketches a theodicy in which he clearly distinguishes between the goods (good*) that the gods give us and the use that we make of them (III. 70, *SVF* II. 341). Plutarch (46–127), for his part, argued against the materialist determinism of the atomists with the Stoic concept of *pronoia* (*Isis and Osiris* c. 45. 369a, *SVF* II. 322).

The concept of *pronoia* was transmitted to theology* by Philo of Alexandria (c. 13 B.C.–54 A.D.). According to his *De opficio mundi,* God created man as "the most familiar and precious being" (§77), and has arranged everything so that nothing is lacking for either his material or his spiritual life*. The same assertion is found in his *De Providentia,* which attributes to the Creator wisdom* and providence, by means of which he takes care of all things (*De Providentia* I. §25). The harmony of the universe is evidence of the universal providence that invisibly moves everything (I. §32) as the soul (soul*-heart-body) moves the human body (I. §40). God created the sun, moon, and planets to provide a rhythm for time and to stabilize the cycles that are useful for the generation of animals and the growth of plants (II. §57). God wanted the Earth to occupy the center of the cosmos. That is why divine providence has given it a spherical shape (II. §62). Air, humidity, and the fixed stars have all been made for a precise purpose (II. §§64, 67, 73, 76, 84). God does not act as a tyrant, but as a king, like a father toward his sons, by adding to the immutable laws of nature the government and preservation of things. God protects the religious man, but also grants the dissolute man the time to redeem himself. In this context, the ideas of providence and divine justice* are linked, inaugurating a connection among soteriology, theodicy, and the doctrine of providence that is typical of Judaism* and Christianity.

Plotinus (205–70) made *pronoia* one of the central concepts of his philosophy* and devoted an entire treatise to it (in two parts, *Enneads* III. 2 and 3). According to him, the belief that the world had a beginning "would imply a foreseeing and a reasoned plan on the part of God providing for the production of the Universe and securing all possible perfection in it" (III. 2. 1). But, given that the world is eternal, providence is "a universal consonance with the divine Intelligence" (ibid.)The soul of the world, according to the supreme Reason* that governs all and makes "harmony and beauty*" reign (III. 2. 17), assigns to each man his role, but it is up to the human actor to play it, and this is why he is responsible for his actions (action*) (ibid.). Vice thus has its usefulness, because punishment for it serves as an example (III. 2. 5), even though evil* in itself is nothing but privation (ibid.). This is clearly a more refined theodicy than that of Cicero. The inequality of various regions of the universe contributes to the harmony of the whole (III. 2. 17). "The universe is organized with the foresight of a general" (III. 3. 2), and each being is perfect in itself inasmuch as it is in accordance with its own nature (III. 3. 3). If a being is less perfect than others, that comes not from a deficiency in its Principle, but from a weakening of the effects of that Principle as it gets closer and closer to matter (ibid.). Beings have no need of equality in order for providence to be equal; what is important is that everything is linked in the universe, "just as in some individual animal, linked from first to last" (III. 3. 5)

(Isnardi Parente 1989). Porphyry (232–304), a disciple of Plotinus, also adopted Stoic anthropocentrism (*De abstinentia* III. 20, *SVF* II. 332).

b) Old Testament and Hellenistic Jewish Circles. The Old Testament gives a central place to man—particularly at the beginning of Genesis—and God's historical action toward Israel*, his chosen people*, is one of its fundamental themes, but the concept of providence is not brought out on its own account. Passages used to support the opposite argument (e.g., in Schmid 1965) are not persuasive. Genesis 22:8–14, for example, does not refer to the concept of providence: the Hebrew term *r'h* ("to see") means "to choose for someone" in verse 8, and in verse 14 "appear," in the sense that God has manifested himself to Abraham. In both these cases the Septuagint (ancient Greek translation of the Bible) faithfully translates using *horaô*. Job 5:18–22 expresses a general concept of God's salvific action at dangerous or difficult moments (Weiser 1980), without using any technical term. In Job 10:12, God "watches with care" over the spirit of Job. The verb *pqd* indeed means "to take care," "to be concerned," but there is no question of an organizing intelligence. In Jeremiah 1:5 it is said that God had chosen Jeremiah as a prophet* even before his birth. The passage is certainly significant because, even in the absence of a technical term, it indicates an idea of prescience and foresight. Proverbs 16:4 is an affirmation of divine omnipotence* (Ringgren and Zimmerli 1980). Psalm 16:8 expresses faith* in the nearness of God. Psalm 145 (verses 8f. and15f.) celebrates God the provider of everything good (*see also* Ps 147:9). Judith 16:3–5 recalls how the Lord used a woman* to defeat the enemies of Israel. In short, there is nothing in these passages that clearly indicates a fully developed concept of providence, even though many of their elements were later adopted and integrated into a theology that inherited the concept of providence from the Greeks.

The case is entirely different in the Wisdom of Solomon, which was written in Greek in Alexandria toward the end of the second century B.C. (Schmitt 1986) in a milieu close to that of Philo. Providence is mentioned in three passages. The first, "for the Lord of all . . . takes thought [*pronoei*] for all alike (Wis 6:7) is the least significant, because the verb *pronoei* may be related to the Hebrew *pqd*. The term *pronoia* appears for the first time, in speaking the ship of Wisdom: "but it is thy providence [*pronoia*], O Father, that steers its course" (Wis 14:3). Interpreters agree in seeing the influence of Greek thought in this verse (*see* note on the passage in the French version of the Jerusalem Bible; Schmitt, 116–17). Finally, Wisdom 17:2 once again mentions *pronoia*.

c) New Testament. The theme of God taking care of human beings even in small matters is well developed in the New Testament (see particularly Mt 6:30–32 and 10:29–31). But in this case too the concept of *pronoia* is not adduced for its own sake.

Acts 2:23 uses the term *prognôsis,* or "prescience"; God knows things in advance and thus "what seems to be free action by Jews and Gentiles (the crucifixion of Christ*) comes to pass because God had foreseen it" (Barrett 1994). Acts 4:28 uses the term *proôrizein* (predetermine, arrange in advance). It is noteworthy that here Luke "is not thinking of determinism in general but of the specific revelation* of God's purposes in the history of Jesus*" (Barrett).

Ephesians 1:4, sometimes invoked as evidence (Schmid 1965), deals with the choice* of the Church* and its members even before creation (Barbaglio 1985; *see also* Jer 1:5 and Acts 2:23).

New Testament writings are concerned principally with what happened with Jesus, and are very far from the concept of *pronoia* or the rational government of the universe (Bultmann 1953). But Hellenistic Christianity soon adopted it, as Hellenistic Judaism had done; this had perhaps already happened by the time of Paul, or in any case shortly afterward. Nevertheless, the first Christian document to use it, probably in 95 or 96, is Clement of Rome's *Epistle to the Corinthians* (SC 167).

2. Patristic Age

The concept of *pronoia* occupies a central place in Christian thought of the first millennium; Christian liberty* was contrasted by the Fathers* of the Church and the early Scholastics to the pagan belief in fate *(heimarmenè).* They emphasized both man's autonomy and freedom in the government of his own life and the voluntary and intelligent action of providence in the government of the universe. Clement of Alexandria (c. 150–c. 215), strongly influenced by Philo, says that "God provides for everything" (*The Pedagogue* I. 8, SC 70) and that God made of man a specially chosen creature (ibid., I. 3). Origen*, a student of Clement, affirms that "the world exists thanks to providence" (*Contra Celsius* IV. 79, SC 136). And he explicitly refers back to the Stoics for the assertion (ibid., IV. 54 and 74) that all creatures exist for man.

Augustine* too inherited the Stoic concept of providence (Flasch 1994). He writes, for example: "I always retained belief both that you are and that you care for us" (*Confessions* VI. v (8); see VII. vii (11). In *The City of God,* speaking of the unequal condition of the rulers and the ruled, he explains that this inequality was not produced by chance but following a clearly determined order, an order arranged by God's sovereign power, which gives earthly or eternal happiness only to those who deserve it (IV. 23; a passage of great interest because it explicitly brings together the theme of providence and the theme of election, hence the predestination* of the just to salvation*). Augustine subsequently refers to a passage already used by Philo and the school of Alexandria*, according to which God has ordered all things "by measure and number and weight" (Wis 11:20). The Creator has thus given form and beauty to everything, and there is therefore nothing outside the laws of divine providence (*City of God* V. 11). In speaking of the beauty of created things and the fact that they reveal divine providence, Augustine refers explicitly to Plotinus (X. 14). In the same passage he quotes Matthew 6:28ff. Contrary to common understanding, Augustine has no notion of the action of providence in history. The succession of peoples and civilizations seems to him to be the result of chance, and unrelated to the problem of human destiny. After the sack of Rome* in 410, he intends to show in *The City of God* the struggle between the two kingdoms and the election of the just, but he attributes to history neither an immanent meaning nor an ultimate direction (Flasch).

At the juncture of Antiquity and the Middle Ages, Boethius* is convinced that God rules the world according to eternal reason (*perpetua mundum rationi gubernas*) (*Consolation of Philosophy* III. 9), and in his definition of providence, he clearly identifies it with divine intelligence:

"Providence is divine reason itself which, established in the one who is the sovereign principle of all things, orders them all—*providentia est ipsa illa divina ratio in summo omnium principe constituta, quae cuncta disponit* (IV. 6). For him it is not chance but the order of things that flows from the fount of providence (*de providentiae fonte*) (V. 1).

3. Middle Ages

Averroës (1126–98) holds that nothing happens by chance and in particular that the Primal Intelligence links what occurs in the sublunary sphere to the movements of the heavenly bodies. Hence, evils either prevent greater evils or are in themselves positive phenomena that accidentally bring about negative consequences. Providence is revealed principally in man, who could not preserve himself without reason. Taking his inspiration from Alexander of Aphrodisias (late second-early third centuries) and Aristotle, Averroës holds that providence has nothing to do with particular things and hence nothing to do with individuals (Baffioni 1991).

For Maimonides (1135–1204), nothing either good or evil happens to a human being if he has not deserved it, because God always acts with perfect justice (*Guide for the Perplexed,* 463–64). It is sometimes "love* that punishes," by inflicting a punishment that causes even greater delight in the future reward (464–65). Against Averroës, Maimonides holds that providence concerns only human beings and not natural events, which are subject to chance; if they affect men, this is because God uses them according to his will and his justice to reward or punish (465–66). Providence is thus in the service of Intelligence (469).

Scholasticism* inherited the problematics of late Antiquity and systematized it. For Thomas* Aquinas providence depends as much on divine knowledge as on divine will. According to him, the good of things consists not only in their substance but also in their being ordered to an end (which clearly depends not only on the will but also on the intelligence of God). Echoing Boethius, Thomas holds that it is necessary that the reason for this order preexist in the divine mind before it is created. This is precisely the definition of providence: *ratio autem ordinandorum in finem, proprie providentia est* (*ST* Ia. q. 22. a. 1). It is not only the universe as a whole that is subject to providence, but also all beings and all particular events (*ST* Ia. q. 22. a. 2). But on the question of whether God provides immediately for everything, Thomas partially follows Averroës in saying that if it is a question of determining the purpose of all things then God provides directly for everything; but in the matter of bringing about those purposes he rules the inferior by means of the superior, in order to give to created beings "the dignity of causality" (*ST* Ia. q. 23. a. 3). Predestination is a part of providence (*ST* Ia. q. 23. a. 1 and a. 4).

4. Modern and Contemporary Periods

a) 16th and 17th Centuries. Modern times raised different sets of questions, particularly because of the influence of Ockham (c. 1285–1349), amplified by the Reformation (Auletta 1995). Ockham's voluntarism* on questions of both ontology and ethics is potentially in conflict with the Greek idea of an ordering intelligence. For him, the concept of providence is generally subordinated to that of predestination* (*Tr. de Predestinatione, Opera philosophica* II, 510–11, 514, 520–26). And because of questions raised by the Reformation, the problem of the relationship between providence and predestination, theodicy and freedom, became central for modern thought. Examples of this can be found in Molina (Bañezianism*-Molinism-Baianism) for Catholicism* and Leibniz* for Protestantism*.

Molina adopts Thomas's distinctions and asserts that providence concerns the relationship of things with God's ultimate purposes; it is an action interior to God, which expresses itself outwardly in the moments of the creation and of the governance of things (*Concordia…* 403). The ends of providence are differentiated: the ultimate end is God himself, but the action of providence is already expressed in the immense variety, the beauty, and the order of finite beings (407), although human beings and angels* occupy a privileged place among them (408). Sin* almost derives from a secondary intention of divine providence (*quasi ad secondariam intentionem divinae providentiae*); having foreseen the sins of human beings and of angels, God has permitted them and integrated them into an order directed toward an ultimate end (408). Although providence is extended to everything, it is most specifically concerned with things in relation to the supernatural* order (415). It is distinguished from predestination, which concerns reasonable creatures insofar as it guides *all* of them toward eternal life ([*Deus*] *vult creaturas omnes mente praeditas salvas fieri*) (426). This is also why the punishment of sinners is only a secondary consequence of providence and predestination (409) and a continuation of the latter (Craig 1988).

Leibniz's position is more complex. Like Molina, he believes that God's providence is expressed in the creation of the greatest possible variety of things, accomplished in the best of all possible worlds, and in their preservation and ordering for an ultimate purpose (*Philosophische Schriften* VI, 445; VII, 358, 391). He also thinks that God permits sin as a secondary consequence (III, 37; VI, 119–21, 162, 198, 200, 313–14, 334, 448). However, he is also convinced that some are predestined to eternal damnation (VI, 275), and as a consequence, the problem of theodicy becomes even more central for him than for Molina. He distinguishes between metaphysical, physical, and moral evil (VI, 115, 261). The first is necessarily consubstantial with created beings, because it is a matter of their finiteness; it is therefore an inevitable consequence of creation (VI, 114–15, 198–200, 230 273). Physical evil is a consequence of metaphysical evil. Moral evil consists in sin understood as the pursuit of an apparent good by a limited created being; in the last analysis, it too can therefore be traced back to metaphysical evil as well (VI, 202–03). However, given that the universe is the providential realization of a perfect order, determined by divine intelligence down to the smallest details (VI, 107–08), it is clear that disharmonies, including sin, are only apparent and in the last analysis contribute to the greater harmony of the All, so that those predestined to damnation are sacrificed for the greater good or the greater beauty of the All (VI, 187–88, 196, 231–32). By asserting in this way that the universe does not have as its sole purpose the happiness of reasonable beings (VI, 169–74), Leibniz radically distanced himself from the traditional anthropocentrism of the concept of providence.

b) 18th and 19th Centuries. Giambattista Vico (1668–1744) was the first to propose a "civil and reasoned theology of divine providence" (*The New Science* 114), that is, a theology of history based on providence. Far from being a simple succession of fortuitous and disordered facts, history has a true purpose; this is why Plato, according to him, was right to say that "human things are ordered by providence" (426). Providence gave laws to "the great city* of the human race" (115), and those laws as a whole make up the "eternal ideal history" (89, 99, and *passim*) that is the framework within which the real history of nations unfolds.

Herder (1744–1803) links cosmological and historical perspectives; the cosmos is the theater of a development toward ever higher forms (*Ideen* ... I. 5. 3), up to the pinnacle represented by human beings. Providence has given human beings a task that goes beyond the earthly realm and for which this life is only a preparation (I. 5. 5). But the fact that human history in the strict sense involves a succession of civilizations experiencing greatness and decadence shows that the only thing that counts for human beings is the acquisition and exercise of reason (III. 15. 3); hence, for Herder, there is no purpose to history itself.

For Lessing (1729–81), revelation is to humanity what education is to the individual (*Erziehung* ...7). It communicates to human beings more quickly, and in a determinate order, truths* that they could in principle have reached by reason, but which in fact they would have had great deal of difficulty in discovering, lost as they were in the labyrinth of idolatry (8). To correct them, God chose not an individual but a people, Israel (8–9). First he showed them his power, then he gave them the idea of the uniqueness of God, and finally taught them the idea of the infinite* (9–10). This was the education of an infant people, who would in turn become the educator of the rest of humanity (11) by means of a special primer, Scripture (13–14, 19–20). The Book of Job and the Wisdom of Solomon already indicate the elevation of this people above earthly goods (14–15); thereafter, under Persian influence, Hebrew thought refined its concept of God and came to the doctrine of the immortality of the soul (17–18). Then came a still better "pedagogue," Christ (21). He is the first teacher of purity* of the heart, the morality that has us pursue virtue* for virtue's sake (22 and 27). But the action of providence does not end there; Lessing adopts the doctrine of Joachim of Fiore on the

three ages to assert the necessary coming of a "new eternal Gospel" (28–29), purely rational, with no Church or dogma*. This will represent the spiritual maturity of the human race. We are thus dealing with a teleological vision of history of which the revelation of the God of Israel is an integral part and that makes the particular history of that people and that revelation a decisive element in God's providential action for all of humanity. In another perspective, this position was also arrived at by the theology of the 19th and 20th centuries, both Protestant (school of Erlangen) and Catholic (school of Tübingen*), with the concept of salvation history (*Heilsgeschichte*).

German idealism tries to integrate the two dimensions, cosmic and historical, of providence. In Schelling*'s early works the creation of finite things appears, in Gnostic fashion, as a fall of God, in whom freedom and necessity coincide (*Philosophie und Religion, SW* VI, 40). Finite things thus cannot return to the Absolute (*SW* VI, 56–57) but, born from the difference between reality and possibility, are subject to temporality. God, however, remains the in-itself of nature through the intermediary of the human soul and is thereby the immediate in-itself of history, which as a whole (and only as a whole) presents itself as the harmony of the freedom and necessity that are in God from the beginning; history is thus the revelation of God (*SW* VI, 57). However, at the end of his philosophical development, Schelling abandoned attempting a definitive reconciliation of cosmos and history and recognized that historical existence is substantially removed from cosmic Reason (Semerari 1971).

For Hegel*, history is a moment of the necessary dialectic of the Absolute (*Encyclopedia* §§483–86). He thus relegates religion and revelation to a subordinate position, where they take their place among other historical moments (§§564–71); and he empties the concept of providence of its meaning, whether on the historical plane, where the idea of providence is reduced to the "cunning of history," or on the cosmic plane, where the cosmos is merely the reflection of the dialectical necessity of the concept.

c) 20th Century. After Hegel we enter a period in which the idea of providence no longer has a place and mechanistic determinism triumphs, for example in positivist interpretations of the theory of evolution*. However, theologians and philosophers have maintained the idea of providence. For example, Franz Rosenzweig (1886–1929) emphasizes the Greek character of the concept of providence. In its universality it does not immediately concern individuals as such (*see* Averroës), but only concepts, species, genera, and the universal interconnection of things that God renews from day to day through a continuous creation (*Der Stern der Erlösung* II, 1). For the Bible*, the world is created and therefore has no sacred character and depends on the protection of providence (II, 3, 216); it is also a cosmos over which man holds stewardship (266–67). Finally, the logic of redemption associates world and man; both are destined to be saved (II, 3, 216).

Karl Barth* relies explicitly on Calvin*, who identifies the concept of providence with the concept of divine rule over the world, and emphasizes the central character of this doctrine (*Inst.* I. 16. 1; *see* Barth, *KD* III/3, 8). He therefore logically subordinates providence to predestination, which consists of the eternal decree through which God chooses his Son to be at the head of his Church and of all created beings, while providence amounts merely to the carrying out of that decree (*KD* III/3, 3). It is thus the rule of God "according to the criteria of his own will" (*KD* III/3, 12). And history in the end has no meaning but the realization of the providential covenant* between God and man (*KD* III/3, 41).

As for the Catholic Church, Pope Pius XII, speaking of a personal God "protecting and ruling the world through his providence" (*DS* 3875), repeated in 1950 what had been promulgated by the First Vatican* Council (1870): "God protects and rules the universe through providence" (*Universa…Deus providentia sua tuetur atque gubernat*) (*DS* 3003). The *CCC* reaffirms belief in " God's action in history" (§2738; see §§302–14) and in the government of the world (§1884; see §§1040 and 2115).

The Judeo-Christian tradition* is thus resolutely opposed to all forms of determinism; there is an intelligent government of the world and human beings are morally responsible for their actions. With these principles posited, theology still has a good deal to do to think providence through to the end. The Lisbon earthquake of 1 November 1755 was able to demolish the optimism of the Enlightenment. The horrible events of the 20th century encourage a view of history that is more tragic than providential. We must still answer Job, and understand the response given to him in Jesus Christ.

Gennaro Auletta

5. Prospects

Reconstructing a theology of providence, on which recent scholarship seems to have maintained an uncomfortable silence, calls for a certain number of precautions:

First, we should recall the obvious fact that we can speak in this context only by presupposing an act of faith (*see* Barth, *KD* III/3, 15). If in fact the modern fate of the concept of providence has been disastrous, this is because a theological doctrine accepted the hospitality offered by philosophies (philosophy) of history, and doomed itself to share their fate. Neither the conditions of that hospitality nor that fate hold any more secrets. According to Vico's axiomatics, in the field of history the true is identical to the fact: *factum et verum convertuntur.* The "fact" itself is defined in terms of positivity and production. Because it is the trace of an action, it refers to that action as a preterite, a concluded reality. And if no fact is the last fact—if there is no history without the prospect of a future, whether we are speaking of a history to be lived or one to be written—the future itself, the fact that is not yet, can only itself be thought of as the strict analogue of what has already been done and well done (Troeltsch). The question of "meaning" or "purpose" is consequently identified with the question of a logos or a spirit, the secret of which is fundamental one of technique, of the "doable." Logos or spirit, this secret has certainly been merchandised in various ways. The philosophy of history may be situated within the assumption of First Cause pursuing an uncompleted grand design through the mediation of secondary causes. It can dispense with that protection, grant human causality the status of first cause, and make its spirit the spirit of a utopia (Bloch, e.g.). But here also, shared presuppositions win out over the variety of particular expressions. If we must still speak of providence, it will have to be commensurate with the facts. And although the "facts," in the *epistemè* presiding over their birth, may have begun by using the language of order, progress, and the possibility of happiness, it is at least certain that they may use another language, and it is also certain that no fact, as fact, will ever be the obvious trace of a divine government of all reality.

But if we may expect an affirmation of divine providence only from faith and its self-referential language, then the logic of the fact is called into question; one can never make of any fact, as such, a speech act arguing in favor of God. Faith is certainly based on the believable, and divine credibility* no doubt implies a certain credibility to the idea of divine providence. The experience of Israel nevertheless indicates that divine government of all things and of all history can be believed only from within a primordial act of faith that God solicits as savior, and then as creator and master of a covenant. God, on the one hand, is not believed because his providence is obvious to us; nor, on the other hand does the believing affirmation of God cause his providence to become obvious. There is providence only for faith, which does not *see* what it *believes.*

Next, we would have to agree about the fulfillment of the divine will. Christian prayer* does not speak of that will in the indicative but in the optative ("Thy will be done"); and then linking God's will to the two obviously eschatological events of the sanctification of the Name* and the coming of the Kingdom, prayer indicates the inadequacy of any speech satisfied with the present prospect or with the prospect of an absolute future congruent with that present. The idea of providence associates the logic of belief with the logic of hope*, and that is what makes it possible to confess divine providence in the tragic element of the present of history. A basic requirement of theological coherence makes it necessary that God be not only a lord of the End—of the *eschaton*—whom man's sin dooms to temporary impotence: God *is* lord. But in order to say that, we must again take leave of the facts. The last fact, after all, is indeed the fact of the impotence of God, the fact of the Absolute crucified. And although the event of Easter prevents that fact from having the last word, so that God *is* today the conqueror of the *world,* it remains true that one can today take part in that victory only in the mode of a promise* whose realization remains inchoate. Since Easter Sunday, the *eschaton* is no longer the ineffable (we can think and speak about it with complete rigor), and it is no longer part of its definition that it has no locus in the history of the world. The End is now no longer the favorite shelter of dream and myth*. However, no anticipation and no promise are engraved in the history of the world, through the experience of Israel and the experience of Jesus, with the force necessary to transfigure that history. Thus, in asking that God's will be done, the person who prays accepts what is trivially obvious, that is, that today it is the will of human beings that is done. And because it is accepted before God, the trivially obvious is *ipso facto* given speculative weight. The will of God is in fact that his will may be done only obscurely in history, where the will of human beings is often done with spectacular brutality.

The difficult articulation between divine power and divine impotence is in this context an indication of the need for a theoretical work that is able, on the one hand, to avoid the fascination that the concept of causality has in the past held for theology; and on the other, in an age of suspicion, to avoid any assimilation of the divine will to a will to power. In its Scholastic form the doctrine of providence is the doctrine of an overall plan that the First Cause realizes through the mediation of secondary causes (sometimes dispensing with that mediation). Philosophies of history have provided secularized versions of this doctrine. But does God really provide for history a "reason" and a "cause," *ratio sive causa?* And is it necessary that the only providence that is thinkable be a calculus of means and ends ready before the foundation of the

world, through which God allows himself what he forbids to human beings as moral: permitting evil in order to promote a greater good? This is really not certain. A calculus of this kind is in fact the work of a divine intellect, the work of a God conceived in the image of the *noûs* of Greek thought, and the theological purity of a conception of this kind is open to question. If love* is in fact not a divine attribute ("God is a God who loves"), but the very name of God ("God is love"), then we must immediately ask what effects can be attributed to a hypostatic love.

Several remarks should be made at this point. 1) On the medieval view the power inherent in love is necessarily an "ordered" power, *potentia ordinata,* and it is not fitting that love be *absolutely* powerful. 2) If the logic of creation is a logic of love, and if it is therefore appropriate to attribute affection to God more certainly than we attribute intellection to him, then we must attribute to created free beings, if they refuse to respond to love with recognition and praise*, the power to render God impotent. It is in the nature of the Good* to give itself. But it is in the nature of the gift to expose itself to rejection. 3) There is, however, one gift that one cannot refuse to receive from the Good, and that is the gift of being. Therefore, despite himself, even the being who refuses to see himself as a being-who-has-been-given manifests the goodness of the gift that has made him be and continues to make him be. A hermeneutics* is thus possible that would attempt to discern wherein lies the trace of an intention and a divine foresight. 4) The Good gives beyond power and impotence. Beyond power, because it wishes for a communion* that excludes any constraint and subordinates its causality to its goodness. But beyond impotence, because it has promised to judge the world, and because that judgment*, for him who has eyes to believe, is already taking place in the world's present.

A viable theology of providence could thus be organized as the doctrine of a love crucified before the eyes of all and whose resurrection* was manifest to only a small number of witnesses. Renouncing the invocation over any present of the transcendental (but not necessarily generous) majesty of a supreme cause, renouncing the onto-theological concept of an Absolute proving its absoluteness by predetermining (meta) physically everything that happens in the world, and renouncing the identification of the Spirit of God with the spirit of universal history, such a theology should abandon any systematic and totalizing claims: to proceed to the conceptual apocalypse of meaning is what it absolutely could not do. Perhaps the classical theology of providence died from being a systematic theology. And perhaps the abandonment of any desire for a system would make it possible to gather and benefit from certain meanings that were lost or neglected under systematization. The classical theology of providence was a *theologia gloriae* capable, it believed, of assigning today a dual meaning to every thing and every event, a proto-logical meaning (knowing reality as it was foreknown by God from all eternity) and an eschatological meaning (knowing the provisional in the evident light of the definitive). We certainly should not abandon the ambition for a paschal hermeneutics of history, but we must also accept that it will never be legitimate except on the critical foundation of a *theologia crucis*. To the element of impotence that the Good takes on in the history created by its generosity corresponds, on its own level, a certain impotence of the rational faculty. And when theology confesses that it cannot give a reason for everything, then it does not sign its own death warrant. It simply admits that it exists in the world as a system of believing and hoping thought that reads in being the trace of a gift and the promise of a fulfillment, but that also knows that the bringing forth of meaning is inseparable from the way of the cross. Obviously, not everything *is* good, beautiful, and true. But even when the work of the theological concept ends in collision with the antinomian connection of *meaning* and the *cross,* all work of thought is not over. It simply leaves to another kind of thought, mystical and a-systematic, the task of rejoicing in the idea that "all shall be well, and all manner of thing shall be well" (Julian of Norwich).

Jean-Yves Lacoste

● Anaxagore, *Témoignages et fragments,* in H. Diels, *Die Fragmente der Vorsokratiker,* Berlin, 1903, 7th Ed., W. Kranz, 1954.

Augustine, *Confessions,* BAug 13–14; *City of God,* BAug 33–37.

K. Barth, *KD* III/3, §48 (*Dogmatique,* Geneva, 1962–63).

Boethius, *De consolatione Philosophiae,* LCL 74.

Catéchisme de l'Église catholique, 1992, §302–24.

William of Ockham, *Opera philosophica,* New York, 1974–.

G.W.F. Hegel, *Enzyklopädie der philosophischen Wissenschaften,* SW 6 (Ed. Glockner), §377–577.

G.G. Herder, *Ideen zur Philosophie der Geschichte der Menschheit,* Berlin, 1784 (*Werke,* Ed. Bollacher et al., vol. 6, Frankfurt, 1989).

G.W. Leibniz, *Die philosophischen Schriften,* C.I. Gerhardt (Ed.), Berlin, 1875–90, vol. 6, 1–471.

G.E. Lessing, *Die Erziehung der Menschengeschlechtes,* 1780, Stuttgart, 1985.

M. Maïmonide, *Le Guide des égarés,* 1190 (French translation by S. Munk, 1866, new Ed. 1970).

L. Molina, *Concordia liberi arbitrii cum gratiae donis, divina praescientia, providentia, praedestinatione et reprobatione,* 1588, Paris, 1876.

Philon d'Alexandrie, *De Providentia,* in *OC,* Ed. R. Arnaldez, C. Mondésert, J. Pouilloux, 36 vols., Paris, 1961–92, vol. 35 (1973).

Plotinus, *Enneads,* III 2 and 3.

Posidonius, I. *Die Fragmente,* II, *Erläuterungen,* Ed. W. Theiler, Berlin-New York, 1982.

F. Rosenzweig, *Der Stern der Erlösung,* 1921, The Hague, 4th Ed. 1976.

F.W.J. Schelling, *SW,* Ed. K.F.A. von Schelling, 14 vols., Stuttgart, 1855–61.

SVF, Ed. J. von Arnim, 3 vols. + index, Leipzig, 1903–24, new Ed. Stuttgart, 1964.

Thomas Aquinas, *ST* Ia, q. 22, 23, 103.

G.B. Vico, *Principi di scienza nuova* (definitive Ed. 1744), Milan, 1992.

♦ R. Garrigou-Lagrange (1936), "Providence," *DThC* 13/1, 935–1023 (useful but old).

J. Maritain (1947), "Bienheureux les persécutés…", in *Raison et raisons,* Paris, 339–50.

R. Bultmann (1953), *Theologie des Neuen Testaments,* 8th Ed. 1980, Tübingen.

M. Pohlenz (1964), *Die Stoa: Geschichte einer geistigen Bewegung,* Göttingen.

J. Schmid, K. Rahner (1965), "Vorsehung," *LThK2* 10, 885–89.

W. Kern (1967), "Zur theologischen Auslegung des Schöpfungsglaubens," in *MySal* II, 464–545.

G. Semerari (1971), *Introduzione a Schelling,* Bari.

P. Geach (1977), *Providence and Evil,* Cambridge.

H. Ringgren, W. Zimmerli (1980), *Sprüche/Prediger,* Göttingen.

A. Weiser (1980), *Das Buch Hiob,* Göttingen.

H. Jonas (1984), "Der Gottesbegriff nach Auschwitz," in O. Hofius (Ed.), *Reflexionen finsterer Zeit,* Frankfurt, 61–86.

G. Barbaglio (1985), *Paolo di Tarso e le origine cristiane,* Assisi.

L. Koehler, W. Baumgartner (1985), *Lexicon in Veteris Testamenti Libros,* Leyden.

E. Jüngel (1986), "Gottes ursprüngliches Anfangen als schöpferische Selbstbegrenzung," in *Wertlose Wahrheit,* Munich, 1990, 151–62.

A. Schmitt (1986), *Das Buch der Weisheit: Ein Kommentar,* Würzburg.

W.L. Craig (1988), *The Problem of Foreknowledge and Future Contingents from Aristotle to Suarez,* Leyden.

M. Isnardi Parente (1989), *Introduzione a Plotino,* Bari.

C. Baffioni (1991), *Storia della filosofia islamica,* Milan.

M. Isnardi Parente (1993), *Introduzione allo stoicismo ellenistico,* Bari.

C.K. Barrett (1994), *A Critical and Exegetical Commentary on the Acts of the Apostles,* Edinburgh.

K. Flasch (1994), *Augustin: Einführung in sein Denken,* Stuttgart.

G. Auletta (1995), *Determinismo e contingenza: Saggio sulla filosofia leibniziana delle modalità,* Naples.

R. Bernhardt (1996), "Vorsehung," *EKL* 4, 1208–11.

T.P. Flint (1998), *Divine Providence: The Molinist Account,* 2nd Ed., Ithaca-London.

R. Swinburne (1998), *Providence and the Problem of Evil,* Oxford.

G. A.

See also **Evil; Justice, Divine; Predestination**

Prudence

a) *Definition.* In ancient and medieval ethics*, *prudentia* was a virtue (virtues*), the developed capacity to deliberate, choose, and act in the right way. It was "right reason" applied to actions, defined by Thomas* Aquinas (following Aristotle) as *recta ratio agibilium* (*ST* Ia IIae, q. 57, a. 4).

This view of prudence must be distinguished from what is understood by "prudence" today. Its sense as "caution," especially in financial matters, is far too restrictive. In moral philosophy, "prudence" has even come to designate motivation from self-interest, and Kant* contrasts it with truly moral motivation, that is, duty. Even in Catholic theology*, where the traditional meaning has never been totally forgotten, legalism has allowed prudence to take on the character of obedience of authority*, often assimilated with conscience*. To avoid all such equivocations, the term *practical wisdom* may be preferred, providing that it encompasses not only deliberation and choice, but also the carrying out of the action. Acting well is indeed the most important part of prudence, and being capable of giving good advice, to others or to oneself, is not enough.

b) *Philosophical Tradition.* The definition of prudence as chief of the cardinal virtues (the others being justice*, fortitude, and temperance) goes back at least to Plato (*Republic* 4, 441–42). Aristotle adds three details to this definition. He distinguishes theoretical wisdom (*sophia*) from practical wisdom (*phronesis*), the first being based on knowledge of universal principles, the second requiring both general principles and knowledge of specific circumstances (*EN* VI, 1141). He analyzes the process of practical reasoning: after establishing a purpose, there is deliberation (*bouleusis*) on the best means for realizing it, followed by the choice of such a means (*prohairesis*) and of the action itself (*EN* III). Finally, he shows how prudence does not exist without other virtues: an intelligent will capable of judicious deliberation but lacking the virtue of justice is no longer a prudential will (*EN* VI, 1142 *a;* 1143 *a* 25–*b* 17).

The Stoics already placed more emphasis on knowledge of universal principles and less on knowledge of circumstances or on rational choice. However, it was during the Renaissance that the notion of prudence changed significantly. In the writings of Machiavelli (1469–1527), for example, prudence is barely anything more than the choice of means, a calculating virtue that seeks a result, rather than right action. Here, there is an authentic anticipation of utilitarianism*.

c) *Scripture and the Theological Synthesis.* At first sight, the atmosphere of the Bible*, in which "The fear of the Lord is the beginning of wisdom" (Prv 9:10), may seem quite different, since it places value on humility and obedience to the divine law, rather than on the quality of reasoning. Yet this obedience is not blind: God*'s instructions must be understood and applied with discernment. Human beings endowed with prudence are so impregnated with the divine law that they are capable of grasping immediately whether a particular way of acting is good or bad. Several of the parables (parable*) of Jesus* ("The kingdom of heaven is like a merchant in search of fine pearls," Mt 13:45f.; "For which of you, desiring to build a tower, does not first sit down and count the cost, whether he has enough to complete it," Lk 14:28ff.; the parable of the 10 virgins in Mt 25:1–13; "build your house on the rock," Mt 7:24–27) highlight traits that combine biblical wisdom with secular wisdom. What matters is that the end should be good, the deliberation well-conducted, the judgment sane, and the action coherent.

The early Fathers* (e.g., Ambrose*) made the four cardinal virtues Christian, but it is Augustine* who most profoundly demonstrates the unity of the virtues in love*. He sees clearly that the need that prudence has for the other virtues can be summed up in the love of God and one's neighbor: Christian prudence is "love choosing wisely" (*amor sagaciter eligens, De moribus ecclesiae catholicae,* 5, 25, BAug 1).

Thomas Aquinas based his theological analysis of prudence on Aristotle's description of practical reason. While Aristotle is vague as to the origin of general principles, and leaves the formation of prudence to education, good examples, and reflection, Aquinas attaches great importance to right will and to obedience to the eternal law (*ST* Ia IIae, q. 19, a. 4). Revelation* provides sure principles for deliberating and judging, although prudence must be capable of recognizing exceptional circumstances in which the customary rules cannot be applied (IIa IIae, q. 51, a. 4). Believers are aided in all this by the light that they receive from the Holy* Spirit (IIa IIae, q. 52, a. 1).

d) Higher Degrees of Prudence. The ordinary domain of prudence is individual conduct, but Aristotle reminds us (*EN* VI, 1141 *b* 29–1142 *a* 10) that the good* of each person cannot exist without a good domestic economy, or in the absence of political organization. Moreover, according to Aquinas the exclusive search for personal good stands in opposition to love (IIa IIae, q. 47, a. 10). There is therefore a political prudence that aims at a higher end than the personal good of the prince, that is, the common good. This is not the concern of rulers alone, for all human beings must govern themselves by reason (IIa IIae, q. 47, a. 12).

There is a link between "prudence" *(prudentia)* and "providence*" *(providentia)* that is not merely etymological. While the highest form of practical wisdom belongs to God, human beings can participate in it if they wish. The actions (action*) that they freely choose allow them to participate in providence if they are in conformity with God's will (Ia, q. 22; Ia IIae, q. 91, a. 2). The disappearance of trust in God is undoubtedly one of the main causes of the modern degradation of prudence into cautious calculation.

- C. Spicq (1933) "La vertu de prudence dans l'Ancien Testament," *RB* 42, 187–210.
- D. Noble (1936), "Prudence," *DThC* 13/1 1023–76.
- A. M. Henry (1948), *Prudence chrétienne,* Paris.
- J. Pieper (1949), *Traktat über die Klugheit,* Munich.
- P. Aubenque (1963), *La prudence chez Aristote,* Paris; id. (1965), "La prudence aristotélicienne porte-t-elle sur la fin ou sur les moyens?" *REG* 78, 40–51.
- R. A. Gauthier (1963), *La morale d'Aristote,* Paris.
- R. Saint-Jean (1985), "Prudence," *DSp* 12/2, 2476–84.
- D. Westberg (1994), *Right Practical Reason: Aristotle, Action, and Prudence in Aquinas,* Oxford.
- P. Pellegrin (1996), "Prudence," *DEPhM,* 1201–7.

DANIEL WESTBERG

See also **Action; Casuistry; Epieikeia; Ethics; Good; Intention; Virtues**

Przywara, Erich. *See* Analogy

Psalms

---

a) Collection. Entitled "book* of praises (praise*)" (Hebrew *Tehillîm*), the Psalter is the canonical collection of the prayers (prayer*) of Israel*. It has been introduced in various forms into Christian liturgies (liturgy*).

A psalm (from the Greek *psalmô,* play a stringed instrument) is a poetic piece composed to be chanted, called *mizemôr* (57 times), from *zimmér,* to chant with accompaniment. Of the 150 Psalms, 28 have come down under the name of Levite brotherhoods and 73 (84 in the Septuagint) were transmitted late under the name of David (12 "titles" evoke a moment of his life, especially his ordeals), an attribution that came to be applied to all of them. The brief concluding ritual formulas of praise (doxologies) found in Psalms 41:134, 72:18–20, 89:52, and 106:48 (*see also* Ps 150) separate the book into five parts. This division, which is very late, incorporates older collections. The most archaic compositions are found between Psalms 3 and 41; we can also distinguish "Elohist" Psalms (42–83); the Passover *Hallél* (Ps 113–118); and the Psalms of "ascent" or pilgrimage* to Zion (Ps 120–134). Psalm 151, found in the Septuagint and at Qumran (Hebrew 11QPsa), claims Davidic origin for the entire collection, a belief attested in the New Testament (Mark 12:35–37 and parallels, Acts 1:16, 2:25, and 4:25, Romans 4:6 and 11:9, and Hebrews 4:7). Caves 4 and 11 at Qumran contain elements of the Psalter; Qumran has its own hymns or *Hôdayôt* (1QH). Under the title *Psalms of Solomon,* there are 18 other noncanonical

Psalms, inspired by the Roman invasion of 63 B.C. Catholic liturgy, having adopted the same numbering of the Psalms as the Septuagint and the Vulgate, is out of step with the numbering employed in the Bibles (Bible*) translated from Hebrew, which are the ones used in most commentaries.

b) Author and Speaker. From the point of view of the origin of the Psalter, the "author" of a psalm (to whom is attributed the conception and composition of the prayer) and the "speaker" (the one who addresses it to God*) may or may not coincide at the outset, but the distinction between them is constant. On the one hand, the text is detached from its author; it belongs to the speaker in whose mouth it is placed. On the other hand, the speaker is necessarily linked to a chain of individuals or groups that the repertory has designated for typical situations. It may happen that a collective prayer is spoken by an individual and conversely, but the text does not lose its formal characteristics. The "title" given to the psalm, if any, does not make it possible to trace the origin of the psalm. It is rather an illustration, attached to David as a type. According to the *Midrash Tehillîm*, (18, 1), "everything that David said in his book he said in relation to himself, in relation to all Israel, in relation to all time*." Hence, Jewish exegesis* attributes Psalm 22 to Esther and sees in Psalm 35:21 the situation of Susanna and the elders.

Modern historians have attempted to identify authors, but, with few exceptions, the identifiable facts referred to by the Psalms are confined to the distant past. It is reasonable to think that a core group dating from the first temple* was preserved and then considerably augmented after the exile. A relationship has been noted (the genealogical order remains subject to debate) between some Psalms and the prayers of Jeremiah, between the Psalms of the reign of YHWH and the hymns of Isaiah 40–55, and between Psalm 51 and Ezekiel. One can often detect within a single piece traces of "rereadings" left by an ancient anonymous chain of poets (A. Robert, R. Tournay).

c) Turning Point in Scholarship. Hermann Gunkel carried out his study of the Psalms between 1904 and 1933 *(Die Psaumen* and *Einleitung in die Psalmen).* By focusing his attention on the literary aspect and the ritual function of the Psalter, in order to discover "forms" or "genres" *(Gattungen),* Gunkel indirectly contributed to the theology* of biblical prayer. The poet calls on every reader, or rather every reciter who will succeed him, to share an experience* that goes beyond him, the experience of the encounter with God. Communication is established through poetry; the Psalter represents an enormous repertory of symbols,

and its language is a vehicle for all corporeal signifiers, sites of sensations, and feelings.

At the same time, the experience is expressed in what Gunkel calls *forms,* in which conventions of language regulate the *composition,* the *motifs* (or themes), and the *style* of a psalm. Neither meter nor stanzaic structure is immediately apparent to us today because the accents and caesurae of the accepted Hebrew text are of medieval origin (E. Beaucamp, *DBS* [1979] col. 158–66). Studies of biblical rhetoric have been concerned particularly with the procedures of composition, such as parallelisms and concentric organization (R. Meynet: P. Auffret; J.-N. Aletti; and J. Trublet).

The interplay between norms and innovations made possible the circulation of the experience in the community. Because the psalter formed a repertory of songs, the psalmist had to identify himself with the psalmists preceding him. This appropriation of the prayer of others became a component of the spiritual experience, corresponding to the essentially liturgical character of the collection. At the same time, the experience made the framework open and available. It elicited a response that was expressed within the book by songs claiming to be "new" (Ps 40:3; *see also* Ps 22:31b and 102:20). The various forms are both rigid and flexible. Each psalm is unique. Finally, in all can be heard not a general truth*, nor only a particular event, but a unique series of events shared between the individual and the community.

Form Criticism *(Formgeschichte)* looks for a sociological foundation for every form, called a *Sitz im Leben,* or situation of the community in the time and place of the composition of a biblical work. However, the classification proposed by Gunkel carries this out incompletely, and is thus inconsistent and disparate. A division into 10 groups of Psalms makes it possible to collate various lists drawn up by Gunkel and his school:

1) The *hymn:* praise addressed to God for his work of creation* and in history*. The tone is one of jubilation; these Psalms may have been intended for choral performance. They normally contain an "introit" ("praise," "sing"), a recitation in the third person of God's deeds, and a conclusion (e.g., Ps 8, 65, and 136).
2) The *enthronement song* or song of the royalty of YHWH, which has in the forefront the acclamation "YHWH reigns" (e.g., Ps 47, 93, 97, and 99).
3) The *songs of Zion,* a category of hymn whose theme is the holy city*, the temple mount, liturgically adapted to a pilgrimage or a festival celebrated in Jerusalem* (e.g., Ps 48 and 87). It is

convenient to add to this group the "Psalms of pilgrimage" (e.g., Ps 84 and certain "Psalms of ascent").

4) *Psalms of thanksgiving,* which some scholars have classed with the hymns; however, being more individual, these make up a distinct group, open to variation (e.g., Ps 18 and 116).

5) *Psalms of collective and national lament,* joining together the description of a misfortune and an appeal to the obligation of YHWH. These may also include, according to circumstances, a confession of sins (sin*) or a protestation of innocence (e.g., Ps 44, 74, and 79).

6) *Psalms of individual lament,* characterized by the triad I-God-the enemy. These frequently include an expression of confidence and in conclusion the promise or the vow to give God thanks. These Psalms may be subdivided into laments from persons suffering persecution who find refuge in the temple or in YHWH (e.g., Ps 11); laments of persons who are ill, and who see their sins as the sources of their sickness (e.g., Ps 6, 31, and 39); and laments of accused innocents who appeal to the tribunal of God (e.g., Ps 7 and 17).

7) *Psalms of confidence,* expressing either calm and peaceful confidence in God, or the effort to strengthen that confidence in times of crisis (e.g., Ps 16, 23, and 27).

8) *Liturgical Psalms,* constructed like ritual acts (real or fictitious) and incorporating indications about the ritual in the text (e.g., Ps 15, 24, and 118).

9) *Wisdom Psalms,* recognizable from their theme, their meditative tone, or their didactic style (e.g., Ps 1, 37, and 49). This group may include Psalms organized as historical meditations (e.g., Ps 78, 105, and 106).

10) Finally, *acrostic Psalms,* organized according to the 22 letters of the Hebrew alphabet (e.g., Ps 9, 10, 25, 34, 111, 112, 119, and 145).

d) From Mowinckel to von Rad. It remains indispensable to consider each psalm as "a unity whose principle is simultaneously of a poetic, a theological, and a religious order" (L. Alonso-Schöckel 1972). Several lines of scholarship by Gunkel's associates, his followers, and sometimes his opponents may be examined in comparison with the impetus and direction given by Form Criticism. Sigmund Mowinckel (*Psalmen-studien* 1921–24) attempted to establish the unity of the *Sitz im Leben* of the Psalms around the annual enthronement of YHWH as king of the cosmos*, in parallel with the Babylonian festival of Akîtu. Dismissed by historians, this approach found support among specialists in mythology, and it long drew attention to the integration of the cosmos* into the prayer and poetry of the Psalms (R. Murray, *The Cosmic Covenant* 1992). The principal interpreters of the Psalms agree today in wishing to take into consideration the specificity of the language and its aesthetics. Claus Westermann has to some degree moved away from the explanatory side of Gunkel's sociology. For him, the pairing of praise and supplication is the principal formula of the book. It is a matter of "what happens in the words." For, he writes, "the bipolar form of speaking to God is the *Sitz im Leben* specific to the psalms" (*Das Lob Gottes in den Psalmen,* 1954). That amounts to positing a "site in the word" and at least provisionally calling into question the principle of classification. An anthropology* of prayer is already taking shape. Gerhard von Rad has been able to show the theological import of the literary schematism of ritual texts, which in a sense call for hyperbole (situations that are always extreme, "the radicalism of description"). In *Theologie des Alten Testaments* (1957, vol. 1), he writes: "We will have to take with the greatest theological seriousness the difference between what is really experienced and the extreme form in which the speaker presents himself before God."

e) David the Prophet (Acts 2:30). It was indeed hyperbole that was given prophetic value in interpretations such as that given by the apostle* Peter* of Psalm 16:10 (Septuagint), from his very first proclamation of Christ* (Acts 2:24–32). This reading according to the extension each generation contributes to the meaning of the Scriptures, with faithfulness, and in an exchange between the individual and the community, opens onto the Christological interpretation of the Psalms, which we see in the New Testament (Lk 24:44). The New Testament contains approximately 80 quotations from the Psalms, amounting to about one-quarter of all its quotations of the Old Testament. About 30 of these are placed in the mouth of Jesus*.

In the background of this exegesis there may be one or another specific psalm (such as Ps 2, 8, or 110) that the period understood as messianic. But primarily there is a reading that is simultaneously contemporaneous and eschatological in the context of prophecy in general (noted in Qumran: *see* the *"pesher"* of Habakkuk and 4Q171, 173, 174), as well as a general inclusion of the Psalms in the genre of prophecy, and finally the place granted to the royal figure of the psalmist David, the embodiment of messianic promises (promise*).

The bipolarity of supplication and praise is then verified in hyperbolic terms (*see* von Rad, above), and it is transcended in the Passion* and Resurrection* of Jesus (P. Beauchamp 1980). The Epistle to the Hebrews uses verses from the Psalms to express directly the secret dialogue uniting Jesus to the Father* (Heb 1:5, 8–13, 2:12a, 5:5–6, and 10:5–9). The early Christians were drawn to pray to God in the language of the Psalms, though they were not thereby prevented from composing their own hymns. The prayers calling for the punishment of the men of violence, calumniators, and those casting evil spells were applied to the forces of evil*, and to the enemy everyone carries within himself. Those who pray today, more reserved in the face of these transpositions, hear in these cries the victims of injustice throughout history* bringing their complaint before God.

• E. Balla (1912), Das "Ich" der Psalmen, FRLANT 16.
H. Gunkel (1926), Die Psalmen, Göttingen; id. (1933), Einleitung in die Psalmen, Göttingen.
L. Alonso-Schökel (1963), Estudios de poética hebrea, Barcelona; id. (1972), "Poésie hébraïque," DBS 6, 158–66; id. (1981), Treinta Salmos: Poesía y oración (annotated bibl., 453–56), Madrid; id. (1989), "Interpretación de los Salmos desde Casiodoro hasta Gunkel," EstB 47, 145–64.
M. Mannati, E. de Solms (1966–68), Les Psaumes, 4 vols., Paris.
E. Lipinski (1968, 2nd Ed.), La Royauté de Yahwé dans la poésie et le culte de l'ancien Israël, Bruxelles.
F. Crüsemann (1969), Studien zur Formgeschichte von Hymnus und Danklied in Israel, WMANT 32.
E. Beaucamp (1976), Les Psaumes, 2 vols., Paris.
M.-J. Seux (1976), Hymnes et prières aux dieux de Babylonie et d'Assyrie, Paris.
C. Westermann (1977), Lob und Klage in den Psalmen, Göttingen.
J. Gelineau (1978), "Les Psaumes à l'époque patristique," MD 135, 99–116.
E. Lipinski, E. Beaucamp, I. Saint-Arnaud (1979), "Psaumes," DBS 9, 2–214.
C. Westermann (1979), "Anthropologische und theologische Aspekte des Gebets in den Psalmen," ThJb, 51–62.
P. Beauchamp (1980), Psaumes Nuit et Jour, Paris.
P. Auffret (1981), Hymnes d'Égypte et d'Israël: Études de structures littéraires, OBO 34.
J. Trublet (1986), "Psaumes," DSp 12/2, 2504–62.
L. Alonso-Schökel, C. Carniti (1992), Salmos, 2 vols., Estella.
K. Seybold et al. (1997), "Psalmen/Psalmenbuch," TRE 27, 610–37.

THE EDITORS

See also **Healing; Kingdom of God; Liturgy; Music; Praise; Prayer; Scripture, Senses of; Soul-Heart-Body; Temple**

Pseudo-Dionysius. See **Dionysius the Pseudo-Areopagite**

Pseudoepigrapha. See **Intertestament**

Pseudo-Macarius. See **Messallianism**

Psychoanalysis. *See* **Freud, Sigmund**

Punishment

---

a) Definitions. Punishment is traditionally defined by the retributive principle, *malum passionis quod infligitur ob malum actionis* ("suffering harm imposed for having done harm"—Grotius). It embraces universal social practices that respond to offense by imposing suffering on the offender, and, in religious terms, the experience of suffering as chastisement of sin*. Every theory of punishment undertakes to make retributive social practices intelligible; a theological theory undertakes to make them morally intelligible in the light of the relation of humanity to God*. The special problematic of punishment in Christian theology* is posed by divine mercy*: if our relations to God are determined by his will to forgiveness and salvation*, what follows for social practices based on the retributive principle? The story of the woman taken in adultery (Jn. 8:2–11) could be taken to challenge them outright. Several answers have been given: some (e.g., Luther*) sharpen the distinction between the order of providence* and that of redemption, assigning punishment to the former domain; others (e.g., Hegel*) find a redemptive element within punishment itself; still others (e.g., Tolstoy) declare the retributive principle to be morally unintelligible. Most theologians, however, have favored moderating tendencies in penal practice, as a witness within the sphere of providence to the horizon of divine mercy.

b) Nature of Punishment. On the social plane, punishment is midway between a purely abstract disapproval of offense and the purely instinctive desire for vengeance; on the religious plane, it is midway between the infinite opposition of divine goodness to sin and the commensurability that exists in an equal exchange. Punishment differs from vengeance in that the retributive principle becomes a principle of reflective public action*, rather than instinctive private action. Punishment is a rational and "expressive" condemna-

tion (Feinberg 1970), a "communication" (Lucas 1993), which presupposes the authority* of those who represent society*. Grotius (*De iure belli ac pacis* On the Law of War and Peace I, 20, 3) holds that from the point of view of natural law, it belongs to a superior, of whatever kind, to punish. Punishment differs from other acts of public judgment in addressing the offense primarily as a challenge to the moral and legal order itself, rather than as an injury to the victim. In law, punishment corresponds to crime, satisfaction (or damages) to tort. Hence, punishment is a public performance, a moral self-definition on the part of a society. On the private plane, as in the family, punishment is adapted to domestic purposes such as education.

Theologians have hesitated over Aristotle's proposal that the justice* displayed in punishment is of the kind "that orders private transactions," the judge attempting "to establish equality by punishment" (*NE* 1131 *b* 25–1132 *a* 10). Thomas* Aquinas recognizes *vindicatio* (public condemnation) as a species of "commutative justice" (*ST* IIa IIae, q. 80, a. 1), but also argues that God can practice only distributive justice (Ia, q. 21, a. 1). For Aquinas, the paradigm of commutative justice is not punishment but restitution (IIa IIae, q. 62). Grotius, who briefly entertains and then rejects the view that the justice of punishment is distributive, classifies it as "satisfactory justice" (*iustitia expletrix*), a category corresponding to commutative justice but without its criterion of equality between the parties, to be distinguished simply by the right that one party has over the other (*De iure belli...*, I, 1, 8; II, 20, 2). The right of punishment belongs, not to the victim, but to whoever is in a position of authority to inflict it.

When God punishes, he demonstrates his relative (*ordinata*) power, not his absolute (*absoluta*) power. Thus, God's punishment of Israel* is the expression of YHWH's faithfulness to the covenant*, contrasted with the destruction of the people* that would follow if he gave free rein to his wrath* (Jer 10:24; Sg 11:21–12 and 27). In Christian theology, punishment is closely interwoven with atonement, understood as an act of divine "jurisdiction" (Grotius, *De satisfactione Christi* On Christ's Atonement) that delivers man from the infinite expression of God's wrath through the sufferings that Christ* has undergone for us.

c) Goods of Punishment. As a public act, punishment makes manifest the nature of the offending action in relation to the social order. The retributive principle becomes part of God's plan by disclosing the truth of human offense. In this way, punishment can be understood, from the theological point of view, as one of the ways in which God preserves and redeems the world, and therefore as a good*. When God himself punishes, the disclosure is a good sufficiently apparent, like every manifestation of God. Only divine punishment is thus self-authenticated (Grotius, *De iure belli...,* II, 20, 4). Human punishment needs to serve ends that demonstrate the divine preservation or redemption of the world; hence, there are "goods" or advantages of punishment, which demonstrate God's goodwill to society in its act of moral self-definition.

Differences of interpretation arise as the emphasis is laid upon the providential or the redemptive aspects of punishment; these are not necessarily the same, and some can appear to be more important than others, depending on the case. A tradition with classical roots identifies three possible beneficiaries of punishment: the offender, the victim, and society. Within Christian thought, the second of these has largely disappeared from consideration. Such personal satisfaction as the victim may take in the punishment of the offender is regarded as morally suspect, a refusal of the commands to love one's enemies and to take no vengeance (Mt 5:44; Rom 12:19). The limited scope given to the "blood avenger " in the Old Testament institution of the cities of refuge (Num. 35:9–28; Deut. 19:1–10) was a means of wresting the initiative in retribution out of private hands. "Retributive" theories of punishment (e.g., Kant*) emphasize the importance of the retributive principle for the integrity of society, rather than for any interest that the victim may have in it.

An emphasis on the benefit to the offender corresponds to the redemptive significance of punishment. The Epistle to the Hebrews speaks of God's treating the churches (church*) as his children in correcting them (Heb 12:5–11). This paradigm controls what is said in the Platonism* of the Fathers* of the Church. For them, as indeed for Plato himself (*Gorgias* 476 a–478 e), punishment is a purgation of the soul*. According to Augustine*, a "benign harshness," which takes thought for the ultimate conversion* of the offender, marks the Christian ruler's actions with paternal affection (*Ep.* 138, 14, CSEL 44). Gregory* of Nyssa applies this to the fires of Hell* (PG 46, 97–101). Only within the church or the family can punishment be understood solely in these terms, for neither institution makes human justice the principle of its action. Alongside this account, therefore, another developed that is not always distinct from it, and that relates punishment to the welfare of the community, whereby "the good live more peaceably in the midst of the evil" (Augustine, *Ep.* 153, 16, CSEL 44). In this regard, Hell becomes "the righteous ordering of the unrighteous" (*De natura boni* On the Nature of the Good 37, BAug 1).

As penitential practice (penance*) developed juridically in the Middle Ages, it afforded a paradigm for punishment directed to the offender's welfare and voluntarily embraced. Nicholas* of Cusa sees it as a mark of ecclesiastical coercion that it is undertaken with consent and for the salvation of the punished (*De concordantia catholica* II, 261). The existence of two jurisdictions, spiritual and secular (church* and state), allowed the two interpretations of punishment to coexist, each in its institutional context. A natural result of the collapse of dual jurisdiction as a result of the Reformation was the attempt to synthesize the two conceptions. This type of theory reaches its highest point in Hegel, for whom the welfare of the offender and that of society converge upon the common need for an "annulment" of the transgression, an effective expression of the inherent nullity of the crime. Punishment fulfills the "implicit will" of the offender, expressing the law that he has recognized by the very fact of his rational action (*Grundlinien der Philosophie des Rechts Foundations of the Philosophy of Right,* §97–100).

In as strong a contrast as possible to this attempt at synthesis, utilitarianism* treats the good of the offender and that of society as irreconcilable; it is therefore necessary to ask which one should prevail. Distinctive to this family of theories is a shift of focus from the practice of punishment to the threat of it. According to Beccaria, punishment is to be introduced as a "motive" into the offender's calculations, a deterrent "annexed" to the law, which may be justified only on the grounds of "general prevention" of crime, to be achieved "at as cheap a rate as possible" (Bentham, *Introduction to the Principles of Morals and Legislation,* 14, 6). Of some alarm to critics has been the comparative inconsequence to this theory of the retributive principle. The actual execution of punishment is necessary only "for the sake of producing the appearance of it" (*Rationale of Punishment* 1, 5). What if some other threat—say, to kill the offender's children—should prove more "economical"? The theory is premised, in effect, upon the *unintelligibility* of the retributive principle, and proposes alternative principles that will save as many of the appearances of punishment as possible. Inevitably, many are unsaved; and so utilitarian theories have contributed to institutional reform, for they discard elements of penal practice that seem to have doubtful deterrent efficacy. In the 19th century, penal reform was driven by an uneasy coalition of utilitarianism with a type of Pietism*, the former seeking to secure the most economic prevention of crime that was possible, the latter to find means to promote the conversion of the criminal (so that illusory hopes were reposed in, e.g., solitary confinement).

d) Proportion in Punishment. As an expressive act, punishment "says something" about the wrong done; as an act within the ordered relativities of human society, it says nothing about the absolute opposition of wrong to divine goodness (as in the limiting case of eternal punishment), but expresses the relation of this wrong to the normal compromises of social life. Hence arises the question of how punishment may be proportioned to the particular wrong. Since Aristotle (*NE* 1132 *b* 21–31), it has been acknowledged that simple retaliation (doing to the offender what he did to the victim) cannot be a basis for just punishment, although Kant influentially championed the *lex talionis* ("law of retaliation," or "an eye for an eye"), seeing it as a logical consequence of the retributive principle (*Grundlegung zur Metaphysik der Sitten*§ 49 E, AA 6 331–37). The *lex talionis* plays a limited role in the Old Testament. It is applied in cases of careless injury to a pregnant woman (Ex 21:23–25), lasting disfigurement (Lv 24:20), and malicious witness (Dt 19:21), this last case being of special interest, in that the *lex talionis* is applied even though the harm is only intended, not executed. The relation of harm suffered to harm done must be a symbolic one; a penal system has the character of a language, and must express itself in comprehensible terms. Montesquieu's observations on "the severity of punishments in different governments" (*L'esprit des lois*, 6, 9) invert the old idea that harsh governments are a form of discipline imposed by God on societies that need them. It is now the moral disposition of a society, its varying inclination to "lenity or pity," that determines how severe the law must be. It is difficult, therefore, for one society to assess the appropriateness of another society's penal practices. Yet the will to impose limits on severity and to avoid the degeneration of the language of punishment into inflated rhetoric can be appreciated in very different penal systems. Thus, the Deuteronomic code limits flogging to 40 stripes, lest…your brother be degraded in your sight" (Deut. 25:3).

To this principle that punishment must be propor-

tionate, Christian thought has added a prejudice in favor of mildness, on three grounds: the judge is himself a sinner in need of forgiveness (*see* Mt. 18:23–25); human judgment is fraught with error (Augustine, *Civ. Dei* XIX, 6); the offender is always addressed by divine mercy, to which human mercy must bear witness. From the fourth century onward, bishops (bishop*) interceded with secular authorities on behalf of those condemned to death, without derogation from the right of punishment (Augustine, *Ep.* 153). In the 16th century, equity (epieikeia*) was appealed to in support of the claims of mercy (Perkins, *Epieikeia, or a Treatise of Christian Equity,* Cambridge, 1604, or Shakespeare, *Measure for Measure*).

e) Capital Punishment. When Ambrose* stated that civil authority "will be excused if it applies capital punishment, and admired if it does not apply it" (*Ep.* 50, 3), he was summing up the main tradition of post-Nicene reflection, still represented by John Paul II (*Evangelium vitae, AAS* 87, 41–522, §56): punishment "ought not to go to the extreme of executing the offender except in cases of absolute necessity." Before Nicaea* I, the church had expressed a hatred of bloodshed, but it had made no positive penal recommendations. The Old Testament's endorsement of capital punishment made it impossible to condemn it without incurring the accusation of Marcionism*, yet it provided no justification for the use of the death penalty by Christian magistrates. Some radical groups in the Middle Ages and the Reformation era criticized the application of capital punishment by Christians as part of a wider case against holding secular office, although they were sometimes prepared to defend its legitimacy "outside the perfection of Christ" (Confession of Schleitheim 1527, 6). Resistance to the Waldensian* heresy* had led Innocent III to insist on this legitimacy, "so long as it is done judicially and without hatred, carefully and not rashly" (*DS* 425).

The ability of a state to minimize the use of capital punishment depends in part upon the existence of a well-organized and humane prison system. Progress in this domain contributed in the 18th and 19th centuries to the revulsion against the abuse of capital punishment in earlier centuries. Contemporary arguments for the categorical immorality of capital punishment—such as those of G. Grisez, who argues that it infringes the rule against doing evil that good may come—have been criticized for viewing the practice outside its political context, although the state must find some means to restrain instincts to vengeance and murder. Opposing arguments, influenced by the views of Kant, which require capital punishment for murder on the basis of the *lex talionis,* have no theological basis.

● C. Beccaria (1764), *Dei delitti e delle pene.*

J. Bentham (1789), *Introduction to the Principles of Morals and Legislation,* Ed. J. H. Burrs, H. L. A. Hart, London, 1970; id. (1811), *Rationale of Punishment.*

H. Rashdall (1907), *The Theory of Good and Evil,* Oxford.

J. H. Yoder (1961), *The Christian and Capital Punishment,* Newton, Kans.

H. B. Acton (Ed.) (1969), *The Philosophy of Punishment,* Oxford.

J. Feinberg (1970), *Doing and Deserving,* Princeton.

D. E. Cooper (1971), "Hegel's Theory of Punishment," in *Hegel's Political Philosophy: Problems and Perspectives,* Ed. Z. A. Pelczynski, Cambridge, 151–67.

O. O'Donovan (1976), *Measure for Measure,* Nottingham.

W. Berns (1979), *For Capital Punishment,* New York.

M. R. Weisser (1979), *Crime and Punishment in Early Modern Europe,* Brighton.

A. Renaut (1986), "Beccaria, *Des délits et des peines,*" DOPol 62–67 (bibl.).

N. Walker (1991), *Why Punish?,* Oxford.

J. R. Lucas (1993), *Responsibility,* Oxford.

M. van de Kerchove (1996), "Pénale (éthique)," DEPhM, 1108–14.

OLIVER O'DONOVAN

See also **Authority; Hell; Justice; Law and Legislation; Penance**

Purgatory

The term *purgatory* does not appear in the Bible* and is not universally used among Christians. It refers to a theological notion developed in Western Christendom in the Middle Ages to define the condition of the souls (soul*-heart-body) of those among the dead who are neither capable of entering immediately into the presence of God*, nor destined to eternal damnation in hell*. It denotes, therefore, a temporary rather than a final condition.

1. Sources of the Doctrine

The notion of purgatory may be related to four biblical themes:

1) The belief in a life after death* and in participation in the Resurrection* of Jesus*: "For since we believe that Jesus died and rose again, even so, through Jesus, God will bring with him those who have fallen asleep" (1 Thes 4:14; *see* 1 Cor 15:20 and Rom 6:8f.).

2) The practice of saying prayers (prayer*) for the dead, carried over from the customs described in the Old Testament. Judas Maccabeus, for example, "made a sacrifice of expiation for the dead, so that they would be delivered of their sins" (2 Macc 12:46). In Christianity such prayers are based on the mediating role of Jesus (Cyril of Jerusalem's fifth *Catechesis Mystagogica* 9–10) and are linked to the Eucharist*. They presuppose that the fate of the dead can undergo some modification even after death.

3) The notion of the purification of the dead in the hereafter. The biblical image adopted by Christians in antiquity was that of fire: "We went through fire and through water" (Ps 66:12). Origen* writes of the time "when we shall have passed into the fire" (*Homélie sur Jérémie* 18, 1, SC 238, 178), and Ambrose* expresses the same idea: "All those who desire to return to Paradise must be tested by fire" (*Expositio in Ps 118,* XX, 12). However, the fire in question is not a punishment but a sign of God's judgment*, and an image of testing and truth*, for one enters into salvation* "only as through fire" (1 Cor 3:15).

4) The very ancient image of a place where the dead wait: Sheol (Jb 30:23); in Hellenistic culture, the Underworld; in certain schools within the Judaism* of Jesus' time, the "bosom of Abraham" (Lk 16:22) or "Paradise" (Lk 23:43). There was thus a common tendency to situate the existence of the dead in the hereafter metaphorically.

2. Establishment and Acceptance of the Belief

Within Western Christendom, the symbolic location of the dead began to be divided, during the 12th century, between hell in the strict sense of the word—the place of damnation—and purgatory, a place of purification. Previously, in East and West alike, the word *purgatory* had been used only in adjectival form, as in "the purgatorial fire" or "purgatorial punishments" (*poenis purgatoriis*). From this time on, however, Christians within the Latin tradition also treated "purgatory" as a noun, linking it to the biblical notion of the location of the dead, and combining with the idea of purification or testing the idea of punishment or expiation*.

a) Cautious Formulations. The notion of purgatory was incorporated into Western medieval theology* in the wake of Bernard* of Clairvaux and Peter Comestor; it appears, for example, in the works of Thomas* Aquinas (*In Sent.* IV, d. 21, q., a. 1). However, the church authorities (magisterium*) were slower to embrace it. At the Second Council of Lyon* (1274) there was no question of anything but "purgatorial punishments" (*DS* 856), and at the Council of Florence (1438) it was simply declared that: "Those who have died in the love of God before they have been made worthy by the fruits of penance are purified after death by purgatorial punishments and benefit from the support of the living" (*DS* 1304).

It was not until the Council of Trent* that the doctrine of the place known as purgatory was explicitly affirmed, first of all in the Decree on Justification (sixth session, 1547): sin entails punishment, which is to be expiated "either in this world or in the next, in Purgatory" (*DS* 1580). There followed a Decree on Purgatory (25th session, 1563; *DS* 1820): "The Catholic Church...has taught...that there is a Purgatory and that the souls that are detained there are aided by the intercessions of the faithful, and, above all, by propitiatory sacrifice at the altar." Bishops (bishop*) are therefore requested to "take every care in order that the sound doctrine of Purgatory may be believed by the faithful, and universally taught and preached" (ibid.). Nevertheless, a certain degree of caution is to be observed: "excessively difficult or subtle questions are to be excluded from sermons addressed to the populace" and the bishops "are not to permit, expound or disseminate ideas that are doubtful or tainted with error. As for those ideas that arouse nothing but curiosity or superstition, or smell of ill-gotten gain, they are forbidden, as being scandalous and injurious to the faithful."

b) A Complex Context. The doctrine was thus established, within quite precise parameters. First, purgatory is a notion limited to Western Christendom, for the Eastern churches have never accepted it. It is also an exclusively Catholic belief. Luther* objects to it on the grounds that it is a nonbiblical notion that encourages extravagant religious practices intended to deliver the dead from purgatory (*Articles of Schmalkalden,* 1537, *BSLK* 442 and 443), while Calvin* writes that "Purgatory is a pernicious fiction of Satan" (*Inst.* III, Ch. 5).

Second, the doctrine of purgatory has been associated with a variety of forms of spirituality and devotion. The desire to provide a spatial symbol for the hereafter is so ambiguous that nowadays most Catholics concur in regarding purgatory as a condition rather than a place. In addition, before the Council of Trent there was a general fascination with death and suffering, and this must have affected the belief in purgatory. Finally, during the 19th century the emphasis placed on praying for "the souls in purgatory" sometimes became excessive, threatening to distort the gospel of pardon freely given in Jesus Christ. The precautions taken by the Council of Trent were not necessarily effective. Within this range of responses we should nonetheless give a place to a tradition of mysticism* that attempted to discern in certain conditions of this life an experience* analogous to that of purgatory. Catherine of Genoa (1447–1510), who wrote a remarkable *Trattato del Purgatorio* (Treatise on Purgatory), led the way in developing this very refined interpretation of purgatory.

3. Contemporary Meanings

a) An Extremely Subtle Affirmation. Given the prodigious success of the image of purgatory within Western Catholicism*, it is astonishing to observe the extent to which it has been effaced today. It is true that Vatican* II refers to the Council of Trent (*LG* 52, n. 22), but it does not explicitly use the word *purgatory,* restricting itself instead to references to "purification" after death: "Certain (of the) disciples...are purified after their deaths" (ibid., 49). The *Catechism of the Catholic Church* (1992) is more explicit, but is relatively restrained: "The Church gives the name purgatory to this final purification of the elect, which is entirely different from the punishment of the damned." (1031) It is indicated that this teaching is based on Scripture, on the decisions of councils, and also on "the practice of prayer for the dead" (1032.). Finally, it is taken as self-evident that purgatory is a "state" (1472).

How should we understand this change in sensibility? First of all, there has been a considerable shift in the way in which the West relates to death, and for many people reference to the hereafter has become a matter of uncertainty. In addition, our era is more cautious than previous centuries were in handling eschatological images, with the result that the notion of purgatory seems excessively concrete. Many Catholics, while they retain their hope* for the final resurrection and still affirm the solidarity, in Christ, of the living and the dead, prefer to abide by the discretion of the Bible. Nevertheless, one might wonder whether such reservations have some drawbacks. After all, the Christian affirmation of the resurrection needs to be accompanied by some conception of the present fate of the dead.

b) A Theological Reformulation. It is this approach that has been taken up within Western theology, notably by Y. Congar, J. Ratzinger, Hans Urs von Balthasar*, and G. Martelet. Once it has been accepted that urgatory is a condition and not a place, it is still necessary to envisage how the present life of the dead may be represented. Their life is involved in the dynamism of the resurrection of Jesus. That life has not yet reached its end, in the form of the final resurrection. It is not primarily a punishment but an experience of truth in relation to life within history. It is an existence in proximity to God and sustained by his Spirit, with an intensity analogous to that of mystical experience.

• R. Guardini (1949), *Die Letzen Dinge,* Würtzburg.
Y. Congar (1951), "Le purgatoire," in Coll., *Le mystère de la mort et sa célébration,* LO 12, 279–336.
H. U. von Balthasar (1960), "Umrisse der Eschatologie," *Verbum Caro,* Einsiedeln, 276–300.
G. Martelet (1975), *L'au-delà retrouvé,* Paris (new Ed. 1995).
J. Ratzinger (1977), *Eschatologie, Tod und ewiges Leben,* Regensburg (6th Ed. 1990).
J. Le Goff (1981), *La naissance du purgatoire,* Paris.
P. Miquel (1985), "Purgatoire," *DSp* 12, 2652–66.
H. Bourgeois (1985), *L'espérance maintenant et toujours,* Paris; id. (1990), "Purgatoire," *Cath.* 12, 304–13.
F. Wolfinger et al. (1995), "Fegfeuer," *LThK*3 3, 1204–10 (bibl.).

HENRI BOURGEOIS

See also **Eschatology; Hell; Judgment; Limbo; Resurrection of Christ; Resurrection of the Dead; Vision, Beatific**

Puritanism

a) Definition. Historians generally regard Puritanism as a very important phenomenon. Max Weber (1864–1920) argued, though on a narrow sociological and historical basis, that the Anglo-American puritan tradition was one of the decisive elements in the formation of the modern world. Others have looked upon Puritanism as the source of the political and social values most cherished by Americans, or even as the forebear of modern science or the contemporary family*. Puritanism also plays a central role in some Marxist analyses of society*. However, it is not easy to define the term precisely. *Puritanism* was originally a pejorative term; it came into use at the time of the social upheavals that accompanied the Reformation in England. "Puritans" were devout Protestants in a religious and social milieu that had not yet been won over to Protestantism*, a religious minority that caused surprise and shock. (A similarly circumstantial origin gave rise to the French term *Huguenot* [Calvinism*].)

b) Elizabethan Puritanism. In principle, what distinguished Puritans from other Protestants—although the distinction was never clear or absolute—was their attitude to what is known as the Elizabethan Settlement, dating from the early years of the reign of Elizabeth I

(1558–1603). The Settlement was a set of fundamentally Protestant arrangements, within which some concessions were made to the religious feelings and customs of the past. These concessions included the preservation of a certain ceremonies, some types of liturgical ornament, and some traditional church furnishings. The earliest Puritans were "nonconformists"—another term that was to have a significant future in the history of English Christianity—and they aroused the hostility of those who supported obedience to the ecclesiastical laws (law*) of the country. The points that caused controversy were in fact "indifferent things" *(adiaphora),* but the Pauline principle of Christian liberty* was at stake in these disputes. In the eyes of the Puritans the Elizabethan Settlement did not go far enough, as was demonstrated, in their view, by the liturgical conservatism of *The Book of Common Prayer.* The Settlement also had practically no effect on the structure of the Church*, since it left the episcopal system (bishop*) in place. For the Puritans, this too was a sign of serious religious indifference.

The most radical Puritans drew inspiration from the ideal example of Geneva and the "better" reformed churches, including that of France, rejecting the episcopate and adopting a position that was later to become known as Presbyterianism. All those who agreed on these grievances and aspirations came to form a sort of "church within the church," which brought together pastors (pastor*), prominent laypeople, and believers who desired to be "simple gospellers." Only a minority among these early Puritans formally separated themselves from the Church of England. At first these separatists were known as "Brownists," from the name of their first theorist, Robert Browne (c. 1550–1633). The Brownists were among those who founded the movement that gave rise in the 17th century to the Baptist* and Congregationalist Churches of England and America.

Those among the Elizabethan Puritans who remained within the Church of England campaigned energetically on behalf of their ideas over the course of several sessions of Parliament, as well as through the periodical press. However, they did not succeed in imposing these ideas, even though they had some political support, primarily because of the opposition of the Queen and of her successor, James I (king from 1603 to 1625), who were supported by two successive archbishops of Canterbury, John Whitgift (c. 1530–1604) and Richard Bancroft (1544–1610).

c) Growth of Puritanism. This defeat did not cause Puritanism to disappear. Blocked on the political level, it deeply penetrated English religious consciousness. In many respects, what historians call "the growth of puritanism" was no more than the full internalization of Protestantism and its values. This only adds to the difficulty of defining Puritanism, for in this sense it was not so much a basis for resistance to the established church, which was officially "Protestant," as a very powerful movement within it.

Not only individuals but the whole nation had to become "puritan," committed to respecting the divine covenant*, and subject to an extreme moralism that placed great emphasis on the Ten Commandments. Typically, there was a special focus on the fourth commandment (according to the Calvinist and Anglican numbering), to respect the Sabbath*, which required the imposition of a Christian form of the Sabbath. The Puritans wanted to make society* moral by suppressing every type of sin*, every form of impious behavior, from violation of the Sabbath to drunkenness, and all the "disorders" associated with popular forms of entertainment. (They were thus opposed to the innovation embodied in the Elizabethan theater.) Their principles were not entirely alien to those of their larger society, but the Puritans pushed them to the extreme.

Essentially, however, Puritanism was a form of spirituality, a religious experience* arising from the heart a of Calvinism that had more or less been imposed as

orthodoxy among Protestants; but this was an extreme form of Calvinism. The Puritans were sure that they were God's elect, clinging to this certainty above all else, and seeking confirmation of it in the spiritual fruitfulness of their lives: their Calvinism was "experiential." They took as their guides in this spiritual enterprise the famous "doctors of the soul" of their day, and some of them were to take this conception of religion with them into New England.

The most representative figure among the nonconformist Puritan preachers is undoubtedly John Bunyan (1628–88). He lacked originality, but his piety, of simple and fervent expression, was ideal for propagation. His most celebrated work, *The Pilgrim's Progress,* a "construction of pious morality" (L. Bouyer) that presents the wanderings of an allegorical hero on a quest for salvation, has enjoyed a success as wide as it is enduring. The evangelical conversion* of Vincent Van Gogh in 1875 (his family belonged to the Remonstrant tradition and the theological tendency known as the Gröningen school; *see* Calvinism) also represents an example of this form of spirituality. His experience was nurtured by two books in particular, *The Imitation of Christ* (devotio* moderna) and *Pilgrim's Progress,* and both remained fundamental to his religiosity, as expressed not only in his preaching but also in his painting.

d) Puritanism and the English Revolution. Puritanism might have been merged into the English Protestant consensus if the Church of England had not also included a tendency hostile to Calvinism, and if this tendency had not been dominant at the start of the reign of Charles I (1625–49). This tendency is sometimes interpreted as an English variant of Arminianism, while others speak of "Laudism" because of the overwhelming influence of Archbishop William Laud (1573–1645). Its supporters identified Puritanism with Calvinism pure and simple, and launched a very broad reaction that contributed to the fall of the monarchy and the English Civil War*. This revolutionary context led to the temporary collapse of the Church of England, and the Puritans acquired the political means to realize their program and take the Reformation to its conclusion. However, once they had come to power, the Puritans succumbed to their own internal contradictions, and to the opposition between the principle of liberty and the principle of discipline. The monarchy and the episcopal church were therefore restored after 1660. Nevertheless, the Puritans, who generally came to be called "Dissenters" from around this time, remained a religious, political and social force, simultaneously the grain of sand and the pearl in the oyster of English life.

- *Elisabethan Nonconformist Texts,* A. Peel, L.H. Carlson (Ed.), 6 vols., London, 1951–70.

Puritan Manifestoes, W.H. Frere, C.E. Douglas (Ed.), London, 1907 (new Ed. 1954).

A Seconde Parte of a Register, A. Peel (Ed.), 2 vols., Cambridge, 1915.

P. Miller (1933), *The New England Mind: The Seventeenth Century,* New York.

♦W. Haller (1938), *The Rise of Puritanism,* New York.

M.M. Knappen (1939), *Tudor Puritanism,* Chicago.

G.F. Nuttall (1946), *The Holy Spirit in Puritan Faith and Experience,* Oxford.

P. Collinson (1967), *The Elizabethan Puritan Movement,* London; id. (1982), *The Religion of Protestants: The Church in English Society, 1559–1625,* Oxford; id. (1983), *Godly People: Essays on English Protestantism and Puritanism,* London; id. (1987), *English Puritanism,* London.

J.S. Coolidge (1970), *The Pauline Renaissance in England; Puritanism and the Bible,* Oxford.

M.R. Watts (1978), *The Dissenters from the Reformation to the French Revolution,* Oxford.

P. Lake (1982), *Moderate Puritans and the Elizabethan Church,* Cambridge; id. (1988), *Anglicans and Puritans? Presbyterians and English Conformist Thought from Whitgift to Hooker,* London.

K. Powers Erickson (1991), "Pilgrims and Strangers: The Role of the *Pilgrim's Progress* and the *Imitation of Christ* in Shaping the Piety of Vincent van Gogh," *Bunyan Studies* 4, 7–36.

F.J. Bremer (Ed.) (1993), *Puritanism: Transatlantic Perspectives on a Seventeenth-Century Anglo-American Faith,* New York.

PATRICK COLLINSON

See also **Anglicanism; Baptists; Calvinism; Congregationalism; Methodism**

Purity/Impurity

I. Anthropological Foundation

The notion of impurity is related to a feeling of repugnance at touching or eating certain things. It appears that the specific things that provoke disgust are culturally determined, but the feeling of repugnance is a universal anthropological given that many religions integrate into their conception of the cosmos*. Impurity is communicated by physical contact and alimentation.

II. Old Testament

1. Contact

a) Sources of Impurity. The following are impure: 1) bodily secretions (Ez 4:12ff.; Dt 23:13ff.: excrement); 2) corpses of humans (Nm 19:11–16) and animals* (pure: Lv 11:21f. and impure: Lv 11:27f., 11:31); 3) a swelling, eruption, or spot on the skin (generically called leprosy, Lv 13; Dt 24:8f.), a case of leprous disease on garments (Lv 13:47ff.) and on walls (Lv 14:34ff.). Certain rites of purification and pardon also render impure (Nm 19:7, 19:10; Lv 16:24, 16:26).

b) Effects. Impurity leads to exclusion from ritual observance (Lv 12:4, 15:31, 1 Sm 16:5). It is canceled by various forms of purification.

c) Biblical Interpretation of the Distinction between Pure and Impure. The sacerdotal document (P) and the code of holiness* (H) Deuteronomy 14:1–21 interpret the dichotomy purity/impurity as a prior condition for holiness. According to these texts it has a value of *imitatio Dei* (Lv 11:44f., 20:25f,). Purity is indispensable for approaching YHWH (Is 6:5ff.), who is surrounded by holiness (Is 6:3).

The cosmos is arranged in three concentric zones: the impure, the pure, the holy. On the outside is the impure, separated from the pure; in the center is the holy, separated from the impure by the *cordon sanitaire* of the pure, which occupies the intermediate zone. In an analogous arrangement foreigners are outside of the people (Lv 20:24ff.; Dt 14:21), lay* Israelites occupy an intermediate position between foreigners and priests, the consecrated priesthood* is at the center. Contact between the impure and the pure pollutes the latter (Hg 2:13f.). Contact between the impure and the holy annihilates the holy (Lv 21:4, 21:11f.), necessitating a new sanctification (Lv 16:19) under threat of a profanation that can lead to death* (Lv 15:31, 22:3; Nm 19:13, 19:20). Contact between the pure and the holy does not modify either one (Hg 2:12), except in certain circumstances where contact with the sacrosanct (*qodèsh qâdâshîm*: Ex 29:37, 30:29; see Ez 44:19) sanctifies the pure (consecration). The impure is never compatible with the holy, the pure is ordinarily compatible except when the sacrosanct raises it to the level of the holy. For the pure, contact with the impure is inevitable in human life, but it should be impossible for the holy (Dt 24:8f.; *see* Ez 22:26).

The divine injunction "be holy" (Lv 11:44f.; Dt 14:1f.) can be interpreted as an extension to all Israel ("democratization") of priestly status, which is the furthest from impurity; this is how the injunction was interpreted at Qumran.

2. Pure and Impure Food

Impure food is limited to impure meat, all vegetables being pure. Impurity stemming from consumption of the impure cannot be rectified. This is why such impurity must be avoided, even at the cost of martyrdom* (2 Macc 6 *Sq*).

a) Pure and Impure Animals. Leviticus 11 (P), Deuteronomy 14:3–21a give two lists of animals with the criteria of purity/impurity.

They represent ancient traditions (tradition*), later completed, organizing all living beings in four groups: large quadrupeds, birds, aquatic creatures, and tiny beasts. The criteria of purity for quadrupeds are cleft hooves and rumination, and for aquatic creatures, scales or gills. There are no comparable distinctive criteria for the other two categories. This was an attempt to rationally organize a complex ancestral tradition by priestly reflection (Ez 22:26).

b) Cultic Immolation and Consumption. Only pure animals are suitable for sacrifice* and, among these, only domestic animals. Impure animals form the outer circle, those that can be immolated form the center, and the intermediate circle is composed of pure animals suitable for consumption. The connection between ancestral eating customs (e.g., grasshoppers, Lv 11:22) and sacrifices with consumption of the meat explains the choice of permitted species.

3. Anthropological Interpretation

a) Cultural Environment. The exclusion of impure animals from sacrifices and from the table is common to Near Eastern peoples, with variations among them as to the species prohibited.

The reason for the impurity of pork, donkey, and dog, domestic animals in the region since at least the Bronze Age (third millennium B.C.), is not known for certain. The pig was never a sacrificial victim in the ancient Near East, except perhaps in the Chthonic cults or funerary rites (*see* Is 66:17, 65:3f.). Dogs scavenge

on garbage and corpses (2 Kgs 9:10, 9:35f.). This dietary habit might explain why predatory animals are considered impure. The absence in the texts of any mention of poultry (except for pigeons), which were raised in Israel* in the first millennium, or of cats and horses, remains unexplained.

b) Symbolic System. The purity/impurity distinction is not founded on reasons related to hygiene, economy (food production), religion (rejection of "idolatry*"), nationality (signs of identity), or cosmic symbolism. These interpretations correspond to real concerns, but do not explain the disgust provoked by the impure, which is an intolerable, aggressive ugliness that provokes rejection and nausea *(tôʿévâh)*. By degrading the sphere of life, ugliness offensive to sight and smell attacks social cohesion, which has a vital need for dignity and decorum in the organization of its life. The purity/impurity distinction preserves a privileged social space separated from nauseating polluting elements; this distinction is the symbolic expression of the harmony of social relations of the group threatened with physical and moral degradation from the surrounding world. On the religious level the discord of impurity attacks holiness. In Israel the refusal of impure food signifies confession of the holy God* of Israel (Tb 1:10ff.; 2 Macc 6f.).

c) Impurity and Sin. By analogy, sin* can be called impurity and vice versa (Is 1:16; Jb 14:4, 15:14; Ps 51:7). In particular, the following are said to be impure in a metaphoric sense: foreign countries (Am 7:17; Is 52:11) where the food is impure (Hos 9:3; Dn 1); the land of Israel sullied by sexual sins (Lv 18:27f.), murder (Nm 35:33), necromancy (Lv 19:31) or the invocation of other gods (Hos 6:10; Jer 2:23, etc.). The behavior of the people (Ez 36:17), and even their good works, can become impure (Is 64:5).

III. New Testament

1. Paul

No food is in itself impure (Rom 14:20): Paul bases this certainty on the authority* of the Lord Jesus* (Rom 14:14), without further explanation of the reference. On the other hand, he knows there are Christians, probably Jewish Christians, who consider that impure meat is forbidden, and he believes that this represents a conscientious obligation for them.

2. Synoptics

In Mark 7:1–23 par. and Matthew 15:1–20 a logion of Jesus (Mk 7:15; Mt 15:11) on impure food is developed. In Mark 7:24–30 par., the synoptic tradition declares through an account of Jesus' action that the Jewish dietary prohibitions are null and void.

3. Acts

In Acts 10:9–16; 11:5–10, the narrative of vision reveals that God abolishes the two parallel distinctions between pure and impure foods and between Israel and pagans in the Church*. In 15:20, 15:29 Christians of pagan origin are ordered to abstain from meat immolated to idols, as from blood, the flesh of strangled animals, and illicit sexual acts. These obligations imposed by the "council" of Jerusalem* seem to correspond to those for *gérîm* (foreign residents, later proselytes): Leviticus 17:8f,, 8:10, 8:13, 18:26. Pagans converted to Christianity are bound by the law of purity as are the *gérîm*.

Qumran extended sacerdotal purity to laymen, whereas the New Testament diminished and sometimes abolished the purity/impurity distinction because many non-Jews were entering the Church and replacing the practice of the law* by faith* in Jesus Christ, in line with Pauline thinking.

IV. Theological Interpretation

The purity/impurity distinction is the symbolic expression of the beauty* of the social space created by God and existing in his presence. It was a way of confessing God in gestures that touched on every aspect of daily Israelite life, expressing Jewish identity in the face of the world.

The New Testament diminishes this symbolic system in favor of faith in Jesus Christ, from whom it expects the energies and impetus that can structure the ecclesial community in beauty, even at the level of everyday life.

- J. Döller (1917), *Die Reinheits- und Speisegesetze des Alten Testaments,* Münster.
R. de Vaux (1958), "Le sacrifice des porcs en Palestine et dans l'Ancien Orient", in *Von Ugarit nach Qumran,* BZAW 77, 250–265.
M. Douglas (1966), *Purity and Danger,* London.
W. Paschen (1970), *Rein und Unrein,* Munich.
M. Weinfeld (1972), *Deuteronomy and the Deuteronomic School,* Oxford.
J. Neusner (1973), *The Idea of Purity in Ancient Judaism,* Leyden.
I. Zatelli (1978), *Il campo lessicale degli aggettivi di purità in ebraico biblico,* Florence.
J. Henninger et al. (1979), "Pureté et impureté", *DBS* 9, 398–554.
J. Milgrom (1983), *Studies in Cultic Theology and Terminology,* Leyden; id. (1990), *Numbers,* Philadelphia; id. (1991), *Leviticus 1–16,* New York.
E. B. Firmage (1990), "The Biblical Dietary Laws and the Concept of Holiness", *in* J. A. Emerton (Ed.), *Studies in the Pentateuch, VT.S* 41, 177–208, Leyden.
W. Houston (1993), *Purity and Monotheism,* Sheffield.
M. Douglas (1993 *a*), *In the Wilderness. The Doctrine of Defilement in the Book of Numbers,* Sheffield; id. (1993 *b*), "The Forbidden Animals in Leviticus," *JSOT* 59, 3–23.
R. Péter-Contesse (1993), *Lévitique 1–16,* Geneva.
H. Harrington (1993), *The Impurity System of Qumran and the Rabbis,* Atlanta.
E. Jan Wilson (1994), *"Holiness" and "Purity" in Mesopotamia,* Kevelaer-Neukirchen.

ADRIAN SCHENKER

See also **Animals; Cult; Expiation; Healing; Holiness; Law and Christianity; Paganism; Sacrifice**

Q

Qualifications, Theological. *See* Notes, Theological

Quietism

Quietism, a polemical term that appeared in French, Italian, and Latin around 1680, designates a school of mysticism* characterized by the "prayer of quiet," as opposed to asceticism and discursive meditation. It has its sources in the Scriptures* (Paul in particular) and in the teaching of the Fathers* (Clement of Alexandria); it is possible to follow its development in the Middle Ages and the Renaissance (Mary Magdalen Pazzi). The mystical renewal contemporary with the Tridentine reforms led in the 17th century to a dissemination of "heroic indifference" (Francis of Sales, *Traité de l'amour de Dieu,* 1619), in which the human will attempts to merge with the will of God*, without nonetheless disappearing: it was, as a matter of fact, in the context of Francis of Sales's thought that the first quarrel concerning "pure love*" occurred, in 1641 (the Jesuit Sirmond, author of *La défense de la vertu,* was opposed to a disciple of Francis of Sales, Monsignor Camus, bishop of Belley, author of *La défense du pur amour*).

The spiritual teaching of the Spaniard Miguel de Molinos (1628–96) was in keeping with a doctrinal context well represented in the *Rule of Perfection* (1608–9) by English Capuchin Friar Benet of Canfield

(1562–1610). Molinos's correspondence and his spiritual guidance* supplied more evidence for his condemnation than his *Guìa Espiritual* (1675). This book, however, contains such an exclusive panegyric of acquired contemplation* as might give rise to some unfortunate consequences: the illusion of "spiritual souls*" who believe they will no longer commit sins; a permanent state of abandonment to God without having to reiterate the act of faith*; or the secondary and discrete nature of any meditation on the Passion* of Christ*. These points were of foremost importance among the accusations that led to his arrest and to his trial in Rome*, in 1685, which culminated in his condemnation to life imprisonment.

A violent campaign against quietism was triggered off at the time, bringing suspicion on a number of mystical authors who until then had been considered orthodox: Benet of Canfield himself, some Italians, and French writers such as François Malaval (1627–1719) and Bernières de Louvigny (1602–59). These were the authors who had cultivated and nurtured the piety of a young widow, Jeanne Guyon (1648–1717). Obsessed by the personality of Jeanne de Chantal, and experiencing mystical feelings and extraordinary trials, Madame Guyon wrote *Les torrents* in the space of just a few days in the winter of 1681–82. This work was the first of a long series of treatises (among which the famous *Le moyen court,* 1685) and of biblical commentaries. Her encounter in 1688 with the theologian Fénelon (1651–1715), the future archbishop of Cambrai, added to her social influence and gave her a doctrinal support that radicalized her teachings. Close to Madame de Maintenon, and introduced into the circle of the Ladies of Saint-Cyr, Jeanne Guyon was denounced and indicted in 1691: she had to defend herself before the bishop* of Chartres, Godet des Marais, and then before Bossuet, bishop of Meaux. The latter's spiritual dynamism and theological rigor were, from the outset, opposed to the lack of constraint that characterized Madame Guyon's teaching and the mystical experimentalism supporting it. In 1695 the difficulty encountered in the writing of a draft agreement (the "Issy articles") led Fénelon to want to justify himself, which he attempted to do with the *Explication des maximes des saints sur la vie intérieure* (1697). This book betrays the prevailing climate of hostility; at times it hardens the positions, and several of its proposals are lacking in nuances. However, the efforts Fénélon makes to define matters are enlightening. He discerns five different ways of loving God. The first two are motivated by self-interest; the fifth is absolutely devoid of self-interest; it is pure love ("It is possible to love God in a way that is pure altruism, and without any motive of self-interest"); the third and the fourth are mixed: "love mixed with hope"* (which does not exclude love of self) and "altruistic love mixed with some remnants of self-interest." The decisive point was a delicate one, and concerned the precise difference between the fourth and the fifth kinds of love. Vehemently attacked by Bossuet and referred to Rome*, Fénelon's book was condemned in 1699. There were two principal objections to it. The first one was its "impossible assumption" that some exceptional souls might renounce their salvation* for the love of God; the second one was the assertion of a state of perfection already attainable during life on earth. Although milder than Bossuet's accusations (the act of pure love was not condemned, and Fénelon was easily able to yield), the brief *Cum alias* (12 March 1699, *DS* 2351 *Sq*) delivered a fatal blow to Catholic mysticism. Taken up in the Germanic countries and Great Britain, Jeanne Guyon's spirituality spread and survived among Protestants such as Pierre Poiret (1646–1719) and Jean-Philippe Dutoit (1721–93), among Anglicans such as Andreas-Michael Ramsay (1686–1743), and even in the Methodist Great Awakening.

Various doctrines have been linked under the umbrella name of quietism: what they unquestionably have in common is the strongly traditional call for the selfless love of God, devoid of any hope for reward. They also have in common the lack of a christological center of gravity, which explains their difficulties. Their differences are important, however, essentially on account of the role given to acquired contemplation. There is a question that has remained open throughout the modern era (including Descartes*, Malebranche, or Leibniz*) right up to our own time, the question of pure love: is it possible to imagine a love of God absolutely devoid of love of self? A theological solution being impossible, the difficulties inherent in this question could not be abolished without having to review radically the egocentric and passionate definition, Cartesian in origin, of love.

● Fénelon (François de Salignac de la Mothe-Fénelon), *OC,* 10 vols., Paris, 1851–52; *Correspondance,* Ed. J. Orcibal, J. Le Brun, 14 vols., Paris, Geneva, 1972–.
Jeanne Guyon: La passion de croire, Ed. M.L. Gondal, Paris, 1990.
Jeanne Guyon, *Le moyen court,* Grenoble, 1995.
Molinos, *La guide spirituelle*[AuQ1], Paris, 1983 (repr. of the first French translation, 1688, from an Italian translation); *Guide spirituel,* Paris, 1997 (French trans. by P. Drochon from the Spanish original, New Ed., J.A. Valente, Madrid, 1989).
♦ L. Cognet (1958 *a*), *Crépuscule des mystiques,* Tournai (2nd Ed., Paris, 1991); (1958 *b*), *De la dévotion moderne à la spiritualité française,* Paris; (1963), "Fénelon," *DSp* 5, 151–70.
R. Spaemann (1963), *Reflexion und Spontaneität,* Stuttgart.
L. Kolakowski (1965), *Chrétiens sans Église: Conscience religieuse et lien confessionnel en France au XVIIe siècle,* Warsaw (French trans. 1969).
L. Cognet (1967), "Guyon," *DSp* 6, 1306–36.
P. Zovatto (1968), *Fénelon e il quietismo,* Udine.
J. Orcibal (1968), "Le procès des *Maximes des saints* devant le Saint-Office," *AISP* 5, 411–536.
J. Le Brun (1972), *La spiritualité de Bossuet,* Paris.
J.-R. Armogathe (1973), *Le q.,* Paris.
E. Pacho (1977), "Molinos," *DSp* 10/2, 2, 1486–1514.
J. Le Brun (1978), "Le quiétisme entre la modernité et l'archaïsme," SHCT 18, 86–99.
B. Llorca (1980), *La Inquisicion española y los alumbrados (1509–1667),* Salamanca.
R. Leuenberger (1985), "*Gott in der Hölle lieben:* Bedeutungswandel einer Metapher im Streit Fénelons und Bossuet um der Begriff des 'pur amour,'" *ZThK* 82/2, 153–72.
E. Pacho, J. Le Brun (1986), "Quiétisme," *DSp* 12/2, 2756–2842.
J.-R. Armogathe (1987), "Quiétisme," *Cath* 12, 370–77.
J.I. Tellechea Idigoras (1987), *Molinosiana: Investigationes historicas sobre Miguel Molinos,* Madrid.
M.L. Gondal (1989), *Madame Guyon (1648–1717)—un nouveau visage,* Paris.
D. Leduc-Fayette (1996), *Fénelon et l'amour de Dieu,* Paris.

JEAN-ROBERT ARMOGATHE

See also **Asceticism; Contemplation; Hope; Love; Mysticism; Prayer; Spirituality, Salesian**

Qumran. *See* Apocalyptic Literature

R

Race

The word *race* refers to a group of people delineated according to a common denominator distinguishing them from other groups or "races." Such a common denominator may be chosen within the group or imposed from outside it, according to religious, anthropological, geographical, biological, or linguistic criteria. One might thus speak of an "Islamic," "white," "British," "black," or "Latin" "race." When membership of a particular "race" is used to secure or deny certain rights or privileges, the term *racism* defines this attitude. Because of this variety of meanings, the word *race* has been used in many ways within theology*, under the influence of concepts taken from Greek or Jewish thought.

a) Greek Philosophy. According to Plato, the virtues* of the ideal citizen are an eager desire for knowledge of real existence, contempt for the pleasures of the body, and indifference to money (*Republic* VI). Although these criteria are presented as universal, they are firmly rooted in the cultural ideal of Plato's Greece. Yet Plato does not explicitly claim the superiority of the Greek "race" over other cultures.

Aristotle agrees in defining the striving for virtue as the highest ideal that could be proposed, but he gives this virtuosity, and the lack of it, a distinctly "racial" connotation, by claiming that some are by nature fit to be slaves (*Politics* I, 1254 *a* 17– 1255 *b* 15). These "natural slaves" are people lacking certain key virtues, such as munificence and magnanimity, and are often,

though not exclusively, non-Greek (ibid.). These dicta have since been used to justify racist oppression and slavery, although it is not Aristotle's suggestion to do so. In the Hellenistic era, it was individual excellence, a gift from the gods, that counted above all in judging the worth of people, rather than "racial" or ethnic origin (Koetzer 1982).

b) Judaism. In the Old Testament, the idea of a "chosen race" plays an essential role. Israel* is the "chosen race," according to the great narrative* beginning with YHWH's promise to Abraham to bless and multiply his descendants, proceeding through the Egyptian enslavement of the people* and their deliverance, and culminating in the conquest of the Promised Land by the descendants of Abraham. One reading of this history contained in theological justifications of racism is that belonging to the Jewish people was conditional on the physical link with Abraham; "race" is then a determinative factor, desired by God* himself, in distinguishing among human beings. However, in another reading of this same narrative, it is faith, and not "race," that is the condition for the membership in question. Thus, a proselyte of any origin at all could receive circumcision and become a member of the Jewish community, and hence an inheritor of God's promises.

c) New Testament. The latter reading is substantiated by the statement of John the Baptist that "God is able from these stones to raise up children for Abraham" (Mt 3:9). This New Testament universalism*, especially plain in Pauline* writings, is generally considered to be a deliberate refutation of the importance of "race" as a category for determining membership in the Church*. Galatians 3:23–29 is often quoted as support, as well as the other Pauline passages where it is claimed that faithful Israelites are united with faithful Gentiles in Christ* (e.g., Eph 2:11–18; Rom 11; Heb 8; see also 1 Pt 2:9 f.).

d) Christian Theology. With regard to "race," Greek philosophy influenced Christian theology in two ways. On the one hand, its inherent egalitarianism strengthened the Pauline relativization of "racial" heritage. On the other hand, the idea that there are natural slaves influenced some theologies in a racist direction.

During the patristic period many writers, such as Tertullian*, Cyprian*, Ambrose*, and Ambrosiaster (fourth century), allowed sin*, whether personal or inherited from our first father, to play a major part in equalizing all human beings. According to Augustine*, too, original sin* places all human beings on the same level before the holiness* of God (*De civitate Dei* II. xiv. 1). Augustine never renounced this egalitarianism, despite his view of "racial" divisions and the resulting breakdown of communication as consequences of sin.

Thomas* Aquinas takes up Aristotle's idea of the "natural" justification of the slavery of certain people, but inverts it by using it to criticize the domination of pure strength over intelligence (*SCG* III, 81). He accepts that in certain cases slavery may be justified, in the interest of the slave as well as of the master, but it is not "natural" in any absolute sense (*ST* Ia IIae, q. 94, a. 5, ad 3; IIa IIae, q. 57, a. 3, ad 2). At the cost of a certain distortion of his ideas, Aquinas's authority was claimed by both sides in the Spanish debate of the 16th century on the status of the American Indians: should they, or should they not, be viewed as natural slaves because they belonged to an "inferior race"? Vitoria (c. 1485–1546) argued against the theological justification of the "natural slavery" of "races" labeled as inferior, and concluded that the "aborigines" have true rights of property* and political autonomy.

Within the work of the fathers of the Reformation, notably Calvin* and Luther*, the importance of "race" and origin was deliberately minimized: for them, as for Augustine, what matters is the radically sinful condition of humanity before God. The humanist optimism of the Renaissance (Christian humanism*) produced theologies that were less pessimistic about human nature and gave new currency to the old Hellenistic ideal of human perfection. As in antiquity, this ideal was used in certain cases as the base for racist theologies

that served to justify colonial expansion. Later, during the 18th century, the age of the Enlightenment, it was seen as the sacred obligation of Europe to enslave and then educate the members of "inferior races" that in principle were "less excellent by nature."

Within the romantic philosophy of the latter part of the 18th century, thinkers such as Herder (1744–1803) stressed the individuality of peoples and "races," seeing the peculiarity of the *Volk* as the very image of the primordial. Hegel* takes up this term *Volk,* if only to accentuate the universal rational criteria that supersede "racial" differences. Thus, according to Hegel, the modern state must accommodate and accord civil rights to minorities, such as Jews, simply because they are human. "Universal reason" can never be the exclusive possession of one particular "race."

The colonial expansion of Europe into Africa, Latin America, Asia, and the Pacific raised the recurring questions about the justification of slavery and the value of different "races." The struggle for the abolition of slavery in America, culminating in the Civil War, focused theological discourse on the issue of racism. In *A Theology for the Social Gospel* (1917), Walter Rauschenbusch (1861–1918) claims that institutions can harbor intrinsically racist tendencies, and that such institutional racism can operate oppressively in any society*. In the wake of the civil rights movement led by Martin Luther King (1929–68), "black theologies" emerged, of which James Hal Cone was one of the main standard-bearers. This racially defined theology is an explicit attempt to do Christian theology from the perspective of people who identify with, and seek to affirm the experience of, the "black race."

Finally, one cannot forget two notorious examples of 20th-century racism, along with the theological justification that could be provided for them, and also the theological opposition that they encountered. In South Africa, Afrikaner Calvinism* sought to justify *apartheid* by appropriating certain Protestant doctrines in a one-sided fashion. By hardening the Reformation notion of "racial" pluralism, and the theology of the autonomy of different social spheres developed by Abraham Kuyper (1837–1920), into a full-fledged racist theology, "racial" divisions were taken to be divinely ordained categories of existence that should be reflected in the structures* of the church and of society. Against this theology, the *Kairos Document* (1986) and the *Belhar Confession* (1986) reaffirmed the universalist message of the New Testament.

Within Protestantism* in Germany in the 1930s, "German Christians" elaborated an extremely dangerous theology of history* to justify Hitler's program of systematic discrimination against and annihilation of the Jews, and thus placed a racist theology in the service of hatred and criminality. Consequently, notably under the influence of Karl Barth*, Protestants who were opposed to this theology constituted themselves as the Confessing Church, and issued the Barmen Declaration (1934).

In the case of South Africa, as in the case of Nazi Germany, the legitimacy of racist legislation was challenged and disputed. State racism was condemned in the name of Christian universalism.

● K. Barth, *Les communautés chrétiennes dans la tourmente,* Neuchâtel, 1943.

Belhar Confession (1986) (Publication of the Dutch Reformed Mission Church in South Africa, 1957–63).

Commission pontificale Justice et paix, *L'Église face au racisme,* Vatican City, 1988 (Paris, 1989).

J. H. Cone, *Black Theology,* New York, 1969.

G. W. F. Hegel, *Grundlinien der Philosophie des Rechts,* §209, 270, and 341–60.

Institute for Contextual Theology, *The Kairos Document: Challenge to the Church,* Johannesburg, 1986.

F. de Vitoria, *Relectio de Indis (Relecciones teológicas del Maestro Fray Francisco de Vitoria),* Madrid, 1933–35.

♦ E. Brunner (1948), *Christianity and Civilization* (Gifford Lectures, 1947), London.

W. J. Carey (1952), *A Christian on the Colour-Bar,* London.

C. G. Campbell (1953), *Race and Religion,* London.

L. Hanke (1959), *Aristotle and the American Indians,* Regnery.

E. W. Blyden (1967), *Christianity, Islam and the Negro Race,* Edinburgh.

C. Hill, et al. (1968), *Race: A Christian Symposium,* London.

F. E. Auerbach (1970), *The A.B.C. of Race,* Johannesburg.

S. Ahlstrom (1972), *A Religious History of the American People,* New Haven.

C. Lévi-Strauss (1972), *Race et histoire,* Paris.

A. Meier (1973), *CORE: A Study in the Civil Rights Movement, 1942–1968,* Oxford-New York.

B. Moore (Ed.) (1973), *Black Theology: The South African Voice,* London.

T. D. Moodie (1975), *The Rise of Afrikanerdom,* Berkeley-London.

C. Vandervelde (1975), *Original Sin,* Amsterdam.

A. Boesak (1976), *Farewell to Innocence,* New York.

H. Koetzer (1982), *History, Culture and Religion of the Hellenistic Age,* New York.

J. W. de Gruchy (1986), *The Church Struggle in South Africa,* 2nd Ed., Grand Rapids, Mich.

M. L. King, Jr. (1986), *A Testament of Hope,* Ed. J. A. Washington, San Francisco.

A. Nolan (1988), *God in South Africa,* Cape Town.

I. J. Mosala (1989), *Biblical Hermeneutics and Black Theology in South Africa,* Grand Rapids.

R. M. Brown (Ed.) (1990), *Kairos: Three Prophetic Challenges to the Church,* Grand Rapids.

A. Chibambu (1990), *Right Is Might,* Zimbabwe.

J. W. de Gruchy (1990), *Liberating Reformed Theology,* London.

J. Evans (1992), *We Have Been Believers: An African American Systematic Theology,* Minneapolis.

J. van Eck (1992), *God, Mens, Medemens, Humanitas in de theologie van Calvijn,* Franeker.

M. Macey (1993), *Christianity, Capitalism and Racism,* Bradford.

C. O'Doherty (1993), *Racism: A Growing Challenge to Christians: Report of a Seminar Presented by Missionaries of Africa (White Fathers),* Dublin.

G. Schutte (1995), *What Racists Believe: Race Relations in South Africa and the United States Today,* London.

D. Schnapper (1996), "Racisme," *DEPhM,* 1247–52.

STEFANUS DU TOIT

See also **Adam; Anthropology; Church and State; Pauline Theology; Person**

Rahner, Karl

1904–84

A. Life

Rahner was born at Freiburg im Breisgau and died at Innsbruck; he was the fourth of seven children of Karl Rahner, a schoolteacher, and his wife Luise, née Trescher. He grew up and went to school in the town of his birth. By the time he made his vows at Tisis (Vorarlberg) in 1922 to become a member of the South German province of the Society of Jesus, his brother had already been a Jesuit for three years. Rahner had previously belonged to the "Quickborn" youth association, especially influenced by Romano Guardini. It was in the context of the post-First World War Catholic revival that he became involved in the activities of the Jesuits: at that time influences from France (H. Bremond) and Belgium (J. Maréchal) were arousing considerable interest in the life of prayer* and spirituality, while the study of sources and documents relating to the origins of the Jesuit order *(Monumenta Historica Societatis Jesu, MHSJ)* was offering religious youth a variety of inspirations and stimulating the revival of the *Exerzitienbewegung* (spiritual exercises) movement. The critical discussions that had begun in Germany (since the *Kulturkampf* and research within Protestantism* undertaken by figures such as H. Böhmer) had led to important historical results (B. Duhr) that would influence the Order's conception of itself.

Along with his brother, Rahner grew interested and became involved in these trends, and he was soon advancing original points of view—as revealed in the short texts dating from these first years. Prompted by this strong interest in Ignatian spirituality*, from 1924 to 1927 Rahner undertook general, scientific, and philosophical studies at the Berchmannskolleg, which the Order had just founded at Pullach near Munich. So deeply involved did he become in these studies that toward the end of this period he decided to devote himself to teaching the history of philosophy* (in particular modern philosophy). However, this ambition did not however have any immediate consequences for the remainder of his training, since he was initially given the job of teaching languages to young members of the Order, and subsequently studied theology* at the Jesuit university of Valkenberg in Holland. He was ordained priest by Cardinal Michael Faulhaber in Munich in the summer of 1932—a summer marked by political unrest due to the rise of National Socialism. He spent his last year of general training in 1933–34 at Sankt Andrä (Carinthia), before returning to his home town to specialize in philosophy. Heidegger* had just resigned as Rector; at Freiburg, Rahner's studies were directed by M. Honecker. Rahner pursued a variety of courses, in particular Heidegger's seminars. He selected as his research topic finite knowledge in the work of Thomas* Aquinas, thus situating his research among the attempts to adapt neo-Thomism to modern philosophy. A number of theses supervised by Honecker approached this problem from different angles. Rahner chose to develop some suggestions made by J. Maréchal and P. Rousselot. His thesis, as it was presented in 1936, was not accepted by M. Honecker, but even before this news had been conveyed to him, Rahner, with the energetic support of his brother Hugo, had turned to church history*, done a theology doctorate at the University of Innsbruck and passed his examination to teach theology. This led to a change of plan: abandoning philosophy, Rahner prepared himself to take up a chair of theology at Innsbruck. At the "Salzburg University weeks" in August 1937 (the last before the Second World War) he presented the ideas

that would later be published under the title of *Hörer des Wortes* (*Hearers of the Word,* 1967); then, at the beginning of the winter term 1937–38, he took up his post at Innsbruck.

Following the Anschluß in the spring of 1938 the faculty was closed by the Nazis (effective the following summer), and Rahner, like the other members of the Order, was forced to pursue his academic work in semisecrecy. Only in 1945 was he able to resume his teaching openly, this time at Pullach near Munich (until 1948). Upon his return to Innsbruck he displayed a tireless energy in a variety of fields, throughout the years of reconstruction and right up until the Second Vatican* Council: the most important fruits of this period, apart from the *Theological Writings,* which originated as occasional texts, were the preparation of the second edition of the *Lexikon für Theologie und Kirche* and the publication of the series Quaestiones Disputatae. Thanks to his university activities and his sensitivity to the numerous challenges encountered by faith* and the church, he became more and more clearly aware of the gulf that separated the traditional presentation of Christianity from the new problems confronting it, and he felt the need for a theology that would truly be able to face up to them. It was in this frame of mind that he accorded increasing importance in his writings to spiritual* direction and began work on the publication of a large *Handbuch der Pastoraltheologie.* While his work was, above all, situated in a German context, Rahner's involvement with Vatican II—initially as an adviser to the Viennese Cardinal Franz König, then as an expert on the theological commission—enabled him to make his voice heard in the universal Church as well. Bishops and theologians discovered a man deeply attached to Catholic tradition*; a man who, concerned for a world that was moving ever further from its former criteria, displayed an incredible ingenuity for discovering new viewpoints.

It was precisely this talent that Rahner hoped to exercise when the philosophy faculty of Munich University asked him to succeed Romano Guardini to the chair of Christian thought. He accepted the offer in 1964, but soon realized that it was just as urgent to revitalize theology so as to ensure the acceptance of the council's decision at local* church level. With this in mind, in 1967 he rejoined the theology faculty of the University of Münster, where he pursued his academic activities until 1971. His services were particularly called on by the Diocesan Synod of the Federal Republic of Germany, which met in Würzburg from 1971 to 1975 and was concerned not only to implement the council's approach in the life of the German church, but also to respond to the spiritual transformations that had taken shape in the meantime. 1976 saw the publication of the *Grundkurs des Glaubens (Foundations of Christian Faith),* in which Rahner again sought to give impetus to the life of faith and to theological training. As discussions took a new direction, he defended the principles of openness and engagement in the face of the ever-stronger tendencies advocating a turning inward and a reassertion of traditional positions. At the beginning of the 1980s Rahner returned to Innsbruck, where he continued his activities until the end of his life. He died soon after his 80th birthday and was buried in the Jesuit Church at Innsbruck. In the last years of his life he displayed a keen interest in young people and the questions they were asking, and made cautious attempts to establish a new dialogue with atheism*, in particular with representatives of the Communist intelligentsia. In this respect, the publication in 1983 of French and Hungarian translations of his *Foundations* represented the culmination and vindication of his work.

KARL HEINZ NEUFELD

B. Theological Outlook

This article deals mainly with Rahner's major insights, and with a few key concepts that give his work its coherence without making it into a system. The continuity of his life and thought, notwithstanding the changes associated with the context of the world* and the church*, justifies a synchronic approach.

1. The Living Source

"In order to free me from the fear which your immensity inspires in me, you must allow your infinite word to be contained within limits, you must make it pass within my narrowness" (*Worte ins Schweigen,* 1938). Rahner's theology is not simply the outcome of lecturing and academic research. It is grounded in a life of faith* and prayer*, of which four aspects should be borne in mind: an Ignatian spirituality*, involving the experience* of God* both on a personal level and through the church; familiarity with the Church Fathers*, leading to a spirituality centered on the mystery* of the Father*, his Word*, and his Spirit; the influence of Origen* and Bonaventure* and the doctrine of "spiritual meanings"; and attachment to the transfixed heart* of Christ crucified, the symbol of infinite Love* and source of the Church.

Rahner's spirituality was based on the incarnate Word, the *Word of the Father;* his life as a believer was lived out in a primordial affirmation of the physical church, the arena of our conversion*, so as to become a "minister of Christ" and "bring succor to souls." For Rahner the mind, forever turned toward the world, was also a self-awareness that could grasp itself, going beyond images and concepts and finding its freedom by seeking the invisible in the visible, listening amid the silence to the words of the beginning (*Urworte*), simple words that bore a secret mystery: the Nameless had come to express itself in human hearts and in the history* of peoples.

This living source of his theology gave an advance unity to his further philosophical and theological research. Destined to teach first philosophy and then theology, Rahner would always see the former as an intrinsic part of his theological research. Between the 1930s and the 1980s, however, his awareness of an insurmountable pluralism prevented him from taking a unified philosophical tradition as the anthropological foundation for a system of theological thought (which had itself become very diverse in the meantime).

2. Philosophical Influences: Maréchal and Heidegger

During his years studying philosophy (1924–27) Rahner studied the fifth *Cahier* in the series by the Belgian Jesuit Joseph Maréchal (1878–1944) entitled the *Starting Point of Metaphysics: Thomism in the Light of Critical Philosophy* (1926). Maréchal's aim was to integrate the truthful portion of modern philosophy (Descartes*, Kant*, Fichte) with Thomas's realism: the mind's thought as receptivity *and activity* in the act of knowing. This subjective impulse of knowledge was not the result of experience or knowledge. Rather, it was always already present in man, and constituted an a priori to which philosophy devoted an inquiry known since Kant as "transcendental": a consideration of the conditions under which experience in general is possible. Following Maréchal, Rahner took up this critical approach that highlights the necessarily subjective impulse of any knowledge, whatever it might be. Along with the Belgian philosopher, however, he emphasized the other aspect of a transcendental approach, which is the mind's urge toward an absolute horizon.

From 1934 to 1936 Rahner worked on a philosophy doctorate at Freiburg and attended Heidegger*'s classes. He would subsequently tend to play down the influence of the author of *Being and Time* upon his thought. The Rahner of the late 1930s is nonetheless indebted to Heidegger—as, indirectly, is the author of the *Foundations of Christian Faith* (*Foundations*, 1976, English trans. 1978) in relation to two themes: the *existential* and *being-in-the-world*. Existentials, according to Heidegger, are the general and formal structures that make up the *Dasein*, in other words, the mode of being proper to man, and their analysis makes it possible to discern in man the locus in which the question of being* *(Sein)* arises, beyond the questions devoted to such and such an entity or group of entities. If being is in question in man, it is because the latter is defined first of all in terms of his openness to the world. Either in advance or straight away, man is "outside himself." As Rahner wrote in 1940, "Man is from the outset open to the totality of the world.... In order to be present to himself, he must externalize himself, and make room in himself for the totality of the world" (*RSR* 1940, 162). Man, in short, is open to being not as a result of theoretical considerations, through the mediation of contingent experiences, but by virtue of a fundamental experience: the anticipation of death*. These themes, echoing Heidegger, would later be developed by Rahner in strictly theological terms.

Rahner's philosophy thesis, "The Mind in the World: The Metaphysics of Finite Knowledge in the Work of Saint Thomas Aquinas" (which was rejected), brought these philosophical considerations to a conclusion and announced some of the questions to come: with Thomas and Heidegger, Rahner conceived of man as a being forever linked to the perceptible, while with Kant and Maréchal, he saw in man a consciousness of self, the mind. It was thus, as both complete openness and impassable finiteness, that man pondered the conditions under which knowledge was possible.

3. Intellectually Honest Faith

As a teacher, an editor, and a preacher, Rahner had one paramount concern: not to gloss over difficulties, whether of the present time or of historical Christianity. He also sought to profit from the *chances of the Christian faith* by making clear that it was not an ideology. Hence the considerable thought he devoted to the relationship of theological method to that of other academic disciplines.

a) Two Ways of Conceiving the Fundamental Relationship between God and Man. Man appeared to Rahner first and foremost as the intended recipient of a possible revelation* in history, and God appeared to him first in his intimate mystery, as he had chosen to present himself to man in his grace* and in his Word made *flesh*. So Rahner formulated a rule intended to clarify any particular theological question: proximity and distance, dependence and autonomy, do not grow in inverse proportion but in direct proportion (*Schr. zur Th.* I, 29, no. 1; *Foundations*). The fullness of heavenly grace was Jesus* of Nazareth, born of a woman*. The fundamental theological law *(Grundgesetz)*, the axiom of all Christian thought, and the christological principle of dogmatics* (*Schr. zur Th.* I, ibid.) was therefore this: in the sight of *Deus semper major*, finitude and contingency are not mere nothingness*, but rather creation*.

Within this theology a place was found for a consideration of the *experience of grace*. Grace was freely offered to all, and every human being could receive and experience it in his daily life, by virtue of the mind's transcendence of any object, even in the absence of a "religious" dimension. Christianity alone could recognize in it an experience of grace. If, however, this experience were not possible for everyone, Christianity could never have found acceptance.

On the basis of these axioms Rahner constructed concepts (or modified the sense of ancient expressions) intended to show how "it is possible to believe today," and did so with one constant goal: that of conceiving of the intimate relationship that God wished to establish between himself and a man created with the capacity to understand a possible revelation; even more, to consider the mystery of the uncreated, which becomes the "most intimate constituent" of its creature.

b) Obediential Power. While Rahner did not invent the expression, he did give new life to the problem. This power characterizes man in two ways: both as an obedient openness (in other words, pure disposition) and as a positive capacity—resolute receptiveness, the *capacity for assumption (Foundations)*. Grace (in other words, God giving himself) must be able to be received *as grace*, transcending all expectation and all desire; but it must also be able to be *received* by man. There must be an affinity between nature* and grace— if this were not the case, Christianity would remain external to the human condition in the universe. Obediential power is man's concrete essence. However, a particular concept of "nature" is thereby implied: the recipient of the free gift must be firm in himself.

c) Supernatural Existential. This second expression is linked to the previous one. While man is destined for a supernatural end, this is not as a result of some kind of legal decree: this destiny corresponds to what man is in his essence, in other words a being focused on the absolute, awaiting a possible revelation. By speaking thus of an "existential," Rahner (following Heidegger) means to denote a structure that precedes any decision. However, by attributing to this existential the quality of being "supernatural*," he makes it clear that the existential is not due, that it is not an attribute of a "pure nature," but rather man's absolute relation to God, the location of grace in the innermost part of man. Every human being lives under a desire for universal and effective salvation*.

d) Self-Communication. This term is a key concept of Rahner's, and serves to express the mystery of God the Father who makes himself the innermost part of man. All metaphysical distance and impossibility are thereby transcended. The human being is then defined as an *event* of God's self-communication, freely given and forgiving: not only as recipient and beneficiary, but also as partner in an act that comes complete from God in such a way that God allows freedom and intelligence to be recipients of it. God becomes the starting point for *man's self-fulfillment (Foundations)*. In this way the "heart of Christianity" (ibid.) is affirmed: the absolute giver (the Father) coincides with the gift (the Word), and it is only thus (as uncreated grace, the Holy Spirit) that he enables man to receive it himself (rather than an idol, the projection of desires)—in other words, the Trinity*. Man's finite nature and fragility are not abolished by such a gift; on the contrary, it gives them all their dignity.

e) Anonymous Christians. Since the human being is created to participate freely in God's vision, and since the grace by which God offers himself freely to man has forever been the *gratia Christi*, Rahner is led to suggest that there must be women and men who, having received and acted upon the offer of participation in the life divine, have "believed" in Jesus Christ without ever having known his name* or belonged to his Church.

The theory of anonymous Christians is first a "theory of consequent grace" (Hilberath 1995). It is linked to two suppositions: the unity of love for God and for one's neighbor; and the idea that the history of salvation and revelation is "coextensive" with human history. It aims to overlook neither the concrete nature of revelation nor the necessity that the "ministerial" church should be a missionary one. The proposition of this theory gave rise to arguments that H. de Lubac partly dispelled: the existence of "anonymous Christians" was not in doubt, but to speak of "anonymous Christianity" would be to misrepresent Rahner's intentions.

f) Economic Trinity Is the Immanent Trinity, and Vice Versa. The history of revelation would lose all its meaning if God did not give himself to man just as he is in himself. Rahner frequently ponders the theological implications of faith in the Trinity. The "economic Trinity" is the revelation of the God who gave himself in his entirety, as the Father, in the life, ministry and Passion* of Jesus his Son, and in the Spirit of filial adoption communicated to mankind. The "immanent Trinity" is the Trinity in itself, independently of the history of salvation: the Father is eternally the sole Uncreated, with his Word and his Spirit.

Rahner's axiom (the economic Trinity is the immanent Trinity, and vice versa) may be interpreted from the starting point of mankind: the latter has access to the divine in-itself only by virtue of its revelation. If God reveals himself as the Trinity, it is because he is so eternally. Revelation *is* the communication through God of his own secret, his identity, in and through the human face of Jesus, the complete fulfillment of revelation in history. Taken from the starting point of God, the axiom signifies that his in-himself is a for-us (divine philanthropy, Ti 3:4). Here Rahner takes a stand against two extremes:

1) Against the separation of the treatise on the triune God from the treatise on the singular God, the latter being dependent on philosophical conceptions and providing prerequisites to any revelation, the former adding a dogmatic complement: a separation according to which the eternal Trinity, cut off from history, can end up resembling a conceptual game. Against such an isolation of the doctrine of the Trinity, Rahner aims to put back at the heart of theology what he calls the "unique Mystery": the self-communication of the personal God, the Father, in the Incarnation* of his Word and in his Spirit's gift of grace.

2) From here the question arises of why one should continue to posit a Trinity in itself, an immanent eternal Trinity. Against the second extreme suggested by this question, Rahner asserts that the Trinity in history would become meaningless if it were not the revelation of God's eternal being. Revelation in history is indeed the self-communication of the Father's secret, but this se-

cret is given precisely *as* inexhaustible. What is at stake here is the *gratuitousness of an infinite Love,* in itself perfect, which has *freely* wished to create another and give itself to that other.

"Vice versa" implies, in short, that the mystery of the living God is not really respected either by a strictly "economic" approach or by a pure doctrine of the "immanent" Trinity. Rahner frequently concludes his reflections with a *reductio in mysterium.* If he insists on "economy," it is certainly not to imply that the Trinity exhausts itself in history. For this reason he is able to conclude his meditation on the Trinity by saying that "God himself, the unending sacred mystery, the incomprehensible foundation of man's transcendent existence, is not only the God of infinite distance, but wishes to be the God of absolute proximity, in true self-communication" *(Foundations).*

g) Sacramental Penitence As "Reconciliation with the Church." An entire volume of the *Schriften zur Theologie* (XI) collects Rahner's historical and systematic studies on penance* in the early church, and the last volume contains another text from 1980 on the status of the sacrament* of penance. This interest came from the wellspring of his thought: the life of faith, worship, the pastoral sense ("he wanted to be a pastor* out of love for mankind," Vorgrimler 1998), the perception of the inner connection between the "loss of grace," conversion*, and the social dimension of our being. Rahner's thinking on penance is an exemplar of his whole theological method: the theology of grace and the anthropology of the *spirit in the world* are united in ecclesiology*.

With a sound knowledge of the history of doctrines and sacramental practices, Rahner frequently detected "forgotten truths." In this particular case, the modern West had lost sight of an ecclesiological truth: "If the Church must be seen not only as an external canonical organization but as God's *holy* people, as a covenant of grace, as Christ's body animated by a Spirit, then *any* sin by a member of the Church contradicts the inner essence of the Church, not just those sins that the Church punishes with excommunication in the strict sense. This also stems from the fact that…any serious sin, before it is sacramentally erased, of itself excludes one from the Eucharist*, from the Church's central mystery, and therefore always has an ecclesiological aspect" *(Schr.* VIII).

Rahner judged the post-Vatican* II reforms to the celebration of the sacrament of penance to be both important and insufficient. While he recognized the value of private confession, he nonetheless felt that community ritual better expressed the penitent sinner's reconciliation with the Church (Vorgrimler 1998).

4. Theologian in a Time of Contrasts

Rahner always aimed to consider faith and the approach to faith as a theologian, in an age characterized by the proliferation and specialization of knowledge—an age, that is, when no one can any longer master everything he really ought to know.

Concerned about the theological training of the laity*, and also of future priests*, he aimed to introduce people to Christianity by starting from its essence, but also in the context of his own time. While no one can ever be sure of everything before embarking on a decision that will shape his whole life (profession, choice of religion, ecclesiastical vocation), an initial "knowledge," as a preliminary to the specialized disciplines, must nonetheless exist, expressing both the most personal self and an openness to human experience in general. So there must exist, as an elementary postulation of all fundamental* theology, a rational justification of Christianity that will take account of the possibility, open to all, learned and uneducated alike, of understanding and believing that Jesus is Lord. As early as 1954 Rahner observed that there was a need to find a catechism for beginners, those whom Augustine called the *rudes (Mission and Grace;* see *Schr.* III,). It was really to this that he was applying himself in the *Foundations of Christian Faith,* in an age when we are all in some sense *rudes.*

The book is structured in nine stages, of which the first four, devoted to mankind, may be read independently of any Christian reference. The central part (a centrality proved by the relationship between the fifth and sixth stages) links the transcendental and categorial aspects of divine revelation, both of which culminate in Christ. The remainder of the book deals with ecclesiology, the life of the Christian, and eschatology*, all the while stressing the link between human experience and Christian revelation.

The attitude of the theologian who, in an age of contrasts, reflects on faith and hope*, can be summed up in one word: patience. This is in no sense resignation. It does all that can be done. It is oriented toward the absolute future, whose seed is already present *in a time of winter.*

Rahner involved himself ever more resolutely in ecumenical work, alongside Protestant theologians such as Eberhard Jüngel, with whom he had already published a pamphlet, *Was ist ein Sakrament?* (1971). In 1983 they published a new tract on patience *(Über die Geduld).* Without yielding to impatience or utopian visions, Rahner maintained, along with his pupil Heinrich Fries, that the unity* of the churches was already possible, around the *fundamental substance* of faith.

From the 1950s Rahner had asserted the right to free speech and the rights of the individual within the church. The "yes to the physical church" (*Schr.* IX) and the respect for its hierarchical structure did not "rule out the right to disagree." On this point Rahner was not always understood, either by the "Romans" or by the "dissidents" (as, for example, in his debate with H. Küng). But the testimony he bore to true Christian responsibility helped many Christians to *follow Jesus* in the Church. More than some of his critical writings, the humor of *The Speech of Ignatius of Loyola to the Jesuits of Today,* or of *The Undying Topicality of the Papacy (Letter of Paul VII to Peppino: A Papal Letter of the Twenty-First Century,* in *Schr.* XVI, 1983) expresses Rahner's realistic support for the hierarchical church, as well as his refusal of lies or injustice in the church. Realism—and even a certain pessimism—is as essential to the Christian life as hope. Christianity does not conceal the reality of failure and death; the Christian proclaims the victory of a death that is *the one entrance to life (Foundations,* 449). Here Rahner takes up some observations from his earlier writings: "You have committed yourself to a perpetual coming. You have taken our state of slavery as the starting point for your coming, which will put an end to that slavery" *(Worte ins Schweigen).* And, echoing Heidegger: "Being resolute in one's 'being-for-death,' this is the fundamental attitude demanded of the *Dasein;* to bear the anguish of nothingness, that is the courage to live" (*RSR* 1940).

● R. Bleistein, E. Klinger (Ed.) (1969), *Bibliographie K. Rahner, 1924–1969,* Freiburg.

R. Bleistein (Ed.) (1974), *Bibliographie K. Rahner, 1969–1974,* Freiburg.

P. Imhof, H. Treziak (Eds.) (1979), "Bibliographie K. Rahner, 1974–1979," in H. Vorgrimler (Ed.), *Wagnis Theologie,* Freiburg, 579–97.

P. Imhof, E. Meuser (Ed.) (1984), "Bibliographie K. Rahner, 1979–1984," in E. Klinger, K. Wittstadt (Ed.), *Glaube im Prozeß,* Freiburg, 854–71.

Schriften zur Theologie, 16 vols. and index, Einsiedeln-Zurich-Köln.

Sämtliche Werke, 32 vols., Freiburg-Köln, 1995–.

♦ P. Eicher (1970), *Die anthropologische Wende: K. Rahners philosophischer Weg vom Wesen des Menschen zur personalen Existenz,* Fribourg.

G. Langevin (1973), "Le pluralisme en matière spirituelle et religieuse selon Karl Rahner," *LTP* 29, 3–18.

B. van der Heijden (1973), *Karl Rahner—Darstellung und Kritik seiner Grundpositionen,* Einsiedeln.

K. Fischer (1974), *Der Mensch als Geheimnis: Die Anthropologie Karl Rahners,* Freiburg.

N. Schwerdtfeger (1982), *Gnade und Welt: Zum Grundgefüge von Karl Rahners Theorie des "anonymen Christen,"* Freiburg.

K.H. Neufeld (1984), "Somme d'une théologie—Somme d'une vie," *NRTh* 106, 817–33.

B. Sesboüé (1984), "Karl Rahner et les "chrétiens anonymes,'" *Études* 361, 521–35.

J. Hak-Piu Wong (1984), *Logos-Symbol in the Christology of Karl Rahner,* Rome.

E.G. Farrugia (1985), *Aussage und Zusage: Zur Undirektheit der Methode Karl Rahners veranschaulicht an seiner Christologie,* Rome.

G. Vass (1985), *Understanding Karl Rahner,* London.

H. Vorgrimler (1985), *Karl Rahner verstehen,* Freiburg.

R. Miggelbrink (1989), *Ekstatische Gottesliebe im tätigen Weltbezug: Der Beitrag Karl Rahners zur zeitgenössischen Gotteslehre,* Altenburg.

K.H. Neufeld (1994), *Die Brüder Rahner: Eine Biographie,* Freiburg.

B.J. Hilberath (1995), *Karl Rahner: Gottgeheimnis Mensch,* Mayence.

T. Knieps (1995), *Die Unvertretbarkeit von Individualität,* Würzburg.

Y. Tourenne (1995), *La théologie du dernier Rahner,* CFi 187.

A. Raffelt, H. Verweyen (1997), *Karl Rahner,* Munich.

H. Vorgrimler (1998), "La théologie du sacrement de pénitence chez Karl Rahner," *MD* 214, 7–33.

YVES TOURENNE

See also **Balthasar, Hans Urs von; Lonergan, Bernard John Francis; Lubac, Henri Sonier de; Spirituality, Ignatian**

Rationalism

Appearing in the 16th century in France as an antonym for *empirical,* the adjective *rationalist* was first used in philosophy. A rationalist is one for whom pure thought has more cognitive power than experience. It was not until the 17th century that the theological history of rationalism began.

a) Protestant Theology. The theological concept of rationalism came into being as a polemical tool. For the Lutheran theologian D. Hoffmann (1538–1611) and his student J.A. von Werdenhagen (1581–1652), their philosophical colleagues who followed Aristotle were *rationistae* or *ratiocinistae* (*RE,* 3rd Ed., 21, 103). P.

Poiret (1646–1719) used the term (associated with *idealism*) in his critique of deism and Socinianism. The term was soon taken up by a strictly theological current. From the publication of L. Meyer's *Philosophia S. Scripturae Interpres* (1666), there was a debate in the Netherlands between "rational" and " nonrational" or "antirational" theologians. In England there was opposition between the "rationalists," the "skeptics," and the "fideists." Whatever its beginnings, rationalism was soon defined in terms of a critical reorganization of the concept of revelation*, in which theology* attempted to respond to the objections of the Enlightenment, particularly in Germany, where the *Aufklärung* did not seem armed with any hostility to Christianity.

Several movements can be distinguished. The *Übergangstheologen* (S.J. Baumgarten [1706–57], J.F. Buddeus [1667–1729], J.L. von Mosheim [1694–1755], and C.M. Pfaff [1686–1760]) defended the harmony of reason* and revelation by emphasizing the fact that revelation could contain nothing in contravention of the natural and rational knowledge* of God. There appeared simultaneously in Switzerland a "rational orthodoxy" among "Switzerland's theological triumvirate" (J.A. Turretini [1671–1737], S. Werenfels [1657–1704], and J.F. Ostervald [1663–1747]). And again in Germany, the Wolffian theologians (J.G. Reinbeck [1683–1741], J. Carpov [1699–1768], and F.A. Schultz [1692–1763]) carried out a systematic organization of dogmas* designed to satisfy the demands of reason. An axiom was linked these movements: revelation is not only capable of justifying itself before the court of reason, it must do so.

Protestant rationalism was most fully developed in the "neologist" theologians (A.F.W. Sack [1703–86], J.F.W. Jerusalem [1709–89], J.J. Spalding [1714–1804], J.G. Toellner [1724–74], J.A. Ernesti [1707–81], and J.D. Michaelis [1717–91]) between 1740 and 1790. Faith* in a revelation remains, but its dogmas may not be supported unless they are subjected to the tests of reason and "moral conscience*." Nothing more (but also nothing less) is revealed than the true content of "natural religion," which leads the theology of the neologists to marginalize a substantial number of dogmatic affirmations (original sin* and the existence of hell*, among others). Kant was not a theologian, but when his *Religion within the Limits of Reason Alone* appeared in 1793 it looked very much like a concluding manifesto to the movement.

The movement thereafter experienced a further radicalization in the form of "Christian rationalism" (H.P.K. Henke [1752–1809], J.F.C. Loeffler [1752–1816], J.F. Tiefrunk [1759–1837], J.A.L. Wegscheider [1771–1849], H.E.G. Paulus [1761–1851]): in their work, what remained of Christianity was a path

toward the truly ethical and religious life. Hegel* was able to say of rationalism that it had emptied philosophy* of its content by "emptying heaven" and by "reducing everything to finite relationships" (*Jubiläumsausgabe* 17. 112). Opposed to rationalism was a "supernaturalist" school (G.C. Storr [1746–1805], K.C. Flatt [1772–1843], F.G. Süskind [1767–1829], G.C. Knapp [1753–1825], and J.A.H. Tittmann [1773–1832]). An intermediate position was held by "rational supernaturalism" or "supernaturalist rationalism" (K.F. Stäudlin [1761–1826], E.G. Bengel [1769–1826], K.L. Nitzsch [1751–1831], and K.G. Bretschneider [1776–1848]), which affirmed a perfect coincidence of the revealed and the rational, while recognizing the divine origin of revelation.

In a theological landscape henceforth dominated by Schleiermacher*, rationalism had to retreat before the "theology of the awakening" or the confessional theology of the school of Erlangen, while its critical concerns were taken up by the Hegelian left. But rationalist theology resurfaced in the form of liberal Protestantism*. The "dialectical theology" created by Barth* wished to draft rationalism's death certificate. Nevertheless, there were always voices as respectable as those of Dilthey, Troeltsch, and E. Hirsch to recall the contributions of rationalism to biblical criticism and to the history of Christian doctrines. Such individuals believed that it had made possible progress in theology itself: "There is a road that leads, through rationalism, to a knowledge of Christian truth* deeper than the truth that rationalism reaches. But there is no road allowing theology seriously to reach its aim by circumventing rationalism or relying only on what precedes rationalism" (Hirsch).

b) Catholic Theology. The influence of the Enlightenment on theology was substantially less in Catholicism* than in Protestantism (influence did occur, however—F.A. Blau [1754–98], J. Danzer [1743–96], J.A. Dereser [1757–1827], and L.B. Werkmeister [1745–1823]). The term *rationalism* did not appear in Catholic theology until the 19th century, and it appeared first of all in official declarations of censure. By opposing rationalism, on the one hand, to the pair formed by fideism* and traditionalism*, on the other, Catholicism articulated its relationship to a philosophy and a critical historiography that had taken shape outside its sphere of influence. The violence of the condemnations is obvious, although the modes of thought condemned did in fact lack maturity.

As early as 1832 Gregory XVI's censure of the theories of Lammenais on religious freedom was presented as a censure of reason relying on its strength alone (*ASS* 4 [1868] 341, 344 *Sq*). The year 1835 saw the posthumous condemnation of the works of G. Hermes (1775–1831). This theologian from Bonn, whose apologetics granted legitimacy to doubt as long as the conceptual work of establishing a foundation had not been accomplished, was said to have taught that reason is "a governing norm and the only means by which man may attain knowledge of supernatural truths" (*DS* 2738). On 9 November 1846 Pius IX devoted a part of his inaugural encyclical, *Qui pluribus,* to the errors of those who "constantly rely on the strength and the excellence of human reason" (*DS* 2775). In 1857 there was another cause célèbre: the condemnation of the Viennese A. Günther (1783–1863), a somewhat confused Gnostic thinker. The "system of rationalism" was dominant in his writings; he attributed "a magisterium to human reason and to philosophy, which in religious matters should not dominate but serve"; he had violated both "the distinction between science and faith and the perennial immutability of faith, which is always one and the same" (*ASS* 8, 446 *Sq*). In 1862 there was a third cause célèbre: the condemnation of J. Frohschammer (1821–93): "The author in fact teaches first that philosophy, if one has a proper notion of it, cannot only comprehend those Christian dogmas that natural reason knows as well as faith…but that even the very sacred mystery* of the Incarnation* of the Lord belongs to the province of human reason and philosophy" (*ASS* 8, 430 *Sq*). In 1863 a theological conference held in Munich and presided over by J.J.I. von Döllinger gave Pius IX the opportunity to recall the submission of science to the magisterium* of the church and the impotence of reason alone in the face of the "infallible and uncreated light of the divine intellect" (*ASS* 8, 438 *Sq*). Finally, in 1864 the *Syllabus* bringing together all the "modern errors" proscribed by the teaching of Pius IX provided the most precise definitions of rationalism. "Human reason, taking no account of God, is the only arbiter of the true and the false, of good* and evil*, it is its own law and can rely on its own strength to benefit men and peoples": this is the way in which "absolute" rationalism was said to speak. "Moderate" rationalism was supposed to say that historical reason could penetrate to the depths of the truths of faith, that philosophy could not submit itself to any authority, that the principles of Scholasticism* were no longer suited to the scientific needs of the present time, and that "philosophy should be practiced without taking supernatural revelation into account" (*ASS* 3, 168 *Sq*).

The canons of the First Vatican* Council gave the condemnation its definitive formulation: "If someone says that human reason is so independent that God cannot command it to have faith, may he be anathema"; "If someone says that divine faith is not distinct from the natural knowledge of God and morality and that, as a consequence, it is not required for divine faith that one believe in revealed truth because of the authority* of God who reveals, may he be anathema" (*COD* 810, 29–34).

It was left to Leo XIII to establish a "proper use of philosophy" by solemnly installing Thomism* in the position of official Catholic philosophy (*ASS* 11, 98 *Sq*). The modernist crisis saw a change in Roman language. In *Pascendi* (1907) it was under the rubric of "agnosticism*" (and also a certain "intellectualism") that modernism*" was condemned (*ASS* 40, 596 *Sq*), In 1950 the errors to be combated (in *Humani generis* of Pius XII, *AAS* 42, 561 *Sq* and 960) were now "idealism," immanentism," "pragmatism," and "existentialism," with the text referring to the *Code of Canon Law* of 1917 (can. 1366, §2) to recall that future priests* should be trained "according to the intellectual method, the doctrine, and the principles of the angelic doctor."

A new perspective appeared with Vatican* II. Rationalism was no longer named; and the fascination that it had long exerted was from now on to be exerted by atheism*. But the new stance was that it was appropriate to engage atheism in a "loyal and cautious dialogue" (*GS* 19–21). A more refined theology of grace* and the supernatural*, along with a more rigorous reception by Catholics of modern philosophies, has made the denunciation of rationalism irrelevant to contemporary theory.

● C.F. Stäudlin (1826), *Geschichte des Rationalismus und Supernaturalismus vornehmlich in Beziehung auf das Christenthum,* Göttingen.

W. Gaß (1862–67), *Geschichte der protestantischen Dogmatik in ihrem Zusammenhange mit der Theologie überhaupt,* vols. 3 and 4, Berlin.

K. Aner (1929), *Die Theologie der Lessingszeit,* Halle.

E. Hocedez (1947–52), *Histoire de la théologie au XIXe siècle,* 3 vols., Brussels-Paris.

E. Hirsch (1949–54), *Geschichte der neuern evangelischen Theologie,* vols. 1–5, Gütersloh.

P. Schäfer (1974), *Kirche und Vernunft: Die Kirche in der katholischen Theologie der Aufklärungszeit,* Munich.

H. Fries, G. Schwaiger (Ed.) (1975), *Katholische Theologen im 19 Jahrhundert,* 3 vols., Mayence.

G. A. McCool (1977), *Catholic Theology in the Nineteenth Century,* New York.

R. Specht (Ed.) (1979), *Rationalismus,* Stuttgart.

E. Coreth, W.M. Neidl, G. Pfligersdorffer (Ed.) (1987), *Christliche Philosophie im katholischen Denken des 19. und 20. Jahrhunderts,* vol. 1, Graz.

W. Schmidt-Biggemann (1988), *Theodizee und Tatsachen: Das philosophische Profil der deutschen Aufklärung,* Frankfurt.

L. Scheffczyk (Ed.) (1989), *Rationalität: Ihre Entwicklung und ihre Grenzen,* Freiburg-Munich.

F.W. Graf (Ed.) (1990), *Profile der neuzeitlichen Protestantismus,* vol. 1, Gütersloh.

JEAN-YVES LACOSTE

See also **Faith; Fideism; Philosophy; Reason; Theology**

Ratramne. *See* Eucharist

Realism

Two senses of the term *realism* may be distinguished: a strict sense, which concerns logic and the ontological status of universals, and a broad sense, which has to do with the relevance of knowledge and also encompasses metaphysical, ethical, and theological considerations. In the first sense, *realism* is opposed to *nominalism*:* it denotes the theory whereby the universal exists in things, while nominalism only acknowledges the reality of singular things. Arising from the tradition of Neoplatonist commentaries on Aristotle, the question was developed in Porphyry's Isagoge, in which he explicitly questioned the object of Aristotle's *Categories*—were they vocal sounds, intellectual constructs, or things *(phonai, noemata, onta)*? It was revived in the Middle Ages by the application of logic to Trinitarian theology* (Trinity*), seeking to explain how the three divine Persons* could be one and the same God*, and how to distinguish between the existence of the one God and the common substance that enables three men to be "men" without being one and the same man. After almost vanishing from philosophical debate during the classical period, the question has once again become a crucial one for contemporary logic and analytical philosophy*.

A. Medieval Questions

---

a) 12th Century: The "Reals." We should begin by noting a terminological difficulty: the word *nominalist* only appeared in the 15th century, from the pen of opponents of nominalism in the modern sense (represented at the time by Ockham and Buridan) (Kaluza 1988, 1995), and the term *realist* seems to have developed in tandem. The 12th-century sources speak of two "schools" *(sectae):* "nominals" and "reals" *(nominales et reales,* according to the translation of Leibniz, *New Essays on Human Understanding* II, 21, §6, Gerhardt), which suggests an initial conception very different from that of the 15th century. Unfortunately, the sources often speak of an anonymous *realis,* or of *antiqui,* rather than mentioning specific individuals, which makes the identification of the theories involved more difficult. They reveal that in the 12th century the ideas of the *nominales* were frequently opposed to those of the *reales,* but often only give us the opponent's viewpoint. Nevertheless, they do tell us something about the content of the ideas that were at that time considered to be realist: the ontological status of the *genus* and the *species,* the distinction between language and reality, the doctrine of the *unitas nominis,* and the conceptions of logical inference.

The *reales* (reals) adhered more or less closely to the position of William of Champeaux (Saint*-Victor), according to whom Aristotle's *Categories* concerned the first things, which implied that genera were things. In this form, realism was the standard doctrine professed during the 12th century and went hand in hand with a theory of the participation of the singular in universal forms. This was why its opponents (the "moderns," *moderni*) considered it the *positio antiqua*. Thus realism maintained that, in a proposition, what is attributed to a thing is a thing *(rem de re)*, while nominalism held that predication predicates a term from a term *(terminus de termino)* (Iwakuma-Ebbesen 1992). More precisely, "some maintain that it is only terms that may be predicated, while others maintain that it is things, in other words that which the terms signify" (anon., *Ars Meliduna*, Oxford, Digby 174, fo 218 vb, cited in Libera 1996).

The problem then was to know whether a complex proposition ("Socrates is a living being") referred to a structure in the order the order of things (the inherence of a form—living being—to a particular thing—Socrates) or whether the two linguistic signs *(Socrates, living being)* referred directly to the same singular thing. William of Champeaux thus maintained that singular men, distinct in themselves, constitute one single being in mankind (in other words they are the same essence—humanity). Singular by virtue of their distinctness, these men were nonetheless regarded as universal by reason of their nondifference and their convergence in one likeness. The ontological consequence of this was that substance was in itself essentially identical, but became diverse through the forms of the beings that came under its universality; in these terms essence was an undifferentiated background, and form was what produced distinctions.

According to Godfrey of Saint-Victor's *Fons philosophiae* (II, 450) and John of Salisbury's *Metalogicon* II, 17 (1159), the reals were apparently grouped into four schools: the followers of Robert of Melun, Albéric du Mont, Gilbert de la Porrée, and Adam of Balsham (Parvipontanus).

According to Albéric du Mont, the universal was both the thing existing by itself and the so-called thing of substance: the *Categories* spoke not only of *voces* and their meaning, but also of *res*. According to the school of Robert of Melun *(Ars Meliduna)*, universals were neither terms, nor things, but the very being* of things: they were neither substances, nor properties, but they had existence in their own right "just like the utterable subjects, time*, vocal sounds, and glory." This clearly corresponds to the status of incorporeals according to the Stoics: the mode of being of objects of discourse, which have no existence of their own. According to Gilbert de la Porrée, the problem was to explain how two men were simultaneously "two" and "men." He justified this convergence by the fact that they shared the same form *(conformitas)*. In the case of collective nouns, such as *a people,* the term denoted merely a collection *(unio),* but "the conformity of singular natures is the full resemblance which causes Socrates and Plato to be considered naturally alike by

reason of the singular humanities which make them resemble one another" (*Summa Zwetlensis,* I, 18, Ed. N. Häring, 1976).

This realism, then, was far from being naïve: paradoxically, it was through the same singular form that two singular things were distinct one from another and that they were consistent with the universal.

At the root of the crisis of realism we find the position of Abelard*'s teacher Roscelin: "vocalism." In his view, words referred to singular things whose qualities were inseparable, to the extent that when one of their parts disappeared the words no longer referred to them, even though they survived as mere vocal sounds *(voces).* Only the whole existed: the word referred to a whole whose parts were indivisible, and the universal was merely a name which referred to a multiplicity of things, while a reality of which a part was lacking was incomplete and no longer deserved the same name. The development of Abelard's nominalism in reaction to this doctrine is a familiar story.

b) Grammar and Theology. Chiefly in the writings of the early 13th century, grammar added to the logical problem the problem of *unitas nominis.* This question played a large part in the debates about the immutability* of divine knowledge (divine science) and about the unity of a faith* expressed at different moments in time (in particular prior to the Incarnation*, among the prophets* and, later, among Christians). For the nominals the unity of the universal resided in the "name": in spite of the case introduced by declension, the three vocal sounds *albus, alba, album* were one and the same "name," since they referred to the same *res significata.* This same unity subsisted in temporal utterances: the same *res* was initially in the future, then in the present, and finally in the past. To say that something was to come, or present, or past, was not to introduce a multiplicity of things signified, but simply a multiplicity of vocal sounds. So the utterance retained the same meaning and remained true. For this reason the nominals held that what had once been true would always be true. This interpretation, similar to the unity of faith through time assumed by Augustine* (*Tract. in Io.* XLV, no. 9, PL 35, 1722), was referred to by Peter of Capua, Prévotin of Cremona (Chenu, Landgraf), and Bonaventure* (*Sentences* I, d. 41, a. 2, q. 2), and sanctioned by Peter Lombard (*Sentences* I, d. 41, chap. 3; I, 293). It implied that God was eternally aware of contingent realities in the past and future, and that Abraham's faith in the coming of the Messiah* was the same as the Christian's after that coming.

Against this interpretation, the reals suggested that God could begin to know something, and that Abraham's faith was not the same as the Christian's: "The *realis* concedes that since it is true that 'I am' *(me esse),* and that this has not always been true, so God knows it at one moment and has not always known it, but that he is not in consequence any more knowledgeable than he was before" (Peter of Capua, *Summa,* cited in Courtenay 1991).

Immutability therefore had to be understood in a different way, as the living unity of a knowledge that changed object and content while remaining the same; and epistemic utterances (those concerning knowledge, belief, or doubt) must be considered as identical despite the contingency and volatility of their objects.

In some 12th-century treatises the realists' doctrine was related to the rules of logical inference. The *Obligationes Parisienses* mention (only to reject it) the rule according to which the acceptance of a false premise makes it possible to accept and prove any contingent thing (De Rijk 1975). According to the anonymous author of the treatise *De communibus distinctionibus,* in the view of the *nominales* anything follows from the impossible *(ex impossibili sequitur quidlibet),* while for the *reales* nothing follows from it *(ex impossibili nihil sequitur)* (De Rijk 1988).

c) 13th and 14th Centuries. By the 13th century the *nominales* and *reales* were a mere memory, mentioned only in the context of the theological problem of *unitas nominis,* and summed up thus by Albert the Great (who regarded nominalists as Epicureans): if one situated universals' property of "being in many" in things themselves, one was a realist; but if one situated it in human thought, one was a nominalist (*De Praedicabilibus* IX, 3; I, 147). Realism triumphed in the great metaphysical and theological works (Albert the Great, Bonaventure, Thomas* Aquinas, Duns* Scotus). Three factors combined to alter the nature of the problem: the rediscovery of Aristotle's *De anima,* in which all the critical debates about the formation of the universal are condensed (II, 5, 417 *b* 23: "The universal exists in the soul"), and also of his *Metaphysics* (Z, 13, 1038 b 9: "The universal, as a universal, is not substance"); and the influence of Avicenna, who offered a coherent formulation of the problem of universals.

According to Avicenna, every being had an essence that made it what it was, independently of its existence or its nonexistence, irrespective of whether it had real existence or the status of being imaginary (*Philosophia prima* I, 5 and V, 1). The essence of a horse was only the essence of a horse, and all other circumstances (existence, singularity, or universality) were incidental to it. This solution established the distinction and correspondence between three statuses of essence: the intelligible *(intellectuale)* in itself, before the thing *(ante*

multiplicitatem), physical realities *(na-turalia)* in the multiple *(in multiplicitate),* and in the intellect after the event *(post multiplicitatem)* (*Logica,* fo 12 ra-va)—recalling the Neoplatonic threefold scheme of "physical," "logical," and "theological" viewpoints. This structure and this correspondence, taken up by Albert the Great in terms of the universal *ante rem, in re,* and *post rem,* influenced the interpretations of Thomas Aquinas. The latter emphasized the importance of the intellect in the constitution of the universal, and thus the disparity between these different levels. Duns Scotus was also influenced, but concerned himself more with intentional correspondence and the persistence of the essence in spite of the diversity of levels (Boulnois 1992). During the 14th and 15th centuries Scotus's position was maintained by the Oxford realists, John Sharpe and John Wycliffe, while that of Albert the Great was recast by his school, notably the Köln neo-Albertists such as Jean de Maisonneuve and Eymeric de Campo (Kaluza 1986). It may thus be said that by the end of the Middle Ages, notwithstanding noetic refinements such as the theory of intuition, the form and content of realism was fixed.

● Albert the Great, *Opera omnia,* Ed. A. Borgnet, Paris, L. Vivès, 38 vols., 1890–99.

Anon., *Ars Mediluna,* partial edition, De Rijk, *Logica modernorum* II, 1: "The Origin and Early Development of the Theory of Supposition," Assen, 291–390.

Anon., *Compendium Logicae Porretanum,* Ed. S. Ebbesen, K. M. Fredborg, L. Nielsen, 1983, *Cahiers de l'Institut du MA grec et latin* 46, 1–113.

Avicenna, *Liber de philosophia prima sive scientia divina,* Ed. S. Van Riet, Louvain-Leyden, 1977; *Logica,* Venice, 1508.

Bonaventure, *Opera omnia,* Quaracchi, 11 vols., 1882–1902.

Gilbert de Poitiers (de La Porrée), *The commentaries on Boethius,* Ed. N. M. Häring, Toronto, 1966.

Godefroid de Saint-Victor, *Fons Philosophiae,* Ed. P. Michaud-Quantin, *Analecta medievalia Namurciensia* 8, Namur, 1979.

Guillaume d'Auxerre, *Summa aurea,* Ed. J. Ribaillier, Grottaferrata, 5 vols., 1980–87.

Heymericus de Campo, *Invectiva,* in G. Meersseman, *Geschichte des Albertismus* 2, DHOP 5, 1935, 112–212; (1496), *Tractatus problematicus,* Köln.

John of Salisbury, *Metalogicon,* Ed. C. C. J. Webb, Oxford, 1929 (English trans. D. D. McGarry, University of California Press, Berkeley-Los Angeles, 1955).

G. W. Leibniz, *Die philosophischen Schriften,* Ed. C. J. Gerhardt, vol. 5, Berlin, 1882.

Peter Lombard, *Sententiae in quattuor libris distinctae,* Grottaferrata, 2 vols., 1971–81.

John Sharpe, *Quaestio super universalia,* Ed. A. D. Conti, Florence, 1990.

♦ *See* the bibliography for **Nominalism** and:

M. D. Chenu (1935–36), "Grammaire et théologie aux XIIe et XIIIe siècles," *AHDL* 10, 5–28.

A. Landgraf (1943), "Studien zur Theologie des zwölften Jahrhunderts, I: Nominalismus in den theologischen Werken der zweiten Hälfte des zwölften Jahrhunderts," Tr 1, 183–210.

L. M. de Rijk (1975), "Some Thirteenth-Century Tracts on the Game of Obligation II," *Vivarium* 13, 22–54.

N. Häring (1976), *Summa Zwetlensis*, Ed. N. M. Häring, BG-PhMA-NF 15, Münster-Copenhagen.

D. M. Armstrong (1978), *Nominalism and Realism: Universals and Scientific Realism,* vol. 1, Cambridge.

Z. Kaluza (1986), "Le *De universali reali* de Jean de Maisonneuve et les *epicuri litterales*," *FZPhTh* 33, 469–516.

L. M. De Rijk (1988), *Some Earlier Parisian Tracts on* Distinctiones Sophismatum, Artistarium 7, Nijmegen.

Z. Kaluza (1988), *Les querelles doctrinales à Paris: Nominalistes et réalistes aux confins du XIVe et du XVe siècle,* Bergamo.

W. J. Courtenay (1991), "*Nominales* and Nominalism in the Twelfth Century," *in* Lectionum Varietates, *Hommage à Paul Vignaux (1904–1987),* Paris, 11–48.

A. de Libera (1991), "Nominaux et Réaux: *Sophismata et con-*

sequentiae dans la logique médiévale," *Rue Descartes* 1, 139–64.

O. Boulnois (1992), "Réelles intentions: Nature commune et universaux selon Duns Scot," *RMM* 97, 3–33.

Y. Iwakuma, S. Ebbesen (1992), "Logico-Theological Schools from the Second Half of the 12th Century: A List of Sources," *Vivarium* 30, 157–72.

J. Jolivet (1992), "Trois variations médiévales sur l'universel et l'individu: Roscelin, Abélard, Gilbert de La Porrée," *RMM* 97, 111–55.

Z. Kaluza (1995), "La crise des années 1474–1482: L'interdiction du n. par Louis XI," *in* Hoenen (M. J. F. M.), et al. (Ed.), *Philosophy and Learning: Universities in the Middle Ages,* Leyden, 293–327.

A. de Libera (1996), *La querelle des universaux,* Paris.

OLIVIER BOULNOIS

B. Modern and Contemporary Questions

a) Realism, Neoscholasticism, and the Theory of Knowledge. In modern and contemporary theology, and in a large part of 19th- and 20th-century philosophy, the term *realism* generally no longer implies the opposite of *nominalism,* but instead usually means the opposite of *idealism,* in a new schema that has arisen within Catholicism. In Neoscholastic parlance the term *realist* was applied to a theory of knowledge aimed at refuting Cartesianism and Kantianism, two philosophies that see knowledge of the world as a knowledge posterior to the proper knowledge of the self (Descartes*), or as a knowledge mediated by the self and its capacity for experience (Kant*). According to J. Kleutgen, who better than anyone codified Neoscholasticism (*see* McCool 1977), it is possible to speak of knowledge only "when the thing is known from the foundation of its being, and consequently when the foundation of being* is the foundation of knowledge" (I, 148). In the context of the new school this idea was developed in two directions, both of which Kleutgen had suggested (McCool 1977).

1) D. Mercier (1851–1926, professor at Louvain, archbishop of Malines-Brussels, made cardinal in 1907) pursued an epistemology aimed at "examining the certainty that the mind has when it is aware that its knowledge is true" (1918): a theory of evidential criteria that ruled out postulating the existence of unknowable noumenal realities. J. Scheuer and J. Maréchal followed Mercier and

refined the project of a "Scholastic* solution to the paradoxes of Kant" (Maréchal 1926), in a manner that took considerable account of Kant's demands. The decision to "go beyond Kantianism from the starting point of Kantianism itself" (ibid.) presumes at least the acceptance of the terms of a question, and Scheuer accepts more than this, seeing Kant as "the Newton of the universe of ideas" (Scheuer 1971).

2) To a realism that might be termed "mediate" there was opposed an "immediate" realism that resolved the problem of knowledge by postulating the "immediate apprehension of things by the mind" (Noël 1925). However, the most serious objection came from Gilson. Realist theories, according to the great historian, all had one original sin in common—that of being theories of knowledge that took Descartes and Kant as their starting point, and which attempted to "find in a particular doctrine [i.e., that of Thomas* Aquinas] the solution to a problem which that doctrine never suspected" (1930). True fidelity to Thomas demanded in practice that one "free oneself from the obsession with epistemology as a precondition of philosophy" (ibid.). Once one had concluded that one "will never obtain from any cogito the justification of Saint Thomas Aquinas's realism" (ibid.), there still remained a mission: "to think from the viewpoint of the object" (ibid.).

Maréchal's realism and "immediate" realism were both influential. The German Jesuits were Maréchal's most energetic followers; and this "transcendental" Thomism* inspired J. B. Lotz's philosophical (and spiritual) project as much as it did K. Rahner*'s theological project—though it should be added that from 1927 the German Neoscholastics judged it necessary to confront the new questions posed by Heidegger*, so that that of realism inevitably receded into the background. In the French-speaking world, and in the faculties of Rome, most notably at the Angelicum, the "immediate apprehension" of being—of the *ens*—by the human mind was an unquestioned dogma, although arguments did arise about the means of this apprehension. Maritain, for example, spoke of intuitive apprehension ("the intuition of being as an analogue"), though few followed him. In any event, Gilson's scheme remains the most exact formulation of the Neoscholastic realist project. Sketches toward its completion are to be found in Gilson's own work, for example in *Peinture et réalité* (1972).

b) *The Real and the Unreal.* The history of Neoscholasticism is not finished, and the concept of realism is still a shibboleth in the circles where it continues. Meanwhile, however, the realist question has been taken up anew, in two contexts.

1) In epistemology and in the theory of knowledge, an argument about realism has been unfolding in the work of English-speaking philosophers who call themselves (or are happy to be called) "unrealists" or "antirealists," and who share a rejection of W. V. Quine's hard realism or physicalism. In the extreme position adopted by N. Goodman, every object is a human artifact, in the sense that it is an object in a "world" whose unity results from its being a system of references, perceptions, preferences, and so on, organized by human beings. In the moderate position taken by H. Putnam, who incidentally cites Kant as an inspiration in his recent texts, we maintain an "internal" realism. Within a coherent structure of experience, knowledge, and theory, the realist demand is valid: an armchair is "real" in the world of life, an electron is "real" in the world of physics. But there is no divine viewpoint or "God's eye view": each thing bears witness to our organizing spontaneity. Mention should also be made of M. Dummett's linguistic unrealism (criticism in Alston 1996): a theory of meaning that uses logic and mathematical intuitionists to link all access to the real to the canonical proof of its reality, which can be provided here and now. Nor should we overlook R. M. Chisholm, the author of works that, on many points, agree with the thrust of Cardinal Mercier's "mediate" realism (*see* Chisholm 1966–89).

2) The debate concerning religious and theological language* that began in the 1930s has continued at the fringes of the recent philosophy of religion* (Phillips and also Cupitt, primarily influenced by Wittgenstein*; *see* Runzo 1993). Here there have been attempts to assert the validity and importance of religious language, while at the same time denying that there is meaning in saying that God "exists" or is "real" independently of and outside these language wordplay: "the distinction between the real and the non-real is not determined in advance of the usage peculiar to different language play" (Phillips 1993). Some recent critics of the onto-theological God at times reach similar conclusions (Levinas, Marion, Lash), but the God they attempt to conceive "without being" or "without metaphysical contamination" is a God outside language. The question is not one of his reality, in an unequivocal sense, but rather of his mode of "being" or reality.

c) *Reality of Higher-Order Objects.* Thus, in the inventory of the world's ontological equipment the debates that occupied people in the Middle Ages concern people just as much today, and still bring into opposition realist and nominalist tendencies. Certain questions are continually being investigated: the status of mathematical objects (the ontological implications of Cantor's work on set theory and mathematical infinity*, the reduction of mathematics to logic in the work of Russell, etc.), the status of wholes and parts (Husserl's *Logical Investigations,* Lesniewski's work on "mereology," etc.), the status of "propositions" (Bolzano's theory of "phrases in themselves" [1837], the theory of "states of the thing," *Sachverhalte,* beginning with Twardowski [1894], Meinong's theory of "higher-order objects" [1913], etc.), the status of "sensory data" (the positivism of Carnap, then A. J. Ayer and J. Austin's criticisms of him, etc.), and others as well (*see* survey in Smith 1994). The key question probably concerns what it means to exist. It was undoubtedly Meinong who had the distinction of formulating it, when he denounced a "prejudice" in the philosophical tradition "in favor of existence" and erected a theory of "objects" (an object being anything about which meaningful propositions may be formulated) intended to take account of the "manner of being" *(Sosein)* of any object, including gold mountains and square circles ("impossible" or "stateless objects"; *see* Chisholm 1982). Long condemned in the wake of

Russell's criticisms (see *Essays in Analysis,* Ed. Lackey, London, 1973: texts by Russell and commentaries by the editor), but rehabilitated in the 1970s, Meinong's theory is an extreme realism, which has been construed as an extreme form of Platonism. It has a counterpart, within recent philosophy, in "reist" theories, which admit the existence only of individual things (*see* Brentano's late texts, Kotarbinski 1929, etc.). The field remains open (*see,* e.g., Chisholm, *A Realistic Theory of Categories,* 1996, and Nef, *L'objet quelconque,* 1998); moreover, the theological reception of these investigations remains to be undertaken.

● F. Bolzano (1837), *Wissenschaftslehre* (2nd Ed., Leipzig, 1929, 4 vols.; repr. Aalen, 1981).

J. Kleutgen (1860–63), *Die Philosophie der Vorzeit vertheidigt,* 2 vols., Münster.

K. Twardowski (1894), *Zur Lehre vom Inhalt und Gegenstand der Vorstellungen,* Vienna (repr. Munich-Vienna, 1982).

E. Husserl (1901), "Zur Lehre von den Ganzen und Teilen," *Logische Untersuchungen,* vol. II/1, Tübingen, 225-93.

A. Meinong (1913), *Abhandlungen zur Erkenntnistheorie und Gegenstandstheorie,* New Ed., *GA* 2, Graz, 1971.

D. Mercier (1918), *Critériologie générale ou théorie générale de la certitude,* Louvain-Paris.

L. Noël (1925), *Notes d'épistémologie thomiste,* Louvain-Paris.

J. Maréchal (1926), *Le point de départ de la métaphysique,* Cahier V: *Le thomisme devant la philosophie critique,* Brussels-Paris.

T. Kotarbinski (1929), *Gnosiology: The Scientific Approach to the Theory of Knowledge,* Oxford, 1966 (original in Polish).

E. Gilson (1930), "Le réalisme méthodique," in *Philosophia Perennis,* Festschrift J. Geyser, vol II, Regensburgm 745-55.

K. Rahner (1939), *Geist in Welt: Zur Metaphysik der endlichen Erkenntnis bei Thomas von Aquin, SW* 2, Düsseldorf-Freiburg, 1996.

R. M. Chisholm (1966), *Theory of Knowledge,* Englewood Cliffs, N.J. (2nd Ed., revised and corrected, 1977; 3rd Ed., revised and corrected, 1989).

P. Scheuer (1971), *Écrits philosophiques,* Ed. L. Wuillaume, Heverlee.

B. Lonergan (1972), "The Origins of Christian Realism," *A Second Collection,* Toronto, 239–61.

N. Goodman (1978), *Ways of Worldmaking,* Indianapolis.

J. B. Lotz (1978), *Transzendentale Erfahrung,* Freiburg.

H. Putnam (1990), *Realism with a Human Face,* Cambridge, Mass.- London.

M. Dummett (1993), "Realism," *The Seas of Language,* Oxford, 230–74.

D. Z. Phillips (1993), *Wittgenstein and Religion,* Basingstoke-London.

R. Runzo (Ed.) (1993), *Is God Real?* New York.

W. P. Alston (1996), *A Realist Conception of Truth,* Ithaca-London.

P. J. K. McCormick (Ed.) (1996), *Starmaking: Realism, Anti-Realism and Irrealism,* Cambridge, Mass.-London (texts by Goodman, Putnam, Scheffer, Hempel).

◆ G. A. McCool (1977), *Catholic Theology in the Nineteenth Century: The Quest for a Unitary Method,* New York.

R. M. Chisholm (1982), *Brentano and Meinong Studies,* Amsterdam.

T. F. Torrance (1982), "Theological Realism," in B. Hebblethwaite, S. Sutherland (Ed.), *The Philosophical Frontiers of Christian Theology: Essays Presented to D. M. MacKinnon,* Cambridge, 169–96.

W. Halbfass, et al. (1992) "Realismus II-III," *HWP* 8, 156–69.

C. Smith (1994), *Austrian Philosophy: The Legacy of Brentano,* Chicago-La Salle.

R. C. S. Walker, J. M. Soskice (1997), "Realismus," *TRE* 28, 182–96 (bibl.).

JEAN-YVES LACOSTE

See also **Chartres, School of; Language, Theological; Nominalism; Saint-Victor, School of**

Reason

Reason is defined in Littré's *Dictionnaire de la langue française* as "the faculty by which man knows, judges, and behaves." Christian theology* has never denied that man is an animal endowed with reason and has always claimed that its own discourse is reasonable, even if it is not first and foremost addressed to the reasonable animal, but to a mortal sinful animal to whom it announces salvation*. The theological problem of reason may be put in Pauline terms. The Greeks seek "wisdom," and the central affirmation of the Christian kerygma can appear as nothing but "folly" to them (1 Cor 1:22 f.). In the field of experience that Paul calls the "world*," human beings live "without God," "atheistically" (Eph 2:12). And if God* remains to a certain extent knowable to the pagan and to pagan reason, the actual reasoning *(dialogismoi)* of the pagans nevertheless shows itself to be "vain" and prevents them from treating God as he should be treated: the use of reason is connected to the life of the heart*, and the pagan's "unintelligent" heart (asunetos) "confuses" his reason (Rom 1:18–22). Therefore the theological status of reason can only be determined with reference to the status of faith*. Faith accomplishes a work of knowledge and can understand itself by way of the logos ("apologetics" is the same as saying logos). But it only knows by virtue of a gift, a "revelation*," that makes accessible to human beings that which is not natively accessible. There is a "natural faith" (our trust in Peter or Paul), and there is a theological faith (faith in God), distinguished from all simply rational knowledge* of God in that it is supernatural: human beings believe by grace*. And faith is not only rational consent, because it involves the will (Thomas* of Aquinas, ST IIa IIae, q. 2, a. 1 and 2).

Once it is granted that there is a faith (pistis) that enables one to know (opens the field of a gnosis), the task of theology can be defined as an "understanding of faith" or a "faith seeking understanding," fides quaerens intellectum. Then the question of the intrinsic limitations of "natural" reason must be a central preoccupation of theology. Augustine* claimed that ignorance is one of the consequences of original sin* (De nat. et grat., BAug 21, 403): the (postlapsarian) nature* of man is defined in terms of wounds, and reason is a wounded reason. The nature assumed by Christ*, says John Damascene, is an "ignorant, servile nature" (De fide orthodoxa II, 21). Bonaventure* formulates a common theological opinion in subsuming the consequences of the first sin under the categories of ignorance and concupiscence. At that time, a consistent strategy of Scholastics* for measuring the exact limits of natural reason was to set up a "protology of reason" and an "eschatology* of reason" that would allow the experiences of faith and rationality to be put in proper perspective. The eschatological destiny of knowledge is the beatific vision*. The first man did not experience this vision, but knew God through the sensible (ST Ia, q. 94, a. 1) and "had knowledge of all things in virtue of species infused by God" (a. 3). Adam* did not have to "believe," but he did not "see" God: his knowledge held to a middle term.

The question of the weaknesses of natural reason occupies an important place in the thought of Luther* (where reason is the "blind prostitute of the devil," WA 40/1, 365) and in Lutheran confessional writings. Rationality remains after the Fall as practical reason that can attain the "justice* of the law*" and as an aptitude to speak of God or render a certain ritual observance to him (BSLK 311, 25 Sq). The emphasis, however, is on a reason that cannot lead to the love* of God: "It is not true…that left to its own unaided force, reason can love God above all and fulfill the law of God" (BSLK

165, 15). The logic of natural reason is not a logic of spiritual life*: "We believe that the intellect, the heart, and the will of unregenerate man left to their own natural forces understand nothing of spiritual and divine things" (BSLK 873, 7). Seventeenth-century Lutheran scholars still speculated on the knowledge of Adam and the knowledge of believers. J. A. Quenstedt (1617–88) believed that Adam possessed a form of knowledge that was "excellent, full, perfect, and such that no man after the Fall could acquire it, either from the book of nature or the book* of Scripture*" (Theologia didactico-polemica II, 6); but after receiving the Holy* Spirit the apostles* knew even more. J. W. Baier (1647–95) gives a good synthesis of the Lutheran position: "As for the intellect, original sin inflicted on it a total deprivation of spiritual light, such that it cannot know God directly nor can it thus perfectly prescribe the way we must adore God.… And even in matters that pertain to natural light, [it inflicts] a certain powerlessness to know God and regulate one's life" (Compendium theologiae moralis, 406–8). However, it would be a mistake to exaggerate the irrational or antirational elements of Lutheran theology. Luther's antiphilosophism was not stronger than that of Bernard* of Clairvaux or Peter Damian; his positions on the "denaturing" of sinful man and his reason are extremist, but this extremism draws on the best traditional cautions—the Council of Trent* was not mistaken in finding absolutely no need whatsoever to rehabilitate reason.

Calvin* unconditionally affirmed the universal possibility of knowledge of God: "We put beyond doubt that men have a sentiment of divinity in them, even of a natural movement. Because God imprinted in all of us a knowledge of himself, so that no one could seek refuge in the name of ignorance" (Inst. I, 3, 1). This argument was not meant to preserve the rights of reason but to establish the guilt of one who knows God and does not honor him. The tone hardens when the confessional texts deal with the consequences of original sin, for example, in the Confession of San Rochelle: even if sinful man "still has some discretion of good and evil, we nonetheless say that his clarity is converted to shadows, when it is a question of seeking God, so much so that he cannot approach him by his understanding and reason" (BSKORK 68). A fundamental hostility toward all natural* theology is certainly a constant feature of Protestant thought, which always counters it with a "more natural" theology (E. Jüngel) organized around divine revelation*. The official Catholic position was not solemnly affirmed until Vatican* I, in a changed context. The Enlightenment proposed a model of "emancipated" reason, which has the force of its natural light alone. In opposition to the

Enlightenment, 19th-century Catholic traditionalism* and fideism* attempted to elaborate a model of rationality that almost completely forgoes natural theology. Its rights were affirmed as clearly as possible by Vatican I. The richest exercise of reason is certainly that of a "reason illuminated by faith." But if "someone says that the one true God, our Lord and Creator, cannot be known for certain by the natural light of human reason, may he be anathema" (*DS* 3026). The antimodernist oath hardened the terms by affirming that the existence of God can be "demonstrated" (*DS* 3538). According to various 19th- and 20th-century Roman Catholic declarations, the existence, immortality, and liberty* of the soul* can also be known by natural reason (*DS* 2766, 2812), and the same is true for natural moral law (*DS* 2866, 3875). "The use of reason precedes faith and leads us to faith with the help of revelation and grace" (*DS* 2813). This thesis, opposed (in 1855) to the traditionalism of Bonnetty, expresses the apologetic strategy dictated to Catholicism by an optimistic concept of "natural" reason. Theism occupies a commanding position on the path that leads from the natural use of reason to the consent reason gives to supernatural truths.

The problems were posed in a different way in the 20th century. The 19th-century Roman Catholic texts defended a possible knowledge in a context that suggested, and even urged, recognizing in certain conceptual systems (specifically those of a reviving Scholasticism) the enduring power to realize that possibility. But in a period when Protestant theology began to show more interest in questions of apologetics or fundamental* theology (E. Brunner, W. Pannenberg, W. Joest), Catholic thought itself was seeking to reorganize the relation between reason and faith. The primarily intellectualist understanding of faith was replaced by a primarily existential understanding, largely under the pressure of contemporary biblical exegesis*. Similarly, the strictly intellectualist understanding of reason seems to be receding. Reason is thought from action according to Blondel*; it is thought in the experience of the communion* of persons according to G. Marcel; while for others intellectual knowledge cannot be dissociated from affective knowledge (e.g., Heidegger*, or more recently M. Henry). The recent appearance of a hermeneutic model of reason favors the (re)birth of the philosophical reading of biblical texts (P. Ricœur, etc.) in which the "hermeneutics* of witness" sometimes seems to serve as "preamble to faith." The existence of a reason pure of all belief is no longer a philosophical article of faith

(e.g., Husserl). Epistemology draws attention to "personal" factors of knowledge that exceed the abstract use of reason. (M. Polanyi). Philosophies of history* can offer theological reason and philosophical reason a more fertile field of dialogue than the one where God the Creator, first named and philosophically named only as such, had to give way to a revealed God of which no philosophy* could provide any precomprehension. The concept of a "philosophy of revelation" (Schelling*) is among those that theology must henceforth take into account. While all the theologies of the end of the 20th century know perfectly well what "belief" means, the identification of "natural reason" has in fact become a problem for them, because it has become a problem for almost all philosophies.

• E. Brunner (1941), *Offenbarung und Vernunft*, Zurich-Stuttgart.
J. Hick (1957), *Faith and Knowledge*, London (2nd Ed. 1988).
B. Lohse (1958), *Ratio und fides: Eine Untersuchung über die Ratio in der Theologie Luthers*, Göttingen.
M. Polanyi (1958), *Personal Knowledge*, London (2nd Rev. Ed. 1962).
J. Baur (1962), *Die Vernunft zwischen Ontologie und Evangelium*, Gütersloh.
H. U. von Balthasar (1965), *Herrlichkeit* III/1/2, Einsiedeln, 943–83.
W. Pannenberg (1967), "Glaube und Vernunft," *Grundfr. syst. Th.* 237–51, Göttingen.
W. Joest (1974), *Fundamentaltheologie*, Stuttgart.
J. Ladrière (1977), *Les enjeux de la rationalité*, Paris.
J.-L. Marion (1977), *L'idole et la distance*, Paris.
G. Ebeling (1979), *Dogmatik des christlichen Glaubens* I, Tübingen, 79–157.
E. Jüngel (1980), *Entsprechungen: Gott–Wahrheit–Mensch*, Munich.
R. Schaeffler (1980), *Die Wechselbeziehungen zwischen Philosophie und katholischer Theologie*, Darmstadt.
T. F. Torrance (Ed.) (1980), *Belief in Science and in Christian Life: The Relevance of M. Polanyi's Thought for Christian Faith and Life*, Edinburgh.
R. Swinburne (1981), *Faith and Reason*, Oxford.
H. Thielicke (1983), *Glauben und Denken in der Neuzeit*, Tübingen.
I. U. Dalferth (1988), *Theology and Philosophy*, Oxford.
G. Hummel (1989), *Die Begegnungen zwischen Philosophie und evangelischer Theologie im 20. Jahrhundert*, Darmstadt.
E. Jüngel (1990), "Glauben und Verstehen: Zum Theologiebegriff Rudolf Bultmanns," *Wertlose Wahrheit*, BEvTh 107, 16–77.
G. Picht (1991), *Glauben und Wissen*, Stuttgart (2nd Ed. 1994).
J. Pieper (1995), *Schriften zum Philosophiebegriff*, WW 3, Hamburg.

JEAN-YVES LACOSTE

See also **Faith; Knowledge of God; Natural Theology; Rationalism**

Reception

a) *Definition.* Most generally, the term *reception* refers to the process by which the church* apprehends, appropriates, and is appropriated by, the gospel*. In recent theological discussions, *reception* more specifically refers to the comprehensive process by which something—a doctrinal decision, a change in the liturgy*, an ecumenical proposal—is accepted by the church and taken into its life. This second sense of the term cannot be understood except in relation to its primary sense. The church is inherently receptive: it exists only because it has received the Holy* Spirit (Jn 20:22; Acts 1:8). The church teaches not what it has invented or discovered, but what it has received (1 Cor. 11:23, 15:3). Even if "the faith...was once for all delivered to the saints" (Jude 3), reception still goes on, as the Spirit leads the church ever deeper "into the all the truth" (Jn 16:13). The church's reception of, for example, the decrees of a council* or the results of ecumenical dialogue should therefore be placed in the context of its continuing reception of the gospel. The subject of reception is thus the church as a whole, rather than merely one part of the church, such as the hierarchy. The reception of the Christology* of Chalcedon*, for example, must be sought not only in the teachings of later councils, but also in hymns, prayers*, icons—the entire spiritual life of the church. Reception is a spiritual reality that cannot be reduced to the official actions of synods* or church leaders. As such, reception cannot be commanded.

The attraction of the concept of reception lies in its complex relations with other important and difficult concepts: the priesthood* of all believers, the teaching authority* of councils and popes*, the indefectibility* and infallibility* of the church, consensus, and the church's continuous conversion* to the gospel.

b) *Reception in the Classic Sense.* In the classic sense (Rusch 1988), *reception* refers to the acceptance and appropriation by the church of authoritative teachings or decisions, such as those of ecumenical councils, synods, or popes. Doctrinal declarations have usually been followed by prolonged periods during which the decisions have been debated and interpreted. Some councils (e.g., Nicaea* I) gave rise to decades of debate before they achieved widespread acceptance. Some other councils were finally rejected by signifi-

cant portions of the Church (e.g., the Eastern Orthodox rejection of Chalcedon). Ephesus II (449), the "Robber Synod of Ephesus," encountered widespread rejection and was overturned by Chalcedon.

Most theologians agree that the church's reception of a teaching or decision is an important sign that it represents the faith. The sheep know the voice of the Shepherd (Jn 10:4, 10:14) and an authentic teaching, related to the very principles of the faith, cannot fail to be received. In the case of the universal Church's acceptance of a teaching or decision by a regional synod (e.g., Antioch 268 rejecting the teachings of Paul of Samosata, or Carthage 418 rejecting Pelagianism*), such acceptance is an important reason for asserting the universally binding character of the teaching. The controversial question concerns the relation between reception (or the lack thereof) and the authority of the teachings of ecumenical councils and popes.

This relation is very important in Orthodoxy* (Hryniewicz 1975). The Russian theologian A. S. Khomiakov (1804–60) and his followers have asserted that reception by the church constitutes a criterion of the infallibility of a council's decrees. While this assertion remains controversial among Orthodox theologians, it expresses the emphasis on reception in Orthodox understandings of authority.

Reception has played a smaller role in Protestant understandings of authority (Protestantism*). The authority of a teaching is more directly tied to its agreement with the gospel or the Scriptures. Nevertheless, Luther* could appeal to universal reception as one reason for accepting the doctrine of Nicaea on Christ*'s divinity (*WA* 50, 554, 4–5) or infant baptism* (*WA* 26, 167, 19–26).

The relation of reception to authority in Catholic theology (Catholicism*) is the matter of continuing debate. On the one hand, Vatican* I stated that *ex cathedra* teachings of the popes are "of themselves, and not by the consent of the church, irreformable" (*DS* 3074). To the degree that *reception* means "consent," the authority of such teachings (and teachings "of the same order" by councils) does not, therefore, derive from their reception. On the other hand, Vatican* II stated that "the congregation of the faithful...cannot be deceived in the faith," since they possess "the supernatural sense of faith" (*LG* 12).

Thus, "the assent of the church can never be lacking" from doctrinal definitions of the teaching office (*LG* 25). Some Catholic theologians and ecumenical dialogues (*see* ARCIC) have sought to understand reception as a sign that true teaching has occurred, although not as a source of the authority of such teaching.

c) Reception in the Ecumenical Sense. The term *reception* has been extensively used in ecumenical discussions. Narrowly, it refers to the Church's receiving the results of the various dialogues and discussions among churches. Such reception includes official responses to their diverse proposals, as well as the entire process of testing results and reshaping church life along more ecumenical lines. More broadly, ecumenical reception refers to the process of the churches accepting or receiving each other in a continuing conversion to the gospel. This presupposes that each church renews the reception of its own traditions*, so that they may become an enrichment for the entire Church.

The discussion and reality of ecumenical reception are still in their infancy. The specific character of ecumenical reception, and its relation to reception in the classic sense, are subjects of contemporary research (Birmelé 1995).

- Y. Congar (1972), "La 'réception' comme réalité ecclésiologique," *RSPhTh* 56, 369–403.
- W. Hryniewicz (1975), "Die ekkleziale Rezeption in der Sicht der orthodoxen Theologie," *ThGl* 65, 250–66.
- ARCIC (1981), *Final Report*, Authority in the Church II.
- W. Rusch (1988), *Reception: An Ecumenical Opportunity*, Philadelphia.
- G. Routhier (1993), *La réception d'un concile*, Paris.
- W. Beinert (1995), "Die Rezeption und ihre Bedeutung für Leben und Lehre der Kirche," in W. Pannenberg, T. Schneider (Ed.), *Verbindliches Zeugnis*, vol. II, Göttingen, 193–218.
- A. Birmelé (1995), "La réception comme exigence œcuménique," in G. R. Evans, M. Gourgues (Ed.), *Communion et réunion: Mélanges Jean-Marie Roger Tillard*, Louvain, 75–94.

MICHAEL ROOT

See also **Authority; Council; Ecumenicism; Magisterium; Sensus fidei**

Reconciliation, Sacrament of. *See* Penance

Redemption. *See* Salvation

Reformation. *See* Anglicanism; Bucer, Martin; Calvin, John; Calvinism; Hus, Jan; Luther, Martin; Lutheranism; Methodism; Protestantism

Reformed Churches. *See* **Calvinism; Zwingli, Huldrych**

Regional Church

In the texts of Vatican* II, the terms *regional church*
and *local church* designate either a diocese, a grouping
together of dioceses, or a regional church with regard
to its rituals or its cultural context. The *CIC* of 1983
never uses *local church* but adopts the term *regional
church* technically and exclusively (can. 386) to designate the diocese and the institutions that the law* assimilates to it: prelature and territorial abbeys;
vicariate, prefecture, and apostolic administration. Personal prelature is clearly distinct about it: thus it is
treated in the section of *The Christian Faithful* (cans.
294–7).

Such a semantic option translates a material fidelity
to Vatican II, where *regional church* predominates for
designating the diocese. However, one cannot come to
theological conclusions from this specialization of
canonic vocabulary from which two questions emerge:
that of the diocese's own consistency and that of the
persistent weakness in the statute of regional churches.

a) Particular Consistency of Regional Churches. To
designate the diocese systematically as a regional
church runs the risk of resulting, at least in the Ro-
mance languages (but the same danger exists in German with *Teilkirche*), in an inadequate understanding
of the articulation between the diocese and the entire
Church. There is in effect a semantic opposition between the particular and the universal, whereas the regional church and the universal Church are the one and
the same Catholic Church. Moreover, *universal* connotes a geographic extension—whose theological
reach is modest—and also a uniformity and abstraction one reaches by stripping them of their particularities, while the unity* of the Church is multiform. As
for the diocese thus designated, the same logic is likely
to make it conceived as a subordinate part to the whole
that alone would have plentitude, while it is a portion
of the people* of God, equipped on the theological

level with all the goods of the whole: the gospel, the
Holy* Spirit, the Eucharist*, and the episcopate (*CD*
11), so that according to *LG* 23 it is "in them and from
them [the regional church dioceses] that the Catholic
Church exists as one and unique." Thus, a number of
theologians prefer their traditional vocabulary to the
systematic option of the *CIC*. Such an option risks
weakening the perception of the ontological Catholicism of the church diocese and reinforces the inadequate image of "an anterior universal Church or
presumably existing in itself, outside of all churches
[local]," that could only be "a being endowed with reason" (Lubac 1971), as if the universal Church were "a
reality ontologically and chronologically precondi-
tioned of any singular regional church" (Sicard 1993).

b) Regional Churches in Catholic Ecclesiology. The
preceding shows that the expression *regional church* is
better suited to the different regional realizations of the
Church that translate its cultural pluralism (such as the
Latin church or the Greek church), or to the canonical
gatherings or the diocese under the form of ecclesiastical provinces, patriarchates*, Catholicosates (patriarchate outside of the Roman Empire), or even national
churches that took shape in undivided Christendom
(e.g., the Gallican church). All these translations of the
gospel in history* and culture, because they are limited, can be called *regional church* without equivoca-
tion.

Vatican II conceived of divine providence* as having
coalesced "in the course of time into several groups organically united,...churches that enjoyed their own
discipline*, their own liturgical usage, and their theological and spiritual heritage" (*LG* 23). The patriarchal
churches are given as an example of this context. The
episcopal conferences might contribute to the new
face of regional churches: the stake is crucial for ecumenism* because a unitarian church is an obstacle to

a unique church, and it is also for a church that exists from as a leaven in all the cultures of humanity.

Because of their restrained national framework and the modesty of the canonical competencies, the episcopal conferences certainly cannot be enough to carry out this wish. The Continental regroupings of the episcopal conferences, combined with the revival (canonically open) of the councils*, can be fruitful in this sense, just as a better articulation between the papacy and the episcopate could be, which cannot be reduced to the problematics of decentralization.

Through the diversity of their historical forms both past and present, regional churches express the catholicity of the Church in its relationship to cultures; and, plenary presence of God's Church in a region, the diocene church is in a relationship of necessary interiority with the entire Church.

● R. Slenczka (1966), "*Ecclesia particularis:* Erwägungen zum Begriff und zur Problem," *Kerygma und Dogma* 12, 310–32.

H. de Lubac (1971), *Les Églises particulieres dans l'Église universelle,* Paris.

H. Legrand, J. Manzanares, A. Garcia (Ed.) (1988), *Les Conférences épiscopales: Théologie, statut canonique, avenir,* Cogitatio Fide 149.

G. Routhier (1991), "Église locale ou Église particulière: Querelle sémantique ou option théologique?" *Studia Canonica* 25, 277–344.

D. Sicard (1993), *L'Église comprise comme communion:* Lettre de la Congrégation pour la Doctrine de la Foi, Paris.

J.-M.R. Tillard (1995), *L'Église locale: Ecclésiologie de communion et catholicité,* Cogitatio Fide 191.

HERVÉ LEGRAND

See also **Bishop; Collegiality; Ecclesiology; Pope; Unity of the Church; Vatican II, Council of**

Reign of God. *See* Kingdom of God

Relation. *See* Being

Relativism

Relativism is a theory that proposes to explain beliefs by claiming that judgments of truth and falsity are not simply influenced by, but are entirely relative to, the temporal and spatial circumstances of those making the judgements.

Although the term dates from the 19th century, the doctrine has much older roots. The father of relativism is often thought to be Protagoras (485 B.C.–11B.C.), al-though he may have maintained only the modest thesis that morality is not immutable, but changes along with institutions. If there was a relativist movement, Sextus Empiricus (third to second century B.C.) would more obviously be its founder; he counseled suspension of judgment in the face of an evident contradiction in behavior or ideas. Montaigne (1533–92), Hume (1711–76), and Nietzsche* are in various ways heirs to this tradition, the last-named even augmenting it by his attempted "genealogy of morals."

Relativism takes different forms depending on three factors: the scope it is alleged to have; the nature of the circumstances held to be crucial in generating various beliefs; and the philosophical presuppositions it may involve. In the first place, relativism may be global or partial, but if it is applied to all judgments of truth* it obviously destroys itself, which hardly makes it plausible. More usually, therefore, it is a thesis about a specific domain, such as science, religion, or morality. Second, there are different forms of relativism, depending on whether one sees the reasons for divergences of opinion in terms of culture, means of production, historical period, or gender. Finally, relativism, whether global or limited, may be either epistemological or metaphysical. It may, for example, be limited to asserting that in relation to a specified domain, we have no means of establishing truth or falsity; but it may go further and claim that this impossibility is explained by the fact that there is no truth of the matter at stake. This radical thesis seems to be an element in some versions of postmodernism* and is maintained, for example, by Richard Rorty.

Although relativism in relation to moral beliefs therefore has a long history behind it, its status as a good explanation of moral disagreement within and between different societies* is open to question. Some critics doubt the existence of fundamental disagreements about moral judgments among human beings: after all, the most radical differences of practice can arise from common moral values. Even where the existence of deep disagreements is admitted, and when these disagreements are explained by reference to social or historical factors, it remains to be shown whether it is impossible to overcome them by rational deliberation. Without that, such disagreements merely show that there is indeed a plurality of moral views. However, to establish this impossibility is by no means a straightforward matter, and "antifoundationalists" such as Alasdair MacIntyre have contended that relativism is justified only if one postulates standards of rationality that no beliefs could satisfy. Antifounda-tionalists acknowledge that moral beliefs cannot be derived from some neutral, self-evident foundation, but necessarily belong within particular traditions of thought and inquiry. They argue, however, that these traditions may be judged to be adequate or inadequate, since they are subject to articulation and to questioning from other traditions.

Belief in moral relativism is often thought to entail pluralism and tolerance; however, since the supposition that moral beliefs cannot be satisfactorily justified also applies to the claim that we ought to respect values and practices other than our own, the alleged justification is clearly fallacious. In his encyclical *Veri-tatis Splendor* (1993, The Splendor of Truth; *AAS* 85, 1128–1228), John Paul II warns that moral skepticism is more likely to lead to oppression than to tolerance, and asserts that humankind may discover the natural law*, and thus acquire valid norms of conduct, by the light of reason* and guided by the magisterium*. What the church* teaches in the name of God* is therefore accessible, in principle, to every intellect, and, accordingly, the church's teaching is addressed to every human being. Within Protestantism*, thinkers such as Barth* (*KD* II/2) or Bonhoeffer* (*Ethik DBW*6) have usually been more ready to suppose that knowledge of good* and evil* is given in and with knowledge* of God. It is thus also revelation—and cannot and should not seek to justify itself against secular thought.

● C. S. Lewis (1943), *The Abolition of Man*, London.
G. Guthrie (1971), *The Sophists*, Cambridge.
J. L. Mackie (1977), *Ethics: Inventing Right and Wrong*, Harmondsworth.
M. Krauz, J. W. Meiland (1982), *Relativism, Cognitive and Moral*, Notre Dame, Ind.
R. Rorty (1982), *The Consequences of Pragmatism*, Brighton.
D. B. Wong (1984), *Moral Relativity*, Berkeley.
J. Annas, J. Barnes (1985), *The Modes of Scepticism*, Cambridge.
A. MacIntyre (1985), *After Virtue*, 2nd Ed., London; (1988), *Whose Justice? Which Rationality?* London.
D. B. Wong (1996), "Relativisme moral," *DEPhM*, 1290–6.

MICHAEL BANNER

See also **Ethics; History; Revelation; Truth**

Relics

In its religious and Christian sense, the term *relics* has two meanings. It refers primarily to the bodily remains of the saints, and secondarily to objects that are directly connected with the life of Christ* (the cross, for instance) or of a saint, or again, to objects that have touched a saint's body. From the earliest times Christians have venerated these remains in a manner consistent with faith* in the Incarnation* and in bodily resurrection, as well as with the Christian rejection of cremation, which was the practice in the Roman world.

In Smyrna, after the bishop* Polycarp's martyrdom in 177, the veneration of his body and tomb had already emerged as an essential component of the cult* rendered to the saint. A particularly important practice in Rome was the cult, attested a little after the year 200, of the "trophies" of the apostles Peter* and Paul (probably their remains). Similarly, in Jerusalem* in the fourth century, the discovery of Christ's cross led to the creation of a cult that would extend to the fragments derived from it. The status of such a cult had to be defined with care and precision, and a distinction laid down by Augustine* (*De Civitate Dei* X, 1) made this possible: adoration is due to God alone (*latreia,* or latry, the opposite of idolatry, which is the adoration of idols), while the saints are owed veneration (*douleia,* dulia). The eucharistic cult, and in another form, the adoration of the cross and the veneration of the Gospels*, belong to the cult of latria (Nicaea* II, *DS* 601).

In the fourth century there began the translation and sharing out of relics (for a long time the Roman church* was opposed to such division), as did the use of a saint's relics at the dedication of a church, when they were placed beneath the altar. During the same period the Fathers* of the Church took a position on the doctrinal validity of the practice.

According to the Basilian homily on Psalm 115 (PG 30, 112), "whoever touches the bones of a martyr shares in the holiness and grace that reside in them." And Gregory* of Nazianzus says of the martyrs: "their very bodies have the same power as their holy souls*" (*Against Emperor Julian* I, 59, PG 35, 589). Finally, at the time of the quarrel with the Gaul Vigilantius, a priest who criticized the cult of relics, Jerome's pamphlet against him *(Contra Vigilantium)* synthesized the state of the practices and justified them.

From the earliest days of Christianity, abuses of the cult of relics were encountered. Such abuses resulted variously from their collectors' credulous naivety or from superstition. In any event, the church's expressed opinion, and especially its practices, were qualified. We cannot know what Vigilantius really thought, but it can be seen that the process of Western Europe's evangelization avoided an uncompromising attitude toward the prior customs of the people (*see* Gregory* the Great to Augustine of Canterbury, *Registrum Epistolarum* XI, 45 [CCHR.SL 140 A, 961]).

The Reformers opposed both the abuses and the very principle of the cult of relics. At the Council of Trent*, on the other hand, the very same decree (DS 1821–5) condemned abuses while reaffirming the legitimacy of the principle of this cult and its consistency with faith in the resurrection of the body (*see* Vatican* II, *SC* no. 111). From the Catholic viewpoint, two obligations stem from this cult: the duty to ascertain the authenticity of relics, and the duty to distinguish carefully between the "objects of the cult," in the general sense of objects used in the cult, and the "object of a cult." And since a relic, in its precise meaning, is an object to which worship is rendered, its intrinsic sacredness implies that it cannot be deconsecrated.

● Saint Jérôme (406), *Contra Vigilantium,* PL 23, 339–52.

C. Mohrmann (1954), "A propos de deux mots controversés de la latinité chrétienne, *tropaeum-nomen,*" New Ed. in *Études sur le latin des chrétiens,* vol. 3, Rome, 1965, 331–50.

K. Schreiner (1966), "*Discrimen veri ac falsi:* Aussätze und Formen der Kritik in der Heiligen- und Reliquienverehrung des Mittelalters," *AkuG* 48, 1–53.

P. Jounel (1989), "Le culte des reliques," "Problèmes relatifs au culte des saintes reliques," *Not* 25, 212–36.

R.F. Taft, A. Kazhdan (1991), "Relics," *Oxford Dictionary of Byzantium,* vol. 3, 1779–81.

W. Klein, A. Angenendt (1999), "Reliquien/Reliquienverehrung," *TRE* 29, 67–74 (bibl.).

PIERRE-MARIE GY

See also **Cult; Cult of Saints; Holiness; Liturgy**

Religion, Philosophy of

I. History

From the very beginning, philosophy* took an interest in religion and its content, but a philosophy of religion was not established in Europe until the 17th and 18th centuries (K. Feiereis). Before that, in its approach to religion, philosophy was itself a theology*, that is, a theory of God* (of the gods, of the divine), whether in the form of rejection, critique, or affirmation. The Enlightenment marked a shift: attention was no longer focused on the deity*, Being*, the One, but rather on man as, and to the extent that, he was in relation with the deity.

Kant summarized the fundamental concerns of philosophy in a question: "What is man?" and this reversal of terms needs more legitimating than can be provided by the fact that it now seems to go without saying. Despite an approach that was still strictly theocentric, Hegel* similarly asserted "the theory of God cannot be understood and expounded except as a theory of religion."

The philosophy of religion thus finds its source in the movement of emancipation that was the Enlightenment, and this has not been without implications for the discipline following the Enlightenment. In attempting to "reach maturity" and depend only on its own rationality, thought has brought about a divorce involving the loss of a fundamental dimension of religion, its relation to authority* and tradition*. This situation, moreover, also characterizes the religious sciences, because even though they themselves developed on the same premises, they are now directly linked to the philosophy of religion.

This is not the place to consider the different factors—intraphilosophical, theological, socioeconomic, political, (inter)cultural, historical (in terms of personal trajectories and scientific developments)—that have affected this development. It remains true that the old certainties have collapsed, and that a fundamental rethinking, that is, a *philosophy* of religion, has become both possible and necessary.

II. Approaches

1. Major Orientations

Three major orientations may be distinguished: 1) the rejection of religion in the name of human freedom and autonomy; 2) the defense of religion (and in the first place of Christianity), that is, apologetics; 3) the theoretical and scientific study of religion, in the perspective of anthropology* or the philosophy of culture.

a)   The rejection of religion is commonly characterized as "(radical) critique." Aside from a usage of the word *critique* that is not accepted by more conservative thinkers, it suggests that apologetics is always uncritical by its very nature. This obscures the fact that the critique of religion has its source in religion itself (R. Schaeffler), in the prophets*, the church fathers*, and the doctors* of the Church.

Those who reject religion see it as a form of false consciousness, whose existence they attempt to explain and whose causes they attempt to treat. Some impute the failing to imperfect knowledge of and control over nature*, or to the development of a civilization that has made us lose the natural sense of existence. As a remedy they count either on the development of science* and technology, or, conversely, on a new adherence to nature, in a restored immediacy of the perception of the senses and "natural" relationships between individuals, and at a higher level in artistic creation and an esthetic view of life. The most ambitious program combines the two perspectives: "Whoever possesses art and science / Possesses religion as well. / May religion come to the aid / Of whoever has neither art nor science!" (Goethe). Others bring in the social perspective. The weakness of the lower classes, fear of thinking, and, among the best educated, self-deception, a lack of political courage, or a deliberate intent to deceive: all these conspire to perpetuate false ideas. The progress of science and reason should thus open the way to the humanization of society*, just as, conversely, social reforms and revolutions* make religious representations superfluous.

With respect to the future that we should expect or prepare for, there are two opposing groups among the adversaries of religion. On the one hand, there are those who hope for a deeper fulfillment of man, either through the restoration of a lost origin (Ludwig Feuerbach) or by the appearance of a new man or superman, as a higher goal of evolution* (Nietzsche*). On the other hand are those who perceive the imminence of a future without illusions (e.g., Freud*).

But at the "end of modern times" (Guardini) it is not so easy to oppose religion to nature or to society. Although it may have been possible 20 years ago to predict the disappearance of religion in modern urban civilization, the century just ended now seems to us to be stamped with religion and religiosity. (In the realm of the history of ideas, one might speak of a victory of Schleiermacher* over Hegel.) Religion has not always benefited in the process, as shown by the emergence of such diverse phenomena as militant fundamentalism* or dubious organizations that adopt the name of "church" for legal and tax purposes.

b) *The defenders of religion* respond by developing and refining, on the basis of the rational nature of human beings, a *natural* theology* with a metaphysical character. But this is at the cost, particularly in deism* and its "natural religion," of a disqualification of history*, despite the fact that (through authority and tradition) it plays an essential role for religion.

Growing out of German idealism, transcendental-subjective approaches (M. Blondel*, J. Maréchal, J. B. Lotz, K. Rahner*) have been added to this objective and metaphysical justification. These approaches justify religion as an open expression of fundamental actions that also condition the possibility of nonreligious attitudes, in both daily life and scientific activity (e.g., in the exercise of judgment).

Finally, the 20th century also witnessed an existential and personalist defense of religion, the roots of which are to be found in the crises and transformations produced by modern wars*. F. Ebner, M. Buber, E. Rosenstock-Huessy, F. Rosenzweig, and R. Guardini are representatives of this dialogical thinking that claims descent from Kierkegaard*. These last two approaches have been criticized for their unhistorical character and their lack of communitarian perspectives. (In Latin America, a philosophy of liberation has recently joined liberation* theology, and the developed countries have even witnessed an attempt, marked by several different tendencies, at a feminist defense of religion.)

c) *The third approach,* which took hold in the course of the 19th century, did not take a position for or against religion, but studied it from an empirical and scientific perspective in its historical, sociological, psychological, and phenomenological dimensions. Neither in themselves nor in the uses to which they were at first put did these works present a philosophical character in the classic sense; they derived rather from the *religious sciences.* They nevertheless require a concept of religion in order to structure their area of study, and to the extent that, for this purpose, they have adopted empirical and inductive approaches, they have themselves entered into the domain of the philosophy of religion, while sharing the formal and general characteristics previously set forth.

A particular form of this approach is the *analytic philosophy of religion.* It adopts, while radically transforming, all the aforementioned points of view. After working out positivist arguments about the absence of meaning in religious statements in a first phase, it is now engaged in methodically "clarifying" their presuppositions, verifiability, rationality, and theoretical and practical justification (L. Wittgenstein, A. Flew, A. MacIntyre, I. U. Dalferth). But in doing so it seems to have left to one side (for the moment?) the central question for religions themselves: that is, of the truth* of what they profess, of the reality of their object. Is it not necessary for any scientific approach to lead finally to a defense or a rejection of religion?

2. Methods

It is more useful to distinguish different ways of proceeding. This is because the philosophy of religion, as a philosophical discipline, has as its primary task the development of an adequate *concept* of religion, on the basis of which it may fulfill its descriptive, comparative, and normative functions in the service of the lived experience* and the scientific or philosophical treatment of religion or religions. Our first typology indeed presupposed a concept of this kind. The methodological criterion also brings out three approaches.

a) *The deductive method* is first of all that of metaphysics (which does not necessarily mean that it proceeds purely a priori, in the sense of the "ontological proof" dismantled by Kant). Having demonstrated the reality of the absolute, it takes the absolute, that is, the supreme Being, as a starting point in order to determine man's relation to it. The deductive method is also used by those who begin with a transcendental hypothesis about the fundamental human faculties and actions in order to offer a reconstruction of religion as the fulfillment of essence and the unconditioned. The philosophy of culture adopts the same program, but bases itself on the human community and not the individual subject. In the final analysis, religion is then defined and judged according to its function, for the individual as for society. In all these forms, the specific "quality" of the religious as such does not seem to be taken into account.

b) *Empirical methods* propose precisely to identify that specificity. They investigate "religious" behavior (prayer* and sacrifice*), distinctive characteristics (moments, places, persons, objects, and instruments), the language used in myth* and ritual, and the speech acts appropriate for contemplation* and for the liturgy*. But in their accumulation of materials and their extension to the "myths" and "rites" of daily life, these analyses end up by losing any substance and become unusable, particularly—but not only—for normative purposes.

c) *Phenomenology,* derived from Husserl, follows a third path. It begins with concrete acts in order to bring out their deep structure and, on that basis, the essential form of the reality toward which they are directed. It thus follows a procedure of transcendental unveiling. Perhaps the most fruitful results can be obtained from this method.

III. Problems

1. Objectivity?

We thus return to the question of content. What would justify the choice of a particular method or a particular concept? Some wish to understand religion in accordance with the idea it has of itself. Others on the contrary attempt to understand it from an extrareligious point of view, showing not so much harmony with the object as the intent to *explain* it.

But neither approach really leads to objectivity. The external perspective, on the one hand, does not see what religious consciousness aims for. In its view, in fact, religion is "in reality" something other than what that consciousness is directed toward: it is "opium" or "the cry of the oppressed," it is an instrument of social stabilization (Durkheim, Weber), a means of mastering contingency (H. Lübbe), and so on. The internal perspective, on the other hand, always includes the observer in the observation, and can therefore only be located concretely within a single religion and must consider the others from outside.

It would be tempting to attenuate the dilemma by hypothesizing that all religions in the end mean the same thing. But if, following a widespread conviction among believers, "any religious knowledge of God is also knowledge given by God, in the sense that its very conception is the work of God" (M. Scheler), then we do not have the right a priori to consider all revelations* as equivalent and equally subject to change: that is, as being in the end a matter of indifference. Moreover, it is hardly possible to reconcile ideas as different as that of successive reincarnations supposed to lead a soul tormented by existence and finitude to a redemptive nirvana, and that of the bodily resurrection* of an individual whom a personal God calls by name.

If we nevertheless wish to follow this path, by trying for example to "put in perspective" and complement each of these views with the other, they can then only be seen as subjective "opinions" (if not as mere figures [K. Jaspers] of a common attitude of flight from the world), and not the manifestation of an absolute Truth, the truth of the Sacred itself. But this position would be no less "dogmatic" and "intolerant" than the truth claims of the competing religions that it alike dismisses. In any event, it is a confusion of levels of discourse to speak of "tolerance" or "dogmatic intolerance," for tolerance does not characterize the relation to truth itself (whether it is the object of real or illusory knowledge), but, in the conflict of convictions about what is true, the relation to a person who thinks differently from us. If the agnostic renunciation of the truth were to become general all tolerance would come to an end. In the meantime the agnostic himself must show tolerance to anyone who confesses "to know whom I have believed" (2 Tm 1:12) and who therefore accepts the customary opposition between "believe" and "know" only with significant qualifications (the problem takes on a different form if instead of the verb *believe,* we use the noun *faith*). If agnosticism* and relativism* are therefore anything but neutral and objective, we must say the same of attempts aimed at reducing various religious doctrines to simple "views" on one or another concrete area of existence or on the deep reality of the world. We do not in any way conform to a material constraint, but to a personal choice and a personal value judgment, when we devalue as mere forms of anthropomorphism* (e.g., G. Mensching) the personal categories of uniqueness, the free promise of faithfulness, and the formal commitment of God, preferring in their place the impersonality of natural images such as the river of life, concentrated energy, the music of the universe, or the lunar sphere, which, though unique, is never reflected in the same way in the moving mirror of the water.

2. Question of the Truth of Religion

The concrete answer to the question of the truth of religion can be given only from within religion, on the basis of faith or a theological position. In a first phase, nevertheless, philosophy also possesses critical competence in this regard, for example in relation to polytheistic views. The philosophy of religion ought to define the essence of religion and distinguish it from its "distortion" (B. Welte), that is, from the many forms of *pseudo-religion* and pseudo-religiosity. Once the philosophically undecidable question of the *truth* of religion is put aside, philosophy should organize a problematics of *veracity* in the religious domain, in order to denounce any unwarranted attribution of the absolute ("divinization," idolatry*) to limited and conditional realities (or the "totalization" of the absolute, the desire to transform God into an idol).

To be sure, no religious act is exempt from distortion. It is therefore necessary to decide whether factual situations of unfreedom—concerning individuals, groups, acts, structures—within a religion are in contradiction with it, and must therefore be judged and abolished on the basis of the religion itself, or whether on the contrary they are the result of that religion. To this extent, the philosophy of religion is in accordance with Hegel's statement: "Religion is the place where a people [a man, a community] defines for itself what it holds to be true." It thus appears that the unavoidable task of the philosophy of religion is to pose the question of the essence of religion while preserving both within and without—in a language shared by believers and nonbelievers—the central truth of the religious phenomenon.

IV. A Concept of Religion?

1. Concept
Before posing the question of the "essence" of religion—what it "really" is—it is advisable to distinguish the level of definition on which that essence must be grasped. The path would be too undefined if we were to begin either with an ultimate value or foundation (Tillich* and his "ultimate concern"), or with things that "are sacred for human beings" (music, love, the nation), or even with the capacity of the human organism to transcend biological nature (T. Luckmann). But on the other hand, the path would be too narrow if we were to settle on the idea of a personal and transcendent God. Even the phenomenon of sacrifice presents an unresolved ambiguity. It is for this reason that R. Schaeffler, for example, calls for an analysis of the language of prayer, which implies both an intentional drive toward transcendence and a demarcation from the profane sphere.

In this context, we can see a combination of phenomenological thematics, transcendental method, and analytic choice of criteria. If we can understand a transcendental theory of God as a hermeneutic* proposition addressed to religious consciousness, then religious discourse—in its reflexivity and its objectivity, in its statements and its speech acts, in its professions of faith, its prayers, and its narratives—provides criteria for identification and evaluation of the religious and thus makes it possible to deal with the themes of a transcendental phenomenology of religion.

2. Quest for Salvation and Adoration of the Sacred
There is today among theologians and specialists in the philosophy and sciences of religion a nearly unanimous consensus in designating the goal and basis of religion with the term salvation*. This is indeed what the divine offers to us "naturally," and what it anticipates that we will expect from it (see Is 7:12–15). But how does one move from that to the noble thanks expressed in the Gloria of the Roman mass: "We thank you for your immense glory*"? Indeed, this is not a despotic glory, but one expressing the goodness of the God of love*. But do we praise that love while looking toward ourselves (confessing his "mercy") or—in total forgetfulness of the self—in looking toward him? Hegel already believed that philosophy now had the task of saving a truth or some truths that "certain forms of theology" sacrificed to the spirit of the age, and philosophical reflection today might again be called on to administer a "fraternal reprimand" to pastoral theology. Before and beyond salvation, it would be necessary to speak of a Good* that is "something other than saving and being saved" (Plato), of a good that does more than doing good (Levinas); it would be necessary to speak of the sacred. The fundamental and final fulfillment of religion would then be not to overcome finitude but to transcend oneself in the adoration of the divine.

It is through religion that things even now (provisionally and in the form of a "pledge" [2 Cor 1:22] of the order to come) find their place in time*. It is through religion that the world finds its order.

● S. von Storchenau (1772), Die Philosophie der Religion, Augsburg.
I. Kant (1793), Die Religion innerhalb der Grenzen der bloßen Vernunft, Königsberg.
F. D. E. Schleiermacher (1799), Über die Religion, Berlin.
G. W. F. Hegel (1832), Vorlesungen über die Philosophie der Religion, Ed. Jaeschke, Hamburg, 1983–85.
L. Feuerbach (1841, 1846), Das Wesen des Christentums and Vorlesungen über das Wesen der Religion, GW 6–8, Ed. Bolin, Stuttgart-Bad Cannstatt, 1960.
F. W. Schelling (1858), Philosophie der Mythologie, Philosophie der Offenbarung, SW 5–6, Ed. Schröter, Munich, 1965.
M. Blondel (1893), L'Action, Paris.
W. Windelband (1902), "Das Heilige," Präludien, Tübingen.
R. Otto (1917), Das Heilige, Munich.
H. Cohen (1919), Religion der Vernunft, Frankfurt.
F. Rosenzweig (1921), Der Stern der Erlösung, Frankfurt.
M. Scheler (1921), Vom Ewigen im Menschen, Leipzig.
R. Guardini (1939), Welt und Person, Würzburg.
K. Rahner (1941), Hörer des Wortes, Munich (2nd Ed. J.B. Metz, 1963).
P. Tillich (1959–), GW I, V, IX, Ed. Albrecht, Stuttgart.
D. M. High (Ed.) (1972), Sprachanalyse und religiöse Sprache, Düsseldorf.
B. Welte (1978), Religionsphilosophie, Freiburg.
H. Schrödter (1979), Analytische Religionsphilosophie, Freiburg-Munich.
I. U. Dalferth (1981), Religiöse Rede von Gott, Munich.
R. Schaeffler (1983), Religionsphilosophie, Freiburg-Munich.
F. von Kutschera (1991), Vernunft und Glaube, Berlin-New York.
♦ J. Hessen (1948), Religionsphilosophie I/II, Essen.

H. Fries (1949), *Die katholische Religionsphilosophie der Gegenwart*, Heidelberg.

A. Flew, A. MacIntyre (Ed.) (1955), *Next Essays in Philosophical Theology*, London (8th Ed. 1972).

C. Bruaire (1964), *L'affirmation de Dieu*, Paris.

K. Feiereis (1965), *Die Umprägung der natürlichen Theologie in Religionsphilosophie*, Leipzig.

K. Riesenhuber (1968), *Existenzerfahrung und Religion*, Mayence.

P. Ricœur (1969), *Le conflit des interprétations*, Paris.

J. Splett (1971), *Die Rede vom Heiligen*, Freiburg-Munich.

R. Schaeffler (1973), *Religion und kritisches Bewußtsein*, Freiburg-Munich.

J. Splett (1973), *Gotteserfahrung im Denken*, Freiburg-Munich (4th Ed. 1995).

C. Elsas (Ed.) (1975), *Religion*, Munich.

K.-H. Weger (Ed.) (1979), *Religionskritik von der Aufkärung bis zur Gegenwart*, Freiburg.

W. Oelmüller (Ed.) (1984–86), *Religion und Philosophie*, 3 vols., Paderborn.

W. Dupré (1985), *Einführung in die Religionsphilosophie*, Stuttgart.

W. Kern, H.J. Pottmeyer, M. Seckler (Ed.) (1985), *HFTh I*.

E. Feil (1986), *Religio*, Göttingen.

H. Lübbe (1986), *Religion nach der Aufklärung*, Graz.

F. Wagner (1986), *Was ist Religion?* Gütersloh.

K.H. Weger (Ed.) (1987), *Argumente für Gott*, Freiburg.

D.Z. Phillips (1993), *Wittgenstein and Religion*, London-New York.

J.-Y. Lacoste (1994), *Expérience et Absolu*, Paris.

R. Trigg (1998), *Rationality and Religion*, Oxford.

JÖRG SPLETT

See also **Atheism; Existence of God, Proofs of; Fundamental Theology; Hermeneutics; History; Knowledge of God; Language, Theological; Mysticism; Negative Theology; Reason; Revelation; Spiritual Theology**

Religion, Virtue of. *See* Cult

Religions, Theology of

1. Concept

The theology of religions may be defined as a systematic study of non-Christian religions, intended to relate their essential contents to the revealed truth* of Christianity. The existence of the Church* and of theology has always been fundamentally linked to the encounter and confrontation with other religions that claimed their own legitimacy. But it has been under the impetus of the Second Vatican* Council, and within the framework of the interfaith dialogue set in motion by the Ecumenical Council of Churches, that reference has become more and more frequent to "religions as a theme of theology" (H.R. Schlette), to a "theology of the history of religions" (E. Benz), or to a "theology of religions" (H. Bürkle). A theological study of non-Christian religions has thus grown up around particular themes, and points in specific directions. H. de Lubac*, for example, studied Buddhism from the perspective of "the origin of religions." Y. Congar was concerned with a clearer perception of "the truth and [the] dimensions of salvation*." J.-A. Cuttat took a primary interest in the spirituality of Asian religions. All these works approach religions from a theological angle and are thereby distinct from studies based on historical, comparative, or phenomenological methods. The theology of religions of course presupposes these kinds of analysis, and others as well (e.g., field studies, the psychology of religion, or the history of civilizations), and it benefits from these in conducting of its own research. But its basis and point of departure are located in the convergences and divergences presented in the light of the revealed truth of Christianity by the different religious paths by which human beings have expressed their "desire for God" (*CEC* §27).

2. Religions in Holy Scripture

The history of the Old Covenant* is already bound up with the encounter and confrontation with religious cults* and beliefs of other peoples. The unique election of Israel* and the unique revelation* received through Mosaic law* and the prophets* are rooted in a certain historical configuration involving spheres of influence external to Israel. But despite the parallels that may be established between Judaism* and other Semitic religions, the exclusive covenant established by God with Israel and the affirmation of his sovereignty over the people of Israel confer a new meaning on these religions. They remain imprisoned by a religion of nature and its polytheistic cults, whereas Israel, through its covenant with the Creator who is the origin of all natural reality, rejects those bonds and frees itself from the power of the divinities of nature. The self-manifestation of God in Israel, on the other hand, takes on a universal character that abolishes all ethnic boundaries; this universality is expressed with particular force in Deutero-Isaiah (Is 45:14 ff.) and in the Psalms*.

The language and the concepts of the New Testament are not derived from the tradition of Israel alone. Greek philosophy* and religion (notably Stoicism and the Gnostic and Neoplatonic traditions) contributed to the theological interpretation of the mystery* of Christ*, as did the Roman imperial cult. The language of myth, ancient cosmology, and Roman aristocratic titles were all put at the service of Christ and his message. "The light that appeared at the heart of human darkness in Greece is nothing but the reflected light of another sun. That sun is Christ" (H. Rahner, *Griechische Mythen in christlicher Deutung* 10). The theological study of non-Christian religions thus finds its New Testament model in Paul's speech before the Areopagus in Acts 17. Before the multitude of altars, in the heart of the great bazaar of systems and beliefs of the time, Paul presents Christ as the goal and the fulfillment of every religious quest. Through the multiplicity of their answers to the question of the foundation and the ultimate goal of their existence, human beings confess that they have not yet experienced divine reality in its depth and completeness ("What therefore you worship as unknown, this I proclaim to you," Acts 17:23). The religious progress of human beings is an expression of their sense of their condition as creatures (R. Otto). In various ways it shows that they are in search of the divine reality on which all of creation* is based and thereby in search of the unity of the human species (Acts 17:26). This common origin already provides a

principle of pre-Christian and extra-Christian solidarity. This is why God, despite the different names* that have been given to him, despite the diversity of paths on which human beings seek salvation, is proclaimed as an absolute who is close to everyone and present to all his creatures (Acts 17:27 f.). Confronting the world of other religions, the New Testament does not call on theology to pronounce their abolition; in these provisional and partial approaches to salvation it is necessary on the contrary to discern the still open demand for complete salvation and respond to it by basing itself on the advent of Christ (Acts 17:30 ff.).

3. Historical Landmarks

The whole history* of the Church is linked to the theology of religions in a more or less intense way depending on the period. The theology of the early Fathers was primarily directed at establishing the New Testament foundation of faith in the face of paganism*, and therefore was obliged to make judgments about the meaning of religions that had preceded Christianity and still coexisted with it in the Roman Empire. In the theology of the *apologists** of the second and third centuries the problem was resolved by a pattern of argument in terms of continuity and difference. Christian revelation did not negate but instead brought to perfection the results, weak and distorted though these certainly were, that paganism had been able to produce in its quest for virtues* and values of use to the human community. The doctrine of the Logos made it possible to deepen this argument, and played an essential role in the confrontation of Christianity with the representatives of the ideas of classical antiquity. For *Justin* (†165), for example, it became a bridge enabling him to link the christological economy of revelation with every action of God prior to Christ and independent of him; thus, it was said of the elements of virtue and wisdom* contained in pre-Christian doctrines that they consisted of "germs" or "seeds" *(spermata)* of the divine Logos revealed in Jesus Christ. *Clement of Alexandria* (A.D. 140), familiar with the mystical* and theosophical movements of late antiquity, was able to recognize in them means of access to the true and authentic mystery of the incarnate Logos: "[He] was able to recognize the element of relative truth [in the] philosophical message [of paganism]. But full and clear knowledge could be found only in the prophets and above all in the Logos itself which leads to all truth" (H. von Campenhausen, *Griech. Kirchenväter* 35).

In the *Summa contra gentiles* (1259–64), Thomas* Aquinas worked out his own theology of religions, and he did so by establishing a close relationship between dialogue and mission*, in order to support the preaching* of his Dominican brothers among the Muslims. In the absence of a sacred text common to the two religions that would make it possible to distinguish between true and false belief, Thomas relied on rational knowledge, by nature common to all human beings. Because faith* could be expressed only by analogy* with the created order *(analogia entis),* Christian truth had to be connected to truths accessible to the non-Christian, hence to truths taken from the sphere of the world of created beings. But only illumination by the Holy* Spirit made it possible to cross the border between nature* and the supernatural *(ST* Ia IIae. q. 109. a.1). The biblical model of divine revelation as prophecy and fulfillment found a new expression in Nicholas* of Cusa, through the link he made between diversity and unity. In his *De pace fidei,* Nicholas presents an imaginary dialogue in heaven concerning the way to institute peace* between religions. The area of tension within which religions are in conflict with one another has as its principle the *explicatio* and the *contemplatio* of God, by virtue of which laws, customs, and religious rites have taken on different forms depending on circumstances. In order to ensure the harmony of religions it is therefore necessary to undertake a "return" to that explanatory diversity in the *complicatio* of the one true God. In this context Christianity enjoys the privileged status of bringing together the elements of an authentic quest for God that appears in a dispersed state in other religions. Those elements converged in Christian faith and found in it their fullest expression in the form of a true love* and a true knowledge* of God.

The Enlightenment and ideas of social evolution influenced some theories of religion, among which the parable of the rings in *Nathan the Wise* by G. E. Lessing (1729–81) provides the most eloquent summary. The concern with revealed truth is replaced by a *quest* for truth and for a truly moral life: "It is not in possessing but in searching for truth that [the] capacities [of man] flourish, and this is how he always progresses further toward his perfection." This philosophical approach to religion and its call for tolerance were particularly influential in non-Catholic theology, and it is now experiencing a renaissance in various theological programs guided by social and ethical concern centered on the human person. It was in this perspective that E. Troeltsch (1865–1923) suggested the idea of a cultural relativization of religions, which would be dependent on the "individual particularities of different cultural and racial spheres" and the "specificity of their unifying religious structures" *(Die Absolutheit des Christentums und die Religionsgeschichte* 78).

This development of liberal Protestantism* was one of the principal targets of the "dialectical" theology that grew up around the young Barth*. Because any natural knowledge of God was radically excluded, Christian faith maintained a relation of pure opposition to religion, which was accused of wishing to make of "man…the creator of God, with God [becoming] in a dubious way the God of man, a predicate of the being and the life of man" *(KD* IV/1, 769). On this basis the theology of religions could have no purpose but to explain the incomparable particularity of Christianity (e.g., in the very Barthian book by H. Kraemer, *Die christliche Botschaft in einer nichtchristlichen Welt* [Zurich, 1940]). Only the encounter with religious traditions of other cultures, within the framework of a broadened ecumenical platform, would make possible the emergence of another perspective, which itself has had consequences in the theological realm.

4. Theology of Religions as Dialogue

Vatican II (1962–65) was able to provide a rich reformulation of the indications supplied by Scripture and tradition* on the relations between Christian revelation and other religions. The groundwork had been laid by an intense work of theological analysis and by the careful examination of the transformations that religions had experienced in the modern world. The doctrine of the council owes a good deal to the contributions and initiatives of theologians such as Y. Congar, H. de Lubac, K. Rahner*, H. Dumoulin, F. König, and others, for whom the swift changes in conditions with which humanity had been confronted had made it possible to recognize the role of non-Christian religions, along with Christianity, in a single task of taking charge of the world. The point of departure of *Nostra Aetate (NA),* the council's declaration on the Catholic Church's relations with non-Christian religions, was thus humanity, considered in its singleness and against the background of the ever closer ties uniting peoples to one another. Between the original unity of the human species, as it was intended by the Creator, and the unity restored in the sight of everyone by the fulfillment of the plan of divine salvation, humanity is in search of a meaning and a direction. By looking in different religions for "the answer to the hidden riddles of the human condition," human beings demonstrate not only their openness to the ultimate reality of God, their religious attitude even expresses a "certain perception *(quaedam perceptio)* of the hidden power" that governs their lives. The council document nonetheless recognizes that religions, as their history shows, also develop in relation to the development of cultures. Far from being static formations, closed off from any outside influence, they are themselves already evolving, to the extent that they attempt "to answer the same questions with more precise notions *(subtilioribus notionibus)* and more complex language."

At the same time, what Vatican II says of different religions outlines the major directions that now govern theological dialogue with the representatives of those religions. The religions of nature and tribal cults are, of course, not expressly mentioned in *NA,* but their particular type of religiosity is obviously alluded to in "the perception of a hidden power" or the "recognition of the supreme Divinity, or even of a Father" (*NA* 2). The theological contributions to the study of these ethnic religions ("primal religions")—in the wake of the work of P. Tempels on Bantu philosophy, which has been widely accepted—deal with the global vision expressed through religious rites and observances, and with the image they present both of man in his knowledge of himself as a created being, and of his group envisaged as a community of the living and the "living dead" (J. S. Mbiti). With regard to Hinduism, the council document refers particularly to "the inexhaustible fertility of myths*," the "penetrating efforts of philosophy," "ascetic forms of life," and the "depth of meditation," all of which makes it possible for the followers of that religion to "examine the divine mystery." Theological dialogue with Buddhism revolves around the "radical insufficiency of this changing world" and the search for a "state of complete freedom" and "supreme illumination." As for Islam, it has the virtue of adoring the "one God," referring to the Old Testament, venerating Jesus* as a prophet, and honoring his mother. Finally, the relationship of Christianity to Judaism is treated separately, by virtue of the common legacy that makes them the two chosen religions.

The impetus provided by Vatican II has given rise to a large body of scholarship that has taken concrete form in a multiplicity of monographs on non-Christian religions. Along with seminars and meetings organized by the Pontifical Council for Interfaith Dialogue, conferences sponsored by the Ecumenical Council of Churches and its program of studies for dialogue with representatives of non-Christian religions and ideologies have, on the Protestant side, contributed a mass of materials and particular contributions. In the face of the divergent developments and tendencies that have appeared in the theology of religions, the doctrinal texts *Redemptoris Missio* (1990) and *Dialogue et annonce* (1991) have, on the Catholic side, recalled the tasks that Vatican II assigned to the discipline.

• O. Karrer (1934), *Das Religiöse in der Menschheit und das Christentum,* Frankfurt.

H. de Lubac (1952), *La rencontre du bouddhisme et de l'Occident,* Paris.

E. H. Schillebeeckx (1952), *De Sacramentele Heilseconomie,* Antwerp.

F. König (Ed.) (1956), *Christus und die Religionen der Erde,* Vienna.

F. König, H. Waldenfels (Ed.) (1957), *Lexikon der Weltreligionen,* Freiburg-Basel-Vienna.

T. Ohm (1957), *Die Liebe zu Gott in den nichtchristlichen Religionen,* Freiburg.

R. Guardini (1958), *Religion und Offenbarung,* Würzburg.

H. Kraemer (1959), *Religion und christlicher Glaube,* Göttingen.

R. Panikkar (1963), *Die vielen Götter und der eine Herr,* Weilheim.

K. Rahner (1964), "Das Christentum und die nichtchristlichen Religionen," *Schr. zur Th.* V, Einsiedeln, 136–58.

J. Ratzinger (1964), "Der christliche Glaube und die Weltreligionen," in H. Vorgrimler, et al. (Ed.), *Gott in Welt: Festgabe für K. Rahner,* vol. II, Freiburg, 287–305.

H. R. Schlette (1964), *Die Religionen als Thema der Theologie: Überlegungen zu einer "Theologie der Religionen,"* Freiburg.

H. Bürkle (1965), *Dialog mit dem Osten,* Stuttgart; Id. (Ed.) (1966), *Indische Beiträge zur Theologie der Gegenwart,* Stuttgart.

Pontificium Consilium pro Dialogo inter Religiones (1965–), *Bulletin,* Rome.

K. Rahner (1965), "Anonymes Christentum und Missionsauftrag der Kirche," *Schr. zur Th.* VI, 545–54.

A. Bea (1966), "Die Haltung der Kirche gegenüber den nichtchristlichen Religionen," *StZ* 177, 1–11.

N. Söderblom (1966), *Der lebendige Gott im Zeugnis der Religionsgeschichte,* 2nd Ed., Munich-Basel.

G. Thils (1966), *Propos et problèmes de la théologie des religions non chrétiennes,* Tournai.

J. Heislbetz (1967), *Theologische Gründe der nichtchristlichen Religionen,* Freiburg.

Secretariatus Pro Non Christianis (1970), *Religions—Fundamental Themes for a Dialogistic Understanding,* Rome-Milan.

H.-J. Margull, S. J. Samartha (Ed.) (1972), *Dialog mit anderen Religionen: Material aus der ökumenischen Bewegung,* Frankfurt.

W. Kasper (1973), "Der christliche Glaube angesichts der Religionen," *Wort Gottes in der Zeit: Festschrift für K.-H. Schelkle,* Düsseldorf, 347–60.

H. Bürkle (1977), *Einführung in die Theologie der Religionen,* Darmstadt.

R. Panikkar (1977), *The intrareligeous dialogue.*

C. H. Ratschow (1979), *Die Religionen,* HST 16.

W. C. Smith (1981), *Toward a Universal Theology of Religion,* New York.

H. Waldenfels (Ed.) (1982), *Theologen der Dritten Welt,* Munich.

H. Küng, et al. (Ed.) (1984), *Christentum und Weltreligionen,* Munich.

D. J. Krieger (1986), *Das interreligiöse Gespräch: Methodologische Grundlagen der Theologie der Religionen,* Zurich.

M. Seckler (1986), "Theologie der Religionen mit Fragezeichen," *ThQ* 166, 164–84.

Commission théologique internationale (1997), *Le christianisme et les religions,* Paris.

HORST W. BÜRKLE

See also **Experience; Inculturation; Judaism; Religion, Philosophy of**

Religious Life

The term *religious life* now principally refers to all forms of church life marked, in Roman Catholicism*, by the profession of the evangelical counsels: "it is the *profession* of those counsels in a stable manner of life recognized by the church* that characterizes the life consecrated to God*" (*CEC* §915). Under this definition fall some hermits, consecrated virgins (and consecrated widows, for the *CCEO*), religious life under its various aspects, the institutes of the secular clergy, and, in a closely related way, the societies for apostolic life. Indeed, since Pius XII's apostolic constitution *Provida Mater Ecclesiae* (2 February 1947), religious life—which also included, according to the *CIC* of 1917, the brothers and sisters of congregations taking simple vows—has been subsumed under the category of consecrated life, which, following Vatican* II, the Code of 1983 describes in terms of following Christ* under the action of the Holy* Spirit (can. 573). The Ninth Synod of bishops of October 1994 saw chastity for the kingdom* as its determining criterion (*Propositio* 3; *see* 13).

There is no lack of doctrinal difficulties connected with this teaching of the magisterium. What is the link between this "particular consecration" (*LG* 42) and baptism*? How is this manner of life related to the New Testament, if the practice of the "evangelical" counsels of chastity, poverty, and obedience does not find its literal basis there? Can it be maintained, along with the recent code (*see* can. 607), that religious life, so abundant and so representative of the "great tree with many branches" (*LG* 43), is characterized by vows, when not all regular clergy are governed by the threefold vow: by communal life, which is now in competition with fraternal communion*; by public profession, when the particularity of the habit, the habitat, and activity are disappearing; or finally by separation from the world*, when it is more urgent than ever to evangelize? In confronting this crisis of concepts—linked, in the West at least, to the confusion of practices—history* is certainly a resource, because many monographs have indicated, particularly with regard to recent centuries, the existence of a spiritual family irreducible to its sociological interpretations (*see* in particular essays devoted to "flight from the world" and to the increased value placed on women). From the very beginning of the Christian era, there did indeed emerge ascetics, virgins, and the continent, who "remain in chastity in honor of the flesh of the Lord" (Ignatius of Antioch, *To Polycarp* V. 2; *see* the *Didache*) while never being assimilated to the Greek, Jewish, Gnostic, or Encratic movements that perhaps anticipated and certainly surrounded them. This commitment was widespread in the third and fourth centuries, as demonstrated by Tertullian*, Ambrose*, Jerome, and Augustine*. The archetype (and its integration into the church) goes back to the *Life of Anthony* by Athanasius* of Alexandria, soon followed by the rules of the first "monks," notably Pachomius and Basil*. From Marseille, Jean Cassian, in his *Institutions,* and especially his *Conférences,* spread abroad the reputation of these Desert Fathers (and Mothers) who had some predecessors in the West. Saint Benedict himself, whose *Rule for Monks* influenced the entire Middle Ages, did not represent an absolute beginning. While Christian ascetics were broken down into hermits, monks, cenobites, canons, and the like, monks became priests*, priests became monks, and their sisters followed them at a distance (deaconesses*, canonesses, beguines*, etc.). This early back-and-forth between the priestly and religious vocations almost led Pope Nicholas II in the 11th century to impose communal life on all priests, who had for several centuries adopted continence and then celibacy. In the East, monastic life, marked by the evangelical practices of continual prayer, healing* of the heart, and compassion for all created beings, has persevered up to the present, with great institutional fluidity, in the humble service of spiritual discernment and fatherhood, in a fraternal community, along with the evangelization of the people.

Irenaeus*, Ambrose, Jerome, and Augustine had thought about the soon-to-be-classic differentiation between precepts* and counsels. In Thomas Aquinas, especially in the *Summa Theologica*, this teaching is set in a doctrinal synthesis: counsels appear as the means best adapted to the ultimate goal, the love* of God and of our neighbor. The economy of the "states of perfection" flows from this, with the bishop* being seen as the *perfector* and religious life, particularly of the mixed variety (joining contemplation* and action), as representing the state of perfection "to be attained." Committing oneself in this form of life to the practice of the evangelical counsels, by devoting oneself to one's neighbor for the love of God, does indeed establish an association with the perfection of the bishops (*ST* IIa IIae. q. 188. a. 6). This also attests to the bond of spiritual life* with the hierarchical priesthood*, the communion of charismatic life with apostolic duty. This balanced manner of thinking (still at work in the *Spiritual Exercises* of Ignatius of Loyola), notwithstanding Francis of Sales and his *Traité de l'amour de Dieu,* was overturned in favor of "monks." Luther*'s radical challenge, and that of the Reformation (despite the persistence in Protestantism* of forms of life that were to make possible the 19th-century revival of a diaconal religious life and even a contemplative life), represented on the doctrinal level, for the monastic vows, a danger of eradication at least as great as the threat that the French Revolution posed to those who actually professed those vows.

Undermined in this way by theological and political egalitarianism, religious life nevertheless experienced an upsurge in the 19th century, particularly among women, that was even greater than that which had greeted the appearance of the mendicant orders in the 12th century, or the regular clergy in the 16th. But recruitment was declining in the West even before the Second World War, and the years since Vatican II have seen the shift of center of powers (not to mention financial resources), first to North America and now to Asia, with Latin America and especially Africa neglected in this regard.

If this history has a meaning, it is to show that the religious or consecrated life is marked by a practice inherent in the life of the church. This practice is by its very nature distinct from the priestly ministry*, and distinct in every respect from its *other,* which is Christian marriage*. Its remarkable persistence, its many forms, its universal extension, and also its variations mean that there is always a risk that any proposed formulations of the essential elements of religious life will be too narrow, although they do exist. As has already been said, celibacy for the kingdom is its lowest common denominator. Most commonly added to this is an agreed manner of living together ("life to be led in common," according to Vatican II; *see PC* 15) and often of working in the vineyard of the Lord (a common apostolate, "corporate action"), as for example in the practice of poverty and obedience. But these fragments shine, among all those who are consecrated, with their full brightness only if we indicate, at the heart of the inexpressible experience* of the paschal mystery*, an immediate encounter with the risen Christ, who, while he certainly brings forth and directs life, also infallibly accompanies it in person (consecration).

● Thomas Aquinas, *ST* IIa IIae, q. 179–89.
M. Luther, *De votis monasticis judicium, WA* 3, 565–669.
♦ R. Lemoine (1956), *Le Droit des religieux, du Concile de Trente aux Instituts séculiers,* Paris.
A.-J. Festugière (1961–65), *Les moines d'Orient,* 5 vols., Paris.
L. Moulin (1964), *Le monde vivant des religieux,* Paris.
A. Perchenet (1967), *Renouveau communautaire et unité chrétienne: Regards sur les communautés anglicanes et protestantes,* Paris.
J.-M.R. Tillard (1974), *Devant Dieu et pour le monde: Le projet des religieux,* CFi 75.
J. Halkenhäuser (1978), *Kirche und Kommunität: Ein Beitrag zur Geschichte und zum Auftrag der kommunitären Bewegung in den Kirchen der Reformation,* Paderborn.
A. Restrepo (1981), *De la "vida religiosa" a la "vida consecrada": Una evolución teológica,* Rome.
C. Langlois (1984), *Le catholicisme au féminin: Les congrégations françaises à supérieure générale au XIXe siècle,* Paris.
P. Brown (1988), *The Body and Society: Men, Women and Sexual Renunciation in Early Christianity,* New York.
A. de Vogüé (1991–), *Histoire littéraire du mouvement monastique dans l'Antiquité, Première partie: Le monachisme latin,* Paris.
C. Dumont (1992), "Spiritualité de religieux et de prêtres diocésains," *VieCon* 64, 344–58.
B. Secondin (1997), *Il profumo di Betania: La vita consecrata come mistica, profezia, terapia,* Bologna.

NOËLLE HAUSMAN

See also **Asceticism; Life, Spiritual; Monasticism; Precepts**

Renaissance

As a period in European history the Renaissance is generally considered to have extended from the beginning of the 15th century in Florence until about the end of the 16th in northern Europe. As a cultural phenomenon, on the other hand, there is no real consensus about its nature, its relationships with the 16th-century schisms collectively known as the Reformation, and there is no agreement about the part played in the Renaissance search for a new educational ideal by renewed recourse to the pagan texts of classical antiquity.

The Renaissance had a central philosophical and theological core, but spilled over into all the arts and sciences, and is often treated primarily as an episode in the history of the visual arts and secondarily also in music. At its heart was a sense of optimism about the dignity of human nature, a dignity that, on account of its diminution or abolition of the effects of original sin, late medieval theological orthodoxy could not accommodate. This optimism was made clear by the excited sense of innovation among those like Erasmus (1467–1536) who, in the wake of Francis Petrarch (1304–74), rallied to the clarion call of *bonae literae* (good learning), and claimed that they were inaugurating the rebirth or reflowering of an antique educational ideal. They created the term *Middle Ages,* which they variously regarded as "dark," "Gothic," or "barbarian," to denote the millennium between 500 and 1500. The diffusion of the cultural change it mediated was powerfully assisted by the technological revolution in communications when the discovery of a metal compound both soft and durable enough to be used for movable type vastly speeded the multiple reproduction of texts.

The early adepts of the new learning were conscious of promoting a new "humanism," understood both as a potential alternative to Scholasticism and in the Ciceronian sense of professing elevated standards of personal morality. At the very end of the 18th century the marquis de Condorcet (1743–94) was to speak of this movement as the revolt of "the sciences and philosophy" against "the yoke of authority," and the 19th-century romantics then built on the view of the Renaissance promoted by Germaine de Staël (1766–1817) in her 1800 *De la littérature,* as a rebellion against an obscurantist past. That view was famously restated by Jules Michelet (1798–1874) in the seventh volume of his history of France (1855, but drafted as early as 1841) and further elaborated in the fundamental work for modern Renaissance studies, the 1860 *The Civilization of the Renaissance in Italy* by Jacob Burckhardt.

Not until the 19th century were Michelet's historical discontinuities seriously attacked, and only toward the end of the 20th did it begin to become clear that the Renaissance was itself neither necessarily secularizing, nor a movement that originated in Italy and fanned out north of the Alps. It may well be that something analogous to the shift in values and attitudes constitutive of the Renaissance on the Italian peninsula occurred against a quite different intellectual, sociopolitical, and religious background, but spontaneously and independently, in France, the Low Countries, England, and northern German-speaking Europe.

Florence under the Medici anchored its new view of human dignity, which demanded a positive reevaluation of attitudes toward the virtuous potential of instinctive human behavior, through recourse in painting, literature, and the arts generally to metaphor, allegory, classical mythology, and the elaborately Plotinian Neoplatonism* elaborated by Marsilio Ficino (1433–99). In northern Europe the pattern of reform, emphasizing more insistently that spiritual fulfillment had to be intrinsic to moral elevation, was modeled on the imitation of Christ, the spiritual doctrine of the *devotio* *moderna* based principally on humility, a devotional ideal derived from the Rhineland* mystics, and the quiet celebration of the domestic virtues of life.

The reciprocal independence of the northern and southern Renaissance must not be over-stressed. Although from the 14th century northern painters clearly derived inspiration from south of the Alps, by the 1470s Italian painters were painting landscape backgrounds and foreground figures in a style derived from Flemish realism. The great painters of the Italian Renaissance painted and were patronized by princes and popes. Sculptors and architects imitated ancient Roman models, while painters concentrated on portraits, frescoes, and altarpieces. The new style of painting in the north, where oil-based pigments originated, was on the other hand developed from miniaturists and manuscript illumination. Northern painters more often painted groups of guild leaders, town councilors, domestic interiors, and scenes of communal emotion, whether joy, sorrow, or fear, but all with a naturalistic precision, which did not differentiate between the significance of details.

Outside the visual arts, it was the Renaissance writers themselves who emphasized their rejection of the Gothic past, which had been intellectually monopolized by Scholastic arguments based on intricate divisions and subdivisions. The Scholastics, primarily north of the Alps, had produced an endless series of irresolvable dilemmas resulting from the hardened precision of categories like intellect and will, nature and grace, body and soul, transcendence and immanence, predestination and free will, which the late Middle Ages had imposed on the legacy of Augustine. Intellectually, spiritually, in his view of history as essentially remote from the present, and in his enthusiasm for Plato and an elegant Latin style, Petrarch is regarded as the first precursor of the full Renaissance change in moral, religious, and literary culture. He consciously modeled himself on Augustine, turning toward Plato and away from the Scholastics' Aristotle, whose philosophy seemed to Petrarch to endanger belief in the immortality of the soul.

Petrarch's advocacy of a new system of values, still tentative and oblique, was taken up by Giovanni Boccaccio (1313–75), and in moral philosophy and Latin style by Coluccio Salutati, chancellor of Florence from 1375. It was Cosimo de' Medici (1389–1464) who had Ficino trained as a scholar and who commissioned from him the translation of Plato. Furthermore, Ficino not only translated Plato, Plotinus, and a miscellany of what he referred to as "Platonic books," but also adapted Plotinian Platonism into a "theology" of the immortality of the soul and, in his adaptation of Plato's *Symposium*, tentatively suggested that ordinary human emotional relationships, not exclusive of physical sexual union, might be the first stage in the soul's ascent to the beatifying love of God.

Ficino's achievement was much enhanced by the influx of Greeks into the Italian peninsula for the 1439 Council of Florence. However sparsely, Greek began to be taught in the West, and there arose an important, bitterly conducted dispute between the advocates of Aristotle and those of Plato, ending with the celebrated defense of Plato by the Greek cardinal Bessarion (1400–72), the *In calumniatorem Platonis* printed at Subiaco early in 1469 on the first Italian printing press. Ficino was to draw on it.

Ficino's literary influence was enormous, and his view of love, for which he coined the term "Platonic love," immediately became widespread and popular, establishing a whole new literary genre, the *trattato d'amore*. But he also became a cult figure among a tiny number of scholars, mostly from France, England, and Germany, who were more interested in the content of his theology. Among those most active in its transmission north of the Alps were Giovanni Pico della Mirandola (1463–94), who spent a year and a half in Paris, and from whom Erasmus derived much, and John Colet (1467–1519), the Oxford theologian who founded Saint Paul's School in London, to whom Erasmus looked for patronage.

Erasmus was himself the single most important intellectual figure of the northern Renaissance to combine classical learning with a desire to promote religious reformation. Like Jacques Lefèvre d'Etaples (†1536) in France, Erasmus became preoccupied with the dissemination of scriptural teaching in the vernacular, although he published the first critical edition of the New Testament in Greek, preceding by several years the more distinguished but less radical Complutensian Polyglot Bible being prepared by the team of scholars gathered by Francisco Ximines de Cisneros (1436–1517) at Alcala. Huldrych Zwingli (1484–1531) was inspired by Erasmus, and although Luther was not himself much concerned with the new learning, his principal lieutenant, Philipp Melanchthon (1497–1560) was an accomplished humanist. Erasmus was also on intimate terms with John Fisher (1469–1535) and particularly Thomas More (1478–1535) in England. He wrote satirical as well as pedagogical works, scriptural translations and commentaries, edited both classical and patristic texts, and wrote thousands of letters; he was at the center of nonschismatic religious reform, and was reluctantly cornered by the papal curia into writing against Luther in 1524. At the high point of his optimism he declared, in a passage to be borrowed by Rabelais, that there was only a "minimal" inclination to evil in the best-endowed human beings.

The new Renaissance attitudes to human nature and potential both permeated the relationship between the church and the new nation states, and changed the way in which the church regarded itself. It had seemed, especially during the pontificates of Julius II (reigned 1503–13) and Leo X (reigned 1513–21), as if the reimposition of papal authority after the conciliar movement had ebbed away depended on the existence of a secular papal state with an income independent of that which flowed from the nation states, on account of the church's sacerdotal sovereignty*. Popes outdid the great Renaissance princes in the magnificence of their building and the lavishness of their artistic patronage.

The first wave of the Renaissance was over by the time the decrees of the Council of Trent were promulgated in June 1564. The council had been called primarily to restore proper ecclesiastical discipline, although it is now best remembered for its strongly reactionary dogmatic decrees. Christendom had been split, and Trent's decrees hardened the divisions. The Renaissance optimism of Rabelais and Erasmus was dimmed, and was further to be challenged by religious schisms and subsequent wars. Nonetheless, it was recognizably from the culture of the Renaissance that modern Europe would eventually emerge.

● W. K. Ferguson, (1948), *The Renaissance in Historical Thought,* London.
M. M. Phillips (1949), *Erasmus and the Northern Renaissance,* London.
R. R. Bolgar, (1954) *The Renaissance Heritage,* Cambridge.
Denys Hay (Ed.) (1961), *The Italian Renaissance in Its Historical Background,* London.
P. O. Kristeller, (1961), *Renaissance Thought,* New York.
A. G. Lehmann, (1984), *The European Heritage,* London.
P. Johnson (Ed.) (1997), *The Papacy,* London.

ANTHONY LEVI

Renewal. *See* Pentecostalism

Resemblance. *See* Analogy; Trace (Vestige)

Resurrection of Christ

A. Biblical Theology

---

a) Acts of Faith. To establish the fact and the sense of Christ*'s Resurrection requires an interpretation of the testimonials, because all claims and statements about the Risen Christ are made with reference to an experience* (known as "paschal"). This has been expressed in three forms: 1) the structured forms of confession of faith, invocation, and hymn; 2) the direct witness of Paul; and 3) the Easter narratives* in the Gospels*.

The earliest acts of faith* belong to the first group. They include: a) participial forms that attribute to God* the act of raising Jesus* from the dead, including Romans 4:24 and 8:11, 2 Corinthians 4:14, and Galatians 1:1; b) the invocation—"Our Lord, come!" in 1 Corinthians 16:22 and "Come, Lord Jesus!" in Revelation 22:20—that calls for the final coming of this Jesus, presupposed Lord of the last times; and c) hymns celebrating the domination over all reality exercised by the man who was seen in his earthly humanity and is now exalted—as in Philippians 2:6–11 and 1 Timothy 3:16.

The second group, the Pauline witness, is especially important, as it is a unique, direct, personal witness of a paschal experience (1 Cor 15:8–10; Gal 1:15–16; and Phil 3:8–11).

The third group includes the accounts of the empty grave (Mk 16:1–8 and parallel passages) and all other narrative passages. Some of these narratives are in the literary form of "narrative of recognition," in which the Risen Christ shows himself, is not immediately recognized, and is finally recognized before he disappears (Lk 24:13–32 and Jn 20:11–17). Others take the form of "narrative of apparition," in which Jesus appears in a marvelous modality, is immediately recognized, and then spends some time with the disciples and entrusts them with a mandate (Lk 24:36–49 and Jn 20:19–23). In Mark 9:2–10 (the Transfiguration) and Mark 6:47–52 (walking on water) the narratives of apparitions of the Risen Christ are projected onto the prepaschal narrative, but this reading is too conjectural.

b) Times and Places. A sequential organization of events (discovery of the empty grave–apparitions–Ascension–Pentecost) was imposed starting from Luke 24 and Acts 1–2, but in fact the testimonials vary. Matthew 28 and John 20–21 diverge on the distinction of the events and their temporal distribution. The structured formulations (confessions of faith, etc.) permit the supposition of a different intelligence of the event. These testimonials are verbal condensations of a complex spiritual experience subject to diverse interpretations by the texts. The apparition of Jesus (1 Cor 15:5–8), his exaltation (Phil 2:9), his enthronement as Son (Rom 1:4), and his assumption in glory (1 Tm 3:16) are acts of the Spirit (Rom 1:4 and 1 Tm 3:16), and the Spirit is a gift to the community. Along these same lines the Risen Jesus, giving witness of himself before Paul, makes Paul an apostle* invested by the Spirit. Vision, hearing, and ecstasy are combined in the paschal experiences. Easter, Ascension, and Pentecost join together. In the later version of John (Jn 14:1–31) they are still present as a unit; in Luke they are projected in a linear succession.

However, this approach does not solve the whole problem. Two questions remain: 1) Should the motif of the "third day" after the death of Jesus (1 Cor 15:4) be seen as a historical fact of the first paschal experience, or a pure theological elaboration? The motif can be traced to Hosea 6:2, or to the idea that the soul* does not completely leave the body until after the third day. The vagueness of these other possibilities argues for treating the motif as a historical fact. 2) How can the apparently contradictory localization of the apparitions in Jerusalem* (Lk 24 and Jn 20) and in Galilee (Mk 16:7; Mt 28, and Jn 21) be resolved? The sequence in John 20–21 is a rewriting. Further, the two localizations have theological bearing in Matthew and Luke. (The same procedure is used in Mk 1:14–39, 9:30, and 14:28; Luke 24:47; and Acts 1:8.) The fact that the disciples were in Jerusalem, where the first community was organized, argues in favor of Jerusalem.

c) Empty Grave. Did the Gospel of Mark, in its primitive version, really end with the women's discovery of the empty grave, adding that the women were "afraid" (Mk 16:8)? It is generally accepted that Mark 16:9–20 is a later addition. This raises a problem: Can the paschal faith be built on the empty grave? An evaluation of Mark 16:1–8 should focus on the fact that the core of the narration is not the empty grave, but the paschal confession pronounced by the angel* (Mk 16:6, Rom 4:24, etc.). In that context, the angel's word responds to the Passion* of Jesus, identified with the suffering of the Just One (*see* Ps 22:23–24 and 69:29–33). The empty grave does not prove the Resurrection of Jesus, but it serves as scenic background to a message unambiguously upheld by other New Testament witnesses, and adequately founded by the encounter with the Risen Christ in person in the apparition experiences. The faith of Easter does not stand on the credibility granted by historians to accounts of the empty grave. The witness of the apparitions comes first, the empty grave, second.

d) Resurrection and Christology. The theological meaning of Easter can be described as follows: the death of Jesus (Gal 3:13; *see also* Wis 2:12–20) and the flight of his disciples (Mk 14:50) showed that Jesus had failed in his self-appointed goal of rendering God totally present to Israel*. The paschal experience opened a new perception: the Jesus put to death for God (Mk 16:6 and Rom 4:24) is recognized by God as his own. The consequences of that recognition are conveyed in the metaphorical language of awakening, resurrection, and exaltation, given descriptive or at least cognitive meaning by the texts. This network of signifiers (death and resurrection) functions first of all to block the hypothesis of an apparent death followed by reanimation.

In the same way that the texts establish the new status of Jesus at Easter, they all, without exception, attest to the reality of his death (1 Cor 15:3–4). The Risen Lord is associated with the celestial reality of God; he himself brings testimony of his resurrection to the disciples. And his paschal status is the starting point of the Christology* that would immediately and forcefully spread, retrospectively casting a new light on Jesus' prepaschal existence. Thereafter it is accomplished: In Jesus, God fixed forever his relation to mankind (1 Thes 1:10, 4:17) and to all that is real (1 Cor 15:20–28 and Rom 8:18–23). Christology would then be elaborated to relate that affirmation. Borrowing concepts from Jewish apocalyptics*, Paul called Jesus "the first fruits of those who have fallen asleep" (1 Cor 15:20), and saw his times as the last times before judgment* and the fulfillment (Rom 13:11).

There was no reflection on the corporeity of the Risen One and his post mortem condition in the earliest texts, which do not go beyond the confession of a corporeal resurrection. In Luke 24 and John 20–21, presence in the world and transcendence to this same world come together at an extreme degree of tension. In 1 Corinthians 15:35–50, Paul uses the vocabulary of corporeity in an argumentation aimed at showing the specifically unworldly nature of the risen existence, an absolute future of the body that exceeds all worldly limits. By the apparitions of the Risen One and the gift of the Spirit, the community of the disciples was founded anew and became the Church* of Christ. Mission* and apostleship were articulated on that new foundation (*see* Mt 28:19–20; Lk 24:46–48; Jn 20:21–23; and Acts 1–2), soon followed by development of the ensemble gospel-faith-salvation (1 Thes 1 and 1 Cor 15). The paschal faith became the foundation of Christian hope*. The God who raised Christ from the dead is the one who will annihilate suffering and death and bring all reality to its ultimate fulfillment (1 Thes 4:13–18; 1 Cor 15; Rom 4:17 and 8:11–12).

● H. Schlier (1968), *Über die Auferstehung Jesu Christi*, Einsiedeln.
Coll. (1969), *La résurrection de Jésus et l'exégèse moderne*, Paris.
X. Léon-Dufour (1971), *Résurrection de Jésus et message pascal*, Paris.

J. Kremer (1977), *Die Osterevangelien—Geschichten um Geschichte,* Stuttgart (2nd Ed. 1982).

L. Oberlinner (Ed.) (1986), *Auferstehung Jesus—Auferstehung der Christen,* Freiburg-Basel-Vienna.

P. Hoffmann (Ed.) (1988), *Zur neutestamentlichen Überlieferung von der Auferstehung Jesu,* WdF 522, Darmstadt.

F. Blanquart (1991), *Le premier jour (Jean 20),* LeDiv 146.

P. Stuhlmacher (1992), *Biblische Theologie des Neuen Testaments* I, §13.

J. Becker (1993), *Das Urchristentum als gegliederte Epoche,* SBS 155, 29 *Sq.*

JÜRGEN BECKER

See also **Apocalyptic Literature; Creation; Creeds; Death; Eschatology; Faith; Gospels; Holy Spirit; Jesus, Historical; Judgment; Passion; Resurrection of the Dead; Soul-Heart-Body**

B. Theological Problematic

The first conviction of Christians is that God tore Jesus* of Nazareth away from death. This explains why the "Lord's day" is a celebration of the victory of the Risen One (Justin, *I Apol.* 67, 7, Ed. Wartelle, 193), why Easter comes first in the liturgical cycle in all Christian churches, why the celebration of the Eucharist* commemorates the Crucified-Risen. (Hippolyte, *Trad. apost.* 4, SC 11 *bis,* 51–53). The memory of the faith* is not connected solely to the ignominious death of Jesus: "On the third day he rose from the dead" was proclaimed by the first Christian authors in christological confessions of faith in which the Resurrection figures prominently, even though Incarnation* or Crucifixion may be the only mentions that gloss the name of the Son in some binary or ternary confessions. The words of Polycarp of Smyrna are a typical affirmation of faith of "those who believe in our Lord Jesus Christ* and in his Father* who raised him from the dead" *(Letter to the Philippians* 12, 2, SC 10 *bis,* 221). Afterward, all church creeds mention in the second article Jesus' Resurrection in the narrative* of the paschal mystery*, with the corresponding general resurrection of the dead following in the third article. It is this "awakening" to life, transcending the precariousness of our world*, that calls to mind his earthly itinerary, including the death sentence. Without this resurgence, Jesus would not be proclaimed the Lord of history*.

1. History

Of course this initial element of Christian faith, already present in Clement of Rome, who saw it as the "premises" of our coming resurrection (*Aux Cor.* 24,1, SC 167, 143), encountered immediate opposition. The Docetic movement of the Gnostics devaluated the sense of the Resurrection by questioning the fleshly reality of Christ. Ignatius of Antioch forcefully declared that Jesus Christ "is truly resurrected from the dead" (*Trall.* 9, 1, SC 10 *bis,* 119) and this resurrection is the most manifest sign of Jesus' divinity (*Ephes.* 7, 2, ibid., 75). But the most radical objections came from the Greeks, who considered the very idea of the resurrection of the dead as nonsense.

The pagan Celsus ridiculed it: "Once that flesh was deposed, did it perhaps become God*? And why not Asclepios, Dionysius, Heracles?" He jeered at the Christian argument that founds the divinity of Christ on the testimony of his resurrection, and he rebuked the Christians for mocking "those who worship Zeus because his tomb is exhibited in Crete" whereas they worship "a man who left his tomb, but they don't know how or why the Cretans do as they do" (*see* Origen's *Contra Celsum,* III, 42–43, SC 136, 101). Origen* retorted that Celsus "criticizes us because we have admitted that our Jesus was buried; but we say that he rose up from his grave, and the Cretans have not yet dared claim as much for Zeus" (ibid., 103). He goes on to show the difference between the mythological legends alleged by his adversary and the undeniable, public nature of Jesus' death. His disciples, who knew him, testified all the more courageously to his resurrection.

Nevertheless, the discourse of second and third century apologists* was centered not on Jesus' Resurrection but on the general resurrection of the dead or the flesh, of which Jesus' Resurrection was the best example. Tatian, Athenagoras, and then Irenaeus*, Tertullian*, and Origen all took major positions on this subject. And it was the basis of speculation on the possibility and the reality of the resurrection of the flesh and on the nature of the risen body. Concerning Jesus himself, his ignominious death on the cross had to be justified first.

Thus, in the fourth century, Jesus' Resurrection became the subject of a "peaceful possession" in the church. The great Christological debates of that time centered primarily on Jesus' Incarnation and human-divine identity. This went so far that some modern thinkers accuse the Greek church fathers*, wrongfully, of shifting the center of gravity of the faith from the Resurrection to the Incarnation (*Jossua* 1968). In fact, the debates at Ephesus* and later at Chalcedon* on the truth* of the being-become-man-of-the Word* of God, in the distinction of his two natures, was meant to found the truth of the paschal mystery—that is, of the death and Resurrection in the flesh of that same Word. "His flesh being resuscitated, we still speak of his resurrection, not that he fell into corruption, but because his body is resuscitated" (Cyril of Alexandria, *DCO* II–1, 111). "Even if the resurrection of the dead is said to have taken place through a man, still it remains that we conceive of this man as the Word born of God and the means by which death was broken" (ibid., 133). The entire argumentation has a soteriologic intention: Christ Risen realizes first in his own body and for us the fullness of life that is the destiny of all mankind that is saved.

However, the Greek Fathers came up against the Hellenistic interpretation of the immortality of the soul* as an obstacle to the scriptural representation of the Resurrection. They made a considerable effort to justify it without denying the radical discontinuity caused by death, resorting to the Creation* and the necessity of assuming in glory the real history of the individual (Origen, *De Principiis,* 1–4, SC 252, 375 ff.; *Comm. Jo., II,* 225–45, SC 157, 519 ff.; Gregory* of Nyssa, *De Anima et Resurrectione,* Paris, 1995).

The situation remained stable in the Middle Ages and up to the dawn of modern times. Thomas* Aquinas treated the Resurrection of Jesus among the mysteries of Christ's life (*ST* IIIa, q. 53–59). He distinguished miracles* that are arguments for the faith from those that are objects of faith, placing Jesus' Resurrection in the latter category. Nevertheless, it also confirms the faith. Thomas particularly emphasized its salvational importance. Just as the Passion* liberates us from our ills, the Resurrection raises us to the goodness of the justification* (*ST* IIIa, q. 53, a. 1). This led Thomas to speculate on the charnel identity of the Risen Christ: his risen body is a real body, the same one he lived in before Easter. But it is also a "glorious" body: continuity must leave room for the rights of discontinuity. Thomas was careful to not transpose this earthly world into the glorified world (because of his theory of the soul as form of the body); his theology* does not contain any revivification of the corpse. However, marked by an overly literal interpretation of scriptural narratives, he granted a largely uncritical credibility to the neotestamentary representations of Jesus Risen, taking

the expression of a transcendent presence for information on a nonearthly state (*ST Suppl.* q. 75–81; IV *Sent.*, dist. 43 and 44). He did, however, pose precise questions on the signs of his resurrection given by Jesus, and their credibility*.

In the 16th century Luther* rejected the complications of Scholastic* speculation and announced the cross and the Resurrection of Jesus as the first event of salvation*. In the 17th and 18th centuries the resurrection of Jesus was put in doubt by a rationalism* wary of all miraculous notions. These doubts raised by the Enlightenment culminated in the 19th century in research on the life of Jesus that tried to account for the Resurrection by seeing it as a lovely myth* (myth being understood as the Other of history), as revelation of a religion of humanity (D. F. Strauss) or, more flatly, as the fruit of hallucinations by Jesus' disciples (E. Renan). Under pressure from these arguments, theology was led to favor an exclusively apologetic treatment of the Resurrection. In the order of reasons adopted by Neoscholastics in the latter half of the 19th century, the Resurrection stands as a supreme historical proof of Jesus' divinity. They tried to found this proof on rational historical arguments, supposedly valid regardless of any presupposition of belief. But these arguments often left out transcendence of the risen body with respect to the empirical order of phenomena, which makes them a bit naïve. At the same time the Resurrection almost disappeared from the field of dogmatic* theology. Soteriology was reduced to an analysis of the sense of the Passion and the cross.

The 20th century deserves credit for restoring the Resurrection of Jesus to its central position in the ordained exposition of the Christian mystery. F.-X. Durrwell's *La résurrection de Jésus mystère de salut* (1950, frequently reprinted), was particularly effective in this restitution. Thereafter, the Resurrection was restored to the heart of soteriology and its eschatological dimension regained a vivid relief. However, in recent decades, critical exegesis* has combed through the New Testament testimonials, bringing dogmatic interest and critical concerns to play in the highly diversified interpretations of the first element of the faith. In the minimalist line already fixed by Schleiermacher* (belief in the Resurrection is second with respect to the first element, God acting in Christ), followed by E. Troeltsch, some interpretations reduced the Resurrection to nothing more than the salvational sense of the cross, as perceived by the faith (Bultmann*'s Jesus risen "in the kerygma"). Other reductive interpretations saw it as the present energy of the faith of Peter*, giving a future to the event of Jesus Christ (W. Marxsen 1968), or as the ever vivifying act of the Spirit (J. Pohier 1977). At the same time, recent research has also produced "maximal" interpretations of the Resurrection as the expression of the salvational act of God for mankind (Barth*, etc.), an eschatological anticipation so radically inscribed in the history of the world that it is a possible object of all historical research (Pannenberg). The Resurrection contains all the keys to interpretation of the faith. One point should not be contested: a correct theological access to Jesus' Resurrection supposes that one has overcome all disjunction between "fact" and "sense."

2. A Fundamental Theological Problem

The dogmatic challenge cannot hide a major difficulty overlooked in the apologetic approaches—paschal kerygma does not speak of an event that belongs entirely to common history; the veracity of this discourse cannot be established on the sole bases of verisimilitude and credibility of the witnesses (X. Léon-Dufour). The death of Jesus is undeniably inscribed in the order of the probable and verifiable. The observation is not limited to the testimony of friends, it goes beyond the circle of his followers, and it does not transgress the verisimilitude of all reasonable interpretation. The same cannot be held (despite Pannenberg) of the Resurrection: Jesus, who is said to have vanquished death, slipped away from the world he had belonged to. Thereafter, he is no longer inscribed within common credibility; he stands apart from all public transmission of information because he only manifests himself, alive, to a few friends and disciples (Acts 10:40–41). And even if the "rumor" (Moingt) of his resurrection soon began to spread, it does not modify the initial form of the witness, which is the word of a self-implicating commitment. (Because of its original ambiguity—resurrection or theft of the corpse?—the account of the empty grave is no less so.) For he who is called to believe and did not see the only possible access to the Resurrection is a hermeneutics* of the testimony. And because the theology of the Resurrection does not treat anything that it is authorized to describe, it must allow the organization of meanings of an event filtered from signs given to it.

3. Systematic Theology

The condition of believer suggests the following arrangement in four periods:

a) *Subdued Victory.* This title refers to the ambiguous nature of experiences that give rise to the two testimonial elements: the empty grave and the play between nonknowledge and recognition of the Resurrection in apparition accounts.

The account of the empty grave is detached from in-

formation that spoke the truth of Jesus' death, condensed in the words of the Apostles' Creed: "He descended into Hell." This account tries to capture both the reality and the strangeness of Jesus' arising. Because it is related, the ambiguity is hard to reject. In fact, the disappearance of Jesus' mortal remains fits more easily with theft than "awakening." Whereas the emphasis on his burial in the grave calls for a clear determination, in the attestation of his resurrection, of what became of his corpse. The affirmation that he is risen in his body is problematical if his corpse can also be venerated. Of course, the presence of his spirit near to God could be maintained, but an essential element of the sense of that "awakening" would be excluded from the experience. Therefore, the ambiguity of the empty grave does not eliminate the importance—both objective and negative—of that signifying trace in backing the attestation of the resurrection of Jesus' body. The "he is not here" (Mk 16:6) indicates the sense of that trace; but the empty grave in itself does not impose a unique, unquestionable interpretation (Moingt 1993).

Nor do the apparitions escape two forms of ambiguity, one emphasizing strangeness (Lk 24:36–37) and the other underscoring the continuity (Mt 28:9 and Jn 21:9–11) with Jesus' earthly existence. First, the strangeness: the visionaries do not recognize Jesus when he appears before them. Then the continuity: Jesus is described as if he belonged once more to this world. He is seen preparing a meal (Jn 21:9–11). His friends know it is him; they recognize him by a sign; their doubt or astonishment is so strong that they cannot ask him to decline his identity (Moingt 1993).

The ambiguity of the account is reinforced by the strangeness and continuity of the personage in the apparitions. Where the author emphasizes the strangeness, we might seem to be dealing with a ghostly apparition (Lk 24:37), a communication with the other world, revealing nothing of the effective result of the resurrection of Jesus, and diminishing the corporeal sign. One thing is sure: he who appears this way escapes the confinement of death, because he can show himself at will. The corporeal sign acts as a necessary representation to make his presence tangible in our world. When the author underscores the continuity, he gives the impression that the risen body has the same status as his prior condition; this would be the same as Lazarus' return to life. However there is an important difference. He who appears in a corporeal form in the narrative has mastery of space, because he makes himself seen where he wants, to whom he wants; Lazarus did not have this ability. The narratives of apparition are ambiguous because they recount a marvelous event as if it were ordinary.

b) The Corporeal Sign. The ambiguous nature of the apparition accounts orients confessions of faith toward the corporeal sign. The motif of the resurrection of the body becomes the central point of the tradition*. The disappearance of the corpse was already an invitation to place emphasis on "the body," which is the locus of all awakening. The apparition accounts—by their insistence on a spatial, convivial presence—are organized around the same concern: the Nazarene not only survives in soul and spirit, he prevailed over death in his totality as a physical human subject.

The allusion to a descent* into hell accentuates the truth of Jesus' death; Jesus went to Sheol, the place where the defunct lead a larval existence. He does not come back from Sheol as a spirit or a soul given permission to communicate with earthlings, such as Samuel with Saul in the conversation at Endor (1 Sm 28:8–20), he awakens from the dead in full possession of that which constitutes the human being. Because the body is not a superfluous element, it is that by which the subject manifests itself, communicates, constructs, and develops itself over time (Pannenberg 1993). To say that Jesus not only survived like the souls that sleep in Sheol but arose from death with his body is to recognize that the body by which he manifested himself to humans, communicated with them, and constructed himself as human subject, was not abandoned like useless remains.

Jesus rose up from hell to live intensely, in a way unknown to us, that which constituted his history; he rose up as a human being. The body is not a simple metaphor to designate the fullness of an awakening to "divine" life, it is the point of incandescence of the life given by God in the victory over death. The specific affirmation of the Christian faith on Jesus is that he lives next to God as an intact human subject. This risen body cannot be described, we have no experience of it, we have only obscure signs of a strangeness that does not exclude a certain proximity. The Word of God does not respond to curiosity, it speaks the plenitude toward which the earthly life of Jesus led, despite the death endured. This plenitude concerns all who believe in Jesus or are called by him.

c) The Universal Vocation. Jesus' rising from the dead is not an unprecedented divine act in his life, it is the seal placed on an itinerary of unconditional opening to the will of God to signify his proximity and love*. The kenosis* (Phil 2:6–11) designates the originality of that prophetic life; it also expresses God's renunciation of the exercise of power. Jesus' liberty* with respect to the law*, and his proximity with the distressed, and it led him to words and deeds whose ambivalence expanded endlessly under the horizon of hopes* borne by the tradition of Israel* (Moltmann, Theissen, Pannenberg). By not hiding the originality of his message or his disinterest for any immediate messianism*, Jesus alienated the crowd without holding off the hostility of the ruling class. His "assassination" is the fruit of his prophetism* and his proximity to sinners, and the outcome of a path he did not want to change, despite the dangers.

Jesus died of our sins* and for our sins, making himself the brother of the poor in all times. This itinerary is universal and negative: rejected by human beings, Jesus went to the extreme of dereliction, believing himself abandoned by God. In the heart of his solitude, Jesus cries out a cry that symbolizes his word with regard to those who kill him: "Father, forgive them" (Lk 23:34). This cry is heard. To the one who did not refuse to give his life for his own, God gave life in plenitude, tearing him out of hell and bringing him into his kingdom without denying his humanity. In his body Jesus devoted himself to others, in his body he felt the force of life. In the gift of himself to humanity, the sense of his existence comes to light: God has it proclaimed that Jesus belongs to him, and designates him Son (Rom 1:4), first born of a multitude of brothers. He died for others a death with universal value; thereafter, he lives, for others, a life with universal meaning. The Resurrection narratives are envoys on mission*.

d) Current Energy. The Resurrection is not an event of the past inscribed once and for all in the immobility of history. A past event is not current, but finished. This is not true of the Resurrection; it functions today, because it is today that the Eternally Living gives the Spirit (Moingt 1993). The Resurrection is operational not only as a chain of actions inscribed in history by virtue of an initial inspiration and witness. It did operate on the level of values and institutions. Believers stood up to realize in part the demand that inhabited his preaching*. Already, in this sense, the initial event of the witness remains actual. But when a believer affirms the present reality of the Risen Christ he is not thinking in the first place of this historical inscription. He thinks of the actual subject of that new existence, that which the Spirit now gives so that others will follow the path he took and attain a similar glory, that which leads history to the fortunate term that Scripture calls the kingdom of God. It is he, the Risen One, who by the constantly given Spirit confronts the recurrent figures of evil* and death. The actuality of the Risen One thus designates his present action, in continuity with that of his life as a prophet*, but different, because it stimulates subjects whose task is to work for a fortunate history, not subject to the judgment* of God, liberated from the "day of wrath."

That is why the Gospel Resurrection narratives are in themselves narratives of mission. The disciples are sent out so that, in Jesus, God reconciles the world (Mk 16:16–20). The order given to the apostles*—to proclaim the gospel over all the earth, to baptize in the name of Jesus, to pardon sins—is heard on the horizon of the active presence of the Living for centuries. The mission of the disciples is the form henceforth taken by the action of the Risen Christ. It is not the only one; in other forms the Risen One gives the Spirit so that human history will not be only a place of violence*, but will be worthy of the one that Dante* called first Love (*Inferno* III, 6). This action is supposed, by reason of the divine will, to save all men (1 Tm 2:3–4). The mission of his disciples and his own mission will not reach their term until Christ has vanquished, in all, death, his enemy, and submitted all to his Father, so that God will be all in all (1 Cor 15:26–28). The actuality of the Risen Christ is inseparable from his eschatological force (Moltmann 1964).

● *See* the bibliography for **Christ and Christology** and:

D. F. E. Schleiermacher (1821), *Der Christliche Glaube*, Berlin, §100–105.

A. Michel (1937), "Résurrection," *DThC*, 13/2, 2565–71.

F.-X. Durrwell (1950), *La résurrection de Jésus mystère de salut*, Paris (11th Ed. 1982).

R. Bultmann (1955), *L'interprétation du Nouveau Testament*, Paris (original French collection of several contributions by Bultmann written at different times).

K. Barth (1959), *KD* IV/3, Zurich.

J. Moltmann (1964), *Theologie der Hoffnung*.

W. Pannenberg (1964), *Grundzüge der Christologie*, Gütersloh.

B. Klappert (Ed.) (1967), *Diskussion um Kreuz und Auferstehung*, Wuppertal.

J.-P. Jossua (1968), *Le salut, incarnation ou mystère pascal*, Paris.

W. Marxsen (1968), *Die Auferstehung Jesu von Nazareth*, Gütersloh.

L. Schenke (1968), *Auferstehungsverkündigung und leeres Grab*, Stuttgart.

G. Martelet (1972), *Résurrection, eucharistie et genèse de l'homme*, Paris.

B. Rigaux (1972), *Dieu l'a ressuscité*, Gembloux.

P. Gibert (1975), *La résurrection du Christ*, Paris.

J. Moltmann (1975), *Kirche in der Kraft des Geistes*, Munich.

J. Pohier (1977), *Quand je dis Dieu*, Paris.

C. Duquoc (1985), *Messianisme de Jésus et discrétion de Dieu*, Geneva.

P. Carnley (1987), *The Structure of the R. Belief*, Oxford.

G. Theissen (1987), *Der Schatten des Galiläers*, Munich.

W. Pannenberg (1991, 1993), *Systematische Theologie*, Göttingen (II, 385 *Sq*; III, 588–625).

J. Moingt (1993), *L'homme qui venait de Dieu*, Paris.

CHRISTIAN DUQUOC

See also **Adoptionism; Barth, Karl; Bultmann, Rudolf; Christ and Christology; Creeds; Descent into Hell; Eschatology; Fundamental Theology; Miracle; Passion; Resurrection of the Dead; Salvation; Word**

Resurrection of the Dead

A. Biblical Theology

---

a) In the Hebrew Bible. Although Sheol* occurs as a common element of Old Testament eschatology, the resurrection of the dead is mentioned infrequently. In this context we need not include those earthly resurrections brought about by Elijah (1 Kgs 17:17–24) and Elisha (2 Kgs 4:31–37, 13:2), which are akin to the healing* of individuals and in no way foretell mankind's ultimate destiny. Linked to the Canaanite agrarian myths, the Israelites' hope, as expressed in Hosea 6:1 ff. ("After two days he will revive us; on the third day he will raise us up," 6:2), a hope of which in any case the prophet does not approve (6:4–6), concerns the nation's restoration. Similarly, the evocation of the dry bones springing back to life (Ezekiel 37), this time based on the Yahwist theme of Genesis 2:7, heralds the revival of Judah after its downfall in the sixth century before Christ.

On the other hand, a passage from the apocalypse of Isaiah, usually dated from the Persian period (sixth century B.C.)—Isaiah 26:19—by use of the verbs *chyh* (to live), *qwm* (to arise), and *héqîç* (to awaken), announces the resurrection of those among the faithful people* of God who had died (death*), while the impious, the oppressors of this people, will vanish for ever

(26:14). Around 165–164 B.C., at a time of fierce persecution, and basing itself on Isaiah 26:14 and 26:19, but also on Isaiah 53:11 (Septuagint and IQIsa) and 66:22 ff., Daniel 12:1 asserts, in an apocalyptic context, the resurrection of the faithful who have died and their transfiguration in the beyond.

The best and most generally accepted interpretation today of this crucial text, which exerted a strong influence on later traditions, is the one proposed by B. J. Alfrink. At the moment of the final intervention by Michael, the guardian angel* of the people of God, the living inscribed in the Book* of Life will escape death and a great many of the dead will reawaken (Dn 12:1–2 a); therefore, only a portion of the living will preserve their lives and a portion of the dead will regain theirs. These are all the faithful, righteous people. The following verse (Dn 12:2) specifies that the latter will be destined for "everlasting life" (life*, eternal) while the others, both those who died during Michael's intervention and those who had died earlier, will not reawaken during this final intervention, but will experience everlasting shame and contempt (see Is 66:24). There is, then, no universal resurrection: only the righteous among those who had already died before Michael's intervention will come back to life. The verse that follows this one (Dn 12:3) concerns the spiritual guides (see Is 53:11) of those mentioned in Daniel 12:1–2a, those who will not die and those who will reawaken: they will be transformed and will share in the luminous and transcendent world of the stars, assimilated to the angels.

b) Supplements to the Septuagint. Written at an uncertain date between 160 and 180, the didactic account of the martyrdom* of the seven sons and their mother (2 Macc 7) develops Daniel's views (12:2) while clarifying them. Faithful unto death to the laws* of the Old Covenant, each one of these martyrs affirms in turn the doctrine of the resurrection. The first son states the scriptural argument: "He [the Lord] will have compassion on his servants" (Dt 32:36, quoted in 2 Macc 7:6). The second son then specifies that "the King of the world will revive us for an everlasting return to life" (7:9). The third, holding out his tongue and his hands, hopes to recover them: thus the body shares in the resurrection (7:11). According to the fourth son, the impious have no share in this resurrection (7:14). As for their mother, proclaiming her faith* in God the Creator, she encourages her sons: "through his mercy* he will restore your minds *(pneuma)* and your lives *(zôè)*" (7:23). Finally, the youngest of the sons states that his brothers have undergone "fleeting pain for the sake of boundless life" (7:36). Nothing is clearly stated about the time of the righteous martyrs' resurrection, since the author is more concerned with the fact than with the date.

The author of Wisdom, a contemporary of the emperor Augustus, does not speak explicitly of resurrection. He only mentions Greek notions of immortality *(athanasia),* of the hope and reward of the righteous subjected to trials (Wis 3:4 ff.), and of incorruptibility *(aphtharsia),* for which man was created (2:23), and which God grants to his faithful by bringing them closer to himself (6:18 ff.). And yet Wisdom's eschatology seems to entail resurrection. The author's silence on this subject arises perhaps from the fact that he is more interested in the final salvation* of the righteous than in the way in which it will happen. Certainly, on the day of judgment* (their "visit") the righteous "will become resplendent" (Wis 3:7, *see* Dn 12:3) and a transfiguration of their being can be imagined. Such imprecision is clarified by Wisdom 19: there, against the backdrop of the Creation*, the author gives a rereading of the episodes leading to the event that founded Israel*. The episodes of the Exodus, for example, where the punishment of the impious and the freeing of the righteous are brought about by means of cosmic elements, strike the author as another creation (Wis 19:6), in which the world's component elements are transformed in order to save the righteous from death (16:24). This history*, which implies a cosmology, founded an eschatology: if the Exodus, the prototype of the history of Israel, was a new creation, eschatology also calls it; therefore one can speak of the physical salvation of the righteous; and the meditation on the Exodus (11–19) illuminates the author's thoughts about the final destiny of the righteous (1–6).

Israel therefore gradually asserted the resurrection of the dead. This began during the Persian period in a historical context marked by the trials endured by its people. It was essential for them to understand how the fidelity of God, the master of life and death, toward his faithful ones did not cease with their deaths, with the gift of their lives which they made him. Resurrection involved only the righteous, for it implied that in the beyond they would be close to the God whom they had served and loved here below; and it was seen collectively, for the individual merged with the community. Moreover, contrary to the Greek body/soul dichotomy, biblical anthropology* could not conceive of the human being without a body; the soul *(nèfèsh)* did not enjoy an autonomous existence: it animated the body, thus making it a living being. Victory over death thus implied a revivification of the body.

c) Intertestamental Jewish Writings. These texts reveal a great diversity in their conception of an afterlife, but in general they accept that in the beyond the righteous will be rewarded for their faithfulness. Even within the same book, diverse conceptions sometimes occur. Some writers derive their ideas from a more Greek conception: 4 Maccabees speaks of immortality (16:13) and incorruptibility (9:22, 17:12). Moreover, the texts are not always as clear as one would like, and this is what explains discrepancies between their commentators. Nonetheless, the idea of resurrection was making progress. Certain of these texts grant resurrection only to the righteous: 1 Enoch 51, first century (controversial date); *Test XII* Judith 25:1–5; *Test Abraham* A (long version) 18:9–11; *Psalm of Solomon* 3:12; *Biblical Antiquities* 3, 10 (?), 19, 13; 2 Baruch 30:1–14, the *Life of Adam and Eve* 13:3 (add.). Others envisage a universal resurrection, before the judgment that separates the righteous from the impious: Test XII Benjamin 10:5–10 (but 10:8 is a Christian gloss); 2 Baruch 49–51; Test Abraham B (short version) 7 and 13–17; *Sibylline Oracles* IV, 179–92; Test Job 4:9; 40:4 (*see* Job LXX, 19:25; 42:17); 4 Esdras 7:32–37; *Biblical Antiquities* 3:10; Life of Adam and Eve 41:3).

As for the texts from Qumran, the controversy continues. Fragments from cave 4 provide the testimony of belief in the resurrection of the sons of light alone: 4 QTestQah 1 II, 5; 4Q Vis, Amr, 1 II, 14; 4Q245 = 4QPs-Daniel, 4 ('), but these texts are pre-Essene. 4Q385 II, 5–9 + 4Q Deutero-Ezekiel (*see* Ez 37) and especially 4 Q 521 2 II, 12 might reveal Essene thought on the resurrection of the righteous.

d) The Jewish Sects in Jesus' time held different opinions. The difficulties raised by the Essene texts have just been mentioned. For the Sadducees, we have at our disposal only the testimony of their adversaries, the Pharisees and the Christians. Despite this fact, their rejection of the resurrection of the body, of retribution after death, and even of any kind of afterlife, can be maintained; for them, there was fundamentally no scriptural argument for such beliefs. Passages from Matthew 22:23–33 (about tithes), as well as Acts 23:6 ff. (Paul before the Sanhedrin) clearly mention the stance of the Sadducees, to which a few scattered Pharisean texts refer (Abbot de Rabbi Nathan, A 5; Misnah Sanh X, 1; TB Sanh 90B-91A).

The Pharisees, on the contrary, made the resurrection of the dead an essential point of their doctrine, and it passed from them into postbiblical Judaism*, but their explanations vary. Although perhaps a few Hellenic influences can be found in it, the roots of Pharisean thought remain deeply embedded in the biblical understanding of the human being. While the Pharisean scholars also searched for scriptural sources (e.g., Dt 32:39; 1 Sm 2:6; Is 26 and 19; Ez 37; Job

10:10 ff.), they concentrated on the body's ultimate fate, sometimes with a realism that contrasted sharply with the spiritualizing trends of the intertestamental writings. In short, although certain Pharisees thought that everyone, both the righteous and the unrighteous, came back to life, ready to meet different fates, the majority held to the resurrection of the righteous alone, and perhaps even of the repentant.

e) New Testament. The restorations to life accomplished by Jesus* (Mt 9:25 par.; Lk 7:15), Peter* (Acts 9:40) and Paul (Acts 20:10), being prophetic signs of the new times (Mt 11:5: "The dead are raised"; *see* Is 26:19), do not belong in the list of resurrections. In opposition to the Sadducees (Mt 22:23–32; Acts 4:1 ff.), but following in the steps of the Pharisees (Acts 23:6, 24:15), Jesus proclaimed the resurrection of the dead *(anastasis [tôn] nekrón);* together with the eternal judgment, it is among the fundamental teachings of Christianity (Heb 6:2). As the work of the power of God, the resurrection transforms: "they neither marry nor are given in marriage, but are like angels in heaven" (Mt 22:30). It is primarily, on the Day of Judgment, the reward of the righteous (Lk 20:35: *anastasis ek nekrôn*), whether Jews (Lk 14:14: "you will be repaid at the resurrection of the just") or pagans (Mt 12:41 ff.; Lk 11:31 ff.). Yet Paul (Acts 24:15) and John (Jn 5:28 ff.) announce the resurrection of the righteous and of sinners, a resurrection that will lead to different destinies. This judgment, which Matthew 19:28 situates at the time of the "new world" *(paliggenesia),* will involve all the nations and will be pronounced by Christ* in his glory (Mt 25:31 ff.). Jesus himself will raise up at the last day whoever believes and shares in his flesh and his blood (Jn 6:39 ff., 6:44, 6:54). More than a simple bringing back to life (*see* Jn 11:39), the resurrection of Lazarus—which Martha assumes will take place on the "last day" (11:24)—is accomplished by Jesus as a sign of the mission he has received from the Father* (11:42): Jesus is the resurrection (11:25). Finally, Luke 13:28 ff., 16:19–31, and 23:42 ff. give us to understand that at death each person's fate is provisionally decided, in expectation of the last judgment.

His Pharisean roots meant that Paul had retained the Jewish and not the Greek view of life after death, but he subsequently based his views on the Resurrection* of Christ, to whom he gave his energies until the end. At the time of the Lord's Parousia (1 Thes 4:15; 1 Cor 15:23)—in his epistles Paul only looks at the position of Christians (except for 2 Tm 4:1)—those who have died in Christ (1 Thes 4:16; 1 Cor 15:18) will come back to life and the living will be caught up together with them (1 Thes 4:16 ff.).

They will all be transformed (*allagèsometha,* 1 Cor 15:51), and will clothe themselves in incorruptibility and immortality (1 Cor 15:53 ff.: a concession to Hellenism?). To return again to our celestial abode we must either be naked (dead) or "put on more clothing" (if we are alive: *ependusasthai,* 2 Cor 5:4). Our raised body *(sôma psychikon)* will become a spiritual body *(sôma pneumatikon,* 1 Cor 15:44): Christ "will transfigure *(metaskhematisei)* our wretched body by making it conform *(summorphon)* to his body of glory" (Phil 3:20 ff.).

Until the time of the Lord's revealing (1 Tm 6:14), those who have died in Christ are nevertheless already united with him (1 Thes 5:10; Rom 14:8; 2 Cor 5:8; Phil 1:23). In order to recount this mystery* (1 Cor 15:51), Paul, while basing himself on the word of the Lord (1 Thes 4:15), resorts to the apocalyptic* (such as Revelation 20 for the universal judgment) and to the analogy* with nature, as in Judaism (*see* 1 Cor 15:36 ff.

and the parable of R. Meir, *TB Sanh* 50 B). Moreover, Paul thinks that the resurrection is anticipated in the present life of all those who, through baptism*, share in Christ's resurrection (Eph 2:6; Col 3:1 ff.).

- B. J. Alfrink (1959), "L'idée de résurrection d'après Dan XI, 1–2," *Bib* 40, 355–71.
- P. Beauchamp (1964), "Le salut corporel des justes et la conclusion du Livre de la Sagesse," *Bib* 45, 491–526.
- R. Martin-Achard (1981), "Résurrection des morts," *DBS* 10, 437–87.
- K. Spronk (1986), *Beatific Afterlife in Ancient Israel and in the Ancient Near East,* Neukirchen-Vluyn.
- E. Puech (1993), *La croyance des Esséniens en la vie future: Immortalité, résurrection, vie éternelle? Histoire d'une croyance dans le judaïsme ancien,* Paris.

MAURICE GILBERT

See also **Anthropology; Apocalyptic Literature; Cosmos; Death; Eschatology; Hell; Judgment; Salvation; Soul-Heart-Body**

B. Historical Theology

Based on the biblical accounts, especially in the New Testament and particularly in the writings of Paul, in Christian tradition* the resurrection of the dead is one of the earliest attested articles of faith*. Its founding formula can be seen in the Apostles' Creed: "I believe in the resurrection of the flesh *(eis [...] sarkos anastasin)*" (*DS* 11) or in the Creed of Nicaea-Constantinople: "We await the resurrection of the dead *[anastasin nekron]*" (*DS* 150). The fact that the resurrection is the resurrection of the body and not only the immortality of the soul* is central in the doctrinal history of this article of faith.

1. Early Christianity

a) The Apostolic* Fathers, although with varying emphases, agreed unanimously on the resurrection of the dead. Clement of Rome (*I Clement 26, 3)* describes it as a resurrection of the flesh*, meaning by *sarx* not the body as distinct from the soul, but the perishable creature, and as such contrasted with divine immutability*. This nondualist meaning of *flesh,* which occurs in the Roman creed, had first of all an exhortatory and ethical force: because salvation* takes place in the flesh, which will be raised and judged, from now on the holiness* of this flesh must be preserved. But

since it must be judged, that means that resurrection is not identified with salvation but has a neutral character rather, which is why the Roman creed mentions "everlasting life," which completes salvation after the resurrection. As for the dead awaiting the resurrection, according to *I Clement* they dwell in a temporary abode similar to the Hades of the pagan poets. On the other hand, according to Ignatius of Antioch *(Epistles)* and *The Acts of the Martyrs,* the righteous—at least the martyrs, who must include the patriarchs and the prophets*—go to meet Christ at once, which can be interpreted as a resurrection at the very moment of death*, since these authors do not express the idea of the survival of the soul (*see* Greschake-Kremer 1992).

b) The Apologist* Fathers (second century), more fully aware of the Platonist tradition and Gnosticism*, have a clearer idea of the distinction between the immortality of the soul and resurrection. But although the former facilitates a certain approach to Christian hope* (Justin), its announcement of resurrection is charged with an originality that it can in no way translate: "If the Savior...had announced as good news only the life of the soul, what new thing would he have contributed compared to Pythagoras, Plato, or other men?" (Ps.-Justin, *De res.* 109). For Irenaeus* of Lyons and

Tertullian*, the resurrection is the decisive criterion that separates Gnosticism from Orthodoxy. While the Gnostics view the flesh—that is the body, the world, and history*—as the creation of a lesser god, a creation from which the soul must be delivered in order to return to its celestial abode, Irenaeus states that all flesh *(pasa sarx)* has been created by God* and is appointed for salvation: "What is more ignominious than dead flesh? On the other hand, what is more glorious than that same flesh once it is raised, having received incorruptibility as its portion?" *(Adv. Haer.* V, 7, 2). Similarly, Tertullian declares that: "the flesh is the pivot of salvation" *(caro cardo salutis, De res.* 8,2). And to oppose Gnostic interpretations that understood resurrection in a purely spiritual sense, these authors insist on the absolute conformity of the terrestrial body to the resurrected body and establish the existence of an intermediary stage that excludes the possibility of salvation for the soul alone. According to Tertullian, for this reason the soul guards the body's effigy in Hades while awaiting the resurrection that will constitute the fullness of salvation: it would indeed be "unworthy of God to grant salvation to only one half of man" *(De res.* 34).

c) Doctors of the School of Alexandria* (Third Century). By *anastasis* Clement of Alexandria and Origen* mean a process of maturation and of ontological ascent that begins in man in this life, through the gift of the Holy* Spirit, and which is completed after death by means of a transfiguration of the body, which becomes a spiritual body *(sôma pneumatikon)*. In his controversial work, which contradicts both those who deny the resurrection of the body and those who confuse it with the reanimation of the corpse, Origen invokes the soul's mediation in order to establish the continuity between the earthly body and the risen body. Although incorporeal by nature, the soul needs the body as a "vehicle" or as "clothing," of which it retains an identical form *(tupos* or *eidos)*, even when the body materially melts away. Through divine grace*, this bodily form will be preserved and transfigured after death: "To inherit the kingdom of heaven and live in a region different from earth, we need spiritual bodies; nevertheless, our original form *(eidos)* will not disappear but will be glorified, just as the form of Jesus* and that of Moses and Elijah remained the same in their transfigurations" *(Comm. in ps.* 1, 5).

Origen emphasizes just as strongly the ecclesial aspect of the resurrection, which will not attain its perfection until Christ's body is constituted definitively: "Abraham still awaits us … and all the prophets await us to receive perfect beatitude* together with us. For there is only one body which awaits its redemption" *(In lev.,* hom. 7, no. 2).

d) Augustine* (fourth–fifth century) can be viewed as a link between theology of the patristic age theology* and medieval theology. Influenced by Neoplatonism, his anthropology* gives priority to the soul in defining man as "a rational soul that uses an earthly and mortal body" *(De moribus eccl.* I, 27, 52). All the same, man's unity remains inconceivable to Augustine without the body, and it is for this reason that the soul preserves after death a "natural appetite" for the body that will be restored to it at the end of time*. This risen body, although made spiritual and immortal, will be absolutely identical to the earthly body. To answer objections from the pagans and certain Christians, Augustine was led to specify that the size, age, organs, and so forth of the raised body would indeed reconstitute the earthly body, but in a state that would make its beauty shine through (see *De civ. Dei* xxii, 12 *Sq)*. It is also noteworthy that Augustine takes the opposite tack from the theological tradition that dominated the battle against Gnosticism and introduces the idea of a resurrection of the soul (ibid., XX, 6) or of a first resurrection: the soul, fallen into sin*, comes back to life in a state of grace from that day forward, while awaiting the second resurrection, that of the body, which will perfect the first one. He therefore follows Origen and the earlier patristic tradition when he recalls that individual resurrection is commanded at ecclesial communion* in the body of Christ: "See, the perfect man, both head and body, composed of all the members who, at the time ordained, will all be present. Every day, however, members join this same body, as long as the Church* continues to develop" [(ibid., XXII, 18). In short, according to the patristic tradition and its followers: 1) Contrary to Platonist and Gnostic interpretations, the resurrection is totally distinct from a simple salvation of the soul or of the "inner man," which results in its deferral to the "last day," when it will be a miraculous event due to divine action. 2) Dependent on the Incarnation* and Christ's Resurrection, the resurrection of the dead fundamentally involves the "flesh," and the creation* taken in its material and temporal aspects. It thus gains a hitherto unknown value and dignity, enabling Tertullian to declare Christianity an "apology of the flesh" *(praeconium carnis)*.

2. Medieval Theology

a) 11th and 12th Centuries. It was generally accepted in the Middle Ages that man was composed of a soul and a body, that the resurrection of the body would set a seal on his eternal fate, and that in this life the immortality of the soul already expressed its destiny. Nonetheless, this eschatological perspective led to an anthropology in which Platonist and Aristotelian references would oppose each other. For theologians influenced by Augustine, the soul alone constituted the human person* (Hugo of Saint Victor), to the point that the human person did not fully appear until the separation of the soul and the body (Abelard*). In these theories, resurrection would seem secondary or even futile were it not required by the biblical data.

Faced with this perplexity, other authors referred to Aristotle's doctrine, according to which the soul was the form of the body; this enabled them to state that man's substantiality was no longer only to the soul, but to the unity of the composite of matter and form. But adoption of this point from Aristotle, for whom the mind *(noûs)* belongs to another order than the compound and comes from outside to lodge in it, seemed to lead to the admission along with him that the form melts away alongside the matter and therefore to an abandonment of the concept of the soul's immortality. The Augustinian aporia of a man who is defined by the soul but cannot be himself except by virtue of the soul's and the body's union was not raised.

b) Thomas Aquinas (13th century) was to solve the problem by conceiving the Aristotelian statement differently. According to him, the soul may be at once an incorporeal substance and immortal (in the Augustinian sense) as well as the form of the body, and this is possible because it transfers its own substantiality to the body. Body and soul are not two separately definable realities, but it is the soul that completely determines the body by appropriating its materiality. Man's nature is such that he is a mind by dint of his bodily relation with the world and with others, and it is not possible to conceive of his perfection without that relation (see *In Sent.* IV, d. 44, q. 1, a. 2, ad 1). Since that is so, death is truly an annihilation of man, since the "separated" soul, deprived of the body, lives on only as a monad without relations and without a world, and therefore in a state that goes "against nature" (*CG* IV, 79), a state in which it has no knowledge beyond that which comes to it directly from God. Arising from this fact, if man is to achieve his purpose, resurrection is a necessity of his nature—which does not mean that it is natural, for through its own means nature has no capacity to effect it: "to speak categorically, resurrection is a miracle*; it cannot be called natural except in relation to its end" (*ST Suppl.*, q. 75, a. 3). However, Thomas's position leaves certain questions open: 1) How is it possible to reconcile the soul's incomplete state when deprived of its body with the assurance of a possible beatitude immediately after death? 2) Is it necessary to state, as Thomas does, following the anti-Gnostic argument (and doubtless in reference to the cult of relics*), that there

is material identity between the earthly body and the risen body, when the material identity of the body is determined by the soul in its quality of substantial form? 3) Does the idea that resurrection does not occur until the end of time necessarily imply the concept of the survival of a separated soul?

3. Modern Theology
The end of the Middle Ages and the beginning of the modern era are characterized by a shift of emphasis, from resurrection to the immortality of the soul. The motives for this shift are both theological and philosophical.

a) Theological Motives. These were related to the preservation of a dualistic concept of man that overvalued the "soul" as against the "body." Although the Council of Vienna* (1312) consecrated the formula "soul, the form of the body," this statement was understood in various ways, often far removed from Thomas Aquinas's understanding, and ways in which the integral unity of the human person was lost. Moreover, Benedict XII's Constitution *Benedictus Deus* (1336) condemned the opinions of his predecessor, John XXII. The latter had laid down that souls in their separated state could not yet know beatitude, though John abjured this thesis on his death bed. Benedict, by contrast, drew attention to the soul's absolute future in a way that tended to push into the background the question of the future of the body.

b) Philosophical Motives. These themes made their appearance with the return to Platonism that characterized Renaissance humanism. This Platonism unfolded in a new context in which the soul was no longer considered a substance but a subject (Marsilio Ficino). This context reached its full expression in Descartes*, for whom the soul was a *res cogitans* (thinking thing) distinct from the body described as a *res extensa* (extensive thing). The growing role of the subject in the philosophies* of mind that were to distinguish modernity and would culminate in German high idealism (Fichte, Hegel*) left little room for any question of the body and its fate. Thus, the Enlightenment philosophers who refined the proofs of the soul's immortality often held resurrection to be a mythic representation. This was the case with Kant*, for example: "The spirit can see no advantage whatsoever in dragging after it for eternity a body which, however purified it might be, must nonetheless still consist of the same matter" (*Religion within the Boundaries of Pure Reason*).

In this climate of thought, theological meditation tended to limit the eschatological problem to the question of the soul, or at least to treat the theme of the resurrection as secondary. The Fifth Lateran* Council (1513), when it condemned Pomponazzi's Aristotelianism influenced by Averroës, concerned itself only with the immortality of the individual soul. It is also noteworthy that from the 17th to the 19th century, the language of popular piety no longer evoked the resurrection of the body and the last day, but rather the salvation of the soul and everlasting life (*see* Althaus 1961). Although theological textbooks still mentioned resurrection, they dealt with it as a speculative question more than as an existential problem (*see* Greschake-Kremer 1992).

4. Contemporary Theology

The renewal in biblical studies and the questions raised by a new scientific and cultural climate have led recent theology to approach the theme of the resurrection of the body in a manner that takes these changes into account. The most important recent trends are summarized below:

a) *Resurrection of the Dead Rather Than Immortality of the Soul.* In reaction against an eschatology* that dampened faith in the resurrection by means of philosophical argumentation that favored immortality, many reformed theologians, swayed by a return to Luther*, reject the idea that one can find in man any residue whatsoever, either spiritual or corporeal, that might ensure the transition between earthly life and revivification. Death therefore seems to be a total annihilation and resurrection a new creation ex nihilo, the identity between mortal man and the risen man being assured only through the fidelity of a God who has both created and saved. What remains in man, at his death, "is neither anything divine nor anything created, but the Creator's action and attitude with regard to his creation" (Barth* 1959). It is in this spirit that O. Cullmann strongly emphasized the opposition between the Greek and the biblical conceptions of death and the beyond: "The biblical conception of death is thus founded on a story of salvation, and consequently it must differ totally from the Greek conception; nothing shows this better than the comparison of the deaths of Socrates and of Jesus" (1956). Catholic theologians do not take to such lengths an argument that fails to explain why God, in the life he himself recreated, would make man answerable for his deeds in his present life, but they agree to emphasize a necessary return to a biblical theme that, insofar as the resurrection is concerned, gives priority to divine action.

b) *Hypothesis of a Resurrection at the Moment of Death.* To avoid the perplexities raised by the survival of the separated soul, certain theologians—following Thomas Aquinas's reasoning about the soul as a subsisting form that determines its own body—propose the hypothesis of a body that would reappear immediately after death, in a shape not physically perceptible: the idea of "resurrection in death" would thus correspond to a conception of the person that would require a relational foundation, not only religious, but also social and cosmic, which would be the equivalent of a "resurrection in death" (*see* Greschake-Lohfink 1978). J. Ratzinger nonetheless bases himself on the "Notice by the Congregation for the Doctrine of the Faith in Everlasting Life and in the Beyond," which gives a reminder of the necessity of belief in the survival of the soul after death, in order to challenge a thesis that "is in no way a possible expression of the common faith, such as it is commonly understood" (1990 [6th Ed.], 218). The hermeneutic* difficulties of the new definition undoubtedly stem from the way it seeks to evade the spatiotemporal framework in which traditional representations have been elaborated.

c) *Stages of a Philosophy of the Body and the Flesh.* While theology once borrowed from philosophy, in particular, the vocabulary of the soul, today it questions philosophy about new ways of speaking about the body. The phenomenological approach to the body as a "transcendental body," as found in the works of L. Landgrebe, M. Merleau-Ponty, M. Henry, and others, could provide a new theological access to the question of the resurrection; B. Welte (1965) and C. Bruaire (1968) have tried to take advantage of this possibility: "A phenomenological and transcendental meditation on corporeity might arrive at a formal concept of resurrection (of the body as flesh) that might go beyond the simple concept of a spiritual and indestructible part of man and refer back to the Christian hope represented by the *resurrectio mortuorum* [resurrection of the dead] as to an image that is at least not unreasonable." (Greschake-Kremer 1992).

d) *Indissoluble Link between the Resurrection of the Dead and Christology.* However, no rational or strictly philosophical approach can afford to forget that, following Pauline* and patristic tradition, Christ is the unique mediator, whose death and Resurrection lead the universe from the first Creation to its completion in the glory* of God (*see* Martelet 1974). This central reference to Christology* must thus serve as a theological criterion when it is a question of determining whether faith in the resurrection of the dead is compatible with beliefs of another nature—for example, with the reactivated thesis of reincarnation (*see* Schönborn 1990).

e) Analogical Value of Representations of Resurrection. If, all things considered, none of the representations of the resurrection and the future life is really adequate, that means that they are attempting to deal with a mystery* that has no common measure with our expressive and imaginative abilities. Like the mystery of God to which it is closely related, the resurrection of the dead is approachable only by means of analogical expressions that serve to support faith, while effacing themselves before the reality they designate.

• P. Althaus (1922), *Die letzten Dinge,* Erlangen, Gütersloh (8th Ed. 1961).

K. Barth (1946), *KD* II/2, Zollikon-Zurich (*Dogmatique,* Geneva, 1958–59).

O. Cullmann (1956), *Immortalité de l'âme ou résurrection des morts?* Neuchâtel.

B. Welte (1965), *Leiblichkeit als Hinweis auf das Heil in Christus,* Freiburg-Basel-Vienna.

C. Bruaire (1968), *Philosophie du corps,* Paris.

G. Greshake (1969), *Auferstehung der Toten,* Essen.

G. Martelet (1975), *L'Au-delà retrouvé,* Paris (New Ed. 1995).

J. Ratzinger (1977), "Zwischen Tod und Auferstehung," in *Eschatologie: Tod und ewiges Leben,* Regensburg (6th Ed. 1990), 211–26.

G. Greshake, G. Lohfink (1978), *Naherwartung, Auferstehung, Unsterblichkeit,* Freiburg-Basel-Vienna.

G. Greshake, J. Kremer (1986), *Resurrectio mortuorum,* Darmstadt (2nd Ed. 1992).

C. Schönborn (1990), "Réincarnation et foi chrétienne," *Com(F)* XV/1, 36–65.

ANDRÉ DARTIGUES

See also **Anthropology; Death; Eschatology; Hell; Hope; Judgment; Life, Eternal; Resurrection of Christ; Salvation; Soul-Heart-Body; Vision, Beatific**

Revelation

The vocabulary of revelation (Greek *apokalupsis, epiphaneia, dèlôsis;* Latin *revelatio, manifestatio*) has existed in Christian literature from the beginning, but Christianity took a long time to provide a structured concept of revelation. What the words designate, in any case, is one of the theologically central facts: God* is known through God. This knowledge, however, arises in several ways. The *Trésor de la langue française,* for example, distinguishes three meanings of revelation in the Judeo-Christian context: 1) "Natural revelation, a manifestation of God who makes himself known through creation* and the consciousness of man"; 2) "Supernatural revelation, a manifestation of God communicating to man, by words addressed to his messengers, the knowledge* of his being*, his will, his plan as it unfolds in history*'"; and 3) "Direct revelation, a communication that God establishes directly with one of his elect, notably through vision or hearing." These definitions provide only a preliminary understanding. In any event, they make possible a perception of the major problem of any theology* of revelation: that is, if revelation must be interpreted in terms of divine spontaneity and human receptivity, and if revelation is therefore a process that includes its audience, then no satisfying concept of it can be proposed that does not do equal justice to subjective and objective factors.

a) Biblical Theology. Faith* in a hidden God occupies the center of the experience of Israel* (Is 45:15). " For the theology of the Old Testament, it is unthinkable that man can know God through his own resources. God can be known only when he allows himself to be known, that is, when he wishes to reveal himself" (E. Haag, *Bibellexikon,* 1968).

God allows himself to be known in many ways: in catastrophic events such as storms or earthquakes, in numinous experiences of his glory, in the prophetic word authenticated by the formula "Word of YHWH." The hidden God reveals himself as a savior God: the theophany* of Sinai is the gift of the law* (moreover, this "gift of the law," *mattân torah,* provided rabbinical Judaism with a technical term to identify divine revelation). God reveals himself in the communication of his Name* (if we agree not to treat Ex 3:14 as an expression of refusal). He reveals himself in the great deeds accomplished for the benefit of Israel. Revelation is bound up with election and reaches the people through chosen mediators, Moses and the prophets*. The witness that God gives of himself ("I am the Lord, the God of Abraham your father and the God of Isaac," Gn 28:13; Ex 6:2, 29; Is 45:5 f.) provides structure for a people that knows the will of God. The theme of veiling and unveiling is certainly not omnipresent in the Old Testament, and the discretion of its presence in the Wisdom writings is striking. Ecclesiastes never refers to a revelation; Ecclesiasticus assimilates its teaching to a prophetic teaching (24:33), but it is the teaching that asks to be heard, and not the word of God. The Wisdom books, however, make their contribution to a theology of revelation by emphasizing the gratuitous character of a wisdom* that, although not "revealed" in the technical sense, comes to man from beyond himself. If God manifests himself through his creation, wisdom is the privileged bearer of that manifestation. And if God does indeed reveal himself to everyone as the Creator, then it is possible to say that the idolatry* of the pagans "is not forgivable" (oude suggnôstoi, Wis 13:8; see Rom 1:20, anapologètoi).

Bultmann*'s judgment of the teaching of Jesus* remains to some extent valid: his word does not communicate "a doctrine of God, a vision of the world, but a call to conversion* in the face of the coming kingdom of God" (1933). Neither the vocabulary nor the fact of unveiling is, however, absent from the New Testament. In Paul the language of mystery* is linked to the language of manifestation (phaneroun, Rom 3:21, 16:26) and of revelation (apokaluptein, 1 Cor 2:10; Eph 3:5). The Johannine Logos is presented as an interpreter or explainer of the invisible Father* (Jn 1:18). The revelation of the Name occupies the same central place in John that it did in the Old Testament (Jn 17:6), linked to the revelation of divine truth* and grace* (Jn 1:17). The word transmitted by the Son seals a history punctuated by many divine utterances (Heb 1:1 f.). Even if God is knowable outside the historical limits of the Covenant*, on the basis of the nature of things (Rom 1:20; Acts 17:22–31), John 14:9 states that he is clearly visible in Jesus. The soteriological focus of the New Testament excludes almost all apocalyptic concerns. The texts do not pretend to provide information about or descriptions of the end of the present age, the kingdom of God, and the like. But although the point of the testimony is to provoke interest not in a theophany or an epiphany, but in the dialogical relation between the savior God and man the sinner, the language of salvation* and conversion cannot be used without also using the language of knowledge—the revelation of the salvific purposes of God calls for faith and elicits praise*, which is inseparable from contemplation*.

b) Patristics. In the theology of the Fathers* of the Church, revelation is generally the object of a subsidiary interest, dependent on the gradually developing organization of Christian discourse. Many themes appear and use various words. Schematically, a few tendencies can be distinguished, all of which, from the period of the Apostolic* Fathers, are present together and intertwined. (The term itself, revelare, was established in Latin beginning with Tertullian*, under the influence of the first Latin translations* of the Bible*.)

The first tendency emphasizes the role of Christ* as master and teacher. The Didache links "life" and "knowledge" to describe Christian experience (19. 3), and 1 Clem. uses the verb paideuein to give an account of Christ's mission (59. 3). This theology adopted conceptual tools from Clement of Alexandria's theory of Christian knowledge (gnôsis). Clement had adopted and Christianized the idea of God as teacher already present in Plato (Laws X 897b), and later in Origen*, according to whom the revelatory activity of God makes it possible for human beings to leave the realm of the "shadow" for the realm of the "image," and thence to the realm of "truth," while at the same time closely linking revelation to the very Person* of the incarnate Word*, autobasileia, "kingdom in person." All truth comes from God through the mediation of his Logos.

Because the God of Jesus Christ is the creator God, a second tendency leads to emphasis on the inherently revelatory function of the creation. The work of the apologists* among the early Fathers contains a first encounter with the God of the philosophers, whose transcendence made the idea of revelation problematic, but this encounter did not produce a sharp distinction between "faith" and "reason*." In Justin, the theory of "seminal reasons" (logoi spermatikoi), adopted from Middle Platonism and Stoicism, makes it possible for pre-Christian wisdom outside the Bible to play a role in the knowledge of God; but as an indirect consequence, the theory devalues the demonstrative role of the incarnate Word. Theophilus of Antioch also speaks of a God knowable on the basis of the order of the world. (Ad Autolycum I. 5). Clement of Alexandria speaks of a revelation (emphasis) of God through nature. Further, philosophy* for Clement is seen as a "gift of God to the Greeks." Philosophy, law, and gospel thus appear as three testaments all authored by the Logos.

By contrast, a third tendency involved a concentration on the history or the "economy" (oikonomia, a term already used by Paul in Eph 1:10, 3:2, and 3:9), in which God saves and makes himself known. Irenaeus* is no doubt the most influential representative of this tendency. He adopts the leitmotif of every biblical* theology of revelation: "God is not known without God.... And all to whom the Son has revealed him know him" (Adv. Haer. VI. 6. 4; see also, e.g.,

Clement, *Strom.* V. 82. 9). He adds major themes that were to structure the later theology of revelation. Against Gnosis*, he denies that secret traditions can have apostolic value. Also against Gnosis, he establishes the criterion of apostolic transmission: the transmission of the truth (which as early as Tertullian begins to occupy a place as important as that of the revelation of the truth) is an act of the church materially guaranteed by the succession of bishops in episcopal sees. The link between Scripture and tradition* does not yet pose any problem, much less any aporias. Emphasis on Scripture (Origen: "The Logos constantly becomes flesh in the Scriptures in order to set up its tent in us"; *Philocalia* XV. 19, PG 14. 1313 B) meets without tension an emphasis on a process of tradition derived from God himself (Tertullian), while Tertullian also sets out a Roman understanding of the argument from authority*. Reduced to almost nothing in Marius Victorinus, who sees revelation only in a philosophical framework, the reference to history by contrast occupies a central position for Augustine*'s mentor, Ambrose*.

A fourth tendency leads to a view of revelation as a process that has been concluded and that is reactualized in the experience of faith. In the *Visions of Hermas* it seems that revelation can still continue to occur in the church*. For Clement of Alexandria, the present of the liturgical and mystical life was conceivable in terms of revelation, and Gregory of Nazianzus also maintained that the church, which lives within the time of the spirit, is experiencing a continued revelation (*Or* 31, 26). But already in the works of Cyprian* (who uses *traditio* for revelation), what he calls *Traditio* is not a permanent possibility but an accomplished fact: it is a present divine revelation that is normative for the church, and of which the apostles* were the authentic channels, and which Christians only need to appropriate. The lack of insistence on what would later be called the revealed "given" did not keep the Latin Fathers from wondering about the human medium of divine revelations—the theology of revelation is organized around the theory of prophetic inspiration, as with Jerome for example; remnants of such an organization can be found in Thomas Aquinas—and on the illumination that allows the believer to welcome divine revelation. There are variations that reflect theological differences generated elsewhere: while the theologians of the school of Antioch* placed a clearer emphasis on the past history of salvation, Cyril of Alexandria continued a conception that already existed with Origen and which states that the proclaimed word must be accompanied at all times by an illumination (which he calls revelation). Augustine uses language close to that used by the Alexandrians, marked by Christocentrism and an increasing interest in the experience of the believer: Christ is present in the one who believes, and fulfills in him a revelatory function. The revealed God of Augustine is a God who is a teacher: "In order for the human mind, moved by the desire for knowledge, not to fall from weakness into the misery of error, it needs a divine magisterium that it may freely obey" (*Civ. Dei* XIX. 14). But this magisterium is not exercised in an extrinsic way. The process of revelation does not take place outside man, he grasps it existentially. Revelation is an "attraction" exerted by God, and it is exerted concretely within a totally sacramental universe in which everything signifies divine will and divine love*.

Patristic thinking about revelation was bound up with doctrinal conflicts. Irenaeus responded to the Gnostic challenge; and, confronting Montanism*, the church had to express its rejection of a revival of revelation. The Arian crisis also made possible a major proposition: in Jesus, it was God himself who manifested himself in order to recreate man in his image (Athanasius*). Finally, against Eunomius, who claimed it was possible to know God as he knows himself, the Cappadocian Fathers explained that there was revelation, but it was of a God who remained strictly incomprehensible.

Finally, a conclusion emerges clearly from the synthesis of Pseudo-Dionysius*: creation and revelation are two aspects of a single divine act calling human beings to an "ecstatic love" and a cosmic contemplation leading to the perception of the traces of divine goodness everywhere. For Maximus* the Confessor, on the other hand, the two are clearly distinct, and there is room for an autonomous *theôria phusikè* providing knowledge of God through the nature of things. For John the Scot Eriugena, the principal transmitter to the West of the writings of Dionysius and Maximus, revelation is theorized in two stages. In itself, the creation is a perfect revelation (Eriugena thus conceives of creation as revelation: *creatio, hoc est in aliquo manifestatio,* PL 122. 455 D); but because of human sin*, revelation also comes in the form of the word.

c) Middle Ages. The tendencies of patristic theology—above all, the search for a balance between historical-objective and subjective-existential factors—were also those of early medieval theology. For Anselm*, Scripture has the status of objective norm, whereas the *intellegentia fidei,* as a subjective norm, always remains in the foreground. Already known to patristics, the neglect of history found a distinguished practitioner in the person of Abelard*, for whom revelation was not only turned over to dialectics, but seemed thoroughly suited to a dialectical treatment. A view of revelation rather analogous to that of Eriugena found an equally distinguished representative in Hugh of Saint-Victor, for whom creation as a whole was the "book of God," but a book that fallen human beings could no longer read, and which Scripture alone could make readable. However, the Middle Ages placed its distinctive mark on the theology of revelation. The vision of Augustine and Dionysius of a totally sacramental universe was replaced with a local meditation on what would later be called "special revelation," the biblical history of salvation, and the sense of a single tradition formed by Scripture and the Fathers of the Church was replaced by a questioning of the revelatory specificity of the Scriptures. In early Scholasticism*, according to M. Grabmann, "Fathers and Scriptures make up a single *Scriptura Sacra*"; creation and revelation were thought of in the generalizing terms of a single economy. But Rupert of Deutz (1075–1129) already had to defend himself against the accusation of adopting those positions. And by the time of William of St. Thierry (c. 1085–1148), a clear distinction had been established: revelation due to creation is one thing, revelation due to the Word spoken in history is another.

It fell to Albert* the Great to produce the first modern synthesis of elements that had previously been dispersed. Albert distinguishes between Scripture, which is "believable," and the church, which is its interpreter. He makes a further distinction between the early time* of revelation and the time of the church (a time directed "toward the exposition of the articles of faith"). In the Aristotelian framework that had become obligatory, Albert's successors extended his work and sometimes proposed modifications and additions. The *Summa Halensis,* for example, made a vigorous attempt to organize a theology of revelation of Franciscan inspiration by integrating the history of salvation as much as possible into the new conceptual apparatus of theology. Bonaventure* explained the relationship between revelation and the sinful condition of human beings: "Because the world has become an unreadable book, the Incarnation* is, as revelation, the commentary that restores readability" (Seybold 1971). He also explained the relationship between objective and subjective factors: faith in revelation arises from the combined action of the external and the interior word, but mainly from inner hearing.

For Thomas* Aquinas, as for most of his contemporaries, the principal theoretical interest was aroused by the problem of prophetic inspiration (*see* his *De prophetia*), which he did not distinguish clearly from revelation. As with Bonaventure, an unquestionable bibliocentrism was associated for Thomas with the analysis of interior facts, and the theology of revela-

tion was closely connected to and sometimes identified with the theology of faith. At the same time, a new notion destined to influence the entire later history of the concept of revelation made its appearance: the action of the savior God who provides human beings with all the truths that are needful and useful for the pursuit of their supernatural* goal. From this it followed that "whoever does not adhere, as to an infallible and divine rule, to the teaching of the church that proceeds from the first Truth* revealed in the Holy Scriptures does not have the 'habitus' of faith" (*ST* IIa IIae. q. 5. a. 3).

Duns* Scotus established just as close a link between Scripture and church and set Scripture even more distinctly at the center of everything: ... [I]n fact, our theology deals with nothing but what is contained in Scripture and what can be inferred *(elici)* from it" (*Op. Ox,* prol. q. 3, Wadding, VI/1, p. 102). Finally, the authoritarianism of William of Ockham led him to set forth with unprecedented bluntness the necessity for revelation, taken as an objective reality. Because his nominalism* could not maintain a necessary ontological structure in divine revelation, that revelation tended therefore to be atomized and restricted to positive information dealing with facts unrelated to one another. The extreme individualization of the events of revelation led to a theology that juxtaposed articles of faith, thus presenting the first distinctive characteristics of a positive* theology, with the earliest glimmerings of a "theory of the two sources" of revelation, Scripture and church tradition. The first signs of the replacement of revelation understood as an action by revelation understood as a "deposit," in the sense something entrusted, also appeared at this time.

d) Reformation, Counterreformation, and Enlightenment. We are indebted to Luther* for the first really new theory of revelation produced since the New Testament, and the subsequent development of a truly systematic theology of revelation. A theologian of the hidden God who remains hidden even in his Incarnation (*Deus in carne absconditus,* WA 4. 7. 1. ff.), a theologian of a God who manifests himself "as his opposite" in the scandal of the cross, Luther attributes to the gospel the distinctive mark that belongs to Christ himself, the *absconditas sub contrario.* There can be no question of revelation through creation. God becomes manifest in the preached Word and only there. The center of interest shifts: the past facts of salvation meet the believer in the existential and dialogical event of the present of conversion and justification*. Only Scripture records those facts; but in the strict sense, it is a transmitter of revelation rather than being itself revelation. And faith cannot be defined as "knowledge of history" *(notitia historiae)* unless it is simultaneously defined as "confidence in the mercy*" of God *(fiducia misericordiae)*. The Word, however, again became "doctrine" in the later works of Luther's best student, Melanchthon. Lutheran confessional texts confirm the absolute sufficiency of Scripture: *sola sacra scriptura judex, norma et regula agnoscitur* ("Holy Scripture alone is recognized as judge, norm, and rule"; *BSLK* 769.7).

Calvin*'s theology shares traits with that of Luther, although it has its own particular emphases. On the one hand, the kenotic motifs omnipresent in Luther give way in Calvin to a more Johannine* contemplation. On the other hand, Calvin maintains a dual knowledge of God *(duplex cognitio)*, through creation and through the Word. Of course, *non…ab elementis mundi hujus, sed ab evangelio faciendum est exordium* ("Our exordium comes not…from the elements of this world, but from the gospel"; CR 51. 10). However, the exordium does not claim to be the entirety of the discourse; the Confession of La Rochelle is completely faithful to Calvin on this point when it asserts that "this God shows himself thus to men, first by his works, by the creation and by the preservation and operation of those works. Secondly and more clearly, by his Word, which at the beginning revealed by oracle, was thereafter set down in writing in the books that we call Holy Scripture" *(BSKORK* 66).

Against the principle of the sufficiency of Scripture that unites all Reformation theologies, the work of the Council of Trent* focused on maintaining the rights of tradition, or more precisely (at a time when the apostolic origin of the Apostles' Creed was still accepted) of traditions transmitted from the beginning but not present in Scripture. These traditions, "which have come down to us, either because the apostles had received them from the mouth of Christ himself, or because the apostles have transmitted them to us as though directly, after receiving them from the voice of the Holy Spirit" (DS 1501) are to be received by the believer with the same piety and affection *(pari pietatis affectu)* as revelation contained in the Scriptures; they too play a revelatory role. The council was also careful not to give Scripture and the traditions the status of two parallel channels: proposed during the debates, the idea of a revelation contained "in part" *(partim)* in Scripture and "in part" in the traditions was rejected in favor of a more cautious formulation.

The 17th and 18th centuries saw both the development of systematic Protestant theologies worthy of the name "Scholastic" and, finally, the Catholicism's development of its own theology of revelation.

Among the Lutherans, J. A. Quenstedt adopted the classical formulations only to shift their meaning toward a conception of revelation as the communication of truths: revelation defined as "a divine act turned toward the outside *(externus)* in which God reveals himself to humankind through his word for its salutary information" *(Theologia didacto-polemica,* I. 32). This indicates a process of doctrinalization of revelation as well as an identification of Scripture and Word, which can be seen even more clearly in Johannes Gerhard. Just as Catholic theology roots Scripture in the tradition of the church, so Protestant theology unilaterally roots the Word in Scripture.

Against Protestant illuminism (the most extreme form of which was presented by Zwingli*, the theoretician of an immediate revelation of God to consciousness), the first task of post-Tridentine Catholic theology was to maintain the sufficiency of a revelation mediated simultaneously by the two objective phenomena of church tradition and the Word. The subjective aspect would of course never be neglected (particularly since this period saw significant refinements in the "analysis of faith" *[analysis fidei]*). M. Cano (1509–60, *Loci,* 1563) firmly maintained the necessity of the "inner cause," that is, a "certain divine light inciting belief." D. Bañez (1528–1604) also focused on the illumination of the subject more than on the revelation of the object. Cajetan (1469–1534) and Suarez*, however, carry more weight in the history of the problem. For Cajetan, revelation is indeed the action of a "God speaking himself," but the emphasis is placed even more on the articles of faith that this God communicates. And Suarez proposes a concept that was to become central, the concept of divine witness. This would lead to the definition of revelation as "divine speech witnessing itself" *(locutio Dei attestans).* Suarez distinguishes two senses of revelation:

First, then, a veil is removed by the revelation of the object of faith, and it is "thus that it becomes in some way knowable by reason of divine witnessing. Also, the infusion of faith removes the ignorance that affected the intellect. And we may speak of revelation in both cases" *(De Fide,* disp. 3, sect. 3, no. 7). But revelation was viewed principally from the side of the object, as the offering of a revealed object to be believed out of regard for divine authority.

Late Scholasticism suffered from a major deficiency, neglecting the Christocentric nature of revelation in favor of a theory of veridical divine communication. For example, for J. de Lugo (1583–1660): "It is requisite for the object of faith that there be divine speech, for that speech is founded on divine veracity*; indeed there is no veracity but in the Word"; and the church is therefore defined as the location of a "mediated locution." There was also Ripalda (†1648), who emphasized "immediate and intellectual revelation." But, whether in Lugo, among the Carmelites of Salamanca, or elsewhere, the general tendency was clear: a doctrine of the event of the Word, which was unquestionably fruitful, pushed into the background and indeed rode roughshod over subjective factors and the historical economy of revelation. The principal themes of baroque Scholasticism became more pronounced during the Enlightenment, when apologetics adopted its classic organization (a sequence of treatises "On Religious Truth," "On Christian Truth," "On Catholic Truth," derived from a schema of P. Charron) and when the treatise *De veritate christiana* (or *De Christo legato divino*) was fully established, with the aim of proving (primarily against deism*) the existence of a revealed religion, a Christianity that was not as old as the creation, and a revelation that said more than natural reason knew (V. Pichler [1670–1736], F. Neumayr [1697–1765], P. M. Gazzaniga [1722–99]). The voices of Enlightenment philosophy were no doubt more prominent than those of the theology contemporary with it. However, the century did have an atypical genius in J. G. Hamann (1730–88), who expressed a violent Christocentric protest barely heard in his time. There was more readiness to listen to the dilemma of G. E. Lessing (1729–81): could eternal beatitude* be based on contingent historical truths? Lessing also secured a willing audience for his thinking about revelation in terms of the education of the human race. J. G. Herder (1744–1803) offered an idea of revelation through nature and history (universal history, a concept containing elements designed to undermine the privileged position of biblical history). Despite all the efforts of apologetics, the *Aufklärung* (Enlightenment) spoke posthumously and authoritatively through Fichte, who said that "only metaphysics, and not history, makes us blessed."

e) 19th Century to Vatican II. The two most characteristic ideas of 19th-century theories of revelation were those of a universal revelation and of a principle of tradition. They are found in the most organized way in the thinkers of the Catholic school of Tübingen*. For Drey, who certainly also owes to Schelling* the idea of a "scientific construction of revelation," the aim of the theory is to go beyond the antinomy between rationalism* and suprarationalism on the one hand, and to establish a correspondence between the outwardness of historical facts and the inwardness of their religious appropriation on the other. Because human beings confront a God who was never not revealed, this appropriation is the most lasting of all possibilities. And because revelation has been an object of transmission from the beginning, the present attainment of knowledge is always an entrance into the community which transmits revelation through time; clear affinities with traditionalism* here tend to ride roughshod over the gratuitous character of divine interventions. Similarly, the principle of "proto-revelation" led Möhler to maintain, against Bautain, the possibility of a natural knowledge of God. For Staudenmaier, too, the theology of the *imago Dei* led to the postulate of the existence of an immemorial relation of human beings to God, but one that could not find expression in the absence of external revelation. For Kuhn, finally, the for-us of revealed truths is indissociable from their in-themselves; a supernaturalist tendency in his work, holding to the letter of Scripture, is combined with a developmental theory that tends to present the process of revelation in terms analogous to that of the development of dogma*. Although no factual influence can be established, Newman*'s interest in history and his acceptance of the idea of a universal proto-revelation unquestionably make his thinking close to that of the Tübingen theologians.

Protestant theology was divided between the predominant influence of Schleiermacher* (for whom the inner event of illumination and revelation tends to absorb into itself any external fact) and the more classic perception of revelation best represented by the school of Erlangen, until liberal Protestantism diluted the idea of revelation in the idea of a supremely moral teaching. The history of Catholic theology is, on the one hand, one of innovative (although unbalanced) attempts and their censorship by the ecclesiastical magisterium, and, on the other, one of the restoration, by the theologians of the School of Rome, of a strictly doctrinal theory of revelation. For Hermes, revelation came to be considered within the strict confines of practical reason. His theory was a much softened version of what the young Fichte had said in his *Attempt at a Critique of All Revelation* of 1792—that God could reveal himself only as the communicator of a moral law, an argument also adopted by the young Hegel*. Conversely, for Günther, the concept of "ideal knowledge" swallowed up any difference between faith and knowledge, or between philosophy and theology, so that the idea of revelation lost any specific substance. The failure of a theological reception of newer philosophies was followed by a reestablishment of the concepts and arguments of the baroque Scholasticism. For J. Kleutgen (1811–83), revelation is a supernatural reality whose "immediate end" is "to increase in us the knowledge of divine things and consequently to enlighten our reason" (*Die Theologie der Vorzeit* [Münster, 1875], V. 143). J. B. Franzelin (1816–86) relied on Suarez and Lugo for the assertion that revelation is "a divine locution, made up of words stating a truth and of facts proving that those words are a divine locution" (*Tractatus de divina Traditione et Revelatione* [Rome, 1896] 618). Another doctrinaire theory of revelation was presented by Scheeben*, who also established a hierarchy of revelations, rising from *revelatio naturae* to *revelatio gratiae,* and culminating eschatologically in *revelatio gloriae.*

Vatican* I was the first council in the history* of the church to take revelation as its theme and indeed to use the word (it was used once at Trent, but in an entirely different sense; *see* Eicher 1977) with reference to what it called a "divine deposit" (DS 3020). It should first of all be noted that revelation was not defined by the council, which was more concerned with determining its modes: natural knowledge of God, scriptural accounts of revelation, and the mediating role of church tradition. The weakness of the council's theory lies in the fact that it placed any personal dimension in the background; revelation was understood as a "that," as a body of *revelata,* rather than as a divine action. Modernism* unjustly caricatured an incomplete but authentically Christian theory: a modernist proposition condemned in *Lamentabili* says that the dogmas that the church treats as revealed are not truths that "fell from heaven," but no official Catholic document spoke of "truths that fell from heaven" (*pace* S. Sykes, *EKL* 3rd ed., vol. 3).

It was left to Vatican* II to provide a corrective to the unilateralism of the declarations of Vatican I. The constitution *Dei Verbum,* which shows the dominant influence of H. de Lubac*, maintains the right to a natural knowledge of God (§6). In particular, it establishes as close a connection as possible between "words" and "acts" *(gesta)*: "This economy of revelation comes about through events and words closely connected to one another" (§2). Further, it provides a first satisfying attempt at a resolution of the modern aporia of Scripture versus tradition: "springing from a single divine source" (§9). "The sacred tradition and Holy Scripture constitute a single sacred deposit of the word of God, entrusted to the Church" (§10). The *revelata* almost disappear in favor of the *revelatio,* itself thought of from the outset on the basis of Christ, "who is both the mediator and the fullness of all revelation" (§2). Vatican II did not of course provide any final word; for example, §10 of *DV* unfortunately juxtaposes "sacred tradition, Holy Scripture, and the magisterium* of the Church"—the awkwardness suggests there is matter for further reformulation.

f) Systematic Perspectives. A central reality of Christian experience, but a concept that was long marginal, revelation certainly appears as an organizing notion of contemporary theology. The organizations over which it presides are many, and they cut across denominational lines. Major tendencies can be clearly identified (Dulles 1983).

A first tendency conceives of revelation as a doctrine and has been given the classic name of "propositional theory of revelation." The Princeton theologian B. Warfield (1851–1921) is perhaps the most classic Protestant representative of the doctrine, although it was expressed quite directly by another American thinker, C. Pinnock: "Revelation is embedded in written accounts, and it is essentially propositional in nature" (1971). Neoscholastic theology uses similar language (R. Garrigou-Lagrange, C. Pesch, H. Dieckmann): "Divine revelation is formally a divine locution addressed to men in the mode of teaching" (Garrigou-Lagrange 1918). Moreover, because this theory is linked to a homologous theory of the development of Christian doctrines (most notably in Marin-Sola, *Le Développement homogène du dogme catholique* [Paris, 1924]), it leads to the conception of this development as an "infinite unfolding of conclusions out of their premises" (Lubac, *RSR* 35, 1948). The image of the "revealed given" is central (A. Gardeil), and as with Thomas Aquinas, the analysis of prophetic experience is also central.

A second tendency conceives of revelation as history. Its most extreme expression is provided by the theory of W. Pannenberg: God reveals himself indirectly by his actions, and by his actions situated in the fabric of universal history as so many events to which any historiography has the right of access, as so many facts that speak for themselves. More cautiously, the theory of O. Cullmann links the fact to its prophetic interpretation, so that the conjunction of the two constitutes the very process of revelation. Among the Anglicans, W. Temple (1881–1944) had used very similar terms: "The essential condition for an effective revelation is the coincidence of events subject to divine control and of minds divinely illuminated to read them correctly" (Baillie and Martin 1937).

A third tendency reduces revelation to an inner experience. French Protestantism of the 19th century had a typical representative of this tendency in A. Sabatier (1839–1901). Revelation "consists of the creation, the purification, and the growing clarity of the consciousness of God in the individual man and in humanity" (1897). German Protestantism had another in the person of W. Herrmann (1846–1922); however, Herrmann qualified the position by positing, on the one hand, that inner experience is revelatory only if it is based on communion* with Jesus, and on the other hand, by purging that experience of any mystical* element in order to see it primarily as a moral experience. But it was Catholic modernism that went the furthest and most systematically down this path. G. Tyrrell (1861–1909), for example, believed that dogmatic formulations had no purpose other than to enable anyone to bring forth and appropriate a founding experience under the influence of the Holy Spirit: "revelation is not a statement, but an experience" (1907).

Against liberal Protestantism, on the one hand, and propositional theories, on the other, the dialectical theology derived from Barth* represents a fourth tendency, marked by a strict christological concentration and a close connection between revelation and salvation—Bultmann coined the word *Heilsoffenbarung,* "salvific revelation." Revelation comes about in order to call into question the pseudo-sufficiency of sinful human beings in any time and place in which the word of salvation is proclaimed: "Each generation has the same primordial relationship to revelation" (Bultmann; *see* the concept of "contemporaneity" in Kierkegaard*). Bultmann's followers refined the theory by thinking of revelation as an "event of language," *Sprachereignis* (E. Fuchs) or as a "process of speech," *Wortgeschehen* (G. Ebeling).

A fifth tendency entails reading the process of revelation as the opening of a new consciousness of the self and the world—as an access to the heart of things. The sacred in this instance tends to replace God, and the experience of the sacred to be the only revelation: "Only what approaches me with the quality of the unconditional is revelation for me" (Tillich* 1927). L. Gilkey radicalizes the idea: religious language "is not discourse about the heavens but discourse about the earth—in reference to its foundation and its ultimate sacred limits" (*Naming the Whirlwind,* Indianapolis, 1969).

A few conclusions can be drawn from a sinuous doctrinal history, marked in the 20th century by a veritable "inflation" of theories of revelation (E. Troeltsch). Against the aporia of propositional theory, the common virtue of various currents (dialectical theology as well as the theology of the Dominicans of the Saulchoir or the "new theology," largely dependent on this point on the *Jésus* of L. de Grandmaison [1928]) was to compel acceptance of what *Dei Verbum* confirmed in 1965: that a concept of revelation must be Christocentric (and soteriological) or it is condemned to death. Against the same aporia, which consists of repressing the "Revealer" in favor of the revealed, and treating the revealed according to the categories of a reifying reason, we must also admit that dialogical reason and the categories of the interpersonal encounter are necessary for the opening of any truly passable road: the merit of R. Guardini (1940) is to have said as much in the most convincing manner. We can then understand that the very term of revelation has fallen into disuse among

thinkers more concerned with divine "self-communication." Two tasks that are certainly not new, but which we see with great clarity, perhaps lie in wait for any future theology of revelation. The first is to preserve the perpetually threatened balance between subjective and objective factors. On this point the theory of subjective and objective evidence that makes up the first part of Balthasar*'s trilogy (1960) manages to provide the conditions for a possible balance. The second task is to not lose sight of the biblical link between revelation and the mystery of God. Despite Hegel, the revealed God is not an obvious God about whom human beings could know everything. God is known as unknown and revealed as incomprehensible. In this respect the theology of revelation cannot fail to lead back to a theology of the liturgy*, partly because the liturgy offers itself as the privileged location in which the Scripture becomes Word, and partly because it reminds us of the sacramental distance separating man from the invisible God, who joins him through ecclesial mediations in the "connatural context in which the revealed unfolds itself in all its dimensions" (Breton 1979).

• L.-A. Sabatier (1897), *Esquisse d'une philosophie de la religion d'après la psychologie et l'histoire,* Paris.
G. Tyrrell (1907), *Through Scylla and Charybdis,* London.
R. Garrigou-Lagrange (1918), *De Revelatione per Ecclesiam Catholicam proposita,* Rome.
P. Tillich (1927), "Die Idee der Offenbarung," *ZThK* 8, 403–12.
R. Bultmann (1933), "Die Begriffe des Wortes Gottes im NT," *GuV* I, 268–93.
J. Baillie, H. Martin (Ed.) (1937), *Revelation,* London.
L. Charlier (1938), *Essai sur le problème théologique,* Thuillies.
R. Guardini (1940), *Die Offenbarung, ihr Wesen und ihre Formen,* Würzburg.
G.E. Wright (1952), *God Who Acts,* London.
J. Baillie (1956), *The Idea of Revelation in Recent Thought,* London.
J. Alfaro (1959), "Adnotationes in tractatum De Virtutibus," copy of lecture, Gregorian University, Rome.
H.U. von Balthasar (1961), *Herrlichkeit,* vol. 1: *Schau der Gestalt,* Einsiedeln.
W. Pannenberg (Ed.) (1961), *Offenbarung als Geschichte,* Göttingen (4th Ed. 1970).
M.-D. Chenu (1964), *La Parole de Dieu,* 2 vols., Paris.
R. Latourelle (1966), *Théologie de la r.,* 2nd Ed., Paris-Bruges.
G. Moran (1966), *Theology of Revelation,* New York.
R. Schutz, M. Thurian (1966), *La Parole vivante au concile,* Taizé.
B. Welte (1966), *Heilsverständnis,* Freiburg-Basel-Vienna.
B.-D. Dupuy (Ed.) (1968), *La r. divine,* UnSa 70, 2 vols., Paris.
A. Dulles (1969), *Revelation Theology,* New York.
F. Konrad (1971), *Das Offenbarungsverständnis in der evangelischen Theologie,* Mayence.
C. Pinnock (1971), *Biblical Revelation, Foundation of Christian Theology,* Chicago.
M. Seybold, et al. (1971), *Die Offenbarung: Von der Schrift bis zum Ausgang der Scholastik, HDG* I. 1. a.
P. Eicher (1977), *Offenbarung, Prinzip neuzeitlicher Theologie,* Munich.
P. Ricœur, et al. (1977), *La révélation,* Brussels.

H. Waldenfels (with L. Scheffczyk) (1977), *Die Offenbarung: Von der Reformation bis zur Gegenwart, HDG* I. 1. b.

S. Breton (1979), *Écriture et révélation,* Paris.

M. Seckler (1980), "Aufklärung und Offenbarung," *CGG* 21, 5–78.

J. J. Petuchowski, W. Strolz (Ed.) (1981), *Offenbarung im jüdischen und christlichen Glaubensverständnis,* Freiburg-Basel-Vienna.

A. Dulles (1983), *Models of Revelation,* Dublin.

H. de Lubac (1983), *La révélation divine,* Paris (New Ed. with hommage to Dupuy, 1968).

G. Scholtz, et al. (1984), "Offenbarung," *HWP* 6, 1105–30.

E. Salmann (1986), *Neuzeit und Offenbarung: Studien zur trinitarischen Analogik des Christentums,* Rome.

C. J. Mavrodes (1988), *Revelation in Religious Belief,* Philadelphia.

B. Welte (1993), *Geschichtlichkeit und Offenbarung,* Frankfurt.

R. Brague (1995), "L'impuissance du verbe: Le Dieu qui a *tout* dit," *Diogène* 170, 49–74.

C. Gunton (1995), *A Brief Theology of Revelation,* Edinburgh.

G. Wießner, et al. (1995), "Offenbarung," *TRE* 25, 109–210.

G. Fackre (1997), *The Doctrine of Revelation: A Narrative Interpretation,* Edinburgh.

O. González de Cardedal (1997), "Actualisación de la revelación," *La entraña del Cristianismo,* Salamanca, 741–78.

JEAN-YVES LACOSTE

See also **Fideism; History; Holy Scripture; Mystery; Rationalism; Tradition; Traditionalism; Vatican I; Vatican II; Word of God**

Revelations, Individual

1. Definition and Scope of the Phenomenon

a) Designation. The expression "special or individual revelations" adopted at the Council of Trent* (session VI, chap. 12) designates manifestations of divine origin that make known hidden truths related to a particular situation of the church*. Their relevance is limited to a precise context, whereas "general revelation*" is applicable to the Church in all times and places. Individual revelations were for a long time called "private revelations," but the expression is unfortunate, because every revelation is intended to be communicated sooner or later and none of them is of strictly private interest, aside from the revelation of personal salvation* (*see* Trent, can. 16 on justification*).

b) Scope of the Phenomenon. Individual revelations refer to a phenomenon that occurs in diverse modes (visions, apparitions, hearing voices, ecstasies, ravishings, messages, letters from heaven, secrets, dreams, clairvoyance, and prophecies*) and is often complex. A verbal message (or one that can be verbalized) is often accompanied by visual or olfactory percepts, and various epiphenomena (radiance, levitation, incorruption, stigmata, and the like). These make of individual revelations a kind of mystical experience* often transcending the purely cognitive realm, and even overshadowing it. Known in most religions, the phenomenon is well attested in Christianity.

The first martyrs were favored with visions (*Didache,* letters of Ignatius of Antioch, the *Shepherd* by Hermas, narratives of the martydom of Polycarp, and of Felicity and Perpetua) modeled on those recorded in the Old Testament (visions of Abraham, Jacob, Moses, Isaiah, Elijah, Daniel, etc.) or even more, those in the New Testament (apparitions of the risen Christ; visions of Stephen, Peter*, Paul, and others). Thereafter, individual revelations never ceased throughout the church's history. Examples can be cited from every period. In late antiquity there was Benedict of Nursia's vision of the cosmos* recapitulated in God* (Gregory* the Great, *Dialogues* II. 35). In the Middle Ages, particularly from the 12th through the 15th centuries, they became a means for exploring dogma* (notably of the last things, by means of "journeys to the beyond" [eschatology*]), and later for union with Christ* (Francis of Assisi, Mechtild of Magdeburg, Julian of Norwich, Birgitta of Sweden, among others). Luther* did not reject all individual revelations but considered visionaries as *Schwärmer* and visions as an encouragement to the pursuit of sanctity by works*, contradicting the principle of *Scriptura Sola.* Calvin* reduced them to the capacity to read Scripture. Post-Tridentine Catholicism* saw a renewed flowering of individual revelations, in tandem with a defense of the cult* of saints and their canonization processes. The visions of Teresa of Avila were in a sense ratified by Gregory XV in his bull of canonization in 1622, and her process was for a long time used as a model for the examination of individual revelations. On the other hand, the revelations of Marie of Agreda were bitterly disputed. Scarce in the 18th century, individual revelations again became numerous in the 19th century (apparitions of Lourdes, the rue du Bac, Pontmain, Fatima) and the 20th century up to the present (Garabandal, Medjugorje). In the last two centuries alone, more than 300 apparitions of Mary* have been counted around the world (B. Billet).

c) Individual Revelations and the Social Sciences. The numerous individual revelations encountered in beatification and canonization processes have always aroused reservations and suspicion among theologians. Analyzed within the framework of the history of mysticism*, apologetics, and hagiography, individual revelations have provoked little interest among theologians during the last half century, with the odd exception (e.g., Laurentin). On the other hand, they have been the subject of much analysis by psychologists (from Jung to Vergote). But at the present time it is historians of religious mentalities (Dinzelbacher, Frugoni) who are most involved in the study of the question, analyzing the circumstances of individual revelations, the identity of the recipients (women, adolescents, etc.), the role of liturgical and ascetic practices, and the influence of social and political factors (social crises and divisions, messianic expectations, tension between the ministerial priesthood and the prophetic function). In any event, the role of individual revelations in history* is significant, by reason of their repercussions in the church (establishment of sanctuaries and pilgrimages*, origin of devotional practices), in politics (the role of such revelations in the decisions of popes and secular rulers with regard to crusades, wars, alliances, and jubilees; and the foundation of religious orders and institutions, not to mention sects such as that of Swedenborg), and in culture (interaction with religious iconography, influence on the liturgical calendar, and the establishment of feasts).

2. The Church and Individual Revelations

Prompted by the proliferation of accounts of apparitions in the late Middle Ages, the church began to legislate on the subject at Lateran* V (1517), by asking that they not be divulged without prior examination and authorization by the local ordinary. Thereafter, it was his responsibility to prepare the file and give his approval before any examination by the Holy See (this division of labor was definitively confirmed by Urban VIII in 1634). Fundamentally, the Latin theology* of individual revelations as derived from Augustine* (evidenced in the writings of David of Augsburg, Cardinal Bona, Eusebius, Amort, and Benedict XIV) concentrated its attention on three questions: 1) the origin and authenticity of individual revelations; 2) their finality (the relationship of individual revelations to general revelation); and 3) the type of adherence that an individual revelation deserves to receive from believers.

a) Origin of Individual Revelations. God and the saints are not the only ones to appear; demons* appear too, not to mention ghosts. The origin of marvelous phenomena may be natural, demonic, or divine, and it is the corresponding discernment that is the primary preoccupation of pastors. The critique of evidence is a task that is all the more necessary because individual revelations made to groups or crowds (Fatima) are very rare. Because he, or more often she, is most often alone, the visionary is exposed to illusion and hallucination. The appetite for visions (against which John* of the Cross warned) and the profusion of pseudo-revelations have brought about an increase in calls for caution, particularly with respect to individual revelations made to women and children. The formulation of negative criteria is easy: insincerity of the visionary, the wish to put oneself forward, challenge of legitimate authority*, a message contrary to faith* or the moral teaching of the church, and the like. The principal positive criteria of discernment enabling the uncovering of counterfeits and arguing in favor of the authenticity (i.e., the divine origin) of an individual revelation, following the nearly unanimous opinion of theologians (an opinion formulated by Cardinal Bona and adopted by Benedict XIV in his *De canonisatione* III. 52, which is still authoritative on the question), are extrinsic criteria, the humility of the recipient and, in general, the various signs in his life of the fruits of the Holy* Spirit (Gal 5:22: charity, joy, peace*, patience, kindness, goodness, gentleness, and so on). If the visionary is a monk or a nun, note should be taken of the reluctance or eagerness to speak of the individual revelations and it should be asked, for example, whether he or she has remained obedient. Other criteria can and should be invoked, in particular some intrinsic criteria such as the harmony of the object and form of individual revelations with Scripture, or extrinsic criteria such as the authority of the church and the opinion of competent people, the psychological health of the visionary, and so on.

b) Finality of Individual Revelations. General revelation having come to an end, individual revelations can provide neither additions nor modifications. On the other hand it is agreed that they can provide an explanation for general revelation. Depending on the circumstances, their raison d'être, clearly set out by Thomas* Aquinas (IIa IIae. q. 174. a. 6: in every age, men have received divine signs to guide them), is to recall or to clarify, in an age tempted to forget it, a particular salutary truth*, even a general truth (e.g., the call to repentance transmitted by the apparitions at Lourdes and La Salette). This reminder can come about in a more or less didactic ("I am the Immaculate Conception") or parenetic form, even if that involves commands bordering on threats (La Salette). Individual revelations are intended to foster sanctity, not as *gratiae gratum faciens,* but as *gratiae gratis datae* (Benedict XIV, III. 52. 2).

c) What Credence Should Be Given to Individual Revelations? Individual revelations are not part of the content of the faith that is to be believed from "divine faith" (theological notes*); but no one can hold them in contempt without being presumptuous. When they have been approved by the magisterium*, it is recommended to believe them from "human faith" (Benedict XIV, III. 53. 12–15). For, although it is true that "Christ is the fullness of Revelation" (Vatican* II, *DV*), individual revelations nonetheless remain a desirable gift (1 Cor 14:1–5) to the extent that they are an integral part of the gift of prophecy that the Holy* Spirit generously bestows on the Church of the apostles*. Indeed, the outpouring of the Holy Spirit cannot be confined to the early days of the church, nor to institutional forms of the church alone. The proof of this lies, historically, in the fact that many individual revelations helped to clarify the content of general revelation. Their influence on the life of the church, notably through the popes*, has been significant.

- Eusebius Amort, *De revelationibus, visionibus et apparitionibus privatis regulae tutae ex Scriptura, Conciliis, Sanctis Patribus aliisque optimis auctoribus collectae, explicatae atque exemplis illustratae,* 2 vols., Augsburg, 1744.

Augustine, *De Genesi ad litteram,* l. XII.

Benedict XIV, *De servorum Dei beatificatione et canonisatione,* 4 vols., Bologna, 1734–38.

John Cardinal Bona, *De discretione spirituum liber unus,* Brussels, 1671; Rome, 1672.

David of Augsburg (†1272), *De exterioris et interioris hominis compositione,* 3 vols., Quaracchi, 1899.

Dominic Gravina, *Lapis Lydius (Ad discernendas veras a falsis visionibus et revelationibus basanistès, hoc est Lapis Lydius),* 2 vols., Naples, 1638.

Thomas Aquinas, *ST* IIa IIae, q. 174, passim and a. 6.

Pierre Thyrée, *De apparitionibus spirituum tractatus duo,* Köln, 1600.

♦ J. de Tonquédec (1937), "Apparitions,", *DSp* 1, 801–9.

K. Rahner (1952), *Visionen und Prophezeiungen,* Innsbruck (2nd Ed. 1960).

L. Volken (1961), *Les révélations dans l'Église,* Mulhouse.

E. Benz (1969), *Die Vision: Erfahrungsformen und Bilderwelt,* Stuttgart.

R. Laurentin (1976), "Fonction et statut des apparitions," in *Vraies et fausses apparitions dans l'Église,* 2nd Ed., Paris, 153–205.

H. F. Fuchs (1978), *Sehen und Schauen: Die Wurzel hzh im Alten Orient und im Alten Testament. Ein Beitrag zum prophetischen Offenbarungsempfang,* Würzburg.

P. Dinzelbacher (1981), *Vision und Visionsliteratur im Mittelalter,* Stuttgart.

F. Boespflug (1984), *Dieu dans l'art:* Sollicitudini Nostrae *de Benoît XIV (1745) et l'affaire Crescence de Kaufbeuren,* Paris.

P. Dinzelbacher (1991), *Revelationes* (Typology of the Western Medieval sources, fasc. 57), Turnhout.

A. Vergote (1991), "Visions et apparitions: Approche psychologique," *RTL* 22, 202–25.

FRANÇOIS BOESPFLUG

See also **Experience; Miracle; Mysticism; Revelation**

Revolution

Until the end of the 18th century, the word *revolution,* which had entered the technical vocabulary of politics in the 17th century, essentially concerned constitutional problems: it referred to the reconstruction of the government, in form or in personnel, by the people or its representatives. In England, the Glorious Revolution of 1688 was aimed at effecting a change in the succession to the crown with minimal disruption to the rest. In this sense, although with more sweeping ambitions, the Constituent Assembly (1789–91) in France conceived the task of reconstructing the French government based on rational ideals as revolutionary. Subsequent events, however, so impressed themselves upon the European imagination as to produce a new concept of revolution, in the light of which the American and French experiences came to be reinterpreted. It was no longer a matter merely of changing the system of government: "historical necessity" had to be obeyed; radical novelty had to be secured; and the whole of society*, and no longer just the government, had to exercise power. As Hannah Arendt put it, "Only where the pathos of novelty is present, and where novelty is concerned with the idea of freedom, are we entitled to speak of revolution" (Arendt 1963). Theology* made a decisive impression on the earlier of these two ideas of revolution; it received equally important impressions from the later of the two.

a) Constitutional Revolution. The idea of constitutional revolution developed in Europe from the Gregorian Reform (11th–12th centuries), according to which the preeminence of the spiritual power gave the pope* the right to depose errant monarchs and absolve subjects from their obedience. It therefore became possible for a subject to defy a prince who no longer had legitimate political authority*. This idea became associated with the classical theme of virtuous tyrannicide. For John of Salisbury (1120–80), the tyrant is absolutely hostile to the common good*, and guilty of a "more than public crime," for he attacks law*, which is superior even to emperors; to slay him, therefore, is equable and right, since it is an action in the service of public order (*Polycraticus* III.11). Thomas* Aquinas, citing Aristotle, adds that the tyrant "seeks his own advantage from rule, not the good of the multitude subject to him" (*De regimine principum* I, 11). From a tyrant no law can be derived (*ST* Ia IIae, q. 95, a. 4), for law is part of the public order, which does not exist in such conditions. Hence, "the overthrow of such a regime does not have the character of sedition" (*ST* IIa IIae, q. 42, a. 2).

However, this idea of the tyrant as a political nullity was too abstract, and subsequent discussions recognized tyranny as a political system. It then became necessary to find a legitimate form for the struggle against it. According to Marsilius of Padua (1290–1342), a distinction can be made between person and office; the law emanating from the office can judge even the person who holds the office (*Defensor Pacis* 18). However, since the removal of a tyrant is no longer an action performed in a political vacuum, there must be criteria for its lawful performance. Here, the Holy Roman Empire provided a paradigm: since the emperor was appointed by the electors, some civil

lawyers argued, he could be deposed by the same electors (a right that the supporters of the empire refused to the pope: e.g., Ockham [c. 1285–1347], *Brev.* II, 9). In the 15th century, conciliarists located this principle within a general doctrine that government is illegitimate if it is not representative: "all legitimate authority arises from elective concordance" (Nicholas* of Cusa, *De conc. cath.* 3, 331). This does not imply a license for anarchy. Christian subjects ought in general to obey tyrannical authorities, since they must consent to political order in principle. Only in the service of a practicable strategy of revolution could defiance be contemplated (Wyclif, *Dom. civ.* I, 28).

Sixteenth-century thought developed from this position. Which law authorized the removal of a tyrant? Opinions varied on the subject. Calvinists preferred to rely on *constitutional law,* by analogy with the empire: certain officials (*ephors,* a term borrowed from Sparta) have the responsibility of correcting, restraining, and, if necessary, removing the supreme magistrate. For Calvin*, this was true merely de facto of certain constitutional arrangements. For his followers (Althusius [1557–1638] or Beza [1519–1605]), the ephorate was a feature of ideal constitutional principle, to which all actual constitutions implicitly aspired. Parliamentary estates were assigned this role. In English thought (Ponet [1516–56]), the authority of *natural law* was invoked; while it was in the name of *divine law* that John Knox (1505–72) summoned the various classes of society to expel the Guises from Scotland.

Constitution or nature: the problem constantly reappeared in the debates over ideas that surrounded the American and French revolutions. Advocates of constitutional revolution argued from ideal theory based upon the "rights of man." Conservatives (e.g., Burke [1729–97]) argued for the extraordinary and extraconstitutional character of revolution, justifiable only in emergency. No one appealed any longer to divine law; in its place stood the notion of "social contract," which held out to advocates of revolution the idea that society could dissolve itself into its elements and reconstitute itself anew if necessity demanded it.

b) Social and Economic Revolution. With Condorcet (1743–94), who wrote at the height of the French Revolution, the idea of revolution was inserted into the philosophy of history* as conceived by Voltaire (1604–1778) or Turgot (1727–81), and it became the premise for the achievement of the goal of history: liberty*. This implied a new vocabulary and new political principles. The word *révolutionnaire,* coined expressly for the French Revolution, could apply only to a revolution that sought liberty on the basis of complete equality of rights (Condorcet, *Oeuvres,* 18, 4 *Sq*). This unique moment called for revolutionary laws and measures, unjust at any other time, to repress counterrevolution (ibid., 16 *Sq*). Nineteenth-century socialists (e.g., Proudhon [1809–65]) developed a broader vision of revolution: the French Revolution had been incomplete, since it had failed to liberate the workers (work*), or to emancipate society from private property*. The dynamic of revolution now came to characterize a whole phase of history.

It was Hegel* who made the revolutionary idea of history into a theodicy: the transformation of the "idea of liberty" into "the reality of the consciousness of liberty" is the justification of God*'s operations in history. The revolutionary dynamic that marks this transformation is an ideal dynamic, the dialectical unfolding of the idea, which expresses itself in concrete historical movements. Hegel interpreted history according to a Trinitarian pattern, derived from Joachim of Fiore (millenarianism*): an age of the Father*, an age of the Son, and an age of the Spirit. The constitutional liberal principles that marked the modern era were the expression of the age of the Spirit, which began with the assertion of subjectivity by the Reformation and developed, itself in a Trinitarian pattern, by way of the rational thought of the Enlightenment. Protestant lands had no need of the violent turmoil experienced in France, since they were already prepared for the constitutional changes required. During the 19th century, Hegel's theological idealism gave rise within Protestantism to all the nuances of optimistic progressivism, embracing at one pole the pantheistic American Transcendentalists (e.g., Emerson [1803–82]) and at the other an orthodoxy clothed with a gradualist eschatology*. The disciples of Albert Ritschl (1822–89), such as Hermann or Forsyth, had a view of history centered on the doctrine of the kingdom* of God. Until the Reformation "ethicized" faith, Christian society had required nothing but conformity to authority and custom; rationalism* was nothing but an empty repudiation of this attitude, which Kant* overcame by establishing the validity of the Reformers' insight into the authority of conscience*. This created the modern mind, which in turn transformed society according to the demands of liberty: "The control of the great and long social revolution must, more than ever before, lie in such a radical spiritual revolution, which God makes and not man" (Forsyth 1913).

With Marx* and Engels (1820–95), the theory of revolution achieved its most developed form. Rejecting the idealism of Hegel, they provide a dialectical interpretation of historical necessity, rendered in terms of various stages in the economic organization of society. The whole of history is to be explained by the struggle between classes over the appropriation of the means of production. The role of a revolutionary movement is to be the self-conscious representative of the revolutionary class. However, a gulf opens up between the exigencies of the revolutionary struggle for power and the dissolution of the state in the achievement of liberty.

Despite the strongly antireligious strain in Marxism, some theologians have seen a correspondence between its revolutionary promise of an end to economic oppression and Jesus*' preaching of the Good News to the poor (e.g., Lk 4:18, 7:22). Liberation* theology also assumed various elements of Marxian theory—class conflict, the dominant role of the economy, knowledge through praxis, and so on—but it has never approximated to a fully Marxian concept of revolution. Lacking a philosophy of history, its revolutionary commitment has not gone beyond struggles against local or regional oppressions. Its concept of liberty is neither liberal democratic nor socialist. At its most revolutionary, it has propounded a constitutionalist model of revolution; experience and disappointment have produced a waning enthusiasm even for this. Nevertheless, its ecclesiology*, fashioned by the idea of the revolutionary movement, has to some extent played a role in recovering a concept of the church* as a critical "countersociety" that functions according to its own laws. We are thus led back to where the idea of revolution began: to ecclesial society as an independent reality, capable of defying unevangelical power structures.

OLIVER O'DONOVAN

● J. Althusius, *Politica methodice digesta,* Ed. C.J. Friedrich, Cambridge, Mass., 1932.

T. de Bèze, *Du droit des magistrats sur leurs sujets,* New Ed. Geneva, 1971.

E. Burke, *Reflections on the Revolution in France, Works,* vol. 15, London, 1815.

M.J.A.N. de Condorcet, "Sur le sens du mot 'révolutionnaire,'" *OC* vol. 18, Paris, 1804.

P.T. Forsyth, *The Principle of Authority,* London, 1913.

G.W.F. Hegel, *Vorlesungen über die Philosophie des Geschichte, Vorlesungen,* vol. 12, Hamburg, 1996, 500–521.

John Knox, *Political Writings,* Ed. M.A. Breslow, Washington, 1985.

John of Salisbury, *Policraticus,* Ed. C.C.J. Webb, Oxford, 1909.

Marsilius of Padua, *Defensor Pacis,* Ed. R. Scholz, Hanover, 1932.

K. Marx, F. Engels, *The Communist Manifesto.*

N. of Cusa, *De concordantia catholica, Opera omnia,* vol. 14, Ed. G. Kallen, Hamburg, 1963.

J. Ponet, *A Short Treatise of Politic Power,* Ed. W.S. Hudson, Chicago, 1946.

P.-J. Proudhon, *Qu'est-ce que la propriété? Œuvres,* vol. 1, Paris, 1865.

Thomas Aquinas, *De regimine principum; ST* IIa IIae, q. 42.

William of Ockham, *Breviloquium de principatu tyrannico,* Ed. L. Baudry, Paris, 1937.

J. Wyclif, *De civili dominio,* Ed. J. Loserth, London, 1886.

♦ K. Martin (1929), *French Liberal Thought in the XVIIIth Century,* London.

H. Arendt (1963), *On Revolution,* New York.

J. Comblin, (1970), *Théologie de la Révolution,* Paris.

J. Comblin (1974), *Théologie de la pratique révolutionnaire,* Paris.

J. Miguez-Bonino (1975), *Doing Theology in a Revolutionary Situation,* Philadelphia.

R. Kozelleck (1984), "Revolution," in O. Brunner, W. Conze, R. Kozelleck (Ed.), *Geschichtliche Grundbegriffe: Historisches Lexikon zur politisch-sozialen Sprache in Deutschland,* vol. 5, Stuttgart.

J. L. Segundo (1984), *Faith and Ideologies,* Maryknoll, N.Y.

G. Mairet (1986), "Marsile de Padoue, *Le défenseur de la paix,*" *DOPol,* Paris, 525–8 (bibl.).

B. Roussel, G. Vincent (1986), "T. de Bèze, *Du droit des magistrats,*" ibid., 85–90. K. M. Baker (1988), "Revolution," in C. Lucas (Ed.), *The French Revolution and the Creation of Modern Political Culture,* vol. 2, Oxford.

A. Rey (1989), *"Révolution": Histoire d'un mot,* Paris.

Paul E. Sigmund (1990), *Liberation Theology at the Crossroads: Democracy or Revolution?* New York.

See also **Authority; Democracy; Liberation Theology; Liberty; Marx, Karl; Society; Violence**

Rhineland-Flemish Mysticism

The mystical* movement known as Rhineland-Flemish mysticism is made up of two distinct factions, often sharing a similar inspiration but sometimes moving in opposite directions: a German tradition represented by the Beguine Mechtild of Magdeburg (1207/1210–1282/1294), author of *The Flowing Light of the Godhead,* and the Dominicans Meister Eckhart of Hohengheim (1260–1328), Henry of Berg, also known as Heinrich Sús or Suso (†1365), and Johannes Tauler (†1361), all of whom wrote in Middle High German; and a Flemish tradition represented by the Beguine Hadewijch of Antwerp (c. 1240), author of *Visions* and *Stanzaic Poems,* the anonymous author of *Poems in Rhyming Couplets* known as Hadewijch II, the Cistercian nun Beatrice of Nazareth (1200–68), author of *The Seven Ways of Love,* Jan van Ruusbroec (1293–1381), and his disciple Jan van Leeuwen (†1378), who wrote in Middle Dutch. Although, despite the differences in language, there is a deep affinity between Mechtild, Hadewijch of Antwerp, and Beatrice, an affinity based on a similarity of culture, experience, social status, and literary expression (favoring poetry), the same cannot be said of Eckhart and Ruusbroec, whose common sources and apparent identity of concerns do more to separate these two than unite them. Further, the distinction between a mysticism that is called "feminine" or "emotional," and a mysticism that is called "masculine" or "speculative" theoretically sets up additional dissonances within each group.

1. Rhineland-Flemish Mysticism As a Cultural and Historical Entity

The "Rhineland mysticism" of Eckhart, Suso, and Tauler existed in a complex social and religious context that has been partially obscured by historiographical categories.

a) Nuptial Mysticism and Mysticism of Essence. It is necessary to reconsider the traditional distinction between the "bridal" mysticism of the women*, Beguines or nuns *(minne-Mystik),* and the "intellectual" mysticism of the men, monks or theologians. The most immediate question has to do with the biblical texts underlying the language of each of them. Two texts can be identified, around which works, practices, and even religious orders were organized: the Song of Songs and the Prologue to the Gospel according to Saint John. Before becoming "feminine," Rhineland-Flemish bridal mysticism was Cistercian, because it was nourished by the works of Bernard* of Clairvaux on the Song of Songs. This source in particular provided one of the central themes of Hadewijch and Beatrice, the "without why" *(sonder enich waeromme)*—a formula that is found from Eckhart to Angelus Silesius—extending Bernard's argument in Sermon 83. 3 on the Song of Songs that "love wishes for no cause and no result other than itself." Speculative mysticism occupied a different literary space, that of the birth of the Word*, as expressed in John 1:11 *(in propria venit,* "he came to his own"), and it was there that was located the theology* of the indwelling of the essence or depths of the soul* *(Seelengrund, abditum mentis)* that played a decisive role for Eckhart and his followers.

b) Spiritual Movements and Heretical Tendencies. Rhineland mysticism derived largely from the encounter between professional theologians charged with the *cura animarum* and their female audiences, nuns and Beguines, often grouped around houses of mendicant friars who guaranteed their protection. Eckhart, for example, had spiritual responsibility for 75 convents of Dominican nuns of the Dominican tertiary order of Alsace and Switzerland and of some 85 Beguine houses of Strasbourg sheltering approximately one thousand women. In parallel to the Beguines*, the rise of Rhineland-Flemish mysticism gave rise to a male movement, the Beghards. In the time of Eckhart, Suso, and Tauler, the Beghards and some Beguines established a powerful movement that spread widely in Germany: the "sect" of the Brothers and Sisters of the Free Spirit and Voluntary Poverty. The doctrines of the Free Spirit, which are known to us through the *Determinatio* of Albert* the Great on the heresy* of Ries (taking a position on a list of 97 heretical theses, which the leader of the German Dominican school traced back generally to Pelagianism* and Manicheanism*), also bring out very clearly the theme that was most widespread in Rhineland mysticism: the "deification" or "divinization" of man. The Free Spirit, however, understood deification as a process of *personal* realization, independent of the sacraments* and of the infused gifts of grace*. Although Eckhart himself was vigorously opposed to the doctrines of the sect, the supporters of the Free Spirit used his authority to spread their ideas. This involuntary sponsorship probably played a role in the Inquisition's proceeding against Eckhart in 1326, which led in 1329 to his condemnation by the Avignon pope* John XXII (constitution *In Agro dominico*). Eckhart's opposition to the Free Spirit cannot be put in doubt. The Free Spirit professed deification without grace (Council of Vienna* VI, 6), in distinguishing the *incipientes*, the *proficientes*, and the *perfecti*. It asserted that once the end had been reached, the perfect were deified and should be the object of a cult* of adoration. Moreover, it reserved deification for a few of the elect, whereas for Eckhart, in contrast, every man should become a son of God* and thus be "by grace" what the Son is "by nature." Eckhart also criticized two other positions of the Beghards: the confusion between blind free will and freedom, and the assertion of the futility of works* (Council of Vienna VI, 2). For Eckhart, works led to eternal beatitude*, and the practice of virtue* was not characteristic of imper-

fect man (contrary to the claims of the Free Spirit). Suso, Tauler, and Ruusbroec repeated and amplified these criticisms.

2. Major Themes of Rhineland-Flemish Mysticism

The originality of Rhineland mysticism lay in its exploration of the theological links between Trinitarian indwelling, the transforming union of the soul with God in knowledge* and love*, and the beatific vision*. The difficulty of this mysticism is thus not that it calls on extraordinary "experiences"; rather, the difficulty is a genuinely theological one. To this is added the difficulty of language and style, the obscurity of certain formulations, and the false impression of homogeneity created by the reading of works that are often linked to one another.

a) Uncreated and Created Grace. The central intuition of Rhineland mysticism is nonetheless clear. It is articulated in a thesis that has become an adage: "God became man so that man might become God." This is the unity of two graces, the grace of the Incarnation* and the grace of indwelling, considered as constitutive of the ontology of the Christian mystery*. This intuition extends the teaching of the Fathers* of the Church, who maintained with Irenaeus* of Lyons that the motive for the Incarnation was the deification of man: "This is the reason for which the Word became man, and the Son of God Son* of man, so that man, by joining himself to the Word and thereby receiving adoptive filiation, might become the son of God" (*Adv. Haer.* III. 19. 1). By "deification" or "justification*," the Rhineland mystics understood the indwelling of the entire Trinity* in the "soul of the just"—what they also called the gift of "uncreated grace." For them, the indwelling was not limited to the gift of "sanctifying" grace, since in the gift they had in mind, the Holy* Spirit, was considered as indwelling man: it was the divine Person* itself that was given to us and not only the gifts of that Person (i.e., "created grace").

b) Meister Eckhart, Johannes Tauler, and Deification. Because it is centered on the two graces of the Incarnation and indwelling, Eckhart's mysticism is essentially Christocentric. Expounded in the theme of the birth of the Word or Son in the soul (theogenesis), it is presented in the form of a "mysticism of Christmas." A spirituality with both a practical and a contemplative orientation, it sees in Christ* the one who brings to preeminent realization all the virtues by which the corresponding deification of the Christian is accomplished: humility, poverty of spirit, inner nobility. Christ, the new Adam*, is the prototype of the Christian, of man restored in the plenitude of a nature brought back to the time before sin*, a prototype of the man renewed by grace in humility, poverty, and nobility. Christ on the cross is thus not at the heart of Eckhart's mysticism. Eckhart's Christ is "beyond joy and sorrow," "detached," and "abandoned" in a genuine "freedom," the freedom of the "depths of the soul" *(Seelengrund)*. What Eckhart proposes as a model to the Christian is less Christ's suffering than his "detachment" *(Abgeschiedenheit)* and his "abandonment" *(Gelâzenheit)* in the heart of all action and all passion. Eckhart's mysticism is thus expressed in a simple formula condensing a whole series of theological developments: the humble, poor, and noble man is a detached man abandoned in the "Unique One" *(Einicein)*. It does not, however, reject any of the common practices or exercises or works supposed to "realize" the life of the Christian: prayer*, the Eucharist*, and the taking of the sacraments (Eckhart wrote an apologia for frequent Communion). The same doctrine is found in the preaching of Johannes Tauler.

c) Suso and the Mysticism of the Passion. Although he defended the most speculative aspects of Eckhart's mysticism in his *Little Book of Truth,* Suso's later works effected a radical change. The heart of his mystical doctrine is given in a new definition of "true abandonment": "An abandoned *(gelassener)* man must be stripped of any form *(entbildet)* recalling created being, be conformed *(gebildet)* to Christ, and transformed *(überbildet)* into the deity*." The change that takes place between Eckhart and Suso has to do with the notion of "conformation." For Eckhart, abandonment, that is, the "transcendence of images," "unknowing knowledge," "poverty of spirit," is the only way to come into "conformity with Christ." For Suso, on the other hand, the way is the way of suffering taken as a sign of total abnegation of one's own will. The *Gelâzenheit* to which Eckhart and his follower Suso both refer thus does not have the same meaning: when Eckhart speaks of "conforming oneself to Christ," he is thinking of his divinity; when Suso speaks of it, he is thinking of his suffering humanity. The "transforming union" does not therefore crown the same kind of structure. According to Eckhart we must abandon ourselves by allowing the Word to be born in the depths of our soul, we must engender Christ in ourselves. For Suso it is necessary "to become an expressive image of the Crucified One." These are two models of mystical theology, one focused on *deification,* the other on the *Passion*.

d) Ruusbroec and Common Life. The watchword of Ruusbroec's mysticism is "common" life. By this expression, Ruusbroec understands the life of the "common man," the man who enters into the eternal communion* of the Trinity with all the saints and tastes there a "fructifying beatitude" in which there are "no distinctions." The common man who lives in the Son, his eternal image, "contemplates and savors the Trinitarian union" in an essential unity with God, which, contrary to some intuitions of Rhineland mysticism, does not point to the "transcendence of God in God." Ruusbroec's mysticism is not a mysticism of the One, but a Trinitarian mysticism: the communion of the Father*, the Son, and the Holy Spirit is the dwelling place of common life, its "reality." It is therefore not surprising, despite their superficial kinship, that Eckhart's and Ruusbroec's mysticism came into conflict. In fact, while Ruusbroec, like the Rhineland mystics, was a determined opponent of the Free Spirit (which he attacked in the person of "la Bloemardinne" and her followers), he showed at least an equal reserve toward Eckhart's doctrines. In the *Spiritual Weddings,* he attacked Eckhart's "emptiness" while denouncing the "natural repose" that a man may reach if he has "succeeded in stripping and abstracting himself from all images," "in detaching himself from all activity in relation to superior powers." In Ruusbroec's view, one reaches this repose "without the grace of God." His denunciation of the "leisure" that "Jews and pagans" may attain, "as well as all men, however bad they may be," clearly indicates his perspective: the "quest for God through desire" and the "encounter with God through the love of fruition," contrasted to a "natural repose" in which Ruusbroec thinks that the loving man neither can nor should stop, "because charity and the inner motion of divine grace are never appeased." It is because he believes that he sees a kind of quietism* or what might be termed today a *natural* mysticism in Eckhart, that Ruusbroec's follower, Jan van Leeuwen, also concentrated his attacks on what he called Eckhart's "false emptiness."

3. Posterity of Rhineland-Flemish Mysticism
Despite the condemnation of Eckhart in 1329, Rhineland and Rhineland-Flemish mysticism had a wide posterity. It influenced Luther* through the *Frankfurt Unknown* (or *Theologia germanica*). It also marked John* of the Cross, who knew the *Spiritual Institutions* of Pseudo-Tauler, translated into Latin by Surius (*Opera Tauleri* [Köln, 1548]) and published in Spanish in Coimbra in 1551. Thanks to the translation of Tauler's *Sermons* by Surius, dedicated to Philip II, which was in fact an anthology of northern mysticism, John became familiar with the theme of the "depths of the soul" *(fondo del alma)* and with most of the other themes of Eckhart and Tauler: the abandonment of powers ("so that the soul becomes absolutely empty,

naked, pure, and separate"); the idea that God is the agent and man the patient, and "that once the obstacles have been removed and the soul is in a state of expectation, God cannot fail to flow into it, placing himself as it were in its power." In Germany the most notable continuation of Rhineland-Flemish mysticism was in the *Cherubic Pilgrim* of Johannes Silesius, in anticipation of the "rediscoveries" made by Schopenhauer in the 19th century and by Heidegger* in the 20th.

● Beatrice of Nazareth, *Sept degrés d'amour,* French trans. J.-B. M. Porion, Paris, 1972.

Eckhart, *Die deutschen und lateinischen Werke,* Stuttgart, 1936–.

Deutsche Mystiker des vierzehnten Jahrhunderts, Ed. F. Pfeiffer, vol. 2: *Meister Eckhart,* Aalen, 1962.

G. Théry, "Édition critique des pièces relatives au procès d'Eckhart contenues dans le manuscrit 33 b de la bibliothèque de Soest," *AHDL* I (1926), 129–268.

Eckart, *Traités et sermons,* French trans. A. de Libera, Paris, 1993.

Hadewijch of Antwerp, *Écrits mystiques des béguines,* French trans. J.-B. M. Porion, 2nd Ed., Paris, 1994.

Mechtilde de Magdebourg, *Offenbarung der schwester Mechthild von Magdeburg, oder das fliessende Licht der Gottheit,* Ed. G. Morel, Regensburg, 1896.

Ruysbroeck [Ruusbroec], *Opera omnia,* Ed. G. de Baere, CChr.CM, 101, 102, 110; *Œuvres choisies,* French trans. J. A. Bizet, Paris, 1947.

Suso, *Œuvres complètes,* French trans. J. Ancelet-Hustache, Paris, 1977.

Jean Tauler, *Sermons,* French trans. E. Hugueny, G. Théry, M. A. L. Corin, Paris, 1991.

♦ E. Filthaut (Ed.) (1961), *Johannes Tauler: Ein deutscher Mystiker, Gedenkschrift zum 600. Todestag,* Essen.

Coll. (1963), *La Mystique rhénane: Colloque de Strasbourg, 16–19 mai 1961,* Paris.

E. Filthaut (Ed.) (1966), *Heinrich Seuse: Studien zum 600. Todestag, 1366–1966,* Köln.

A. de Libera (1984), *La Mystique rhénane: D'Albert le Grand à Maître Eckhart,* Paris (2nd Ed. 1995).

G. Épiney-Burgard, É. Zum Brunn (1988), *Femmes troubadours de Dieu,* Turnhout.

N. Largier (1995), "Meister Eckhart: Perspektiven der Forschung, 1980–1993," *ZDP* 114/1, 29–98.

A. de Libera (1996), *Eckhart, Suso, Tauler et la divinisation de l'homme,* Paris; (1998), *Maître Eckhart et la mystique rhénane,* Paris.

ALAIN DE LIBERA

See also **Beguines; Christ and Christology; Contemplation; Deity;** *Devotio moderna;* **Intellectualism; Mysticism; Vienna, Council of; Voluntarism**

Richard of Saint-Victor. *See* **Saint-Victor, School of**

Richer, Edmond. *See* **Gallicanism**

Ricoeur, Paul. *See* **Hermeneutics**

Rigorism. *See* Alphonsus Liguori; Casuistry

Rites, Chinese

The "rites argument" troubled the world of missionaries in China for a century, from 1643 to 1742. It was at the confluence of many theological and philosophical debates (up to Malebranche's *Entretien d'un philosophe chrétien et d'un philosophe chinois* of 1708) in a Christian Europe that had been challenged by its encounter with an older culture, one whose self-sufficient wisdom demanded that it be approached with caution and respect. A break with missionary Europeanism had to be made.

In reality the rites argument was concerned with two principal questions: the name* of God* in Chinese and Confucian rites. Everything had begun in the Middle Kingdom with the Jesuit missionary Matteo Ricci (1552–1610). After becoming an expert among learned men, he had slowly developed a method for the cultural adaptation of Christian discourse by relying on Confucian humanism. He thought he could detect in the Confucianism of Chinese antiquity a natural religion (deism*) still bearing the traces of the primitive Adamic revelation*; elsewhere, he acknowledged that Confucian rites had a purely civil character. His successors developed his method, which was characterized in particular by the choice of divine names taken from the Chinese classics and by authorization given to Christians to participate in certain familial and social rites.

Dominican missionaries began appearing in China in 1632, soon followed by Franciscans. Having access to less cultivated segments of society that were more inclined toward superstitious practices, they were soon accusing the Jesuits of tolerating participation by Christians in "Chinese rites" suspected of "idolatry*." In 1643 the Dominican J.-B. Morales sparked the rites dispute by informing the Congregation De propaganda fide. The debate stirred intellectual Europe in the 17th and 18th centuries. In Paris the Jesuit L. Le Comte defended the cause of "Chinese rites" against the objections of the Sorbonne. In 1700 he attempted to explain that these rites had no purpose but to "render honor to the dead, to Confucius." In them, according to Le Comte, there was "not a feeling of religion," but a "spirit of gratitude." Finally, on 11 July 1742, after many hesitations, with alternating prohibitions and concessions, Benedict XIV condemned Chinese rites in the bull *Ex quo singulari,* rescinded the earlier permissions, and manifested his express intention to demand obedience by requiring that missionaries take an oath that they would no longer tolerate such practices.

It was only two centuries later, in 1939, that the instruction *Plane compertum* of Pius XII recognized that the rites belonged to the "civil" realm, thereby nullifying the 1742 decision. The rites dispute witnessed the confrontation of different conceptions of salvation*, involving the conflict between nature* and grace* and between humanism and prophetism. In its concern to integrate with the Chinese ritual order, did the humanism of the Jesuits alter the dynamism of grace? Pascal* thought so, and in the fifth of his *Lettres provinciales* went so far as to accuse the Jesuits of "suppressing the scandal of the cross." The Leibniz* of *Novissima Sinica,* for his part, defended the Jesuit cause. The rites dispute represents a typical, but not novel, case of the tension inherent in any attempt at inculturation*. If the proclamation of the gospel can make itself heard only by becoming a cultural fact, how far short of the limits of cultural embodiment must it be kept in order not to compromise the integrity of the Christian message?

• L. Le Comte (1696), *Nouveaux mémoires sur l'état présent de la Chine,* Paris.
G. W. Leibniz (1697), *Novissima Sinaca…,* Hanover.
G. W. Leibniz (1716), *Lettre… sur la philosophie chinoise à M. de Rémond,* in *Epistolae ad diversos,* Ed. C. Kortholt, Leipzig, 4 vols., 1734–42; repr. in *Discours sur la théologie naturelle des Chinois* (with the document "Écrits sur la question religieuse de Chine"), Ed. C. Frémont, Paris, 1987.
N. Longobardi (1701), *Traité sur quelques points de la religion naturelle des Chinois,* Paris.

J. Brucker (1905), "Chinois (rites)," *DThC* 2/2, 2364–91.

R. Étiemble (1966), *Les Jésuites en Chine: La querelle des rites (1552–1773),* Paris.

J. Gernet (1982), *Chine et christianisme: Action et réaction,* Paris.

G. Minamiki (1985), *The Chinese Rites Controversy, from Its Beginning to Modern Times,* Chicago.

É. Ducornet (1992), *Matteo Ricci, le Lettré d'Occident,* Paris.

ÉTIENNE DUCORNET

See also **Deism and Theism; Idolatry; Incultura-tion; Mission/Evangelization; Name; Natural Theology; Religions, Theology of**

Romanism. *See* Ultramontanism

Rome

a) Origins of the Roman Church. The first uncon-tested evidence of the presence of Christians in the capital of the Roman Empire is the letter addressed by Paul in 55–58 to the believers of the city *(urbs).*

The testimonies cited in order to locate in the 40s the first references to Christianity in Rome are more doubtful: thus, Suetonius (*V. Claudii* 25, 4) mentions the expulsion from the city—in 49, during the reign of Claudius (Orosius, *Hist.* VII, 6, 15)—"of the Jews who were fomenting trouble at the instigation of Chrestus." Could this be seen as a way of alluding to Christian preaching*? This is a hypothesis that Acts 18:2–3 would seem to corroborate—provided at least Aquila and Priscilla had adhered to the new faith* prior to their encounter with Paul. It is a possibility. On the other hand, it does not seem acceptable to link Peter*'s liberation from the prison of Herod Agrippa I, some time between 41 and 44 (Acts 12:17), and his coming to Rome, on the basis of Jerome's *Chronique* (GCS 47, Ed. R. Helm, §179), which places that arrival in 42.

The Epistle to the Romans does not allow us to de-termine with accuracy the characteristics of the first Roman community: initially, the first Christian implant must certainly have occurred within the large, active, and very mobile Jewish diaspora of the city. The themes of the letter (the relationship between Jews and Christians of the nations) and the onomastics of Paul's

correspondents (at least if Romans 16, where he greets by name 26 "brothers and sisters," is indeed part of that letter) testify to this, but there is no indication whatsoever as to the way this community is organized. In any case, when chronology is examined rigorously (*see* Ambrosiaster, *Ad Romanos,* CSEL LXXXI, p. 6, l. 13–16), it is clear that neither Paul nor probably Peter (who is not mentioned at all in Romans) were present at the origin of the Roman church*.

Paul arrived in Rome a few years after having writ-ten the Epistle to the Romans. He remained there con-fined to his house for a period of two years, during which he was able to instruct his visitors (Acts 28:30–31), and, according to a hypothesis suggested by a few exegetes, he composed a certain number of the "captivity epistles" (Colossians, Ephesians, Phile-mon?); and if so, perhaps together with the evangelist Luke (Col 4:14; Phlm 24; 2 Tm 4:11). This stay in Rome, followed perhaps by a resumption of traveling, either toward the Iberian peninsula or the East, started to inspire, in the second century and among Eastern Christian communities, hagiographic accounts that were quick to compensate for the silence of Luke's ac-count (Acts of Paul). Peter, also, was at the center of comparable narratives which showed him being chal-lenged by Simon Magus on the banks of the River Tiber (Acts of Peter). It is not known when the apostle* reached Rome. There he wrote—or rather, most probably inspired—his First Epistle, a letter addressed to the Christians of Asia Minor. In a tone that is, in some aspects, close to that of Romans, this Epistle devotes itself to defining clearly the foundations and the content of life in Christ*. Mark may have gathered at that moment, directly from Peter's mouth, some recollections that he used for the composition of his Gospel* (Papias *ap.* Eusebius, *HE* III, 39, 14–17). In any case, Peter, like Paul, suffered martyrdom* in Rome, most probably at some point between the major fire of the city in 64—which Nero blamed on the Christians—and Nero's death in 68.

If Peter's stay in Rome was an uncontested fact in ancient times (*see* Clement of Rome, *Ep. ad Cor.* 5, 3–7; Ignatius of Antioch, *Ad Rom.* IV, 3; Dionysius of Corinth *ap.* Eusebius of Caesarea, *HE* II, XXV, 8), that was not to be the case in some Waldensian* circles. From the second third of the 13th century, under the umbrella of a vigorous criticism of the Constantinian church (J. Gonnet - A. Molnar, *Les vaudois au Moyen Age,* Turin, 1974), these circles started casting doubt on the truth of Peter's presence in Rome. Their skepticism found an echo with Marsilius of Padua, then later with some Reformed Christians, and even with a few historians of the first half of the 20th century. Today the debate is closed, having been decided in favor of the ancient accounts (Cullmann 1953).

As far as Roman memory is concerned, it is the martyrdom of the two apostles that signals the founding of the church in the city. There is evidence that in 258, on 29 June, there occurred for the first time a celebration marking in common the martyrdom of both Peter and Paul, who were thus associated, on the same day, in this supreme event.

b) Emergence of Self-Representation of the Roman Church (Second and Third Centuries). On the basis of the double apostolic martyrdom, a sort of very special self-consciousness was born and grew quickly in the Roman community, in a way that had no identifiable parallel in any other Christian community whatsoever, at least as far as available sources are concerned; the case of Jerusalem* is poorly documented. We are considering here a mere sketch in a developing process that would require a thousand subtle nuances for a proper description: indeed, an ecclesiological conviction can occur only when speeches and ecclesial practices come into play inseparably (internal evolution of each church, and first of all that of Rome; changes in relations between the various churches; and the relationships of churches to political, social, and cultural shifts). With the church of the martyrdom of Peter and Paul—from around 200, a first monumental-

ization of the "apostles' trophies" (Gaius *ap.* Eusebius, *HE* II, XXV, 7) inscribed in the Roman topography the founding gesture—the community of the city believed itself to be entrusted with a particular sort of authority*, understood first, in its Latin meaning, as "the power to authenticate and to increase the scope of an account" (Pietri 1976), in this case that of the apostles. The Christian groups of the *urbs* were of a great diversity and vitality in the second century and at the beginning of the third: the fame of the Roman church (*see* Origen* *ap.* Eusebius, *HE* VI, 14, 10) and the prestige of the "imperial city" converged to attract to Rome peripatetic theologians and preachers, originating mainly from the Greek East (Valentinus, Cerdo, Marcion, Theodotus, Justin, Tatian, Hegesippus, Praxeas, Aberkios, etc.). And in this "great laboratory" (G. La Piana), the notions of apostolic tradition* and succession underwent a remarkable development. Out of this came the elaboration of a list of incumbents in the *episkopè,* a concomitant, or almost, of the establishment of the monoepiscopate around the middle of the second century (*see* Irenaeus, *Adv. haer.* III, 3, 2–3). A sole president succeeded a collegial administration of the community in the city; the incumbent of that presidency could rightfully be called bishop*. From then on, the burgeoning Roman belief in the church of the city as the authorized trustee of the apostolic tradition and as its interpreter par excellence, found the pastor* of this community to be its most zealous spokesman. Reading *Ep. ad Cor.* by Clement of Rome, then a letter by Dionysius of Corinth to his Roman namesake (*ap.* Eusebius, *HE* II, XXV, 8 et IV, 23, 9–11), and finally the record of the conflict between Victor of Rome and Polycrates of Ephesus regarding the way of determining the date of Easter (Eusebius, *HE* V, 24) is useful in this respect: it allows us to measure the distance covered in one century by the assertiveness of the Roman church in its hold on the essential responsibility it was demanding: it wanted to be a privileged center of reference for the control of ecclesial unity*, and to that effect it made use of circumstances and solicitations of all sorts. Similarly, reading these documents allows us to be informed on the obvious resistance that was aroused among the Eastern Christian communities by the claims of the Roman church. That resistance resulted from the fact that the Eastern Christian communities could often boast equally well of their own apostolic foundation.

The third century played a fundamental role in the forming of the legacy of arguments, themes, and images meant to support the assertiveness of the Roman church. There was an increasingly frequent use of Matthew 16:18 f. in a number of churches, which was intended to legitimize episcopal authority (Tertullian*,

De pudicitia 21, 9–10; Cyprian*, *Ep.* 33, 1; 43, 5, 2; 75, 16, 1). As a probable consequence of this, Peter became the main source of the Roman apostolic succession, which meant that in the long run he came to be considered as the first bishop of the city. The debates from 250 to 257 regarding the matter of the *lapsi* who had left the church at the time of the persecutions and who were asking to be readmitted (Novatian crisis), and principally those debates pertaining to the validity of the baptism* of these schismatics, brought the Roman bishops into particular conflict with the African bishops, who were led by Cyprian of Carthage. This was a decisive moment. Stephen of Rome, pastor of a community that constituted by far the most important association in the city (Eusebius, *HE* VI, 43, 11; Cyprian, *Ep.* 55, 9, 1), defended the Roman position with increasing firmness. That position claimed that "the unity of faith and church finds diversity inappropriate and takes unity of discipline more or less for granted" (Pietri 1976). This position necessarily implied that the apostolic tradition should be closely tied to the Roman tradition, but that was not all: Stephen of Rome wanted to monopolize Matthew 16:18 f. to the sole profit of the Roman see. From then on, the concept of the Roman primacy *(primatus)* was launched (*see* Firmilian of Caesarea *ap.* Cyprian, *Ep.* 75; the two writings by Cyprian of *De unitate ecclesiae* 4–5).

c) On the Way to the Triumph of Roma Christiana *(from Constantine to Leo the Great).* The "new Constantinian context," which manifested itself in the period after the persecutions by Diocletian and the battle of the Milvian Bridge (28 October 312), meant, for the Roman church, an exceptional contribution by the emperor and by his family toward the material establishment of Roman Christendom (Lateran Cathedral and Baptistery, basilicas at the tombs of Peter, Paul, Lawrence, Agnes, and Marcellinus and Peter). These new developments, followed by episcopal and private initiatives, allowed the bishop of the city to create, in a very pragmatic way, a pastoral system that, in the West, was increasingly taking on the appearance of a missionary model: this was based as much on the old division of the urban space into ecclesiastical regions as on the meticulous inventory of the martyrs' holy bodies dispersed in the cemeteries *extra muros* (*see* the action of Damasus, bishop from 366 to 384). The appearance in Rome—one of the principal crucibles, from the third century, for the invention of a specifically Christian imagery—of a body of figurative representations showing the gesture of Peter, who was often assimilated to Moses, guide of the Hebrew people* during the Exodus) is a silent commentary on the progress accomplished by Christianization in the *urbs*.

With the unfolding of events, the Roman church adapted to the customs of the Christian empire, from the Roman arbitration at the time of the early signs of the Donatist exile in 313, through the first Imperial Council* of Arles in 314, and up to the exile, in 356, of Liberius, victim of Constantine II's caesaropapism. Although invited to the Arles council, Pope Sylvester I took no part in it, except through his legates; he thus inaugurated the kind of attitude toward these gatherings that would continue to be that taken by the Roman bishops in the fourth and fifth centuries. The various episodes of the Arian crisis, in which Rome was closely involved from 338, as well as the highly varied demands of the churches and the imperial authorities, contributed to the outlining—not without twists and turns, should conflicts arise among persons with rival ambitions and sometimes rival ecclesiologies—of the features, both real and theoretical, of a Roman primacy that was variously exercised and perceived depending on the occasion and on the Christian communities concerned and their traditions. From the time of Damasus the primacy was assisted by the establishment of a pontifical chancery, by the development of a true "theology of law*" (Pietri), and by bringing together dossiers of *dicta probantia* regarding one or other question. The first decretals (*Ep. ad Gallos*; Innocent, *Ep. ad Decentium*), intended for the promotion of the discipline of the "Apostolic See"—this designation appeared under Liberius (352–66) and gradually became general—are one of the major illustrations of this.

The multifaceted and decisive rise enjoyed by the Roman church saw its climax during the episcopate of Leo the Great (440–61). The unprecedented success obtained by the dogmatic canons of Chalcedon* (451) was echoed by the transfiguration that Leo effected in the *urbs* with his sermons: the city was no longer the Babylon excoriated by 1 Peter 5:13; it was no longer the city born from fratricide; it had become the "holy nation, the Chosen People, the priestly and royal city*, the head of the universe, thanks to the Holy See of the blessed Peter (*Serm.* 82, 1). In this unifying rereading of the history of the *urbs*, , by reworking many of the themes mentioned above, Leo celebrated the wedding of the city and the church, the triumph of *Roma Christiana*.

● L. Duchesne (1886–92), *Le* Liber pontificalis, *texte, introduction et commentaire,* Paris (New Ed. with added materials by C. Vogel, Paris, 1957).

H. Lietzmann (1927), *Petrus und Paulus in Rom,* Berlin.

E. Caspar (1930–33), *Geschichte des Papsttums* I-II, Tübingen.

F. Dölger (1937), "Rom in der Gedankenwelt der Byzantiner," *ZKG* 56, 1–32.

O. Cullmann (1953), *Pierre, disciple, apôtre et martyr,* Neuchâtel.

H. Chadwick (1959), *The Circle and the Ellipse: Rival Concepts of Authority in the Early Church,* Oxford.

H. Fuchs (1964), *Der geistige Widerstand gegen Rom in der antiken Welt,* Berlin.

M. Maccarrone (1976), *Apostolicità, episcopato e primato di Pietro: Ricerche e testimonianze dal II al V secolo,* Rome.

C. Pietri (1976), *Roma christiana: Recherches sur l'Église de Rome, son organisation, sa politique, son idéologie, de Miltiade à Sixte III (311–440),* Rome.

M. Simon (1981), "Remarques sur les origines de la chrétienté romaine," in *Religion et culture dans la cité italienne de l'Antiquité à nos jours, Actes du Colloque du Centre interdisciplinaire de recherches sur l'Italie (8–10 November 1979),* Strasbourg, 40–50.

C. Pietri (1990), "Rome: Histoire et archéologie," *DECA* II, 2182–91.

M. Maccarrone (1991), *Romana Ecclesia Cathedra Petri* I, Rome.

P. Levillain (Ed.) (1994), *Dictionnaire historique de la papauté,* Paris.

M.-Y. Perrin (1996), "La papauté héritière de saint Pierre et de la romanité (des origines à 604)," in Y.-M. Hilaire (Ed.), *Histoire de la papauté: 2,000 ans de mission et de tribulations,* Paris, 19–117.

R. Klein, et al. (1999), "Rom," *TRE* 29, 352–79 (bibl.).

MICHEL-YVES PERRIN

See also **City; Jerusalem; Peter; Political Theology; Pope**

Roscelin of Compiègne. *See* **Anselm of Canterbury; Realism; Tritheism**

Rosmini-Serbati, Antonio. *See* **Ontologism**

Ruusbroec, Jan van. *See* **Rhineland-Flemish Mysticism**

S

Sabbath

1. Biblical Theology

The sabbath is a day that should be "sanctified" (*qdsh*), "kept" (*shmr*). Assimilated in the Torah with the seventh day (*yôm shevî'î*), the sabbath is a day of rest on which all work is prohibited; breaking the sabbath is punishable by death* (Ex 31:15; *see also* Nm 15:32–36). The prophets* and the Chronicler often associate the sabbath with the new moon (*chodesh*) and warn against its profanation (*chillel*). In the New Testament, the sabbath enters into competition with "the first day of the week" (Acts 20:7).

a) Philology. The etymology of the Hebrew term *shabbât* (feminine) is obscure. Genesis 2:2–3 seems to connect it to the verb *shâvat,* "to be idle, to stop working" (*see* Ex 31:17; Lv 23:32), but the derivation is philologically unexplainable, as is the derivation based on the figure seven (in Hebrew, *shèva'*). The Aramaic *shabbât* has been compared to the Acadian *shapattu,* designating the full moon; to the Aramaic *shb,* "revolve"; and to a verb *shbb* attested in Arabic with the meaning "to grow," but no consensus has been reached on these possibilities. The late term *shabbâtôn* is sometimes associated with *shabbât* (Ex 31:15; Lv 23:3). In this form or alone, it also applies to certain days of rest associated with holy days—for example, Yom Kippur (Lv 16:31; *see also* Lv 23:24–39). *Sabbaton* in Greek is a transposition of the Hebrew. It also designates the week.

b) History. Since the Old Testament leaves us in ignorance as to the origin of the sabbath, various hypotheses are advanced. Attempts to explain it by a direct foreign influence (Babylonian, Canaanite, Kenite) have turned out to be unsatisfactory; the sabbath has no parallel in the ancient Orient. Though the weekly sabbath day of rest is cited in all the codes of law*, the institution is not necessarily very ancient. Today, two periods are generally distinguished; it is supposed that before the exile (sixth century B.C.), the sabbath designated the holiday of the full moon, matching the neomenia, or new moon, with which it frequently appears in texts from that period (Hos 2:13; Am 8:5). During the period of exile, according to this theory, the sabbath became the weekly day of rest. There may have been a day of rest for humanitarian reasons before the exile (Ex 23:12; Dt 5:14). If this is so, it would suggest a fusion of the two practices. Whatever the case may be, priestly elements were essential in the development of the sabbath as a central institution of Judaism* (Is 56:1–7; Neh 13:15–22). Sabbath observance was the subject of a casuistry* in first-century Judaism, which left traces in the New Testament and in Talmudic writings. The first Christians continued to practice the sabbath until Sunday* was imposed.

c) Meanings. The essential nature of the precept* of the sabbath is indicated by its central position in both versions of the Ten Commandments (Ex 20:8–11; Dt 5:12–15), with different meanings in each version.

In Exodus 20:11, the interruption of work* is related to God*'s resting on the seventh day of creation* (Gn 2:2–3). The Creator stopped working and assumed a limitation, showing that his power is gentle by mastering his own mastery. And by withdrawing, he liberated a space for that which is other—the universe and especially mankind. In this sense, the sabbath is the day when man shows that he renounces his illusions of superpower and makes room for alterity and the possibility of justice in relations.

In Deuteronomy 5:15, the sabbath is a memorial of the liberation from bondage in Egypt. The seventh day is the day when the Israelite stops working to manifest the liberty* received from YHWH. But this day of rest is also valid for his dependents (Dt 5:14); on the sabbath, man puts his power in the service of the liberty of others, as YHWH used his power to favor the liberty of Israel*. To honor God is to limit one's action by refusing to make one's own house a house of servitude. The practice of sabbatical and jubilee years has a comparable meaning (Lv 25).

Consenting to limits of power and the profits and prestige it produces and recognizing the Other seem to be central elements of the sabbath symbolism. They are the two essential parameters of all covenants*. Thus, it is no surprise that the sabbath is presented as the sign of the covenant between Israel and YHWH. The fact that breaking the sabbath is punished by death emphasizes that the practice of the spirit of the sabbath is vital (Jer 17:19–27; Ez 20:12–13). Conversely, observance of the sabbath opens the door of the chosen people even to foreigners (Is 56:2–7, 58:13–14).

In the New Testament, while retaining the profound meaning of the sabbath as the day when man honors God by working for the dignity and the liberty of his brothers (Mk 1:21–28; Lk 13:10–17; Jn 5:17), Jesus* revitalizes the institution as such (Mk 2:27–28). Hebrews 4:1–11 does the same in offering an eschatological reading of sabbath rest in which it is a sign and prediction of a repose that God constantly offers to his own (commentary on Ps 95:11). The Christian Churches* gave preference to Sunday, the first day of the week, the day of Christ's resurrection*.

● E. Lohse (1960), "Jesu Worte über den Sabbat," in *Judentum, Urchristentum, Kirche,* BZNW 26, Berlin, 80–89.
M. Tsevat (1972), "The Basic Meaning of the Biblical Sabbat," *ZAW* 84, 447–59.
N. Negretti (1973), *Il settimo giorno,* Rome.
P. Grelot (1975), "Du sabbat juif au dimanche chrétien," *MD* 123, 79–107 and 124, 14–54.
Ch. Dietzfelbinger (1978), "Vom Sinn der Sabbatheilungen Jesu," *EvTh* 38, 281–98.
J. Briend (1985), "Sabbat," *DBS* 10, 1132–70.
E. Spier (1989), *Der Sabbat,* Berlin.
L. Laberge (1992), "Sabbat: Étymologie et origines. Étude bibliographique," *ScEs* 44, 205–20.
R. Goldenberg (1998), "Sabbat. I: AT; II: Judentum," *TRE* 29, 518–25.
B. Schaller (1998), "Sabbat. III: Neues Testament," *TRE* 29, 525–27.
J. Kaiser (1998), "Sabbat. IV: Christentum," *TRE* 29, 528–33.

ANDRÉ WÉNIN

See also **Decalogue; Ecology; Jesus, Historical; Law; Scripture, Fulfillment of; Time; Work**

2. History and Systematic Theology

The sabbath, a Jewish cultural institution from which the preaching* of Jesus* took away meaning rather than add to it—to say the least—does not figure in an obvious, necessary way among Christian theological objects. The Jewish origin of the first Christian communities, combined with an autocomprehension that the new "Way" had nothing to renounce in that origin, explains why these communities respected the sabbath. Nonetheless, Christian time* is a "dominical" time that borrows its meaning in that of the commemoration of death* and resurrection and that is organized weekly around Sunday*, which is both the "eighth day," the first day of the week, the day of the resurrection, and the day of Eucharistic *synaxis*. Christian liturgies* hardly kept any memory of the sabbath that is the last day of the Jewish week, and theologians pointedly criticized the vetero-testamentary institution of the sabbath. Referring to John 5:17 it is asserted that the God* of Jesus Christ worked without interruption. It was said that the sabbath was given to the Jews because they are hard-hearted; it was unknown to the patriarchs (*see,* e.g., Justin, *Dial.* 9, 6; 27, 3; 46, 2–3). The sabbath's essential cultual content is henceforth extended to the totality of Christian time (Tertullian*, *Adv. Jud.* 4, 1–5). Or, arguing from Colossians 2:16, the Jewish sabbath was described as but a "shadow" (or "type" or "image") of the eschatological sabbath (e.g., Origen*, *part. Hom. in Num.* 23, 4).

The Christian Church, outlawed or barely tolerated, had to wait until the Peace of the Church and the decision of Constantine in 321 to make Sunday a day of rest on the Jewish model. Although they could do nothing to change it, some in monastic circles, hostile to all laziness, were reticent about this development (Jerome, *Ep.* 108, 20, 3; Palladius, *Hist. Laus.* 59, 2; Benedict, Reg. 48, 22). In fact, the sabbath turned from an "image" into a model for the Christian Sunday (Eusebius of Caesarea, *Comm.* in Ps 91 [92]; John Chrysostom, In *Gen. Hom.*10, 7; Eusebius of Arles, Sermo 16, etc.). By the sixth century an equivalence was established between the sabbath and Sunday (Césaire d'Arles, *Sermo* 10, 3, 5, 2nd Mâcon synod, can. 1, Narbonne synod of, can. 4).

Sunday was seen first as a day of rest, compulsory rest, inscribed in the laws of the Church and the empire as well. Of course the liturgical meanings and exigencies were never obscured. Because Sunday is the day when profane and laborious relations are suspended, it is the day when the Christian can and must "attend to God." The precept* itself remained rather thin: abstain from "servile works"* and participate in the eucharistic assembly (see *CEC* 2192–93). This rudimentary legislation explains why Christianity never developed a casuistry* of Sunday comparable to the Jewish casuistry of the sabbath. But it was not until recent theology* that the eucharistic meaning of Sunday predominated over its sabbatical meaning.

A remarkable case of sabbatization arose in English and Scottish Protestantism*. In 1595, N. Bound, in *The True Doctrine of the Sabbath,* strongly argued in favor of strict application of the vetero-testamentary precepts, or "sabbatarianism" (see Cox 1853). The argument was widely accepted in Puritan circles. Lengthy public controversies followed in the course of which the Puritan sabbath was imposed three times by the legislature (in 1644, 1650, and 1655), with regulations prohibiting all forms of entertainment on Sunday. The Puritan Sunday was attenuated by Charles II in the Restoration, practiced in extreme forms in Scotland, and did not really fade out until the end of the 19th century.

Finally, in the 20th century, two factors—liturgical renewal in Catholicism* and a new theological interest in the Jewish experience in all Christianity—led to a fine distinction of eucharistic meanings and sabbatical meanings, a rejuvenated theology of Sunday as the eucharistic day, and a first Christian reception* of the Jewish spirituality of the sabbath. Whereas medieval theology treated the sabbath only within the elaboration of criteria for defining elements of Jewish law that remain valid and those that are no longer binding on Christians (the solely "ceremonial" precepts), the contemporary rediscovery of Israel*, ratified and stimulated by the Second Vatican Council, is a discovery of the mystery* of Israel, and with regard to the sabbath, it is primarily a question of spirituality.

Under the powerful influence of Abraham Heschel, the sabbath no longer appeared as a tissue of legalistic constraints. Distinct from the pagan *otium* or *ataraxie,* a theological experience of the day of rest lends itself to development in such a way that Christianity can adopt it

as its own (Sales 1994). Some Christian communities, generally issuing from charismatic renewal, adopted a sabbath liturgy conceived as a vetero-testamentary preparation of the neotestamentary joy of Sunday (e.g., the community of the Beatitudes; *see* Doze 1993).

Though a Christian theology of time is commonly organized by the temporal horizons of the eucharistic celebration (memorial, anticipation, and sacramental presence of the eschaton), the thematic of the sabbath seems indispensable for the appearance of other temporal horizons—such as that of life created and blessed by God, which man can enjoy peacefully in praising the gift that gave him to himself (*see* J.-Y. Lacoste, *RMM* 100 [1995], 198–200; *CEC* 2169–72). Then the sabbath is not seen as a Jewish reality replaced by the Christian reality of Sunday or as a vetero-testamentary rough version of the Christian Sunday but as an ensemble of meaningful gestures that can be received by Christians with respect for its specific religious intention. Moreover, respect for the sabbath is inscribed in a decalogue* where theology classically sees the expression of a "natural law" that obliges all men as men. Therefore, the sabbath gives food for thought not only to liturgical theology and the liturgical pastoral but more broadly to the philosophy of religion* and the theology of religions.*

● R. Cox (1883), *Sabbat Laws and Sabbat Duties,* London.
A. Heschel (1951), *The Sabbath*: *Its Meaning for Modern Man,* New York.
H. Huber (1958), *Geist und Buchstabe der Sonntagsruhe: Eine historisch-theologische Untersuchung über das Verbot der knechtlichen Arbeit von der Urkirche bis auf Thomas von Aquin,* STMP 5.
W. Rordorf (1962), *Der Sonntag. Geschichte des Ruhe- und Gottesdiensttages im ältesten Christentum,* Zurich, 79–171.
W. Rordorf (1972), *Sabbat et dimanche dans l'Église ancienne,* Bern-Neuchâtel (coll. of patristic sources).
S. Bacchiocci (1984), *Du sabbat au dimanche,* Paris.
W. Rordorf (1990), "Dimanche" et "Sabbat," *DECA* I, 690–93, II, 2204–5.
E. Haag (1991), *Vom Sabbat zum Sonntag,* Trier.
E. Bianchi (1992), *Le jour du Seigneur: Pour un renouveau du dimanche,* Paris.
A. Doze (1993), *Joseph, gardien du Shabbat,* Nouans-le-Fuzelier, 19–30, 38–40, and passim.
P. Haudebert (1993), "Sabbat," *Cath* 13, 238–40.
M. Sales (1994), "L'accomplissement du sabbat," *Com(F)* XIX/1, 11–30.
B. Schaller (1994), *Jesus und der Sabbat,* Münster.
C. Körting et al. (1999), "Sabbat," *TRE* 29, 518–33 (bibl.).

GALAHAD THREEPWOOD

See also **Cult; Sunday; Time; Work**

Sabbelianism. *See* Modalism

Sacrament

---

1. *The Semantic Field of* Mustèrion *and* Sacramentum

The Greek word *mustèrion,* translated in the Latin Bibles* by its Latin cognate *mysterium* or by *sacramentum* (e.g., Eph 5:32), is at the origin of our word *sacrament. Mustèrion* is relatively rare in the Old Testament (appearing approximately 15 times); it is found only in late works coming out of either apocalyptic* literature (nine times, e.g., in Daniel), in which it designates the revelation by God*, through dreams and visions, of his secret purpose for the definitive establishment of his kingdom, or from the tradition of wisdom* texts (three times in the Wisdom of Solomon), where we can detect a Hellenistic transposition of the term that comes from the language of the mystery cults to integrate itself into the language of the initiation into *sophia.* The 28 occurrences of the term in the New Testament depend principally on the Jewish apocalyptic usage: the disciples (Mt 13:11; Mk 4:11) or Paul (Eph 3:2–6) are the recipients of the revelation* of the "mystery*" of God in the world in the person of Jesus Christ, which authorizes Paul to assimilate "the mystery of Christ*" to the "mystery of God" (Col 2:2; Eph 5:32); furthermore, he can extend the term to the Church*, to the Church as spousally united to Christ (Eph 5:32) and as eschatologically gathering the peoples in him by the reconciliation of Jew and Gentile (Eph 3:5f.). As a result, although "mystery" still to some degree connotes a secret of God concerning his "benevolent purpose" for the world* (Eph 1:9), it is no longer intended, like the pagan mysteries, to be hidden. On the contrary, it is the subject of a public proclamation (Rom 16:25f.), and it is now made visible even among the Gentiles (because the mystery is "Christ among you"; Col 1:27); and the apostolic ministry* has precisely no other purpose but "to proclaim the mystery of the gospel" (Eph 6:19), in the ministers' capacity as "stewards of the mystery of God" (1 Cor 4:1).

It is notable that "mystery" is never used in the New Testament in a cultic sense; the mystery is entered into by "the grace* of God" (Eph 3:2, 8) and not through the activity of a master mystagogue. Nevertheless, its essential link to the person* of Christ, as well as to the body of the Church, because of that entity's dependence on Christ, or even (at least indirectly) to the apostolic ministry, left the door open to a broader usage, encompassing the mediations through which mystery is proclaimed by the Church*, principally Baptism* and the Eucharist*. Nevertheless, it was to the Scriptures*, as the fundamental mediation of the revelation of God in Christ, that the fathers* of the church first applied the vocabulary of mystery. Indeed, the Scriptures contain a multiplicity of *mustèria/sacramenta* relating to Christ, to the Church, to moral life, and to eschatological consummation, which patristic exegesis* endeavored to decipher down to the smallest details. "*Sacramentum,* that is, any saying of the sacred writings" (Augustine*, *Ep.* 55. 38); "every term contains a *sacramentum;* in each word there is a *mysterium*" (Jerome, *Tract. in Ps.,* ed. Morin, *Anal. Mar.* 3, p. 33). All the Fathers, Greek as well as Latin, whether from Antioch or Alexandria, could have adopted these formulations. All of them read the great moments of the divine story narrated by the Scriptures (creation*, flood, sacrifice* of Abraham, story of Joseph, Exodus, and so on) as so many "mysteries" or "sacraments." And all of them did so following 1 Corinthians 6:11, which stood as the fundamental principle for a Christian hermeneutics: all those events were a "figure" of the realization that would come in Christ.

The application of the vocabulary of mystery to the ritual activities of the Church was slower in coming. It was initiated, with a good deal of caution, early in the third century (Clement of Alexandria, *Strom.* IV. 1; see *Protr.* 12. 20) and went through a much greater development in the following century. This caution can probably be explained by the risks of confusion with pagan mysteries; there was at the time a tendency "to exclude words that in one way or another were related to contemporary pagan cults" (Mohrmann 1958), which were in any case easily accused of being nothing but diabolical counterfeits of Christian rites (Justin, *1 Ap.* 25–27; 68). In the fourth century, on the other hand, a period when Christians adopted many symbols and metaphors from a paganism* that had lost its social force (*see* Jourjon, *MD* 119, 1974), "mystery" or "sacrament" (often equivalent terms for the Latin Fathers, e.g., in Augustine; *see* C. Couturier, *Études augustiniennes,* 1953) very commonly designated not only the Scriptures but also Christian cult*, whether a ceremony as a whole (baptism, Eucharist, ordination*) or one particular element in it (anointing with holy oil*, sign of the cross, rite of salt, and so on).

It was Tertullian* who gave the Latin *sacramentum* official Christian status as a translation of the Greek *mustèrion.* However, *sacramentum* added a new legal color to the Greek (the first sense was a surety deposited in the temple by each of the two parties to a trial and the oath accompanying this deposit). It could easily be applied to Christian rites, beginning with baptism, the sacrament of the swearing of faith (*sacramentum fidei*). On the other hand, it brought along with it legal connotations that risked gradually cutting it off from the semantic domain of the "Word*," whereas the Greek *mustèrion* had sufficient semantic strength to keep alive its relation to the *mustèria* of the Scripture.

This danger of distortion, however, became obvious only at the end of a long process of development. For during the first millennium (and even beyond), the feeling of the relation between the ritual mysteries and the biblical mysteries was so vivid that there was a constant movement with no discontinuity from Scriptures to liturgy, with ritual, to a large extent, seen as the presentation of the *sacramenta* of the Scriptures. The sacraments were also included within the vast and dynamic economy of salvation* attested to by the Scriptures; through the Holy Spirit*, they actualized that economy in a salvific event.

In the Syriac Churches, the term *raza* (plural *razé*), frequent in the fourth and fifth centuries in Aphraate, Ephrem, Theodore of Mopsueste, and Narsaï, went through a development rather similar to that of the Greek *mustèrion,* with perhaps a greater emphasis on the dimension of the "hidden" or the "enigmatic" on the one hand and the eschatological dimension on the other (Dalmais 1990).

2. The Controversies over Baptism and Ordination

There were no controversies during the patristic period over what would later be called the efficacy of the sacraments. Whether we read the *Apologies* of Justin or the eucharistic writings of Irenaeus* in the second century, Tertullian's treatise or Cyprian*'s letters in the third century, or the mystagogic catecheses* of the Greeks or Latins in the fourth century, it appears everywhere that baptism, "sealed" by the laying on of hands* and/or chrismal anointing by the bishop* and completed by participation in the eucharistic body of Christ, marked the passage from the kingdom of death* and sin* to the kingdom of life and grace. Controversies had to do with other points, with the two major ones concerning the ecclesial conditions of this salvific efficacy and the question of infant baptism.

The first debate took place in the time of Cyprian, in the middle of the third century. Cyprian, followed by all the bishops of Africa, considered baptisms or ordinations carried out by schismatic or heretical groups (Novatians, Montanists, and so on) that had set themselves up as separate communities to be invalid. His argument was not on moral but on ecclesiological grounds: there was no Holy Spirit but in the Church, and without the Holy Spirit, no salvation was possible; therefore, those who had cut themselves off from the Church (who had broken the *unitas* or the *pax ecclesiae*), not having the Holy Spirit, could not bestow it: they had removed themselves from the possibility of salvation (*see* particularly *Ep.* 69, 70, 73). Therefore, those who returned to the *Catholica* had to be rebaptized (or reordained). As firm as Cyprian was in this position, Stephen, the bishop of Rome*, took the opposite position. He criticized the Africans for adopting a position that was not traditional: "there should be no innovation except according to what has been transmitted." For someone returning from heresy*, it was enough to lay on hands "for penance"—"that he might receive the Holy Spirit" was a clarification made by the Council* of Arles in 314 (can. 8), whereas the Council of Nicaea (325) assumed the rebaptism of those who had been baptized with an orthodox formula interpreted in a heterodox way (can. 19) (*DS* 123, 127–28).

The controversy resumed in the fourth century with the Donatists (Donatism*), who proclaimed, relying on Cyprian, the invalidity of baptisms and ordinations conferred outside their Church. The theological problem was resolved by Augustine* by means of a threefold distinction: 1) between Christ, who alone has the *potestas* to save and the baptizer who exercises only a simple *ministerium,* so that Christ acts "even through a bad minister"; 2) between the *sacramentum* and its effect (its *virtus*), so that the sacrament can be true (*non vacuum, non inane*—"valid" in the late Middle Ages in a more legalistic perspective) even if not spiritually fruitful; and, finally, 3) between the Church as "sacramental communion*" (*communio sacramentorum*) and the Church as "spiritual communion" (*societas sanctorum,* communion of saints). The Donatists belonged to the former, and their sacraments were therefore "true," and Augustine could say to them, "You are our brothers." But they did not belong to the latter, which alone was animated by the Holy Spirit, and their sacraments were therefore unfruitful, devoid of salvific effects (*see* Congar 1963). The problem of ordination was treated according to the same principles.

Augustine's contribution was twofold. On the one hand, he made it clear that the gift of God in the *sacramenta* is supremely free because it does not depend on the subjective dispositions of the minister or the receiving subject and, on the other, that the reception of this gift as a gift (its fruitfulness) depends on the personal dispositions of the subject: "Each one receives according to his faith*," he writes, in this case speaking about baptism. The clarity of this position nevertheless has another side: can personal dispositions be totally separated in this way from the "validity*" of the sacrament? (On the views of the Greek Fathers, *see* Villette 1959.)

3. Isidore of Seville (Seventh Century) and the Sacrament as Secret

Particularly noteworthy in the early Middle Ages was the connection of *sacramentum* to *sacrum secretum* in the *Etymologies* of Isidore of Seville (VI. 19), whereas Augustine had associated it with *sacrum signum.* The fact is important because Isidore's definition was to govern Latin theology* until early in the 12th century and because it drew attention not to the revelatory aspect of the Augustinian "sign" but to the aspect of a mystery hidden under the veil (*tegumentum*) of the sacrament.

It is precisely this sensitivity to the sacramental "veil" that explains the first controversy in history* on the presence of Christ in the Eucharist. In the ninth century two monks of Corbie, Paschasius Radbert and Ratramnius, disputed this point. The problem arose because the latter began with a theory of knowledge according to which *veritas* is "the designation of an unveiled thing," whereas *figura* designates the thing in a veiled way. Hence, the sacraments, defined as a "veil" hiding an *aliquid secretum,* are necessarily "figures"; and if Christ is indeed "truly" present in the Eucharist, it is *in figura* and not *in veritate.* This controversy would have had only limited consequences had it not been taken up again in the 11th century by Berengar of Tours, whose dialectical rationalism*, linked to certain theories of the grammarians of the period and in reaction against the then dominant "sensualist" or ultrarealist representations,

was no longer able to understand the "truly in figure" of Ratramnius except as meaning "not really." It is clear in any event that the theory of the sacraments needed to be refined.

4. The Development of the Concept of Sacramentum *in the 12th Century*

The refinement was the work of the Scholasticism of the 12th and 13th centuries. At the time, *sacramentum* had become the generally prevalent term in ritual language. But in this field alone the theologians of the first half of the 12th century enumerated, variously and with no intention of establishing an exhaustive list, four (Lanfranc), five (Abelard*), 10 (Bernard* of Clairvaux), and 12 (Peter Damien) *sacramenta.* Thanks to the new technique of the *quaestio,* the new *scolares* implemented what was the entire program of the century: "faith developing into science" (M.-D. Chenu, *La Théologie au XIIᵉ siècle,* 1956). The "symbolic mentality" (ibid.) of the Romanesque age was certainly still very much alive, but it was gradually controlled and organized. And under the impetus of this new cultural imperative, there arose the hitherto unknown need to explain the "specific difference" of the sacraments strictly speaking and, by the same token, to provide an exhaustive list of them.

Three major milestones can be identified in this complex operation: 1) The Augustinian definition of sacrament as *sign* recovered its primacy over Isidore's definition of sacrament as *secret* (Alger of Liège, c. 1120). 2) A distinction was then made between "major" and "minor" sacraments (the latter beginning to be called "sacramentals" in the 1140s), depending on whether or not they were directly concerned with salvation (Abelard, Hugh of Saint Victor). 3) But because this criterion of finality with relation to salvation was insufficient—according to it, indeed, Jewish circumcision belonged to the major sacraments and marriage* to the minor—recourse was made to the criterion of causality, which was so important in the Aristotelian philosophy* that invaded the intellectual life of the West from the 1160s. There is nothing at all surprising in this because "the notion of cause is no doubt the most significant aspect" of the great project of the time for a theology* adopting a "scientific" apparatus (Chenu).

The criterion of causality was therefore decisive with respect to the "sacraments of the old law," such as circumcision or the sacrifice* of the paschal lamb*. It came to be said that these *sacramenta* certainly justified our Jewish fathers, but they did so only *ex opere operantis* (through the work of the acting subject, i.e., through his subjective dispositions to faith). Thus, "they merely signified the grace of Christ but did not cause it," whereas the "sacraments of the new law*," "effecting what they figure," "contain it and confer it" (Thomas* Aquinas, *ST* IIIa q. 62 a. 6; and before him Peter Lombard, *Sent.* IV. d. 1. 5, PL 192. 839). These sacraments do so *ex opere operato* (Trent*, *DS* 1608), through their innate virtue, which comes to them from Christ. This expression, of course, does not imply anything mechanical or magical; on the contrary, it means, negatively, that the gift of salvation remains totally free on the part of God with respect to any merit or lack of merit in the individual (minister or receiver) and, positively, that the sacramental act of the Church is an act of Christ himself. Shortly before 1160, Peter Lombard provided a list of the seven rites of the Church, which, as "signs" and "causes" of the grace of God (*Sent.* IV. d. 1. 2), "properly" deserve the name of sacrament (d. 2. 1). It is this list, mentioned at Lateran IV* in 1215, that was adopted dogmatically by Lyon II* in 1274 (*DS* 860), Florence* in 1439 (*DS* 1310), and finally Trent in 1547 (*DS* 1601).

The establishment of the seven sacraments (baptism, confirmation*, the Eucharist, penance*, extreme unction, holy orders, and matrimony) was, however, not simply or even firstly, the result of an intellectual operation. The practice of the Church was as decisive as theory. For example, penance and matrimony fit very badly with the new theory because a number of 12th-century theologians considered that God granted his forgiveness as soon as the sinner turned toward him in a movement of contrition and that marriage constituted more a "remedy for concupiscence" than a source of grace properly speaking. And although, despite these theoretical difficulties, the theologians of the time (with some notable exceptions) recognized them as belonging to the seven, this was because of the importance that the Church in fact attributed to them in its liturgical practice (an excellent example of the adage "*lex orandi, lex credendi*"). A rite that effectively proclaimed the forgiveness of God that was always offered to sinners could not be considered secondary. And as for marriage, recognized by Paul as a *sacramentum* (according to the Vulgate) of the faithful love* of Christ for the Church (Eph 5:32), it too could not fail to be accepted as a genuine sacrament, whatever the theoretical difficulties that that acceptance might otherwise entail. These theological themes would not, however, have been able to prevail if the dispensation of these two sacraments by the Church had not at the same time adopted a stronger framework (shift to private penance in the 12th century, with an emphasis on precise identification of serious sins to the priest*; increasing importance during the same period of the role of the priest as official witness of the Church in the ritual of matrimony) and if the Church

had not simultaneously invested in them its intention to exercise social control.

It does not appear that the symbolism of numbers played a role in the organization of the seven sacraments. It was only afterward that the Scholastics permitted themselves considerations of this kind that nevertheless did appeal to them: there were seven sacraments, just as there were seven deadly sins, seven gifts of the Holy Spirit, and seven principal virtues (three theological and four cardinal). But they did not make this into a principle of deduction; they saw it rather as an opportunity, according to a more or less natural inclination at the time, to provide allegorical interpretations for the seven sacraments that had already been accepted.

5. *Some Specific Points*

a) An Analogical Concept. It is appropriate to point out first that the concept of sacrament is analogical. On the one hand, this is not held to be equally true in respect to each of the seven sacraments. Following patristic tradition, two "principal" sacraments are recognized: baptism (which, early on, included a special rite associated with the Holy Spirit, this being later called "confirmation") and the Eucharist. (This point is obviously not without ecumenical significance today because the churches that came out of the Reformation recognize these two sacraments.) Note particularly that it is the sacraments of Christian initiation*, those through which one becomes a full participant in the paschal mystery of Christ through the Holy Spirit, that constitute the fundamental sacraments. By the same token, it is in relation to them that the others must be understood, whether they are retrospective (penance, extreme unction) or whether they consecrate the path of life on which each person, according to his or her specific vocation, is called to assume those sacraments: a particular function in the Church (ordained ministries* of bishop, priest, or deacon*) or state of life (marriage and religious profession, the latter, of course, not one of the seven sacraments because it merely extends baptismal consecration into a more fully developed logic, but it should nevertheless be understood as a sacramental and can in any event be understood only in a sacramental framework).

On the other hand, the fact that the medieval concept of sacrament was produced through the manifestation of two specific differences, with the sacraments "of the old law*" on one side and the sacramentals on the other, requires that we not isolate the seven sacraments from the larger world of the sacramental. Analogy* makes it possible to understand the seven sacraments, themselves hierarchically differentiated and "not equal among themselves" (Trent, can. 3, on the sacraments in general, *DS* 1603), within a larger gradation of the sacramental, either from the point of view of the unique biblical economy of salvation (the Scholastics, as we have seen, had no hesitation in speaking of New Testament *sacramenta*) or from the point of view of their relation to "sacramentals." We must of course acknowledge that the somewhat anxious search for the specific difference or the relevant characteristic that defines the sacraments properly speaking has fostered a kind of fascination with the seven rites that, alone, "cause what they signify," the seven then tending to eclipse the general sacramentality within which they find their meaning.

b) Sacramentals. The *Code of Canon Law* defines sacramentals as "sacred signs through which, in a certain way which imitates the sacraments, primarily spiritual effects are signified and obtained at the prayer* of the Church" (can. 1166; *see* Vatican II*, GS 50 §1).

Two characteristics are worth noting: sacramentals exist in a relation of analogy to the sacraments, of which they are, as "sacred signs," a kind of "imitation." And their efficacy is linked to "the prayer of the Church." These then are signs that can be said to be instituted by the Church and not by Christ, and they do not act *ex opere operato* like the sacraments but *ex opere operantis Ecclesiae,* which means that their efficacy is not tied primarily to the personal dispositions of subjects but to the prayer of the Church itself. This shows itself perfectly clearly in the perspective of Thomas Aquinas, who "never speaks of sacramentals except on the occasion of the sacraments to which they are related," as indicated by the term *sacramentalia,* which does not mean "little sacraments" or "imitations of sacraments," but "things related to the sacraments" (Roguet 1951).

This is the perspective in which theologians have considered, in the case of baptism, prebaptismal unction, exorcisms*, or the blessing* of water, and in relation to the Eucharist, the consecration of an altar. Sacramentals "dispose us toward the sacraments," wrote Thomas (*ST* IIIa q. 65. a. 1. ad 6; q. 66. a. 10).

More broadly, we can consider as belonging to the sacramentals, and even in their first rank, certain recognized rituals in which the Church reveals itself in its pure form, according to its function of intercession or praise*, for example, the taking of religious or monastic vows, the institution of a lay ministry, the communitarian celebration of reconciliation without absolution, the prayer of the divine office, and Christian funeral rites. These various celebrations, although not sacraments in the strict sense, are nevertheless weighted with the "sacramental," and they may be of great importance in the spiritual life of persons and even in the life of the Church as a whole. In a perspective of spiritual and ecclesiastical life, the degree of importance given to particular liturgical celebrations is not determined in relation to the boundary, however precious and indeed indispensable, between what is a sacrament in the strict sense and what is not. We are rather dealing with a kind of sacramental nebula, with a central kernel that is denser (the sacraments of initiation crowned by the Eucharist), and, orbiting around its gravitational mass, sacramentals of lesser density. The Eastern Churches, with a tradition and a sensibility not very inclined toward the precision of the Latins, fit rather well into this perspective. For example, the Orthodox Churches also recognize seven sacraments, but for them the theory hardly plays the role it does in the Latin Church. In any event, if we do not think of the sacraments primarily in the register of "things" (as the Greek Fathers tended to do when they focused attention on the sanctification [*théiopoièse*] of matter and as Isidore of Seville later tended to do) but rather in the register of action (liturgical action); or, in the language of Thomas, if we do not rely primarily on the notion of efficacy but on the notion of "sign," we are then invited to integrate into the world of the sacramental not only the seven sacraments but also sacramentals and to think of all these liturgical gestures, as the fathers of the church did, in the relationship of "fulfillment" that links them to the New Testament sacraments. We thus attain an "organic and systemic representation" (Roguet 1951) of the sacramental.

c) The Institution of the Sacraments by Jesus Christ. This question was not posed as such in the early Church. Reference was simply made, as to a practical norm, to the gestures and words of the Lord acting in the rites of his Church, as we can see in Irenaeus (baptism: *Dem. praed. ap.,* 3; the Eucharist, against the Gnostics: *Adv. Haer.* IV. 17. 5) or in Cyprian (the Eucharist, against the Aquarians: *Ep.* 63. 14). More profoundly, John Chrysostom* (*Cat. bapt.* 3. 17) and Augustine (*In Io. Ev.,* tract. 120) saw in "the water and the blood" that flowed from the side of Christ "asleep" on the cross the source of baptism and the Eucharist and hence of the Church.

It is precisely the conviction that Christ and therefore God is the life-giving source of every sacrament that constitutes the significance of the problem of their institution. What is in question here is not primarily the determination of the exact words (the "form") and the materials to be used (the "matter"); it was not until the 16th century, in the context of the polemic with Reformation thinkers, that Catholic controversialists pursued this kind of demonstration. But in the Scholastic period, to say that Christ was the *institutor* of the sacraments was to say that he was their *auctor,* a term to be understood in the strong sense of "author-actor." According to Thomas's formulation, this meant that, "because the virtue of the sacraments comes from God alone, it follows that God alone instituted the sacraments" (IIIa q. 64. a. 2), more precisely, Christ as God (ibid., ad 1). With this principle established, it was then possible to accept "easily an institution that was mediately divine" (Y. Congar, *Conc[F]* 31, 1968) in such a way that the precise determination of the matter and the form might have been left by Christ to the Church aided by the Holy Spirit (*see,* e.g., Bonaventure*, *Brevil.* VI. 4. 1). For the Scholastics, in any event, the institution of the sacraments by Christ was the subject of a theological conclusion, and the controversialists of the 16th century ran into a dead end by attempting to make it into the subject of a historical demonstration.

In 1907 the decree *Lamentabili* condemned the modernist proposition that asserted that "the sacraments owe their origin to the fact that the apostles* and their successors interpreted the thinking and intention of Christ stimulated by the pressure of circumstances and events" (no. 40). But the proposition was considered false principally because it presupposed that circumstances and events randomly imposed an "interpretation" and the appearance of an institution and that other circumstances would have imposed other interpretations that were just as legitimate (*see* Rondet 1972). In any event, this question has now been settled because it has been dealt with on its proper, theological grounds and in the framework of the general sense of the Church as sacramental (*see* K. Rahner* 1960).

d) Character. Heir to a doctrine that had become common in the Scholastic period, the Council of Trent affirmed that "the three sacraments of baptism, confirmation, and holy orders instill into the soul a character, that is, an indelible spiritual mark which makes it impossible to repeat them" (*DS* 1609). The fathers of the church had frequently applied to baptism and anointing the Pauline image of the spiritual "seal" (1 Cor 1:21f.), a seal authenticating an official document or a mark of belonging as indelible as a mark (*spragis, character, signaculum*) branded on an animal's skin or a tattoo set by a pagan mystagogue on an initiate into the "mysteries" of a divinity or by a military leader on the bodies of his soldiers. The Scholastics, however, did not see in this indelible character merely a mark of definitive belonging to the "flock" or to the "army" of Christ. They distinguished it by the name *res et sacramentum* from sanctifying grace properly speaking (*res sacramenti*), which is the essential gift of the sacrament. Joined to an idea derived from Augustine (*see* 2

above), this distinction helped them differentiate the valid reception of a sacrament and its spiritual fruitfulness: it is possible to have received baptism or orders in full truth and therefore to be marked with the corresponding "character" even though these sacraments may not be subjectively fruitful. If the subject later returns to God through conversion*, he does not need to be baptized, confirmed, or ordained again: the sacrament recovers its normal efficacy that had earlier been prevented by the evil inclinations of the subject (question of the "revival" of a sacrament: Thomas, *In IV Sent.,* d. 4. q. 3. a. 2. qª 3; *ST* IIIa q. 69. a. 10).

6. The Reformation of the 16th Century and the Council of Trent

The principal motive behind the reaction of Reformation thinkers was an excessive concentration by the Church on the sacraments at the expense 1) of a "word of God" that deserved precedence (the principle of "Scripture alone," *Scriptura sola*) and 2) of the subjective commitment of believers. The restoration of the importance of the Scriptures as *norma normans* of the faith of the Church led them as a result to retain only two sacraments, baptism and Holy Communion, and to exclude as "human inventions" the other alleged five, the practice of which was not based on Scripture. (That said, Luther* hesitated over penance, and Melanchthon explicitly acknowledged it as a "sacrament properly speaking" in 1531; and in 1562 Calvin* declared his readiness to acknowledge that the laying on of hands for ordination could "be called a sacrament when it was performed properly:" *Inst.* IV. 19. 31.) In other respects, Reformation writers saw the sacraments as events in the preaching* of the Word: the sacraments, according to Calvin, served to "sign, confirm, and certify [it] more strongly" (ibid., IV. 14. 3). As a result the emphasis was necessarily placed on the faith by which subjects responded to the word promising the remission of sins so that "it is not the sacrament but faith in the sacrament that justifies" (Luther, *WA* 57, 169). This was the point that provoked the principal reaction from the Council of Trent: to assert that God bestowed the grace of salvation not through the sacraments as such but "through faith alone" (can. 4), a faith that their sole purpose was to "foster" (can. 5), amounted to denying that they "contain the grace that they signify" and that they "bestow it on those who place no obstacles in the way" (can. 6) (*DS* 1604–6).

7. Contemporary Perspectives

a) Ecumenicism. As indicated by the numerous documents setting out agreements on the doctrine of the sacraments that have been signed by various Churches over the course of the past 30 years, most points of discord have now been overcome. The difference of liturgical traditions between Orthodox and Catholic Churches in no way prevents theological unanimity on the essential question. Between the Churches that came out of the Reformation and the Roman Church, two questions remain particularly difficult: first, the question of ministries, and, second, the question of the Eucharist (although the theologies of the eucharistic presence have sometimes become extremely close, particularly among Catholics, Anglicans, and Lutherans). Besides, a document such as *Baptism, Eucharist, Ministry* (known as the Lima document, 1982), worked out by the Ecumenical Council of Churches, shows very clearly the convergences of faith that exist among Churches on these questions without in any way concealing the real problems that remain, notably with respect to ministries (*see* the reactions to the *BEM* by representatives of various Churches in *MD* 163, 1985).

b) Rediscoveries. Catholic sacramental thinking substantially shifted in the course of the 20th century, first of all because of influences from within the Church. The revival of biblical and patristic studies in the Church, as well as of studies of the history of the liturgy and of ecclesiology*, played a significant role. While not in any way denying the medieval and early modern past of the Church, Vatican II presented to it the principal results of that movement. We may point to at least four: a return to liturgical action itself (celebration) as the first "locus* theologicus" of thinking about the sacraments; a recentering of the liturgy as a whole on the paschal mystery of Christ (death, resurrection*, and parousia*), of which the sacraments are the "memorial" (*see* particularly eucharistic anamnesis); a counterbalancing of the christological principle, predominant in Latin liturgy and sacraments, with a pneumatological principle that has always been a moving force in the East as well as in the Calvinist tradition (invocations of the Holy Spirit—epicleses*—for the sanctification of baptismal water and the bread and wine of the Eucharist or for the ordination of bishops, priests, and deacons are significant in this respect); and an understanding of the sacraments within the general sacramental character of the Church (a point that sometimes raises difficulties for Protestant theologians, however, because they have a different understanding of the Church and its role in the mystery of faith).

c) Openings. There have also been important contributions from outside the Church, notably in the influence of the social sciences and the philosophy of language. The work of ethnologists and analysts of rituals has made it possible to discover that ritual activity

constitutes a specific form of expression, with its own ancient basis, following particular laws and producing vital symbolic effects in social, institutional, and psychological contexts and in the search for identity. Sociology has shown the importance of the legitimacy of roles, functions, procedures, and institutional mediations in the processes of identification and the attribution of various statuses. Psychoanalysis has made it possible to grasp ceremonial staging as a reactivation of the hidden order of desire. For its part, linguistics has led analysts of the sacraments to an awareness of the wide variety of speech acts in the liturgy. Although not professional members of these various disciplines, many theologians have become sufficiently familiar with them to derive from them conceptual tools suited to a renewal of liturgical and sacramental theology and pastoral care. This nevertheless requires on their part a particular epistemological vigilance in order to avoid methodologically inappropriate "recoveries" and to remain on their own ground: to propose a discourse whose subject is indeed God and the "salvation" that he brings through Jesus Christ and in the strength of the Holy Spirit through the sacraments.

● A. Michel (1939), "Sacrement," *DThC* 14/1, 485–644.
A. M. Roguet (Ed.) (1951), *Thomas d'Aquin, Somme théologique*: *Les sacrements*, Paris-Tournai-Rome.
Chr. Mohrmann (1958, 1965), "'Sacramentum' dans les plus anciens textes chrétiens," dans *Études sur le latin des chrétiens*, Rome, vol. I, 233–44; vol. III, 181–82.
L. Villette (1959, 1964), *Foi et sacrement*, vol. 1: *Du NT à saint Augustin*, vol. 2: *De saint Thomas à K. Barth.*
K. Rahner (1960), *Kirche und Sakramente*, Fribourg.
E. Schillebeeckx (1960), *Le Christ, sacrement de la rencontre de Dieu*, Paris.
Y. Congar (1963), "Introduction générale à Augustin," *Traités anti-donatistes*, vol. I, BAug 28, 7–133.
D. Michaelides (1971), *Sacramentum chez Tertullien*, EAug, Paris.
H. Rondet (1972), *La vie sacramentaire*, Paris.
Y. Congar (1975), *Un peuple messianique: L'Église, sacrement du salut*, Paris.
R. Didier (1975), *Les sacrements de la foi: La Pâque dans ses signes*, Paris.
J. Ambaum (1980), *Glaubenszeichen: Schillebeeckx' Auffassung von den Sakramenten*, Ratisbonne.
Y. Congar (1980), *Je crois en l'Esprit Saint*, vol. III: *Le Saint-Esprit et les sacrements*, Paris, 279–351.
J. Finkenzeller (1980, 1981), *Die Lehre von den Sakramenten im allgemeinen*, vol. 1: *Von der Schrift bis zur Scholastik*, vol. 2: *Von der Reformation bis zur Gegenwart*, HDG IV/1 a and IV/1 b (standard reference).
M. Jourjon (1981), *Les sacrements de la liberté chrétienne selon l'Église ancienne*, Paris.
J.E. Desseaux (1982), *Dialogues théologiques et accords œcuméniques*, Paris.
A. Ganoczy (1984), *Einführung in die katholische Sakramentenlehre*, Darmstadt.
A. Duval (1985), *Des sacrements au concile de Trente*, Paris.
J. Guillet (1985), *Entre Jésus et l'Église*, Paris.

L.-M. Chauvet (1987), *Symbole et sacrement: Une relecture sacramentelle de l'existence chrétienne,* CFi 144.

H. Vorgrimler (1987), *Sakramententheologie,* Düsseldorf.

I.-H. Dalmais (1989), "Sacrement," *DSp* 14, 45–51.

I.- H. Dalmais (1990) "*Raza* et sacrement," in P. De Clerck, E. Palazzo (Eds.), *Rituels: Mélanges offerts à P.-M. Gy O.P.,* Paris, 173–82.

L.-M. Chauvet (1992), "Sacrement," *Cath* XIII, 326–61.

G. Colombo (1997), *Teologia sacramentaria,* Milan.

F. J. Nocke (1997), *Sakramententheologie: Ein Handbuch,* Düsseldorf.

H. Meßner (1999), "Sakramentalien," *TRE* 29, 648–63.

G. Wenz et al. (1999), "Sakramente," *TRE* 29, 663–703.

LOUIS-MARIE CHAUVET

See also **Anointing of the Sick; Baptism; Eucharist; Initiation, Christian; Liturgy; Marriage; Mystery; Ordination/Order; Penance**

Sacramentals. *See* Sacrament

Sacred Heart. *See* Heart of Christ

Sacrifice

I. Old Testament

The foundation of every primitive society, as René Girard (1972) has demonstrated, sacrifice is at the heart of the religion of Israel*. It is rooted in the context of the covenant* of Sinai, both as gift and as demand. In the visions of Ezekiel 40–48, the temple* and its sacrificial cult* are at the center of the future Jerusalem*.

The importance of sacrifice is confirmed by the numerous occasions on which it is performed. It is offered to God* both by individuals and by communities, as an obligatory and habitual sacrifice or as a spontaneous one; and it is offered both in moments of distress as an ultimate recourse and in moments of joy. Sacrifice can therefore not be reduced to a rite of individual piety or interpreted in psychological terms.

Sacrifice is basically a theophanic rite. The consequence of a breakdown, it expresses the desire to restore communication with God (Gn: 20ff.). Its purpose is to provoke the coming of God with a view of obtaining his blessing* (Ex 20:24) and to responding to his presence in the midst of his people (Ex 29:38–46).

1. Three Kinds of Sacrifice

a) Offering of First Fruits (e.g., Dt 26:1–11) and of the Firstborn (e.g., Ex 13:11–16). These are dues paid to God as owner of the land and hence of its resources. Firstborn children, on the other hand, are redeemed by an animal* (e.g., Ex 13:13b; *see* Gn 22) or by a sum of money (Nm 18:15f.).

b) Burnt Offerings (Lv 1), Sacrifices of Communion* (Lv 3), the Most Important of Which Are Sacrifices of Praise*, tôdâh (Lv 7:11–15), Vegetable Offerings (Lv 2), and Libations. These sacrifices are made up exclusively of edible products and, more precisely, of products characteristic of stock raising (large and small cattle) and of agriculture (grain, olive oil, wine), put together in the form of a meal. The meal is entirely offered to God, a sign of particularly deferential hospitality (burnt offering, libation), or shared between God, the priest, and the person making the offering (sacrifice of communion), whom it unites by commensal bonds (Marx 1992). The priestly code attributes a special place to the vegetable offering, which it associates with the priesthood* and which evokes early vegetarianism and its values (Gn 1:29f.). All these sacrifices are said to have a "pleasant odor" for God (Marx 1994).

c) Sacrifices for "Sins" (Lv 4:1–5:13) and Sacrifices of Reparation (Lv 5:14–26). These sacrifices are present only in the priestly code, in Ezekiel, and in the writings of the Chronicler. Arising from an acute consciousness of the sanctity of God and of the requirement of purity* that is consequent on the presence of God among his people, they are prescribed in a certain number of precisely defined circumstances. Sacrifice for "sins" is generally considered a ritual for the absolution of sins* and/or as a rite of purification. It is fundamentally a blood ritual performed in situations of passage. It serves to reintegrate into the community the man or woman who has sinned inadvertently or negligently (Lv 4:1–5:13) or who has become impure through illness (Lv 14; 15) or from giving birth (Lv 12). But it is also required in the context of rituals of consecration (Lv 8; Nm 8) and deconsecration (Nm 6) and at the principal turning points in the liturgical year (Nm 28–29) (Milgrom 1976b; Schenker 1994). As for the sacrifice of reparation, it is chiefly required of anyone who has been guilty of harming the property of God or his neighbor and is made up of a reparation given to God as the ultimate owner of all goods (Milgrom 1976a). These sacrifices play the role of *kappér,* expiation*, never directed toward God but toward the beneficiary of the rite.

In every case the immolation of the victim is only a preparatory ritual intended to liberate the sacrificial material and not the central rite, which contradicts all forms of the theory of vicarious satisfaction (including Girard's theory).

2. Communion and Expiation

Sacrifice attests to the presence of God among his people, enabling Israel and each individual to establish communication with God and enter into a companionate relation with him and authorizing, under certain conditions, the person who is condemned by sin or impurity* to reintegrate with the community. In these ways, existing as it does between the two poles of communion and expiation*, sacrifice gives Israel an indispensable feeling of confidence.

Like any form of cult, the sacrificial cult is threatened by the danger of formalism. Its critics do not seek its abolition but recall that sacrifice cannot dispense with the requirement of social justice (Is 1; Am 5:21–27; Mi 7), and they emphasize both the honor of God that the sacrificial cult ought to express (Mal 1) and the inner attitude (Ps 51:19). But the contrasting of sacrifice with the love* and knowledge* of God (Hos 6:6) with obedience (1 Sm 15:22), with the offering of the lips (Hos 14:3), and with praise (Ps 50:14) prepares the way for a spiritualization.

II. Qumran and New Testament

1. Essenes

This spiritualization occurred at Qumran. The Essenes, at odds with the official cult, formed a community there that understood itself as the true Torah (1QS VIII, 4–10), awaiting the restoration of a pure cult in Jerusalem. In the everyday life of this community-as-Torah, two rituals took on fundamental importance: purification baths, linked with the notion of forgiveness of sins (1QS III, 4–12) and thereby assuming the position of expiation, and the communal meal, made up of elements constituting the vegetable offering, prepared by a priest, offered by him to God, conceived as an anticipation of the eschatological feast (1QS VI, 4–5; 1 QSa II, 17–21), and thereby giving a privileged position to communion. Even though this may have been a substitute liturgy* in a situation that it was hoped was provisional, a turning point had been reached: sacraments* were replacing sacrifice.

2. New Testament

The same is true of the movement initiated by John the Baptist. The baptism* to which he called the crowds replaced the rites of the Torah. Indeed, it seemed to be a mediation making possible the granting of divine forgiveness.

Jesus*' proclamation of the forgiveness of sins with no precondition or rite (Mk 2:1–12 and parallel passages; Lk 7:36–50) in a sense replaces John's baptism. But if Jesus does not baptize (or no longer baptizes), this is because he feels authorized to proclaim the forgiveness of sins with no ritual support. In this perspective his companionship with sinners, which seems to be an anticipation of the Kingdom* and the eschatological feast, assumes its full meaning. It allows, with no ritual preliminary, the institution of a communion, which marks the end point of the sacrificial cult. As a result, it is as though, in Jesus' preaching*, the Good News of the emergence of the kingdom of God replaces the Torah and its rites. As long as the Bridegroom is present with the wedding guests (Mk 2:19), there is a near immediacy in relations with God. There is no other mediation but the presence of Jesus alone, and all who meet him are invited to the feast. Later, mediations and rites will again be necessary (Mk 2:20), but at this point all distance between God and his envoy has been abolished.

The words of institution of Holy Communion (Mk 14:22–25 and parallel passages) (Eucharist*) can be interpreted in terms both of expiation (motifs of the body and the shedding of blood; the theme of "for you") and of communion (the perspective of eschatological companionship in the kingdom of God), and they call for an understanding of the gift made by Jesus of his own life as a recapitulation of the two poles of the sacrificial cult. Further, Jesus is establishing a rite that will be both a place of memory (of his life and his death for his people) and the place of hope* within the early Church*.

The death* of Jesus was in fact understood as recapitulating the entire sacrificial cult. The ancient confession of faith* of 1 Corinthians 15:3 already affirms that Jesus died "for our sins." Other traditions* that are just as old interpret his death in relation to the major Jewish festivals. They make him not only the paschal lamb* (1 Cor 5:7) but also the *hilastèrion,* the Ark of the Covenant, the location of both the mysterious divine presence and the annual sprinkling of blood carried out in the very heart of the Holy of Holies by the high priest on Yom Kippur (Rom 3:25). By thus recognizing that the eschatological Yom Kippur had taken place on Good Friday, at Golgotha, the early Christians were indeed confessing that the sacrificial cult had been recapitulated. But they also made the most of the fact that it was by that very act abrogated.

This line of interpretation of the death of Jesus was adopted and developed in the New Testament, principally by Hebrews. From the fundamental affirmation that Christ* is risen and has opened for all the path of communication to God, Hebrews derives the following consequence: the sacrificial cult has been abolished because what it was supposed to procure (namely, expiation and communion) has been bestowed once and for all and in an entirely different manner, one that recapitulates the old order while simultaneously making it unnecessary. In Hebrews as in Paul, "the New Testament representation serves as a type to attest to the antitype, which itself transcends the type, and the proper meaning of which comes not from the type but from itself and is merely manifested by the type" (Merklein 1990).

In the perspective that emerges here, it seems that, at the level of ritual, baptism and communion specifically replaced sacrifice in the early Church and constituted the antitype of sacrifice in the way the death of Jesus did. The forgiveness of sins now finds its place in baptism, whereas Holy Communion, an anticipation of the eschatological rest, realizes the vegetarian utopia of the priestly code but through the detour of the tragedy of a life offered at the heart of the dynamics of the coming kingdom.

● O. Betz (1959), "Le ministère cultuel," in *La secte de Qumrân et les origines du christianisme,* Bruges, 163–202.
R. Girard (1972), *La violence et le sacré,* Paris.
J. Milgrom (1976a), *Cult and Conscience,* Leiden.
J. Milgrom (1976b), "Israel's Sanctuary," *RB* 83, 390–99.
J. Starcky (1979), *DBS* 9, 996–1006.
M. Hengel, "Der stellvertretende Sühnetod Jesu," *IKaZ* 9, 1–25, 135–47.
H. Merklein (1990), "Der Sühnetod Jesu," in *Versöhnung in der jüdischen und christlichen Liturgie,* Fribourg, 155–83.
W. Kraus (1991), *Der Tod Jesu als Heiligtumsweihe,* Neukirchen.
C. Grappe (1992), *D'un Temple à l'autre.,* Paris.
A. Marx (1992), "Familiarité et transcendance," in A. Schenker (Ed.), *Studien zu Opfer und Kult im AT,* Tübingen, 1–14.
I. Willi-Plein (1993), *Opfer und Kult im alttestamentlichen Israel,* Stuttgart.
A. Schenker (1993), "Interprétations récentes et dimensions spécifiques du sacrifice *hattat,*" *Bib* 75, 59–70.
C. Grappe (1994), "Cène, baptême et ecclésiologie du Nouveau Temple," *RHPhR* 75, 35–43.
A. Marx (1994), *Les offrandes végétales dans l'AT: Du tribut d'hommage au repas eucharistique,* Leiden.
♦ Bibliography by V. Rosset in A. Schenker (Ed.) (1992), *Studien zu Opfer und Kult im AT,* Tübingen, 107–51.

ALFRED MARX (OT) AND CHRISTIAN GRAPPE (NT)

See also **Animals; Eucharist; Expiation; Lamb of God/Paschal Lamb; Mass, Sacrifice of the; Passion; Passover; Priesthood; Purity/Impurity; Scapegoat; Scripture, Fulfillment of; Temple; Theophany**

Saint Victor, School of

The period of fruitfulness and brilliance of the school of Saint Victor was essentially confined to the 12th century. The origin of the establishment can be traced to 1108, when William of Champeaux, archdeacon and head of the schools in Paris, left his position and retired with a few students a short distance from the city to an old *cella* (hermitage) that bore the name Saint Victor. But, encouraged by Hildebert of Lavardin, he continued to teach. In 1113 William became bishop* of Châlons, and Saint Victor was established as an abbey for regular canons, thereby taking its place in a movement of church* reform that had begun in the 11th century. It was from the outset a learned abbey that, in various aspects, was to play an important role in the 12th-century renaissance, some of whose principal characteristics it illustrated. Until close to the end of the century it included *magistri* of great quality: Hugh (†1141); Achard, abbot from 1155 to 1161, then bishop of Avranches; Prior Richard (†1173); and Andrew (†1175). We might also mention Walter, Godfrey, and Adam, names that will recur. From the point of view of Church organization, Saint Victor began by spreading its reform to a certain number of communities. But it was never the center of a network of monasteries, and its expansion did not go so far as actually founding any new ones; it seems that the order did not survive beyond the 13th century. The material conditions necessary for the life of an active and productive school had been assembled: proximity to Paris, with its intellectual resources and urban activity; the continuous exercise of teaching; and the creation and growth of a large library. From all this came a thoroughly individualized, though not entirely homogeneous, culture. It can therefore be described thematically rather than through the enumeration of names and works.

a) The Didactics of Saint Victor. The spirit of Saint Victor, a place of study and teaching, can be approached through the *Didascalicon* of Hugh, the first of the great teachers of the abbey. He proposes to teach "what to read, in what order, and how" in the area of "arts," that is, secular disciplines (Part I, in three books). Gathering all the primary arts in "philosophy*," Hugh fits together a certain number of didactic blocks inherited through various channels from antiquity. For example, the arts of the *quadrivium* (arithmetic, music, geometry, astronomy) make up "mathematics," included by Aristotle, along with theology* and physics, under the heading of "theoretical philosophy." Similarly, at the other end of Hugh's classification, argumentative methods, divided and subdivided, together constitute "the art of reasoning," which, along with grammar, reconstitutes the *trivium* (grammar, dialectics, rhetoric), here called "logic." Between these two major parts of philosophy (the theoretical and the logical) come "practical philosophy," divided as in Aristotelianism (individual, private, public), and "mechanics," a group of seven sciences concerned with "the work of the artisan," the nomenclature of which owes a good deal to Isidore of Seville. That mechanics makes up one of the four major parts of philosophy is a fact that has often been noted, and it certainly evidences an interest in practical life and technique, even though these "sciences" are called "bastard" (by association of *moecha* with *mechanica*) and their description hardly reflects the material civilization of that time and place.

The second part of the *Didascalicon* treats of the "holy" or divine "Scriptures." The "theology" of the first part was defined there as contemplation* of God*, of the spirit, and of spiritual creatures, and here there is reference to the "books of the pagans" where there are things that might be accepted—an attenuated but genuine reflection of the spirit of Abelard. The principal interest of the second part lies in books V and VI, which constitute a brief treatise on exegesis*: involving a threefold understanding of Scripture, according to history*, allegory, and *tropology* (senses* of Scripture); revival of the Augustinian doctrine of "things that signify" in sacred history; and recall of the rules of Tyconius, which had been adopted by Augustine* and Isidore. History has to do with events (person, action, time, place), and knowledge of it must precede knowledge of allegory, a veiled expression of divine mysteries* to which it is not possible to accede without a certain maturity; and tropology has to do with the "dignity of morals," "natural justice" that is learned "by contemplating what God has done." In the Latin tradition these distinctions between the senses of Scripture goes back to Jerome and Gregory the Great*, and it is one of the principles on which the theology of Saint Victor is based. Finally, it is worth noting that in several places in the book, Hugh raises the subject of rules of life and of the virtues* associated with reading, both secular and religious, an aspect of the spirituality of an order that devoted itself to study at a time when there was new interest in the legacy of antiquity. A few decades after the *Didascalicon*, the *Fons philosophiae* by Godfrey of Saint Victor reiterated its didactic program in verse.

b) Aspects of the Theology of Saint Victor. The various forms of theology practiced in the 11th and 12th centuries were present in Saint Victor, as can be observed from the works of its leaders, beginning with the founder. We have a certain number of theological maxims by William of Champeaux in which he deals with various problems: trinitarian appropriations*, also found in Abelard*; the Son as the Wisdom* of God*; the Holy Spirit* as Love* (*caritas*); *translatio*, by which one attributes to God the human qualities of which he is the author, such as justice; a refutation of the eternity of the world ("against those who say that there were always created beings with the Creator," "that the Creator never existed without some effect"); on providence* and contingency (with traces of the *Peri hermeneias* of Aristotle); on evil* and sin*; and on the "two natures" of the inner man (*anima, spiritus*). Other questions are of a philosophical order: form and matter (including those of men and of angels), nature, and substance. We know that William and Abelard had been opposed on the question of universals (nominalism*) and that William had in succession supported two forms of realism. In addition, we also know his commentaries on works of rhetoric: on Cicero's *De inventione* and the *Rhetoric to Herennius*, also attributed to Cicero. His commentary on the *Topics* of Boethius* was also published, as well as a certain number of works on grammar, rhetoric, and dialectics, attributable either to him or to his school. All this does not come directly under theology but cannot be separated from it in the culture and actual practice of the 12th-century teachers.

We have seen that Hugh of Saint Victor did not consider access to allegory and tropology in the reading of the Bible* possible until after a precise understanding of the *historia*, of the text taken in its literal and hence "historical" sense, especially in the case of the Old Testament books. In his major treatise, "Of the sacred signs (*de sacramentis*) of natural and written law*," he sets out a theology articulated according to the twofold development of "constitution," *conditio*, and "restoration," *restauratio*. The first moment, *opus conditionis*, runs from creation* to the Fall, to sin, to the law; the *opus restaurationis* begins with Christ, continues with the Church and its sacraments*, and concludes with the last things. The content of Christian faith is thereby organized in a genuinely historical fashion, following a process of *exitus* and then *reditus* seen in the text of the Bible, according to "the succession of times*, the succession of generations, and the stipulation of precepts*."

Like Hugh, Richard of Saint Victor insisted on the importance of the literal sense, and he adopted the schema of the two "works," constitution and restoration. He was original, however, in his profound capacity for contemplation and speculative meditation, for which Dante* compared him to the angels* (*Riccardo/Che a considerar fu piu che viro*). He is the author of *De Trinitate*, which can be compared, at least for its spirit, to the *Monologion* of Anselm*. In it he emphasizes the necessity of always driving the "intelligence" of divine things further in order to find in them "ultimate sweetness, infinite delectation." He thus seeks "necessary reasons" for the Trinity*. He first does this at the conclusion of a metaphysical combinatorial analysis by distinguishing what is eternal from what has begun, what is by itself from what is by another (aseity*): the Father* is eternally and by himself, the Son and the Holy Spirit are eternally and by another. Then he considers God as supreme love who communicates what he has: God must have, in order to love him, another who is supremely lovable, "a person equal (*condigna*) to the person," and this is the Son, who is God. A third person shares this love and brings it to completion: the Holy Spirit, who receives the "wave of love" (*affluentia amoris*) emanating from the Father and received and diffused by the Son.

c) Spirituality of Saint Victor. The centrality of love in the structure of the Trinity is consonant with the spirituality of Richard, particularly as expressed in his *Four degrees of violent charity, Benjamin minor,* and *Benjamin major.* Among the many spiritual works of Hugh, we should mention his commentary on the *Celestial Hierarchy* of Pseudo-Dionysius*, which played a major role in the diffusion of the thought of Dionysius in the West. Rooted in this movement were the glosses and commentaries on Dionysius by Thomas Gallus (†1246), who was trained at Saint Victor and in the 13th century went to Italy, where he extended the period of Victorine fruitfulness. We must also include within the spirituality of the school the more obscure but daily practices of liturgical life, the measured austerity in sleeping and eating, and the availability for pastoral activity in the spirit of the rules for regular canons and the rule known as the Rule of Saint Augustine. We should also note that the members of Saint Victor produced many sermons, not only Hugh and Richard but also Garnier, Achard, Gautier, and Godfrey. Hugh, Richard, and anonymous others also developed a doctrine of sin that locates its constitutive moment in an inner movement of the sinner, which represents another encounter with Abelard.

d) *Exegesis.* We have already noted a principal characteristic of the exegesis of Saint Victor: an insistence on the *littera* (the literal sense of Scripture). We must add that William of Champeaux had been associated with the biblical scholarship undertaken in Laon by Anselm and his school. The systematic collection of glosses on Scripture was also a characteristic of the theological work of the 11th and 12th centuries. But in the school of Saint Victor the principal figure in the area of exegesis was Andrew, whose work covers a large part of the Old Testament. He carries the principle established by Hugh to its final consequences by seeking particularly for the original meaning of the text, the *hebraica veritas,* beyond the Latin translations. He certainly did not know enough Hebrew to determine this meaning, but he found many elements of it in various sources of the Latin tradition. And it is also very probable that he had contact with Jewish scholars, at the risk of ignoring christological interpretations—he was at least criticized by Richard for doing so. Many traces of his exegesis can be found in writers of the second half of the 12th century. Also with reference to exegesis, mention should be made of the *Gregorianum* of Garnier of Saint Victor, a compilation of allegorical interpretations gleaned from the works of Gregory* the Great.

e) *Metaphysics, Poetry, Reaction.* We must finally mention two members of the school whose works, or some of them, lie outside the areas mentioned thus far. First is Achard, abbot in 1155 and bishop of Avranches in 1162. In addition to his sermons and a brief work, "On the soul, the *spiritus,* and the *mens,*" he wrote a treatise, *On the unity of God and the plurality of created beings,* in which his editor, E. Martineau, has pointed out an entirely singular metaphysical theology. The multiplicity of created beings has as a principle, even beyond ideas, an original divine plurality, also distinct from that of the persons and essentially linked to unity. Then there was Adam of Saint Victor, who died toward the middle of the century. He was the author of liturgical poems, a "very excellent versifier" who might have been "the greatest poet of the Middle Ages" had he not lacked "a little of the elevation of mysticism" (R. de Gourmont). There was thus poetry and Platonism*, which, with the aspects previously described, make of Saint Victor an image faithful in almost every way to the spirit and energy of the 12th century and its doctrinal innovations. But toward the end of the century there appeared in Saint Victor a "narrow traditionalism*" (J. Châtillon) represented by Gautier, who, around 1177, in his *Contra quatuor labyrinthos Franciae,* attacked several innovative theologians of the time: Peter Abelard, Peter Lombard, Peter of Poitiers, and his disciple, Gilbert de la Porrée.

● Achard, *Sermons inédits,* Ed. J. Châtillon, Paris, 1970.
Achard, *L'unité de Dieu et la pluralité des créatures,* Ed. E. Martineau, St-Lambert-des-Bois, 1987.
Adam, *A. de Saint-Victor: Liriche sacre,* Ed. G. Vecchi, 1953; *Adam von Saint-Victor: Sämtliche Sequenzen,* Ed. and translated in German by F. Wellner, 1955.
André, *Expositionem super Heptateuchon,* Ed. C. Lohr, R. Berndt, Turnhout, 1986; *Expositio super Danielem,* Ed. M. Zier, Turnhout, 1990; *Expositiones historicas in libros Salomonis,* Ed. R. Berndt, Turnhout, 1991.
Gautier, "Le 'Contra quatuor labyrinthos Franciae' de Gauthier de Saint-Victor," Ed. P. Glorieux, *AHDL* 19 (1952); *Galteri A Sancto Victore et quorundam aliorum: Sermones ineditos triginta sex,* Ed. J. Châtillon, Turnhout, 1975.
Godefroy, *Microcosmus,* Ed. P. Delhaye, Lille, 1951; *Fons philosophiae,* Ed. P. Michaud-Quantin, Namur-Louvain-Lille, 1956.
Guillaume de Champeaux, O. Lottin, *Psychologie et morale aux XIIe et XIIIe siècles,* V, Gembloux, 1958.
Hugues, PL 175–77; *Didascalicon: De studio legendi,* Ed. C. Buttimer, Washington, D.C., 1939; *Didascalicon: L'art de lire,* translated in French by M. Lemoine, Paris, 1991; *Six opuscules spirituels,* Ed. and translated by R. Baron, Paris, 1969.
Richard, PL 196; *Sermons et opuscules spirituels inédits,* Ed. J. Châtillon, trans. J. Barthelemy, Paris, 1951; *Les quatre degrés de la violente charité,* Ed. and translated by G. Dumeige, Paris, 1955; *La Trinité,* Ed. and translated G. Salet, Paris, 1959; *Trois opuscules spirituels inédits,* Ed. J. Châtillon, Paris, 1986.
♦ Notes on Achard, Adam, André, Garnier, Gautier, Godefroi, William of Champeaux, Hugues, Richard, with bib. (editions, studies) in *Dictionnaire des lettres françaises: Le Moyen Age,* 2nd Ed., Paris, 1992. Also: R. de Gourmont (1930), *Le latin mystique,* 2nd Ed., Paris, 283–94.
J. Châtillon (1952), "De Guillaume de Champeaux à Thomas Gallus," *RMAL* 8, 139–62, 247–72.
F. Lazzari (1965), *Il contemptus mundi nella scuola di S. Vittore,* Naples.
R. Berndt (1991), *André de Saint-Victor (1175) exégète et théologien,* Paris-Turnhout.
J. Longère (Ed.) (1991), *L'abbaye parisienne de Saint-Victor au Moyen Age,* Paris-Turnhout.
J. Châtillon (1992), *Le mouvement canonial au Moyen Age: Réforme de l'Église, spiritualité et culture,* Paris-Turnhout.
D. Poirel (1998), *Hugues de Saint-Victor,* Paris.

JEAN JOLIVET

See also **Chartres, School of; God; Scholasticism; Scripture, Senses of; Spiritual Theology**

Salvation

A. Biblical Theology

I. Generalities

1. Terminology

The Bible* expresses the idea of salvation by many different terms in Hebrew and in Greek. The basic substantives are formed from verbs. The main Hebrew etymologies are the following:

The verb *yâsha'*, form *hiphil: hoshî'a* "tear away, liberate, save," gives the meanings of "salvation," *yésha'* or *yéshoûa'*. *Pâdâh*, "redeem, liberate," gives the abstract *pedoût*, "liberation," and the concrete *pedoûyim* (or *pideyôn*), "ransom price." *Gâ'al*, "claim, redeem, affranchise," namely in the present participle *go'él*, expresses the personal notation of "savior"; it can also refer to the substantives derived from *yâsha'*. The synonyms of these verbs are also found in the form *yâça'* (*hiphil*), "extract, lead outside, send out," and *'âçal*, "take out from, separate," of *'éçèl*, "flank, sides." In the Septuagint, the abstract *sôtèria* (fem.) "salvation, conservation, security," and the concrete *sôtèr* (masc.) "savior, protector, liberator," are derived from *sôzein*, "save, preserve, care for." In New Testament Greek, in addition to terms proper to the Septuagint, other terms restricted to the social register acquired theological value, such as *lutron*, "liberate against ransom, affranchise," from which come the substantives *(anti)lutron*, "ransom (price)" and "*apolutrôsis*, "redemption, untying (of bonds)." Similarly *(ex)agorazein*, "acquit, redeem," and especially *eleutheroun*, "liberate," give the abstract *eleutheria* (fem.), "liberty*," and the personal adjective *(ap)eleutheros*, "free."

2. Negative Situations

The evils from which the beneficiaries of salvation escape can be seen on two levels: material or moral. 1) Negative material situations include slavery (Ex 20:2: "I am the Lord your God, who brought you out of the land of Egypt, out of the house of slavery"; Mi 6:4); persecution or oppression, either by enemies (2 Sm 22:18; Ps 106:10, etc.) or the impious (Ps 71:4, 140:2, etc.); illness (Mk 5:28: "If I touch even his garments, I will be made well") or death* itself (2 Cor 1:10: "He delivered us from such a deadly peril, and he will deliver us"); and, in general, the present worldly condition (2 Tm 4:18: "The Lord will rescue me from every evil deed and bring me safely into his heavenly kingdom"). 2) On the moral and spiritual level, the condition that calls for redemption is evil* in general (Mt 6:13: "Deliver us from evil"); but here the Greek term can also mean "wickedness" and especially sin* (but here salvation is usually expressed by other verbs: "forgive, expiate, forget, cover over, efface, wash away"; however, *see* Romans 8, 2: 9 ("The law of the Spirit of life has set you free in Christ Jesus from the law of sin and death"). Salvation liberates us from the law* that sin used against us (*Rom* 7:7–13; 1 Cor 15:56; *see* Gal 3:13: "Christ redeemed us from the curse of the law"). Further, it is escape from eschatological condemnation (Lk 13:23: "Lord, will those who are saved be few?"; Rom 5:9: "Much more shall we be saved by him from the wrath of God*"; 1 Thes 1:10: "Jesus who delivers us from the wrath to come").

3. Salvation and History

A fundamental observation ought to be made here: the biblical concept of salvation should be clearly distinguished from all forms of Gnosticism. Man's salvation is not understood simply as his becoming aware of himself and his own original divine identity (should it be restored by a revelator come from on high for this purpose). Salvation is the intervention of God in history*, to establish a new dialogical relationship with man; and in this relationship, man remains fully himself in the face of a God who is distinct from him (*see* the exodus from Egypt and the death of Jesus on the cross, respectively).

II. Old Testament, Intertestament

The Bible does not envisage an autonomous salvation of man (autosoteriology); whether salvation comes directly from God or God gives judgment through the intermediary of human agents, salvation always presupposes the intervention of an alterity.

1. God as Savior

Numerous texts attribute to God alone the possibility of an effective intervention in favor of human beings, whether they are faced with illness (2 Kgs 5:7: "Am I god, to kill and make alive?"; Ps 146:7ss: "The Lord sets the prisoners free...opens the eyes of the blind...lifts up," etc.) or are trapped in the eschatological ordeal (Is 35, 4: "Behold, your God...He will come and save you"; *see* the theme of the *Day of the Lord*). God is the sole and unique "savior," *môshîa'* (Is 43:11: "Besides me there is no savior"; 45:15, 45:21, 63:8), or "redeemer," *go'él* (Jb 19:25; Ps 19:15; Is 41:14, 43:14, 44:6, 44:24, 47:4, 48:17, 49:7, 54:5 [59:20; derived from the right of the levirate: *see* Dt 25:5–10]). He bears exclusive responsibility for ensuring the conduct of Israel*, as affirmed in Isaiah 63:8–9: "And he became their Savior...The angel of his presence saved them"; *see* Deuteronomy 26:8 and the Passover* Haggadah (*see also* Ex 15; Ps 77–78). The theocentrism of the history of salvation is thus clearly safeguarded, to the point of directly invoking God himself: "Oh that you would rend the heavens and come down!" (Is 64:1).

2. Mediators

However, other citations can be found which contradict the foregoing assertions: "He will send them a savior and defender, and deliver them" (Is 19:20). A series of envoys figure in the Old Testament, acting in varied ways in favor of the people. Abraham intercedes for the inhabitants of Sodom (Gn 18:16–33); through his intercession, Israel and the whole of mankind are blessed by God (Gn 12:1ff., 15:1–6). And, above all, Moses, "chosen among all the living" (Sir 45:4), who acts as mediator between God and Israel, as leader and liberator from Egyptian oppression (Ex 3:9–20; Nm 11:10–15), as spokesman of God at Sinai and legislator (Ex 19:7f.; 33:11; 34; Neh 9:14; Sir 45:5). He is declared "faithful in all my house" (Nm 12, 7) and the greatest prophet* of Israel (Dt 34:10). The judges are also cited as saviors (Jgs 3:9; *see* 2:16, 3:15–31, 8:22, 9:17, 13:5). Another prominent figure is David (2 Sm 3:18): "By the hand of my servant David I will save my people Israel"; his dynasty is chosen to defend and protect the people (Ps 72:4): "May he defend the cause of the poor of the people." The figure of the king gradually becomes the symbol of the privileged envoy of God; he will fill his role to perfection in the last days when, as "messiah*" (*oint*), he will punish the wicked and exalt the chosen (Is 11:4ff.). A particular picture of the savior is drawn by Deutero-Isaiah (Is 42:1–7; 49:1–6; 50:4–11; 52:13–53, 12): a mysterious "servant of the Lord," a prophet and especially a man of suffering, is invested by God with the very special role of carrying justice to the nations (Is 42, 1), "to bring Jacob back to him" (Is 49:5), "to sustain with a word him who is weary" (Is 50:4), and on whom "the Lord has laid...the iniquity

of us all," so that "his soul makes an offering for sin," and he will "make many to be accounted righteous" (Is 53:4, 53:10–11; *see* v. 5: "With his stripes we are healed*"). The divine Wisdom* itself is personified for a mission of assistance and guidance for the people (Sir 24:18–21; Sg 10–19; Bar 3:37–4, 1).

In intertestamentary (intertestament*) literature, a whole series of eschatological mediators appears: the Son of man (1 Hen 48, 4: "He will be a staff for the holy and the just...and will be the lamp of peoples and the hope for those who suffer in their souls"), a sacerdotal messiah (Test.Lev. 18, 10: "He will open the door of Paradise, and the sword held over Adam will be thrust aside"), and even *Melchizedek*—the freedom promised to prisoners in Isaiah 61:1 is attributed to this personage, who is charged with proclaiming to them "who are freed from the debt which they have incurred through their iniquity" (11*qmelk* 6).

3. Conclusion

The idea of a purely interior, moral, or spiritual salvation does not exist in Israel; salvation always includes a material if not a directly national dimension, implying peace* and prosperity on earth (Dt 33:29: "Israel...a people saved by the Lord"). Possession and usufruct of the land are an integral part of this promise (1 Kgs 4:25: "And Judah and Israel lived in safety, every man under his vine and under his fig tree"). However, the spiritual component of a salvation that rests on God's unfailing love* (Is 49:13ff., 54:1–10) is not forgotten. This explains these words attributed to God: "I, I am he who blots our your transgressions for my own sake" (Is 43:25) and the pressing calls for conversion* as return to the Lord (Jer 2:1–4, 4; Hos 2). These two components are found together in the eschatological perspective of salvation: on the one hand, the horizon of a new heaven and a new earth (Is 65:17) manages to integrate the corporeal resurrection* of the dead (Dn 12:1ff.; Is 26:19), and, on the other, eschatological salvation purifies all impurities*, giving man a new heart and a new spirit (Ez 36:25ff.; Jer 31:31) to the point that "whoever calls on the name* of the Lord will be saved" (Jl 3:5).

III. New Testament

1. Act of Grace

Christianity, from its very beginnings, has been aware of living qualitatively at the end of times (Lk 16:16; Acts 2:16f.; 1 Cor 10:11; 1 Pt 4:7; 1 Jn 2:18). Indeed, "The time is fulfilled" (Mk 1:15); "the fullness of time" has come (Gal 4:4; Heb 9:26; 1 Pt 1:20). This is why not only are humans "being guarded through faith for a salvation ready to be revealed in the last time"

(1 Pt 1:5), but already, "by grace you have been saved," (Eph 2:5–8; the Greek *sesôsmenoi,* meaning "perfect," can also mean "the accomplished"). The fact is that God's approval of the plan of salvation took shape" in the present time" (Rom 3:26) by way of a precise historical modality consisting in the death of Christ on the cross and in the faith* in him which is its consequence: "It pleased God through the folly of what we preach to save those who believe" (1 Cor 1:21; *see* Eph 1:5, 1:9); in this way, human beings are both object and recipient of his ultimate *eudokia* (benevolence) (Lk 2:14).

a) Jesus the Savior. There is only one historical savior in the New Testament, and that is Jesus of Nazareth, not so much because of the literal meaning of his name (*Yehoshoûa'* or *Yéshoûa',* "YHWH saves") but because the entire process of salvation is connected to him as indisputable protagonist: "There is salvation in no one else, for there is no other name under heaven given among men by which we must be saved" (Acts 4:12). The title that so fundamentally belongs to God (*see* Lk 1:47: "God my Savior") is now prevalently attributed to Jesus (16 times; *see* 1 Jn 4:14: "The Father has sent his Son to be the Savior of the world").

b) Jewish Roots. The affirmation in John 4:22 that "salvation is from the Jews" (Is 2:3) attests the basic connection of Christianity to Judaism*. The former depends on the latter, both from a historical viewpoint and from the point of view of ideas: the Christian discourse on salvation would not employ a language or a concept if it did not perpetuate the tradition of Israel (Rom 9:1–5).

c) Nature of the Action of Salvation. The central event of salvation presupposes the thaumaturgical activity of the earthly Jesus. (*see* Mt 9:22: "And instantly the woman was made well"). It is related to the integral gift of self realized by Jesus himself: it qualifies the act he desired (Lk 19:10: "to save the lost") and is effectively accomplished in his death on the cross (Rom 3:25; Eph 1:7: "in him we have redemption through his blood") and crowned by his resurrection* (*see* 1 Cor 15:17: "And if Christ has not been raised, your faith is futile and you are still in your sins"). It is necessary here to rectify a long-standing legalistic interpretation of redemption, whereby God, by way of a penal substitution, is given satisfaction for outrages endured, as if in Jesus God had wanted to chastise all sinners. The idea of a chastisement of the *Servant* for the sins of others does exist in Isaiah 53:5. However, the case of Jesus goes far beyond this. He "he died for (*huper* does not mean "in the place of" but "in favor of" or "be-cause of" or "in relation to") our sins" (1 Cor 15:3; *see* Gal 1:4; 1 Cor 6:20: "You were bought with a price"; 1 Tm 2, 6: "Christ Jesus, who gave himself as a ransom for all"; 1 Pt 1:18f.). That is, Jesus' death was essentially a personal act of love on the part of Jesus himself (Gal 2:20: "the Son of God, who loved me and gave himself for me"; Eph 5:2; Jn 13:1) or of God (Rom 8:31: "If God is for us, who can be against us?"). The basic schema for understanding the saving event of the Passion* is analogous to the exodus: God acts sovereignly and freely as he did then "with a strong hand and long arm" for the love of his people (*see* Is 15:13: "Guide with your favor this people whom you have redeemed"; Dt 7:7: "The Lord set his love on you and chose you…because the Lord loves you"; Is 63:9: "In his love and in his pity, he redeemed them""). It is in the same way that God has intervened, in the immolated Christ as the new paschal lamb* (1 Cor 5:7) "because of the great love with which he loved us" (Eph 2:4; 2 Cor 5:19).

d) Efficacy of the Gospel Proclamation. Inextricably linked to the objective event is its announcement, the proclamation—that is, the gospel: "The word of the cross…to us who are being saved…is the power of God" (1 Cor 1:18); "The Gospel…is the power of God for salvation to everyone who believes" (Rom 1:16); "the Gospel…which you received, in which you stand, and by which you are being saved, if you hold fast to the word I preached to you" (1 Cor 15:1f.). It could be said, in particular for Paul, that the gospel proclamation, if it is received in the faith*, contains the very power of the salvation proper to the cross and the blood of Christ. Conversely, the proclamation is taken as scandal and folly by those who reject it (1 Cor 1:18–31).

e) Effects of the Action of Salvation. The explicit vocabulary of salvation is rarely used to express the anthropological impact of the cross and its announcement: "For with the heart one believes and is justified, and with the mouth one confesses and is saved" (Rom 10:10; *see* Eph 2:5, 2:8). Ordinarily another vocabulary is used, at least by Paul, bringing together various metaphors: "redeem" (Gal 4:5), "deliver" (Ti 2:14), "free" (Rom 6:18), "reconcile" (2 Cor 5:18ff.), "make peace" (Col 1:20), "expiate" (Heb 2:17), and especially "justify" (Rom 5:1; *see* 8:1) and even "re-create" (2 Cor 5:17: "Therefore, if anyone is in Christ, he is a new creation"; *see* Eph 4:24). Notions of life, joy, and peace* also have their rightful place in this semantic constellation. The variety of the vocabulary reflects the inexhaustible wealth of the fact. Here it should be emphasized that the notion of salvation presupposes the notion of "sin." And, according to the New Testament, this concerns not only actual personal sins but also a basic situation implicating all human beings, even before they consciously believe. This appears in Romans 1:18–3, 20, and especially 5:12–21 (in opposition to Adam), in the context of the theme of the gratuitous intervention ("justice") of God in the redemptive death of Christ.

2. Eschatological Salvation

The specific vocabulary of salvation is essentially used to designate eschatological novelty. This is clear in Paul: "justified by his blood, much more shall we be saved by him from the wrath of God" (Rom 5:9; *see* 13:11). Jesus will be revealed as the sole savior in the eschatological future (Phlm 3:20f.; *see also* Heb 9:28: "So Christ, having been offered once to bear the sins of many, will appear a second time, not to deal with sin but to save those who are eagerly waiting for him"; *see also* Rev 7:10, 12:10). For, according to the New Testament and the Bible in general, there is no complete salvation without the total reintegration of man in all his created identity, which is made not only of a soul but also and no less of a body and therefore of relation to the world. So the notion of resurrection* is an integral part of the notion of salvation from both a Jewish and a Christian perspective.

3. Hope

This results in a paradox of salvation in the Christian sense: it is already a given fact, and yet it must be completed. This antinomy can be expressed by the motto, "already and not yet" (or, conversely, "not yet, but already now"). Romans 8:24 (Greek *tè gar elpidi esôthèmen*) can be translated several different ways, literally, "In hope (or, so that we may hope) we were saved," but, more exactly, "Our salvation is object of hope" (*BJ*) or, even better, "because we were saved, but it is in hope" (TOB). Thus, hope comes to the foreground. It rests henceforth on the redemption wrought by Christ, giving us the certainty of a new eschatological identity. Hope itself, which projects human beings toward a later fulfillment, is not canceled by it: it "does not put us to shame" (Rom 5:5) because it originates less in subjective uncertainty than in the objective fact that founds assurance for the future: "waiting for our blessed hope" (Ti 2:13; *see* Col 1:5: "because of the hope laid up for you in heaven"). The attitude that characterizes it in the history of our day is patience (Greek *hupomonè*), resistance, and perseverance in the ineluctable trials that are more particularly the lot of believers (*see* Lk 21:19; Rom 5:3; Rev 1:9).

IV. The Dimensions of Salvation

1. Antinomy between Gratuity and Commitment

If salvation is fundamentally a gratuitous gift from God (*E*ph 2:8–9: "For by grace you have been saved through faith. And this is not your own doing; it is the gift of God"), it nonetheless implies a responsible activity on man's part: "Work out your own salvation with fear and trembling" (Phlm 2:12). The act of receiving the gift of God goes with a constant effort to lead a life worthy of the gift that is given (Rom 14:19; 1 Cor 9:24–27; Phlm 1:27; 1 Tm 6:12). The same antinomy is already inscribed in the Old Testament decalogue*: gratuitous liberation from Egypt (Is 20:2) founds and demands observance of God's will (Is 20:3–17). And the question asked of Jesus on the number of the saved (Lk 13:23) receives this apparently evasive answer: "Strive to enter through the narrow door" and so on (Lk 13:24).

2. Individual and Community

Moreover, salvation not only concerns the individual, who nevertheless remains the immediate beneficiary (Rom 7:24–25a; Gal 2:20), but often includes a communitarian dimension. This is already true for the people of Israel, who benefit completely from God's saving intervention of (Ex 3:7f.) and who, as a single whole, will enjoy eschatological salvation (Rom 11:26, and in the *Mishnah Sanh.* 10, 1: "All Israel will be saved," notwithstanding all the exceptions listed). Analogously, the Christian community, qualified by Paul in its totality as "the body of Christ" (1 Cor 12:27; *see* Rom 12:5; Gal 3:28), owes its existence to the blood of the cross (Acts 20:28; Eph 2:14–18: "that he might create in himself one new man in place of the two [Jews and Gentiles], making peace, and might reconcile us both to God in one body through the cross") and is completely turned toward eschatological consummation (symbol of the bride in Rev 19:7f., 21:2).

3. Universal and Cosmic Dimension

Further, salvation has a universalist dimension, in a double sense: 1) inasmuch as it is the destiny of all people and that all people are at least called (*see* 1 Tm 2:4; Rev 7:9: "Behold, a great multitude...from every nation, from all tribes and peoples and languages") and 2) in that it is turned not only toward the human race but also toward a renewal of the entire created world (*Rom* 8:21: "The creation itself will be set free from its bondage to decay"; 2 Pt 3:13: "We are waiting for new heavens and a new earth in which righteousness dwells"). Because no man is an island and every individual is connected to the cosmic context, salvation must be the negation of all individualism and spiritualist escape; it must bring full communion* not only with God but also with human beings and the world.

- H. Crouzel (1957), "Le dogme de la Rédemption dans l'Apocalypse," *BLE* 58, 65–92.
W. Foerster, G. G. Fohrer, "*Sôzô, sôtêria,*" *ThWNT* 7, 966–1024.
S. Lyonnet, L. Sabourin (1970), *Sin, Redemption and Sacrifice: A Biblical and Patristic Study,* AnBib 48.
L. Alonso-Schökel, "La Rédemption œuvre de solidarité," *NRTh* 93, 449–72.
P. Grelot (1973), *Péché originel et rédemption examinés à partir de l'épître aux Romains,* Paris.
N. Lohfink (1973), *Heil als Befreiung in Israel: Erlösung und Emanzipation,* Fribourg.
S. K. Williams (1975), *Jesus' Death as Saving Event,* Missoula, Mont.
E. Beaucamp (1978), "Aux origines du mot "rédemption": Le "rachat" dans l'Ancien Testament," *LTP* 34, 49–56.
J.-C. Filteau (1981), "La racine *ysh':* Une des expressions du salut dans l'AT," *LTP* 37, 135–57.

A. Schenker (1982), "Substitution du châtiment ou prix de la paix? Le don de la vie du Fils de l'homme en Mc 10, 45 et par. à la lumière de l'Ancien Testament," in *La Pâque du Christ, mystère de salut: Mélanges F.-X. Durrwell,* LeDiv 112, 75–90.
P. Nesti (Ed.) (1985), *Salvezza cristiana e culture odierne,* 2 vols.; id., vol. 1, *Salvezza e annunzio,* Turin.
J. Ernst (1992), "Das Heil der Schöpfung," *Cath (M)* 46, 189–206.
G. G. O'Collins (1992), "Salvation," *AncBD,* 907–14.
P. Ternant (1993), *Le Christ est mort "pour tous": Du serviteur Israël au serviteur Jésus,* Paris.
J. Timmer (1993), *Le salut, de la Genèse à l'Apocalypse,* Aix-en-Provence.

ROMANO PENNA

See also **Cosmos, Creation; Death; Expiation; Gospels; Healing; History; Hope; Justification; Law; Liberty; Passion; Sacrifice; Sin**

B. Historical and Systematic Theology

Because human distress has many faces, biblical texts, as we have seen, use many different images to evoke salvation (liberation, redemption, reconciliation, resurrection*, new creation*, etc.). Over the centuries, theology* too has developed very different notions on the subject. However, beyond all divergence, Christian thought has always lived by the central profession of faith*: salvation comes through Christ*. Theology has not been content with simply adopting the New Testament formula; it has also struggled to understand why God* did not operate the salvation of human beings directly from the heavens, by his power and mercy*. The answer to the question "why is a mediator needed?" has remained essentially the same through countless cultural changes, as attested by the following citations from three authors who, at intervals of nearly 1,000 years, were all deeply marked by the Christian doctrine of redemption.

Against a background of Greek thought and with regard to the way in which the devil can be vanquished, Irenaeus* taught, "Because if it were not a man who had vanquished the enemy of man, the enemy would not have been vanquished in full justice*. Further, if it were not God who had bestowed salvation on us, we would not have received it in a stable way. And if man had not been united with God, he could not have received incorruptibility in participation. For it was necessary that the mediator between God and men, by his

relationship with each of the two parties, should lead one and the other to friendship and concord in such a way that, at one and the same time, God received man and man offered himself to God" (SC 211, 365–66).

Anselm* of Canterbury, questioning himself in the Germanic context on the way in which man could give satisfaction to God for his sins*, concluded, "If then it is necessary ... that the city* above be led to perfection with men, and if that is not possible unless the above mentioned satisfaction is made, that none can make but God, and none owes but man, it must be done by a God-man" (Corbin, ed., 3, 409).

Finally, in the modern framework of a dramatic understanding of history* and its conflicts, Balthasar* reflects, "In this place an entirely different pathos must intervene in the dramatic story, the pathos of God. He does not come on stage sneering at his broken adversary but, in an act unforeseeable for man, places himself by the side of his adversary and helps him from within to reach justice and liberty*.... As long as the world lasts, the question *Cur Deus homo* remains always current" (*Theodramatik,* III, 186).

Because it is human beings who brought perdition into the world* by their sinfulness and weakness, it is up to them to vanquish evil*; but they cannot do it. God saves them and preserves their dignity by giving them a mediator who is both human and divine to help them accomplish what they cannot accomplish by their own might. In the mediator the divine efficacy from on high encounters the human action from below, and together they lead human beings to a salvation that in the last instance should be understood as participation in the life of the Trinity*.

In the course of history Christian thought variously put the emphasis on one or the other of these two axes while essentially maintaining the balance between them. Theologians of the first millennium emphasized the divine efficacy by understanding salvation first from the incarnation* and including by way of analogy*—against a Platonist background—the whole of humankind in the humanity of Christ. During the second millennium the action of human nature rising up to God was foregrounded (through the proclamation of the royalty of Christ and, in the first place, his offering on the cross). But these two perspectives cannot be separated because the transcendent God does not act as a worldly cause. Nowhere better than in the figure of Christ can it be more clearly seen how God operates by decreeing man to act turned toward him. All statements on the saving action of God through his mediator Jesus Christ should be understood in this double sense.

Despite the interest in Christ as sole mediator, the history of Christian theology and dogma* includes highly diverse representations of salvation arising from varied cultural presuppositions and divergent notions of the human condition. Balthasar (1961) notes that in Maximus* the Confessor's doctrine of salvation in Christ, his "anthropology* of original sin*" is developed "with almost geometrical rigor." In fact the same could be said of all the great authors. B. Catâo (1965) wrote of Thomas* Aquinas, "His vision of salvation is inseparable, on the one hand, from the sin from which we need to be delivered and, on the other hand, from the mission of the Son of God come to the world expressly to accomplish that work."

1. Economy of Salvation and History of Salvation

The church* fathers* often evoked in a very vivid way how Adam*, created in the image of the eternal Logos, fell into disobedience and how the human beings who came after him sank into a history of sin and idolatry* (see Athanasius*, SC 18 bis, 53–149). They contrasted this picture with the vision of a global economy of salvation in which God, through a long history, by way of his covenant* with Abraham and Moses and through the prophets*, prepared humankind for the coming of his Son. According to Irenaeus of Lyon, who was the first to develop this idea, Christ is above all "the sole truthful teacher" (SC 294, 289; SC 211, 363) who wants to use "counsel" and not "force" to bring human beings back to the straight path (SC 153, 19–20) and

who, by his obedience, positively "recapitulates" the whole history of disobedience (SC 211, 371 and 445). He offers a luminous moral example for the human race to imitate. As the true teacher and model, he is at the same time the "light" of the eternal Father* for human beings: "In the flesh of our Lord burst forth the light of the Father, then, shining out from his flesh it came into us, and thus man acceded to incorruptibility, enveloped as he was by the light of the Father" (SC 100, 631).

In this way, Irenaeus and most of the Greek Fathers were able to attach the biblical image of Christ as the true teacher (Mt 11:27, 23:10; Mk 1:22) and the light of the world (Lk 2:32; Jn 1:4f., 9:5, 12:46; Acts 13:47; Eph 5:14) to the notion of paideia (education), central to Greek philosophy and culture.

Because divine paideia could not, in a world delivered up to tribulation, bring the salvation announced by the Old Testament messianic promises, most second-century theologians awaited the advent of a millennial reign of Christ on earth. This expectation was soon spiritualized (Origen*, Augustine*) and related to the Church. In the Middle Ages, Joachim of Fiore (1130–1202) expounded a new vision of the history of salvation, which he understood as being composed of three ages: the age of the Father up to the coming of Christ, the age of Christ corresponding to the hierarchical Church, and the age of the Holy Spirit* which will see the establishment of a purely spiritual Church. In a secularized form this dynamic vision of history exerted a determining influence on the modern belief in progress and revolutionary ideas (see Lubac* 1979).

The German Aufklärung (Enlightenment) adopted the theme of education, in interpreting the Judeo-Christian revelation* as a divine intervention destined to educate the human race in a superior morality. G. E. Lessing (1729–81) begins The education of the human race with these words: "what education is for individuals, revelation is for the whole of mankind." Kant*, despite his doctrine of radical evil, interpreted the New Testament announcement of the kingdom* of God in an analogous sense. Under his influence, liberal 19th-century Protestant theology saw Jesus Christ especially as the teacher of a new morality. The descending perspective of divine action is no longer articulated around the incarnation but is reduced to the general level of providence*.

In an entirely different context, over the past few decades political* theology and the theology of liberation* have shown renewed interest in the saving action of God in history. However, they see Jesus* not as teacher but as the prophet of new social structures. His saving action is essentially manifest in his proclamation of the imminent reign of God and his solidarity with the poor, the dispossessed, and the persecuted, something that makes Jesus himself the victim of the powerful in his turn.

But the cross, the resurrection, and participation in divine life cannot find full expression in a theology of education or social transformation, and Church doctrine has never contented itself with this approach. The conviction that evil is a power that cannot be overcome by education alone has been perpetuated down through the tradition*.

2. Christ Triumphant Who Liberates from the Powers of Evil

In the New Testament the ultimate power of evil is the devil or Satan (Mk 1:13, 4:15; Lk 10:18; Jn 8:44, 13:2; Acts 5:3; Rom 16:20; 2 Cor 2:11, 11:14; Rev 12:9, 20:2, 20:7), reduced to impotence by Christ through his death* (Heb 2:14). The idea of Christ's struggle against Satan was important in the patristic period (see Aulén 1930). Irenaeus was already speaking of the just victory over the Enemy (SC 211, 365 and 447; 153, 261–79); after Origen there was added the idea that the devil had a right over human beings because they had voluntarily delivered themselves to him. In this approach the soul of Christ was the "prix" (1 Cor 6:20, 7:23; Col 2:14) or the "rançon" (Mt 20:28; Mk 10:45; 1 Tm 2:6) paid to the devil. But the Enemy was duped because he could not conserve this "prix," and yet he lost those he had held in his power (GCS 40, 498–99). Although Gregory* of Nazianzus was vigorously opposed to such notions (PG 36, 653), the idea of the devil's rights found an echo in the writings of several Fathers (Basil* [PG 29, 437]; Gregory of Nyssa; John Chrysostom [PG 59, 372–73; 60, 514]; Ambrose* [PL 16, 1115]; Leo the Great [PL 54, 196 and 353]; Gregory* the Great [PL 76, 680]).

Gregory of Nyssa went so far as to systematically develop the idea of the devil's rights in order to justify the incarnation of the Logos and the necessity of the cross. Like Irenaeus he started from the idea that the devil was to be vanquished not by divine power but in full justice. He had no problem admitting that the victory is that of one kind of cheating (Christ's) over another kind (the devil's). Just as the devil used the good* as bait to catch people on the hook of evil, Christ hid the hook of his divinity under the deceiving bait of his humanity. Seeing this man's prodigious exploits the devil accepted to take him as ransom for all men. But in swallowing this "prix," he got caught on the hidden hook of the divinity (PG 45, 47–63). Similar ideas are found in Augustine (CChr.SL 50 A, 399–408; 46, 76).

The theory of the devil's rights and his guileful eviction includes a subtle but decisive error of reasoning:

from the fact that human beings, because of their sins, legitimately fell under the power of Satan, it does not follow that Satan has any rights over them. In fact, since Anselm of Canterbury criticized the theory at the beginning of Cur Deus homo (I, 7), it has disappeared from rationalist theology, even if the devil continues to play a role.

Not all the Fathers drew on the theory of the devil to resolve the question of the "price" paid by the blood of Christ. Among divergent ideas on this subject, that of Athanasius is noteworthy. He argues that the evil from which human beings must be delivered is the "sentence" and the curse of the law because sin has given death a "right" and a "legal power" over humankind. God did not have the power to lift this sentence pronounced against Adam (Gn 2:16f.) because this would have been a failure of truth*. In order that human beings could be saved but that the sentence should nonetheless be executed, the incarnation of the eternal Word was necessary. He could endure the sentence of death in his body and in our place and yet by virtue of his immortality triumph over death by his resurrection and offer us eternal* life (SC 199, 283–97). John Chrysostom (PG 61, 652–53) and Maximus the Confessor pursued similar lines of thought. However, the latter held, more clearly than Athanasius, that the right to death is not an indeterminate right but, as a consequence of sin, has been directly engraved in human nature as "suffering" and "punishment."

3. Reconciliation with God in Christ

By the intervention of the one mediator, human beings are given to participate in the life of the divine Trinity. The most fundamental obstacle that stands in the way of salvation thus defined is the separation caused by sin. In this context the saving action of Christ is first understood as a reconciliation by which he carries out a penance*, an expiation*, and a satisfaction for sin; brings justification* to human beings; and offers God a perfect sacrifice*. The terms "penance," "expiation," and "satisfaction" are closely related and often used interchangeably. They derive from representations widespread in traditional societies* where the evildoer had to "do penance." The suffering that he had provoked called for a suffering in return (expiation) and the harm done had to be erased by a reverse harm or a compensation (a satisfaction) (see Verdier 1980).

a) Expiation. In the Old Testament, men cannot escape the judgment* incurred for grave shortcomings except by a system of expiation established by God himself (sacrifices rituals, scapegoat*, day of Atonement) (Lv 16–17). Since blood was central to this system, the New Testament could in some cases adopt the term expiation in the metaphorical sense to describe the death of Christ (*hilastèrion* [Rom 3:25]; *hilaskesthai* [Heb 2:17]; *hilasmos* [1 Jn 2:2; 4:10]) without developing a clear and coherent doctrine of expiation.

The same linguistic usage prevailed in the patristic period. The idea of a social mechanism often remained attached to the word "expiation" when the Fathers used it to designate the blood of Christ without clearly indicating the metaphorical level at which they were speaking.

In the Old Testament the prayer of intercession was already an important element of expiation (*see* Nm 14:13–19; Dt 9:25–29). Of the Servant who gave his life in expiatory sacrifice (Is 53:10), it is also said that he "makes intercession for the transgressors"; Is 53:12). In the same way, the Epistle to the Hebrews underscores that Christ learned obedience in prayer* and tears, and thus he became "the source of eternal salvation" (Heb 5:5–10). Eternal high priest, he brought "perfect freedom," with his blood he appeared "in the presence of God on our behalf" (Heb 9:11–28) and acted in our defense (*see* 1 Jn 2:1) (*see* Lyonnet 1959). The church fathers extended these perspectives and saw in the Eucharist* primarily a participation in Jesus' great prayer of intercession, by which reconciliation is offered to sinners. Cyril* of Alexandria saw in the Jewish rite of the two goats on the Day of Atonement a prefiguration of Christ, who both brought a sacrifice for our sins and brought our sins before God to intercede on our behalf in heaven (PG 69, 588–89).

b) Satisfaction. This is a secular concept introduced into theology through the penitential system of the Church. Anselm made of it the key to his doctrine of redemption (*Cur Deus homo*). Working from principles of Germanic law, he argued that all harm done calls for a punishment or a satisfaction. This should correspond to the importance of the loss or even surpass it, to compensate the suffering of the wronged person. Sin, which wrongs an infinite God, is an infinite evil, which therefore calls for a satisfaction of infinite value. No human being can offer this because all are finite and guilty. This is why the act of Christ was necessary: his sacrifice on the cross presented an infinite value because he was God and at the same time man. Anselm's reasoning deeply influenced subsequent theology and spirituality. The doctrine of infinite satisfaction became a central theme of Christian theology, though Anselm's step-by-step transformation of Germanic notions was lost from sight.

Confronted by the testimony of God's infinite mercy in Holy Scripture*, Anselm took on the task of conceiving of a mercy that fully integrates justice and

thus shows itself—beyond all human projections—truly divine. He begins by explaining that God, being infinitely good, cannot in himself be offended. The demand for satisfaction is founded only in the exterior glory of God or in the order of creatures, which coincides in the last instance with the dignity and liberty of human beings. This implies that they act by themselves and thus vanquish by their own forces the evil within them. But in their most intimate being they are turned toward this God beyond whom nothing greater can be conceived and who is truly glorified as God, rather than being secretly transformed into an idol, only by loving him for himself—which is exactly what human beings, entirely corrupted by sin, can no longer do. But Christ, in whom God sends them unlimited love*, offered himself by pure love to the heavenly Father in the place of sinners, thus instituting a form of offering (a satisfaction) that all can assimilate in the Eucharist. In this way they become able to love God by themselves and for himself. So the satisfaction was not necessary in order to bring God an infinite compensation of a purely material order, foreign to the sinner. The decisive fact is that the act of Christ brought human liberty in its deepest root to the God who gives himself (*see* Corbin, ed., 3, 11–163).

The subsequent tradition did not understand how much the Anselm himself had transformed and "converted" the language of his times. Thomas* Aquinas, who did not develop a systematic doctrine of the redemption, again made satisfaction a sort of assistance supplied externally to human beings on the path of merit. However, he explained that the efficacy proper to the passion* of Christ lay in his love which, as the love of a God-man, has superabundant value (*see* Catâo 1965). With the Council of Trent* the concept of satisfaction was officially adopted in the dogmatic language of the Catholic Church without giving rise to new clarifications. On the subject of the "meritorious cause" of justification, the council echoed Thomas Aquinas, speaking of the "meritorious cause, the beloved only Son of God, our Lord Jesus Christ, who, "while we were enemies" (Rom 5:10), because of the extreme love with which he loved us (*see* Eph 2:4), merited our justification by his most holy passion on the wood of the cross and made satisfaction for us to God the Father" (*COD* 673, 21–24).

This formula allowed theologians to present a simplified version of Anselm's doctrine of expiation as the Catholic doctrine par excellence. In the view of J. Rivière, the dogma clearly teaches that Christ, by his passion and death, rendered satisfaction for the sins of humanity and especially for the crucial sin of Adam. But Rivière also acknowledges that "Catholic theology was never so narrow and superficial as to stop at this sole consideration. If Christ had not suffered, he would nonetheless have redeemed us by the perfection of his love, which offered God the perfect homage he deserves and the only kind that can please him" (Rivière 1931).

Others interpret the death of Christ more brutally, following the criminological principle that every offense demands reparation: "The criminal, indebted first to the one he offended, is subject also to the executioner who inflicts the punishment. Here it is God who is offended, and the executioner is the devil, to whom God allowed man to deliver himself by sin in separating from his true master.... To whom should be paid the price of redemption? Obviously to the one who is the master of the slave and who was offended.... If there was a ransom to pay, it was to God alone, not to Satan. And so we say that Jesus Christ offered his blood as the price of our redemption not to the devil but to God his Father" (Hugon 1922).

Such notions could also be associated with the cult of the heart* of Christ. This form of devotion insists on the human love of Jesus Christ but at the same time cultivates—most often without explanation—the theme of the expiation and the image of the blood that was shed. The suggestion is that God could accept the reconciliation only at this price; this idea has provoked a negative reaction in modern thought (see Leites 1982). The misunderstanding arises from the fact that human representations have been uncritically transposed in speaking of the accomplishment of the redemption so that the metaphorical nature of certain central biblical statements has been lost sight of. The transcendent God does not speak or act directly like a person within the world; he operates through the his intermediary creatures, such that his words are always also human words adapted to the realities of this world and its sins. Consequently, as shown by the progress from the Old Testament to the New, they must undergo a profound "conversion" in order to be a true expression of God and his works. If this is ignored and the words that evoke the redemption are understood in immediate human terms, this will necessarily lead to misunderstanding or even a real "deconversion" (Sesboüé 1988). The danger is particularly great when only the action of Christ and the heavenly Father is retained in the dramatic event of the cross, neglecting the role of the "third partner," sinful murderous humanity. This occultation necessarily leads to a profound perversion, "which consists then in making the violence pass from one pole to the other and presenting as a good what is first of all the deed of evil, sinful human beings, the bloody execution of Christ on the cross. [One] simply forgets that there is nothing salutary about the murder as such, that death as death cannot be the object of

God's plan" (Sesboüé 1988). We will see that the danger of such a "deconversion" is no less where the wrath* of God is concerned.

c) The Wrath of God and the Justification by Christ. Luther* broke with the whole previous tradition and developed a new notion of the passion of Christ. The crucified, he argued, not only suffered in the inferior powers of his soul, as acknowledged by the great tradition (*see* Thomas Aquinas, *ST* IIIa, q. 46, a. 8), but was also stricken to the very depths of his being by the divine wrath. Christ on the cross could no longer offer himself to the Father in an act of love because he felt he was being cast into hell*. That salvation is accomplished precisely in this reprobation we are told only by the word* of the gospel on which faith is founded. The cross reveals the strange conjunction of saving wrath and love from which the divine act proceeds. God completely conceals his bounty behind the judgment, which leads the believer too to understand himself as simultaneously just and a sinner. Luther speaks of a "marvelous exchange." Our sin passes entirely onto Christ, and his righteousness is granted to us in the faith as a foreign gift. Luther certainly acknowledges a second righteousness, coming from a person's own works* (sanctification). But he rigorously distinguishes this from the justice of Christ, which alone renders us righteous in the eyes of God and which, even if it becomes ours in the faith, we can never discover in ourselves. Because faith in the justificatory work of Christ is decisive, confidence in salvation is not put into question by possible future sins (there is "certainty of salvation").

This notion of justification discloses a new notion of evil. Luther particularly struggled with God and often felt his wrath. He denied that a person had free choice with regard to salvation, and he broke with Augustine in not granting any theological significance to freedom, not even Adam's freedom, and in defending a more rigorous doctrine of predestination* than that held by the bishop of Hippo. Thus, he was led to distinguish in God the *deus absconditus* (predestinating God) and the *deus revelatus* (preached God). The first is an absolutely ungraspable and terrifying being and can be wicked for human beings; we have to flee from him and put ourselves entirely in the hands of the God revealed on the cross. Therefore, the dialectic of the cross, that of justice and wrath, not only results from the tension between human sin and the sanctity of God but operates in God himself. Fortunately, the reformer did not systematize this backdrop of his theology (*see* Schwager 1986).

Currents vigorously emphasizing human liberty and the moral life soon developed in Protestant theology in reaction against Luther. The whole history of the Protestant doctrine of redemption in the Germanic region was in fact determined by the problematic of a subject who finds "in the recourse to the self-aware ego the ultimate foundation of a theory of the truth*" (Wenz 1984). For the new current of thought, fascinated by the autonomy of the subject (liberty, morality, self-awareness), the idea of a justification by way of an intermediary was unacceptable (Socinianism, Kant*). This vision even attracted defenders of the traditional doctrine, as shown, for example, by the theory of the expiatory suffering of Christ (*satisfactio passiva*). According to this line of thought, Christ, by his death, did indeed endure in our place punishment for our sins and delivered us from them, but in his active obedience he could be only a model for us because on this level the idea of vicarious substitution is incompatible with the autonomy of virtue (J. G. Töllner, 1724–74; G. C. Storr, 1746–1805).

This theological tradition, directly or indirectly dominated by the idea of an autonomous subject, must have caused a sharp reaction in Barth; resolutely rejecting any notion of man's recourse to his subjectivity, he brutally confronted the sinner enclosed in himself with the word that God sent from outside. However, Barth did not call for a return to authoritarian objectivism; he attempted to think God as subjectivity and communication of self, by which alone an authentic human subjectivity can be constituted. To preclude any self-affirmation by sinful man, Barth took as the starting point of his theology the eternal choice of the grace* of God (predestination*) as manifest in the cross and the resurrection of Christ and even placed it ahead of the doctrine of creation and providence. In a "primitive founding act" (*KD* II/2, 25 and 82), God makes a decision with regard to himself because in "choosing man, he not only disposes of him but also originarily of himself" (*KD* II/2, 1; *see* 89 and 96; IV/2, 92). Barth discovers at the cross that the eternal election has a double content. God vows himself to suffering and reprobation for the sake of humanity. Since God in Christ takes entirely on himself the wrath and the "no" of condemnation that weighs on all human beings, each and every person and not just a certain number of the chosen is called to salvation ("predestined"). In this approach, Christ's humanity risks becoming a passive grandeur, and one might ask where the wrath comes from if the cross precedes (logically) the creation and the fall of man by the will of God. This is where Barth introduces his difficult doctrine of the "void" (*das Nichtige*), which constitutes a third mode of being aside from created being as such and nothingness, a mode of being that of course finds its concrete form in human sinfulness but represents

much more than that. The void appears—as what one might call an indirect consequence—in God himself in the eternal election: "It is precisely because the act of God is founded on election that it is always an act of zeal, wrath, judgment. God is always holy, but that also means that his being and his act are always produced in a determined opposition, that they always include real negation, defense, aggression. The Other from which God is separated, with regard to which he affirms himself and imposes his positive will, is the vain" (*KD* III/3, 405).

Balthasar* adopted essential elements of Barth's thought and no less resolutely than Barth rejected all theological subjectivism. Starting from Christology*, he makes the distinction between person and spiritual nature ("subject-spirit") and understands man, insofar as he is a creature, as a simple "subject-spirit" who awaits in the very depths of himself a supplementary determination. This comes from Christ, whose mission is identified with his personal being and includes in itself all humankind. Countering the whole Enlightenment tradition, for which the profound being of the moral subject cannot be the object of any delegation, Balthasar founds the vicarious act of Christ on his mission (i.e., his person), which also raises all other human individuals to the dignity of persons. This substitution culminates for Balthasar—as for Luther and Barth—in the event of the cross, which sees Christ stricken in our place by the divine wrath and, like the damned, abandoned by God, so that he can infiltrate universal sin to its fullest extent. As opposed to Barth, however, Balthasar clearly relates moral evil to the wayward liberty of creatures. He acknowledges a hope* of universal salvation but at the same time insists on the ultimate mystery* inherent in the encounter of divine grace and human liberty.

d) Sacrifice. The liturgy* often speaks of the sacrifice of Christ on the cross, making this idea particularly important for Catholic theology. The *Catechism of the Catholic Church* (1992) interprets the life and death of Christ almost exclusively by means of this concept. But sacrifices also play a central role in the domain of religions, giving rise to widely divergent interpretations. Many animal sacrifices figure in the Old Testament also, and one of the essential duties of the priests was to immolate the victims.

In the New Testament, despite numerous figurative allusions, the idea of sacrifice is rarely applied to the death of Christ. Only the Epistle to the Hebrews develops a theology of the sacerdotal service and the "the blood of Christ, who through the eternal Spirit offered himself without blemish to God" (Heb 9:14). Nevertheless, everything that separates this from the Old

Testament order is emphasized in Hebrews. The decisive originality, which gives the concept of sacrifice an entirely new sense, lies in the fact that in cultual sacrifice those who kill are sacrificers, whereas in the crucifixion of Christ, they are murderers. This reversal led the first Christian authors to use the term with several different meanings. With regard to the offering of the gifts in the Eucharist*, they speak—drawing on Malachi 1:11—of a pure sacrifice of nourishment, offered in all places (Daly 1978). The concept of sacrifice when related to the act of Christ was, on the other hand, highly spiritualized. Augustine writes, "Then true sacrifice is all good works that contribute to uniting us with God in a holy society, meaning all work related to that most supreme grace in which we can truly be happy (*City of God*, X, 6).

This is the definition used by Thomas when he speaks of the passion as a sacrifice (*ST* IIIa, q. 48, a. 3). However, in this ethical acception, we are not given to understand why the sacrifice of Christ had to involve his brutal bloody death and could not be limited to his love for God. Augustine and the church fathers sought to remedy this defect by completing their doctrine of sacrifice with the theme of victory over the devil; Scholastic theologians put the doctrine of expiation to the same purpose. These artificial complements show that an important factor had been neglected: the role of the subconscious in sacrificial representations, as expressed in the materiality of the rite.

Because the idea of sacrifice, despite its spiritualization, inevitably evokes blood and the blood of Christ did flow on the cross, there was a temptation from the patristic era to recognize in the "sacrifice of Christ" an act of putting to death or annihilation. Consequently, the murderers of Jesus could be made the instruments of the eternal Logos (Eusebius, Athanasius, Gregory of Nyssa) or the Heavenly Father (Barth). This entailed the risk of considering the sacrificed Christ as the indirect author of his own death or the victim immolated by the Heavenly Father. Gregory of Nyssa explained that Christ was not dead according to the laws of nature; the Logos, by his plenary power, had separated the soul and the body of his humanity (killing himself directly) to offer the sacrifice (Jaeger II, 132, 7–14; III/1, 152, 30–154, 14; IX, 286, 23–288, 8).

Athanasius added a notion of exchange to the idea that the Logos sacrificed his humanity: "The Word himself took upon himself that which is ours, brought the sacrifice of it, and thus destroyed it in order to clothe us in that which is his" (PG 26, 1061).

Such ideas inevitably led to the "deconversion "of concepts referred to above. The specific role of the murderers was obscured, and the notion of sacrifice repeatedly fell into archaic representations. This is the starting point of the contemporary critique by R. Girard, whose interpretation of ritual bloody cults, which makes a clear distinction between sacrificial representations (myths*) and the sacrificial act (rite), may be useful to theology. Although Girard acknowledges that sacrificial representations developed and were spiritualized throughout the history of religions, he consistently interprets bloody sacrifice in its ritual materiality as a collective aggression directed against a "victim." From this perspective he resolutely refuses to see the death of Christ as a sacrifice. That which in the history of religions was a bloody sacrificial act is revealed in the Gospels* as a sin, the collective act of murderous human. There the figure of the "victim" takes on an entirely different meaning because the offering to the divinity, as expressed in sacrificial representations, is made by the victim himself and not by those who kill or sacrifice.

Moreover, the narrative* of the Fall shows that as soon as human beings become guilty of transgression, they rush to project blame for their act on others: Adam accuses Eve, and Eve accuses the serpent (Gn 3:12f.; *see* Gn 4:9). Cain, devoured by jealousy, tries to find solace by killing his brother, and he too starts by projecting the blame (Gn 4:3–9). Furthermore, in the narratives of the lives of the prophets and in the psalms of lamentation, we see how criminals constantly join forces to calumniate and persecute people of prayer and justice (Jer 26:7–9; Mi 4:11; Za 12:3; Ps 2:2f., 22:13–17, 31:14, 38:13, 38:20, 41:8, 69:5, 118:10–13). And so we understand how many different groups in Israel*, both Jewish and Gentile, combined against Jesus (*see* Acts 4:27f.).

Anselm of Canterbury reasoned that a mercy that draws a veil over evil without restoring the captive liberty from within is unworthy of God as of man. This reasoning is important but in itself insufficient. If transgression implies that the blame is cast on others, turning them into victims, then evil is not fully vanquished until the victims are rescued. In fact, as God's revelation progresses from the Old Testament to the New Testament, he appears ever more clearly as the one who takes the side of the victim. We understand then how Jesus accepted by obedience to become such a victim. Because, like the good shepherd, he was always looking for sinners, he discovered that as soon as he came near them, they placed their blame on him. They made him their "scapegoat," not in the ritual sense as some theologians (Estius, Cornelius a Lapide; H. Lesêtre; E. B. Allo; *see* Sabourin 1961) have believed—on the grounds that God or the Logos, like the high priest in the rite of the scapegoat, deliberately transferred the sin to humankind—but in the sense of the Psalms*, which, moreover, correspond to the approach of modern social psychology. Blinded by sin, people instinctively projected their transgressions on the innocent man, making him the carrier of their sins (1 Pt 2:24) or the scapegoat. God did not directly wish for the death of his Son, but he wanted the Son's total devotion to hardened human beings who would, in the name of the law, identify him with sin (2 Cor 5:21) and a curse (Gal 3:13). As victim of sin, Christ did not answer violence and lies with violence but bore the evil in a nonviolent love; this is the meaning of the "lamb of God" image. By a "mysterious alchemy" (Sesboüé 1988), he was able to transform evil into good. Having simultaneously identified with all the victims (*see* 2 Cor 5:15), he could implore God in their name from this world of perdition and call on the saving power of the resurrection through the coming of the Spirit (*see* Schwager 1990). Here modern theology emphasizes that sending the Spirit must be understood as an autonomous act by which God communicates salvation and not a simple appropriation (*see* Mühlen 1963; Congar 1979–80; Coffey 1979).

e) Transcendental Reconciliation. The central theme of reconciliation was reformulated by Rahner*. The point of departure of his theology is the universal will to salvation in God; he understands revelation as an act of divine self-communication that has repercussions right down through history (transcendental revelation). But Rahner also sees Christ as the absolute savior because it is in him that this divine act, which takes place everywhere in an invisible way ("existential supernatural," "anonymous Christians"), has become historically incomprehensible. Rahner contemplates the question of death from the point of view of liberty and decision. However, the violent death of Jesus does not play any particular role in his reasoning. That is why the theme of evil and sin remains vague in the doctrine of transcendental reconciliation (*see* Rahner 1976).

4. From the Resurrection of Jesus to the New Creation in Christ

According to the narrative in Genesis, God judged after each act of the creation that his work was good and, finally, very good (Gn 1:4, 1:10, 1:18, 1:21, 1:25, 1:31). But on the eve of the deluge, "Now the earth was corrupt in God's sight, and the earth was filled with violence" (Gn 6:11). God's first observation, when the waters recede, is that "the intention of man's heart is evil from his youth" (Gn 8:21); similar grievances are repeated throughout the Old Testament. All the moral admonishments and prophecies* shattered on "that execrable stubbornness" (Jer 3:17, 9:13, 11:8, 13:10, 16:12, 18:12, 23:17). Jesus' proclamation met with the same resistance. That is why, according to

Paul, the "old man" must die with Christ, to share in his resurrection and become a "new man": and a "new creation" (Rom 6:1–11, 8:1–17; 2 Cor 5:17; Gal 6:15). The death of Christ is salutary only because it leads to the resurrection and the new creation (*see* Durrwell 1950).

The theme of the resurrection and the new creation was treated in various ways by the church fathers. They saw in the Eucharist a "remedy for immortality" (Ignatius of Antioch, *Letter to the Churches of Ephesus* 20:2). But the idea of man's deification is what allowed them to explain that the sinner must be renewed in his very nature*. Athanasius argued that man, by the Fall, called down on himself a double misfortune: he is condemned for his transgression and falls into the state of perdition of a creature separated from God (SC 199, 275–79). Having escaped from participation in the Word* and no longer being "such as he had begun to be," he loses the gift of the promised incorruptibility and is brought down to the simple condition of a creature drawn out of nothingness*. He finds himself subject to a power of natural destruction that is rigorously exercised against him since the transgression and must face the death with which he was threatened. It is to eliminate this double misfortune and vanquish the extreme inconstancy of human liberty that man must be naturally bound to God by the incarnation of the Logos: "For he made himself man so that we would be made God" (ibid., 459). We are liberated from sin and deified. The cross manifests the humiliation of the Logos, the resurrection shows the glorification and the new creation of humanity. This notion of an exchange between God and humanity was very important in theology (*see* Thomas Aquinas, opusc. 57, *in Festo Corp. Chr.* 1) as in the liturgy.

Certain Fathers (Origen, Gregory of Nyssa, Maximus the Confessor) replaced the idea of the double misfortune with the doctrine of the double creation. After Philo of Alexandria, they distinguished between a creation prior to the Fall and a creation after the Fall. The first included impassibility, an angelic condition, and an eternal existence; the second includes suffering, death, and procreation with concupiscence (Gregory of Nyssa, SC 6, 151–72; Maximus, CChr.SG 10, 138–39). Man, destined by God to an ideal angelic condition, sinned from the first instant of his existence: he was no sooner created than he was miserable. Sin is inscribed, with all its consequences, in the concrete reality of the creation itself, and it can be vanquished only by a radical transformation, by death and resurrection.

The doctrine of the double creation was not adopted by the Western Church, which taught, with Athanasius, that the creation as such was extremely precarious and that only Adam's preternatural gifts had allowed him to exist briefly in an ideal condition. No doubt man could have avoided sinning (Augustine); however, his "ability to sin" carried the threat of fatality. In both these approaches the moral evil has its condition of possibility and therefore to a certain extent its deep roots in the creation itself, beyond all act of an ethical or political order. Salvation demands a transformation of the "old" creation. That is why the whole tradition insisted on the corporeal nature of the resurrection and presented it as a new creation in view of eternal life and not a return to the precarious existence before the Fall. Only in the second-century Gnosis (see Orbe 1976) and in modern theology did converse movements develop. Whereas Gnosis often subjected the material world to an inferior God and conceived salvation as an elevation out of this world, certain currents of modern theology tend to reduce the resurrection to a process of conversion within believers themselves (Bultmann*, W. Marxen). In both cases there is a risk of losing sight of the important theme of the new creation.

In an attempt to make the idea of precarious creation accessible to a modern sensibility, P. Teilhard de Chardin (1881–1955) made an interpretation based on the theory of evolution*. In some texts he describes "original sin" as a phenomenon coextensive with the whole of evolution: "Original sin is the essential reaction of the finite to the creative act" (Œuvres, v.X, 53). He counts on a transformation of the creation that looks beyond man to the Omega point, the full revelation of Christ. He was taken to task for neglecting the question of moral transgression in his notion of original sin. Even if the specific role of human liberty remains to be clearly defined, today it seems fully justifiable to attempt, as does Teilhard, to place in an evolutionist context the precariousness of the creation, already taught by the Fathers. This leads into the idea that the resurrection of Christ is not only a sign of hope for all people but also the indication of a future transformation of the whole extrahuman creation.

5. Conclusion

The Old Testament messianic texts expressed the hope of an earthly plenitude of salvation (Is 11:1–16, 65:16–25; Am 9:11–15; Mi 4:1–5). Jesus also proclaimed the kingdom of God as a reality already partially accomplished. But the approach of the new world inevitably multiplied the resistance of the old forces. This is why Jesus' fidelity to the kingdom of God led him, beyond his violent death and his resurrection, toward the world of the new creation and authentic salvation. Remembering the distance covered with the help of the Holy Spirit and in its efforts to im-

itate Christ, the Church proclaims the beginning of salvation in this world though knowing that the time of misfortune, suffering, and persecutions is not over. This is why the Church understands itself to be the sign and instrument of a profound metamorphosis of human beings, who are destined for union with God and with each other (LG 1). Since the Church itself is not exempt from sin, iniquity, and suffering, the unambiguous signs of the awaited salvation are found only in the symbolic structure of its sacramental life. Whereas secular societies need to distinguish themselves from foreigners and enemies and can establish their own unity only at the expense of some scapegoat, it is quite a different sort of community that sketches itself in the eucharistic celebration. It is rooted in the conversion* of all the participants and confesses that God made the one who was excluded and rejected by men the "source of eternal salvation" (Heb 5:9), the "cornerstone" of a new community (Acts 4:11), the "food that endures to eternal life" (Jn 6:27). The eucharistic celebration on earth thus becomes the sign of the fullness of the salvation hoped for in eternal life with the divine Trinity.

● Anselm of Canterbury, Œuvres, Ed. M. Corbin, vol. 3, Paris, 1988.

Athanasius of Alexandria, Against the Pagans, SC 18 bis; On the Incarnation, SC 199.

Augustine, De Civitate Dei, BAug, 33–37.

Gregory of Nyssa, The Creation of Man, SC 6.

Irenaeus, Adversus haereses, SC 100 (2 vols.), 152, 153, 210, 211, 263, 264, 293, 294.

♦ J. Rivière (1914), Le dogme de la Rédemption: Étude théologique, Paris.

E. Hugon (1922), Le mystère de la rédemption, Paris.

G. Aulén (1930), Den Kristna försoningstanken, Lund.

J. Rivière (1931), Le dogme de la Rédemption: Études critiques et documents.

K. Barth (1932–67), KD, I–IV + index (1970) (Dogmatique, 26 vols., Geneva, 1953–74, + index, 1980).

F. X. Durrwell (1950), La résurrection de Jésus mystère de salut, Le Puy (11th Ed., Paris, 1982).

S. Lyonnet (1959), "Expiation et intercession," Bib. 40, 885–901.

L. Sabourin (1961), Rédemption sacrificielle, Paris.

H. U. von Balthasar (1961), Kosmische Liturgie: Das Weltbild Maximus' des Bekenners, 2nd Ed., Einsiedeln.

H. Mühlen (1963), Der Heilige Geist als Person, Münster.

B. Catâo (1965), Salut et rédemption chez saint Thomas d'Aquin: L'acte sauveur du Christ, Paris.

J. Galot (1965), La rédemption, mystère d'alliance, Paris.

H. U. von Balthasar (1973–83), Theodramatik, 5 vols., Einsiedeln.

N. Brox (1973), "Soteria und Salus, Heilsvorstellungen in der alten Kirche," EvTh 33, 253–79.

A. Orbe (1976), Christología gnostica: Introducción a la soterología de los siglos II y III, 2 vols., Madrid.

K. Rahner (1976), Grundkurs des Glaubens, Fribourg-Basel-Vienna.

R. Daly (1978), Christian Sacrifice: The Judaeo-Christian Background before Origen, Washington, D.C.

R. Girard (1978), *Des choses cachées depuis la fondation du monde*, Paris.

D. Coffey (1979), *Grace: The Gift of the Holy Spirit*, Sidney.

Y. Congar (1979–80), *Je crois en l'Esprit Saint*, 3 vols., Paris.

H. de Lubac (1979–81), *La postérité spirituelle de Joachim de Flore*, 2 vols., Paris.

R. Verdier (texts compiled by) (1980), *La vengeance*, 2 vols., Paris.

R. Girard (1982), *Le bouc émissaire*, Paris.

N. Leites (1982), *Le meurtre de Jésus, moyen de salut,?* Paris.

M. Seils (1985), "Heil und Erlösung IV, Dogmatisch," *TRE* 14, 622–37 (bibl.).

B. Studer (1985), *Gott und unsere Erlösung im Glauben der alten Kirche*, Düsseldorf.

G. Wenz (1984–86), *Geschichte der Versöhnungslehre in der evangelischen Theologie der Neuzeit*, 2 vols., Munich.

R. Schwager (1986), *Der wunderbare Tausch: Zur Geschichte und Deutung der Erlösungslehre*, Munich.

Th. Pröpper (1988), *Erlösungsglaube und Freiheitsgeschichte*, Munich (3rd Ed. 1991).

B. Sesboüé (1988–91), *Jésus-Christ, l'Unique Médiateur*, vol. I: *Essai sur la rédemption et le salut*, vol. II: *Les récits du salut*.

R. Swinburne (1989), *Responsibility and Atonement*, Oxford.

R. Schwager (1990), *Jesus im Heilsdrama*, Innsbruck.

B. Sesboüé (1990), "Salut," *DSp* 14, 251–83.

J. Sobrino (1991), *Jesucristo liberador*, Madrid.

C. Porro (1992), *Gesù il Salvatore*, Bologna.

RAYMUND SCHWAGER

See also **Beatitude; Eschatology; Jerusalem; Messianism/Messiah; Millenarianism; Scripture, Fulfillment of; Son of Man; Temptation; Vision, Beatific**

Satan. *See* **Demons**

Savior. *See* **Christ/Christology; Salvation**

Scandal/Skandalon

In modern English and French usage, "scandal" (Fr. *scandale*) in the most general sense means an offense to moral sensibility. In a more precise sense, the word refers to the occasion of moral lapse provided by such behavior. In moral theology*, the term translated by *scandale* in French signifies a word, deed, or omission that, because it is wrong or appears wrong, could be an occasion for sin*.

The origin of the notion lies in the Bible. In the literal sense, a scandal is a trap or stumbling block (*skandalon;* the spring that sets it off is *skandàlithon*) or an offense or stumbling (*proskomma*). In the religious or ethical sense, it is anything that is the occasion or cause of temptation* or falling. For example, Israel* is warned against consorting with the people remaining in the promised land lest the latter become "a snare and a trap" to them (Jos 23:13). In the New Testament, the term refers primarily to the ways, utterly different from human expectations, in which God* saves the world*. Jesus* himself is an "offense to" a sinful and self-righteous world (Mk 6:3; *see* Lk 2:34). He is "a stone of stumbling, and a rock of offense" (Rom 9:33; 1 Pt 2:8). By reason of his association with sinners, his freedom from traditions, and his attitude to the Sabbath*, Jesus offends the Pharisees (Mt 12:14), and his death is "a stumbling block to Jews and folly to Gentiles" (1 Cor 1:23). He is the focus of the decision for belief or unbelief. Thus, *skandàlon* is a matter not primarily of ethics* but of faith*. On the other hand, Jesus is recorded as condemning offense in the strongest terms: "Woe to the one through whom they [temptations to sin] come!" (Lk 17:1; *see* Mt 18:6f.).

The Christian must not soften the offensive, or scandalous, aspect of faith. However, as Paul says with regard to food sacrificed to idols, truth* should not be made an occasion of moral lapse for a brother (1 Cor 8:4–13; Rom 14:13–21). Paul refers here to actions that are not evil but that could cause others to sin in certain cases.

Jesus' statement that "Temptations to sin are sure to come" (Lk 17:1) led to questions concerning the sense in which offense is necessary. Does this mean that, if the gospel is preached in its fullness, it is inevitable that some will be scandalized? What is the significance of Jesus' challenge to Peter*: "Get behind me, Satan, you are a hindrance to me" (Mt 16:23)? According to Thomas Aquinas*, *skandàlon* in this case means "obstacle" and not "offense" (*STh* IIa IIae, q. 43, a. 5, ad 1).

Aquinas defines "scandal" (*STh* IIa IIae, q. 43) as "the less right *minus rectum* in word or action giving the occasion of a fall" (a. 1). An act is *minus rectum* when it is wrong or when it has the appearance of sin (example from 1 Cor 8:9ff., loc. cit. a. 1, ad 2). A scandal is an occasion, not a cause, of sin since nothing can be sufficient cause of sin except one's own will.

Scandal may be *per se* or *per accidens*. It is *per se* when a person has an intention* to lead another into sin or when the deed or word is such as to induce another to sin. It is *per accidens* when a person's deed or word, without the deed or the intention being evil, is the occasion of sin for someone who is already disposed toward it. Scandal may be "active" (from the perspective of the one who occasions it) or "passive" (from the perspective of the person who is scandalized; ad 4). Careful discernment is required when the deed is good and legitimate but may occasion a fall by those who are weak. Spiritual goods must sometimes be abandoned in order to avoid scandal. It is obviously forbidden to sin mortally in order to save another. However, there are some spiritual goods that are not necessary for salvation*. In such cases, it is necessary to distinguish between those who are scandalized out

of malice and those who are scandalized because they lack understanding. The former wish to prevent the good effects of what they reject, such as the Pharisees who were scandalized by Christ* (Mt 15:12). It is necessary to take the weakness or ignorance of the latter into account and to take the time to explain what is at stake; if they persevere, this arises from malice and should be ignored.

These ideas were adopted by the manuals of moral theology and repeated, with some variations, for centuries. The work of Alphonsus* Liguori is representative of the manualist tradition (*Moral Theology* 1, 2, 3, 5). Causing an active scandal is always prohibited. As for other types of scandal, the authors engaged in detailed discussions of the circumstances in which one may or may not do something that could be an occasion of sin. It was taken for granted that one may never perform an intrinsically evil act or intend to lead another into sin, but there were cases in which passive scandal could be permitted for a proportionate reason. While this tradition has been accused of legalism, these older authors were intensely aware of the paradoxical allure of the forbidden and the intricate web of relationships between persons.

The manualists formulated what is today the official Catholic position: direct scandal is always wrong, but indirect scandal, caused by an action good in itself, can be justified in certain circumstances on the basis of the principle of double effect (intention*). Direct scandal is equated with seduction, which is the deliberate effort, overt or disguised, to lead another into sin. Seduction is not only a matter of individual acts, nor is it solely to do with sexuality: there can also be cultural, social, political, or economic seduction (e.g., propaganda). The seducer may directly corrupt the moral character or faith of the victim: here the adjective "diabolical" is appropriately used. The seducer may also be need personal satisfaction, or companionship in evil*. Seduction is therefore a radical perversion of friendship.

The theological analysis of scandal sees it as having an objective element, the nature of the scandalous words or deeds, and a subjective element, the culpability of the individuals occasioning or taking scandal. In moral theology, scandal is closely linked to seduction and to complicity in evil. The common context is the relational structure of the moral life. A moral act is to be both an expression of personal authenticity and a witness of the moral life to others, especially in view of the fact that one does not always act alone. Traditional moral theology explored in detail the complexities of what was called "cooperation in evil." The importance of the relational structure of the moral life was expressed in requiring that the entirety of the moral life be informed by the love* of charity. Scandal, seduction, and complicity are profound violations of love as well as of specific virtues*, such as justice*. They contradict the responsibility that we have for the salvation of others (Häring 1978), hence the necessity to make reparation if one has become guilty of scandal.

While the manuals did not ignore political, cultural, and economic realities, they were intended principally for the use of confessors and had a largely individualistic notion of sin. To correct this bias, contemporary theology appeals to the notion of "structural sin."

Supporters of proportionalism* have challenged the theory of scandal, in particular, the idea that there are acts that are intrinsically wrong, the distinction between direct scandal and indirect scandal, and even the validity of the principle of double effect. For many proportionalists, only those acts that in their very meaning include the intending of moral evil, such as deliberately inducing others to violate their consciences* or do what they judge to be immoral, are intrinsically evil (Schüller 1979).

The application of the principle of double effect becomes especially problematic when it comes to choosing between two evil acts. Traditionally, committing an evil act, even if it is the lesser available evil, was never permitted. Today, by contrast, it seems obvious to some that one should *choose* the lesser of two evils. The problem is that, in counseling the lesser evil, one is still persuading someone to do a bad act. A contemporary instance of this problem is the debate over condoms: should one counsel persons who are incapable of abstinence to use condoms so as to avoid AIDS? Would that not be a cause of scandal? Alphonsus Liguori, who is far from being alone in this, thought that when the other is already determined to sin, one may counsel him to perform a lesser sin.

Earlier, Augustine* had argued that divorcing an adulterous wife in order to marry another would be less sinful than killing her for the same purpose since one sin is better than two (*De conjugiis adulterinis* 2, 15). This gave rise to a certain number of quibbles in the manuals that have seemed implausible to contemporary critics who see them as one more confirmation of the inadequacy of the theory of double effect.

Critics of this type of moral theology charge it with narrowing the biblical notion of scandal and its primary reference to faith. The possibility that the Church itself might be an occasion of scandal is not addressed, although the manualists were well aware of the scandalous behavior of some members of the clergy. What Paul says about scandalizing the weak should not be made into an absolute principle: the need to avoid scandal and protect the "weak" has sometimes been invoked to resist necessary changes in the Church and in society*. Avoiding scandal has sometimes also been a means of protecting the reputation of the Church's institutions and personnel.

Finally—and this is an entirely different aspect of the matter—some contemporary theologians speak of the scandal of creation*, arguing that much of contemporary atheism arises from the scandal of the suffering of the innocent. How, then, are we to understand the "necessity" of scandal?

- Alphonsus de Liguori, *Theologia Moralis,* Ed. L. Gaudé, Rome, 1905.

Augustine, *De conjugiis adulterinis,* BAug 2, 101–233.

Jérôme, *Comm. sur saint Matthieu,* SC 242 and 259.

Thomas Aquinas, *ST* IIa IIae, q. 43; IIIa, q. 42, a. 2.

- U.S. Bishops (1989), "Called to Compassion and Responsibility: A Response to the HIV/AIDS Crisis," *Origins* 19, 429.

Jean-Paul II (1994), "Aux pharmaciens catholiques," *OR* 30 January.

La commission sociale des évêques de France (1995), *Sida, la société en question,* Paris.

◆ G. Stählin (1930), *Skandalon: Untersuchungen zur Geschichte eines biblischen Begriffes,* Gütersloh.

N. Jung (1939), "Scandale," *DThC* 14, 1246–54.

A. Humbert (1954), "Essai d'une théologie du scandale dans les synoptiques," *Bib* 35, 1–28.

X. Léon-Dufour (1962), "Scandale," *VThB* 1000–1003.

G. Stählin (1964), "Skandalon," *ThWNT* 7, 338–58.

R. Schnackenburg (1970), "Scandal," *Encyclopaedia of Biblical Theology,* London.

J.M. McDermott (1977), "Luke 12, 8–9: Stone of Scandal," *RevBib* 84, 523–37.

E. McDonagh (1977), "Le jugement de scandale," *Conc(F)* 127, 117–24.

B. Häring (1978), *Free and Faithful in Christ,* vol. 2, New York.

B. Schüller (1979), "Direct Killing/Indirect Killing," *Readings in Moral Theology No. 1,* Ed. C.E. Curran, R.A. McCormick, Mahwah, N.J., 138–57.

BRIAN JOHNSTONE

See also **Casuistry; Intention; Temptation**

Scapegoat

The scapegoat is an animal* that plays a particular role in the ritual of the Day of Expiations* or Day of Atonement. This ritual, drawn from Jewish liturgy,* is described in Leviticus 16, though the name of the holiday is not given there. However, in Leviticus 23:27f., it appears in a liturgical calendar that makes this a day of fasting and rest. The holiday is celebrated on the 10th day of the seventh month, the month of Tishri (September–October) of the Babylonian calendar.

Centered on the idea of purification, the celebration includes two distinct rituals that were combined, no doubt at a late period: a sacrificial ritual composed of sacrifices* for sin*, holocausts, and a nonsacrificial ritual. Aaron the priest (sacerdoce) receives from the community of Israelites two goats, takes them, and places them before YHWH at the entry of the sanctuary. A goat is chosen by drawing lots and designated "for YHWH," the other "for Azazel." The first serves as a sacrifice for the sin of the people. The second, placed alive before YHWH, will be sent into the desert (Lv 16:5, 16:7–10). Aaron places his hands on the head of the living goat, charging it with all the transgressions of the Israelites, and then sends the goat into the desert led by a man who stands ready for this mission (Lv 16:20ff.).

The second goat did not bear the name of "scapegoat"; this was given after the Vulgate translation*, *capro emissario,* which refers to the fact that the animal was sent out, and is meant to be a translation of Azazel. In the Septuagint translation it is no longer the "goat for Azazel" but a goat *"casting away"* (*apopompaios*) sins. The name of Azazel must have created a problem for the translators. It is of course maintained in the rabbinical tradition* but interpreted as the name of a place (*Midrash Yoma* VI, 18). Rashi (commentary on *Leviticus*) saw it as the name of a steep mountain. Azazel, named four times in Leviticus 16 and no where else in the Old Testament, is the name* of a divine being, more exactly a demon* who lives in the desert like the goats or satyrs in Isaiah 13:21 and 34:14. The name Azazel was the subject of numerous discussions, but it can be explained as *'z'zl* from a root *'zz,* evoking force, by a conscious metathesis of *'z'zl* (Azazel) with the intent of eliminating the theophoric element *'el.*

The rite of the scapegoat shows that it is not an offering to a divinity, even an inferior one, and even less a sacrifice because there is no immolation and use of the blood. The animal is sent alive into the desert. The sole function of the goat is to represent symbolically the spatial removal of the transgressions of Israel*. In itself, the goat is neither innocent nor guilty; it serves as a symbolic vehicle.

Illustration-in-act of the purification of the community, the rite of the scapegoat is integrated into a whole that is meant to signify the return to full communion* with God*. In Leviticus 16 the rite is yahwized, but it is ancient or even archaic, and similar rites have been found. The most suggestive, despite the differences, is the rite of purification of the *cella* of the god Nabu in Esagil, the temple* of the god Marduk in Babylon. This rite took place on the fifth day of the Babylonian New Year. A ram was decapitated, and a priest used its body in a ritual destined to purify the sanctuary and its immediate surroundings. The animal's body was then thrown into the river along with the head; the priest and the person who had killed the animal retired to the country until the end of the holiday (D. Wright). The comparison is all the more interesting in that the Babylonian rite is connected with the New Year festival, while the Day of Expiations, before it was set in the seventh month, was celebrated in the first month of a calendar on which the year began in the autumn.

In the New Testament, the goat sent into the desert on the Day of Expiations is never mentioned in relation with the death* of Christ*. Hebrews 13:12, where Jesus* is presented as having "suffered outside the gate," might have contained a reference to the rite of Expiations, but the precision "outside the camp" in Leviticus 16:27 concerns the combustion of animals offered in sacrifice. Similarly, when the texts evoke "Christ having been offered once to bear the sins of many" (Heb 9:28; 1 Pt 2:24), the expression refers rather to Isaiah 53:12 than to Leviticus 16. So it must be recognized that the Christian typology of the scapegoat was not developed before the *Epistle of Barnabas* (7, 1–10), a second-century A.D. writing.

When the expression "scapegoat" is used in everyday language (R. Girard), it has no direct relation with the ritual in Leviticus.

● R. Martin-Achard (1974), *Essai biblique sur les fêtes d'Israël,* Geneva, 105–19.

R. Girard (1982), *Le bouc émissaire,* Paris.

D. P. Wright (1987), *The Disposal of Impurity: Elimination Rites in the Bible and Hittite and Mesopotamian Literature,* Atlanta.

J. Milgrom (1991), *Leviticus 1–16, AncBD* 3, New York.

R. Peter-Contesse (1993), *Lévitique 1–16,* CAT III a, Geneva.

R. Girard (1994), *Quand ces choses commenceront,* Paris.

JACQUES BRIEND

See also **Exorcism; Expiation; Laying On of Hands; Purity/Impurity; Sacrifice; Salvation; Sin; Wrath of God**

Scheeben, Matthias Joseph

1835–88

Scheeben was born in Meckenheim, near Bonn, and died in Köln; he studied theology* and philosophy* in the *Collegium Romanum* from 1852 to 1859. His teachers included in particular Carlo Passaglia, Clemens Schrader, and Johann Baptist Franzelin, who were then seeking to renew Catholic theology through contact with the Fathers* of the Church ("the Roman School"). In the *Collegium Germanicum,* where Joseph Kleutgen taught rhetoric, Scheeben also entered into contact with that eminent representative of the budding Neoscholastic movement. Scheeben was ordained priest* in Rome* in 1858. On his return to Germany he was first rector and catechist for the Ursulines in Münsterfeld; from 1860 he taught in the diocesan seminary in Köln, first as tutor and then as professor of dogmatics* and moral theology.

Scheeben's first important publication dealt with Marian piety (*Marienblüten aus dem Garten der heiligen Väter und christlichen Dichter,* Schaffhouse, 1860). In the area of dogmatics he dealt with the question of the relation between nature* and grace*, one of the fundamental problems of 19th-century theology, and did so in terms both of the theory of knowledge and of ontology. While dissociating the order of nature from the order of grace, Scheeben argued for a subordination of the former to the latter (*Natur und Gnade,* Mainz, 1861). This work was set in the framework of internal theological discussion, but Scheeben also undertook a popularization of his thought in a reworked translation of a work of piety by the Jesuit Eusebius Nieremberg, *Del aprecio y estima de la divina gracia* (Madrid, 1638). This book went through several editions during his lifetime (*The Wonders of Divine Grace* [*Die Herrlichkeiten der göttlichen Gnade,* Freiburg,

1862; final edition revised by the author, 1885]) and allowed Scheeben to widen his audience. In *The Mysteries of Christianity* (*Die Mysterien des Christentums,* Freiburg, 1865), Scheeben started out from the mystery* of the divine Trinity* in order to set forth a general vision of Christian faith* and was intent on bringing out the internal coherence of and the connection between the different mysteries. His *Dogmatics* remained unfinished (*Handbuch der katholischen Dogmatik,* 3 vols., Freiburg, 1873–87; vol. IV, 1–3, is by Leonhard Atzberger [1889–1903]). Scheeben founded the journals *Pastoralblatt* (which first appeared in 1867 and is still published today) and *Das ökumenische religiösen Konzil vom Jahre 1869* (3 vols., 1870–72; the publication continued from 1873 to 1882 under the title *Periodische Blätter zur wissenschaftlichen Besprechung der großen religiösen Fragen deer Gegenwart*).

Scheeben aligned himself with the movement of renewal of Catholic theology brought about by the rediscovery of the treasures of the tradition*, and his work is probably the most original expression of the movement. His principal merit lies in an organic vision of the mysteries of faith, which he interprets on the basis of the central mystery of the Trinity and the Incarnation* as pronouncements bearing on the participation of man in divine life. He follows his teachers Passaglia and Schrader in not interpreting the dwelling of the Holy Spirit in the believer in terms of trinitarian appropriation*. The central place he attributes to Mary* is evidence of the spiritual perspective in which his theology is rooted. Although Scheeben had no direct disciples, he exercised a lasting influence on Catholic theology, an influence that only increased with the publication of his complete works. This in turn gave rise to many critical works. His ideas in certain areas (the doctrine of the Trinity, pneumatology, the doctrine of grace, Mariology) were taken up in the manuals of theology.

● *Gesammelte Schriften*, Ed. J. Höfer et al., 8 vols., Fribourg, 1941–67.

Les merveilles de la grâce divine, Paris-Bruges, 1940 (3rd Ed. 1948).

Le mystère de l'Église et de ses sacrements, Paris, 1946 (2nd Ed. 1956) (excerpts from the following work).

Les mystères du christianisme, Bruges, 1948 (2nd Ed., Paris, 1958).

La mère virginale du Sauveur, Paris-Bruges, 1953 (2nd Ed., Paris, 1956).

Nature et grâce, Paris, 1957.

◆ K. Eschweiler (1926), *Die zwei Wege der neueren Theologie: G. Hermes–M. J. S. Eine kritische Untersuchung des Problems der theologischen Erkenntnis*, Augsburg.

H. Schauf, A. Eröß (Eds.) (1939), *M. J. S. Briefe nach Rom*, Fribourg.

H. Schauf (1941), *Die Einwohnung des Heiligen Geistes: Die Lehre von der nichtappropriierten Einwohnung des Heiligen Geistes als Beitrag zur Theologiegeschichte des neunzehnten Jahrhunderts unter besonderen Berücksichtigung der beiden Theologen Carl Passaglia und Clemens Schrader*, Fribourg.

A. Kerkvoorde (1946), "La formation théologique de M. J. S. à Rome (1852–1859)," *EThL* 22, 174–93.

B. Fraigneau-Julien (1958), *L'Église et le caractère sacramentel selon M. J. S.*, Paris-Bruges.

W. Bartz (1959), *Die lehrende Kirche: Ein Beitrag zur Ekklesiologie M. J. Scheebens*, Trèves.

M. Valkovic (1965), *L'uomo, la donna e il matrimonio nelle teologia di M. J. S.*, Rome.

N. Hoffmann (1967), *Natur und Gnade: Die Theologie der Gottesschau als vollendeter Vergöttlichung des Geistgeschöpfes bei M. J. S.*, Rome.

E. Paul (1970), *Denkweg und Denkform der Theologie von M. J. S.*, Munich.

K. L. Klein (1975), *Kreatürlichkeit als Gottebenbildlichkeit: Die Lehre von der Gottebenbildlichkeit des Menschen bei M. J. S.*, Bern-Frankfurt.

E. Paul (1976), *M. S.*, Graz (selected texts).

K.-H. Minz (1982), Pleroma Trinitatis: *Die Trinitätstheologie bei M. J. S.*, Frankfurt-Bern.

F. J. Bode (1986), *Gemeinschaft mit dem lebendigen Gott* (Communicatio Vitae Trinitatis*): Die Lehre von der Eucharistie bei M. J. S.*, Paderborn.

Coll. (1988), *M. J. S. teologo cattolico d'ispirazione tomista*, Vatican City.

N. Trippen (Ed.) (1988), *Das Kölner Priesterseminar im 19. und 20. Jahrhundert*, Siegburg.

H. Hammans, H. J. Reudenbach, H. Sonnemans (Ed.) (1990), *Geist und Kirche: Studien zur Theologie im Umfeld der beiden Vatikanischen Konzilien. Gedenkschrift für Heribert Schauf*, Paderborn.

G. Tanzella-Nitti (1991), *La SS: Trinità e l'economia della nostra sanctificazione ne "I misteri del cristianesimo" di M. J. S.*, Rome.

W. W. Müller (1994), *Die Gnade Christi: Eine geschichtlich-systematische Darstellung der Gnadentheorie M. J. S. und ihrer Wirkungsgeschichte*, St. Ottilien.

PETER WALTER

See also **Newman, John; Thomism; Tübingen, Schools of**

Schelling, Friedrich Wilhelm Joseph von

1775–1854

Friedrich Wilhelm Joseph von Schelling was born in Leonberg, Germany, the son of a pastor*. He initially intended pursuing an ecclesiastical career and studied in the seminary of Tübingen along with Hegel (1770–1831) and Friedrich Hölderlin (1770–1843). By 1794 his calling as a philosopher had been awakened under the influence of J. G. Fichte (1762–1814). On the recommendation of J. G. Goethe (1749–1832), he was a professor at the University of Jena from 1798 to 1803 and then at Würzburg from 1803 to 1806. From 1807 to 1820 he was general secretary of the Academy of Fine Arts in Munich. He resumed teaching in Erlangen in 1821 and was then called to the new University of Munich in 1827. He served with distinction there until 1841, when the Prussian government invited him to succeed Hegel in Berlin. He subsequently resigned in 1846 and died in Ragaz, Switzerland, in 1854. His work may be divided into four periods: 1794–1800—Schelling gradually breaks with Fichte and develops a philosophy* of nature; 1800–1808—the philosophy of identity; 1809–27—the search for efficacy in God*, sometimes called the philosophy of liberty*; and

1827–54—the late philosophy. The study of the theological aspects of his work follows this classic division without adhering to it in every detail.

1. Under the Sign of Exegesis

The very first writing by Schelling, *De prima malorum humanorum origine* (1792; this was his master's dissertation), is a commentary on Genesis 3. Three aspects of this work, which has been little studied (note, however, Jacobs 1993) should be emphasized here: 1) The choice of this passage of the Bible*, fraught as it is with all the theological interpretations of original* sin, is significant in itself; by advocating exegesis* in the tradition of the Enlightenment as well as of the Reformation, Schelling is in fact criticizing a certain practice of theology*. Evil*, according to Schelling—who was able to take historical arguments from J.G. Eichhorn (*Urgeschichte,* Leipzig, 1779)—is not primarily or essentially moral evil but above all physical evil. Schelling thus plays off history against dogma* and can lay claim to the legacy of Kant (*Mutmaßlicher Anfang der Menschengeschichte*). No more than Kant does Schelling wish to destroy what he criticizes but rather to understand it thoroughly, with presuppositions in reading that have to be made explicit. 2) Indeed, Genesis 3 cannot be understood as the narrative of an event but rather as a myth* and must therefore be compared with the many myths of the golden age, particularly that of Pandora. Schelling's interest in myths was to persist. Mythic representations are not irrational but the signs of a still fledgling reason*; and precisely on that account they can with complete legitimacy be translated into a conceptual language. Genesis 3 thus contains a *doctrine* of human nature. The emphasis on the tree of knowledge allows Schelling to assert that it is the awakening of human wisdom*, the first knowledge of the difference between good* and evil, that is the cause of the unhappiness but also of the progress of man. Again with reference to Kant, the dissonance present in man must in fact be resolved at the end of history*. 3) The comparison of Genesis with other narratives dealing with origins is possible only on the supposition of the unity of reason, which thereby imposes certain limits on the understanding of the plurality of its manifestations. Thus, according to an idea that recurs in Schelling's late philosophy, Judaism* cannot be fundamentally distinguished from other religions, and moreover there is no privilege for the Jewish people in the perception of monotheism*. And Schelling insists, through the analysis of the two divine names*, the plural Elohim and the singular YHWH, on a gradual movement from polytheism to monotheism, which holds as true for the Jews as for others.

This first work is thus noteworthy for the intent to criticize the founding texts of religion, that is, to evaluate them by bringing out the truth* they conceal, first in the light of a reason inherited from the *Aufklärung,* then in the light of a philosophy more specific to Schelling himself.

2. Christianity according to the Philosophy of Identity

The ambition of this philosophy is to establish itself in the absolute, for which the identity A = A (a formulation inherited from Fichte, who applied it to the Ego) is the privileged expression. It also has the aim of understanding through the absolute the world* as a whole, which is nothing other than the composition, at various levels, of the two poles of the ideal and the real. All productions of the mind, all human activities, and nature as well must be understood in the light of the absolute, that is, with the help of philosophy. Religions are thus expressions of the absolute; but from this point of view, they are not necessarily privileged over art or, specifically, over philosophy.

In particular, Schelling on two occasions focused on the meaning of Christianity (*Philosophy of Art, SW* V, 355–736; *Lectures on the Method of Academic Study, SW* V, 207–352). Christianity can be understood only in relation to Greek polytheism, and it is important to recognize in both different expressions of the absolute. Through the Greek gods is manifested the union of the infinite* and the finite in the finite: "The universe is intuited as nature" (*SW* V, 430). Christianity, for its part, wishes to abolish the finite for the benefit of the infinite, an abolition that can occur only through history understood as providence*. Since the infinite can be proclaimed only by the finite, the finite has no other reality but that of being an attempt at identification with the infinite; but such an attempt can occur only sequentially, hence historically. The philosophy of identity is obviously not concerned with understanding the absolute itself in a historical manner; it is eternally already itself, and it cannot be thought of in terms of any kind of becoming. "Each particular moment of time* is a revelation* of a particular aspect of God*, who remains absolute through each one of them; what Greek religion possessed simultaneously, Christianity possesses sequentially" (*SW* V, 288). The absolute thus manifests itself first in the preponderance of the real in nature, then through the preponderance of the ideal pole in history.

Schelling then defends a "speculative" conception of theology that understands the principal dogmas* of Christianity in the light of philosophical knowledge of the absolute. This is not an avatar of the rational religion of Kant, who, contrary to what Schelling intends to do, eliminates the positive or historical aspect from Christianity. The concept of theology developed in the ninth of the *Lectures* is, however, primarily critical. Schelling rejects theology as it practiced in his own time. The excess of exegetical (exegesis*) and hence philological concerns—should this be seen as a distancing from his dissertation?—but also of psychological interpretations of the sacred books*, the tendency to retain from Christianity only a morality close to domestic economy, all, according to Schelling, made it particularly urgent to distinguish within theology between what was simply empirical and touched on the letter of Scripture on the one hand and, on the other, "knowledge in and for itself," that is, the philosophical consideration of theology, obviously for that very reason having little likely future among theologians. The Schelling of 1802 was thus harsh toward Protestantism*, which he considered to be at the origin of these exegetical and empirical tendencies; it was accused of having replaced living authority with the authority of dead books, a "much more restrictive" authority, a "much more abject slavery" (*SW* V, 301). It was, however, not until the *Philosophy of Revelation,* and a very different conception of the absolute, that Schelling interpreted "speculatively" the principal dogmas.

3. From the Absolute to God

It is customary to say that in 1809, the year in which *Studies on the Essence of Human Freedom* (*SW* VII, 333–416) was published, Schelling decisively distanced himself from the philosophy of identity. It is true that this work, along with the three versions of the *Ages of the World* (1811, 1813, 1815), shows us a Schelling in search of a "living God" (*SW* VII, 346) who would make it possible to understand not only what, in the finite, had until then been left in the shadows as illusory because detached from an infinite that alone was real but also how efficacy and life came to being in God himself, now another name for the absolute. It is also worth noting that this change of direction seems to have coincided with Schelling's discovery of Jacob Böhme (1575–1624) and, through or along with him, of Germanic theosophy*.

However, although it is undeniable that the work of 1809 no longer fits into the philosophy of identity, it does not represent a break but is rather the result (although partial and unsatisfactory on many points) of questions on the status of the finite already present in the philosophy of identity. A work of 1804, *Philosophy and Religion* (*SW* VI, 12–70), had already attempted to provide an answer to these questions by calling on the idea of a fall of the finite out of the infinite and, following on from that, on the idea of human freedom. As

for the influence of theosophy—principally, but not exclusively, of Böhme and Oetinger—it has been shown (Marquet 1973, appendix) that it had perhaps been present in the earliest works, certainly in the philosophy of identity, particularly in the philosophy of nature (*see also* Tillich* 1959).

It is, however, quite certain that theosophical speculations attempting to think about a life in God came into their own when Schelling resolved to take into account the finite in all its efficacy (perhaps not deducible) while not falling into any kind of dualism, which he constantly rejected. The *Studies* thus attempted to think of the origin and development of evil on the basis of what, in God, is not God—what Schelling calls the foundation (*Grund*), without which, however, evil could not exist—and on the other hand on the basis of human freedom, defined at the outset as a power "of good and of evil" (*SW* VII, 352). There is, to be sure, a tendency toward evil in the underpinning, noticeable in certain phenomena of nature, but what is to be shown is that its implementation depends on man and man alone. Heidegger* (*Schellings Abhandlung über das Wesen der menschlichen Freiheit,* Tübingen, 1971) emphasizes the originality of this theodicy, which gives to evil, through the *Grund,* a nonethical origin. We have traveled far from the dissertation, which can be accused of having reduced evil to the level of a necessary means for a good end.

In 1810, in the *Stuttgart Lectures* (*SW* VII, 421–84) and in *Clara* (*SW* IX, 3–110), Schelling's philosophy still relies on a distinction in principle between ideal (or spiritual) pole and real (or natural) pole. Affected by the death* of his wife, Schelling also meditated on the world of spirits, on its relations of "sympathy" with the world of the living, and finally on the possible history that would lead it to the last judgment* and then to the apocatastasis*.

The *Ages of the World* leads directly to the late philosophy. It attempts to think of a beginning in God and then to think of the position of a world outside God while preserving his sovereign freedom. Schelling's three successive attempts and his final dissatisfaction are explained by the ambition of the project; in fact, he had to go beyond the idea, strongly affirmed in 1813, according to which necessity is present in God in the form of nature and to develop a philosophy of creation* that preserved divine freedom.

4. Positive Philosophy

a) Principle of Positive Philosophy and the Two "Aspects" of Philosophy. Explicitly articulated for the first time in Munich in 1827, positive philosophy is based on the indeductibility by reason of certain facts that it is obliged to recognize. Although, notably in the *Introduction to Philosophy* of 1830, Schelling characterizes this philosophy as empiricism (37–38), this must be in a very special sense because the founding fact is nothing other than the divine decision to create and hence to reveal himself. Schelling always maintained that there were two directions, then two aspects, in a philosophy that remained single for all that. On the one hand, philosophy can always begin with itself and with a desire for the positive latent in each of us, and it then becomes difficult to distinguish the aspiration to positive philosophy from the aspiration to religion (*Exposition of Purely Rational Philosophy, SW* XI, 564 and 566). On the other hand, a tendency that is at first "regressive" and then, with an undeniable change in meaning, "rational" cannot fail also to assert itself. Reason is always tempted to find its own foundation in itself—this is nothing but a repetition of the initial turning in of man on himself by means of which he willed himself to resemble God. In this way rational philosophy is the inevitable and "negative" consequence of error. Schelling's critique of the ontological argument (proofs* of the existence of God) is especially meaningful in this context. Indeed, it is not enough to wish to prove God to place oneself in positive philosophy; on the contrary, if God *were* by virtue of his nature, he would succumb to the greatest necessity, and it would no longer be possible to think of the existence in him of will, freedom, and creation. Hence, the only way of providing a "continued proof of the existence of God" is through that philosophy that shows that the necessary existent, as it imposes itself on reason from the outset rather than being deduced by reason, is God (*Philosophy of Revelation, SW* XIII, 160–65).

Although Schelling refused to call positive philosophy a "Christian philosophy" (*SW* XIII, 133ff.), it is nevertheless true that it constitutes a philosophy of Christianity since mythology itself can be understood only as a preparation for revelation. Schelling's ambition, however, was always philosophical since his concern was never to justify an orthodox interpretation of dogmas (*SW* XIV 80, 233) but rather to show that they can be understood on the basis of the principles of his philosophy.

b) Schelling's Treatment of Mythology and Christianity: A Free and Creator God through the Interplay of Powers. Subject, object, subject-object; in-itself, for-itself, balance of the one and the other: these are the two possible expressions of the powers that constitute inseparable moments of the divine being, the origin of which must be sought in the philosophy of nature. Through these expressions Schelling is able to think of a progression immanent in the divine being that is not,

however, the becoming of a nature that the *Ages of the World* had had so much difficulty in ruling out. It is necessary to find in God the foundation or the possibility of creation, that is, the position outside the self of the being-other, without, however, denying God's freedom. Schelling emphasizes throughout the late philosophy an idea already embryonically present in the *Erlangen Lectures* (Ix, 225): divine freedom is free only if it can posit that which denies it and run the risk of allowing there to be an efficacy for which the return to God remains the act of another freedom.

Mythology is the consequence, foreseeable but not necessary, of a monotheism that is not reduced to an absolute and uniform singleness but posits the unified totality of the three Persons. The Trinity* properly understood, according to Schelling, cannot be very far removed from tritheism* (on Schelling's documentation with reference to these theological controversies, *see* Tilliette 1969). As for polytheism, it is evidently caused by the error of man who forgets that he can be *like* God only on condition of dwelling in him (*SW* XIV, 349–50). In believing himself master of the powers, man can thus break the bond patiently woven between them only through the creation of the world. He then arouses again the primary power, divine wrath*, the jealous and destructive God; and it is then necessary that there begin again, but now within the human spirit, a process of appeasement of creation that is the always conciliatory work of the second power (for which Dionysus is the mythological figure). Mythological representations are thus only representations, without reality outside the mind, but they constitute the only reality for man. He is possessed by this slow process of division and healing of his consciousness; his life, through rituals—and particularly those rituals that have an element of cruelty—is only the manifestation of that process. This interpretation aims at explaining mythology through itself, and it rejects assimilation to a poetic or euhemerist treatment of myths; it is a representation of the formation of consciousness. Yet mythology acquires its independence only against a background of dependence and must be subordinated to divine revelation, which culminates in Christianity; according to Ernst Cassirer (1953), this reflects Schelling's inadequacy, whereas the attempt to affirm the independence of consciousness (conscience?) constitutes his glory.

Christ: From the Second Power to the Second Person. Schelling's Christ* "is not the master, . . . He is not the founder, but the *content* of Christianity" (*SW* XIV, 35). Schelling examines the principal dogmas in order to understand how they reveal the action of overcoming and reconciliation characteristic of the second power. In Christ this second power becomes a divine person; that is, it acquires such independence from the Father* that it could institute an autonomous and rival reign. Christ is, however, the one who freely chooses to obey the Father and to return to his hands the restored creation. The New Testament is therefore intelligible as a whole only if we accept the status of the Son during the mythological period (and especially at the end of that period), that is, his possible independence from the Father, designated by the form of God that Christ chooses to abandon (*SW* XIV, 39–41; detailed commentary on Phil 2:6–8). The "divine form" that he is able to reassume is nothing other than the expression of his reign over human consciousness, and this reign is possible only because of the mythological overcoming—ultimately, because of man's sin. It is in this sense that Christ may be called "Son* of man."

This interpretation of the Incarnation* (and the pre-existence of the Logos that it presupposes) clearly shows the limits of an orthodoxy with which Schelling was certainly little concerned but with which he generally conformed, with this important exception. Arguing against W. Kasper, X. Tilliette (1969) notes that we can characterize this intermediate status only as that of a demigod. There is, however, a theologically more fruitful consequence of this abandonment of the *morphè theou*: the Incarnation is inevitably kenosis*, divestment, alienation. In relation to traditional theory, this represents an innovation on Schelling's part, although he cannot be classed among the theologians of the "kenotic" movement (*see* Tilliette 1969). We might also note, among other things, Schelling's interpretation of Satan's role, as the contradictor, the one who throughout history forces man to choose, to break out of indecision, to manifest his freedom (*SW* XIV, 241–78). Without ever really contradicting Scripture, Schelling returns here to the broad outlines of the understanding of evil present in the *Studies*.

The Three Churches. The three powers are also at work in the history of Christianity. The Church* of Peter*, that of the founder, the Roman Church, is the reign of the "substantial" principle, and it was its role to be the first to assert its authority* and its rootedness in time (Schelling read the passage traditionally invoked in favor of the primacy accorded to the successors of Peter, Mt 16:18f., as attributing priority, not definitive and exclusive superiority, to Peter [*SW* XIV, 301]). The Church of Paul is its successor. This is none other than Protestantism*, the calling into question of all authority. However, it is itself only a moment in the totality of historical development; and it is the Church of John, the ultimate but still historical form of the Church to come, that will usher in the reign of the Holy Spirit*, the reign of the universal and scientific knowledge of Christianity. This notion of the Johannine Church, the "Church of the Holy Spirit," was already

common among his fellows in Tübingen. And Schelling, who knew Joachim of Flora, was pleased to find in him a confirmation of his theory (Tilliette 1969; Lubac* 1979). We should make it clear that the three powers are at work in all stages of the process of creation and redemption. But each one predominates in succession in the history of revelation.

5. *Influences and Similarities*

Schelling's contribution to theology is summed up in the *Philosophy of Revelation.* Its point in common with the interpretation of Christianity proposed in the philosophy of identity lies in the fact that both are undeniably christological. But the difference in context is no less remarkable. In the late works, indeed, Christ and the history in which he manifests himself are no longer deduced of necessity from a philosophical construction; revelation, taken in the broad sense as beginning with creation, is not deducible. It is positive. It can be conceptualized only because it has taken place. Schelling was obviously not unaware of the christological and critical orientations of his time, but it seems that only the *Glaubenslehre* of Schleiermacher* was definitely one of his sources.

As for the posterity of Schelling's theological thought, if we are to believe W. Kasper (1965), we should speak of similarities and affinities rather than influences. Comparisons are possible with Kierkegaard* (absolute paradox, divine irony), Barth* (predestinarianism), the school of Tübingen (Drey on protorevelation; *see* Th. Wolf *PhJ* 98 [1991], 145–60), Rahner*, Bultmann*, Tillich*, and Cullmann (Tilliette 1969). But it is probably necessary to conclude with the particularity of Schelling's thought. Within a philosophical framework elaborated in the course of a long philosophical journey, he rediscovered dogmas and theological discussions bequeathed by the tradition*, and he was even able to anticipate certain speculations of contemporary theologians.

● (1855–61), *SW*, Ed. K. F. A. von Schelling, 14 vols., Stuttgart.
(1927–28), *Schellings Werke*, Ed. Schröter, 12 vols., Munich (replicate, in spite of a different organization, the pagination of the preceeding edition, which is still cited).
(1976–), *Historisch-kritische Ausgabe*, Stuttgart.
(1947), *Die Weltalter* (1811 and 1813), Ed. Schröter, Munich.
(1990), *System der Weltalter, Münchner Vorlesungen 1927–1928*, Ed. S. Peetz, Frankfurt; (1989), *Einleitung in die Philosophie*, Ed. W. Ehrardt, Stuttgart–Bad Cannstatt.
♦ E. Cassirer (1923), *Philosophie der symbolischen Formen*, vol. 1: *Einleitung.*
K. Leese (1927), *Von Jakob Böhme zu S. Zur Metaphysik des Gottesproblems*, Erfurt.
K. Jaspers (1955), *S. Größe und Verhängnis*, Munich.
W. Schulz (1955), *Die Vollendung des deutschen Idealismus in der Spätphilosophie Ss*, Stuttgart.

P. Tillich (1959), *Mystik und Schuldbewußtsein in Ss philosophischer Entwicklung,* in *GW,* vol. I, Stuttgart.

W. Kasper (1965), *Das Absolute in der Geschichte,* Mayence.

K. Hemmerle (1968), *Gott und das Denken nach Ss Spätphilosophie,* Fribourg.

X. Tilliette (1969), *S., une philosophie en devenir,* 2 vols., Paris (2nd Ed. 1992).

J.-F. Marquet (1973), *Liberté et existence,* Paris.

H. de Lubac (1979), *La postérité spirituelle de Joachim de Flore,* vol. I, Paris.

E. Brito (1987), *La création selon Schelling,* Louvain.

M. Maesschalck (1989), *Philosophie et révélation dans l'itinéraire de Schelling,* Paris-Louvain.

W. G. Jacobs (1993), *Gottesbegriff und Geschichtsphilosophie in der Sicht Ss,* Stuttgart–Bad Cannstatt.

M.-C. Gillet-Challiol (1998), *Schelling, une philosophie de l'extase,* Paris.

X. Tilliette (1999), *Schelling Biographie,* Paris.

MARIE-CHRISTINE GILLET-CHALLIOL

See also **Evil; Existence of God, Proofs of; Hegel, Georg William Frederick; Kierkegaard, Soren Aabaye; Philosophy; Schleiermacher, Friedrich Daniel Ernst; Theosophy; Tillich, Paul; Tübingen, Schools of**

Schism

Today, in Catholic canonical law*, schism refers to a refusal to submit to the pope* or to join the community of Church* members grouped together under his authority* (*CIC* 751). Schismatics are punished by excommunication (*CIC* 1364). Conceptually speaking, schism can be differentiated from heresy* or apostasy since in principle it does not entail any dogmatic error or any willful break with the faith*. But, in practice, hardly any trace of difference between schism and heresy can be found since in the Catholic Church the pope's primacy is considered a dogmatic principle.

Despite this problem, the canonic distinction between heresy and schism can prove fruitful as far as theology and ecumenicalism are concerned—for instance, when it is stated that such and such a sister Church is schismatic but not heretical or that the 14th-century Schism of the West (the Great Schism) did not destroy the Church's doctrinal unity*.

In the New Testament, schism refers to divisions, or scissions (Jn 7:43, 9:16, 10:19; 1 Cor 1:10, 11:18, 12:25). The "schisms" mentioned in 1 Corinthians do not seem for the most part to be dogmatic divisions but are simply related to the faithful regrouping around different masters. The distinction made in 1 Corinthians 11:18–19 between heresy and schism, even if it is not among Pauline theology's main traits, was to play an important role in any case in these concepts' later history. Particularly in the Apostolic Fathers*, one can read that love* knows no schism (*1 Clement* 49:5) and that believers should avoid schism (*Didache* 4:3). In the ancient Church, before Constantine, a clear distinction between schism and heresy is rarely found.

The phenomenon of the schism as an external division existed from the earliest Christian times. Primitive Christianity also had to keep its distance from Judaicizing tendencies and gnosis*. Starting in the fourth century, Donatism* and Arianism* were condemned as schismatic and heretical movements. Since 1054 the separation between the Orthodox Church and the Catholic Church has often been called the Schism of the East, while the Schism of the West covers the period from 1378 to 1417 or 1449, during which time two or even three popes battled for power.

According to Yves Congar (1972), two main periods are distinguishable in the Catholic theology of schism. Until the end of the 11th century, the bishop* of the regional Church* was the guardian of unity. It was through communion* with the bishop that the faithful were linked to the whole Church, and they took communion everywhere at the same altar. The schismatics, on the contrary, "set altar against altar" and thus broke their ties with the regional bishop. From the 12th century on, schism was understood primarily as an attack on the whole Church's unity, and it was the link with the pope as the *episcopus universalis* that became the deciding factor.

For a long time, the Russian Orthodox Church was divided by the schism of the Old Believers, excluded by excommunication in 1666. The Council of Moscow's lifting of the condemnation in 1971 represents an important precedent in the efforts of modern Churches to eliminate schisms. The annulment of reciprocal sentences of excommunication by Pope Paul VI and the patriarch of Constantinople, Athenagoras, in December 1965 was a step in the same direction.

Despite numerous actual schisms, Protestantism only rarely mentions schism, and modern Protestant dogmatics is no more inclined to approach this issue. E. Schlink (1983, 680–81) distinguishes between necessary divisions and unnecessary divisions to conclude that the innumerable schisms between the Christian Churches are often based on reasons other than theological ones. It is impossible to single out a fixed criterion in the divergences about which the Churches have separated during the course of history*. The only justified motive, in Schlink's eyes, would be that a part of the Church had turned away from Christ*.

While following Schlink, Wolfhart Pannenberg (1993, 451) thinks that excommunication cannot be motivated by particular deviations related to the dogmatic norm, only by manifest apostasies or, in certain cases, by disguised ones—that is, by an abandonment of the whole faith. In addition, Pannenberg deems that when heterodox Christians are disposed to maintain ecclesial communion, the Church for its part should also show greater indulgence toward them.

In the ecumenical movement, it is above all the different confessions' "separating" characteristics that provide the subject of theological discussions. When sufficient agreement has been reached and confirmed by ecclesial reception*, the Churches are in a position to state that the historical doctrinal excommunications and condemnations no longer trouble the contemporary partner. Doctrinal dialogues can thus serve to eliminate the theological causes of interconfessional divisions.

● Y. Congar (1939), "Schisme," *DThC* 14, 1286–1312.
Coll. (1967) *Le schisme, sa signification théologique et spirituelle,* Lyon.
D. Baker (Ed.) (1972), *Schism, Heresy and Religious Protest,* Cambridge.
Y. Congar (1972), "Das Schisma," *MySal* IV/1, 415–26.
B. C. Butler (1979), *The Church and Unity,* London.
E. Schlink (1983), *Ökumenische Dogmatik,* Göttingen, 626–708.
W. Pannenberg (1993), *Systematische Theologie,* vol. III, Göttingen, 442–52, 551–59.

RISTO SAARINEN

See also **Ecclesiastical Discipline; Heresy; Jurisdiction**

Schleiermacher, Friedrich Daniel Ernst

1768–1834

a) Life. Friedrich Daniel Ernst Schleiermacher was born in Breslau on 21 November 1768 into a family that had been devoted to the service of the Church for several generations. His parents, supporters of pietism*, sent him to be educated at the Moravian institutions of Niesky (1783–85) and of Barby (1785–87). His heart was opened to pietist ardor, but in his mind he harbored doubts about Christ*'s vicarious satisfaction and his divinity. His personal questioning led him to leave Barby, but he did not renounce his intention of becoming a pastor*: He went to Halle to study theology* and was influenced by J. S. Semler, J. A. Eberhard, and F. A. Wolf. After his ordination* he became a vicar in Landsberg (1794–96); then in Berlin, where he was chaplain in a hospital, he became involved with representatives of the first German Romantic movement and with the intellectual elite. In 1799 he published his *On Religion: Speeches to Its Cultured Despisers* and in 1801 a first volume of *Sermons.* His involvement with the Romantic circle and the "pantheist" thrust of his *Speeches* aroused mistrust among some strict Protestants. In 1803 Schleiermacher published *Grundlinien einer Kritik der bisherigen Sittenlehre* and in 1804 the first part of his major translation of Plato. Appointed professor at the university of Halle, he taught philosophical ethics*, the theological encyclopedia, dogmatic* theology, Christian morality, and New Testament interpretation. On his return to Berlin (1807) he helped create the university (1810), where he was appointed professor of theology and taught almost all theological disciplines. However, he published only two works, a textbook

(*Brief Outline of the Study of Theology,* 1811) and a vast dogmatics* (*The Christian Faith,* 1821–22). Moreover, his philosophical interests extended to almost all fields (except philosophy* of nature), and he played a pioneering role in certain domains (philosophy of religion* and hermeneutics*). He died on 12 February 1834 (Dilthey 1870).

b) On Religion. Schleiermacher never renounced his *Speeches* (Seifert 1960). Rather, he was content to reedit the new editions published in 1806, 1824, and 1831. After having proposed to defend religion as he understood it (first speech), he defined pure and living religion by separating it from metaphysics and morality (second speech). The essence of religion, he believed, was neither thought nor action but rather feeling and intuition directed toward the world, that is, toward the physical world and the human world in terms of its being and future. For Schleiermacher, feelings of respect, humility, love*, and so on, which we often attribute to morality, belong in fact to religion. In the third speech, Schleiermacher stresses that religious feelings spring from the depths of the soul: since they stem from spiritual growth, one is unable to create them in a violent or mechanical way. In the fourth speech, Schleiermacher deals with the relationship between religion and the community and proposes an image of the Church that is strongly influenced by romanticism and pietism. Seeing religious society* as an organ of mutual communication, Schleiermacher opposes the small, fervent communities to the great Church. But for all that, he does not want this Church to disappear since it continues to be the link between those who live faith* and those who seek it. The last speech considers the plurality of religions as a necessary thing: within religion, there is a principle that forces it to become independent. Schleiermacher argues against natural religion, to which he prefers positive religions: they are the specific forms under which infinite religion manifests itself in the finite. Schleiermacher therefore grasps the central intuition of Christianity in the inseparable connection between corruption and redemption; everything that is finite needs multiple mediations—including Christ*'s—in order to be linked to divinity. The *Speeches* so strongly emphasizes the Christian future and its "palingeneses" that the Holy Spirit* appears detached from Christ. Later, however, Schleiermacher would have reservations about Joachimism (millenarianism*) (Lubac 1979).

c) Religiosity and Philosophy. Schleiermacher's important letter to philosopher F. Jacobi (3 March 1818) clarifies the relationship between philosophy and piety.

Jacobi considered himself "a total pagan in terms of understanding, but, at heart, a Christian." Against this, Schleiermacher answered, "The pagan and the Christian oppose each other on the same ground, that is, on religious grounds" (Cordes 1971). Religion is the interpretation of religious feeling through understanding; if the feeling is Christian, the understanding cannot "be Pagan in interpretation" (Flückiger 1947).

In Schleiermacher the difference between piety and understanding—indeed between dogmatic theology and philosophy—is understood as a contrast: it is in the oscillation between Christian piety and understanding that the life of the spirit is formed. Therefore, Schleiermacher can state that his philosophy and his dogmatic theology, far from contradicting each other, become closer and closer (Scholtz 1984). Both share faults and strengths: religious feeling is indeed realized, but it is not pure; in contrast, the philosophical intuition of God* is never realized but is free from all foreign elements. Schleiermacher therefore excludes the idea that religion goes beyond philosophy or that religion is subordinate to philosophy. Nevertheless, these two fields are not heterogeneous: philosophy includes religion as one of the forms of the spirit's victories amid nature; moreover, religion immediately understands the unity between the ideal and the real that makes philosophy possible (Simon 1974).

d) Hermeneutics. It is especially Schleiermacher's hermeneutics* that has drawn the attention of scholars in our time. He distinguishes between two complementary aspects in the hermeneutic task: "grammatical" interpretation, which strives to understand discourse based on the totality of language, and "technical" interpretation, which considers the same discourse as an individual act of thought production (*Hermeneutik,* Ed. Kimmerle). This main division includes a second contrast: the "comparative" process, which progressively clarifies the obscurities of text in the light of what is already known (in particular, the meaning of words), is opposed to the "divinatory" process, which intuitively understands the meaning and coherence of the text. Without this comparison, divination remains uncertain; without divination, the comparison lacks unity (Simon 1987). According to Schleiermacher, hermeneutics as a general science applies to all discourse (Ricoeur 1986): it would therefore be out of the question to reserve a particular interpretation for the Holy Scriptures*.

e) Conception of Theology. In his *Brief Outline of the Study of Theology,* Schleiermacher defines theology as a "positive science." Its unity stems from its task, which is that of directing (in the general sense) the

Church. The specificity of the totality of theological disciplines thus lies in its link to the mission of the Church. As a science, however, theology is subjugated to the laws and the ideal of knowledge that are proper to all the sciences. According to Schleiermacher, theology can be divided into three parts: philosophical, historical, and practical. Philosophical theology brings together elements of philosophical ethics and the philosophy of religion that seem important for the theological task. Historical theology is the main body of theological study and has three sections: exegetic theology, Church history*, and historical knowledge of the present state of Christianity. The last part is divided into dogmatic theology (dogmatic theology, strictly speaking, and moral theology) and "statistics" (i.e., the knowledge of the internal constitution and the external relationships of the ecclesial society). Although all theological disciplines aim to direct the Church, the latter constitutes the favored theme of practical theology.

f) Doctrine of Faith. According to the famous introduction to the *Doctrine de la Foi,* the basis of all ecclesial societies is piety, which is "neither a Knowing, nor a Doing, but a modification of Feeling or of immediate self-consciousness" (*Der Christliche Glaube* [*GL*]; Offermann 1969). Feeling does not signify something vague or ineffectual; it is the immediate presence of all existence, both perceptible and spiritual.

The notion of absolute dependence constitutes the essential part of the concept of religion developed in this introduction: "The common element in all howsoever diverse expressions of piety, by which these are conjointly distinguished from all other feelings, or, in other words, the self-identical essence of piety, is this: the consciousness of being absolutely dependent, or, which is the same thing, of being in relation with God" (*GL*).

Our consciousness of not having an absolute liberty* is, in and of itself, a consciousness of absolute dependence (*schlechthinniges Abhängigkeitsgefühl*). And the representation carried by the word "God" expresses the most immediate reflection on the feeling of dependence (*GL* I). Schleiermacher goes beyond evoking the individual essence of religious societies and considers the various degrees (fetishism, polytheism, monotheism*) of the historical development of religion (*GL*). Christianity is, according to him, the purest expression of teleological piety (*GL* I). Such piety also characterizes Judaism* but to a lesser degree; in contrast, Islam, although monotheistic, belongs to the esthetic type (*GL* I).

Schleiermacher intends to lead to the complete understanding of the tenets of faith and attempts to determine the reasons for their differentiation. He moreover divides each part of *The Christian Faith* into three parts. It is a question first of all of the states of man, then of the modifications of the world in their relationship with the feeling of absolute dependence, and finally of divine attributes in their relationship with man and the world (*GL*). Thus, the first part of *The Christian Faith* first analyzes pious self-consciousness as such, then certain divine attributes (eternity*, omnipresence*, omnipotence*, omniscience), and finally the original perfection of the world. The first aspect of the second part first presents sin* as a state of man, then the condition of the world in relationship to sin, and finally the divine attributes that relate to consciousness of sin. The second aspect of the second part first deals with the state of the Christian, then the condition of the world with regard to redemption, and finally the divine attributes (love, wisdom*) as they relate to salvation*. For Schleiermacher the anthropological perspective is the *Grundform* without which, on the one hand, the cosmological approach deviates toward natural sciences and, on the other, the doctrine of God runs the risk of being confused with metaphysics.

Schleiermacher initiates both christocentric theology and the ecclesiological concentration of pneumatology in the 19th century. He stresses that Christ is different from all men "through the constant vigor of his divine consciousness, which was an authentic being of God in him" (*GL;* Tilliette 1986). But in order to exercise his lordship over the receptivity and the activity of the Church, Christ, according to Schleiermacher, had in a certain way to disappear into the "common spirit" of the Church (*GL;* Brandt 1968). Schleiermacher is right to consider divine mystery* on the basis of the temporal missions of the Son and the Spirit; but in his return to Sabellian modalism* he is doomed to understand God only as an undifferentiated unity (*GL* II; Brito 1994). Moreover, in his *Dogmatics,* the final word is not about the self-manifestation of the Trinity* but about the "divine attributes," whose content is limited to the modification of piety (*GL;* Beisser 1970).

g) Theology of Culture. Schleiermacher interprets the development of culture as an ethical process that, through the human domination of the earth, fulfills the union between reason* and nature (*Ethik,* Ed. Birkner; Jorgensen 1959). His *Christian Ethics* stresses that each structure essential to human nature must become the organ of the divine Spirit. This implies a vast theology of culture. Such a theology does not signify a pure identification of Christianity and culture, but Schleiermacher rather underlines that human culture can survive only on condition of its remaining open to the Spirit of Christ (Birkner 1964).

h) Posterity. Schleiermacher's influence is not limited to the school of the "theology of mediation" that explicitly draws on him (C. I. Nitzsch, A. Twesten, J. Müller). He also influenced R. A. Lipsius's concept of religion, the dogmatic method of A. Schweizer, and the ethical thought of R. Rothe as well as influencing Hegelian authors (E. Zeller). In our time, despite the warnings of dialectical theology (Barth*), some theologians, including leading ones (G. Wobbermin, R. Otto, Tillich*), retained a positive relationship with Schleiermacher. In the immediate aftermath of World War II, Protestant theology tended to draw again from Schleiermacher, and, a little later, Catholic theology began to discover him anew (Stalder 1969).

● T. N. Tice (1966), *S. Bibliography,* Princeton, N.J. (*Updating and Commentary,* Princeton, N.J., 1985).
(1835–64), *Sämmtliche Werke,* 30 vols., Berlin.
(1980), *Kritische Gesamtausgabe,* Ed. H.-J. Birkner et al., Berlin–New York.
(1910), *Kurze Darstellung des theologischen Studiums,* Ed. H. Scholz, Leipzig.
(1959), *Hermeneutik,* Ed. H. Kimmerle, Heidelberg.
(1958), *Über die Religion. Reden an die Gebildeten unter ihren Verächtern,* Ed. H.-J. Rothert, Hamburg.
(1960), *Der christliche Glaube* (*GL* I-II), Ed. M. Redeker, Berlin.
(1981), *Ethik,* Ed. H.-J. Birkner, Hamburg.
◆ X. Dilthey (1870), *Leben Ss,* Berlin.
G. Pünjer (Ed.) (1879), *F. Ss Reden über die Religion,* Braunschweig.
E. Cramaussel (1909), *La philosophie religieuse de S.,* Paris.
F. Flückiger (1947), *Philosophie und Theologie bei S.,* Zurich.
P. H. Jorgensen (1959), *Die Ethik Ss,* Munich.
P. Seifert (1960), *Die Theologie des jungen Ss,* Gütersloh.
H.-J. Birkner (1964), *Ss christliche Sittenlehre,* Berlin.
W. Brandt (1968), *Der Heilige Geist und die Kirche bei S.,* Zurich.

H.-J. Birkner (1969), "Philosophie et théologie chez S.," *ArPh* 32, 179–205.
D. Offermann (1969), *Ss Enleitung in die Glaubenslehre,* Berlin.
R. Stalder (1969), *Grundlinien der Theologie Ss,* Wiesbaden.
F. Beisser (1970), *Ss Lehre von Gott,* Göttingen.
M. Cordes (1971), "Der Brief Ss an Jacobi," *ZThK* 68, 195–212.
M. Simon (1974), *La philosophie de la religion dans l'œuvre de S.,* Paris.
G. Ebeling (1975), *Wort und Glaube* III, Tübingen, 60–136.
Th. H. Jorgensen (1977), *Das religionsphilosophische Offenbarungsverständnis des späten Ss,* Tübingen.
H. de Lubac (1979), *La postérité spirituelle de Joachim de Flore,* vol. I: *De Joachim de Flore à Schelling,* Paris-Namur.
E. Schrofner (1980), *Theologie als positive Wissenschaft: Prinzipien und Methoden der Dogmatik bei S.,* Frankfurt-Bern.
G. Schultz (1984), *Die Philosophie Ss,* Darmstadt.
P. Ricoeur (1986), *Du texte à l'action: Essais d'herméneutique, II,* Paris.
X. Tilliette (1986), *La christologie idéaliste,* Paris.
M. Eckert (1987), *Gott—Glauben und Wissen: F. Ss philosophische Theologie,* Berlin–New York.
M. Simon (1987), *Introduction à F. S., Herméneutique,* Paris.
P. Demange (1991), *L'essence de la religion selon S.,* Paris.
E. Brito (1994), *La pneumatologie de S.,* Louvain.
F. Schleiermacher [1963], *The Christian Faith,* English translation of 2nd German Ed., Ed. H. R. Mackintosh, J. S. Steward, New York and Evanston, Ill.

EMILIO BRITO

See also **Calvinism; Experience; Hegel, Georg William Frederick; Hegelianism; Kant, Immanuel; Kierkegaard, Soren Aabye; Lutheranism; Marx, Karl; Nietzsche, Friedrich Wilhelm; Schelling, Friedrich Wilhelm Joseph von**

Scholasticism

Scholastic theology is not simply medieval theology (by contrast with patristic theology) but the theology of the "school," that is, the theology of the university, an original institution that appeared in the Latin West in the early 13th century (Verger 1996). It is thus to be distinguished both from monastic theology (Leclercq 1957; Anselm* of Canterbury, Bernard* of Clairvaux) and from other forms of the search for an "understanding of the faith*" (*intellectus fidei*), powerfully orchestrated by dialectics and developed in the urban theological schools* of the 12th century.

Scholastic theology is scholastic not only in its institutional location but in its methods, its objects, and its program itself, which is inseparable from the Aristotelian idea of science (Christian Aristotelianism*). It is in fact characterized by its desire to be a science, not simply an art, and especially not a mere defensive apologia for religion, as is the case, for example, with the *kalâm* in Islam. This choice of science was linked to the rediscovery of the Aristotelian corpus, accompanied by Arabic philosophical and scientific texts, all of which supplied concepts, tools, and new procedures. But it was also tied to progress accomplished in the Latin world itself, in the area of the arts of language in general as well as in the area of logic in particular. Scholastic theology was the offspring of the *logica modernorum,* of semantics, and of the philosophy* of language that had developed since Abelard*. It was also linked to the expansion of methods of discussion specific to the pedagogical world of the university, with its parade of *disputationes, quaestiones,* and *sophismata.* Scholastic theology was thus not a monolith. It went through breaks and changes in scientific paradigms comparable to those experienced generally by the university age.

How can it be characterized? One possible angle of approach is the relationship between theology and philosophy or indeed between the faculties of theology and philosophy as revealed in university statutes, academic censures, and condemnations (McLaughlin 1977). And from this point of view the various measures taken against the teaching of Aristotelian natural philosophy—the "high point" being the Parisian condemnations in 1277 (Hissette 1977)—form an integral part of the history of Scholastic theology by outlining the stages of a journey that led from the proscription to the prescription of Aristotle (Bianchi 1990). Given the link between logic and theology, we can also base ourselves on the development of logic and that of scientific modes of thought resulting from or caused by that development to distinguish between theological periods. In this context the appearance of the *subtilitates anglicanae* (Murdoch 1978) would be in the foreground, with the hegemony of those "English" techniques and problematics that were to come under attack from Luther* (in his *Disputatio contra theologiam scolasticam*) and from the Italian humanists (in their invectives against the "Breton barbarians"). These two periods of Scholastic theology, the "Aristotelian" age and the "English" age, were not sequential: they were at the heart of the opposition between the *Via antiqua* and the *Via moderna.* They can thus be found in various forms, depending on the nature of the problems under consideration: the conflict between realists and nominalists, which ran through the entire 15th century, was one of those forms (Kaluza 1988; nominalism*). Whatever interpretive grid is imposed on the history of Scholastic theology, one observation is certainly necessary: historians no longer consider valid the discredit formerly accorded to the 14th century, considered as a period of disintegration of the "Scholastic synthesis" reached in the 13th century, the golden age of the *Summas* of theology. And the automatic association of the late Middle Ages with the notions of "criticism" and "skepticism" is no longer regarded as incontestable.

I. Nature and Specificity of Scholastic Theology

Scholastic theology was not a Christian philosophy. The Scholastic theologian was trained in philosophy (which was part of his formation program during the 10 years he spent in the faculty of arts). He might broach the questions of philosophy (the converse being forbidden by university statutes). He was endowed with a certain scientific culture and frequently relied on the tools of philosophy. But he nevertheless did not adopt the philosopher's point of view. Theology had its own questions, its own universe, that of "intentional providence*," not that of "natural providence." It is nevertheless tempting to rely on what the relation between philosophy and theology was in the late Middle Ages to provide a view of the history of theology and to draw from this the principle of a periodization that would make it possible to explain the break that occurred between the 13th and 14th centuries.

1. The Relation between Philosophy and Theology according to Étienne Gilson: Problems of Periodization

The central element in Gilson's argument is the importance that he attributes to the Parisian condemnation of 1277, conceived as a condemnation of Averroism (naturalism*). According to him, it was this condemnation—which P. Duhem, for his part, saw as the birth certificate of modern science—that separated the two paradigmatic theological figures of the late 13th century, Thomas* Aquinas and Duns* Scotus, thereby opening the way to later developments. The condemnation of 219 philosophical theses by the bishop* of Paris, Étienne Tempier, meant, according to Gilson, that after that date theologians no longer had confidence in philosophy. The sign of this change was provided by the way in which Thomas Aquinas and Duns Scotus related to their philosophical sources. Gilson says that Thomas Aquinas broke with Averroes "as a philosopher and in the area of philosophy," whereas Duns Scotus "broke with Avicenna as a theologian, by reproaching him for having unduly adorned metaphysics with the plumage of theology" and "by reducing to the minimum the limits of validity of natural* theology." In this way, Thomas Aquinas "did not despair of philosophy because he transformed it; his work is a victory of theology *in* philosophy"; but Duns Scotus despaired of pure philosophy "because he took cognizance of it as of a fact": his work could only be a "victory of theology *over* philosophy." The philosophical disenchantment of Duns Scotus thus ended a phase of history; and the "revolution of the fourteenth century," in Ockham and his disciples, had as a consequence an intensification of "the separation between philosophy and theology." Ockhamism, moreover, made it possible to go beyond the purely negative aspect of this antiphilosophical reaction of theologians temporarily disarmed by Thomism*: attacking philosophy by philosophy, it in fact proposed strong and coherent philosophical reasons for not submitting the divine essence to the speculative analyses of natural reason*. The 14th century was thus dominated either by Ockhamism, a *theological separatism,* or by Averroism, a *philosophical separatism* that had come unscathed out of the condemnations of 1277 (Gilson 1944).

2. New Historical Paradigms

Two readings have made it necessary to modify Gilson's picture of Scholastic theology:

1) The first reading takes into account the interaction between theological development and the progress of the sciences, particularly of logic. It brings to the fore the powerful renewal in methods, objects, and problems contributed by English theology of the late Middle Ages while at the same time emphasizing the remarkable interaction that existed between disciplines. Indeed, theology provoked a rapid development of logic by confronting Aristotelianism with nonstandard situations and entities, and it benefited in return from the innovations carried out in the area of the logic of variation (in regard to the theological question of the precise moment of transubstantiation and that of the local movement of angels*), in deontological logic (in regard to the theory of imperatives contrary to duty), and in epistemological logic (in regard to reflection on the contents of belief). From this point of view the 14th century no longer appears as an age of "disintegration," and the ideal of "synthesis" illustrated by the *Summas* of the 13th century is no longer seen as a unique or indeed absolute model.

2) Another perspective, which does not exclude the first, consists in reevaluating the plurality of schools and traditions (Courtenay 1987; Trapp 1956), the study of institutional and intellectual contexts in which utterances were shaped and circulated, and the study of the reproduction of texts and the creation of other tools of knowledge. The history of Scholastic theology then becomes the history of the faculties of theology and of the research centers (*studia*), of the statutes organizing community life, of censures, and of relations with political and religious authorities.

II. Scholastic Method

Since the pioneering work of M. Grabmann, *Histoire de la méthode scolastique* (1904–11), several pictures have been proposed to describe the emergence of theology as a science. M.-D. Chenu has isolated some of the factors that made it possible for the Latins, from around 1150, to move from the assimilation of the philosophical and theological givens of late antiquity to the production of new languages, methods, and problems (Chenu 1969): in the area of pedagogical techniques, the shift from *lectio* to *quaestio;* with reference to literary genres, the shift from the anthology and the gloss to the summa; and in epistemological practice, the shift from the *defloratio* of authentic data (*authentica*) to the determination of authoritative solutions (*magistralia*). This early development, however, accounts for only some aspects of 13th-century Scholastic theology, and it leaves almost entirely unexplained the Scholastic theology of the 14th and 15th centuries.

1. Birth of Scholastic Theology

The first decisive element for the emergence and later development of Scholastic theology was the use of dialectics in theological knowledge, begun in the 11th century by Anselm* of Canterbury (Cantin 1996) and vigorously pursued in the 12th by Abelard* (Jolivet 1996).

a) Introduction of Dialectics into Theology. The submission of theology to logical discussion, as it was carried out by Abelard, was specific to the Latin West; the timid efforts of John Italus around 1055 and of Eustratus of Nicaea around 1100, in Byzantium, were short lived. It was the challenges posed to sacred texts by the tools of logic, practiced on a grand scale from the 1220s on in Western universities, that ensured the expansion of Scholastic theology and of its academic ritual, with its hierarchy of vigorously argued demonstrations (the ordinary *disputationes,* the quodlibetic questions), engendering new ways of thinking.

b) Development of Manuals: The Sentences *of Peter Lombard.* If Abelard provided the first formulation of the method of Scholastic theology, it was another 12th-century thinker, Peter Lombard (†22 July 1160), who provided the opportunity to exercise it by composing the manual that served as the basis for the teaching of theology throughout the late Middle Ages: the *Sentences.* Divided into four books, the *Sentences* break down the knowledge accumulated in patristic theology following a thematic order and in the form of questions. The plan of the work, which presents in sequence the mystery* of the Trinity* (book I), the problem of creation* (book II), the Incarnation* and the action of the Holy Spirit* (book III), and the sacraments* (book IV), served as a kernel for the theological *Summas.* Its role was not limited to that; by the 13th century the principal work of the university theologian was to comment on the *Sentences.*

c) Formation of Axioms and Scientific Method. The *Regulae caelestis iuris,* by a third 12th-century writer, Alain of Lille, opened the way for this Aristotelian definition of a scientific status for theology that marked the first period of Scholastic theology. The central argument of the *Regulae* is that "every science uses rules and principles as foundations that are specific to it" and by means of which it arrives at conclusions. But this argument establishes not only the possibility of theological science expounded in the *Summas;* it also provides a foundation for the theology of conclusions, *conclusiones,* which took hold of the literature of maxims in the 14th century and made the preparation of "syntheses" unnecessary. Alain of Lille's axiomatics thus marked the division of the two ages of Scholastic theology. And it also inspired Eckhart's project of an *Opus propositionum* gathering together the thousand theses necessary to present theological knowledge in axiomatic form.

2. Literary Genres

The model introduced by the *Sentences* of Peter Lombard gave rise to two forms of theological scholarship: the first, which endured, was the commentary on the *Sentences;* the second, limited to the 13th century, was the theological summa.

a) The Genre of Commentary on the Sentences. As early as 1922, Heidegger* (*Phenomenological Interpretations of Aristotle;* Mauvezin 1992) tied any possibility of "understanding the scientific structure of medieval theology, its exegesis, and its propensity toward commentary" to the study of a hitherto neglected genre, the commentaries on the *Sentences* of Peter Lombard. Considered unrealizable at the time, this project has received heightened attention from medievalists (Vignaux 1976). It is far from having borne all its fruit. The *Repertorium commentariorum in Sententias Petri Lombardi* established by F. Stegmüller in 1947 contains more than 1,400 entries, and almost all the documents remain to be published. The importance of the genre of

commentaries on the *Sentences* is not only statistical; it also expresses a veritable theological way of thinking. One of the characteristic traits of Scholastic theology was, in fact, to have gradually substituted commentaries on the work of Lombard for explication of the Bible*, a paradigm that Roger Bacon was almost alone in the 13th century in denouncing as one of the "seven sins*" of theological studies in the University of Paris. The importance of the genre was also methodological: the formal development of commentaries, from the 13th to the late 15th century, was the most reliable indicator of changes occurring in theology.

b) Theological Summa. Another derivative of the *Sentences,* the theological summas articulated in their very structure the demand for a disciplinary ordering (*ordo disciplinae*) that presided over the formulation of a science conceived in the mode of a questioning of texts: books, *quaestiones,* and articles integrated the oral moment of the argument into the framework provided by Lombard (Biffi 1995). This quasi-architectural form was for a long time the one that was most studied. All the great Scholastics of the 13th century contributed to it: Alexander of Halès, Albert* the Great, and Thomas Aquinas. The *Summa aurea* (III. 3. 1. 1) of William of Auxerre (†1231) deserves special mention, for in it was formulated for the first time the principle of a theological science in accordance with the Aristotelian criteria for scientific status: articles of faith are to theology what self-evident principles are to demonstrative science. The general method of theology flows from this principle; it consists of reasoning about the invisible on the basis of the self-evident (the article of faith, which derives its *evidence* from *God** himself, sole *cause* of our assent). With William, faith is no longer only in search of understanding, as for Anselm; it tends by its very *nature* to develop into an argument by following an axiomatic method (*probatio credendorum per rationes*), for it is less a matter of proving the object of a belief (the article of faith) by means of reasoning than of proving the entire object of theology (the *credenda*) on the basis of that object of belief.

III. Contents of Scholastic Theology

It is not possible to enumerate here all the patristic problems or topics developed by the Scholastic method. We will limit ourselves to noting those that are especially tied to the method by which it works out its arguments.

1. The Subject of Theology

The delimitation of the subject of theology is a classic question of Scholastic theology (Biffi 1992). Its point of departure is the doctrine of Peter Lombard, with a dual distinction (inherited from Augustine): on one hand, between "things" and "signs," on the other, between the "things that one enjoys" (the Father*, the Son, the Holy Spirit) and those "that one uses" (the world and what is created in it). From that starting point, various opinions confront one another. According to the first, the subject of theology is everything with which it deals, in other words, "things and signs"; or, in another formulation, the "Head and the limbs," that is, the "total Christ*" (*Christus integer*), "the incarnate Word* and his body, which is the Church*" (Ruello 1987). According to the second, the subject is what is "principally sought for in theological science": God. According to a third, it is the "believable" (*credibile*), and theology is distinct from other sciences in that it presupposes "the inspiration of faith" (Bonaventure*). According to others, it is the works of restoration of salvation (and "the works of the first creation" provide the subjects for the other sciences). According to yet others (Thomas Aquinas), it is "the divine being knowable through inspiration."

In the 14th century this problematics of the subject—in the sense of "matter" (*materia subiecta*)—was rethought in epistemological terms, in a "propositional approach" characteristic of nominalism, by using Ockham's distinction between the object (*obiectum*) of a science, understood as any of the propositions demonstrated in it ("the object of science is the proposition alone insofar as it is true"), and the subject (*subiectum*) of science, that is, the subject of each one of those propositions. Articulated by Ockham (*I Sent.* Prol., q. 9), the principle according to which "however many subjects for conclusions, there are so many subjects for a science" accompanied the "formal" revolution carried out in the system of *conclusiones* at the leading edge of the theology of the late Middle Ages. This is what explains why the theory of the *significabile complexe* (Gregory of Rimini and Ugolino of Orvieto, a theory that saw the object of science in the "complexly signifiable," i.e., the proper and adequate signified of a proposition) was worked out primarily in a theological context. It may be thought that this epistemological advance risked dissolving the material unity of the subject of Scholastic theology. It was in any event parallel to the development occurring at the same time in the problematics of the subject of metaphysics.

2. Status of Theology

If the idea of theology as a science constitutes the defining perspective of Scholastic theology, the scientific status of theology itself was redefined as the idea of science moved from a model of Aristotelian logic to a formally more powerful model, directly derived from the semantic and epistemological work of theologians. This development was accompanied by other questions on the very purpose of the knowledge that had thus been achieved. Was theology a theoretical science, directed toward the *speculatio* or the *contemplatio veritatis,* or a practical science, directed toward the *operatio recta?* Or, more radically, *must* theology be a science? Thomas's answer consisted of making theology a practical and theoretical science (*I Sent.*, prol., q. 1, a. 3), ultimately oriented toward "theory" to the extent that it has the same purpose as human existence, the beatific* vision, itself understood as intellectual contemplation*. This thesis seemed to destroy the idea of a primacy of emotion and of love* in the present condition of man, to compromise the universal character of the gospel message by isolating the theologian from the rest of a community composed principally of *illiterati,* or simply to leave out of account human actions* in favor of a study of *res divinae* alone, and other answers could not fail to make their appearance (voluntarism*). Some, particularly among the Franciscans, supported the idea of Bonaventure: theology is a *wisdom*, and in this respect it is neither purely theoretical nor purely practical. Others attacked more directly the very idea of science, for example, William de la Mare, for whom theology was in the strict sense a law* (i.e., a body of prescriptions) and not a science (i.e., a body of verifiable or falsifiable statements). Others, such as Giles of Rome, saw in theology an "affective" science with charity as its object. Still others, such as William de Ware, saw it as a "contemplative" science directed toward "the love of God" (Putallaz 1996). Finally, others, such as Albert the Great and Meister Eckhart, made mystical* knowledge the end point of the theological faith proper to man on his pilgrimage. And thereby overcoming the opposition between the love of God *in via* and the knowledge* of God *in patria*, they also overcame the opposition between practical science and theoretical science (Rhineland-Flemish Mysticism*).

3. New Objects

Scholastic theology brought to a point of near theoretical perfection several sets of problems that had been considered earlier. This is true for Pseudo-Dionysius*'s consideration of divine Names, the treatment of which it worked out by using the semantics of reference (*suppositio*) and of meaning, in the framework of terminist logic and speculative grammar. This was also true for a related question, the interpretation of the Name* of "Being*" revealed to Moses (Ex 3:14). Scholastic theology also gave great theoretical prominence to the question of transubstantiation and made the theology of the Eucharist* a major area of innovation, both for the philosophy of language (with the discovery of the realm of the "performative") and for logic and physics. By scrutinizing the problem of the body of Christ* during the paschal *triduum,* it made possible a blossoming of reflection on the empty referent that transformed the framework of philosophical semantics. It will perhaps be objected that these contributions have more to do with philosophy than with theology. Nothing could be further from the truth. The Scholastic development of trinitarian theology, of a theology of "divine missions," of grace*, and of gifts; the Scholastic formulation of various models of absolute and ordered divine omnipotence (Oakley 1984; Randy 1987); Scholastic views on freedom (Putallaz 1995) and on poverty (Burr 1989); and so on, was all work that made possible authentic *theological* breakthroughs. The originality of Scholastic theology is precisely that of offering both a set of assets both philosophical and theological, of having contributed to rationalism* in general by contributing to religious rationality in particular. For lack of the possibility of presenting in detail each of its contributions to Christian theology, it is this indirect effect that should be emphasized since it firmly establishes Scholastic theology in a history of the conditions of reason. This strong version of theology was attacked, as early as Petrarch, by the supporters of a "weaker" theology. By choosing "the good pious old woman" against the professional thinker, Petrarch articulated a redistribution of roles that in fact corresponded to a hidden tendency of theology beginning in the middle of the 14th century: the critique of privileges granted to the "scientific" (Bianchi-Randi 1993). This confrontation of the *vetula* and the theologian was to be sanctioned in the 15th century by the rejection of the *theologus logicus.*

• M. Grabmann (1906–11), *Geschichte der scholatischen Methode,* 2 vols., Fribourg.
É. Gilson (1944), *La philosophie au Moyen Age: Des origines patristiques à la fin du XIVe s.,* Paris (2nd Ed. 1962).
D. A. Trapp (1956), "Augustinian Theology of the XIVth Century: Notes on Editions, Marginalia, Opinions and Book-Lore," *Aug(L)* 6, 146–274.
J. Leclerc (1957), *L'amour des lettres et le désir de Dieu,* Paris.
H. A. Obermann (1963), *The Harvest of Medieval Theology: Gabriel Biel and Late Medieval Nominalism,* Cambridge, Mass.
M.-D. Chenu (1969), *La théologie comme science au XIIIe s.,* Paris.
P. Vignaux (1976), *De saint Anselme à Luther,* Paris.
R. Hissette (1977), *Enquête sur les 219 articles condamnés à Paris le 7 mars 1277,* Louvain-Paris.
M. M. McLaughlin (1977), *Intellectual Freedom and Its Limitations in the University of Paris in the Thirteenth and Fourteenth Centuries,* New York.
J. Murdoch (1978), "*Subtilitates Anglicanae* in Fourteenth Century Paris: John of Mirecourt and Peter Ceffons," in M. P. Cosman, B. Chandler (Ed.), *Machaut's World: Science and Art in the Fourteenth Century,* New York, 51–86.
F. Oakley (1984), *Omnipotence, Covenant and Order: An Excursion in the History of Ideas from Abaelard to Leibniz,* Ithaca-London.
W. J. Courtenay (1987), *Schools and Scholars in Fourteenth-Century England,* Princeton, N.J.
E. Randi (1987), *Il sovrano e l'orologiaio: Due immagini di Dio nel dibattito sulla potentia absoluta fra XIII et XIV secolo,* Florence.
F. Ruello (1987), *La christologie de Thomas d'Aquin,* Paris.
Z. Kaluza (1988), *Les querelles doctrinales à Paris: Nominalistes et réalistes aux confins du XIVe et du XVe s.,* Bergame.
D. Burr (1989), *Olivi and Franciscan Poverty,* Philadelphia.
L. Bianchi (1990), *Il Vescovo e i Filosofi: La condanna pariginia del 1277 e l'evoluzione dell'aristotelismo scolastico,* Bergame.
I. Biffi (1992), *Figure medievali della teologia,* Milan.
L. Bianchi, E. Randi (1993), "Le théologien et la petite vieille," in *Vérités dissonantes: Aristote à la fin du Moyen Age,* Fribourg-Paris, 123–29.
I. Biffi (1995), *Teologia, Storia e Contemplazione in Tommaso d'Aquino,* vol. 3, *La Costruzione della Teologia,* Milan.
F.-X. Putallaz (1995), *Insolente liberté, controverses et condamnations au XIIIe s.,* Fribourg-Paris.
A. Cantin (1996), *Fede e Dialettica nell'XI secolo,* Milan.
J. Jolivet (1996), *Abelardo: Dialettica e Mistero,* Milan.
F.-X. Putallaz (1996), *Figure Francescane alla fine del XIII secolo,* Milan.
J. Verger (1996), *Istituzioni e Sapere nel XIII secolo,* Milan.

ALAIN DE LIBERA

See also **Intellectualism; Mysticism; Philosophy; Rhineland-Flemish Mysticism; Theology; Voluntarism**

Science of Christ. *See* Christ's Consciousness

Sciences of Nature

Science attempts to give a complete rational interpretation of all natural phenomena. Its relationship to theology* varies, depending on whether the two are considered as complementary or as contradictory (Torrance 1969) and based on the conception of the relationship between hypothesis, observation, theory, and interpretation.

a) Origins. The Middle Ages underwent the influence of a Christian Platonism*, which saw the material world as secondary, and a Christian Aristotelianism*, which recognized the importance of perceptible experience but in practice favored deduction at the expense of all observation. Nonetheless, there appeared in the work of writers such as Robert Grosseteste (1175–1253), Roger Bacon (c. 1210–92), Nicholas Oresme (c. 1310–82), and, later, Nicholas* of Cusa the type of empirical, mathematical, and speculative thought that was to bear fruit in the work of Copernicus (1473–1543), Tycho Brahe (1546–1601), Johannes Kepler (1571–1630), Galileo Galilei (1564–1642), and Sir Isaac Newton (1642–1727). It has often been suggested (Hooykaas 1972; Jaki 1978) that Christian thought made possible the development of modern science in that the opposition between God*'s liberty* and deductive logic led to a study of the world with the aim of seeing how it really behaved, and a belief in God's rationality and constancy led to the expectation that nature would conform to regular laws.

b) Newtonian Synthesis. From the scientific standpoint, the modern period can be held to begin with Copernicus's defense of heliocentrism (*De Revolutionibus,* 1543). Fifty years later, Galileo, who championed Copernicus's ideas, had the genius to draw the correct conclusions from the existing data but was so rash as to defend his views undiplomatically in publications, thus alienating him from the Church*, though the Church had initially been receptive to his ideas (Robert Bellarmine*; *see* Gingerich 1993). This recklessness had tragic consequences for both theology and science.

In his *Principia,* Newton offered a vision of the world unprecedented in its mathematical harmony, which he saw as reinforcing rather than undermining the idea that the universe was the work of a supremely

rational divine power. But neither Newton nor his successors accepted dogmas such as that of the Trinity*, and their concept of God was based on a natural theology* close to Stoic ideas and not on revelation—a fact that was to play a key role in deism*.

The link between atheism* and science dates from the 18th century, at which time David Hume (1711–76), Jean Le Rond d'Alembert (1717–83), Paul Henri Dietrich d'Holbach (1723–89), and the other philosophes all used science as an argument against theology: since Newton and his successors had explained the world so completely, God had no role to play in the universe—a view epitomized by the famous comment of Pierre Simon de Laplace (1749–1827): "I do not need this hypothesis." Kant*'s rejection of rational proofs* of the existence of God further widened the gulf between theology and science.

The 18th century looked to physics and philosophy* for a way to dispense with God; with Charles Darwin (1809–82) and evolution*, the debate shifted toward biology. Since Copernicus, man had no longer been at the center of the universe. With Darwin, it was biology's turn to justify the idea that the universe had not been made for man alone (Emerton, in Rae et al. 1994). Throughout the 19th century, determinism denied liberty, while the random nature of genetic mutations and natural selection made humanity appear a product of chance. Deterministic physics rendered God impotent; statistical biology made him superfluous (Monod 1972; Peacocke 1986).

c) Modern Science. At the end of the 19th century, the electromagnetism of James Clark Maxwell (1831–79) was already implicitly moving away from mechanism, and there was a belief that all scientific problems were about to be solved. However, in 1895, the discovery of X-rays by Wilhelm Conrad Röntgen (1845–1923) was the first in a series of events that were to transform physics and with it our whole understanding of the universe. With the theory of relativity, at first limited (1905), then general (1915), Albert Einstein (1879–1955) changed our conception of space and time*. For Newton, space had been absolute, three-dimensional, and Euclidean; it had been the "sensorium" of God in which the stars moved without depending on it. After Einstein, it was impossible to separate the movement of non-Euclidean geometry from a four-dimensional space-time, and the universe had to be conceived as both finite and limitless.

The general theory of relativity gave rise to models of the past, present, and future of the universe. They include the big bang theory, which locates the origin of the universe in a singularity (Drees 1990); the concept of an expanding universe and the idea of heavy bodies known as black holes, whose gravitational field is so great as to prevent even light from escaping them (Hawking 1988); and the theory that the universe will either suffer a thermodynamic death* or collapse under its own gravity (Barrow and Tipler 1986). Cosmology has often challenged theism* explicitly, notably regarding the Creation*, providence*, and eschatology*.

In 1900, Max Karl Ernst Luwig Planck (1858–1947) solved a problem inexplicable in terms of classical physics by proposing the idea that energy might exist only in the form of "packets" or precise quantities—quanta. In so doing, he laid the foundations of the quantum mechanics developed by Niels Bohr (1885–1962) and Werner Karl Heisenberg (1901–76). Quantum theory has a remarkable capacity to explain physical phenomena but raises difficult philosophical questions that contradict all our evidence concerning reality, causality, and the relationship of the observer to the observed.

In 1953 the discovery of the double-helical structure of DNA by Francis Harry Compton Crick and James Watson ushered in a period of unprecedented progress for biological research that has enabled an understanding of, among other things, the structure of the human genome and the causes of hereditary diseases and has led to speculation as to the possibility of creating artificial species by genetic manipulation. The workings of the brain, the mystery of consciousness, and artificial intelligence will surely be the major questions of the 21st century and will give rise to new theological problems concerning human nature, the soul, and immortality (Puddefoot 1996).

d) Epistemology and Philosophy of Science. The way in which theologians reacted to Newtonian physics and the ideas of Darwin upheld the frequent criticism that they use God to explain what cannot be explained (*God of the Gaps*), so that when science advances, theology must of necessity retreat. However, the changes in our understanding of space and time, causality, the relationship of the observer to the observed, and the nature of life and of human intelligence have actually enriched theology by providing it with new conceptual tools.

The most interesting area in the debate between science and theology undoubtedly concerns the problems of epistemology (Popper 1959). All the nonintuitive consequences of relativity and quantum theory, the unexpected developments (Prigogine 1979) of nonlinear classical mechanics and thermodynamics (chaos theory), the complexity of perception and language, and the effects of environment and culture on our conception of truth* (Kuhn 1962) gave a new lease on life to problems that were assumed to have disappeared. Theorizing about God and theorizing about the world are activities of a similar order. Both involve responding to fundamental questions about truth, knowledge, and being*. Reasons, explanations, and even the facts themselves are what they are only by virtue of the interpretation a culture gives them according to its values and the way in which it conceives the world. We are unable to stand outside our own minds and enjoy a God-like view of things, free of all the distortions and decisions that stem from our personal viewpoint. There exist complex relationships between data, hypotheses, theories, facts, beliefs, and values, which form the linguistic, social, and cultural background to knowledge. The mind is inevitably implicated in the interpretation of facts and the construction of theories (Polanyi 1958).

Some scientists, however, continue to interpret the scientific explanations of the universe in a way that echoes the agnosticism* and atheism of the 18th century (Monod, Atkins). But such stances are outside the province of science, and there is nothing insurmountable in the conflict between science and faith* (Peacocke 1990). Even Darwin, as much in *The Origin of Species* (1859) as in *The Descent of Man* (1871), considered that natural selection was not incompatible with the idea of a divine plan.

- M. Polanyi (1958), *Personal Knowledge,* London (2nd Ed. 1962).
K. R. Popper (1959), *The Logic of Scientific Discovery,* London.
T. S. Kuhn (1962), *The Structure of Scientific Revolutions,* Chicago (2nd Ed. 1970).
J. D. Watson (1968), *The Double Helix,* London.
T. F. Torrance (1969), *Theological Science,* Oxford.
R. Hooykaas (1972), *Religion and the Rise of Modern Science,* Edinburgh.
J. Monod (1972), *Le hasard et la nécessité,* Paris.
S. L. Jaki (1978), *The Road to Science and the Ways to God,* Edinburgh.
I. Lakatos (1978), *The Methodology of Scientific Research Programmes,* Cambridge.
I. Prigogine, I. Stengers (1979), *La nouvelle alliance,* Paris.
P. W. Atkins (1981), *The Creation,* Oxford.
J. C. Polkinghorne (1984), *The Quantum World,* London.
J. D. Barrow, F. J. Tipler (1986), *The Anthropic Cosmological Principle,* Oxford.
A. Funkenstein (1986), *Theology and the Scientific Imagination from the late Middle-Ages to the XVIIth c.,* Princeton, N.J.
A. R. Peacocke (1986), *God and the New Biology,* London.
J. C. Puddefoot (1987), *Logic and Affirmation,* Edinburgh.
S. W. Hawking (1988), *A Brief History of Time,* London.

W.B. Drees (1990), *Beyond the Big Bang,* La Salle, Ill.

A.R. Peacocke (1990), *Theology for a Scientific Age* (2nd ed., London, 1993).

W.L. Craig, Q. Smith (1993), *Theism, Atheism, and Big Bang Cosmology,* Oxford.

O. Gingerich (1993), "Hypothesis, Proof, and Censorship," *Colloquium* 25, 54–66.

M. Rae, H. Regan, J. Stenhouse (Ed.) (1994), *Science and Theology: Questions at the Interface,* Edinburgh.

J.C. Puddefoot (1996), *God and the Mind Machine,* London.

W.M. Richardson, W.J. Wildman (Ed.) (1996), *Religion and Science: History, Method, Dialogue,* London.

C.B. Kaiser (1997), *Creational Theology and the History of Physical Science,* Leiden–New York–Köln.

JOHN C. PUDDEFOOT

See also **Creation; Evolution; Fundamentalism; Rationalism; Reason; Truth**

Scripture, Fulfillment of

The concept of the fulfillment of the Holy Scriptures originates in the Old Testament. Human beings, fulfilling the Scriptures*, means executing a will (precepts* of Law*). For God*, it means keeping a promise* or realizing an oracle (Prophets*) and also the carrying through of a plan that the biblical narrative draws from Creation*. The words of Jesus*, "Do not think that I have come to abolish the Law or the Prophets; I have not come to abolish them but to fulfill them" (Mt 5:17), apply to these three aspects.

1. Old Testament

a) The Reports of Fulfillment. The fulfillment of the prophecy is not expressed by a specific word. God "will do," "does," but more frequently "has done" according to what he had said. He keeps his word* (literally, he "lets it rise": *héqim*), or he "fulfills" it (1 Kgs 2:27, 8:15, 8:24; Jer 29:10; Dn 9:2; *see* Tb 14:4). He "brings it about," it "occurs," it "does not fail to occur," what he had said "is." These expressions are useful to the Deuteronomy historian for interpreting the successive stages of his narrative: entrance into the promised land (Dt 9:5; Jos 21:43, 23:14); eviction from the sacerdotal line of Shiloh (1 Kgs 2:27; *see* 1 Sm 2:30–36); construction of the temple* (1 Kgs 8:15, 8:20, 8:24), which is, for this particular school, more important than the royal dynasty; division of the two kingdoms (1 Kgs 12:15; *see* 1 Kgs 11:29–39); successive exterminations of the ephemeral lineages of Northern kings (1 Kgs 15:29, 16:12, etc.); fall of their kingdom (2 Kgs 17:23); and then fall of the Southern kingdom, with the exile (2 Kgs 22:16, 24:2) and the re-turn from exile (2 Chr 26:22; Ezr 1:1). In short, everything occurs in fulfillment of the divine word.

Reporting an occurrence generally follows the formula "according to (one or several words)." The event has occurred "in order that" the word might be verified (Dt 9:5; 1 Kgs 2:4, 2:27, 9:2; Ezr 1:1). Thus, an inexplicable human hardening* is first announced, then delivered by God (1 Kgs 12:15; *see* the case of Pharaoh in Ex 7:3). There is a quite systematic emphasis on prophecies of doom (2 Kgs 22:16; Jer 28:8f.). After the pronouncement of an oracle, some limited fulfillments usually occur as a sort of guarantee regarding the final result (1 Kgs 13:26, 13:32, 14:15, 14:18). The impact is cumulative, which explains the use of formulas of recapitulation such as "my (his) servants the prophets" (2 Kgs 21:10, 24:2; *see* 2 Kgs 17:23: "all"); or [I had said] "every day," "without growing weary": Jeremiah 7:25 ("all"), 25:4 ("all"), 29:19, and 35:15 and 2 Chronicles 36:15. The destruction of the temple is such a terrible calamity that it is said to have been foretold "since ancient days" (Jer 28:8; Lam 2:17).

b) The Eschatological Horizon. In its final form the book of Jeremiah represents a turning point: the proclamation of doom is confirmed but is followed by proclamations of salvation*, the main one being of the return from exile (Jer 25:11f., 29:10); the theme of the restoration of the temple comes from a later writing still (Jer 33:14–26). A threshold is being crossed when the prophetic word, which has been uttered "since the beginning of time," is understood as forming a unity with that which created the world. This is the moment of the "Deutero-Isaiah" (Is 40–55). If the category of fulfillment, with the distinction of "first things" and of "new things" (Is 42:9, 48:3, 48:6f.), looks promising as a hermeneutical key for understanding all the words of God, it can be said to have originated with this author. From now on, fulfillment stands out on the horizon of eschatology*. The book of Daniel's rereading of the Jeremiah prophecy (Dn 9:2) is another turning point: the 70-year wait it was heralding becomes a wait of 70 weeks (of years) before "vision and prophecy are sealed together" (Dn 9:24). The fulfillment is accompanied here by a revealed interpretation (revelation*) that carries the letter of the Scriptures to the level of the extreme.

2. The New Testament

The New Testament writers place the coming of the Messiah* within the framework of their sole Bible*, the Jewish Scriptures; and the Gospels* trace this way of reading the Scriptures back to Jesus himself. In this way these writers testify of his founding values in their own faith. The imposing body of biblical quotations in the New Testament is therefore only the visible part of a consciousness of fulfillment and should not make us forget other evocations. They are more diffuse, like the innumerable similarities of language between the two testaments; they are more concealed when the experience* of the novelty of Christ* revisits the great narrative moments of the Old Testament: the story of the Fathers, Easter, the gift of manna, the cycles of Elijah and Elisha (compare, e.g., Jn 6:8–14 and 2 Kgs 4:42–44), and so on. That anamnesis gives first place to the Pentateuch; it is an occasion for an inchoative theory of the "meaning of the Scriptures." More radically still than at the time of the exile, the present turns toward the past, only to deliver it from its archaism.

a) The First Testimonies of Faith. The rooting of the New Testament in the Old is reflected in the testimony of faith* formulated by Paul after a catechesis* that he had first received himself: "I believe that Christ died for our sins* in accordance with the Scriptures; that he was buried, that he was raised on the third day in accordance with the Scriptures" (1 Cor 15:3f.). For the New Testament narrators the Christ event occurs, as in the Old Testament, "in order that" the Scriptures (almost always prophetic) can be fulfilled (Mt: nine times; Jn: nine times). Without this anteriority of the word of God with regard to the moment of Jesus, he would not be perceived in his full dimension. A formula of the type "in order that the Scriptures be fulfilled" puts the emphasis mainly on the Passion* and is invested with several modalities: the Scriptures are quoted in detail by Matthew (11 times) and more generally by Luke and Acts ("all": Lk 18:31; Acts 3:18;

13:27; the whole Scriptures: Mt 26:54; Lk 21:22, 24:44; see Mk 14:49; Jn 19:28, 19:30; Acts 13:29). John places his emphasis on the Passion, when Christ departs into solitude: "Though he had done so many signs before them, they still did not believe in him," fulfilling a prophecy of Isaiah (Jn 12:337–38). There is only one occurrence in Mark (14:49), but it comes at the decisive moment when Jesus gives himself into the soldiers' hands At several crucial moments (Mt 13:14; Lk 4:21) and above all at the last moment (Lk 22:37; Jn 13:18, 15:25, 17:12, 19:28), the announcement of a fulfillment of Scripture is placed in Jesus' own mouth. By this he acknowledges that he has witnessed the fulfillment of the Scriptures and that all is as he has desired (Mt 5:17, 26:54; Mk 14:49; Lk 8:31).

b) Jesus as Agent of the Fulfillment. Facing death, Jesus shows "obedience" (Rom 5:19; Phil 2:8; Heb 5:8): he fulfills the "will" of his Father*. His Father reveals it to him, but Jesus also belongs to the history of humankind, and he knows the will of God because he learned how to find it in the Book*. The Scriptures justify more than once the "it must be so" or "it had to be so" of the Passion (Mt 26:54; Mk 8:31; Lk 22:37, 24:26, 24:44; Jn 3:14). That "it must be so" belongs to the formula of the apocalypses (Dn 2:28 LXX; see Rev: six times). Hence, does the necessity of the fulfillment by the cross have to be understood as the fate to which God's "plan" subjects his Son (filiation*)? The inescapable doom of such a terrible event is certainly emphasized rather than blurred or obscured. But if Jesus "teaches" (Mk 8:31) the correspondence between his tragic death and the Scriptures, this means that he finds there is "light" in it (Mt 16:21: he "shows"). There is indeed the inescapable necessity of the impact of sin. But what is new in this instance is that God does not interrupt the process. He refrains from doing so precisely "in order" to overcome it finally instead, and consequently forever, but away from "mankind's" sight (Jn 14:22). Jesus' participation in the act of fulfillment takes the form of his lived, ongoing consent to his Father's plan.

c) The Two Aspects of Fulfillment. In New Testament Greek, the root *plèr-* implies a happy outcome, but the root *tél-* implies the outcome aimed at or the cut that separates the outcome from the process. This lexical distinction functions in the various formulations of fulfillment because Jesus Christ suffered "in order that" fulfillment may occur. Full realization is plenitude. It is nuptials (Mk 2:19 par.; Rev 21:2, 21:9, 22:17). It is a kept promise since the risen body of Christ is the first stone of the new temple that is being built. The Resurrection (Resurrection* of Christ) fulfills the Scriptures

(Lk 18:31, 24:26, 24:46; Jn 2:22, 20:9; Acts 2:31, 26:22f.; 1 Cor 15:54f.); along with the Passion, it had been taught in advance (Mk 8:31, 9:31 par). Certain texts describe the social and religious divisions that existed at the time of Christ (Eph 2:11–17, 3:6). Implied is the obligatory reconciliation of Jews and Gentiles, something that was expected in the early Church*. In contrast with that plenitude, Creation wails (Rom 8:22f.). In the face of Israel's resistance, Paul is torn (9:2); in him, the Passion remains unfinished (Col 1:24). The unheard-of nature of the blessing that Jesus Christ brought to the world, as well as the extension of that blessing (the entire and unreserved admission of all nations into the people of God), made it indispensable to redefine the status and the rules of this people. They were gradually obliged to choose between circumcision and Baptism*, between the temple of Jerusalem* and the body of Christ, between separation and sharing in a communal life, according to whether the Mosaic law was observed. The most beautiful expression of fulfillment is surely present in the following words of the prophet Malachi (beginning of the second temple era), found in both testaments: the prophet predicted to come "will bring back the fathers' hearts towards their sons and the sons' hearts towards their fathers" (Mal 3:24; *see* Lk 1:16f.). For us today, this prophecy shows also the extent of what has remained unfulfilled.

• S. Amsler (1960), *L'Ancien Testament dans l'Église,* Neuchâtel.
J. A. Fitzmyer (1960–61), "The Use of Explicit Old Testament Quotations in Qumran Literature and in the New Testament," *NTS* 7, 297–333.
G. von Rad (1964), "Antwort auf Conzelmanns Fragen," *EvTh* 24, 113–25.
K. Stendahl (1967), *The School of St. Matthew and Its Use of the Old Testament,* 2nd ed., Lund.
A. H. J. Günneweg (1977), *Vom Verstehen des Alten Testaments. Eine Hermeneutik,* Göttingen.
P. Lenhardt (1978), "Voies de la continuité juive: Aspects de la relation maître-disciple d'après la littérature rabbinique ancienne," *RSR* 66, 489–516.
P. Beauchamp (1979), "Comprendre l'Ancien Testament, by A. H. J. Günneweg," *RSR* 67, 45–58.
P.-M. Beaude (1980), *L'accomplissement des Écritures: Pour une histoire critique des systèmes de représentation du sens chrétien,* Paris.
P. Beauchamp (1990), *L'un et l'autre Testament,* vol. II, *Accomplir les Écritures,* Paris.
H. Hübner (1992), "New Testament, O. T. Quotations," *AncBD*
P.-M. Beaude (1995), "Judaïsme rabbinique et christianisme: Deux modèles d'accomplissement," in *"Ouvrir les Écritures,"* LeDiv 162, 285–306.
P. Gisel, "Variations sur l'accomplissement," in *"Ouvrir les Écritures,"* LeDiv 162, 327–48.
A. Obermann (1996), *Die christologische Erfüllung der Schrift im Johannesevangelium: Eine Untersuchung zur johanneischen Hermeneutik anhand der Schriftzitate,* Tübingen.
Ch. M. Tuckett (Ed.) (1997), *The Scriptures in the Gospels,* BEThL 131, Louvain.

PAUL BEAUCHAMP

See also **Apocalyptic Literature; Bible; Canon of Scriptures; Holy Scripture; Eschatology; Exegesis; Hermeneutics; Jesus, Historical; Mystery; Promise; Prophet/Prophecy; Scripture, Senses of**

Scripture, Senses of

The Scriptures* have more than one sense. This notion of many senses is never very far from the thoughts of theologians. In the Fourth Gospel*, Jesus*, in speaking of Moses, says, "If you believed Moses, you would believe me, for he wrote of me" (Jn 5:46; *see also* Jn 8:56 regarding Abraham). "We have found him of whom Moses in the law and also the prophets wrote, Jesus of Nazareth, the son of Joseph" (Jn 1:45): such a global certainty, reaffirmed in other forms throughout the New Testament, implied or inevitably led to a revolution in the reading of the "Old Testament," which at the time were the sole "Scriptures." A sense unnoticed until then was discovered therein. Of course, it had to be based on ancient sources: it could not simply contradict the previously recognized sense, nor could it be completely detached from it. For the new sense could not leave out genealogy: Jesus could not be revealed as the Son without referring to the traces the Father* had left in history*. It is for this reason that the hermeneutics* of the Old Testament are inseparable from the first steps of Christian theology*.

The procedure of applying to a text a key that was unknown to the text's author was already current outside Israel*. It was used in interpreting Greek philosophers, such poets as Homer and Virgil (who were thought to receive their inspiration from a higher source), and "all those who have dealt with divinity, the Barbarians, and the Greeks" (Clement of Alexandria, *Stromata,* V, 4, 21, 4). The specificity of the Christian interpretation of the Bible* is not in allegory but in the fact that allegory is entirely determined by the experience* of a moment in history held to be unique and is therefore subordinate to the message that announces it (*kerugma*). This is why the doctrine of a plurality of senses in Scripture was applied first to a Christian reading of the Old Testament for which the New Testament provided the model. It is above all the Old Testament that has a multiplicity of senses.

I. Principal Concepts

The terms used to designate the "senses" of Scripture have frequently changed their acceptation, going so far as to take on an opposite content. They are still evolving, but it remains possible to unravel the main sources of convergence or divergence in standard contemporary theological usage.

1. Literal Sense

a) There exists a traditional, negative acceptation, attributed to Paul: "The letter kills" (applied above all to the commandments of the law); it is linked to the limitative or deprecatory usage of "flesh*".

b) "Literal" also designates what is taken as the received sense in the context of daily communication: the immediate or "obvious" sense (*prokheiron*). From another point of view, to interpret something "by the letter" is to adopt the material sense: the "literal sense" is thus the opposite of the "metaphorical sense" and is used above all when referring to a word or a brief syntagma. To interpret a metaphor literally would be a misinterpretation (a "missed sense").

c) On the basis of the technical use of the modern exegesis*, the literal sense is that in which communication occurs or should have occurred between one who destines a message and those to whom *he himself* destined it. It belongs to a "contract of communication," delimited by convention and the possibilities of the era when the message was formulated. This refers above all to a *text* rather than to a word or a formula.

2. Allegory

Today, *allegory* (from the Greek, *alla-egorein:* "to say something else") has a more limited sense than it did in early exegesis. Allegorical language is coded: in a series, each *concept* is replaced by an *image.* Concepts come in succession, but images can be discontinuous (in Zec 5:7–8 a woman is seated in a basket covered with a leaden weight). Incoherence can even forewarn the recipient of the nature of the message. When intended by the author, the allegorical sense is considered to be the "literal sense," in present-day parlance (*see* above, 1 c). Even in ancient times this was occasionally understood so.

3. Typical or Figurative Sense

Tupos is a rich term that designates a mark solid enough for its impression to be long lasting—a matrix. It is less the copy or reproduction of a model (celestial or otherwise) than a model of that which remains to be produced ("antitype") and which will be even greater in dignity (Goppelt). In addition to relationship, it suggests a difference, like that between "hollow" and "full," "mold" and "statue." It can be replaced in Greek by *schema* and is translated in Latin by *figura.* One speaks of a "typical," "figurative," or "representational" sense. The narrative thread of the Bible (narrative*) weaves through types or figures that look to the future: one might say they are drawn by that future. And if the future has a resolution determined by Christ*, it might be said that when the future comes, it leads to the fulfillment of types and figures. Since attraction is a form of participation, thought can examine the relation between accomplishment and principles and origins: there will therefore be an interaction between the typological exegesis and speculative theology. On another level, the principle of typology can easily be recognized by semiotics and narrative analysis, which are attentive to the recurrence of schemas.

4. Spiritual Sense

Provided it is taken strictly as a technical term of theological exegesis and on the basis of its Pauline origin, the adjective *spiritual* designates the new sense revealed by the action of the Spirit. Spiritual interpretation is a novelty in action and in preaching*, the vehicle for so much patristic commentary. The Bible teaches that spiritual understanding comes with the defeat experienced by hardened hearts when they attempt to rely on their own righteousness. The characteristic of the "spiritual sense" interpreted in this way is its radical nature. With the same words, everything is changed in the text, everything is changed in the world. This type of reading acknowledges that the Spirit it is imbued with comes from Christ and, as such, maintains its allegiance to history but grants little importance to its phases.

The ancients often gave other names to the "spiritual sense," including *allegorical, mystical* (from *mystery**), and even *typical* when dealing with the truths of faith*. *Mystical* could also be applied to the journey of the soul. *Tropological* (synonym of *moral*) is directed toward an action and *anagogical* toward the ultimate goals (*see* III, 5).

5. Plenary Sense

The expression *plenary sense* spread among Catholics, particularly in the years following *Divino Afflante Spiritu* (1943), where it was not even used. It acceded to the very ancient principle that the Bible is explained through the Bible as a whole. The plenary sense follows the expansion of the meaning of words. Thus, "life" has always been promised, but tradition overburdened the meaning of the word when the hope of eternity (eternal* life) arose, long before the New Testament. The plenary sense nevertheless did not go so far as to question the specific originality of the New Testament.

II. The Plurality of Senses in the Bible

The origins of biblical typology are biblical, present even in the Old Testament. The process was already a dialectical one. Similarity could be refuted only once it had been stated.

For Deutero-Isaiah, the new act of God reveals him as being present from the beginning. Calling his people* back from exile, God gave them a new memory; the return from exile reproduced the Exodus and caused it to be forgotten (Is 43:18f.). According to Jeremiah 16:14–15, "it shall no longer be said" that the Lord "brought up the people of Israel out of the land of Egypt," but it shall be said that he brought them up "out of the north country [after exile] and out of all the countries where he had driven them." The founding stories (the family structure of the patriarchs, Passover, and the wandering in the desert) have the status of archetypes, interpretive keys of the new developments of which the exile would be the most important. Thus, the fulfilled Sarah represents Jerusalem* repopulated (Is 51:2f. and 54:1). The experience is portrayed as a revelation*: "To this day the Lord has not given you a mind to understand or eyes to see, or ears to hear" (Dt 29:2f.). Psalm 78:2 sees ancient history as "dark sayings from of old" (applied to Jesus' parables* by Mt 13:35). The Wisdom of Solomon 19 transforms the cosmic miracles* of Exodus into a message of a final salvation* of the departed just.

The New Testament, a fortiori, gives new sense to the Old Testament. Romans 4:17 rereads Genesis 15 by placing the emphasis on continuity: the impulse through which Christians believe in resurrection* had already inhabited Abraham, and Paul is not concerned with what Abraham knew about it. 1 Corinthians 10 sees Christ as already present (but hidden) in a reality

experienced by Israel before the Incarnation*. This is a model of typology. Another process, declared "allegorical," underlies Galatians 4:24. Its artificial side acquired a following. For the evangelists, even the details of the life of Jesus (places where he stayed or passed through) represented the fulfillment of prophecy. But the elements drawn from the Old Testament are most revealing when the evangelists do not identify them and simply describe the acts of Jesus by superimposing them over the acts of Moses, Elijah, and Jeremiah without saying so. The narrative is characterized by the certainty that divine intention is leading all of history and that it left traces that can be deciphered only through a resolution in the gospel. The fourth gospel is the only one that makes this strategy explicit: Jesus is the bronze serpent, the manna, the vine of Israel, the temple* not built by human hands. Since, in this perspective, the characters of the story are personally directed toward the individuality of the incarnate Word*, the typology remains historical at its core.

1 Corinthians 10 outlines the hermeneutics. The reach of the ancient narrative is dogmatic, parenetic, eschatological; it is already a subdivision of the spiritual sense. 2 Corinthians 3 introduces the theme of a veil over the hearts of the sons of Israel "whenever Moses is read" (v. 15). We should note that, on the one hand, the obscurity does not spring from the text being read, nor, on the other hand, does the lack of light necessarily signify darkness. The Letter to the Hebrews compares the new covenant* with the old one using the categories of *tupos* (type), *hupodeigma* (leading schema, framework), *homoiotes* (similitude), *eikon* (image), and *skia* (shadow). Everything is directed toward the *ephapax*, the "once and for all" that brings an end to repetition.

III. Tradition

During the first two centuries of the Christian era, Christian exegesis was carried by a rich and continuous flow (e.g., Barnabas, Clement of Rome, Justin, Tertullian*, and Irenaeus*). We will limit our examination to a few examples of originality and faithfulness brought by several participants in this movement.

1. Origen

Origen (c. 185–c. 251, Alexandria, then Caesarea) has been compared with another great son of Alexandria, Philo (c. 25 B.C.–c. A.D. 40), since allegorization was a source of prolific invention for both men, though more so for Origen. There was few codification in his interpretation. At its core was the current and radical transformation of the carnal world* through the incarnate

Word. Through its action and through the gift of the Spirit, the stages of the history of the world have become contemporaneous within the soul. Theology and the reading of the Bible are completely coextensive in this case and are addressed to an audience for the sake of its own progression. This form of exegesis begins with the sustained endeavor to find the true text, which was the aim of Origen's *Hexapla* (*see* Translations* of the Bible), and in this respect it deserves to be called literal. Origen is sufficiently critical to say that the law could not have been carved in stone in its entirety and to allow that the evangelists might have "added to Scripture, in the form of a sensible thing, the spiritual notion that their spirit had conceived" (*In Jo* 10:5). But this form of criticism is not a major concern for Origen; he does not seek the truth* in verisimilitude, even if he is a firm believer in history. His adversaries are those who refuse to allow the mystery revealed by the New Testament to inhabit any text: "For us, both of the Testaments are new" (*Hom Num.*, IX, 4). Taken literally, even the life of Jesus does not reveal its entire sense.

Allegorical exegesis frequently makes use of definitions. For example, for the preparation of offerings, Leviticus (7:9) prescribes an oven, pan, or griddle, and this calls for a spiritual interpretation: but it must first specify a particular property for each tool. As a result, it is usual to find an apt attention to all sorts of reality in this form of exegesis.

Origen's list of the senses of Scripture—which does not necessarily cover all his work—is expressed in triadic form: either *historical, moral* (the milk), *mystical* (meat); or *historical, mystical, spiritual* (in reverse order to 1 Thes 5:23's "spirit and soul and body"; *see also* the *trissos* [tripling] in the Septuagint translation of Prv 22:20). The mystical sense is that which deals with the revelation of the mystery of faith, which concerns both the husband and the wife, Christ and the Church*, and their relation in the history of salvation. This sense is the objective condition of the "spiritual" sense, which specifically concerns the soul of the reader. The "moral" sense also leaves room for truths or virtues*, which are more than supernatural.

The allegorical exegesis practiced by Origen and many others was supported by their perception of biblical discourse, whose logic usually seemed deficient to them, lacking *akolouthia,* or continuity. This was for two reasons: the biblical mode of composition was poorly understood, and people failed to take into account that many works had been written in several stages, whence a tendency to justify these shortcomings by resorting to a sense that, until that point, had remained hidden. By making allegory into a global principle, it was no longer necessary to set it apart

from typology, or the "typical" sense. It is impossible for contemporary readers to take Origen's exegesis simply as it is; for him, every physical sign could be transposed. The rule he applied, of taking any incongruity as a sign of hidden meaning, is untenable, even if it does not belong to Origen alone. What may seem excessive or even mechanical (and that may, in any case, be put down to the fact that he was preaching every day in Caesarea) can be distracting, but the richness of his vision of the renewed world is enlightening. Origen himself did not seek an adhesion to science or even, continuously, to dogma*. That which he gives can be received, which it was through the tradition handed down to Origen himself, but we do absolutely have need of that which he does not give us. He sees the witnesses of Israel in the mystery of the Church (Lubac*, *Histoire et Esprit*), but does not bring them close enough to their people. Even though he set great store by them, he had not only insufficient means but also insufficient interest to reconstitute the spiritual path of Israel.

2. The Exegetes of Antioch

The exegesis practiced in Antioch*, in contrast to that of Alexandria* and a century after Origen, represents another pole. Diodorus, the bishop* of Tarsus in 378, was the teacher of Theodore of Mopsuestia. John Chrysostom* belonged to this school. Antioch sought a "systematic quarrel" (Jay 1985) with Alexandria. Hellenism was kept at a distance, and the emphasis was placed on realism and history. Thus, Theodore of Mopsuestia (350–428) is said to have refused to apply any other sense than a literal one to the Song of Solomon. However, insofar as the spiritual sense of the Old Testament is founded in the affirmations and practice of the New Testament, it was received in Antioch along with what were already its traditional applications. But there were no attempts to add more: there was some mention of Christ in the Old Testament but only intermittently. Origen, on the contrary, said with common sense that if there were "a few cases," it was in order that they might spread to others (*in Hom. Ex.* 5, 1).

John Chrysostomos clearly defined the "type": "Prophecy through the mode of types is a prophecy* of facts (*pragmaton*)" (*De Poenitentia,* hom. VI, 4; PG 49, 320). But for the school, the relation between the two testaments was based first of all on the prophets since prophecy was understood as a prediction or an anticipated vision of a miraculous nature. The vision might be presented on several levels: the same text, in particular in the case of the "prophet" David (*see* Acts 2:30), was applied to the event announced in Israel and its future realization in Christ, the prophet having had this double vision before writing it down. Hyperbole was seen as a sign that the event had come about, for it was the realization that made the hyperbole truthful: this was a position shared by all schools of thought, but in this particular case it was more methodical. Those texts that served as proof had privileged place: the tendency was to seek assurance by confirming a *theoria,* that is, an anticipated vision of future events.

3. Augustine

What was new about Augustine*'s approach was that he conceived of a plurality of senses, either on the basis of a philosophical reflection on signs or on the basis of revelation or by bringing both of these elements together. "The letter kills, the spirit gives life": these words, handed down through Ambrose*, are the starting point of his hermeneutic journey. His classifications of senses are variable; this is the world of a *grammaticus.* Thus, signs are "unknown," "suspect," "literal," or "figurative" (*De Doctrina christiana,* II, III), and it is necessary to distinguish between various metaphors (*verba translata*). The classifications of senses can be understood on two levels (*De utilitate credendi,* III, 5): the "historical" and "etiological" sense (what is the cause of a *dictum* or a *factum*?), "analogical" ("the two Testaments are not opposed"), and "allegorical" (certain texts are meant to be taken not literally but figuratively). The etiology in this case depends, according to circumstances, on reason* or faith, on explanation or interpretation. The "cause" being sought might be literary, logical, or mystical. Augustine demonstrates great freedom, in part because he is not a philologist, but there were even better reasons for this. First, exegesis is a quest that is both regulated and urgent, and it resolutely renders all meanings of texts subordinate to a truth that surpasses not only the author of the text (be it Moses himself) but even the text and its interpreter. That truth is God's truth. It is also the truth of things, whence the necessity of knowing "the properties and nature of those which are used as a basis for comparison." *De Doctrina christiana* outlines this program. Meaning also implies openness: the Bible does not close one in but is itself to be found in a territory without limits. This truth will finally be Augustine's truth, insofar as he never tires of questioning it with confidence. Second, the spiritual sense is, as such, the harmony of several meanings—it causes humanity, Israel, Christ, his Church, and each reader to speak in unison: "Who is speaking? . . . It depends upon you to be the one whom you seek" (*In Psalmos,* 42 [41hb], PL 36, 464). But the reader is with Christ: "Do not venture to say anything without him any more than he will say anything without you" (ibid., 86 [85hb], PL 37, 1 082). It is also

"the entire city* which is speaking, since the time of the blood of Abel" (ibid., Ps 62 [61hb], PL 36, 731). Third, all of Scripture proceeds from charity and leads to it. Charity takes our weakness into account, and it unites the author with the readers and the readers to each other. There are two sorts of disagreement, one relating to the truth of things the other to the intention of those who express those things. As for the second point, "I cannot distinguish it as well" (*Confessions* LXII, chaps. XXIII–XXIV), but, "if I had been Moses, I would have liked to write in such a way" that all opinions that diverged but were not false could be understood in the text, for all that is true "unites in charity," and that is something that Moses obtained (ibid., chaps. XXVI, XXX–XXXI). Rarely has the "figure of the reader" (A.-M. Pelletier 1989) been so highly honored.

4. Jerome

The craftsman of the Latin Vulgate fought for the rule of the *hebraica veritas.* His originality is not in his respect for the literal sense but in his aptitude for seeking it out, both in Origen's *Hexapla* and in the erudition of the Jews of his time, whose scrolls he was shown. He was an indefatigable student of *historia* and *realia* (geography, natural sciences). A prolific and enthusiastic author as well as a master rhetorician, Jerome was also a reader who was sensitive to the workings and quality of a text. His concept of the sense of Scripture was initially taken from Paul: the "letter" kills if it is received *carnaliter,* but the basic principle is that the spiritual edifice rests on the *fundamentium historiae.* The "type" and the "figure" are synonymous for Jerome. Occasionally the figure might be a figure of rhetoric, a trope—the boundary between oblique meaning (metaphors, *translatio*) and spiritual sense is not self-evident. Relying heavily on Origen, Jerome was better able than him to distinguish between the "types" of allegory, about which he had some reservations. He was well aware of the ambiguity of the term *allegoroumena* in Galatians 4:24 (Jay). The spiritual interpretation (*spiritalis*) was to be found on the level of the mystery; it had to follow the "coherence (*ordinem*) of history" and not interpret each word in isolation as allegory did. On many occasions Jerome would follow the common practice of suggesting a spiritual sense where coherence was lacking: "That does not make any sense at all. Therefore, one must resort to the mystical interpretation" (*In Ps,* 95 [hb96], PL 26, 1 112). The incongruity of Hosea 1–3 obliges one to classify it as allegorical. In Jerome's work there can be found tropology, often with a psychological and ascetic coloring, and *anagogè,* which he uses either as an equivalent to the "spiritual sense" or in the sense of an elevation of the soul to a higher level or more rarely in the sense of an application to "future realities," a sense that was later to become dominant.

5. The Distich of the Four Senses and Thomas Aquinas

Littera gesta docet, quid credas allegoria/moralis quid agas, quo tendas anagogia: "The letter teaches that which took place; allegory, that which you must believe; the moral (tropological) sense, that which you must do; and the anagogical sense, that which you must strive for." Augustine of Dacia, a Dominican, is said to have composed (c. 1260, with the variant *quid speres* for *anagogia*) this famous distich (where the triple use of "you" should be noted) to sum up the doctrine of Thomas Aquinas*. In keeping with tradition (*Summa Theologica* Ia, q. 1, a. 10 resp.), Aquinas recalled that "the literal or historical sense" was the foundation of the spiritual sense, which was divided into three: "allegorical, moral, and anagogical." While *littera* only designated words, "the literal sense" was used to refer to what the author meant to say (*quem auctor intendit* or *quod loquens per verba vult significare*): it might deviate from the immediate meaning of the words. The meaning intended by the (divine) author could go beyond what the (human) author meant to say (ibid., ad 1). Another case: Psalm 29 (hb 28), verse 2, was metaphorical for David but literal for Jesus, for Jesus alone was released from the sojourn among the dead (*In Psalmos Expositio*). This objective fulfillment was not necessarily that of a prophecy. Sometimes it was; the ancients believed "A Virgin shall conceive" and we believe "A Virgin has conceived"—same meaning and same faith (Ia Iiae, q. 103, a. 4). One could sense an imminent enrichment of the literal sense. If it was the foundation of the spiritual sense, was this not already on the condition that it was a *sense*? The biblical "mode" was called *narrativus signorum* (*Sent.* I, prol. q. 1, a. 5). Ia, q.1, a. 10 returned to the classical doctrine of typology: an earlier *res* was, by divine disposition, the "type" of a later *res,* in a movement tending toward the ultimate. But was the *res* separable from the words that expressed it? The gap between the signifier and the signified rested on a paradoxical "agreement": Ia, q. 1, a. 9 relied on the Pseudo-Dionysius* in order to state that the most sensible or the lowest was also the most apt to signify that which was most spiritual and least accessible. Alexander of Hales (*Summa Theologica Prolog.* c. IV, a. 1) already called this sensible thing the "form of the unformed" and the "figure of that which has no figure." Although this warranted the legitimating of theology as a science by authorizing it on the basis of the Bible, the widespread acceptance of the literal sense

had been sufficiently affirmed for the task of exploring it to have conquered its autonomy.

IV. The Renaissance and the Reformation

When Lefèvre d'Étaples (c. 1460–1536) found a spiritual sense in the entire Psalter (*Quincuplex psalterium,* 1509, 1st ed.) (psalms*) and decided to call this the "literal sense" because it represented the intention of the prophet David, it became apparent that a coming together of the two dimensions was already being felt. This simplification did not yet lead to significant innovation. The shock came with Luther* when he offered a similar sort of maxim: the literal sense is the Christic sense, "to transfer onto Christ the literal interpretation." His theory contained several elements. Here we will concentrate on the dimension of the word*: the priority he granted to the word was unprecedented. The cross of Jesus would have served no purpose if it had not been made an object of belief through the verbal message. Celestial things could only be *annuntiari verbo.* If John, Romans, and Galatians precede the rest of the New Testament (preface to his 1522 translation), it was because they were conveyors of a message rather than of a story. "He who has words through faith has everything, albeit in a hidden manner" (*WA* 4; 376, 15 *Sq*) We have nothing but words and promises*" (*WA* 4; 272, 16 *Sq*). This "word" however, which has two senses (*sensus in dorso, sensus in facie*), has its own consistence through which that which would be the weakness of a fusion between the literal sense and the spiritual sense is conjured. The word is interposed between the two meanings in the manner of a wall that cannot be seen as convex unless it is also seen as concave, depending on where the viewer stands. Critical science ought not to have to dictate this choice, but ought to clearly trace the line. It separates death and life.

What will become then of the "shadows" of figures? That is the problem of this hermeneutic. Luther often makes one think that the shadow "is night" (Ebeling, *Lutherstudien*) but not always. First of all, he discovered that the letter that kills goes to that extent so that the movement will turn into a promise: the reader must find the way for himself. Later, in reexamining the positions that his advances might seem to have left behind, Luther conceded the legitimacy of a transitional category: the Old Testament also spoke of "the letter and the spirit together"; the just prayed so that *"veniat Christus et transeat Moses"* ("let Christ come and let Moses pass away"; *WA* 4; 310, 38f.). This *transeat* was valid for the Church, situated without stability *inter veterem et novam legem* ("between the old and the new law"; ibid.). Thomas Aquinas shared this opinion. According to Ebeling (op. cit., 51), Luther managed to weave together the opposition "letter of death" and "spirit of life" with a more homogeneous arrangement of the four senses but within a "deafening whirlpool" (*einem verwirrenden Strudel*). To those who reiterated that the Incarnation and the Cross were historical facts, Luther replied that yes, but a fact is only that which is known to be a fact: *quod cognoscitur esse factum* (3; 435, 37–39). Ebeling remarked, "Christ is now the text." We understand this to mean he has the status of a text. Henceforth, it was the word itself that brought about a crisis of representation, a crisis that was both cognitive and ethical*.

V. From the Renaissance to Modern Times

It has been noted on more than one occasion that Luther's interpretation abolished the distance of time*. Commenting later on the obedience of Abraham, Kierkegaard* eliminated any intermediary stage: the substance of the relation with the Father seems indeed to be the same before, during, and after Christ, whether one is dealing with Abraham or a Christian. What matters is the "contemporaneity" of the Christic act, declared absolute after the Incarnation, whereas the period that preceded it had no definite status. Bultmann*, later still, would reveal the way in which the law/gospel pairing, while remaining independent of the relation between the two testaments, was perpetually current. As for the words of the Old Testament, he conceded *in extremis* and certainly without sharing Luther's ardor that faith could legitimately "take hold of the Old Testament, and in its power and within its rights, dare to direct towards us words which were not uttered for us" (*GuV,* 1933, 373), given the "inviolable" condition that these words had been properly understood *and* that the difference between the two situations had been grasped.

Luther's era opened the way to a reconstruction of the letter (to the work of those whom Richard Simon would praise as "grammarians"), but it would be with Galileo, after Luther, that the reconstruction of history would expand, on the border where physics (natural sciences*) and human history overlapped. Calvin* felt that Scripture "carried its credence within" (*Inst.* I, VII, 5), a trait from which he excepted no miracles (ibid., I, VIII). Pascal* was the last significant witness who could apply his genius to reviving the classic division of senses in the Bible without questioning and without even being unduly concerned with the veracity* of the text. The workings of language interested him in the same way it interested the residents of Port-Royal. He knew that charity and cupidity were to be found in the same word (nothing "so similar," nothing

"so contrary": *Pensées,* Brunschvicg 629). The testaments showed "everything doubled, and the same words remaining" (ibid., 862): he did not go any further than the enigma of sense and not only under the aspect of faith. But exegesis would not return to this topic until the long and ineluctable detour imposed on it by the question of historicity had been completed. Pascal, more than others, also offered for consideration the ethical and metaethical dimensions of interpretation: the veil that obscures the meaning of the gospel parables or of the Old Testament is a product of our refusal rather than of our ignorance.

In the centuries that followed, the classical question of the "senses of Scripture," that is, of the relation between the two testaments, would lose the predominant position that it had hitherto occupied in discussion of the Bible. The dominant trend is to study the two testaments separately: the scope and the potential of biblical theology* are thereby diminished.

It was in part due to the progress of history and comparative studies that there emerged the category of literary genre*, which would have such an impact in the 20th century. Gunkel, at the turn of the century, without any theoretical contributions but with talent, would bring about a renewal of the old question—one that opened the *Summa* of Thomas Aquinas—of the relation between poetry and truth. E. Auerbach (*Mimesis,* 1946) emphasized the singularity of a literature that, while never ceasing to be literature, "demands to be believed and "requires to be interpreted." There is no longer the belief in Europe that myths* are childishness. Attention is being focused not so much on content as on the relation between biblical form and mythical form.

Where Catholics are concerned, the issue of the sense of Scripture was reformulated in 1943 in an encyclical of Pius XII, *Divino Afflante Spiritu.* The encyclical outlined the primary task of biblical exegesis as being that of searching for the "so-called literal, and above all, theological sense" since that was the intention of its inspired author. The encyclical gave priority to the interpretations that had the clear support of science and in which science discerned potential for future development. The "theological sense" is discovered not by taking the shortest path but, as has been said repeatedly, by studying "the manner, form, and art of reasoning, telling, and writing" used by the authors of the Bible. The "spiritual sense" (understood as the typical or figurative sense of the Old Testament) is adopted in the form of a concession, not out of any concern to provide a warning (it had never been so little honored), but with the undoubted intention of obliging one to be rigorous about taking the investigation into the literal theological sense as far as it would go: "Certainly, spiritual sense cannot be altogether excluded from Holy Scripture" (*EB* §552). The magisterium* could not deny, and immediately recognized, that the Old Testament "signified in advance, in a spiritual way, that which should come about under the new covenant of grace*" (ibid.). It is easier to see in retrospect that the aim was not only to "adapt biblical studies to the needs of the era" but also to find common ground with Protestant exegesis. And there was also a realization that the path of historical spiritual sense was the one where the Bible of Israel would be revealed to Christians on the basis of its own merit. More explicitly ecumenical, Vatican II* opened a wider door to typology and thus came more fully in line with contemporary research. This research maintains in particular that there is a way to support the typology of the Old Testament through a better knowledge of the means of expression but also, on a more basic level, through a better knowledge of what speech can mean. Exegesis might thus join the leading edge of an anthropology* of a humankind created in the image of God.

- R. Lowth (1758), *De sacra poesi hebraeorum praelectiones academiae oxonii habitae,* Göttingen (1835, Leipzig).
J. Guillet (1947), "Les exégèses d'Alexandrie et d'Antioche. Conflit ou malentendu?," *RSR* 34, 257–302.
H. de Lubac (1947), "Typologie et allégorisme," *RSR* 34, 180–226.
H. de Lubac (1950), *Histoire et Esprit: L'Intelligence de l'Écriture d'après Origène,* Paris.
G. von Rad (1952), "Typologische Auslegung des Alten Testaments," *EvTh* 12, 12–25.
G. Martelet (1956), "Sacrements, figures et exhortations en 1 Cor 10, 1–11," *RSR* 323–59.
G. von Rad (1957), *Theologie des Alten Testaments,* Munich (4th Ed. 1962).
H. de Lubac (1959–64), *Exégèse médiévale: Les quatre sens de l'Écriture,* 4 vols., Paris.
P. Grelot (1962), *Sens chrétien de l'Ancien Testament: Esquisse d'un traité dogmatique,* 2nd Ed., Paris.
L. Goppelt (1966), *Typos: Die typologische Deutung des Alten Testaments im Neuen,* Darmstadt.
M. van Esbroeck (1968), *Herméneutique, structuralisme et exégèse,* Paris.
G. Ebeling (1971), *Lutherstudien,* vol. 1, Tübingen.
P. Beauchamp (1977), *L'un et l'autre Testament: Essai de lecture,* Paris.
T. Todorov (1978), *Symbolisme et interprétation,* Paris, 91–124.
P. Jay (1980), "Saint Jérôme et le triple sens de l'Écriture," *REAug* 26, 214–27.

M. Fishbane (1985), *Biblical Interpretation in Ancient Israel,* Oxford.
P. Jay (1985), *L'exégèse de saint Jérôme d'après son "Commentaire sur Isaïe,"* EAug.
J. Molino (1985), "Pour une histoire de l'interprétation: Les étapes de l'herméneutique," *Philosophiques,* vol. XII, 1, 73–102; 2, 282–314.
A.-M. La Bonnardière (Ed.) (1986), *Saint Augustin et la Bible,* BTT 3.
J. Pépin (1987), *La tradition de l'allégorie de Philon d'Alexandrie à Dante: Études historiques,* Paris.
G. Dahan (1988), "Les "figures" des juifs et de la synagogue: L'exemple de Dalila. Fonctions et méthodes de la typologie dans l'exégèse médiévale," *RechAug* 23, 125–50.
A.-M. Pelletier (1989), *Lecture du Cantique des Cantiques: De l'énigme du sens aux figures du lecteur,* AnBib 121.
G. Bedouelle, B. Roussel (Ed.) (1989), *Le temps des Réformes et la Bible,* BTT 5.
J.-N. Guinot (1989), "La typologie comme technique herméneutique," *CBiPA* 2, 1–34.
J. Delorme (1992), "Sémiotique," *DBS* 12, 282–334.
G. Dorival, M. Dulaey, P. Gibert, Ch. Theobald, P.-M. Beaude (1992), "Sens de l'Écriture," *DBS* 12, 423–536.
M.-D. Chenu (1976), *La théologie au XIIe s.,* 3rd Ed., Paris.
P. Beauchamp (1990), *L'un et l'autre Testament,* vol. 2: *Accomplir les Écritures,* Paris.
H. Graf Reventlow (1990), *Epochen der Bibelauslegung,* vol. 1: *Vom Alten Testament bis Origenes,* Munich.
P. Beauchamp (1992), "Le Pentateuque et la lecture typologique," in P. Haudebert (Ed.), *Le Pentateuque: Débats et recherches,* LeDiv 151, 241–57.
G. Dahan (1992), "Saint Thomas d'Aquin et la métaphore: Rhétorique et herméneutique," *Medioevo: Rivista di storia della filosofia medievale* 18, 85–117.
P. Beauchamp (1993), "Exégèse typologique, exégèse d'aujourd'hui?," *Connaissance des Pères de l'Église,* 51, 19–20.
M. Pesce, "Un "bruit absurde"? Henri de Lubac di fronte alla distinzione tra esegesi storica e esegesi spirituale," *ASEs* 10/2, 301–53.
L. Panier (Ed.) (1993), *Le temps de la lecture: Exégèse biblique et sémiotique. Hommages pour J. Delorme,* LeDiv 155.
P. Ricoeur (1994), *Lectures 3. Aux frontières de la philosophie,* Paris.

PAUL BEAUCHAMP

See also **Alexandria, School of; Augustine of Hippo; Biblical Theology; Exegesis; Fathers of the Church; Hermeneutics; History; Intertestament; Language, Theological; Luther, Martin; Myth; Narrative; Origen; Saint-Victor, School of; Scripture, Fulfillment of; Tradition**

Secularization

a) Definition. The term *secularization* is derived from the Latin *sæculum,* a word used in the Vulgate to translate the Greek *aiôn* (*see* Rom 12:2; 1 Cor 1:20; etc.), the age or world* that Pauline* theology identifies with the domain of sin*. The word denotes in the first place the process of laicization undergone by a monk who leaves his order and returns to the *world.* It also describes the dispossession of Church* property, most commonly to the benefit of the state, or the passing of activities and institutions (e.g., schools and hospitals) from the Church's sphere of influence into other domains that exclude religious references or values. More broadly still, the concept of secularization denotes the process, which has only recently been clearly observable, by which activities hitherto totally or in part dependent on religion have become desacralized. Art, politics, technology, ethical* behavior and standards, and even the various disciplines of science are accordingly understood as being either explicitly opposed to any religion whatever (this is termed secularism) or indifferent to religious norms.

Secularization thus denotes the complete autonomy of a world that is to be understood intrinsically on its own terms. Defined in this way, it calls for interpretation. Inasmuch as the growing autonomy of the world with respect to religion is seen by some as totally unjustifiable (in that it leads to atheism*) and by others as a task that should be worked at in order to complete mankind's emancipation from superstition and/or religion, it is important to grasp the link between secularization and faith*. Ought faith to be concerned at the world's growing self-assurance? Is secularization nothing more than a movement of escape from faith? How is it made possible by faith itself? Is it possible to conceive of a theology of secularization?

b) Historical and Sociological Interpretation. Although it has only recently become clearly perceptible, the movement toward the autonomy of the world has identifiable historical roots, some of which are worth emphasizing at this point. From an interpretation of the Greek roots of modern culture, it might be concluded that secularization is the product of an understanding of the world based not on myth* but on rational discourse; and in fact this understanding of the world, originating with the Presocratics and given new impe-

tus by the Socratic approach, did lead indirectly to a desacralization of knowledge and—especially through the gradual development of the idea of natural law*—to a tendency to free community life from theological standards. But how is one to explain how this emancipation remained latent, becoming established as a principle only more than 15 centuries later? Here a second factor comes into play: the end of the Renaissance corresponded in the West to a redefinition of the idea of nature. Seen from the viewpoint of scientific knowledge, nature appeared divested of the magical powers, forces, and sentient qualities that some medieval philosophers had ascribed to it. By homogenizing nature through the identification of matter with extent and by developing the principles of a geometrical approach to reality, Descartes* then made possible an understanding of the world dependent only on the methodical order adopted by the conscious subject. Science was no longer the *theôria* of the Greeks but the production of knowledge by the thinking subject and must develop its potential while leaving aside final causes, the knowledge of which was God's alone.

In parallel with this development there emerged political philosophies, descended from the nominalism* of William of Ockham (c. 1290–1350), according to which the legitimacy of state power was based on a contract freeing the sovereign people from any external authority. It was thus, on the basis of the newly established separation of nature and finality, that Thomas Hobbes (1588–1679) established a conception of the state that forcefully emancipated it from any theological foundation and placed the free individual at its center (Strauss 1953). Finally, Protestantism*, in particular its Puritan wing, developed a remarkable justification of work* and economic activity. In his search for the "spirit of capitalism," M. Weber (1864–1920) suggested in this connection that the distinction between faith and works* on the one hand and the Calvinist theory of predestination* on the other had given rise to such anxiety as to the certainty of salvation* that some preachers were led to present work* and the success of human enterprise as *signs* of divine election. Thanks to this justification, earthly activities were liberated from the religious references that had made them possible and helped bring about a secularized world given over to the pure interplay of economic conflicts and interests and to be understood according to its own legality. According to Weber, this movement (for which, it may be admitted, even Calvin*'s theology was not responsible) concluded the process of the world's "disenchantment" (*Entzäuberung*) and brought to completion the gradual "elimination of magic as a means to salvation."

c) Theological Interpretations of Secularization. A theological interpretation of secularization has first to go beyond a categorical condemnation of the process by which the world has become emancipated from the Church in particular and from Christianity in general. A condemnation of this sort, whose echoes can even be felt in the First Vatican Council*'s constitution *Dei Filius*, was developed by the French traditionalist* thinkers L. de Bonald (1754–1840) and J. de Maistre (1753–1821). It attributed Western society*'s gradual estrangement from Christianity to the development of rationalism* and to a characteristically Protestant manner of envisaging mankind's relationship with God*. In Protestantism the refusal of authority and the magisterium was balanced by an appeal to the subjective conscience* of the individual, leading to a loss of the Church's influence in the world. To assess the value of these condemnations, one must first consider the clear-cut distinction they make between faith and secularization and their inability to see that secularization is a phenomenon made possible by faith itself.

Emphasizing the world's desacralization, the concept of secularization in effect harks back to the condemnation of idolatry*, endlessly repeated by the prophets* of Israel*. By adoring the work of his own hands, man fills the world with a multiplicity of deities and turns away from God, who alone is holy. Judaism*, however, by asserting the existence of both a single God and a relationship of creation* between the world and God—a relationship that distinguishes them from one another while linking them to one another—provided itself with a novel means of understanding the world both on its own terms and in its relation to its Creator. The world is not God, but nevertheless it is not a force hostile to God, for the world speaks of him who made it and proclaims his glory* (*see* Ps 19:1). Idolatry thus consists of shutting the world in on itself and not apprehending its autonomy as a created autonomy.

Turning to Christian theology, the Incarnation* leads to a confirmation both of the dignity of the world and of its difference from God. In this light, secularization may be seen as the temporal continuation of a dedivinization of the world by God" (Geffré 1976) situated at the heart of Judaism and as a gradual disclosure of the distance that exists between the world and God. This world is itself delivered into mankind's charge. It

must, therefore, be understood in terms of objective causes, organized politically through the intermediary of the state, exploited by means of technology, and so on. Because they recognize man's responsibility toward the world, Judaism and Christianity constitute a "religion of the escape from religion" (Gauchet 1985).

From this perspective, two theological modes of thought stand as emblematic of an understanding of secularization as the result of a logic intrinsic to faith. Dietrich Bonhoeffer*'s approach involves taking account of modern nihilism: men are no longer even idolaters. On the other hand, the nihilist tendency to think of everything *etsi deus non daretur* shows that mankind has become adult and freed itself from its tutors (*Widerstand und Ergebung*). However, this independence, newly acquired and only lately made clear, is not in contradiction of faith: "By becoming adult, we are brought to a true recognition of our situation before God. God makes known to us that we must live as men who succeed in living without God.... Before God and with God, we live without God" (ibid.). The true name of God, from this standpoint, is revealed by the suffering servant*: his kenosis* reveals his divinity. To take on God's suffering in the world—in other words, the independence of the world—is the Christian's vocation: to be human and to be so to the fullest degree. In this way secularization frees the Christian from a "false image of God...to lead him to the God of the Bible*, who gains his power and his place in the world through his impotence" (ibid.).

F. Gogarten (one of Barth*'s colleagues in the early years of dialectical theology) also recognizes that secularization is "a situation brought about by the Christian faith" (*Verhängnis und Hoffnung der Neuzeit*); its point of departure is to be found in faith, and it appears as a duty of the human individual. The theological basis of Gogarten's position resides in the distinction, *drawn by faith itself,* between faith and the works of the law*. Since salvation comes from faith and from faith alone, the world and earthly matters are entirely in the hands of mankind. Nonetheless, the world is not self-sufficient. Through the intermediary of man, it must enter into the dual relationship of creation and filiation* that links man to God. Sin, therefore, consists in turning the world back on itself and in inverting the relationship of Creator to creature that underpins everything that is. This theory has two notable consequences. 1) By virtue of the distinction between faith and works, mankind enjoys a dual liberty* (ibid.): faith frees man from works and releases him from the law. Thus, "All things are lawful" (1 Cor 10:23). Within faith, however, man must answer before God for his works and thus for the world, for "not all things are useful" (ibid.). Faith is thus indebted to secularization inasmuch as it has the effect of maintaining its purity and making man responsible for himself. 2) As a result, faith has nothing to fear from secularization but much rather from secularism—in other words, the desire to Christianize the world by proposing, for example, a Christian morality (ibid.). To take up a distinction of Barth's, faith turns into religion and undertakes prescriptions that are alien to it.

d) Secularization as a Problem. It remains for these interpretations of secularization to be countered by at least three difficulties that have been well defined by C. Geffré. They are as follows.

1) Any theory of secularization must begin by avoiding the stumbling block of the ideological discourse, which justifies in an indirect and veiled manner the impotence or even the obliteration of faith and the Church: "Without even being aware of it the theorists of secularization 'produce' the ideology that the Church needs in order to justify its future—that is to say, its growing marginalization" (Geffré 1976). So the theologies of secularization congratulate themselves on the fact that, bombarded by the criticisms of modern atheism, the Christian is forced to enter into the adulthood of faith—in other words, a world without God. Religion, though, does not seem to have disappeared from this allegedly atheistic modern world, which remains haunted by magical forces and, sometimes unwittingly, revives customs that are purely pagan.

2) By separating faith completely from religion, these theologies cut faith off from its anthropological roots and from an "original sacred" that is at work in every human being. Without religion, faith runs the risk of becoming a mere abstraction and neglecting that part of humanity that genuinely turns to God in a "religious" attitude. Without faith, secularization, understood as the movement by which the world becomes more worldly, runs the risk of obliterating the created dimension of the world itself and merging into paganism. There is thus a dialectic linking faith and secularization. As it unfolds, and by dint of its critical force, secularization questions and reveals that which in faith might be considered pure abstraction or a negation of the world. Conversely, faith, even in its "religious" dimension, can play a critical role toward secularization. It can denounce the world's idolatrous turning in on itself, question a secularization that leads only to the negation of God, and finally purify and raise toward God a desire that, without it, is in danger of becoming blind or simply merging with emotion.

3) By giving the world back to itself, the theologies

of secularization confine faith within the sphere of private life and thereby make it impossible for the Church to comment pertinently on the world. The very fact of secularization, however, refers the Church back to itself and the mission that is specific to it: "Confronted with a society*, which the Church has left to itself in its secular and pluralist condition, the Church—precisely because it cannot manipulate the concrete decisions of that society in a fundamentalist, doctrinaire and juridical way—has an entirely new task, which one might term prophetic" (Rahner* 1967). The Church should not lament the passing of a former historical situation, nor should it immediately impose a set of definitive truths*, which, in any case, it does not have in its possession but which it develops over time. What is important is for it to find the means to respond to the human anticipation of God.

In this respect Vatican II*'s judgment regarding the phenomenon of secularization seems to steer a middle course. While recognizing a "proper autonomy of terrestrial realities" (*LG,* §36), the council emphasizes that "created things and societies themselves have their own laws and values, which man must little by little learn to know" (*LG,* §36.1). This autonomy, however, does not mean that the creature is independent of the Creator. It is up to the Christian conscience "to engrave the divine law in the earthly city*" (*LG* §43.2).

● M. Weber (1904), *Die protestantische Ethik und der Geist des Kapitalismus, Gesammelte Aufsätze zur Religionssoziologie* I, 4, 1–236, Tübingen.
D. Bonhoeffer (1953), *Widerstand und Ergebung,* Munich.
F. Gogarten (1953), *Verhängnis und Hoffnung der Neuzeit: Die Säkularisierung als theologisches Problem,* Stuttgart.
L. Strauss (1953), *Natural Right and History,* Chicago.
E. Levinas (1963), *Difficile liberté,* Paris.
K. Rahner (1967), "Theologische Reflexionen zur Säkularisation," *Schr.zur Th.* 8, 637–66, Einsiedeln-Zurich-Köln.
J. B. Metz (1968), *Zur Theologie des Welt.*
C. Geffré (1976), "La fonction idéologique de la sécularisation," in E. Castelli (Ed.), *Herméneutique de la sécularisation,* Paris, 121–40.
E. Jüngel (1980), "Säkularisierung—Theologische Anmerkungen zum Begriff einer weltlichen Welt," in *Entsprechungen: Gott—Wahrheit—Mensch. Theologische Erörterungen,* Munich, 285–90.
M. Gauchet (1985), *Le désenchantement du monde: Une histoire politique de la religion,* Paris.
G. Marramao (1992), "Säkularisierung," *HWP* 8, 1133–61.
U. Barth, B. Schwarze (1999), "Säkularisierung," *TRE* 29, 603–38 (bibl.).

THIERRY BEDOUELLE

See also **Barth, Karl; Bonhoeffer, Dietrich; Creation; Ethics, Autonomy of; Modernism; Political Theology; Traditionalism**

Sensus Fidei

a) Definition. By "sensus fidei" is meant a capacity given by the Holy Spirit* to the believer to perceive the truth* of faith* and to discern what is contrary to it. More broadly, it is a gift to all the members of the Church* that enables them to recognize the object of faith, to confess it, and to live from it in truth. This *subjective sense* derives from an older objective sense: *what the Church holds to be true.* But because the *ecclesia* is a living subject, the objectivity of faith cannot go without the inwardness of the believer for whom communion* with the Church guarantees an inner sense of what he believes. Without confusing them, sensus fidei can be related to similar expressions developed in the 16th-century works of doctrinal criteriology by Cano, Bellarmine*, and Suarez* (*instinctus fidei, consensus fidelium, sensus fidelium*) that designate the external and objective content of the faith confessed by believers, that is, the sensus fidei as it is made general by the entire *ecclesia.* We may also speak of *phronèma ekklèsiastikon* (sense of the Church). The Council* of Trent* (*DS* 1367) speaks of a "consensus of the faithful," or a "universal sense of the Church," manifested in the assent given to a truth of faith. After Vatican II* (*LG 1* 12), finally, sensus fidei is characterized as a supernatural* "feeling" brought forth by the Holy Spirit, from which the whole people* of God profit in order to receive the word* of God, to adhere to it unfailingly, to deepen it, and to put it into practice.

b) Justification. Sensus fidei finds its strongest scriptural support in the conception of a *priestly people* (1 Pt 2:9), who has the *mind of Christ** (1 Cor 2:16), the *eyes of the heart* (Eph 1:18), the *spirit of truth* (Jn 14:17; 16:3), and *spiritual understanding* (Col 1:9). And the ancient formulation of it that is most often quoted is found in the canon of Vincent of Lérins on "what was believed everywhere, always, and by everyone" (*Comm.* can. 23). Its theological elaboration goes back to the analyses of the subjective act of belief provided by 13th-century Scholasticism*, Guillaume d'Auxerre, Albert* the Great, and Thomas* Aquinas. The latter writes, for example, that *"per lumen fidei vident esse credenda"* ("Through the light of faith they see what must be believed"; *ST* IIa IIae. q. 1. a. 5. ad 1). In this context, sensus fidei deeply guarantees the coherence of a Christian existence capable of a certain "co-naturality" (see *ST* IIa IIae q. 45. a. 2).

The argumentation was developed by M. Cano in the context of a discussion about tradition* and the authority* of the Church (see *De logis theologicis* 3.3; 4.4), and sensus fidei appears there principally as a source of theological knowledge. In 1848, J. Balmes referred to an *instinct of faith.* John Henry Newman* (1870) speaks of a "sense of inference," or "illative sense" (see *Grammar of Assent,* chaps. 9 and 10), which makes possible real assent in matters of faith and conscience*. And drawing the conclusions from his work on Arianism*, in which he had observed that ordinary Christians had shown a faithfulness of which the hierarchy* had not been capable, he also proposed a theory of the *consensus of the faithful (On Consulting the Faithful in Matters of Doctrine,* pt. 3). J. A. Mölher and M. J. Scheeben* also integrate sensus fidei into their conception of faith.

In the 20th century, two problems have fostered a deepening of the notion: on the one hand, the problem of a justification for Marian dogmas and, on the other, the problem of the role of the laity* in the Church. In his presentation of a theology* of the laity*, Y. Congar, for example, points to the link between sensus fidei and the prophetic function in which everyone who has been baptized participates (*see also* John Paul II, *Christifideles Laici,* 30 December 1988, no. 14). A similar intent to explain the role of the baptized is present in the documents of Vatican II, which refer to the idea of sensus fidei and related notions, *Catholic sense, Christian sense of the faithful, Christian sense, religious sense, sense of God, sense of Christ** and the *Church, instinct* (*LG* 12; *PO* 9; *AA* 30; *GS* 52; *AG* 19). The idea is also implicit in *DV* 8, with reference to the development of dogma*.

c) Theological Value. The interpretation of sensus fidei has been the subject of a clarification by the Congregation for the Doctrine of the Faith, which begins by quoting *LG* 12 and goes on to define the *supernatural sense of faith:* "The totality of the faithful, having the unction that comes from the Holy Spirit (1 Jn 2:20, 27), cannot be in error in its faith; and this particular gift that it possesses it shows through the *supernatural sense of faith,* which is that of the whole people when, from the bishops* to the must humble lay believer (*see* Augustine*, *De Praed. Sanct.* 14. 27), it expresses its unanimous consent in the realm of faith and morals"

(Declaration *Mysterium Ecclesiae* no. 2, AAS 63 [1973], *DC* 1973, 644–70). The Council of Trent spoke of a *universus ecclesiae sensus* (*DS* 1367) enabling the believer to distinguish the true faith from heresy*. And if all those who are baptized take part in the prophetic function of Christ, they may therefore, in certain conditions, offer an expression of faith free from error. As an experience* of faith and its truth gone through by all the faithful living from the Holy Spirit, sensus fidei provides a criterion for theological knowledge. As for the magisterial function fulfilled by the ecclesiastical hierarchy, it is in the service of sensus fidei while also carrying out its educational mission. Three conditions have to be satisfied in order to claim infallibility in sensus fidei: it must really be the expression of universal consent, it must bear on the content of Christian revelation*, and it must be recognized by the magisterium* (see *DV* 8, 10; *LG* 12, 25). In this situation, the role of the magisterium is not limited to sanctioning an already expressed consent, for it may prepare for and request that consent. And because it is inseparable from the *sentire cum Ecclesia,* sensus fidei cannot possibly create tension between the magisterium and the Christian people. Clearly understood, the notion of sensus fidei is a tool at the service of a balanced ecclesiology* (*see* International Theological Commission, *DC* 73 [1976], 662–65). We should no doubt go on to say that a theology of *reception** can be viable only if it is based on the reality of sensus fidei.

● Y. Congar (1953), *Jalons pour une théologie du laïcat,* chap. 6: "Les laïcs et la fonction prophétique de l'Église," Paris, 367–453.
Y. Congar (1963), *La tradition et la vie de l'Église,* Paris, 62–64.
J.-M. Tillard (1982), "Magistère, théologie et *sensus fidelium,*" *Initiation à la pratique de la théologie,* Paris, vol. 1, 163–82.
W. Beinert (1987), "Glaubenssinn der Glaübigen," *Lexikon der katholischen Dogmatik,* Fribourg, 200–201.
R. Latourelle (1988), *Vatican II: Bilan et perspectives,* Montreal-Paris, vol. 1, 157–70.
S. Pié-Ninot (1992), "Le sens de la foi," *DTF,* 1131–34.
B. Sesboüé (1992), "Le *sensus fidelium* en morale à la lumière de Vatican II," *Le Supplément,* no. 181, 153–56.
J.J. Burkhard (1993), "*Sensus fidei:* Theological Reflexions since Vatican II," *HeyJ,* 34, 41–59, 123–36.

GILBERT NARCISSE

See also **Faith; Loci theologici; Magisterium; Notes, Theological**

Septuagint. *See* Translations of the Bible, Ancient

Servant of YHWH

1. Old Testament

According to literary and sociological contexts, the term *'ébèd* means either a slave or a servant, whose function varies according to his position and his master. When the term is applied to man's relations with God*, his "Lord (*'adôn),*" it does indeed entail complete humbleness and availability but also a possible worthiness to receive the Master's confidences, even to share in divine deliberations. This respected role is attributed in particular to Moses (Nm 12:7; Dt 34:5), to Joshua (Jos 24:29), to David (2 Sm 7, 8–11), to the prophets* (2 Kgs 9:36, 14:25), and so on. It describes very aptly the character presented in the four Songs of the Servant, which from the time of B. Duhm (1892), exegesis* has detached from the whole text of Isaiah 40–55. When linked together, this series of four pieces (Is 42:1–9, 49:1–9, 50:4–10, 52:13–53:12) form a little book in which are described a mysterious servant's itinerary and fate. Jesus* and the primitive Church* would refer to it.

a) Problematics.   The interpretation of the Songs of the Servant presents one of the most disputed points in exegesis. Questions are raised about their exact number of these poems, their precise boundaries, their literary form, and the history of their creation. More radical critics even deny the existence of a distinct sequence. The theological problems are no less thorny. They bear particularly on the servant's identity. Does he represent an individual or a group? Which group— the people as a whole (which is the meaning in the other passages in Is 40–55), or Israel* the faithful, or Israel the ideal, or the righteous remnant (Is 10:22; Zep 3:12–13)? Which individual—a character from the past (such as Ezekiel or Josiah), a contemporary (Cyrus or a master of wisdom*) or a Messiah* to come? In what form should he be conceived—as prophet, king, or a new Moses? How can his precise role toward Israel and the pagans be determined? In what way does he represent a covenant* with the people (Is 42:6)? Does his death* correspond to an expiation?

b) A Conjecture.   Since everyone has to take a stance in this wide-open debate, we shall try, by means of a genetic approach, to go beyond the aporias and particularly beyond the antinomy of the "individual or group." In their present context, the four songs can mean nothing but the community of Israel; it is Israel that the other passages from Isaiah 40–55 describe as a "servant." But this reading clashes with certain facts: the servant boasts of a mission* with regard to Israel (Is 42:1–4), he suffers for "the multitudes" (Is 53:11–12), and he bears the sins* of those who contemplate him (Is 53:4–5). More than in the rest of the book*, the character's traits are specifically individualized. Above all, these poems form a unit insofar as they recount in a sequential and logical way the enigmatic servant's personal itinerary. This little book could be the work of one of the second Isaiah's disciples who, starting with his master's autobiographical fragments (Is 49:1–6, 50:4–5) and reusing the oracles attributed to Cyrus (Is 42:5–9; *see* Dion 1970), together with materials invented by himself (Is 42:1–4, 52:13–53:12), might have traced an ideal servant's spiritual journey, a servant whose model might be the second Isaiah himself. This little group of poems might have been disassembled, then distributed over chapters 40 to 55 by their editor, who might have given the servant a general, collective connotation.

c) Messianic Figure?   It would be at the level of the autonomous little book containing the four poems that the possibility of a messianic orientation might emerge. Basing himself on the experience* and testimony of the second Isaiah himself, this disciple might have proclaimed thus his hope* for a humbled servant, crushed but in the end triumphant beyond death. It will be noted that in Isaiah 53, the verbs that envisage the far side of death are in the future tense. In the first song (Is 42:1–9), YHWH in person introduces *his* servant, entrusted by the mind of God with a universal mission of salvation* and liberation, which is meant to reach the ends of the earth. In his turn (second song: Is 49:1–9), the servant evokes his intimacy with YHWH, his call from when he was in his mother's womb, and specifies his mission. That mission is identified with his person. Will he not be "the people's covenant" (Is 49:8) or "that of the multitude of nations" (Is 42:6)? From the outset, this work of salvation encounters hostility. The first song depicts the servant as "a bruised reed" that "will not break" and "a dimly burning wick" that "will not quench" (Is 42:3; *see* Renaud 1990, 102–3). He remains determined to bring his mission to a good end. The second song affords glimpses of an inner crisis (Is 49:4), but the servant is suddenly relaunched on a new stage (Is 49:5–6). Soon persecution (Is 50:4–10) will lead him to the most humiliating death (Is 53:1–9). But, amazing paradox, these sufferings and this death assume the value of a expiatory sacrifice, or *'âshâm* (Is 53:10; *see also* 53:4–5). They are the source of justification* and of salvation of "many" (Is 53:11–12), and they win this servant high exaltation (Is 52:13) and satisfaction in his work (Is 53:11).

d) History of Influence.   The text had a history* after to its final editing, a "history of its influence" (*Wirkungsgeschichte*), which was exerted particularly on the late Old Testament writings. Although its interpretation in a collective sense had monopolized both Palestinian and Hellenistic Judaism*'s exegetic efforts (*see* Septuagint), in the Old Testament a few traces still linger of its being understood in an individual sense. This is the case of the mysterious man "whom they have pierced" in Zechariah 12:10–13:1 (Beauchamp 1989). Likewise, the discreet allusions to Isaiah 52:14 and 53:2 in Daniel 1:4; to Isaiah 52:13 in Daniel 11:33, 12:3, and 12:10; and to Isaiah 53:11 in Daniel 12:3–4 prepared the way for the New Testament identification of the Son* of man and of the suffering servant in the person of Jesus.

2. New Testament

a) Jesus' Declarations.   Describing Jesus as a "servant" cannot be considered a "title" on the same level of that of Son of Man or of Son of God, not even in Acts 3:13–26 and 4:27–30 and Matthew 12:18. It is not even certain that these descriptions always refer to the poems in Isaiah. In Acts 3:26, for example, the title might identify Jesus as the new Moses. All the same, there is an impressive number of quotations from the poems and allusions to them. First of all, Jesus himself read into them a sort of sketch of his own destiny (Mt 15:24 reflects Is 53:6, Mk 14:24 and Mt 8:17 refer to Is 53:12, and Mk 10:33–34 evokes Is 50:6). These reminiscences from Isaiah, associated with the logions concerning the Son of man, cast the latter figure in quite a new light—that of the humbled and suffering servant. Thus, beyond the collective sense adopted by Judaism, the Gospels* revived the individual connotation. The early Church was to extend its perception of its Lord to the group of four songs. According to Luke 24:25–27 and 24:44–45, the appearances of the risen Christ* were "the first source of Christian hermeneutics" (P. Grelot), by giving a new meaning to Isaiah 53.

b) Isaiah 53 and Jesus' Passion and Resurrection. Thus, Isaiah 53 represents the starting point of Christian rereading. Confirmations of this are found in the oldest texts of the New Testament—in the narrative* about the Last Supper, evoking the blood "poured out for many" (Mk 14:24; Mt 26:28; *see also* 1 Cor 11:23–25); in the predictions of the passion* (Mk 10:34); and in the ancient professions of faith* (1 Cor 15:3–4; Rom 4:24–25). Similarly, the discourses from Acts 3:12–26 and 4:24–30 make the three lines about royal messianism, the prophetic ministry*, and the suffering servant converge (*see* 1 Pt 2:21). The use of this fourth song made it possible to cast light on the theological sense of Jesus' death. Standing firm with his people, the servant Jesus gave his life for the many. Therefore, it is not surprising that Paul took up these allusions to Isaiah 53 in his soteriological phrases (Gal 2:20; 2 Cor 5:16–6:2; Romans 5:1–9; *see also* 1 Pt 3:18). The lyrical commentary from Isaiah 53 in 1 Peter 2:21–25 superimposes the images of the royal Messiah and of the servant from Isaiah 53.

c) The Group of Four Songs and Jesus' Mission. From that moment on, the Christian community would extend the scope of the four songs to Christ's earthly mission. The quotation from Isaiah 42:1–6 in Matthew 12:17–21, quite strange in its present context, aimed to encompass evocatively Jesus' ministerial activities—less to prove that Jesus was authentically the servant than to reveal and determine his function. In a more precise way, Matthew 8:17 based itself on Isaiah 53:4: Jesus bore human physical sufferings not only in order to undergo them but also to heal us. From this fact, Matthew bound Jesus' thaumaturgic function tightly to his person's influence. John 1:29 made a similar trans-

position by introducing "the Lamb* of God who *takes away*" and no longer *bears* "the sin of the world!" The ambiguity of the Hebrew verb made this reinterpretation possible. In Luke 2:30–32, Simeon summed up Christ's whole mission in the light of Isaiah 42:6 and 49:6, which proclaimed the servant "a light to the nations" (*see also* Is 42:1–4).

d) The Poems and the Disciples' Ministry. In John 12:38–39, the declaration from Isaiah 53:1, associated with Isaiah 6:9–10, focused on the foretelling of the cross and its proclamation by the disciples, identified with the "we" of the poem and who ran up against the chosen people's incredulity. This group of disciples thus found itself involved in this mystery* of cross and glory. Therefore, the group came quite naturally to apply the servant's experience to the witnesses of the gospel. On several occasions (*see* Gal 1:15; Acts 26:16–17), Paul referred to Isaiah 49:1, completed by Jeremiah 1:5–10, and to Isaiah 42:1–7 to clarify his own vocation. His call, anterior to the revelation on the road to Damascus, led him to realize the program of Isaiah 42:1–7 (Acts 26:16–17). Not that Paul identified himself with the servant. Jesus was the one who remained, without any possible confusion, the servant, the "light to the nations" (Acts 26:22–23; *see* Is 42:6). But Christ in glory performed his ministry through the apostolic activities of Paul, who, like his master, had to face the same mystery of incredulity (Rom 10:16, which cites Is 53:1; *see also* Jn 12:38). On the base of Isaiah 52:15, Paul thus confirmed his certainty of being heard by the pagans to whom he was sent (Rom 15:21).

3. Writings of the Fathers

In the first centuries of Christianity, the christological interpretation of the Songs of the Servant would become a topic of debate between the "synagogue" and the "Church." In their dialogue with the Jews, the Fathers clashed with the rabbinical interpretation, in which the servant represented a collective and which rejected any allusion to the Messiah's suffering and passion (e.g., Justin in his *Dialogue with Trypho* and Origen in his *Contra Celsus*). The debate would, therefore, bear above all on the meaning of the fourth poem. The Jews would apply it to the just and to Israel suffering in exile—only a single text imagined that the Messiah might have taken on himself our griefs and our sorrows (*TB Sanh* 98 b). The Christians would read unanimously into these songs, particularly into the fourth one (Isaiah 53), a christological and soteriological testimony.

● P.-E. Dion (1970), "Les chants du Serviteur de Yahweh et quelques passages apparentés d'Is 40–55," *Bib* 51, 17–38.

P.-E. Dion, (1970), "L'universalisme religieux dans les diverses couches rédactionnelles d'Is 40–55," *Bib* 51, 161–82.

P. Grelot (1981), *Les poèmes du Serviteur: De la lecture critique à l'herméneutique,* LeDiv 103.

P. Beauchamp (1989), "Lecture et relectures du quatrième chant du Serviteur," in *The Book of Isaiah/Le livre d'Isaïe: Les oracles et leurs relectures,* J. Vermeylen (Ed.), BEThL 81, 325–35, Louvain.

B. Renaud (1990), "La mission du Serviteur en Is 42, 1–4," *RevSR* 64, 101–13.

P. Grelot (1994), "Serviteur de YHWH," *DBS* 12, 958–1016.

BERNARD RENAUD

See also **Christ; Expiation; Israel; Jesus, Historical; Messianism; Passion; Prophet; Sacrifice; Salvation; Scripture, Fulfilment of**

Severius of Antioch. *See* Monophysitism

Sheol

Peculiar to Hebrew and of uncertain origin (*sh'l,* "to investigate," or *sh'h + l,* "place of devastation and noise"), the word "sheol" (Hebrew *she'ol*), without an article and generally feminine, denotes the abode of the dead, 66 times in the Massoretic text of the Bible, especially in a poetic context. Both the Septuagint and the New Testament translate the term as Hades ("invisible"—popular etymology). By contrast with heaven, Sheol is located in the subterranean depths (Is 7:11), to which all the dead descend (*yârad*), both the just (Gn 37:35) and the ungodly (Nm 16:33).

A dark place (Jb 17:13) of dust (17:16) and silence (Ps 115:17), Sheol is sometimes characterized by destructive waters (Jon 2:3–6). It has gates and guards (Jb 38:17; Is 38:10). Forgotten by all (Ps 88:13), the dead lead a spectral existence there: "or work, or thought, or knowledge, or wisdom*" (Eccl 9:10). Nobody returns from there (Jb 7:9), nobody praises the Lord there (Ps 6:6), and nobody there trusts in him (Is 38, 18). Job wished to shelter there alive while waiting for God*'s wrath* to pass (Jb 14, 13), but in vain, since "Sheol is naked before God" (Jb 26:6; *see* Prv 15:11). God can command it (Is 7, 11); anyone who forces an entry there will be removed (Am 9:2). Moreover, it is God who sends people down there and brings them up again (1 Sm 2:6).

While Sheol is open to the wicked (Prv 5:5; Ps 31:18; Jb 24:19), God prevents the just man from languishing there (Ps 18:6, 86:13; Jon 2:7); the believer is thus spared from death* and the tomb. Sheol is sometimes personified and identified with the personification of Death (Ps 18:6; Hos 13:14; Heb 2:5) or with the grave (Ps 16:10; Is 38:18; Ez 31:16; Jon 2:7). *Abaddôn,* Perdition, perhaps an ancient deity of the underworld, also personifies Sheol (Jb 26:6; Ps 88:12; Prv 27:20).

The fate of the just in Sheol preoccupied ancient Israel*, however. Psalms 49:15—"God will ransom my soul from the power of Sheol, for he will receive me"—offers a glimpse of a different fate for the just man. 1 Henoch 22:2 ff., followed by 4 Ezra 4:35 and 4:41 and perhaps Jb 23:30 b f., divides Sheol into compartments: the ungodly are located in one, in which they will be punished forever, while the just reside temporarily in another "where the spring of light arises" (1 Hen 22:9) while awaiting the Resurrection* and the Last Judgment*, which will seal the fate of both groups—Gehenna or Paradise (4 Ezr 7:35f). The parable* of Lazarus the poor man (Lk 16:19–31) presumes such an explanation.

Christ*'s descent into hell* attests to the reality of his death and the universal nature of the salvation* that he brings (*see* Eph 4:9; 1 Pt 3:19, 4:6—disputed interpretation).

● G. Gerleman (1976), "*she'ol*," THAT 2, 837–41.
C. Perrot (1980), "La descente aux enfers et la prédication aux morts," in *Études sur la première lettre de Pierre,* Paris, 231–46.
T. Podella (1988), "Grundzüge alttestamentlicher Jenseitsvorstellungen: *sheol*," BN 43, 70–89.

W.J. Dalton (1989), *Christ's Proclamation to the Spirits: A Study of 1 Peter 3, 18–4, 6,* 2nd Ed., Rome.
T.J. Lewis (1992) "*she'ol*," AncBD 2, 101–5.
L. Wächter (1992), "*she'ol*," ThWAT 7, 901–0.

MAURICE GILBERT

See also **Death; Eschatology; Hell; Limbo; Soul-Heart-Body**

Siger of Brabant. *See* Naturalism; Truth

Sign. *See* Miracle

Simon, Richard. *See* Biblical Theology

Simplicity, Divine

1. Attribute of Divine Simplicity

a) Simplicity defines the divine essence as opposed to divine persons. Bernard* of Clairvaux discussed it in his *On Consideration* (*De consideratione* 5:16). In his *Proslogion* (23), Anselm* said that divine simplicity "did not multiply in the three divine persons."

b) "Simplicity"—that is, "the lack of a compound nature"—described the divine *esse* (essence) in its absoluteness and its transcendence. On this account, for

Thomas* Aquinas, *simplicitas* was God's prime attribute* (*Summa Theologica* Ia, q. 3; *see also* q. 11, a 4, and q. 30, a 3, on unity and simplicity). In God there was no compound nature either of matter or of form (a. 2), as was the case with man, nor of essence or existence (a. 3), as was the case with the angels*. In God, essence was *idem essentia et esse,* the same thing as existence (a. 4); the divine *esse* was absolutely single. Therefore, God is defined not by saying what he is (*quid est*) but by saying "in what ways he is not" (*quomodo not sit*)—in other words, "by taking away from him what could not be proper to him." Divine simplicity was, therefore, examined according to the negative* method or the negative theology.

c) For Meister Eckhart, simplicity described God, "infinite* in his simplicity and simple in his infinity" (*Sermo* 4:2), but it also described the soul, which was without divisions or partitions (*einfaltig, Pred.* 85 and 86). The soul owed its simplicity to its essence, or to the "nakedness" of its being; and its beatitude* derived from that simplicity and that "nakedness" (*Pred.* 39).

The soul's simplicity was also its trait of direct and undivided intention, according to the biblical sense of the Hebrew word *tam* and according to the evangelic logion about the eye in Matthew 6:22–23 and Luke 11:34–36. The 14th-century writers John Tauler and Jan van Ruysbroeck would accept the Judeo-Christian meaning. For them, simplicity was primarily the attribute of the intention, and it was that idea of purity or of simplicity of intention that would be found in the 16th- and 17th-century spiritual writers John* of the Cross in Spain (*Spiritual Canticle* A 18, v. 4) and Francis de Sales in France (*Entretien,* 12).

2. Problem of Divine Simplicity

a) How can divine simplicity and the plurality of form of the divine attributes be reconciled? This question had already drawn Thomas Aquinas's attention. He dealt with the multiplicity of the attributes of the divine essence's simplicity in his *Summa Theologica* (Ia, q. 3, a. 3): "If one says that deity, or life, or that anything similar at all is in God, the diversity of the terms thus singled out should be related only to our mind and its way of conceiving, not to any actual diversity." And (q. 13, a. 2–4), "in the same way that a unique single Principle corresponds to the creatures' diverse perfections…so, something absolutely one and simple, grasped imperfectly by means of its diverse conceptions, corresponds to our minds' multiple and diverse conceptions." In this way Thomas refuted simultaneously Maimonides' agnostic solution and Gilbert de la Porrée's excessive realism (condemned at the Council of Rheims in 1148). Nonetheless, it was not until the 14th and 15th centuries that the problem would figure at the center of theological debates (Guichardin 1933).

b) For the Greek and Latin world the difference between the essence and the divine attributes presented itself differently. Thomas Aquinas distinguished between a real distinction and a rational* distinction, the latter being capable either of having a real base—which made it a virtual distinction—or of not possessing one—which made it a purely rational distinction, and that second distinction was the one that should be made between the divine attributes so as not to harm divine simplicity. John Duns Scotus* also distinguished between the real distinction and the rational distinction, the real distinction being itself, or else entitative (strictly real), or else formal (*ex parte rei*). It was the latter distinction, therefore, that preceded any intellectual act, that existed between divine attributes. However, Scotus (see *Ordinatio,* 1, I, dist. 8 §209) preferred to speak of "a formal non-identity rather than of "a formal distinction" (Grajewski 1944).

c) For Greek theology*, the distinction (*diaphora*) was either "through the thing" (*tô pragmati*), a distinction perceptible to the senses, or "through the thought" (*kat'epinoian*), a distinction perceptible to the intellect. It was the latter distinction, *kat' epinoian,* that corresponded to the rational distinction of the Latin world in 14th-century Byzantium. For Gregory* Palamas, the problem of the simplicity of essence and the plurality of attributes became the problem of the divine essence and the divine energies. In his *Hagioritic Tome* (1339–40), Palamas proclaimed that "the divinity which was three-fold in persons has a single, non-compound, uncreated, invisible, incomprehensible nature" (1228B). In his *Against Akindynos* (1343–47), he stated that a distinction existed between divine workings and divine essence but that this distinction did not harm God's simplicity. The divine essence was the source of the workings and superior to the workings, and it remained imparticipable, while divine workings, although uncreated, were nonetheless participable. Uncreated energies, Palamas added in his *Homilies on the Transfiguration* (1355–59), were nothing but the light that enveloped Christ* on Mount Tabor. And if objections were raised that the distinction between the essence and the energies seemed to create a division in God, Palamitism replied that it was not so, for this distinction was only an effect of the human intellect. In Latin theology, the "light of glory" was created and had its abode in the human intellect; in Palamitism, on the contrary, the light of Tabor was uncreated and had its abode in God.

● D. Petau (1644–50), *Dogmata theologica,* vol. 1, l. I, c. 12, and *De Dei simplicitate* (new Ed., Vivès, 1865–67).
S. Guichardin (1933), *Le problème de la simplicité divine en Orient et en Occident aux XIVe et XVe siècles: Grégoire Palamas, Duns Scot, Georges Scholarios,* Lyon.
J. Grajewski (1944), *The Formal Distinction of Duns Scotus: A Study in Metaphysics,* Washington, D.C.
Y. de Andia et al. (1990), "Simplicité," *DSp* 14, 892–921.
E. Salmann (1995), "Einfachheit Gottes," *LThK3* 3, 542–43.

YSABEL DE ANDIA

See also **Attributes, Divine; Eternity of God; Immutability/Impassibility; Justice, Divine; Knowledge, Divine; Omnipotence, Divine; Omnipresence, Divine**

Sin

a) Old Testament. In the Old Testament, sin (*châtâ*) is conceived primarily as failure to keep the commandments of God* or to honor God in our actions. Sin may be a conscious or an unconscious failure (Lv 4, 5), but even in the case of an "unwitting" sin, sacrifice* is required as reparation. The emphasis is on the objective character of an act or a failure to act; there is no interest in motivation, and the idea of "guilt" (*'âsham*) is not psychological but rather the definition of a state into which an agent enters purely in virtue of what has happened. The word *'âshem* should be translated as "under obligation to offer reparation" (to God, by sacrifice), not as "guilty." Despite this, there is an increasing emphasis in the texts on the individual character of the liability incurred by the sinner: according to Deuteronomic tradition* (e.g., Dt 24:16), echoed in Ezekiel (e.g., Ez 18:1–29), it is clear that this liability is not inherited. Only the individual agent is to be punished for his or her sin. This is not the case in an older and harsher tradition (e.g., Jos 7), according to which the contagion of sin affects a whole kinship group, who are all liable to punishment. Something of this survives in the story of the murder of Uriah (2 Sm 12). David repents his crime and is forgiven by God (his liability is removed), but his child dies, as if to remind the reader that the consequences of sin are more than individual and cannot be wholly annulled.

In addition, however, there are texts (above all Ps 51 [50]; *see also* Hos 4:7, 10:9) in which sin is more like a moral atmosphere. As such, it can surround a person from his or her earliest days or characterize the entire history of a nation. It becomes less the *effect* than the *cause* of all wrongdoing. Some of the Dead Sea scrolls show evidence of this perspective, particularly the *Hôdayôth* (*see* especially 1QH4), where the language of Psalm* 51 is repeated. Whatever the levels of individual liability, all human beings live in a general climate of moral impotence. We may not inherit a true liability from our ancestors, but we certainly inherit such a great burden of failure that we can only aspire to the divine intervention that will free us from it. This is why one also sees in these texts the introduction of the idea of the intercession of the righteous on sinners' behalf.

b) New Testament. The strongest sense of the impotence resulting from sin and of universal human involvement in sin is found in Paul. Sin is almost personified, particularly in the Epistle to the Romans, which contains an unparalleled number of uses of the word "sin" in the singular (*hamartia*) and as the subject of active verbs. Sin is above all a form of enslavement: we are bound by sin, our options are foreclosed by sin, sin "dwells" in us, sin repays our compliance with death*. We are in a different atmosphere here from the analysis of sin as activity that pollutes (but is capable of being purged) or even as culpable failure or error: for Paul, sin is not deliberate weakness of will or failure in perception but that which disables both will and judgment. If sin leads to death, it is not because we are being held responsible by a hostile or unjust God for actions* that we never chose to perform but because the consequence of our condition is the destruction of our capacity to live with God.

This appears at first sight to be rather at odds with the perspective of the Gospels*, and it is true that Paul's perspective is more deeply and consciously tragic. In fact, however, if one looks more closely, the preaching* of Jesus* in the synoptic Gospels shows signs of the same somber climate. Those listening to Jesus have neither the opportunity nor the capacity to satisfy what is required to purge their guilt or their impurity. Because there is only a short time before the intervention of God to restore his rule, Jesus offers such "sinners" the possibility of forgiveness through their acceptance of his fellowship. All that is needed is the recognition of how serious one's condition is—as in the case of the tax collector in the famous parable* in Luke 18:9–14 or indeed of Peter* when he is confronted with Jesus' miraculous authority* (Lk 5:8). The love* that becomes manifest in the sinner's friendship with Jesus is the mark of forgiveness and perhaps also the ground or opportunity for forgiveness (Lk 7:47f.). Thus, in the Gospels, especially Luke, sin is overcome not by reparatory sacrifice or even by personal repentance but by entry into the community of those who are welcomed by Jesus. This is not far from Paul's scheme. Paul goes further, however, when he identifies Jesus' death as a reparatory sacrifice offered on everyone's behalf. There are hints of this in the synoptic tradition (Mk 10:45 par.), but it is Paul for whom it becomes central. The roots of such an understanding may lie in the saying attributed to Jesus at the time of the institution of the Eucharist*, when he speaks of the shedding of his blood as establishing a new covenant*, that is, as sealing the coherence and identity before God of the new community.

c) Early Church. Although other New Testament writers share something of the Pauline* vision (e.g., Jn 8:34), the first Christian theologians generally exhibit a more atomized and prosaic view. Sins are acts of disobedience to God, and salvation is made visible in the power of Christians to keep the commandments. In much second-century literature, there is concern about sins committed after baptism*: can they be remitted, or is it necessary to hold fast to the ideal of baptism as delivering believers from sin once and for all? Debates on this subject became especially acute in the Church of Rome*. The *Shepherd of Hermas,* written early in the second century, envisages the legitimacy of postbaptismal penance* but on only a single occasion. Even this earned the scorn of rigorists such as Tertullian*. Adultery, apostasy, and murder were widely regarded as being beyond absolution by the Church*, although God might pardon them in the world to come. In the first half of the third century, Origen still maintained the position that sin after baptism is a repudiation of Christ* as serious as that of the Jews who cried out for Christ's crucifixion (*Contra Celsium* IV, 32) and appears to identify postbasptismal sin with the sin against the Holy Spirit* mentioned in Mark 3:29 and parallels (*De principiis,* I, 3, 2 and 7). However, other passages in Origen suggest that he modified his views on this or at least restricted his reference to postbaptismal apostasy. Athanasius (*Ad Serapionem* IV, 9–10) records Origen's views on sin against the Holy Spirit, assuming that he did identify this with *any* postbaptismal sin; by this time, such a position had become eccentric, and Athanasius set out to refute it. The various crises provoked by Christians lapsing under persecution eventually led to a twofold outcome. On the one hand, the Church came under pressure to relax its discipline in pastoral emergencies. On the other, rigorist schisms* occurred, maintaining the older severity (no absolution for apostasy or at least no full rehabilitation) for the sake of defending the purity of the Church.

The theme of sin as pollution thus becomes very powerful once again in early Christianity, especially in separatist groups such as the Novatianists and Donatists. The pollution is not of a single agent but of an entire community, echoing such Old Testament texts as Joshua 7. Although not all grave sins are sexual, the metaphors used are often strongly sexually charged: postbaptismal sin compromises the virginal innocence of the community. In these discussions, we can also see the emergence of differentiation among sins, which would later give rise to the distinction between "mortal" sin and "venial" sin. The notion of "mortal sin," that is, sin that destroys the moral substance of the agent, looks back to 1 John 5:16f. Origen distinguishes between sins that represent the death of the soul and sins that are a weakness in the soul, implying that there are sinful acts that do not proceed from deliberate rebellion against God and so are not fatal perversions of the will. The distinction was developed in the Latin tradition from Augustine* on. Augustine maintains that human life cannot be lived without certain minor sins, arising from our congenital weakness of will, not from deliberate willing of evil*; the unavoidability of these "venial" sins is itself a consequence of original sin*.

d) From Augustine to the Reformation. It was Augustine who restored to Christian theology something of Paul's tragic sense, returning to an analysis of sin as an existential state or a bondage. Although his opposition to Manicheanism* ruled out any idea of absolutely inevitable sin, sin in which free will plays no role, he was increasingly convinced that we cannot understand sin in purely individual terms: our liberty* is neither full nor complete, and our minds, in our fallen condition, are incapable of perceiving the true good*. Evil will is always the ultimate cause of sin, as Augustine argues in his early work *De libero arbitrio,* but the evil will consists of wanting what is not good for us, and this radical error about good is not itself something that anyone chooses. It is the effect of original sin (*see De agone christiano* XI). This is the theme that he elaborates with ever greater pessimism in his treatises against Pelagius and his followers, for whom sin can be reduced (as was done in the second-century literature) to specific acts of rebellion that good habits can overcome.

Although 16th-century Protestant theology often accused late medieval Catholic theology of Pelagian tendencies (Pelagianism*), the Latin tradition was always formally faithful to Augustine, maintaining that sin has to be voluntary to be culpable, that the condition of sin can be objectively present without any specific individual act of disobedience to God, and that one can only be delivered from sin by grace* (on all these points, *see* Thomas Aquinas*, *STh* Ia IIae, q. 71–89).

In places where the Reformation prevailed, the structures of the penitential system were largely dismantled, but many groups restored strong ecclesial discipline* based on primitive models. For some, the radicalness of the Lutheran version of Augustinian pessimism rendered moot any attempt to establish a "diagnostic" of sins. There were even debates in certain Protestant circles as to whether all sins were equally grave in God's eyes, which caused great disquiet among those who sought to identify the unforgivable sin against the Holy Spirit. However, Calvinism* and Anglicanism* developed increasingly sophisticated moral and pastoral theology in which the "diagnostic" found a crucial role (*see*, e.g., the writings of the Anglican Jeremy Taylor [1613–67], especially *Unum Necessarium* [1655] and *Ductor Dubitantium* [1660]).

The list of seven deadly sins (pride, lust, anger, gluttony, avarice, envy, and sloth) was essentially although not exclusively Catholic and seems to be nonexistent in the Eastern Christian tradition except where Latin influence can be discerned. The origins of the list, however, lie in the diagnostic developed in Greek monasticism* for the identification of the major sources of sinful behavior (asceticism* 2[b]). John Cassian, in the fifth century, writes in his *Monastic Institutes* of eight "vices," and a brief digest of his teaching on these circulated widely in Eastern monastic houses, finding its way eventually into the classic anthology published in the 18th century, the *Philokalia* (prayer*). Cassian's list included gluttony, fornication, avarice, anger, dejection, accidie (spiritual weariness), vainglory, and pride. Its purpose was not to provide a structure for self-examination before confession, as was generally the case in the Western tradition, but to offer a method of spiritually combating each vice.

e) Modern Times. Modern discussion of sin has frequently returned to Paul's sense of the priority not of individual choice for evil but of a controlling atmosphere in which choices are always already corrupted. Something of this can already be discerned in Schleiermacher*, but this perspective comes into its own in 20th-century theologies influenced in one way or another by existentialism. For Sartre or Camus, we are imprisoned in a condition that lacks "authenticity" and sets us at odds with ourselves by failing to enable choices that are really our own; for Heidegger* and his school, our habitual state is "estrangement" from being*. Thus, Paul Tillich* and, in a slightly different framework, Rudolf Bultmann* treat sin as essentially the self-alienated condition of human beings who have not yet heard the liberating word* of God. Tillich, in the second volume of his *Systematic Theology,* attempts to clarify this by defining "sins," chosen acts of "turning away from that to which one belongs," as the expression of "sin," the state of estrangement from God, self, and others. For Karl Rahner*, for whom again Heidegger is in the background, sin is the state in which we cannot realize what we are because we are cut off from the self-communication of God. In this perspective, sin is a fundamental frustration before it is a deliberate rejection of God.

Other modern theologians of our era, however, such as Karl Barth* and Hans Urs von Balthasar*, disagree with this view. Our problem is not that we are victims before we are offenders. Certainly, there is a tragic dimension to our condition, but at its heart lies a refusal of meaning or of love*. To say that we are not what we could be might suggest that salvation* is ultimately a matter of returning to our true being, and for Barth in particular this is unthinkable. We acknowledge ourselves as sinners only in the light of our having been conquered by grace, in knowing ourselves to be both sinners and redeemed sinners. Discourse about sin is thus always soteriological and christological: the self that recognizes itself as sinful and capable of forgiveness or self-transcendence is a self *already* re-created by hearing the Word. For both Barth and Balthasar, sin remains a mystery*, an impulse of self-destruction corroding our moral identity rather than simply holding it back.

Political theology* in Europe and the various schools of the theology of liberation*, including feminist theology, appeal to the concept of "structural" sin. This type of sin stands somewhere between individual acts of evildoing and the general condition of humanity: we are morally and spiritually imprisoned by specific kinds of injustice built into the way in which power and economic liberty are distributed in society*, and the work of salvation involves a challenge to this situation and a summons to transform it. This may mean revising language: some theologians have pointed out, for example, that the definition of pride as the greatest of the mortal sins has often worked against the development of proper authority and self-esteem. The primary sin for an oppressed person is not pride but the lack of self-love and self-trust.

It is clear that the awareness of sin as a pervasive condition remains a theological priority: sin damages the structure of our moral and spiritual (and therefore *social*) being and is not simply an act that leads to a "debt" to be paid. Absolution is part of active healing*, the restoration of relation with God and God's people*, rather than the cancellation of a payment due. However, this does not rule out the need for a "diagnostic" of sin, such as is represented by Cassian's analysis. There is still a task to be performed of identifying those patterns of behavior that, whatever the degree of consciousness with which they are chosen, render a person incapable of a vivifying relation with the truth*, that is, with God.

● K. Barth (1932), *KD* I/1, 11–1 (*Dogmatique*, Geneva, 1953).
R. Niebuhr (1942), *The Nature and Destiny of Man*: *A Christian Interpretation*, New York.
P. Tillich (1957), *Systematic Theology*, vol. 2, Chicago.
W. Pannenberg (1962), *Was ist der Mensch? Die Anthropologie der Gegenwart im Lichte der Theologie*, Göttingen.

H.U. von Balthasar (1963), *Das Ganze im Fragment,* Einsiedeln.

K. Rahner (1970), "Die Sünde Adams," *Schr.zur Th.* 9, Einsiedeln, 259–75.

G. Gutierrez (1971), *Teología de la liberación: Perspectivas,* Lima.

J. Moltmann (1971), *Mensch,* Stuttgart-Berlin.

P. Schoonenberg (1975), "Der Mensch in der Sünde," *MySal* II, 845–936, Einsiedeln.

J. Pohier (1985), *Dieu: Fractures,* Paris.

L.G. Jones (1995), *Embodying Forgiveness: A Theological Analysis,* Grand Rapids, Mich.

ROWAN WILLIAMS

See also **Adam; Anthropology; Conscience; Conversion; Demons; Expiation; Good; Hesychasm; Justice; Justification; Law; Mercy; Passions; Penance; Scandal; Temptation; Wrath of God**

Sin, Original

The expression "original sin*" was coined by Augustine* (PL 40, 106) to designate the sin that "came into the world" (Rom 5:12) by the transgression of Adam* and that affects all human beings by the very fact of their birth (PL 40, 245). Later this would be called "originated" original sin as opposed to the "originating" original sin of Adam himself. The theological analysis of original sin is always connected to reflection on free will, grace*, and concupiscence (or covetousness).

1. Elaboration of the Notion

a) Scripture. The narration* in Genesis 2–3 reinterpreted in Song of Songs 2:23 and Sirach 40:1 refers more to the unfortunate consequences of Adam's sin than the transmission of this sin. Several texts stress that human beings are sinful from birth (Ps 51:7; Jb 14:4, 15:14ff.) and that sin is universal (Ps 14:2f.).

Jesus* underscores the illusion of those who flatter themselves by saying they are just (e.g., Jn 8:39; Lk 18:9–14); he affirms that all need to be saved (Mk 16:15f. par.). And he says that it is from the heart that comes all that makes a person impure (Mt 15:19). But the true scriptural foundation of the doctrine of original sin is found in the parallel established by Paul between Adam and Christ* in Romans 5 (Paulinian* theology). Jesus, source of life and righteousness, is opposed to Adam, who thrust humanity into sin and death*.

b) Church Fathers. During the first four centuries after Christ, the church fathers* unquestionably accepted the historicity of the narrative in Genesis and the connection between Adam's fall and the condition of the human race. Although they were in agreement on our condition as beings fallen from grace, they diverged in their analyses of that fall. Irenaeus* saw it as disobedience (*Adv. Haer.* V, 16, 3), but others identified it with the weakness and ignorance of the mortal condition and did not envisage a real participation in the sin of Adam. Gregory* of Nazianzus considered that an unbaptized person who had done no wrong could deserve neither glory nor punishment (SC 358, 248), and John* Chrysostom claimed that Romans 5 means not that human beings are sinful but that they are condemned to suffering and death (PG 60, 477).

In 397, 15 years before the anti-Pelagian controversy, Augustine's doctrine was already fully developed (*Ad Simplicianum,* PL 40, 101–48). Because of Adam's transgression, all human beings are marked by original sin. This is the true sin, which brought down on us temporal punishment (death and desire) but also eternal punishment (separation from God*). Original sin is propagated by carnal generation and the desire that goes with it.

Because of his confidence in free will, Pelagius minimized the difference between the primitive state of humanity and its present state. On the one hand he affirmed that the first man was created mortal, while on the other he rejected the idea of a weakening of free will subsequent to Adam's sin. To combat this doctrine, Augustine invoked the practice of infant baptism*. Since the purpose of baptism is the remission of sins, children must bear in themselves a sin that they did not commit but was transmitted, precisely original sin. Against Pelagius, the Council* of Carthage (418) affirmed that Adam's death was the consequence of his sin (*DS* 222) and that the original sin of infants is true sin (*DS* 223). The Council of Orange (529) specified that Adam transmitted to his descendants a true sin and a spiritual slavery (*DS* 371–72). Augustine's influence on these councils and on the subsequent official teaching of the Catholic Church* is undeniable. However, the definitions of that Church should be distinguished from the numerous elements of Augustinian doctrine that were the subject of free debate in Catholic theology*: the fate of children who died without baptism, the problem of limbo*, the way original sin is transmitted, the relationship between original sin and sexuality, the measure of the disorder introduced by original sin, the eventual immortality of the first man if he had not sinned, and so on.

c) Middle Ages.   Considered as a whole, Scholastic* thought on original sin was an effort to interpret and add nuance to Augustine's doctrine.

In defining original sin as loss of original righteousness (*Œuvre* 4, 197), Anselm* explained how it is propagated: if Adam had retained righteousness, he would have transmitted it to his descendants, but he could not transmit that which he had lost. Peter Lombard (c. 1100–60) took up a traditional exegesis* of *Lk* 19, 30 to mark the difference between the gratuitous gifts that had been stripped away from man and the nature* that had been wounded. Alexander of Hales (c. 1186–1245) introduced a distinction that would become classical: in its formal aspect, original sin is the loss of justice, and as such it is a true sin; in its material aspect it is covetousness, which is not a sin but the punishment for sin. This analysis was adopted by Thomas* Aquinas as by Bonaventure* and their respective schools*. Thomas reasoned that man has a participation in the divine light that cannot be destroyed by original sin. This idea of the natural light of reason* leads to a less pessimistic perception of mankind's fall from grace, even if human nature is corrupted by sin, and man without grace cannot resist covetousness permanently (though he can resist for a certain length of time; *ST* Ia IIae, q. 109, a. 8). It should be noted that on this point, Duns* Scotus agreed with Thomas (*Op. Oxoniense* II, d 29, a. 1).

2. Divergent Interpretations

a) Reformation.   For Luther*, theology is not a form of abstract speculation on man's relations with God. It rests on an experience: the word* of God transmitted in Scripture comes to liberate human beings enslaved to covetousness. Rejecting by this the "sub-

tleties" of the Scholastics, Luther made of original sin a "total loss of all the uprightness and all the power of all the forces of the body as of the soul of man altogether, inner and outer" (*WA* 56, 312). In opposition to the humanism of a thinker such as Erasmus (c. 1469–1536), he affirmed the radical corruption of fallen man and the impotence of the free will to do good. Calvin* also denied that sinful human beings had the power to do good of their own free will. The Augsburg Confession (a. 2) affirms that original sin is a true sin but does not distinguish the loss of righteousness from covetousness. As a consequence, Melanchthon (1497–1560) reduced the grace of baptism to the nonimputation of original sin. (*Apologie*, §36); this was unacceptable to Catholic theology (Dubarle 1983).

b) Council of Trent.   Trent* took up the teachings of former councils and reaffirmed, in opposition to the Reformers, the distinction between covetousness and sin strictly speaking; only the loss of justice is an authentic sin that is effaced by baptism (*DS* 1520).

From that time on, the debate on the question of original sin was connected, in the Catholic Church, with the problem of what we mean by "human nature." Baius rejected the Thomist notion of grace added on to nature* and saw in original sin a radical corruption of human nature; in the name of a return to Augustinianism*, he concurred with Luther's understanding of original sin. In order to oppose this pessimistic conception of fallen nature, the great majority of Catholic theologians radicalized the Thomist doctrine of created grace and defended the idea that, without grace, human nature is preserved in its essential principles and in particular in its free will. Here we can see the development of the hypothesis of a pure nature endowed with a natural telicity distinct from the beatific* vision. The advocates of this argument thought in general that man was raised to the supernatural* order at the time of his creation* and that sin had the double consequence of making him fall from grace and leading to a disorder in his sensibility. This hypothesis, which facilitated the understanding of the doctrine of Trent, was adopted by the majority of Catholic theologians after the condemnation of Baius (1567) and Jansenius (1653). However, it was not unanimously accepted. Some Augustinians, such as H. Noris (1631–1704), rejected it without nonetheless being condemned. H. de Lubac* (1946) demonstrated that it is not in harmony with the Thomist doctrine of the natural desire to see God.

c) Eastern Theology.   The Eastern Church was not touched by the Pelagian crisis; it remained true to the earlier understanding of human nature oriented toward divinity. Consequently, Eastern theology thought of Adam's sin not as the loss of created grace (Lossky 1944) but as the perversion of nature. All human beings are united with Adam and come into the world with this fallen nature.

d) Philosophical Approaches. The way in which the doctrine of original sin sheds light on the human condition found an echo with a number of philosophers. Pascal* leads his reader to a radical questioning of man become incomprehensible to himself. The Christian mystery* recapitulated in Adam and Jesus Christ (*Br* 523) answers this questioning. J.-J. Rousseau made property* rights responsible for the corruption of a humanity assumed to be naturally good. Kant* saw in the propensity to evil* that man discovers in himself a "radical evil" over which he must triumph by deciding to make his life conform to moral law*. Hegel* stressed that man, in discovering himself to be evil, also discovers himself to be responsible (Pottier 1990). For Kierkegaard*, whose *The Concept of Anxiety* was meant to be a "clarification...of the problem of original sin," this dogma* presupposes that human beings in the state of innocence can choose between good* and evil without knowing what they are. This is where individuals experience the anguish of nothingness*: to choose one is to not choose the other. Through anguish, each of us is awakened to his own liberty*.

3. Contemporary Thought

P. Ricoeur (1969) vigorously expressed the grounds on which Augustinian teaching on original sin can provoke rejection: "Pseudo-rational speculation on the almost biological transmission of an almost legal guilt for the transgression of another man going back to the beginning of time, somewhere between *Pithecanthropus* and Neanderthal man."

Even if one finds this judgment excessive, one cannot deny the reality of the discomfort it conveys. It is clear that this discomfort has stimulated contemporary theology in its search for a renewed formulation of original sin.

a) Exegesis. To read Genesis 2–3 correctly, it is necessary to take the story's literary genre into consideration. It is an *etiological* legend (Dubarle 1958). By way of an imagistic representation of our origins, the author seeks to describe the psychology of sinful man and to show that moral evil is prior to human misfortune. Further, the theme of solidarity* in sin is, as shown by Ligier (1959), a perspective familiar to authors of the Bible*. As for the meaning of the word *eph'ô* in Romans 5:12, which has been widely discussed, it seems that it means "due to the fact that"

"death spread to all men because all sinned" (*see* Lyonnet 1966).

b) Patristics. In studying the church fathers we can rediscover forgotten perspectives. Irenaeus, for example, stresses that man was not created perfect from the beginning (*Adv. Haer.* V, 38, 1). Several of the Fathers, including Augustine, did not hesitate to see in Adam, beyond the individual, the human community as a whole, dislocated through sin (Lubac, *Catholicisme*, 1938). From this viewpoint we have a better understanding of the transmission of original sin: man comes into the world born into a community torn apart from its origin, and so he necessarily participates in this rupture.

c) Systematic Theology. Beyond confessional differences, contemporary theologians can be divided schematically into three groups. There are those, such as Villalmonte (1978), who believe that an inherited sin is a contradiction, every sin being necessarily personal. Others strive to think original sin in terms of the sin of the world, as brought to light by Ligier. The sin is not only the act of the one who turns away from God but also the influence exerted by that act on another liberty. Here Schoonenberg (1967) speaks of situation and specifies that this situation may concern a human being before he is engaged in his existence. He suggests we speak in this case of an "existential" situation (by opposition to the "existentiel" situation in the face of which my liberty can react). Original sin is such an existential situation that comes to weigh on every child born in a world marked by sin. And the *CCC* (408), for example, considers that the loss of original justice should be carefully distinguished from the sin of the world, which is the consequence of original sin and of all personal sins. It is with respect to this position that some have defended a strict monogenism*. Rahner* (1967), however, showed that the Catholic dogma* of original sin does not require monogenism but demands the affirmation of a real unity of humanity as its source. Others, such as Fessard (1966), think that the sin of the origins refers to a supernatural historicity that should be clearly distinguished from natural historicity. Bold opinions in the same direction have been proposed by Léonard (1987), who places Adam and Eve in "a preternatural world that is real but does not coincide with the actual universe."

Original sin is not the most profound element of Christian faith*, which is hope* in God rather than despair over transgression. But if all human beings are united in sin, that means two things: a unity of humanity more ancient and more fundamental than all its divisions and the extension of salvation to all those who want it: "For God has consigned all to disobedience, that he may have mercy* on all" (Rom 11:32).

● Anselm, *De conceptu virginali et de originali peccato: Œuvre*, vol. 4, Paris, 1990.

Augustine, *Writings against the Pelagians*, BAug 21–24.

Calvin, *Inst.*, l. II, 1–3.

Luther, *Comm. de l'épître aux Romains*, WA 56.

Kant, *Die religion innerhalb der Grenzen der blossen Vernunft*, AA VI.

Kierkegaard, *Le concept d'angoisse*, OC, vol. 7, Paris, 1973, 105–258.

J.-J. Rousseau, *Discours sur l'origine et les fondements de l'inégalité parmi les hommes*, Part II.

Thomas Aquinas, *De malo*, q. 5; *ST* IIa IIae, q. 81–83.

♦ A. Gaudel (1933), "Péché originel," *DThC* 12/1, 275–606.

M. Jugie (1933), "Péché originel dans l'Église grecque après saint Jean Damascène," *DThC* 12/1, 606–24.

W. Lossky (1944), *Théologie mystique de l'Église d'Orient* (2nd Ed. 1990), 123–29.

H. de Lubac (1946), *Surnaturel*, Paris.

M.M. Labourdette (1953), *Le péché originel et les origines de l'homme*, Paris.

A.-M. Dubarle (1958), *Le péché originel dans l'Écriture*, Paris.

L. Ligier (1959, 1961), *Péché d'Adam et péché du monde*, 2 vols., Paris.

P. Ricœur (1960), "Le "péché originel": Étude de signification," *EeT* 23, 11–30, repr. in *Le conflit des interprétations*, Paris, 1969, 265–82.

J. Gross (1960–72), *Geschichte des Erbsündedogmas*, 4 vols., Munich.

G. Siewerth (1964), *Die christliche Erbsündenlehre*, Einsiedeln.

G. Fessard (1966), *La dialectique des Exercices spirituels de saint Ignace*, vol. 2, Paris.

S. Lyonnet (1966), "Péché (in the NT)," *DBS* 7, 486–567.

P. Schoonenberg (1966), *Theologie der Sünde*, Einsiedeln; (1967), "Der Mensch in der Sünde," *MySal* II, 845–938.

K. Rahner (1967), "Erbsünde und Evolution," *Conc(D)* 3, 459–65.

H. Rondet (1967), *Le péché originel dans la tradition patristique et théologique*, Paris.

A. Sage (1967), "Péché originel: Naissance d'un dogme," *RE Aug* 13, 211–48.

J.L. Connor (1968), "Original Sin: Contemporary Approaches," *TS* 29, 215–50.

K.A. Weger (1970), *Theologie der Erbsünde*, Fribourg.

M. Flick, Z. Alszeghy (1972), *Il peccato originale*, Brescia.

A. de Villalmonte (1978), *El peccado original; veinticinqo años de controversia (1950–1975)*, Salamanca.

H. Häring (1979), *Die Macht des Bösen: Das Erbe Augustins*, Gütersloh-Zurich-Köln.

H. Köster (1979, 1982), *Urstand Fall und Erbsünde in der Scholastik*, HDG II/3/b; *U. F. u. E. von der Reformation bis zur Gegenwart*, HDG II/3/c.

L. Scheffczyk (1981), *U. F. u. E. von der Schrift bis Augustinus*, HDG II/3/a, first part.

M. Sievernich (1982), *Schuld und Sünde in der Theologie der Gegenwart*, Frankfurt.

A.-M. Dubarle (1983), *Le péché originel: Perspectives théologiques*, Paris.

G. Martelet (1986), *Libre réponse à un scandale*, Paris.

A. Léonard (1987), *Les raisons de croire*, Paris, 177–231.

B. Pottier (1990), *Le péché originel selon Hegel*, Namur.

L. Scheffczyk (1990), "Die Erbsündenlehre des Tridentinums in Gegenwartaspekt," *FKTh* 1, 1–21.

A. Vanneste (1991), "La nouvelle théologie du péché originel," *EThL*, 1991, 249–77.

P. Grelot (1994), "Pour une lecture de Rm 5, 12–21," *NRTh* 116, 495–512.

Louis Panier (1996), *Le péché originel: Naissance de l'homme sauvé*, Paris.

R. Schwager (1997), *Erbsünde und Heilsdrama: Im Kontext von Evolution, Gentechnologie und Apokalyptik*, Münster.

K. Rahner (1998), *Der Mensch in der Schöpfung*, SW 8 (cours d'Innsbrück), 263–511.

LAURENT SENTIS

See also **Adam; Augustinianism; Banezianism-Molinism-Baianism; Jansenism; Justification; Pelagianism**

Situation Ethics

Situation ethics* designates an ethics for which moral qualification cannot be attributed to human actions without a hermeneutics of the situation in which the agent finds or found himself: good* and evil* are good in this situation and evil in that situation. Standard philosophical treatments of the concept of situation can be found in philosophies of existence (Heidegger, Jaspers) and in philosophies of dialogue (Buber, Levinas).

Catholic theology* has given a place to the concept of situation in a way that has provoked extreme reservations on the part of the Roman magisterium* (*See* Pius XII, speeches of 23 March and 18 April 1952, and the directive of the Holy Office of 2 February 1956, *DS* 3918–21). Situation ethics is not among the theories condemned in the encyclical *Splendor Veritatis* of John Paul II (1993). The taking into account of situations is, moreover, in common doctrine, an indispensable element in the evaluation of moral actions. Catholic doctrine is expressed, for example, in the *CEC* §1757: "The object, the intention, and the circumstances constitute the three 'sources' of the morality of human actions." The existence of intrinsically wrong actions is also the subject of long-lasting Catholic teaching (e.g., *Splendor Veritatis* §80). The debate over situation ethics seems to be closed.

● M. Honecker (1990), *Einführung in die theologische Ethik,* Berlin.
F. J. Wetz, U. Laucken (1995), "Situation," *HWP* 9, 923–37.
G. Outka (2000), "Situationsethik," *TRE* 31, 337–42 (bibl.).

Jean-Yves Lacoste

Skepticism, Christian

The New Testament does not mention the philosophical current known as skepticism. However, Pilate, who expects no answer after asking Jesus* "What is truth?*" (Jn 18:38), might appear as the archetype of the skeptic. Principally characterized by the suspension of judgment (*epokhè tès dianoias*) on opinions or dogmas* (hence the terminological equivalence of skeptics, epechists, and pyrrhonists [from Pyrrhon, 365–275 B.C., the originator of skepticism], which also include the Academics, because of the New Academy, a school founded by the skeptic Carneades, 214–129 B.C.), skepticism has an ambivalent theological status. Insofar as it rejects any dogmatic affirmation, it may appear as the enemy of faith*. But to the extent that it recognizes that human reason* is the norm for no truth (the different assertion according to which no truth can be attained by the strength of human reason alone would be fideism*), it may have a role as a preparation for faith. This ambivalence marks the attitude of Augustine* toward skepticism, then reappears in the modern period, before decaying into fideism.

a) Ancient Skepticism. It does not seem that ancient skepticism ever denied the existence of the gods or any particular god: "Taking life as a guide, we assert without dogmatism that the gods exist, that we venerate them and pay them homage" (Sextus Empiricus, *Outlines of Pyrrhonism* III. 2). An enemy of philosophies* (this is why it has no equal when it comes to destroying that wisdom*, which, according to 1 Cor 1, is madness before God), it is presented as a mortal opponent of religion, notably in Cicero, only by adherents of a religion founded on rational proof, such as that of the Stoics, whereas it is a weapon in the service of traditional religion (*De natura deorum*). Before the diversity of beliefs and cults* (*see* 10th mode of suspension of judgment of Ænesidemus [80–130 B.C.], *Pyrrhonian Discoursest* I. 37) and the inability of philosophers to decide questions on the nature of God, the existence of providence*, and the conflict between divine omnipotence* and divine goodness or between evil* and liberty*, the ancient skeptics practiced suspension of judgment.

Augustine criticized this position in book III of *Contra academicos* and again in book XIX of *De civitate Dei,* considering it dangerous for wisdom as much as for faith. It was by highlighting the "intentional character of the mind"—that is, by acceding to a formal truth anterior to any material truth—that he avoided suspension of judgment (*Contra academicos* III. 5. 1), thereby anticipating the transcendental status of truth (*De libero arbitrio* II 9. 26 and 12. 34). Augustine's quarrel with skepticism had two aspects, philosophical and theological: 1) It was in order to answer arguments of the skeptics that Augustine first set forth what would be called after Descartes* the *cogito* and thus made immaterial the very possibility of error or deception (*Soliloquies* II. 1. 1; *De libero arbitrio* II. 3. 7; *De civitate Dei* XI. 26; *De Trinitate* X. 10. 14); but by the same token he recognized the initial experience of doubt, from which he begins in order to attain the certainty of his own being* and then that of the existence of God. 2) Augustine confessed that he had gone through a skeptical phase—"the Academics long held my rudder in the midst of the waves struggling against all the winds" (*De beata vita* 1. 4)—even at the time when he was a catechumen. "I kept my heart from giving any assent, and in that state of suspended judgment

I was suffering a worse death" (*Confessions* VI. iv [6]), for "I wanted to be as certain about things I could not see as I am certain that seven and three are ten." Academic probabilism (which in no way called into question the existence of God and providence, only his substance and the means of access to him, VI. v [7–8]) led him to this status of provisional catechumen, "until some clear light should come by which I could direct my course" (V. xiv [25]). Faith was thus conquered in the tension between the need to believe and the fear of believing in error (VI. v [7]). The fact remains that skepticism presented two essential advantages: 1) it made it possible to escape from Manicheanism* (III. vi [10–11]; V. xiv [25]), which claimed to impose nothing without rational justification (Augustine would use skeptical arguments against the Manichees [*Contra Faustum*]), and 2) it showed that, incapable of finding truth by ourselves by means of clear reasoning (Vi. v [8]), it makes us rely on the authority of holy Scripture and tradition*. The latter argument, which shows both the preparatory function of skepticism and its usefulness against heresies*, established what we may call skeptic apologetics, which was not the least paradoxical form of Augustinianism* in the modern period.

b) *Skeptic Apologetics.* Arguing against the *Theologia naturalis sive liber creaturarum* of Sebond (posth. Ed. 1487; French trans. by Montaigne 1581), Montaigne's project in the "Apologia of Raymond Sebond" is to propose a risky apologetics for philosophers, that is, relying on the lack of arguments, which determined an essential aspect of Pascal*'s projected *Apologia* (many of Pascal's reflections have their source in Montaigne: "Pyrrhonism is the truth," "Pyrrhonism serves religion," "It is by lacking proofs that they [the Christians] do not lack sense"). Since Montaigne considers "man deprived of any revelation*" (Pascal), his skepticism "presents man naked and empty, recognizing his natural weakness, fitting to receive from above some external power, devoid of human knowledge, and all the more likely to house the divine within himself, abolishing his judgment to make more room for faith" (*Essays* II, 12). This radical apologetics is based on recognition of the omnipotence of God, which can in no way be conditioned by any finite rationality. But it also has an ecclesiological aspect because it allows Montaigne to take a position against the Lutherans. The same passage goes on: "neither unbelieving nor establishing any dogma against common observances [i.e., the tradition*], sworn enemy of heresy*, and consequently escaping from the vain and irreligious opinions introduced by false sects. This is a blank slate prepared to take from the finger of God whatever forms it may please him to engrave on it." It is because

human reason cannot be the norm for divine doctrine that Montaigne also opposes translations of the Bible* into vernacular languages ("Of Prayers" I, 56, an argument repeated by Francis de Sales) and the Protestant use of logic that makes us see a contradiction in the real presence (II, 12).

Contemporary with the *Essays* and like them very dependent on the *De disciplinis* of Juan-Luis Vivès (1492–1540), the *Quod nihil scitur* (1581) of Francesco de Sanchez (†1623) used nominalist arguments for skeptical purposes and constituted a powerful weapon against the Aristotelian *organon*. A disciple of Montaigne in *La sagesse* (1601), Pierre Charron reconciled apophaticism and skepticism in *Les trois vérités* (1593) and the *Discours de la Divinité* (1604). To a great extent the relationship between what has been called "erudite libertinage" (Gassendi, Naudé, Diodati, La Mothe Le Vayer) and Christianity was established in the wake of the *Essays* and evidences the objective alliance between one form of nominalism* and skepticism. The idea of "preparation" for faith, for example, can rely on the skeptical apologetics of La Mothe Le Vayer (1588–1672), who, in his dialogue *De la Divinité* (1632), also used the works of Pseudo-Dionysius to make skepticism the exemplification of Paul's expression *Noli altum sapere* (Rom 11:20; a large number of scriptural references, relying particularly on 1 and 2 Cor, is aimed at demonstrating that Paul was a skeptic) and a "perfect introduction to Christianity": "Skepticism does not have any drawbacks for our holy Theology*, but even…properly understood, its *epochè* may serve as a useful preparation for the gospel." Jean-Pierre Camus (1584–1652), a close friend of Francis de Sales and bishop of Belley, published an *Essai sceptique* in 1610 and then went on to invent the pious novel (writing more than 50 of them, including *Élise ou l'innocence coupable,* 1621; *Palombe,* 1625; *Callitrope,* 1628).

c) *From Critique to Fideism.* With the appearance, in the midst of the Reformation crisis, of a Christian skepticism aimed at avoiding the fratricidal quarrels of religious sects by taking refuge in tradition, skeptical arguments led to an alternative. Either, as in the libertine current, they destroyed religious belief for the elite, with religion remaining necessary for the people at large only in order to maintain social order, or, as for Bayle, they demonstrated the innate weakness of reason and fostered the impulse to take refuge in the bosom of Scripture and to "take every thought captive to obey Christ" (2 Cor 10:5). Skepticism in Catholic circles gave rise to an emphasis on the respect due to tradition, on the grounds that human reason is too weak to resolve dogmatic conflicts (Huet [1630–1721], bishop of Avranches). In Protestant circles it led to pre-fideist positions (Bayle [1647–1706]), to the defense of an art of ignorance as well as of knowledge, of doubt and suspension of judgment as well as of belief (Castellion [1515–63]), and thereby prepared the way for defenses of the "errant conscience*" of good faith (Grotius [1583–1645], Bayle), which played a decisive role in thinking about religious tolerance in the age of classicism.

Hume gave skepticism a critical function with respect to knowledge and used it in particular to examine beliefs that he considered the least justified, namely, those based on witnesses and especially miracles* (*An Enquiry concerning Human Understanding,* 1748). But the opposition of the *Dialogues concerning Natural Religion* (1779) to any form of religion, especially natural religion, makes it impossible to include Hume among the Christian skeptics. Kant* opens the *Kritik der reinen Vernunft* with the opposition between dogmatism and skepticism, an old impasse from which only critique provides an exit, but he recognizes that skepticism had set forth the *bounds* of reason, whereas critique determines its *limits* (*Kritik der reinen Vernunft* A 761/B 789). In the broad sense of critical function (*skepsis*) or limitation of rationality, Kantianism constitutes perhaps the final avatar of Christian skepticism—the late 19th and early 20th centuries saw it as a form of fideism. In condemning fideism, tolerationism, and indifferentism, the Church did not mention skepticism.

● Cicero (45 av. J.-C.), *De natura deorum.*
Sextus Empiricus (IIe s.), *Hypotyposes pyrrhoniennes.*
Augustine (386), *Contra Academicos, De beata vita*; (394–95), *De libero arbitrio*; (397–401), *Confessions*; (413–27), *De civitate Dei*; (409–22), *De Trinitate.*
J.-L. Vivès (1531), *De Disciplinis,* Antwerp.
S. Castellion (1560), *De arte dubitandi et confidendi, ignorandi et sciendi.*
Montaigne (1580), "Apologie de Raymond Sebond," *Essais* II, 12, Bordeaux.
F. Sanchez (1581), *Quod nihil scitur,* Lyon (new Ed. and French trans., Paris, 1984).
P. Charron (1593), *Les trois vérités,* Bordeaux.
P. Charron (1601), *La Sagesse,* Bordeaux.
P. Charron (1604), *Discours de la Divinité,* Paris.
J.-P. Camus (1609–10), *Essai sceptique,* in *Diversités,* vol. IV, Paris.

H. Grotius (1611), *Meletius,* Leiden, 1988.
P. Gassendi (1624), *Exercitationum paradoxicarum adversus Aristotelos,* Grenoble (vol. I; vol. II, in *Opera omnia,* Lyon, 1658; new Ed., Stuttgart–Bad Cannstatt, 1964).
F. La Mothe Le Vayer (1631), *De la divinité,* in *Dialogues faits à l'imitation des Anciens,* Frankurt, 1506 (*sic*) (new Ed. by A. Pessel, Paris, 1988).
M. Schoock (1652), *De skepticismo pars prior, sive libri quatuor,* Groningue.
B. Pascal (1670), *Pensées sur la religion...,* Paris.
P.D. Huet (1679), *Demonstratio evangelica,* Paris.
P. Bayle (1696), *Dictionnaire historique et critique,* III (Éclaircissement sur le pyrrhonisme), Rotterdam.
P.-D. Huet (†1721), *Traité philosophique de la faiblesse de l'esprit humain,* Paris, 1723.
D. Hume (1748), *Philosophical Essays (An Enquiry,* 1751) *concerning Human Understanding,* London.
D. Hume (1779), *Dialogues concerning Natural Religion,* London.
E. Kant (1781), *Kritik der reinen Vernunft,* Riga.
♦ E. Saisset (1865), *Le scepticisme: Aenésidème-Pascal-Kant,* Paris.
R. Jolivet (1931), *Essai sur les rapports entre la pensée grecque et la pensée chrétienne,* Paris.
R. Pintard (1947), *Le libertinage érudit dans la première moitié du XVIIe siècle,* 2 vols., Paris.
P. Courcelle (1950), *Recherches sur les "Confessions" de saint Augustin,* Paris.
M. Testard (1958), *Saint Augustin et Cicéron,* 2 vols., Paris.
R. Popkin (1960), *The History of Skepticism from Erasmus to Spinoza,* Assen.
A. Flew (1961), *Hume's Philosophy of Belief,* New York.
T. Gregory (1961), *Scetticismo ed empirismo: Studio su Gassendi,* Bari.
J. A. Mourant (1966), "Augustine and the Academics," *RechAug* 4, 67–96.
A. Comparot (1983), *Amour et vérité*: Sebon, Vivès et Michel de Montaigne, Paris.
M. Screech (1983), *Montaigne and Melancholy,* London.
P. Dibon (1990), "Skepticisme et orthodoxie réformée," in *Regards sur la Hollande du siècle d'Or,* Naples, 721–55.
J. M. Maia Neto (1995), *The Christianization of Pyrrhonism: Skepticism and Faith in Pascal, Kierkegaard and Shestov,* Dordrecht-Boston-London.
T. Gregory (1999), *Genèse de la raison classique, de Charron à Descartes,* Paris.

VINCENT CARRAUD

See also **Augustine of Hippo; Augustinianism; Deism and Theism; Existence of God, Proofs of; Fideism; Humanism, Christian; Natural Theology; Pascal, Blaise; Stoicism, Christian; Truth**

Slavery. *See* Liberty

Society

From the theological point of view, human society is a community of persons who share lasting and organized relationships; society is oriented toward a common good* and unified by bonds of interdependence, love*, authority*, and law*. While the concepts of authority and law are of doubtful applicability to the divine society of the Trinity*, the Trinity remains the archetype of all human society, being the source and end of love, communion*, and the very personhood of human beings.

Important theoretical issues regarding society have arisen historically within ecclesiology* and political theology* whenever it has been necessary to define the ways in which the Church* and the political community are societies. The contemporary problematic in this arena can be understood only in this context.

a) Ecclesiological Issues. These have focused on the nature and operation of authority and law in binding believers together into one society. Authority and law in the Church are christological and eschatological in nature but are embodied in juridical and disciplinary structures. The primary issue is whether jurisdictional authority and positive law truly express the Church's spiritual essence of faith*, liberty*, and love. The medieval Church presented the most complete integration of spiritual and legal-political society, its members being incorporated into the mystical body of Christ* through a legally articulated structure of sacraments*, institutions, practices, and precepts*. The doctrine that the pope*, as the Church's supreme lawgiver and judge, was the earthly embodiment of Christ's spiritual headship undergirded the seamless transposition of divine authority, law, and judgment* onto ecclesial structures*. This conception of a supernatural* juridical-spiritual corporation gave impetus to a conception of civil society as at once a community of fellowship and virtue and a political and legal structure.

By contrast, Luther* saw the Church as a purely spiritual community, whose purely divine and charismatic internal essence had nothing to do with legal or social forms. This view inspired the anarchist and antinomian experiments of the more extreme Protestant sects (Anabaptists*) and more generally encouraged a proclivity for apolitical theories of ecclesial society, especially among German philosophers and theologians, from Friedrich Schleiermacher* to Paul Tillich*, Karl Barth*, and Jürgen Moltmann. (Unlike Luther, Calvin* never divorced the spiritual community of the Word* from the visible polity of "constitutions" and "offices.") Today, it is not Hegel*'s synthesis of spiritual freedom and political structure but rather the Marxist rejection of the bourgeois state that attracts the sympathy of the Lutheran Moltmann and his Catholic contemporary Johann Baptist Metz, leading them to identify political power with oppression and positive law with systems of idolatrous self-justification. For Moltmann, the Church, which participates in the "messianic mission, the representative self-giving, and the liberating lordship of Christ" (1975), is a charismatic community of brotherly love, fellowship, and service, free from jurisdictional structure, whether of monarchical episcopate (bishop*), clerical aristocracy, or democracy* (ibid.). While he recognizes "gifts of rule" as among the charismata, these are powers of fraternal leadership exercised within the community, not powers of authority over it (ibid.).

In response to these spiritualizing Protestant ecclesiologies, modern Catholic theology* has come back to a long-standing issue that concerns the divinely appointed structure (rather than the authenticity) of jurisdictional authority. Since Vatican II*, charismatic and sacramental images of the Church have drawn inspiration from the rehabilitation of conciliarism* (*see* Paul de Vooght or Hans Kung). The 15th-century conciliarists sought to relativize the model that made Peter* the summit of jurisdictional authority; for them, it was rather the entire Church, as a mystical corporation, that held the authority of its head, Jesus Christ. They presented the spiritual communion of Christ's body as a latent political society possessing a divinely given (for some, naturally given) right to self-government, exercised through the structure of clerical offices but supremely through the agency of the universal council*. By anchoring the Church's external political unity* in a communal spiritual totality, they contributed decisively to the emergence of theories of the state that derive it from and subordinate it to a prior social totality.

To summarize, there are thus at least three historically influential models of Church society: as a seamless spiritual and legal hierarchy; as a nonjurisdictional spiritual communion, christologically and eschatologically defined; and as a divine/human spiritual totality articulated in corporate political structures.

b) Issues in Political Theology. If there are, as Augustine* says, two incompatible cities*, the *civitate dei* (city of God) and the *civitas terrena* (earthly city) (*Civ. Dei,* XIX), one may question the sense in which relations belonging to the *saeculum,* the passing order of the world*, could comprise a true society. In Augustine's view, in any case, the secular *res publica* is not a true community, knit together by charity and consensus about the good*, for that can exist only where faith in Christ and obedience to his law of love bind persons together. It is rather a fragile and shifting union that targets limited categories of earthly goods in the midst of a sea of moral disorder and personal and collective hatreds (*Civ. Dei* XIX, 5–7, 14, 17, 21).

Subsequent thinkers, concurring with Augustine's pessimism, proposed various solutions to this situation. Gregory VII and his medieval successors located the sole means of salvation of the temporal order from its disintegrating impulses in its thorough subordination to the ecclesiastical order, particularly in the subordination of royal government to priestly government and of civil law to canon law. By contrast, between the 14th and the 17th centuries—the period of the emergence of centralized states—imperialist, royalist, and republican thinkers located the resolution of social conflicts in an authoritarian political order. Power and law, in their view, were to be erected either on the divine right of a royal will (absolute monarchy) or on the natural right of popular will (popular sovereignty) and/or on the foundational contract of individual wills, with their respective rights (contractualism). Skepticism about the capacity of "natural" or "sinful" wills to remain unified on the one hand and growing confidence in the resources of the human mind on the other—these two factors led to the antinaturalist political systems of such theorists as Jean Bodin (c. 1529–96), Hobbes (1588–1679), Spinoza (1632–77), and Pufendorf (1632–94).

In reaction to political formalism, 18th- and 19th-century liberals wanted to define nonpolitical principles of social unity while conceding the individualism of each member of society. Thus arose a plethora of "social theodicies." Political economists, such as Benjamin Franklin (1706–90), Adam Smith (1723–90), and Frédéric Bastiat (1801–50), conjured economic and social equilibrium out of the self-interested choices of individuals by means of mechanistic market forces. Jeremy Bentham (1748–1832) and the English utilitarians (utilitarianism*) derived social harmony from the pursuit of private desires by sufficiently socialized individuals. Marx* saw social integration in the classless society arising from the cooperation of autonomous individuals working to maximize their expressive and productive freedoms. During the 20th century, the depoliticizing of social theory has been carried forward by liberal sociologists (largely in the tradition of Max Weber [1864–1920]) who invoke impersonal social mechanisms such as universal bureaucratization or instrumental rationality to explain the harmonization of interests, values, and passions*. Ironically, sociological marginalizing of the properly political order has gone hand in hand with a diffuse politicizing of the social whole, as theories claim that everything is political.

For some contemporary theologians, the sociological conception of society has exacerbated the Augustinian problem of whether a community is possible in the *saeculum.* The social *system* is by definition a structure of external determination, which thus denies individual liberty; it is also a means of domination insofar as its mechanisms can be manipulated. Thus, both Lutheran and Catholic liberation theologians regard salvation* as preeminently emancipation from social necessity in a movement of theological negation (i.e., Moltmann's *theologica crucis* ["theology of the cross"] or Metz's *memoria passionis* ["memory of the passion"]), which opens up a sphere of personal spontaneity and authentic communication (eschatological life in the Spirit*). However, when negation of any particular systematic oppression, injustice, or dehumanization is also negation of society itself (as predictable, institutional regularity), it is difficult to restore community, that is, to give stable practical, moral, or social content to the "new man in Christ." The frequent Hegelian-Marxist response of liberationists to this impasse is to appeal to the historical dialectic of freedom and to the progressive realization of self-conscious reflection and action by the masses. This, however, is essentially an appeal to the contemporary status quo, to the philosophy and public discourse of liberal, democratic, pluralistic, and technological polities. In fact, aspirations to maximize freedom of choice, equality of opportunity and participation, and, above all, the realization of subjective rights lead to the politicization of the social fabric, which is then subjected to increasingly restrictive organization.

The alternative theological answers in the West to the Augustinian problematic are the Thomist rejection of it and the Calvinist transformation of it. Both answers share an attachment to the "spiritual-legal" model of society, which retains the juridical character of social unity.

Under the influence of Aristotle, Thomas Aquinas* exchanged the Augustinian conception of a conflictual secular society for a more organic conception of the social order. Certain institutions were traditionally regarded as having already existed before the Fall (original sin*), such as marriage* and the family*, while others, such as private property* and political authority, were thought to have come after it. Aquinas minimized the spiritual distance between them, and this enabled him to have a more unified view of social life. He viewed sinful society as retaining the harmony of a hierarchy of natural ends and functions, each part having its place within the teleological whole. With no internal division, especially as between political and nonpolitical communities, the whole constitutes a real social totality whose common will is directed toward the common good. For Aquinas, the hierarchical harmony and functional integration of society does not make government useless; rather, through legislating, governments creatively define the order of public and private benefits constituting the common good and organize society to pursue them.

Modern Catholic social thought has drawn on non-Thomistic sources, such as Otto von Gierke (1841–1921) and the German historical school, the dialectics of Hegel and Marx, or the antirevolutionary social mysticism of Joseph de Maistre and Louis de Bonald (traditionalism*). However, the Church's official social teaching since Leo XIII has been a concerted attempted to adapt Thomistic social theory to industrialized, technologically advanced, and pluralistic societies. Two concepts have been important: solidarity* and subsidiarity. Originally, "solidarity" referred to the common interests uniting members of the working class but has come to refer to the binding of people together, whether by intimate relationships or by the fact of belonging to the human species (*see* John XXIII, *Pacem in Terris;* Paul VI, *Populorum progressio;* John Paul II, *Laborem exercens* and *Sollicitudo rei socialis*). As for subsidiarity, this principle allows for a balance within any one society between the unity of the whole and the diversity and freedom of the parts. It originated in Leo XIII's declaration (*Rerum Novarum* 28) that the state must not interfere with individuals' and families' pursuit of their own interests, unless protection of the common good requires juridical action. Today, the principle has the more general twofold meaning that 1) societies should not usurp functions performed competently by individuals and 2) societies of a higher order should not usurp functions performed adequately by those of a lower one (*see* Pius XI, *Quadragesimo anno* 78–80; John XXIII, *Mater et magistra* 54–55, 117, 151–52; *Pacem in Terris* 138–40). For the past century, both official and un-

official Catholic thought has articulated the two principles in terms of the natural and legal rights of individuals and collectivities.

After the Reformation, Catholic social theory placed the universal, spiritual society of the Church above civil society. The earlier "Gelasian" dualism (from Pope Gelasius I, fifth century), which conceived a single Christian society with two governments, was replaced by the conception of two self-sufficient societies, ordered to higher and lower, supernatural and natural ends (*see,* e.g., Leo XIII, *Immortale Dei, Libertas praestantissimum, Rerum Novarum;* Pius XI, *Divini illius magistri, Quadragesimo anno*). Since World War II, neo-Thomistic social thinkers, influenced by Jacques Maritain (1882–1973), have attenuated this dualism by making civil society superior to the state from the moral, cultural, and religious point of view. Because the body politic lacks cultural, religious, and social unity, it can be integrated only through the purely "civic or secular faith" that is "the democratic charter," which articulates the rights and duties of the political society and its members (Maritain 1951). The Church does not exercise the claims of a *societas perfecta* ("perfect society") over the secular polity: rather, its claims are mediated through the consciences* of Catholics, its rights being the natural political rights of Catholics as citizens. Conversely, as a social institution, the Church is an integral part of the body politic, enjoying the same public (juridical) recognition as other associations and corporations that contribute to the common welfare.

Unlike Aquinas, Calvin responded to the Augustinian problematic with a reorientation rather than a displacement. For Calvin, the disorder of sinful social relations could not be mitigated by an appeal to natural social teleology but required a different conception of social order as a more exclusively political/juridical order. Such an order was directly based on God's providential rule and conceptualized with ideas (largely borrowed from the Old Testament) of covenant*, divine commandment, and divinely established offices. The unity of civil as well as ecclesiastical society depend on their institutional structuring by God's commandments, which define the rights and duties of every "office" as a vehicle of his revealed law. The common core of Calvinist social thought, in both its English and its American strands, has been an awareness of the diversity, independence, and equality of all social institutions and offices as vehicles of God's law as well as of the covenantal basis of all communities.

In America, however, the covenantalist-pluralist tradition has passed over into increasing political formalism and individualistic voluntarism*. Under the influence of "scientific" political theory (e.g., James

Harrington [1611–77], Montesquieu [1689–1755], and David Hume [1711–76]), American constitutionalism (*see The Federalist*) replaced the Puritan structure of offices with a contrived balance of powers and interests regulated by largely procedural laws, with the result that procedural consensus has come to be considered the key to the political integration of radically diverse social material. In addition, a virulent political contractualism has encouraged the growth of an economic or commercial model of political order wherein rights-bearing consumers contract with elected officials to provide specific services (*see* Robert Nozick's work). By contrast, in Europe, Protestant social theory favors a corporatist Christian pluralism. Against the background of Calvinist Germanic federalism (Althusius, 1557–1638), Dutch "antirevolutionary" neo-Calvinism (G. Groen van Prinsterer [1801–76], Abraham Kuyper [1837–1920], and Herman Dooyeweerd [1894–1977]) has proposed a nonhierarchical, antinaturalist, and evangelical theory of society; the ideas of "sovereignty" and of the functional interdependence of the different social spheres created by God rely on faith in God's sovereignty through Christ. As with the more conservative Catholic statements of social pluralism, the regulative rights of institutions and communities are deemed as important as those of individuals for creating harmony in political society.

● Augustine, *De Civitate Dei*, BAug 33–37.

J. Calvin, *Inst.*, Ed. J. D. Benoît, 5 vols., Paris, 1 957–53, IV, 20.

H. Dooyeweerd, *Vernieuwing en Bezinning om het Reformatorisch Grondmotief*, ed. J. A. Oosterhoff, Zutphen, 1959.

The Federalist, Ed. E. G. Bourne, New York, 1937.

O. von Gierke, *Rechtsgeschichte der deutschen Genossenschaft*, vol. I of *Das deutsche Genossenschaftsrecht*, 4 vols., Berlin, 1868–1913.

G. Groen van Prinsterer, *Ongeloof en Revolutie*, Amsterdam, 1847.

G. W. F. Hegel, *Grundlinien der Philosophie des Rechts*, Ed.

Gans, *Hegels Werke* 8, Berlin, §257–360.

John XXIII, *Mater et magistra* (15 May 1961), *AAS* 53, 401–64.

John XXIII *Pacem in terris* (11 April 1963), *AAS* 55, 257–304.

Leo XIII, *Immortale Dei* (1 November 1885), *Leonis XIII P.M. Acta* V, 118–50.

Leo XIII, *Libertas praestantissimum* (20 June 1888), *Acta* VIII, 212–46.

Leo XIII, *Rerum Novarum* (15 May 1891), *Acta* XI, 97–144.

M. Luther, *Von weltlicher Obrigkeit, wie weit Man ihr Gehorsam schuldig sei*, WA 11, 245–80.

J. de Maistre, *Oeuvres Complètes*, 14 vols., Lyon, 1884–87.

J. Maritain, *Man and the State*, Chicago, 1951.

J. B. Metz, *Glaube in Geschichte und Gesellschaft*, Mayence, 1977.

J. Moltmann, *Kirche in der Kraft des Geistes*, Munich, 1975.

Nicholas de Cusa, *De concordantia catholica*, in *Nicolai Cusani Opera omnia* XIV, Hamburg, 1963.

Pius XI, *Quadragesimo anno* (15 May 1931), *AAS* 23, 177–228.

Thomas Aquinas, *ST* Ia IIae, q. 90, 92, 95, 105, a. 1 and 2; IIa IIae, q. 50, a. 1–3.

Thomas Aquinas, *De regimine principum ad regem Cypri*.

◆ H. X. Arquillière (1955), *L'augustinisme politique*, Paris.

S. S. Wolin (1960), *Politics and Vision*: *Continuity and Innovation in Western Political Thought*, Boston.

R. A. Markus (1970), *Saeculum*: *History and Society in the Theology of St. Augustine*, Cambridge.

P. Riley (1982), *Will and Political Legitimacy*: *A Critical Exposition of Social Contract Theory in Hobbes, Locke, Rousseau, Kant and Hegel*, Cambridge, Mass.

M. Fédou (1986), *Augustin: La "Cité de Dieu,"* 413–26, *DOPol*, 31–40 (bibl.).

S. Stephens (1986), *"Le Fédéraliste," DOPol*, 225–230 (bibl.).

L. Boff (1987), *A Trinidade, a Societade e a Libertaçao*, Petrópolis, Brazil.

J. Milbank (1990), *Theology and Social Theory: Beyond Secular Reason*, Oxford.

J. W. Skillen, R. M. McCarthy (Ed.) (1991), *Political Order and the Plural Structure of Society*, Atlanta.

Pierre Manent (1994), *La cité de l'homme*, Paris.

L. Bégin (1996), "Société," *REPhM* 1411–18.

JOAN LOCKWOOD O'DONOVAN

See also **Augustinianism; Authority; Church and State; Kingdom of God; People**

Socinianism. *See* Unitarianism

Solidarity

The term *solidarity* belonged to legal and philosophical vocabulary before it entered more recently the language of theology.* In the 19th century, social solidarity was no longer viewed as a deed but as a virtue, as the object of a duty (A. Comte, P. Leroux), and as the secular substitute for Christian charity, then as the foundation of morality (L. Bourgeois's *solidarism; see* Debarge 1994).

a)   In its kinship with charity, the term *solidarity* has formed part of the Church*'s social teaching since Pius XII (*Summi Pontificatus*); John XXIII (*Mater et Magistra*); Vatican II*, which made it an important theme in the Pastoral Constitution on the Church in the Modern World; *Gaudium et Spes* (*see* 31:2, 32, 46, 57, and 85:1); and Paul VI (*Populorum Progressio*). Vatican II stressed that through his whole way of life, Christ had chosen to join in the interplay of human solidarities (*Gaudium et Spes* 32:2 and 32:5). Solidarity among men is founded on the unity and equality of their creation*, on their vocation, and on the redemption achieved in Jesus Christ, which makes all men members of his mystic body. In our time, "the duty of solidarity" should be practiced to benefit the undernourished (John XXIII), to favor humanity's development as a group in solidarity with each other (Paul VI), and by choosing to favor the poor (John Paul II). This duty should be performed at all levels of society*, given the globalization of communications (Coste 1990). The Christian call to solidarity was heard vigorously in the theology of the Liberation and in the Polish Solidarnosc Movement.

b)   In Christian dogma*, the principle of solidarity is illustrated by the doctrine of original sin* (the negative solidarity of all men in Adam*) and by that of the redemption (the affirmative solidarity of all men in Christ*). The traditional theological term that most closely corresponds to solidarity is the communion* of saints, for "the achievement of liberty* involves a cohesive order of liberties" (Kasper 1974). Individuals act on each other, not only in the material sphere but also through the influence of their spiritual decisions.

In the realm of soteriology (salvation*), the theology of solidarity has increasingly replaced that of substitution. Both ideas are meant in the biblical idea of representation (a single person represents all by assuming their fate), which can in fact develop to become either substitution (a single person acts in the place of all) or solidarity (a single person acts in the name of those with whom he has assumed by free choice a solidarity of fate). "The faith*'s future will depend to a great extent on the way in which we succeed in reconciling the biblical idea of representation with the modern idea of solidarity" (Kasper). The admirable exchange between Christ and us of justice* and sin* (Gal 3:13; Phil 2:6–9; 2 Cor 5:14, 5:21), of divinity and humanity (fathers* of the church), is founded on the perfect solidarity of the Word* incarnate with God* on the one hand and with men on the other. It is for this reason that Christ is the mediator.

● W. Kasper (1974), *Jesus der Christus,* Mayence.
J.B. Metz (1977), *Glaube in Geschichte und Gesellschaft,* Mayence, (5th Ed. 1992).
H. Peukert (1978), *Wissenschaftstheorie, Handlungstheorie, Theologie,* Frankfurt, 300–10.
H.U. von Balthasar (1980), *Theodramatik III: Die Handlung,* Einsiedeln.
N. Hoffmann (1981), *Sühne: Zur Theologie der Stellvertretung,* Einsiedeln.
E. Tischner (1983), *Éthique de solidarité,* Limoges.
B. Sesboüé (1988), *Jésus-Christ l'unique médiateur,* vol. 1, Paris.
R. Coste (1990), "Solidarité," *DSp* 14, 999–1006.
L. Debarge (1994), "Solidarité," *Cath* 14, 246–50.
C. Hungar (1995), "Solidarität," *EKL* 4, 277–80.
W. Kerber (1995), "Solidaritätsprinzip," *HWP* 9, 1115–17.
A. Wildt (1995), "Solidarität," *HWP* 9, 1004–115.

BERNARD SESBOÜÉ

See also **Justice; Love; Market Economics, Mercy; Moral; Scapegoat; Society; Virtues**

Solovyov, Vladimir

1853–1900

An eminent figure in Russian religious philosophy* and ecclesiologist, moralist, and poet, Solovyov was born in Moscow and died in Uzkoe, near Moscow. The son of a famous historian and the grandson of a priest, he first completed his higher education in the natural sciences and then obtained his doctorate in philosophy. For political reasons his university career lasted only a few years (1876–82). His work can be divided into three periods, each characterized by their main emphases: from 1870, sophiological interests ("Sophia" is seen as a person and constitutes the foremost referent of Wisdom*, of the Virgin, and the Church*; there is also a sophia of the world*); from 1880, preoccupation with ecumenism* and theocracy (harmony of Church and state*); and from 1890, investigations into ethics*, aesthetics, and eschatology*. Intellectual heir to the Slavophiles, Solovyov wanted first to found a twofold philosophical critique—a critique of both positivism and idealism—on the basis of the revealed unity between the material world and the spiritual world (or between the created and uncreated), which he called *unitotality.* In order to define this concept he referred both to hermetic writings and to Plotinus (see *Ist.,* 1992). The sophiology developed by Solovyov was not just theoretical; it was also practical, or "incarnate." It rested on religious experience* (essentially of Christ) and on the use of the notion of "divino-humanity" as the key to interpreting the real. Solovyov was reproached for having greatly borrowed from Gnosticism during this period.

Although Solovyov's early Christology* was distinguished by Sophian thought and influenced by Schelling*, it became more classical after *Lectures on Divine Humanity* (1877–81) and the *The Gospel as the Foundation of Life. Dogmatic Development of the Church* (1886), the first part of *The History and Future of Theocracy,* subsequently expressed Solovyov's ecclesiological intuitions and his ecumenical impulses. Their significance was not really recognized until our own time. Evaluating the ecclesiological positions of the contemporary Russian Church, Solovyov considered that they were marked by the tragic crisis of Raskol, who ended up punishing those who rejected Byzantine influences on the Church (see *Great Controversy,* chap. V). During these same years, Solovyov eagerly sought to distinguish the reasons for separation between the Eastern and Western Churches, and he emphasized that they had no direct, dogmatic foundation. He therefore thought that as a Russian Orthodox he was not in the least separated from Rome—but he carefully distinguished between "Romanity," which was the fundamental ecclesiological principle, and "Latinity," which was a purely cultural reality. Consequently, he did not link himself at all to the Catholic Church: for him, it was sufficient that his Orthodox faith* linked him to the faith of Catholics. His thoughts on the history of Christianity also led him to take a keen interest in Judaism*, Islam, and Buddhism. Solovyov had learned Hebrew and had studied the Talmud and the Kabbala. He also confirmed himself as a Christian moralist with *The Justification of the Good* (1894–96). He also wrote important works of aesthetics. Between 1892 and 1900 he was responsible for the "philosophical section" in the great Russian encyclopedic dictionary *Brockhaus and Efron,* for which he himself wrote almost 200 articles.

At the end of his life Solovyov saw Christian history* in its entirety as a manifestation of the judgment* of God* on the world and the Church. He then expressed a great vision of the end of time, of the return of Christ*, and of the coming of the Kingdom, in the "Court Récit sur l'Antéchrist," which ends his *Three Conversion on War, Progress, and the End of History* (1899–1900). A utopian and a visionary, Solovyov was also a polemicist. He formulated a pertinent critique of the Church of the Middle Ages and of the Church of the modern age in *The Crisis of the Medieval Worldview* (1891) and *On Counterfeits* (1891).

Strictly speaking, Solovyov did represent a school of thought, but he deeply influenced young philosophers such as N. Berdiaev, S. Boulgakov, P. Florenski, A. Losev, N. O. Lossky, S. Troubetskoï, and others. After 60 years of being blacklisted, the heritage of his thought is today in the process of being rediscovered and is generating many studies in Russia and in the West.

• *Oeuvres Complètes,* 10 vols., Saint Petersburg, 1911–13; phototype repro, Brussels, 1966.
French Translations: *Les fondements spirituels de la vie,* 1932; *La crise de la philosophie occidentale,* 1947; *Conscience de la Russie* (14 articles or article excerpts arranged in five categories: 1) Dostoyevski and the vocation of Russia;

2) Poland and Russia; 3) the Russian problem; 4) East and West; 5) The Path of History, Montreux, 1950); *La grande controverse*, 1953; *La Sophia et les autres écrits français*, Lausanne, 1978; *Trois entretiens*, 1984; *Le sens de l'amour, Essais de philosophie esthétique*, 1985; *Le développement dogmatique de l'Église*, 1991; *Leçons sur la divino-humanité*, 1991; *Le judaïsme et la question chrétienne*, 1992; *La justification du bien*, 1997.

♦ F. Rouleau (1990), "Vl. S.," *DSp* 14, 1023–33.

D. Stremooukhoff (1935), *Vl. S. et son œuvre messianique*, Paris, new Ed. s.d., Lausanne.

H.U. von Balthasar (1962), *Herrlichkeit* II/2, Einsiedeln, 647–716.

S.M. Soloviev (1982), *Vie de Vl. S. par son neveu*, Paris.

A. Losev (1983), *Vl. S.*, Moscow.

A. Besançon (1985), *La falsification du bien*, Paris.

G. Przebinda (1992), *Wlodzimierz Solowjow*, Krakow.

M. Tenace (1993), *La beauté, unité spirituelle dans les écrits esthétiques de Vl. S.*, Troyes.

S.V. Soloviev (1994), *Œcuménisme et eschatologie selon S.*, Paris.

M. Herman (1995), *Vie et œuvre de Vl. S.*, Fribourg.

BERNARD DUPUY

See also **Ecumenicism; Intercommunion; Orthodoxy, Modern and Contemporary**

Son of God. *See* Filiation

Son of Man

The epithet *Son of man* is the only one to be placed exclusively in Jesus*' mouth (with the exception of Acts 7:56, where Stephen uses it). It is an enigmatic title, for no trace of it can be found in the Pauline body of writings or in any other New Testament texts outside the four Gospels*. It does appear independently nine times in Matthew and 10 times in Luke, in four passages that are common to both Matthew and Mark (i.e., a total of eight times), and another time in Matthew, which is paralleled in Mark but without the term "the Son of man." In addition to these 28 occurrences, it is found in eight texts that are common to all three synoptic Gospels (Matthew, Mark, and Luke), adding up to another 24 times, and in eight texts common to Matthew and Luke (probably taken from the Q source of the Gospels*), for an additional 16 times. This brings the total number of occurrences in the synoptics to 68. The Gospel of John, in its turn, uses the term 13 times. In all cases, the term is accompanied by the definite article: *the* Son of man.

1. Origins of the Term

The term *Son of man* found favor among the Greek-speaking Christian communities, even though it seems to have derived from Semitic circles and to have resulted from a merger between Psalm 110:1 (quoted in Mk 12:36) and Daniel 7:13. Its formation may have been influenced by its usage in Psalm 8:4 and by exegetic processes analogous to those that were in use in Qumran.

Ezekiel is named 93 times "son of man" (Hebrew *ben 'adam*, i.e., "man"), an expression without an article. In Daniel 7:13, "like a son of man" (Aramaic *bar-nasha*) is closer to "the Son of man" because it refers to the celestial man, a collective body personifying the saints, perhaps the ideal Jewish people. "The Son of man" sometimes replaces a personal pronoun: *me, thou*, or *him*. For a long time, Enoch's *Parables* were used, as was Daniel, to decipher the meaning of "the Son of man." But insofar as the parables began to be regarded as Christian by numerous researchers, they are no longer retained in this study. The messianic Son of man does not appear in the texts in Qumran. In 4 Esdras the expressions "son of man," "like sons of men," "like sons of man," and "likenesses of man" have taken on a messianic sense, meaning the true man of the beginning or of the end of time.

2. The Son of Man and Jesus

Jesus used the term *the Son of man* in the third person as if he were making someone other than himself speak: "The Son of man has come not to be served, but to serve." This epithet (which makes it possible to avoid using either the phrase "Son of God*" or the term "Messiah*") is not a creation of the early churches but goes back to Jesus himself.

In Luke 6:22, those who are persecuted "on account of the Son of man" are said to be blessed, an expression that Matthew 5:11 words differently: "on my account." The Son of man can also be the equivalent of a personal pronoun, as in Ezekiel. The line in Mark 8:38 is a good example of interplay between the pronoun "me" and "the Son of man": "For whoever is ashamed of me... of him will the Son of man also be ashamed." Nonetheless, Jesus never said, "I am the Son of man," and the early communities never proclaimed him as the Son of man. Matthew and Luke have sometimes enlarged and sometimes specified the usage Jesus is supposed to have made of the term *the Son of man,* particularly in the texts that describe his sufferings. For example, Mark 9:1 and Luke 9:27 have "the kingdom of God," whereas Matthew 16:28–29 uses "the Son of man."

3. Range of the Expression

a) Synoptics. The words referring to the Son of man can be divided into three groups. The first group consists of the maxims on the Son of man's actual deeds and authority: forgiveness of sins* (Mk 2:10) and Lordship over the Sabbath* (Lk 6:5). The second group is made up of the declarations that announce that the Son of man must suffer and be spurned. These declarations are absent from the Q tradition found in Matthew and Luke and cannot derive from Judaism*; certain ones may go back to Jesus. The third group is composed of mentions of the Son of man's advent on earth and of the Parousia*. To a great extent the thought they contain corresponds to the apocalyptic expectation in Daniel 7:13–15, where the Son of man is lifted from the earth with the clouds to be given au-

thority by the Ancient of Days. In the apocalyptic passages of the synoptic Gospels (Mt 24; Mk 13; Lk 17, 21) and in passages describing Jesus' appearance before the Sanhedrin, the words "like a son of man" (Dn 7:13) become "the Son of man." Flexible and imprecise, the term *the Son of man* can designate just as easily *the Son* as it can *the man* and cover the other christological epithets.

b) The Fourth Gospel. The Son of man's role is highlighted in John 1–13: the heavens always open on the Son of man (Jn 1:51) and point him out as the bearer of the new and constant covenant*. The only one to have come down from heaven, he will be lifted up on the cross and rise next to the Father* (Jn 3:13–14). The Father gives him the authority of judgment* in his time (Jn 5:27) because he is the Son of man. He bestows everlasting life* (Jn 6:27; *see also* 6:53, in which eating "the flesh of the Son of man" bestows life). Thus, John created an original eucharistic usage.

The Son of man is also the revealer: "When you have lifted up the Son of man, then you will know that I am he" (Jn 8:28). To the man born blind who was healed, Jesus said, "It is he [the Son of man] who speaks to you" (Jn 9:37). At the Last Supper, after Judas departs, Jesus* predicts his death* on the cross: "Now is the Son of man glorified, and in him God is glorified" (Jn 13:31). Pilate's words "Behold the man!" (Jn 19:5), as he brings Jesus out to the crowd, doubtless have a link to the term *the Son of man,* but this epithet could not be put into a pagan's mouth. John also stressed the Son of man's traditional role while accentuating his human role as the new humanity's leader in a descending and ascending movement.

• S. Légasse (1977), "Jésus historique et le Fils de l'homme, aperçu sur les opinions contemporaines," in coll., *Apocalypses et théologie de l'espérance,* Paris, 271–98.
F.J. Moloney (1979), *The Johannine Son of Man,* 2nd Ed., Rome.
B. D. Chilton (1992), "The Son of Man: Human and Heavenly," in *The four Gospels (Festschrift F. Neirynck),* Louvain, vol. 1, 203–18.
M. D. Hooker (1992), "The Son of Man and the Synoptic Problem," in *The four Gospels (Festschrift F. Neirynck),* Louvain, vol. 1, 189–202.

MAURICE CARREZ

See also **Adam; Apocalyptic Literature; Intertestament; Jesus, Historical; Johannine Theology; Messianism; Parousia**

Sophiology

A philosophical and theological movement originating in Russia that continued in émigré circles, sophiology consists of speculations about divine wisdom* ("sophia"), seen as a factor in the union between God* and man or, more generally, between God and His creation*. The principal representatives of the movement were V. Solovyov* (1853–1900), S. Bulgakov (1871–1944), and P. Florenski (1882–1937). The influence of Schelling* is clear. Sophiology cultivates antinomic or paradoxical characterizations of Wisdom: it is both created and uncreated, it is the fourth hypostasis, it is the eternal femininity of God, and so on. Sophiology's principal adversary was V. Lossky (1903–58), who violently attacked its Gnostic tendencies, taking Bulgakov as his chief target. The latter was subjected to censure by the Moscow patriarchate.

• S. Boulgakov (1933), *Agnets bojii*, Paris.
S. Boulgakov (1936), *More about Sophia: Divine Wisdom*, Paris (in Russian).
V. Losski (1936), *Debate on Sophia: 'Memorandum' from S. Boulgakov and the sense of judgment of the Moscow Patriacharte*, Paris (in Russian).
A. Litra (1950), "La 'Sophia' dans la création selon la doctrine de Serge Boulgakov," *OCP* 16, 39–74.
P. Florenski (1975, French trans.), *La colonne et le fondement de la vérité*, Lausanne, 209–54, "La Sophie."
W. Goerdt (1995), "Sophiologie," *HWP* 9, 1063–69 (bibl.).
R. Williams (Ed.) (2000), *Sergii Bulgakov*, Edinburgh.

JEAN-YVES LACOSTE

See also **Orthodoxy, Modern and Contemporary; Solovyov, Vladimir; Wisdom**

Soteriology. *See* Salvation

Soul-Heart-Body

A. Soul (Biblical Theology)

Our concept of the spiritual soul can barely be found in the Bible*: indeed, the Hebrew *nephesh* and the Greek *psukhè* have different meanings.

1) Nephesh in the Old Testament
The term *nephesh,* widely used in the Masoretic Text (755 3), has many meanings.

a) *The Throat, the Seat of Vital Needs.* The concrete sense of "throat, gullet," in Akkadian *napishtou* and in Ugarit *npsh* is not known in Hebrew (Is 5:14; Ps 69:2). The place where food is absorbed (Ps 107:5; Eccl 6:7), seat of need, appetite (Is 29:8), the *nephesh* asks to be filled, satisfied (Prv 6:30); taste is located here (Nm 21:5; Prv 27:7). The throat is also the organ of breathing; thus, *nephesh* sometimes means breath (Jb 41:13), the absence of which is a sign of death* (Gn 35:18; 1 Kgs 17:21). This is what the verb *nâfash* means, "to respire, to breathe" (Ex 23:12; 2 Sm 16:14).

b) Desire and Feelings. From the idea of a being that needs to eat and breathe, we are not far from the idea of desire, even of greed or envy (Prv 10:3, 12:10). From the root *wh* (to desire) or the verb *ns* (to rise), *nephesh* is human desire, man's aspiration for material things (Mi 7:1), human realities (2 Sm 3:21; Jer 22:27), actions (1 Sm 20:4), for God* himself (Ps 25:1, 42:2f.); even evil* is not excluded from this desire (Hos 4:8; Prv 21:10).

On desire, which is like the driving force of human beings (Prv 16:26), depend certain feelings and states of soul, which are thus linked to *nephesh:* hatred (2 Sm 5:8), sadness (Jer 13:17), bitterness (1 Sm 1:10, 1:15), confusion (Ps 6:4), anguish (Ps 31:8), pain (Is 53:11); but *nephesh* can also know love* (Sg 1:7), hope* (Ps 130:5f), joy (Ps 86:4), calm (Jer 6:16), delight (Prv 2:10), consolation (Ps 77:3), and praise* (Ps 35:9, 103:1f.). Impatience (Jgs 16:16) and patience (Jb 6:11) are also part of *nephesh*. In this respect, poetic language speaks of the *nephesh* of God in order to express his desire or feelings (Jgs 10:16; Jer 12:7; Jb 23:13).

c) Life Itself. More broadly, *nephesh* is the life of the individual, often confronted with fragility, limitation, and, in particular, death (Ps 30:4; Prv 8:35f.). Several phrases invoke the term. "To seek" *nephesh* means wanting a person's life, threatening them (Ex 4:19; Ps 35:4) with a view to their annihilation (Gn 37:21; Ps 26:9). "To save" *nephesh* is to save a life from the threat of death (verbs of deliverance: Jos 2:13; 1 Sm 19:11; Ps 34:23). "To keep" *nephesh* is to preserve life, to keep it away from danger (Ps 25:20; Prv 13:3). Life in this sense always has a physical aspect (including for animals: Lv 24:17f.); so *nephesh* can be understood as linked to blood as the symbol of life (Gn 9:4f.; Lv 17:11).

d) Living Being. In later texts, *nephesh* means a human person, an individual; this is so in casuistic laws (Lv 2:1; Nm 15:30) and lists of descendants (Gn 46:15; Ex 1:5). The word is even used for a dead person (Lv 21:1; Nm 6:6) and for living beings other than human (Gn 1:20–24; Ez 47:9). For an individual, *nephesh* with a possessive suffix is often used with the personal pronoun—"my *nephesh* = "myself" and so on—an indicator that *nephesh* has to do with an individual's identity (Gn 19:19f.; Jgs 16:30; Ps 54:6). Approximately a quarter of the uses of *nephesh* can be translated in this way. It is useful to verify these occurrences to see which of the word's meanings are actually in effect.

2) Psukhe *in the Septuagint and the New Testament*

a) Septuagint. For the Septuagint, *psukhe* must have best matched the various nuances of *nephesh* since it has been overwhelmingly adopted in this translation.

Consequently, if we disregard the uses influenced by Platonism, the semantic field of *psukhe* is greatly similar to that of *nephesh,* meaning respiration, life, the seat of desire and of the feelings, the person. Thus, for Lys (1966), *psukhe* represented an adequate translation from the Hebrew, avoiding a body-soul dualism.

In Hellenistic Judaism there was a shift in meaning: with regard to death, the immortality of the *psukhe* seems to have been preferred to a Palestinian belief in resurrection* (Wis 2:22f; 3:1–4; 4 Macc 18, 23). *Psukhe* in this sense would be clearly distinct from its corporeal envelope (Wis 9, 15): the anthropological unity of the human individual found in the Hebrew *nephesh* would be sacrificed in favor of a less tragic vision of death.

b) New Testament. Most of the uses of *psukhe* in the New Testament reflect the meaning used in the Old Testament. It is the individual physical life of human beings (Mt 6:25; Acts 20:10) and animals (Rev 8:9), life that can be given (Jn 10:11, 13:37), killed, or saved (Mk 3:4). The word designates the person (Acts 2:41; Rom 2:9) and also has the sense of a personal pronoun (Mt 11:29; 2 Cor 1:23). The *psukhe* is still the seat of human feelings (Mk 14:34; Jn 12:27; Acts 14:2).

The term sometimes seems to describe the authentic and complete life that the believer experiences in the presence of God (3 Jn 2). In Mark 8:35ff. par., *psukhe* could designate the person himself whose life is the supreme good*. But the text seems to refer to the restoration of this life after death (*see* Jn 12:25): life is not limited to the life experienced in the earthly body (Lk 21:19, 23:43; Heb 10:39), which does not exclude a certain bodily state after death (Lk 16:22; *see* 24:39). The *psukhe* thus seems different from the body (Mt 10:28), even if this distinction does not exactly reflect the dualism of mortal body and immortal soul. This conception is not opposed to the belief in the resurrection of the person (Rev 6:9, 20:4).

Paul hardly uses *psukhe,* except to mean "natural life," or "person." With the adjective *psukhikos* it defines man as left to own vital forces alone, without the gift of the Spirit of God (1 Cor 15:44–49; *see* Jas 3, 15).

● D. Lys (1959), *Nèphèsh: Histoire de l'âme dans la révélation d'Israël,* Paris; (1966) "The Israelite Soul According to the LXX," *VT* 16, 181–228.

E. Schweitzer et al. (1973), "*psukhè,* etc.," *ThWNT* 9, 604–67.

H. W. Wolff (1973), *Anthropologie des AT,* Munich, 25–48.

C. Westermann (1979), "*næfæsh* Seele," *THAT* 2, 17–96.

R. Lauha (1983), *Psychophysischer Sprachgebrauch im AT. Eine strukturalsemantische Analyse von leb, nefesh und rûah,* Helsinki.

H. Seebass (1986), "*næpæsh,*" *ThWAT* 5, 531–55.

E. R. Brotzman (1988), "Man and the Meaning of *nepesh,*" *BS* 145, 400–409.

ANDRÉ WÉNIN

B. Heart (Biblical Theology)

The heart, in Hebrew *lév* or *lévâv* and in Greek *kardia,* represents a central concept of biblical anthropology*. The semantic field is almost the same in the Old and New Testaments.

1) Biblical Meaning of Heart

Aside from a few passages that mention the physiological heart (2 Sm 18:14; Hos 13:8), the biblical terms refer to the notion of the interior: the heart denotes what is hidden within (*qèrèv:* 1 Sm 25:37; Ps 64:7) and what only God* can see (1 Sm 16:7; Ps 44:22). From this comes the parallel with the kidneys (Jer 11:20; Ps 26:2) and the figurative use of the word (Dt 4:11; Jon 2:41; Mt 12:40).

a) Seat of the Emotions. As with us, but even more so, the Hebrews located different human emotions in the heart: joy and sadness (1 Sm 1:8; 1 Kgs 8:66; Acts 14:17; 2 Cor 2:4), love and hatred (Lv 19:17; Dt 6:5; Phil 1:7), desire, confusion and fear (Dt 20:8; 1 Sm 13:14; Jn 14:1; Rom 10:1), anxiety and irritation (Dt 9:6; Jer 12:11; Acts 7:54), confidence and vanity (Ez 28:3; Ps 57:8), and so on.

b) Seat of the Intellect. Quite clearly, the heart has intellectual and rational functions; in this sense, it is closer to what we call the mind. Thus, the heart is the organ of knowledge and understanding (Dt 8:5; Is 6:10; Prv 15:14), linked by this function to the ear (1 Kgs 3; Prv 18:15). It is also the place of attention (Eccl 1:13), of memory (Dt 6:6; Is 57:11; Lk 2:51), of conscious thought (Jer 19:5; Ez 38:10; Mt 9:4; 1 Cor 2:9), and of meditation (Ps 19:15; Prv 15:28). Thought, moreover, is what one "says in one's heart" (Gn 17:17; Dt 7:17; Mt 24:48). The heart remains the place of knowledge (Dt 8:5), of reason* (Hos 7:11; Eccl 10:3), and of wisdom* (1 Kgs 3:12; Jb 9:4).

c) Seat of Will. If the heart is the organ of thought, it is also the place where intentions are born (2 Sm 7; Is 10:7), where plans and projects ripen (Gn 6:5; Ps 20:5; 1 Cor4:5), where decisions are made (1 Sm 14; 1 Cor 7:37; "to speak to the heart," is, according to Wolff [1973], "to incite one to make a decision"; Jgs 19:3; Hos 2:16f.) and from where one can draw courage to complete an action (2 Sm 7; Ps 27:14). We are not far here from moral choices (Is 57:17; Eccl 11:9), from ethical and religious commitment in which the human heart is revealed: the straight (Ps 7:11) and pure (Ps 51:12; 1 Tm 1:5) heart of the one who is "wholeheartedly" bound to the Lord and his law* (Jos 22:5; Jl 2:12f.; Acts 11:23) or, on the other hand, the hardened heart (Ps 95:8) of the one who refuses the word* of God (Is 6:10; Mk 16:14). In this way the heart is linked to one's speech and one's hands, for it is essential that an attitude be without duplicity, in agreement with the heart (Ps 28:3; Sir 12:16; Lk 6:43ff.).

The heart, therefore, represents the center of being, the place where individuals face themselves, with their feelings, their reason, and their conscience, and where they assume their responsibilities by making decisive choices for themselves, whether these are open to God or not. So it is not surprising that the word designates the person (Ps 22:27; Prv 23:15; Col 2:2) and that it is used as an equivalent to a personal pronoun (Ps 27:3; Mk 2:6; *see* section A).

2) Theologically Significant Uses of "Heart"

A major concept in biblical anthropology, the heart is used in particular to describe certain aspects of the relationship between a human being and God. Thus, God knows the heart of human beings. He is the one who probes the kidneys and the heart (Ps 7:10; Prv 15:11; Lk 16:15; Rom 8:27), a theme that can be found in Wisdom literature. However, it is in their hearts that human beings accept God or do not (Dt 6:5f.; Lk 8:15).

a) Hardened Heart. In the Exodus traditions, the hardening* of the heart is Pharaoh's obstinate refusal in the face of YHWH's desire to liberate Israel (Ex 7:13, 8:32).

His stubbornness is reinforced by God's determination in such a way that the narrator can say that YHWH hardens the heart of his adversary (9:12, 14:4). The narrator thus describes the negative consequence of God's desire for salvation* for a heart whose rebellion finally contributes to the revelation* of divine glory* (7:3ff.). For the prophets* and in the Gospels*, this motif is used in order to denounce the refusal of the word of God (Is 6:9f., cited in Mt 13:14f. par.; see Ps 95:8; Mk 3:5), the stubbornness of an evil heart that does not want to listen (Jer 3:17; Ez 3:7; see Za 7:12; Mk 6:52).

b) Conversion of Heart and a New Covenant. If the sin* of a people is thus engraved onto its heart (Jer 17:1), it is the heart that must be transformed by conversion* (Jl 2:12f.). Here the Bible draws on several images: the circumcision of the heart (Dt 10:16; Jer 4:4; Rom 2:29), whose infidelity represents a refusal of the covenant* made to Abraham (uncircumcised heart: Lv 26:40f.; Jer 9:25; Acts 7:51), the inscription of the Law on the heart (Jer 31:33; see Heb 8:10) or the gift of a new heart, a heart of flesh* instead of a heart of stone (Ez 11:19; see Jer 32:39f.). It is the integral renewal of the being that is thus linked to the promise* of a new covenant. This is why Paul situates in the heart the place where the Holy Spirit* comes to dwell (Rom 5:5; 2 Cor 1:22; Gal 4:6).

c) Heart of God. "Heart" has similar meanings in the Old Testament when it is applied anthropomorphically to God (26 times). The place of his desire, of his pleasure and his will (1 Sm 2:35; Jer 32:41), of his plans (2 Sm 7:21; Ps 33:11), his memory (Jer 44:21), and his secret deliberations (Gn 8:21; Jb 10:13), the heart of God beats to the rhythm of his feelings for man: solicitude (Jb 7:17), affliction (Gn 6:6), regret (Lam 3:33), and compassion (Hos 11:8; see Mt 11:29).

● P. Dhorme (1923), *L'emploi métaphorique des noms de parties du corps en hébreu et en akkadien*, Paris, 109–28.
F. Baumgärtel, J. Behm (1938), "kardia," *ThWNT* 3, 609–16.
H. W. Wolff (1973), *Anthropologie des AT*, Munich, 68–95.
R. Lauha (1983), *Psychophysischer Sprachgebrauch im AT. Eine strukturalsemantische Analyse von leb, nefesh und rûah*, Helsinki.
P. Mourlon-Beernaert (1983), *Cœur—langue—mains dans la Bible* (CEv 46), Paris.
H. J. Fabry (1984), "leb lebab," *ThWAT* 4, 413–51.

ANDRÉ WÉNIN

C. Body (Biblical Theology)

In the Old Testament, the horizon of promises* for a long time remained internal to this world, where bodies live. This perspective began to change right before the New Testament until the radical threshold that it crossed with the bodily resurrection* of Jesus*. But no period in biblical history stopped seeing the body as the site of salvation*.

1) Old Testament

a) A Corporeal Horizon. Without being absolutely denied, the afterlife (sheol*) is of no interest to the people of the Old Testament (Ps 6:6, 115:17; Is 38:18). Obedience to the Torah is conditioned by corporeal benefit or harm (Lv 25; Dt 28), hence the intensity of the life of the righteous.

Stories and poems make strong feelings resound. There is no word for "body," but parts of the body express feelings or gestures (*feet:* moving, *see* Is 52:7; *hand* or *arm:* action, *see* 53:1; *nose:* anger, *see* Ps 30:6; *face:* presence; *bone:* substance, *see* Gn 29:14; 2 Sm 5:1, etc. [Dhorme 1923; Wolff 1973]).

The believer can verify the promises only in the time-space of his body. He transcends the body only through his offspring, something that is in itself very uncertain (sterility, death in family, conflicts). Family* and nation (also understood as family) extend the body outside itself (Wheeler Robinson 1936), but community fractures and enmities—the typical forms of which are found in the Psalms*—reduce the individual body to its solitude: "I can count all my bones" (Ps 22:17). A place is thus made for the word of the prophet*.

b) Sphere of the Commandments. Some extracts from the Torah are applied to the body (Ex 13:9; Dt 6:8). A large part of the commandments focuses on the sphere of the body: purity* or impurity of food, clothing (Lv 17:15; 19:19c; Dt 22:5, 22:11f.), hair (Lv 19:27), hygiene (Lv 13; Dt 23:13ff.), environment (Dt 22:6f.). To observe these commandments promotes health (Dn 1:1–15). The dominant theme of one of these codes is "sanctity" (Lv 17–26): since no body is profane, boundaries are placed between bodies, between bodies and things, between Israel* and other people. With the risk of ritualism and sometimes magic, this includes an ethics* of respect. These codes point to a strong feeling of modesty. Moreover, sexual shame only emerged after sin (Gn 2:25, 3:7, 3:11). Poems show the body of man (Sg 5:10–16) and woman (Sg 6:4–7, 7:2–7) without inhibition.

The law* of the new covenant* (Jer 31:31–34) is, of course, to be inscribed in hearts (v. 33): not because this will regulate internal dispositions but because bodily gestures will henceforth be dictated by transformed hearts instead of by an external being.

c) Body and Its Origins.   Creation* makes God* responsible for the whole sensible world and therefore the body. He who is at the origin (Ps 139:3f.) assures it of specifics (Ps 104, 148:8f.), such as nourishment, respiration, and propagation. Although human beings are similar to animals*, they mostly resemble God (Gn 1:26f.: "image" means more than the capabilities of the soul) and were the only ones to receive God's breath (Gn 2:7). Nevertheless, the difference (Gn 2:20b) between human beings and animals (heart of ethics) connects to their solidarity (Gn 6:18–7, 3; 9:9ff.; Ps 36:7; Jon 3:7f.).

d) Fate of the Body.   Biblical man does not take a stoical view of his ultimate bodily fate: he rather sees in it something that can move God to pity (Ps 89:48, 39:6f.). He does not defy death*. It was only later that the annals took an interest in this form of heroism, or even in suicide (2 Macc 14:37–46), in the face of the enemy. In particular, it would be a long time before death was preferred to disobeying the Torah (1 Macc; 2M; Dn). The Psalms do not record the fate of the individual God allows to die; only the saved are spoken of. Also later, the book of Esther tells of the plan to annihilate the whole of Israel at once (Est 4:6–13). After many martyrs had responded to a forced Hellenization, a light appeared: the Creator restored the bodies of those who had lost them by remaining loyal to him (2 Macc 7:9–14, 22–36; 12:44; 14:46; *see* Dn 12:2).

2) New Testament

a) Healing Bodies.   The signs that Jesus, questioned by John the Baptist, gives to announce the coming of the Messiah* appear in the healing* of bodies (Mt 11:4f.). He is never seen avoiding bodies for any kind of spiritual reason. However, each story discreetly orients sufferers and witnesses toward healing "the whole man (*holon*)" (Jn 7:23). After the resurrection of Jesus the disciples continue to perform the acts of the Master (Acts 5:15, 19:12). For the evangelists, miracles* proceed from the resurrection of Jesus, whether they come before it or after it.

b) Teaching.   In the Sermon on the Mount ethical attitudes are represented by actions (Mt 5:24, 5:40, 5:47; 6:6, 6:17, etc.). If it might be necessary to lose an eye or a hand rather than sin (Mt 5:29f.), this would be in order to avoid losing "the whole body" (v. 30). Notwithstanding such amputations, it can be noted that, among the demands made in Matthew 5–7, that of sacrificing one's life is not one. Food and clothing should not be a cause of anxiety since priority is given to the Kingdom* (Mt 6:33). This does not represent a contempt for these needs because we are certain that God will take care of them, down to the very hairs on one's head (Mt 10:30). Jesus is reproached for not being an ascetic (Mt 11:18; *see* Mt 9:14). His most urgent commandments have to do with caring for the bodies of others: naked, hungry, imprisoned (Mt 25:31–46). Matthew 10:28 implies the possibility of a person losing his body without losing his "soul."

Jesus does not rush toward his death; certain martyrs were less horrified by it than him. He surrenders himself to death only when he sees that the "hour" has arrived, having escaped death until that moment (Jn 7:30, 8:20, 8:59, 10:39). He says openly that a violent death threatens the disciples (Mt 10:21f., 23:34, 24:9; Jn 16:2). This will not be provoked but will come only from the hate of the world* for those who manifest the truth*. Before dying, Jesus leaves not only his words but his very body to nourish his disciples.

c) Paul and John.   Paul sees the body in the perspective of creation: the body that dies is a seed (1 Cor 15:36ff., 42ff.), what is revived is not the spirit but "a spiritual body" (*pneumatikon:* 1 Cor 15:44). The image of the seed speaks of a kinship: the original body is therefore not evil. The words "body of sin*" (Rom 6:6; *see* 6:12ff.) point to historical subservience and not to the body's nature* as such. To "pommel" the body," to "subdue it" (1 Cor 9:27), is to tear it away from what denatures it. The specifically Pauline distinction between "body" and "flesh*," despite inevitable but instructive superimpositions, is a good lead. Flesh (especially in Rom 7–8) is not the inanimate body but the body outside of the spirit. The flesh also includes the "psyche." But it was precisely in this flesh (Rom 8:13) that Christ* was sent, to meet our "body of flesh" (Col 1:22). The sharing of the bread and the cup—of Christ's body and his blood—is the principal site for the Pauline doctrine of the body. "You are the body of Christ" (1 Cor 12:27): these words can be spoken to a group but never to an individual. The Christian is a "member" (*melos:*

Rom 12:5; 1 Cor 6:15, 12:12, 12:27) of this body. There is truly a body to the extent that each member fully performs a specific function. Christ's unicity (the "head": 1 Cor 11; Eph 1:22; Col 1:18; etc.) grounds that of the members: this teaching corrects the syncretic notions favored by the Corinthians and imposes on each member the whole force of his or her own calling. This body of Christ lives in time* and grows over time. (Eph 4:16).

The fourth gospel designates the body of Christ as being, from the beginning, the true Temple* (Jn 2:21). In the water that comes out of the wounded side (Jn 19:34) is recognized the river that Ezekiel saw coming out of the temple (Ez 47:2). The bodily signs that Jesus gives through healing (Bethesda, Siloam) and through feeding foreshadow the post-Easter sacraments*.

● P. Dhorme (1923), *L'emploi métaphorique des noms de parties du corps en hébreu et en acadien,* Paris.
H. W. Robinson (1936), *The Hebrew Conception of Corporate Personality,* BZAW 66.
W. H. Schmidt (1964), "Anthropologische Begriffe im Alten Testament," *EvTh* 24, 374–88.
E. Schweizer (1964), "*sôma,*" *ThWNT* 7, 1024–91.
H. W. Wolff (1973), *Anthropologie des Alten Testaments,* Munich, chap. I (4th Ed. 1984).
Coll. "ACFEB" (1983), *Le corps et le corps du Christ dans la première épître aux Corinthiens,* Paris, especially D. Lys, "L'arrière-plan et les connotations vétérotestamentaires de *sarx* et de *sôma,*" 47–70.

PAUL BEAUCHAMP

See also **Animals; Anthropology; Creation; Death; Ethics; Flesh; Healing; Miracle; Pauline Theology; Resurrection of Christ; Resurrection of the Dead; Sacrament; Sheol; Temple**

D. Historical Theology

1) Patristic Origins

a) The first Christian writings focus primarily on holding together the major affirmations of faith*: man created in the image of God*, Christ* as the incarnate Son, and the resurrection* of the dead. For this they borrow concepts and categories of thought from contemporary Judaism* but also from philosophies* of the time, especially Stoicism*. This explains how authors of this period differ in part from ancient biblical anthropology* and from its notion of the heart, teaching that man is composed of a soul and a body while nevertheless avoiding a Platonic-like dualism. They never consider man's corporal condition as a fall or the result of sin.

b) During the second and third centuries the debate between Gnosis* and Platonism* forced orthodox writers to specify more clearly what it was that the Christian doctrine of the soul and body explained.

Gnostics, Platonic thinkers, and Hermetists declared that human souls (at least some of them) were divine by nature, that they existed separately from the body, and that their embodiment represented a fall from their true condition. Man, that is the soul, therefore has to separate itself from matter in order to return to the divine world, which corresponds to his real nature. For Gnostics the corporeal universe was not the work of the supreme God but of a demiurge, identified as the God of the Old Testament, and resulted from a metahistorical fall that occurred in the world of the divine "eons."

Justin rejected the idea that the soul could have an affinity with the divine in such a way that a person could seize it and find happiness by means of the intellect alone (*Dial. Avec Tryphon 4*). He clearly affirmed the innovative character of the Christian message concerning bodily resurrection: "If the Savior only proclaimed eternal* life for the soul, what would he bring us that was different from Pythagoras, Plato, and others? In reality he came to bring man a new, extraordinary hope*. Was it not extraordinary and new that God promised, not to preserve immortality to immortality, but to make what was mortal immortal?" (*De la Résurr.* 10, Holl 109). Irenaeus* of Lyons was, at the end of the second century, the main defender of the tradition* of the Church in the face of Gnosticism. His teachings revolved around the unity of God and his plan for salvation*: the transcendental God is himself the creator God who, thanks to his two "hands," the Logos (Word*) and Spirit, persons* different from himself, but who are coeternal and one with him, made the world and performed the whole economy of salvation. Human beings are creatures, and do not have any element in themselves which is divine by nature. They are composed of a body (corruptible but call to incorruption) and a soul (the breath of life that animates the body), created "in the image and likeness of God," that is, in the image of the coming incarnate Logos. Nevertheless, the divine "likeness" will be realized in human beings only if, by consenting to divine grace*, they receive in themselves a third element, that of the Spirit.

The anthropology of Irenaeus is not trichotomist: the Spirit is not an element of man's nature but a free participation in divine life. Nevertheless, it is not a gift that is simply added to nature since for Irenaeus man is not really what he should be, a "perfect man" according to the design of the Creator, unless he has this divine gift within him, which is necessary to reach true life, the vision of God.

It should be noted that the conflict of orthodox theology with Gnosis cannot be reduced to anthropology: an entire Christology* and a cosmology are also at stake, which clearly shows that debates concerning the soul and the body cannot be separated from other theological questions. Irenaeus's synthesis (by referring to the divine project of creation*, or to the recapitulation in Christ) is a prime example.

c) Tertullian* teaches an anthropology similar to that of Irenaeus. He also focuses on the unity of the human compound, in which the soul blends with the body in a "complete mixture," *mixis di'holôn.* Like Irenaeus he distinguishes the divine breath (*afflatus*), which constitutes the human soul, from the divine Spirit (*spiritus*) given to those who are worthy of it. The Spirit is not a constitutive part of human nature, but the body and soul "are worthless" without it. The decisive formula *caro salutis cardo* ("the flesh is the axis of salvation," *Res.* VIII 2) sheds light both on Tertullian's Christology (treatise *De Carne Christi*) and on his anthropology (the entire treatise *De Resurrectione Carnis* is an apologia for the flesh—e.g., "It is in flesh, with flesh, and by flesh, that the soul contemplates all that the heart contemplates"; XV, 3).

d) With the Alexandrians Clement of Alexandria and Origen*, theology was influenced by Platonism. Inspiration, however, remained fundamentally Christian; and if it drew from philosophy, this was both with a missionary purpose and in order to enrich Christian thought with secular elements that were deemed convergent. Clement himself proved to be not very systematic and continued to borrow much from Stoicism. For him, the tension between body and soul belongs to the unity of man: "Certainly, the best part of man is the soul, and the body is inferior. But the soul is not good by nature, and neither is the body evil by nature. Man is created in the world of senses; he is made by the synthesis of different things, which do not, however,

contradict each other: the soul and the body. All things come from one same God" (*Strom.* 4, 26; PG 8, 1373–76) Origen's work is more speculative. In order to understand it, one really has to study the context in which *Peri Arkhôn* was written, that is, the conflict with Gnosticism, and at its primary intention, which is the recounting of a story of salvation in which the freedom of the creature is given its full place. According to Origen, the concrete condition of each spiritual creature results from a prior choice made by his free will. In *Peri Arkhôn,* therefore, he discloses that from all eternity God created a world of spirits united to subtle natural bodies, ethereal creatures, equipped with free will, and all equal. Sometimes they sin out of negligence, and they turn away, through satiety, from divine contemplation*. Depending on the seriousness of their sin, their bodies assumed a more or less thick and obscure form. Those who sinned less gravely retained bodies that were relatively subtle and became angels*; they were allowed to remain close to God and to form his court. Finally, the ethereal bodies of those who had committed a sin of medium gravity would be transformed into human bodies, into the form they take in our current world. Through practice of the Christian life and through contemplation, human beings can, however, free themselves from the weight of their earthly condition and find again something of their original condition. At the end of time, risen bodies will find their subtle condition and become spiritual bodies (*see* 1 Cor 15:42–49).

Origen's texts require very careful interpretation. In substance, H. Crouzel (*Origène,* Paris, 1985) offers the interpretation adopted here. But many hold to the exegesis that was already championed by Origen's first adversaries, which claims that the corporeal condition, without being evil in itself, was only a temporary medicinal punishment between the fall and the final restoration (apocatastasis*), and it was no longer possible to speak of a salvation of the flesh. Man has three elements: body, soul, and spirit. The spirit is the divine element in man, a free gift from God that leads the soul toward good. The soul has a superior and an inferior part. The former is the intellect (*noûs*) or the hegemonic faculty (*hègemonikon*); in biblical contexts, Origen also calls it the heart (*kardia*). The intellect is the center of free will and of spiritual sensibility. It alone is created in the image of God, of the Logos (and not the body, as Irenaeus, who retained Judeo-Christian categories, believed). If it submits itself to the Spirit, it becomes spiritual, contemplative, and reaches "resemblance"; it then even spiritualizes the inferior part of the soul, added to the soul after the fall and which corresponds to *thumos* (irascible appetite) and *epithumia* (appetite of concupiscence) of Platonic psychology. As for the body (*sôma*), it is a characteristic element of all creatures, and only the Holy Trinity* is entirely incorporeal. But the body can assume various states: earthly (human beings here below), diabolical, or ethereal and luminous (the angels or the righteous after the resurrection). With regard to this spiritual condition of the body, one can speak of relative "incorporeality." Terminological hesitation over this point explains the various interpretations offered of Origen's thought.

His theology and anthropology, clarified by elements that could not be incorporated into the orthodoxy of the following centuries, was to have a great influence on Christian thought and spirituality, in the churches* of both East and West. The earthly body and the sensible (world) are not condemned, but they are relativized. Created by the one God, they constitute the world in which the "true realities"—the celestial and eschatological mysteries*—are embodied and are symbolized according to the modalities that belong to the temporary and fallen condition of intelligent creatures. And these creatures, instead of stopping there, must, via these modalities, rise up toward the true realities in and of themselves. The tension between soul and body can therefore serve to describe the spiritual* life as the elevation of man.

e) Origen's contribution was clarified by the works of the Fathers* of the fourth and fifth centuries, in particular the great Cappadocians Basil* of Caesarea, Gregory* of Nazianzus, and Gregory* of Nyssa, at a time when Christian thought was achieving form through combating the major Trinitarian and christological heresies*. The highlighting of the saving role of Christ's flesh and the insistence on the corporeal union between the risen Christ and Christians, who had become his members through communion* in the eucharistic body, went to explain, contrary to all Platonism, the dignity of the body and its participation in salvation. The Fathers were able to construct an anthropological synthesis that obviously varied greatly depending on the author but that might be systematized in the following way:

It is man, and not a part of man, who is in the image of and resembles God. And it is all of man that is saved (in accordance with the principle: all that was assumed by Christ is saved; *see*, e.g., Gregory of Nazianzus, *Ep.* 101, PG 37, 181). The human soul, while being intellectual and immortal by nature, is not divine by nature: it is only capable of being gradually deified, through the free participation that God grants it (man, through grace, becomes what God is by nature; *see*, e.g., Gregory of Nyssa, *Orat. In beat.*, PG 44, 1280 d). Matter, which is also created by God, is good and able to take

part in the deification of the soul. The bodily condition of man does not result from sin, from a fall, but is the effect of a positive disposition of God. One can often note in the Fathers, especially in their commentaries on the creation story, an amazement before the material creation and the perfection of the human body.

Nevertheless, the Fathers distinguish two successive states in material creation and in the human body: the earthly, "psychic" condition and the eschatological condition, which came first in God's plan of creation. The eschatological condition alone corresponds to the primitive will of God over a creation of which it is (by virtue of this correspondence) the "true nature." In its earthly state, dependent on the sin* of the first parents, the human body is "animal," psychic," and corruptible. It dons "garments of skin" (patristic exegesis* in Gn 3:21): it needs to nourish itself, to sexually reproduce, and is subject to suffering and death*. In fallen man there is a tendency to give in to the senses in a way that is opposed to the Logos, to the creative thought-will of God. Yet even in this condition marked by the fall, the role of sensible realities and of the body is far from being purely negative. Creatures reveal the Creator and, sanctified by the Church, become "mysteries," "sacraments." The body can and must become an auxiliary of the soul in its spiritual battle and in its search for God, through an ascesis of transfiguration and not of destruction. The body is thus felt, in its present state, as an ambiguous reality, "both friend and enemy" (Gregory of Nazianzus, *Disc. 14;* PG 35, 865 *bc*). After the resurrection the body will be a spiritual and glorious body, transfigured by the power of the Spirit.

This patristic anthropology, marked by the habits of Platonic thought, remains essentially Christian. Nevertheless, the theology of the Fathers did not limit itself to correcting philosophy, even if this correction was considerable, as in the case of the reevaluation of the body. The originality of its understanding of man presupposes another perspective: to consider man, that is, the soul-body unity, in the horizon of salvation (which is quite clearly shown by the eschatological motif of the resurrection of the flesh) and of liberty (which implies a spiritual life and the possibility of union with Christ).

f) We must mention here a whole spiritual tradition and at its head the mysterious author of the *Homilies* attributed to Macarius of Egypt. This tradition adopts a psychophysical conception of the heart and one that is closer to the biblical notion. It thus touches on certain trends of Greek medicine and philosophy, especially Stoicism, which made the physical heart into the organ and center of the *noûs*. The heart then appears as the unifying center of the person, the organ of the intellect and of profound desires that gives man's life its fundamental orientation. "Grace, once it seizes the heart's pastures, reigns over all members and thoughts. For, it is in it that the spirit and all the thoughts of the soul and its hope* are located. Through it, grace spreads to all the members of the body" (Macarius, *Homilies* 15, PG 34, 589). This notion also belongs to the great Eastern spiritual thinkers, for whom the heart is the place of the highest spiritual experiences; and it can be found again in the 13th and 14th centuries in the Hesychasm* of the Athos monks. It inspired the psychophysical method of prayer*. The prayer of the heart also reveals an understanding of man.

2) Western Tradition

a) Augustine's work had its origins in his response to Manicheanism* and in a Christian reinterpretation of Platonic tradition. His vast output was bound to have a deep influence on Western theology and spirituality. In terms of the soul, it implied elaboration and modification.

First, Augustine established the notion of a completely immaterial intellectual substance that he calls "spirit." He clearly maintains the distinction between the uncreated spirited and the created spirit but emphasizes the kinship between them—this is why he represents the beginning of a less apophatic theology than that of the Greek Fathers. The traditional theme of man in the image of God is developed in an original manner in the form of an analogy* between the soul and the Trinity. In the *Confessions* (XIII, 11) the soul is likened to the Father, the Son, and the Spirit, respectively, through its being, its understanding, and its will. The *De Trinitate* extensively describes another threefold scheme, that of memory, intellect, and will.

The privilege of the soul over the body is now certain: it is by turning inward that the soul discovers God. "It is in the inner man that truth* lives" (*De Vera Religione* XXIX, 72), but this link between introspection and conversion* concerns only the soul. Because God and the soul are of the order of spirit, there is no question of an actual deification of the body: Augustine saw the eschatological glorification of the resurrected body much less as its transformation by the Spirit than did Ambrose* of Milan and the Greek Fathers. His pessimistic conception of the bodily condition is found in his thoughts on the original* sin and can also be explained, perhaps, by the polemical character of many of his writings on grace and freedom*. As for the deification of the soul, he considers it intentional union (on the order of knowledge) rather than the energetic compenetration proposed by the Greek

Fathers, who readily compared the process to the penetration of a branding iron by fire.

b) It was particularly Aristotelianism* that Thomas* Aquinas used to construct theology as a "sacred science," and his anthropology is differentiated from Platonism. Thomas's theology developed in an intellectual climate in which beatitude* was understood as contemplation of God, beatific* vision. However, this emphasis never yields to a division of man: Thomas's anthropology is deeply unifying. The link between the soul and body is not the compound of two substances that can survive by themselves. The soul is the form of the body, an Aristotelian formula that nevertheless calls for an original interpretation: the soul is form of the body (and remains one with it), but this form is also the spirit of man, an individual spirit (and does not come from the outside, from an impersonal spirit, like the Aristotelian *noûs* that comes "through the door").

In this context Thomas cannot retain the fullness of the biblical meaning of the word "heart": for him it is only a metaphorical equivalent of will. However, Thomist psychology does not ignore the realities evoked by the biblical notion; it simply analyzes them through categories other than the heart (e.g., *intellectus* and *voluntas ut natura*).

c) Spiritual writings would also have genuine repercussions in anthropology. Such was the case in the 17th century with the work of Cardinal Bérulle*, who developed a devotion to the humanity of Jesus* and to his heart. All the states that Jesus experienced as a man express his perfect adoration of God. These states, which belong to his inner life, where divine and human activity mingle, are now perpetually present in Christ, and the contemplative life allows the believer to interiorize and adhere to them. Bérulle's work is nourished by the great patristic and mystical tradition and would inspire the entire French school of spirituality (devotion to the Sacred Heart of Jesus).

Other examples can be cited, also belonging to the 17th century, of a spirituality of the heart that comes close to the biblical concept. In the school of cordial prayer, represented by Jean Aumont, Maurice Le Gall de Querdu, and the members of the Breton missions, the notion of the heart approximated that of the Byzantine Hesychastic tradition: contrasted with cerebral reflection is the deep inner life of the reunified being, which is seated in the heart. During the same century, Pascal*'s anthropology also attests to the importance of the heart.

d) The problem that modern thought poses to theological anthropology is that of the distance that it places between itself and theological anthropology's central themes. In the first place, the theme of the heart managed to persist during the Enlightenment and beyond only by submitting itself to certain emphases and inflections that deprived it of its biblical resonances. Pietist theology is a theology of the heart, which sets itself the task of an "affective transposition of [Christian] doctrine" (J. Pelikan), but its emotional a priori never helped it develop a Christian logic of affectivity (J. Edwards* provided the only exception to the rule, within the context of the "great awakening"), no more than it led Shleiermacher* to do so, despite the primacy that he gave to feeling. The theme of the body, on the other hand, was subject to many evolutions during the 18th century: there was a rejection of the modified hylemorphism that had allowed Thomas Aquinas to express the fundamental affirmations of Christian anthropology as well as a Cartesian reduction of the corporeal to an "extended thing" that can be put aside without altering the essence of the self (the indirect consequence that is possible for a materialism in which man, like animals in Descartes*, is, in fact, only an extended thing). Finally, the soul, in terms of the various concepts used—a thinking thing, monad, spirit—appears more and more as a worldly principle of rationality and not as an index in man of an eschatological destiny: moreover, it is rather introverted (as, e.g., with the Leibnizian monad), so that the idea of a salvation promised to the body no longer gives rise to great theological interest.

- A. Guillaumont (1950), "Le sens des noms du cœur dans l'Antiquité," in *Le Cœur, Et Carm,* 41–81, new Ed., in *Études sur la spiritualité de l'Orient chrétien,* SpOr 66, 13–67.
- J. Chatillon (1952), "*Cordis affectus* au Moyen Age," *DSp* 2/2, 2288–300.
- L. Cognet (1952), "Le cœur chez les spirituels du XVIIe s.," *DSp* 2/2, 2300–2307.
- A. Guillaumont (1952), "Le 'cœur' chez les spirituels grecs à l'époque ancienne," in "*Cor et Cordis affectus,*" *DSp* 2/2, 2281–88.
- Cl. Tresmontant (1961), *La métaphysique du christianisme et la naissance de la philosophie chrétienne: Problèmes de la création et de l'anthr., des origines à saint Augustin,* Paris.
- F. Chirpaz (1965), *Le corps,* Paris.
- W. Biesterfeld (1974), "Herz," *HWP* 3, 1100–1113.
- P.J. van Schaick (1974), "Le cœur et la tête: Une pédagogie par l'image populaire," *RHSp* 50, 457–78.
- H. de Lubac (1979), "Morale e mistica: L'antropologia tripartita nella tradizione cristiana," in *Mistica et Misterio cristiano,* Opera omnia, vol. 6, Milan, 59–117.
- A. Vergote (1979), "Les corps: Pensée contemporaine et catégories bibliques," *RTL* 10, 157–75.
- T. Borsche et al. (1980), "Leib, Körper," *HWP* 5, 173–85; "Leib-Seele-Verhältnis," *HWP* 5, 185–206.
- B. Sesboüé (1982), "La résurrection du Christ et le mystère chrétien du corps: Points de repère théol. en forme de propositions," *Les quatre fleuves* 15–16, Paris, 181–203.
- Pl. Deseille (1984), "Introduction," *Les "Homélies spirituelles" de saint Macaire,* SpOr 40, 22–26.
- H. Sonnemanns (1984), *Seele-Unsterblichkeit-Auferstehung,* Fribourg.
- E. Behr-Sigel (1989), *Le lieu du cœur: Initiation à la spiritualité de l'Église orthodoxe,* Paris.
- A. Sauvy (1989), *Le miroir du cœur: Quatre siècles d'images savantes et populaires,* Paris.
- R. Beulay (1990), *L'enseignement spirituel de Jean de Dalyatha, mystique syro-oriental du VIIIe s.,* Paris, 459 s.
- X. Lacroix (1992), *Le corps de chair: Les dimensions éthique, esthétique et spirituelle de l'amour,* Paris.
- F. Ricken et al. (1995), "Seele," *HWP* 9, 2–89.

PLACIDE DESEILLE

3) Contemporary Viewpoints

It is first of all to philosophies of the body that recent theology owes its concern for reorganizing a biblical vision of man as well as the conceptual means for undertaking this reorganization. In the corporeal experience of effort, Maine de Biran had already discerned an affirmation of the self that was as elementary and fundamental as the Cartesian *cogito* (*see* Henry 1965). Husserl's inquiries (*see* Franck 1981) were to bring him to posit a fertile distinction between the "organic body" (*Körper,* the human body as object) and the "body itself" or "flesh" (*Leib,* the body as experienced by a subject). Whether pursued by M. Merleau-Ponty or by M. Henry, philosophical consideration of the body had three benefits: 1) it brought to an end the unsatisfying representation of a self that "has" a body; 2) replacing it with the concept of a self that "is" a body/flesh and of a body that is a self, thus allowing a consideration of the transcendence of the self in relation to the domain of objective realities; henceforth, 3) the phenomenological approach allowed a renewed affirmation of the soul (e.g., Henry 1966, 1987), one that was capable of reappropriating the principal meanings of Thomist theory without falling back on the concepts of a metaphysics of substance. A notably different approach, neo-Hegelian in nature, also allowed Claude Bruaire (1968) to develop a philosophy that was able to accept the idea of a salvation intended for the body while proceeding (1983) toward an affirmation that was separate from the being of the spirit. Because they avoided the twofold reduction of the self to a thinking thing and of the body to an object, these contributions could not avoid disagreeing with the discourses that classically identified the essential self with intellectual activity. In a period in which theology could no longer take for granted that the Greek concept of the *noûs* truly accounts for divine life, philosophy could no longer take for granted that man exists first of all in a noetic mode. In *Being and Time,* Heidegger* attributes to "existence," to the "there," two modalities of the same origin and importance, one being understanding (*Verstehen*) but the other being the *Befind-*

lichkeit, which in fact designates fact the foundation of emotional life and is similar to the Augustinian concept of *affectio.* Interpreting what he does not call "existence" but "life," understood as original immediacy, M. Henry (1963) was brought to posit the unconditional primacy of pathos and emotion. And it is possible that another way to consider immediacy, in the manner of E. Levinas, is to consider the privilege of emotion; in fact, ethics*, which constitutes the first philosophy because of the demands that the other person lays on the self simply because his face appears before me, can understand only because it is aroused by pathos. Here as elsewhere (e.g., in M. Scheler's meditation on the *ordo amoris* and his explicit reference to Pascal*), it is toward an anthropology of the heart that the concepts are tending.

The theological repercussions of such forms of inquiry could hardly fail to be beneficial ones: 1) For theologies in which the resurrection of the body appeared in effect to be an appendix to a more fundamental doctrine, that of the immortality of the soul, a more precise perception of the egological dimension of corporeity certainly allowed for an anthropology that was more faithful to the basic theoretical demands of Christianity. A theology of the resurrection, moreover, calls for a theology of death* that goes further than interpreting it as an event outside the essential reality of the self but that can articulate carnal finitude and eschatological vocation. An absolute future is promised to man, in the personal unity of his flesh* and spirit, but this future is the object of faith* and hope: man can be one with himself only by being one with God. But if this absolute future is believed in and hoped for, there is the possibility of a theologal relationship between man and his body (*see* Brague 1980)—and with the adoption of an eschatological horizon, we see here also the foundation of a sexual* ethics, of a liturgical anthropology, of a theology of asceticism, and even of a Christian interpretation of art. 2) The same period, which questioned the primacy of noetic activities in favor of emotional ones, underwent a significant renaissance in terms of a speculative interest in mystical experience, and the two facts were certainly linked. Whether or not these interests were strictly philosophical (as in the case of J. Baruzi), philosophico-theological (G. Morel), or purely theological (M. Huot de Longchamp—to name only three studies of John* of the Cross), it is at least clear that it is in the experience of suffering that one can find what is most human in man. Mysticism can be more than the trace of a boundary or the paradox of an excess; it can, for example, shed light on the fine word ipseity (*see* Henry 1963 on Eckhart). Proceeding with caution, this kind of clarification does not disqualify all experience of

God* that involves the intentionalities proper to *theôria.* But this clarification undeniably responds to the modern crisis of theories of contemplation and to the uncertainties that surround the concept of "vision of God" by adopting ancient notions of the *apex mentis,* or "the spark of the soul," that make their appeal to a logic of affectivity that is more innate than any logic of the intellect. 3) It is not surprising, therefore, that disagreement about the classic conceptualizations is typically formulated in the name of a theme of charity that is meant to be a critique of the themes of being* (Laberthonnière early on, J.L. Marion) or reason*. A theology that attempts to "de-Hellenize" the basic concepts used to speak of God (e.g., Pannenberg, *Syst. Theol.* I, 401–15) necessarily asks that the same approach be applied to concepts used to speak of knowledge* of God. If God is more suitably and radically *agapè* than supreme intellect, knowledge of God is rooted in the demands of *agapè* more essentially than in the demands of *gnôsis* (e.g., Marion 1978). And just as the theologies of "God's transcendental subjectivity" seem to be inadequate for analyzing divine life, theological anthropology seems committed to leaving behind conceptual systems in which man had intervened, in many ways, as the *subject.* If the final principle of all reality is the act of loving more than the act of being, this entails consequences for theological anthropology. 4) The many references to the lexicon of the "person" and the "personal," passed on to theology by a philosophy that had itself borrowed them from a formerly theological vocabulary, reveal here their true meaning, which is a task that is more important than the often murky and redundant conceptual content of this lexicon. Strictly speaking, the notion of the human person adds nothing to the notion of the human being. The term, half descriptive and half evaluative, nevertheless ceases to appear as (merely) the fruit of a rhetoric of the concept if one is aware that in contemporary usage it serves to name this human being in its existing totality. There is no shortage of reasons for attributing a being to the body as such or to the soul as such or for drawing a strict distinction between the laws of the intellect and the laws of emotion and so on. But to describe man as person is to relativize these distinctions and attributions in the name of a promise of eternity addressed to the concrete reality of the self. The interest in what is most noble in man, such as has been manifest in all philosophical anthropologies, therefore requires a theological corrective. Here and now, man appears to us to be under the condition of a mortal finitude, which, according to Christianity, does not definitively reveal his humanity. The definitive itself, which the resurrection* of Jesus allows us to consider and in a certain way to represent, is not available to us. But one thing is certain: the "personal" reality of a salvation jointly and severally destined for all of humanity. Whether in speaking of man we use the lexicon of the body, that of the soul/spirit, or that of the heart, nothing of that which we name is free from eschatological meanings. And if theology speaks of sanctity, it is in fact anticipating these meanings.

● G. Siewerth (1953), *Der Mensch und sein Leib,* Einsiedeln.
C. Fabro (1955), *L'anima: Introduzione al problema dell'uomo,* Rome.
M. F. Sciacca (1959), *Morte e immortalità,* Milan.
M. Henry (1963), *L'essence de la manifestation,* Paris.
M. Henry (1965), *Philosophie et phénoménologie du corps,* Paris.
A. Görres, K. Rahner (1966), *Das Heil und der Leib,* Mayence.
M. Henry (1966), "Le concept d'âme a-t-il un sens?," *RPL* 64, 5–33.
Cl. Bruaire (1968), *Philosophie du corps,* Paris.
P. Geach (1969), *God and the Soul,* Bristol (2nd Ed. 1994), 1–85.
Cl. Tresmontant (1971), *Le problème de l'âme,* Paris.
A. Pfänder (1973), *Philosophie auf phänomenologischer Grundlage,* Munich, 82–104 (posthumous texts from the years 34–36).
J. Seifert (1973), *Leib und Seele: Ein Beitrag zur philosophischen Anthropologie,* Salzburg.
J.-L. Marion (1978), "De connaître à aimer: L'éblouissement," *Com(F)* III/4, 17–28.
J. Seifert (1979), *Das Leib-Seele Problem und die gegenwärtige philosophische Diskussion,* Darmstadt (2nd Ed. 1989).
R. Brague (1980), "Le corps est pour le Seigneur," *Com(F)* V/6, 4–19.
D. Franck (1981), *Chair et corps: Sur la phénoménologie de Husserl,* Paris.
Cl. Bruaire (1983), *L'Être et l'Esprit,* Paris.
C. A. Bernard (1984), *Théologie affective,* CFi 127.
R. Brague (1987), "L'âme du salut," *Com(F)* XII/3, 4–17.
M. Henry (1987), "Représentation et auto-affection," *Com(F)* XII/3, 77–96.
J. Seifert (1989), *Essere e persona: Verso una fondazione fenomenologica di una metafisica classica e personalistica,* Milan.
J.-L. Chrétien (1992), "Le corps et le toucher," in *L'appel et la réponse,* Paris, 101–54.
X. Lacroix (1992), *Le corps de chair,* Paris.
Th. De Koninck (1995), *De la dignité humaine,* Paris, 81–114, "L'âme et le corps."
W. J. Wainwright (1995), *Reason and the Heart: A Prolegomenon to a Critique of Passional Reason,* Ithaca-London.
R. M. Chisholm (1996), *A Realistic Theory of Categories,* Cambridge, chap. 12, "Persons and Their Bodies: Some Unanswered Questions."
J.-L. Marion (1997), *Étant donné,* Paris.

JEAN-YVES LACOSTE

See also **Adam; Anthropology; Heart of Christ; Knowledge of God; Person; Resurrection of the Dead**

Sovereignty

In the modern world the exercise of sovereign authority through legal systems conferring jurisdiction has in practice to be bounded by systems of "human rights" for which there does not exist a precise and fully developed moral theology or even clear moral norms to which secular law should conform.

Ultimately, in modern societies, insurrection, anarchy, and lesser forms of social disorder are avoided by the imposition of a sovereignty exercised through legal systems that confer jurisdiction and depend on a large measure of public acceptance, not always aptly described as consent. In political systems regarded as democratic, mechanisms have been developed to ensure that public consensus does eventually impose limits on the exercise of sovereignty. Because there are theological principles at stake in the definition of human rights, the rights and duties of the churches in their interaction with secular sovereignties must be considered, whether they are personal or corporate, and particularly if, as is increasingly the case, they do not acknowledge the ultimate derivation of all human authority from God.

From pre-Christian Roman antiquity, when the Church was a branch of the state and the *ius sacrum* a branch of the *ius publicum,* offenses against the community had in many societies been regarded indifferently as crimes against the state or sins against the deity, and throughout history trial by ordeal in civil matters has invariably been viewed as an appeal to the judgment of God. Natural law theory, whatever it may owe to the utilization of the ancient Roman legal codes by the medieval canonists, did not find its firm theological foundation much earlier than the 13th century, when Aquinas proposed that law was the promulgation of rational norms for the common good. Scotus was immediately to argue that the Thomist view compromised God's transcendence of his own creation, constraining him to legislate in accordance with the norms of the divine reason, *ratio divina,* from which human reason derived and in which it participated. Human reason could therefore, at least in theory, generate "natural" law in accordance with God's own eternal law, the *lex aeterna.* Divine law, for Aquinas, had not been the unfettered promulgation of an arbitrary divine will, and secular legal systems, however sovereign, were bounded by natural law.

Even before Aquinas, "natural law" was considered by Gratian to have been generated according to the rational principles of the eternal law. By the 13th century, however, after the 11th-century investiture controversies decided in favor of deriving episcopal authority from ecclesiastical rather than secular sources, early Christian attempts at separating episcopal and princely authorities, like those made in the late fifth century by Gelasius I, had been replaced by theories in which the secular authority was subordinated to the ecclesiastical. This situation often sought its justification by recourse to the "donation of Constantine," a document that purported to be Constantine's transfer of civil power into ecclesiastical hands and that was revealed as a forgery only by Valla (c. 1405–57) in the 15th century. Constantine himself, as emperor, had felt himself entitled to appoint the bishops of Rome, that is, the popes.

From the time of the 16th-century schisms, Western Christendom was no longer simply synonymous with Rome's hierarchical Catholicism, and the ability of princes or, in the empire, town councils to enforce the various forms of sectarian Christianity to which they themselves adhered quickly led to the notion of state religious allegiances in which the state followed the religion of the sovereign: *cuius regio eius religio.* At least in matters of external conformity, this provided a practical solution to which some surprising major political theoreticians and literary figures such as Bonaventure des Périers (c. 1510–c. 1543), Jean Bodin (1529/30–96), and even Erasmus (1467–1536) and Justus Lipsius (1547–1606) came near to giving philosophical justification.

Indeed, it was not until after World War II, when Catholic theology was in turmoil on so many major issues, that John Courtney Murray could definitively argue that the imposition of state Catholicism in Spain could be justified only by reference to some relationship between Catholicism and *Hispanidad* rather than to any ecclesiastical right. But by the 17th century it had already become clear that absolutist concepts of civil sovereignty could be supported both with recourse to a divine origin of civil authority, as in Jacques-Bénigne Bossuet (1627–1704), and without it, as in Thomas Hobbes (1588–1679), who derives civil authority from a social contract between sovereign and people. Whether theoretically derived from divine law or not, a theological basis for political authority in western Europe, as to some extent later in America, was shown to be compatible with the whole spectrum of political attitudes from extreme forms of absolutism to extreme liberalism.

In fact it was not until the 17th century that Grotius (Huigh de Groot, 1583–1645), in his *De iure belli ac pacis* of 1625, elaborated an ethical system in which human rights, duties, and obligations—personal, national, and international—were established without any reference to their derivation from the law of God. Grotius's philosophy of law was codified by his disciple Samuel Pufendorf (1632–94) and transmitted, largely through the pedestrian handbook *Principes du droit naturel* (1747) of the Genevan Jean-Jacques Burlamaqui (1694–1748), to Montesquieu (1689–1755). The latter proclaimed in the opening sentence of his celebrated *De l'esprit des lois* (1748) that laws, far from being a promulgation of God, were "the necessary relationships deriving from the nature of things." God was himself constrained by laws. Montesquieu's work is the source from which all modern theories of international law derive, and they invariably, like Montesquieu, fail to acknowledge the divine will as the source of all authority. By the 18th century both the American *Declaration of Rights* (1774) and Thomas Paine's (1737–1809) *The Rights of Man* (1791–92) were to derive essentially from Montesquieu despite the illiberal tyranny that resulted from the French Revolution, which Paine sought to defend against the criticisms of Edmund Burke (1729–97).

The three great religions originating in the Middle East, Judaism, Christianity, and Islam, have all had the greatest difficulty in accommodating their theologies to purely secular concepts of sovereignty. The laws contained in both the Pentateuch and the Koran are only partly religious, and religious regulations are mixed with exclusively secular injunctions, as they notably also were in Puritan England, Calvinist Geneva, and Presbyterian Scotland. The admixture of religious authority in secular legal systems is still apparent in the importance attached in many parts of the modern world to the taking of oaths, whether in civil courts, on the bestowal of offices, or in the coronation ceremonies of kings and queens, still often clearly showing clear signs of derivation from episcopal consecrations.

In retrospect it can be seen that attempts by the ecclesiastical powers of both Catholic and Protestant Europe from the 16th century on to favor theologies linking sacerdotal and secular authority were for practical as well as religious reasons doomed to fail. The separation of the realms of God and Caesar proclaimed by Jesus (Mt xxii, 21) was to prevail. It happened, however, only gradually in the wake of the sectarian divide that opened up in the 16th century.

In 1570, Pius V both excommunicated and attempted to depose Elizabeth of England, thereby asserting even in political affairs a direct papal sovereignty superior to that of national sovereigns. The decree of deposition had no effects other than to make more certain the execution of Mary, Queen of Scots; to make life harder for English Catholic recusants; and to antagonize Spain, France, and the empire. No further attempt to depose a Protestant monarch on grounds of heresy was ever again made by a pope. When in 1585 Sixtus V declared Henri de Navarre incapable as a heretic of succeeding to the French throne, he had recourse not to any primacy of political sovereignty but to his spiritual power to absolve vassals from oaths or other obligations of allegiance. The effect aimed at was the same as that which Pius V had intended to achieve in England and in practice was equally nugatory, but a new theology of sovereignty had been developed.

When in 1625 Urban VIII sent his nephew, Francesco Barberini, to Paris to urge acceptance of the papal refusal to permit France to subject the Catholic population of the upper Adda valley to the three Grison leagues, forming together a Swiss Protestant *Bund,* he justified his interference in Europe's political arrangements by insisting that France's commitment to the Protestant Grisons was abrogated because a Catholic sovereign could not contract or inherit an obligation to heretics. Claims to the spiritual power to dispense civic obligation as well as a direct and superior sovereignty had now been abandoned in favor of effectively denying moral rights to Protestant sovereignties. Barberini's argument was regarded as derisory, and direct assertions of the dependence of civil legitimacy on the consent of the spiritual power were gradually abandoned.

The modern theology of sovereignty crystallized in the 19th century, when Napoleon's subjugation of restored state Catholicism to the civil power came to a head with the appointment of Cardinal Maury (1746–1817) to the archbishopric of Paris against papal wishes. It drove Lamennais (1782–1854) into his strongly ultramontane position and eventually into his strenuous 1826 defense of the separation of spiritual and temporal powers. Impelled by the desire to impede civil tyranny in the name of political autonomy, Lammenais also held the papal right to decide what was the law of God and what pertained to the purely temporal realm. It was Lamennais's liberal attack on the untrammeled authority of the temporal power in matters concerning civil liberties, unwelcome to the papal curia on account of its alliance with the czar of Russia against the 1830–31 Polish insurrection, that finally brought about the open concession by Rome of total sovereignty to the civil sovereign in civil matters.

The papal encyclical *Etsi multa luctuosa* of November 1873 was finally to lay down Rome's acceptance of a distinction between a natural power of secular sovereignty and a supernatural ecclesiastical authority ordained for the salvation of souls, the final step in the development of the Catholic theology of sovereignty.

ANTHONY LEVI

See also **Authority; Canon Law; Law; Religious Freedom; Traditionalism; Ultramontanism**

Spiritual Combat

The notion that spiritual progress, growth in the *habitus* of charity, is necessarily a lifelong combat or even that the love of God involves lifelong effort is not systematically to be found in the spiritual doctrine of the Gospels, where at best it is implied by some of the reported sayings of Jesus. Saint Paul clearly shared the view that moral life involves combat, but it originated in Plato, who expounds it in the *Phaedrus* (246, 253, and 256) using the parable of the charioteer and his two horses, with its distinction between noble, obedient affections and wild, disobedient ones. It is borne out by the distinction in the *Republic* between rational and appetitive parts of the soul (Book IV, 441a) and the ascription in the *Timaeus* (69d) of different functions of the soul to different parts of the body.

It was popularized by Cicero in the *Tusculan Disputations* (Book 1, chaps. 10 and 33), and Origen was to import it systematically into Christian spiritual doctrine. During the Renaissance, Pico della Mirandola took up the idea from Origen and used it in what we know as the *Oratio de hominis dignitate*. Erasmus also used it in the *Enchiridion* (chap. 7). He had expressed the spirituality of the conflict in terms of an anthropology also taken from Origen, although more commonly found in the Antiochene Fathers, exploiting Saint Paul's trichotomist psychology in 5 Thessalonians 23, which sees rational human beings as composed of spirit, soul, and body. *The Spiritual Combat* itself starts with a quotation from 2 Timothy 2:5 referring to the suffering to be endured in the career of arms of the soldier of Christ.

The idea that spiritual progress arises out of victory in a spiritual combat had become a common in spiritual writing, certainly by the end of the first decade of the 16th century, and a dozen years after that is fundamental to the spirituality of Ignatius of Loyola. The classic exposition of spiritual progress in terms of a combat is, however, the short book first published anonymously in Venice in 1589 under the title *Il combattimento spirituale,* with 24 chapters. A second edition of the same year has 33, and the 1598 edition had grown to a total of 60 chapters. There were at least 60 editions by the time of Scupoli's death in 1610. The definitive Theatine edition, published in 1657, has 66 chapters, with the final six added from a work on preparation for death.

The work, whose authorship was once disputed, is now universally ascribed to Laurence Scupoli, a Theatine from Padua. It is likely that Scupoli gave a copy to Francis de Sales, who was studying law in Padua in 1590. He recommended Scupoli's book more frequently than anyone else did, keeping a copy on his person for 18 years and reading from it daily. The book saw numerous editions and was translated into German in 1591, French in 1595, and English in 1598. Translations also swiftly appeared in Latin, Castilian, and Catalan. It was notably influential among the lead-ing figures of the "Catholic revival" in early 17th-century France.

In content *The Spiritual Combat* defines spiritual perfection in terms of knowledge of God's greatness and goodness and of our own nothingness and inclination to evil and in the love of God and the hatred of ourselves. It consists in perfect submission to the will of God for his own sake. The four arms to be used are the mistrust of self, confidence in God, the striving for virtue through the conquest of the passions by the higher faculties of the soul, and prayer. It is necessary to beware of the tricks and illusions of the devil and to acquire virtues or overcome vices one at a time. The combat lies essentially in the battle between the higher and the lower parts of the soul, is fought under the standard of Christ, and admits of no relaxation of effort.

The principal weapon is prayer. Scupoli describes various forms of mental prayer and, while noting the importance of devotion to the Blessed Virgin and of intercession also to the angels and saints, holds that the major subject of contemplation should be the passion of Christ. Prayer becomes efficacious and invincible chiefly through the Eucharist, and Scupoli warns against the dangers of discouragement in spiritual aridity or of trust in the sensible warmth of feelings of devotion. The Christian warrior must rely on the examination of conscience and never give up before the moment of death.

As expounded by Scupoli, *The Spiritual Combat* is a, or possibly even the, classical statement of Renaissance Christian spirituality, whose principal elements can be traced back to the *devotio moderna* through Ignatius of Loyola, Erasmus, and such contemporaries of Erasmus as Battista Carioni da Crema (†1534) and Serafino da Fermo (†1540). Scupoli is certainly familiar with Cassian and Augustine. Christ, as for Ignatius and Zwingli, is the military leader under whose banner the Christian battles. Scupoli's book differs from other mainstream forms of Christian piety only in the Theatine emphasis it places on disinterest, the cultivation of the unattainable "pure" love of God for his own sake, but it shares with the contemporary spiritualities of which it is a synthesis a strong insistence on following the suffering Christ along the path to which we are called.

ANTHONY LEVI

Spiritual Direction

It would be excessive to claim that Christianity invented the role of director of conscience*. Aristotle had already written to Nicomachus that a profligate fell very far indeed "if he lacked a master's direction." On the other hand, "if he found someone to guide him, he was not incapable of attaining the golden mean and of acquiring the sense of duty" (*EN* IV, 35). Seneca, too, was convinced that we could not achieve virtue* if no one gave us a hand to free ourselves from our weaknesses. The guide constantly pleads the cause of good*. This was the spirit in which the Stoics would deal with the great themes such as peace of mind and the brevity of life.

From a Christian point of view, direction inquires about the relationship between the soul and revealed God*. It is a difficult task, and Gregory* of Nazianzus asserted that directing that strange animal that is man was "the art of arts" (PG 35, 426); Gregory* the Great was later to adopt his expression (PL 77, 14).

The fathers* of the church* saw direction as an essential pastoral duty. In his monastic rule, Basil* urged no concealment of any secret impulse of the soul: the heart's mysteries must be divulged to those appointed to care for the weakest. This was veritable therapy (PG 31, 987). Augustine* would write to Paulinus of Nola and his wife Theresia, who were experiencing difficulties about how to conduct themselves in society, "Talk about it to some doctor of the heart (*cum cordis medico*) who is compassionate" (PL 33, 355).

In the Middle Ages it would be said that it was foolhardy to appoint oneself one's own guide and to spurn the ministry* of those in the Church who had the mission of directing souls. Bernard* wrote that by deciding to be one's own master, "one makes oneself a fool's disciple" (PL 182, 215). By refusing to give one's hand to a guide, one took the hand of a seducer. And William of Saint-Thierry offered this advice to a Carthusian (PL 184, 324): "If you want to get well fast, require yourself to do nothing on your own initiative, without having consulted your physician; and if you need his treatment, you should, without false shame, always reveal your ulcer to him."

Somewhat closer to our own time, treatises and letters of direction were to proliferate. Too often, through generalizations based on certain abuses, these texts are presented as the director taking in hand the soul of the person directed. In fact, directors did not lack respect for the other. Today we would say that their aim was to encourage an awareness of the affective behaviors that condition the individual's disposition before God. But they were not seeking to put a soul "under such restraint" that it was made powerless to make a mature judgment. Bossuet (1627–1704) deplored the fact that, because tastes and feelings were overanalyzed, souls no longer dared to receive any gift from God. This author would tell the "genuine directors" to set souls free: "As much as you can, get them to become less in need of you and, through the rules of conduct you give them, to proceed as if by their own accord" (*Méditations sur L'Evangile* II, 56th day).

In 1707, Fénelon (1651–1715) would write to Madame de Montberon that "the frequent scrutinizing of the anatomy of one's own heart makes for a dangerous remedy of self-love." And M. Olier (1608–57) had already advised a pious person against thinking so much about themselves: under the pretext of making oneself more holy, one looks at oneself with satisfaction (*Lettres,* 297). It is therefore unfair to make a general charge of tyranny against directors or to treat their directives as "the pretentious prose of hygienists of the soul." Francis de Sales urged Madame de La Fléchère "not to make her dear conscience sting any more."

All the same, spiritual direction remained necessary. And Fénelon summed up the problem in his *Lettre sur la direction,* which condemned the hidden inclination to flatter oneself (OC, vol. 5, 731): "Your most subtle temptations come from you yourself; you are your own worst enemy; you need someone who has neither made your mistakes nor indulged in your passions*, someone at a distance from you who will help you to free yourself from them."

There has also been much discussion about the *spiritual father.* This person is not primarily a master who negotiates with his disciples: it is because of what he is that he reaches the other. M. Legaut (1974) writes, "Spiritual filiation and paternity come in their own good time, at a privileged meeting between two beings who have already been secretly prepared." One imagines that such an attitude is somewhat dangerous, and Dr. C. H. Nodet is right when he says (*Encyclopédie médico-chirurgicale,* 1955), "Psychologically, a man who by nature should have been the head of a household should not accept too easily remaining all his life the *son* of a religious *father.*" True paternity encourages the *son* toward increasing autonomy.

Today the emphasis is on *spiritual companionship,* and it is not always a priest who provides this. The companion must possess an inner sensitivity that allows him to recognize God's action in another. He does not walk ahead of the other, nor does he follow him: he points out the obstacles. He constantly helps to put bring human activity into harmony with the Spirit's urging to the extent that that impulse can be discerned in our hearts. Companionship is walking side by side, and both partners benefit from this journey, for each one of them is invited to undergo a continual conversion*.

There is therefore a similarity with what the reformed pastoral tradition calls the *cure of souls.* This *cure* is a search for signs of the Holy Spirit within a biblical perspective. Souls are followed in their winding progress, with respect being shown for each one's individual inspiration. Protestant* theology stresses that the Holy Spirit is the real director: it is therefore important to help a soul be receptive to this guidance. The soul will be urged to distance itself from any anxious kind of searching and to avoid imprisoning itself in false security and illusions (J. D. Benoît 1940). The cure of souls will never demand a dependent state: it is a form of mutual aid supplied by two people who are on a journey together.

The *Christian East* does not use the word *direction,* at least not in the abstract sense of the term. The *starets* (elder) teaches above all how to turn one's heart constantly toward God and therefore how to persevere so as to receive "the charism of prayer* and psalmody" (Evagrius Ponticus). One progresses from sensible impressions to spiritual prayer, which unfolds within the heart, for the heart plays a central role in the life of prayer. Isaac the Syrian was to say, "Apply yourself to going into your inner room and you will see the celestial room." Nonetheless, the practice of the virtues* is not neglected, especially the virtues of humility, discretion, and charity. These three virtues guarantee the cohesion of the spiritual structure. Now, to attain such stability a companion's help is sometimes very useful, especially at the beginning. John Climacus asserted that "the cenobite often needs a brother's support (in Gouillard 1979).

Lastly, religious literature has often stressed what the spiritual master *is not.* His role is to lead others onto a mystical path. This guide is not necessarily a saint, although he should radiate virtue. Above all, it should be said that he is not primarily a scholar giving a course on what he has learned and what he knows. His desire is not to pass on his own knowledge but to orient his neighbor toward a certain way of life. It should be noted, however, that the Catholic "director" cannot be unaware of an ethic* that corresponds to the Church's teaching. Faced with a concrete situation, the adviser has the task of answering in the spirit of the Scriptures and of tradition* the one who asks how to act. Theresa of Avila particularly wanted "erudite" directors, and she said, "I have always sought learned confessors, because those who were only half-educated have done the greatest harm to my soul" (*Life,* V).

Depth psychology would later reveal all the ambiguities of human motivations. We know that Paul Bourget's eponymous disciple (1889) had a "precocious liking for inner dissection" and pushed his examinations of his conscience to the point where they became "acts of secret torture": his directors did not notice these excesses, calling them childish. What was needed was such as Abbé A. Huvelin, advising everyone not to analyze themselves too much and not to be continually telling their own story to themselves.

When R. Guardini (1885–1968) dealt with melancholy (*Schwermut*), he thought that it found its last refuge in the anxiety provoked in us by the proximity of the eternal. He added, "That is what makes man happy and, at the same time, is a threat to him, *Beseligung und Bedrohung zugleich*" (*Vom Sinn der Schwermut,* 2nd Ed., Graz-Wien-Munich, 1951). Perhaps it is the chief mission of spiritual direction to make it understood, in the light of the Gospels, that this proximity of the Absolute is primarily a source of peace* at the "fine point of the soul".

● F. de Fénelon (1848–52) *Œuvres complètes,* Paris.

J.-J. Olier (1885), *Lettres,* Paris, vol. I.

P. Bourget (1889), *Le Disciple,* Paris.

François de Sales (1892–1964), *Œuvres,* Annecy, 27 vols.

R. de Sinety (1934), *Psychopathologie et direction,* Paris.

J.D. Benoît (1940), *Direction spirituelle et protestantisme,* Paris.

E. Thurneysen (1946), *Die Lehre von der Seelsorge,* Zollikon-Zurich.

Coll. (1951), *Direction spirituelle et psychologie,* EtCarm.

E. Ringel, W. van Lun (1953), *Die Tiefenpsychologie hilft dem Seelsorger.*

I. Hausherr (1955), *Direction spirituelle en Orient autrefois,* Rome (2nd Ed. 1981).

F. Vandenbroucke (1956), *Direction spirituelle et hommes d'aujourd'hui,* Paris.

E. des Places *et al.* (1957), "Direction spirituelle", *DSp* 3, 1002–1214.

C. Huvelin (1959), *Écrits spirituels,* posthumous Ed., Paris.

J.-P. Schaller (1959), *Direction des âmes et médecine moderne,* Mulhouse.

T. Merton (1960), *Spiritual Direction and Meditation,* Collegeville, Minn.

A. Godin (1963), *La relation humaine dans le dialogue pastoral,* Paris.

J. Laplace (1965), *La direction de conscience ou le dialogue spirituel,* Paris.

Coll. (1968), *Relation pastorale (La)*, Paris.
M. Légaut (1974), *Un chrétien de notre temps*, Paris.
J.-P. Schaller (1978), *Direction spirituelle et temps modernes*, Paris.
A. Gouillard (Trans.) (1979), *Petite Philocalie de la prière du cœur*, Paris.
A. W. Barry, J. Conolly (1982), *The Practise of Spiritual Direction*, New York.
Y. Raguin (1985), *Maître et disciple: La direction spirituelle*, Paris.

P. Hadot (1987), *Exercices spirituels et philosophie antique*, Paris.
J. J. Maison (1989), *La direction spirituelle d'Alexandre Vinet*, Mont-sur-Lausanne, 2 vols.
A. Louf (1992), *L'accompagnement spirituel*, Paris.

JEAN-PIERRE SCHALLER

See also **Casuistry; Hesychasm; Monasticism; Spiritual Theology; Spirituality, Ignatian; Spirituality, Salesian**

Spiritual Paternity. *See* Spiritual Direction

Spiritual Theology

I. Definitions

1. Relationship to Other Kinds of Theology

The term "spiritual theology," like the term "mysticism," is modern and marked by the crisis in culture that can be traced back at least to the later Middle Ages and the Reformation. The term is used in practice to mark out a distinction from the rest of theology*. *Dogmatic* *theology* is regarded as too cerebral and remote from actual Christian life, and while spiritual theology is keen to retain its roots in *biblical* *theology,* it still sees it as necessary to wrest theology from the "critics." In this way, it has given a hostage to an anti-intellectualism that is itself one of the responses of modern theology and culture to the crisis. Spiritual theology, like mysticism, seeks its roots in a tradition* that can be traced back to the patristic period, if not the Bible* itself, where it is claimed there can be found a theology that is free from the disjunctions of modern culture.

2. Notion of the "Spiritual"

Such an approach to spiritual theology is too bound up with what it is rejecting to be of lasting value. Here, we shall attempt a fresh start by engaging with the notion of the "spiritual," in the two senses of the word. "Spir-

itual" can refer to the Holy Spirit* and be concerned with a lived engagement with the Spirit. Spiritual theology, then, attempts to understand what this means for our relationship with God*. However, "spiritual" can also refer more directly to a dimension of the human person that is often called the "heart": the soul, inwardness, the capacity to engage with God. In this sense, spiritual theology consists in exploring the world that is opened up when one becomes aware of these realities, in a process that can be called "discovery of the heart." These two ways of conceiving spiritual theology partially overlap and can mutually interpret each other, but they are fundamentally different. One has its roots in the biblical understanding of the Spirit of God and the dogma* of the Trinity*; the other is more philosophical and has affinities with Platonism*. The term "heart," which is biblical, may perhaps reconcile these perspectives.

II. Outlines of a Spiritual Theology

1. The "Spiritual" and the Spirit

The first approach therefore involves starting out from what Scripture tells us and especially from deepening one's understanding of Johannine* and Pauline* notions: the indwelling of the Spirit within us (Jn 14–16), worship in the spirit (Jn 4:24), and the Spirit moving within the baptized Christian, incorporating him into the Son, and awakening a sense of communication with the Father* in prayer*, all this in solidarity with the whole cosmos* (*see* Rom 8). The church fathers* applied the term "mystical" (Bouyer 1986) to this hidden reality of the Christian life that is made manifest by the Spirit. The "mystical" meaning of Scripture is therefore its inner meaning, revealed by the Spirit, in which the Church* enters into intimate communion* with the incarnate Word* to whom the whole of Scripture points. Similarly, the "mystical" meaning of the sacraments*, especially the Eucharist*, is their inward reality, realized by the invocation of the Spirit. A further dimension of this "mystical" life is the Christian's life "hidden with Christ in God" (Col. 3:3), which is the real state of the baptized Christian. The object of spiritual theology, thus understood, is not merely personal inwardness but the inward reality of the Church's engagement with Scripture and its liturgical life. This inward reality is sometimes described as paradise, the state in which and for which God created human beings. One can become aware of paradise only through "spiritual senses" that complement and in some way surpass the normal five senses.

2. The "Spiritual" and the Inward

The other form of spiritual theology explores inwardness more philosophically and from a more unambiguously individualistic perspective. Nonetheless, its conception of inward reality has profoundly influenced traditional Christian understanding of the spiritual life. The soul is regarded as being divided into two parts, the rational and the irrational. Within the former there is found the *nous,* the mind, capable of pure awareness of ultimate reality. The latter is itself divided in two: the incensive part, the source of psychic energy, and the desiring part, which is closest to the body. This analysis of the soul has provided the framework for the definition of the virtues* that make for the beauty of the Christian life and the vices (originally temptations) that mar it. It also permits a definition of the goal: a state of tranquillity (*apatheia*) in which the *nous* is no longer disturbed by the turbulence of the lower part of the soul and can contemplate the reality of the cosmos and, ultimately, God himself.

3. The Heart

a) Scriptures. The notion of the heart (Hebrew *lev,* Greek *kardia,* Latin *cor*) is of particular importance in spiritual theology. "Heart" is a biblical term,

referring to the center of the person. It is not what modern languages understand by "heart" but something deeper and broader than affectivity. In the Psalms*, the heart is a place of gladness (Ps 4:8; 15[16]:9) and sorrow (Ps 12[13]:3); but it also meditates (Ps 18[19]:15, 48[49]: 4, etc.), seeks God (Ps 26[27]:8), can incline toward him and his testimonies (Ps 118[119]:36, 111ff., etc.), can be troubled (Ps 54[55]:5, 108[109]:22), and can be broken (Ps 50[51]:19). Indeed, a broken heart will not be set at naught by God, and one can beg for a new heart (Ps 50[51]:12). It is not just an organ of feeling; it is also an organ of decision, of pondering, but above all it is that part of the person that is at the center of our dealings with God. The heart *prays:* that is the deepest aspect of the heart. In this sense, to refer to the "heart" is to refer to the inwardness of the person: what is meant by the soul or, better, the *nous* in the philosophical tradition outlined here but without the intellectualism of that tradition. Because the heart is physically at the center of the body and essential for life, this language not only avoids intellectualism* but also shows that one must not forget the unity of the human being.

b) Christian Thought. The theme of the heart is treated in a whole spectrum of ways in the historical development of spiritual theology. In the writings of Origen* and Evagrius, for example, the heart is simply a biblical term for the intellect: heart and *nous* are used interchangeably, the choice being probably determined by context (*see* Evagrius, *Practical Treatise* 47). At the other extreme, in the *Homilies* of Pseudo-Macarius, for instance, the heart is a much more comprehensive notion than the soul, and the expression "the depths of the heart" (*see Hom.* 43, 9; 15, 32) represents an inwardness that extends far beyond consciousness, including longings and passions* that are unknown to the conscious mind and are capable of affecting one's behavior in unpredictable ways. Understood like this, the heart is the center of the person, but it needs to be discovered, for as a result of original sin* we have lost contact with ourselves, we deceive ourselves about our longings and passions, and we are incapable of self-knowledge or self-control. The heart is thus an arena of conflicting tendencies, open to the assaults of both demons* and the influence of grace*. It is a place of discernment, a place of struggle, a place of prayer: purity* of heart entails self-knowledge and awareness of the unconscious and releases the person to love God and one's neighbor. The struggle to achieve pure prayer is often seen as a search for the heart: the later techniques of Hesychasm*, which aim at pure prayer, are explicitly seen as ways of finding the true place of the heart.

4. The Spiritual Senses

Another traditional theme of spiritual theology is that of the spiritual senses (Rahner* 1932, 1933). Just as Paul distinguished between the inner man and the outer man, so we find a distinction being drawn, from the time of Origen on, between the five senses that belong to the outer man and the spiritual senses that belong to the inner man. It is the inner man that is created in the image of God and so can know union with him in love*. The outer man is the human being turned outward, toward the world perceived through the senses; the inner man is the human being turned inward, toward the world perceived through the spiritual senses. Through these spiritual senses we perceive the spiritual world, the realm of God, the angels*, and souls that have woken up to spiritual reality. Sin and the Fall have turned human beings outward—turned them inside out, in fact—so that they pour themselves out into the external world, which is not so much the physical world as a world valued in terms of external things, a world of reputation and ambition, possession and consumption. Most human beings are so committed to this world that the world of spiritual reality is foreign to them, or, rather, they are foreign to it. If they turn inward, if they allow themselves to hear the call of God, they will begin to wake up *within,* so to speak, to the spiritual world. As they become accustomed to this inner world, their spiritual senses will come to life. This inner world is sometimes conceived after the model of Plato's realm of the Forms, where truth* is essentially immaterial. At other times, and more profoundly, this inner world is the whole created order, seen in its true worth as created, a transfigured world perceived through spiritually transfigured senses. Maximus* the Confessor sees this transfiguration being effected both through the presence of the Spirit in the sacraments, especially the Eucharist, and through the purification of the heart through the simultaneous action of asceticism* and the grace of the Holy Spirit (*Ambigua* 41, *Mystagogia* 1–7, 24).

III. Emergence of Spiritual Theology in the West

1. The Heart and the Feelings

From around the 12th century, the conditions for the emergence of the modern notion of spiritual theology were put in place in the West, in particular a shift in the understanding of "heart." It was increasingly seen as the seat of the emotions, and the biblical emphasis on the heart was taken to entail a contrast with the intellect. The already ancient idea that God is unknowable was taken to mean that God cannot be known but can be loved and that love of God is what is meant by knowledge* of God: *amor ipse intellectus est* (William of Saint Thierry, *Epistula aurea* 173). Alongside this change in the understanding of the heart (itself bound up with *fin amor* "refined love" and the beginning of the modern notion of romantic love), there was also a change in the understanding of the Church.

2. Emergence of the "Mystical"

a) Shift in Notion of the Church.   Until the 12th century, the expression *corpus Christi* ("body of Christ") designated the Church: from that time on, in the West, *corpus Christi* came to mean the eucharistic body of Christ (specifically, the consecrated host), and the Church came to be referred to as the *corpus Christi mysticum* ("mystical body of Christ"). Certeau has developed this insight to show how this change laid bare a division between the priesthood*, which alone has the power to consecrate the Eucharist, and the hidden reality of the Church ("hidden" is the traditional meaning of *mysticus*). It is to this reality that claim was made by those who had special graces manifest in contemplation*, increasingly understood to be a supernatural* form of prayer (Prayer* IV 2b), and in extraordinary phenomena such as visions, levitation, the stigmata, and so forth. Such experiences, which began to be called "mystical," provided supernatural validation of a source of authority that could challenge the institutional authority of the priesthood (authority* A). It was also open to those, especially women, to whom the priesthood was denied (Bynum 1987). The contrast between intellect and heart was reinforced by this contrast between the institutional hierarchy* and claims to direct mystical experience. Many of the spiritual writings of the later Middle Ages thus set up a clear distinction between the intellectual theology of Scholasticism* (itself the preserve of the priesthood) and an often overtly anti-intellectualist theology of the spiritual* life (see *The Cloud of Unknowing* and the *Imitatio Christi*).

b) Taming of Spiritual Theology.   This theology of the spiritual life was not left in peace by Scholastic theologians or at least those theologians trained in Scholastic methods. While the supernatural claims of mystical prayer were conceded, vigorous attempts were made to limit such claims. Thus, for example, at the beginning of the 15th century the chancellor of the University of Paris, Gerson, attacked the Flemish mystic Ruusbroec. The development of spiritual theology from the 16th century on can be read as a conflict between claims to inherent authority on the part of those who possessed spiritual experience and the hierarchy's concern to see that such claims were conceded only where its ultimate authority was recognized. The condemnation of Molinos in 1685 and, still more, Bossuet's securing of the censure of Madame Guyon in 1694 and of Fénelon in 1699, because of their doctrine of "pure love" (quietism*), can be seen as instances of this conflict. Although the notion of "spiritual theology" had now clearly emerged, it was with a more complex terminology: and such complexity is also evidence of this struggle. Not only was it explicitly called "spiritual theology" during this period, but it was divided into "ascetic theology" and "mystical theology." Ascetic theology was concerned with those practices that foster prayer and devotion and with all those matters over which human beings could have control. In respect of prayer, it was therefore concerned with vocal prayer (especially the recitation of the divine office) and meditation. The latter was understood as thinking about passages of scripture and the mysteries* of faith*, aimed at encouraging affective prayer. Meditation also covered matters of fasting and ascetic practices. These were all things that human beings could achieve by their own endeavors. "Mystical" theology was concerned with "supernatural prayer," or contemplation, which God alone could grant. This was regarded as something rare that only a few could hope to experience (and those few confined in enclosed convents for "contemplatives"). Such an approach to spiritual theology became the norm in the Catholic Church after the Council of Trent*: it is found in Scaramelli's two treatises of 1754, *Il direttorio ascetico* and *Il direttorio mistico,* and is still manifest in A. Poulain's *Des grâces d'oraison* (1901), which is described as a "treatise on mystical theology."

3. Modern Problems

a) Dissolution of the Old Consensus. At the beginning of the 20th century there was considerable controversy about whether contemplation is something that any devout and earnest Christian might expect to achieve. Poulain continued to regard contemplation as a rare grace, while others, such as Saudreau (1900) and Arintero (1908), regarded it as an attainment of the life of prayer of every baptized Christian. In reality, the whole controversy was overtaken by broader changes in Catholicism*, for two reasons in particular. On the one hand, there was a growing awareness, not least among those touched by modernism*, of the authenticity of the spiritual life of many outside the Christian dispensation. This is found in the work of Friedrich Heiler (1892–1967), R. Otto (1869–1937), Friedrich von Hügel (1852–1925), Evelyn Underhill (1875–1941), and others. On the other hand, there was also the rediscovery of the fathers* of the church, most notably as a result of the labors of Henri Sonier de Lubac*, Hans

Urs von Balthasar*, and J. Daniélou (1905–74), and the impact on Western theology of Orthodox émigrés such as Vladimir Lossky (1903–58) and Myrrha Lot-Borodine (1882–1957). The growing use of the term "spiritual theology" today has much to do with the collapse of the conflict implied in the terms "ascetic" and "mystical" and greater openness to the spiritual resources of other religious traditions.

b) Future Prospects. The future is open. One strand sets spiritual theology against the dogmatic traditions of the different Christian traditions and indeed religious traditions altogether, seeking in spiritual theology something that transcends what is perceived as the divisiveness of all dogmas. On the other hand, for Christians of the Orthodox tradition and those attracted to it, spiritual theology does not entail disregard for the dogmatic tradition of the Church but rather explores the life of prayer and communion* with the God who has revealed himself in those ways explored by the dogmas of the Church. It is noted that patristic theology does not easily yield to the later Western distinctions. For instance, the notion of God's infinity (infinite*) is explored by Gregory* of Nyssa both in an explicitly dogmatic context, when he is defending the Trinity against Eunomius, and in his writings on prayer and the spiritual life, where God's infinity and the soul's experience of darkness are seen as complementary. In the treatises of Maximus the Confessor, flights of speculation, analysis of theological terms, and discussion of prayer and contemplation are found side by side. Even in the 14th century, when questions were raised about methods of prayer on Mount Athos (Hesychasm*), arguments in their defense were based mainly on the dogmatic distinction between the essence and energies of God. All this points to a theological balance that we should be seeking to recover while ceasing to regard spiritual theology as something to be contrasted with, or even opposed to, dogmatic theology.

● Anonymous, *The Cloud of Unknowing* and *The Book of Privy Counselling,* EETS 218, London, 1944.

Evagrius, *Practical Treatise,* SC 170–71.

J. Gerson, *De mystica theologia,* Lugano, 1958.

William of Saint-Thierry, *Lettre aux frères du Mont-Dieu (Epistula aurea),* SC 223.

Macaire, *Die 50 Geistliche Homilien...,* PTS 4.

Maximus the Confessor, *Ambigua,* CChr.SG 1.

Maximus the Confessor, *Mystagogia,* PG 91, 657–717.

J. van Ruusbroec, *Opera omnia,* CChr.CM 101, 102, 110.

Thomas a Kempis, *Omnia opera,* 7 vols., Fribourg, 1902–21.

♦ G.B. Scaramelli (1754a), *Il direttorio ascetico, nel quale si insegna il modo di condurre le anime per le vie ordinarie della grazia alla perfezione cristiana,* Venice.

G.B. Scaramelli (1754b), *Il direttorio mistico, indirizzato ai direttori di quelle anime che Iddio conduce per la via della contemplazione,* Venice.

A. Saudreau (1900), *La vie d'union à Dieu et les moyens d'y arriver d'après les grands maîtres de la spiritualité,* Paris.

A. Poulain (1901), *Des grâces d'oraison,* Paris.

J. Arintero (1908), *Evolución mistica,* Madrid.

F. von Hügel (1908), *The Mystical Element of Religion, as Studied in Saint Catherine of Genoa and Her Friends,* 2 vols., London.

E. Underhill (1911), *Mysticism: A Study in the Nature and Development of Man's Spiritual Consciousness,* London.

R. Otto (1917), *Das Heilige,* Stuttgart.

F. Heiler (1918), *Das Gebet: Eine religionsgeschichtliche und religionspsychologische Untersuchung,* Munich.

C. Butler (1927), *Western Mysticism: The Teaching of Ss. Augustine, Gregory and Bernard on Contemplation and the Contemplative Life. Neglected Chapters in the History of Religion* (2nd Ed. with added "Afterthoughts"), London.

H. Bremond (1929–33), *Histoire littéraire du sentiment religieux en France depuis la fin des guerres de religion jusqu'à nos jours,* 11 vols., Paris.

K. Rahner (1932), "Le début d'une doctrine des cinq sens spirituels chez Origène," *RAM* 13, 113–45.

K. Rahner (1933), "La doctrine des 'sens spirituels' au Moyen Age, en particulier chez saint Bonaventure," *RAM* 14, 263–99.

Vl. Lossky (1944), *Essai sur la th. mystique de l'Église d'Orient,* Paris.

H. de Lubac (1944), Corpus Mysticum: *L'Eucharistie et l'Église au Moyen Age,* Paris.

A. Stolz (1947), *Th. de la mystique,* 2nd. Ed., Chevetogne.

R. A. Knox (1950), *Enthusiasm: A Chapter in the History of Religion with Special Reference to the XVII and XVIIIth Centuries,* Oxford.

H. U. von Balthasar (1961), *Herrlichkeit: Eine theologische Ästhetik,* vol. I, Einsiedeln.

M. Lot-Borodine (1970), *La déification de l'homme,* Paris.

M. de Certeau (1982), *La fable mystique: XVIe–XVIIe siècles,* Paris.

O. Clément (1983), *Sources: Les mystiques chrétiens des origines,* Paris.

L. Bouyer (1986), *Mysterion: Du mystère à la mystique,* Paris.

C. W. Bynum (1987), *Feast and Holy Fast: The Religious Significance of Food to Medieval Women,* Berkeley.

ANDREW LOUTH

See also **Asceticism; Contemplation; Mysticism; Prayer**

Spirituality. *See* Life, Spiritual; Spiritual Theology

Spirituality, Franciscan

The outlook and attitudes characteristic of Franciscan spirituality originate with the experience of Francis of Assisi (1182–1226)—his character, life, and aims. This spirituality has undergone a variety of developments and emphases over the centuries.

1. The Founding Figure and His Originality

a) Our knowledge of Francis and his vision is based on two sorts of ancient documents: the *hagiographical narratives* (around eight appeared in the 40 years after his death) and the *writings of Francis* himself (around 30 texts of varying length and content). To these should be added the feminine contribution of Clare of Assisi (1194–1253) in terms of both her writings and her life.

b) The originality of Franciscan spirituality resides in the unusual, if not unique, fact that it derives from the Christian experience* of a lay* person without a clerical education (he referred to himself as *ignorans et idiota*). While he borrowed some features from the mendicant movements of the 12th and 13th centuries, Francis was scarcely influenced by the intellectual and spiritual trends of the time. He drew his vision of God*, man, and the spiritual path from a fresh and immediate overall grasp of the gospel message. An astonishing balance enabled him to avoid fundamentalism* in his interpretation. Presented without any systematic conceptual development, his "doctrine" nonetheless has a theological and spiritual breadth that is closer to the desert Fathers* than to Scholasticism*.

2. Key Themes of Francis's Spirituality

The hagiographical narratives present and interpret Francis as a historical figure, but it is his own writings that best reveal the vision that occupied him and the spiritual attitudes that it implied. The following themes appear to constitute the framework of that vision.

a) Gospels as First Point of Reference. Francis does not refer to existing spiritual currents, their conclusions, or their practices. What he offers is "the life of the gospel of Jesus Christ," understanding the gospel not selectively but in terms of its whole breadth as the revelation* of God's love* in Jesus Christ and of the new life that issues from it.

b) "God Desirable above Everything." Francis underwent a profound experience of the mystery* of the Trinity. While he is reticent about its subjective repercussions, he commends it insistently to every believer, inviting them to "love, honor, adore and serve, praise and bless God, desirable in his entirety above everything." His view of God has something Johannine* about it: the Father* is preeminent, the Son is the revealer of his Father's Name*, and the Holy Spirit* alone gives us knowledge of it. The Son is contemplated in the humility, frailty, and poverty of his abasement; his words, often quoted, are "spirit and life"; and he is present in the context of the Church* through the Eucharist*.

The believer is invited always to have "his heart turned towards the Lord," in an attitude above all of adoration, wonder, praise*, and thanksgiving.

c) Complete Poverty of the Individual. "The good words, good deeds and all the good* that God does or utters in man or through man belong to God alone and must be restored to him in thanksgiving. Only man's vices and sins* are his own. Therefore, he can glory only in his own weaknesses and bear Christ*'s cross every day. In this is to be found true joy, true virtue*, and the salvation* of mankind." The material poverty that Francis proposes in his Rule (but not in the texts addressed to the laity) is an eloquent symbol of this complete poverty of the individual before God. From this follows the necessity of behaving as children ("minors"), submissive to everyone and servants of everyone, not as lords and masters.

d) "Maternal" Love for All Mankind. Another person, whether he be "a blessed friar, a friend or an enemy, a thief or a brigand, should be welcomed with kindness, spiritual joy, and respect. Even if he sins a thousand times, we should never stop loving him, without wishing him to become a better Christian for our comfort." All human relations must be governed by such a degree of trust "that each may make plain his need to the other, like a child to its mother. For each of us must cherish and nourish his brother like a mother her son."

e) Presence of Brotherhood, Peace and Joy. Francis describes the maintenance of a fraternal bearing toward all mankind in these terms: "May they avoid disagreements, verbal quarrels and negative judgements, and display gentleness, peace*, serenity, benevolence, humility, and courtesy to all people." This kind of evangelical utopia is not applicable to mankind alone: it extends to the world of matter and to cosmic realities, which he refers to as brothers and sisters. Paradoxically (since Francis has a rather gloomy vision of mankind), it assumes a fundamental optimism, that of the creation* and of salvation. It is the basis of the desire to be everybody's "brother" and of the concern to create harmony, reconciliation, and peace.

3. Franciscan Tradition and Its Developments

a) Francis's spiritual influence was not restricted to the circle of his religious disciples. It extended to lay Christians, for whom Francis wrote a scheme of life, the *Letter to the Faithful.* The content of his message was presented over the centuries with a variety of emphases. The figure of the saint is central, and there is an insistence on his most striking aspects: the completeness of his poverty, his stigmata, and his palpable devotion to Christ's humanity.

b) Two periods particularly rich in their contributions and developments may be singled out within the tradition: the 13th century and the 15th to 17th centuries.

1) The 13th century saw the continuation on the one hand of a current close to Francis's own thinking and approach and represented by figures who were close to him: the friars Richer of Muccia (†1236), Egidius of Assisi (†1274), and Roger of Provence (†1310) and the nun Angela of Foligno (†1309). This current was marked by strong mystical tendencies and expressed itself in simple language, without any systematization.

In parallel with this, a learned tendency linked to Scholasticism* asserted itself, composed of theologians and Spirituals: Bonaventure* (†1274),

Petrus Joannis Olivi (†1284), Ubertino of Casale (†1329), and Ange Clareno (†1337). They developed syntheses that incorporated Francis's great intuitions into systematic frameworks that were marked by the intellectualism of the period and by contemporary preoccupations (such as the conflict over poverty).

2) During the period between the 15th and 17th centuries inclusively, after preachers such as Bernardino of Siena (†1444), a succession of figures appeared who were to give an impulse to Rhineland-Flemish* spirituality while stamping it with the Franciscan imprint. The Belgian Henri Herp (Harphius, †1477) was its most distinguished representative. His *Theologia mystica* was disseminated across southern Europe and, by way of the Spanish Franciscans Francisco de Osuna (†1541) and Bernardino Laredo (†1540), was to influence Carmelite spirituality through Teresa of Avila. A similar development occurred in France in the 17th century: the *Rule of Perfection* by the Capuchin Benet of Canfeld (†1610) was to play an important part in the origins of the French school and inspired continuations by Franciscans in France and Belgium. There was thus a strange affinity linking the extremely abstract Northern spirituality with a Franciscan approach that valued love above any concept. At the end of this period, a female Capuchin, Saint Veronica Giuliani (†1727), is evidence of the persistence of the mystical tradition* at the heart of Franciscan spirituality.

c) Even today "the spirit of Assisi" retains its fascination. It draws on the figure of Francis himself and on various features of his message: kindness, universal brotherhood, peace, reconciliation, a certain (poetic) lightness of being, and love and respect for nature. Most important, however, is the root of all these values, without which they would be neither meaningful nor possible: the need to take the whole gospel seriously, the profound experience of God, and the complete poverty of being.

● K. Esser (1976), *Die Opuscula des Hl. Franziskus von Assisi,* Rome.
François d'Assise (1981), *Écrits* (SC 285).
Claire d'Assise (1985), *Écrits* (SC 325).
E. Menestó (Ed.) (1995), *Fontes Franciscani,* Assisi.
♦ H. de Lucerne (1924), *L'idéal de saint François d'Assise,* Paris.
A. Gemelli (1935), *Le message de saint François au monde moderne,* Paris.
E. Longpré (1966), *François d'Assise et son expérience spirituelle,* Paris.
K. Esser, E. Grau (1967), *Antwort der Liebe,* Werl/West.
K. Esser (1975), *Origini e inizi del movimento e dell'Ordine francescano,* Milan.
A. Rotzetter (Ed.) (1982), *Un chemin d'Évangile, l'esprit franciscain hier et aujourd'hui,* Paris.
Th. Desbonnet (1983), *De l'intuition à l'institution,* Paris.
O. van Hasseldonk (1985), *La Lettera e lo Spirito,* vol. 1, 351–479, Rome.
M. Bartoli (1989), *Chiara d'Assisi,* Rome.
D. Flood (1989), *Francis of Assisi and the Franciscan Movement,* The Franciscan Institute of Asia, Quezon City.
Coll. (1991), *La sp. de saint Fr. d'Assise,* Paris.
A. Cacciotti (1992), "Amore e conoscenza nel francescanesimo, alcuni aspetti," *Anton.* 67, 305–29.
G. Iammarone (1993), *La spiritualità francescana,* Padua.
Th. Matura (1996), *François d'Assise, "auteur spirituel,"* Paris.

THADDÉE MATURA

See also **Beguines; Bonaventure; Carmel; Devotio Moderna; Imitation of Christ; Rhineland-Flemish Mysticism**

Spirituality, Ignatian

Ignatian spirituality is not linked to a particular theological viewpoint but to a "way of proceeding" (*modo de proceder*) in order to seek God* in everything, to help souls, and to serve the Church*. Nonetheless, this conduct implies some theological presuppositions.

I. Ignatius Loyola (1491–1556)

His conversion* in Loyola and his solitude in Manresa (1522) awakened Ignatius to the discernment of spirits and opened his intellect to the mysteries of the Trinity*, the creation*, the Incarnation*, and of Christ*'s presence in the Eucharist* *(Autobiography,* no. 30): "He understood and knew many things, spiritual things as much as matters of faith* and learning, with so great an illumination that everything seemed new to him."

1. The Spiritual Exercises

a) Sources. The writing of the text, completed in Rome, where it received pontifical approval in 1548, was enriched by the exercises being put into practice and by Ignatius's studies at the University of Paris. But the main part dates from Manresa, where he had already noted down what might be useful to others. Strongly affected by his readings of the *Flos sanctorum* *(The Golden Legend)* by Jacobus de Voragine (†1298) and of the *Vita Christi* *(Life of Christ)* by Ludolphus of Saxony (†1377), which played a part in his conversion at Loyola, he became dependent in Manresa on the *devotio* moderna through the *Imitation of Christ* and through the *Compendium breve,* which was compiled from the *Exercitatorio de la vida espiritual* by the abbot Garcia de Cisneros (†1510) and was the manual for retreatants at Montserrat. These texts display the convergent influence of Franciscan tendencies (the devotion to Christ's humanity in Bonaventure's *Meditations)* and Augustinian ones (meditation according to the soul's three powers: memory, intellect, will) as well as the influence of the desert Fathers, filtered through Cassian (discernment of spirits).

b) Originality. Nadal, Ignatius's witness and interpreter, says, "The *Spiritual Exercises* contain almost nothing which does not appear in other books." But it is all reworked through the intuition that informs the whole operation, that of the central contemplations* of the Reign and of the Two Standards (the call from the eternal King to work with him to establish his kingdom* and to fight Satan), and through their link to the rules of election and discernment. The goal of the *Spiritual Exercises* is that of preparing a given individual, through an intense four-week process, for an experience* of union with God, sufficiently structured to lead to the fully free decision that decides a fate. They thus enlighten the conscience* as it grapples with a fundamental problem of modernity, "that of historical topicality, and of the free decision by which both social and individual human reality can create itself in it" (G. Fessard). In this sense, they propose a *spirituality of the decision,* or, again, a mysticism* of service, according to Ignatius's insistence that "God must be sought in all things," which Nadal interpreted in terms of being "contemplative in action."

c) Influence. Following the *devotio moderna* and in a more radical way, the *Spiritual Exercises* extend Christian spirituality to all walks of life. By their focus on election and their adaptability they aim at integration of existence in a life lived according to the Holy Spirit*. They would therefore be rapidly extended not only to the reform of monks and the training of the clergy but to the laity* of every rank, in particular to those within the Marial congregations. Many institutions called "Ignatian" would adopt the exercises as the focal point of their spirituality or as an element in an original synthesis. Francis de Sales was directly inspired by them, especially in his doctrine of indifference. Many other founders or reformers performed the spiritual exercises (Charles Borromeo, Bérulle*, and so on). These exercises became Church property, as is shown today by the practice of the examination of conscience and reference to the *Rules for Discernment.*

2. Other Writings

Ignatius's correspondence (6,800 letters), the *Autobiography* (also called *A Pilgrim's Journey),* the *Constitutions,* and the *Spiritual Journal* also form part of the founding documents.

II. The Ignatian Tradition

The tension between prayer and action constantly preoccupied Ignatius. Even though Ignatius, himself a man much given to prayer, demonstrated a preference for searching for union with God through the service of neighbor—whence his insistence on the "examination"—clear contemplative tendencies (Balthasar Alvarez, Cordeses, Alvarez de Paz) arose from the first generations. In 1590, General Aquaviva's letter on prayer annulled the debate: prayer should always tend toward a practical goal and not come to a halt at the joys of contemplation*, given that apostolic needs urge action. One must go to God with an upright intention that transforms action into prayer and that moreover presumes the habit of prayer. This develops Nadal's doctrine of the "circle of prayer and action," which would endlessly be commented on.

The mystical tendency would receive its classical form in the 17th century with Louis Lallemant, Jean-Joseph Surin, Jean Rigoleuc, and Jean-Baptiste Saint-Jure amid the abundance of innumerable spiritual treatises published in Spain, Italy, Germany, Poland, Lithuania, and the Netherlands. The other more ascetic tendency won out with the condemnation of Molinos in 1687 and of quietism* in 1699. Tested by this "twilight of the mystics" (Louis Cognet), then by the rationalism* of the Enlightenment, the Ignatian balance would be saved from voluntarism* only through a few exceptional masters (Jean-Pierre de Caussade, Pierre-Joseph de Clorivière in the 18th century) and through the mysticism of service put into effect in the missionary and instructional epic of the 19th century. The contemporary period, from 1950 on, has seen a real renaissance of the Ignatian spirit through the rediscovery of the *Spiritual Exercises* and of discernment, thanks particularly to publications of the Ignatian *Writings,* to the work of theologians (H. and K. Rahner*, F. Varillon, G. Fessard), and to the sharing of the Ignatian charism within religious and lay communities.

III. Characteristic Features

1. Seeking God's Will

Human beings do not unite with God through prayer or through action but through the union of wills, and that union presupposes a state of inner freedom* that makes it possible to "seek and find the divine will in the organization of one's life" (Exercise 1). This indifference, guided by a desire for conformity with Christ, brings about the discernment of inner impulses (spiritual feelings) that rise up when faced with the alternatives. In this sense, the spiritual* life operates at that point where prayer* and action are no longer two separate activities but join together in a single free act that wants what God wants.

2. Following Christ in His Mission

The growth of this freedom can be understood from a Christocentric viewpoint. The *Spiritual Exercises* cause a desire for "inner knowledge* of the Lord who for me became a man, so as to love him better and follow him." Ignatius's contemplation of Christ becomes an absorption in the mission that Christ received from the Father*; and in the call Christ issues to all, to work "with him" to establish the Kingdom* by fighting the forces of evil*. Union with Christ is seen not in terms of nuptial symbolism but as a *sequela,* an apostolic companionship.

3. In the Midst of Creatures

Ignation indifference has nothing in common with Buddhist detachment. Rather, it is the principle of an action that is all the more incarnate in that it is disengaged from "disordered affections" and rectified by the "right intention." In a letter of 18 July 1548, Ignatius writes, "[God in fact] wants to be glorified and served with what he gives us as Creator, which is nature*, and with what he gives us as the author of grace,* which is the supernatural*." This is why Ignatius does not propose only contemplation of the evangelical mysteries*, sacramental fidelity, and meditation on the commandments and on the counsels but also discernment of spirits, which makes it possible to "feel" what the spirit of Christ urges in existential situations. This im-plies that the Creator speaks to the creature through what he is composed of as a creature (sensitivity, memory, intelligence, will). And it also leads to the Ignatian rule of action as defined by Hevenesi (1705) and commented on by Fessard: "Have faith in God as if success depended entirely on you and not at all on God. However, set every means in motion as if you had nothing to do, and God everything."

4. In Obedience

Obedience is founded on the Church's sacramental nature, the mystical body of Christ organized as a hierarchy. Obedience to the pope* for the missions, the fourth vow that the Jesuit makes during his solemn profession, is, according to Pierre Favre, "our principle and main foundation." True obedience, in fact, "does not look to whom it is given but for whom. And if it is given for our only Creator and Lord, it is him, the Lord of "all, that one obeys" (*Constitutions,* 84). Therefore, it is "blind" provided only that it is not dumb since, as stated in *Constitutions* (92), "It is more than very important, it is capital that the superior should have full knowledge of the inclinations and impulses of those for whom he is responsible." The most audacious initiative might come from below. That is why obedience also concerns the superior.

● *Monumenta Historica Soc. Jesu, Fontes Narrativi,* Rome (1894–).

I. de L. (1991), *Écrits,* Paris. (The series "Textes" from the coll. "Christus" has the main basic texts.)

M. Ruiz Jurado (1965–90), *Orientaciones bibliographicas sobre san I. de L.,* Rome.

♦ E. Przywara (1938–40), Deus semper major, *Theologie der Exerzitien,* Augsburg.

J. de Guibert (1953), *La spiritualité de la Compagnie de Jésus,* Rome.

G. Fessard (1956, 1966, 1984), *La dialectique des Ex. spirituels de saint Ignace de Loyola,* 3 vols., Paris.

K. Rahner (1958), "Die Logik der existentiellen Erkenntnis bei I. von L.," in *Das Dynamische in der Kirche,* Basel.

H. Rahner (1964), *Ignatius von L. als Mensch und Theologe,* Fribourg.

Coll. (1990), *Chercher et trouver Dieu: Lectures des Ex. spirituels d'Ignace de Loloya, Christus,* 124 HS, Paris.

H. U. von Balthasar (1977), *Christlicher Stand,* Einsiedeln.

H. U. von Balthasar (1993), *Texte zum ignazianischen Exerzitienbuch,* Einsiedeln.

J. Servais (1994), "Une théologie de l'obéissance ignatienne," *NRTh* 116, 353–73; (1996) *Théologie des Ex. spirituels: H. U. von Balthasar interprète saint I.,* Brussels.

A. de Jaer (1998), *Faire corps pour la mission: Lire les Constitutions de la Compagnie de Jésus,* Brussels.

H.P. Kolvenbach (1998), *Fous pour le Christ: Sagesse de Maître Ignace,* Brussels.

CLAUDE FLIPO

See also **Asceticism; Carmel; John of the Cross; Mission/Evangelization; Spirituality, Franciscan; Spirituality, Salesian**

Spirituality, Salesian

a) *Francis de Sales (1567–1622).* The eldest of 10 children, Francis de Sales was born in Thorens into an old Savoyard family. His education, first at La Roche and Annecy and then, from 1582 to 1588, with the Jesuits at the Collège de Clermont in Paris was that of a future noble. He was to stay close to the Society for the whole of his life. From 1588 to 1592 he studied law* in Padua, notably with Panciroli (1523–99), while entrusting his soul to the Jesuit Possevin (1534–1611). It is possible that he met the Theatine Scupoli (1530–1610) in Padua; in any event, it was there that he discovered Scupoli's *Spiritual Combat,* a forerunner to *Introduction à la vie dévote,* which would immediately become his bedside book. On his return, and despite his father's reservations, he set his heart on the priesthood* and was ordained in 1593. After having successfully directed the Catholic reconquest of Chablais in 1599, he was appointed bishop-coadjutor of Geneva. Before his episcopal ordination, a diplomatic stay in Paris in 1602 put him in contact with the French court and with Madame Acarie's circle (Bérulle, Carmel*). Ordained bishop on his return, he reestablished his diocese, which had been undermined by Calvinist penetration and was concentrated around Annecy (since all hope of returning Geneva to Savoy and to Catholicism* had been abandoned at the start of his episcopacy). In 1604 he met Jeanne de Chantal (1572–1641), with whom he would found the Order of the Visitation in 1610. Back in Paris in 1618, he met Vincent de Paul, Richelieu, and Angélique Arnaud, who was to place herself under his spiritual direction*. He died in Lyons on 28 December 1622.

b) *The Key to Salesian Thought: Crisis of 1586.* Eager to understand his faith, Francis wanted to take advantage of his studies in Paris in order to initiate himself into theology*. The quarrels of the time drove him to a crisis that would be decisive for his future: tormented by Baius's theses on predestination*, he thought himself damned and sank into deep despair. The temptation* of his era—believing, like Calvin* and Jansenius, in the small number of the elect—imposed itself on him with full force. Then, quite suddenly and definitively and without however giving his full support to Molinism, he was relieved of his torment by abandoning himself to Providence*, an act inspired before the statue of Our Lady of Deliverance. Even if there was only a single elected person, it depended only on himself to be that one through a sincere and total faith, everything else being nothing more than false problems from false theologians. Henceforth, that confidence would dominate his whole inner life, but he would retain from his trials the conviction that to prepare one's salvation* was the only thing that mattered in this world.

It is noteworthy that the two people whom he directed, Jeanne de Chantal and Angélique Arnaud, would have to face the same temptation; the solution for the former would be found in the Order of the Visitation; for the latter, the completely different path of the monastery of Port-Royal, once Francis's death had left the field clear there for Saint-Cyran (Jansenism*).

c) *Salesian Humanism.* From his studies in Paris and Padua, Francis was to retain a thorough classical culture, a love of speaking well and writing well, and above all a deep-seated humanism; "I am so much a man as to be nothing more than a man!" (XII, 330). All ideas interested him, and his thinking progressed continually under the eyes of the masters, both ancient and modern (among them Montaigne), whom he cited with a certain pride. At the height of his pastoral activities he would think it important to found in 1606 a literary academy in Annecy. By temperament he had confidence in the human race ("There is not a soul in the world which attaches itself more warmly, tenderly, and lovingly than I "; XX, 216).

Was he therefore optimistic? If so, rather less than has been claimed. His correspondence reveals him to have been anxious to save whatever could be saved in "the outside world," but he never failed to stress how fragile this salvation was and how much simpler was the monastic life. His *Introduction à la vie dévote* (1608) represents the codification of this encouragement to a sanctity in the world for "those whose circumstances oblige them, to all appearances, to live an ordinary life" (III, 6)—but only for those because deep down he would always hesitate about the salvation of the others. But the fact remains that, independently of the number of the elect, this guidebook to the Christian life would have the merit of setting down for generations to come (the work has gone through more than

1,000 editions in all languages) the rules of a baptismal spirituality exposed to every outside influence, where Christian order no longer holds sway. All the same, the emphasis was laid more on the transposition within society of the means to a religious life than on a more modern evaluation of temporal duties as such.

d) A Man Rather Than a Work. It would be futile to try to systematize Salesian thought. Francis's spiritual doctrine is certainly valid in itself; the density and depth of his *Traité de l'amour de Dieu,* well thought out over a 10-year period and published in unfinished form in 1616, make it an important work of reference for an understanding of the inner life. From the meditation of beginners to the precise description of the death of love*, the treatise is consistent, ordered, and complete. Nonetheless, Salesian spirituality lies elsewhere: in the way of anticipating souls, of revealing them to themselves, and of removing one by one the obstacles that hinder them. This supernatural teaching would be the common foundation of the whole Salesian family from the Order of the Visitation to the numerous congregations that would identify themselves with Francis. Providing an antidote to an ever more influential Jansenism*, it would shape the pastoral work of reforming bishops* such as J.-P. Camus (1583–1652) or A. Revol (1548–1629). His rules are few and uncumbersome but are repeated over and over and pressed to their logical conclusion.

- "God* is the God of the human heart" (IV, 74). A disciple of Bernard* and of Augustine* (the most frequently quoted of his masters), Francis locates the pivot of the spiritual life* in the heart of man, in his ability to love, which made him a sharer in the Love that God is in himself. Therefore, perfection would be to "do everything by love and nothing by force" (XII, 359). Achieving this was just a matter of leaving everything to God, that is, of allowing the active expansion of a love that came from him and that advanced toward him: "Devotion [i.e., perfect love] is not a thing that one must win by force of arms; one must really work at it, but the real toil depends on having trust in God" (XX, 133). In practice, that means "ask for nothing, refuse nothing" (advice that occurs dozens of times in his works): without either repugnance or inappropriate zeal, do things one at a time because each event expresses God's good pleasure, and this without regret for the moment just passed, without anxiety for the moment to come, and with one's attention constantly focused on the God who is present.

- Go forward "gently." No opportunity is too small for a soul that wants to advance: "From wherever good comes, we must love it" (XX, 348). The minimum of means is always most desirable to Francis. He writes, "I have always thought that the spirit of the Order of the Visitation was one of a deep humility towards God and a great gentleness towards one's neighbor… . The spirit of gentleness is so much the spirit of the Order of the Visitation that whoever wanted to introduce more austerity into it would destroy it at once" (VI, 229).

- "I leave you the spirit of liberty*, the spirit that excludes force, doubt, or haste" (XII, 359). Salesian gentleness is not sickly sweet ("I like independent souls, vigorous ones that are not weaklings"; XX, 216) but naturally and supernaturally* calm, by means of which true love and true liberty progress at the same pace: "Grace is so gracious and so graciously seizes our hearts to draw them that she noways does offends the liberty of our will; she touches powerfully but yet so delicately the springs of our spirit that our free will suffers no violence from it" (IV, 127).

● François de Sales, *Œuvres…,* Annecy, 27 vols., 1892–1964.

J.-P. Camus (1624), *Dévotion civile,* Paris

J.-P. Camus (1640), *Théologie mystique,* Paris.

◆ H. Bremond (1912), *Sainte Chantal,* Paris.

A. Gazier (1915), *Jeanne de Chantal et Angélique Arnauld,* Paris.

H. Bremond (1916), *Histoire littéraire…,* I, 68–127.

J. Calvet (1938), *La littérature religieuse de François de Sales à Fénelon,* Paris.

F. Trochu (1946), *Saint François de Sales…,* Lyon-Paris.

Cl. Roffat (1948), *A l'écoute de saint François de Sales,* Paris.

L. Cognet (1951), *La Mère Angélique et saint François de Sales, 1618–1626,* Paris.

J. Dagens (1952), *Bibliographie chronologique de la littérature de spiritualité et de ses sources (1501–1610),* Paris.

V. Brasier et al. (1956), *Bibliographia salesiana,* Turin.

P. Sérouet (1958), *De la vie dévote à la vie mystique,* Paris.

A. Ravier (1962), *Saint François de Sales,* Lyons.

P. Sérouet (1963), "François de Sales," *DSp* 5, 1057–97.

L. Cognet (1966), *La spiritualité moderne,* t. 1: *L'essor: 1500–1650,* Paris.

E.-J. Lajeunie (1966), *Saint François de Sales: L'homme, la pensée, l'action,* Paris.

H. Bordes, J. Hennequin (Eds.) (1994), *L'univers salésien: Saint François de Sales hier et aujourd'hui,* Paris.

MAX HUOT DE LONGCHAMP

See also **Banezianism-Molinism –Baianism; Humanism, Christian; Life, Spiritual; Spiritual Direction; Spiritual Theology; Spirituality, Ignatian**

State. *See* **Church and State**

Staudenmaier, Franz Anton. *See* **Tübingen, Schools of**

Stoicism, Christian

In the Hellenistic world, Stoicism had influence more as a moral philosophy* than as a metaphysics. It provided rich intellectual resources for the Christian theology* of the first centuries, and its influence was to be felt once again at the beginning of the modern era.

a) Stoicism of the Church Fathers.   Stoicism left its deepest mark on the Greek Fathers*, notably Clement and Origen*, because of the importance of the Stoic school in Alexandria. However, Stoicism also made an impact among the Latin Fathers, from Tertullian* on, for they took from it not only the theme of exhortation (*parenesis*) and the rhetorical genre of consolation but also other materials. Thus, Ambrose* of Milan was inspired in writing his *De officiis ministrorum* (389) by Cicero's *De vita beata* (Seneca, Augustine*). Nevertheless, two separate periods and two different attitudes should be distinguished.

In the earlier of these two periods, certain Fathers took from Stoicism, as well as from Platonism*, those philosophical ideas that seemed to them to be pertinent for expressing Christian experience* or teaching. These included notions of the unity and transcendent nature of the divine Logos, the single filiation of the whole of humanity, and the organic conception of the universal society* of humankind. Ambrose, for example, states in *De officiis ministrorum* (III, 19), "It is the natural law that links us to the whole of humanity, so that our relations, one with another, are like those of

the parts of a body." The Stoics' notion of conflagration (*ekpurosis*) was conflated with the idea of the apocalypse, although Origen (*Contra Celsum* VIII, 72) contrasted the cyclical repetition of this catastrophe to the regeneration offered once and for all by the savior Logos. Through a similarly facile conflation between the Stoic *logos* and the Johannine* *logos*, such formulas as "to follow nature is to follow God" or "only the honest are good" seemed to be acceptable in a Christian context.

Very quickly, however, the incompatibility between Christian belief and certain fundamental ideas of Stoicism, such as its thoroughgoing corporealism, led the Fathers to retain Stoic phraseology rather than Stoic ideas and to underline those points on which Christianity and Stoicism differed. The god of the Stoics, the principal organizing agent of the cosmos*, is not a creator god or a savior god, and divine impassibility* (*apatheia*) does not exclude either the goodness or the wrath* of God* (Lactantius, *De ira Dei*). God's wisdom*, the source of a well-ordered world*, implies a specific providence*, concerned with the good* of each individual, in contrast to the impersonal and deterministic providence of Stoicism, which underpinned its hostility to astrology and divination. The Stoics' affirmation that humanity and the universe share a single nature (the "microcosmic" human being of Numenius of Ephesus) influenced Basil*, but Gregory* of Nyssa (*De hom. op.* XVI, PG 44) emphasized the inadequacy of this type of naturalism in handling the creation* of human beings in the image of God.

The divergences between Christianity and Stoicism also had consequences for ethics*. It is right to follow nature (Cicero, *Off.* I, 100), but "to make oneself as much like God as possible" implies more than an ever greater development of rationality. Christians took over the Stoic terminology of the soul (hegemonic), but, apart from Tertullian*, they denied that it could be corporeal in nature. Nevertheless, the morality of "imperial" Stoicism attracted such favor that it was possible to interpret a plagiarized version of Epictetus's *Manual* as a Christian text and, in the fourth century, to find readers for a false exchange of letters between the apostle* Paul and Seneca. Thus, Christians adopted Stoic formulas for the analysis of the passions* and the determination of moral norms, although the right of the wise man to commit suicide (Augustine, *De Civitate Dei* I, 22–29) and the self-sufficiency of the wise man remained stumbling blocks. Indeed, Seneca's argument that the wise man is superior to God because he owes his virtues* to his own efforts rather than to nature* was to give rise to a Christian critique of Stoic pride. However, the ideal of *ataraxia* was taken up within monastic asceticism*, notably in the form of the notion of "holy indifference" (by Meister Eckhart in particular).

b) Modern Era. Stoicism survived into the Middle Ages as a naturalistic morality that emphasized form and intent rather than content and that presented itself as a rival to Aristotelianism*, then dominant. However, from the Renaissance on, there was an increasing number of moral anthologies influenced by Stoicism, such as the *Flores Senecae* compiled by Erasmus* (1534). Thus, Christian Stoicism entered a new period of influence, first in morality and philosophy and then, as a result, in theology*. Calvin*, for example, wrote a commentary on Seneca's *De clementia* (1532), only to end up opposing a conception of destiny and patience that seemed to him to be an expression of obstinacy and pride (*Inst.* XVII).

Seneca's ideas were rediscovered and put into popular form by Justus Lipsius (1604), who presents a Stoic version of theology in his *Physiologia Stoicorum* (1604), an introduction to Seneca's *Naturales quaestiones*. His conception of a transcendent and immanent God, the principle of all life and order, prefigures the God of deism* while avoiding disputes over the Trinity* and Christology*. By forging links between the single, good, and omnipotent God; universal providence; and individual destinies, the Stoic theory of providentialism provided a rationalist explanation for the existence of evil*. Understanding the destiny of each individual as a determinate system of causes, among which (in the case of human beings) free will participates as the decisive cause, made it possible to justify the inevitability of whatever happens and to enfold a series of events within a rational process. This process was understood to be good because desired by God, even though its meaning and its justness would not become apparent until it ended.

Pierre Charron (1541–1603) and Guillaume Du Vair (1556–1621) took from Stoicism the fundamentals of a model of moral wisdom and of impassibility in the face of public misfortunes. Charron insisted on the intrinsic worth of nature and with one blow reduced the role of original sin*. Human perfection once again became a matter of following nature, as in Charron's *De la Sagesse* (II, 3; On Wisdom): "The good, which is the goal and purpose of human beings, and in which are to be found their rest, their liberty, and their contentment—in a word, their perfection in this world—is to live and to act according to nature when whatever is most excellent within them commands them, that is, reason; true prudence is a strict and firm disposition of the will to follow the counsels of reason."

God's grace* is undoubtedly also needed, as the wind that makes the organ on which human virtue plays produce a tune. However, this "relief" for natural virtue, which makes it worthy of an eternal reward, is not a constituent element of beatitude* but an addition to it. Prudence takes the place of charity as the architectonic virtue that organizes and sums up all the other virtues.

During the 17th century, treatises influenced by Stoicism were presented as preparations for Christianity: "Stoic philosophy is the handmaiden of Christian wisdom" (Gaspard Scioppius [1575–1649], *Elementa*, §167). Such treatises set out an easy and accessible way in which every person might reach Heaven (Jean de Bona [1609–74]) or upheld a "natural religion," distanced from superstition, grounded in the recognition of a provident God, and accepting the plurality of churches* (Mackenzie, *Religio stoici*). Stoic indifference (*apatheia*) was understood as "disciplining of judgment" and was seen as being useful for encouraging resignation in the face of divine providence. Nevertheless, there was a danger that such indifference could be mistaken for the proud attitude of one who believes that it is possible to penetrate, by reason, "the counsels of nature, as if making laws for it" (Yves de Paris [1593–1678]).

In general, references to Stoic naturalism invited the reproach, as in the case of Leibniz*, that it led only to "patience without hope" and promoted fatalism and hence a drift into the naturalism* of Spinoza. This is why the morality proposed by Descartes, who eliminated the notion of final causes, was compared to Stoicism. Even before that, S. Goulart, who translated works by Seneca into French, had emphasized in his *Vie de Sénèque* (1595, §XII) that there is an abyss separating pagan philosophy, however suitable it might be for reforming behavior, from revealed religion: "There is nothing in his [Seneca's] writings or in his death that comes close to Christian belief and confession. On the contrary, in my opinion, Stoic philosophy is directly opposed to the true religion, for, while the former teaches human beings to glory in themselves, the latter teaches them to renounce themselves and glory in God."

Pascal*, in his *Entretien avec M. de Saci* (1655, published 1728), objected to Montaigne's skepticism*: after that, Stoicism could no longer be regarded as the philosophical language of Christianity. The Stoic philosophy of the power of human beings had been accurate in its presentation of human grandeur but mistaken in its one-sidedness and its neglect of human wretchedness. It had made what it misunderstood into a philosophical principle, and it therefore came to be seen as a reprise, within theory, of original sin itself. More fundamentally, in treating nature as strictly homogeneous, Stoic naturalism was completely inhospitable to any idea of the supernatural* or of nature as fallen. Finally, the Stoics' conception of time*, centered as it was on the present moment, made it impossible for them to conceive of a personal and collective salvation* embedded in history* and linked to an eschatology*.

● A. de Riveaudeau (1567), *La doctrine d'Épictète stoïcien, comme l'homme se peut rendre vertueux, libre, heureux,* Poitiers.
Juste Lipse (1584), *De Constantia,* Anvers.
Juste Lipse (1604), *Manuductio ad stoicam philosophiam; Physiologia stoicorum,* Anvers.
S. Goulart (1595), *Œuvres morales et meslées de Sénecque,* Paris, 3 vols.; in vol. 3, *Ample discours sur la doctrine des stoïques* (4th Ed., 1606, Geneva).
G. Du Vair (1590), *Traité de la constance et de la consolation es calamités publiques,* Paris; (1600), *De la sainte philosophie,* Paris.

P. Charron (1601), *De la sagesse,* Paris (rev. Ed., Paris, 1604).
G. Scioppius (1606), *Elementa philosophiae stoicae moralis,* Mayence.
Yves de Paris (1638), *De l'indifférence,* Paris.
J. de Bona (1658), *Manuductio ad coelum,* Köln.
P. Du Moulin (1661), *Traité de la paix de l'âme et du contentement de l'esprit,* Paris.
A. de Sarasa (1664), *Ars semper gaudiendi ex principiis divinae providentiae et rectae conscientiae deducta,* Anvers.
G. Mackenzie (1665), *Religio stoici with a friendly adresse to the Phanaticks of all sects and sorts,* Edinburgh.
J. Abbadie (1693) *L'art de se connaître soi-même,* Rotterdam.
♦ G. Verbeke (1945), *L'évolution de la doctrine du* pneuma *du sto. à saint Augustin,* Paris.
E. von Ivanka (1964), *Plato christianus.*
M. Spanneut (1969), *Le stoïcisme des Pères de l'Église,* 2nd Ed., Paris.
J.-C. Fredouille (1972), *Tertullien et la conversion de la culture antique,* Paris.
G. Verbeke (1973), "Le stoïcisme, une philosophie sans frontières," *ANRW* I, 4, 3–42.
Julien-Eymard d'Angers (1976), *Recherches sur le stoïcisme aux XVIe et XVIIe siècles,* Hildesheim.
G. Abel (1978), *Stoizismus und frühe Neuzeit,* Berlin–New York.
J.-C. Fredouille (1981), "Les normes morales du stoïcisme chez les Pères de l'Église," *StMor* XIX, 2, 153–75.
M. L. Colish (1985), *The Stoic Tradition from Antiquity to the Early Middle Ages,* 2 vols., Leiden.
H. Gouhier (1987), *L'anti-humanisme au XVIIe siècle,* Paris.
A. Jagu (1989), "La morale d'Épictète et le christianisme," *ANRW* XXXVI, 3, 2165–99.
V. Carraud (1992), *Pascal et la philosophie,* Paris.
J. Lagrée (1994), *Juste Lipse et la restauration du sto.,* Paris.
G. Olivo (1994), "Une patience sans espérance? Descartes et le stoïcisme," in *Le stoïcisme aux XVIe et XVIIe siècles,* Ed. J. Lagrée, CPPJ 25, 131–46.
T. Gregory (1999), *Genèse de la raison classique, de Charron à Descartes,* Paris.

JACQUELINE LAGRÉE

See also **Alexandria, School of; Aritotelianism, Christian; Deism; Erasmus, Desiderius; Origen; Pascal, Blaise; Platonism, Christian; Providence; Tertullian**

Strauss, David Friedrich. *See* **Tübingen, Schools of**

Structures, Ecclesial

The notion of ecclesial structures indicates that the Church* of Jesus Christ* constitutes an organized entity. Different kinds of structures have appeared in the course of history*. Simplifying, we may distinguish between the following structures: *primatial,* which depends on a supreme pontiff; *episcopal,* centered on the ministry* of the bishop*; *synodal,* in which responsibility is exercised collegially; *congregational,* in which each particular community holds complete power; and *consistorial,* marked by its administrative character. In reality, however, none of these types appears in its pure state. Ecclesial constitutions never allow one of these elements to dominate without also accepting others. The task of the theologian in this area is to determine whether the factors of the organization are based on the positive function of the Church as it was instituted by God* (*iure divino*), on the "natural law*" willed by divine ordinance, or on a purely historical necessity (*iure humano*).

1. History

The problematic considered here was already present in the earliest developments of the Church. According to the New Testament the Church is the mystery* of the salvific action of God, which operates in time* and space through the Word* and the sacraments*. As such, it transcends the institutional order, but at the same time it can accomplish its historical task only by means of an organization and with the help of institutions that always fall short of its essential reality. This is what is expressed by the founding images by which the Church is designated in the New Testament: the relation to God (the Trinitarian God) is always emphasized there, but this is also so for a given structural element, which may not necessarily coincide with another element valorized in other conceptions. The notion of *people* of God, for example, implies a relationship of equality among all its members, whereas the image of *body of Christ* may give rise to a hierarchical interpretation, and the image of the *temple of the Holy Spirit** signifies both equality (all have received the Holy Spirit) and the episcopal structure of the Church (apostolic succession*). There are thus several models of ecclesial structure as early as the New Testament period. In the Pauline communities, rigorously subject to the authority* of the apostle*, the

functional division of tasks according to differences of gifts predominates (*see* 1 Cor 12:4–31a, with the reference to the body of Christ). In the Greek communities we find a collegial organization of the Church (Phil 1:1: bishops and deacons*; Ti 1:5: presbyters*; Acts 20:28: presbyters and bishops). Presbyterial organization was the rule in Jerusalem*.

It was not until the second century that the episcopal structure, with the hierarchical triad of bishop, priest, and deacon, was established in communities (local* churches) as well as in assemblies of local churches; these were governed by the synodal principle, and each bishop represented his church. After the establishment of the imperial church (381) and through the increased authority of the pontifical see in Rome*, constitution assumed a metropolitan and patriarchal character. From the fourth century, monastic communities and religious orders were able to develop their own structures with relative independence. The Eastern Church, for its part, was organized around a threefold principle: the eucharistic basis of the local (episcopal) church, the pentarchy (primacy of the five oldest patriarchates*: Council of Nicaea*, can. 6–7), and the "symphony" between the Church and the (Byzantine) state (Council of Chalcedon*, can. 17).

In the West a strongly centralized system took shape from the 11th century on. Its principal elements were the almost absolute primacy of the pope* (in a history running from Gregory VII in the 11th century to Vatican I* in the 19th), the unification of canon law* (by Gratian in the 12th century), and the insistence on "inequality" between clergy and laity*. Synodal elements survived only through the rights of participation of cathedral and collegial chapters as well as in the institution of the council. In the late Middle Ages this concentration of power provoked opposition (mendicants, conciliarism*, secularization of Church property by monarchs) that through the Reformation was to give rise to new confessions organized on the synodal (Lutheranism*), presbyterial (Reformed Churches), or congregational (Free Churches) model. The 20th century has seen the development of worldwide, continental, and national confessional alliances (confessional* families) as well as a World Council* of Churches bringing together the principal churches other than the Roman Church. The council has not, however, introduced any organizational principle into the community of its members.

2. Ecclesial Structures in Contemporary Christian Churches

a) The Catholic Church. It sees itself as the visible community of believers, not absolutely identical, however, to the Church of Christ (*LG* 8). All believers who are in communion* with it participate in its mission. Some are members of the clergy, others of the laity; this difference is based on the sacrament of orders*. Authority* inheres essentially in the clergy, which has a dual structure: a vital structure based on the ordination* that links bishops to the apostles (apostolic succession), priests, and deacons by integrating them into the apostolic succession and a legal structure based on the power of jurisdiction invested in the pope—who holds supreme and absolute legal authority—and in the bishops. The latter, in communion* with the pope (*communio hierarchica*), exercise power in the universal Church and in the dioceses (local church). This primatial-episcopal structure is complemented by synodal characteristics (the system of councils, worldwide as well as in a single parish) as well as by congregational elements (which restore importance to the role of the laity and of local communities and affirm the fundamental rights of the Christian).

b) Orthodox Churches. The basis for the Orthodox ecclesial structure is the independence of the local church, centered on the sacrament of the Eucharist* and subject to the authority of the bishop, who is placed in the apostolic succession. There is no primatial jurisdictional body, for all local churches are equal, and all bishops participate in the same apostolic succession. Because the Eucharist is also the same everywhere, the different local churches, and hence the different bishops, are united by the bond of communion, which is realized and manifested primarily in the councils*. The synodal principle is thus the real structure of the Eastern Church. But it also includes primatial elements in the patriarchal system as well as congregational elements in the emphasis on reception*, particularly in Russian theology* (modern and contemporary Orthodoxy*) since Khomiakov (the principle of *sobornost* as participation of all believers in the life of the Church).

c) The Churches of the Reformation. The Churches that came out of the Reformation or that have been established since then have very diverse ecclesial structures. They nevertheless all share a strict rejection of the primatial principle and an emphasis on the synodal, congregational, and also very broadly consistorial aspects of their constitutions. In the Scandinavian Churches, in the Anglican communion, and in part also in the United States, episcopal structures have been maintained or, as in Germany after 1918, reestablished. These Churches also maintain very different relations with the political authorities. Sometimes the sovereign has the status of *summus episcopus;* sometimes the Church is a state church, with the head of state as a structural element; and sometimes, on the contrary, church and state* are rigorously separated.

● A. Khomiakov (1870), *Die Einheit der Kirche,* Berlin.
K. Küng (1960), *Strukturen der Kirche,* Fribourg-Basel-Vienna.
A. Dulles (1967), *Models of the Church,* Dublin.
W. Aymans (1970), *Das synodale Element in der Kirchenverfassung,* Munich.
H. Frost (1972), *Strukturprobleme evangelischer Kirchenverfassung,* Göttingen.
W. de Vries (1974), *Les structures ecclésiales vues dans l'histoire des sept premiers conciles œcuméniques,* Paris.
E. Wolf, E. Thul (1975), "Kirchenverfassung," in *Evangelisches Staatslexikon,* 2nd Ed., Stuttgart-Vienna, 1248–93.
G. Alberigo (1981), *Chiesa conciliare,* Brescia.
K. Walf (1984), *Einführung in das neue katholische Kirchenrecht,* Zurich.
A. Jensen (1986), *Die Zukunft der Orthodoxie: Konzilspläne und Kirchenstrukturen,* Zurich-Einsiedeln-Köln.
A. Anton (1989), *Conferencias episcopales—instancias intermedias,* Salamanca.
H. Frost (1989), "Kirchenverfassungen," *EKL3* 2, 1192–202.
H.J. Pottmeyer (Ed.) (1989), *Kirche im Kontext der modernen Gesellschaft: Zur Strukturfrage der römisch-katholischen Kirche,* Munich-Zurich.
M. Kehl (1993), *Die Kirche,* 2nd Ed., Würzburg.
R. Puza (1993), *Katholisches Kirchenrecht,* 2nd Ed., Heidelberg.
W. Aymans (1995), *Kirchenrechtliche Beiträge zur Ekklesiologie,* Berlin.

WOLFGANG BEINERT

See also **Catholicism; Church and State; Collegiality; Gospel; Government, Church; Hierarchy; Jurisdiction; Orthodoxy; Protestantism; Salvation; Synod**

Suarez, Francisco

1548–1617

Suarez was a Spanish Jesuit, theologian, philosopher, and jurist who became known as the *Doctor eximius* ("distinguished doctor").

a) Life and Writings.   Born in Granada, Suarez entered the Society of Jesus in 1564 while he was studying canon law* at the University of Salamanca. He studied theology* from 1566 to 1570. He began teaching in 1571, first, as was customary, in philosophy* and then, from 1574, in theology, notably at the University of Valladolid, where he wrote a commentary on the first part of the *Summa Theologica* of Thomas Aquinas*. In 1580 he was called to teach theology at the Roman College. He also wrote a commentary on the questions in parts IIa and IIIa of the *Summa* while he was in Rome*. Having returned to Spain health grounds in 1585, he went to the University of Alcala to replace Gabriel Vasquez (1549–1604), the other great Jesuit theologian of the time, with whom Suarez openly disagreed on a number of questions. Vasquez himself took Suarez's place in Rome. At Alcala, Suarez continued his teaching on the questions in part IIIa of the *Summa.* He then published his *Commentarium ac disputationum in tertiam partem Divi Thomae tomus primus* (Alcala, 1590, Vivès XVII–XVIII).

After Vasquez returned to Alcala, Suarez departed for the University of Salamanca, where, not being required to teach, he devoted his energies to publishing his writings, based on his course notes. During this period he revised and expanded his first volume on part III of the *Summa* and published a second volume (Alcala, 1592, Vivès XIX) and a third (Salamanca, 1595, Vivès XX–XXI). He also started writing his *Disputationes metaphysicae,* which is partly based on the philosophy courses that he had taught in the first years of his teaching career and which was intended as an introduction to the study of his theology. Having been made a doctor of the University of Evora, Suarez was invited to Coimbra in 1597 by King Philip II of Spain-Portugal to occupy the famous chair of principal professor. It was also in 1597 that Suarez published the *Disputationes metaphysicae* (Salamanca, Vivès XXV–XXVI). The fourth and fifth volumes of his commentary on part IIIa of the *Summa* appeared some years later (respectively, Coimbra, 1602, Vivès XXII, and *De censuris,* Coimbra, 1603, Vivès XXIII).

The concilium *de auxiliis* (Bañezianism*) began around the same time, and Suarez had to break off his work on his commentary in order to address the relations between grace* and freedom. The texts he wrote during this period were collected in the *Opuscula theologica sex* (Madrid, 1599, Vivès XI): they include, in particular, *De concursu et efficaci auxilio Dei ad actus liberi arbitrii necessario, De scientia quam Deus habet de futuris contingentibus,* and the memorandum *Brevis resolutio quaestionis de concursu et efficaci auxilio Dei ad actus liberi arbitrii necessario.* This memorandum served as a manifesto for a number of Jesuit theologians in Castile along with *Disputatio de justitia qua Deus reddit praemia meritis et poenas pro peccatis.* The latter is an argument against Vasquez, who did not accept that divine justice* has anything to do with rewarding merits, on the grounds that such rewards are due exclusively to divine goodness and that divine justice has no role to play other than in the punishment of sins*. The *Opuscula* were criticized by Bañez, and Suarez defended them in a memorandum that was not published until 1859 (by Monseigneur Malou in Brussels): *Patris Francisci Suarez gravis epistola ad Clementem VIII pontificem maximum et epistolae subjuncta ejusdem Apologia, seu responsiones ad propositiones de auxiliis gratiae notatas a M. Dominico Bannez.* In this same context we should also mention Suarez's *Tractatus theologicus de vera intelligentia auxilii efficacis ejusque concordia cum libertate voluntarii consensus,* which was also published posthumously (Lyon, 1655, Vivès X).

Suarez did not take part in any of the concilium *de auxiliis,* but he had great influence over the debates through those of his pupils and followers who did take part as well as through his presence in Rome from 1604 to 1606. This was due to the necessity of defending his argument, expounded chiefly in *De paenitentia* (*Disputatio* XXI, §IV, Vivès XXII), for the sacramental nature of confession for one who is absent, which makes confession at a distance possible. (This argument was to reappear during the 19th century, when the question of confession by telephone was raised.) Despite Suarez's efforts, the argument was prohibited by Rome in a decree dated 7 June 1603 (*DS 1994–95*).

After his return to Coimbra, Suarez went on teaching until 1615 and published or prepared for publication his commentaries on part Ia of the *Summa: De Deo* (Lisbon, 1606, Vivès I), *De angelis* (Lyon, 1620, Vivès II), and *De opere de sex dierum* (Lyon, 1621, Vivès III). He also worked on his commentaries on part Ia IIae, *De gratia* (first and second parts, Coimbra, 1619; third part, Coimbra, 1651; Vivès VII–X) and *De legibus* (Coimbra, 1612, Vivès V–VI). He wrote *De virtute et statu religionis*, which concerns part IIa IIae, not on the basis of his own teaching but at the request of the Jesuit General Father Aquaviva. This commentary was published together with a treatise on the religious life in the Society of Jesus (4 vols., Coimbra, 1608–9, and Lyons, 1624–25, Vivès XIII–XVI). It was during this period that Suarez changed the method he used in his commentaries on Aquinas. Several polemical treatises also date from this period, including *Defensio fidei catholicae et apostolicae adversus anglicanae sectae errores…* (Coimbra, 1613, Vivès XXIV), which was written at the request of Pope Paul V in opposition to two texts by King James I of Great Britain. Such writing and publishing works were brought to an end with Suarez's death on 25 September 1617. After his death, his friend Father Balthazar Alvarès (1561–1630) undertook to publish not only those works that were ready for publication but also the course notes that Suarez had not yet revised. In addition to the posthumous publications of the 17th century that we have already mentioned, Alvarès published *De anima*, a philosophical treatise that dated from Suarez's youth but that had been partially revised before his death in order to make it part of his theological system (Coimbra, 1621, Vivès III). Alvarès also published part of a commentary on part Ia IIae of the *Summa*, based on lectures given in Rome, which had also probably been partly revised by Suarez (Lyon, 1628, Vivès IV), and part of a commentary on part IIa IIae (Coimbra, 1621, Vivès XII). However, neither Alvarès nor, two centuries later, Malou was able to complete the publication of Suarez's writings.

b) Suarez's Characteristic Method and Arguments. Suarez's works are distinctive primarily because of the style of his commentaries on texts by Aquinas and Aristotle. Indeed, he systematized a new form of commentary. Instead of closely following the letter of the text being commented on, the succession of arguments within it, or even the order in which questions are addressed in it, his commentaries are organized as autonomous treatises providing systematic treatment of the questions at stake and invoking the text being commented on solely to insert excerpts from it in their original order. Thus, each of his commentaries progresses in line with the passage reproduced at the beginning, and there is no further reference to it other than to indicate concordance with the questions. This new style of com-

mentary, more concerned with doctrine than with text, was undeniably "modern," representing a break away from the traditional practices inherited from medieval Scholasticism*. Suarez adopted this approach in his philosophical works from the outset, with *Disputationes metaphysicae,* but only at a later stage in his theological works, at the time of his first period in Coimbra (from 1606). As a result, two different methods are applied in his commentaries on the *Summa Theologica.*

Suarez was also innovative in his way of handling the relationship between philosophy and theology. Even though he accepted the traditional view of philosophy as the handmaiden of theology, Suarez believed that metaphysics was prior to any doctrine, including theology. Theology is discursive and develops on the basis of natural principles that it takes to be understood, while the function of metaphysics is to establish and explain these natural principles. Accordingly, metaphysics has value as a universal foundation, its prior status is equivalent to independence from theology, and this independence is required precisely so that it can best perform its role as handmaiden (*see Disputationes metaphysicae, prooemium,* vol. XXV, and *De divina substantia, prooemium,* vol. I).

Suarez's approach to metaphysics is distinctive for five main reasons. 1) He regards metaphysics as the study of real being, *ens in quantum ens reale.* 2) He divides studies in metaphysics into two distinct disciplines: the common determination of being (covered in the first volume of *Disputationes metaphysicae,* vol. XXV) and then (as in the second volume of that work, vol. XXVI) the determination of the different species of being, in other words, the specific determinations of being. This division would lead, following Suarez, to the distinction between *metaphysica generalis* and *metaphysica specialis.* It allowed Suarez to argue for a double primacy within metaphysics: on the one hand, the primacy of being understood in terms of its largest and most universal determination, which constitutes the sufficient and principal object of metaphysics, the being of God*, and, on the other hand, the primacy of being from the point of view of the study of the specific determinations of being. 3) Suarez subjected God to metaphysics. He studied God as primary object, but only as *praecipua pars entis,* not as deity*. One may therefore speak of Suarez's metaphysics as having an ontotheological structure. 4) As against Aquinas, Suarez refused to treat the being* of a real being as an act distinct from essence. This refusal is manifested in particular in Suarez's concern to exclude from metaphysics every datum that is resistant to reason*. 5) Finally, Suarez affirmed the primacy of the univocality of the objective concept of *ens* over the analogy* itself (*Disputationes metaphysicae* I–III).

In theology Suarez often distanced himself from the

Thomist tradition (Thomism*), in particular on the following questions: 1) the motive for the Incarnation* (*Commentaria in tertiam partem* …, vol. XVII), 2) the role of the express species in knowledge and its consequences for the conception of the beatific vision* (*De Divina substantia*, l. II, c. 11 and 12, vol. I), and 3) the tendency to supplement Aquinas's intellectualism* by taking greater account of the will, whether in the determination of beatitude* (*De ultimo fine hominis*, d. VII, vol. IV), in relation to the question of the origin of civil society* (*De opere sex dierum*, l. V, c. VII, vol. III), or in defining law* (*De legibus*, l. I, c. V, vol. V). It was on the question of the definition of law that Suarez entered into controversy with Vasquez.

Along with certain other Jesuit theologians of his time, Suarez accepted the hypothesis of pure nature* (*De ultimo fine hominis*, d. IV, s. III) and of the type of relationship between nature and the supernatural that results from it. He also accepted, albeit after some reflection, the idea of intermediate knowledge. However, he differed from the Molinists on the problem of predestination*, for he adopted Bañez's solution to it and succeeded in reconciling it with the notion of intermediate knowledge: it is because God has predetermined us that he can infallibly foresee our consenting to receive grace (*De concursu, motione et auxilio Dei*, vol. XI).

In the moral domain, Suarez played an important role in the development of casuistry* at the turn of the 16th and 17th centuries by contributing to the formulation of what was to be called moderate probabilism (*De bonitate et malitia…*, d. XII, vol. IV). On questions of politics and law, what is most noteworthy is Suarez's insistence on the specific nature of the purpose of civil life (*De legibus*, l. III, c. XI, vol. V) and the consequences of that specificity for the treatment of two questions: the relationship between Church and state* and the limits of political authority. Suarez applied these considerations to the case of James I (*Defensio fidei*, vol. XXIV). We should also mention the role that Suarez played in the establishment of the natural law tradition, even though his ideas were then developed in an antitheological spirit opposed to his intentions, as well as his contribution to the definition and development of modern international law.

The exceptional breadth and diversity of Suarez's writings ought not to distract us from the originality and firmness that he brought to the exposition of his ideas or to his independence of spirit. His importance within theology and philosophy throughout the 17th century cannot be exaggerated. It was assumed that Suarez was a Thomist, and from the 17th century on, his writings became the main reference point for philosophy and theology within the Society of Jesus. By another irony of history, this Counter-Reformation Jesuit also had considerable influence on the development of the "Scholastic metaphysics" that dominated Lutheranism* in German-speaking countries during the 17th century. Suarez's influence even extended into Greek and Russian Orthodox theology, which was undergoing its "Babylonian captivity" at that time and depended exclusively on borrowings from the Latin West. Suarez's ideas also played a leading role in the "neo-Thomism" that was encouraged in the late 19th century by Leo XIII's encyclical *Aeterni Patris* (4 August 1879). The Thomist manuals published at that time were inspired by late Scholastic commentators (John of Saint-Thomas and the *Salmanticenses; see* Thomism*) and especially by Suarez. The history of "Suarezism" was thus extended into the early years of the 20th century, when it was represented most notably by P. Descoqs and G. Picard.

- *Opera omnia*, Paris (Vivès), 1856–78, reprises the edition of the *Opera Omnia*, Venice, 1740–51. Suarez's correspondence and other writings are not included in this edition and reamin unpublished.

R.P. Francisci Suaresii Opuscula sex inedita, Ed. Mgr Malou, Paris-Brussels, 1859. To be published in *Bibliotheca hispanica de filosofia*, Madrid.

♦ K. Werner (1889), *S. und die Scholastik der letzten Jahrhunderte*, Ratisbonne.

R. de Scorraille (1912), *François S., de la Compagnie de Jésus*, 2 vols., Paris.

A. Gemelli (Ed.) (1918), *Scritti varii pubblicati in occasione del terzo centenario della morte di F. S.*, RFNS X/1.

E. Rivière, R. de Scorraille (1918), *S. et son œuvre, à l'occasion du troisième centenaire de sa mort*, Toulouse.

L. Mahieu (1921), *F. S. Sa philosophie et les rapports qu'elle a avec sa théologie*, Paris.

P. Descoqs (1925), *Institutiones metaphysicae generalis*, Paris; 1926, "Thomisme et suarézisme," *ArPh* 4, 82–192.

M. Grabmann (1926), "Die *Disputationes Metaphysicae* des Franz S.," *Mittelalterliches Geistesleben*, vol. I, chap. XVII, Munich.

E. Conze (1928), *Der Begriff der Metaphysik bei Franciscus S.*, Leipzig.

J. B. Scott (1933), *S. and the international community*, Washington, D.C.

P. Mesnard (1936), *L'essor de la philosophie politique au XVIe siècle*, Paris.

P. Monnot, P. Dumont, R. Brouillard (1941), "S.," *DThC* 14/2, 2638–728.

É. Gilson (1947), *L'être et l'essence*, Paris.

G. Picard (1949), "Le thomisme de S.," *ArPh* 18, 108–28.

S. Castellote Cubelles (1962), *Die anthropologie des S. Beiträge zur spanischen Anthropologie des XVI. und XVII. Jahrhunderts*, Fribourg-Munich.

R. Wilenius (1963), *The social and political theory of Fr. S.*, Helsinki.

J.-L. Marion (1980), *Sur la théologie blanche de Descartes*, Paris.

J.-F. Courtine (1990), *S. et le système de la métaphysique*, Paris.

B. Neveu (1993), *L'erreur et son juge*, Naples.

M. G. Lombardo (1995), *La forma che dà l'essere alle cose: Enti di ragione e bene trascendentale in Suárez, Leibniz, Kant*, Milan.

LAURENCE RENAULT

See also **Analogy; Authority; Bañezianism-Molinism-Baianism; Being; Casuistry; Grace; Law; Predestination; Supernatural; Vision, Beatific**

Substance. *See* Being

Subordinationism

The term "subordinationism" covers the different forms taken, in particular before the Council of Nicaea* in 325, by the tendency to make the Son* dependent on the Father* and to place him therefore in a certain position of inferiority in relation to the Father. And while subordinationism is centered primarily on the person of the Son, it may also be compared with different types of modalism*. Before Nicaea the christological definitions of the Fathers*, who were concerned with preserving the integrity of the monotheistic affirmation and above all with avoiding any ditheism in relation to the Son, could avoid the risk of subordinationism only with great difficulty. Certain verses of the New Testament, particularly in the Saint John's Gospel, also lent support to a hierarchical presentation of the Father, the Son, and the Spirit. Thus, alongside expressions indicating the equality of Father and Son (Jn 10:30; 14:7, 9; 17:10, 21), there could also be found "The Father is greater than I" (Jn 14:28), which was rarely applied by the Fathers to the humanity of the Word* alone but also to its divinity. The influence of the emanationist schemas of the Gnostic type also influenced the various currents of theology* of the Logos in the second and third centuries (Simonetti 1993); the divinity of the Son is a divinity of participation, and only the idea of a subordination of the Son to the Father can allow one to distinguish them from each other (*See* Novatian, *De trin.* 31, 192). Several passages in the works of Justin might lead us to view this apologist* as a subordinationist: in his desire to fully maintain the unity of God and the monarchy of the Creator, he speaks of the Logos as the "most powerful and most just prince we know, *after* God who engendered him" (*First Apology* 12, 7; *see also* the *Dialogue with Trypho* 56, 4; 61, 1). Irenaeus*, however, avoided any form of subordinationism in two ways: first, in refuting Gnostic systems he took care to insist on the difference between rational "emissions" of eons and the generation of the

Son, which was an ineffable event (*Adv. Haer.* 2, 28, 6); second, and even more important, the connections he established between theology and economy preserved both the full equality of the Persons within the Trinity* and the order of their manifestation.

Subordinationism is still a live issue in the work of Origen (Rius-Camps 1987). His position may seem contradictory, and according to the texts he holds that the Son is both equal and subordinate to the Father. "There is no time where the Son did not exist," he affirms on several occasions (*Treatise of Principles* I, 2, 9 and IV, 4, 1; *Commentary on the Romans* I, 5); and as Athanasius* (*De decretis nicaneae synodi*, PG 25, 465), he refers to the Greek text of the *Treatise of Principles* (IV, 4, 1), it is out of the question to consider the affirmation as an addition due to the Latin translator Rufinus. Other formulations in Origen's work do, however, imply (e.g., *Commentary on John* XIII, 25, 151) that the Son is inferior to the Father, thus lending support to the idea of subordinationism; but it is the question of the order of the Persons* that is dealt with in this way, and the Father's superiority is a result of the fact that he is the Father, the source of divinity. Origen's exegesis* of John 14:28 in the *Contra Celsum* (VIII, 14–15) aimed above all at refuting the idea—which Origen attributed to Celsus—that the Son, the Logos, could be more powerful than the Father. Elsewhere (*Commentary on John* XIII, 151), using the meaning of "logos" as a proportion, he asserted that the Son, like the Spirit, "transcends all creatures...but is himself transcended by the Father as greatly or even more than he himself or the Holy Spirit transcend other beings."

The only subordinationism that was truly heretical was that of Arius and his successors, who refused the Nicaean *homoousios* (consubstantial*) and considered the Son to be a creature. The debate on the concept of engendering during the Arian crisis was thus a lasting reflection of the subordinationist position, to which the

Christology* of the Athanasius's *Defense against the Arians,* written between 338 and 350 (PG 26), was a response.

● G.-L. Prestige (1955), *God in Patristic Thought,* London.
W. Marcus (1963), *Der Subordinatianismus,* Munich.
J. Doré (1982), "Monarchianisme et sub.," dans *Initiation à la pratique de la théologie* (coll.), II, 1, Paris, 209–16.
J. Rius-Camps (1987), "Subordinacianismo en Origenes," in L. Lies (Ed.), *Origeniana Quarta,* Innsbruck-Vienna, 154–86.

H. Crouzel (1992), *Origène et Plotin,* Paris, 123–33.
M. Simonetti (1993), *Studi sulla cristologia del II e III secolo,* Rome.
G. U. Bilbao (1996), *Monarquia y Trinidad: El concepto teologico "Monarchia" en la controversia "monarchiana,"* Madrid.

HENRI CROUZEL

See also **Arianism; Christ/Christology; Docetism; Johannine Theology; Modalism**

Substance

Philosophical Greek from Aristotle on commonly uses substance in two senses. Substance is, on the one hand, individual reality, the this or the that, a man, a god, a stone: we are then speaking of "first substance," *prôtè ousia.* Substance is, on the other hand, what members of the same species have in common: we are then speaking of "second substance," *deutera ousia.* Peter and John are each a first substance. But they are both men and therefore have a second substance (a nature) in common. The vocabulary of substance made its solemn entry into Christian language when the Council of Nicaea* defined the consubstantiality of the Father* and the Son, so that they are one and the same God*: consubstantiality thus as one and only one first substance (if "substance" had been used in the sense of second substance, the council would have asserted that the Father and the Son have divinity in common, as the gods of Olympus do, that is, as participants in a single nature). The language of substance was later used by the bishops* present at the Council of Chalcedon* in a confession of faith formulated in an equivocal way, calling Christ* "consub-stantial with the Father in His divinity" (first substance) and "consubstantial with us in His humanity" (second substance). Another Aristotelian distinction, that between substance and accident, was appropriated for theology in the Scholastic* doctrine of the Eucharist*, in which appeared the notion—monstrous in terms of Aristotle's physics, which the Averroists hastened to point out—of transubstantiation (a first substance, bread and wine, is converted into another first substance, body and blood of Christ, but the accidents of the first substance remain). It should be added that the most solemn formulations of the Catholic doctrine of the Eucharist speak of substance and "species," not substance and accidents.

● C. Stead (1977), *Divine Substance,* Oxford.
J. Halfwassen et al. (1998), "Substanz; Substanz/Akzident," *HWP* 10, 495–553.
H. Seidl (2001), "Substanz," *TRE* 32, 293–303 (bibl.).

JEAN-YVES LACOSTE

See also **Being; Chalcedon, Council of; Consubstantial; Nicaea I, Council of**

Suicide. *See* Death

Sunday

a) *Origin of Sunday.* The New Testament states that the Christians gather together on the first day of the week, the day on which Christ* was resurrected (Acts 20:7–12; 1 Cor 16:2; *see also* Jn 20:26). In Greek this day received the name of "the Lord's day" (Rev 1:10), in Latin *dominica dies,* whence derived the Spanish *domingo* and the French *dimanche* and so on (while the Germanic languages kept their reference to the sun's day). The Slavic name for this day means "resurrection*."

According to the old law* (Ex 20:8), the Jews reserved the Sabbath* (seventh day) for the Lord God*—an observance whose legalistic aspects were annulled by Jesus* when he declared that he was the Lord of the Sabbath (Mt 12:8). It is difficult to tell whether the early Christians (or certain ones among them) observed both the Sabbath and Sunday or whether in the early days the gathering on the first day of the week took place according to the Jewish way of counting the days, the evening of the day before (therefore on Saturday), or whether, on the contrary, from the outset it took place on the morning of the resurrection. In any event, from the beginning of the second century, according to Ignatius of Antioch (*Letter to the Magnesians* 9), it seems that there are two incompatible rationalizations, and Pliny the Younger's epistle to Trajan (112) certainly seems to indicate that the Sunday gathering was a fundamental practice of the Christians.

Justin Martyr's *First Apology* has left us the first description of a Sunday eucharistic assembly. For the martyrs of Abitinae in Tunisia (304), this assembly was a requirement of their faith*, even though an imperial edict forbade it to be held. Contrary to the previously mentioned imperial edict, Constantine was to favor the pagan cult of the sun at the same time as Christianity when he made the first day of the week a day of rest (321).

b) *Theology.* In the theology* of the fathers* of the church*, Sunday was the day on which the resurrected Christ was present in the midst of his disciples as he was during the meals that followed Easter*, and it would also be the day of his return at the end of time. It is the first day of the week, and it thus commemorates the creation* of the world, and it is the eighth day, the day that comes after the Sabbath, therefore the day of the world to come. The theme of the resurrection is

perhaps stressed more strongly in the ordinary Byzantine liturgy* for Sundays (as it was already in Jerusalem* in the fourth century, when one of the Gospels* about Christ's resurrection was read at the nocturnal vigil), while the Roman liturgy pays more attention to the sequential unfolding of the Word* of God during the course of the year.

Early Christians laid great stress on two distinctive symbols in the dominical liturgy: the absence of fasting and the practice of praying standing up and not on one's knees since standing prayer* symbolically represented Jesus raised from the dead. From the Constantinian era on, the fact that Sunday was a day of rest gave the Sunday holiday an importance that, despite the difference in meaning, was not without analogy with the Old Testament attitude to the Sabbath. According to the Catholic discipline (*CIC,* can. 1247), the dominical obligation mainly involved participation in Holy Communion; theologians have striven to bring out the full importance of the principle of this obligation. It is a participation in a gathering of the Church, which ensues from the Church's very nature as an assembly. Moreover, when Mass is not accessible, a liturgy of the Word is strongly recommended in Church or among family circles (*CIC,* can. 1248). The religious traditions to which the Protestant Reformation gave birth make no provision for an obligation on this point; on the other hand, certain people strive to put a higher value in the Sunday service on celebration of the Eucharist*, which is quite often still restricted to four Sundays per year (because the Reformers did not allow Holy Communion without communion).

● W. Rordorf (1981), "Ursprung und Bedeutung der Sonntagsfeier im frühen Christentum: Der gegenwärtige Stand der Forschung," *LJ* 31, 145–56.

H. Auf der Maur (1983), *Feiern im Rythmus der Zeit I, Herrenfeste in Woche und Jahr,* Ratisbonne, 35–49.

P. Jounel (1983), "Le dimanche," in A.-G. Martimort (Ed.), *L'Église en prière,* new Ed., vol. IV, Paris, 23–41.

MD 166 (1986), *Le lectionnaire dominical de la messe.*

Congrégation pour le culte divin (1988), "Directoire pour les célébrations dominicales en l'absence de prêtre," *Not* 24, 366–78.

P. Bradshaw (1995), *La liturgie chrétienne en ses origines,* Paris, 217–19.

PIERRE-MARIE GY

See also **Cult; Easter; Liturgical Year; Mystery; Shabbat**

Superessential. *See* Supernatural

Supernatural

The concept of the supernatural is a theoretical tool that enables us to envisage the union of man with God*. At the intersection of anthropology* and theology*, it relies on the idea that man is by nature* oriented toward God: man has a natural desire for the vision of God, an aspiration that nature cannot accomplish by itself and that only a supernatural gift can satisfy. Just as grace* fulfills the ends of nature by raising it beyond its natural power, the supernatural completes nature and gives meaning to human history*. Through the vicissitudes of the supernatural, one may grasp all the difficulties of Christian anthropology.

a) The Word and the Thing. "Supernatural" was used at first to designate substances superior to nature. Following Plato (*Republic* VII, 509*b*), the apologist Justin designates God as living "beyond every essence (*epekeina pasès ousias*)"; others locate Him beyond the world or beyond heaven. For Gregory* of Nazianzius, God is "above essence" (*Sixth Discourse,* chap. 12; PG 35, 737 B). Didymus the Blind sees in God the "superessential essence" (*hupeousios ousia, De Trin.* II, 4; III, 2, 47), as does Gregory of Nyssa (*Contra Eunomes*). Pseudo-Dionysius* adopts the vocabulary of Proclus in order to celebrate divine transcendence, the "superessential Jesus*" (*Mystic Theology* I, 3; PG 3, 1033 A), which is beyond all heavenly essences, the God above nature (*huperphuès, Divine Names* I, 4, 589; II, 9, 648; 13, 3, 980 3 CD; 981 A). Maximus* the Confessor, his commentator, calls God "the superessence of essences" (*On Divine Names,* chap. 1, PG 4, 193 B). These expressions were translated as *ultra substantiam* (Jan Scotus, *In opuscula sacra Boetii* Rand 40, Munich, 1906), *supersubstantialis,* and *superessentialis* (id., PL 122, 154b)—all terms designating the transcendent in its absolute separation, in a purely static sense.

However, within the world but in a dynamic sense, *huperphuès* also means the operations of God that are outside the ordinary course of nature: immaculate conception, incarnation*, Eucharist*, miracles* (Maximus, *Expositio orationis dominicae,* PG 90, 8793 B). *Huper phusin* (above nature) has the sense of transcendent, but it is sometimes associated with *para phusin* (against nature) in an allusion to Paul: the Church* of the pagans is grafted onto Israel* like a wild olive branch onto a cultivated olive tree—"against nature" (Rom 11:24). This allegory has always posed a dilemma for interpreters. For some, the doctrine of the incarnation implies that God wills nothing against nature (nor against reason*), for that which is against nature is the realm of disorder and evil*: "None of the things made by God can possibly be against nature,... [but] there are things that are above nature: they are those things that God can do by raising man above human nature" and uniting him with divine nature (Origen*, *Against Celsus* V, 23). For other interpreters, what is against nature designates the abasement and the incarnation of Christ*.

The confrontation with philosophy* (Christian Aristotelianism*, Platonism*, and Stoicism*) made necessary an articulation between these realms. It was presented as early as Leontes of Byzantium: it can be said that operations in accordance with nature are simply human, those that go against nature are depraved, but that whoever elevates himself extends his capacity and attains, thanks to God, to acts above nature (*Contra Nestorianos et Eutychianos* I, 2; PG 86, 1333 AB). The gifts received by man elevate him above his nature and unite him with divine nature. Salvation*, deification, and the gift of the Spirit occur according to grace and not according to nature, not by destruction or negation of nature but by raising it above itself.

The Latin term *supernaturalis* seems to make its first appearance in Rusticus, as a translation of *huperphuès* in a work of Isidore of Pelusium (R. Aigrain 1911, *Quarante-neuf lettres de saint Isidore de Péluse* 44). It assumed prominence notably in the Carolingian translations of Dionysius, Hilduin, and John the Scot

Eriugena (c. 810–c. 877) and then in the latter's own works. A synonym of "spiritual" or "pneumatic," it means primarily the theological transcendence of the divine principle, but it also indicates that, in the economy of salvation, that divine principle leads man to deification in a way that fulfills his aspirations and goes beyond his capacities. The union of the human and the divine is accomplished in the union of nature and the supernatural.

b) Problem of the Supernatural: The Desire of God and the End of Man. Without using the word "supernatural," the fathers* of the church consider that man was created in the image of God, in Christ and for Christ: he has received the divine prerogatives of thought, freedom*, immortality, and the domination over nature; and he is made in light of the full resemblance to God, which will complete that image. He is destined to live eternally in God, to enter into the movement of Trinitarian life, and to draw all creation* into that life. Augustine* is convinced that man was made with an eye to the vision of God face to face: "You made us for you and our heart is without rest until it rests in you" (*Confessions*). But he also knows that in order to reach his goal, beatitude, man needs the external help of God, which is grace. Thus, it is God who raises man to a blessed condition, one that he has not merited by his works*. Better yet, man has no merit in himself: it is divine grace that bestows it on him. To be sure, eternal* life is the recompense for good works (*Enchiridion*, chap. 107; *De correptione et gratia*, n. 41), but these good works have value for God only because they themselves are engendered by grace (*De correptione et gratia*, n. 41; *De diversis quaestionibus ad Simplicianum* I, n. 3). Man is saved by an overflowing of divine generosity that owes nothing to no one. He attains the completion of his humanity thanks to the help of God.

Grace is thus not simply indispensable to man in order to restore to him his nature from before sin*, it is also necessary to raise his nature, before original sin* as well as afterward. Before sin, Adam had no less need of grace than sinful man, but he needed it only as an aid making it possible for his freedom to persevere. After sin, on the other hand, it gives him both the strength to avoid evil and the strength to exercise his freedom for the good*. Existence before sin thus did not consist of greater independence from God. The term took on a problematic cast when it came to integrating this theological tradition into a vision of nature created by God in which the world was seen no longer as a pure miracle dependent on divine power but as one in which natural laws have their own coherence; and this was even more so when nature was thought

about with the help of Aristotle's metaphysical concepts in the 13th century. For Aristotle, in fact, the relationship to the divine is entirely natural: the divine is the unmoved mover of the cosmos*, but it is possible to raise oneself toward divine life by an ethical fulfillment of the self.

It was first necessary to agree about terms. Although the commentators on Aristotle say that the divine is supernatural in itself, this is in the static sense in which it belongs to separate, transphysical realities (Thomas Aquinas*, *In I Metaphysicae*, Prooemium). How is a supernatural movement to be introduced into our world? Aristotle knows of only two kinds of movement, natural and violent (against nature) (*Physics* V, 6, 230 a18–b9): it is thus difficult to integrate the action of grace into nature without reducing it either to a natural fulfillment of the goals of nature or to a violent reversal of nature against itself. The solution came from the study of the relationships between nature and art in Aristotle. Art imitates nature, which means that it fulfills it in the human realm: the human works of mechanical arts, ethics*, and politics lead human nature to its perfection. Medieval writers thus think of the supernatural following the model of art, as a gift that fulfills the goals of nature while remaining of divine origin. The supernatural thereby no longer characterizes primarily a transcendent object (a separate nature) but rather designates the way in which God acts on the finite world.

Thereafter, it was necessary to agree about the goal. For Aristotle, all men wish to know, particularly the highest causes: the contemplation* of God is the goal of man, the act that most radically fulfills his essence. For the theological tradition* as well, the vision of God is the goal of human destiny. There is thus agreement on the final goal. The question lies with the means. And to answer this question, a distinction must be made between the felicity of the philosophers, accessible here below in the exercise of morality and speculation, and heavenly beatitude, reserved for the beyond and dependent on the gift of divine grace.

It is here that the theologians of the Middle Ages separate themselves from the philosophers. For Thomas Aquinas, it is true that every being attains its goal according to the order of its nature. But in man the natural desire for the divine vision is a determination that belongs exclusively to his essence (*De malo*, q. 5, a. 1; *CG* III, 50; III, 147; *ST* Ia IIae, q. 3, a. 8). Thus, "every intellect naturally desires the vision of the divine substance" (*CG* III, 57, 2334); and this desire can be satisfied because "it is possible for the substance of God to be seen through the intermediary of the intellect, both by intellectual substances and by our souls" (*CG* III, 51, 2284). God thus raises up nature in order to make it capable of receiving the vision of God. Our final goals go beyond the grasp of our nature. Man thus has for Thomas a *paradoxical* destiny, which even surpasses the capacities of his nature. The paradox of intellectual nature is to desire what it does not have the power to acquire and to be able to attain, through another, a perfection that no creature can acquire by itself (*ST* Ia IIae, q. 5, a. 5 ad 2um). This poverty makes up the grandeur of man. The supernatural increases the dignity of his nature. The natural desire to see God opens out into a Christian humanism*.

In a more technical manner, Duns Scotus* dissipates a possible ambiguity between two senses of natural that naturalism* tends to confuse. Within a single nature, the natural is opposed to the violent and to the neutral (Aristotle). In the relationship between two natures, on the other hand, the natural is opposed to the supernatural. And in this case, supernatural designates merely a relationship between two terms: the action of an agent who is not by nature the one who imprints that action on that agent is supernatural (*Ordinatio*, Prologue, §57). The supernatural comes from a superior free agent who does not follow the ordinary course of nature. For Duns Scotus as for Thomas, the natural desire of man is for the vision of God. And the opposition between philosophers and theologians is already at this point built around the supernatural. "Philosophers assert the perfection of nature and deny supernatural perfection": they think that the dignity of nature is to be able to attain its own perfection. But "the theologian knows the defect of nature and supernatural perfection" (*Ordinatio*, Prologue, §5), for he knows the sinful degeneracy of our nature as well as the grandeur of man when he receives grace. The theological goal of man, beatitude, is greater than philosophical felicity, for that is only an abstract knowledge* of God. This is why only theology knows the dignity of man, a creature naturally able to receive the supernatural in order to attain a good beyond the means of his nature. For Duns Scotus, however, a single act changes value in the eyes of God according to whether it comes from a subject in a state of grace, "informed" by charity, "supernaturalized" by divine election (*Quodlibet* 17, a. 2, §[4] 7). As a result, the intrinsic content of the act is in danger of being devalued and replaced by the extrinsic presence of grace. In this theology, which exalts the absolute power of God, the present, instituted order of salvation is contingent: God could save without the Church and without the sacraments*.

The nominalism* of Ockham (c. 1300–c. 1350) goes further: there is no permanence of the habitus in man; it is thus the act itself that is salvific and not the corresponding habitus (*Sentences* I, d. 17, q. 1 and 2).

Thus, God could save man even without a habitus of charity, *without grace:* "No form, whether natural or supernatural, can constrain him" (*Sentences* I, d. 17, q. 1; *Opera theologica* 3, 455). God does not require that one already have grace in order to save. He saves without conditions and gives His grace as He wills. Ockham thus hopes to be at the opposite end of the spectrum from Pelagius.

But if one begins from man, not from divine power, here too Ockham's position implies that man can be saved without grace. It thus appears Pelagian to his opponents: "If God accepts a work that is purely natural as meriting eternal life*, His will that accepts it finds dignity and value in nature, and this is the heresy* of Pelagius" (Lutterell, art. 14, Koch ed., *RthAM*, 1935–36). The freedom of divine power is thus reflected outside itself in an anthropology* of nature alone. And one can understand the reaction of Gabriel Biel, positing a harmony between nature and grace. No work is good, according to Biel, as long as it has not been made acceptable by divine charity. But to whoever does good, God does not refuse His grace: "God gives grace to whoever does what is in his power, by immutable necessity and by hypothesis, for He has arranged immutably to give grace to whoever does what is in his power" (*Collectorium* II, d. 27, q. 1, a. 3, dub. 4). Through the covenant established with man, God has committed Himself necessarily to giving His grace to ratify the free acts of man. This gift is necessary, but it is not constrained, because God submits Himself to an obligation that he has freely ratified—a conclusion in which Biel, against his will, is closer to Pelagianism* than all his predecessors (Vignaux 1935).

The violent opposition of Luther* to this interpretation is well known. He expresses it by rejecting the very problem of harmony between the natural and the supernatural, for he recognizes no unity in nature except in the form of a corrupted reality (and an illusion maintained by the philosophers). The activity of the creature is nothing other than the realization of the present omnipotence of God. There is thus no longer any finite free will (*WA* 18, 719).

c) Pure Nature, or Anthropology Detached from Theology. In Scholastic* theology, which focused more on the study of nature than on the history of salvation, it seemed necessary to organize anthropology and to scrutinize the relationship between the nature of man and the supernatural independently of the breach opened up by sin. In order to study the supernatural in its pure state, it was necessary to study nature in its pure state, before sin, in Adam*. Opinions on this point were diverse. For Bonaventure (*Sentences* II, d. 29, q. 1, a. 2) and for Duns Scotus, man was created at first without grace, but for Prévotin of Cremona and Thomas Aquinas, this could not have been the case. Gilles of Rome supported the position of Prévotin and Thomas with arguments that were transposed to human nature as a whole: "There was a necessity, a debt through which human nature had to be created with a supernatural and gratuitous gift" (*Sentences* II, d. 30, q. 1, a. 1; Venice, 1581, 408–9). But the question was on occasion raised in terms of the history of salvation. In order to move from a historical stage to a state of pure nature, it was in fact necessary to reverse Augustine's perspective, something that 13th-century Scholasticism declined to do, although the Scholasticism of the 15th century had no such scruples.

Dionysius the Carthusian (1402–71) limits the natural desire of man to the capacity of his nature, thereby opposing Thomas Aquinas (*De puritate et felicitate naturae,* a. 55; *Opera omnia,* vol. 40). In a universe made of a stream of emanations coming from the Principle in an ontological gradation, every intelligence naturally has as a final goal to be joined to the intelligence immediately superior to it, as in the theology of Avicenna. And only this goal is naturally desirable because natural desire tends toward a natural goal. Cajetan reiterates the same separation among the orders, but he inserts it into his commentary on Thomas. He introduces the hypothesis of pure nature in the name of an Aristotelian principle: nature does nothing in vain; it cannot have an aspiration that it would be unable to fulfill through its own means. Hence, if there is in man a desire for God, this desire is not natural but added on by God in a gratuitous act of His omniscience and His will. De juris, nature is self-sufficient (this is the theory of pure nature); and if, de facto, man always desires God, this is simply because God so wishes and because He substitutes Himself for the order of nature. It is thus by virtue of an ""obediential" power (a power that can be actualized only by the gratuitous intervention of God) that man desires God and not because of his nature as man. Cajetan thereby makes possible both a humanism without God (which can subsist without the supernatural) and a theology imposed from outside, destructive of human nature, antihumanist (*see* Boulnois 1993, 1995; Lacoste 1995). Molina adopts the same hypothesis, with more caution (*Concordia* [1588], 1876 Ed.). For Suarez* (*De Gratia,* Proleg. 4, chap. 1, n. 2; Vivès, 7, 179), man is made for a natural beatitude by virtue of his creation; and if he pursues a higher goal, this has been added on. In the state of pure nature, contrary to what Augustine may have said, man would not be troubled but at peace (*De ultimo fine hominis,* Vivès Ed., vol. 4, 156). Instead of opening onto the infinite*, man is closed in on his nature. Created nature is considered as perfect in itself,

not, to be sure, without grace but as though grace did not open it up to the beyond and did not raise it above itself. It is no longer oriented toward union with God.

The position of Michel de Baye (Baius) reverses perspective on the subject to such a degree that it is with reference to him that "supernatural" appears for the first time in a document of the Catholic magisterium* (Pius V's bull condemning Baius in 1567; van Eijl 1953). Reacting against the hypothesis of a pure nature, Baius asserts that it is empty. By virtue of his created nature, in fact, man must receive grace, and he even, in complete fairness, has a right to it, for God has freely committed Himself to giving His grace to the man who obeys the laws of his nature. Following this reasoning, grace no longer intervenes except as the means enabling man to merit his recompense (*De meritis operum* I, 2). Nature's goal remains commensurate with its created requirements, and the means to attain it are due to the creature. Grace was due to the pure nature of innocent man (Adam) and confirmed his freedom (proposition 21: "The elevation and exaltation of human nature with divine nature was due to the integrity of its original condition; it must therefore be natural, not supernatural"). But after original sin, in the state of fallen nature, the will is powerless: it is determined either by grace or by its own corruption. By thus emphasizing the corruption of nature, Baius is led to misconstrue the question of freedom and the origin of sin. The grace that he deals with is extrinsic; it is due to intact nature, but it reigns from the outside over fallen nature.

Jansenius was influenced by Baius on several decisive points. In Baianism*, grace is due to the nature of innocent man and enables him to act, but optimism concerning created nature—where sufficient grace abounds—is associated with a pessimistic vision of the state ensuing on sin: not to attribute everything to grace would be to presume on what remains of will in sinful man. Jansenist refutations of Baianism are based on the system of pure nature, in fact taking their place on the same terrain as their opponent, and they thus cannot carry conviction. Jansenism is thus confined to asserting that fallen man has the power of accomplishing at least some morally good actions because pure nature, free will, and morality were not destroyed by original sin. Grace is thus reduced to an adventitious status. The supernatural order appears as contingent and external, whereas the natural order is presumed sufficient and appropriate for man.

Theologians of the classic period were distributed among all these positions. Bérulle agreed with Augustine that "the nature of man was not created to remain within the terms of nature; it was made for grace" (*Opuscule* 1323, 2; Rotureau, p. 389). Leibniz*, in contrast, subjects God to the necessity of the various kinds of nature, among which His will is confined to recognizing which combination is the best; grace supervenes to confirm and strengthen that choice but not to exalt and transport the kinds of nature beyond their limits. Despite a few noteworthy exceptions, the supernatural is thus dissociated from the aspirations of nature, and whereas the supernatural is exiled far from human nature, that nature seems capable of attaining its own goals without recourse to a grace that appears as an extrinsic, if not alienating, superstructure. In this perspective, rationalism* and traditionalism* appear as deformations of the same paradox of the supernatural: rationalism by supposing that, in the state of created nature, man would know God without revelation*, traditionalism (L. de Bonald) by supposing that revelation provides man with his initial store of natural knowledge. In the first case, nature is sufficient unto itself; in the second, the supernatural is for nature and nature not for the supernatural.

This set of questions and the challenges they pose had been generally obscured by Neoscholasticism, and the principal credit for bringing them to the fore lies with H. de Lubac*, under the influence of M. Blondel* and despite violent opposition from neo-Thomist circles. When K. Rahner* (1962) reiterated "calmly the concept of obediential power" in order to establish a theology on the basis of the presence of a "permanent existential supernatural preordained for grace," despite a vocabulary taken from Cajetan, he was engaged in perceiving in the fundamental structures of existence a mediation between the nature of man and grace, the interface making possible the desire for God. Closer to the church fathers, H. Urs von Balthasar* (1966) is important in this debate principally because he emphasized that Christianity is neither a philosophy of nature nor an anthropology but the revelation of God in the figure of Christ: "Revelation does not run counter to any human aspiration...[but the] heart [of man] understands itself only if it has first of all perceived the love*, turned toward it, of the divine heart pierced for us on the cross." Lubac thus rediscovered a very old principle: if all men are called to salvation, divine grace acts within each one of them. The whole cosmos* was created with a view to the recapitulation (Irenaeus* of Lyon) of all things in man and in Christ. The human spirit is a nature that desires God but can receive Him only as a free and gratuitous gift. For God deposits the aspiration in nature itself. "This desire is nothing other than His call" (Lubac 1946).

● H. Bouillard (1944), *Conversion et grâce chez saint Thomas d'Aquin,* Paris.
H. de Lubac (1946), *Surnaturel, Études historiques,* Paris (2nd Ed. 1991).
H. Rondet (1948), "L'idée de nature pure au XVIe siècle," *RSR* 35, 481–521.
E. van Eijl (1953), "Les censures des universités d'Alcala et de Salamanque et la censure du pape Pie V contre Michel Baius (1565–1567)," *RHE* 48, 767–75.
K. Rahner (1954), "Über das Verhältnis von Natur und Gnade," *Schr.zur Th.* 1, 323–45.
É. Gilson (1955), "Cajetan et l'humanisme théologique," *AHDL* 22, 113–36.
H. Bouillard (1964), "L'idée de surnaturel et le mystère chrétien," in *L'homme devant Dieu, Mélanges H. de Lubac,* vol. 3, Paris, 153–66.
S. Dockx (1964), "Du désir naturel de voir l'essence divine d'après saint Thomas," *ArPh* 63, 90–91, 93–96.
É. Gilson (1965), "Sur la problématique thomiste de la vision béatifique," *AHDL* 32, 67–88.
H. de Lubac (1965), *Le mystère du surnaturel,* Paris.
H. Urs von Balthasar (1966), *Glaubhaft ist nur Liebe,* Einsiedeln.
H. de Lubac (1980), *Petite catéchèse sur nature et grâce,* Paris.
L. Weimer (1981), *Die Lust an Gott und seiner Sache,* Fribourg.
I. Bochet (1982), *Saint Augustin et le désir de Dieu,* Paris.
B. Sesboüé (1992), "Le surnaturel chez Henri de Lubac," *RSR* 80, 373–408.
O. Boulnois (1993), "Puissance neutre et puissance obédientielle: De l'homme à Dieu selon Duns Scot et Cajetan," in B. Pinchard, S. Ricci (Eds.), *Rationalisme analogique et humanisme théologique: La culture de Thomas de Vio "Il Gaetano,"* Naples, 31–70.
O. Boulnois (1995), "Les deux fins de l'homme: L'impossible anthropologie et le repli de la théologie," *Henri de Lubac et la philosophie, Eph,* no. 2, 205–22.
J.-Y. Lacoste (1995), "Le désir et l'inexigible: Préambules à une lecture," *Eph,* no. 2, 223–46.
A. Vanneste (1996), *Nature et grâce dans la théologie occidentale: Dialogue avec H. de Lubac,* Louvain.

OLIVIER BOULNOIS

See also **Anthropology; Banezianism-Molinism-Baianism; Beatitude; Grace; Life, Eternal; Nature; Vision, Beatific**

Suso, Henri. *See* **Rhineland-Flemish Mysticism**

Symbols of Faith. *See* Creeds

Synderesis. *See* Conscience

Synergy

Synergy is a key concept in the Orthodox theology* of grace*, where it designates the cooperation (the Greek *sunergeia* is a synonym of the Latin *cooperatio*) of man in the work of salvation* carried out in him by God.* The Christian East almost entirely escaped the Pelagian crisis: the concept of synergy is the object of an untroubled affirmation that enables the avoidance of the distinctions and refinements introduced from Augustine* on into the Latin theology of grace. Catholic theology has no objection to make to the synergism of the Eastern Church: it is itself a theory of "cooperation" (*see* the documents of the Council of Trent*, *DH* 1529, 1554, 1559). In Luther*, the Protestant theology of grace was set forth as a protest against synergism. But as early as the generation of Melanchthon (1497–1560), a moderate synergism found a place in Lutheranism*.

JEAN-YVES LACOSTE

See also **Augustine of Hippo; Grace; Pelagianism; Works**

Synod

The word *synod* (from the Greek *sun-hodos,* "a deliberative meeting," with the same etymology as "council*") means an assembly of lawful and competent representatives of the Church*, called for the purpose of achieving ecclesial unity* by means of resolutions about theological, disciplinary, and legal matters. The synod is the institutional concretization of the structural principle of the *communio* (community), which, by virtue of the fundamental equality of all the Church members through baptism*, also extends the responsibilities of the regional communities to the level of the universal Church.

1. Development of the Synodal Institution

Modeled on the Council of the Apostles* (Acts 15), the synodal institution was created during the second century at a time of local and regional crises (involving Montanism*, concerning the date of the Feast of Easter*). This first synods aimed to bring about a resolution of the internal conflicts by harmonizing the faith* of a Church held to be one in time* and space (Vincent of Lerins, *Commonit.* 2, 3; 3, 20–23). The criteria the synod had to meet were, therefore, the lawfulness of the participants (mostly bishops* but also priests, deacons*, and laity*), faithfulness to tradition*, freedom of speech, publicity, the people's participation, and the Church's reception*.

Synods were held at the provincial level (provincial, eparchial, or metropolitan synods, whose sittings the Council of Nicaea*, in canon 5, had prescribed as biannual). They were held in the provinces of patriarch* (in Constantinople, once a year, in addition to the *sunodos endèmousa,* convoked piecemeal—in 448 for the first time—and composed of all the bishops present in the town). They were also held in ecclesiastic regions—either regions of a particular nation or regions of the whole Western Church. (The Roman synod held in 376 was thus called a *sunodus dutikè.*) On the scale of the empire (*sunodus oikoumenikè*), by tradition the synod adopted the name of (*ecumenical*) *council.* The synodal element has endured through all the ecclesiastical constitutions, but it works in various ways according to the ecclesiologies*.

2. Particular Forms

a) Catholic Church. On account of its structure*, the synodal and communal element of the Catholic Church finds itself in a contradictory relationship with the primatial and hierarchical element and can therefore be evaluated only in comparison with itself. The Second Vatican Council, whose aim was to stress communion* within the Church, strove to reinforce that aspect. According to the Code of Canon Law of 1983, that communion is revealed in the episcopal synod (cans. 342–48), in the full and provincial synod (cans. 439–46), in the episcopal conference (cans. 447–59), in the diocesan synod (cans. 460–68), in the presbyterial council (cans. 495–502), in the pastoral diocesan council (cans. 511–14), and in the pastoral parish council (cans. 536). In every case, however, these assemblies have only an advisory function in their relations with their hierarchic superiors, the bishop or the priest.

b) Orthodox Churches. In the eyes of the Orthodox Churches, since their ecclesiologies center on the

regional* Church and its eucharistic foundation, the synod is the only authentic decision-making body; it demonstrates what all the regional Churches live and believe. It meets on the regional and provincial levels and then on the levels of the patriarchate and the autocephalous Churches before reaching its highest expression at the ecumenical councils. At each level, the synod generally represents the supreme authority regarding doctrinal affairs, the liturgy, and spiritual life* but also regarding all questions concerning the attribution of responsibilities and external representation. The validity of its resolutions depends mainly on their reception* by the believers. It may be composed only of bishops, or it may bring together various levels (bishops, members of the clergy, monks, or laity); however, the bishops always have primacy.

c) The Church Born of the Reformation. The synodal principle followed a specific development in these Churches after their rejection of the Roman pontifical and episcopal hierarchy*, thought to be an instrument of domination. The synods are composed in various ways that range from the direct administration by the Church to simple parishional representation. There is no single set of rules regarding relations between clergy and laity in the synod, the directorship (which may be entrusted to a bishop or to a layperson), the possibility of admitting supplementary members, or the ecclesiastic authority's right to admonish. Its powers are no less variable. They generally include legislation, electoral and budgetary management, and doctrinal questions.

The first Lutheran synodal rules—establishing a structure formed of pastors* and elected members, entrusted with administrative tasks and supervision—were laid down in 1526 for the state of Hesse. In Germany, until well into the 20th century, they retained a certain skepticism about this system, which presupposed ordination*.

The Reformed Church's first synodal constitution was introduced in Paris in 1559 to settle ecclesiastical questions of doctrine and discipline; it granted equal rights to pastors, to elders, and to deacons. It exerted an influence over the presbyterial constitutions of Scotland (1561), of the Netherlands (1571), and of the Rhineland (1610).

● L. Coenen (1953), "Gemeinde und Synode," *ZevKR* 3, 74–86.
J. Hajjar (1962), *Le synode permanent (sunodos endèmousa) dans l'Église byzantine des origines au XIe siècle,* Rome.
P. Duprey (1970), "La structure synodale de l'Église dans la théologie orientale," *POC* 19, 123–43.
H. M. Biedermann (1971), "Die Synodalität," in L. Hein (Ed.), *Die Einheit der Kirche,* Wiesbaden.
D. Staniloae (1971), "Dogmatische Grundlagen der Synodalität," OS 20, 3–16.

Pro Oriente (Ed.) (1975), *Konziliarität und Kollegialität als Strukturprinzipien der Kirche,* Innsbruck.

W. Brandmüller (Ed.) (1977), *Synodale Strukturen der Kirche,* Donauwörth.

W. Beinert (1979), "Konziliarität der Kirche," *Cath (M)* 33, 81–108.

N. Närger (1988), *Das Synodenwahlrecht in den deutschen evangelischen Landeskirchen im 19. und 20. Jh.,* Tübingen.

H. J. Sieben (1990), *Die Partikularsynode,* Frankfurt.

La synodalité (1992), *Actes du VIIe Congrès international de droit canonique,* 2 vols., Paris.

G. Routhier (1993), *La réception d'un concile,* Paris.

G. Alberigo (1994), "Synodalität in der Kirche nach dem Zweiten Vatikanum," in W. Geerlings, M. Seckler (sous la dir. de), *Kirche sein,* Fribourg-Basel-Vienna, 333–47.

WOLFGANG BEINERT

See also **Catholicism; Collegiality; Council; Government of the Church; Jurisdiction; Orthodoxy; Protestantism**

T

Targums. *See* **Translations of the Bible, Ancient**

Tatian. *See* **Apologists**

Tauler, John. *See* **Rhineland-Flemish Mysticism**

Teilhard de Chardin, Pierre. *See* **Evolution; Eschatology**

Tempier, Etienne. *See* **Naturalism; Truth**

Temple

The temple is the house of God*. God lives in the midst of his people* and makes himself present to the faithful. In the biblical world the temple stands at the center of religious life and the life of the nation of Israel, bearing a strong symbolic charge.

a) Various Denominations of the Temple. The Hebrew word for *temple* is *hêkâl,* which corresponds to the Acadian *ekallu* and the Sumerian *E-GAL,* meaning "big house." The word can refer to a palace, the temple, or the main room of the temple later called the Sanctuary. Because the temple is the house of God, it is often designated by the common word for house, *baît,* as in Bethel, "House of God" (Gn 28:19).

The term *mishekân* also pertains to the register of habitation. However, it is used in a more specialized sense in the description of the sanctuary in the desert, alternately with *'ohél,* "tent," and *'ohél mô'éd,* "tent of meeting." The term *mâ'ôn* applies to God's celestial abode (Dt 26:15) and his earthly abode (2 Chr 36:15–16). If the place where Moses stands is holy ground (Ex 3:5), the generic term "place," *mâqôm,* is sometimes a parallel to *baît,* with the meaning of "temple," given that in the thought of Deuteronomy it is the place chosen by the Lord to place his name* (1 Kgs 8:29; see also Dt 12:5).

For Ezekiel and the priestly writers, the dwelling place of the Lord that is filled with glory is the tabernacle, *miqedâsh* or *qodèsh* (Ex 40:34), which participates in a privileged way in the very sanctity of God. Solomon had been chosen to build "a house" as sanctuary (1 Chr 28:3). The psalmist concisely includes several different elements of this vocabulary, stating: "Lord, I love the habitation *[mâ'ôn]* of thy house *[baît],* and the place *[mâqôm]* where thy glory *[kâbô]* dwells *[mishekân]*" (Ps 26:8).

b) The Temple and its Symbolic Function. In the Ancient Near East, the temple was built by the king at the request of the divinity, according to plans revealed by him. The earthly house of God is a replica of his celestial abode. David had planned to build a temple (2 Sm 7:1–3), but he was rejected because he had shed too much blood (1 Chr 28:10). It was left to Solomon to accomplish this great project.

The temple built and consecrated by Solomon (1 Kgs 6:1–8:66 and 2 Chr 1:18–7:22) stood until the fall of Jerusalem* in 586 B.C. In a grandiose utopian vision, Ezekiel and his disciples envisaged the future Israel* symmetrically arranged around a new temple (Ez 40–48). Restoration of the temple cult* was a priority for the repatriated; the second temple was built between 520 and 515 B.C. under the leadership of Ezra (Ezr 5:1–6:22). The priestly writings describe at length the erection of the tent of meeting in the wilderness, which owes a great debt to the structure of the temple (Ex 25–31 and 35–40). Herod the Great's building, erected between 19 B.C. and A.D. 27, represented an authentic reconstruction of this temple (though since ancient sources referred to as Herod's temple as still being the "second temple," there was presumably some structural continuity with Ezra's post-exilic building).

The architecture* of Herod's temple reflected the hierarchical organization of Israel's religious society*. After the square of the pagans comes the square of the women, and then the square of the men. The altar of the holocausts was located in the courtyard of the priests. The building was made up of the vestibule, the Sanctuary containing the altar of incense, and then, separated from the Sanctuary by a veil, the Holy of Holies, where the high priest entered only once a year on the Day of Atonement. Each room had its specific minister, its rites, its decoration.

Symbolically, the temple exercised an irresistible force of attraction on Israel. It was, first of all, the affirmation of the presence in the midst of his people of a God who allowed himself to be approached by his believers. "And the name of the city henceforth shall be, The Lord is there," proclaims Ezekiel at the end of his vision (Ez 48:35). It was also the sacred place where God manifested his sanctity, and each person participated according to his standing, having access to a given part of the temple. The temple, in receiving the heritage of the temple of Silo where the Ark (1 Sm 1–3) was kept, and the ark of Mount Sinai on Mount Zion, became the focal point of Israel's traditions. Just as the ancient temples were conceived as true microcosms, the symbolism of the temple extended ultimately to the cosmic order (cosmos*).

c) The Temple in the Life of Israel. However, such a strong institution was not unanimously approved. At first it appeared as a foreign and, consequently, pagan import. By its sedentary conception, the temple could seem to traduce the nomadic roots of Israel, which went back to a time when God walked with Israel without asking for a "house of cedar" (2 Sm 7:7). Even worse, was the temple not a discredit to the transcendence of God, who has heaven for a throne and the earth for a footstool (Is 66:1)? To obviate this possibility, the temple had to be described as the place that God had appointed as the abode of his name or his glory.

As the center of religious life, the temple exerted considerable influence. The masses converged there for the great pilgrimage* festivals. The complex ritual of sacrifices* was developed at the temple in response to the profound aspirations of the Israelite soul: total offering, communion, expiation. From the temple the praises of Israel rose joyfully up to God, as testified by the Psalms* and the Chronicles. Love of the temple inhabited the piety of Israel (Ps 26:8).

In addition to prayer*, the temple always exercised an educational function. After the period of exile Israel existed as a religious community centered around the temple. And the priests (priesthood*) who governed the temple enjoyed authentic political power. The temple was an economic and financial power. It also functioned as a relief committee.

But there were fissures in the imposing edifice. The prophets* had already warned against the formalism (Jer 7:4) of worship at the temple. The infidelities of its governors, already denounced by Nehemiah in the fifth century B.C., diminished its prestige. With the approach of the Christian era, a group of Essenes questioned the legitimacy of the temple and ultimately seceded, taking refuge in Qumran. The allegiance of the priestly aristocracy to the Roman authority led to additional discord. This loss of credibility coincided with the development of the institution of the synagogue. Centered on a liturgy* of the word*, it ensured the survival of Judaism after the destruction of the second temple in A.D. 70.

d) Jesus and the Temple of Stone. Jesus knew the temple of Herod in all its splendor (Mk 13:1). In Greek, *hieron* designates the whole of the edifice and *naos* the part where the divinity resides, next to more unusual appellations: the place *(topos)*, the holy place or Sanctuary *(hagia).* Luke gives particular prominence to the temple. His Gospel* begins with the announcement to Zechariah, which takes place in the sanctuary, or *naos,* and ends, after the Ascension, with the unceasing prayer of the disciples in the temple, or *hieron* (Lk 24:53). This is where Jesus* is revealed, whether by Simeon (Lk 2:27–32) or by his own words (Lk 2:40–51). As John points out in various passages, Jesus attended the temple during the great pilgrimage festivals. It was there that he taught (Lk 19:47), and there that he debated with his adversaries (Mt 21:23–27). When he entered Jerusalem he purified the temple (Mt 21:12–27). His announcement of the coming destruction of the temple (Mt 24:2) was held against him by those who were the most bent on his ruin, as it would later be held against his disciples.

e) From the Temple of Stone to the Temple of the Body. With his prophetic gesture of driving the merchants from the temple, Jesus demonstrated his concern for an authentic cult. His claims went even further, when he declared "something greater than the temple is here" (Mt 12:6). The edifice that Jesus would rebuild would not be man-made (Mk 14:58). The new temple is his risen body (Jn 2:20f.). As he "dwelt among us," or literally, "pitched his tent among us" (Jn 1:14) he was God present among men. "And what is becoming obsolete and growing old is ready to vanish away" (Heb 8:13). The Christians would not be taken by surprise by the destruction of the temple in A.D. 70; this temple had been part of the old economy that had been nullified by Christ's sacrifice.

In Christian thought, the community had become the temple of God. God henceforth abides within believers sanctified by the offering of Christ. A construction founded on the apostles* and prophets, with Jesus as cornerstone, the Church forms "a holy temple *[naos]* in the Lord" (Eph 2:21). Paul reminds the Corinthians that they are the temple of God and the Spirit abides in them, "for God's temple is holy, and you are that temple" (1 Cor 3:17). In their very existence, believers live the sanctity demanded of an abode of God. Their consecration signifies unfailing adherence. Since their bodies are temples of the Holy* Spirit, they do not belong to themselves anymore (1 Cor 6:19). Because they are the temple of the living God, they must accept the necessary separations, as the new covenant* obliges (2 Cor 6:16–18).

f) The Heavenly Sanctuary. Jesus entered once and for all into the heavenly sanctuary (Heb 9:12). The temple of stone and its cult pertain to the image and the replica (Heb 9:23), the figure, the parable (Heb 9:9–10), destined to be effaced when the reality is fulfilled. Penetrating beyond the veil, Jesus has sat down on the right-hand side of his Majesty's throne in the heavens, and he is the minister of the true sanctuary (Heb 8:1–2). Always ready to intercede for human beings, he is their way to the Father*. In the Epistle to the Hebrews the community is presented as being on the move, overcoming all difficulties, aiming for the heavenly fatherland where it will live in intimate, permanent union with God.

The Book of Revelation is informed by this liturgy of praise* and acclamation celebrated in the heavenly temple. The chosen stand before the throne of God and "serve him day and night in his temple" (Rev 7:15). What is this temple in reality? In the new Jerusalem, John, the visionary of Revelation, does not see any temple, "for its temple is the Lord God the Almighty and the Lamb" (Rev 21:22).

In the final analysis, behind the image of the temple it is the history* of the presence of God among human beings, and the presence of human beings to God, that is being played out. The temple of stone is only the figure of a spiritual reality. And yet, paradoxically, the Jews did not rebuild the temple after its destruction in A.D. 70, whereas the Christians, notwithstanding their awareness of being the temple of God, went on to build many places of worship.

● G. Schrenk (1938), "To hieron," *ThWNT* 3, 230–47.
J. Daniélou (1942), *Le signe du Temple,* Paris (2nd Ed. 1991).
O. Michel (1942) "Naos," *ThWNT* 4, 884–95.
B. Gärtner (1965), *The Temple and the Community in Qumran and the New Testament,* Cambridge.
L. Gaston (1970), *No Stone on Another,* Leyden.
E. Jenni (1971), "Baît," *ThWAT* 1, 308–313.
M. Ottoson (1974), "Hékal," *ThWAT* 2, 408–415.
M. Haran (1978), *Temples and Temple-Service in Ancient Israel,* Oxford.
V. Hurowitz (1992), *I have Built you an Exalted House,* Sheffield.

JOSEPH AUNEAU

See also **Architecture; Soul-Heart-Body; Church; City; Creation; Cult; Holiness; Jerusalem; Liturgy; Praise; Priesthood; Sacrifice**

Temptation

A. Biblical Theology

a) *Vocabulary.* In Hebrew, the verb *nissâh* means "to tempt," in the sense of "to put to the test" (synonyms: *bâchan,* "to test," and *châqar,* "to examine") in order to show, to see, to know something not apparent. Sometimes, the verb means "to experiment in order to find out" (1 Sm 17:39 and Eccl 2:1). In Greek, "temptation" is rendered by words derived from the root *peira* (the verb *[ek]peirazô,* "to try, to attempt, to test" and the substantive *peirasmos,* "attempt" and "temptation").

b) *The Archetype: Temptations in the Desert.* In the Old Testament, alongside profane uses (1 Kgs 10:1 and Wis 2:17; see also Acts 9:26; and Heb 11:29), two syntagms stand out: "God* tempts X" and "X tempts God." A sort of shuttling between one and the other, linked with the material benefits and the law* given by Yahweh, appears in the narratives* of Israel*'s sojourn in the desert.

The gifts of water and manna are a proving point for Israel, a sort of test: will Israel resist the temptation of seeing them as nothing but things to be taken to satisfy its needs? Or, on the contrary, will it see them as a sign, an invitation to freely acknowledge the giver? Its way of undergoing this "test" says much about the people's fidelity (Dt 8:2). In this test, the law intervenes like a word spoken against covetousness, separating the need from the thing in order to give a chance to the sign and to the faith* that imbues it. (Ex 16:4; see also Ex 15:25). Both the gift (Dt 8:16) and the law (Ex 20:20; see also Sir 4:17) are components of the test-temptation, as Genesis 2–3 recounts. Likewise, in Genesis 22:1, Abraham's test consists of an order given by God about his gift, Isaac. In its way, the gift of the Promised Land will be a test: the pagans' presence could tempt Israel to turn away from the law (Jgs 2:22).

The people's resistance to this test of voluntary acknowledgement of God is also called temptation: Israel tempts God. When the goods bestowed happen to fail and nothing more is available than the narrative's or the law's words, lack of faith is expressed in murmurs, in challenges (Ex 17:2–7). This rebellious attitude involves forgetfulness of the signs already given, refusal to listen to the Word* and to have confidence, contempt for God (Nm 14:22–23 and Ps 78:41). It is the opposite of faith and fear* of God (Dt 6:14–17; see also Jdt 8:12–13), for it puts God into the position of having to show his proofs by confirming his presence (Ps 95:9); it also reveals a people enslaved by covetousness and, hence, by death* (Nm 11; see also Ps 106:14–18). The New Testament takes up this theme again (1 Cor 10:9, Heb 3:8–9, and Acts 15:10), a theme maintained by the tradition of the wise (Wis 1:2 and Sir 18:23). With this as a background, the Pharisees' mistrust, which they show by their putting Jesus* to the test, takes on an enhanced meaning (Mk 8:11 and parallels, Mk 12:15 and parallels, and Jn 8:6).

c) Development of the Theme: The Temptation of Man. In the late wisdom literature and in the New Testament, it is during the testing by suffering that the just (the Christian) finds himself tempted to abandon his fidelity. If God tests the just/believer, of whom Abraham is the archetype (Sir 44:20 and 1 Macc 2:52, and Heb 11:17), it is through the painful situation in which the latter finds himself because of his faith (Sir 2:1, Wis 11:9, and 1 Pt 4:12–13). In this crucible, faithfulness may increase (Sir 4:14, Wis 3:5–6, Jas 1:2–3 and 1:12, and 1 Pt 1:6–7), thanks to God's protective presence (Sir 33:1, Mt 6:13, 1 Cor 10:12–13, and 1 Pt 5:8–9). The test here has a more educative aspect (see already Dt 8:2–6). In apocalyptic* literature the tribulations at the time of the end are sometimes seen as the decisive test (Dn 12:10 and Rev 3:10).

The theological narrative of Jesus' temptation renews its links with the archetypical narratives, evoked by the biblical quotations with which Jesus counters the tempter. Proclaimed Son of God (Filiation*) and Messiah-servant at his baptism* (Mt 3:17 and parallels), Jesus confronts the temptation of being son and servant just as Israel had been when in the desert—taking the benefits and forgetting the word, challenging God to furnish proofs, preferring power and glory to service of the One (Mt 4:1–11 and parallels). But Jesus responded with the word of the law, which is the presence of the Other (see Dt 8:3, 6:16, and 6:13) to the fiction of a desire that destroys all covenants. In this way his true fidelity shone through, fidelity to himself, to his Father*, to his mission*, a fidelity from which he never deviated (Mt 16:16–23), not even in the face of death (Mt 26:36–44). In that situation, Jesus is the new Adam* (Mk 1:12–13; see also Heb 4:15).

d) God or Devil? Quite late, Satan (the enemy), or the devil (demons*) gradually assumes the tempter's role. Supporting texts include: 2 Samuel 24:1–2, 1 Chronicles 21:1–2, Wisdom of Solomon 2:24 (which glosses Gn 2–3), Matthew 4:1, 1 Thessalonians 3:5, and 1 Peter 5:8. The text of Job 1:8–12 reveals an intermediate position. James 1:13–14 establish the problem's anthropological base more firmly, starting with Genesis 3:1–5 (see also Rom 7:7–11 and 1 Tm 6:9–10): the temptation corresponds to the possibility of corrupting desire to turn it into covetousness. The test that forms the handling of desire may end either in growth or in a fall, an alternative reflected by the variation of the subject God-devil in the "mythological" type of presentation.

● H. Seesemann (1959), "Peira…" *ThWNT* 6, 23–37.
J. Dupont (1968), *Les tentations de Jésus au désert,* Bruges.
M. Tsevat (1973), "Bchn", *ThWAT* 1, 588–92.
P. Beauchamp (1976), *L'un et l'autre Testament: Essai de lecture,* Paris, 44–50.
J. Le Du (1977), *La tentation de Jésus ou l'économie des désirs,* Paris.
F. J. Helfmeyer (1986), "Nissah", *ThWAT* 5, 473–87.

ANDRÉ WÉNIN

See also **Demons; Evil; Faith; Good; Jesus, Historical; Law and Christianity; Miracle; Passion; Sin**

B. Spiritual Theology

Following the New Testament, Christian authors give the words *peirazô* and *peirasmos* not only the Old-Testament meaning of test, but above all, in a quasi-technical way, the precise meaning of temptation, of soliciting to do evil*, in particular, in the way in which they understand the sixth request in the Lord's Prayer, to which they generally give the meaning of "Protect us from agreeing to temptation" (see J. Carmignac, *Recherches sur le "Notre-Pere,"* Paris, 1969).

a) Patristic Theology of Temptation. The idea of the struggle against temptation in the Christian's life had already been suggested by the theme of the two paths that the *Didache* and the *Epistle of Barnabas* had inherited from the literature of Qumran. But the phenomenon of temptation only reveals its full meaning when compared to the patristic conception of redemption, envisaged as Christ*'s victorious combat against the forces of evil (see G. Aulén, *Christus Victor, la notion chrétienne de la rédemption,* Paris, 1949).

Irenaeus* of Lyons was one of the first representatives of the above conception, which the whole of Greek patristics would adopt. For him, Christ's temptation in the desert held a central place in the plan of salvation*. It "recapitulated"—that is, it took up again, while inverting it—the temptation and Adam*'s fall. Adam, by using his freedom* badly, had yielded to the tempter and fallen into the grip of sin*, death*, and the demon*. In essence, the second Adam, Christ, was the Son of God*, the conqueror of the enemy who had conquered man. His temptation in the desert thus revealed the whole meaning of the redeeming incarnation. For Irenaeus, the Church* relived this struggle between Christ and Satan, fortified through his example and clothed in the power he had passed on to it. Like Christ, Christians are tempted to worry about their material survival instead of counting on divine Providence*. They are capable of yielding to pride, which leads to heretical interpretations of the Scriptures, and of capitulating before the earthly powers, which drive them to martyrdom* or to apostasy. In the last days, this struggle would culminate in the assaults of the Antichrist, in whom would be distilled all the Enemy's malice.

This theme recurred in Origen*, whose thought would exert such a strong influence on the development of theology* and spirituality. For Origen, too, redemption was above all a victorious combat of cosmic dimensions, a combat between Christ and the evil powers that hold man captive. This battle raged during the whole of Christ's earthly life, until the resurrection*, but the triple temptation in the desert was its crucial moment.

Through baptism*, which involves a radical conversion*, Christians participate in Christ's victory. But temptation accompanies Christians the whole length of their spiritual lives*. By renouncing the seduction of the heretics' scriptural arguments, the Christians of his time relived Christ's second temptation, and by resisting as far as martyrdom the pressures of the Roman state's paganism*, they shared in the third.

Very aware of Christ's ontological union with the Christians and of that of the Christians among themselves, Origen taught both that it was Christ himself who continued in the faithful his battle against Satan, and that any victory won by a Christian was a victory of the whole Church (Steiner 1962).

As Henri de Lubac* remarked (*Histoire et Esprit,* Paris, 1950), the idea that the spiritual combat was a continuation of the battle that won redemption and that the images of Christ's military campaign and the two enemy cities*, which would be found in the 16th century in Ignatius's reflections on the Kingdom and the two banners, really went back for the most part to Origen.

After the edict of Milan, which brought peace* to the Church in 313, the idea that in the martyr's person* it was Christ himself who suffered and fought—for instance, in the case of the martyrs of Lyons in 177 (Eusebius of Caesarea, *History of the Church* V, 1, 23; SC 41, 12)—was transposed onto the monk's fight against diabolic temptations (for instance, in Athanasius* of Alexandria's *Life of Anthony,* 7, 1; SC 400, 151).

b) Spiritual Combat in Ancient Monastic Literature. The main reason for the first monks' retreat into the desert was a search for *hèsukhia,* for the silence and solitude needed for contemplation*. But the desert was also the place of temptation for them, and their asceticism* held traits of a fight against Satan.

Evragius Ponticus classified the Desert Fathers' doctrine about spiritual combat. He translated their experiences into the categories established by Alexandrian* philosophy and Origen. His teachings were spread in Greek Christianity by the majority of later spiritual writers, and in the Latin world by John Cassian who, before his foundation of two monasteries in Marseilles, had been Evagrius's companion in asceticism in the deserts of Egypt.

Evagrius stressed the usefulness of temptations. By giving us the opportunity to demonstrate our preference for Christ and to preserve our humbleness, temptation played a positive role in spiritual life: "Suppress temptations and no one will be saved," says one of his *Apothegms* (Evagrius, 5). According to Evagrius temptation began with a simple suggestion, then the soul "entered into a dialogue" with it, either to offer good arguments against it, or to begin to let itself be seduced. Then came the consent, which, by repetition, engendered passion, then captivity, a veritable obsession, an irresistible urge against which the will was powerless.

We also owe to Evagrius the catalogue of the eight evil thoughts, or demons, which attack the soul: gluttony, lust, avarice, anger, dejection, acedia (sloth), vanity, and pride. This list is the source of the Western catalogue of the deadly sins, as it was fixed by Gregory* the Great, in which laziness replaced acedia, envy replaced dejection, and vanity merged with pride. But this catalogue of sins represents the moralist's point of view; the ancients spoke of demonic tempters and of evil "thoughts." That was the view the spiritual father, for whom discernment had to apply itself to the suggestions before consent occurred.

Indeed, Satan was skillful at disguising himself as "an angel of light" (2 Cor 11:14), giving rise to the importance to the spiritual father of spiritual discernment and of the manifestation of the "thoughts." Finally, Evagrius and the ancient masters discoursed at length on battle strategies against temptations, particularly on the guarding of one's heart (*see* soul*-heart-body) and of recourse to short and ardent prayer*, which were the chief defenses against them.

c) Spiritual Authors.   With variants and transpositions adapted to each milieu and each epoch, the first Desert Fathers' teachings about temptation and spiritual combat were adopted by all spiritual writers. In Greek Christianity, these teachings can be found in the great classics such as John Climacus's *Ladder of Divine Ascent,* or *Ladder of Paradise,* and in the *Philocalie,* an anthology compiled by Macarius Notarus of Corinth and Nicodemus of the Holy Mountain. In Western Catholicism* *The Spiritual Combat* by Lorenzo Scupoli the Theatine deserves particular mention.

● Evagrius Ponticus, *Practical Treatise,* SC 170 and 171; *Thoughts,* SC 438.
François de Sales, *Introduction à la vie dévote,* part IV, chap. 3–10.

John Climacus, *Klimax,* Ed. Sophronios (1970), Athens.
Philokalia tôn Hierôn Nèptikôn (1957–61), 5 vols., Athens.
A. Rodriguez (1609), *Ejercicio de perfeccion y virtudes christianas,* 2, tr. 4.
G.B. Scaramelli (1754), *Direttorio ascetico,* tr. 2, art. 10, Venice.
L. Scupoli (1589), *Combattimento spirituale,* ch. 13–33, 61–66.
Fr. Suarez, *De Angelis,* l. VIII, chap. 18–19.
Thomas Aquinas, *ST* Ia, q. 48, a. 5, ad 3; q. 114; IIa IIae, q. 97; IIIa, q. 41.
◆ A. Eberle (1941), "Über die Versuchung," *ThPQ* 94, 95–116 and 208–232.
J. de Guibert (1943), *Leçons de théologie spirituelle* I, Toulouse, 278–87.
A. and C. Guillaumont (1961), "Évagre le Pontique," *DSp* 4/2, 1731–44.
Coll. (1961), *La Tentation, LV(L),* no 53, 1–100.
M. Steiner (1962), *La tentation de Jésus dans l'interprétation patristique de saint Justin à Origène,* EtB 50 (on Irenaeus, 44–80; on Origen, 107–192).
J. Dupont (1968), *Les tentations de Jésus au désert,* Bruges.
A. Grun (1990), *Aux prises avec le mal: Le combat contre les démons dans le monachisme des origines,* Bégrolles-en-Mauges.
J.-Cl. Larchet (1991), *Thérapeutique des maladies spirituelles,* Paris.

PLACIDE DESEILLE

See also **Adam; Anthropology; Conscience; Passion; Prayer; Spiritual Direction**

Ten Commandments. *See* **Decalogue**

Teresa of Avila. *See* **Carmel; Contemplation**

Terminism. *See* **Nominalism**

Tertullian

c. 160–c. 225

At the turn of the second and third centuries, Tertullian dominated the Christian community in Carthage by the force of his strong personality (31 treatises have come down to us, and many others have disappeared). An African with a double Greek and Latin education, trained in the areas of rhetoric and law, he converted in his adult years. The question of whether he remained a layman or was ordained a priest has not been decided, but, in either event, he filled the role of a Doctor within the Church, which at that time of rapid expansion was also faced with myriad troubles, including persecutions by the Roman state, propaganda campaigns by Gnostic sects, and internal conflicts.

a) Apologetic Works. His chief work, the *Apology,* is an energetic defense, in the name of justice* and freedom* of thought, of a Christianity reputed to be "an illicit religion." But also, with its form of an exhortation to conversion, this book stresses the originality of the "Christian truth" (compared to that of Judaism*, the philosophers, and heresies*). Tertullian set forth the contents of his *Apology* from the triple angles of a "faith*" (monotheism*, the doctrine of the Word*, and the doctrine of the Incarnation*), of a life of "love*" (practice of the faith and moral conduct), and of a "hope*" (eschatological promise of the resurrection*). This book assumed the heritage of the Greek apologists*, amplified their views, and distinguished itself from them by its passionate tone and its challenging voice. Thus, one of the phrases proclaims: "The Christians' blood is a seed" (*Apology* 50:13). One of Tertullian's most original themes, summed up by the exclamation "Oh, testimony of the naturally Christian soul" (*Apology* 17:6), was developed in his *De testimonia animae.* Questioning the soul*, which is cognate with God* because it was made in his image before it was corrupted by the world and the education received therein, Tertullian discovered in current popular expressions (such as "good God!" and "Great God!") authentic perceptions of the divinity, God's attributes*, and the beyond. His remodeling of the Stoic proof by *consensus omnium,* together with the cosmological proof, allowed him to define a natural way of acceding to knowledge* about God, a way that preceded the supernatural path through revelation* in the Scriptures.

b) Conception of the Christian Life. For Tertullian, Christian life was a break with the world, corrupted by the ubiquity of idolatry* in civil society *(De idololatria).* He stressed the importance of penitence and baptism*, closely allied, since the first was the necessary condition for obtaining the second *(De paenitentia, De baptismo).* Having fallen into the power of the devil* and of death* through Adam*'s transgression, man had been snatched from this slavery by Christ's work, which baptism reactualized by restoring to the repentent sinner his status as a son of God. Even though his baptismal theology was quite ambiguous, juxtaposing affirmations of the efficacy of the holy water and of the quasi-exclusive importance of the inner state of mind, it nonetheless brought out clearly the sacramental originality of this "seal of faith," which guaranteed man's regeneration. Through the acceptance of the Holy* Spirit, baptism opened the doors to a life of perfection and holiness*, whose every action was both a gift from God and a voluntary response from man. The work of personal sanctification dedicated itself to divine will in total commitment to Christ's service, in a spiritual combat and a search for purity* and rigor, which was realized through the most perfect imitation* possible of God's holiness as manifested in Jesus* *(Patienta* 3:2–11). This work should normally end with the acceptance of martyrdom*, the acceptance that "baptism by blood", the crown of Christian patience, gives direct access to heaven.

c) Controversy with the Gnostics. It was during the course of this dispute that Tertullian developed his theological thought. Although he was a detractor of philosophy*, in which he found the roots of Gnostic speculations, he was not that champion of anti-rationalism that he has been regarded as for so long. His famous *credo quia absurdum* ("I believe what is absurd") is inauthentic, and his somewhat similar expression (see *De Carne Christi* 5:4) did no more than extend the Pauline paradox of 1 Cor 1:25 by combining it with a rhetorical argument drawn from a commonplace phrase, which juggled with concepts of likelihood and unlikelihood. Moreover, Tertullian was capable of drawing extensively on the arsenal of a philosophical thought based on Stoicism. The Monist materialism of the Pontus also tinged certain of his images (the corporality of God, of the soul). Certainly he answered his adversaries, at first, in an authoritative way, the refusing to engage in any discussion, based on the principle that, since they had come later, they had no rights over the Scriptures; only the Church, their keeper, could legitimately interpret them according to its "rule of faith" and its "apostolic tradition" *(De praescriptionibus haereticorum)*.

But Tertullian put this negative attitude behind him in order to refute theological, christological, and anthropological conceptions with rational* arguments, especially the arguments of Valentinus and Marcion. He applied his main efforts to attacks on their Docetism.* Following Irenaeus*, he reacted against their contempt for a "flesh" that they excluded from salvation. In his *De Carne Christi* and his *De resurrectione mortuorum,* as well as in his erudite treatise *De anima,* Tertullian established the interdependence of soul and body in man's condition and in the history of salvation* by basing himself on Scripture as well as on an argument that involved power, justice, and God's goodness. Thus, the true incarnation of the Son—so true and so complete that it excluded Mary's virginity *in partu* and *post partum (De Carne Christi* 23:3–5)— became the principle and guarantee of an eschatological resurrection.

d) Controversy with Modalism. Tertullian answered Praxeas, who insisted on strict monotheism and rejected the growing idea of the Trinity*, by recalling the concept of a plan, or of the divine being's inner disposition to refine his doctrine of the Word. The "perfect generation" of the Word for the work of creation* (*Adversus Praxean* 7:1–1) made him the Son of God and a second person without, nevertheless, denying his eternity* (ibid., 5:2). The term "person*" made possible the expression, inside God's essential unity ("substantial"), of a distinction without separation in the three divine beings who manifested themselves in the achievement of the plan of redemption and creation. A subordinating inflection can be seen in his term *gradus* ("step"), which his Trinitary analysis associated with *persona,* and also in his images of the root, of the spring of water, and of the sun, on which he based his conception of the "planning" of the outflow of the Father*'s divine being, who retained it in all its plenitude, to the Son, "derivation" and "portion," and finally to the Holy Spirit (*Adversus Praxean* 8:5–6 and 9:2). But in fact this language aimed above all to highlight participation and coexistence in the difficult expression of a mystery* in which identity of substance was accompanied by the otherness of the Three. Tertullian also elucidated through a precise expression (*Adversus Praxean* 27: 11) the hypostatic*

union, according to which Christ Jesus' two component elements, God and man, were united, without merging, in a single person in whom each substance retained its specificity *(proprietas)*.

e) Adhesion to Montanism. As far as discipline was concerned, Tertullian's demand for rigor gradually forced him into increasingly intransigent positions that distanced him from the orthodoxy of his times. For instance, on ascetic practices (fasts), on the remarriage of widows and widowers, and on penitence after baptism—from which he ended by excluding, in his *De pudicitia,* certain categories of sinners (those guilty of the irredeemable sins* of idolatry, adultery, and homicide). He adopted—and tried to justify in opposition to the Carthaginian Church, which he disdainfully described as "psychic"—the "new prophecies" and conceptions of the Montanist trio (Montanus, Priscilla, and Maximilla). This trio had claimed to have received the Spirit of truth, of the Paraclete promised by John 14:16, and, in a climate of "pneumatic" exaltation, they had established stricter disciplinary and religious rules. Under this influence, Tertullian's ecclesiology* hardened without changing. He saw in the church, an exclusively spiritual group, the Trinity's extension and earthly image, and he set against the hierarchical Church *(numerus episcoporum)* the Church of the Spirit, the only one to which he reserved the right, through the intermediary of a spiritual man, to forgive sins (*Pud.* 21:16–17). In the end, this attitude was to make him a schismatic (the sect of Tertullianists?). Moreover, the impression of living in the last days seems to have exacerbated his expectation of the Parousia*, and particularly of the thousand-year reign that was foretold for the just and that was supposed to precede the Last Judgment*, but he emphasized its purely spiritual character (*Adversus Marcion* 3:24 and 5–6).

f) Influence. Despite certain anomalies in his doctrine and his final faltering, which earned his work a condemnation in the *Decretum Gelasianum,* Tertullian played an essential role in the history of Western theology*—and not only through the intervention of Cyprian*, who called him "the master." Through several of his perceptions—particularly in the domain of Trinitary and christological thought—Tertullian anticipated the dogmatic wordings of the great Councils* of the fourth and fifth centuries. He was able to create a firm and precise theological vocabulary by adapting and adjusting Latin materials to the expression of a thought whose roots went back to the Bible*. He guided this theology toward a more moral and philosophical religious form, more voluntaristic than speculative, less inclined to construct rational syntheses than anxious to respect the revelation given by exploring it more deeply, and by insisting on salvation's historic and eschatological realities.

● CChr.SL 1 and 2. *Apology* (CUFr). In SC: *To his Wife* (273); *Against Marcion* 1, 2, 3 (365, 368, 399); *Against the Valentinians* (280–81); *Patience* (310); *Prescription against Heretics* (46); *Exhortation to Chastity* (319); *The Flesh of Christ* (216–17); *Monogamy* (343); *Repentance* (316); *Modesty* (394–95); *The Shows* (332); *The Apparel of Women* (173); *Baptism* (35); *The Veiling of Virgins* (424).
◆ A. d'Alès (1905), *La théologie de Tert.*, Paris.
S. Otto (1960), *Natura und dispositio: Untersuchung zum Naturbegriff und zur Denkform Tertullians*, Munich.
W. Bender (1961), *Das Lehre über den Heiligen Geist bei Tertullian*, Munich.

R. Cantalamessa (1962), *La cristologia di Tertulliano,* Par. 18, Fribourg.
R. Braun (1962, 1977), Deus Christianorum: *Recherches sur le vocabulaire doctrinal de Tert.*, Paris.
J. Moingt (1966–69), *Théologie trinitaire de Tert.*, Paris.
J.-C. Fredouille (1972), *Tert. et la conversion de la culture antique*, Paris.
G. L. Bray (1979), *Holiness and the Will of God: Perspectives on the Theology of Tertullian*, London.
C. Munier (1990), "Tert.," *DSp* 15/1, 271–95.
R. Braun (1992), *Approches de Tert.*, Paris.

RENÉ BRAUN

See also **Asceticism; Eschatology; Existence of God, Proofs of; Gnosis; Millenarianism; Modalism; Montanism; Sacrament; Schism; Stoicism, Christian; Subordinationism; Tradition**

Theism. *See* **Deism and Theism**

Theodicy. *See* **Evil; Providence**

Theodore of Mopsuestia. *See* **Antioch, School of**

Theodoret of Cyrrhus. *See* **Antioch, School of**

Theological Schools

In a cultural universe in which the two phenomena were closely connected, Christianity appeared not only as a religious movement but also as a school of thought, a *hairesis*. Thus the apologist* Justin offers the perfect example of philosophical research culminating in a conversion* to Christianity, without any renunciation of his original interests (*Dial.,* prologue). It was, however, within Christianity itself that schools were soon to arise, splitting the unsystematic jumble of New Testament teachings into a multiplicity of theologies. The New Testament already refers to the existence of groups that almost deserve the title of schools: Pauline* and Johannine* theology are not merely the work of individual thinkers. Our corpus seems to include texts written by disciples of these thinkers (in the case of the deutero-Pauline texts) and texts that suggest the presence of a circle and its theological options, such as the community of the Beloved Disciple.

It was, however, necessary for theology to become increasingly understood as a systematic discourse, or exegesis* of the Scriptures, and moreover for it to adopt a general policy of borrowing from the dominant philosophies* of late Antiquity, before well-differentiated schools appeared. These schools could already be linked to a teaching institution. The rise of Alexandrian philosophy, which was prominent from Clement to Cyril* of Alexandria, was due in part to the *didaskaleion,* or "catechetical school," founded by Pantaenus about 180. Some schools may also have owed their fundamental outlook to one or more founding masters.

The doctrinal debates of the fifth and sixth centuries were to demonstrate the contribution of the theological schools to the formulation of Christian dogma*. They would also compel the Church hierarchy* to arbitrate the debates that set one school against another—in this case the schools of Alexandria* and Antioch*. In the patristic age, a number of characteristics of theology can be clearly seen: 1) The supreme teaching bodies of the Church*, the Ecumenical Councils*, can accord the status of official Christian doctrine to a particular theology. Examples include the canonization of Alexandrian Christology by the Council of Ephesus* (in 431) and of neo-Chalcedonian Christology by the Second Council of Constantinople* (553). 2) The procedure by which the Church defines its confession of

faith* never concludes a discussion without giving rise to new debates. The concept of dogmatic definition is not that of a "last word." 3) It is also possible for a particular theology to be unable to fit on its own terms into Christian doctrine as it has developed. The tumultuous history of Antiochene Christology is that of a theoretical tendency whose orthodox intentions were quite clear. It was able to offer a valuable corrective to the extremist interpretations of Cyrillian Christology, but it was hard, in the period between Ephesus and Constantinople II, to reconcile fruitfully with the defined orthodoxy. 4) Arbitration is sometimes achieved, not by canonizing the theory of one school, but by proposing a *via media,* which has never itself constituted the opinion of a school. Thus the Christology promulgated at Chalcedon* (in 451) was largely that of Pope* Leo I's *Tome* to Flavian, which may be thought of as an innovative contribution inspired by the desire to quell the debate in which Alexandrian Christology was opposed to Antiochene Christology.

While Byzantine theology from the sixth century experienced disagreements that did not really oppose one school with another (with the exception of the conflict between the hesychastic tradition and the Latin-speaking philosophical movement), the Latin Middle Ages witnessed the development of a system of theological working in which the schools played a more dominant role than ever. Two important phenomena bear on to the interpretation of this: 1) the existence of centers of theological research linked with monastic communities or cathedral churches; and 2) the rise of specific theological traditions within the religious orders.

1) The history of medieval theology up until the 12th century must be considered as the history of a number of centers of teaching. An abbey where a well-known master taught would attract monks eager to acquire the best theological training. Anselm, for example, became a monk at Bec because of Lanfranc's prestige. At Chartres, Laon, and elsewhere, theology was taught and created at the very heart of diocesan life and under the patronage of the bishops*. Thus, traditions arose that in general handed down not so much theologoumena, or "opinions" peculiar to each school,

as a certain style composed of shared references, common usage of the same sources, and a shared conception of theology.

2) Scholasticism* in the strict sense was characterized by the institution of universities and of study-houses *(studia)* for monks, most notably those of the mendicant orders (Franciscans and Dominicans). A new way of teaching and producing theology developed within the framework offered by the institution of the university. From then on, theology would be the theology of the *schola,* the school, more than of any particular school, and that school would always be known as a school of theolog*ies* (in the plural). Consequently, no medieval university can be regarded as a single school.

Tradition in the university only extended as far as the discipline and the course of study. Thus theological schools in the 13th century emerged from the process in which the newly founded religious orders established their own theological heritage by according special authority to their principal doctors. This did not however make Albertism or Thomism the exclusive property of the Dominican order, nor Bonaventurism or Scotism the sole property of the Franciscan order. The great monastic doctors began by teaching at universities alongside secular masters, where their influence went beyond the confines of their religious families. Some religious families (for example, Carmel*) never acquired a theological tradition of their own, but made do with borrowings. A religious family such as the Franciscans, on the other hand, counted among its numbers so many original thinkers, with such a variety of fundamental outlooks, that it is hardly possible to identify a homogeneous Franciscan school after Alexander of Hales, Bonaventure*, and Duns* Scotus (and also Ockham).

In any event, what is important is that there was a diversity. On the one hand, some theological theses became more or less the exclusive property of one school. For example, there was a Thomist solution to the problem of the reason for the Incarnation*, and there was also a Scotist solution; there were also Thomist and Scotist positions on the question of the immaculate conception of Mary*, and so on. On the other hand—and this second fact is probably more significant—the schools proved to be the heirs and transmitters of an idea of theology itself, and so the "scientific" view of theology would become a rallying-cry for the Thomist tradition, while the tradition of Bonaventure can always be recognized by a "practical" and wisdom-based outlook largely inherited from Augustine*. Moreover, since each school made its

voice heard beyond the zones of influence assured it by its own teaching centers, its discourse—geared to the demands of academic work and constantly open to questioning, especially in the forum of the *disputatio*—could maintain its individuality while continuing to aspire to the universal. The theological schools were not theological chapels.

The theological schools that arose in the 13th century did not merely continue through the later Middle Ages, but to some extent survived beyond them; the history of Thomism* or Scotism cannot yet be regarded as complete. A new factor came into play, however. As a result of the theological confrontations of the Counter-Reformation, founding systems gave rise to schools that—because of prevailing circumstances—were condemned to a rather sterile repetition of their defining theories. The dispute that most troubled Catholic theology from the Council of Trent* to the 18th century was a far-reaching debate on grace*, in which theses and systems confronted one another violently. This was, above all, a debate that Rome* wished vainly to bring to a close. While the heterodoxy of Baianism (*see* Bañezianism*-Molinism-Baianism) and Jansenism* was evident and was clearly condemned, the inconclusiveness of the congregations *de auxiliis* entrusted with investigating Bañezianism and Molinism was more than anything an acknowledgement of impotence. (Rome failed to reach a decision despite nine years of theological discussions; the opposing parties were forbidden to anathematize one another; and further publications on the subject were prohibited.) There may have been a difference of perspective between the opposing theories (to which could be added the later Augustinianism of Norris, Berti, and Bellelli, declared lawful by Benedict XIV in 1749 in a bull that encouraged the existence of theological schools), but there were also contradictions. Incapable of offering a judgment (but suggesting by that very fact that the debate concerned theological constructs and not the confessed faith of the Church), Rome obliged all parties to stand their ground. Consequently, neither Molina's theory nor that of Bañez was able to benefit from a constructive reception*. The Bañezian theory of "physical premotion," which had originated in the Dominican order, became a shibboleth of that order until the 20th century, as did Molina's "moderate science" for the Jesuits. Both systems, however, were handed down just as they had been formulated, with a fidelity that did not permit them to develop a history. As for Jansenism, this "wayward Augustinianism*" (H. de Lubac) was never in a position to give rise to a school—its fundamentalist relationship to the *Augustinus* restricted its existence to that of a party within the Church.

The history of theological schools since the 18th century has been characterized by unity of place, unity of founding influences, a unified conception of theology, and the defense of a school's own theological theses on subjects that the Church's official doctrine leaves open to debate. All or some of these distinctive characteristics occur regularly in the recent history of theology. The schools of Tübingen*, the (Protestant) school of Erlangen, and the Roman school clearly show the continued importance in the 19th century of a thriving intellectual center in which theological production is in part a communal activity—the Dominican school of Saulchoir and the Jesuit school of Fourvière are contemporary examples of the phenomenon. Recent tendencies, such as liberation* theology and feminist theology, have proved durable enough, and have brought together authors with enough in common, to make it likely that they will take their place in the history of theological schools, even though they lack unity of place.

Neoscholasticism, an institutionalized offshoot of the Roman school that was declared the official Catholic theology (and philosophy) by Leo XIII, has presented itself as a reincarnation of the School (of Thomism alone, in point of fact) persistently enough, with a clear enough sense of its theoretical aims, and with enough of a monopoly over certain teaching centers, to qualify by right as a theological school. Two reservations must be stated, however. On the one hand, the most important theologians of the 20th century (Barth*, Balthasar*, Lubac*, Rahner*, and so on) have exerted their influence without founding schools. (Barth was considered the founder of a school, but "dialectical theology" was no more than a temporary grouping of several theologians whose paths were very soon to diverge. Lubac was a figure in the theology of Fourvière, but his teaching career was interrupted in circumstances that turned him into a solitary researcher, and so on.) On the other hand, the academic authority that during the Middle Ages ensured a perpetual confrontation between the opinions of different schools, and which thus prevented the schools from degenerating into cliques or lobbies, has more or less ceased to fulfill this role in recent theology. There seems to be no common language (or metalanguage) that would enable a critical evaluation of points of view and positions. The appearance of theological *modes* is no novelty. One characteristic is new, however, and that is the lack of any methodical comparison of discourses—those that claim to be new, those that claim to be very old, those that declare themselves "different," and so on.

The history of theological schools offers striking confirmation of several fundamental truths: 1) the fact that theology has its concrete existence in the multiplicity of "discourses, fragile every one, and all destined to become outmoded, which the Church of necessity accumulates over the centuries in order to express the truth of Scripture" (Chapelle 1973); 2) the fact that this multiplicity has its secondary origin in the "vexations" inherent in the Scriptures, and its ultimate source in the incomprehensibility of God*'s mystery*; and 3) the fact that "the universality of truth proves always to be defined and thus partial, and at the same time defining and thus at the mercy of the current of history*" (ibid.). Nor is it necessary to prove that each particular theology derives from a community whose viewpoints and "familiar interests" (J. Habermas) it expresses. It is equally clear that membership of a group defined in terms of its own style and project does not prohibit a writer from donning the (modern) garb of the "author," but represents the necessary background from which any real originality must differentiate itself.

Admitting all this must in any case lead to a reappraisal of the phenomenon of theological schools, several of whose typical characteristics deserve more than archaeological attention: 1) theological projects capable of bringing together communities both synchronically and diachronically; 2) projects able to give form to the ecclesiastical practices of these communities (whether contemplative, apostolic, or both) while allowing the latter to sustain them in return; 3) contextual projects (limited to one time, one place, or one circle) that go beyond the limits of the discourse demanded by that time or place and attempt an overall contribution to the understanding of the faith; 4) projects that can exist only in the plural, in a perpetual debate whose terms may alter when the Church officially defines its faith, but which is set off anew whenever a new definition opens the way to a new *undefined;* and 5) projects that can only be termed theological by accepting the dual status of Church and scientific matters. So two dialectics harbor the permanent sense of what every theological school reveals in part: the dialectic between tradition* and creativity, and the dialectic between theological experience and community experience.

● K. Eschweiler (1926), *Die zwei Wege der neueren Theologie,* Augsburg.

G. Paré, A. Brunet, P. Tremblay (1933), *La renaissance du XIIe siècle: Les Écoles et l'enseignement,* Paris and Ottawa.

M.-D. Chenu (1937), *Une école de théologie, le Saulchoir,* Paris (2nd Ed. 1985).

E. Hocédez (1947–52), *Histoire de la théologie au XIXe siècle,* 3 vols., Paris and Brussels.

A.M. Landgraf (1952–56), *Dogmengeschichte der Frühscholastik,* I/1–IV/2, Regensburg.

M.-D. Chenu (1957 *a*), *La théologie au XIIIe siècle,* Paris; (1957 *b*), *La théologie comme science au XIIIe siècle,* 3rd Rev. Ed., Paris (1st Ed., 1927, *AHDL*, vol. 2, 31–71).

R. Aubert (1961), "Aspects divers du néothomisme sous le pontificat de Léon XIII," in G. Rossini (Ed.), *Aspetti della cultura cattolica dell'età di Leone XIII: Atti del convegno tenuto a Bologna il 27–28–29 dicembre 1960,* Rome, 133–227.

Y. Congar (1963), *La foi et la théologie,* Paris.

K. Rahner (1969), "Le pluralisme en théologie et l'unité du credo de l'Église," *Conc.(F),* no. 46, 93–112.

A. Chapelle (1973), *Herméneutique,* copied course, Institut d'études théologiques, Brussels.

P. Eicher and D. Schellong (1985), "Neuzeitliche Theologien," *NHThG* 4, 128–44.

A. Le Boulluec (1987), "L'école d'Alexandrie: De quelques aventures d'un concept historiographique," in *Alexandrina: Mélanges offerts à Claude Mondésert,* Paris, 403–417.

A. Orbe (1987), *Introduccion a la teologia de los siglos II y III,* Rome.

R. Marlé (1990), "La question du pluralisme en théologie," *Gr* 71, 465–86.

H. Crouzel (1993), "Le discussioni su Origene e l'origenismo," *Storia della Teologia, I. Epoca patristica,* Casale Monferrato, 215–20.

G. Pelland (1994), "Le phénomène des écoles en théologie," *Gr* 75, 431–67.

JEAN-YVES LACOSTE

See also **Hermeneutics; History of the Church; Theology**

Theologumen

Term originating in Protestant exegesis* and introduced into Catholic theology by K. Rahner*. A theologumen is "a proposition consisting of a theological assertion that should not be treated immediately as a magisterial teaching of the Church or as a dogmatic pronouncement imposing a commitment of faith*" (*Lexicon für Theologie und Kirche* 10, 80). Theologumen means a fragment of a theological theory, a theorem, but a fragment that has not been subject to a definition (or the condemnations generally accompanying definitions).

THE EDITORS

See also **Theological Schools; Theology**

Theology

Explaining Christian faith*, speaking coherently of the God* to whom the Scriptures bear witness, or speaking of all things in their relation to God, *sub ratione Dei* (Thomas Aquinas): these formulas, which are only introductions and are by no means exhaustive, spell out the program of theology. This program is, in a sense, already accomplished in the Scriptures themselves: theology, in fact, is founded upon the Scriptures as a body of texts that are already theological, and its highest ambition is to render them totally comprehensible. Furthermore, this is the program adopted by the Christian Church*: theological writings are answerable to a community of believers, whose faith the writings wish to interpret and transmit; they engage their authors more as "people of the Church" than as individual thinkers. Finally, the theological program is realized in a multiplicity of discursive and textual practices that are always historically determined: it is therefore only in the exposition of this multiplicity and its history that theology demonstrates its essential features.

1. Terminology

"Theology," from the Greek *theologia,* or "discourse on divine matters," is a pre-Christian term. It first appeared in Plato (*Republic, 379 a*), in a passage that poses the question of the pedagogical use of mythology. Aristotle used the term, but modified it: the theologians are Hesiod or Homer, who are considered distinct from the philosophers (*Met.* I, 983 b 29, II, 1000 a 9, etc.), but two passages from the *Metaphysics* (V, 1026 a 19, and X, 1064 b 3) use the expressions "theological philosophy" and "theological knowledge" to designate the third highest of the theoretical sciences after mathematics and physics. It was thanks to Stoicism, however, that the term "theology," and all words of the same family, became established in philosophy: theology became explicitly a philosophical discipline as early as Cleanthes (*SVF* I, 108, 12), then with Panaetius. The complicity of theology and mythology certainly endured and the Stoics took note of it: a famous passage by Varro, abundantly quoted in Christian literature (Augustine*, *Civ. Dei* VI, 5–10, etc.), distinguishes three kinds of theology: the mythical theology of poets, the "physical" theology of philosophers, and the political* theology of lawmakers. It was not until the advent of Neoplatonism that we could see philosophy somehow annexing theology (Proclus)—but that was at a time when Christianity had already taken possession of the term.

Prior to finally taking possession of the term, Christianity had shown little eagerness to appropriate it; this may have been due to the association of theology with pagan mythology. Appropriation of the term by Christianity did not really begin until the thinkers of the School of Alexandria*. Although Clement and Origen* still mentioned "the ancient Greek theologians" and the "theology of the Persians," they in fact claimed that the term "true theology" should be applied only to Christian discourse. Orpheus is mentioned as a theologian by Clement, but so is Moses (*Strom.* V, 78, 4); and the same Clement makes a distinction between the "theology of the eternal Logos" and the "mythology of Dionysus" (*Strom.* I, 57, 6). The term *theology* did not, however, entirely lose its association with pagan religiosity until the *Ecclesiastical Theology* of Eusebius of Caesarea (and the political triumph of Christianity over paganism*); it was only then that *theology* really became a Christian term. Theologians, henceforth, were no longer the pagan mythologists; they were the prophets* of the Old Testament; they were Paul, or particularly John the Evangelist. Theology was defined by the Christian faith; the term could even serve to designate the Christian Scriptures (as, for example, in Pseudo-Dionysius*, *Ecclesiastical Hierarchy* IV, 2). The usage of the term took shape and became clearer as the Trinitarian and christological debates evolved, and as a result, *theologia* and *theologein* became qualifiers to describe orthodoxy*. An extra terminological point came authoritatively into the picture, starting with Eusebius (*HE* I, 1, 7): from then on "theology" was to designate knowledge of the Trinitarian mystery*, and that knowledge was to be distinguished from "economy," from the doctrine of salvation*. At the same time, an existential meaning came to be attached to the term in ascetic literature (Evagrius Ponticus, Maximus* the Confessor), where "theological contemplation*" represented the third and highest level of the mystical life. Finally, in the work of Pseudo-Dionysius, the christianization of the concept of *theolog* achieves completion: the distinctions made between "cataphatic" (affirmative) and "apophatic" (negative*) theology, between mystical and "symbolic" theology, would bear, from then on, only on the internal articulations of Christian discourse and on its intrinsic coherence.

This Christian appropriation of a term of Greek origin received, for a long time, a marginal response in the Latin West. Latin theology, although aware of Greek terminology, adopted other terms instead: *doctrina sacra* (Augustine), *sacra scriptura, sacra eruditio, sacra pagina, sacra doctrina.* However, Latin thought did take from Boethius* the Aristotelian tripartition of theoretical work (physics, mathematics, philosophy/theology, see *Met.* E 1, 1025 b-1026 a) and remained attached to it. Later (dating from the ninth century), with the spread of the *Corpus Areopagiticum* and the influence of John the Scot Eriugena, the term *theologia* became more common. In the work of Abelard* it received a meaning which was even more precise, and which heralded the "scientific" theology of Scholasticism*. But the term *sacra doctrina* would still be the one most commonly used by Thomas Aquinas. It was not in fact until late Scholasticism that *theology* became the sole term used.

2. The Patristic Discourses

From the very beginning of Christian preaching* a certain number of contexts and authoritative analyses came into play, and these determined in a definitive manner what theology was going to be. Theology became the discourse of the Church; it was a discourse aimed at existing communities, in their own churches; it was also meant as a missionary discourse, with the purpose of defending *(apologia)* the faith of the Church against the pagan world, thus allowing the spread of that faith.

a) Catecheses and Exegeses. Being an intra-ecclesial discourse, theology follows the cultic rhythm of ecclesial life. Christian initiation*, in which sacramental rites presuppose catecheses*, is a primary site for discursive production; the eucharistic celebration, during which the Scriptures are read and commented upon following the pattern of synagogal preaching, is another; and both are inseparable. The first problem that theology had to resolve was an exegetical one—that of the realization in the person of Jesus Christ of the hopes* of Israel*—and the treatment of this problem is discernible across the whole corpus that would eventually be called the "New Testament." Likewise, it was under the privileged form of exegesis that patristic theology became organized. Theology deals with events, and it does so by interpreting texts that have been acknowledged as canonical, and which enjoy the status of normative evidence. It is therefore not surprising if the largest part of the corpus of patristic writings is made up of scriptural commentaries, whether or not these derive from preaching. And it is also not surprising that the theological theory that received the earliest sophisticated treatment was precisely the theory of the senses of Scripture.

b) *Apologetic Discourses.* The first theology that had claimed for itself the dignity of embodying a figure of the logos was, however, that of the apologists*. Theology bears a Greek name, and that name begs a question. The early apologies composed in favor of Christianity raised less the question of its rationality than that of its morality. Nevertheless, the question of its rationality was already a central issue for Justin. And when we come to the masterpiece of patristic apologetics, Origen's *Against Celsus,* rationality and truth* (Origen was replying to Celsus's *True Discourse*) occupy center stage. Theology here assigns itself the function of defending the coherence and credibility* of Christianity against the religious and philosophical reasoning of paganism. But this defensive discourse is also a creative discourse: the defense of Christianity is accompanied by an elucidation, thanks to which a number of important and enduring concepts take shape.

c) *Internal Requirements of Faith.* If exegesis and catechesis gave rise to the production of new words that commentary or initiation into the mysteries demanded; and if apologetic discourse could not be organized without instigating work on the articulation and conceptualization of the reasons for Christianity, theological work also appeared as early as the patristic era as the fruit of an internal exigency of faith. By distinguishing between faith *(pistis)* and knowledge *(gnôsis)* on the one hand, and by discerning, on the other hand, the fact that the latter is achieved via the former,

Clement of Alexandria supplied the founding charter of a theology whose purpose was nothing other than to meet the believer's intellectual requirements. Neither Clement's *Stromata* nor Origen's *Principles* reflect any cultic or apologetic context whatsoever. In these works theology develops (loosely with Clement, systematically with Origen) as an effort of speculative intelligence. It certainly acquires no autonomy from its scriptural sources and from the exegetical treatment they receive; however, a new organization of theology does seem to emerge.

d) *Theology and the History of Definitions.* Theology is meant to be "Gnostic"; but we cannot separate the speculative self-understanding of faith, with its conceptual basis, from the doctrinal history that constitutes the context in which the conceptual work of theologians is inserted. Indeed, a first intra-ecclesial discourse, that of Christian initiation and of preaching, is linked to a second intra-ecclesial discourse, that of the defense and illustration of faith within the Church itself. The history of theology is also the history of theological crises within the Church, and it is through these crises that the Church forges its official language, even if it means always borrowing it from individual thinkers. Speculative theology thus came to be part of the history of doctrinal definitions, and in this way a superior mode of theological discourse was being reached: the "magisterial" word. By introducing a non-biblical term ("consubstantial*") into the Church's public profession of faith, the First Council of Nicaea* proved as solemnly as it could that theological work is more precisely a work *of* the Church than a work *in* the Church. It also proved that this work is subject to the constraints of a history* in which the Church constantly clarifies its language.

The plurality of discourses and of their authors can thus be coordinated with some clarity. On the one hand, theology, understood in the broadest sense, accompanies all of the Church's experience: here we speak of theology as an evangelizing word referred (symbolically or really) to the cultic practice of Christian communities. This theology is not of a strictly technical kind, but through it the "event of the Word*," which founded the Church, is perpetuated. On the other hand, because this evangelizing word is committed to manifesting some coherence and means to be the true word among all words, theology is also committed to meeting technical demands: the foundation of the catechetical school *(didaskaleion)* of Alexandria by Pantaenus (c. 180), or before him (see Eusebius of Caesarea, *HE* VI, 3, 3), and probably the foundation of other similar centers, represent the "birth certificate" of the "theologian" (it must be said, however, that the

Christian East will always be reluctant to confer such a title, and will reserve it for John the Theologian—known in English as John the Divine, author of the Revelation and usually identified with John the Evangelist—Gregory* of Nazianzus, and Symeon "the new theologian"). The theologian is thus understood as being entrusted with an intellectual responsibility within the Church. The coming of a theology that is more conceptual and more systematic needs finally to be understood in two ways: it is an instrument that allows the Church to fine-tune its creed of faith, and it also meets the demands of a faith in search of "gnosis." Theology is a constraint born from the deployment of doctrines; it also reveals an unquestionable complicity of Christian faith with the needs of reason*. A complex system thus takes shape; its organization will vary with time, but its essential elements will endure.

3. Scholasticism: Scientia et Quaestio

The closing of the philosophical school of Athens by Justinian (in 529) may have had only a certain symbolical value, but it nonetheless signaled the advent of an age during which (within the Christian world) theology ruled incontestably over the organization of knowledge. The theory of that rule is older than the Middle Ages and as old, in fact, as Christianity. The gnoseology of Augustine probably provides the best patristic illustration, inasmuch as it rigorously reduces all other knowledge to the status of prolegomena to faith. Later, an opuscule by Bonaventure* was to give the most compact version of that theory (*De reductione artium ad theologiam*, Q. V, 319–325—the title is editorial). The Latin Middle Ages and the Greek Middle Ages knew how to practice other discourses than that of theology and they conferred the status of knowledge on these other kinds of knowledge. However, the Latin Middle Ages happened to be—and this point is of the utmost importance—the very time and place when theology was being defined in a privileged manner by its position in the structure of knowledges. This was the time when theology came to be defined first of all as a science and as a discipline within a teaching curriculum. The establishment of teaching institutions, from Alcuin (730/735–804) to the creation of the abbatial and cathedral schools, and then of the universities, represented the major external factor in the history of medieval theology. The plurality of discourses may endure—catechetical and homiletic discourse, magisterial discourse, and so on—but the lexis, as well as the history of ideas and of institutions, confirm that theology was defined from then on above all by the place it occupied in the codified organization of the institutions in charge of transmitting knowledge. When the expression *facultas theologica* ("discipline"

or theological "science") appeared at the University of Paris in the first half of the 13th century, it confirmed a long but steady process, in the course of which theology had become the business of professors of theology and of students in theology.

On the other hand, this process saw the emergence of a system of education that owed most of its characteristics to the successive receptions of Aristotle in the West. Several distinctive features emerged in a schematic manner: 1) Known primarily through the early translations of his work in logic, Aristotle supplied theology with the means newly to define itself as a rigorous discourse. Under the influence of the *Organon*, theology was thus practiced and thought out within the canons of dialectic. The victory of the "dialecticians" (of whom Abelard may be regarded as the patron) over the anti-dialecticians (Peter Damian, Bernard* of Clairvaux) did not mean, despite the extreme nature of the anti-dialecticians' remarks, that theology became subject to procedures that were irrelevant to theology's intentions. This victory did mean, however, the advent of a new rationality. The logos of theology and the logos of philosophical logic were linked from then on. The latter gave the former the required tool for carrying out its reasoning; theology could claim to be true by tying its fate to the most rigorous language. 2) This language found its exact expression in the adoption of the "question," *quaestio*, as the basic tool of theological reasoning. Devoted to the study of the patristic "authorities," who were known directly or via anthologies, early medieval theology did not "question." When Peter Lombard composed his *Sentences*, his aim was still to provide the student with an organized compendium of these authorities. Between the didactic account of the compilations and the dialectic brought forward in the "questions," the transition was therefore the one that led to a heuristic notion of theology. 3) The consequence was an obvious relegation of biblical commentary to the background. Higher Scholasticism did not neglect biblical studies—the scriptural commentaries of Thomas Aquinas are among the best of his writings—but it marginalized them, or it made them in any case preliminary to the speculative work of the "question." Readily defined from then on as a "science," on the Aristotelian model of the "subaltern sciences," theology could no longer give any centrality whatsoever to scriptural exegesis.

A certain unity in the practice of theology does not mean that Scholasticism enjoyed any type of unanimity concerning the nature of the knowledge it was thus practicing. Theology was thematized as science (*scientia*) by Thomas Aquinas and his descendants; Franciscan theology, as illustrated by Bonaventure and his descendants, will be understood more readily as wisdom*, *sapientia.* In Thomist thinking, theology was considered as a theoretical understanding of God subordinate to the knowledge of God by God himself and by the blessed; in Franciscan thinking it was more readily considered as practical knowledge related to charity. It may seem, however, that the differences between schools of thought are less important than the *organization* of each of these theologies, which merit the precise name of "scholasticisms," and that the unity of a method is more important than the uses to which it was put, because all of the schools did in fact belong to *the* School. The patristic theologies did not develop anarchically, any more than did post-patristic Greek theology. With the organization that the Latin West gave to theological studies, it may seem, however, that method weighed more heavily. This gave rise to consequences that signaled the precariousness of the medieval synthesis. Practiced as an academic discipline, Scholastic theology saw the unraveling of the ties that, during the patristic period, had linked the systematic/speculative discourses to the ascetic and mystical ones. Scholastic theology was first constituted to meet the needs of "faith seeking understanding" (it certainly did not discover those needs); and even in those of its traditions that were the least intellectual in character, it was a theology for intellectuals, losing almost any connection with preaching and with the kerygmatic activities of the Church. The focus of Christian experience* was certainly never out of sight; but in a discipline where the heuristic dimension was of foremost importance, the theological consequences tended to occupy a place that was considerably more important than the recalling of the articles of faith.

4. Reformation and Modernity

Theology owes its modern face to a plurality of heterogeneous factors: Luther*'s protest against Scholasticism; the growth of historical disciplines; a reorganization of the relations between philosophy and theology; the tension that finally erupted between "science" and "Church."

a) Luther furnished his program, on the one hand for a theology with a firmly biblical orientation, and on the other hand for one that was firmly existential. The Protestant watchword, *scriptura sola,* did not at all mean that Protestant theology was to follow only the way of scriptural commentary, or that it was to give it clear preference. Indeed, from Melanchthon onwards, and especially in the 17th century, Protestant theology was to organize itself in a way that was as systematic as the Catholic theology of late Scholasticism, and in many respects it was to be neo-Aristotelian. Nonethe-

less, Luther himself was first of all a professor of Old Testament exegesis, and his notion of theology was based on a return to a biblical "reading" and a vigorous rejection of any influence coming from philosophical reasoning. "It is an error to say that it is not possible to become a theologian without Aristotle," states the *Disputatio contra scholasticam theologiam* of 1517 (*prop.* 43). This theology that wants to be free from any philosophical influence is a theology that has been brought back to its focus, namely the crucified Christ* of Pauline* theology. The theology of the cross, *theologia crucis,* which Luther opposes to a "theology of glory*," *theologia gloriae*—the latter desirous of contemplating the divine majesty as it governs all things—is then developed as an experiential theology. "It is not through understanding, reading, or speculating" that one becomes a theologian (*WA* 5, 163, 28), but through true faith, felt by personal experience. Some well-known formulas express, along with his lack of interest in theological speculation, Luther's focus on the experience of salvation: "Christ is not named Christ because of his two natures. Why should that matter to me? But he bears the name of Christ, a name which is magnificent and comforting, because of the ministry* and of the task he has assumed; that is why he is given that name. His being by nature man and God, that is for himself; but his having assumed his ministry, his having poured out his love* to become my Savior and my Redeemer, that is where I find my solace and my well-being" (*WA* 16, 217–218).

Lutheran theology speaks of God indeed and does not limit itself to being a science of belief. It is certain in any case that it is not the discourse of a faith seeking understanding: it is the discourse of faith seeking the certainty of salvation.

b) The post-Reformation era was an age of theological specializations. *Moral theology* (ethics*) was born as a distinct discipline toward the end of the 16th century; at the same time there was also the advent of *positive* theology,* which was to develop fully during the 17th century. The latter was a theology concerned with its own history. From the patristic era the recourse to authorities had been an accepted theological procedure. But with the rise of humanism, that recourse had become critical. It is often difficult to decide where the dividing line is between a positive theology defined as a theological discipline, and a history of the Christian doctrines that would not have any theological concern. In any case it is a major fact that theology was influenced by historical disciplines that had themselves been developed for the writing of histories other than that of theology. In both the Catholic and Protestant realms, and in a process that accelerated up until the end of the 19th century, theology was written as it wrote its own history. The debates prompted by the historian J. J. I. von Döllinger (1799–1890) in the run-up to Vatican* I constitute perhaps the perfect example of this: from that time onward the Church had to take into account the critical history of its sources and include it in its magisterial discourse.

c) Theology has always known that it is not alone in speaking of God. But if enough thinkers acknowledged the factual coexistence of a "theologians' God" and a "philosophers' God" to allow for a basic philosophy to find its place within the classic framework of theological constructions, something new emerged in the 19th century: a philosophy nourished in its turn by theological motifs. Whether in Hegel*'s works, or in Schelling*'s later philosophy, or in Kierkegaard*, the discourse does not claim to be theological, but it mobilizes theological arguments. Delivered as lectures in university philosophy departments (Hegel, Schelling) or privately, the discourse was in fact marginal as far as theology was concerned. It would certainly give rise to theological responses but would not be considered as belonging fully to the history of theology. Although operating at the margins, this discourse did, however, inaugurate a new practice in theological reasoning, which was thenceforth at work within the realm of philosophy itself. Philosophy could become a "philosophy of revelation*," or even include a Christology* and an idea of the Trinitarian God. A christological sketch could present itself, in Kierkegaard's work, under the title of *Philosophical Fragments*. In any case, two major phenomena must be taken into consideration. On the negative side, theology, in part, ceased to be a primarily ecclesial discourse and underwent (in Hegel and Schelling, but not in Kierkegaard) a certain annexation; a line of thought that did not explicitly claim any doctrinal or intellectual authority in the Church took over the content of ecclesial preaching and partially subjected it to its laws. On the positive side, the Biblical God entered (as such) the realm of philosophy, which required an expansion of theology's traditional boundaries. On the one hand, the standard frontier between theology and philosophy became blurred. On the other, the juxtaposition of the philosophical and the theological was being replaced by theological work done within the framework of the philosophical.

d) If contemporary theology is starting to perceive the benefits of such a reorganization, its dangers were evident rather sooner. Can theology keep its name and its ambitions while ceasing to be a discourse of the Church? Medieval theology was of the university and

of the Church. The hypothesis of a university theology that would no longer be ecclesial emerged clearly during the 19th century in the Protestant world. The question was raised particularly acutely by C. A. Bernoulli's book, *Die wissenschaftliche und die kirchliche Methode in der Theologie* (Freiburg, 1897). The book's main interest was that it brought to a conclusion a trend that had persisted throughout virtually the whole of the century. From the Middle Ages to the 19th century, the requisites of scientificity changed; the idea of a scientific theology became at least problematic. Between the demands of academic work and those of ecclesial faithfulness, between university and Church, there was henceforth a field of "tension" (for example Seckler 1980). That tension was bound to arise once critical history was earning its place in theology, and the position of theology itself was becoming less secure among the university disciplines. Medieval theology had been able to take the form of an academic theology without losing its ecclesial identity—even though it is true that the upheaval of the Reformation was not due only to the spiritual experience of a monk, Luther, but also to that monk's revolt in his capacity as a university professor, "Dr. Martin." The 18th century had already given good examples of a crisis situation: the birth of "enlightened" and anti-authoritarian theologies, and of a "neology" (rationalism*) that criticized the traditional doctrinal formulas, because of its sustained desire to become emancipated from the magisterial authority* of the ecclesiastical ministry; and symmetrically, the polemic of pietism* against the "theology of the non-regenerated," which stated it was impossible to practice the profession of theologian where the demands of theological life were not met. During the 19th century, and still in the Protestant world, the crisis became more acute because the scientific status of theology became less certain. As a result, the aporia occurred quickly, under the form of a division. On the one hand the Church uttered the discourse of its confessions of faith and of its catecheses; on the other hand the university faculties of theology faced the temptation of ensuring their scientific respectability by freeing themselves of all ecclesial constraints. Theology wanted to organize itself as a science, albeit a science with a new meaning—and it could do this only by assuming the role of an authority that criticizes any form of theological speech other than "scientific" speech.

5. Contemporary Reorganizations

University theology of the 19th century was not entirely cut off from the daily life of the Church; nonetheless, reestablishing a close connection was one of the main problems it had to face in the 20th century.

The prime inspiration of the "dialectical theology" of the young Barth*—a pastor who subsequently became a professor——was the avowed need to create a theology that could be preached; and the mature Barth responded to Bernoulli's dilemma by giving his main work the title of *Kirchliche Dogmatik* (*Church Dogmatics*). As the ecclesial structures of Catholicism* could not have allowed such a dilemma to be raised, Catholic theology had not been subjected to the temptations of Protestant university rationalism*. But because this theology had been deployed continuously as a university theology since the Middle Ages, and because Neoscholasticism, officially established at the end of the 19th century, had probably exacerbated the problems already raised by the syntheses of higher Scholasticism, analogous efforts had to be made. A theology that could be preached, a university discourse that would not be separated from the languages of worship and preaching; this is precisely what would eventually be requested, a few years after Barth, by "the theology of preaching" *(Verkündigungstheologie),* as proposed by people such as J. A. Jüngmann and H. Rahner. The Protestant answer to Bernoulli's question was a neo-orthodoxy capable of taking up again, in a significant manner, the central themes of Christian preaching; the Catholic response probably came with the renewal of patristic studies. The aporia of theology was hidden, in a certain sense, in the notion of progress. Organized as a science, medieval theology and its posterity could not but produce the ambition of enriching a body of knowledge: if theology, thus conceptualized, had to have a history, it could not be any other than the progress of knowledge—and the progress of knowledge is not achieved only through its accumulation, but also through the refinement of the technical language in which knowledge is expressed. History cannot be undone. It is, however, through a rereading of sources, rather than because of any ambition for progress, that 20th century Catholic theology has made its most noteworthy contribution to the understanding of faith. To the rediscovery of patristic writings, with all their power to fertilize theological discourse, might be added another factor: the reappearance of Orthodox theology amid the totality of Christian theologies, due to the emigration that followed the 1917 Russian Revolution. The adversaries of the "new theology" (Lubac*; see *TRE* 24, 668–675) were not entirely wrong about what was at stake. The founders of *Sources chrétiennes* and those around them (though with other words) wanted to replace a heuristic/deductive theology with a hermeneutic one. A science of conclusions had to be replaced by a return to the sources; without the study of these sources, conclusions would have no meaning; any conclusion was in fact only to be drawn after a close interpretation of the sources. It was indeed a matter of refusing the endemic progressivism of Neoscholasticism.

There was probably more to this: the connections between contemporary Catholic theology and the "liturgical movement" were a major new fact. Theology is liturgical in essence, but it had probably reached a point where it had become so only in the most attenuated way. The rediscovery of liturgy as a site of speech and meaning, which had been heralded in Guardini's program (published under the title *L'essence de la liturgie* in 1918, one year prior to Barth's first commentary on the Epistle to the Romans), goes beyond the limited framework of the theory of Christian worship and generally concerns any theory of Christian discourse. The theologian's profile thus changes significantly. Nowhere is it said that reflection and critical activity are being refused the right to exist, but on the other hand, theology is being taken back to its source. Theology deals with the mystery of God, it deals with it in a Church that also celebrates "mysteries," and in a Church for which this mystery offers itself to thought in an economy of presence and event—in a Church, therefore, whose religious practices provide the first matrix for speaking *about* God by offering a language in which to speak *to* him. And if that is the basis of a Catholic as well as of an Orthodox theology, it should probably be added that hermeneutics*, to which a significant current of Protestant theology has committed itself (E. Fuchs, G. Ebeling), is in a certain way a genuinely liturgical theology—a theology of words that become Word, and eminently so in the act of preaching.

These tendencies are those of an existential theology, of which Balthasar*'s article (1948) on "Theology and sanctity" gives us probably a complete manifesto. It is not possible to respond to the question of theology without evoking the person of the theologian. Theological language* is a believing language, self-implicating, which cannot be understood separately from those who speak it. Theology cannot therefore be entirely defined without discerning in it the efforts of a faith in search of charity, of a faith already prompted by charity. And if, on the other hand, we go back to the patristic identification of theology and the highest contemplation*, then it will be necessary to observe that theology takes form in the experience of the saints as certainly as (or even more certainly than) it does in academic work; in this case the theologian appears not just in the form of a professor, but also in the features of a Theresa of Lisieux, or an Elizabeth of the Trinity, or a Silouan of Athos. None of this is new, but this classical view revives a tradition* forgotten over the centuries during which the theological contribution of the mystics had been considered scientifically negligible.

This does not mean that a theology understood first of all to be *sapientia* can eliminate all scientific concern from its field of research. If theology is an experience, it is simultaneously a discourse among all the discourses that aspire to be true, and the matter of its validity has permanent value. During the 20th century this matter was approached in several ways: 1) Faced with the modern redefinition of the field of "science," it was not possible to reaffirm the rationality of the theological by isolating theological language in the realm of cultic languages in such a way that all communication would be broken off: it was necessary to integrate theological language into the general economy of language without denying it its own specificity, but also without condemning its logic to be a merely "regional" logic. Whether in relation to logical reason (e.g. Breton, 1971) or the philosophy of language (e.g. Ladrière, 1984), theology had therefore to prove that its experience is indeed the experience of the logos; it also had to recall what patristic teaching tells us, namely that the divine Logos is not separable from the logos present in human beings. 2) Again because of the modern redefinition of the field of "science," theology was bound to respond by justifying its own epistemic competence. Beyond the classical theories concerning theological knowledge (e.g. Scheeben*), the production of a theological epistemology that would take into account this redefinition in the framework of a dialogue with the sciences represented a necessary moment (Torrance 1969). The concept of "theological science" then reappeared in order to reintegrate theology into the community of knowledges that aspire to the highest rigor, and to prove that it does have at its disposal cognitive procedures as well-founded as those of other branches of knowledge. 3) Missionary concerns required that theology responded to the requests for critical rationality inherited from the Enlightenment by arguing for (and from) the immediate intelligibility of its statements. The necessity for existential relevance is thus added, in Bultmann*'s opinion, to the necessity for critical judgment: theology can exist in the element of the logos only by conducting within itself a critical analysis of any mythical residue; and inasmuch as its own vocation is to have its words heard and its central texts read, theology cannot meet these necessities (and permit those texts to become word) unless it decodes the texts for modern man, deciphering them in such a way that the eternal meaning of the gospel appears from beneath the alluvium of a bygone cultural context.

Whether a circle or a field of tension, the connection between *scientia* and *sapientia* remains the constitutive problem of theology. Fully given back to the context of ecclesial life, theology cannot, without risking ruin, lock itself up in the joys of liturgy* or in the satisfactions provided by a precritical reading of the Scriptures. On the one hand, theology owes it to the world to express itself in a rigorous language: the apologetic moment is constitutive. On the other hand, it owes it to itself to be able to conduct its own self-criticism. Theology may fashion for itself an ideal image of what it is, the image of the word proclaimed and commented upon liturgically by the ministers of the Church; and that image, with which eucharistic ecclesiology* is familiar (N. Afanassieff, A. Schmemann, J. Zizioulas; *see also* Marion, 1982), no doubt has its truth: theology is mystagogical. There is, however, another image, which does not contradict the previous one, but reveals another aspect: here theology appears as a perpetual quest for the most accurate language, and thus it enters the debate in which *all* the languages that aspire to be true participate. The demand for proper criticism does not contradict the mystagogical or doxological demand; it actually proceeds from it. Theology is plural by nature, And the plurality of discourses leads to a tenuous equilibrium. If theology were only liturgical in nature, it would cease to meet the missionary demands of *apologia*. Should it instead be only scientific in nature, it would cease to meet the demands of the spiritual lives of believers. The complex history of theology shows the aporias that constantly threaten it. It also demonstrates the conditions of theology's loyalty to its own logos and its own functions.

Theology best seizes these conditions when it conceptualizes the ecclesiological status of its discourses. The Church as such is then the very subject of theology. It is so in various ways: as Church determining solemnly its rule of faith; as Church commenting liturgically upon its Scriptures; as Church bringing its own discourse into an encounter all the religious discourses of the world; as Church guaranteeing reflexively the rigor of its discourse; as Church discovering in the process of reasoning the means to deepen faith. No ecclesial function could therefore exhaust the practice of theology, and no simple definition could exhaust its meaning. The status of the theologian is multifaceted: neither the bishop*, nor the professor, nor the mystic could suffice as such to realize the whole essence of the theological. Theology is a historical discourse produced by a Church that is never entirely absorbed by a single one of its tasks; that never claims to have delivered the final commentary on the events from which it was born; and that does not entrust any one person among its members with the exclusive responsibility of issuing commentary. The unity of theology is discovered only in the articulated plurality of theological discourses. And the good articulation of these discourses—a good division of theological labor—is perhaps the essential task of the Church.

• K. Barth (1924), *Das Wort Gottes als Aufgabe der Theologie*, Munich.

E. Peterson (1925), "Was ist Theologie," *Theologische Traktate* (Repr. Ausgewählte Schriften 1, Würzburg, 1994, 3–22).

M.-J. Congar (1946), "Th.," *DThC* 15/1, 341–502.

H. U. von Balthasar (1948), "Th. und Heiligkeit," *WuW* 3, 881–96, new revised edition in *Verbum Caro*, Einsiedeln, 1960, 195–225.

B. Welte (1965), "Die Wesensstruktur der Th. als Wissenschaft," in *Auf der Spur des Ewigen*, Freiburg-Basel-Vienna, 351–65.

J. Macquarrie (1967), *God-Talk: An Examination of the Language and Logic of Theology*, London.

R. Bambrough (1969), *Reason, Truth and God*, London and New York (2nd Ed. 1979).

T. F. Torrance (1969), *Theological Science*, Oxford.

S. Breton (1971), *Foi et raison logique*, Paris.

J. Pelikan (1971–89), *The Christian Tradition*, 5 vols., Chicago.

G. Sauter (Ed.) (1971), *Th. als Wissenschaft*, Munich (classic articles by Troeltsch, Tillich, Peterson, Barth, Gogarten, etc., with a rich historical and systematic introduction).

B. J. F. Lonergan (1972), *Method in Theology*, New York.

F. Mildenberger (1972), *Theorie der Th.*, Stuttgart.

K. Rahner (1972), "Th. als Wissenschaft", *Schr. zur Th* 10, 11–112.

W. Pannenberg (1973), *Wissenschaftstheorie und Th*, Frankfurt.

W. Joest (1974), *Fundamentalth*, Stuttgart, not. 135–255 (2nd Ed. 1981).

P. Eicher (1980), *Th.: Eine Einführung in das Studium*, Munich.

E. Jüngel (1980), "Die Freiheit der Th." and "Th. in der Spannung zwischen Wissenschaft und Bekenntnis," in *Entsprechungen*, Munich, 11–51.

R. Schaeffler (1980), *Glaubensreflexion und Wissenschaftslehre*, QD 82.

M. Seckler (1980), *Im Spannungsfeld von Wissenschaft und Kirche: Th. als schöpferische Auslegung der Wirklichkeit*, Freiburg.

T. F. Torrance (1980), *The Ground and Grammar of Theology*, Belfast and Charlottesville (2nd Ed., Edinburgh, 2001).

G. Wainwright (1980), *Doxology: A Systematic Theology*, London.

G. Bof and A. Stasi (1982), *La teologia come scienza della fede*, Bologna.

J.-L. Marion (1982), "Du site eucharistique de la th.," in *Dieu sans l'être*, Paris, 197–222.

J. Ladrière (1984), *L'articulation du sens*, 2 vols., Paris.

G. A. Lindbeck (1984), *The Nature of Doctrine, Religion and Theology in a Postliberal Age*, Philadelphia.

D. Ritschl (1984), *Zur Logik der Th.*, Munich.

W. Kasper (1987), *Th. und Kirche*, Mainz.

M. Seckler (1988), "Th. als Glaubenswissenschaft", *HFTh* 4, 179–241.

F. Wagner (1988), "Zur Theologiegeschichte des 19. und 20. Jahrhunderts", *ThR* 53, 113–200 (bibl.).

J.-Y. Lacoste (1994), "Urgence kérygmatique et délais herméneutiques: Sur les contraintes élémentaires du discours théol.," *RPL* 92, 254–80.

A. Dulles (1996), *The Craft of Theology*, New York.

D. Lange et al. (1996), "Theologiegeschichte des 19./20. Jh.s", *EKL* 5, 774–853.

Coll. (1997), *Les Pères de l'Église au XXe siècle*, Paris.

JEAN-YVES LACOSTE

See also **Being; God; Language, Theological; Philosophy; Scholasticism; Theological Schools**

Theology, Dialectical. *See* **Barth, Karl; Lutheranism**

Theology, Feminist. *See* **Woman**

Theology, Monastic. *See* **Bernard of Clairvaux**

Theology, Moral. *See* **Ethics**

Theology, Mystical. *See* **Negative Theology**

Theophany

I. Old Testament

1. Vocabulary: "To See," "To Be Seen," and "Vision"

"Theophany"—from *theos,* "God," and *phanein,* "to appear" or "to make oneself seen"—is not found in biblical vocabulary. Its content belongs to the semantic field of "seeing" and "vision" (*see* Vetter, 1976). It had been granted to man to "see" God*, or at least be witness to one of his manifestations. When a human being "sees" God, however (simple mode, or "QAL" from the verb *ra'ah*), it is not simply a matter of sensory perception (Vetter), and it is God who "makes himself seen" (reflexive mode or *niphal*). Likewise, the "vision" *(mare'eh, châzôn...)* goes beyond ordinary human capacities. God's transcendence is maintained thanks to mediations, such as that of "the angel* of the Lord," or through terms such as "Name*" *(shém),* "face," *(pânîm)* or "glory*" *(kâbôd),* which contain an element of anthropomorphism*.

These changes in formulation correspond to a tension that can be felt in a number of narratives*. YHWH "manifests himself" to Abraham (Gn 18:1), but Abraham only sees three men (verse 2). Similarly, the angel of the Lord appears to Moses (Ex 3), but the burning bush, which is not consumed (v. 2), is all that is visible. In Judges 13 the angel of the Lord is taken at first for a "man of God" and later recognized (v. 20), then Manoah goes so far as to say, "We have seen God" (v. 22). The texts often give the Word* as the only means of divine communication. But we will see that some individuals qualified as "seers."

2. The Texts

Theophany is frequently a sign of divine favor, confirms a promise*, or accompanies help given.

a) Narrative Traditions: Local Manifestations (Sanctuaries). From the relation (not always explicit) between theophany and localized sanctuaries, modern exegesis* has uncovered "cultual legends" or narrative traditions* maintained by the guardians of various localities. Thus in Exodus 20:24: "In every place where I record my name, I will come to you and bless you." To the divine initiative, the human response is that of building an altar. Thus explains Abraham in Sichem (Gn 12:7) and Isaac in Beersheba (Gn 26:23ff.). Genesis 16:1–16 is the story of manifestation that completes 13:18 (construction of an altar). The angel of the Lord comes to the aid of Hagar (Gn 16:8ff.) at Lahai Roi, whose name suggests that she could have seen God (or the god) who sees her (vv. 13f.)

In the Jacob cycle, the tradition of Bethel (Gn 28:10–22) combines several features: vision in a dream, angels (v. 12), the promise of the Lord (vv. 13ff.). Jacob recognizes him to be present "in this place" (vv. 16ff.), which will be a "house of God" (elements of a ritual in verse 18); he names it "bethel" and will later build the altar there (Gn 35:1, 35:8). Elsewhere, the name of Peniel or Penouel clearly emphasizes that Jacob was able to see God without dying (Gn 32:31) while he was struggling against the mysterious "man" (Gn 32:25–32).

A cultual legend seems to be behind Exodus 3:1–6. The site, which an addition identifies to be at Horeb-Sinai, was protected as a holy place: "Don't approach…take off your sandals" (v. 5). The "bush," *senèh,* suggests Sinai, a supreme place of divine manifestation. In Judges 6:11–24, theophany legitimizes both Gideon and an altar (v. 24).

God was also manifest in places that were already recognized as holy, and where there was a temple*, such as Gabaon (1 Kgs 3:4–15), where Solomon had come to make a sacrifice (v. 3).

b) Theophany as the Legitimization of a Role. The theophany that Moses experienced (Ex 3:1–4, 17) coincided with his being sent on a mission*. He even received the revelation* of the name of the Lord (3:13ff.; 6:2f.) and would be able to make use of signs of credibility (3:12; 4:1–9). The case of Gideon is similar (Jgs 6:1–10, 6:14). The sign requested (v. 17) and granted (vv. 18–24) is comparable to Exodus 3:12 and 4:1–9. To this might be added the case of Samuel (1 Sm 3:10, 3:21) and Solomon (1 Kgs 3:4–15), although no mention of the prophets* will be made at this time.

c) Prophetic Traditions: "Seers," Prophets, and Vision. According to Numbers 12:6ff., while God manifested himself to prophets through visions or dreams, he spoke in the presence of Moses, and Moses "saw the form of the Lord." Visions and dreams were therefore the usual means of revelation to the prophets. However, the prophets were first and foremost men of the "word." Even if stories of vocation could be ac-

companied by theophany (Is 6; Ez 1–3), this was not always the case (Is 40:1–9; 61:1ff.; Am 7:14f.).

1–2 Samuel and 1–2 Kings feature prophets, "seers," or "men of God." The Lord can be consulted through their mediation (*see* 1 Sm 9:5ff.; 1 Kgs 14). Gad, the prophet (1 Sm 22:5; 2 Sm 24:11) is declared "seer of David" (2 Sm 24:11). Oracles are announced in writing as "visions" (*see* Is 1:1; 2:1; 13:1; Am 1:1; Mi 1:1; Na 1:1; Hb 1:1), something that is verified only in certain passages (*see* Am 7:1–9; 8:1ff.; 9:1–4; Jer 1:11ff.). Ezekiel is the great visionary and prepares the way for apocalyptic theology.

d) The Theophany of Sinai and Cultual Traditions. The theophany par excellence is that of Sinai (Horeb), associated with the covenant* and the Ten Commandments (Decalogue*). It is accompanied by cosmic phenomena (Ex 19:16–19). The texts bring together several traditions.

In spite of Exodus 19:13b (*see* 24:1f., 24:9–11), Moses alone approaches the mountain. But according to Exodus 19:17, the people go with him as far as the foot of the mountain. From that spot, so that they will not be afraid, it is Moses who will speak to them (Ex 20:18–21). Moses speaks with God (Ex 19:19), and preserves the "words (*debârîm*) of the Lord" (Ex 24:3; see 20:1f.), which are related to the covenant (Ex 24:3–8; 32:10, 32:27f.).

By means of a sort of return to the source, it is again at Horeb, another name for Sinai (1 Kgs 19:11) that God promises Elijah that he will pass in front of him, as in an earlier time when the glory of the Lord passed before Moses (Ex 33:21ff.; 34:5–8). A powerful wind, an earthquake, and a fire (1 Kgs 19:11) precede the advent of a light breeze: Elijah understands then that God will "pass" and he veils his face as he stands at the entrance to the cave (v. 12f.). God then speaks to him and gives him a few orders (vv. 13–18).

In the sacerdotal traditions, the theophany of Sinai is relayed by the meeting tent, which in turn anticipates the temple of Jerusalem* (Ex 24:15b–18a; 25–31; 35–40). The "glory" of the Lord (*see* Ex 24:16f.; or the pillar of cloud: Ex 33:6–11) comes to reside there (Ex 40:34f.). The temple of Jerusalem, where the ark is kept, is also where the Lord, "who presides over the cherubim," can be found (1 Sm 4:4; 2 Sm 6:2; 2 Kgs 19:15; Ex 37:16; Ps 80:2; 99:1; 1 Chr 13:6). The arrival of the ark and of the presence of the Lord amount to the same thing (*see* 1 Sm 4:7f.). If the temple was built in the "name" of the Lord (*see* 2 Sm 7:13; 1 Kgs 8:17–20, 8:43, 8:48; Dt 12:5, 12:11, 12:21, etc.), it is his "glory" that, accompanied by the cloud, comes to inhabit it (1 Kgs 8:11). One day Ezekiel would see the "glory" leave the temple (Ez 8–11). For the faithful in the Old Testament, the temple was the place of divine manifestation (Ps 63:2f.).

3. The Eschatological Manifestation

The definitive intervention of God in favor of his people, which radically changed the course of history*, has the traits of a theophany presented above all in an apocalyptic genre (*see* literary* genres). God reveals his power over the cosmos* according to the model—somewhat amplified—of the major episodes of the holy war, sometimes described as cosmic cataclysms (Ex 14:29; 15:1–12; Ps 106:8–12). It is thus that in Deuteronomy 7–12 one finds several colorful descriptions. The apocalyptic discourse of Jesus* in the synoptic gospels* (Mk 13 par.) also uses the conventions of this language.

4. Who Can "See God" and How?

a) "One cannot see God and stay alive." "You cannot see my face, for no man can see my face and live" (Ex 33:20). This axiom was etched into the consciousness of the people (Ex 3:6; Jgs 6:22; 13:22, etc.; *see* Is 6:5). Manoah's wife, however, does notice that the message received is incompatible with the threat of death* (Jgs 13:23). Sometimes the Lord himself is reassuring (Jgs 6:23; *see* Is 6:6f.).

b) Exceptions. The major exception is Moses. God spoke to Moses "face to face, as one man speaks to another" (Ex 33:11), and Moses knew the Lord face to face (Dt 34:10), whence his superiority over other prophets. Numbers 12:6ff. is particularly explicit. There are diverging traditions.

In Exodus 33:18–23, Moses asks to see the "glory" of the Lord (v. 18). The answer he receives does not seem homogeneous: unlike what is said in v. 11, Moses cannot see the "face" of the Lord (v. 20); and it is only when hidden by the Lord's hand that he will be able to see his "back parts" (vv. 21ff.).

Other than Moses, it was granted to few individuals to "see God": for example, along with Moses, there were Aaron, Nadab, Abihu and seventy ancients in Exodus 24:1f.; 24:9ff. The text is not straightforward.

If the peak of the story is to be found in vv. 10ff.—Moses and his companions were able to contemplate God without risking death—the 2nd verse diverges. The same discordant note, in the case of an entire people, is found in Deuteronomy 5:4f. According to verse 4, an older verse, the entire nation listened to the Lord face to face (without any explicit mention of the word "vision"), but verse 5 introduces Moses's mediation. This is in fact a correction, for verses 23 ff. repeat the line from verse 4: the people no longer want to communicate with the Lord without Moses as intermediary.

c) Writings of Wisdom. Elements of theophany are frequent in the Psalms*; they even appear, from time to time, in wisdom* writings. In the Psalms, divine manifestation disrupts nature (Ps 29:5–9; 68:2f.; 78:13–16; 97:2–5; etc.). God appears before Job in the middle of a hurricane (Job 38:1; 40:6) and Job recognizes his own error: "I had only heard of you by word of mouth, but now my eyes have seen you" (42:5).

II. New Testament

1. Vocabulary

The authors of the New Testament followed to a large degree the path opened to them by the translation of the Old Testament into Greek, the Septuagint (LXX). *Horâo* and *horama,* with their synonyms, are important. The related vocabulary, "to see" and "vision," has therefore a privileged place. But the LXX, to mention only this work, had used *epiphaneia* and *epiphanein* on numerous occasions, often to restore the *r'h* to the *niphal.* It is therefore not surprising to come across them also in the New Testament (see Lv 1:79; Acts 27:20; Ti 2:11; 3:4, for the verb; 2 Thes 2:8; 1 Tm 6:14; 2 Tm 1:10; 4:1, 4:8; Ti 2:13, for the noun).

2. Revival of Old Testament Traditions, and New Elements

It was through Jesus that God appeared in a decisive manner. And from one Testament to the other there is both continuity and development.

a) Continuity. In some cases the way in which God is made manifest or revealed is nearly the same as in the Old Testament: God guides Joseph (Mt 1:20; 2:13, 2:19, 2:22) or Paul (Acts 16:9f.; 18:9; 23:11; 27:23) by using dreams. Luke repeats the idea of Joel 3:1: dreams are an eschatological manifestation of the Holy* Spirit (Acts 2:17). God also manifests his will through angels: the annunciation of the birth of Jesus to Joseph (Mt 1:20) and to Mary (Lk 1:26, 1:38), and of the birth of John to Zachariah (Lk 1:11ff., 1:19). In Matthew 1:20 the angel of the Lord appears in a dream; in Luke 1 the apparition of Gabriel is more immediate. Angels assist Jesus (Lk 22:43; see Mt 4:11; Mk 1:13) or announce his resurrection* (Mt 28:2; Lk 24:4, 24:23; *see* Jn 20:12). The baptism* of Jesus (Mk 1:9ff. par.) gave rise to a sort of theophany: the skies open, the Spirit descends, a voice proclaims: "This is my beloved son." The episode of the transfiguration contains several comparable features (Mk 9:2–9 par.).

b) Development. The new element in the New Testament relates to the resurrection of Jesus (Mk 16 par.; *see* 1 Cor 15:5–9), made known above all through his appearances. But the aspect of theophany is more evident in the vision of Stephen (Acts 7:55f.; see Lk 22:69), or that of Paul on the road to Damascus (Acts 9:1–19; 22:4–21; 26:9–18). The risen Jesus is contemplated in the features of the Son* of Man by the seer of the apocalypse (Rev 1:9–20). The event of the resurrection was unique insofar as it was a definitive manifestation of the grace* of God for the salvation* of humankind (Ti 2:11, etc.); likewise, our hope* is found in the expectation of the "manifestation *[epiphaneia]* of the glory" of Christ* (Ti 2:3): this would become the definitive theophany.

3. "To See" in the Fourth Gospel

Jesus, Theophany of the Father. John emphasizes the aspect of theophany in the incarnation* and in the mission of Jesus. In the incarnate Word* we are given the possibility of contemplating the glory of the only Son (Jn 1:14), even though Jesus, before his death, speaks of a glory yet to come: (Jn 13:31f.). Philip asks: "Master, show us the Father" (Jn 14:8)—thus, Jesus is the theophany of the Father: "Whoever has seen me, has seen the Father" (v. 9). Through Jesus, the invisible God is made visible (Jn 1:18). Faith*, therefore, is received through what the first witnesses "saw" (*see* Jn 20:29) and that faith nourishes one's expectations of

contemplating Jesus in his glory (*see* Jn 17:24). We live from that certainty: "We see him as he is" (1 Jn 3:2; *see* Rev 22:4) and we too shall be glorified with him (*see* Col 3:4).

● E. Jacob (1955), *Théologie de l'Ancien Testament,* Neuchâtel and Paris, 58–68.
W. Michaelis (1959), *Horaô,* etc., *ThWNT* 6, 713–73.
F. Schnutenhaus (1964), "Das Kommen und Erscheinen Gottes im Alten Testament," *ZAW* 76, 1–22.
J. Jeremias (1965), *Theophanie,* Neukirchen.
O. García de la Fuente (1971), *La búsqueda de Dios en el AT,* Madrid.
E. Zenger (1971), *Die Sinaitheophanie,* Würzburg.
J.E. Alsup (1975), *The Post-Resurrection Appearance Stories of the Gospel Tradition,* Stuttgart.
D. Vetter (1976), "R'H-sehen", *ThWAT* 2, 692–701.
H. Haag, J. Guillet (1985), "Révélation," *DBS* 10, 586–618.
R.J. Tournay (1988), *Voir et entendre Dieu avec les Psaumes,* CRB 24.
T. Hiebert (1992), "Theophany in the Old Testament," *AncBD* 6, 505–511.
H. Cazelles (1993), "La théophanie au désert: Montagne de Dieu, Sinaï, Horeb", in *Tradició i Traducció de la Paraula (Hommage to G. Camps),* Montserrat, 19–32.

JOSÉ LOZA VERA

See also **Angels; Anthropomorphism; Cosmos; Eschatology; Glory of God; Prophet and Prophecy; Resurrection of Christ; Revelation; Temple**

Theophilus of Antioch. *See* Apologists

Theosophy

The use of the term *theosophia* is unknown before Porphyry, for whom the *theosophos* was an ideal being who could be both philosopher and poet. Proclus used *theosophia* in the sense of doctrine, and according to Clement of Alexandria the *theosophos* was a man driven by divine knowledge. In the Middle Ages

theosophia became synonymous with *theologia;* but from the end of the 16th century the term came to be used to denote an esoteric movement. It may have been in Arbatel's *De magia veterum* (Basel, 1575), a short work on spiritual magic, that it was used for the first time in a sense close to the 17th-century one. Its usage spread thanks to the editors of Boehme's works.

a) Dawn and the First Golden Age of the Theosophical Movement. One esoteric movement among several that had appeared since the Renaissance (including neo-Alexandrian hermetism, Christian cabbala, Paracelsianism, and "spiritual" alchemy), theosophy was in part inspired by these, and became established in Germany as a specific spiritual movement. Among the proto-theosophists, mention should be made of Valentin Weigel (1533–88), who combined Rhineland*-Flemish mysticism with Paracelsianism, which was both a mode of thought concerning nature and a cosmology composed of medicine, alchemy, chemistry, and complex theories about the networks of interrelations that united the different levels of the reality of the universe. Also important were Heinrich Khunrath (1560–1605), whose *Amphitheatrum Sapientiae Aeternum* (1595 and 1609) was to exert a lasting influence on various later esoteric movements, and Johann Arndt (1555–1621), who in his *Vier Bücher vom wahren Christenthum* (vol. 4, 1610) attempted to fuse medieval mysticism, the neo-Paracelsian inheritance, and alchemy.

From Silesian Lutheran Jacob Boehme's first book (*Aurora,* 1610) the theosophical movement acquired its definitive characteristics, or nearly so—only *Der Weg zu Christo* (1622) appeared in Boehme's lifetime; *Aurora* (1634), *De Signatura Rerum* (1645), *Mysterium Magnum* (1640) and his other works were published subsequently. Boehme and his successors exhibit little doctrinal unity, but three common characteristics can be discerned in the movement: 1) The "triangle" of God*, man, and nature—a visionary theory concerned at the same time with the nature of the deity* (including intradivine processes, etc.), with nature, and with mankind's origin, place in the universe, and role in the economy of salvation. 2) The primacy of myth. The theosophist's creative imagination is presumed to be based on revelation*, but emphasizes its most mythic aspects, such as are to be found in Genesis, the vision of Ezekiel, and the Revelation. Thus such themes and figures as Sophia, the angels*, the primitive androgyne, and the successive falls of Lucifer and Adam* are presented. Theosophy is a kind of theology* of images. 3) Direct access to higher worlds. Man has the ability to place himself in an immediate relationship with the divine world or that of higher entities, the *mundus imaginalis* or imaginal world (Henry Corbin), and can thus hope to bring about an interpenetration of the human and the divine, and to "fix" his spirit in a body of light for a "second birth."

Six factors contributed to the success of this type of experience*: 1) Lutheranism* permitted free enquiry, which in the case of some mystics assumed a prophetic bias. 2) Theosophy was characterized by a mixture of mysticism* and rationalism*, and the theosophists gave expression to inner experience, while conversely also paying attention to pre-existing discourses in order to transform them into inner experience. 3) A hundred years after the Reformation, the spiritual barrenness of theology was at times keenly felt. 4) Many believers expressed the need to turn their interest toward a prophetic type of activity, in reaction to a magisterium* that was often intolerant of this. 5) The period witnessed an intensification of desire for unity between sciences and ethics*, and theosophy was in its very essence all-embracing. 6) The appearance of mechanism gave rise to a reaction that reaffirmed the place of the microcosm within the macrocosm—in other words, the idea of universal correspondences.

The following authors are attached to this current of theosophy: In Germany, besides Boehme, Johann Georg Gichtel (1638–1710), *Theosophia Practica,* published 1722; Quirinus Kuhlmann (1651–89), *Külpsalter,* 1677; and Gottfried Arnold (1666–1714), *Das Geheimnis der göttlichen Sophia,* 1700. In the Netherlands, Johann Baptist Van Helmont (1577–1664), *Aufgang der Arzneikunst,* 1683; and Franziscus Mercurius Van Helmont (1618–1699), *The Paradoxical Discourses Concerning the Macrocosm and the Microcosm,* 1685. In England, Robert Fludd (1574–1637), *Utriusque Cosmi Historia,* 1617–26; John Pordage (1608–81), *Theologia Mystica, or the Mystic Divinitie of the Aeternal Invisibles,* 1683; and Jane Leade (1623–1704), *The Love of Paradise, Given Forth by Wisdom to a Translated Spirit,* 1695. In France, Pierre Poiret (1646–1719), *L'Économie divine, ou Système universel,* 1687; and Antoinette Bourignon (1616–80), *Œuvres* (edited by Pierre Poiret, 1679–1684). To these is added a rich theosophic iconography. At the end of the 17th century, theological writings appeared that gave a key place to theosophy, but which either criticized it or condemned it, such as Ehrgott Daniel Colberg's *Das Platonisch-Hermetische Christenthum,* 1690–91.

b) The Transitional Period. In the first half of the 18th century a new theosophical movement arose, in which two main tendencies can be distinguished. One tendency, which remains close to the original Boehmian corpus, is characterized by William Law (1686–1761) in *An Appeal to All that Doubt, The Spirit of Prayer* (1749–50), and *The Way to Divine Knowledge* (1752); Dionysius Andreas Freher (1649–1728), an interpreter of Boehme; Johann Georg Gichtel in *Theosophia Practica* (1722); the German Douzetemps in *The Mystery of the Cross* (1732); and by the Swiss Hector de Saint-Georges de Marsais (1688–1755), an associate of the spiritualists of Berlebourg, in the *Explication de la Genèse* (1738). This theosophy no longer exhibits the visionary outpouring that was characteristic of the movement in the 17th century. It is more intellectual and, while it is true that it remains "all-embracing," it is hardly based on a *Zentralschau,* or central vision, of an illuminative type.

The same goes for the second strand of early-18th-century theosophy, a "magical" tendency that showed a Paracelsian and alchemical bias. It was represented by Georg von Welling (1655–1727), also known as Salwigt, in *Opus mago-cabbalisticum et theosophicum* (1719); by A. J. Kirchweger (†1746) in *Aurea Catena Homeri* (1723); by Samuel Richter, also known as Sincerus Renatus, in *Theosophia Philosophica Theoretica et Practica* (1711); and by Hermann Fictuld in *Aureum Vellus* (1749).

This period also saw a proliferation of treatises on theosophy, most of them highly critical, such as those by Friedrich Gentzken's *Historia Philosophiae* (1724), Johann Franciscus Buddeus's *Isagoge* (1727), and above all, Jakob Brucker's *Kurtze Fragen* (1730–36) and *Historia critica philosophiae* (1742–44). Diderot's article in the *Encyclopédie,* "Theosophes" (1758 and 1763), which plagiarizes Brucker, is however relatively favorable.

c) From Pre-Romanticism to Romanticism, or the Second Golden Age.

The theosophical movement underwent a revival in the 1770s, enjoying a second golden age that lasted until the middle of the 19th century. Several significant factors contributed to this: 1) the importance of the idea of the "inner" or "invisible" Church*, independent of denominational structures; 2) an increasingly widespread interest in the problem of evil*, and particularly in the myth* of the fall and reinstatement; 3) the agreement between science and knowledge, which became a major issue at the same time as experimental physics was being popularized, with its capacity to stimulate the imagination by offering a glimpse (thanks to electricity and magnetism) of a life or fluid that seemed to permeate all the kingdoms of nature; and (4) eclecticism, which took more varied shapes than ever—some became interested in little-known civilizations, some attempted to reconcile apparently very distinct traditions.

Within the theosophical scene that extends over these eight decades, three currents can be discerned. First, there was a theosophy that continued to be influenced by Boehme, and that is represented by a figure still considered to be the greatest theosophist in the French language, Louis-Claude de Saint-Martin (1743–1803). Saint-Martin's first book, *Des Erreurs et de la Vérité* (1775), was inspired by the teachings of his mentor Martines de Pasqually (1727–74), the author of a *Traité de la Réintégration des Êtres créés dans leurs primitives propriétés, vertus et puissances spirituelles divines.* Among Saint-Martin's other major works are the *Tableau naturel des rapports qui unissent Dieu, l'homme et l'univers* (1781), and those inspired by Boehme, such as *L'Homme de Désir* (1790) and *Le Ministère de l'Homme Esprit* (1802). In French, too, there appeared *La Philosophie divine appliquée aux lumières naturelle, magique, astrale, surnaturelle, céleste et divine* (1793) by Jean-Philippe Dutoit-Membrini (1721–93), also known as Keleph Ben Nathan. In Germany the two most important figures were the Swabian Friedrich Christoph Oetinger (1702–82), an interpreter of Boehme, Swedenborg, and the Cabala in *Lehrtafel der Prinzessin Antonia* (1763) and *Biblisches und emblematisches Wörterbuch* (1775); and Franz von Baader of Munich (1765–1841), one of the major representatives of German Romantic *Naturphilosophie* (*Complete Works,* 1851–60).

The second current is epitomized by the name of a single author, the Swede Emanuel Swedenborg (1688–1772), who seems to owe nothing to earlier or contemporary theosophy. Swedenborg's output included *Arcana Coelestia* (1745–58), *De Nova Hierosolyma* (1758), *Apocalypsis revelata* (1766), and *Apocalypsis explicata* (published posthumously, 1785–89). This body of work, produced during the previous period, is less dramatic and tragic than the other productions of the same movement in that it puts little emphasis on the foundation of Judeo-Christian myth and the complexities of hierarchy; but the doctrine of "universal correspondences," which it expounds at length, has influenced many writers, including Balzac and Baudelaire.

The third current involved a number of initiatory societies of an esoteric nature. These served to transmit part of the content of the two previous currents with the help of rituals that were often rich in symbolism. This was particularly true of several high-degree Masonic rites, including the Corrected Scottish Rite (1768), the Golden Rose-Cross (1777), the Brothers of the Cross (1777), the Initiated Brothers of Asia (1779), the Illuminated Theosophists (around 1783), and the Ancient and Accepted Scottish Rite (1801).

d) Eclipse and Persistence.

The Occultist Movement, which made up a major part of the esoteric scene in the late-19th and early-20th centuries, was hardly of a character to secure the continuance of theosophy. It did, however, help to ensure its transmission, thanks to its very eclecticism. The second half of the 19th century also witnessed the success of the idea of a "primordial tradition," which was assumed to lie behind all humanity's religious traditions. Theosophy tended rather to take root and develop within a specific tradition (the Judeo-Christian*), and the appeal to a parent "tradition" easily led to quite abstract speculations. The work of René Guénon (1886–1951) also helped to stifle the theosophical movement.

The birth of the Theosophical Society, the first mass esoteric society in the modern West, was contemporary with the rise of occultism, in which it was partly rooted. The Society was founded in 1875 by Helena Petrovna Blavatsky (1831–91), and according to its constitution had three aims: 1) to form the nucleus of a universal brotherhood; 2) to encourage the study of all religions, philosophy*, and science, and 3) to study the laws of nature as well as the psychic and spiritual powers of mankind. The cultural and spiritual influence of the Theosophical Society brought about a shift of meaning. In the minds of a vast section of the public, this is what the word *theosophy* typically conjures up, rather than the quite different esoteric movement that arose at the turn of the 17th century.

The theosophical current has not altogether dried up during the period running from the mid-19th century to the present day. It had a profound influence on the thought of such Russians as Vladimir Solovyov* (1853–1900) and Nicolas Berdyaev (1874–1945). It is present in the works of the Austrian Rudolf Steiner (1861–1925), the founder of the Anthroposophical Society—including his *Goethe als Theosoph* (1904) and *Theosophie* (1904)—as well as in the works of the German Leopold Ziegler (1881–1958), in the *Meditationen über die grossen Arcana des Taro* (1972) by the Baltic writer Valentin Tomberg (1901–73), and in the *Ésotérisme de la Genèse* (1946–48) by France's Auguste-Édouard Chauvet (1885–1955).

Over the past 70 years, studies of the theosophical movement, or rather of some of its representatives, have been far commoner than what could strictly be termed new theosophical works. Mention should be made, however, of Henry Corbin (1903–78), a respected Islamist, who put "Abrahamic theosophy" at the heart of an investigation that combined scholarship and spiritual research to introduce Islamic theosophy to the West. In this work, Corbin also attempted to lay down the foundations of a "comparative theosophy" of the Biblical religions—in spite of the obvious differences separating the Western theosophical movement from what one might call the theosophies of Islam.

- A. Viatte (1928), *Les sources occultes du Romantisme: Illuminisme-Théosophie,* 2 vols., Paris.
A. Koyré (1929), *La philosophie de Jacob Boehme,* Paris.
E. Susini (1941), *Franz von Baader et le Romantisme mystique,* Paris.
S. Hutin (1960), *Les disciples anglais de Jacob Boehme,* Paris.
A. Faivre (1965), *Kirchberger et l'Illuminisme du XVIIIe siècle,* The Hague.
R. Le Forestier (1967), *La Franc-Maçonnerie templière et occultiste aux XVIIIe et XIXe siècles,* Paris.
J. Trautwein (1969), *Die Theosophie Michael Hahns und ihre Quellen,* Stuttgart.
B. Gorceix (1970), *La mystique de Valentin Weigel (1533–1588) et les origines de la théosophie allemande,* Lille.
A. Faivre (1973), *L'ésotérisme au XVIIIe siècle en France et en Allemagne,* Paris.
A. Faivre (1974), *Mystiques, théosophes et illuminés du XVIIIe siècle,* Hildesheim.
B. Gorceix (1974), *Johann Georg Gichtel, théosophe d'Amsterdam,* Paris.
R. Breymayer and F. Häusserman (1977), edition of *Lehrtafel der Prinzessin Antonia* by F. Ch. Oetinger, Berlin and New York.
Coll. (1977), *Jacob Boehme,* Ed. A. Faivre, Paris.
B. Gorceix (1977), *Flambée et agonie: Mystiques du XVIIe siècle allemand,* Sisteron.
Coll. (1979), *Jacob Boehme ou l'obscure lumière de la connaissance mystique,* Paris.
P. Deghaye (1985), *La naissance de Dieu ou la doctrine de Jacob Boehme,* Paris.
J. A. Santucci (Ed.) (1985–), *Theos. H.*
Coll. (1988), *Swedenborg and his Influence,* Bryn Athyn.
R. Larsen (Ed.) (1988), *Emanuel Swedenborg: A Continuing Vision,* New York.
J.-F. Marquet and J.-L. Vieillard-Baron (Ed.) (1988), *Présence de Louis-Claude de Saint-Martin,* Tours.
J.-L. Siemons (1988), *Théosophia: Aux sources néoplatoniciennes et chrétiennes,* Paris.
P. Koslowski (Ed.) (1993), *Die Philosophie, Theologie und Gnosis Franz von Baaders,* Vienna.
J. Godwin (1994), *The Theosophical Enlightenment,* Albany, NY.
N. Jacques-Chaquin (1994), "Le théosophe Saint-Martin et la sorcière: deux imaginaires du monde des signes," thesis, University of Paris VII.
A. Faivre (1995), *Philosophie de la Nature (Physique Sacrée: Théosophie, XVIIIe et XIXe siècles),* Paris.
A. Faivre (1996), "Théosophies," in *Accès de l'ésotérisme occidental,* vol. II, 43–167, Paris.

ANTOINE FAIVRE

See also **Lutheranism; Mysticism; Myth; Nature; Orthodoxy, Modern and Contemporary; Philosophy; Platonism, Christian; Rhineland-Flemish Mysticism; World**

Theotokos. *See* **Ephesus, Council of; Mary**

Theresa of Lisieux. *See* **Childhood, Spiritual**

Thierry of Chartres. *See* **Chartres, School of**

Thomas à Kempis

1379/80–1471

The importance of Thomas à Kempis, who was born in 1379 or 1380 at Kempen, near Zwolle in the Rhine delta (now in the Netherlands), derives from a probability bordering on certainty that he was the author, and not just the copyist or final editor, of the four spiritual treatises known as *The Imitation of Christ.* These treatises constitute by far the most influential work of Christian devotion to have been published during the second Christian millennium and, although their genesis has been the subject of academic dispute, opinion has increasingly hardened behind à Kempis's authorship. The controversy was reviewed at length in 1968 by R. R. Post (*The Modern Devotion: Confrontation with Reformation and Humanism,* Leyden 1968) who argues with apparent conclusiveness for à Kempis's authorship, in the wake of studies by L. M. J. Delaissé (*Le manuscrit autographe de Thomas à Kempis et "L'Imitation de Jésus-Christ,"* Paris/Brussels/Antwerp/Amsterdam 1956) and P. Debongnie (*L'auteur ou les auteurs de l'imita-*

tion, Louvain 1957). The academic controversy may yet be rekindled, but modern editions now universally ascribe the *Imitation of Christ* to à Kempis. The assumption is that the work arose in the context of à Kempis's development of his own spiritual life, as he jotted down the aphorisms and insights on which it was based.

À Kempis was sent, like his brother John ten years earlier, to the famous chapter school at Deventer, where he arrived around 1392–94. He was still attending school in 1399, and in that year he traveled to Zwolle to see his brother, by then prior of the new monastery of Canons Regular of the Windesheim congregation at St Agnietenberg. At Deventer he had been received by Florens Radewijns (1350–1400) into the hostel of the Brethren of the Common Life, founded by Geert Groote (1340–84), of whom Radewijns was the successor, in the spirit of his popular and widespread spiritual movement known as the *devotio* moderna.*

À Kempis himself probably entered the monastery in 1399 and was invested there in 1406. In 1413–14 he was ordained priest. The Windesheim congregation of monasteries was a further foundation of Groote's followers, also based on his spiritual tradition, the *devotio moderna,* of which the *Imitation of Christ* is by far the best known, if not necessarily the most central exposition. The spirituality of the *Imitation* deviates from that central to the *devotio* only because it contains elements and emphases peculiar to à Kempis's own personal meditation as his spiritual life developed.

À Kempis was the monastery's "procurator," but his indifferent success in that office led in 1429 to his appointment instead to the post of sub-prior. With only two short periods of absence, he remained at St Agnietenberg until his death in 1471, by which time he had become superior. The canons, like the non-monastic and non-ordained Brothers and Sisters of the Common Life to whom their spirituality related them, earned their living as experts in the copying and binding of manuscripts, and À Kempis himself became a renowned copyist, producing at least two full ten-volume bibles as well as choir books and missals. He was however also an author of spiritual treatises and such other works as the lives of Groote, Radewijns, and other brethren, and of the history of St Agnietenberg. He was also in charge of transmitting Groote's spiritual legacy to the younger members of the community.

The four treatises of the *Imitation of Christ* circulated separately, and were probably not intended to form a single work. When they appear in a manuscript together, their order is sometimes different. They are known in over 700 manuscripts and 3,000 published editions in 95 languages. There is an unsigned autograph of nine of à Kempis's spiritual treatises, including the four that make up the *Imitation of Christ,* dated 1441. The treatises deal with matters central to Groote's spirituality, the life and passion of Jesus, the moral virtues, and spiritual exercises. They are essentially practical, oriented toward performing God's will on earth in such a manner as to augment spiritual perfection and to gain heaven, and are characteristic of the movement away from an emphasis on Christ's glory and the idealized depiction of Jesus' life and passion, which reflected the generally liturgical, monastically based devotion of the high Middle Ages. They are also concerned with the "purgative" and "illuminative" stages of devotional life, rather than the final "unitive" phase of ecstatic union with God. In this à Kempis differed from what had been the preoccupation of some earlier members of the Windesheim community, such as Hendrik Mande (c. 1360–1431) and Gerlach Peters (1378–1411). They had developed the more purely mystical doctrine of Groote's own model, Ruusbroec,

although without totally neglecting the need to overcome the reality of sin.

Outside the *Imitation,* à Kempis's other spiritual treatises, such as *The Garden of Roses* or *The Valley of Lilies,* continue to use the allegory common in medieval works of devotion. They are written as an encouragement to cultivate the virtues taught as well as exhibited by Christ. Even in the *Imitation,* in which the new religious sensibility of the *devotio* makes Jesus clearly vulnerable and his agony an encouragement to his followers to bear their own anguish, the title is somewhat misleading.

The word "imitation," which in the context means "following" or "discipleship of Christ," is taken from the opening sentence of the first treatise, and must be understood as indicating the need to follow Christ's teaching and example. The consideration of his agony, as a means for arousing compunction, is still secondary. The need to "conform one's whole life to Christ" is stated in the first chapter, but leads to an extended meditation on the nature and acquisition of virtue. Christ's human agony had gradually become a principal focus of Christian devotion in Bernard* of Clairvaux (1090–1153) and Francis of Assisi (1182–1226). It was firmly established north of the Alps by the date of the great folio of meditations known as the *Life of Christ* by Ludolph the Carthusian (†1378) in the late 14th century, and had become the basis for the popular lay devotion propagated by the *devotio* generally. À Kempis exploits the compassion engendered by the tortured Jesus to motivate his readers to the arduous effort needed to overcome the vanity of earthly ambition and sensual desire.

The first treatise of the *Imitation* cannot be later than 1424, and the others not later than 1427. The work is unpretentious and disordered, written in rhythmic, clear, simple Latin for personal use. The first three books could be arranged in any order, like the chapters within them, which follow no consecutive pattern or argument. The work reads like a personal handbook of annotated and expanded spiritual aphorisms, such as the devout were encouraged to compile from their own and others' experience, and to use for their personal spiritual profit.

The first book starts with the medieval theme of contempt for worldly vanities and contains short chapters on mostly passive virtues, such as humility, truthfulness, prudence, and obedience, and on the avoidance of vices such as arrogance, inordinate affection, loquacity, and rash judgments. Only by freeing itself from the desires of the flesh can the soul attain peace. The moral stoicism of the ancients, adopted and christianized by the Middle Ages, has been transformed into a genuinely Christian spirituality. From the beginning the importance of learning is emphatically deflated. Indeed, "the more thou knowest…so much the heavier will thy judgment be, unless thy life be also more holy." What is important is the acquisition of virtue. "Study to wean thy heart from the love of visible things, and to betake thee to the things unseen…" There are chapters on resisting temptation, on the uses of adversity, on the monastic life, and on the examples of the fathers, with reflections about death, judgment, and the amendment of life. The aim, which is the promotion of an essentially lay piety, explains the recurrent emphasis on moral virtue as something to be striven for, and its acquisition as the purpose of life on earth. The aim of the devout life is to "win" Christ.

The interiorization of religious devotion in the *devotio moderna,* the relatively slight importance it attached to sacraments outside the Eucharist, and the relative indifference to sacramental piety and the hierarchical nature of the Church outside the Eucharist was to allow it to blend easily into the spirituality promoted by Lutheran theology when the time came. But there still remains in à Kempis a central insistence on a spiritual progress that could be achieved only by effort. Virtues have to be acquired little by little, and through constant effort: "If every year we rooted out one vice, we should soon become perfect men." Together with compassion for the suffering Christ, in the pursuit of virtue à Kempis invokes the fear bred by contemplating death and judgment. The spirituality is rigorously individualistic.

The second book holds up the example of interior virtue and exhorts to companionship in the life and sufferings of Jesus, again emphasizing the need for effort and its reward. The personal assimilation of Christ's moral virtues, to which the *Imitation* is intended to guide the reader, depends on as complete as possible an imaginative identification with Jesus himself, and the union with Christ in which perfection consists is even taken to the extent of stimulating a desire to share his sufferings.

The third and fourth books are a dialogue between God and the devout soul. They strongly reflect the characteristic spirituality of the lower Rhineland in the early 15th century, with its sharp distinction between the spiritual and the material, the internal and the external. Learning is still treated with suspicion, as likely to lead more easily to vanity than to humility. True peace and happiness lie in renunciation, abnegation, and endurance. The fourth book is devoted entirely to the Eucharist. During Mass the faithful should meditate on Christ's self-immolation as a preparation for receiving him. The spirituality is personal and ascetic rather than social or apostolic. It is concerned with the private acquisition of virtues, particularly those fostering abnegation and humility. It both paved the way for the Reformation (for which in the early 16th century it speedily made way), and was the basis—although transformed—for the piety of Erasmus and, a little later, of Ignatius of Loyola and the Jesuits. Its central message is "Endure with Christ and for Christ, if thou wouldst reign with Christ."

● Thomas Hemerken a Kempis, ed. M.J. Pohl, (1922) *Opera omnia,* 7 vols., Freiburg.

H. A. Oberman (1963), *The Harvest of Medieval Theology,* Cambridge, MA.

R. R. Post (1968), *The Modern Devotion,* Leyden.

ANTHONY LEVI

Thomas Aquinas

c. 1224–1274

---

1. Life and Works

Thomas was at first a Benedictine Oblate at Monte Cassino, where he received a solid initiation into the study of Augustine* and of Gregory* the Great. In Naples from 1239 on, at a time when, under Frederick II, that city was a center of intense cultural activity, he familiarized himself with the natural philosophy* and metaphysics of Aristotle and of his commentators. When Thomas became a Dominican (1244) he was sent to Paris (1245–48) to study under the direction of Albert* the Great, who introduced him in particular to the works of Dionysius* the Pseudo-Areopagite. He deepened his knowledge of Aristotle's ethics* and he appropriated the expository methods of the Masters of Arts, whose courses he appears to have taken. With Albert he went to Köln, where he completed his training (1248–52). Having become, by the end of that period, "Bachelor of Biblical Studies," he lectured on Isaiah and on Jeremiah.

Teaching in Paris (1252–59), Thomas Aquinas was at first a bachelor and for two years (1252–1254) he lectured on the *Sententiae* by Peter Lombard. His text (completed in 1256 or slightly after) allows for his personal opinions, as well as the marked influence of Albert and of Bonaventure* (this is less apparent in his later books). *On The Principles of Nature* and *On Being and Essence* were also from that period. As Master in Theology* (1256), Thomas Aquinas participated in philosophical dispute and wrote the questions *On Truth* (truth and knowledge: q. 1–20; good* and the appetite for good: q. 21–29), the *Quodlibetal Questions* VII–XI, and the commentary on Boethius*'s *The Trinity* (in particular the epistemological aspects). Against the secular masters of Paris (Guillaume de Saint-Amour and his supporters), he undertook the defense of the mendicant orders, of their right to study and teach, and he published a book, *Contra Doctrinam Retrahentium a Religione.*

In Italy (end of 1259–68) Thomas resided first in Naples (? 1259–61), then in Orvieto (1261–65), where he occupied the functions of conventual lecturer, and completed two major works. The *Summa Contra Gentiles* (the first 59 chapters were written before he left Paris), had the double objective of explaining the Catholic faith* and of rejecting contradictory errors. It was organized according to a plan in which the subject matter is divided in four books, and which already looked forward to that of the *Summa Theologica:* (1. God*; 2. the "procession" of creatures; 3. their return to God; 4. the truths that elude philosophy: the Trinity*, the Incarnation*, the sacraments*). At the same time, Thomas wrote a commentary on Job, a good example of literal exegesis* at the service of a doctrinal reflection on the suffering of the just and innocent man, and on divine Providence*. At the request of Pope Urban IV, he started the "Chain of Gold" *(Catena aurea),* a commentary followed by the four Gospels*, by means of extracts from the fathers* of the church (*On Matthew* was completed in 1264). Several responses to theological consultations and numerous opuscules date from that period (*Contra Errores Graecorum; On the Divine Names* by Pseudo-Dionysius; *Officium etiam of corpus Christi fecit,* and so on).

In Rome* (1265–68) Thomas started the *Summa Theologica,* whose First Part was composed at that time (1266–68). He completed the "Chain of Gold" (*Mark, Luke, John),* and engaged in philosophical dispute or wrote on this whole series of questions: *On Divine Omnipotence, On the Soul, On Human Souls and Angels.* At that time he also wrote the *Compendium Theologiae* (unfinished). Aside from numerous talks, he commenced his activity as commentator of Aristotle with *Sententia Super De anima* (direct collaboration with Aristotle's translator, Guillaume de Moerbeke, was hardly probable).

In Paris once more (1268–72), Thomas taught the commentaries *On Matthew* (1269–70) and *On John* (1270–72), debated and wrote the questions *On Evil,* the *Quodlibets* I–VI and XII. He also continued his commentaries on Aristotle (*Physics, Comets, Posterior Analytics, Ethics, Politics,* and so on), as well as writing the Second Part of the *Summa* (1271–72). The reawakening of the quarrel with the seculars prompted him to write *The Perfection of Spiritual Life* and *Against those who Hinder Entering into Religion,* which reveal his passionate nature, the religious ideal of his order as well as his own. His commitment in doctrinal quarrels is indicative of a moderate Aristotelian position: against the "Augustinians," *On the Eternity of the World* recognizes that only the Christian doctrine on creation* can lead to an affirmation that the world had a beginning. And *On the Unity of Intellect* refutes the "Averroist" thesis of a unique intellect possible for all mankind, by declaring it contrary to the teaching of Aristotle as well as to the Christian faith (Libera 1994).

In Naples, at the beginning of the summer of 1272, Thomas directed the Dominicans' new center for study, continued writing the Third Part of the *Summa* (on Christology* and the sacraments), and he probably gave a course on the Epistle to the Romans, and on the Psalms (1–54). A number of repeated mystical experiences* and great fatigue forced him to stop his writing and his teaching around 6 December 1273. Summoned by Gregory X to the Second Council of Lyon*, he fell ill during the journey and died on 7 March 1274, at the Cistercian abbey of Fossanova. Canonized by Pope John XXII in 1323, Thomas Aquinas was proclaimed a Doctor* of the Church by Pius V, on 15 April 1567.

2. Sources and Methods

The Thomist synthesis relies on a large number of philosophical ideas, ranging from Stoicism (through Cicero and Ambrose*) to Neoplatonism (through Augustine and Pseudo-Dionysius). Aristotle is, however, the dominant authority, together with his Arabic (Avicenna, Averroes) and Jewish (Avicebrón, Maimonides) commentators. From the theological viewpoint, one notices the predominant influence of the Bible* and of the fathers of the church.

a) "Master in Holy* Scripture," and bound by this ti-tle, according to the university statutes, to "read" the Scriptures every teaching day, Thomas Aquinas con-tributed several commentaries on the Old Testament (Isaiah, Jeremiah, Job, and Psalms) and on the New (Matthew, John, and all of Paul's writings). That im-portant part of his complete works must be read and made use of as well as the systematic accounts; but the latter also give an important and decisive place to the Scriptures (25,000 biblical quotations in the *Summa* alone), since it is not merely one authority among many, but really the source and the framework of the theological accounts. This cannot be ignored without misapprehending Thomas in his capacity as theologian (Valkenberg 1990). His commentaries are more or less developed depending on what they are meant to be: "a cursory reading (Isaiah) or a masterly and authoritative exposition" (Job). In order to appreciate them it has to be realized that they are often *reportationes,* that is, notes taken by listeners published after having been put in order. They may be faithful and reliable, but the fact remains that they have not had the benefit of a fi-nal editing. Isaiah (handwritten in part) is an exception to this, as are Job (composed), John, and Romans (re-viewed). Depending on the genre being used, the Thomist exegesis abounds in distinctions and recon-structs what the author is saying in order to accentuate the deep theological intention. Conscious of the limits of allegorical exegesis, Thomas favors the literal meaning, which he finds to be the only one that is adapted to theological argumentation—but he includes in it the spiritual meaning (Spicq, Verger, Smalley 1983 and 1985).

b) Thomas Aquinas had a good knowledge of both the Latin and the Greek Fathers (the "Chain of Gold" quotes 57 Greeks and 22 Latins), and of the history of the Ecumenical Councils, being the first Western theo-logian who used the complete corpus of the first four Ecumenical Councils (Geenen 1952). He gave an emi-nent example of what would later be called positive* theology. Among his favorite authors, the following should be mentioned: Gregory the Great (2,470 in-stances; Portalupi 1989), John Chrysostom* (in the scriptural commentaries), but above all Augustine, whose influence, considerable and constant (1,000 quotations in the *Sentences;* 2,000 in the *Summa,* "which was written in an uninterrupted dialogue with Saint Augustine," Elders 1987), can be clearly identi-fied, particularly with respect to the following: the di-vine ideas (transposition of a Platonic theme), the Trinity, the appropriateness of Incarnation, the nature of the soul*, beatitude*, the law*, grace* and sin*, and so on. This Augustinian heritage, when added to

Thomas Aquinas's meditation in *Nicomachean Ethics,* and perhaps also to the controversies of 1270, would help him to correct, during his mature years, the exces-sive intellectualism* of his youth.

The influence of Pseudo-Dionysius is less great (1,702 quotations in all of the works put together, and among these quotations 899 come from the *Divine Names*), but this author was, with Augustine, one of the means through which Neoplatonism counterbal-anced, for Thomas Aquinas, the influence exercised by Aristotle. This anonymous theologian, who wrote at the junction of the fifth and sixth centuries and who at-tempted to evangelize the Neoplatonic system, had as a particular contribution the fact that he acclimatized, in Christian theology, the theory of the three means leading to the knowledge* of God (causality, negation, eminence). His works, known in the West since Gre-gory the Great's time, were already available in four translations at the time of Thomas Aquinas (Hilduin, 827–35; John the Scot Eriugena, 852; the translation of John Sarrazin, from the middle of the 12th century, was the first satisfactory one, and was to enjoy a wide distribution; and finally the translation of Robert Gros-seteste, 1240–43). His supposedly apostolic authority did not impose itself in an absolute manner on Thomas Aquinas. Although the construction of the *Summa* may have owed something to Pseudo-Dionysius, Thomas did not adopt Dionysius's theory of the knowledge of God without reservations. The apophaticism, for ex-ample, of the *Divine Names* represents in Thomas only a moment, a stage, in what is a more global thought process, where positive knowledge is certainly analog-ical, but also real (see O'Rourke 1991; Humbrecht 1993; analogy*). The Dionysian influence is felt in the treatment of numerous other questions, for instance in angelology and in the use of the category of sign in sacramental theology (listed in Pera or Turbessi 1954). It is, however, carefully criticized in respect of some key points: for Thomas, God is not beyond being*, but very well the *ipsum esse subsistens* (being himself sub-sisting); being has primacy over good, and the axiom *bonum est diffusivum sui* (good tends to spread) is in-terpreted in an Aristotelian sense.

c) These sources, however, were no more than mere materials, and sometimes even mere instruments at the service of a theological project perfectly unified by the reality whose understanding is at issue. The subject of theology is God himself, and all the rest must be viewed in a perspective dependent upon him. Devel-oped in particular regarding Boethius's *The Trinity,* and in the Summa Theologiae Ia, q. 1, the theory of theology brings out two major features: it is insepara-bly speculative and practical. Its contemplative *(specu-*

lativa) orientation places it in the line of the *intellectus fidei* of Augustine and of Anselm*, but, to achieve this end, Thomas uses two elements derived from Aristotle, although he does transform them deeply before making use of them (Torrell 1994).

The notion of "science" is verified as soon as there is "speech", that is when two truths are being related to one another by means of reasoning: the first truth, being better known, plays the role of explanatory principle, and the other one, the second, is dependent and plays the role of explanatory conclusion (thus the resurrection* of Jesus Christ in its relationship to that of Christians). Gradually, step by step, the totality of the given that is revealed thus gets organized according to its internal relations into a coherent synthesis that reproduces in a human mode something of the intelligibility of the divine design concerning the world and the history of salvation*.

The theory of subordinationism*, also received from Aristotle (who, in fact, gave it only a minor place) is of capital importance for the status of this science, which is unique in its way: indeed, it expresses the dependence in which theology is positioned in relation to revelation*. As a result of this dependence, theology is connected through faith to the knowledge God has of his own self (Torrell 1994). Theology is thus situated on the very path leading from faith to blessed vision: the purpose of this *scientia* (named also *sacra doctrina*) is the "contemplation*" of first truth* in the celestial fatherland (*Sent.* I, Prol., q. 1, a. 3, sol. 1; Chenu 1957; Torrell 1971). This knowledge, however, is also practical. It exercises a directing influence on human conduct, which it enlightens in such a way as to orient it toward its final end, namely God himself. The *Summa*, therefore, does not consist only of a dogmatic* reflection directly centered on the mystery* of God; it also develops an important moral theology.

3. The Thomist Synthesis

a) The work of Thomas Aquinas is ample and varied, and can by no means be reduced to the Summa. But the Summa does provide a fair idea of the whole. The author's topics are strong enough that they can be found over and over again in all of his works, but there are also indications that his ideas have gone through some evolution on several points (for instance on the manner in which the gifts of the Holy* Spirit are distinct from the virtues*, Ia IIae, q. 68, and particularly on the gift of science, IIa IIae, q. 9; on the necessity of grace* in order to persevere in the direction of good, Ia IIae, q. 109; on the motive and necessity of the Incarnation, IIIa, q. 1, a. 1–3; on the acquired science of Christ*, IIIa, q. 9, a. 4; on the notion of satisfaction in the the-

ology of redemption, IIIa, q. 46, a. 2, ad. 3; and on the causality of the sacraments in the production of grace, IIIa, q. 72). The Summa can be read with profit only if the reading is accomplished in the perspective of a probing mind. Ignoring this point would entail transforming into a rigid system what the author has intended certainly as a rigorous synthesis, but an open one as well.

b) This fact is already apparent in Thomas's plan. He took inspiration from a circular pattern that pulls his reader into the dynamic of "exit" *(exitus)* of creatures from the first Principle, the Creator of all things, and of their "return" *(reditus)* toward him. A Neoplatonic influence is not to be excluded, but the fact that it is here a question of emanation through free creation indicates that this influence should not be overestimated. Rather, Thomas found his inspiration in the contemplation of the God of the Bible*, the Alpha and Omega of all things (Rev 1:8). Although the circular vision was not exclusively Thomas's (he found it in fact in Albert, and to a lesser degree in Bonaventure), he did, however, put it to a more systematic use in several of his works. It allowed him to incorporate in his philosophical construction all the contingencies of the history* of salvation, in particular of the Christ who is "born from God and going toward God" (Jn 13:3), and through whom the effective return to the origin takes place (Émery 1995).

c) As for its content, therefore, the Thomist synthesis starts with the study of God and of his creative work: the angels*, the world*, and Man. The latter received privileged treatment, because he was created in the image of God (Gn 1:27), who associated him with himself as a secondary cause in the government of the universe. That was the object of the first part. Despite the classical division into second and third parts, one has to understand everything that follows as describing in all its fullness the return of the image to its divine example. From the outset, Thomas gives special consideration to what occupies first place in the order of desired aims, to what is the ultimate *purpose* of the enterprise, namely God as beatitude of Man, the supreme Good who satisfies fully all the aspirations of his creatures (Ia IIae, q. 1–5). That is the goal to be reached. All the rest are simply the "means" which are employed to achieve that goal. It is, first of all, a matter of dealing with human action, voluntary and free, through which human beings proceed toward this goal or turn away from it (second part); then it becomes a matter of the "means" par excellence, "the only Mediator between God and men" (1 Tm 2:5), Jesus Christ, who in his humanity is the way to beatitude (third

Thomas Aquinas

part). The "circle" closes finally with the study of the blessed life in which human beings enter at the end of time, following the risen Christ, but Thomas died before he could write this part (the supplement), which completes some editions of the *Summa Theologica* (it was written by his disciples using his *Commentary* of the "Sentences," and so does not reflect the final state of his thinking).

d) The components of this large philosophical construction were not all equally new. Indeed, it presented in organized form the essential theological heritage of the preceding centuries. But the metaphysical premises that underlay the whole construction provoked very lively reactions at the time. In 1279, barely five years after Thomas's death, the Franciscan Guillaume de la Mare published a catalogue (*Correctorium,* Glorieux 1927) of 118 Thomist theses reputed to be dangerous. In this same work he also published the censures, which those theses had received from the Church, proposing both a critique and a refutation of them. The most famous of the censures concern the following: the manner through which God will be known in the beatific vision (without any created concept, said Thomas, but according to his very essence, Ia, q. 12, a. 2); God's knowledge of future contingents (in the present of his eternity, Ia, q. 14, a. 13); the eternity of the world (its contingent nature is in itself separable from its beginning in time*, something that can only be affirmed by faith, Ia, q. 46, a. 2); the hylomorphic composition (matter and shape) of the angels and of the human soul (which Thomas replaced with a composition of *quod est* and *quo est,* essence and existence, Ia, q. 50, a. 2 and q. 75, a. 5); and the unique nature of the substantial shape in Man (whereas Bonaventure accepted a plurality of hierarchically arranged forms—spiritual, sensitive, vegetative—Thomas thought that these three functions were exercised by the same soul: simple and indivisible, it accepted no pluses or minuses, Ia, q. 76, a. 3). Though apparently very abstract, these theses in fact had quite concrete repercussions in theology. They brought with them other deep differences regarding knowledge (intellectual illumination or abstraction based on senses) and the primacy of intellect over will. These differences were immediately reflected in the way theology itself was regarded (for Thomas, it was primarily speculative; for Bonaventure, practical) and they persisted in the voluntarist or intellectualistic premises that would later mark the history of theology so strongly.

e) The principal merit of the *Summa* resided (as it does today) in the fact that it highlights the internal intelligible connections between the elements of faith with a vigor that would be hard to surpass. For those who know how to dissociate the pedagogical value of the Thomist synthesis from the outdated "physics"—which can easily be separated anyway—or from those elements which have aged too much since Thomas's time, that synthesis has kept its pedagogical value. It does indeed remain, even in our own time, a brilliant introduction to the Christian mystery. Some of its elaborations have become absorbed into standard Catholic theology: the treatise on God, in particular the five "paths" which lead to the establishment of his existence, the divine names and the Trinitarian relations; the creation; the ontology of Christ and the instrumentality of his humanity; and the relationship between human freedom and God's omnipotence, as seen in the light of the theology of grace. These are no doubt the most salient points.

It seems two things should be highlighted more than they usually are. The first one concerns moral theology as a whole, in respect of which it is possible to notice something genuinely new on two major points. Putting together in a single, organically structured work all of the dogmatic and moral theological materials is, on the one hand, a way of standing out against the usual approach of the manuals of that time (Boyle 1982); and thus ethics finds itself freed from the limitations of voluntarism*, and we go from a morality of obligations to one of virtues and beatitudes, with a deeply evangelical inspiration (Pinckaers 1985; Schockenhoff 1987). On the other hand, the unified treatment of all human behavior in the light of the ultimate end comes under the same necessity that links closely the moral theology of the *Summa* to the contemplative finality of all theological knowledge. It could not be otherwise, because "the basic truth, which is the object of our faith, being also the aim of all our desires and all our actions, will act through charity, in the manner of speculative intellect which becomes practical by extension, according to Aristotle." (Ia IIae, q. 3, a. 2, ad 3).

Influenced by theological virtues, moral theology can therefore extend itself into a spirituality in which the central themes are easy to identify: the Trinitarian vocation of Man, who has been made in the image of God, and is restored to the image of the first-born Son through God's first gift, the omnipresent and active Holy Spirit. And since grace does not destroy nature*, it is also possible to envisage a spirituality of creation in which can start to blossom the glorious freedom of the children of God (Torrell 1991 and 1996).

The second point to be highlighted is the treatment of Christology. Theologians rightly took advantage of a Thomist notion, which for the first time in the West included the components of the christological councils—but the most original contribution may be found perhaps in the questions devoted to the "mysteries" of the life of Jesus Christ (IIIa, q. 27–59). Thomas Aquinas was, in fact, the first and the only theologian of the Middle Ages to speak not only of the main events marking the human existence of the incarnate Word (the *acta et passa Christi in carne*) from his birth to his death*, but to treat them in a structured piece of work conceived as an integral part of a speculative Christology (Biffi 1994; Scheffczyk 1986; Torrell 1994 and 1996). Each one of these events is highlighted in a soteriological perspective, but also in that of an ontological and moral exemplarity. These pages, in which Thomas questions himself methodically, and with a deep knowledge of Scripture and of the Fathers, about the role of the humanity of Christ in the work of salvation, already provide an outline of what is being sought under the name of narrative Christology in contemporary research. Aside from their theological interest they also have an evident bearing on the spiritual application of theology (Torrell 1991 *b*). The causality exercised by each of the mysteries of the life of Christ on those who receive it opens highly creative perspectives for Christian life: because grace is not only Christic, but also Christoconformist.

● Detailed catalogue of the editions and translations in J.-P. Torrell, *Initiation*, Paris and Fribourg, 1993, 483–525.

S. Thomae Aquinatis…Opera omnia… Rome, 1882– and Paris, 1992– (monumental critical edition called "leonine"; 28 vols. already published).

Somme de théologie, bilingual French and Latin edition, "Revue des Jeunes" (68 vols., Paris, 1925–1971).

Bref résumé de la foi chrétienne, Compendium theologiae, translation only, Paris, 1985; *Opuscules de saint T. d'Aquin,* Latin and French, 7 vols., Paris, 1984.

Questions disputées sur le mal, Latin and French, 2 vols., Paris, 1992.

L'unité de l'intellect contre les averroïstes… (bilingual French and Latin edition and important commentary, by A. de Libera), Paris, 1994.

◆ J. Durantel (1919), *Saint T. et le Pseudo-Denis,* Paris (always useful).

P. Glorieux (1927), *Les premières polémiques thomistes: I. Le correctorium corruptorii "Quare,"* Kain.

P.A. Walz et al., "T. d'Aquin (saint)," *DThC* 15, 618–761 (older, but a must).

C.G. Geenen (1952), "En marge du concile de Chalcédoine: Les textes du IVe concile dans l'œuvre de saint T.," *Ang.* 29, 43–59.

J. Turbessi (1954), "Denys l'Aréopagite", 3, "Saint T. d'Aquin," *DSp* 3, 349–56.

M.-D. Chenu (1957), *La théologie comme science au XIIIe siècle,* 3rd Ed., Paris.

M.-D. Chenu (1959), *Saint T. d'Aquin et la théologie,* Paris.

J.-P. Torrell (1971), "Théologie et sainteté", *RThom* 71, 205–21.

E. Gilson (1972), *Le thomisme: Introduction à la philosophie de saint Thomas d'Aquin,* Paris.

M. Corbin (1974), *Le chemin de la théologie chez T d'Aquin,* Paris.

J.A. Weisheipl (1974), *Friar T. d'Aquino: His Life, Thought and Works,* Garden City, NY (2nd Ed. 1983).

G. O'Daly (1981), "Dionysius Areopagita," *TRE* 8, 772–80.

L.E. Boyle (1982), *The Setting of the Summa Theologiae of St. T.,* Toronto.

B. Smalley (3rd Ed. 1983), *The Study of the Bible in the Middle Ages,* Oxford.

J. Verger (1984), "L'exégèse de l'université," in P. Riché and G. Lobrichon (Ed.), *Le Moyen Age et la Bible,* Paris, 199–232.

S.-Th. Pinckaers (1985), *Les sources de la morale chrétienne,* Fribourg and Paris (3rd Ed. 1993).

J. Verger (1985) *The Gospels in the Schools c. 1100–c. 1280,* London and Ronceverte.

L. Scheffczyk (1986), "Die Stellung des T. von Aquin in der Entwicklung der Lehre von den *Mysteria Vitae Christi*," in M. Gerwing and G. Ruppert (Ed.), *Renovatio et Reformatio,* Münster, 44–70.

L. Elders (1987), "Les citations de saint Augustin dans la *Somme théologique* de saint T. d'Aquin," DoC 40, 115–167.

E. Schockenhoff (1987), Bonum hominis: *Die anthropologischen und theologischen Grundlagen der Tugendethik des T. von Aquin,* TTS 28.

E. Portalupi (1989), "Gregorio Magno nell'Index Thomisticus," *BPhM* 31, 112–146.

V.G.B.M. Valkenberg (1990), *"Did Not our Heart Burn?": Place and Function of Holy Scripture in the Theology of St T. Aquinas,* Utrecht.

F. O'Rourke (1991), *Pseudo-Dionysius and the Metaphysics of Aquinas,* STGMA 32.

J.-P. Torrell (1991 *a*), "T. d'Aquin", *DS* 15, 718–773; (1991 *b*), "Imiter Dieu comme des enfants bien-aimés. La conformité à Dieu et au Christ dans l'œuvre de saint T.", in C.-J. Pinto de Oliveira (Ed.), *Novitas et veritas vitae,* Fribourg and Paris, 53–65.

B. Davies (1992), *The Thought of Thomas Aquinas,* Oxford.

T.-D. Humbrecht (1993–94), "La théologie négative chez saint T. d'Aquin", *RThom* 93, 535–66; 94, 71–99.

J.-P. Torrell (1993), *Initiation à saint T. d'Aquin: Sa personne et son œuvre,* Paris and Fribourg.

I. Biffi (1994), *I misteri di Cristo in Tommaso d'Aquino,* vol. 1, Milan.

G. Émery (1995), *La Trinité créatrice: Trinité et création dans les Commentaires aux "Sentences" de T. d'Aquin et de ses précurseurs Albert le Grand et Bonaventure,* Paris.

J.-P. Torrell (1995), "Le thomisme dans le débat christologique contemporain," in *Saint T. au XXe siècle:* Actes du Colloque du centenaire de la *RThom,* Ed. S.-Th. Bonino, Paris, 379–93.

J.-P. Torrell (1996), *Initiation à saint T. d'Aquin,* vol. 2: *Thèmes spirituels,* Paris and Fribourg.

R. McInerny (1997) (Rev. Ed., 1982), Ethica Thomistica, *The Moral Philosophy of Thomas Aquinas,* Washington, D.C.

Coll. (1998), "Thomas d'Aquin," *RIPh* 52, 203–328.

J. Finnis (1998), *Aquinas,* Oxford.

JEAN-PIERRE TORRELL

See also **Albert the Great; Aristotelianism; Augustine of Hippo; Bonaventure; Duns Scotus; Dyonisius the Pseudo-Areopagite; Scholasticism; Thomism**

Thomism

The adjective "Thomist" has been applied since the 14th century to followers of Thomas* Aquinas. Since around 1950 it has been in competition with a new word, "Thomasian," although this coinage has not been accepted everywhere or by everyone. "Thomasian" is sometimes used to refer to what relates directly to Aquinas, and the literal exegesis of what he wrote, while "Thomist" and "Thomism" are used to refer to his followers.

While Thomism has had an unbroken history, we can distinguish three periods when it has been particularly important: 1) the 150 years following Aquinas's death in 1274; 2) the efflorescence of neoclassical and baroque Scholasticism* from the 16th to the 18th century; and 3) the revivals of Thomism that preceded and followed Leo XIII's 1879 encyclical *Aeterni Patris* (Garrigou-Lagrange, Pesch, and Weisheipl). The philosophical distortions that Thomism has undergone have been described fairly frequently, but here we shall concentrate on the theological aspect, which is much less well known.

1. Beginnings

Nascent Thomism was vigorous, but already on the defensive. On 7 March 1277 Étienne Tempier, bishop of Paris, issued a list of 219 heterodox articles subject to prohibition, some of which were indirectly targeted at Aquinas (*see* naturalism*). There were also some direct official attacks on Aquinas's teaching, but once the investigation had been transferred to Rome* it was halted. In 1323 John XXII, expressing his personal admiration for Aquinas and seeking to hinder Franciscan spirituality, canonized Aquinas and praised his writings on doctrine. In 1325 another bishop of Paris, Étienne Bourret, declared that his predecessor's condemnation did not apply to Aquinas (Torrell 1993).

a) Opposition to Aquinas continued nonetheless. It had begun, even before Aquinas's death, with Robert Kilwardby and John Pecham, and was carried on by Guillaume de La Mare in his catalogue (1279) of 118 Aquinas's propositions that were regarded as dangerous. This *Correctorium* stimulated a series of refutations by the Dominicans Richard Knapwell, Robert of Orford, Jean Quidort (also celebrated for his writings on ecclesiology), William of Macclesfield, and Rambert of Bologna.

Alongside these authors, the first generations of Thomists in England, France, and Italy also included Thomas Sutton, a relatively independent follower who wrote an impressive body of work; Bernard of Trilia, who was more subservient to Aquinas; Peter of Auvergne, who was more eclectic; Hervé Nédellec, who rejected the real distinction between essence and being*; and Remy of Florence, who had been taught by Aquinas himself. Meanwhile, in Köln, the influence of Albert* the Great remained predominant.

All these writers have been recognized as Thomists because of their acceptance of Aquinas's major theses (Weisheipl 1967), but in addition they soon came into opposition to Duns* Scotus and to the doctrine of the Immaculate Conception of the Virgin Mary*, for, while Aquinas had believed in the sanctification *in utero* of the mother of Christ*, he had not accepted that she was free from original sin*. The Thomists also adopted a common position on the subject of theology* (God*), its speculative purpose, and its subordination to the knowledge of God and the blessed. Like Aquinas himself they made a clear distinction between the respective domains of faith* and reason*, and believed that reason cannot provide proofs in matters of faith (Torrell 1996). In defending Aquinas they highlighted their master's texts, following the formula *Thomas suiipsius interpres* ("Thomas interpreted by himself"). Their repetitiveness was a sign, not only of their faithfulness to the original teaching, but also of the ossification that was to follow.

b) This initial period of efflorescence was followed first by a relatively latent period, and then by revival in the 15th century. The latter was evidenced by the growing number of Thomist teachers, as more new universities were created throughout Europe; the growing number of manuscript copies of Aquinas's writings; the translations of the *Summa Theologica* into Greek and Armenian; and the sound knowledge of Aquinas displayed by the Italian Renaissance humanists (Kristeller 1967, Swiezawski 1974, Memorie 1976).

Jean Capréolus (1380–1444), *princeps thomistorum,* is the most notable of the Thomist writers of this period. His *Defense of the Theology of Saint Thomas* (1433) demonstrates his profound understanding of his master's work, which he defended against a whole series of opponents. He recognized that it was possible to develop Aquinas's conclusions, and was inclined to emphasize those elements in Aquinas's teaching that were derived from Augustine*. Several abridged versions of the *Defense* ensured that it became an influential work, and it was to Capréolus that Cardinal Cajetan (discussed below) owed the best part of what he knew about the first generations of Thomists and the controversies that had marked the beginnings of Thomism (Grabmann 1956, Bedouelle 1996).

During this same period, Antonin of Florence (1389–1459) undertook some innovative extensions of Aquinas's morality into the domain of economics, while Johannes of Turrecremata (1388–1468) stood out among ecclesiologists as a moderate papalist. In 1473 Peter of Bergamo published his *Tabula aurea,* which remains a valuable reference tool.

2. Expansion

The Dominicans had never ceased to read the *Summa Theologica,* but it was only in Köln, where Henry of Gorcum (†1431) had consolidated a form of Thomism, that commentary on the *Summa* took the place of commentary on the *Sentences.* There had already been some commentaries on the *Summa*—for example, Johannes Tinctoris (†1469) had commented on Parts Ia and Ia IIae—but the practice received official authorization in 1483. Conrad Köllin published his commentary on Part Ia IIae in 1512. In Paris Pierre Crockaert, a Flemish nominalist who had joined the Dominicans and been converted to Thomism, started teaching the *Summa* in 1509.

a) The most celebrated of the commentaries that follow Aquinas's texts article by article is that of Tomaso de Vio, Cardinal Cajetan (1465–1534). He taught the *Summa Theologica* at the University of Pavia from 1497 to 1499, but he did not start writing his commentary until 1507. He finished it in 1522, by which time he had already been head of the Dominican Order, then a bishop* and a cardinal (Iserloh-Hallensleben 1981).

Cajetan was an innovator who introduced many changes, both in terminology and in content. His essentialization of Aquinas's *esse* led him to give up any attempt to provide a rational demonstration of the immortality of the soul* (Gilson 1953, contested on this point by Reilly 1971 and Hallensleben 1981). His doctrine of analogy* was close to that of the Scotism he was combating. He also developed new theories about the formal constitution of the personality, original justice*, the sacrifice of the Mass*, the causality of the sacraments*, and other questions. Cajetan's interpretation of the natural desire to see God led him to develop a theory of the capacity for obedience that is far re-

moved from that of Aquinas (Boulnois 1993). Reviving one of Aquinas's own practices, he also wrote commentaries on the Bible*, adopting some daring views that caused him to be censured by the Sorbonne. As a moralist, Cajetan supplemented his course on Part IIa of the *Summa Theologica* with his own *Small Summa of Sins,* to be used by confessors, in which he addressed the pastoral problems of his day, although in doing so he revived a practice that Aquinas had sought to move beyond. Pius V ordered Cajetan to publish an expurgated version of his commentary on the *Summa Theologica* alongside the first complete edition of Aquinas's writings (the *Piana,* Rome, 1570).

Cajetan's contemporary, Francesco Silvestri of Ferrara (1474–1528), distanced himself from him and put forward his own ideas. Silvestri's commentary on Aquinas's *Summa contra Gentiles* was printed later, alongside Aquinas's text, in the so-called "Leonine" edition (see below).

b) In Spain the main centers of Thomist activity were the universities of Valladolid and Salamanca (Andrès 1976–77), to which the practice of writing commentaries on the *Summa* had been introduced from Paris by Francisco de Vitoria (c. 1485–1546), a former student of Crockaert's. While he did not neglect philosophy*, Vitoria treated Scripture and the church fathers* as the basic building blocks of theology. Attentive to the problems of political morality that were being raised by the colonization of the New World, Vitoria laid some of the foundations for modern international law*, and he was more restrictive than Aquinas had been in defining the conditions for a just war*.

Vitoria's followers played leading roles in the Council of Trent*, and Thomism reached its apogee: the Council's decrees on justification* and the sacraments were strongly influenced by Aquinas's teachings. Vitoria's followers included Domingo Soto (1494–1560), who took an active part in the writing of the decree on justification, and Melchor Cano (1509–60), who is best known for his *De Loci Theologicis* (1563), a text that exemplifies the practice of a theology newly concerned with sources. Drawing inspiration from Aquinas (*Summa Theologica* Ia, q. 1, a. 8, ad 2), Cano proposed a method of research and appreciation *(inventio)* of the propositions that serve as the basis of theological speculation. This method inaugurated the various positive specialisms that were soon to declare their independence, and led to a disastrous separation between the various branches of theological learning that Aquinas had kept united through his *sacra doctrina.*

Cano's pupil Domingo Bañez (1528–1604) wrote a commentary on the first two parts of the *Summa Theologica* in a spirit of synthesis and approached problems by the summit. In opposition to Cajetan, he understood the role of the *esse* in Aquinas's philosophy. Whatever else may be said about it, Bañez's doctrine of nature* and grace* was not unfaithful to Aquinas. His concept of "physical premotion" means nothing more than the priority in nature (not in time) of the real efficacy of grace over the human action* that it sustains. The opposition that this concept aroused was an indication of a climate of "pre-Molinism" (Duval 1948; and *see* Bañezianism*-Molinism-Baianism).

c) The last of the great Thomists of this period, John of Saint-Thomas Poinsot (1589–1644), inaugurated the era of *Disputationes:* he no longer followed the letter of Aquinas's texts in detail, but, like the *Salmanticenses,* undertook wide-ranging discussions of a selection of major problems. Like Cajetan, John of Saint-Thomas has been seen both as an emblematic figure and a symbol of contradictions (Fabro 1989). Jacques Maritain denounced his "complications, so typical of baroque Scholasticism," the limitations of his polemic, and his lack of attention to the scientific renaissance. Since he was not concerned with history, John of Saint-Thomas had little interest in internal criticism. Thus, he accepted the apocryphal *Summa totius logicae* as authentic, asserted that Aquinas had not rejected the notion of the Immaculate Conception, and placed the formal constituent of the divine essence within the *intelligere subsistens,* thereby demonstrating that he had failed to perceive the force of Aquinas's *ipsum esse subsistens.* According to John of Saint-Thomas the true disciple is not content merely to follow Aquinas, but extends his ideas. Accordingly, he frequently and deliberately put forward his own conceptions, and so became one of the first to define the object of theology as the deduction of new conclusions. John of Saint-Thomas wrote a fine treatise on the gifts of the Holy* Spirit, which was rediscovered in the 20th century (R. Maritain 1950, Sese 1989), and his genius, along with his position in history*, allowed him to play a crucial role in the diffusion of a popularized form of Thomism, as the immediate source of works that were to have considerable influence, including writings by J.-B. Gonet (†1681), A. Goudin (†1695), V. L. Gotti (†1742), and Ch.-R. Billuart (†1757).

d) Following the wishes of its founder, Ignatius Loyola, the members of the Society of Jesus were required to study and teach in accordance with the *Summa Theologica* (Tolet, Le Jay). However, Ignatius and his successors also wanted a theology that would be capable of reconciling Thomists, Scotists, and nominalists. This Jesuit eclecticism found its most outstanding representatives in Francisco Suarez* and Gabriel Vasquez (1549–1604), both of whom, like Cano, displayed a concern to return to the sources. The doctrine of grace developed by Luis de Molina (*see* Bañezianism-Molinism-Baianism) became the focus of an interminable dispute between the Jesuits and the Dominicans, which popes Clement VIII and Paul V had to leave unresolved despite all the efforts of the congregations *de auxiliis* (1598–1607). From 1656 onward both schools were also divided over the question of probabilism, a theory initiated by the Dominican Bartolomé de Medina (1528–80).

e) The Carmelites of Salamanca—the *Salmanticenses*—initiated a major collective project that included a textbook on "Scholastic" theology, published between 1600 and 1725, a textbook on moral theology, and a manual of philosophy (*Complutenses*). Long hailed as a monument of fidelity, this project is in fact a monument to the Thomism of its time. The authors' lack of a historical sense led them to neglect sources and omit certain treatises (IIIa, q. 27–59), while their separation of dogma* from morality contradicted both the letter and the spirit of Aquinas's work. Thus, they studied the sacraments in moral terms, but, since the reflexive questions that morality raised were allocated to "Scholastics," there soon remained little for morality to cover apart from casuistry*. The *Salmanticenses* failed to perceive the distinctiveness of the theological method—they did not comment on the section in the *Summa Theologica* (Ia, q. 1) concerning the *sacra doctrina*—and their rational elaboration of Thomism attained a level of dialectical refinement that it would be difficult to surpass (Deman 1939).

The Thomism of the 17th and 18th centuries deserves to be better known than it is. Many of the Thomist writings that appeared in France (by Contenson, Gonet, Goudin, and Massoulié), Flanders (Billuart), Italy (Maurus, Gotti), and Austria (the Benedictines of Salzburg) were influenced, for the worse, by the philosophical climate of the time. Yet they have some merits, chiefly in their having maintained a living tradition, evidenced by new editions of Aquinas's own writings: there were eight editions of his complete works during these centuries, of which the last (1775–86) was edited by B. de Rossi (or De Rubeis) and was the second to be published in Venice.

3. Revivals

a) The 19th-century revival of Thomism in Italy, made possible by a movement that had begun in the early 18th century, resulted from numerous painstaking efforts by secular priests* as well as by Jesuits and

Dominicans—most notably by M. Liberatore, one of the founders of *Civiltà Cattolica* (1850); L. Taparelli d'Azeglio, who introduced Goudin into the Jesuit college in Naples; T. Zigliara, the first chairman of the commission established by Leo XIII to prepare a critical edition of Aquinas's works; and V. Gatti, F. Xarrié, and N. Puig, all three of whom taught at the Dominican college of the Minerva. Among the Jesuits active in this movement, two should be mentioned. J. Kleutgen wrote the first draft of the encyclical *Aeterni Patris,* as well as a reinterpretation of the history of theology and philosophy, the *Theologie* and *Philosophie der Vorzeit* (1853–63), which was directly inspired by Cano and Suarez, and which had a great deal of influence; J.-B. Franzelin (1816–86) tried in vain, despite his considerable learning, to reconcile Aquinas with Suarez and Lugo.

b) Leo XIII's encyclical *Aeterni Patris* (1879), with its call for "Christian philosophy to be restored according to the spirit of St. Thomas," was to have a decisive impact (StTom 1981). Several scholarly institutions and periodicals made their appearance in its wake: *Divus Thomas,* at Piacenza (1880); the Academy of St. Thomas in Rome (1879); the Institute of Philosophy (D. Mercier) and the *Revue néoscolastique de philosophie* (1894) at Louvain; the University of Fribourg (1889); the *Revue thomiste* (Toulouse-Fribourg, 1893) and the *Revue des sciences philosophiques et théologiques* (Paris and elsewhere, 1907); the *Rivista italiana di filosofia neoscolastica* (Milan, 1909); and *Ciencia tomista* (Salamanca, 1910). From the outset, differences in terminology indicated differences in approach: thus, while some, such as Mercier or Sertillanges, were happy to call themselves "neo-Thomists," others, including Mandonnet and Maritain, wanted to be known simply as "Thomists."

In 1914 Pius X acted against modernism* by ordering the publication of a list of 24 philosophical propositions, written by a Jesuit, G. Mattiussi, which was intended to promote a purer form of Thomism (*Enchiridion Symbolrum*, 3601–24; see Régnier 1984). All but one of these propositions were opposed to Suarez, but the General of the Jesuits secured from Benedict XV a degree of flexibility in their application. In 1917 the obligation to teach Thomism was incorporated into the new *Codex Iruis Canonici* (no. 1366, §2), and manuals saturated with an unconscious rationalism* were used to spread a repetitious doctrine that referred to Aquinas only by way of later commentators, and that caused some disaffection.

c) Meanwhile, Leo XIII's call for the restoration of Christian philosophy was being answered by more in-

dependent thinkers. At the very least, we should mention the "transcendental Thomism" promoted by J. Maréchal (1878–1944), who came up against a marked degree of distrust because he was thought to be tainted with Kantian idealism. Nevertheless, he inspired such men as Karl Rahner* and Bernard Lonergan*, who were to have considerable influence, as well as J. B. Lotz and E. Coreth (Puntel 1969, Verweyen 1969). We might also mention G. Siewerth, who attempted to draw comparisons between Thomism and the ideas of Martin Heidegger*, and E. Przywara (*see* analogy), a profound thinker in whose writings the inspiration of Aquinas is combined with a number of other approaches (Coreth, Neidl, Pfligersdorffer 1990).

Jacques Maritain (1882–1973) deliberately based his speculative version of Thomism on the work of the major commentators, yet he did not hesitate to introduce innovations (*Les degrés du savoir,* 1932). His writings on art and poetry, and his political and social philosophy, were widely influential. Adopting a more historical approach, É. Gilson (who was accompanied in this regard by C. Fabro and L.-B. Geiger, notably on participation) denounced the "betrayals" of the Thomists (Bonino in *Revue thomiste,* 1994). In addition to his book *Le Thomisme* (fourth and decisive edition, 1941), he also wrote on Augustine*, Bonaventure*, and Duns Scotus, and was thus enabled to situate Aquinas more accurately within his milieu. Gilson and Maritain assembled a body of followers in Canada and then in the United States, with the foundation of the Institute of Toronto by Gilson (1929), and of the Institute of Ottawa and Montreal by M.-D. Chenu (1930), which brought about a declericalization of Thomism and medievalism, and was something Leo XIII had not foreseen when he launched his initiative.

This tendency may be illustrated by the work of A. Gardeil and R. Garrigou-Lagrange in apologetics and mystical theology; that of L. Billot, R. Schultes, N. Del Prado, and F. Marin-Sola in dogmatic theology; and that of H. Noldin, D. Prümmer, and B. H. Merkelbach in moral theology. In some of these cases the original Thomist inspiration was perceptibly modified by other influences, but one also finds theologians who have stayed closer to Aquinas, such as J. M. Ramirez or M.-M. Labourdette (Bonino 1992). The inspiration of Thomism may also be traced in the ecclesiology* of Ch. Journet.

d) The single most important factor in the revival of Thomism has been the historical and critical research of medievalists, starting with the work of H. Denifle, F. Ehrle, M. Grabmann, P. Mandonnet, P. Glorieux, and other pioneers. Following the foundation of the *Bul-*

letin thomiste and the *Bibliothèque thomiste,* the school of Saulchoir inaugurated a historical and critical form of Thomism that was still developing at the end of the 20th century. Research by Y.M.-J. Congar and M.-D. Chenu (*La théologie comme science au XIIIe s.,* first published 1927, third edition 1957), and publications by M.-R. Gagnebet (*La nature de la théologie spéculative,* 1938), have been decisive in reconstructing the precise conception of Aquinas's *sacra doctrina.*

Two new editions of Aquinas's *Opera omnia* (Complete Works) appeared during the 19th century (Parma, 1852–73; Paris, Vivès, 1871–80), but both have now been surpassed because of the exceptionally high standard of the critical edition known as the "Leonine" edition, based most notably on the work of Constant Suermondt, J. Perrier, the brothers H. and A. Dondaine, P.-M. Gils, R.-A. Gauthier, L.-J. Bataillon, and B.-G. Guyot. Alongside the research by Franciscans on Bonaventure and Duns Scotus, and that of other scholars on a multitude of other medieval authors, these studies of Aquinas have helped to bring about a far-reaching renewal of approaches to Aquinas's teachings.

4. Appreciation

a) It has now become clear that "Thomism" and "Thomist" are analogical terms, sometimes bordering on the equivocal, for Aquinas's originality has sometimes been poorly understood. On the other hand, it is also certain that Aquinas's historical authority owes a great deal to his followers, who adapted and extended his teachings in a variety of ways, and thus kept them alive. Their greatness lies in their having brought Aquinas into eras other than his own; their tragedy lies in their having unconsciously projected the categories of these eras onto their master's ideas. Nevertheless, it is not possible to dismiss the contributions made by Vitoria and his followers, or those of Cajetan and John of Saint-Thomas.

b) Many questions continue to be subject to debate (*see* Pesch 1965); here we shall focus on theology alone. Misinterpretation of the *intellectus fidei* has led some to treat theology as a "deductive" discipline that aims to arrive at new conclusions. Yet Aquinas himself wanted theology to be "ostensive," with the aim of "showing" the internal coherence of what has been revealed by relating it to the *articuli fidei.* The doctrine of grace has also given rise to numerous differences, with the idea of pure nature, complications in vocabulary, and the proliferation of entities unknown to Aquinas. In Christology* the theory of the "subsistence" and the *unum esse* of Christ represents a shift away from Aquinas, as does the declining interest in the important section on Scripture (27 questions) and Aquinas's account of it.

However important these particular questions may be, it appears that from the 17th century onward it was quite common to regard Aquinas, erroneously, as a philosopher first and foremost. Yet he was above all a theologian, who made use of philosophy—or, better, philosophies—but recognized them as having an authority that is "alien and merely probable" (*Summa Theologica* Ia, q. 1, a. 8, ad 2). There has also been a tendency to emphasize his Aristotelianism, although in fact it was heavily influenced by Neoplatonism and other schools of thought, and Aquinas never felt that he was tied to Aristotle on decisive questions. During the baroque era those who wrote commentaries on Aquinas believed that they could construct a Thomist philosophical system distinct from theology. By insisting on the necessity of restoring Aquinas's *philosophy,* Leo XIII inadvertently accentuated this tendency, to the detriment of his formal, theological intention. The requirements of the era also made Thomism into a weapon in the war of apologetics, following on from the theodicy (Leibniz*, Kant*) developed in the preceding centuries. As a result, too little attention was paid to Aquinas as disciple of the church fathers, and of Augustine in particular, and to Aquinas as commentator on the Bible, even though, in Aquinas's view, scripture is "the soul of theology" (*Dei Verbum* 24).

c) Thomism retains its inherent diversity in our own time. Some of the more rigid views developed within neo-Thomism have not entirely disappeared, but historical research has resulted in a tendency to return to Aquinas with more caution and more attention to the letter of his writings. The commentaries left to us by his followers are less important than they used to be, and greater care is being taken to avoid projecting the concerns of posterity onto the master's own texts. The sources of Aquinas's ideas are better understood, in all their diversity, as also are his relations with his teachers (Albert*) and contemporaries (Bonaventure). Tracing what he owes to them or shares with them also makes for a better grasp of his originality.

Nowadays, Thomist philosophy, which is vigorous and well informed about its own history, seems to have more life in it than Thomist theology does. Nevertheless, there are good grounds for hoping that Aquinas's strictly theological ambitions may be rediscovered. The unity of theological knowledge is moving into the foreground once again, and efforts are being made to follow Aquinas's example and to combine the "speculative" with the "positive," "dogma" with "morality."

There has also been a revival of interest in the spiritual dimension of theology (Torrell 1996), and its link with pastoralia and the Christian life. However, despite the large number of detailed studies undertaken from this new perspective, much still remains to be done in order to present all the riches of Aquinas's works to a new generation of readers.

- *Bulletin thomiste,* Étiolles (1924–1965), then *Rassegna di letteratura tomistica,* Rome (1966–).
- R. Garrigou-Lagrange (1946), "Thomisme," *Dicitionnaire de theologie catholique* 15, 823–1,023.
- O. H. Pesch (1965), "Thomismus," *Lexikon für Theologie und Kirche* 10, 157–67.
- J. A. Weisheipl (1966), "Contemporary Scholasticism," *New Catholic Encylopedia* 12, 1,165–70; (1967), "Thomism," *New Catholic Encylopedia* 14, 126–35 (best overviews).
- ♦ T. Deman (1939), "Salamanque (Theologiens de)," *DThC* 4, 1,017–31.
- A. Duval (1948), "Bañez (Dominique)," *Cath* 10, 1202–4.
- Coll. (1949), *Jacques Maritain: son œuvre philosophique,* *Revue thomiste* 48 (special number).
- R. Maritain (translation) (1950), *J. de Saint-Thomas, Les dons du Saint-Esprit,* Paris.
- É. Gilson (1953), "Cajetan et l'existence," *Theologie und Philosophie* 15, 267–86.
- É. Gilson (1955), "Cajetan et l'humanisme théologique," *Archives d'histoire doctrinale et littéraire du Moyen Age* 22, 113–36.
- M. Grabmann (1956), "Johannes Capreolus O.P., der *Princeps Thomistarum* (†1444), und seine Stellung in der Geschichte der Thomistenschule," in *Mittelalterliches Geistesleben* III, Munich, 370–410.
- P. O. Kristeller (1967), *Le thomisme et la pensée italienne de la Renaissance,* Paris and Montréal.
- R. Laverdière (1969), *Le principe de causalité: Recherches thomistes récentes,* Paris (bibl.).
- L. B. Puntel (1969), *Analogie und Geschichtlichkeit: Philosophiegeschichtlich-kritischer Versuch über das Grundproblem der Metaphysik,* Freiburg-Basel-Vienna.
- H. J. Verweyen (1969), *Ontologische voraussetzungen des Glaubensaktes: Zur transzendentalen Frage der Möglichkeit von Offenbarung,* Düsseldorf.
- J. P. Reilly (1971), *Cajetan's Notion of Existence,* The Hague and Paris.
- S. Swiezawski (1974), "Le thomisme à la fin du Moyen Age," *StTom* 1, 225–48.
- Coll. (1976), *Memoire Domenicane 7, Tomismo e Antitomismo* (studies on L. Valla, A. Nifo, B. Spagnoli).
- M. Andrès (1976–77), *La Teologia española en el siglo XVI,* 2 vols., Madrid.
- Coll. (1981), "L'enciclica *Aeterni Patris,*" StTom 10–12.
- E. Iserloh, B. Hallensleben (1981), "Cajetan de Vio," *Theolgische Realenzyklopadie* 7, 538–46.
- M. Régnier (1984), "Le thomisme depuis 1870," in Y. Belaval (Ed.), *Histoire de la philosophie,* vol. 3, 483–500, Paris.
- B. Hallensleben (1985), Communicatio. *Anthropologie und Gnadenlehre bei Thomas de Vio Cajetan,* Münster.
- C. Fabro (1989), "Il posto di Giovanni di S. T. nella scuola tomistica," *Angelicum* 66, 56–90.
- J. Sese (1989), "Juan de S. T. y su tratado de los dones del Espiritu Santo," ibid., 161–84.
- E. Coreth, W. M. Neidl, G. Pfligersdorffer (1990), *Christliche Philosophie im katholischen Denken des 19. und 20. Jahrhunderts,* vol. 3: *Moderne Strömungen im 20. Jahrhundert,* Graz.
- G. Prouvost (Ed.) (1991), *É. Gilson - J. Maritain, Correspondance 1923–1971,* Paris.
- S.-Th. Bonino (1992), "Le thomisme du P. Labourdette," *Revue Thomiste* 92, 88–122.
- O. Boulnois (1993), "Puissance neutre et puissance obédientielle: De l'homme à Dieu selon Duns Scot et Cajetan," in B. Pinchard and S. Ricci (Eds.), *Rationalisme analogique et humanisme théologique: La culture de Thomas de Vio "Il Gaetano,"* Naples, 31–70.
- J.-P. Torrell (1993), *Initiation à saint T. d'Aquin: Sa personne et son œuvre,* chap. 15, Paris and Fribourg.
- Coll. (1994), *Autour d'Étienne Gilson,* Études et documents, *Revue Thomiste* 94, 355–553.
- S.-Th. Bonino (1995), "Historiographie de l'école thste: le cas Gilson", in *Saint T. au XXe siècle:* Conferences and Acts in the centenary of the *Revue Thomiste,* Paris, 1994, 299–313.
- G. Bedouelle, R. Cessario, K. White (Eds.) (1996), *Jean Capréolus (†1444) en son temps,* Paris.
- G. Prouvost (1996), *Saint T. d'Aquin et les thomismes,* Paris.
- J.-P. Torrell (1996), "La scienza teologica in Tommaso e nei suoi primi discepoli," in G. d'Onofrio (Ed.), *Storia della Teologia,* vol. 2: *Medio Evo,* Casale Monferrato.

JEAN-PIERRE TORRELL

See also **Bonaventure; Duns Scotus, John; Grace; Loci Theologici; Lonergan, Bernard John; Lubac, Henri Sonier de; Rahner, Karl; Scholasticism; Suarez, Francisco; Thomas Aquinas**

Tillich, Paul

1886–1965

1. Life and Works

Born in Eastern Prussia, a Lutheran pastor and son of a Lutheran Pastor, Paul Tillich taught systematic theology* and the philosophy of religion* in Germany. In 1933 he emigrated to the United States because of his membership in the religious socialists' movement. From this time on, he became a professor of philosophical theology at the Union Theological Seminary in New York, and then taught at Harvard from 1952 and from 1962 in Chicago, where he died.

2. Theology

The principal objective of Tillich's work was to reconcile religion and culture by unveiling, in particular, the divine present at the very foundation of all reality. In order to do this, Tillich initially implemented a method known as "correlation."

a) Correlation and Theology of Culture. Tillich's theology, like his life, was always situated "on the frontier" between two worlds or two versions of reality. But this frontier was not so much a dividing line as an element joining two versions of reality that contrived, appropriately, to enter into a reciprocal correlation. Thus the two worlds of Christian faith* on the one hand and culture on the other, far from being opposed, were called on to provide mutual illumination and reveal their full reciprocal potential. There is a religious basis to any cultural endeavor, an aspiration to touch "the very foundations" of things and of life, the foundation of the "being*." This is why "the existential concept of reality also concerns...the relation between religion and culture. Religion, insofar as it is an *ultimate concern,* is the substance that gives culture its meaning. And culture is the sum total of forms through which the fundamental concerns of religion can be expressed. In sum, religion is the substance of culture, and culture is the form of religion" (*The Theology of Culture*).

b) The Depth of Being and Ultimate Reality. The truths of faith also provide an answer to the existential questions that characterize the human condition. God* "is the answer to the question underlying human finiteness. This answer cannot be derived from an analysis

of existence.... If the notion of God appears...in correlation with the threat of non-being implied in existence, one must call God the power of infinite* being, which resists the threat of non-being...the infinite basis of courage" (*Systematic Theology* I). God appears, therefore, as the very depth of one's being—of all beings—a depth that both founds and eludes in an almost limitless way *(ground of being).* God is seen as the ultimate reality on which everyone feels dependent; God "approaches us unconditionally," and all aspire to him.

c) Jesus, the Christ and the New Being. Tillich's Christ* is the one who will deliver man from the alienation to which all human existence is subject. Christ accomplishes this first of all by opening the existence of the historical individual who was Jesus* of Nazareth to a new reality that transcends and transfigures that existence—that of Christ, or the New Being, who also opens the door to whomever shares his experience*. "To experience *the New Being in Jesus as Christ* is to understand that this power does not depend on our good will, but is a gift, a present, a grace*" (*Systematic Theology* II). In this way, "the New Being that is Christ is neither that which he does, or suffers, or says: It is his entire being, with his corporeal and social dimensions...bringing renewal to all those who partake of him, and he ushers them into the sphere of the New."

d) The Courage to Be, Faith, and Love. The new life, revealed in Christ and made manifest through his spirit, is fully displayed in faith and in the power of reconciliation that animates it. "Faith, indeed, is the act of being seized by spiritual presence, of being open to the transcendent unity of a nonambiguous life. In relation to the christological affirmation, one might say that faith is the fact of being seized by the New Being as it is manifested in Jesus Christ." (*Systematic Theology,* III). On an individual level, this reconciliation deflects anxiety and enables the courage of being to assert itself as faith and unfold as love*. On a cultural level, this same appearance of the new being is manifested by the power of a symbolic language, restoring what alienation had destroyed, and through the union of art and religion, it transfigures reality and opens it to its ultimate meaning.

3. Influence and Posterity

Tillich was very influential, particularly in the United States, where he managed to arouse interest in theology among scientists and people in the cultural domain, who often had no prior interest in theology. Nor can one deny the synthetic impact of his work. Relayed by certain elements of *Process* Theology*, Tillich's ideas are, in some respects, comparable to those of Teilhard de Chardin (1881–1955). But, as with de Chardin, they were seen to be too distant from the radical questions raised by atheism* or the persistence of evil* as revealed in contemporary agnosticism* to truly provide an answer. And yet these questions continue to demand an urgent response.

- (1959–1990), *GW*, 14 vol., Stuttgart (vol. XIV of this ed. is called: *Bibliographie, Register und Textgeschichte des Gesammelte Werke: Schlüssel zum Werk von Paul Tillich*); (1973–83), *Ergänzungs- und Nachlaßbände*, Stuttgart; (1956–64), *Systematic Theology*, 3 vols., Chicago.
- H. Zahrnt (1966), *Die Sache mit Gott: Die protestantische Theologie im 20. Jahrhundert*, Munich.

J.-P. Gabus (1969), *Introduction à la théologie de la culture de Paul Tillich*, Paris.

W. and M. Pauck, *Paul Tillich: His Life and Thought. 1. Life*, New York.

J.-C. Petit (1974), *La philosophie de la religion de Paul Tillich: Genèse et évolution: la période allemande 1919–1933*, Montréal.

J. P. Clayton, *The Concept of Correlation: Paul Tillich and the Possibility of a Mediating Theology*, New York and Berlin.

M. Michel (1982), *La théologie aux prises avec la culture: De Schleiermacher à Tillich*, Paris.

R. Winling (1983), *La théologie contemporaine (1945–1980)*, Paris.

R. Albrecht and W. Schüssler (1986), *Paul Tillich, sein Werk*, Frankfurt.

R. Albrecht and W. Schüssler (1993), *Paul T., sein Leben*, Frankfurt.

R. Gibellini (1994), *Panorama de la théologie au XXe s.*, Paris, 93–118.

JEAN-FRANÇOIS COLLANGE

See also **Barth, Karl; Bultmann, Rudolf; Experience; Religion, Philosophy of; Revelation**

Time

While Greek philosophy* first considered time in terms of its cosmic and cyclical reality, the Christian experience is that of a time organized into a history* by divine initiative and reflected as such in the experience of a "stretched" consciousness (Augustine*) between present, past and future. Caught between a sequence of founding events (the *absolute past* of an inaccessible "sacred history") and an *absolute future* (eschatological fulfillment) promised and anticipated in Christ*'s Resurrection*, the believer's present is defined in the first place by an act of memory, which provides its historical coordinates, and in the second place by an act of hope*, which refers it to this absolute future. Thus the theological meaning of the present consists of its envelopment by an originating past and its yearning for the perfection of all things, represented in theology by the "kingdom* of God."

The liturgical experience fixes and expresses the chief characteristics of this envelopment and this yearning. On the one hand, the believer's memory is strongly expressed in the liturgy as a *commemoration*. Going beyond the mere order of remembrance, the original past is endlessly represented in a sacramental practice that feeds on presence (but not Parousia*) rather than defying an absence, and which regards the experience of salvation* in the present (for example, O. Casel). On the other hand, the present of the liturgy* is presented as an anticipation of the *eschaton*: the eternal rewards are already at the Church*'s disposal while it acts in hope. Hence, the relationship with the absolute future is experienced in the form of extreme proximity. Just as Jesus* began his preaching* by announcing the imminence of the Kingdom, so the Christian experience lives out this imminence as the secret of its relationship to the *eschaton*. All presents are liturgically equidistant from the final summation, just as they are equidistant with (or "contemporary" with, in Kierkegaard*'s description) the origin. Thus the present earns the designation of *kairos*, the favorable time able to accommodate fully the relationship between man and God. "In this daily existence which we receive by your grace*, eternal life has already begun" (*Roman Missal*, sixth preface to the Sundays of ordinary time).

Trapped in the time of this world, contained in the consciousness like any present, never free from the pressures of anguish and boredom, and caught in the irrefutable logic of a *time leading toward death**, the present of faith and hope is nonetheless experienced at the boundary between the world and eschatology. This fact may itself be reflected in the intrinsic style of temporalization. The proposition of original experiences corresponds to a time necessarily bursting with eschatological meanings. The concern here, in which a philosophical analysis can discern the secret of time (Heidegger*), centers on the proposition of a *nonchalance*, which entrusts the direction of the future to God alone and thus experiences the present in its own terms, in the fullness of its meaning. By virtue of the essential imminence of fulfillment, the present can be lived as a *vigil* that refuses to speculate on the postponements of history. And in this nonchalance and this vigilance, a *filial* temporality is established, in the image of Jesus' pre-Resurrection time (Lacoste 1990).

Admittedly, the theological and eschatological meanings do not rule out the existential logic of a Christian time that is in the first instance a human time comparable to any other, but they do give rise to a divergence. Thanks to its kairological content, this time also structures itself by subverting the logic of any purely worldly temporalization. It is thus desirable to qualify, by means of a christological conception of the question of time, in relation to God's eternity*, that which eternity controls and judges (Barth*). And if the divine/human person* of Jesus must, therefore, be regarded as "the concrete *analogia entis*" (Balthasar*), if human time and God's eternity can assume a relationship of analogy*, human time ultimately ceases to be defined in terms of being-in-the-world, and instead defines itself in terms of an eternal relation to God, an eternal movement of the finite spirit toward God (Gregory* of Nyssa's "epectasis"). In speaking of the resurrection of the flesh, theology necessarily speaks also of a resurrection of time. The believer thus experiences, in his mortal flesh, a time leading *toward* death that is not a time intended *for* death.

● M. Heidegger (1927), *Sein und Zeit, GA* 2, Frankfurt, 1976.

E. Husserl (1928), *Vorlesungen zur Phänomenologie des inneren Zeitbewußtseins,* Husserliana X, The Hague, 1966.

G. Delling (1940), *Das Zeitverständnis des Neuen Testaments,* Gütersloh.

K. Barth (1948), "Der Mensch in seiner Zeit," *KD* III/2, 524–780.

E. Levinas (1948), *Le temps et l'autre,* Montpellier (2nd Ed. 1979).

H. Conrad-Martius (1954), *Die Zeit,* Munich.

J. Mouroux (1962), *Le mystère du temps: Approche théologique,* Paris.

R. Schaeffler (1963), *Die Struktur der Geschichtszeit,* Frankfurt.

M. Bordoni (1965), *Il tempo valore filosofico e misterio teologico,* Rome.

J. Barr (1969), *Biblical Words for Time,* revised edition, SBT 33, London.

B. Welte (1971), "Meditation *Über die Zeit*", *ThQ* 151, 289–99

B. Welte (1982), *Zwischen Zeit und Ewigheit,* Freiburg-Basel-Vienna, 25–42, 251–60.

P. Ricoeur (1983–85), *Temps et récit,* 3 vols., Paris.

H. Bourgeois, P. Gibert, M. Jourjon (1986), *L'expérience chrétienne du temps,* Paris.

G. Lafont (1986), *Dieu, le temps et l'être,* Paris.

J.-Y. Lacoste (1990), *Note sur le temps,* Paris.

M. Baude (1991), *Théologie du temps,* Paris.

B. Leftow (1991), *Time and Eternity,* Ithaca.

M. Theunissen (1991), *Negative Theologie der Zeit,* Frankfurt, esp. 13–86 and 197–377.

D. Janicaud (1997), *Chronos: Pour l'intelligence du partage temporel,* Paris.

JEAN-YVES LACOSTE

See also **Eschatology; Eternity of God; History; Life, Eternal; Liturgy**

Tolerance. *See* **Deism and Theism**

Trace (Vestige)

The Latin term *vestigium,* translated as "vestige" or "trace," belongs first of all to the problematic of representation. It is thus related to the symbol of the line, proposed by Plato in Book VI of the *Republic,* in which the tangible world appears as the reflection of the intelligible world*. Philo used the Greek *mimèma,* translated into Latin by *vestigium,* to define the tangible world, a degraded image or vestige of the *Logo*s; he also applied it to man insofar as he is part of that world (*De opif.* 145 ff.). The term was adopted in the patristic and medieval periods, not solely in reference to the problematic of the image, but in order to express an orientation toward likeness and, more broadly, the relationships between the cosmos*, man, and God*. To recognize the trace of God in created beings is to contemplate the author through his work, to ascend from the cosmos to its creator and thereby unify cosmology and symbolic theology*. The concept of trace, used in this way, is at the basis of all Christian aesthetics.

It was in Augustine that *vestigium* was given decisive direction as well as a non-disparaging sense. If he adopted it to designate the world, this was with the idea that the world was the expression of its creator. In Book X of the *Confessions* and in the Commentary on Psalm 41, for example, Augustine introduces a *prosopopeia* of the Creation*, in order to show that everything that exists is not God, but has been created by him, and is, therefore, fundamentally good and refers to its creator.

More radically, Augustine makes the soul* the quintessential *vestigium,* for it is in the image of the Trinity*. This image, however, is not of the same nature as its creator, and this is why Augustine offers analogies* in order to express it: soul, knowledge, love* (*De Trinitate* IX); memory, intelligence, will (X); memory, inner vision, will (XI). Offered in order to show that the soul expresses the Trinity, these analogies are created to give a positive meaning to the concept of vestige. They are echoes of the Trinity in the human being. Augustine, however, emphasizes that the Trinity infinitely transcends the traces it has left in us, and goes on to say: "If the Trinity of the soul is the image of God, this is not because it remembers itself, understands itself, and loves itself; but it is because it can still remember, understand, and love Him by whom it was created" (*De Trinitate* XIV. 12. 15). The image of

the Trinity in the soul is thus not static, but dynamic; it realizes itself only in relation to the Creator, and this relation constitutes for it a kind of continuing creation.

As for the theme of *resemblance,* Augustine does not offer a detailed treatment of the theme of likeness but implies it in his analysis of the dynamics of the image. Understood thus as a vestige, the Creation is seen as a theophany*. Visible images express the primordial nature of things and recount the glory* of God and the regeneration of the cosmos through salvation*. Imitative of the Creator in various forms, these primordial natures carry on among themselves a harmonious relationship, and each one resembles the others in accordance with constant rhythms.

In this context, Dionysius* the Pseudo-Areopagite is another important source. Because for him God is absolutely unknowable and can be characterized only by an absolute negativity, it would be deceptive to believe that he can be attained by means of noble images, which would necessarily be inadequate. On the contrary, it is better to have recourse to figures "drawn from the most lowly earthly realities," and to represent God "with images that do not resemble Him in any way" (*Celestial Hierarchy* I §3, PG 3. 140 D). The dissimilar symbol is thus a better theological instrument than the image, to the extent that it declares its own insufficiency and impels the soul again in its ascent toward God. John the Scot Eriugena, who considered nature as an immense allegory of the divine, adopted this theory. And because human art can do nothing but imitate divine art, art itself then takes on an anagogic dimension (*see* senses of Scripture*). This is the meaning of the plastic representations, even the most monstrous of them, decorating Romanesque churches, and of the stained glass windows of the Gothic cathedrals (*see* Suger, *De consecratione,* ed. G. Binding, Köln, A. Speer, 1995).

Although Augustine's analogies had many imitators, as shown, for example, in Richard of Saint*-Victor, the Augustinian understanding of *vestigium* was of short duration, except in Anselm* and John* of the Cross, who both present the created being as a vestige of the Creator. In the 12th century, in fact, the term tended to resume a Platonic tonality and to be rationalized. In the *Summa de Anima* (p. 147), Jean de la Rochelle opted for a variation on the Augustinian scheme, *vestigium,* *imago,* and *similitudo,* but *vestigium* is defined as a "distant, obscure, and individual representation," far from the *similitudo,* which is an immediate, complete, and clear representation. The concept of trace nevertheless maintained a decisive role in the reflection on nature. For example, beginning in the 12th century, encyclopedias developed the theme of the "mirrors of nature"—means of knowing the invisible attributes* of God on the basis of His work. In an analogous way, Cistercian art also used a symbolism of nature and made the cloister, for example, a figure for paradise.

In the following century, Bonaventure* adopted a similar perspective, but he introduced some nuances. First of all he differentiated the image, the traces of which can be found in nature, and likeness, the privilege of man alone. In his Commentary on the *Sentences* (I. d. 3. p. 1. c. 1. q. 2. ad 4) Bonaventure proposes a distinction not among vestige, image, and likeness, but among shadow, vestige, and image. The *shadow* is a distant and confused representation, based on the immediate causality of Creation. The vestige is a distant representation, but one that is distinct and based on a threefold causality (efficient, formal, and final) as well as on the transcendentals (the One, the True, and the Good). As for the *image,* it is a close and distinct representation and belongs only to intellectual nature, as that nature is structured by the three faculties of the soul that had been recognized since Augustine.

In the fourth of the *Questions on the knowledge of Christ,* Bonaventure applies the scheme *vestigium, imago, similitudo* in order to define the degrees of being* of created beings and the mode by which God cooperates in their action. He explains: "As a vestige, [the created being] is related to God as to its principle, as an image, it refers to Him as the object of its activity (of intellect and love). But as a likeness, it is directed to God as to the innate gift that He makes of Himself. Hence, any created being coming from God is a vestige of Him; any created being who knows God is an image of Him; but only the created being in whom God dwells is His likeness."

An analogous procedure can be found in the *Itinerarium,* in which the soul gradually rises to the contemplation* of God. Bonaventure clearly distinguishes between vestiges, which are the first stage of this ascent, and the image of God, which represents the second stage. And he explains (ch. I §2) that "among created beings, some are vestiges and others the image of God; some are corporeal, the others spiritual, the former temporal, the latter intemporal; some are outside us, the others within." But although the *Itinerarium* at first proposes a path toward contemplation through and in the vestiges of God in the world, it then advocates a return to inwardness, through the intermediary of the image of God that is in us, and at that point, unlike Augustine, Bonaventure does not speak of vestiges. The Sermon on the threefold witness of the Trinity (n. 7), finally, adopts a broader point of view, but does not give the soul a special place. Thomas* Aquinas also defined a hierarchy of created beings in accordance with the scheme *vestigium, imago, similitudo* (De Potentia q. 9. art. 9 c; *Summa Contra Gentiles* IV. 26; *Summa Theologica* Ia q. 4. a. 3; q. 45. a. 7; q. 93. a. 2, 6).

Although the vestige is an important moment in the dialectic of being, it is in itself only a simulacrum in which likeness is only partial. This is perhaps the reason for which Meister Eckhart (*see* Rhineland*-Flemish mysticism) said that, left to themselves, created beings are "pure nothingness*," but that there is "something in the soul" through which they are more than a simple vestige.

This symbolic understanding of the world and of "vestiges" was replaced by a more ontological interpretation in Duns* Scotus and John of Ripa. In the 17th and 18th centuries, it was necessarily called into question by the appearance of mechanist and rationalist arguments. Some recollections of Augustine, such as the "mark of God on his work" in Descartes*, are all that modern times preserved of the problematics of the vestige.

A reflection on the theme of the trace, however, has been resumed in the 20th century, not referring to the world but to others, in the work of E. Levinas (*En découvrant l'existence avec Husserl et Heidegger,* Paris, 1982): "Being in the image of God does not mean being the icon of God but finding oneself in his trace. The revealed God...does not show Himself through his trace, as in chapter 33 of Exodus. To go toward Him is not to follow that trace, which is not a sign, but to go toward others who are standing in the trace."

- É. Mâle (1898), *L'art religieux du XIIIe siècle en France,* Paris.
- M.-D. Chenu (1957), *La théologie au XIIIe siècle,* Paris.
- G. de Champeaux and S. Sterck (1966), *Le monde des symboles,* La Pierre-qui-Vire.
- R. Javelet (1967), *Image et ressemblance au XIIe siècle,* 2 vols., Paris.
- W. Beierwaltes (1977), "*Negati affirmatio*: Welt als Metapher. Zur Grundlegung einer mittelalterlichen Ästhetik durch Johannes Scotus Eriugena," in coll., *Jean Scot Érigène et l'histoire de la philosophie,* Paris, 263–76.
- M.-M. Davy (1977), *Initiation à la symbolique romane (XIIe siècle),* Paris.
- M. Mentré (1984), *Création et apocalypse: Histoire d'un regard humain sur le divin,* Paris.

MARIE-ANNE VANNIER

See also **Anthropology; Beauty; Creation; Images**

Tradition

A. Catholic Theology

a) The Idea. The *idea* of tradition, which initially referred to the act of transmitting material objects, was eventually applied to the perpetuation of religious doctrines and practices, handed down from one generation to the next by word of mouth and living example. From there, the term was extended to the whole of the contents thus communicated. In that sense the Catholic Church* considers itself to be the constitution of living tradition and justifies its message and role through the transmission of the Christian faith*, of which it is, in its own eyes, a component element. However, this claim must not be viewed as concerning merely a specific confessional trait, but as an essential element of Christianity itself. By putting the accent exclusively on the Holy* Scriptures, the Reformers cut themselves off from that tradition, which they made a collective term to denote all the exterior biblical manifestations of Christian life and thought since the time of the apostles* (apostolic tradition). The widest meaning of the term *tradition,* including the Holy Scriptures, however, is the oldest one, while the antonym Scripture/Tradition became current only from the time of the Reformation and Counter-Reformation onward.

b) Origins and Development of Christian Tradition. In the daily lifestyle and the history* of the Jewish people, tradition did not at first give rise to any discussion. It was lived as an obvious fact. The only difficulty came from the concrete means that had to be adopted or developed gradually in order to ensure its continuity and growth and to thus make it the object of a conscious relationship. The beginnings of the Christian movement lie entirely within that context; it was a matter of taking the measures and creating the institutions that seemed necessary for the community's protection. These measures and institutions were based on the authority of the gospel*—that is, on the word of the Lord, who by this means ensured his living presence in the world*. The first elements of an explicit awareness of tradition appeared with the "rule of faith" and the links it created—links with the canon* of Scripture and links with the idea of the succession of bishops* and presbyters*. So many reference points and institutional means made it possible to reject doc-

trinal errors, schisms, and the founding of illegitimate communities.

It took some time before particular traditions came into being, and then an explicit awareness of tradition. In 1 Thessalonians 4:16–17 we find Paul still announcing the imminent dawning of the day of the Lord—which, moreover, did not exclude but, on the contrary, presumed the missionary work of the spreading of the Word*; in Romans 9–11, however, Paul has already developed the lines of force of a history of salvation*, understood as a temporal process in which the work of its transmission is embedded and of which he, Paul, is the instrument, as he states particularly in 1 Corinthians 11:23 and 15:3. Here can be observed the appearance of a central aspect of the gospel message, which would finally be given an official definition under the technical term "deposit of faith," and which coincides at bottom with the idea of an obligatory "rule of faith."

In the process of the composition and interpenetration of New Testament testimonies, Luke, the evangelist and the author of the Acts of the Apostles, is credited with a particular influence on the creation of tradition and the idea of tradition (*see* Lk 1:1–4 and Acts 1:1–2). This is why, in the perspective of systematic exegesis, elements of a "proto-Catholicism" have been seen. It is only because of its account of the life of Jesus Christ that John's narrative was inserted in the New Testament between Luke's Gospel and Acts, and this interpolation has obscured the impression of the original cohesiveness of these two texts. It is often thought that Luke's project was only made possible by neglecting the eschatological meanings of Jesus*' message or by his reinterpretations oriented toward a contemporary eschatology*. But although it is true that the time frame determines the conception that we form of concrete tradition, the New Testament texts show that these two realities can be linked in various ways. A consistent eschatological approach to the Gospels can also make room for mission* and tradition. The fact remains that, faced with the attacks and challenges of the period that followed, attempts were clearly made to extract from it principles and institutions intended to reinforce tradition.

It was above all the Gnosticism* of the second century (but also Marcionism* and other movements) that necessitated measures capable of ensuring the solidarity of the faithful and the cohesion of communities. For example, in his *Against Heresies,* Irenaeus* of Lyons assembled all the established doctrinal elements in order to develop a coherent and consistent view, in which the individual references might reinforce each other. Tertullian*, for his part, defended the Christian faith by means of judicial rhetoric, thus adding a new facet to the kinds of argument deployed by Irenaeus in the field of salvation history. Henceforth, it was easier to define not only the contents of Christian tradition but also the way in which these contents ought to be transmitted. However, a fear of innovation ended up casting suspicion on Christianity's vital activity, as is clearly shown by the use made of the expression by which Vincent of Lerins has summed up the principle of tradition. Only "what has been believed everywhere, always, and by everyone" (*Commonitorium,* c. 23) was to be accepted as Catholic, with the risk this presented of trapping the Church in a unilateral relationship with the past. Only as long as Christianity experienced its faith, in the main, as a lifestyle that was still self-evident, did this conception present no difficulties. The significance of the *Commonitorium* for the history of dogma* was not recognized until the 16th century.

The nominally Christian world of the end of Antiquity and the Middle Ages did not see its own Christianity challenged, except at the margins. Tradition belonged to a natural environment, so to speak; it did not raise any real problems, and even if the validity of such and such a particular tradition happened to be disputed, in its totality it was accepted without argument.

c) The Reformation. In the end, even the Protestant Reformation's reactions against certain particular traditions challenged tradition as such only in the name of Scripture, that is, relative to the whole to which Scripture belonged (see *Enchiridion Symbolorum: Definitionum et declarationum de rebus fidei et morum* 1501). By his demand for conformity with Scripture, Luther* introduced an element of tradition and a specific method of transmission. In his own way, therefore, he himself invoked tradition. The question was, who was following the *best* tradition? What the Reformer rejected was certain individual traditions—that is, concrete points of Christian practice and particular convictions that, according to him, derived from other sources than the testimony recorded in the texts of the Gospels. He therefore restricted the domain from which traditions might be drawn, only acknowledging the legitimacy of those that seemed to him to be confirmed in Scripture. Likewise, the Council of Trent put up less of a defense of tradition per se than it defended certain particular conceptions, dispositions, or customs. Therefore, the "Decree on the Acceptance of the Holy Books and the Tradition of the Apostles" (*Enchiridion Symbolorum* 1501–5) was intended for the most part to clarify the Catholic understanding of Scripture. It states: "This truth* and this principle are contained in the written books and the non-written traditions that, received by the apostles from the mouth of Christ* himself or transmitted as if hand-to-hand by the apostles under the Holy* Spirit's dictation, have come down to us." The fact that this definition later gave birth, in catechesis and theological commentary, to what has been called the "theory of the two sources" of revelation, is explained by a desire to oppose the Reformation's progress and by the (imagined) demands of apologetics. On this point the quarrel did not break into the open until just before Vatican* II, notably in the famous controversy that pitted J. R. Geiselmann (Tübingen) against H. Lennerz (Rome). This confirms that it is only in the modern period that the problem of *Tradition* has become a completely separate issue from the question of *traditions* (in the plural).

d) The 19th Century Debate about Tradition. It was the Enlightenment's radical challenge to authority as well as the progress of historicism during the previous century that finally led Catholic and non-Catholic thinkers to ask themselves explicitly the question about tradition. French *traditionalism* (Bonald, J. de Maistre and so on) tried to base the whole of religious thought on the principle of tradition, while the Catholic school of Tübingen* was bent on putting this principle into practice in the framework of a discussion founded on constituted orthodoxy*. The "Roman school" (G. Perrone, C. Passaglia, Cl. Schrader, and J. B. Franzelin), also moved by a desire for theological revival, likewise stressed the principle of tradition, without nonetheless falling into a traditionalism excluded in the meantime by the Magisterium*. At Vatican* I, recourse to tradition took on such importance that Pope Pius IX is supposed to have uttered the questionable phrase: "I am Tradition." The classic summary of the position of the Roman school was put forward by J. B. Franzelin in his *Tractatus de Divina Traditione et Scriptura* (lithographed in 1867–68, printed in 1870). The reversal of views that had occurred is evident from the title of the work, where tradition preceded the Holy Scriptures, which seem more like a collection of "writings," in the plural, subordinate to the unity of tradition. The interest of Franzelin lies in the fact that he introduced into the concept of tradition a differentiation that authorized a new approach to the problem. A tradition existed *before* the testimonies that record their contents in writing; and there is a tradition *after* the testimonies, a tradition whose work is to translate, to interpret, to bring these testimonies up to date—in short, to bring them alive in the present time. In this way Franzelin could deal first with the essence of the divine tradition, then with its preservation, and lastly with its relationship to Scripture and the interpretation of Catholic doctrine. After this first part he tackled Scripture by examining first of all the inspiration of the whole, then the way in which the inspired books are known to us. He continued by looking at the role of the canon of Scripture in the tradition of the Catholic Church and at the authenticity of the Vulgate. Finally, in an appendix he described, in a way characteristic of the whole work, the relation between human reason and divine faith, which clearly showed that he was not aiming merely at a formal examination of tradition. Typically he relied, above all, on linguistic observations and data, whose historical character was not lost sight of either in establishing the facts or in their interpretation, even if this aspect had not yet been treated with all the technical tools that later research would make available.

e) After Vatican I. The neo-Thomism of the following period, on the other hand, viewed thought as a system existing outside time *(philosophia et theologica perennis);* it therefore evaded the problem of a living tradition while leaving the field open to properly historical research. However, in assigning to the latter the task of upholding and confirming already validated truths, independent of tradition, neo-Thomism placed itself at perpetual risk of seeing in their results nothing but threats of relativism*. The crisis of Modernism* showed that the problem could not be solved in this way (see *Enchiridion Symbolorum* 3458–66 and 3494–98, as well as 3873). Naturally, it was not without reason that there was some hesitation about making a commitment to an in-depth and systematic examination of the question of tradition. Indeed, no discussion can restore the nature of "evidence" derived from a reality actually lived. On the contrary, discussion only distances it further, at the risk of breaking the tie, which in the last resort sustains the spirituality of a faith and of the reflection it inspires.

In the period since World War I, and in order to counter the dichotomy introduced by Thomist Neoscholasticism, certain Catholics have put the emphasis on the whole, which encompasses the factors thus dissociated. In so doing they have reminded the faithful of the central aspects of the traditions of Christian life, whether in the activities that express the Church's concrete reality (divine service/liturgy*, charitable works, teaching, *actio catholica, participatio actuosa,* counsel, synods* and so on), or in Christian thought in general, or again in theological reflection. At the very beginning of the 20th century, in his *Histoire et dogme* (1904), Blondel had stressed the importance of this task. The immense amount of historical material released in the interval needed to be integrated into the Christian spirituality of the time so as not to remain merely soulless knowledge. From another angle, the philosophy of life and the philosophy* of existence emphasized the need for a new practical commitment.

f) The "Living Tradition." Sustained by the memory of the Catholic school of Tübingen and of Scheeben* (one of the great representatives of the "Roman school"), the "living tradition" movement was one of the sources of spiritual renewal that was to make it possible for theological thought to act beyond the borders of its own field. In place of a quantitative view of tradition it substituted a qualitative view, through which revelation seemed above all to be a communication and a self-communication. Dialogic and hermeneutic* thought drew from this movement a new impetus and materials. Research on orality as the unsurpassable form of tradition and as the original testimony's mode of expression, revealed the fact that the writings can only intervene in this process in an indirect and secondary way. Since a new reality cannot be born (whatever its continuous ties with the past) unless a reciprocal action is necessarily established between the present and tradition, a reciprocal action that is immediately translated on the social level, the theme of orality influenced the debate about the foundations of the historical sciences, the controversies about the abandonment and the loss of tradition, as well as the thinking about the validity for later eras of the testimony about tradition. Certainly, the first consequence of the problematization of tradition was to show that the approaches, the descriptions, and the attempts at rational explanations were incapable of solving by themselves the problem of the distance that separates a tradition—lived or fixed in the evidence—from the discourse held about it. But can a tradition be genuinely appropriated through learning, knowledge, and thought in the specific meanings that these terms have taken on today in the Western context? A theory of tradition is not, and cannot itself be, a living tradition, even if theory as such is an inseparable part of human tradition—that aspect of the problem would have to be treated in a discussion about "fundamentalism*," because it is wrong to say that realities experienced and ways of life cannot be better transmitted and preserved than by theoretical teaching.

g) Vatican II. By its stress on the *pastoral* nature of its elucidations, developments, and resolutions, Vatican II rejected a view of historiography understood as an accumulation of knowledge, and as a simple matter of intellectual çomprehension, in favor of a more all-encompassing, qualitative approach. It thus linked its own conception of tradition with the points of view introduced in the new discussions on history (*see DV* in *Enchiridion Symbolorum* 4207–14). The question of the limits of historical science, as it had been practiced until then, did indeed provoke a fundamental debate from which might emerge a new view of history, closer to traditional Christian conceptions, but one in relation to which these traditional Christian conceptions might themselves also undergo some modification. In any event, it could no longer be a question of indefinitely accumulating information and results, with these becoming so numerous as to render the mind incapable of taking a global view and organizing these disparate elements into a meaningful sequence. From this there arose the problem of the legitimate abandonment of a tradition, a problem that until then had scarcely been glimpsed, and even less analyzed in any convincing way. An awareness developed of the difficulty of the selection that must inevitably be made between various traditions, of the need to distinguish between the important and the secondary. Moreover, this question had already been raised in the old context. In any case, from the Christian point of view, a clear and plausible definition of what is called salvation history was lacking (*see LG* in *Enchiridion Symbolorum* 4122–24 and 4130–41), a concept that certainly involves differentiation in the historical material, but that must not give support to the false idea that history contains separate parts or fields. It remains to find agreement once more about the means that a theological history of traditions could properly use, because a great number of criticisms addressed today to religion and the Church are aroused by institutional blockades that tradition is accused of having put in place. The idea of tradition's essentially "living" nature does not refer only to the effects of the truth of the gospel but also to the method of transmitting this truth, which is based in a decisive way on communication and reciprocity. The rediscovery of this living aspect could be seen as the real transformation of tradition, a tradition that, for far too long, had been understood in terms of an anxiety to preserve with the least possible change a treasure or a capital conceived as a material entity. But then the critical potential of this living material must also be reckoned with. In that sense, Vatican II was not only the result of a new way of thinking about tradition but also the starting point for forms of research that, in the interests of the Christian faith, need to be pursued today.

● Y. Congar (1960), *La Tradition et les traditions,* 2 vols., Paris.
J. Feiner, M. Löhrer et al. (1965), "Die Vergegenwärtigung der Offenbarung durch die Kirche," *Mysterium Salutis: Grundriß heilsgeschichtlicher Dogmatik* I, 497–783.
J. Hasenfuss, F. Mussner, J. Ratzinger (1965), "Tradition," *Lexikon für Theologie und Kirche 2* 10, 290–99.
P. Lengsfeld (1965), "Tradition innerhalb der konstitutiven Zeit der Offenbarung," *Mysterium Salutis: Grundriß heilsgeschichtlicher Dogmatik* I, 239–87.
K. Rahner, J. Ratzinger (1965), *Offenbarung und Überlieferung,* Freiburg.
K.-H. Weger (1969), "Tradition," *Sacramentum Mundi: Theologisches Lexikon fur die Praxis* 4, 955–65.
J. Ratzinger (1982), "Anthropologische Grundlegung des Begriffs Überlieferung," in *Theologische Prinzipienlehre,* Munich, 88–105.
P. Ricoeur et al. (1984), *La Révélation,* Brussels.
W. Kasper (1985), "Tradition als theologisches Erkenntnisprinzip," *Dogmengeschichte und katholische Theologie,* Würzburg, 376–403.
S. Wiedenhofer (1990), "Grundprobleme des theologischen Traditionsbegriffs," *Zeitschrift für katholische Theologie* 112, 18–29.
D. Wiederkehr (1991), *Wie geschieht Tradition?,* Freiburg.
Th. Langan (1992), *Tradition and Authenticity,* Columbia, MO.
K. Schori (1992), *Das Problem der Tradition,* Stuttgart.

KARL HEINZ NEUFELD

See also **Canon of Scriptures; Holy Scripture; Loci Theologici; Magisterium; Revelation**

B. Protestant Theology

1. Great Historical Movements

Protestantism* maintains a critical but not a negative relationship with the notion of tradition. Its consistent principle of acknowledging the sole authority* of the Scriptures leads it to reject the idea of any authority belonging to tradition (whether Fathers*, Councils*, or Magisterium*). When summoned to abjure before the Diet, Luther refused and declared: "Unless they can convince me by testimony from the Scriptures or by obvious reasons—for I have faith neither in the pope* nor in councils alone, since it is clear that they have often been in error and have contradicted themselves—I am bound by the scriptural texts that I have cited and my conscience* is held captive by the word* of God; I cannot nor do I want to retract anything, for it is neither sure nor honest to act against one's conscience" (Discourse of Worms, 18 April 1521: *Luther's Works*, vol. 7, 832–38 [*Works*, vol. 2, Geneva, 1960]). This critical principle is well in evidence in the three great movements that arose from the "Teaching Reformation"— that is to say, Lutheranism*, Calvinism*, and Anglicanism* (the polemical aspect would be radicalized if we extended the presentation to the various movements of the radical nebula, such as Anabaptists*, Spiritualism, Unitarianism*, or Millenarianism*).

a) Lutheranism. The critical principle was adopted in the symbolic texts of Lutheranism. Melanchthon tried to express it in a conciliatory way by specifying at the end of the first part of the *Augsburg Confession* (1530): "We did not... want to give or transmit to our children and our descendants another doctrine than the one which conforms to the pure word of God and Christian truth*. If therefore this doctrine is clearly based on the Holy Scriptures, and if, in addition, it is neither in contradiction nor in opposition to the Christian Church*, not even to the Roman Church—as far as one can ascertain from the writings of the Fathers— we consider that our adversaries cannot be in disagreement with us as regards the articles below."

The Book of Concord (1577) specifies that the writings of the Fathers or the theologians should never be placed in the same category as Holy Scripture, that they are subordinate and that they can only state to what extent and in which places the doctrine of the prophets* and the apostles has been preserved in its integrity (*Epitomé* I). The Scriptures are consequently the only yardstick of faith*. Other doctrinal writings should be subordinate to them and no ecclesiastical tradition contrary to their teachings could be accepted. However, if the conformity of a doctrine is judged by reference to the Scriptures, nothing prevents theologians from adding to their presentation proofs drawn from tradition and from the Fathers.

The Lutheran attitude consists of tolerating tradition when it is not in disagreement with the Bible*. Above all, it is a question of repudiating anything that might seem likely to veil the principle of justification* by faith alone.

b) Zwinglianism and Calvinism. In the Zwinglian-Calvinist or reformed movement the same insistence

on the sole authority of the Scriptures can be found. The first *Helvetic Confession* (1536) makes clear distinctions. First there are the Scriptures, which should not be "interpreted and explained except by means of themselves, according to the principle of faith and charity." Then there are the Fathers* and the Doctors, who, as long as they have kept to the Bible, are recognized "not only as interpreters of the Scriptures but also as chosen instruments through whom God has spoken." Lastly there are the doctrines and tradition of men, which, "however beautiful and venerable they might seem, and however ancient they are... turn away from God and the true faith" (articles 2–3–4).

The *Confession de foi des Eglises réformées de France* (1559) specified that the biblical canon, which constitutes the rule of faith, finds its legitimacy "not so much through the common accord and consent of the Church as through the testimony and inner conviction provided by the Holy* Spirit."

The word contained in the books of the Bible is untouchable, so much so that: "Men, or even the angels*, are not allowed to add to, subtract from, or change it. Whence it follows that neither Antiquity, nor custom, nor the masses, nor wisdom, nor judgments, nor rulings, nor edicts, nor laws, nor councils, nor visions, nor miracles* should be opposed to these Holy Scriptures." Conformity with the Scriptures does not however preclude the assumption of a heritage from the past, and particularly not the acceptance of the great symbols of the faith (articles 4–5). The "Reformed Church Principle" consists in retaining only the doctrines and practices that are established by the Scriptures.

c) Anglicanism. In the Anglican family there is both a great anxiety to maintain the link with the usages, particularly the liturgical ones, of the undivided Church and a desire to give the different Churches a certain latitude in the observation of the rites. Therefore, article 6 of the *Thirty-Nine Articles* stipulates: "The Holy Scriptures contain everything necessary for salvation*: everything which is not contained in them or which cannot be proved by them cannot be considered a requirement for anyone as an article of faith and could not be considered indispensable or necessary for salvation." But in practice the position is more moderate, as stated in article 34: "It is not necessary for traditions and ceremonies to be the same in all places and on all points; for in all ages they have been diverse and can vary according to the diversity of the countries, eras, and customs, provided that nothing is established contrary to the word of God."

Anxious to allow the coexistence of a certain practical plurality alongside the Church's unity*, Anglicanism tries to establish a distinction between the fundamental truths (convictions or institutions) and those that are secondary: the balance is maintained according to a "calculated combination"—different according to each movement—between the Scriptures, tradition, and reason*.

2. Theology

a) The Principle of Sola Scriptura. The Protestant position needs to be related to the distinction it imposes between the original norm, which is the Scriptures *(norma normans)* and the derived norms *(normae normatae),* which consist of the symbolic texts (confessions of faith and catechisms). Doctrinal, liturgical, and ecclesiological traditions do indeed exist within Protestantism, but no actual authority is conferred on the texts which testify to them: they derive their normative value from the Scriptures, which they seek to mirror. That is what is specified by the conclusions of certain symbolic texts that do not feel bound by the form that the expression of faith takes (1st Confession of Basel, 1534): "In this Confession, if something happened to be lacking, we are ready, God willing, to present more ample information in conformity with the Scriptures [*Augsburg Confession*]. In the last place, we wish to submit to the judgment of the divine Scriptures this Confession which is ours, and, to this end, we have sworn that if we learn anything better at the instigation of the Holy Scriptures, that we are willing to be obedient to God and to his holy Word at all times and with a great act of grace."

In the period when the controversy was at its height (16th and 17th centuries), whatever their confessional family*, the Protestants attacked Vincent of Lerins's adage according to which, in the Church, truth was whatever had always been believed everywhere and by everyone. They delved into patristics and the notion of antiquity: on the one hand, contrary to what the Roman position leads one to believe, the Fathers have not all and not always taught the same doctrine, for example, with regard to the Eucharist* or images* (for instance, J. Daillé, *Traité de l'emploi des saints Pères,* 1632); on the other hand, a statement's antiquity cannot constitute a criterion of its truth (for instance, J. Mestrezat, *Traité de L'Ecriture Saint,* 1633). From the 17th century onwards and into the 18th, the progress of the *critica sacra* provoked a crisis of scriptural reference: L. Cappel (1585–1658), J. Locke (1632–1704), J. Le Clerc (1657–1736). Since that was so, unless it proceeded to a fundamentalist type of reading, or acknowledged along with Catholicism* that an official authority was needed in order to settle the senses of the Scriptures*, Protestantism had to take the historical aspect into its hermeneutics*. In the 20th century, Bult-

mann*'s thinking is decisive. According to it, preaching* and the sacraments* belong to the traditions of Christ, not in the sense that he might have established them but because they are the means by which his kerygma is delivered to believers: "Tradition is part of the very event which is contained within it." In addition, scientific exegesis becomes aware of the historical nature of every doctrine and text—that is, of the influence that various traditions exert over the writing of the biblical books. This is why Protestant theology* insists on both the distinction and the necessary link between the word of God—the heart of the message— and its form, which is the Scriptures.

b) The Ecumenical Dialogue. By distinguishing the tradition of the Gospels from the traditions belonging to each Church, the IVth World Conference on Faith and Constitution (Montreal, 1963) made possible a theoretical convergence of the confessional positions. The conference defined tradition as the transmission of the gospel in and by the Church, its updating, its being made current through preaching and the administration of the sacraments, the liturgy, theological teaching, mission*, and witness. It questions and challenges particular traditions. Even if this distinction does not in practice abolish the divergences—as shown by certain reactions from Protestant theologians to the document *Baptism, Eucharist, Ministry* (Lima, 1982; *see*, for example *Etudes théologiques et religieuses* 58, 1983/2)— it made it possible to go beyond the past antagonism between Scripture and tradition. Protestant theology revealed itself willing to "rehabilitate" tradition, not as an example of dogmatic authority, but as a point of mediation where, in the act of transmission, individual faith accepted its historical and community dimensions (*see* G. Ebeling, P. Gisel). Far from ensuring the continuity and the repetitiveness of the statements of faith, tradition then constitutes a starting point for a constantly renewed realization of the Christian witness in the world*. This point of view goes back to the distinction—a founding distinction in the Protestant family—between Law* and Gospel: the truth is not attested by the form of the statement but by the relationship—between man and God—that gives rise to the daring expression of faith.

- *The Book of Common Prayer and Administration of the Sacraments…According to the Use of the Church of England,* Oxford (s.d.).
Bekenntinisschriften der evangelisch-lutherischen Kirche.
Bbekenntinisschriften un Kirchenordnungen der nach Gottes Wort reformierten Kirche.
L. Vischer (1968), *Foi et Constitution 1910–1963,* Paris and Neuchâtel, 172–85.
R. Stauffer (1980), "La confession de Bâle et de Mulhouse," in *Interprètes de la Bible,* Paris, 129–52.

◆ F. Chaponnière (1882), "Tradition," in F. Lichtenberger (Ed.), *Encyclopédie des sciences religieuses* vol. 12, 191–199, Paris.

R. Bultmann (1933), *Glauben und Verstehen* I, Tübingen, 153–87.

R. Snoeks (1951), *L'argument de tradition dans la controverse eucharistique entre catholiques et réformés français au XVIIe siècle*, Louvain.

G. Ebeling (1962), "Tradition: VII. Dogmatisch," *Die Religion in Geschichte und Gegenwart 3*, 6, 976–84; (1971), *Einführung in die theologische Sprachlehre*, Tübingen.

G. Gassmann, V. Vajta (1972), *La tradition dans le luthéranisme et l'anglicanisme*, Œc. 1971–1972.

J. Solé (1985), *Le débat entre protestants et catholiques français de 1598 à 1685*, Paris.

P. Gisel (1986), *Croyance incarnée: Tradition-Écriture-Canon-Dogme*, Geneva.

K. Ware (1991), "Tradition and Traditions," *Dictionary of the Ecumenical Movement*, Geneva, 1013–17.

HUBERT BOST

See also **Calvin; Ecumenicism; Zwingli, Huldrych**

Traditionalism

The word "traditionalism" refers first of all to a school of thought that appeared at the beginning of the 19th century and to its continuation up to the present day, and also to a theological error that was censured on numerous occasions and finally condemned by Vatican* I.

a) Historical Origins. Having witnessed the damage caused to the Church* and to theology* by the French Revolution, certain Catholics set about renewing apologetics. At the very moment when Paris was celebrating the Concordat signed by Pius VII and Napoleon, François-René de Chateaubriand (1764–1848), the father of Romanticism, published his *Génie du christianisme* (1802). Diverging from the usual perspective, this work sought to show not that Christianity is excellent because it emanates from God*, but that it "comes from God because it is excellent"; it endeavors therefore to prove in every domain the wealth and beauty of its dogma*, its morality, and its worship.

The three "founders" of traditionalism proposed another path: despite differences in style and doctrine, Joseph de Maistre (1754–1821), Louis de Bonald (1754–1840), and then Felicité Robert de Lamennais (1782–1854) came together to denounce the rationalism* and individualism of the 18th century which had led to a generalized skepticism. On a political and social level, the Revolution was the fruit of the Enlightenment, the current of thought made famous by French and German philosophers. According to the light of divine providence*, these founding thinkers averred, it was an expiation* of the fathers' forgetfulness of religion, and punishment for the struggle led against Catholicism* and royalty, which it was important should be restored (J. de Maistre, *Considérations sur la France*, 1796; *Soirées de Saint-Pétersbourg*, 1821). Wanting to reestablish religion and the monarchy by restoring the notions of authority* and by placing God once again at the summit of society*, Bonald reflected upon the constitution of society and the origins of power: the perfect form of religious society, Catholicism alone corresponded to the social nature of man (*Théorie du pouvoir politique et religieux dans la société civile, démontrée par le raisonnement et par l'histoire*, 1796; *Législation primitive considérée dans les derniers temps par les seules lumières de la raison*, 1802). A formula by Lamennais summed up these doctrines: "Without the pope, there is no church; no church, no Christianity; no Christianity, no religion and no society; such that the life of European nations has…its sole source in pontifical power" (*De la religion considérée dans ses rapports avec l'ordre politique et civil*, 1826). Maistre demonstrated the existence of a logical link between sovereignty and infallibility (*Du pape*, 1822).

The anarchy in the political and social order was an expression of the skepticism that reigned in the order of thought: the question of the origin of power was inseparable from that of the origin of ideas. What authority could enable one to attain certainty, if not that of infallible reason*? This was the issue that Lamennais raised in his famous *Essai sur l'indifférence en matière de religion* (vol. I, 1817; vol. II, 1820; vol. III and IV, 1821–23). In this essay he denounced all forms of indifference, and rejects philosophy*, which made individual reason the judge of what man ought to believe—hence universal skepticism. The authority of proof must be replaced by the proof of authority, according to Bonald, who underlined the link between thought and word, and again asked the question, already raised in the 18th century, regarding the origins of language: for Bonald, it is a gift from God, similar to the ideas given by the Creator to his creatures (*see* creation*) in a primitive revelation.

Traditionalism can be summarized in two interdependent theses: 1) Individual reason left to its own devices is incapable of attaining moral and religious truths, and in particular of knowing them with certainty. 2) These truths have their origin in a primitive revelation that infallibly transmits tradition*: thus, the general assent of the human race—or common sense—has become the sole criterion of all certainty. Maistre was the precursor of this traditionalism, Bonald its father, and Lamennais its herald (Hocédez, vol. I). Similar but subtler theses were posited during those years by Catholic theologians in Tübingen (Drey, Möhler).

b) Developments, Censure, and Condemnation. The encyclicals *Mirari vos* (1832) and *Singulari nos* (1834) condemned Lamennais's ideas, particularly his liberalism. The influence of his traditionalism continued to be felt among certain disciples such as P. Gerbet (1798–1864), or an Italian cleric who came to France, J. Ventura (1792–1861), as well as in an entire sector of the French clergy, including in particular Monsignor Doney, bishop* of Montauban (1794–1871). In 1855 the founder and director of the *Annales de la philosophie chrétienne*, A. Bonnetty (1789–1879), who held that revelation and faith* alone were capable of leading man to the knowledge of natural religious truths, had to sign four propositions recalling the doctrine of the Church on the origins, capabilities, and use of reason. In Louvain, G. Ubaghs (1800–74) would contribute to the development of a traditionalist current that differed from the French current on the question of certainty; in 1866, Rome* called for a halt to the teaching of what it regarded as a dangerous doctrine. Several provincial councils—Rennes and Avignon in 1849, Amiens in 1853—condemned rationalism*, but also warned against the theses of traditionalism on the powerlessness of reason and on the exaggeration of the authority of tradition at the expense of reason.

The First Vatican Council's constitution *Dei Filius* (1870) condemned the errors of traditionalism by asserting that "God, the principle and goal of all things, can be known with certainty through the natural light of human reason on the basis of the created things"; but it also acknowledged, in accordance with the doctrine of Thomas* Aquinas, that "it is thanks to divine revelation that all humankind, in the present condition of the human race, needs must know with ease, and with a solid certainty and no traces of error, that which in divine things is not in and of itself inaccessible to reason" (see *DS*, 1785–86).

c) Traditionalism in the 20th Century? While much of the early-19th century debate has been forgotten, certain political theses of traditionalism regarding the Revolution, the monarchy, and the *ancien regime* were revived by Charles Maurras (1868–1952) and the Action Française.

Monsignor Lefèbvre and his *traditionalist* movement rejected Vatican* II in the name of tradition, viewed as the preservation of a religious past established by the council of Trent* and the reforms of Pius V. The reform of the liturgy* was thus impugned in the name of a sacral conception of immutable rites; the religious freedom* of persons*, in the name of the rights of an irreformable doctrinal truth; and ecumenism*, in the name of the one true Catholic Church. Such attitudes demonstrated the absence of a sense of history, whereas the Council reiterated that "the Church is a social reality of history*" (*GS* §44). The rejection of the Revolution and of democracy* underscored the affinities of the movement with Action Française and the political theses of the founders of the traditionalist school in the 19th century.

The paradox of traditionalism has been emphasized: it does not take into account the authentic tradition of the Church regarding the capacity of reason and the necessity of revelation. Along with Jaroslav Pelikan one might conclude: "Tradition without history homogenized all the stages of development into one single statically defined truth; history without tradition produced an historicism which relativized the development of Christian doctrine in such a way that it seemed arbitrary to make a distinction between an authentic growth and a cancerous aberration.... Tradition is the living faith of the dead; traditionalism is the dead faith of the living" (*The Christian Tradition: Development of Christian Doctrine*, vol. I).

R. Aubert (1945–50), *Le problème de l'acte de foi*, Louvain and Paris.

● E. Hocédez (1947–52), *Histoire de la théologie au XIXe s.*, 3 vols., Brussels and Paris.

L. Foucher (1955), *La philosophie catholique en France au XIXe s. avant la renaissance thomiste et dans son rapport avec elle (1800–1880)*, Paris.

R. Spaemann (1959), *Der Ursprung des Soziologie aus dem Geist der Restauration: Studien über L. G. A. de Bonald*, Munich.

J.-R. Derré (1962), *Lamennais, ses amis et le mouvement des idées à l'époque romantique, 1824–1834*, Paris.

B. Reardon (1975), *Liberalism and Tradition: Aspects of Catholic Thought in Nineteenth-Century France,* Cambridge.

L.F. Múgica (1988), *Tradición y revolución: Filosofía y sociedad en el pensamiento de Louis de Bonald,* Pamplona.

CLAUDE BRESSOLETTE

See also **Fideism; Freedom, Religious; Modernism; Political Theology; Rationalism; Tradition; Vatican II, Council of.**

Traducianism

Traducianism is the hypothesis according to which the human soul* is transmitted by way of carnal generation. After having been linked to the question of original sin*, this hypothesis progressively disappeared in favor of *creatianism* (not to be confused with *creationism,* the fundamentalist* position opposed to the evolution* of species). According to creatianism, each human soul is directly created by God*.

According to Jerome (c. 347–419), who seemed, for his part, to be partial to creatianism (PL 23, 1112), the question at the beginning of the fifth century was as follows: "Did the soul fall from the sky as thought Pythagoras, all the Platonists, and Origen*; does it emanate from God's own substance according to the Stoician or Manichean hypothesis...? Or, are souls created each day by God and sent into bodies...or [are they born] by propagation *(ex traduce)* as Tertullian*, Apollinarius*, and most of the Occidentals claimed?" (PL 22, 1085–86). Probably under the influence of stoicism, Tertullian saw the soul as a subtle body that propagated at the same time as the material body. Augustine* vigorously rejected this materialistic traducianism (PL 33, 1861), but considered the possibility of a spiritualistic traducianism according to which God created one soul, that of Adam*, from which are drawn all the souls of the men who are born (PL 32, 1299). According to him, this hypothesis allows one to understand the doctrine of original sin, by which all men sinned through Adam. Thus, Julian of Eclana (around 386–454), for whom true faith* imposes creatianism, concluded that this doctrine is indefensible. To better reject it, he nicknamed his partisans *traduciani* (PL 45, 1053) and so we owe him the word *traducianism.* Augustine responded by maintaining his stance: on the one hand the question of the soul's origin is a very difficult one to resolve, on the other hand the adopted hypothesis should not bear on the doctrine of original sin.

In 498, Pope Anastasius II rejected materialistic traducianism (*DS* 360) and emphasized that creatianism did not question the transmission of the original sin. Up until the 13th century, many authors hesitated to clearly condemn spiritualistic traducianism, out of respect for Augustine. Scholasticism, however, took to Peter Lombard's affirmation (c. 1100–60) that the Catholic Church* was teaching creatianism (II *Sent* d. 18). For Thomas* Aquinas, "it is heresy to say that the intellective soul is transmitted with the seed," because this would render it so interdependent of the body that it would disappear with it (Ia q. 118, a. 2). This doctrine was confirmed in 1341 by Benedict XII (*DS* 1007).

Calvin* rejected traducianism more firmly than Luther*. Bellarmine* thought that the argument of tradition* could be invoked against traducianism. H. Noris (1631–1704) countered him on this point by recalling that Augustine remained in uncertainty. Traducianism saw a renewal of interest in the 19th century with authors such as Jacob Frohschammer (1821–93) or Antonio Rosmini (1797–1855). Of the last, in 1887 the Holy Office rejected an affirmation suggesting the multiplication of souls by generation (*DS* 3221).

● A. Michel (1949), "Traducianisme," *DThC* 15 1350–65.

V. Grossi (1990), "Traducianisme," *DECA* 2475.

L. Sentis (1995), "Qu'est-ce que l'homme pour que tu penses à lui?" *Éthique* 18, 116–22.

LAURENT SENTIS

See also **Original Sin**

Transcendence, Divine. *See* **Analogy; Infinite**

Translations of the Bible, Ancient

---

1. The Septuagint and Other Greek Translations

a) Origin and Name. The name "Septuagint" (Latin, *septuaginta,* "seventy," and for that reason often rendered by the shorthand "LXX"), originates in the legendary meeting of 70 (or 72) independent translators. The term appears as early as the second century A.D. and refers to the earliest Greek translation of the Old Testament and, more precisely, of the Pentateuch. Only later did the term come to denote the Greek translation of the entire Hebrew scripture, as well as the deuterocanonical books* written originally in Greek. Ben Sira (Ecclesiasticus) was included in this category until manuscripts of the book in Hebrew were found at the Cairo Geniza and at Qumran.

According to the "Letter of Aristeas" (probably second century B.C.), the Greek translation of the Pentateuch was due to the request of Philadelphos Ptolomeus (Ptolemy II, reigned 285–246 B.C.) for a copy of the Law* to be placed in the library at Alexandria; according to tradition, the team of 70 translators worked in seclusion on the island of Pharos. It is much more likely, in fact, that the Septuagint represents translations by the Jews in Egypt for their own use, perhaps as early as the end of the third century B.C.

b) The Translation. The Septuagint indicates a Hebrew (or in some cases Aramaic) text that differs from the Masoretic text. Each book or group of books has been translated somewhat differently, and the vocabulary represents Jewish philosophical thinking of the second and first centuries B.C.. Since the Septuagint is the form of the Old Testament most frequently quoted in the New Testament, its vocabulary helped to shape the Christian theology* of the first centuries.

c) Revisions of the Septuagint. The Greek text was apparently revised several times, in the first century B.C.

and in the first century A.D., with further revisions or re-translations from the Hebrew text during the second century, as well as Lucian's revision in the fourth century. In the case of 1 and 2 Samuel, and 1 and 2 Kings, Lucian's recension was based on a pre-Masoretic Hebrew text that bears certain similarities to texts of 1 and 2 Samuel from Qumran, and to citations in Flavius Josephus and Justin. In addition, this recension bears occasional resemblance to the *Vetus latina* (Old Latin) translation of the second century A.D.. All this suggests that Lucian's text was based on a much earlier revision, possibly from as early as the first century B.C.

The Greek text of the Minor Prophets* contained in a scroll from the Dead Sea (c. 132 A.D.) was clearly brought closer to the Masoretic text. According to Barthélemy (1963), this text was part of a larger recension of almost all of the Old Testament. Calling this the "*kaige* recension" (based on translating the Hebrew *gam* by the Greek *kai ge*), or R recension, Barthélemy found evidence of this in some sections of the texts of Samuel and Kings in the Codex Vaticanus, as well as in Lamentations, the Song of Songs, Ruth, Judges, Theodotus's recension of Daniel, parts of Job and Jeremiah, and the Psalms in the fifth column of Origen*'s *Hexapla* (1963). This same first-century recension seems to be at the basis of a later translation attributed to Theodotus.

d) Other Greek Translations. In the second century, some rabbis became dissatisfied with the Septuagint, since it had been taken over by the Christians as the text of their scriptures. This prompted attempts to re-translate the Old Testament from the Masoretic text. In about 130, Aquila (probably to be identified with Onkelos) produced a slavishly literal translation, of which only fragments are in existence today. However, the Greek version of Ecclesiastes incorporated into the Septuagint has been attributed to Aquila (Barthélemy 1963). The best source for Aquila's translation is what remains in the *Hexapla,* whose third column contained Aquila's text.

During the same century, Symmachus produced another translation. As with Aquila, he followed the Hebrew text closely, but he was more careful to write in a good Greek style. As with Aquila, the best source for this translation is the little that remains of it in the fourth column of the *Hexapla.*

Aquila's translation was used by communities of Hellenized Jews until the Middle Ages. In 553, Justinian's *Novella* 146 *(Peri Hebraion)* officially authorized its use in the liturgy* of synagogues.

2. The **Vetus Latina**

a) Origin. Most scholars agree that the *Vetus latina* ("Old Latin") translation originated in northern Africa. Tertullian* states that in his time (c. 160–c. 225) the language of the churches* in Africa was Latin. This is confirmed by Cyprian* and, later, by Augustine*. There may have been a pre-Christian Old Latin translation of the Old Testament current in Africa, but this has been categorically denied (J. Gribomont, "Latin Versions," *IDB Supp.*). Latin was also the language of the churches in northern Italy, Spain, and Gaul. Novatian (first half of the third century) cites a text that is not African, which suggests a rather rapid multiplication of Latin translations, corresponding to the rapid expansion of Christianity in Europe. These texts, which today are called "European," correspond to what Augustine called the *Itala,* a name that, until recently, was used to refer to the Old Latin translations in general. The variety of locations accounts for the various forms in which the *Vetus latina* is found in the manuscripts today.

b) Nature and Importance. The *Vetus latina* is a translation from the Greek of both the Old and the New Testaments. For the Old Testament, it is a valuable witness to what the Greek text was before it underwent Origen's recension. For the New Testament, the underlying Greek text represents the western tradition. As with the Greek, the Latin text must be studied individually for each book, since no pandect (manuscript containing the entire Bible) dating from before the seventh century has been found. The *Vetus latina* is not merely of interest in relation to textual criticism: it has the same importance in relation to the theological language* of the earliest Latin theologians that the Septuagint has in relation to that of Christian authors who wrote in Greek.

3. The **Vulgate**

a) Jerome (c. 347–419). Jerome, who had very quickly come into contact with both secular and Chris-

tian literature, traveled around the Empire and mixed as much in Roman aristocratic circles (as witness his correspondence with Marcella, Paula, and her daughter Eustochium) as with the monastic communities of Syria, Egypt, and Palestine. Endowed with knowledge of Hebrew and Greek—he was a *vir trilinguis,* "a trilingual man"—and benefiting from his acquaintance with Jewish masters, he became an advocate of *hebraïca veritas,* "the Jewish truth," which explains his preference for the translations of Aquila, Symmachus, and Theodotus. Although he quarreled and broke with his friend Rufinus of Aquileia, who had translated Origen's writings, Jerome shared Rufinus's admiration for the Alexandrian master. Jerome's exegetical labors also became the occasion for an exchange of letters with Augustine.

b) In 383, Pope Damasus entrusted the revision of the Latin text of the gospels* to Jerome. Jerome went on to revise the Psalms* according to the Greek, creating what is known as the "Roman Psalter." After his arrival in Palestine, he undertook a revision of the Old Testament based on the Greek text of the *Hexapla:* he had access to a copy of Origen's text in Caesarea. His Psalter from this time is known as the "Gallican Psalter" because it was adopted for liturgical use in Gaul during Charlemagne's reign. Around 390, Jerome abandoned this project and set about a fresh translation of the Old Testament based on the Hebrew text. In 391, he published his translations of the prophets; this was followed, some time before 395, by Samuel and Kings, the Psalter *juxta Hebraeos* ("according to the Jews"), Job, and Ezra and Nehemiah. Two years later, 1 and 2 Chronicles appeared, and in 398 the "books of Solomon": Ecclesiastes, Proverbs, and the Song of Songs. Finally, in 405 his translation of the Octateuch (Genesis to Ruth) appeared, along with Esther. In the meantime, Jerome had also translated Tobit and Judith from the Aramaic. The remaining books (Wisdom, Ecclesiasticus, 1 and 2 Maccabees, and Baruch) were incorporated into the Vulgate in the text of the *Vetus latina,* since Jerome never translated or revised these "deuterocanonical" texts.

It is still debated today to what extent Jerome revised or translated the New Testament beyond the gospels. Many scholars think that the translations of Acts, the Epistles, and Revelation are to be attributed to Pelagius or his circle, or to Rufinus the Syrian, one of Jerome's followers. In the New Testament, the Vulgate clearly differs from the *Vetus latina.*

The text of the Vulgate had authority* in the Latin church (Decr. 1–2 of the fourth session of the Council of Trent*) until the publication of the "Neo-Vulgate" in 1979 (Const. apost. *Scripturarum thesaurus* of 25

April 1979, *AAS* 71 1979, 557–59). It was therefore crucially important for Catholic liturgy and theology.

4. Syriac Translations

a) Old Testament. Nothing is known for certain concerning the translation of the Bible into Syriac, commonly known as the *Peshitta.* It is suggested that it dates from the third century, but it is not clear whether the translators were Jews or Christians. If they were Christians, the translation may have been done in Edessa or Adiabene. In any event, the first mention is found in Aphraate in the fourth century. The *Peshitta* was translated from the Hebrew in a form close to or even the same as the Masoretic text. The publication of a critical edition of the Old Testament is under way in Leyden.

b) New Testament. The New Testament was translated into Syriac at least five times during the first six centuries of the Christian era. It is disputed whether the first effort was Tatian's, in his *Diatessoron* (a fusion of the four gospels into one, c. 170) or the Old Syriac version (extant today in two manuscripts from the fifth century). The *Peshitta* of the New Testament became the official translation in Edessa in the fifth century, but it was already the common text of the churches that used Syriac, the Nestorians and the Jacobites, before their successive separations at the Councils of Ephesus* and Chalcedon*. Its text fluctuates between agreement with the Byzantine text and with the western text.

5. Targums

According to Nehemiah 8:8, as early as the time of the return from the exile there was a need for an Aramaic translation of the scriptures from the Hebrew, which was no longer spoken currently by the people. The "targums" are translations intended for the reading of the scriptures in the synagogues.

There are targums of all the books of the Hebrew scriptures except Daniel, Ezra, and Nehemiah. Fragments of what are probably targums of Job and Leviticus have been found at Qumran. For the Torah, the *Targum Yerushalmi* (fragment TJ2) is the oldest; it is based on oral traditions in Galilee from the second century A.D. onward. It was known only in fragments until A. Diez Macho found a complete manuscript in the Vatican Library (1956). The *Targum Onkelos,* close to the Hebrew text, was given an official status in the third century A.D. (*Targum of Babylon*). It may be of Palestinian origin. The *Targum Yerushalmi* I (*Pseudo-Jonathan*) is a late composition, dating from the late Middle Ages. As for the Prophets, the *Targum Jonathan* contains Joshua, Judges, 1 and 2 Samuel, 1 and 2 Kings, Isaiah, Jeremiah, Ezekiel, and the 12 "minor prophets." It is written in the same Aramaic dialect as the *Targum Onkelos* and generally follows the Hebrew text closely. The "Megillot" targums include the Song of Songs, Ruth, Lamentations, Ecclesiastes, and Esther, and the "Writings" targums include Psalms, Job, Proverbs, and Chronicles.

The targums constitute a reflection of what Judaism* was in the early centuries of the Christian era, as well as an indication of how the Scriptures were understood. They also clarify some of the formulations and beliefs in the New Testament.

● a) Sources
The Old Testament in Greek, Ed. A.E. Brooke, N. McLean, Cambridge, 1906–40.
Septuaginta: Vetus Testamentum Graecum, Göttingen, 1922–.
Septuaginta, 2 vols., Ed. A. Rahlfs, Stuttgart, 1935.
La Bible d'Alexandrie (French trans. Ed. M. Harl) 1. *La Genèse,* 1986; 2. *L'Exode,* 1989; 3. *Le Lévitique,* 1988; 4. *Les Nombres,* 1994; 5. *Le Deutéronome,* 1992.
Lettre d'Aristée à Philocrate, SC 89.

b) Secondary Literature
H. B. Swete, R. R. Otley (1914), *An Introduction to the Old Testament in Greek,* 2nd Ed., Cambridge.
H. St. J. Thackeray (1921), *The Septuagint and Jewish Worship,* London.
P. Kahle (1947), *The Cairo Geniza,* London.
D. Barthélemy (1953), "Redécouverte d'un chaînon manquant de l'histoire de la LXX," *RB* 60, 18–29; (1963), *Les devanciers d'Aquila,* Leyden.
S. Jellicoe (1968), *The Septuagint and Modern Study,* Oxford.
E. Tov (1981), *The Text-critical Use of the Septuagint in Biblical Research,* Jerusalem.
P. M. Bogaert (1985), "Les études sur la Septante: Bilan et perspectives", *RTL* 16, 174–200.
M. Harl, G. Dorival, O. Munnich (1988), *La Bible grecque des Septante: Du judaïsme hellénistique au christianisme ancien,* Paris.
P. M. Bogaert, B. Botte (1993), "Septante et versions grecques," *DBS,* fasc. 68, Paris, col. 536–691.
M. Hengel and A.M. Schwemer (Eds.) (1994), *Die Septuaginta zwischen Judentum und Christentum,* Tübingen.

2. a) Sources
Bibliorum sacrorum latinae versiones antiquae, Ed. P. Sabatier, Reims, 1739–43; Paris, 1751.
Vetus latina: Die Reste der altlateinischen Bibel, ed. B. Fischer, Freiburg, 1949–.
La Vetus latina *hispana,* ed. T. Ayuso Marazuela, 1953.
Itala, *das Neue Testament in altlateinischer Überlieferung nach den Handschriften,* ed. A. Jülicher, 1938.

b) Secondary Literature
F. C. Burkitt (1896), *The Old Latin and the* Itala, Cambridge.
H. von Soden (1909), *Das lateinische Neue Testament in Afrika zur Zeit Cyprianus.*
B. Fischer, H. Frede, M. Thiele (1972), *Die alten Übersetzungen des Neuen Testaments.*
C. Pietri (1985), *Le monde latin antique et la Bible,* Paris.

3. a) Sources

Biblia sacra iuxta vulgatam versionem, 2 vols., Ed. R. Weber et al., Stuttgart, 1969.

OT only: *Biblia sacra iuxta latinam vulgatam versionem* (Ed. abbaye de Saint-Jérôme), Rome, 1926–94.

NT: *Novum Testamentum Domini nostri Iesu Christi latine secundum editionem S. Hieronymi,* Ed. J. Wordsworth, H.J. White, H.F.D. Sparks, Oxford, 1889–1954.

b) Secondary Literature

S. Berger (1893), *Histoire de la Vulgate pendant les premiers siècles du Moyen Age,* Paris.

H. Quentin (1922), *Mémoire sur l'établissement du texte de la Vulgate,* part 1: *Octateuque,* Rome and Paris.

F. Stummer (1928), *Einführung in die lateinische Bibel,* Paderborn.

R. Weber (1953), *Le psautier romain et les autres anciens psautiers latins,* Rome.

B. Fischer (1963), "Bibelausgaben des frühen Mittelalters", *Settimane di studio del centro italiano di studi sull'alto medioevo* X, 519–600.

B. Fischer (1965), "Bibeltext und Bibelreform unter Karl dem Großen," in *Karl der Große, Lebenswerk und Nachleben II: Das geistige Leben* (Ed. B. Bischoff), Düsseldorf, 156–216.

B. Fischer (1972), "Die Alkuin-Bibeln," in *Die Bibel von Moutiers-Grandval,* Bern, 49–98.

T. Stramare (Ed.) (1987), *La Bibbia "Vulgata" dalle origini ai nostri giorni,* Vatican City.

P. M. Bogaert (1988), "La Bible latine des origines au MA," *RTL* 19, 137–59 and 276–314.

4. a) Sources

Vetus Testamentum Syriace, *The Old Testament in Syriac According to the* Peshitta *Version,* Leyden, 1966–.

Quatuor Evangeliorum Syriace, recensionis antiquissimae, atque in Occidente adhuc ignotae quod superest, Ed. W. Cureton, London, 1848.

Remains of a Very Ancient Recension of the Four Gospels in Syriac, ed. W. Cureton, London, 1958.

Evangelion da-Mepharreshe; the Curetonian Syriac Gospels, New Ed., 2 vols., Ed. F. C. Burkitt, Cambridge, 1904.

The Old Syriac Gospels, or Evangelion da-Mepharreshe, Ed. A. S. Lewis, London, 1910.

b) Secondary Literature

B. M. Metzger (1977), *The Early Versions of the New Testament: Their Origin, Transmission, and Limitations,* Oxford.

P. B. Dirksen (1989), *An Annotated Bibliography of the* Peshitta *of the Old Testament,* Leyden.

P. B. Dirksen (1993), *La* Peshitta *dell'Antico Testamento,* Brescia.

5)

R. Bloch (1955), "Note méthodologique pour l'étude de la littérature rabbinique," *RSR* 43, 194–227.

R. Le Déaut (1963), *La nuit pascale,* Rome (2nd Ed. 1975).

R. Le Déaut (1965), *Liturgie juive et Nouveau Testament,* Rome.

R. Le Déaut (1966), *Introduction à la littérature targumique,* Rome.

J. Potin (1971), *La fête juive de la Pentecôte,* Paris.

A. Diez Macho (1973), "Le Targum palestinien," *RevSR* 47, 169–231.

P. Grelot (1986), *Les Targoums: textes choisis,* Paris.

STEPHEN PISANO

See also **Bible; Canon of Scriptures; Exegesis; Fathers of the Church; Gospels; Hellenization; Intertestament; Origen**

Treasure of the Church. *See* Indulgences

Trent, Council of
1545–1563

Starting with the early years of the Reformation, some theologians who had remained faithful to the Church of Rome* provided their viewpoint, supported by relevant arguments, in reply to the assaults of the Protestant reformers; this was done mainly in Paris, Köln, and Louvain. There was, however, one single manner to reaffirm solemnly the dogmas* that were being challenged: only the meeting of an ecumenical council* could defend those dogmas and could suggest a larger vision of the Church's reform, as had been highly proclaimed by Lateran* V. There had not been, however, sufficient political and religious will to bring to fruition the wish proclaimed by Lateran V; that is why an ecumenical council, that is, a general one, appeared to be in order.

1. The Historical Framework

The council meeting that eventually became the Council of Trent was expected and announced for decades; it was delayed by political and ecclesiological disagreements, and it was finally convened in the northern Italian city of Trento (Trent), an imperial city where many people spoke both German and Italian—the choice of venue was a compromise to satisfy both the emperor's and the pope*'s demands. The council brought about a reform in depth of the Catholic Church. It also provided the Church with a vision that remained, roughly speaking, valid until Vatican* II. It also supplied, albeit not exclusively, a doctrinal basis that served as the framework within which Catholicism* was to model its thinking and its action during four centuries.

It is essential to recall the chronology of the council's events, which stretched over almost twenty years.

a) The Early Period: 1545–47. The council was convened by Pope Paul III; its members assembled, in a modest fashion, for the first time on 13 December 1545; 34 Fathers had voting privileges. There were eight meetings in all at Trent, then two more in Bologna, after the transfer there (25 March 1547) of a majority of the Fathers. Their departure from Trent was motivated by a plague epidemic, but it was also due to the papal desire to resist the strong pressures coming from the emperor.

b) Second Period: 1551–52. At the end of the year 1550, pope Julius III reconvened the council; it opened on 1 May 1551 at Trent. Being in the course of a political conflict with the pope, King Henry II of France did not allow the French bishops* to attend. There were six sessions during that second stage of the council. One of the major events, although it had no practical impact, was the presence of some Protestant delegations, in particular from Württemberg and from some imperial cities; they were able to present their confessions of faith* (*See* creed*). The council was suspended "for two years" on 28 April 1552, on account of the threats coming from the Protestant armies.

In fact, ten years passed before the council could

meet again. The sudden death of Pope Marcellus II Cervini, then in 1555 the election of Paul IV Carafa, who was convinced that the reform of the Church had to be preceded by those of the Curia and of the diocese of Rome, and finally the abdication of Emperor Charles V in 1558, had prevented the council's resumption. When peace in Europe was re-established with the treaty of Cateau-Cambrésis in April 1559, Pius IV of Medici, elected pope at the end of that same year and assisted by his nephew, Cardinal Charles Borromeo, convened the council to pursue the work that had been started. Emperor Ferdinand and the king of France, Charles IX, would have preferred a fresh start based on new foundations; their preference was motivated by the dogmatic decrees already voted on, which they found unacceptable for their Protestant subjects. Up to that point, the first two periods had been most strongly influenced by the emperor, but from then on, the pope was determined to assume responsibility for the council, in particular the task of carrying it to fruition.

c) Third Period: 1562–63. Opening again on January 18, 1562, the council of Trent had nine more sessions, thus bringing the total to 25. Following the failure of the colloquium of Poissy, then the violence of the opening encounters of France's religious wars* (April 1562), the French bishops arrived on November 13, 1562, led by Cardinal de Lorraine. The number of conciliar Fathers assembled in session reached its maximum on 11 November 1563, with 232 voting members out of an episcopate estimated to be approximately 700 in total; the maximum number of members present at the two earlier periods had reached only 71.

On 4 December 1563, the Council of Trent came to a close with the approval of all the texts that had been previously accepted by vote. These measures entrusted the pope with numerous tasks, such as the preparation of a catechism and the revision of the instruments of a Catholic reform, breviary, missal, and index of forbidden books.

The theological work had been carried out by experts, for the most part members of religious orders. Among these, the early Jesuits, the companions of Ignatius of Loyola, distinguished themselves. They held their meetings in commissions that were open to the Fathers who wished to attend. As for the bishops, they would meet in "general congregations," or in smaller groups, before the ultimate step of text ratification in solemn "sessions." The work done by the theologians was considerable, especially during the quiescent periods such as 1547–48 and 1553, during which they accomplished work that became preparatory tools for the ensuing period of meetings.

2. The Doctrinal Work

The following question was raised from the outset (it became a doctrinal stake per se, or at least an ecclesiological one): should dogmatic matters be dealt with first, or should priority be given to reforms? The pope could hardly have accepted giving priority to reform, which would have been interpreted as a tacit acceptance of the conciliarist point of view according to which the council could act as an apparatus of the government* of the Church rather than limit itself to the defense and affirmation of the faith; the lack of accepted solution to the ecclesiological problem regarding the relations between pope and council had an impact on the whole sequence of events at Trent. Realizing that doctrine and reform were fundamentally linked, the council decided on 22 January 1546 that they should not be dissociated, but that the council's work should always start with the theological foundation.

a) *Revelation.* In their wish to be methodical, the legates decided first to examine the matter of revelation*, to make it "the foundation of what was to be discussed subsequently." The first decree (*Sacrosancta, DCO* 1350–1355), dated 8 April 1546, is constructed in two parts. The second is simply borrowed from the decree of 1442 regarding the Jacobites, and is a list of biblical books* making up the canon* of Scriptures that had been passed down. The first part of the text lists the manners through which the "gospel" was passed down, a term deliberately generic. It distinguishes three steps: the promise* announced by the prophets*, the promulgation coming from the very mouth of Christ*, and finally the preaching* done by the apostles*. "The gospel is the source of every salutary truth and every moral rule." Truth* and rule *(disciplina)*—meaning dogma and moral standards—are contained in the Scriptures, and they are also present in the traditions that can be called "apostolic." These Scriptures and traditions have been passed down and been revered "with the same feeling of piety and respect."

The council of Trent is therefore not opposed to Scriptures and tradition*. On 12 February 1546, cardinal Cervini had proposed formulations that made such an opposition possible: divine revelation is "transmitted partly by the Church *(partim)* through the Scriptures which are present in the Old and in the New Testaments and partly *(partim)* by mere tradition passed down from hand to hand" *(CT* V, 7–8). The Fathers refused that proposal (though the refusal was probably not seen by the compilers as the determining factor it was later said to be; *see* J. Ratzinger, "Ein Versuch zur Frage des Traditionsbegriffs," in Rahner-

Ratzinger, *Offenbarung und Überlieferung,* Freiburg, 1965).

In any case, the position of the council is not what the church later adopted when it came to establish the theory of the "two sources" of revelation. It is clear as well that the council did not want to describe, or even list, the ecclesiastical traditions that were, nonetheless, mentioned by the summatory Tridentine profession of faith of Pius IV in 1564. The council of Trent wanted to reject the Protestant insistence on *sola Scriptura* as the source of authority by emphasizing the common origin of the whole revelation, which is God* himself, and it invited the Church to "preserve the purity of the gospel."

b) *Original Sin.* Once the foundation of revelation had been reasserted, the council of Trent tackled the dogma of the original sin*, the interpretation of which had so many repercussions on the debates with the reformers. That was the object of the decree of 17 June 1546, *Ut fides nostra (DCO* 1354–1359), and its anathemas. The decree recalled, against the Pelagians, that the original sin of Man is not the imitation of Adam*'s sin by everyone, but its hereditary consequence *(propagatio),* and as a result it cannot be overcome by human strength alone. However, the decree clarified, against the Lutherans, that this sin is not to be confused with concupiscence, which is only an inclination toward sin. Concupiscence subsists, even after baptism*, as a "source" of sin *(fomites),* and the Fathers acknowledge that it is even sometimes called "sin" by Paul, but divine grace* allows the believer to overcome it in a real fight *(ad agonem).* Trent did not pronounce itself on the nature of original sin, but it did reassert its existence according to the beliefs of tradition: the council thus avoided ratifying the opinions of any school of thought and did not decide who was to be favored, whether it be Thomists or Augustinians. Having opted against two extreme doctrines, Trent then devoted a canon to a defense of the baptism of infants (against the Anabaptist* thesis that only a baptism consciously sought by its recipient was spiritually effective), by following the common interpretation of Romans 5:12, "All have sinned in Adam." The proposal to include a paragraph on the Immaculate Conception of the Virgin Mary* was found to be inopportune and was not passed (14 June 1546).

Taken as a whole, *Ut fides nostra* was christological in essence because each canon repeated the role of grace and of the merits of Christ "who reconciled us with God through his blood." It was thus an anticipation of the decisive wording of the decree on justification*, which began to be debated immediately after the vote on *Ut fides nostra.*

c) *Justification.* The decree *Cum hoc tempore* was adopted during the 6th session, on 13 January 1547 (*DCO* 1366–87). Divided into 16 chapters, it is followed by 33 canons. After implicitly rejecting the first draft, (calling it a "sermon rather than a decree"), the legate Cervini asked Seripando, general of the Augustinians, for a new wording. Seripando had participated in 1541 in the interdenominational colloquium of Ratisbon (Regensburg), where an agreed position on justification was found between Catholic and Protestant theologians. Seripando thus introduced in his text a chapter on the double justice*, which had, as a matter of fact, been the very foundation of the Ratisbon accord. Cervini eliminated that chapter and he even took the opposite position in a second draft. Seripando, however, vigorously defended his own thesis of a distinction between imputed or extrinsic justice, which was Luther*'s opinion, and an inherent justice, identical to sanctifying grace, to which Seripando linked the doing of good works* (*CT* II, 431, 23–27). The majority of Fathers refused that division, which meant an obligation to resort to a new application of the merits of Christ (the sanctifying grace brings in fact the internal justice of man in an intimate relationship with that of Christ), whose sole cause is the justice of God. The discussion that ensued did not re-establish, however, the double justice, but at least its condemnation was not requested. The Fathers finally adopted the fifth draft of the text. From the starting points of reasserting the original sin and of bearing in mind the reality of free will—which is not completely wiped out, but whose strength is weakened and turned aside *(attenuatum et inclinatum)*—Trent spoke of a new birth, brought about by the "regenerative bathing" of baptism, thanks to which redemption and remission of sins are granted.

The description of the process of justification adopted by the council was as follows. It is brought about by the conjunction of two factors: grace, and man's free will *(libera voluntas).* With Evangelical preaching, man starts preparing for this new life that he will get through baptism, and through baptism he receives a justification that "is not mere remission of sins but also sanctification and renovation of internal man through the voluntary reception of grace and gifts." These gifts are received through the mediation of Jesus Christ in whom man is present *(cui inseritur);* these are faith, hope*, and charity (love*). Under a language of rather technical theology, Trent proposed therefore a real Christian anthropology*. The process being described pursues its course by asserting that the certainty of justification is never actually given to man ("unlike what the heretics conceitedly trust"); but it also asserts that this does not at all prevent increased

justice through observance of the commandments (Decalogue*) and perseverance. A few lines finally remind the theologians of the soberness to be observed regarding predestination*. Chapter 16 of the decree develops a theology of merit. "Our personal justice…is said to be ours because it is inherent in us, it justifies us, and it is also the justice of God because it is God who injects us with the merit of Christ." As Franco Buzzi has put it (1995): "Against the Pelagians, the council wanted to remind us that our justice is that of Christ; and against the Protestants, that the justice of Christ has become ours."

As with its formulation on original sin, the council aimed here to reinforce the major features of a Catholic theology of grace without having to engage in Scholastic disputes (even if chapter 7 uses the vocabulary of causes).

d) *Sacramental Doctrine.* On 3 March 1547 (7th session), Trent laid the first foundations of its sacramental doctrine (*DCO* 1392–95) before dealing with baptism and confirmation*—showing remarkable theological coherence given the political difficulties of the situation in which the debates were conducted; these were particularly difficult where the councilors were pursuing discussions on points of doctrine in parallel with the explorations of the Reformers. Dealing with the sacraments* in general, Trent had to ensure theological continuity with their preceding decrees: "In order to crown the salutary doctrine on justification, it seemed to be in order to deal with the sacraments…it is through them that all true justice begins, that it grows after having started, that it can be repaired when it has been lost."

In a first step, the council reasserted the Catholic doctrine in reply to the negations of the Protestants, who, since Luther, had been asserting that there were not seven sacraments, nor had they been instituted by Christ. In very sober canons, Trent reasserted the septenary by the authority of its acceptance in tradition without, as modern theologians do, entering into the history of its formation. Without making any allusion to the distinction observed in medieval thought between "mediate" and "immediate" institutions, the council declared that the sacraments were instituted by the Lord himself. While the Protestants did not believe that baptism, confirmation, and ordination* imprinted any "character" (*see* sacrament section 5) d), Trent stressed the "spiritual and indelible mark" they leave, and it used, in canon 8, the famous expression *ex opere operato,* the meaning of which has already been given by canon 6: sacraments convey the grace they signify to those who do not make obstacle to them. Canon 12 proposed an illustration of that: a minister who is in a state of mortal sin, but who observes what is essential in the conferment of a sacrament, does indeed confer it validly. The principles of the sacramental doctrine are then brought into play for each of the sacraments; in the following paragraphs, baptism and the Eucharist* will be discussed.

Trent did not propose strictly speaking any dogmatic account on baptism. In a new series of canons, it went straight to what is essential: "if somebody says that baptism is free, meaning that it is not necessary to salvation*, it is a case for anathema" (canon 5). Canon 13 stated its opposition to the Anabaptists by asserting that young children, even though they are incapable of a personal act of faith, are part of the body of believers, on account of their baptism; in other words, it makes them part of the Church. Trent devoted only three canons to confirmation, stressing that it is a true sacrament, and not merely a catechetic profession at the time of adolescence. The minister who may administer it is "ordinarily" a bishop; this qualification was included so as not to condemn the Greek Orthodox custom of accepting the administering of this sacrament by priests.

The theology of the Eucharist can be fairly said to have been a constant theme during the three periods of the council's deliberations. It was first introduced in 1547—mainly among the theologians—and they returned to the subject in 1551. On 10 October 1551, Trent decided to hold off discussion of some points (reception of the Eucharist and small children's receipt of communion) until the arrival of the Protestant delegation. These points were taken up again in 1562, when Trent specified that reception of the bread "is sufficient for salvation" and that receiving communion is not a "necessity" for small children.

In the 13th session, which began on 11 October 1551, Trent voted to adopt a lengthy text with 11 canons (*DCO* 1410–21), which recalled that the Eucharist—a sacrament so contested and controversial—was in fact established by the Lord precisely "because he wanted it to be a symbol of the unity* and the charity binding Christians to each other." At the end of the text, in an appeal "from the depths of God's mercy*" (Lk 1:78), the council begged Christians to unite around that symbol of concord. Nevertheless, they must agree on a sole interpretation: "After the consecration of the bread and the wine, our Lord Jesus Christ, true God and true man, is really present, truly and in substance under the appearance of these realities felt by the senses." The text rejected the ubiquitarian position of Luther (who had argued that the body of Christ cannot be present in the Eucharist since a body cannot be in many places at once; only in the sense that Christ, as God, is everywhere—ubiqui-

tous—can he be said to be present). For Trent, however, "there is no contradiction" between Christ being seated at the right hand of the Father* while his body is simultaneously present in the Eucharist. Chapter 2 described in sober terms the riches of the sacrament (memorial, nourishment, remedy, guarantee of our future glory*, sign of unity).

Chapter 4 declared that the change of substance in the Eucharist receives "justly and exactly [*convenienter et proprie*]" the name of transubstantiation in the Catholic Church. This is why it must be said that Christ, present in the Eucharist, is being eaten "sacramentally and really [*sacramentaliter ac realiter*]" as well as spiritually (canon 8). Furthermore, the council recalled that the cult* of the Blessed Sacrament legitimately offers to God the cult of latria (supreme worship) which is owed to him.

As far as the possibility of a "concession to the laity" in certain countries was concerned, it was left up to the pope to decide. This text, which the council adopted on 15 July 1562, also reasserted that the Church legitimately has the power to decide and to organize the administration of the sacraments, their "substance being safe" as it is.

There was still left to reassert the sacrificial character of the Mass; it became the object of the 22nd session's text, on 17 September 1562 (*DCO* 1488–97). The theological difficulty raised by the Protestant position was twofold: it was necessary to clarify the connection between mass and the Lord's Supper by maintaining that there is a unique sacrifice and by establishing simultaneously a connection between the Lord's Supper and the cross. Did Christ offer himself in sacrifice* on Maundy Thursday? Having discussed this matter, the Fathers came round to the following position in a dense passage: "On the night he was handed over, the Lord wanted to leave to the Church, his beloved spouse, a visible sacrifice...in which would be shown the bloody offering that was about to be performed one single time on the cross, a sacrifice whose memory would last till the end of time, and whose salutary properties would be applied to the redemption of our daily sins" (chapter 1).

From its theology regarding baptism and the Eucharist, the council went on to deduce somehow its teaching on penance*, on ordination, and on extreme unction. As for marriage* (*Tametsi* decree), Trent worried a great deal about clandestine marriages and about the problem adultery posed for the principle of the indissolubility of marriage (Mt 19:9). And although it declared that this sacrament was instituted by Christ and that it conferred grace, Trent did not solve either the question of matter and form or that of the minister.

The theology of Trent is thus marked by two characteristics: the concern to give a clear answer to the Protestant Reformers, which was an ever-present background to the discussions; and a consistently cautious approach to all fundamental questions of theology. This prudent position was undoubtedly the cause of the debates on grace which went on to trouble the Church during the subsequent two centuries, but it also allowed the teaching of the council to become a doctrinal reference for the Church regarding a real Catholic reform.

• *Concilium Tridentinum: Diariorum, actorum, epistolarum, tractatuum nova collectio* (CT) (1901–80), Freiburg.
COD, 657–799 (*DCO* II/2, 1339–1624).
◆ H. Jedin (1951–1975), *Geschichte des Konzils von Trient*, Freiburg, 3 vols.
G. Dumeige (Ed.) (1975 and 1981), *HCO* 10 and 11.
A. Duval (1985), *Des sacrements au concile de Trente*, Paris.
F. Buzzi (1995), *Il Concilio di Trento (1545–1563)*, Milan.

GUY BEDOUELLE

See also **Baptism; Conciliarism; Eucharist; Justification; Lateran V; Pope; Sin, Original; Protestantism; Revelation; Sacrament**

Trinity

A. Theological History

The Trinity is the mystery* of a single God* in three persons*—the Father*, the Son, and the Holy* Spirit—recognized as distinct within the unity of a single nature, essence, or substance (*symbole Quicumque,* DS 75; Lateran* IV, DS 800; Dumeige, 9 and 29). Two errors should be avoided from the point of view of this paradoxical "monotheism*." The first error is tritheism*, which means to privilege the number and represent three distinct consciousnesses in God, three centers of activity, three concrete beings (the "three little figurines" mocked by Calvin). The second error is modalism*, which is seeing nothing more in the Father, the Son, and the Holy Spirit than three ways in which God presents himself to us. The Trinitarian mystery can be known only by revelation*. It distinguishes Christianity from the two great monotheistic religions, Judaism* and Islam. It is the source of the notion of the person, distinguished from that of nature. It leads to the idea that being* (or beyond being) in its highest form is gift, sharing, relation, love*. The Trinity is a fundamental article of faith* for every Christian.

The confession of the Trinity is a major paradox, not only because it holds that God is simultaneously "one" and "three," but because the second of these three persons—Christ*—is at the same time a man. This introduces a new element of alterity in God, all the more so in that this man is inseparable from his "body," which is the Church*.

A further paradox: the theologian claims that the dogma* of the Trinity is found in Scripture; this is not obvious. And in fact the idea of the Trinity, in its present form, took hold gradually, and at the cost of numerous controversies.

1. Scriptural Foundations

a) Old Testament. From the beginning of the Bible*, God appears as a mysterious being who does not exclude in himself a certain plurality, as noticed by the church fathers*: Genesis 1:26 ("Let us make man"), Isaiah 6:3 (Trisagion), theophanies* (identity and nonidentity between the angel* of YHWH and YHWH himself). In the Hellenistic period there arose the personification of Wisdom* (Jb 28; Bar 3:9–4, 4; Wis 1–9; Sir 24; Prv 8) and of the creative or redemptive Word* (Gn 15:1; Am 5:1–18; Ps 32:6, 32:9, 147:18; Wis 28:14–25). The theme of the Word and Wisdom occur in John (Jn 1:1–18) and Paul (1 Cor 1:24 and 1:30), where it is associated with the redemptive cross.

b) New Testament. While suggested in the Old Testament, for the theologian the Trinity is explicitly revealed in the New Testament; but this revelation is indirect, and takes place in the context of a particular approach that consists in a new reading of everything in the light of Christ's resurrection*. Pentecost (Acts 2), where Luke places the first official proclamation of this resurrection (paschal kerygma), already takes on a Trinitarian dimension. Other narratives* also feature the Father, the Son, and the Holy Spirit: the annunciation to Mary* (Lk 1:35); the baptism* of Christ in the Jordan (Mt 3:13–17); the words of Christ addressed to God as his Father, with the occasional mention of the Holy Spirit; the jubilation of Christ in Luke (Lk 10:21); the farewell speech in John (Jn 14–17).

c) Matthew 28:19. One of the most important texts for the history of the Trinitarian dogma is the baptismal formula in Mt 28:19: "Go therefore and make disciples of all nations, baptizing them in the name of the Father and of the Son and of the Holy Spirit." The three "persons" are coordinated in the formula *(and, and)* placing them on equal footing, but in a definite order, starting with the Father. The triple nomination goes together with a singular expression: "in the name of." Elsewhere the order to baptize is associated with the order to teach and with a gesture of salvation* (baptizing) that will become a sacrament*, in a certain sense reproducing the figure three by a triple interrogation and a triple immersion (*see below*). The surprising nature of the formula inspired doubt in critics, but they could be told in reply that nothing justifies a challenge to the authenticity of the formula (Lebreton 1910; E. Cothenet, *Tr. et Liturgie,* 1984).

d) The First Summaries of the Faith. The New Testament contains an initial series of brief proclamations of the paschal kerygma that amount to professions of faith in a Trinitarian dimension (Sesboüé 1994). A second, enumerative series with Trinitarian content, sometimes includes two terms (1 Cor 8:6; 1 Tm 2:5f., 6:13), sometimes three (1 Cor 12:4ff.; 2 Cor 13:13, Eph 4, 4ff., and, naturally, Mt 28:19). Both series were freely adopted by the first Fathers in formulas that establish them, the kerygmatic sequence being attached to the second article of the Trinitarian formula (Sesboüé, ibid.).

2. The Second Century

a) By the end of the first century, Clement of Rome was using a ternary formula: "Do we not have a single God, a single Christ, a single Spirit of grace that was poured out upon us?" (*Epistle to the Corinthians* 46, 5–6: *SC* 167; *see* Ignatius, *Epistle to the Magnesians* 13, 1: *SC* 10; *see* Justin, *Apologies* I, 48; I, 61: Ed. Wartelle, 1987; *Dialogue with Trypho* 30, 3; 76, 6; 85, 2: Ed. G. Archambault, 1909). Irenaeus*, c. 180, proposed the first developed exposition of Trinitarian faith (*Against Heresies* I, 10, 1–2: *SC* 264) and a "rule of faith" that he explicitly associated with baptism

(*Demonstration of the Apostolic Preaching* 5–7: SC 62 and 406).

b) In its origins the rite of baptism was the usual means whereby faith in the Trinity was transmitted. According to the *Didache* (1st century), baptism should be done by a triple immersion in running water (with reference to the baptism of Christ in the Jordan; *Did.* 7, 1–3: *SC* 248). Triple immersion remained a constant in subsequent centuries. *The Apostolic Tradition* (*SC* 11 b), an early-third-century liturgical document, relates that before each immersion three questions are put to the person being baptized. Three times they reply: "I believe" and three times they are immersed (ibid., 21 = *DS* 10). The content of the questions, grouped in a declarative account, corresponds to the ancient form of the Roman creed (*DS* 11). Thus is manifest the baptismal and Trinitarian structure of the "symbols of faith" confessed in every baptism, including in the East, where triple immersion is most clearly attested.

c) Recourse to Theophanies and the Logos. In the second century, apologists* were asked to explain their faith in the Trinity. Called upon by the Jew Trypho to explain how he could say that Christ is "another God" beside the one God, Justin gave a double reason. Referring to theophanies when God was understood to be manifest, he argued that this God could not be the Father: "No one, no matter how weak his mind, would dare to claim that the author and Father of the universe abandoned the supracelestial regions to appear on a corner of the earth, (*Dial. with Trypho* 59 and 127). Here a philosophical principle tacitly accepted by Trypho himself intervenes (*Dial.* 60): because of his own transcendence, God himself cannot appear. Justin concludes that the God who did appear was none other than the Son, Word (logos) of the Father, his envoy, his angel*. Thus the Son, going back to the Old Testament, is the visible manifestation of the Father, who remains invisible. This is what distinguishes him from the Father. This argument continued to be used until the Council of Nicaea* (Aeby 1958).

Justin's second argument was to admit that there is in God a Logos that, paradoxically, knows two successive states: it exists as immanent word in God for all eternity *(logos endiathetos),* and as word "woven onto" *(logos prophorikos),* as Son at the time of the creation* (Justin, *Dial.* 61; Theophilius of Antioch, A Autolycus II, 10 and II, 22: SC 20). *Logos,* a word borrowed from Greek (perhaps especially Stoic) culture, here acquires a Judeo-Christian content (showing the influence of Philo of Alexandria), with the endlessly invoked reference to Prv 8:22. The Word is understood as a living being, assisting the Father in the work of creation. This theology* belongs to middle-Platonism in so far as it recognizes in God a certain creative power from which the world comes into being, a power that the philosophers identified with the nature of God. But it is more deeply inspired by Christian preaching*, in that the Logos is understood as a personal being, identified with the Christ of the Gospels* (Daniélou 1961). This theology of the two states of the Logos, which was not retained and which Origen would rectify, includes some part of the truth in that it affirms a certain link between the generation of the Word and the "creation," a link whose nature remained to be defined (this would be done by Athanasius of Alexandria in the following century).

d) Trinity and Economy. Irenaeus refused to speculate on the origin of the Son in God. Arguing against the Marcionites and the Gnostics, who teach about the existence of "two Gods," he defended the thesis of the one God, the Father, while nonetheless upholding the existence of the Son and the Holy Spirit, who are like "two hands." To this end he had recourse to the "economies." The word "economy," used either in the plural or singular, designates here and subsequently God's plan with regard to humankind, and the multiform workings out of that plan in the temporal sphere. In the fourth century it would be distinguished from "theology," designating the mystery of God considered in himself.

3. Third Century

a) Adoptionism, Modalism, Subordinationism: The Posing of the Problem. At the beginning of the third century the confession of Christ as God was not self-evident even within the Christian community, which wondered how to reconcile such a notion with the monotheistic "dogma." Two parries, subsequently disavowed, were attempted: 1) adoptionism*: denying that Christ is truly God, considering him a man adopted by God as his son (Ebionites, Artemon, Paul of Samosata). 2) modalism: denying that Christ is really distinct from the Father, considering him simply as a mode of God's being. The Son and the Spirit are but two faces *(prosôpa)* of the one God, two ways for him to enter into relation with the world. This opinion was attributed to Sabellius (Rome, third century). "Sabellianism" subsequently denoted any opinion accused of insufficiently affirming the distinction of persons within the Trinity. In the early third century it was preceded by a primitive form of unitarianism according to which it was the Father himself who, in Jesus, had become incarnate and had suffered (patripatian-

ism). This opinion, held by the Monarchians (defenders of the divine *monarchia: DECA* 2, 1663–64), was not at all Trinitarian because it did not allow for any alterity in God. Third-century theologians were able to safeguard number in God against this and other more developed forms of modalism only at the cost of a subordinationism* for which they would later be reproached: the Son and the Holy Spirit are distinguished in the Father to the extent that they are in some way inferior to him (see Sesboüé 1994 on that non-heretical subordinationism, which is clearly distinguished from Arianism*).

b) The Christian Paradox. Hippolytus (early-third century) believed that God, is "one and yet multiple" *(Contra Haeresin Noeti.* 10). For Tertullian* († c. 225), "God is one (or unique), and yet he is not one (alone)." *(Adversus Praxean* 5, 2). "It is proper to the Judaic faith to believe in one sole God, refusing to add the Son and after the Son the Holy Ghost.... What is the substance of the New Testament if not that henceforth the Father and the Son and the Holy Spirit are believed three to be compared to one only God? God wanted to innovate his Testament so as to be believed unique in a new way: by the Son and the Spirit." (ibid., 31, 1–2).

Adversus Praxean is the first treatise on the Trinity. Tertullian uses the word *trinitas* ten times in a theological sense (out of a total of 15 times; R. Braun, *Deus Christianorum,* 1977). He too distinguishes two phases in the birth of the Word: the exteriorization, which is the *nativitas perfecta (Prax.* 7, 1), and a logically prior phase, in which God, imagining the creation, engenders in his spirit *(ratio)* a word/project *(sermo),* "stirring it in himself" (ibid., 5, 7).

c) Orthodox Ante-Nicene Subordinationism: Origen. Origen* (†254) was the first to affirm the eternal generation of the Son: "There was not a [time] when the Son was not" *(De princ.* I, 2, 9: *SC* 252; IV, 4, 1: *SC* 269). Countering Monarchianism and the first forms of modalism, he used the expression "three hypostases" *(treis hupostaseis: Commentarii in evangelicum Joannis* [*CommJo*] II, §75: *SC* 120) to affirm the existence proper of the Son and the Spirit. Against middle Platonism he maintained that God, because he is love, is not impassible *(Homiliae in Ezechielem* VI, 6: *SC* 352); however, he went along with its assertion that the image is, by definition, inferior to the model *(De principiis* I, 2, 13; see *SC* 253, 53, n. 75) and that he who gives is superior to he who receives (Plotinus, *Treatise* 38, 17, 2–4, 49, 15, 1–7). Another difference: God is absolutely "one and single" *(hen kai aploun),* whereas Christ is and becomes a "multiplicity" *(polla ginetai)* for the salvation of other beings *(geneta)*, of which he is the firstborn *(CommJo.* I, §119). The relation one/multiple is thus admitted into the very heart of the Trinitarian mystery. Whereas Plotinus related this only to the level of the "second hypostasis" (Plotinus himself does not speak of "three hypostases," *see* Aubin 1992), in which only the Spirit *(noûs)* unfolds in a plurality of forms (Plotinus, *Treatise* 38, 17; *see* Hadot, ibid., intr. 32–33 and 42), in such a way that the "One" does not have a connection with the "Spirit" *(noûs)*, in Origen the Father does not go without the Son (see *SC* 279, 13), to the extent that the infinite* *(apeiron)*, the "not-limited" *(aperigraptos)*, does not go without the "limitation" *(perigraphè)*, which is the Son (Daniélou 1961). This theology in which the Son remains inferior to the Father who is "greater than him" *(see* Jn 14:28) would be a problem for the tenants of the Nicaean orthodoxy—but it is fundamentally Christian, both because it preserves the connection between the Father and the Son and because it respects the existence of a connection between the Father and the "creatures" *(geneta)*. Other aspects of his thought make him an interesting witness of ante-Nicene theology, for example his long-suspected effort to achieve a spiritual understanding of the generation of the Son *(Princ.* I, 2, 6: *SC* 252; *Diologus cum Heraclide* 2–4: *SC* 67). By making room for a concept of *donation* in God, Origen's theology (notably his thesis of the *epinoiai* of Christ: *see* J. Wolinski, in *Origeniana Sexta,* Louvain, 1995) perhaps situates us in the heart of the Christian mystery; as opposed to Hellenistic thought, in which the One does not know, and even if it overflows and gives, does not give of itself (Plotinus, *Treatise* 38; J.-L. Chrétien, *ArPh* 43, 1980).

4. The Arian Crisis and the Nicaean Council (325)

a) Heterodox Subordinationism. Arius (Arianism*) followed the lines of Origenist subordinationism, but subjected it to a radical modification. Origen considered the Son inferior to the Father but eternal like him because engendered by him. Arius believed that the Son is inferior to the Father because, as Son, he began to exist. Arius's key affirmation was: "There was [a time] when [the Son] was not" (Thalia, cited by Athanasius, *Orationes contra Arianos* [*Car.*] I, 5; *see* G. Bardy, *Recherches sur Lucien d'Antioche et son école,* 1936). He argued that affirming the eternity of the engendered *(gennètos)* Son is in contradiction with the unanimously accepted affirmation of the unique "unengendered" *(see Urkunden* and 6: Opitz, *Athanasius Werke* III, 1934). Three other theses complete the Arian doctrine. 1) The absolutely immaterial nature of God, which excludes all generation according to sub-

stance, allowing solely for generation/creation by an act of will. 2) The superiority of the "Son" with respect to other creatures; the Son is a "perfect creature, and not like one of the other creatures" *(Creed,* Urk. 6, Opitz III, 13; *see HCO* 1, 253). 3) The cosmological function of that generation/creation: God created the Son so that he could, through him *(see* Jn 1:3), create all the rest *(Thalia According to Athanasius,* Car. I, 5: *see HCO* 1, 254 and Arian fragment cited by Athanasius in *Car.* II, 24). Thus, a three-phase schema is established: at the top, a solitary God who can have no equal; at the bottom, the creature; between the two, an intermediary, inferior to God but superior to the creatures, making a bridge between the two. The paradox of the Christian God as "one and yet not one (alone)" is abandoned in favor of the Greek notion of a God who is *only* one "who does not communicate with humankind" (Irenaeus, *Haer.* III, 24, 2; III, 11, 1: *SC* 211; Augustine, *De Civitate Dei* VIII, 18: Baug 34, with reference to Plato).

b) The Nicaea Council (325) and the Thesis of "God the Father." Against the heresy* of Arius the Nicene Creed declared: "We believe in one God, the almighty Father, creator of (the universe) visible and invisible; and in one Lord Jesus Christ, the Son of God, engendered from the Father *[ek tou patros]*, that is, from the substance of the Father *[toutestin ek tès ousias tou patros]* as only Son, God of *[ek]* God, Light of *[ek]* Light, true God of *[ek]* the true God, engendered and not created *[gennèthenta ou poièthenta]*, consubstantial* with the Father *[homoousion tô patri]*..." (*DS* 125). Contrary to the theses of Harnack (*Lehrbuch der DG* I, 1931, 250) and H. Küng (*see* A. Grillmeier, in J.-R. Armogathe, Ed., *Comment être Chrétien?* 1979), Nicaea did not represent a Hellenization of the evangelical message by the introduction of philosophical elements into the dogma, but a reaction against the influence of philosophy* on Arius's thought, in order to return to Scripture, according to which God is, above all, Father *(see* Athanasius, *CAr.*I, 30 and 34: PG 26, 73 A-B and 81–4). The need to give their true meaning to the words "father" and "son" (an altogether original juxtaposition that is appropriate only for God) motivated a response that combined precision with philosophical appeal: "that is of the substance of the Father" from which it follows that the Son is "true God [born] of *[ek]* the true God, consubstantial with the Father."

c) Homoousion ("consubstantial"). Nonetheless, Nicaea initiated a new era of Christian discourse insofar as the term *homoousion,* foreign to Scripture, encouraged thinkers to conceive the relation between the Father and the Son in itself, independently of the "economy." The word literally means "of the same substance" (*homos* = of the same, common to two; *ousia* = substance or essence). It at least expresses the specific unity of a substance considered in the abstract (*ousia* as "second substance"), which is sufficient to establish, with a hint of tritheism, the equality of the Son with the Father. It can also mean the numerical unity of a substance considered concretely (*ousia* as "primary substance"). This is the meaning given to it in contemporary theology, in liaison with the reciprocal immanence of the two (the Son is in the Father and the Father in the Son: *see* Jn 14:10; circumincession*). Other explanations are proposed (C. Stead, *Divine Substance,* 1977, Oxford; A. de Halleux, *Patrologie et œcuménisme,* 1990). Under the influence of Athanasius, the Council of Nicaea and its *homoousion* became the very expression of Christian faith, in a manner comparable to the message of the apostles themselves (H. J. Sieben, *Die Konzilsidee der alten Kirche,* 1979).

d)   In the fourth century, besides a small number of strict Nicenes or *homoousians,* several currents can be distinguished: an extreme Arian trend, which claimed that Christ is "dissimilar *(anomoios)* from the Father" (Anomians, disciples of Eunomius); others who believed him to be no more than similar (*homoios:* Homoians, adepts of a mitigated Arianism, which is the historical Arianism); and a party formed around Basil of Ancyra in 358, who professed that Christ is "similar to the Father according to the substance" *(homoiousios),* which gave them the name Homoiousians. Some, who accepted the divinity of the Son but not that of the Spirit, were sometimes called Semi-Arians (Mayeur et al. 1995).

e)   Athanasius*, eyewitness of the Council of Nicaea, defined the meaning of the *homoousion* from the reciprocal immanence of the Father and the Son. (Jn 14:10; 14:9 and 10:30). The two are "one" because the fruit of generation in God is not placed "outside God," but in him (*CAr.* III, 3–4). Questioning the Neoplatonic principle of the inferiority of the image to the model, he maintained that the divinity that passes entire from the Father into the Son, without implying any loss on the Father's part, is indivisible and single, to the point that "it is said of the Son what is said of the Father, but for the appellation of Father" (ibid., III, 4). The Father having given all to the Son (Jn 16:15 and 17:10), it is in the Son that he possesses and acts, doing all "through him," interpreted as the Son (Jn 1:3: *CAr.* II, 41–42; III, 36). Elsewhere, in reaction to the Arian interpretation of Jn 1:3, Athanasius declared: "Even if God had judged better to not produce, he still would

have had his Son" (*Car.* II, 31). Here he touches on the link between the generation of the Son and the creation. This link being admitted, Athanasius clearly affirmed the independence of the Trinity with respect to the creation, and the gratuitousness of the creative act. But that act does not terminate on the periphery of God. Having introduced, in the name of the *genitum non factum* (*DS* 125) of Nicaea, an absolute distinction between the Son and creatures, between existence by creation (*genesthai*) and existence by generation (*gennasthai),* Athanasius transgressed this limit by saying, in a second step, that those whom God first created, he later called "Son" in the sense that he engendered them (*CAr.* II, 59; *see* I, 56).

f) *Other Councils.*   Other councils dealt with the Trinitarian mystery, after the First Council of Constantinople* (381), which was devoted to the Holy Spirit (*DS* 150; see Decree of Damasus of 382, *DS* 155–77, and later the creed *Quicumque,* known as the Athanasian Creed, fifth/sixth century: *DS* 75), the Councils of Toledo (particularly the sixth and the 11th centuries), the Fourth Lateran* Council (1215), the two councils of union, Lyon* II (1274) and Basel*-Ferrara-Florence (1339–44: *see* notably *DS* 1330 sq). In the 20th century, the Trinitarian faith was set out once again in Pope Paul VI's *Profession of faith* (Dumeige, no 52) and the *Catechism of the Catholic Church* (1992).

5. Continuation of Arianism up to Augustine

a)   The Cappadocians (Basil* of Caesarea, Gregory of Nyssa, Gregory of Nazianzus) adopted the Athanasian interpretation of Nicaea, but in the Origenist perspective of the "three hypostases," arriving at the formulation, "A single substance [or essence] in three hypostases" (Gregory of Nyssa; *see* S. Gonzalez, *AnGr* 21, 1939). Basil was the first to give form to this "neonicenism," distinguishing that which is common *(to koinon)* and that which is proper *(to idion)* to the three (*Eph* 214:4; 210:4–5). Coming from a Stoic point of view, he used *ousia* only in its first, concrete, meaning. In another perspective, Gregory of Nyssa opposed *ousia* and *hupostasis* as the second *ousia* and the first *ousia* of Aristotle, *ousia* designating the generic concept of the divinity and *hypostase* the concrete reality of the "persons." In the eyes of the old Nicenes, and of modern commentators, this placed him under suspicion of tritheism. But he explicitly affirmed the numerical unity in God, in a language that held together propositions which were irreconcilable from the standpoint of reason* (*see Treatises, GNO* III/1). This theology reached its height with Gregory of Nazianzus, "the

Theologian." On the eve of the First Council of Constantinople he gave a masterful exposition of the entire mystery in *Five Theological Orations* (Orat. 27–31: SC 250), explaining why the revelation of the Trinity was not made in stages (*Orat.* 31, 25–26). He inspired the entire Byzantine period, notably the theology of Maximus* the Confessor (†662) and John Damascene († c. 749).

b) Augustine (†430) dealt with the Trinity from his earliest writings. He first did so in an anagogical perspective drawn from Neoplatonism, speaking of an "entry into oneself" and, from there, an ascent toward God. He subsequently considered the Trinity in an analogical perspective (O. du Roy 1966). The major work here is *De Trinitate*. It is marked by Nicaea from the first page. Augustine asked the question: if the Father is God, if the Son is God, and if the Holy Spirit is God, how can it be said that there are not three Gods but one only God? (*Trin.* I, 5, 8). To answer this question he develops the "psychological analogy." Starting from Genesis 1:26 ("Let us make man in our image"), he sees in man's inner life (his "psychology") the most important of the vestiges left in the creation by a single operation (*see inseparabiliter operari: Trin.* I, 5, 8), which, in its unity, bears the trace* of the Trinity. Among these vestiges of the Trinity he notes the triads *esse, nosse, velle* (*Conf.* XIII, 11, 12), *mens, notitia, amor* (*Trin.* IX, 2–5), *memoria, intellegentia, voluntas* (ibid., X–XV). He argues that the "three powers" of the soul* are implicated in each other without being confused with each other. Unity is certainly developed there. But he acknowledges that the same does not hold true for the distinction: it is one and the same who remembers, knows, and loves. Augustine recognizes this at the end of *De Trin.*; it rings like an acknowledgment of failure (*Trin.* XV, 22, 42). He is just as mistrustful with respect to the word *persona* (ibid., V, 9, 10; VII, 6, 11–12). After a systematic study of Latin vocabulary—and Greek (ibid., V, 8 and 9, 10; VII, 4–6)—he shows that the word is inadequate to the mystery it is meant to express, and he accepts it for lack of better (ibid., V, 9, 10; VII, 6, 11). The new language was to take hold in the West, which would particularly appreciate finding there a new way to speak of the Holy Spirit, identified in several different ways with love. But Augustine's major contribution remains having generalized in the West a recourse to the notion of relation (see below).

6. Trinitarian Vocabulary during the Patristic Period

a) Substantia *and* Persona. Tertullian "established at the outset if not the sense at least the usage of *substan-*

tia" in the Trinitarian domain (Moingt 1966). The Father is the totality of the divine substance *(summa substantia, tota substantia)*, communicated indivisibly to the Son who is its derivation *(derivatio totius et portio: Contre Prax.* 9), and to the Spirit. As for *persona,* this word designates that which is "numerous" and distinct in God, but does not yet signify it, metaphysically speaking. Tertullian's contribution concerned the distinction between the unity of the substance and the Trinity of the persons, as he attempted different ways of expressing that which is common and that which is unique in God, and that which is distinct and that which is numerous (Moingt 1966). The expression "one single substance in three that hold together" (*Contre Prax.* 12) has an "economical" bearing: the Three are associated in the same work of creation (*see* Sesboüé 1994). Elsewhere, the expression "to be in cohesion" *(cohaerentes)* has an ontological dimension, testifying to a deliberate use of the word "person" (Moingt 1966).

b) Ousia, Hypostasis, Prosôpon. The Council of Nicaea used *ousia* and *hupostasis* interchangeably (*DS* 125). At the Council of Alexandria in 362 some people spoke of "three hypostases," and others of a single one, and Athanasius accepted both usages (*Tomus ad Antiochenos* 5–6: *see HCO* 1, 271–72). The Cappadocians imposed the expression "a single *ousia* in three hypostases." The word *prosôpon* (literally "mask," "face," and then "role") designated the one in Scripture in whose name this or that word is pronounced (*ek prosôpou tinos*). In the fourth century it was favored by the Sabellians (see the *poluprosôpon* attributed to them by Basil: *Letter* 210, 3), but Gregory of Nyssa also began to use it against those he accused of "tritheism." The word did not take on a strong meaning until Chalcedon* (451), once associated with hypostasis (*DS* 302).

c) Trias, trinitas. Applied to God, the word *trias* appeared for the first time in the work of Theophilus of Antioch (*A Autolycus* II, 15), and later in Hippolytus (*Contra Haeresin Noeti* 14). Tertullian's *Adversus Praxean* (v. 213) inaugurated the use of *trinitas* in a discourse on God that began to connect the idea of number with the idea of unity, yet without expressing the Trinitarian mystery as such. It was often used in Latin translations of Origen, but in Origen's Greek *trias* occurs only three times (H. Crouzel, *SC* 253, 58, n. 3; once in Clement of Alexandria: *Strom.* V, 103, 1: *SC* 278). Its use around 260 by Pope Dionysius (*DS* 112–15) may be a heritage of Tertullian. It is absent from Nicaea, Constantinople I, and Chalcedon, but was imposed after Athanasius who, having used it incidentally in the orations *contra Arianos* (I,17–18 and III, 15), systematically adopted it in the *Epistula ad Serapionem* (v. 360). *Trias* became common currency with the Cappadocians. Marius Victorinus composed a hymn to the Trinity (*O beata Trinitas*, SC 68, 634–53; *see* Augustine, *De beata vita* 4, 35). Augustine commonly used the expression *Deus-Trinitas*, which replaced the *Deus Pater* of Scripture and became a new way of speaking of God.

d) Perichoresis, circumincession *(see Florence, DS 1331)*. The word *perikhôrèsis*, initially used in Christology*, did not enter Trinitarian theology until Pseudo-Cyril (in the sixth century) and Maximus the Confessor (in the seventh; *see* Prestige 1936) but the theme of the reciprocal immanence of the Father and the Son appeared from the early third century. The Latin equivalent of the more dynamic Greek word was *circumincessio* and later *circuminsessio*.

e) *Relations.* As shown in Nicaea, Trinitarian theology rested primarily on the idea of relation, inscribed in Scripture itself by the appellation of God as Father, a name* which in itself implies that of Son. Tertullian already wrote: "The Father must necessarily have a Son in order to be a Father, and the Son a Father to be Son" (*Contre Prax.* 10). The theme is present in the (Gnostic) *Tractatus Tripartitus*, in Origen (*see SC* 279, 13–14), and in Dionysius of Alexandria (*Refutation and Apology* II, PG 25, 504 C). Arius rebuked those who invoked "related beings" (*ta pros ti: see* Aristotle, *Cat.* VII, 7 b 15; Arius: *Creed*, Urkunden 6, H. G. Opitz, *Athanase Werke* I, 3, p.13). The theme was taken up by Athanasius and the Cappadocians: "Father is neither a name of substance, nor a name of action, it is a name of relation" (Gregory of Nazianzus, *Orat.* 29, 16: SC 250). Augustine, answering an objection of Eunomius, argued that beside the names attributed to God as accident and the names attributed as substance, there was a third possibility of attribution: as relation (*dicitur…ad aliquid: Trin.* V, 5, 6). Against anomianism, he distinguished in God the absolute names, which apply to the three persons and are used in the singular (such as the titles God, great, good); the relative names "*ad intra*," which distinguish the persons from each other (such as the names Father and Son); and the relative names "*ad extra*" (*Trin.* V, 11, 12), which express an original relation between God and the creature and are at the foundation of the theology of missions (ibid., IV, 20, 28; V, 16, 17; previously Athanasius: *CAr.* II, 14; *see* A. Michel, *DThC* 15, 1830–34). From Augustine, the theology of relation passed to Thomas Aquinas (Chevalier 1940).

f) *Greek and Latin Trinitarian Schemas.* It is commonly accepted that Eastern theology first focused on the multiplicity of hypostases before turning to the unity of the divinity, while Western theology went from the single substance to the search for a way to distinguish the persons within it. This systematization, popularized by Th. de Régnon (1892), remains useful (e.g. Halleux, op. cit., 31) but should not be exaggerated (see the violent protest of A. Malet, 1956, *Personne et amour* 14–20). We may also distinguish a Greek Trinitarian schema, in which everything comes "from the Father, through the Son, in the Holy Spirit," and conversely goes "in the Holy Spirit, through the Son, to the Father," as opposed to a Latin schema known as Augustinian. In the latter case the Father, the Son, and the Holy Spirit are placed on the same plane, from which flows a single "activity" common to the three, which goes toward the creature, understood as exterior to the Trinity. The first schema sets forth the distinction of the persons and their implication in the economy of salvation, but may be used in a subordinationist sense. The second clearly establishes the equality of the three persons, but does not show the relation of the creature to each of them, or the originality of the invisible missions that do not terminate "outside of God" but lead to man's participation in intratrinitarian life (*see* Athanasius, *CAr.* III, 22–4). (Recent theology works with a different conceptual pair: *Trinity of the economy of salvation* and *immanent Trinity, see* Rahner 1967.)

7. Synthesis in the Scholastic Period

a) *The Trinity in the West, 6th–12th Century.* From the sixth century onward the Trinity is mentioned in sermons, royal documents, donation charters, scriptural commentaries. After the Carolingian period, Trinitarian theology was affirmed during the pre-Scholastic period (11th–12th century) by Anselm* of Canterbury (†1109), Bernard* of Clairvaux (†1153), Richard of Saint Victor († c. 1173), who insisted on the love in God as a principle of alterity (*Trin.* III and VI), and P. Lombard (†1160), whose *Sentences* was used as a source in succeeding centuries (but who still did not distinguish between the *De Deo uno* and the *De Deo trino,* to the great regret of A. Michel, *DThC* 15, 1719). It reached its height in the West with 13th-century Scholasticism* (see a detailed survey of this vast body of literature in ibid., 1702–62). It was led by two masters of the Franciscan school—Alexander of Hales (†1245) and Bonaventure* (†1274)—and by the Dominicans Albert* the Great (who introduced Aristotelianism* in the West) and Thomas* Aquinas (†1274).

b) *Thomas Aquinas.* Thomas Aquinas broached the question of the Trinity several times (see ibid., 1741), but it is the synthesis in the *Summa Theologica* (*ST* Ia, q. 27–43) that left its mark for posterity. Breaking with the method of P. Lombard in the *l.I* of his *Sentences,* Thomas treated first, and separately, the question of the *De Deo uno,* a mystery that man can know by reason alone, and then the mystery of the *De Deo trino,* known only by revelation. He envisaged successively the emanations, the relations, and the divine persons.

1) Emanations. The first emanation is a generation by mode of knowledge. It is an act of intellect, immanent to the Father, placing the Word at the interior of the latter. The second emanation is a spiration, an act of will, that follows the operation of the intelligence and presupposes it, "because nothing can be loved that is not first known" (*ST* Ia, q.27, a.3). It is identified with the Holy Spirit. This systematization, the result of a long process of Christian thought, constitutes an unavoidable heritage of the Catholic tradition*. It is extremely rich, for example in the presentation of the Holy Spirit as the mutual love of the Father and Son, and as the principle in man of a filial movement that brings him from the condition of slave to that of "son" (e.g. *CG* IV, 21). However, developed in the perspective of Augustine's psychological analogy it does not adequately take into account Augustine's own reservations with respect to its modalist flavor (*Trin.* XV, 22, 42). God engenders in knowing himself and breathes forth *(spirat)* the Spirit in loving himself (e.g. *CG* IV, 23; *ST* Ia, q.37, a.2, ad 3: *see* H.-F. Dondaine, Thomas Aquinas, *Trinity,* 1962).

2) Relations. There are four real relations in God: the Father to the Son (active generation, or paternity), from the Son to the Father (passive generation, or filiation), from the Father and from the Son to the Holy Spirit (active *spiratio* or "breathing forth"), and from the Holy Spirit to the Father and to the Son (passive *spiratio*). But there are only three persons in God, because the active *spiratio,* common to the Father and the Son, does not constitute a fourth person. The relations identified with the divine essence constitute the divine persons, called "subsistent relations" (*ST* Ia, q.29, a.4). They exist in a mutual relation among themselves, but also in themselves and for themselves (*DThC* 13, 2151–53).

3) The persons. The person is defined, following Boethius, as an "individual substance of a ratio-nal nature" (*persona est rationalis naturae individua substantia, ST* Ia, q. 29, a.1; IIIa, q.2, a.2), which implies: a) individuality, with its character of incommunicability; b) a belonging to the order of that which effectively exists, in equivalence with the instruments (as subject of the essence) and the hypostasis (as subject of accidents); c) rational nature, which gives the person his nobility and makes him a responsible subject. Here might be grafted the modern notion of "person" as a free being, being of relation, and subject of a history* (Hegel). Obviously the notion of person applies to God only by analogical transposition (*ST* Ia, q.29, a.3; q.13, a.5; *De Potentia,* q.9, a.1).

In the Thomist tradition the following elements are also distinguished: 1) personal properties (Lateran IV, *DS* 800)—paternity, filiation*, passive *spiratio*—constitutive of each of the persons; and 2) notional acts—the act of knowledge that constitutes the Son and the act of will that constitutes the Spirit—which are at the base of the emanations. The notional acts are in fact identified with the personal properties and distinguished from the essential acts common to the three persons. To sum up, according to Bartmann (1905), it can be said that there is: 1) one God, a single divine Being in a single act of essence; 2) two emanations and two notional acts; 3) three persons, three opposed relations, three personal properties; 4) four real relations; 5) five notions... And the author concludes: "The doctrine of the Trinity should revert to unity. Unity is our primary truth, the Trinity is a secondary truth" (ibid.; *see* Nicolas 1985, 3rd Ed. 1991).

Further, the following points belong to this heritage: 1) the thesis that in God all is one if there is no opposition of relation (Florence, *DS* 1330); 2) the principle of the unity of action of the three persons outside of themselves (see Augustine's *inseparabiliter operari*); 3) the theory of appropriations*, by which attributes* or activities common to the three are "attributed" to one of the three to manifest certain of his properties; and 4) the theology of missions (i.e. the "sending" of the Father and the Holy Ghost) (*see DThC* 15, 1830–41).

8. Modern and Contemporary Periods

a) The Reformation and Its Consequences. The first reformers (Luther*, Melanchthon, Calvin*) remained faithful to the traditional Trinitarian dogma, considered as the foundation of Christian salvation; however, they increasingly insisted on the "for us" of this mystery. Luther, in his own particular perspective, gave new value to the great principle dear to the Cappadocians by which God is revealed to us *sub contrario,* that is, in contradiction with what human beings spontaneously expect of him (*see* Chrétien 1985). However, the abandonment of reference to the authority* of the Church, together with the influence of erudite humanism and the difficulty of finding in Scripture the classical Trinitarian formulas, soon favored antitrinitarian reactions (Michel Servet: *Christiana restitutio,* 1553, criticizing the "*tritoïstes,*" Fausto Socin [†1604] and the Socinians, whose ideas, transposed to England and the United States, produced Unitarianism*). Some authors accepted the hypothesis of a Trinity but detached it from the Christian revelation and gave it a personal interpretation: this was true of certain philosophers (*DThC* 15, 1783–90).

b) Kant*, in the 18th century, questioned the possibility of knowing "the thing in itself" independently of the a priori categories of the human mind, and showed the importance of freedom in the process of knowledge. He profoundly influenced the way the question of the Trinity was approached outside the Churches and by certain theologians. Kant himself did not broach the Trinitarian mystery, but Fichte, Schelling*, and Hegel* did so. Hegel, a former student of Lutheran teachers, sanctioned the idea of a certain becoming in God: the absolute Spirit (thesis: the Father) is more fully accomplished by self-denial (antithesis: kenosis* of the Son and creation of the world), in order to reassert himself in a greater way when alienation is at last overcome (synthesis: the Holy Spirit; Piclin, *Les philosophies de la Triade,* 1980). This perspective of novelty and progress was opposed to the logic of essences (or ideas) laid out by ancient Greece, but in accord with certain aspects of the paschal mystery (unlike the resurrection of Lazarus, the resurrection of Christ is not a return to the starting point but an entry into a radically new way of existing). However the thesis of the "becoming" of God was incompatible with the traditional notion of his perfection.

c) Early 20th century theology was troubled by modernism*, which rejected the idea of objective revelation and advocated an evolutionary notion of religious truth* in line with Hegel (*DThC* 15, 1799).

Schleiermacher* argued that the dogma of the Trinity did not exist outside of man. It was nothing but a way of describing and explaining certain phenomena of the Christian consciousness. An illusory, objective Trinity must be sacrificed in favor of the Trinity as revealed in the history of the human spirit. The so-called "semi-rationalist" reaction of certain Catholic theologians (Hermès, Günther, Frohschammer) who attempted to show that the dogma of the Trinity can be partially demonstrated, provoked reprobation from the Catholic hierarchy* (ibid., 1792–97). In line with Schleiermacher, Harnack in Germany and Sabatier in France adopted the traditional formulas to expound their own notions of God and the Trinity.

d) Early in the 20th century Karl Barth*'s severe reaction against so-called liberal theology (see Schleiermacher, Harnack et al.), restored to honor the absolute primacy of God and revelation. This became the very heart of a new presentation of the Trinity not as a simple fact in itself, cut off from the world, but as God in the mystery of his self-revelation to the world. The one God made himself known according to three "modes" corresponding to the three "persons" recognized by faith (Barth accepts the word "person" even though he finds it inadequate). The Father is God as he reveals himself; the Son is God as the revelation offered to man in the act of reconciliation; the Holy Spirit is God as revelation received in man in the working out of his redemption.

e) 20th Century Trinitarian Theology before Vatican II. The return to the primitive texts, interpreted in a new critical spirit, was initially felt as an attack by science on faith, but turned out to be beneficial for theology, with the works of d'Alès, Lebreton, Cadioux and others. In 1936 and 1937 H. U. von Balthasar* published two articles presenting Origen in a new light (*The mysterion of Origen,* RSR 26, 514–62 and 27, 38–64), soon followed by H. de Lubac* and J. Daniélou, in the same perspective. In 1951, on the occasion of the 15th centennial of the Council of Chalcedon, K. Rahner* invited theologians to restore the trinitarian dogma to its rightful central place *(Theological Investigations).* Further, he launched the *Grundaxiom:* "The Trinity of the economy of salvation is the immanent Trinity, and vice versa" (ibid.; *see* Rahner, 1967). The "vice versa" was subject to debate (G. Lafont: *Peut-on connaître Dieu en Jésus-Christ?,* 1969).

f) From the 19th century onward the Orthodox tradition participated in this renewal with the works of A. Khomiakov, Vl. Solovyov*, S. Boulgakov, and in the 20th century with Vl. Lossky, P. Evdokimov, O. Clément, B. Bobrinskoy, Kallistos Ware, C. Yannaras, and J. Zizioulas (*see* Bobrinskoy 1986). Characteristics: attention to the mystery (*apophaticism,* advancing the uncreated energies as expression of God's transcendence in the line of Gregory* Palamas), stress on the eminence of Scripture and the Fathers, a theology rooted in liturgy* and ecclesial communion*

(Zizioulas). All of this went with a constant attention to the paschal reality, seen as already at work in human beings, as evoked in the liturgy with the *Hymn to the Cherubim:* "We who mystically represent the Cherubim, and sing to the vivifying Trinity the thrice holy hymn, let us divest ourselves of all earthly concerns" (*Liturgia* of John Chrysostom).

g) After Vatican II the classical division into treatises, inspired by Melchior Cano (*De Locis theologicis,* 1567) and imported into manuals of dogmatics* from 1680 onward, was maintained. Theological courses separated Christology from the study of the Trinity, but interaction among the treatises had become commonplace, and the Trinity even found a place in courses on morality. It was accepted from this time that the New Testament message is not reducible to the content of the Nicene *homoousion* (Cardinal Franzelin: *see* B. Waché, Mgr Duchesne, 1992). Greater importance was given to the first centuries and to theologies prior to Thomas, notably the church fathers and Anselm (e.g. M. Corbin 1992), and this engendered a renewed approach to the God of revelation. Besides the attributes of the *nature* of God, the believer tried to consider the object of God's *free choice,* his "eternal counsel," his "personal pleasure" as made manifest in Christ, in Scripture, and in the destiny of human beings. At the core of these manifold approaches, whose variety recalls the ante-Nicene period, we can discern a movement that seeks a greater attentiveness to the advances of a God who freely decided to "not be without man, but *with* him and *for* him" (K. Barth, *The Humanity of God*). This God the Father carried within himself the great mystery of the Son, the Lamb* foreknown from before the ages (1 Pt 1:20), today made manifest: "There was conceived in a time before the ages a union of the limited and the limitless, of measure and without-measure, of the term and the without-term, of the Creator and the creation, of stability and motion. This union came in Christ manifest in the last times, itself giving plenitude to the designs of God." (Maximus the Confessor, *A Thalassios,* q. 60: PG 90, 621 B-C). This perspective in its way reconnects with the "Christian paradox" of a God who is at the same time one and so diversely multiple—a paradox received and transmitted, for better or worse, by Christians from the earliest days of their history.

•1. Encyclopedic Works
A. von Harnack (1886–90), *Lehrbuch der Dogmengeschichte,* 3 vols., Tübingen (5th Ed. 1931–32; (1889–91), *Grundriss des Dogmengeschichte.*
Th. de Régnon (1892–98), *Études de théologie positive sur la Sainte Tr.,* 4 vols., Paris.

A. von Harnack (1902), *Das Wesen des Christentums.*
B. Bartmann (1905), *Lehrbuch der Dogmatik,* Freiburg (8th Ed. 1932).
J. Tixeront (1905–1912), *Histoire des dogmes,* 3 vols., Paris (9th Ed. 1927).
J. Lebreton (1910), *Histoire du dogme de la Tr,* 2 vols., Paris (3rd and 8th Ed. 1927–28).
G.L. Prestige (1936), *God in Patristic Thought,* London and Toronto.
G. Bardy, A. Michel (1950), "Trinité," *DThC* 15/2, 1545–1855.
L. Ott (1954), *Grundriss der Dogmatik,* Freiburg.
J.N.D. Kelly (1958), *Early Christian Doctrines,* London.
K. Rahner (1976), *Grundkurs des Glaubens,* Freiburg.
J.-H. Nicolas (1985), *Synthèse dogmatique,* Paris (3rd Ed. 1991).
B. Bobrinskoy (1986), *Le mystère de la Trinité,* Paris.
B. Sesboüé, J. Wolinski (1994), *Histoire des dogmes* I: *Le Dieu du salut,* Paris.

2. Patristic Sources
J. Quasten (1950–60), *Patrology,* 3 vols., Utrecht.
J. de Ghellinck (1961), "Le dogme trinitaire," in *Patristique et Moyen Age,* vol. 3, 152–162, Paris.
J. Doré (Ed.) (1992), *Introd. à l'étude de la théologie,* vol. 3, 262–67, Paris (bibl.).

3. Patristic Studies
I. Chevalier (1940), *Saint Aug. et la pensée grecque: Les relations trinitaires,* Fribourg.
H.U. von Balthasar (1942), *Présence et pensée* (on G. of Nyssa), Paris (New Ed. 1988).
J. Daniélou, (1944), *Platonisme et théologie mystique,* Paris.
H. de Lubac (1950), *Histoire et Esprit* (on Origen), Paris.
G. Kretschmar (1956), *Studien zur frühchristlichen Trinitätstheologie,* Tübingen.
G. Aeby (1958), *Les Missions divines, de saint Justin à Origène,* Fribourg.
J. Daniélou (1958), *Théologie du judéo-christianisme,* Paris (2nd Ed. 1991).
M. Harl (1958), *Origène et la fonction révélatrice du Verbe incarné,* Paris.
A. Orbe (1958–66), *Estudios Valentinianos,* 5 vols., Rome.
J. Daniélou (1961), *Message évangélique et culture hellénistique,* Paris (New Ed. 1990).
H.U. von Balthasar (1962), *Herrlichkeit* II, Einsiedeln.
J. Moingt (1966 and 1969), *Théologie trinitaire de Tertullian,* 4 vols., Paris.
O. du Roy (1966), *L'intelligence de la foi en la Trinité selon saint Aug.: Genèse de sa théologie trinitaire jusqu'en 391,* Paris.
E. Boularand (1972), *L'hérésie d'Arius et la "foi" de Nicée,* 2 vols., Paris.
M.-J. Le Guillou (1972), *Le Mystère du Père* (on Irenaeus), Paris.
R. Lorenz (1979), *Arius Judaizans?,* Göttingen.
Ch. Kannengiesser (1991), *Arius and Athanasius,* Aldershot.
P. Aubin (1992), *Plotin et le christianisme,* Paris.

4. Council History and Documents
Acts: *ACO* or Mansi
Decrees: *COD (DCO); BSGR; HCO; DS; DH.*
Dumeige (Trans. of the main documents from *DS*).
J.-M. Mayeur, C. and L. Piétri (Eds.) (1995), *Histoire du christianisme,* vol. 2 (years 250–430), Paris.

5. On the Middle Ages

K. Barth (1931), Fides quaerens intellectum: *Anselms Beweis der Existenz Gottes im Zuzammenhang seines theologischen Programms, GA* II/2, 1981.

É. Gilson (1948), *Le thomisme,* Paris.

M.-D. Chenu (1954), *Introduction à l'étude de saint Thomas d'Aquin,* Paris.

A. Malet (1956), *Personne et amour dans la théologie trin. de saint Thomas,* Paris.

M. Corbin (1974), *Le chemin de la théologie chez Thomas d'Aquin,* Paris.

M. Corbin (1992), *Prière et raison de la foi: Introduction générale à l'œuvre d'Anselme de Cantorbéry,* Paris.

6. General or Systematic Approaches

K. Barth (1932), *KD* I/1, 311–514.

Vl. Lossky (1944), *Essai sur la théologie mystique de l'Église d'Orient,* Paris.

F. Bouillard (1960), *Connaissance de D.,* Paris.

J. Moltmann (1964), *Theologie der Hoffnung,* Munich.

K. Rahner (1967), "Der dreifaltige Gott als transzendenter Urgrund der Heilsgeschichte," *MySal* II, 317–405.

J. Moltmann (1972), *Der gekreuzigte Gott,* Munich.

F. Varillon (1974), *L'humilité de D.,* Paris.

A. Brunner (1976), *Dreifaltigkeit: Personale Zugänge zum Geheimnis,* Einsiedeln.

E. Jüngel (1977), *Gott als Geheimnis der Welt,* Tübingen.

J.-L. Marion (1977), *L'idole et la distance* (2nd part), Paris (New Ed. 1991).

H. Wipfler (1977), *Grundfragen der Trinitätsspekulation,* Regensburg.

J. Moltmann (1980), *Trinität und Reich Gottes,* Munich.

W. Kasper (1982), *Der Gott Jesu Christi,* Mainz.

H. U. von Balthasar (1985), *Theologik II, Wahrheit Gottes,* Einsiedeln.

J.-L. Chrétien (1985), *Lueur du secret,* Paris.

B. Forte (1985), *Trinità come storia,* Rome.

W. Pannenberg (1988), *Systematiche Theologie I,* Göttingen, 283–364.

T. F. Torrance (1988), *The Trinitarian Faith,* Edinburgh.

G. Greshake (1997), *Der dreieinige Gott: Eine trinitarische Theologie,* Freiburg-Basel-Vienna.

JOSEPH WOLINSKI

B. Systematic Theology

How can we speak in a true way about the God* whom Christian faith celebrates as "friend of men" (Ti 3:4) and "greater than our heart" (1 Jn 3:20)? How can we attest, following the Scriptures*, that he is three times differently the same in being "the Father, the Son, the Holy* Spirit" (Mt 28:19) and that this "repetition of eternity in eternity" (Anselm*, *Ep. de Incarnatione* XV; 33) is the superabundant effusion of that unique eternity upon every man? The Father, revealed in the death* and resurrection* of Jesus*, his "well-beloved Son" (Mt 3:17), is above our thoughts, even our highest thoughts. If he is not only beyond being but beyond all grasping by image or concept, such that nothing greater can be thought, this is not in order that he might remain withdrawn in some kind of superlative solitary perfection, but so that he might give himself freely, coming closer to man than man is to himself. Theology* seeks understanding of this coincidence of the more than essential distance and the more than lavish donation. Naming the Unnamed beyond all name, theology transforms its own weakness into a blessed wound from which springs forth the overflowing gift of which theology is not the source. Accepting that the infirmity of its reasons may appear to the unbelieving as a failing of truth*, it refuses all absolute knowledge and knows itself to be provisional.

For the one who sees that in the Thing itself "are hidden higher reasons" (Anselm, *Cur Deus Homo* II, XVI; 117), no pretension to completeness is possible. Countless are the Trinitarian doctrines that have tried to show that the unity of God is beyond what we call one and multiple. Escaping all efforts at unification in a synthesis, they show the "manifold wisdom of God" [Eph 3:10] But if all the thought of faith is first apology (1 Pt 3:15), a defense of the resurrection against ideologies that call it an unrealistic utopia, how can we not be wounded when Feuerbach argues *(The Essence of Christianity)* that faith is the illusion of an unhappy conscience? Shall we answer these accusations of alienating projection by a "rational" proof of God's existence*? Meant to be anterior to faith, it would be an idea that arose in our hearts of a Supreme Being who reigns complacently at the summit of being. This is precisely the theism that gave rise to atheism*. Then will we remember that God revealed himself, that he is a Trinity of persons* in the unity of a single nature, and that this paradox, this *summa concordia* of apparently contrary elements, dislodges our reason* from the temptation of placing itself above its origin? Certainly! The proof that "God shows his love for us" (Rom 5:8) lies in the death of his Son, whence flows the Spirit of filiation*. But is this respected by the conventional expositions? The following declaration can be read in the *Catechism of the Catholic Church* (§253–55): "We do not confess three gods, but one single God in three persons: the 'consubstantial Trinity' [Constantinople* II]. The divine persons do not share the unique divinity; each of them is wholly God....Each of the three persons is that reality, that is, the divine substance, essence, or nature [Lateran* IV]....God is unique but not solitary [Fides Damasi]." "Father," "Son," and "Holy Spirit" are not simply names designating modalities of the divine being, because they are really distinct from each other: "He who is the Son is not the Father, and he who is the Father is not the Son, and he who is the Holy Spirit is neither the Father nor the Son" (Toledo IX). They are distinct from each other by their relations of origin: "It is the Father who engenders, the Son who is engendered, the Holy Spirit who emanates" (Lateran IV). Because it does not divide the divine unity, the real distinction of the persons from each other lies solely in the relations that refer them to each other: 'In the relative names of the persons, the Father is referred to the Son, the Son to the Father, the Holy Spirit to the other two; when one speaks of these three persons in considering the relations, one believes nevertheless in a single nature or substance" (Toledo XI). "Because of this unity, the Father is wholly in the Son, wholly in the Holy Spirit; the Son is wholly in the Father, wholly in the Holy Spirit; the Holy Spirit is wholly in the Father, wholly in the Son [Basel*-Ferrara-Florence]."

This language, borrowed from Greek philosophy*, is no longer audible to us because of the shift in meaning of the words. The citations underscore the absence of reference to the Fathers* and Scripture. Even more serious: this language does not speak of the paschal event of Jesus Christ, or of the Church* brought forth by this event. Obsessed with the compatibility of the one and the three, it forgets the believing subject and allows itself to be dominated by the notion of objective representation, so dear to the West since Thomas* Aquinas adopted Aristotle's thought. It postulates the divinity as an Object with a capital O, confined in his solitary perfection. How far from the Fathers, who are so attentive to Scripture, and to the signs by which the founding event is displayed in existence! As an example we may cite Ambrose*'s *Sacraments* (VII, 20–3). Making a connection between the unity of the Trinity and the way baptism* is conferred, procuring forgiveness of sins* and divine filiation, it identifies the divinity of God in a concrete sign by which man participates in what he says. It makes the Trinitarian confession (*see* creed*) the symbol of the faith, incorporates the speaking subject into that which he speaks, marks the connection between the paschal event and the confession of the Father, the Son, the Holy Spirit. At baptism, it is Christ* who comes down to a level more intimate than man, to make him new after this submersion in water: "You came to the font. You entered. A priest* came to you. You were asked: 'Do you renounce the Devil and his works?' You answered: 'Yes, I renounce.'...The name of the Father, the presence of the Son and the Holy Spirit were invoked, and you were asked: 'Do you believe in God the almighty Father?' You answered: 'I believe.' You were immersed in the water, that is, you were buried. A second time you were asked: 'Do you believe in Jesus Christ our Lord and in his cross?' You replied: 'I believe' and you were immersed. Thus you were buried with Christ, and he who is buried with Christ, with Christ also rises. A third time you were asked: 'Do you believe in the Holy Spirit?' You replied: 'I believe.' And again you were immersed so that the triple profession would destroy the multiple falls of the past....Thus, you received the sacrament* of the cross on which Christ was nailed. And so you are crucified with him, attached by the nails that were his. May they hold fast, those nails of Christ! May your weakness not pull them out! And then you came up from the font and you received white clothes to show that you are divested of your cloak of sin*, and you were clothed in the light of the resurrection." This is the kind of thing with which the apology of the faith should concern itself, with producing texts like this, where the anamnesis of the paschal event is not separated from the exhortation to live accordingly. But how can we recover the plenitude of such texts without a deconstruction of the rationalist and representational strata that have covered and deformed them?

1. The Nativity of the Son

a) Trinity and Supereminence of God. The Trinitarian doctrine is not found as such in the Scriptures, despite the ternaries they contain that attest that the Christian God is "in an inalterable unity the same, but also in an inalterable diversity, three times differently the same." It is "a document of the theology of the Church" (Karl Barth*, KD I/1, §8), an interpretation meant to guard against all reduction of the imminent newness of God, by using other words than those of the Bible* in order to come closer to the sense. In using Greek philosophy, which had no knowledge of the gift, so as to express that which surpasses it, there was an undeniable risk of concealing the word* of God beneath layers of interpretation. Thomist thought succumbed to it in the hope of reconciling faith and Aristotelian reason, though without undertaking a true critique of the latter. It divided the doctrine of God into two treatises: a *De Deo uno* with a hierarchical schema of natures in which perfection degrades as it gets farther away from the *summus vertex;* and a *De Deo trino* that overdetermines this graduated hierarchy without changing it, adding the category of relation, which "multiplies the Trinity," to that of substance, which "contains the unity" (Boethius*, *De Trinitate* 6; PL 64/1255 A), approaching the distinctions *secundum rem* of the three persons from the distinction *secundum rationem* of the perfections of the one being, positing a Trinity in itself before the economy in which God is for us. Should these defects be corrected, or should other notions be sought in order to develop the parallel that Thomist thought presupposes but does not thematize between the Trinity beyond the one and the many and the supereminence "beyond all negation and affirmation" (Dionysius* the Pseudo-Areopagite, *Mystical Theology* I, 2; PG 3/1000 B)? Two points contradict this. If Thomas was not able to get beyond the modalism* that disjoins the being and the revelation* of God (*see* M. Corbin, *La Trinité ou l'Excès de Dieu,* Paris, 1997), it is because the paschal economy belongs to the divinity of God that, far from excluding his humanity and ours, includes them. This connection between the eternal and the economic distinctions is stated in the *Apocalypse:* "the mystery of God would be fulfilled" (Rev 10:7). Moreover, the sequence on the three moments of the naming of God—affirmation, overriding negation, supereminence—is both a meditation on the path of man toward a God who is endlessly "more divine" (Pseudo-Dionysius, op. cit., I, 1) and a repetition of the "word of the cross" (1 Cor 1:18), which transforms the weakness of the cross into a strength greater than the strong. This believing reversal of the illogical, which traces a logic that is more than logical, is explained thus: "Not only does God overflow with wisdom* and 'of his comprehension there is no limit,' but he surpasses all reason, all wisdom, all intelligence. Paul marvelously understood it when he said: "For the foolishness of God is wiser than men" [1 Cor 1:25]. . . . Because it is the custom of theologians to reverse all positive terms so as to apply them to God under their negative aspect. . . . Applying the same method, the Apostle, according to the texts, praises the divine folly on the basis of what appears paradoxical and absurd in it in order to rise to the unutterable truth that surpasses all reason. . . . Thus divine things must be understood in a divine way. When one speaks of the unintelligence or the insensitivity of God, this negation must be understood as excess and not as deprivation. Thus . . . we call ungraspable and invisible Darkness the 'unapproachable light' [1 Tm 6:16] because it surpasses visible light." (*Divine Names* VII, 1–2; PG 3/865 B- 869 A).

If associating the Trinity and supereminence leads us back to the paschal event, no one can dissociate the Trinitarian doctrine from christological statements; and this impossibility, by repudiating all representative strata concerned about a foundation prior to the incarnation*, demands a deployment of the paradox by which to speak of supereminence is only to trace, by the Son and in the Holy Spirit, a path to the Father who "is greater than all" [Jn 10:29].

b) Economy and Theology. An important though little-noted contribution of Thomas Aquinas is the division of the articles of faith into two classes: truths accessible to natural reason, and inaccessible truths that, exceeding and overdetermining that reason, are nonetheless to be justified before its tribunal (*CG* I, III). In Trinitarian matters it leads to two treatises between which no demonstrable link is possible, because "*the creative virtue of God is common to the whole Trinity,* it belongs to the unity of essence, not to the distinction of the persons" (*ST* Ia, q.32, a.1). The italicized phrase comes from the confession that opens Augustine*'s *De Trinitate:* "The Father, the Son, and the Holy Spirit attest, by the inseparable equality of a single and identical substance, their divine unity; that in consequence they are not three gods but one God, even though the Father engendered the Son in such a way that the Holy Spirit not be the one that is the Father, that the Son was engendered by the Father in such a way that the Father not be the one who is the Son, and that the Holy Spirit be neither the Father nor the Son but only the Spirit of the Father and the Son, also equal to the Father and the Son, belonging to the unity of the Trinity. And yet it is not the Trinity itself that was born of the Virgin Mary*, that was crucified and buried under Pontius Pilate, that was raised on the third day and rose up to heaven, but only the Son. It is not this same Trinity that descended in the form of a dove on Jesus when he was baptized, or that, on the day of Pentecost, after the ascension of the Lord, amidst a heavenly uproar like unto a hurricane, came to rest in distinct tongues of fire on each of the apostles, but only the Holy Spirit. And it is not the Trinity who said from heaven: 'You are my beloved Son' [Mk 1:11] when Jesus was baptized by John, when the three disciples were with him on the mountain, or when the voice resonated saying: 'I have glorified it [the name of God] and I will glorify it again' [Jn 12:28], but only the Father speaking to the Son, though the Father, the Son, and the Holy Spirit work inseparably as they are inseparable. Such is my faith because such is the Catholic faith" (I, IV, 7).

The schema that governs this text has three adversative articulations that play between four poles: the consubstantial unity of the Trinity, the distinction of the Three, the diversity of the theophanic signs, the unity of the divine work. They are united two by two on two parallel lines: above, the *ad intra* relations that precede history*; below, the signs given *ad extra* to reveal the divine persons. Between these horizontal lines runs the vertical line of the relation between man and God where all differences between the Three disappear. Not being distinguished by their relation to time*, they "work inseparably" and use effects created by their one being to teach that they are Three *despite* the inseparability of their being. Also, as it is not said that the relation of the voice to the Father, of the dove to the Spirit is not that of man to the Son—the Son of God and Son* of man in one person—Christ becomes the simple *sign* and not *the sign and the reality* of a greater God. Between signified and signifying, between being and revelation, there is a separation that symbolizes the impossibility of superimposing the horizontal lines and the vertical line. It preserves the pagan presupposition of a God enclosed in himself, and authorizes the notion of *vestigia Trinitatis in creatura,* psychological images disconnected from the paschal event.

In the West this schema seems self-evident, and a proper interpretation of the Nicene Creed (325): "We believe in one God, the almighty Father, creator of all things visible and invisible. And in one Lord, Jesus Christ, the Son of the Father, born of the Father as only Son, that is, of the substance of the Father, God of God, Light of Light, true God of true God, begotten and not created, consubstantial with the Father, through whom all things were made, that which is in heaven and that which is on earth, who for us men and for our salvation, descended, took flesh, made himself man, suffered, was raised on the third day, went back up to the heavens whence he will come to judge the living and the dead. And in the Holy Spirit."

The schema *De Trinitae* is not Augustine's; it is monotheistic by its first affirmation, because "one God" does not designate the Trinity but the Father *fons omnius Trinitatis, Pantocrator,* king of the new universe. The second affirmation concerns first the Son, though its first element attaches this filial moment to the Father, but "one Lord Jesus Christ," whose path among us the second element recalls. Wishing to be faithful to Scripture, the symbol safeguards their *lectio difficilior* by using expressions that are not in Scripture. That Jesus, son of God, is "of the substance of the Father," that his generation is a true generation in the strict meaning of the word, implies that he is "begotten, not created." The corollary of this negation is that he is "consubstantial* with the Father." The word *homoousios,* being composed of the adjective *homos* and the substantive *ousia,* has the same meaning as *hupostasis,* "that which is placed in existence." The Son then has the same substance as the Father from which he comes by true birth.

There is another dimension to the gap between Augustine and Nicaea*. It appears in the development of the article on the Spirit at the First Council of Constantinople (381): "[We believe] in the Holy Spirit, who is Lord and who gives life; he emanates from the Father; with the Father and the Son he receives the same adoration and the same glory; he spoke through the prophets*. In the Church, one, holy, Catholic and apostolic. We confess one single baptism for the forgiveness of sins; we await the resurrection of the dead and the life of the century to come" (DS 150). The Spirit is connected to the Church, and the formulas concerning him do not employ the linguistic register of substance that is used for the Son. They are rooted in the liturgy* that gives thanks and glory* to God.

To objections that a gap exists between the Creed and the New Testament, one may reply:

1) The word *theos* is used of the Son only six times: Jn 1:1; 1:18; 20:28; Rom 9:5; Ti 2:13; 1 Jn 5:20. All the other occurrences of the word, the vast majority, designate the Father of Jesus, and none of them the Holy Spirit.

2) All the groups of verses in which the ternary Father, Son, Holy Spirit figure, in whatever order, coordinate these three names with the event of the paternal "loving kindness" [Ti 3:4]. Whatever the context, it is never omitted that the Church welcomes the Spirit of the promise* that configures with the Son, the only path to the Father. If any distinction is made it is not between a God *in himself* and a God *for us,* but between that which remains *hidden* and that which is *manifest;* the Father being hidden and the Son who reveals him in fullness being manifest by the Spirit who spreads his wealth in the Church.

After disqualification of all strata classifying the Father, the Son, and the Holy Spirit within a received notion of the divine derived from ancient philosophy, what can be done but to seek a schema more faithful to the Scriptures, whose extraordinariness the councils* wanted to safeguard? Here is the one given by Basil* of Caesarea: "When, under the influence of an illuminating force, we fix our eyes on the beauty* of the Image of the invisible God and, through it, we raise ourselves up to the ravishing sight of the Archetype, the Spirit of knowledge is inseparable from it, that in itself gives to those who love to see the Truth the strength to see the Image." It does not have to be discovered from without; it is within one that it is recognized. Just as "no one knows the Father except the Son" [Mt 11:27] thus "no one can say 'Jesus is Lord' except in the Holy Spirit" [1 Cor 12:3].... Thus it is "in him that he shows the glory of the Only-Begotten and in him that he gives to true worshippers the knowledge of God. The path of the knowledge* of God goes from the Holy Spirit who is ONE, through the Son who is ONE, to the Father who is ONE. In the opposite direction, native goodness, sanctity [holiness*] according to nature, dignity follow from the Father through the Only-Begotten to the Spirit. Thus the hypostases are confessed without destroying the orthodox doctrine of the *monarchia*." (*Treatise of the Holy Spirit.*, SC 17 *bis*, XVIII, §47).

There is no longer a distinction between God's *esse* and *operari,* but a single vertical line that goes from bottom to top as the path of knowledge, and from top to bottom as the flow of goodness. The Spirit and the Church are indissociable. The mission of the Spirit with regard to the Son is to illuminate from within that which Jesus said and did for us; it is placed in parallel with the mission of the Son with respect to the Father: that of showing his image. The Father is the source of this Triad; his monarchy is administered by "his two hands" (Irenaeus*, *Adv. Haer.* IV, VII, 4), the Son and the Spirit; this is not a matter of treating successively a common nature and the relations that diversify, but of praising a communication of which the Father is the principle of unity: "ONE God the Father, ONE the Only-Begotten Son, ONE the Holy Spirit. Each one of the hypostases is stated in isolation, and if there should be a need to number them together, one does not, by an unintelligent numbering, give in to a polytheist conception." (op. cit., XVIII, §44) The eternal distinction of the hypostases not being numbered with the vertical arrows that articulate the temporal relation of man with the Father, Basil conceives the path of man in a Trinitarian manner, as a potential of living in the Spirit—the route that the Son traced "through his flesh" [Heb 10:20] to the Father.

c) Resurrection of the Son and Higher Promise of God. If the liturgy, in praying to the Father through the Son in the Spirit, accords with what is discerned in the Bible, does Basil's schema open this connection between the Trinity and the supereminence—putting theism and atheism back-to-back as equally mistaken figures? And yet, if there is a unity between the economy that concerns our salvation* and the theology that celebrates the divinity, does the distance from God not disappear when his donation is underscored? Is God not made so dependent that his absoluteness would vanish in taking his being from a relation? To show that the coincidence between donation and distance preserves God's providence (Rom 11:35) better than any representation of some foundation prior to the creation*, we have only to quote Basil's narrative: "As I was praying with the people, and I was finishing in this double way the doxology to God the Father, now "with" *[meta]* the Son, now "with" *[sun]* the Holy Spirit, now "by" *[dia]* the Son "in" *[en]* the Holy Spirit, some of those present accused us, saying that we had used foreign, contradictory expressions." (op. cit., I, §3) The first doxology, held by the heresy* for a *subnumeration* supposing median terms on a line, speaks of *mediation* between God and man. The second is known as theology. Declaring equality of honor among the Three, the inseparability of their dignity, it extends to the Spirit (though with different words) what Nicaea affirmed of the Son. Is a doxology a representation? The justification of the *connumeration* of the Spirit transposing that of the consubstantiality of the Son, the reply is given in Basil's explanation that the doxologies are not contradictory but complementary: "If one looks at the grandeur of the nature of the Only-Begotten and the supereminence of his dignity, one testifies that it is with the Father that the glory comes to him. If one thinks of the bounty that he goes out of his way to procure for us, or of our personal access to God, our entry into his familiarity, it is through him and in him that one confesses having received that grace. Thus one of the two phrases—with whom—is proper for proclaiming the doxology and the other— through whom—better for giving thanks." (op. cit., VII, §16)

To speak of princely grace* and supereminent glory to render to the Son turned to the Father, is to read Paul's indictment against the idolatry into which all men fell in Adam*: "For although they knew God, they did not honor him as God or give thanks to him, but they became futile in their thinking" (Rom 1:21). It is to reap what the Easter event restored, to enter into the filial relation to the Father, who is beloved in all and more than all. Sung in the Psalms*, this relation is by turns supplication, thanksgiving, and praise*. Overcome by the Spirit who makes him cry out: "Abba, Father!" (Rom 8:17) the Christian makes his own the prayer* of Jesus. With him, he knows himself poorer than the bird that God nourishes. Though he needs many goods, he does not simply take them where he finds them. Acquiring them by his labor, he asks for them every day from the Father. And he receives his bread with no care for the morrow, and this bread truly nourishes him because it is received as a gift of God. It is bread and more than bread, taken in Eucharist* as the gift of a giver who makes it a sign of his bounty and promises even greater signs. It is a "our daily bread" (Mt 6:11), eaten with gratitude as a gift from a benefactor who is praised as such in the doxology, with the assurance that his communion* is better than all the goods flowing from this encounter. For the believer who does not seek the upper hand, whose intention goes toward the origin, the supplication for bread and the praise* of the Name* are not two separate things. In saying: "Our Father in heaven, hallowed be your name" (Mt 6:9) he knows that his request is fulfilled because he recognizes in God his Father and acknowledges his holiness. He receives his prayer as a relation that can only be exercised in desiring more ardently, as a good among others, that which surpasses them and integrates them in his thrust toward the Other, with no separation between Eucharist and doxology, flow of goods and path of knowledge. Then *dia* and *meta* are united, because there is neither a more loving praise of the giver without thanksgiving for the gifts, nor Eucharist without a doxology confessing his *ousia* as an inexpressible stock of gifts ever more worthy of his bounty. Here the usual, representative meaning of the words *essentia* or *substantia* diverges from the original meaning given to them by the Fathers, for example, Gregory of Nyssa: "Supposing that someone approaches [a natural spring]. He will admire these infinite waters that endlessly spring forth and spread. But he could not say that he had seen all the water; how can he see what is still hidden in the bowels of the earth? No matter how long afterwards he remains close to the spring, he will always be at the beginnings of his contemplation of the water. Because the water never stops spreading and forever begins to spring forth. And so it is for the one who looks at the limitless divine beauty: that which he endlessly discovers manifests itself to him as being absolutely new and astonishing with regard to that which he has already grasped; and he admires that which, every second, is revealed to him and he never stops desiring more of it, because that which he awaits is even more magnificent and more divine than what he has already seen" (*11th Homily on the Song of Songs,* PG 44/997 C -1000 C).

When the paternal *ousia* is received as the hidden source of the more divine overflowing that reveals it, it follows that the more the Eucharist grows the more praise is rendered: "When the Apostle Paul offers thanks to God through Jesus Christ [Rom 1:8] and says he has received through Jesus 'grace and apostleship to bring about the obedience of faith for the sake of his name among all the nations' [Rom 1:5], or when he says that we have had access through Christ 'into this grace in which we stand' [Rom 5:2], he shows what are the gifts of the one who now dispenses to us through the Father the grace of good things, and now brings us, through himself, to the Father's side.... But when we recognize grace at work, from him to us, do we subtract something from his glory? Is it not rather true to say that all enumeration of benefits is an appropriate theme of doxology?" (op. cit., VIII, §17) To unmask Arianism*, Basil could have simply invoked the names of Jesus proper to his divinity: Only Son, Word*, Omnipotence and Wisdom* of God. But would he then have shown the venom of the heresy? So that the *kharis* coming from the Father by the Word did not make his flesh appear exterior to his *phusis,* but its overflowing, he added to the first class of names that express the glory, a second that make of grace a "characteristic of nature": "Scripture does not transmit the Lord to us under a single name, nor under those that only reveal the divinity and the grandeur, but also under the characteristics of his nature. For it knows how to say 'the name that is above every name' (Phil 2:9) the name of Son, and to call him true Son, only-begotten God, power of God, Wisdom and Word. But elsewhere, again, because of the multiformity of the grace offered to us, which, in the richness of his bounty, he offers according to the infinite variety of his wisdom to those who ask him for it, the Lord is designated in Scripture by many other names: here pastor, there king, and elsewhere doctor and even spouse, road and door, source, bread, axe, stone. These names evoke not the nature but the multiform character of the energy granted by mercy... according to the particularity of each need, to those who ask for it." (op. cit., VIII, §7).

The word nature being in the singular, it is not a question of the two natures of Christ, but of a blossoming of the nature in multiple benefits, of an outpouring of the *ousia* as overflowing plenitude of multiple *energeiai*. For such is the bond of *meta* and names praising the nature, of *dia* and names gathering the diverse energies. In this second class, destined to prove the supereminence designated by the first, emerges the name doctor (Mk 2:17), a name that presupposes illness and the possibility of remedy. An illness: the arrogance and falsity, envy and violence* that deformed the image of God when Adam tried to "seize equality with God by force." A remedy: the deliberate lowering of the Son who "did not count equality with God a thing to be grasped" but emptied himself of the form of God where he abided to take the "form of a servant" (Phil 2:6–7), the disfigured figure of the Crucified, condemned in the name of the law*, "becoming a curse for us" (Gal 3:13). Revealing and destroying sin, revealed by the paschal exaltation, the kenosis* of God is celebrated in the words "the weakness of God is stronger than men" (1 Cor 1:25). Source of all conversion*, gracious dispensation of love*, it is the radiating center where, beyond all thought, service and royalty are united: "Every time that [Jesus] can receive a soul* tormented by the mean blows of the devil and cure it of the grave weakness of sin, he is given the name Doctor. Does such solicitude for us invite humble thoughts? Does it not provoke astonishment before the great power and tenderness of the Savior, that he could bear to sympathize with our weaknesses and come all the way down to our weakness? Neither heaven nor earth nor the vast seas, the inhabitants of the waters nor the guests of the earth, the plants, nor the stars, the air, the seasons, nor the multiform harmony of the universe, nothing so proves his supereminent force than letting himself, God, he whom space cannot hold, impassively letting himself entwine with death, through the flesh, in order to favor us, by his own passion, with impassibility." (op. cit., VIII, §18).

There is no lack of similar texts in the tradition*. For example, Gregory of Nyssa: "That God lowered himself to our baseness, this shows his overflowing power that knows no shackles, even in conditions against his nature" (Catechetical Orations).

And Maximus* the Confessor: "If he deliberately delivered himself up to death, wanting himself guilty in place of us who should have suffered for our [own] guilt, it is clear that he loved us more than himself, we for whom he delivered himself up to death, and—even if the expression is daring—that he who is more than good chose insults, at the moment required by the economy of our salvation, preferring those to the proper glory of his nature, as being more worthy. Surpassing the dignity of God and overflowing the glory of God, he made the return to him of those who had drifted away an outpouring and a greater manifestation of his own glory. Nothing is more proper to the principle of his glory than the salvation of men." (Letter 44, PG 91/641 D sq).

And then there is Anselm, who conjectures about the "necessary reasons" for the incarnation: "Of the three persons of God, none 'emptied himself of himself' more opportunely 'in taking the form of a slave,' to subdue the devil and intercede for man who, by theft, had claimed a false resemblance with God; none more than the Son, splendor of the eternal light and true image of the Father, who did not believe that he in himself should wish to be equal with God [Phil 2:7] but by true equality and resemblance, said: 'I and the Father are one' (Jn 10:30) and: 'Whoever has seen me has seen the Father' [Jn 14:9]" (Ep. de incarnatione Verbi X).

This uses a variant of the name given in the Proslogion: "We believe that You are something such that nothing greater can be thought" (II; 101). It has long been the practice to read this as expressing the idea of the most perfect being. But it is a proposition of faith. It does not say that God is, nor what he is. It is simply a negation: it is impossible to conceive of greater than him or to circumscribe him, impossible to place oneself above him as if he were an object representable in being, impossible to confuse him with the idols of

which greater can always be imagined because they are the work of our hands (see M. Corbin, Prière et raison de la foi, Paris, 1992). Coming from revelation (Jn 15:13), it returns to it by negatively signifying it as the event, such that no fiction about an eventual salvation and or any new idea of a foundation in self can surpass it. A prohibition of the idol, it is the opposite of the overriding of our thought and it keeps from all grasp the more than positive donation signified by that other name: "You are something greater than can be thought" (XV; 112). Here is designated the superabundance of the Spirit flowing from the pierced side of Jesus (Jn 19:34), and the cross as that "something" of our history that exhibits our sin and traces a cross on our attempts to inscribe it within the horizon of our human possibilities. The same goes for the name of doctor. We must be saved from the idols that have falsified the face of God in us, cured of the illness that has presented him to us as a rival to dethrone, liberated from the alienating projection that has pushed us to deify wisdom or power. As a work of superlative power would have plunged us more deeply into that night, giving reason to the devil who would suggest that God wanted to "make them know his power" (Mk 10:42), there was no better remedy for our disdain than the non-power of the cross, the mad love, disarmed love, wiser than the wisest, stronger than the strongest. The impersonation of the good had lost us in Adam; nothing was more suitable for us to find ourselves than the appearance of evil in Jesus's cross.

And yet it is but half the truth, because if nothing suited our illness better than the remedy of the cross, nothing better suited the bounty of God than that free promise of mercy*, for we who had such great need, and that overflowing love, "kept secret for long ages but now...disclosed" (Rom 16:25–26). This impossibility of thinking a bounty more divine than the humble tenderness that adapts its remedies to our illness, undoes our dreams of omnipotence, destroys all vision of graduated natures, destroys the notion of God that governs Arianism. The proclamation of a "God man, an Immortal who dies, an Eternal who is buried...a God who comes from a man, an Immortal from a mortal, an Eternal coming out of a tomb" (Hilary, De Trinitate I, PL 10/35 B) goes beyond intuition to cast doubt on a quantitative logic in which the signs "equal to" and "greater than" are excluded. In fact, when man wants to "seize by force equality with God," he masks his illusion of being the strongest, his need to dominate, which comes from his fear of being dominated, under the alibi of a claim to equality. But that pride that would abase the other is vanquished by the humility that holds the proud one himself for the greatest; it is overcome by the love that empties itself (Phil 2:6) of equality with God even unto the curse of the cross; a love that knocks at the door, saying: "If anyone hears my voice and opens the door, I will come in to him and eat with him, and he with me" (Rev 3:20). Of course, for one who does not seek understanding in this place where praise opens the way, where "more divine" is the perfect image of "divine," the one who wants to represent the distance in which God holds sway and to forget that to place an object before a subject is to deny the donation, it is scandalous to think that in taking personal pleasure in considering man, in washing his feet, God demonstrated and brought forth that which is most properly divine, that "love" (1 Jn 4:8) whose eternity is beyond time and eternity, that impassive charity whose freedom transcends the arbitrary and the necessary. But in blessing the Father who "chose us in him [Christ] before the foundation of the world" (Eph 1:4), Paul teaches that the being of God is more than necessary because it "belongs to his essence to be superabundant, to extend, overflow, and diffuse itself externally" (Barth, KD II/1, §28); that the being of God is higher than the necessary being of metaphysics, because it binds his glory to our remaking in charity. Paul learned it from Jesus who said: "There will be more joy in heaven over one sinner who repents than over ninety-nine righteous persons who need no repentance" (Lk 15:7).

Basil and Gregory of Nyssa expressed this coincidence-without-confusion of nature* and grace, by naming *parousia* the superabundance of *ousia*. Anselm did it by superimposing the kenosis on the eternal equality of the Son with the Father. On the cross the Good* beyond all good was revealed in its true form. All accept the equivalence between "God" and "resurrection" that appears in a saying of Jesus': "They are equal to the angels and are sons of God, being sons of the resurrection" (Lk 20:36); and in a speech of Paul's: "This he [God] has fulfilled to us their children by raising Jesus, as also it is written in the second Psalm, 'You are my Son, today I have begotten you' (Acts 13:33). They see that there is no higher salvation than the cross; not because they limit the divine power by not making the incarnation a possible among others, but because that power is the power of the love that gives being to the other, in overflowing communion, and because God alone can reveal what he wishes. They say that nothing is more proper to the glory of God than his free grace for us, that to receive the name of the Father, of the Son, and of the Holy Spirit is neither projecting a supreme object—because God is God in overflowing the dignity of God—nor seeking a representation, but standing in a filial relation to the Father—so that what they say is advanced only as a support for a prayer that listens to

the Word. That is the only answer to the Arian modalist heresies that know only TWO or ONE but never the donation opening the communion where one is ONE while remaining TWO. Because, far from denying nature by the creation of a dependence, or adding itself to nature as an appendix, grace is its overflowing repetition. And, far from denying *meta* (with) that praises the equality between Father and Son, *dia* (by) that receives the mediation of Jesus is all the more interior to the Father in that it unveils his eternity and grants his overabundance. Basil writes it in the names of the being of the Son with the Father: "'Whoever has seen me has seen the Father' [Jn 14:9]: not the figure or the form of the Father, because the divine nature is pure of all composition, but the bounty of the will that, coincidental with the essence, is seen as similar and equal or, even better, as the same in the Father and the Son. Which means: 'He humbled himself by becoming obedient' [Phil 2:8]? And: 'He [God] gave him [his Son] up for us all' [Rom 8:32]? Which comes from the Father, the bountiful action of the Son for men" (op. cit., VIII, §21).

It is impossible to speak of the Father and the Son without hearing Jesus say that "the Father is greater" (Jn 14:28) and that he is "ONE" (Jn 10:30) with the Father. The essence communicating from the Father to the Son like an inexhaustible promise of bounty "coincides" with a will to tenderness, "which is sustained through all eternity in the manner of a form reflected in a mirror" (op. cit., VIII, §20). And the Son is perfect resemblance to the Father, eternal "image of the invisible God" (Col 1:15), in the work of his passion where his mad love is sign and reality of the paternal love. Whence these words: "Glory is common to Father and to Son, and it is with the Son that we offer the doxology to the Father" (op. cit., VII, §16). This has two meanings: it is with the Son that we give thanks and glory to the Father; it is to the Father and the Son, from whom all good things come, that we offer the doxology. This means that the relation of the Son to the greater Father is all the greater in that it is the path that carries us, and all the better dispenser of the Father's good in that it is traced in his heart like the secret that abides in us and surpasses us.

2. The Effusion of the Holy Spirit

a) The Baptismal Confession. It still remains to celebrate the Holy Spirit in a way that honors the mediation of the Son, to receive that wound which opens our heart to the Good that passes all thought because it binds his future to ours. If it means a greater opening, we cannot forget that Thomas Aquinas named the spirit when he considered (*CG* IV, XXI)

1) The friendship inaugurated between God and ourselves, as the reciprocity of the love that bears God to us and us to God, as the indwelling of God in us and ourselves in God (Jn 14:23).

2) The sharing of the secrets of God as Spirit illuminates from within that which Jesus revealed in the Father's name (Jn 16:13), plumbs the depths of God (1 Cor 2:11), manifests the mystery, and brings forth in the believer a prophetic word.

3) The communication of the bounty of God: our creation (Ps 103:30), our purification, by the taking from us of our idols and filth (Ez 36:25), our vivification by a more than intimate presence (Wis 1:7), our sanctification in the truth (2 Thes 2:13), our introduction into filiation (Rom 8:17), our consolation in the contemplation* of God (2 Cor 3:18), our future resurrection (Rom 8:11).

4) Our free obedience of the commandments (Decalogue*) of God, the Gospel of grace (Eph 2:8) being that of liberty* (Gal 5:13).

"God's love has been poured into our hearts through the Holy Spirit" (Rom 5:5), and this is the love of God for us and our love of God, the Spirit supplying us with that which springs forth from us. Thomas interprets (op. cit., XIX) its effusion as a coming "by its own substance" and "by its effects." He approaches this synergy of grace and liberty with the texts in which Augustine recalls that Scripture often attributes to the cause what goes for the effect, God making himself our refuge when we take refuge in him. It is enough to say that God gives himself as the hidden principle of our path to him for it then to follow that, because the Spirit reminds us of what Jesus said and did for us (Jn 14:26), because he receives the good of the Son to share it with us and glorify him (Jn 16:14) by showing us that "Jesus is Lord" (1 Cor 12:3), since he makes us sons who assume the prayer of the only Son (Gal 4:6), he is named when the way of Jesus to his greater Father overflows to more intimate than our most intimate. He gives us to understand what the Father and Son say to call us to life; he inscribes "on their hearts" (Jer 31:33) the charity that is the "very substance of God" (Bernard* of Clairvaux, *Traité de l'amour de Dieu* XII, §35); and he is named when we say: "It is no longer I who live, but Christ who lives in me" (Gal 2:20). Because to decenter oneself toward the Higher, "to love more ardently than one feels oneself loved before being able to love" (Bernard, *Sermon 45 sur le Cantique,* §8), is to live a relation given and ordered in the Spirit, to be taken under the shadow (Lk 1:35) of him who effaces himself under our own effacement. If then the Spirit is inseparable from Jesus, the "one mediator between God and men" (1 Tm 2:5), and if the

mediation of the Son is all the more interior to the Father in that it better manifests his bounty, the mediation of the Spirit is that of the *interiorization,* to depths greater than our depths, of what was done by the Father and the Son before we knew it. And to confess the Spirit of the Father and the Son is to receive the more than essential deity that makes itself the being of our being: it is to praise *Deus intimior intimo meo et superior summo meo* ("God more inward than my most inward part, and higher than my highest being").

Basil often reminds us that we must distinguish the "objective" mediation of the Son from the "subjective" mediation of the Spirit, who is the inner light illuminating both the image that is offered and the eye invited to rejoice in it: "He, like a sun taking hold of a very pure eye, will show you in himself the Image of the Invisible and, in the wonderful contemplation of the Image, you will see the unutterable beauty of the Archetype....As limpid, transparent bodies sparkle when touched by a ray, and of themselves reflect another gleam, so those souls which bear the Spirit also become spiritual and reflect grace on others." (op. cit., IX, §23) The Spirit offering in himself to see ourselves the Son speaking of the Father, his mediation is all the more inseparable from the Father and the Son in that it gives us to become the only Son turned toward the Father. But, if the Spirit opens by faith the way to the Father that the Son sealed in his Passion, and the knowledge of the bounty incorporated and given in excess in God's sending of Jesus, the line that, rising from the Spirit by the Son toward the Father, descends toward the Church must leave room for another figure. It draws the parallel between the two turnings of the Son toward the Father of whom he is the exegete and of the Spirit toward the Son whose path it illuminates, but does not show the difference between the two mediations or the direct connection of the Spirit to the Father from which it "proceeds" (Jn 15:26). But, if the Spirit given by the Father and the Son is their mutual love, their peace*, if his effusion opens us to the inner presence of the Father and the Son, to the mystery of *Deus intimior intimo meo,* if the Spirit that is given is not separated from the Church that receives it, it must be recognized as the overflow of the overflowing communion of the Father and the Son, or the overflowing communion of the Father and the Son overflowing on ourselves who believe, *exundantia plenitudinis [Christi]* (Anselm, *Cur Deus Homo* II, XIX; 131), and it is no longer possible to speak of a communion between the Three, because this *perichoresis* or *circumincession** would play between the Father, the Son, and their communion itself. In the *connumeration* of the Three, a difference must be noted between sayings about the Father and the Son and sayings about the

Spirit. It can be found in Hilary* of Poitiers's discourse on the baptismal commandment in which "Name" is in the singular though Three are named:

The Lord said: "Go therefore and make disciples of all nations, baptizing them in the name of the Father and of the Son and of the Holy Spirit, teaching them to observe all that I have commanded you. And behold, I am with you always, to the end of the age" (Mt 28:19–20). What is there in the mystery of "human salvation that is not contained there, or left aside, obscure? Everything there is plenitude, as coming from the one who is plenitude and perfection: simultaneously, the terms are indicated, the realities posed, the problems situated, the nature explained. He commanded that baptism should be given 'in the name of the Father and of the Son and of the Holy Spirit,' that is, by professing faith in the Source, in the Only-Begotten and in the Gift. The source of all things, single, because there is only one God the Father 'from whom are all things,' one Only-Begotten, Our Lord Jesus Christ 'through whom are all things' [1 Cor 8:6] and 'one Spirit' [Eph 4:4], gift in all things. All things are ordered according to their virtues and merits; single is the power from which comes all things, single his offspring by whom are all things, single the Gift [munus] of perfect hope. And nothing will be found lacking in such a perfect accomplishment: in the Father, the Son, and the Holy Spirit are found infinity in the Eternal, beauty in the Image, and enjoyment in the Present" (De Trinitate II, §1; PL 10/50 C-51 A).

Expressions applied to the Spirit are reversed with regard to those that designate the Father and the Son. While the expression "in whom are all things" is used to designate the Spirit, we read:

1) "Who is in all things," which means the deity flows as communion where thanksgiving and praise originate.
2) "Present of perfect hope," which refers to the universal groaning for "the freedom of the glory of the children of God" (Rom 8:21).
3) "Enjoyment in the Present," which does not primarily express the mutual enjoyment of the Father and the Son, but our own jubilation in being given as brothers to the Son and in having a Father for whom we exist.

The Spirit is venerated three times over, as the over-abundant Gift that the Father bestows us in giving us his only Son, and which the Son bestows, in freely giving us his given life.

b) The Restitution of the Glory. This profuse gift to all is treated in Hilary's exegesis* (op. cit., III, §9–16; PL 10/80 C-85 C) of the prayer pronounced by Jesus in Jn 17:1–5, and this is all the more surprising in that the prayer does not mention the Spirit, but its fruits: love, joy, knowledge of the "Name," glory, unity. Here is the introduction: "Witness for us from our own [goods] of divine things the Son of God could, through the infirmities of the flesh, preach to us a God the Father, to us the infirm and carnal. In which he accomplished the will of God the Father, according to his saying: 'I have come down from heaven, not to do my own will but the will of him who sent me' [Jn 6:38]. Not that he himself does not do his own will but because in doing the paternal will he manifests his obedience, himself willing to fulfill the will of the Father." (III, §9) To defend the *nativitas Dei* which is communication of the *natura* and nature communicated, Hilary recalled Cana, and the multiplication of the loaves, and explained that in these miracles* of gratuitous, inexplicable superabundance, Jesus had no "need of us to adorn his ineffable works with praises, as if he lacked them" (§7). He cited the word of the cross that reverses folly into more than wisdom. Before reading the prayer of Jesus in the light of a paradox opening on superabundance, he emphasized that the Son manifests his free will to obey the will of the Father, not to "make us feel the omnipotence of God in the creation of things," but to announce to us that "God is the Father of this Son who speaks to us" (III, §22). Transcribing the first verse: "Father, the hour has come, glorify your Son that your Son may glorify you" (Jn 17:1), showing that it is a question of the passion and the resurrection, he notes a circularity: the Father will glorify the Son who will glorify him. This refutes the Arian heresy, which saw an inferiority of nature in the fact of being glorified: "There it is, the hour when he prays the Father to glorify him, so that he himself may glorify the Father. What is it? If he waits to be glorified before glorifying, asks for an honor before giving it, would he need that which he in turn is going to give? . . . The Lord said: 'Father, the hour has come.' He designated the hour of the passion, because it is when he was right there that he spoke this way. After which he added: 'Glorify your Son.' But how was the Son to be glorified?" (III, §10)

If the Son asks for an honor that he will render to the Father, how can he need that which he is going to give, not have it when he asks? The representative sense of the comparative "greater" attributed to the Father by Jesus and the immediate reversal of the "greater" for the Father in "smaller" for the Son have already been hinted at. But how can it be said without seeing how the Father glorifies the Son in that passion which contradicts his glory? It suffices to read the narratives* of Good Friday:

"When the centurion and those who were with him, keeping watch over Jesus, saw the earthquake . . . they were foiled with awe and said, 'Truly this was the Son of God!'" (Mt 27:54). "Creation frees itself of having to intervene in this crime, the stones do not keep their force and solidity, those who had put him on the cross confess him truly the Son of God. The effect goes with the supplication because the Lord had said: 'Glorify your Son.' He had testified that he is not only the Son by name but also by property as expressed by the word 'your'"(III, §11). Thus, the Son is glorified by the Father when the man at the foot of the cross recognizes him as true Son, "by origin and not by adoption," delivered by the Father as the most princely of gifts, united to the Father in a more than unutterable union, that of origin. This glorification by the Father is also the glorification by the Spirit (Jn 16:13), who makes the wondrous reception of the gift unfold in our hearts that were closed. Because there is no true gift but a gift received. Does that imply the inferiority of the envoy with respect to the one who, sending him, fulfilling him, glorifying him, is more powerful? Can Arius cite the word of Jesus: "The Father is greater than me?" Will he be answered by the classical distinction: Jesus is equal to the Father as Son of God, smaller as Son of man? But do we know what "greater" means when we say it of God to man? The majesty of God "surpasses all understanding" (Phil 4:7), including our images of height and grandeur. And do we know, of ourselves, about God and about man? We learn it on the "path" (Jn 14:6) that Jesus traced to the Father. There we discover better and better, with no possible halt, the desired truth. The usual reply should be extended by studying the whole of the accusatory verse: "You heard me say to you, 'I am going away, and I will come to you.' If you loved me, you would have rejoiced, because I am going to the Father, for the Father is greater than I" (Jn 14:28). By repeating "I am going away, and I will come to you," what does Jesus announce if not the passion when, ascending to the Father, he encounters those who are his? By inviting them to rejoice, what does he promise if not the Spirit that is the fruit of his departure? He will no longer be present by their sides, but in a more noble way, *in* them, in the Spirit which he received from the Father in order to distribute "without measure" (Jn 3:34). The Gospels* could not have emerged without this Spirit that "will guide you into all the truth" (Jn 16:13), nor could the disciples recognize the free self-abasement of their master and discover in the Spirit that Jesus is "the same" (Heb 13:8) in his humility of a servant and his kingly elevation. The gospel being the fruit of the passion, he who declares that "the Father is greater" is Jesus on whom God has bestowed "the name that is above every name" (Phil 2:9), and who says: "I am in the Father and the Father is in me" (Jn 14:10). This produces the paradox whereby nativity and glorification are superimposed: "The Father is greater since he is the Father, but the Son, since he is the Son, is not smaller. The nativity of the Son constitutes the greater Father; but the nature of that nativity does not allow that the Son be smaller. The Father is greater, since he is prayed to render glory to the man assumed; the Son is not smaller, since he regains glory at the Father's side. This is how the mystery of the nativity and the economy of incorporation are accomplished. Because the Father is greater, since he is Father and now glorifies the Son of man; at the same time, the Father and the Son are ONE since the Son born of the Father is glorified in this Father after he has taken on an earthly body" (op. cit., IX, §56, PL 10/327 A-B).

This is to attest the reversal brought about on the cross. Instead of reiterating the sin of Adam by imagining himself "a greater" and wanting to dominate by seeking "equality with God," in masking his wish to dethrone him, to make himself greater, under a claim to equality, Christ freely "made himself nothing" (Phil 2: 6–7). Loving us more than himself in loving the Father more than himself, he caused to radiate and overflow, in counter-image, the bounty of the Father and, in that kenosis in which love is again more lovable, in this free obedience that allows him to be greater because he is source, the Father recognized his true resemblance, allowed the overflowing of his own superabundance. Then, when Jesus prays to the one he calls "greater," his equality of glory and his unity of nature appear. His glorification is that of the Father: "'May the Son Glorify you.' The Son, he who must render like in the fact of glory once he has been glorified, is not weak. But if he is not weak, what did he have to ask for? One asks only for that which is lacking. Is it possible that the Father might also be weak? Or had he been so prodigious with his goods that the Son must render them to him in glorifying him? But the one is lacking nothing, and the other does not desire, and yet they make a mutual gift to each other. To ask for the glorification to give, to render in return, this takes nothing from the Father and does not weaken the Son, but shows in both the same power of divinity, because the Son prays the Father to glorify him, and the Father does not disdain to be glorified by the Son. This shows the unity of power in the Father and the Son by reciprocity in the gift and restitution of the glory" (III, §12).

If the glorification of the Son implied his inferiority, due to a need, that of the Father would imply the same inferiority. But the Father "is not served by human hands, as though he needed anything, since he himself gives to all mankind life and breath and everything" (Acts 17:25). Therefore the Son lacks nothing and, far from signifying a mutual need, the circularity of the glorification between Father and Son indicates a superabundance of desire beyond all need: "They will make each other a mutual gift." Can such a superabundance not be at the heart of their communion? The Other being promise of more, can it not overflow on the others as gracious effusion of "the reciprocity in the gift and the restitution of the glory?" Yes, divinity is without need without change, it IS that which it IS, and its eternity is subject to "neither flaw nor improvement, neither advancement nor loss" (III, §13). But if the Father and the Son are glorified by each other, how do they recover what they never lost and receive that which is not lacking to them? The question prohibits all image of God as self-sufficiency enthroned at the summit of being. It refers to the immutability of the source that gives itself, to the more divine overflowing of a love equal to itself in its fidelity. The Son showed its blessings.

Such was the glory: the Son received from the Father "power over all flesh" (v. 2).... The glory is not added to God. None had "left him to return and be added. But through the Son he is glorified in the midst of us, the boors, the deserters, the wretched, the hopeless dead, the lawless creatures of the night. He is glorified in that the Son received from him power over all flesh, to give to it eternal life*. There they are, the works of the Son who glorified the Father. Thus, the Son, because he received all, was glorified by the Father; conversely the Father is glorified, because all is done by the Son" (III, §13).

If the Son is glorified by the Father when we recognize him as true Son, the Father is glorified in turn when the Son, receiving all from him, gives us the life that resides in the knowledge of the Father of "the one [he] sent" (v. 3). This glorification is not made in a "new construction," as if God began his creation again from the start, but in the "sole knowledge of God," in the discovery that the truth of the creation is a recreation that surpasses it, an entry into the divine filiation. It is in us that the Father and Son glorify each other in an overflowing of glory that adds nothing to theirs. But if life consists in recognizing the Donator, "present in the beginning and the end, above all and within all" (I, §6, PL 10/29 B), is it not the fruit of the Holy Spirit? Are we not those that the Father gives to the Son and the Son leads to the Father by decentering himself toward the Greater, in giving them the Spirit so that they will do "the same works" and "even greater ones" (Jn 14:12)?

Of course, faith in the Spirit was not Hilary's main concern. Rather, he wanted to show that there is "neither interval nor solution of continuity in the confession of faith," that Father and Son are "one single something" though they are "two someones" (III, §14). But elsewhere he says that the Spirit is *res naturae* (VIII, §22, PL 10/252 C), "thing of nature," "even affair" of God who wants to "prepare us for the gift that he is himself" (Meister Eckhart, *Spiritual Instructions*). The following explains this liaison of the Spirit with the overflowing of the *natura* in *gratia* of which we cannot speak in making the substances objective, except in a posture of reception: "All praise of the Father comes to him from the Son, because that in the Son which is worthy to be praised will be praise for the Father. He "accomplishes" everything the Father wanted. Son of God... he is nailed to the cross, but on the cross of the man, God triumphs over death. Son of God, Christ dies, but in Christ all flesh receives life. Son of God, he is in hell, but he, the man, is raised to the heavens. The more this is praised in Christ, the more will follow the praise for the one by whom Christ is God. These are the ways in which the Father glorifies the Son on earth, and by which the Son in turn, in the face of the ignorance of the nations and the folly of the world*, glorifies, in virtue of the works of his powers, the one from whom he takes to be himself. This exchange of glorification does not concern an advancement in divinity but the honor received at being known to the ignorant. For, in what did the father lack abundance, he from whom all things come, or what was lacking to the Son, he in whom God took pleasure in making his plenitude abide? The Father is then glorified on earth because this, his work that he commanded, is accomplished" (III, §15).

This reflection on the mutual gift of the Father and the Son radically poses the paradox: on the one hand, the exchange of glory is not an advancement in God; on the other, the more the economy of our salvation is praised in Christ, "the more follows the praise" for the Father. There is juxtaposition of an affirmation—greater praise comes to God because we are living—and an overriding negation: his divinity is without need. Distinguishing nature and glory, this juxtaposition is not an exteriority between economy and theology, because the nature is understood according to the praise as a more than unutterable promise of bounty, as a personal pleasure such that there cannot be greater, as inexhaustible source where we can drink our fill. In this attention, moments in apparent contradiction are the two wounds from which flows and is celebrated the supereminence, as new as eternal, of love accepting to receive something from us who receive everything from him. Though he is without lack, God awaits the fruit that, in the Spirit, we must bear. Because Jesus said: "By this my Father is glorified, that you bear much fruit" (Jn 15:8). The proof of this *summa concordia* is offered in the verses that amplify the initial prayer: " 'Father, glorify me near to your glory which I had near you before the world was made' (v. 5). What does he expect of the Father as glorification? That which he had by his side before the world existed. He had the plenitude of divinity. He has it, because he is the Son of God, but he who was the Son of God had begun also to be the Son of man: 'the Word became flesh' [Jn 1:14]. He had not lost what he was, but began to be what he had not been. He did not lack what was his, but took what is ours. Thus he claimed for what he had taken a progress in that glory that he was not lacking. Also, because the Son is the Word, the Word was made flesh, the word is God, close to God in the beginning, because the Word was Son before the constitution of the world, the Son who now was made flesh prayed that the flesh would begin to be for the Father that which he, the Word, was; for that which was within time would receive the glory of what is outside of time and, transformed into the force of God, in the incorruptibility of the Spirit, the corruption of the flesh was swallowed up. This is why he prayed to God. This is what the Son proclaimed facing the Father; it is what the flesh begs for. And thus it is that all will see him on the day of judgment*, transpierced, marked by the cross, as he was prefigured on the mountain, as he was brought up in the heavens, as he is seated on the right hand of God, as he was seen by Paul, as he received the homage of Stephen" (III, § 16).

Without this unsurpassable prayer, for which Hilary lets the movement reign without seeking any explanation, we cannot say that Jesus became on Easter day that which he always was, nor reverse the contradiction between the absence of need and the surplus of praise aiming at a logic more than logical, that of the Love that IS. When Jesus beseeches the Father to reinstate him in the glory he enjoyed "at his side before the world was made," it is an equal glory and a greater glory for which he asks. Equal because it is that of the love that surrenders itself, of the Lamb* "foreknown before the foundation of the world but...made manifest in the last times for your sake" (1 Pt 1:19–20), of the Christ in whom we are "chosen" "before the foundation of the world" (Eph 1:4). Greater, because the wounds of the Son shown on Easter evening like "royal finery" (N. Cabasilas, *Life in Christ* VI, §15, SC 361) are the wounds we inflicted on him, which he made a remedy, such that anything better adapted to our illness and more appropriate to the mercy of God cannot be conceived. It is " transpierced" that we will see him, in the great promise of his tenderness, the day when, through him and in the Spirit, we will have a transfigured flesh and will become for the Father what the Son is from all eternity. Thus, at Easter:

1) God is revealed as more divine, and this "even more" that remains more than can be thought, is his undivided divinity.

2) There comes what IS: the communion of God and man, which is not separate from, nor is it confused with, the communion of the Father and the Son, because it stands on this *totus homo totus Deus* (IX, §6, PL 10/285 B), who says more than God alone while saying his truth, more than man alone while saying his truth.

3) The man no longer being "closed on high" nor God "below" (K. Barth, *The Humanity of God*), the superimposition of the nativity and the resurrection of the Son unfolds in the Spirit in our deepest depths, as the being of our being "has not yet appeared" (1 Jn 3:2), but already identical to that which is coming: "That God may be all in all" (1 Cor 15:28.)

If the greater glory given on Easter morning to the Word made flesh is the restored glory equal to that of the Word turned toward God in the beginning, it is impossible to imagine that God would be first of all *in himself,* enclosed in his *phusis,* and then *for us,* the author of a *kharis* that does not commit his being. Of course a distinction is made between *phusis* and *kharis, natura* and *sacramentum,* by way of showing that God loves us freely, that his personal pleasure precedes us; but far from leading to the representation of a supreme Object, this distinction honors the manifestation of that which has been forever hidden (Mk 4:22). It disposes us to the coming of that which is, to the reception of superabundant goods that the Father reserves for us, he who has no other reason to let them flow than the overflowing of his gracious bounty. Impossible also to identify the hidden and the manifest by way of a loop that would be closure on an object, forgetting that the source never stops outpouring, ever more clear, in the hands that the word of Jesus hold open.

c) God is Spirit. Is it in conformity with the Scriptures to connect the Spirit of the Father and of the Son to the mutual gift they give each other, to call it the superabundant Gift of the superabundant communion of the Father and the Son, the Spirit of the passion opening us to the surplus of the Other who chooses us for abode? Hilary's words on the Spirit assure us (II, §29–35; PL 10/69 A-75 A): "As to the Holy Spirit, it is not necessary to hold one's tongue nor is it necessary to speak.... The question of his being is not to be treated.... If someone requires the sense of our intelligence, he reads as we do in the Apostle: "And because you are sons, God has sent the Spirit of his Son into our hearts, crying 'Abba! Father!' [Gal 4:6].... It follows from that that he is, that he is given, possessed, and that he is God ... If now he asks through whom he is, for which and for what he is, our answer might displease him because we say: he is the one through whom and of whom are all things, and he is the Spirit of God, a gift made to the faithful" (II, §29). Three paradoxes are present here:

1) We must not talk about the Spirit because he is the unsurpassable witness of the Father and the Son, and we must not remain silent because some have not yet received. "Now we have received not the spirit of the world, but the Spirit who is from God, that we might understand the things freely given us by God" (1 Cor 2:12). It should be noted that the Spirit escapes from the category of substance, which our utterance can never do without, and to make it an object before a subject would be denial of the Gift that it is.

2) "He IS because also he is GIVEN." This brief phrase rejects all separation of *phusis* and *kharis.* Identifying "being" and "being given," it joins the Spirit to the overflowing repetition of the *natura* in the *sacramentum,* as if naming the Spirit was receiving the very bond of the same essence and the superabundance, this "more remaining more" that is the eternal divinity, without separation between its being and its personal pleasure. We only speak of the Spirit in the Spirit, in the communion it establishes.

3) "It is given and obtained." If it stimulates a move on our part, a "merit," the Spirit gives us that which comes from ourselves. Creator, it makes us partners of the covenant*, in freedom.

These paradoxes are brought together as follows: "Some, I think, remain in ignorance and doubt because they see the third term, that is, the Holy Spirit, is frequently understood of the Father and the Son. But there is nothing there that should shock: the Father, like the Son, is just as much Spirit as Holy." (II, §30)

The Spirit is named by the conjoining of the two words most appropriate to the Father and the Son, though their conjunction never be attributed, and this proves that it *is,* that it is given by them as their overflowing communion. Spirit not having a proper name but being signified by a thousand names, it is like the force driving toward the Other, or the decentering that constitutes the person in his unity. Creating and recreating us, it effaces himself before our free response, itself made of effacement before the Greater. But some refuse to speak of it as "enjoyment and gift." They confuse it with that which is common to the Father and the Son, deny that their communion subsists and

is distinct from it, cite the word of Jesus: "God is Spirit" (Jn 4:24). How shall we answer them if not that they do not read the words in their context, as Jesus's reply to a woman who sought a geographical place where she could worship God? "To say: 'God is Spirit' does not preclude speaking of the Holy Spirit and making it a gift. For he replied to the woman who wanted to enclose God in a temple, on a mountain, that everything is in God, that God is in himself, that the Invisible, the Incomprehensible must be worshipped in that which is invisible, incomprehensible. Thus is the nature of the present and of the homage signified by this teaching: God-Spirit must be worshipped in Spirit. That shows the freedom and the knowledge of the worshippers as well as the infinity of the Worshipped" (II, §31).

If God is such that nothing can contain him, present in all and overflowing all, the true worship that recognizes in him the Father of Jesus is made only in a place that corresponds to that excess of being and goodness, in the Holy Spirit who is distinguished from the Father and the Son who are God-Spirit, and whose unutterable superabundance responds to the inexhaustible communion of the Father and the Son. In the Spirit we worship the Father who gives us his Son and the Son who gives us to the Father; the Spirit who worships is not separated from the "freedom" and the "discernment" of the worshippers that we are: "The Holy Spirit is everywhere one, illuminating all the patriarchs, the prophets, all the choir of the Law, inspiring also John in his mother's womb, and given to the apostles, to the other believers to make them recognize the truth that was granted" (II, §32).

In the Spirit, donation of the donation, God abides in us and by the reciprocity of this indwelling his donation is at the same time our response to the love that goes ahead of us and surpasses us: "Let us use that which is so freely given to us, let us ask to use of this very necessary present. The Apostle says: 'Now we have received not the spirit of the world, but the Spirit who is from God, that we might understand the things freely given us by God' [1 Cor 2:12]. We receive it in order to know. [If our soul] has not drawn by faith the gift of the Spirit, certainly it will have a nature made to recognize God, but it will not have the light of knowledge. This gift made in Christ is accessible, single, and entirely ours; that which is nowhere lacking is given in the measure in which each one desires to receive it, and retained in the measure that each one desires to merit it. This is what is with us up to the consummation of the ages" (II, §35).

Just as it is not possible to see without light illuminating both the thing and the eye, so we cannot be that for which we are made if we do not draw, by the faith that is its fruit in us, "the living water" (Jn 4:10) of the encounter. To draw this water is to make our own response to the gift through a desire that "asks, merits, and keeps." Then are found prayer, filial relation to the Father, a posture drawing itself more upright, *epectasis* (yearning) (Phil 3:13) toward higher and higher goods "by beginnings that have no end" (Gregory of Nyssa, *Homily on the Song of Songs*). It is carried so deeply inward, so overwhelmed by that of Jesus, that the Spirit fills our hearts to overflowing and makes them overflow.

Must we question ourselves on the notions of essence and person? As the first word does not designate a metaphysical foundation, but the plenitude of love and life that is given, the "good measure, pressed down, shaken together, running over" promised to those who follow (*Lc* 6, 38), it is better to make the second word a second auxiliary concept making up for the impossibility of thinking and saying what are the Three as three: "If we ask: three what [*tres quid*]? human words are at pains and totally impoverished. We do say three persons, not to say but in order not to say nothing." (Augustine, *Trin.* V, IX, 10, Baug 15). "It is better to meditate on the heart of the faith: "God is love. God manifested his love for us in that God sent his only Son into the world so that we would live through him. This is what the love consists of: it is not we who loved God, it is he who loved us and sent his Son as propitiatory victim for our sins. Beloved, if God so loved us, we too must love each other. No one has ever contemplated God. If we love each other, God abides in us, in us his love is made complete. By

this we know that we abide in him and he abides in us: 'He has given us of his Spirit'" (1 Jn 4:8–13).

Is this a definition? So that we will understand behind "God" the Father of Jesus and our own, not a supreme self-sufficiency, John reminds us that God "sent his Son" and "gave of his Spirit." So that we will understand behind "love" the free superabundance of the source, not an objectified principle, he tells how that love "manifested itself": in the most wise folly of the cross. So that we will leave behind our errors of representation, he tells us that "no one has ever seen God." To keep us from concluding from this that he is unknowable, he invites us to know him by obeying a new commandment. Thus, for a knowledge of God according to sight, which seeks to grasp his reality through image or concept, John substitutes knowledge according to love, which consists in our loving one another as Jesus loved us, and in allowing God to dwell in us as an ever more lovable Father, "to be born of God" (v.7) in the Spirit. Of these two kinds of knowledge, one claims to inscribe the secret within the vaster horizon of our possibilities and place itself above him: it is the root of all heresy. The other understands the prohibition of idols by the cross as the most beneficial event that could be. It receives it as the underside of the princeliest donation that could be thought. It reaches up with gratitude toward the source, obeys the timeless call of Jesus: "If anyone thirsts, let him come to me and drink" (Jn 7:37).

MICHEL CORBIN

See also **Being; Christ/Christology; Father;** *Filioque;* **God; Holy Spirit; Word**

Tritheism

a) Patristics. In anti-Christian polemics the accusation of Tritheism reveals a misunderstanding of the Christian Trinity*, by which the polemicists see only a troika of divine beings. And as a term in heresiology, *Tritheism* refers to a Trinitarian theology* that gives each of the three divine persons* an existence conceived in the same way as the existence of an individual. Taken to its logical conclusion, a Trinitarian theology of this kind so slackens the link between the divine persons that the accusation of Tritheism does no

more than draw the final conclusions. The various forms of Tritheism are all dependent on particular philosophical conceptions about what is common to the three persons (that is, their nature*).

In the third century, the opponents of Monarchianism (Modalism*) were accused of Ditheism or Tritheism. Indeed, Justin († c. 165) used the expression *heteros theos* when he spoke of the Word*. Even among the Cappadocians, certain passages lend themselves to an interpretation in terms of Tritheism. Basil*

(c. 330–79) in fact conceived the hypostases as subsisting essences defined by particular properties *(idiotetes)* and suggested between the divine *phusis (ousia)* and the three hypostases, *treis hupostaseis (prosôpa),* the same relationship that exists between abstract human nature and the individuals in whom it proliferates *(Ep.* 236, 6, PG 32, 884; *Ep.* 214, 789; *see DThC* 5, col. 1671). In the sixth century, inspired by the philosophy of Aristotle (Christian Aristotelianism*), the neo-Chalcedonian Leontius of Byzantium († c. 543) tried to define precisely the meaning of the terms *hupostasis* and *phusis.* Under his influence the idea spread in the schools of Edessa, Constantinople, and Alexandria* that there were three hypostases in God*, each one requiring a concrete nature; whence came the conclusion that there were three natures in God, which was equivalent to professing Tritheism. Those who followed this doctrine found their theoretician in the person of John Philoponus († c. 565), a grammarian and philosopher from Alexandria. In his book entitled *Diaitetes e peri henôseôs,* (*The Arbitrator, or On Union, see* Nicephore Calliste, PG 147, 424–28), Philoponus asserted that all existing nature was necessarily individual and that it could be realized only in and through a hypostasis, for the good reason that hypostasis and individual merge. And from this fact he concluded that since there were three persons in God, there were also three divine natures. According to the testimony of Leontius of Byzantium, Philoponus taught that in the Trinity there were three *merikai ousiai* and a common *ousia* (PG 86, 1233). Philoponus's Tritheist views were opposed by the monks of the period. Among the adepts of ancient Tritheism can also be named Stephen Gobar, who was writing in Egypt or in Syria under Justin II (565–78).

b) Middle Ages and Modern Times. Tritheism took on a new form in the 11th century under the influence of dialectics (Scholasticism*). His dialectic approach and his Nominalism* led Roscelin of Compiègne (1050–1125), professor of dialectics and later Canon of Tours, to the implicit affirmation of the existence of three Gods.

The works of Anselm* are our main historical source for this medieval Trinitarian heresy*. In 1090, while still an abbot, Anselm was alerted by the monk John to the doctrine of a "cleric in France," whose essential points he reported to him in these terms, "If three persons are a single thing and are not three things in themselves, like three angels* or three souls*, in such a way that in their will and power they are completely identical, the Father* and the Holy* Spirit became flesh along with the Son" (*Ep.* 128, ed. Schmitt, III).

In his reply (*Epistles* 129; Schmitt, III) Anselm sketched a solution: if the cleric in question meant by the three *res,* three relationships, it was futile for him to have said what he did. If, on the other hand, he used the three *res* to name the three persons and each person was God, a dilemma ensued: either he wanted to establish three gods, or else he did not know what he was saying. Therefore, from the beginning, Anselm denounced Tritheism as a logical consequence of Roscelin's position, and later he drew up a fuller refutation that was unfinished, entitled *Epistola de Incarnatione Verbe* and addressed to those who "cultivate the Catholic and Apostolic faith."

Anselm's second contribution was motivated by the unchanged attitude of Roscelin, who had not stopped spreading his heterodox views, although he had abjured his errors at the Council of Soissons (1092 or 1093) for fear of being killed by the people. The situation grew more complicated by the fact that in order to defend himself Roscelin tried to compromise Lanfranc in this doctrinal matter and claimed that Anselm himself had preached similar views. In his letter addressed to Fulcon, bishop* of Beauvais (*Epistles* 136, Schmitt, III), Anselm protested against these allegations by solemnly confessing his orthodox faith.

The main points of Roscelin's arguments are based on a postulation: each of the three persons must be a *thing* if one wants to avoid the absurd conclusion of the incarnation* of the Father and of the Holy Spirit. Roscelin therefore deduced from this the existence of three complete *res* in the Trinity, but he maintained however that the three persons had a common will and power (the first sketch of what the 20th century would call a "social" conception of the Trinity). The stumbling block in his dialectical approach was the ambiguous meaning of the term *res.* In his criticism Anselm made a distinction: if Roscelin meant by three *res* the three relations *(relatio),* his position could be accepted. But if *res* was understood in the sense of substantial or essential, it became logically impossible to avoid the absurd conclusion that there were three Gods, which compromised the simplicity and eternity of the divine nature. According to Anselm's interpretation it was therefore through drawing the consequence that Roscelin professed Tritheism.

After Anselm's death the polemic flared up again between Roscelin and his disciple Abelard*. The poisonous relations between the two antagonists is recounted in a letter from Roscelin addressed to Abelard, who, in his *De Unitate et trinitate divina* (PL V, 178, col 39), violently reproached Roscelin for his Tritheism.

A new form of implicit Tritheism reappeared in the nineteenth century in the theological system of Anton Günther, who was condemned in Pius IX's bull *Exi-*

miam tuam (1857). Günther proposed a conception of the human person—identified with his awareness of his ego and with his external actions—which, when applied to God, led Günther in fact to consider the three divine persons as three consciousnesses, and therefore, as three substances or three realities absolutely distinct from each other.

Of the two main trends of contemporary Trinitarian theology, one seems to have made all the concessions to Modalism which are possible without abandoning orthodoxy (Barth*, Rahner*); while the other seems to supply a version, which is also orthodox, of a thinking inclined towards Tritheism; an instance of the latter being seen in the extreme psychologization or personalization to which H. U. von Balthasar* subjects the divine hypostases.

• A. Günther (1829), *Vorschule zur speculativen Theologie des positiven Christentums,* Vienna, vol. I, 104, 119, 352, and vol. II, 291, 535–39.

A. Günther (1833), *Janus Köpfe für Philosophie und Theologie,* Vienna, vol. II, 272–79, 334–40.

Justin (1909), *Dialogue avec Tryphon,* Ed. G. Archambault, p. 56, col. 597 b.

A. Sanda (1930), *Opuscula monophysitica J. Philoponi* (syr. text with Lat. trans.), Beirut.

F. S. Schmitt, *S. Anselmi Cantuariensis Archiepiscopi Opera Omnia,* Seckau-Edinburgh-Rome, 1938–1961 (6 vol.), see *Ep.* 128, Schmitt, III, 270–71; I, I, 2, p. 282, 5–8; II, II, p. 6, 10–7, 2; II, II, p. 5, 1–4.

♦ R. Stolzle (1891), *Abaelards 1121 zu Soisson verurtheilter, Tractatus de unitate et Trinitate divina,* Freiburg.

M. de Wulf (1896), "Le problème des universaux dans son évolution historique du IXe au XIIIe siècles," *AGPh,* 427–44.

E. Kaiser (1901), *Pierre Abélard, critique,* Fribourg.

J. A. Endres (1906), "Die Dialektiker und ihre Gegner im 11. Jahrhundert," *PhJ* 19, 20–33.

B. F. Adlhoch (1907), "Roscelin und S. Anselm," *PhJ* 20, 442–56.

A. Porée (1909), "L'école du Bec et saint Anselme," *RevPhil* XV, 618–38.

A. Reiners (1910), *Der Nominalismus in der Frühscholastik,* BGPhMA VIII/5, Münster.

F. Picavet (1911), *Roscelin philosophe et théologien d'après la légende et d'après l'histoire: sa place dans l'histoire générale et comparée des philosophies médiévales,* Paris.

A. von Harnack (1923), "The *Sic et Non* of Stephanus Gobarus," *HThR* 16, 205–34.

A. Wilmart (1931), "Le premier ouvrage de saint Anselme contre le trithéisme de Roscelin," *RThAM* 20–36.

M. de Corte (1934), *Le commentaire de J. Philopon sur le 3e livre du "Traité de l'âme d'Aristote,"* Liège.

F. S. Schmitt (1939), "Cinq recensions de l'*Epistola de incarnatione verbi* de saint Anselme de Cantorbéry," *RBen* 51, 275–87.

G. Bardy (1947), "Le florilège d'Étienne Gobar," *REByz* 5, 5–30.

C. Mews (1992), "Nominalism and Theology before Abaelard: New Light on Roscelin of Compiègne," *Vivarium* 30, 4–33.

C. Mews (1996), "St Anselm, Roscelin and the See of Beauvais," in D. E. Luscombe, G. R. Evans (Eds.), *Anselm: Aosta, Bec, Canterbury,* Sheffield, 106–19.

C. Viola (1996), "Authority and Reason in Saint Anselm's Life and Thought," ibid., 172–208.

COLOMAN VIOLA

See also **Consubstantial; Modalism; Monotheism; Trinity**

Tropology. *See* Saint-Victor, School of; Scripture, Senses of

Truth

A. Biblical Theology

When the New Testament speaks of "truth" (*aletheia* in Greek; *veritas* in Latin) within a theological perspective, as is the case particularly with Paul and with the Johannine corpus, it is throwing a bridge between the Hebraic-biblical basis and Greco-Hellenist thought. The rapprochement had already begun in the third century B.C. when the Septuagint translators chose to use the Greek *aletheia* to convey the words *emounah* (trust, loyalty) and above all *emet* (solidity, permanence) in the Hebrew Bible*, as Hebrew did not have a specific term to express the notion of truth.

a) Etymology and Meaning of Aletheia.   A derivative of *lanthano/letho* (see the Latin *lateo*), which means "to be hidden," preceded by the privative "a-," the word *aletheia* designates a thing that is shown as it is, as well as the precision of the discourse (logos) that states it. Neither the everyday use nor the classical philosophical use of the term departed from this initial acceptation (E. Heitsch): during the classical era, *aletheia* signified truth in the sense of a non-dissimulation and openness of the manifest being (Heidegger*)—that is, a reality which rose above appearances, opinions, and prejudices—but also the precision of what is stated about that reality. On the subjective level, *aletheia* could also designate the "truthfulness" of a person*.

b) Truth in the Hebrew Bible.   The Hebrew word *'emet* and the Greek *aletheia* do not cover the same semantic field, and in order to render the Hebrew term the Septuagint also had to resort to the words *pistis* (trust, loyalty), *dikaiosune* (justice), and so on. The words *'emet* and *'emounah,* as well as the *amen* of the Christian cult, derived from the verbal root *'mn* (to be solid, resistant). As a result, truth, in Hebrew, was that which was solid, something one could rely upon with full confidence. The meaning of *'emet*—"which, more than any other derivative of *'mn*... has taken on the sense of 'truth'" (H. Wildberger)—was structured around a certain number of definitive uses. For example: 1) Jeremiah (28:9) declares: "The prophet* which prophesied of peace, when the word of the prophet shall come to pass, then shall the prophet be known, that the LORD hath truly [in truth, *'emet*] sent him"; to the false prophet Hananya he says: "thou makest this people to trust in a lie [or: 'be lulled by illusions']" (Jeremiah 28:15). It is therefore the future that causes truth to break forth, and the future is its touchstone. The opposite of truth is not so much illusion as disillusion (H. von Soden). Where truth is to be found, duration and permanence are also to be found (Proverbs 12:19). 2) The term *'emet* is not therefore applied only to words that are presented as being worthy of trust (2 Sm 7:28; 1 Kgs 17:24, 22:16). Exodus 18:21, for example, speaks of "men of truth" to designate energetic individuals who have played a felicitous role in the past and in whom one can place one's trust in the

future. *Emet* asks not only to be known, but requires above all that it be put into practice (Gn 47:29; 2 Chr 31:20; Neh 9:33). Truth is therefore an action, which produces definite results, by means of which an individual can obtain the trust of his fellows. Truth can be found only within a human community. 3) When applied to people, *'emet* can take on the meaning of "loyalty" (Jos 2:14; Prv 3:3). But insofar as truth is constitutively linked to a future reality, *emet* often also means "trust" and is similar to *emounah*. 4) All these uses are based upon the proclamation of the "God of *'emet*" (Ps 31:6), as found in particular in the Book of Psalms*: "The work of his hands are *'emet*" (Ps 111:7); "All the Lord's ways are faithful and *'emet*" (Ps 25:10; *see also* Ps 54:7)—that is, signs of his truth and his loyalty, on which Israel* can be built. But this God worthy of trust is not one God among others; he is the sole and true God (Jer 10:10). An astonishingly vast perspective is opened in Psalm 146, where the *'emet* of the Creator is realized through his action in favor of the oppressed and the hungry (v. 6f.).

On the whole, early Judaism* adopted the biblical concept of truth (*see* e.g. Tb 1:3; Ps 3:6, 14:1, 4; Ezr 5:1, etc.). The new element was that there was now a dualistic relation of antithesis between divine truth and mendacity, as in the manuscripts of Qumran, where the members of the sect, designated as "men of justice" (1QS IC, 5.6; XI, 16; 1QH VI, 29 and passim*),* are opposed to the "sons of iniquity" who do not belong to the group (1QS V, 2. 10, etc; *see also Test Jud* 20, and so on). "To do the truth" is a formula that appears regularly in the manuscripts of Qumran (1 QS I, 5; V, 3; VIII, 2, etc.), even though it no longer refers to the totality of the Torah as a rule of action, but to the correct interpretation given by the sect, that is, to truthful doctrine.

c) The Bible of the Septuagint.   The Septuagint translation inflected the notion of "truth" on several occasions. Indeed, if the Israelites attributed a fundamental importance to the close link between truth as *knowledge* and trust as *practical behavior,* the Greek language on the other hand kept the two notions separate, right from the lexical level, by expressing truth through *aletheia* and trust through *pistis*. It is significant, for example, that Psalm 26:3 (" I have walked in thy truth") is translated in the Septuagint (25:3) by "I found happiness in your truth": it was the gnoseological dimension of the concept that prevailed in this case (K. Koch 1965, with other examples).

d) The New Testament.   The historical Jesus* did not make truth a theme of his proclamation. It was only after the resurrection* that the "truth of the Gospel" (Gal

2:5, 2:14) became an important element to be defended in the face of objections and errors of interpretation. Thus Paul and the Fourth Evangelist were the two primary witnesses of this new method of debate, which made increased use of the term, without however rendering a clearly structured idea of "truth."

The "truth of the Gospel" in Galatians 1:5, 1:14 (*see also* 5:7) introduces a theme. It designates the logic of the gospel, which Paul develops all through his epistle in order to show that in liberating the pagans from the Torah he is not departing from the gospel. In 2 Corinthians, *aletheia* is used on several occasions in an absolute sense (2 Cor 4, 6:7, 13:8, etc.), but always in relation to the gospel, on whose victorious strength the apostle* can rely. *Aletheia* in this case signifies the functioning reality of God, as manifested in his Word*, and virtually presents the features of a power of salvation*: "Because we can do nothing against the truth, but for the truth" (2 Cor 13:8). It is revealing that in Romans 1:18 the *aletheia* of God, held "captive" by the impiety of mankind, is immediately associated with "divine justice*," whose saving action is displayed in the Gospels (Rom 1:16f.). Occasionally used in the sense of "veracity" (2 Cor 7:14; Phil 1:18) or within the framework of a homiletic formula (2 Cor 11:10; Rom 9:1), the word *aletheia* still carries for Paul (in Rom 3:7 and 15:8) the theological impact of the Old Testament *'emet,* implying loyalty to a covenant*. In this respect the truth of God is his loyalty to Israel, which he would show at the end of time by fulfilling his "promises* to the Fathers" and by saving all Israel (*see* Rom 11:25ff.). The Epistle to the Hebrews also seems to refer to 1 Cor 13:6, where *aletheia,* opposed to "injustice," evokes a form of human behavior.

For John, *aletheia* is a central concept designating the revelation* of the reality of God through his Son Jesus, insofar as this is authentically communicated to the believer in the Holy Spirit; the notion here belongs to a Trinitarian structure. The specific emphasis of John's Christology* intended for the theocentric line to be dominant in this case: as God's envoy, Jesus "says" and "attests" the truth that he "had heard from God" (John 8:40, 8:45f.). This is why he "came into this world" (18:37). The fact that *aletheia* is preceded by the definite article (as is generally the case in John) indicates that it is not the content of a particular revelation that is at issue here, but the very reality of God: this reality, according to Johannine dualism (*see* e.g. John 8), is absolute reality, "because it is life and gives life"; whereas the illusory reality of this world is "a usurped reality which opposes God, being a vain reality, a bearer of death" (Bultmann* 1941). But the Johannine Jesus is not satisfied with merely bearing

witness, verbally, to this divine reality: he is, in his very person, the gift that the God of life offers to human beings. For this reason the Fourth Gospel on occasion, and in certain decisive terms, identifies Jesus himself with God's truth (John 14:6 but also 1:14–17). The "Spirit of truth" (John 14:17, 15:26, 16:13) would reveal this reality to the disciples after Easter, as would, from different perspectives, the verses of the Paraclete. "The true worshipers of God" would worship the Father "in spirit and in truth" (John 4:23f.).

In the Fourth Gospel it is clearly the Greek concept of truth as an unveiling of reality that takes precedence—with, it is true, a specifically theological emphasis (Hübner 1980). The place of dualism—Johannine truth/lie (John 8:44f.)—in the history of religion remains controversial to this day (must it be connected to a biblical basis? To the Qumranian tradition? To Gnosis*?) In any case, the expression "doeth truth" (Jn 3:21; 1 Jn 1:6) is permeated with the Judaic spirit. The author of the First Epistle of John insists, moreover, that Christian ethics* are rooted in the truth revealed by Christ: it is the known truth that determines concrete action in love* (*see also* Eph 4:15).

● M. Heidegger (1927), *Sein und Zeit,* Halle.
R. Bultmann (1933), "Alêtheia," *Theologisches Worterbuch zum Alten Testament* 1, 239–51; (1941), *Das Evangelium des Johannes,* Göttingen.
H. von Soden (1951), "Was ist Wahrheit?", in *Urchristentum und Geschichte* I, 1–24, Tübingen.
Ch. H. Dodd (1955), *The Fourth Gospel,* Cambridge.
F. Nötscher (1956), "Wahrheit als theologischer Terminus in den Qumran-Texten", in K. Schubert (Ed.), *Vorderasiatische Studien,* 83–92, Vienna.
H. Boeder (1959), "Der frühgriechische Wortgebrauch von *logos* und *alètheia,*" *ABG* 4, 82–112.
E. Heitsch (1962), "Die nicht-philosophische *alètheia,*" *Hermes* 90, 24–33.
J. Blank (1963), "Der johanneische Wahrheitsbegriff", *BZ-NF* 7, 163–73.
J. Lozano (1963), *El concepto de verdad en San Juan,* Salamanca.
J. Becker (1964), *Das Heil Gottes,* Göttingen.
K. Koch (1965), "Der hebraische Wahrheitsbegriff im griechischen Sprachraum," in H.-R. Müller-Schwefe (Ed.), *Was ist Wahrheit?,* Göttingen, 47–65.
H. Wildberger (1971), "'Mn," *Theologisches Handworterbuch zum Alten Testament* 1, 177–209.
Y. Ibuki (1972), *Die Wahrheit im Johannesevangelium,* Bonn.
A. Jepsen (1973), "'Mn," *ThWAT* 1, 313–48.
I. de La Potterie (1977), *La vérité dans saint Jean,* Rome.
H. Hübner (1980), "Alètheia," *Exegetisches Wörterbuch zum Neuen Testament* 1, 138–45.

MICHAEL THEOBALD

See also **Covenant; Faith; Hermeneutics; Knowledge of God; Promise; Revelation; Veracity; Wisdom; Word of God**

B. Historical and Systematic Theology

a) Antiquity and Middle Ages. It is not because of an error, says Paul, that Christian teaching was rejected by Jews and pagans, but because of stumbling blocks and folly (1 Cor 1:23). This does not imply, however, that early Christianity did not experience truth as a reality and as a problem. The reality was initially Christological. In Jesus* of Nazareth, Christian catechesis* confessed that the loyalty and constancy of God*, his *emet,* had taken on the face of a man; Origen* would say of Christ* that he is "truth itself," *autoaletheia* (*In Jo* VI, 6). Because the life, passion*, and resurrection* of this man involved what was most important of all—salvation*—the Christological kerygma ("Jesus is Lord") takes on the character of a fundamental assertion, and since the kerygma can be contradicted, of a fundamental truth. Truth assumes a double meaning: as the presence of God who reveals himself, and as the human testimony of that revelation*. The revelation is paradoxical (it was through its opposite that God manifested himself on Good Friday), and the testimony given contains no apodictic evidence, whether in regard to the messianic expectations of the Jews, or to pagan soteriologies. The apology was therefore a necessity to show how the hopes* of Israel* were fulfilled in the person of Jesus as were, symmetrically, the expectations of the nations. Addressed to the Jews, the apology would be based on scriptural hermeneutics*: proving that what Christians said was true was equivalent to proving that the "event of Jesus Christ" was the ultimate referent of Jewish Scripture. Addressed to the pagans, the apology would be based on a theology* of mythology (and of philosophy*) which saw "particles of truth" or "preparations for the gospel" in the religious traditions of paganism: proving that Christians were telling the truth was to prove that the idolatry* of the pagans was an implicit reflection of a destination determined for the covenant* and for the worship in spirit and in truth; it was to prove that a desire for God impelled paganism. The first *demonstratio christiana* surely owed its potential to the existence of a shared language, on the one hand, and to that of an "available believable" (P. Ricoeur), on the other. The words used by Christianity were endowed with meaning before they were used, whether in Judaism* (Messiah*/ Christ, resurrection), in the paganism of late Antiquity, or in both (god, salvation); there was no lack of anticipated understandings. And even if there was some debate about the meaning that Christians attributed, or were forced to attribute, to certain words, that debate also shed light upon a vision of the world shared by

Christians and non-Christians alike (E. Miura-Stange, *Celsus und Origenes, Das gemeinsame ihrer Weltanschauung,* Giessen, 1926; *see also* E.R. Dodds, *Pagans and Christians in an Age of Anxiety,* Cambridge, 1965): a vision of a world in which, among other things, the message of salvation enjoyed a certain a priori credibility*. Anticipated understandings did not require comprehension; the language of Christianity was also a hard—*skleros*—language, (John 6:60; *see* J.-Y. Lacoste, *Revue philosophique de Louvain* 1994, 254–80, in particular 261–69), and broke with all the discourse which had prepared it, necessitating an original rereading of what would then become the "Old Testament"; and it contradicted all known rationality by demanding that one have faith* in a God who identified his cause with that of a crucified man. It must, however, be conceded to the apologists* that whatever the division separating Christian Christology* from Jewish messianic beliefs, and whatever the even more brutal discontinuity separating the Christian experience* from the pagan one, it was indeed a *sensible* discourse that Christianity offered. A language, therefore, which could be true.

From the first centuries until the scholastic era, the Christian history of truth might be summed up simply as that of an ever-increasing interpretation in theological terms of what was true. Truth was a matter of logos, but even more than that, it was a Christian matter, since Christianity was based upon the revelation of the divine Logos. Truth was a matter of communication and unveiling, and Christianity was defined as the holder of the secrets of God. Theology would never deny that other true discourses existed besides its own, nor would it ever forget the requirement of a justification of its pronouncements with regard to Judaism and paganism. But amid all the words and propositions that claimed to be true, it was primarily as an ultimate measure of truth that it would become preeminent; the language of theology would therefore acquire the epistemological privilege of confirming or invalidating the claims to truth that informed non-theological language.

There was no lack of theoretical methods for ensuring the reign of theological language by other means than the simple argument from authority*, by resorting to universally accepted concepts of truth. In the work of both Albert* the Great and Thomas* Aquinas, truth would be defined in theologically neutral terms: *adaequatio rei et intellectus.* And it was also in theologically neutral terms that medieval ontology asserted that what was true was transcendental, a transcategorical name for being. The first theory was valid for all acts of knowledge, the second for all being. Certainly, both lent themselves to a theological use insofar as their refinement had been the work of theologians rather than philosophers, but both could be received as strictly philosophical. And truth only really became a burning issue when the idea of a division of the concept of truth arose, such that what was (said to be) theologically true need not be philosophically true.

More a product of Étienne Tempier's experts, who condemned it in 1277, than of the spirit of the Aristotelian and Averroist philosophers, the theory of the "double truth" constituted the first serious challenge to theological reasoning. Did there exist a "philosophical truth" that contradicted theological truth (in affirming the eternity of the world or the existence of one single collective soul for all of humankind) and that all the while left to theology the right to assert, at its own level, the creation* of the world and the existence of individual souls*? Neither Siger of Brabant, nor Boethius of Dacia, nor any of the thinkers involved in the censure of 1277 actually affirmed this (*see* R. Hissette, *Enquête sur les 219 articles...* Louvain and Paris, 1977). But from the *maîtres ès arts* of Paris in the 13th century to the last Averroists in Padua, the history of philosophy was one of an ever-increasing tendency toward autonomy in relation to theology—and this autonomy was taking shape through a conflict between philosophical truth (strictly rational truth) and theological truth (truth founded upon the authority* of Christian revelation). A solution to the conflict was sought by separating truth from probability, as the dogma* of the Church was true by virtue of divine authorization, and philosophical (Aristotelian) terms, founded upon experience and induction, were considered merely probable. This distinction was not, however, viable. And it was perfectly logical that Paduan Averroism would draw further censure upon itself (condemnation of Pomponazzi at the Fifth Lateran* Council, *COD* 605–6); the principle of contradiction was valid for the relations of the theological and the philosophical. Truth could only be one.

b) Modern Times. It is not truly "modern" to doubt theological truths, since doubt was contemporary with the reception of Aristotle into the Christian world. But what is modern is the production of concepts of truth that in and of themselves cannot be the subject of any theological reception whatsoever. When he established the primacy of practical reason*, Bacon adopted a pragmatic concept of the truth: *quod in operando utilissimum, id in scientia verissimum* (*Novum organum* II, 4). The concept of "fact," moreover, would

help Vico to provide the elementary formula of a new ontology that was strictly worldly and historical in outlook: *factum et verum convertuntur.* And finally, if the concept of "experience," along with the idea of experimental verification, was not originally used to deny the existence of a theological truth but to found a new field of knowledge, the evidence acquired through this knowledge would eventually label theological realities as totally lacking in proof. The desire to safeguard the cognitive claims of faith was certainly often present, in Descartes* or Kant*, for example. But from Descartes to Kant the domain that philosophy abandoned to theology would diminish dramatically. Henceforth, theology would have to learn from philosophy the canons of true knowledge; its task was no longer merely to tell the truth, it would also have to prove the truth of what it said. The era of a new apologetic (whose name would change, as one would eventually speak of fundamental theology) had arrived, the task of which would be to display the truth of religion, of Christianity and (in some cases) of the outlook of a particular confessional family* such as Catholicism*, either by having recourse to the permissions granted by reigning philosophies or by resorting to medieval conceptual instruments (in baroque Scholasticism and Neoscholasticism).

The same period witnessed the birth of a new polemic whose aim was no longer to dispute the truth of theological discourse but to dispute its veridicality. From Fontenelle to Nietzsche* there would be a gradual refinement in the nature of the accusation, but its substance remained the same. Christianity speaks of faith, but it lives off people's credulity. Christianity speaks of truth, but in fact speaks only to serve, unconsciously, the interests of a social class (Marx*). An ascetic priest* might claim to live for his desire for truth, and to bring others to live for that truth, but his practice and his preaching are merely symptoms of resentment (Nietzsche). What remains to be said is that in reality theology is moved only by archaic impulses and memories (Freud*). The question of the possible truth of theology would no longer even be raised; it was no longer what theology might say that occupied philosophy, but *why* it said it.

Corresponding in a remarkable way to the "death of God" is a certain "death of truth," and the theories generally accepted during the 20th century have had certain traits in common: they are modest theories, where no transcendence is at stake, and all are careful not to appeal to a "primary truth." They achieve this in two distinct ways: 1) Semantic theory (Tarski 1933) provides a means of linking words and things in a precise way ("*p* is true"; *p*), but in no way determines the nature of things. According to the theory of coherence

(Neurath 1931 et al., *see* Puntel 1990), a term is true if it can be integrated within a system of terms already accepted as being true; and if theory can be used to render metaphysical or theological language illegitimate, such a use does not necessarily prevail as the only possible one. According to "critical rationalism*" (Popper), no term can be a candidate for inclusion in the category of true terms if no falsification whatsoever of it is conceivable—but it is a logic of scientific research that provides the criterion of what is falsifiable, and nothing implies a priori that the criterion is valid elsewhere than in the physical world. Similarly, the various analytical interpretations of truth (Ramsey 1927; Strawson 1949; Davidson 1967 et al.) make no metaphysical decisions, nor does an interpretation in terms of communication and intersubjectivity (Habermas 1973). 2) It would be up to logical positivism, however, in due time, to exclude from the domain of truth any term with metaphysical or theological pretensions; for only the tautologies of logic on the one hand, and empirically verifiable terms on the other, are true (e.g., Ayer 1935). Only that which can lend itself to verification is true; to say precisely what this "verification" implies, one would resort to exemplary procedures such as those used by science; and, since what is false provides its own auto-definition in terms of verification/falsification, one will describe that which is neither true nor false as being devoid of meaning.

Whether they were non-theological, atheological or formally atheistic, such theories called for a theological response. And indeed they would give rise to a lengthy debate in Anglo-Saxon countries on theological language*, a debate inaugurated by J. Wisdom ("Gods," *Proceedings of the Aristotelian Society,* 1944/1945, 185–206), and which can now be considered closed. The answer to the question of verification was that theological givens called for an "eschatological verification" (J. Hick 1960 and 1978); another response was to emphasize the trivial nature of the concept of "facts" utilized by the positivists ("Facts, like the telescope and men's wigs, are a creation of the 17th century": A. MacIntyre). One response to the relegation of religious language to the domain of the "emotive" (e.g., Ayer 1935) was that the positivist definition of cognitive languages was unduly restrictive. One response to the theories that held that formalized language was the measure of all other languages was the practice of a Wittgensteinian strategy of defense and the illustration of "language games" used in the everyday speech of natural languages (e.g. D. Z. Phillips), or by an elucidation of the auto-implicative nature of religious language (D. D. Evans 1963, *see* Ladrière 1984, vol. 1). Theological language

was certainly a "foreign" language—but it was constructed, and well constructed, to correspond to experiences that were in their own way foreign (Ramsey 1957).

c) For a Theological Theory of Truth. The reason why theology should be measured against linguistic and logical theories of the truth is simple: theological language is a language, and there are no strategies of immunization which might exempt it—since it makes claims to truth—from being subjected to the tests elaborated to verify the coherence and pertinence of any language. Theology can, incontestably, be developed within a plurality of discourses of varying degrees of rigor, and one cannot require of homilies or baptismal catechism a strict obedience to the canons of a "scientific" theology: therefore it is possible (and for the theologian, necessary) to defend equally a scientific practice of theology (Torrance 1969; Carnes 1982, etc.) and the looser terms in which Christian faith expresses itself. Efforts at legitimization undertaken in the 1940s would, however, come up against an obstacle. Undoubtedly, theology can do no less than be true in a semantic/propositional sense. But it would be to misunderstand the specific style of its own language if the matrix provided by the biblical texts were to be neglected. And if one examines these texts, one is obliged to adopt a concept of truth that adapts to its diction in metaphors, parables* and stories, and even goes so far as to find therein its most accurate expression. The logic of truth must therefore be linked to a rhetoric of truth (thus, Jüngel 1980; McFague 1983; Soskice 1985, etc.), with a theological theory of the story (narrative* theology), with a theory of discourse through parables (Via 1967; Crossan 1975, etc.), and, in a more general fashion, with a theory of language through images (Biser 1970). From this time on, philosophical references of theology would not fail to change. More than formalized or formalizable language, and more than the "ordinary language" of analytical philosophy, the Heideggerian hermeneutics of speech has provided the greatest food for thought in recent theology (Fuchs 1968 etc.) Truth is not meant to be only a relation between words and things, or merely a relation of coherence between them; it is also the revelatory power of each specific word spoken through the mediation of the texts where it figures (*see* Tugendhat 1967): truth of an "event of the word"—*Sprachereignis* for Fuchs, *Wortgeschehen* for G. Ebeling—constituting the living center of theology.

Theological language is propositional, but the true problem of a theological theory of the truth resides in the impossibility of reducing the "revelation" that it professes to a mere system of propositions. And just as the propositional theory of revelation—a theory that can now be regarded as obsolete—was destined to found itself on a propositional theory of truth, each non-propositional theory of revelation is necessarily founded on a congruent theory of truth. Wherever one means by "revelation" a historical process that is coextensive with universal history*, but which has already been realized in advance in the life, death*, and resurrection of Jesus, then the truth is thought of as a *last event* that is taken as a *last word* (e.g. Pannenburg, *Grundfr. Syst. Th.* 202–222). Wherever one means "revelation" as the work of a word* that frees human liberty* by opening it to an existence of belief that is "authentic," one also thinks of the truth as an event, as the content of an "eschatological" experience (of a *last experience)* (Bultmann* etc.). In cases where one considers the revelation to be a divine self-communication corresponding "categorically" to an opening to God and to a "transcendental" expectation of God, the question of truth refers back to a "mystery*" with which all of human consciousness in the act of knowledge (Rahner*) is confronted. And finally, whenever the revelation is interpreted in terms of a unique global event whose "figure," *Gestalt,* can be perceived in a mode analogous to that of a work of art (Balthasar* 1961), then truth must be considered to be the revealing feature of the entire event of Jesus Christ, taken in its integral dimensions.

A theological theory of truth must include the following items: 1) Theology is organized within the memory of a past that it considers closed ("the closed nature of revelation"), but whose meaning has been adopted and placed at the heart of a *Wirkungsgeschichte* (Gadamer 1960, notes 284–90) that is basically open and where no one, by definition, can lay claim to a final interpretation or a final perspective. Moreover, the foreclosed facts and texts whose memory is revived by theology constitute neither a fully unified story nor a continuous commentary of a truly homogeneous history. And the most normative documents known to theology—the Gospels*—use a plurality of testimonies that is irreducible (but that can certainly be coordinated) to deconstruct prismatically the founding events, which are accessible only through this refraction. The true word can thus be defined as faithful memory; the criterion of fidelity will not consist of a fetishistic respect for the signifiers, but in the ("hermeneutic") service of meaning (*see* Lacoste, *Revue philosophique de Louvain* 1994, 268ff.); and since it will always be determined by the present-day views of interpretation, no theology will ever be organized into absolute knowledge. 2) The perpetual necessity of reinterpretation does not prevent theological terms from being purely and simply true (and contradictory

terms from being purely and simply false). This is the exemplary case of dogmatic terms. Since they are formed in natural languages, and not in formalized languages, the allocation of a value of truth goes hand in hand with the right to a constant reaffirmation of such terms (which will call for a hermeneutic task). However, in the (historical/cultural/philosophical) field of meaning where a dogmatic term was produced, and provided it can be translated into other contexts of meaning (but not *any* other), the term is simply true. A linguistic theory of truth is indispensable to a theological theory of truth. 3) The history of theology does not comprise a discontinuous succession of interpretations that are correct one moment and then rapidly grow obsolete; it must appear as a single continuous process of enunciation. Henceforth, the truth of theological speech can only be confirmed within a double framework, synchronic and diachronic; it is through a reading of the development of Christian doctrines that current theological discourse can truly express what it wishes to say, and that it can say it well. 4) The propositional and (more largely) discursive reality of theological truths cannot, however, offend the essential requirements of negative*, or "mystical" theology, insofar as it attributes a meaning to silence itself. Whether the language of theology is affirmative ("cataphatic"), negative ("apophatic"), or takes the path of "eminence," in all three cases it is a practice of the discourse. However, the true problem of theology resides in the inexpressibility that constitutes what is both the first and ultimate property of God. What is beyond language and veridicality is not, however, beyond what is true: on the contrary, the inexpressible God actually proves that it is not simply in the act of speech that he confronts humankind, and that it is not only by themselves echoing these words that human beings pay the most appropriate homage to God; divine truth is also a truth to be honored in silence. 5) One cannot speak the language of truth without speaking that of evidence, which is defined precisely as the "experience of truth." And if one wonders what evidence theology claims as its own, the answer must be in the terms of an analysis of the act of faith, reiterating that the God who reveals himself solicits intellect and will indissolubly—that his truth, therefore, will exercise no constraints upon human beings. Theology must preserve the memory of this absence of constraint, and integrate it into its theory of the truth, on the one hand, and into its practice of veridicality, on the other. Theology is truthful in suggesting a truth, which is not only truth-for-the-intelligence (the old theory of truth as an "appropriateness of the thing and the intellect" can no longer be applied), but also truth-for-the-will or truth-for-the-emotions. The "believable," moreover, is not a deficient mode in the rendering of truth: it is the truth as it is rendered when it calls for acquiescence. "To each fundamental mode of objectivity…belongs a fundamental mode of evidence" (Husserl, *see* Tugendhat 1967, §5). Classically, faith is distinct from "vision"— but its element is not, for all that, one of a lack of evidence.

The demands that burden faith and its theology thus demand a concept of truth as rich and complex as the complexity of their calls for truth. Theology undoubtedly has better things to do than contribute to the progress of epistemology. But it may be, in passing, an actual favor to any potential knowledge if there is an obligation to articulate the propositional meaning of truth, its phenomenological meaning, its ontological meaning, and its reference to an Absolute known as *veritas prima*. And when philosophy happens to suggest an existential concept of truth, and to affirm that "truth exists" (Heidegger*, *GA* 27, 158), such a suggestion cannot help but collect theological memories and bring to mind the New Testament's identification of the truth with the person* of Jesus. A theology of the truth must include a Christology of the truth.

• F. P. Ramsey (1927), "Facts and Propositions," in *Philosophical Papers,* Ed. H. Mellor, Cambridge, 1990, 34–51.

O. Neurath (1931), "Soziologie im Physikalismus," *Erkenntnis* 2, 393–431.

A. Tarski (1933), "Le concept de vérité dans les langages formalisés," in *Logique, sémantique, métamathématique,* vol. 1, Paris, 1972, 157–269 (original in Polish).

A. J. Ayer (1935), *Language, Truth and Logic,* London.

M. Heidegger (1943), "Vom Wesen der Wahrheit" and "Platons Lehre von der Wahrheit," in *GA* 9, 177–202 and 203–38.

P. F. Strawson (1949), "Truth," *Analysis* 9, 83–97.

H. G. Gadamer (1960), *Wahrheit und Methode,* Tübingen.

J. L. Austin (1961), "Truth," in *Philosophical Papers,* Oxford, 85–101.

G. Siewerth (1962), *Philosophie der Sprache,* Einsiedeln, 65–148.

G. Pitcher (Ed.) (1964), *Truth,* Englewood Cliffs (collection of classic Anglo-Saxon articles).

D. Davidson (1967), "Truth and Meaning," *Synthese* 17, 304–33.

E. Tugendhat (1967), *Der Wahrheitsbegriff bei Husserl und Heidegger,* Berlin.

A. C. Danto (1968), "Truth," in *Analytical Philosophy of Knowledge,* Cambridge, 243–65.

J. Habermas (1973), "Wahrheitstheorien," in *Wirklichkeit und Reflexion: W. Schulz zum 60. Geburtstag,* Pfullingen, 211–65.

N. Rescher (1973), *The Coherence Theory of Truth,* Oxford.

L. B. Puntel (1978), *Wahrheitstheorien in der neueren Philosophie,* Darmstadt.

L. B. Puntel (1990), *Grundlagen einer Theorie der Wahrheit,* Berlin-New York.

W. P. Alston (1996), *A Realist Conception of Truth,* Ithaca.

♦ D. Bonhoeffer (1943), "Was heißt die Wahrheit sagen?" in *Dietrich Bonhoeffer: Werke* vol. 16, 619–29.

A. Flew, A. MacIntyre (Eds.) (1955), *New Essays in Philosophical Theology,* London.

B. Mitchell (Eds.) (1957), *Faith and Logic,* London.

I. T. Ramsey (1957), *Religious Language,* London.

J. Hick (1960), "Theology and Verification", *ThTo* 17, 12–31.

H. U. von Balthasar (1961), *Herrlichkeit* I, Einsiedeln.

D. D. Evans (1963), *The Logic of Self-Involvement: A Philosophical Study of Everyday Language with Special Reference to the Christian Use of Language about God as Creator,* London.

D. O. Via (1967), *The Parables,* Philadelphia.

E. Fuchs (1968), *Marburger Hermeneutik,* Tübingen.

R. Bambrough (1969), *Reason, Truth and God,* London-New York (2nd Ed. 1979).

T. F. Torrance (1969), *Theological Science,* Oxford, chap. 4.

E. Biser (1970), *Theologische Sprachtheorie und Hermeneutik,* Munich.

W. Pannenberg (1973), *Wissenschaftstheorie und Theologie,* Frankfurt.

J. D. Crossan (1975), *The Dark Interval: Towards a Theology of Story,* Niles, IL.

J. Hick (1978), "Eschatological Verification Reconsidered," *Religious Studies* 13, 189–209.

M. Corbin (1980), "L'événement de Vérité," in *L'inouï de Dieu,* Paris, 61–107.

E. Jüngel (1980), "Metaphorische Wahrheit: Erwägungen zur theologischen Relevanz der Metapher als Beitrag zur Hermeneutik einer narrativen Theologie," in *Entsprechungen,* Beiträge zur evangelischen Teologie 88, 103–57.

I. U. Dalferth (1981), *Religiöse Rede von Gott,* BEvTh 87.

J. R. Carnes (1982), *Axiomatics and Dogmatics,* Belfast-Dublin-Ottawa.

S. McFague (1983), *Metaphorical Theology,* Philadelphia-London.

J. Ladrière (1984), *L'articulation du sens,* vol. 1, *Discours scientifique et parole de foi,* vol. 2, *Les langages de la foi,* CFi 124 and 125.

R. Brague (1985), "La vérité vous rendra libres," *Com(F)* X/5–6, 9–23.

J. M. Soskice (1985), *Metaphor and Religious Language,* Oxford.

J. D. Zizioulas (1985), "Truth and Communion," in *Being as Communion,* Crestwood, NY, 67–122.

E. Jüngel (1990), "Wertlose Wahrheit: Christliche Wahrheitserfahrung im Streit gegen die 'Tyrannei der Werte'," in *Wertlose Wahrheit,* BEvTh 107, 90–109.

J. Ladrière (1993), "Interprétation et vérité," *Laval théologique et philosophique* 49, 189–99.

B. Neveu (1993), *L'erreur et son juge: Remarques sur les censures doctrinales à l'époque moderne,* Naples.

M. Henry (1996), *C'est moi la vérité: Pour une ph. du christianisme,* Paris.

JEAN-YVES LACOSTE

See also **Faith; Hermeneutics; Language, Theological; Naturalism; Philosophy; Theology**

Truths, Hierarchy of

The expression *hierarchy of truths* was formulated in number 11 of the decree of Vatican* II on ecumenism*, *Unitatis Redintegratio (UR):* "As they compare doctrines, they [Catholic theologians] will recall that there is an order or a "hierarchy" of truths in Catholic doctrine, by virtue of their varying relations with the foundation of Christian faith*." This declaration was greeted by Cullmann as very important (*see* "Comments on the Decree on Ecumenism," *ER,* 17 April 1965, 94): even if it was still subject to varying interpretations within and outside of Catholic theology, it enabled one in fact to discern the effects of a hermeneutic* principle of great ecumenical fruitfulness.

1. Historical Antecedents of the Idea

a) The formulation is new, but an idea of the organic nature of Christian faith and of an articulation of the truths of faith around a center could be found in the most ancient patristic traditions (Valeske 1968). The very notion of *regula fidei* implies a distinction between the fundamental truths of the Creed* and less important truths. For the Fathers*, all the truths of faith were organized around a center, the salvation* granted by God* through Jesus Christ. They also distinguished a hierarchy of heresies*, the most serious being those that compromised Trinitarian faith. In the Middle Ages, Bonaventure* and Thomas* Aquinas spoke of the distinction between *articula fidei* and *alia credibilia.* And at the very heart of the articles of faith Thomas discerned those truths of faith that had a direct relationship with the object of revelation* and those that had only an indirect relation by virtue of the relation with the preceding ones (*ST* Ia IIae, q. 106, a. 4, ad 2). Subsequently, theology would often speak of the "truths necessary to salvation" contained in Scripture and in tradition*, and would make a distinction between these and secondary truths. After the Council of Trent*, however, the insistence upon the normative character of the truths of faith, as stipulated by the ecclesiastical authorities*, would consign to oblivion the very idea of an order or a hierarchy among truths.

b) The notion of a hierarchy of truths not only had antecedents in the history of Christian thought but also

equivalents in other fields besides that of dogma*. In exegesis*, for example, it was usual to state that all the Scripture was of divine inspiration, whereas its discrete parts had diverging relations with a single center, which was the mystery* of God and of Christ* viewed in all its depth (Col 1:26; Eph 3:4). Or again, that all western Christian confessions gave priority to the first seven ecumenical councils, or that a number of theologians didn't hesitate to establish a hierarchy among them depending on how close their relation to the mystery of Christ and of the Trinity* actually was. Or again, that the sacramental septenary offered a perfect example of "hierarchy" within a single order of realities directly concerned with faith, insofar as the other sacramental acts were linked to the two "great sacraments*," which were baptism* and the Eucharist*. Finally, all the feasts of the liturgical calendar and the feast days of the saints were linked to the center or foundation constituted by the paschal mystery (Easter).

2. Attempts at Interpretation

From September 1985 the study group that brought together the Catholic Church and the World Council of Churches began organizing several consultations on the hierarchy of truths. This endeavor concluded in January 1990 with a study document whose aim was to "understand and interpret the intentions of the Second Vatican Council regarding the hierarchy of truths." Although it has not dispelled all the ambiguities, the document (GMT) published by the Pontifical Council for the Promotion of Unity among Christians (number 74, 1990) can help in discerning the Council's true intentions and avoid any misinterpretations.

a) The Intentions of Vatican II. Counter to a juridical understanding where all the truths of faith would be on an equal level by virtue of a formal point of view provided by an obligation to believe, the Council presented the content of faith as an organic whole within which each truth sustains a different relationship with the foundation of faith. In a *modus* that directly inspired the preparation of number 11 of *UR,* Cardinal Koenig expressed his wish that the truths of faith be the subject of an *evaluation* rather than an enumeration. The principle of the hierarchy of truth was proof of a concept of truth* that favored its character of attestation over its strength of obligation. And it was possible to establish a hierarchy of truth from two perspectives: an objective perspective of the content of faith, and a perspective regarding its reception* by the Church*.

From an objective perspective. This concerns the various links *(nexus)* with the foundation of faith. "We must see the importance or the 'weight' of each truth in relation to the foundation of faith in the existential relation of Christians with their communities" (GMT 26). Dogmas constitute a structured whole, and each dogma refers to every other dogma and asks to be interpreted on the basis of its relation to the foundation of faith as well as mutual ties (Kasper 1987). From this point of view, a legitimate comparison can be made between the hierarchy of truth of Vatican II and the *nexus mysteriorum* or "analogy of faith" of Vatican* I.

From the perspective of reception by the Church. In this case one considers not only the various relations of each truth to the foundation of faith but also the Church's *varying reception* of the same faith according to the era. The dogmatic perspective, which was peculiar to a given moment in history, must be understood from the point of view of its dynamic relation to the truth that it is trying to express (*see* Thomas Aquinas's formula: "The act of faith does not terminate in a proposition, but in reality *(res),*" *ST* IIa IIae, q. 1, a.2, ad2). Despite its permanent value, the vocabulary of transubstantiation, for example, is not the only way of expressing the mystery of the "real presence" (Tavard 1971). And there are also several legitimate ways of explaining the relation of the Holy* Spirit and the Son within the Trinity (Congar 1982).

b) Erroneous Interpretations. The idea of the hierarchy of truths does not represent a simple return to the controversial question of "fundamental articles" rejected by the popes Pius XI *(Mortalium animos)* and Pius XII *(Orientalis ecclesiae),* something that was also abhorrent to the Orthodox tradition. For the Orthodox Church, "there exist no distinctions between principal truths and secondary truths, between essential doctrines and non-essential doctrines" (GMT 16). For the Orthodox, as for the Catholics, it is the Church itself that ensures the continuity of doctrine and not any given truth. For the Reformed Churches however, it is the fundamental truths that ensure the continuity of the Church. But if one takes into account the material content of faith (and not only the formal motif, that is, the authority* of God revealing himself)—which

seemed to be the intention of number 11 of the *UR*—one is forced to concede that there are, in the tradition, the beginnings of a theory of "fundamental articles," if only in the consensus that can be established between the Churches with regard to the first seven ecumenical councils.

In any case the conciliar idea of the hierarchy of truths cannot be reduced to the old qualifications used to determine the importance of theological theses: *de fide definita; de fide; proximae fidei;* and *theologice certae.* On the contrary, by resorting to the idea of the hierarchy of truths, it seems there was a desire to go beyond a concept where faith was too narrowly considered within the juridical and disciplinary mode, that of the obligatory or the optional (Marlé 1986). It would also be erroneous to try to bring the principle of the hierarchy of truths closer to the distinction between the three categories of truths, as set out in the *Profession of Faith* required since 1989 from those who exercise a function in the name of the Catholic church (*DC* 1989, 378–79) and as stated (number 23) in the *Instruction of the Congregation on the Doctrine of Faith* on *The Ecclesial Vocation of the Theologian* of 24 May 1990. (In this text, indeed, the classification of truths was established in the name of the degree of authority of the magisterium* and the degree of obligation for the believer.)

3) Ecumenical Impact Insofar as the churches strive for full communion* with each other, the principle of the hierarchy of truths provides a hermeneutic criterion that is extremely fruitful for ecumenical dialogue. While lacking the expression itself, a similar concern can be found in the Orthodox tradition and in the Reformed churches. "Orthodox theologians have suggested that the notion of the hierarchy of truths could help to distinguish the permanent and shared teachings of faith, such as the symbols [credos] proclaimed by the seven ecumenical councils and other confessions of faith, from teachings which have not been formulated or sanctioned by the authority of the councils" (GMT 16).

Similarly, it was in relation to the gospel, the core of faith, that the Protestant churches established a certain hierarchy among the truths of faith. The Catholic notion of the hierarchy of truths and the Lutheran concept of the "center of the gospel" are not identical, but they are close (*see Malta Report,* 25). There is at present a broad consensus among distinct groups of Christians over the issue of the free gift of salvation in Jesus Christ, but the place occupied by the doctrine of justification* in relation to the foundation of faith varies depending on the particular church. Thus in mutual dialogue the principle of the hierarchy of truths provides a criterion, which helps to "make a distinction between the different concepts of the truths of faith which are points of conflict and other differences which should not exist" (GMT 28).

During bilateral or multilateral dialogues, Churches tend to reach a certain consensus on the fundamental truths. In any case they are better able to discern the divergences that depend on historical and cultural factors and the differences that concern the foundation of faith. It is certain, for example, from a Catholic perspective, that the fundamental concept of the Church and the nature of its instrumentality directly concern the bases of faith, while this is not the case with Protestants. The very future of ecumenical dialogue however hinges on the shared conviction that consensus is, after a fashion, "more fundamental" than fundamental differences (Birmelé 1986). On the occasion of the 450th anniversary of the *Augsburg Confession* on 25 June 1980, Pope John Paul II referred to a fundamental consensus between Catholics and Lutherans on the core truths of the Christian faith (*DC* 1980, 696).

● H. Mühlen (1966), "Die Lehre des Vaticanum II über die Hierarchia veritatum und ihre Bedeutung für den oekumenischen Dialog," *TuG* 55, 303–35.

U. Valeske (1968), Hierarchia veritatum: *Theologiegeschichtlich Hintergründe und mögliche Konsequenzen eines Hinweises im Oekumenischen-dekret des II Vatikanischen Konzils zum zwischenkirchlichen Gespräch,* Munich.

G. Tavard (1971), "*Hierarchia veritatum:* A preliminary investigation," *TS* 32, 278–89.

W. Hryniewicz (1978), "La hiérarchie des vérités: Implications œcuméniques d'une idée chrétienne," *Irén* 51, 470–91.

G. Thils (1979), "*Hierarchia veritatum:* décret sur l'œcuménisme no 11," *RTL 10,* 208–15.

Y. Congar (1982), *Diversités et communion,* Paris.

A. Birmelé (1986), *Le salut en Jésus-Christ dans les dialogues œcuméniques,* Paris.

R. Marlé (1986), "L'idée conciliaire d'une 'hiérarchie' des vérités de la doctrine catholique," *Doc. épisc.* 13, 1–6.

W. Kasper (1987), *Theologie und Kirche,* Mainz.

CLAUDE GEFFRÉ

See also **Ecumenicism; Magisterium; Notes, Theological; Vatican II**

Tübingen, Schools of

The University of Tübingen in Württemberg was founded in 1477, restructured in 1534, placed under the Kingdom of Württemberg's political authority* in 1811, and endowed with a faculty of Catholic theology* in 1817. It owes a major part of its fame to its two faculties of theology, Protestant and Catholic, from which arose at the end of the 18th and the beginning of the 19th centuries several movements, each of which became known under the name of *School of Tübingen.*

In order of appearance, the first was the one called the "Old Evangelical School of Tübingen." It came into being under the influence of the philosopher and theologian Gottlob Christian Storr (1746–1805), who taught at Tübingen from 1775. Next came the Catholic School of Tübingen. Its birth resulted from the 1817 merger of the Friedrichs-Universität of Ellwangen (a Catholic establishment founded in 1812) with the Eberhard-Karls-Universität of Tübingen, and from the foundation in 1819 of the periodical *Tübinger Theologische Quartalschrift,* which is still in publication. A

full decade later, in the Protestant faculty, among the pupils of the dogma* and Church* historian Ferdinand Christian Baur (1792–1860, professor in Tübingen from 1826) the New School of Tübingen was founded. Unlike the preceding one, it had a relatively brief life. It was considered dissolved even during Baur's lifetime, in about 1858.

a) Old Evangelical School of Tübingen. As many university professors as influential people from the regional Church of Württemberg belonged to the Old Evangelical School of Tübingen, which was also known by the name of its founder, Gottlob Christian Storr. Apart from Storr himself, its most eminent members were the brothers Johann Friedrich and Karl Christian Flatt (1759–1821 and 1772–1843 respectively), Friedrich Gottlieb Süskind (1767–1829), Johann Christian Friedrich Steudel (1779–1837), Christian Friedrich Schmid (1794–1852), and above all Ernst Gottlieb Bengel (1769–1826). In addition to the various monographs published by the professors in this group, for the most part this school set forth its positions in three periodicals: *Magazin für christliche Dogmatik und Moral* (1796–1816), *Archiv für die Theologie und ihre neueste Literatur* (1815–1826, from 1822 onwards under the title *Neues Archiv für Theologie)* and the *Tübinger Zeitschrift für Theologie* (1828–1840).

At its core, the Old Evangelical School of Tübingen's chief trait was a marked supernaturalism or biblicism, which meant in practice that it based itself on the Lutheran principle by which revelation* was concerned only with faith* and not with reason*. Consequently, it broke with both Enlightenment thought and with Protestant biblical criticism. Surprisingly, to support this fundamental thesis the school invoked Kantian criticism, which it drew on in its defense of divine revelation as the Bible*'s authority, placing the Bible beyond the realm of rationalization. However, that did not prevent the school from having recourse to this very rationalization to interpret the biblical texts, which gradually put it in a contradictory position with its own supernaturalism. Bengel and Steudel, therefore, slanted their positions toward rationalism*. The same contradiction was often to provoke criticisms, thanks to which this theological movement still enjoys a certain notoriety today. Hegel*, Schelling*, and Hölderlin, who were occasionally fellow students at Tübingen between 1788 and 1795, issued criticisms, and so did D. F. Strauß, who taught at the famous seminary *(Stift)* of Tübingen in 1832–35.

b) Catholic School of Tübingen. Contemporary editions and research by J. R. Geiselmann (1890–1970), St. Lösch (1882–1966), M. Seckler (1927–), R. Reinhardt (1928–), E. Klinger (1938–), A. P. Kustermann (1944–), and others have made it possible to trace the Catholic School of Tübingen's history precisely. It turns out that the idea of a "Catholic School"—one that followed a theological movement that was particularly oriented toward speculation—began to take root (if we omit certain occasional or polemical usages to which it might have given rise) only under the influence of A. von Schmid and the historical work of C. Werner, dating respectively from 1862 and 1866, and that the idea was not adopted by the Tübingen theologians themselves before 1898.

Unless it is taken in its broadest meaning the name Catholic School of Tübingen makes no sense. In fact, the school did not only furnish an umbrella title for the extremely mixed history of a faculty and its various adherents, but also permitted the grouping together under a common title of erudite efforts by numerous scholars who differed in many ways, including both

their intellectual orientation and their political attitudes toward the Church. Moreover, the title also covered theologians who, although they were in contact with the University of Tübingen, were not actual members of it—such as, for instance, Franz Anton Staudenmaier (1800–56), Anton Berlage (1805–81), Wenzeslaus Mattes (1815–86), and Franz Xaver Dieringer (1811–76). If this broad definition of the term is accepted, a number of points can be agreed upon from an historical, then a systematic viewpoint.

In its history's first phase, which ran from about 1817 to 1831, the Catholic School of Tübingen was strongly influenced by the Enlightenment—already, it is true, with that touch of German Romanticism characteristic of the Catholic sphere, which can also foster a criticism of the Enlightenment, provided in this case by J. M. Sailer (1751–1832), J. H. A. Gügler (1782–1827), I. H. von Wessenberg (1774–1860), and others. The chief representatives of this period were Johann Sebastian Drey (1777–1853, professor at Tübingen from 1817–46), Johann Baptist Hirscher (1788–1865, professor at Tübingen from 1817–37), Peter Alois Gratz (1769–1849, professor at Tübingen from 1817–19), Johann Georg Herbst (1787–1836, professor at Tübingen from 1817–32), Andreas Benedikt Feilmoser (1777–1831, professor at Tübingen from 1820), as well as Johann Adam Möhler (1796–1838, assistant at Tübingen from 1823 to 1826, then professor from 1826 to 1835). For these scholars it was just as much a matter of revising theology in conformity with the epistemological principles of biblical criticism and idealist philosophy* as it was of reforming the Church (its constitution, its pastoral practices, and its spirituality). To those aims should be added a tolerant attitude toward other confessions.

The second phase, covering the period 1831–57, began with J. A. Möhler's change of stance. He turned away from Enlightenment ideas to embrace a more classical ecclesiology*. Convinced that under all circumstances the Church remained faithful to its essence and that its reforms could, therefore, have only a purely external character, he was gradually led to reject the principle of a criticism conducted according to criteria derived from outside the Church or outside theology, as well as to reject any tolerant attitude toward the non-Catholic confessions' views. Möhler's evolution was going to decide the Catholic School of Tübingen's fate and would long affect the next generation, as much in its theological orientation as in its political position with regard to Rome*.

Among this new generation were Karl Joseph Hefele (1809–87, assistant at Tübingen from 1835–40, professor from 1840–69, then bishop* of Rottenburg), Johann Evangelist von Kuhn (1806–87, professor at Tübingen from 1839–82), Martin Joseph Mack (1805–85, professor at Tübingen from 1835–40), Benedikt Welte (1805–85, professor at Tübingen from 1838–57), and Anton Graf (1811–67, professor at Tübingen from 1841–43). However it would be wrong to reduce all these theologians to the position of defenders of a "papist, Jesuit, curialist, and ultramontane system," as has often been done in the heat of polemical debate. Thus Franz Anton Staudenmaier (J. S. Drey's pupil and a coach at the *Wilhelmstift* of Tübingen from 1828–30, then professor in Gießen and in Freiburg) tried, just as did J. E. von Kuhn, to enter into open yet critical discussion with Hegel's philosophy. Nonetheless, from the political angle, this second phase ended with an undeniable ultramontane victory.

The third phase, which should be sited between 1857 and 1900, began when K. J. Hefele and J. E. Kuhn distanced themselves from this ultramontane trend, not only on account of internal quarrels in the diocese of Rottenburg, but also because of the quarrels about the dogma of papal infallibility* at the First Vatican* Council. This development set the Catholic School of Tübingen against the Neoscholastic movement, which at this period had committed itself to a total rejection of modern thought and tried to subject all scholarly and cultural activities to the Church's doctrinal authority. On the contrary, not only J. E. Kuhn, but also the professors of the third generation strove to maintain a balanced discussion with the knowledge of their times—especially Moritz von Aberle (1819–75, professor at Tübingen from 1850–66), Franz Xaver Linsenmann (1835–98, professor at Tübingen from 1867), Anton Koch (1859–1915, professor at Tübingen from 1894), Franz Xaver Funk (1840–1907), professor at Tübingen from 1875), and Paul Schanz (1841–1905, professor at Tübingen from 1876). They met, however, with only a limited response. More serious still—because of their reticence with regard to the reforming tendencies in Germany—the Tübingen theologians did not participate in the theological conference held in Munich in 1863, which displeased Rome, nor did they figure among the representatives of German "reforming Catholicism." In addition, on account of the promulgation of the encyclical *Aeterni Patris* (1879), which introduced Neoscholasticism into all ecclesiastical establishments, the Catholic School of Tübingen found itself increasingly isolated.

The Catholic School of Tübingen approached the modernist* period on the horns of a dilemma, wishing, on the one hand, to adopt a positive attitude with regard to modernity, and attempting, on the other, to show its own orthodoxy and its allegiance to Neoscholasticism (a chair of Scholastic* philosophy was specially created in 1903). This rift revealed itself in 1911, when the bishops insisted on a signing of the Declaration of Breslau, by which German Catholic professors of theology had to adhere to an antimodernist oath. After internal discussions within the faculty, the Tübingen theologians went along with the declaration only with reservations and after making important changes to the text. It is not surprising that, as a result, the school as a whole, as well as certain of its individual representatives, were thereafter suspected of modernism.

While it is already difficult to speak in the narrow sense of the term of a "school" of Tübingen in the 19th century, it is quite impossible to do so in the 20th century. It can only be said that numerous faculty members developed their great predecessors' thought. Their chief contribution was to have highlighted the latter's work—chiefly that of Drey, Hirscher, Möhler, Kuhn, and Staudenmaier—following the founding research of the theologians Josef Rupert Geiselmann and Stephan Lösch. It was these historical works that made it possible for the School of Tübingen to enjoy the theological impact that it deserved. Certain of its members were thus acknowledged as precursors of the Catholic theology of the 20th century, which opened the way to the Second Vatican* Council.

As these studies show, it is not easy to give an unequivocal description of the Catholic School of Tübingen with regard to its theological positions and its intellectual orientation. Here one comes up against the difficulties already met in isolating the very idea of a "School of Tübingen." Nonetheless, it is possible to point out certain traits common to all the School's members, however varied might have been their stances on particular issues and their political attitudes towards the Church.

Contrary to Neoscholasticism, the School of Tübingen tried to conduct a constructive dialogue with the culture of its times. Its critical openness replaced Neoscholasticism's apologetic attitude. That meant that it strove to reword the Christian message while preserving the absolute intangibility of revelation and its ecclesial deep-rootedness in theology. It managed to do this by having recourse both to tradition* and to the knowledge of its time, on both of which it cast the same selective and appraising eye. While appropriating fundamental concepts or principles from Christian tradition—the Enlightenment, Romanticism, Idealism, biblical criticism, Protestant theology, Traditionalism*, and still other movements—it managed in that way to follow an independent path that avoided the positivist approach to revelation, supernaturalism, and political idealization, just as it did the different attempts that aimed to reduce Christian truth to a purely natural and human scale.

The school's achievement must be recognized in having given the historical phenomenon a central place in Catholic theology. It succeeded there by basing itself, in the first place, on the organic view of history* developed by Romanticism, and in the second, on Hegel's speculative dialectics. It is true that it meant endorsing the hypothesis of a certain traditionalism and a certain occasional underestimation of man's role in history, but in this way the school also managed to show that it was proper to consider in terms of history (of salvation*) not only revelation as such, but above all its consequences in Church tradition. It thus gave a new and deeper interpretation of these matters, which was to prove itself extremely fruitful, as much on the dogmatic* as on the ethical, pastoral, and spiritual levels. This evolution was closely akin to a reevaluation of the theology of the Kingdom* of God, and therefore to a rehabilitation of the history of dogma, which became thereafter a central subject in theology.

Finally, the School of Tübingen strove to create a new system of erudite theology, thus opening the way to contemporary fundamental* theology. The origins of this movement are found in the progress of historical exegesis* in the increasing autonomy of certain theological disciplines (for instance, moral theology), and in the idealistic attempts made to organize all the particular branches of knowledge into a new systematic whole. It was history again—as an aspect of divine revelation—that was to furnish the principle of this system. Certainly revelation could not be grasped adequately except through a combination of the historico-critical method and the speculative-theological method. The former had to recognize an historically determinable singularity; the second had to integrate this singularity organically into an accessible whole on a super-individualistic level. This whole seemed to be both the content of revelation and the meaning of the whole of history: it was the establishment of God's Kingdom.

c) New Evangelical School of Tübingen. Among the scholars who considered themselves, or who were considered by others, to be members of the "New," or "Critical," or "Historical" School of Tübingen, only a few—aside from their founder F. Chr. Baur—occupied a chair of theology or taught in Württemberg. Therefore, this school had no institutional affiliation except during Baur's period of teaching as the chair of history of the church and dogma in the evangelical faculty of Tübingen (1826–60) and in its periodicals *Theologische-Jahrbücher* (1842–57) and *Zeitschrift für wissenschaftliche Theologie* (1858–1914). Among its at least temporary members stood David Friedrich Strauß (1810–74), Friedrich Theodor Vischer (1807–87), Gustav Pfizer (1807–90), Christian Märklin (1807–49), Wilhelm Zimmermann (1807–78), Albert Schwegler (1819–57), and Eduard Zeller (1814–1908), as well as

two thinkers who would later become its most virulent critics: Albrecht Ritschl (1822–89) and Franz Overbeck (1837–1905). Aside from these theologians, philosophers, and historians, Otto Pfeiderer (1839–1908), Kuno Fischer (1824–1907), Adolf Hilgenfeld (1823–1907), Carl Holsten (1825–97), Heinrich Julius Holtzmann (1832–1910), and Baur's successor, Karl Heinrich Weizäcker (1822–99) felt close to the School.

This New School of Tübingen's characteristic trait was its consistent application of the historico-critical method to the study of primitive Christianity (especially the New Testament) in particular, and to the history of the Church in general. D.F. Strauß was to draw radical results from it, by approaching the Gospels* as a collection of myths* that might have developed around an historical, but now indiscernible, kernel. However, the majority of the school did not follow Strauß in such a destruction of tradition. On the contrary, it clung firmly to Baur's opinion, in which the historico-critical method was insufficient to reconstruct history without a speculative-philosophical apparatus capable of integrating the facts discovered into a global historical context.

This integration took place in the spirit of Hegelian dialectics. The evolution of dogma was viewed as the objective conscience that produces from itself such a global context, and the history of Church theology or faith was interpreted as the subjective conscience that corresponds to the history of dogmas and, together with that, materializes the spirit of humanity struggling to accede to an absolute awareness of itself. This School's relatively brief existence can be explained as much by this Hegelian influence as by the rapid devaluation of its historical discoveries. However, it exerted a considerable influence on theology, on historiography (through A. Schwelger), and on philosophy—especially neo-Kantian philosophy (through E. Zeller and K. Fischer). It is chiefly thanks to this School that the historico-critical method has managed to establish itself in exegesis and the history of the Church, and that historiography has managed to become aware of its systematizing work with regard to historical facts.

- E. Vermeil (1913), *Jean-Adam Möhler et l'école catholique de Tübingen,* Paris.
- Peter Hünermann (1962), *Trinitarische Anthropologie bei F.A. Staudenmaier,* Freiburg.
- W. Geiger (1964), *Spekulation und Kritik,* Munich.
- J.R. Geiselmann (1964), *Die katholische Tübinger Schule. Ihre theologische Eigenart,* Freiburg-Basel-Vienna.
- Katholisch-Theologische Fakultät an der Universität Tübingen (Ed.), *Theologie im Wandel: Festschrift zum 150 jährigen Bestehen der Katholisch-Theologischen Fakultät an der Universität Tübingen 1817–1967,* Munich-Freiburg.
- E. Klinger (1969), *Offenbarung im Horizont der Heilsgeschichte,* Zurich-Einsiedeln-Köln.

F. Wolfinger (1972), *Der Glaube nach J. E. v. Kuhn,* Göttingen.

F. Courth (1975), *Das "Leben Jesu" von D. F. Strauß in der Kritik J. E. Kuhns,* Göttingen.

M. Brecht (Ed.) (1977), *Theologen und Theologie an der Universität Tübingen: Beiträge zur Geschichte der Evangelisch-Theologischen Fakultät Tübingen,* Tübingen.

G. A. McCool (1977), *Catholic Theology in the Nineteenth Century,* New York.

A. P. Kustermann (1988), *Die Apologetik J. S. Dreys,* Tübingen.

U. Köpf (1994), *Historisch-kritische Geschichtsbetrachtung: F. Chr. Baur und seine Schüler,* Sigmaringen.

A. P. Kustermann (ed.) (1994), *Revision der Theologie-Reform der Kirche,* Würzburg.

HEINRICH SCHMIDINGER

See also **Exegesis; Hegel, Georg Wilhelm Friedrich; Hegelianism; Kant, Immanuel; Schelling, Friedrich Wilhelm Joseph von; Supernatural; Thomism**

Tutiorism. *See* **Alphonsus Liguori; Casuistry**

Typology. *See* **Scripture, Senses of**

U

Ubiquity, Divine. *See* **Omnipresence, Divine**

Ultramontanism

Until the 19th century one did not speak of "Ultramontanism" but of "Ultramontanes," a term that designated those defenders of that conception of the papacy that was current on the other side of the Alps and that Gallicanism opposed. The modern variant has taken on an abstract and ideological aspect revealed in various forms of behavior. The common factor in the different forms of Ultramontanism, contrasting with nationalist views, is the desire for an absolute fidelity at the heart of Catholicity, a concern that inspires the defense not only of Roman prerogatives or a pyramidal ecclesiology* but of a certain form of supranational Catholic (Catholicism*) identity. In this sense it represents a resistance to the rise of the modern states and a defense of an ideal of Christianity. In addition, its emotional conception of religion was destined to facilitate the Christianization of the masses. And from that angle, the continuity is greater than generally admitted between the "Romanism" encountered under the old monarchy and the Ultramontanism of modern times.

1. Romanism
Strongly encouraged by the papacy, the trend toward change and reform that followed the Council of Trent* could do no other than favor the links that united local churches to the See of Rome. In a certain number of cases, especially in France, the presence or proximity of a Protestant minority incited the church* to emphasize its essential elements, and thus to accentuate its "Romanism." Contrary to long-held opinions therefore, on the religious level the first part of the 17th century in France was undeniably "Ultramontane." This explains both the Gallican reaction of Richer and the obstacles he encountered in expounding his ideas. It also explains the fact that all the reforming prelates (Du Perron, La Rochefoucauld, Solminihac) based their actions on strong relations with the Holy See and the nuncios who represented it. This same attitude was found among the reformers belonging to religious orders, or among the founders of new forms of discipleship: Bérulle*, Jean Eudes, Vincent de Paul, and Jean-Jacques Olier were "Romans" in the sense that they stressed the papacy's greatness and authority* and encouraged its interventions. The Jesuits, and the education they offered, undoubtedly favored these views, but in the majority of cases such views found easy acceptance. Far from being a Gallican* bastion, the Faculty of Theology in Paris, where the elite of the

French clergy were trained, was a battleground during the whole of the 17th century between a "Roman" majority and a Gallican or Richer-influenced minority, which only won out thanks to pressures from the political authorities.

In its relation to the growth of Gallicanism, this "Romanism," which has been studied unilaterally but not as a whole, seems to have been quite moderate in its theological expression and prudent in its political views. It expressed itself little, and often when it did so it was in an antagonistic climate, with the Jansenist crisis and Gallican polemics in the background. But its visible characteristics reveal it as a widespread and relatively homogenous movement.

a) It had a strong hierarchical conception that defended Roman prerogatives and tried to extend them (*De Monarchia divina ecclesiastica* by M. Mauclerc, 1662). Papal primacy together with the exclusivity of doctrinal judgment were clearly maintained. It often presented the privilege of infallibility* in a very broad manner, basing it on a form of inspiration rather than conceiving it as a protection against error (M. Grandin). On the juridico-ecclesiological level, the *Tractatus de Libertatibus ecclesia gallicanae* (1682), a refutation of the Four Articles of 1682 by A. Charlas, is the best example of this viewpoint. It also developed important theological aspects, of which the notion of dogmatic progress is not the least important.

b) Ultramontanism represented clerical and authoritarian Christianity, an aspect thoroughly studied in the works of B. Chédozeau (1990). By adopting the Index's *regulae,* this movement rejected all translation: not only of the Bible* but also of the liturgy*, and even of theology (texts of the Council of Trent). It therefore adopted a position diametrically opposed to that of the "Jansenists," who strove to facilitate the access of laypeople to the spiritual life.

c) Ultramontanism favored a festive and associative Christianity. The clear differentiation between the duties of a cleric* and those of a layperson was offset by the duty everyone had to the mission of the church. This commitment was demonstrated through membership of particular groups, congregations, associations, and companies, such as the famous Company of the Blessed Sacrament, and through the organization of a religious life centered on the group's identifying activities: a chapel, a patron saint, a particular pilgrimage*.

d) Ultramontanism also embraced a fervent and charitable Christianity. Group life was the starting point of a work of personal and community sanctifica-tion, by turns educational, moralizing, and charitable. We have knowledge of this dimension of Ultramontanism through the works devoted to the congregations and *The Europe of the Devoted.* This contained traces of an "Ultramontane" piety, that is, of a piety influenced by southern Europe. Marian devotion and membership in the "cordicoles" (Heart* of Christ) were encouraged.

e) Finally, it was an expansionist Christianity that combined strong opposition to any tolerance of error with an effort of conversion. We find in it a reconquering spirit vis-à-vis Protestantism*, but also a great concern with the "propagation of the faith." It is no coincidence that the work of the Paris foreign missions should have come to birth in this milieu. We should certainly be careful about viewing each of the elements defined above as the characteristics of a homogeneous ideology. It is clear that the official adoption in France of the Gallican Four Articles, together with the extension of regalism and the progress of Jansenism* in the other Catholic countries, hampered the growth of this Romanism, sometimes forcing it to disguise itself, but without destroying it. It survived the suppression of the Society of Jesus extremely well and expressed itself in sometimes very violent attacks on the "Jansenism" of the Enlightenment. Rome misunderstood this and failed to support it (*see* Pius VI's tour of Austria and Germany). All the same it was the French Revolution that, by discrediting the Gallican model and destroying the ecclesiastical structure, made an aggressive upsurge of Ultramontanism possible.

2. Ultramontanism

The advances made by anti-Roman theories during the 18th century were not accepted with complete passivity, and the defenders of papal authority, chiefly in Italy (Zaccharia, Cucagni, Marchetti, Anfossi, Ballerini, Cappelari), distinguished themselves in their more or less apologetic refutations, which would exert an influence over the movement in the 19th century. Moreover, the popes attempted to ensure their future by issuing specific condemnations of attacks against their jurisdiction (*Responsio super Nunciaturis,* 1789; censure of Febronius, 1764, of the Synod of Pistoia, 1794). But it was among the younger generation that the main trends emerged that were to express new forms of Ultramontanism. Attacking the principles of the French Revolution, in which they saw the end result of a negative movement launched by the Reformation and orchestrated by the Enlightenment, the traditionalists (Bonald, Maistre) declared the necessity of an unassailable authority, which they identified with the papacy. For its part, through their attachment to the liberal principles of the Revolution, the group that had gathered around Lamennais opposed Gallicanism and pinned its hopes on a regenerated papacy. As for L. Veuillot's group, which mainly expressed itself in the pages of *L'Univers*, it stood closer to a classical and popular Ultramontanism, which the trials of the Revolution had only enriched. The condemnation of Lamennais (1832), his defection, and especially the encyclical *Quanta Cura* (1864) caused the exodus of a whole section of the liberal Catholics, who then drew closer to a neo-Gallicanism with Episcopalian tendencies. The others joined forces with the Ultramontane movement and imbued it with a deep ardor. Encouraged ever more explicitly by the Roman circles, they launched an offensive in order to disavow, and then to condemn, the remnants of an ecclesiological Gallicanism: they abandoned local liturgies in favor of the Roman rite, and revised or rewrote textbooks of ecclesiastical history and of theology. On this matter, the encyclical *Inter multiplices* (March 1853) indicated the papacy's personal commitment, by disavowing all resistance to the centralizing movement. This intervention corresponded to a general expectation as well as to the personality and success of Pope Pius IX, whatever may have been the reservations of bishops and theologians, who had only a limited influence. This passion for Romanism, cleverly orchestrated and encouraged by pontifical entreaties, thus inspired what has been called a neo-Ultramontanism, to distinguish it from the doctrine that was to be imposed with Vatican* I. It principally involved an extreme exaltation of the Roman pontiff, combined with a notion of infallibility that was close to that of inspiration. It was found in all the Catholic countries, and had a character of intransigence and intolerance of which *The Universe* provides a good example. Despite its constraints and limitations, the discussion of these themes at Vatican I permitted a degree of healthy exchange. The constitution *Pater aeternus,* by explaining the Roman pontiff's primacy and setting limits to his infallibility, adopted the chief demands of the Ultramontanes while integrating them into a process of theological reflection, which would be deepened in subsequent pontificates.

Four main aspects of 19th-century Ultramontanism can be distinguished:

a) Ecclesiology. We can note an impoverishment in comparison with classical Ultramontanism, particularly with regard to the "mystic" and supernatural conception, well evidenced by the supporters of the Roman school—Passaglia, Schrader, Franzelin, and Perrone—whose conciliar plans were rejected. The emphasis was placed on the theme of unity, but according to a juridical interpretation: the church is founded on the pope, who is the principle of its unity.

b) Spirituality. The term "Ultramontane piety" has been used to define a popular and festive religion that accentuated certain features of the baroque piety of the previous centuries. It sought to integrate local traditions, which had been earlier branded as superstitious and pagan, and promoted a new veneration of miracle-working saints (Saint Anthony of Padua) and the cult* of relics* (Saint Philomena). It also furthered devotion to the Blessed Sacrament, to the Sacred Heart, and to the Virgin, expressed with "warmth and display of feelings" (Gadille 1985), but also in a spirit of penitence (penance*) and of reparation. We see generally a greater interest in the supernatural*, often associated with marvels, and a massive recourse to indulgences* and papal blessings*. Similarly, pilgrimages to both historic and new sites enjoyed great success.

c) Morality. Liguorism (Alphonsus* of Liguori), which contrasted with "Jansenist" rigorism, spread very rapidly (*Justification de la théologie morale du B.A.M. de Ligorio* by Th. Gousset, 1832), encouraged decisively by the fact of Bailly's theology being placed on the Index. Its influence favored more frequent recourse to the sacraments of penance and the Eucharist, perceived as sources of spiritual strength and as nourishment for the apostolate.

d) Apostolate. Under very diverse forms, the commitment of laypersons and clerics, monks and nuns, revealed a global perception of Roman Christianity, which was both universalist and expansionist—a perception heightened by improvements in the means of communication.

Henceforth, Ultramontanism can only be discussed in an analogical way, in order to designate "integralist" notions, more political than theological, which developed during the 20th century; or to describe, for instance, the challenges to the rejuvenated theology of the episcopate, which would result in Vatican II's constitution *Lumen gentium.*

● J. Vidal (1936), *Documents sur M. de Caulet, évêque de Pamiers,* vol. 3, *Antoine Charles directeur du séminaire et vicaire général de Pamiers, 1634–1698,* Castillon-de-Couserans.
A.-G. Martimort (1953), *Le gallicanisme de Bossuet,* Paris.
J. Orcibal (1955), "L'idée d'Église chez les catholiques du XVIIe siècle," *Relazioni del X Congresso Internazionale di Scienze Storiche,* vol. IV, 111–35.
M. Nédoncelle et al. (1960), *L'ecclésiologie au XIXe siècle,* Paris.
H. Raab (1962), "Zur Geschichte und Bedeutung des Schlagswortes 'Ultramontan' im 18. und frühen 19. Jahrhundert," *HJ* 81, 59–173.
J. Guerber (1973), *Le ralliement du clergé français à la morale liguorienne: L'abbé Gousset et ses précurseurs (1785–1832),* Rome.

H. J. Pottmeyer (1975), *Unfehlbarkeit und Souveränität: Die päpstliche Unfehlbarkeit der ultramonten Ekklesiologie des 19. Jahrhunderts*, Mainz.

R. F. Costigan (1980), *Rohrbacher and the Ecclesiology of Ultramontanism*, Rome.

J. Gadille (1985), *Les Ultramontains canadiens français*, Montreal.

A. Gough, *Paris and Rome: The Gallican Church and the Ultramontane Campaigne, 1848–1853*, Oxford.

L. Chatellier (1987), *L'Europe des Dévots*, Paris.

B. Chédozeau (1990), *La Bible et la liturgie en français*, Paris.

B. Neveu (1993), *L'erreur et son juge: Remarques sur les censures doctrinales à l'époque moderne*, Naples.

JACQUES M. GRES-GAYER

See also **Gallicanism; Infallibility; Jansenism; Traditionalism; Vatican I, Council of**

Unicity, Divine. *See* **God; Monotheism**

Unitarianism/Anti-Trinitarianism

"Unitarianism" refers to doctrines that challenge the dogma* of the Trinity*; accordingly, it is generally synonymous with "anti-Trinitarianism," and the term "Unitarian" can be applied to all anti-Trinitarians, whatever their divergences, although it may give rise to ambiguities. Three main types of Unitarianism, each unrelated to the others, may be distinguished: the anti-Trinitarianism of antiquity; Socinianism; and the doctrine of the Unitarian churches of England and North America.

a) Anti-Trinitarianism in Antiquity. The modalist anti-Trinitarianism (modalism*) of the second and third centuries was condemned as a heresy* at the first Council of Nicaea* and at the first Council of Constantinople*. The various forms of modalism treated the Son and the Holy* Spirit as "modes" of the Father*, while monarchianism denied the existence of the Trinity in order to emphasize the unity of God* (monotheism*, tritheism*), and Sabellianism regarded the three Persons* as no more than "appearances" of the single deity. The subordinationist heresies (Arianism*) were also anti-Trinitarian.

b) Anti-Trinitarianism from the 16th Century Onward: Socinianism. The words "anti-Trinitarianism" and "Unitarianism" have polemical connotations, making it possible to assert a connection between the ancient tradition* and a current of thought that arose from the Reformation, and thus to claim that this current of thought was a revival of Arianism. The connection was made by its opponents, who sought to insert it into the catalog of ancient heresies and to disregard its originality.

It was in this way that the term "Unitarian" came to be applied to Giorgio Biandrata (1516–88), who opposed Calvin* and contributed to the development of Unitarianism in the Italian-speaking region of Switzerland, as well as to Michael Servetus (1511–53), on the grounds that he rejected the Trinity. However, Servetus did so in the name of a speculative philosophy that owed a great deal to Plato, and still more to the *Poimandrès,* and he seems in fact to have been a Gnostic. Later writers sympathetic to Unitarianism, including Voltaire in the seventh of his *Lettres anglaises,* and Jacques-André Naigeon in an important article on *"unitaires"* in the *Encyclopédie,* preferred to assimilate Unitarianism to deism*, which had positive connotations for them. Thus, Naigeon called the Unitarians "hidden deists." Unitarians themselves always indignantly rejected the reduction of Unitarianism to a form of Arianism revived after 12 centuries of oblivion (as Voltaire put it), but the anachronistic and reductive attribution of deism does not fit either.

Indeed, Laelius Socinus (1525–62) and his nephew Faustus Socinus (1539–1604) had introduced a wholly new doctrine, rejecting the dogma of the Trinity in accordance with their own reinterpretation of Scripture. They found followers, some gathered in churches and some not, primarily in Poland but then also throughout the rest of Europe. Thus was born a movement—that is, a continuous historical phenomenon united in doctrine and activity—that still exists today, both in the Old World and in the New. Neither Voltaire nor Naigeon were wrong, for both equated anti-Trinitarians with Socinians, yet neither Laelius Socinus nor Faustus Socinus had liked the word Socinianism, which transformed them into the leaders of the movement. Faustus Socinus was content with his "position" as an adviser to the *Ecclesia minor,* the Minor Reformed Church, also known as the Polish Brethren, without ever claiming a leadership role for himself. Supporters of adult baptism*, the Polish Brethren had been founded by Gregory Paul in 1562. They enjoyed some initial success but were expelled in 1638 from their main center at Rakow, and were forced to leave Poland altogether in 1658, after the triumph of the Counter-Reformation there.

Nevertheless, Socinianism inevitably became the dominant form of Unitarianism, precisely because of its doctrinal innovation, however inaccurately that was to be interpreted by contemporaries and by posterity. In analyzing that innovation, we shall focus on two principal questions: the reinterpretation of the prologue of John's Gospel; and the critique of the conception of Christ*'s Passion* conceived as a sacrifice.

1) John's prologue has to be interpreted separately from the first chapter of Genesis, which was traditionally seen as its parallel. While Genesis 1 has an obvious significance as cosmogony, the prologue refers only to the beginning of the preaching* of the Word* by Jesus, without implying the eternal existence in God of a consubstantial* Son, existing before the creation*; nor does it imply that there has been an incarnation* of a divine principle. By rejecting Jesus' unique possession of a double nature, this "hermeneutic rupture" (Marchetti) reduces him to being nothing other than a human being. The immediate advantage of this rupture is that it eliminates the difficulties associated with the communication of idioms, but it introduces new problems, notably concerning what precise function was fulfilled by a Christ who was no longer also God.

2) In 1578, on the occasion of the discussion with J. Covet that led to the writing of *De Jesu Christo servatore* (published 1598), Faustus Socinus challenged certain Catholic interpretations of the idea of "satisfaction" (Anselm* of Canterbury), as well as the Calvinist interpretation. According to these interpretations, God's wrath* toward sinful humanity, in consequence of original sin*, cannot be appeased except by the sacrifice of an adequate victim. A God made into a man can counterbalance God the Father, but this role can only be taken by God's own Son; and God thus enters into a dialectical relationship capable of redeeming created humanity by abolishing its sin. According to Socinus, however, the effect of such interpretations is to make the relationship between God and humanity into an economic transaction, which is unworthy of the divine glory because it is barbaric. God is not a creditor who can be appeased by the blood of his debtor, and it is difficult to understand how a human being could be capable of such an operation. Hence, it follows that Christ's Passion was not a sacrifice offered to satisfy an angry God. Christ's death was that of an exceptional human being, and it earned him exceptional merit: death was vanquished for the first time, and through this victory a human being was then, and only then, granted powers, as priest and as king, over those who believe in him. Of course, such a human being deserves special honor—not adoration, in the strict sense of that term, but rather piety and veneration. Clearly, this approach deprives both the Catholic Mass and the Lord's Supper of the Calvinists of any value, real or even symbolic.

Nevertheless, while the Son of God is no longer regarded as the Second Person* of a Trinity, given in sacrifice to save all human beings, the God of the Unitarians is not simply the supreme principle of some form of rational Christianity, despite Naigeon's conclusion in his article in the *Encyclopédie* that "there is only an imperceptible difference between Socinianism and deism, and only one step need be taken from one to the other." While deism relies on reason*, Unitarianism relies on faith alone. Faustus Socinus insisted that "natural religion" did not exist, on the grounds that there were peoples, in Brazil for example, who had no notion of such a thing. Accordingly, salvation*—that is, immortality ensured by the human Christ—is a matter for Christians alone. Unitarianism is not a philosophy, but remains a form of religion, "a new type of Christianity" (Voltaire, "Divinité de Jésus," in the *Dictionnaire philosophique*). This is made clear in the *Religio rationalis*, written by Faustus Socinus's grandson Andreas Wiszowaty (†1678). It is because Unitarianism is a religion that this particular product of the "radical Reformation" has been capable of surviving into our own time, notably in English-speaking countries.

c) Unitarian Churches of England and North America. Voltaire saw Isaac Newton and Samuel Clarke as Unitarians (but not Socinians), while others have applied the term to the puritan poet John Milton (1608–74) and to John Locke (1632–1704). However, it was Theophilus Lindsey (1723–1808) who founded the Unitarian Church in England (1778). He went on to write *Conversations upon Christian Idolatry* (1790), in which "idolatry" refers to belief in the Trinity. Around the same time, the chemist Joseph Priestley (1733–1804) also established a Unitarian community (1780–91, first in Leeds and then in Birmingham). Priestley argued against Anglicanism*, criticizing in particular the doctrines of the Trinity and redemption, in more than 70 volumes of religious writings (e.g., *History of the Corruption of Christianity*, 2 vols, 1782; *History of Early Opinions Concerning Jesus Christ*, 2 vols, 1786; and *General History of the Christian Church*, 4 vols., 1792–1803).

In 1794 Priestley emigrated to the United States, where he came into contact with "liberal Christians," dissenters from the Episcopalian Church of New England (Boston) who also denied the existence of the Trinity. They included William Emerson and, later, his son, the writer Ralph Waldo Emerson (1803–82), William Ellery Channing (1780–1842), and Theodore Parker (1810–60). However, Unitarianism spread mainly among the Congregationalists rather than the Episcopalians, and came to be characterized above all by tolerance and absolute liberty* of belief. The sentimental moralism that grew out of American Unitarianism encouraged the development of philanthropic activities and led most Unitarians to take an active part in the campaign to abolish slavery.

● *Nowy Korbut*: Bibliography of Polish Literature, Old Poland, 3 vols., Warsaw, 1965.
Catechism of Cracovie, 1605 (Polish Ed.), 1680 (Latin Ed.).

Bibliotheca Fratrum Polonorum I and II, Amsterdam, 1656 (source of the principal texts of Faustus Socinus and his successors; some of which are translated in Osier [1996]).
C. Sand (Sandius), *Bibliotheca Antitrinitariorum,* Amsterdam, 1684 (New Ed., Warsaw, 1967).
A. Wiszowaty, *Religio rationalis,* Amsterdam, 1684 (New Ed., Warsaw, 1960).
S. Lubieniecki, *Historia Reformationis polonicae,* Freistadt, 1685 (New Ed., Warsaw, 1971).
Acta synodalia ecclesiarum Poloniae reformatarum I (1550–1559), Ed. M. Sipayllo, Warsaw, 1966.
Laelio Sozzini, *Opere,* Ed. A. Rotondo, Florence, 1986.
♦ Henry Allen (1894), *A History of the Unitarians in the United States,* ACHS 10, New York.
G. Bardy (1929), "Monarchianisme," *Dictionnaire de théologie catholic* 10/2, 2193–209.
D. Cantimori (1946), *Per la Storia degli Eretici italiano del secolo XVI,* Rome.
W. E. Morse (1946), *A History of Unitarianism: Socinianism and Its Antecedents,* Cambridge, Mass.
L. Christiani (1950), "Unitariens," *Dictionnaire de théologie catholic* 15/2, 2162–72.
R.H. Bainton (1953), *Michel Servet, hérétique et martyr,* Geneva.
J. Lecler (1954), *Histoire de la Tolérance au siècle de la Réforme,* vol. 1, Paris (New Ed. 1994).
A. Pirnat (1961), *Die Ideologie der Siebenbürger, Antitrinitarier in den 1570en Jahren,* Budapest.
G.H. Williams (1962), *The Radical Reformation,* Philadelphia.
L. Chmaj (1963), *Faust Socyn,* Warsaw.
Z. Ogonowski (1966), *Socynianizm a Oswiecenie,* Warsaw.
A. Rotondo (1974), *Studi e Ricerche di Storia Ereticale italiana del Cinquecento,* Turin.
V. Marchetti (1975), *Gruppi Ereticali Senesi del Cinquecento,* Florence.
M. Firpo (1977), *Antitrinitari nell'Europa orientale del' 500,* Florence.
Coll. (1980), *The Polish Brethren* I and II, HThS 30.
V. Marchetti (1980), *Italia, Venezia, Polonia,* Florence.
A. Pirnat (1982), *Antitrinitarianism in the Second Half of the 16th Century,* Budapest-Leyden.
J.-P. Osier (1983), *D'Uriel da Costa à Spinoza,* Paris.
J.-P. Osier (1984), *L'Évangile du ghetto,* Paris.
J. Pelikan (1984), *The Christian Tradition,* vol. 4: *Reformation of Church and Dogma (1300–1700),* ch. 6.
J.-P. Osier (1996), *Faust Socin ou le christianisme sans sacrifice,* Paris.

JEAN-PIERRE OSIER

See also **Anabaptists; Anglicanism; Arianism; Calvinism; Deism and Theism; Gnosis; Modalism; Monotheism; Tritheism**

Unity of the Church

1. Definitions and History

Christians confess the church* as being one, holy, catholic, and apostolic (creed of Nicaea-Constantinople, 381). As unity is a fundamental characteristic of the church, the unity of the church occupies an essential place in theology* and ecclesiology*. It is an inalienable gift of God*; however, it is constantly threatened by schisms*. It is up to the church to give visibility to this unity and to attain it in history.

a) Beginning with the New Testament, the apostle Paul spoke of the Church of God in Corinth, Rome*, and so on (1 Cor 1:2; 2 Cor 1:1; etc.), and the first assembly (council*) of Jerusalem showed both the diversity and unity of the church. Local churches were, in their plurality, representations or realizations in particular places of the one Church of Christ. The diversity of geographical, cultural, and historical contexts determined the life of the churches, their preaching* and spirituality, their community and cultural life, and their doctrinal and confessional identity. Ecclesial plurality became an ecumenical problem when diversity caused separation and division. The communion between the various churches was broken, and mutual condemnation no longer allowed one church to recognize another as a full and authentic expression of the Church of Christ. Theological stakes (heresies*) and nondoctrinal issues were the cause. In the Gospels*, Jesus* prays for the unity of his followers (Jn 17), and the New Testament epistles warn against the rivalry and tension that threaten the unity of the church (Rom 12:3ff.; 1 Cor 3:4ff., 12:4ff.; Phil 2:2ff.; Eph 4:3ff.; Jude 19).

b) The first schisms occurred in the early church over the date of Easter, over discipline and the ascetic life (Donatism*, Novatianism*), and then above all over issues of Christology* and Trinitarian theology (Arianism*, Monophysitism*, and Nestorianism*). Synods* and councils condemned heretics; and state power, for its part, intervened in order to preserve the unity of the church and that of the empire after 313 (antiheretic legislation).

c) Reasons of ecclesiastical policy and theological questions (*Filioque*, Trinity*) led to the great schism between East and West in 1054. Efforts to reestablish the unity of the church during the Second Council of Lyons* (1274) and the Council of Florence (1438–39) failed and also came up against the problem of the primacy of the pope.

d) With the Reformation the problem of the unity of the church was amplified by the plurality of movements that broke off from the Roman Church (Lutheranism*, Anglicanism*, Calvinism*, etc.). Religious and political efforts (Diet of Augsburg in 1530, the peace of Augsburg in 1555, etc.) were unable to prevent the violent outbreak of a series of religious wars in Europe. Protestantism*, for one, was divided, despite various efforts to preserve its unity (Marburg Colloquy in 1529).

e) Despite Pietism* and the Enlightenment, it was not until the 19th century that there appeared the first movements seeking to reestablish the unity of the church. Their 20th-century successors would create the World* Council of Churches. The ecumenical movement insists on the necessity of renewal and the conversion of all churches as a prerequisite of the visible manifestation of the unity of the church. The Second Vatican* Council fully agreed with this sentiment (decree on ecumenism*, *Unitatis redintegration [UR]*, 6). The unity of the church can in no way be separate from the other essential features (or "marks") of the church: its apostolicity (truth*, authenticity, and continuity of faith*), its catholicity (fullness of communion, universality of mission* and testimony), and its holiness* (service to and responsibility for all humanity). These various aspects characterize contemporary ecumenical endeavors.

2. Contemporary Conception and Models of Church Unity

As a gift of God, the unity of the church is anchored in the unity of the Trinitarian God and his work of salvation (Eph 4:4–6; 1 Cor 12:4–6; Jn 17:21). This conviction is the basis of the contemporary understanding of the unity of the church summed up in the declaration of *Faith and Constitution* (a body to which the Roman Catholic Church and all the other confessional families belong), which was approved during the General

Assembly of the World Council of Churches in Canberra (1991): "The unity of the Church to which we are called is a *koinonia* given and expressed in the shared confession of apostolic faith, in a shared sacramental life to which we gain access through a single baptism* and which we celebrate together in mutual recognition and the reconciliation of the ministries*; finally, it is expressed in the mission through which together we become the witnesses of the gospel of the grace* of God upon all and in the service of the whole of creation*. The goal of our search for full communion will be attained when all the churches will be able to recognize in all of the others the Church which is one, holy, catholic, and apostolic in its fullness. This fullness of communion will be expressed on a local and universal level in the conciliary forms of life and of action."

This declaration gave proof of a number of invaluable achievements on the part of the contemporary ecumenical movement:

a)   Unity and diversity are not contradictory notions. To seek the unity of the church does not imply uniformity. The diversity rooted in theological traditions and differing cultural, ethnic, or historical contexts belongs to the very nature of ecclesial communion. This diversity does, however, become wrongful and divisive when it prevents shared confession and celebration of the gospel. The unity of the church does not require that differences be overcome, but that the nature of those differences be transformed: divisive differences must, through dialogue and shared commitment, lose their divisive dimension. Thus, the classical opposition between Protestants and Catholics in the understanding of salvation* has now lost its divisive nature, and the options of the different traditions are no longer mutually exclusive (without for all that being perfectly identical). One must note, however, that some see divisive differences in what others consider to be legitimate diversity; this is valid above all in the domains of ecclesiology, for example—that of the ministries, where Protestantism accepts and defends a diversity that is unacceptable to Catholicism*.

b)   All the traditions agree in saying that the unity of the church requires full communion in the preaching of the gospel (the shared confession of faith), in the celebration of the sacraments*, and in the mutual recognition of the ministries, the means of grace through which God builds up and sustains his church. Division, for which there were many reasons, had always been historically expressed and concretized by a rupture at the level of these essential features. Preaching*, the Eucharist*, the ministries of other traditions, or even sometimes baptism were rejected as invalid even if in other cases a number of common foundations had been preserved (reference to Holy* Scripture and to the confessions of faith of the early church).

c)   More recently there has been an awareness that ethical divergences could also break the unity of the church. The implication of certain churches in situations of oppression or injustice poses to all Christian traditions a question of ethical heresy. Thus, in the early 1980s world organizations of Protestants excluded those member churches from white South Africa that supported apartheid.

d)   The unity of the church could never be an exclusively spiritual or even abstract reality. It requires a certain visibility and demands a structural expression. From the beginning the ecumenical movement has debated what have been called "models of unity." After an initial period where some pleaded for a fusion or a return of dissidents into the fold of a hypothetical undivided church, three models in particular were proposed: 1) At the World Council of Churches there was enduring support for a form of *organic union* that, by putting an end to traditional confessions and identities, would be founded upon a shared confession of faith, an agreement on the sacraments and ministries, and the adoption of a uniform structural organization. For essentially cultural and geographical reasons, churches would remain different from each other. On the local level, however, they would indeed be united. All of these churches would be gathered into a universal council that would represent the final authority (*see* the vision of a *conciliary community* put forward by the General Assembly of the World Council of Churches in Nairobi in 1975). 2) Anglicans and Catholics both spoke for a *corporative union* in which specific identity would be maintained, and unity would be achieved through a shared episcopal constitution and the shared exercise of the episcopate. 3) *Unity in reconciled diversity* is based on the fact that almost all churches nowadays are organized into world communions (confessional families), and proposes reconciliation and full mutual recognition among the different traditions, which would retain their legitimate diversity even on a local level. However, this would not mean maintaining the status quo, for mutual recognition implies the transformation and conversion of traditional identities and their integration into an ecumenical communion of all churches. These three complementary models are still being debated but have also been applied in various places, depending on the opposing partners.

e)   The spiritual dimension remains essential and is a prerequisite of all the other efforts toward church unity. This unity will be attained wherever believers of diverse origins come together to pray and to worship, something that will prepare them for testimony and shared service in the world (ecumenism*), and from which a more structured unity of churches can in no way be dissociated.

3. Dialogues between the Churches
Examples of church unity are numerous and complementary. They touch all areas of the life of the churches. A particular place, however, is reserved for theological dialogue: over the last 30 years, this has enabled many traditional controversies to be overcome.

a) Dialogue can occur on every level (local, national, international), in a bilateral or multilateral form. Multilateral dialogue on a global level *(Faith and Constitution)* has managed to reach a broad convergence on *Baptism, Eucharist, and Ministry* (Lima Text, 1982, *BEM*). Bilateral talks have been held between almost all the confessional families that have commissioned them officially. The two forms are complementary: bilateral dialogue seeks to overcome the particular disagreements that have divided two specific traditions, and to obtain the necessary and sufficient consensus for mutual recognition and entry into full ecclesiastical communion. Multilateral talks define the general framework and guarantee the compatibility of the various bilateral meetings.

b) The first phase of the theological dialogue between churches has been largely accomplished at the present time. All traditions have had mutual exchanges, have become better acquainted, and have voiced their consensus, or their differences, on specific doctrinal themes. Given the reasons for division, the central questions have been those concerning Holy Scripture, salvation, sacraments, ministries, and church authority. There have been significant convergences, even if ecclesiological issues remain a stumbling block between Roman Catholics and Orthodox, and between these two traditions and the confessional families that emerged from the Reformation.

c) In a new phase, it will be necessary to move from a group of those who have reached consensus to a consensus of the whole. The doctrinal agreement generally obtained on an international level must be translated into a new form of communion among the churches concerned. The churches that emerged from the Reformation of the Western world have been able to accomplish the most significant progress in this respect. Among others, one should mention the Leuenberg Concord (1973) between Lutherans and reformed churches

in Europe; the Meissen (1988) and Porvoo (1993) declarations, between some reformed churches and European Anglicans; the Concord between Lutherans and Episcopalians in the United States (1993); and the agreement between Methodists, Lutherans, and reformed churches in Europe (1994). The dialogue of these churches with Catholicism and the Orthodox* church has brought about an improvement in the quality of communion, even if communion itself is not yet total, as mutual recognition remains partial.

d) All such dialogue will remain sterile if it is not received at all levels of the church's life. This reception is still too partial and must figure at the heart of subsequent endeavors. Moreover, a methodology must be developed to overcome the nondoctrinal factors that have contributed to division (ethnic, social, and cultural factors; issues of majority-minority; and so on) and that often remain a stubborn obstacle to church unity. The unity of the church has no finality in itself; it is based on the promise of Christ, who through the Holy* Spirit sustains his church and sends it out into the world. The full visibility of the unity of the church and its full accomplishment are matters for eschatology*. The contemporary ecumenical movement is progressing in stages. Progress varies according to location, region, and ecclesiastical tradition.

- G. Thils (1962), *Histoire doctrinale du mouvement œcuménique,* Louvain.
- (1966), *Actes du concile Vatican II: Décret sur l'œcuménisme,* Paris.
- H. E. Fey (Ed.) (1970), *A History of the Ecumenical Movement,* vol. 2: *1948–1968,* Geneva.
- J. Hoffmann (1983), "La recomposition de l'unité," in B. Lauret and F. Refoulé (Eds.), *Initiation à la pratique de la théologie,* vol. III, Paris, 343–72.
- A. Birmelé (1986), *Le salut en Jésus-Christ dans les dialogues œcuméniques,* Paris.
- K. Lehmann, W. Pannenberg (Eds.) (1986), *Lehrverurteilungen-Kirchentrennend?* Freiburg-Göttingen.
- K. Blaser (1990), *Une Église des confessions,* Geneva.
- B. Sesboüé (1990), *Pour une théologie œcuménique,* Paris.
- N. Lossky et al. (Ed.) (1991), *Dictionary of the Ecumenical Movement,* Geneva.
- M. Westphal (Ed.) (1991), *Signes de l'Esprit: Rapport officiel: Septième assemblée Canberra,* Geneva.
- O. Cullmann (1992), *Les voies de l'unité chrétienne,* Paris.
- R. Frieling (1992), *Der Weg des ökumenischen Gedankens,* Göttingen.
- A. Birmelé, J. Terme (Eds.) (1995), *Accords et dialogues œcuméniques,* Paris.
- Jean-Paul II (1995), *Ut unum sint,* Vatican City.

André Birmelé

See also **Catholicism; Ecumenism; Family, Confessional; Orthodoxy; Protestantism; World Council of Churches**

Universalism

Jesus*' disciples, schooled in Judaism*, preached a religious universalism in fulfillment of the Old Testament. While the Jewish camp insists on its election and the Christian camp on its universalism, both have always had to cope with the tension between these two extremes.

a) Old Testament. Israel* frequently protected itself against the surrounding paganism*. Its consciousness of election, however, brought with it a complex relationship with the nations. Quite gratuitously (Dt 7:7f.), because "the whole world belongs to him" (Ex 19:5), God* had chosen himself a people*. He could go back on that choice if his chosen ones were to become proud and self-important as a consequence (Am 3:1f., 9:7). The universalism of the Old Testament is based on faith in a "very good" (Gn 1:31) creation*. Despite the fact of human sin*, the narrative* of the beginning (Gn 1–11) is shot through with blessings* (Gn 1:28, 9:1) and a covenant* with the whole of humanity (Gn 9:9–17). Admittedly, the myth of Babel (Gn 11) condemns human excess; but while Abraham, the ancestor of the Davidic dynasty, finds himself chosen by God, this is only so that "the tribes of the earth," Israel's vassals, may receive divine blessings (Gn 12:3).

The Old Testament's universalism is also rooted in the Ten Commandments, seen as the basis of a universal wisdom* (Dt 4:5ff.) and ethics*. Thus the prophetic oracles against the nations denounce the murderous policies of neighboring peoples (*See* Am 1:2–2:3). Israel must practice social universalism by helping the unfortunate (Prv 14:31) and the foreigner (Dt 10:19). So a royal ideology emerges: God is the supreme ruler. He pronounces just laws according to his will (Dt 10:17f.), from the Temple at Jerusalem*, whose magnificence attracts foreigners (1 Kgs 8:41ff.). The psalms of the Kingdom (Kingdom* of God) (Ps 47, 93, 95–100) celebrate his universal influence and call on the nations to submit to his power (Ps 96:1f., 96:7). Upon return from exile the Deutero-Isaiah (Is 40–55) exploited this vein of worship in particular.

There was a whole prophetic tradition that saw the end of time as a pilgrimage* of the peoples to Jerusalem (Jeremias 1956): God would summon the nations that had survived his judgment*, in the wake of the scattered Israelites; and all, in endless bliss, would obey the king of the universe (*see* Is 2:2ff.; Hg 2:7; Zec 8:20–23; Is 60; Tb 13; Is 25:6ff.; Zec 14:6–19). However, as a result of the misfortunes that befell the chosen people, this tradition sometimes dwindled to a simple hope that the scattered Jews would come together and take revenge on their oppressors (*see* Is 45:14–19; Jl 4:9–17 disputes Is 2:2ff.).

How then could God's universal triumph be conceived without lurking thoughts of revenge (Ps 47:4)? Messianism* was not free of these urges toward domination (Ps 72:10f.). Nonetheless, there were ironic voices that celebrated a universalism that mocked nationalistic pretensions. A late prophecy of the Book of Isaiah (19:16–25) imagines an Egypt converted and blessed by God, on an equal footing with Israel and Assyria (A. Feuillet, *Mélanges J. Lebreton,* 1951). In the book of Jonah the pagans appear much riper for conversion* than Israel (E.J. Bickerman, *RHPhR* 45, 1965). Malachi 1:11's tirade opposes pagans to Jerusalem's religious halfheartedness.

This openness found expression in the existence of "proselytes" (*see* Acts 2:11, 13:43). This word, invented by the Septuagint, did not imply a misplaced pursuit of converts, but merely the admission into the Jewish community of pagans who "came towards" it (this being the etymology of *pros-èlytos*). In antiquity political, ethnic, local, and religious identities were closely linked (H.C. Brichto, *HUCA,* 1973). So religious conversion entailed naturalization (Will and Orrieux 1986), even if Israel sometimes exploited the motivations of faith* to integrate foreigners in spite of sociocultural obstacles (*see* Jdt 14:10: the circumcision of a pagan, in contravention of Dt 23:4).

In addition to these periodic assimilations, Israel accepted that some pagans had "the fear* of God" (Gn 20:10–17) and that YHWH could be honored by foreigners (2 Kgs 5:17ff.). What is more, the Old Testament pays attention to the wisdom, ethics, and philosophy of the other nations, to deepen its understanding of divine revelation* (Prv 8–9; Sir 24; Wisdom).

b) Ancient Judaism. After the exile the Jews were intermingled with the nations to a greater extent, above all in the Diaspora, and subject to Hellenistic domination. They began to question the universalism of their traditions, and this gave rise to a rich Judaeo-Hellenistic literature that foreshadowed the inculturation of the Gospels*. Around the second century B.C., Jewish authors such as Eupolemus and Artapanus engaged in the literary rivalry in which every Eastern people attempted to prove to the others the antiquity of its civilization (see G. L. Prato, *RivBib* 34, 1986). *Sibylline Oracles* III recasts the ethical and eschatological message of the Prophets* for the benefit of the Greeks. The moral sentences of Pseudo-Phocylides (first century?) draw on both Stoicism and Mosaic law.

A great many of these writings appeared among the important Jewish community at Alexandria. In particular, it was here that from the third century B.C. the Bible* was translated into Greek in the version known as the Septuagint (ancient translations), which openly emphasizes God's universalism (see Am 9:12, LXX) and attempts to find religious terms comprehensible to the Greeks.

The symbiosis that was sought between Greek thought and the traditions of Israel focused on the shared elements on which a faith in the unicity of God could be based, and which would promote an ethics of quality. In this way it presented the message of the Bible as capable of being received by other cultures. Along with the Septuagint, Philo of Alexandria (born between 15 and 10 B.C.) remains a key witness to this dialogue, "of which, however, Christianity was to be the chief beneficiary" (R. Le Déaut, *DSp* 8, 1947).

The fathers of the church drew on this heritage for their apologetics, while the Jews were to discard it. In the year 70, Israel lost its Temple and its national institutions. In order to safeguard its identity, the People regrouped around the law and the languages of the Holy Land (Hebrew and Aramaic). It was no longer a time for openness, but for a strict awareness of election, and the Hellenistic heritage became more than anything a threat. Judaism even abandoned the Septuagint, which Christians took for their Bible.

c) New Testament. As the final messenger of God's kingdom (see Mt 4:17), Jesus speaks to everyone. The testimony of the Gospels is in agreement: his encounters were subject to no barriers, even where foreigners were concerned (see Mt 8:10;,15:28; Lk 17:18; Jn 4). In this respect, going against the rules of purity* that some made the condition of election, he opposed the sectaries of Qumran, dissociated himself from the Pharisees who strove for the purity of all the people (Mt 23), and resembled John the Baptist, who addressed all people without distinction (see Lk 3:10–14). Unlike the latter, however, Jesus showed a pronounced tenderness toward the excluded and marginalized.

God's universalism, revealed in Jesus, does not do away with election. The Lord's journeys beyond Israel remain rare, their narratives questionable (Legrand 1988). The keynote of the mission "the lost sheep of the house of Israel" appears authentic, even if transmitted by way of Judaeo-Christian particularist circles. Jesus wanted to reform his people who, under the guidance of the 12 disciples (see Lk 22:30), would become a shining beacon for humanity (Mt 5:14ff.) and enable God to unleash his universal salvation in a new pilgrimage of the nations (Lk 13:29). By comparison with this Old Testament symbolism, however, a radical new idea appears: salvation no longer resides in the safe conduct represented by membership of the chosen people, but in the faith that one displays in God's messenger, irrespective of one's origins (see Mt 8:11f.).

Jesus' fidelity to the election of Israel and to divine universalism met with rejection (see Lk 13:34f.); but for those who had been won over by his message (see Jn 6:68), Calvary (see Mk 15:39) and the Paschal experience (Lk 24:33ff.) represented a beginning, a new departure.

In this context the theme of universalism is linked to that of the Christian mission*. The first disciples came from a variety of social and religious backgrounds (see Jn 1:35ff.; Acts 6:1, 6:7b, 15:5)—hence the differences in their interpretations of Jesus' message (see F. Voüga, *ETR* 59, 1984) and of the relationship to be established between Christianized Jews and converted pagans.

The assembly at Jerusalem (C. Perrot, *RSR* 69, 1981) ran through various possibilities: the circumcision of pagan Christians, as new proselytes in the Jewish Church* (Acts 15:5); no circumcision, but a minimum of Jewish practices to seal the association between the two groups (15:19ff.); or their complete freedom as regards Jewish law (15:10f.). This last position won the day, through the influence of Saint Paul (see Gal 2). What, indeed, was the point of insisting that pagan Christians be naturalized as Jews, when by the grace* of Christ they were freed from their sins and enjoyed the gifts of the Holy* Spirit? At this point, however, the controversy revived. Could Judaism accept a universalism of this sort, which seemed to scoff at the story of the election? Gradually the church would become for the most part pagan-Christian (see Acts 28:28), benefiting from the opening that Judaism had made into Hellenistic culture.

● J. Jeremias (1933), "*Anthrôpos*," *ThWNT* 1, 362–69.
K. G. Kuhn (1935), "*Prosèlutos*," ibid. 2, 727–44.
J. Jeremias (1956), *Jesu Verheißung*, Stuttgart.
R. Martin-Achard (1959), *Israël et les nations*, Neuchâtel.
R. North (1966), "Centrifugal and Centripetal Tendencies in the Judaic Cradle of Christianity," in H. Cazelles (Ed.), Populus Dei, *Festschrift Ottaviani*, Rome, vol. 1, 615–51.
P.-E. Dion (1975), *Dieu universel et peuple élu*, LeDiv 84.

G. Lohfink (1982), *Wie hat Jesus Gemeinde gewollt?* Freiburg.

M. Perez Fernandez (1984), "La apertura a los gentiles en el judaísmo intertestamentario," *EstB* 41, 86–106.

E. Will, C. Orrieux (1986), *Ioudaïsmos-Hellènismos: Essai sur le judaïsme judéen à l'époque hellénistique,* Nancy.

H. Legrand (1988), *Le Dieu qui vient: La mission dans la Bible,* Paris.

CLAUDE TASSIN

See also **Choice; Creation; Decalogue; Hellenization of Christianity; Inculturation; Israel; Jerusalem; Messianism/Messiah; Mission/Evangelization; Paganism; Translations of the Bible, Ancient; Wisdom**

Universals. *See* Nominalism; Realism

Universe. *See* Cosmos

Universities

The European universities originated in different ways. Some of the earliest, like Paris, were originally groups of peripatetic masters who gradually came together in the late 12th century. They centered themselves around one or more of the seven or eight existing cathedral or monastic schools in the town and formed associations that allowed them to claim the guild privileges of protection and exemptions accorded to groups of immigrant craftsmen or businessmen. The student groups were divided into "nations," at Paris comprising a French nation for Italians, Spaniards, and Greeks; a Picard nation, including students from the Low Countries; a Norman nation; and an English nation, which included German speakers. The masters had to obtain a license to teach, at first exclusively granted by the ecclesiastical authorities.

The term "university" denotes the corporate aspects of the *universitas* or corporation of masters and scholars, virtually apprenticed to a master and generally sharing accommodation with him. Those Paris masters not licensed to teach theology specialized in "logic" or "dialectic," which, while pretending to leave theological matters to the theologians, simply transposed the theological problems into philosophical debates, the triune nature of the one God into questions about the extramental validity of concepts. To escape the jurisdiction of the chancellor of Notre-Dame and the bishop, some peripatetic masters, such as Abelard, were obliged to remain as close to Paris as they could to attract pupils, while staying outside the jurisdiction of the Paris authorities. The Parisian masters themselves successfully bid to escape local jurisdiction and put themselves under direct papal control in 1246.

At Oxford, the university was probably founded by English scholars forced by political tensions to return from Paris in 1167. Since the university did not grow out of a group of existing schools, the ultimate authority remained the king, although successive monarchs delegated the ordinary exercise of jurisdiction to the bishops of Lincoln. As the privileges of the masters and scholars became abused, friction between town and gown led to reprisals between the conflicting parties, and a particularly severe dispute in 1209 led to the departure of the group that founded the university at Cambridge.

The law school at Bologna, already celebrated in the early 12th century, was established on a different model, and never developed into a proper *studium generale,* teaching the arts curriculum. Elsewhere the practical arts of the *quadrivium,* arithmetic, music, geometry, and astronomy, were abandoned in the early 13th century, and the role of the disciplines comprising the *trivium,* logic, grammar, and rhetoric, was modified by the elimination of rhetoric. The result was an institutional pattern with wandering masters licensed to teach anywhere as well as wandering scholars, and a single compulsory undergraduate discipline known simply as arts. Thereafter the universities trained for the practical disciplines in four graduate faculties: civil law, which made no distinction between lawyers and administrators, canon law, theology, and medicine. Much of the arts teaching, lectures, and repetitions, often in individual halls or in a university's constituent colleges as they came to be founded, was undertaken by graduate students preparing for doctorates.

The universities took over the training of priests from the cathedral and monastic schools. By the end of the 13th century there were 22 universities with the right, constitutive of a *studium generale,* to grant their own degrees and to confer on masters the right to teach anywhere. Five of these were on the Iberian peninsula, two in England, five in France, and 10 on the Italian peninsula. Paris was the most important center of teaching and study north of the Alps. It had attained a self-sustaining mass, offering the largest audiences to masters and the greatest concentration of masters and potential employers to students. Very nearly every one of the important scholastic theologians of the 13th century either studied or taught there.

While the monasteries continued themselves to train those who were destined to join their own community, having only intermittently agreed since the ninth century to train those not destined to become monks, the new orders of regulars—Dominicans, Franciscans—established their own *studia generalia* alongside or within the established universities, vying for chairs against nonregulars and against one another. It has been estimated that by 1200 there were probably between three and four thousand students in Paris, perhaps a 10th of the town's population, with about 150

masters, of whom 100 taught in the arts faculty, with 20 each in civil law and medicine, and eight in theology. From the beginning Paris had excluded civil law, having no desire to train students in the constitutional principles of the late Roman Empire. The result was to be particularly flourishing civil law schools in Orléans, Angers, and Bourges.

Quite early, universities were founded or exploited for political purposes. Reggio, Vercelli, Modena, Vicenza, and Padua arose independently of any official positive civil or ecclesiastical initiative and without charters, but in 1225 the emperor Frederick II founded the university of Naples to provide for training in the arts, theology, jurisprudence, and medicine on his own territory. In the 14th century Köln and Heidelberg were sponsored by the Roman popes on German-speaking territory to reduce the advantages enjoyed in Paris by the Avignon popes. Poitiers and Caen universities were offshoots of the English hegemony in northern France, and were intended to buttress it. Specifically sectarian institutions were established in the wake of the 16th-century schisms, and the politicization of the universities is reflected in the fact that in 1533 all the European canon law faculties voted without exception on the validity of the marriage between Henry VIII and Catherine of Aragon in accordance with the political interests of the territorial sovereign. The only ripple of dissent came from Paris, where 40 theologians voted against the ruling supporting the political policy of François I that Henry VIII's argument for nullity was stronger than that of his opponents against it.

As powerhouses of theological teaching the university theology faculties were naturally subject to the church's *magisterium.* Indeed, for centuries it was disputed whether they had delegated authority to exercise the magisterium and jurisdiction to enforce it by the imposition of ecclesiastical penalties. Paris, in particular, acted as if it did have delegated jurisdiction to decree on matters of faith, a mode of behavior in which it was followed notably by Louvain and Köln.

Heresy, in most countries a purely ecclesiastical *crimen*—although not in Spain, where the Inquisition was a civil court—was everywhere easily enough remitted to the secular authorities as the secular crime of blasphemy. As such it was subject to civil penalties, at certain times and places notoriously including the death penalty. There was therefore a serious question about the ecclesiastical authority and jurisdiction of theological faculties as well as a generally clear, although sometimes blurred distinction in theory, but frequent collusion in practice, between ecclesiastical and secular jurisdiction and the penalties appropriate to each realm.

It was because the theology faculties regarded themselves as custodians of divine revelation that their conservatism was so pronounced and that, for instance, they defended the faulty Vulgate Latin text of the Bible, repudiating Renaissance efforts to establish trilingual colleges, where Greek and Hebrew permitted access to the original scriptural texts, and where vernacular translations of them might be made for the laity.

With the emergence of the larger nation-states of the late 15th century there arose the question of the transfer of ecclesiastical wealth to secular states, which deemed it appropriate to take over de facto responsibility for education. This was typically achieved in Ingolstadt, later transferred to Landshut and now the Ludwig-Maximilian University of Munich. The university, originally founded by a bull of 1459, was not in fact opened until 1472, when a new brief was required. Using the statutes and procedures adopted by Vienna as a model, it was proposed to make the Ingolstadt church of Saint Mary's collegiate, and to make its canons into the university's professors. In this way ecclesiastical income could legitimately be used for secular university purposes. Unfortunately the endowment turned out to be insufficient.

A different pious bequest, supporting its beneficiaries to hear a stipulated number of masses for the benefit of the souls of the dukes of Bavaria, had to be used instead. Its sequestration was sanctioned by the bishop of Eichstatt in 1454 and by Paul II in 1465. One of two professors of theology was probably a prebend of Eichstatt. There were three chairs of jurisprudence, one of medicine, and six of arts. What had been accomplished at Ingolstadt was characteristic of what was happening more widely in the world of university teaching, as at Wolsey's Cardinal College at Oxford. The monasteries whose income was used by Wolsey for his foundation were suppressed by his exercise of full papal jurisdiction as the pope's *legatus a latere*. The ecclesiastically legitimatized transfer of ecclesiastical wealth to secular purposes in accordance with the concomitant transference of sovereignty in late medieval Europe was taking place by the series of concordats and other arrangements between the papacy and the sovereign states. From the early 14th century, universities were typically founded by secular princes and, at their request, granted charters by popes.

Theologically, the attachment of the universities to the churches lingered until at least the late 19th century, when separate institutions of higher education for theologians were added to the Tridentine seminaries with an emphasis on pastoral training. In England it was not until 1877 that legislation loosened the connection between the universities and established church. In 1873 religious tests and declarations of faith for positions at Trinity College, Dublin, were abolished. In France the hostility of the movement to secularize education in the late 19th century resulted in the foundation of the Institut Catholique, and even today theology faculties, although often without formal sectarian affiliation, can retain strong sectarian coloring, as at Strasbourg or Saint Andrews.

The earliest U.S. universities began as theological colleges, but with syllabuses broader than those in Europe, including classical culture, logic, rhetoric, and mathematics, and never confining admissions exclusively to those of some determined denominational affiliation. At first, religion, if not theology, had played a more important part in American universities than in equivalent European institutions, but from the late 18th century onward the American university system veered toward the training of qualified professionals in colleges with an appropriate bias—religious, agricultural, military, or, from the mid–19th century, technological. They followed Newman's *Idea of a University* and developments in Germany in keeping research separate from teaching, the latter being considered the proper function of a university. The study and teaching of theology, except in the older anglophone universities of both sides of the Atlantic, is now on the whole undertaken in separate specialist institutions. Most of them have reforged the connection between teaching and research.

● Hastings Rashdall, *The Universities of Europe in the Middle Ages,* Oxford, 1936.
International Dictionary of University Histories, Ed. Carol Summerfield, Mary Elizabeth Devine, Chicago-London, 1998.

ANTHONY LEVI

Univocity. *See* Analogy

Utilitarianism

"Utilitarianism" refers both to a movement for social reform and to an ethical theory. Jeremy Bentham (1748–1832) championed many legal and political improvements, and also developed the first modern utilitarian system. John Stuart Mill (1806–73) and Henry Sidgwick (1838–1900) provided significant corrections and a certain degree of philosophical rigor. There is, however, no single theory of utilitarianism, but rather a theme with common motifs.

Utilitarianism belongs among "teleological" theories, that is, those that base morality on the ends or consequences of actions*. A classic form of teleology brought together Greek thought and Christian theology*, founding an ethic* on ends inherent in human nature, a supernatural* last end, and divine law (Thomas* Aquinas). This was rejected by philosophers of the Enlightenment, and utilitarianism replaced it with a purely secular teleology of results. It is claimed that this substitution has proved to be a failure (Alasdair MacIntyre). "Deontological" theories (Kant*), in contrast, are founded on duty or law and hold that the morality of at least some acts is independent of their consequences. Consequentialism embraces all theories that accept consequences as determinative of the moral value of actions, and thus includes utilitarianism. The latter, however, has a more specific character, in that it evaluates consequences according to particular criteria. Classical utilitarianism took as the standard the amount of happiness produced and claimed that there is only one moral principle: to seek the greatest happiness for the greatest number. Accordingly, acts are right when they promote happiness, wrong when they produce the reverse. Happiness in this sense does not mean individual happiness, but the greatest amount of happiness altogether. According to Bentham, happiness means pleasure, without any distinction whatever. Mill sought to correct Bentham by introducing qualitative distinctions between pleasures. Most contemporary utilitarians have relinquished the pleasure criterion. Where earlier exponents interpreted utility or welfare in terms of states of consciousness (such as pleasure), more recent authors look to the satisfaction of desires or preferences. Contemporary utilitarianism still retains an essential feature of the theory, namely, that what is valued ought to be maximized. The question is, therefore, which action, among those that are possible, produces the greatest amount of that which is valuable, whether that be the satisfaction of desires or the fulfillment of interests. Those actions may be considered to be morally required or defensible that promote happiness. This relationship is typically expressed in terms of "rightness" (of actions) and "goodness" (of what is intrinsically valued). "Act utilitarianism" applies these ideas to specific acts of individuals. "Rule utilitarianism," on the other hand, focuses on the general patterns of behavior that are capable of promoting the welfare of the community. Right conduct, therefore, is that which accords with useful rules.

Utilitarianism has had a strong appeal, especially in English-speaking countries. Its attractiveness can be explained on several grounds. Utilitarianism does not make any appeal to tradition or to religion, or indeed to anything transcending human life. This can be seen as a great advantage in pluralist societies where there is no commonly accepted religious ethic. The basic good or ultimate end that it proposes, such as happiness or well-being, may be accepted by all as a reasonable aim. Utilitarianism provides a means to resolve moral problems by calculation of the consequences, a method that cannot but have an appeal in a technological culture. Utilitarianism makes it possible to provide a common currency for moral debate: whatever different individuals or groups may aim at, all can be reduced in every case to an amount of happiness. Different amounts of happiness can then be compared according to their respective weights. Thus, all moral disagreements are, in principle, capable of being resolved. Finally, utilitarianism looks to the happiness of all. The wide diffusion of the works of Peter Singer (1993) is evidence of the contemporary influence of utilitarianism.

However, the criticisms of utilitarianism have been many. Persons do, in fact, pursue happiness, but it does not follow that they *ought* to do so. Nor is it explained why we ought to promote the happiness of *others*. Strictly applied, utilitarianism could justify actions that we normally consider wrong, such as murder. Accordingly, utilitarians frequently add constraints to the theory in order to exclude such acts. Rule utilitarians argue that, even if such behavior might maximize aggregate benefits, we should follow generally useful rules and thus abstain from it. However, critics claim that rule utilitarianism is in fact reducible to act utilitarianism, and so cannot provide any acceptable limiting rules. In consideration of such difficulties, a two-level theory, combining the two types of utilitarianism, has been proposed (Hare 1981). Further, on the scale by which values are measured, the satisfaction of one person counts for as much as that of any other: what one loses can be offset by what is gained by others. Thus, one person may be sacrificed for the good of others. By focusing solely on aggregating value, utilitarianism leads to injustice toward individuals. Utilitarianism has also been ambivalent concerning human rights. Those who follow Bentham are skeptical in regard to moral rights. Others, in the tradition of Mill, seek utilitarian reasons to support the idea of rights.

According to utilitarianism, values can be ranked in order on a single scale. Thus, utilitarianism must hold that all values are commensurable, and that there are no incommensurable values, not even human life. Utilitarianism as such does not provide a direct reason for not committing murder. Contingent desires or preferences may count against it, but there is no necessary contrary reason inherent, for example, in the wrongness of an attack on an innocent person.

There are still further difficulties. How can one calculate the long-term results of one's actions when these depend on, among other things, the free choices of other persons? Even if these choices could be foreseen, how can the different values that they embody be measured on a common scale? Utilitarianism calls for universal and impartial benevolence, and to many this appears both impossible and misguided. According to utilitarianism's doctrine of negative obligation, we are as responsible for what we allow as for what we do: a notion that some critics find unrealistic or even opposed to integrity. Dissatisfaction with utilitarianism has led to the development of important alternative theories (Rawls 1971).

Although utilitarianism is fundamentally secular, some of its proponents invoke religious parallels. Mill wrote that Jesus' golden rule reflected the spirit of utilitarianism. J. Fletcher, the popularizer of "situation ethics" in the 1960s, upheld the primacy of the biblical principle of love*, while translating it into a form of act utilitarianism. R. M. Hare claims that utilitarianism is an extension of the Christian doctrine of *agape*. Finally, critics claim to find some of the features of utilitarianism in proportionalism*.

- J. Bentham, *An Introduction to the Principles of Morals and Legislation,* Oxford, 1789 (Ed. J.H. Burns, H.L.A. Hart, London, 1970).
J.S. Mill, *Utilitarianism,* London, 1863 (Ed. J.M. Robson, Toronto, 1969).
H. Sidgwick, *The Methods of Ethics,* London, 1874 (Indianapolis, Ind., 1981, preface by J. Rawls).
C. Audard (Ed.), *Une anthologie historique et critique de l'ut. Les utilitaristes: Leurs précurseurs et leurs critiques. De Shaftsbury à Moore (1711–1903),* Paris, 1995.
♦ É. Halévy (1901–04), *La formation du radicalisme philosophique,* 3 vols., Paris (New Rev. Ed., Paris, 1995).
D. Lyons (1970), *Forms and Limits of Utilitarianism,* Oxford.
J. Rawls (1971), *A Theory of Justice,* Cambridge.
J.J.C. Smart and B. Williams (1973), *Utilitarianism: For and Against,* Cambridge.
R.M. Hare (1981), *Moral Thinking*: Its Levels, Method, and Point, Oxford.
A. MacIntyre (1984), *After Virtue,* Notre Dame, Ind.
P. Singer (1990), *Animal Liberation,* 2nd Ed., London.
P. Singer (1993), *Practical Ethics,* Cambridge.
M. Canto-Sperber (1994), *La philosophie morale britannique,* Paris.
C. Audard (1996), "Utilitarisme," *DEPhM,* 1563–70.

BRIAN JOHNSTONE

See also **Authority; Justice; Relativism; Society**

V

Valentinians. *See* **Docetism; Gnosis**

Validity

On the edge between theology* and canon* law, there were certain specific cases encountered in the early Church* where a sacramental act (for example a baptism*, Holy Communion* or ordination*) was carried out in such a way as to be considered invalid. Gradually, over the centuries, these particular situations were clarified on several levels: 1) The necessary conditions for the fulfillment of each sacramental action were established, both where the action itself was concerned as well as the intention required on the part of the person carrying out the action. 2) It was stipulated that, depending on the case, such actions would require a minister recognized by the Church (see theology of sacraments* and the debate between Augustine* and Donatism*), particularly in the case of ordination, or at the very least "the intention to do what the Church does" (a formula which appeared in theology at the beginning of the 13th century and then became official in the Catholic Church with the decree to the Armenians issued by the Council of Florence [1439, *DS* 1315]). 3) After the mid-12th century this line of thought was developed, in the West, to take into account the clarifications arrived at on the number of the seven sacraments. 4) Finally, at the end of the Middle Ages and around the time of the Council of Trent*, theology and canon law, drawing in this case on the contribution of Roman law, gave an increasingly clear outline to the sacramentarian and juridical category of validity. In the case of marriage* an equivalent notion of nullity was used. As for the notion of "hierarchical acts," it did not concern the domain of sacramental validity, but belonged to the sacramentarian theology of Pseudo-Dionysius* (*Ecclesiastical Hierarchy* 5) and of the theologians who were inspired by him (e.g., Thomas* Aquinas, *ST* IIIa, q. 65, a. 1).

Recent research into the history of Christianity's ancient institutions (Vogel 1983) has endeavored to make a distinction between two issues regarding ordination: on the one hand, recognition by a Church that accepts it as a valid act, and on the other hand, the intrinsic conditions of the act. In 1976, with regard to episcopal ordinations that had been carried out in an invalid way by a Catholic bishop*, the Church of Rome officially stated that it considered the acts to be illegitimate, while refraining from making a declaration about their validity (*AAS* 68, 1976, 623).

1663

The theology and discipline of Eastern Orthodoxy* would adopt a different perspective from that of the Latin West; thus, a distinction can be made (particularly following a response by the Patriarch Photius of Constantinople in Amphilochia, PG 101, 64–65) between a strict canonical attitude and ecclesiastical "economy": in imitation of the divine benevolence, the latter attitude attenuates the rigor of the former, and aims to reassert the validity of the canon, while nonetheless demonstrating a benevolent and pedagogical exception to its rigid application. In practice, however, the concept of "economy" is interpreted in different ways by the various authors (Thomson 1965). Questions of validity, important for all of the sacraments, deserve special attention where baptism and ordination are concerned, as well as Holy Communion and marriage.

● F. J. Thomson (1965), "Economy: An Examination of the Various Theories of Economy Held within the Orthodox Church, with Special Reference to the Ecumenical Recognition of the Validity of Non-Orthodox Sacraments," *JThS* 16, 368–420.

P.-M. Gy (1978), "La validité sacramentelle: Développement de la notion avant le concile de Trente," *Mélanges J. Gaudemet, RDC* 28, 193–202 (reprinted in P.-M. Gy, *La liturgie dans l'histoire*, Paris, 1990, 165–75).

C. Vogel (1983), *Ordinations inconsistantes et caractère inadmissible*, Turin.

On Marriage

Coll. (1976), "Portée et limites de l'acte de déclaration de nullité du mariage," *RDC* 26, 2–99.

P.-M. Gy (1977), "Le sacrement de mariage exige-t-il la foi? La position médiévale," *RSPhTh* 61, 437–42.

Mgr Pierre L'Huillier (1991), "Economy," in N. Lossky et al. (Ed.), *Dictionary of the Ecumenical Movement,* Grand Rapids, 320–22.

PIERRE-MARIE GY

See also **Canon Law; Donatism; Intercommunion; Sacrament**

Vatican I, Council of

1869–1870

Vatican I was the 20th ecumenical council of the Catholic Church (*see* Catholicism*), but it was the first one to take place in the Vatican. It was convened by Pius IX more than three hundred years after the 19th ecumenical council, the Council of Trent*. It opened on 8 December 1869, and was suspended on the 20 October 1870 after the Italian occupation of Rome*.

1. Preparing for the Council; the Events; the People Involved

a) The Controversies and the Roman Reaction: The Syllabus. The pontificates of Gregory XVI (1831–1846) and of Pius IX (1846–1878) were punctuated with the condemnation of systems that opposed each other in respect of the knowledge* of God and the relations between reason* and faith*: the semi-rationalism of G. Hermès (1775–1831) was condemned in 1835, and of A. Günther (1783–1863) in 1857; the fideism* of L. Bautain (1796–1867) in 1840; the traditionalism* of A. Bonnetty (1798–1879) in 1855; and the ontologism* of A. Rosmini (1797–1855) in 1861. These problems were linked to controversies pertaining to the freedom of theologians (condemnation of J. Frohschammer [1821–93] in 1862) and to their method. Furthermore, by condemning the ideas of F. de Lamennais (1782–1854) in 1832, Rome challenged the liberal ideology, the anticlericalism, and a certain indifference that combined to contest the privileged position of the Catholic Church in modern societies. Finally, at the moment when, in France, Gallicanism* and Ultramontanism* were opposed to each other, and as Napoleon III was threatening the temporal authority of the pope, Pius IX published, on 8 December 1864, the encyclical *Quanta cura* and the *Syllabus,* the latter being a list of the 80 errors of the modern world.

b) Preparing for the Council. The pope announced the assembling of a council that would do for rationalism* what the Council of Trent had done for Protestantism*. The bishops were consulted, but did not overwhelmingly adhere to the project of defining papal infallibility* and of adopting the *Syllabus* as a working ground. After some hesitation (due particularly to the Austro-Prussian war of June 1866), and persuaded by Mgr F. Dupanloup (1802–78), Pius IX announced the council on 26 June 1867. The commissions in charge of the relevant preparations then started to work in strictly guarded secrecy.

On 29 June 1868, the bull *Aeterni Patris* convened the council for 8 December 1869. On 8 September 1868, the Eastern bishops who were not united to Rome were invited to "rejoin unity" in order to take part in the council. The letter met with a contemptuous silence. The convening of the Protestants and of the Anglicans (Anglicanism*) was not done until the 13th: this invitation was perceived as a provocation, particularly in Germany.

c) The Controversies Surrounding Infallibility. On 6 February 1869 an article written by two priests who were friends of L. Veuillot (1813–83) appeared in the *Civiltà cattolica,* the unofficial organ of the Holy See: it expressed in particular the wish that infallibility be defined by acclamation. The considerable emotion caused by this article provoked various stands, from the violent reaction of J. von Döllinger (1799–1890) to the moderate response of Mgr V. Dechamps (1810–83), archbishop of Malines, and to the Ultramontane position of Archbishop H. Manning (1808–92) of Westminster. In September, at Fulda, the German bishops found the definition of infallibility to be inopportune. In France, aside from the work of Archbishop J. H. Maret (1805–84; *Du concile général et de la paix religieuse,* September 1869), which adopted a Gallican stand concerning the rights of the bishops, there was an article by A. de Broglie (in *Le Correspondant*) which judged that there was no call for a definition of infallibility that would cover the political acts of previous popes. On 11 November, in his *Observations sur la controverse,* archbishop Dupanloup pronounced himself for inopportuneness.

d) Composition of the Conciliar Assembly. Some 1,000 bishops were convened to the council; 750 participated. All parts of the world were represented: one third of the Fathers came from non-European countries, but all of them had either been born in Europe or had received a European training. Italy was overrepresented (35 percent); a proportion of two thirds of the consultors, as well as all the secretaries and all the presidents of the commissions, were Italian. It is true that the secretary of the council, Mgr J. Fessler (1813–72), was Austrian, but the five chairmen, after the death of Cardinal K. A. von Reisach, were Italian,

and hostile to liberal ideas; they were inclined, however, to conciliation. The supervising congregation was made up of five, then of nine cardinals; it was assisted by five specialized commissions composed of experts. The doctrinal commission, with three Jesuit fathers, J. Perrone (1794–1876), J. B. Franzelin (1816–86) and C. Schrader (1820–75), dealt with the important subjects by using the *Syllabus* as their working basis. The other commissions (on ecclesiastical discipline, on religious orders, on the missions* and Eastern Churches, and on politics) prepared drafts. Few of these drafts made it to the discussions of the council.

2. Unfolding of the Council and Principal Debates

a) From the Opening of the Council to the Suspension of Proceedings (22 February 1870). The council opened on 8 December 1869. The elections to the commissions on 14 December revealed the existing division among the council fathers, which was emphasized by the maneuvering of the supporters of infallibility. The majority was driven by Cardinal L. Bilio (1826–84) and prelates such as H. Manning (Westminster), V. Dechamps (Malines), K. Martin (1812–79, Paderborn), L.-D. Pie (1815–80, Poitiers), J. Fessler (1813–72, Sankt Pölten in Austria). An "international committee" maintained cohesion in the minority groups around Cardinals J. O. von Rauscher (1797–1875, Vienna), F. of Schwarzenberg (1809–85, Prague), and C. Mathieu (1796–1875, Besançon). The members of that international committee were the primate of Hungary, Cardinal J. Simor (1813–81), and Bishops L. Haynald (1816–91, Colocza), J. J. Strossmayer (1815–1905, Diakovar), W. E. von Ketteler (1811–77, Mainz), G. Darboy (1813–71, Paris), Dupanloup (Orléans), and Maret (dean of the Sorbonne).

Distributed on 10 December, the draft of a dogmatic* constitution, *De doctrina catholica,* was poorly received: it attracted only criticism during the public discussion on 28 December. As early as 4 January 1870, Mgr Martin, speaking in the name of the Deputation of the Faith, recognized that a complete revision was in order.

In the meantime the council Fathers had to study a variety of subjects: the duties of bishops (residence, pastoral visits, and so on), a vacancy, clerical life, the catechism. They complained about the labyrinth of canonical questions presented to them without order or perspective. Beyond minor subjects, there were important ecclesiological problems regarding the structure of the Church, the respective roles of the pope, of the bishops, and of the Curia, the rights—and not just the duties—of the bishops. All this criticism stirred up a reaction among the defenders of the pope's prerogatives; division deepened among the Fathers. There were discussions on the methodology, on the length of successive speeches where there was no link between them, and on the deplorable acoustics. The sessions were suspended on 22 February to allow for the refitting of the council's assembly hall. There were also changes in the rules in order to accelerate the debates, though a minority was against the fact that a debate might be ended at the request of ten fathers, and that a simple majority might be sufficient for the adoption of a constitution.

b) The Question of Infallibility. Not on the agenda at the outset, controversies called for the definition of the pope's infallibility. On 21 January a new draft dogmatic constitution was distributed: *De Ecclesia Christi.* The first ten chapters explained the nature of the Church: it was a mystical body and a visible society with its own government, independent from civil societies and with its own characteristics, immutability, and infallibility: a hierarchical society, it was governed by the pope, whose primacy is explained at length (chapter XI), and whose temporal sovereignty is asserted (chapter XII). The last three chapters treat the subject of the relations between the Church and civil society. The Fathers appreciated the nuances that were brought to the saying that 'there is no salvation* outside the Church'; *and* the fact that ecclesiology* does not amount solely to the matter of the pope; but the text is silent regarding the bishops, and appears to show an imbalance in favor of the pope. The press and the chanceries detected theocratic claims in this outdated notion of the relations between Church* and State. The recasting of the schema was entrusted to J. Kleutgen (1811–83), but the new formulation of the text was not made available before the final suspension of the council on 20 October 1870.

On account of contradictory petitions, Pius IX was at first hesitant, but then, on 6 March 1870, he announced that the question of infallibility would become part of the agenda, and on 27 April, he decided to anticipate the debate. The constitution *De Romano Pontifice* was distributed on 9 May. Waiting for that debate, the council took up again the study of the revised decree on the catechism; adopted on 4 May (by 491 votes to 56, with 44 *placet juxta modum*), it was never promulgated.

c) The First Dogmatic Constitution, Dei Filius *(24 April 1870).* Starting on 10 January, a sub-commission chaired by Mgr Dechamps, and attended by Mgr Pie, C.-L. Gay (1815–92), Mgr Martin, and the Jesuit Father Kleutgen, revised Franzelin's text, *De doctrina*

catholica: the first four chapters, devoted to religious knowledge, constituted a draft of a constitution distributed on 14 March.

Presented on 8 March by Mgr Simor, the draft constitution did not invite serious criticism. The prologue recalled the errors that had been made since the Council of Trent. Chapters I and II treated the matter of the existence of God and of the natural knowledge of God and revelation*; chapter III was devoted to faith and supernatural virtue*, to the gift of divine grace* and man's free will, to the signs of revelation and to the credibility inherent in the Church; chapter IV dealt finally with the relations between reason and faith, two distinct modes of knowledge that helped each other mutually. After a first vote, which consisted of 83 *placet juxta modum,* 35 Anglo-Saxon bishops managed to secure an emendation whereby, in order to avoid any ambiguity from an Anglican point of view, the formula *Sancta romana catholica Ecclesia* should be changed into *Sancta catholica apostolica romana Ecclesia.* At the solemn meeting of 24 April the 667 fathers voted unanimously for the constitution *Dei Filius,* which Pius IX ratified immediately.

d) The Second Dogmatic Constitution, Pastor aeternus *(18 July 1870).* The general discussion started on 13 May. The minority insisted on the theological and historical difficulties surrounding the definition; it also weighed the pastoral and political drawbacks, as well as the consequences for relations with non-Catholics. The majority justified the doctrine and the timeliness of its definition by arguing this was not a neo-Ultramontane position, but the traditional doctrine of Thomas* Aquinas and Robert Bellarmine*. The discussion was closed on 3 June.

The prologue, chapter I, and chapter II, which dealt with the institution and the perpetuity of primacy, did not raise any difficulties. Chapter III, on the nature of primacy and on the powers it implies, raised questions regarding the terms used for pontifical jurisdiction: *episcopalis, ordinaria, immediata.* But there were fears: of abusive interventions by Rome in the life of local Churches, with the bishops' opinions not being taken into account; of the creation of obstacles likely to prevent reunification with the Eastern Orthodox Church; of difficulties in reconciling the jurisdiction of the pope and that of the bishops (which is also *episcopal, ordinary,* and *immediate*). These fears were allayed with the following arguments: history shows that the intervention of the pope is exceptional, that it serves the Church well, and that the word *ordinary* is to be taken, not in its most common and usual sense, but in the canonical sense of *not delegated.* At the request of Pius IX, however, a formula was added that excluded any restriction, inspired by Gallicanism, to the pope's *plenitudo potestatis.*

Numerous bishops saw the complexity of the notion of infallibility (chapter IV) and wished to reach an agreement between majority and minority, in order to reject the Gallican thesis (which subordinated the infallibility of a definition pronounced by the pope to a subsequent agreement of the episcopate), while avoiding the assertion that "the pope is the Church," or that he may take no account of the faith of the Church, of which the bishops are the authorized witnesses. In the name of the minority, Cardinal Rauscher proposed the formula of Antoninus of Florence, who made the distinction between the pope acting in his own personal name and the pope calling upon the universal Church; with this distinction, he would be infallible only in the latter case. Cardinal F. M. Guidi (1815–79), who was part of the majority, pointed out that the pope must inform himself by consulting the bishops regarding their opinions; he felt that this would allow the pope to be enlightened on the content of tradition*, but he was reprimanded by Pius IX.

On 11 July, in a long report of a highly theological nature, Mgr V. Gasser (1809–79) explained the changes made to the text: the rights of the bishops and the close union between pope and Church were safeguarded, but the recourse to the episcopate as a *sine qua non* condition for the pope's infallibility was excluded. On 13 July one quarter of the assembly expressed its disagreement. The negotiations resumed. The pope approved a letter by Mgr C.-E. Freppel (1827–91) clarifying the formula *ex sese irreformabiles,* in order to avoid any Gallican allusion to a recourse to the episcopate. On 16 July the addition *non autem ex consensu Ecclesiae* was adopted. Final initiatives taken by the leaders of the minority were in vain. Rather than voting *non placet,* 55 bishops informed Pius IX that they were abstaining and they left Rome. On 18 July the constitution *Pastor aeternus* was approved by the 535 Fathers present, except for two who eventually rallied to the opinion of the majority immediately after the ratification by Pius IX.

3. The Aftermath of the Council

The fall of Napoleon III's empire on 4 September 1870 following France's defeat in the Battle of Sedan against the Prussians allowed the Italian government to occupy Rome on 20 September (French troops had previously occupied the city). For want of an agreement with the pope, Italy annexed Rome and the adjacent provinces. Judging that the freedom of the council was no longer assured, Pius IX adjourned it *sine die* (20 October). In fact it never resumed session. When measured against the standard of the heavy agenda it had been planning at the time of its announcement, and against the expectations it had raised, the council appeared to be a failure to many of its contemporaries, who were hardly convinced of the usefulness of the dogma* of infallibility. With the passing of time, however, it is easier to measure its importance.

a) The Constitution Dei Filius. According to R. Aubert the whole text of *Dei Filius* "constitutes a remarkable piece of work, which puts forward against pantheism*, against materialism, and modern rationalism, a dense and crystal-clear exposition of the Catholic doctrine regarding God, revelation, and faith." Against atheism* and traditionalism the council affirmed man's capacity to know God's existence and perfections, thanks to the natural lucidity of his reason; against deism* it stated that the assistance of revelation was necessary for the knowledge of God's existence to be indeed accessible to all, and without error. That doctrine unquestionably marked post-conciliar teaching by the Church. It does not, however, allow for the tackling of questions raised by the new religious sciences in the biblical and historical domains (exegesis*).

b) The Constitution Pastor aeternus. *Pastor aeternus* clarified the definition of primacy; it encouraged the strengthening of centralization in the Church, as well as the interventions of the Holy See. The serious discussions on infallibility allowed the Church's thinking in this area to evolve; the main error that had been aimed at was Gallicanism; and yet, at the end, the very terms of the definition excluded the excessive theses of the neo-Ultramontanists. The council put an end to the quarrels between Ultramontanists and Gallicans, and it strengthened the role of the Holy See in its missionary expansion. It allowed the bishops to discover the problems of Catholicism* on a world scale; the missionary bishops, above all, spoke out on their experience and curbed the evolution of the Propaganda congregation, which was too focused on the Near East.

Despite the fact that numerous disciplinary schemata planned for adoption did not reach the voting stage, the preparation involved and the study that ensued provided precious documentation for the reform of the code of canon law. The council, however, could not conceal the insufficiencies of an ecclesiology that was much too juridical and hierarchical (hierarchy*), and that remained in favor for decades.

c) Papacy and Secularization. At a time when it was losing its temporal power, the papacy saw its spiritual authority strengthened by the council. Already during the unfolding of the sessions, Pius IX's interventions had left an increasing mark on the discussions and the decisions. The council fathers had indeed enjoyed a real freedom of dialogue, of expression and of vote during the council; they had, however, been submitted to external pressures coming from the press; and of course, those fathers who were in the minority had to bear the law of the majority, which was supported by the pope.

For the first time in its history, the Church assembled in council was free as far as governments were concerned. Left unfinished on account of the circumstances, the council did nonetheless condemn some grave errors, but it was unable to face up to a phenomenon much larger than heresies*, a phenomenon which some fathers had seen coming: indifference. The council was not sufficient in itself to prepare the Church to face up to the secularization of culture and of society, which soon became obvious, mainly in France, through the modernist crisis and the antagonistic separation of Church and State.

● Acts: Mansi (1923–27), vol. 49–53.
Decrees: *COD* 801–16 (*DCO* II/2, 1627–59).
♦ A. Vacant (1895), *Études théologiques sur les constitutions du Concile du Vatican*, 2 vols., Paris.
R. Aubert (1952), *Le problème de l'acte de foi*, Louvain.
U. Betti (1961), *La costituzione dommatica* Pastor aeternus *del Concilio Vaticano I*, Rome.
R. Aubert (1964), *Vatican I, HCO*, vol. 12.
H.J. Pottmeyer (1973), *Unfehlbarkeit und Souveränität: Die papstliche Unfehlbarkeit im System der Ultramontanen Ekklesiologie des 19. Jahrhunderts*, Mainz.
L.M. Bermejo (1990), *Church, Conciliarity and Communion*, Anand.

CLAUDE BRESSOLETTE

See also **Council; Dogma; Existence of God, Proofs of; Infallibility; Modernism; Ontologism; Rationalism; Traditionalism**

Vatican II, Council of

1962–1965

The second council to have taken place at the Vatican was the 21st ecumenical council of the Catholic* Church, and the first in history to have brought together bishops* of all races and from all continents: up to 2,650 Fathers assembled in St. Peter's basilica in Rome*. The council was opened by Pope John XXIII on 11 October 1962, and concluded under Paul VI on 8 December 1965, after four sessions.

1. Preparation of the Council and Composition of the Assembly

On 25 January 1959 John XXIII, who had been elected pope three months earlier, made the surprise announcement of three decisions: the convening of a Roman synod*, the convening of a council*, and the revision of the code of canon* law.

a) Preparation of the Council. Pius XI and Pius XII had not convened a council. The initiative taken by John XXIII was due to a profound evolution of the Church. This was marked, mainly in Europe, by a renewal of studies in the Bible* and in the Fathers* of the Church (coll. Christian Sources, encyclical *Divino afflante*, 1943); by research into liturgy (encyclical *Mediator Dei*, 1947); and by Pius XII's reform of Holy Week and of the breviary. Alongside neo-Thomism a "new theology*" had grown, which paid attention to the problems related to morality, religions, and contemporary society. The encyclical *Humani generis* (1950) condemned the false interpretations that could potentially result from this. Catechetical and pastoral initiatives, together with the experience of *Action catholique* and of the missions*, favored a notion of the Church that was less juridical and less hierarchical (hierarchy*), more community oriented and more mystical* (encyclical *Mystici corporis*, 1943). The collection *Unam sanctam* went along with this transformation.

From January to June 1960 a vast consultation with all the bishops, with major superiors, and with Catholic universities obtained 2,150 responses (76.4 percent of the questionnaires that had been sent out). Ten preconciliar commissions were created: nine of them were chaired by the prefect of each of the dicasteries of the Roman Curia; the tenth being that of the apostolate of the laity*. There were also three secretariats; one of them was devoted to the unity* of Christians; it was entrusted to the Jesuit A. Béa, who was created a cardinal. The central commission, chaired by the pope, coordinated the activities and prepared the rules. Eventually, 70 schemas were retained. On 25 December 1961 the bull of indiction, *Humanae salutis,* appeared: it outlined the objectives of the council. The pope promulgated the regulation on 6 August 1962, and on 11 September he delivered to the world a message of hope. The opening was to take place on 11 October 1962.

b) Composition of the Conciliar Assembly.   Coming from 136 nations, and belonging to 93 nationalities, the 2,650 bishops (including 80 cardinals and 7 patriarchs) represented a great diversity of churches. Also present were 97 superiors of religious orders, with a right to speak. Vatican* I, with 750 members, had been mostly European; what was striking about Vatican II was its "global massiveness" (A. Dupront), with western Europe now representing no more than 33 percent of the Fathers present. In relation to the number of believers, Europe and the Americas were underrepresented, a fact which enhanced the weight of the young churches; out of 289 bishops in missionary countries, 151 were French.

A clear division emerged among the Fathers with the debate on the schema of *De Revelatione.* The supporters of a conceptual classical theology, alert to all the risks of "modernism*," found themselves opposed by those who were attached to the biblical and patristic sources of tradition*, who were sensitive to historical evolution and wished to take into account the problems of a world that had undergone considerable change through secularization*.

Aside from the bishops' experts—one of whom was J. Ratzinger, working with Cardinal J. Frings—more than 400 official experts in the council were appointed: H. de Lubac* and Y. Congar, at the pope's request, along with K. Rahner*, J. Daniélou, G. Philips, P. Delhaye, P. Haubtmann, J. Courtney Murray, and others. Invited by John XXIII, 31 *observers,* subsequently 93, represented 28 other churches and denominations. Their presence in the *aula* was symbolic. With a similar status, some *guests* were invited personally by the pope: R. Schutz and M. Thurian from Taizé, O. Cullmann, and Jean Guitton, the first layman. Paul VI introduced some lay *listeners* (29) and some *lay and religious women listeners* (23).

2. The Great Debates during the Four Sessions

a) In Search of Unanimity: The Action of the Popes. John XXIII's inaugural speech, on 11 October 1962,

caused a sensation, because of the spirit it succeeded in communicating regarding the work to be done by the council. The pope was opposed to the "prophets of doom," who idealize the past and stigmatize the present; he preferred mercy* to condemnation and he invited the members of the council to make a distinction between the deposit of the truths of faith* and the form under which these truths are presented. The council should present its doctrinal work in a manner "that meets the demands of our time," with a "teaching that is mainly of a *pastoral* character." It was thus that the *aggiornamento* of the Church* became clear. On 29 September 1963 John's successor, Paul VI, opened the second session by stating the four goals of the council: "knowledge or consciousness of the Church, its renewal, the reestablishment of the unity of all Christians, dialogue of the Church with the men of the present day." The first encyclical of Paul VI represented a continuation of this opening speech and of John XXIII's last encyclical (*Pacem in terris,* 11 April 1963): *Ecclesiam suam* (6 August 1964) was a "charter of the dialogue" between the Church and all human beings, basing itself on the revelation of God* to all. Such an overture was to be confirmed by Paul VI's first three journeys (to the Holy Land in January 1964, Bombay in December 1964, and the United Nations in October 1965).

b) First Session (11 October–8 December 1962).   Following the *Message of the council to all men,* voted upon on 20 October, the study of the schema on the liturgy* started on 22 October; it was written with renewal in mind. The outline of the text was approved with virtual unanimity on 14 November (2,162 votes to 46). On the other hand the schema *On the sources of revelation,* inspired by a narrowly classical and anti-Protestant viewpoint, ignored all the work done in the area of exegesis*. Although much criticized, this schema was not rejected, because the majority did not reach the required two-thirds (1,368 votes to 822). John XXIII averted the crisis by withdrawing the text, which was transmitted to a commission co-chaired by cardinals A. Ottaviani and Béa; the Secretariat for Unity, under the direction of a biblicist, was linked with the Holy Office. Following the quick examination of two mediocre schemas (on the means of social communication and on the union with the Eastern church), the council began studying the best text from the theological commission, *De Ecclesia.* With the pope's agreement and the support of cardinals P. E. Léger and G. B. Montini (soon to become Pope Paul VI), Cardinal L. J. Suenens suggested putting in order the multiple schemas. Applied to the Church, the distinction *ad intra* and *ad extra* facilitated the classification of the subjects to be treated.

c) *Second Session (29 September–4 December 1963)*. Following the precise speech given by Paul VI, the council devoted one month to the new schema on the Church, redrafted under the direction of G. Philips of Louvain. An agreement was reached to reverse the order of the chapters, the chapter on the people* of God being placed ahead of the chapter on the hierarchical constitution of the Church. On 29 October, and going against that group of Fathers who wished to magnify the privileges of the Virgin, the introduction of a schema on Mary* in the schema on the Church was secured (by 1,114 votes to 1,074). On 30 October the moderators appointed by Paul VI (cardinals G. Agagianian, J. Döpfner, L.J. Suenens, and G. Lercaro) asked four questions: on the sacramental character of episcopal ordination*, on the participation of every bishop in the episcopal college, on the supreme power of the college, and on the divine right it is entrusted with. In spite of the fears manifested by the "curialists" that the jurisdiction* and the primacy of the pope might be reduced, the votes were massively positive (ranging from 2,123 to 34, to 1,717 to 408). A fifth vote accepted the restoration of the permanent diaconate (deacon*) (by 1,588 to 525). These votes led to the complete revision of the schema on the government of dioceses; the Melchite patriarch Maximos IV protested against the predominance of the Roman Curia, and a sharp controversy erupted between Cardinal J. Frings and Cardinal A. Ottaviani regarding the Holy Office.

The schema on ecumenism*, presented by the Secretariat for Unity, prompted a constructive debate. The moderators deferred discussion on chapter IV (on the Jews), written by Cardinal Béa, and chapter V (on religious freedom*), defended by Mgr E. de Smedt.

On 21 November the pope enlarged the commissions, a measure requested by the majority, and he announced the abolition of numerous limits imposed by canon law on the powers of bishops. The constitution on the liturgy, approved with virtual unanimity (by 2,147 to 4), was promulgated on 4 December 1963, as well as the decree on the means of social communication.

At the end of this second session the "Döpfner plan" proposed to structure the work done by the commissions around six main texts, the other seven being more modest in scope. During the summer the encyclical *Ecclesiam suam* insisted on dialogue; the pope wanted to win over the minority by toning down the expression of episcopal collegiality* and reinforcing that of pontifical primacy.

d) *Third session (14 September–21 November 1964)*. A concelebration by the pope and 24 bishops, representing a first application of the liturgical reform, opened this session, during which all the texts were examined.

Some of the debates were very productive—for instance on the Church (chapter on Mary and eschatology*), on revelation (the doctrine of the two sources was abandoned), on ecumenism, and on the pastoral responsibilities of bishops. Other debates were more stormy (for example on the Eastern churches). The texts on religious freedom, on the Jews, and on non-Christian religions were tackled too quickly. While the draft regarding lay people was accepted for further amendment, that regarding priests was considered too superficial and was rejected. As for the draft on people in religious orders, it was deemed too juridical and too Western in nature, and required revision. Schema XIII brought the "prophets" into conflict with the "politicians" on burning issues: birth control, limits on property rights, use of the atomic bomb, obligations of rich nations to those of the developing world; the text of the schema needed to be completely rewritten.

Wishing to reduce the opposition of the minority, Paul VI took some initiatives that were variously received, such as the insertion, in the constitution on the Church, of an *Explanatory Note* in chapter III on the connection between primacy and collegiality. On 21 November three texts were promulgated with a near-unanimity of votes: the dogmatic* constitution on the Church, and the decrees on ecumenism and on the Eastern churches. The pope announced measures that were favorable to collegiality, such as the creation of an advisory synod to be convened at regular intervals; he proclaimed Mary "Mother of the Church" and justified this title, which had not been retained by the council.

During the last intersession, and despite pessimistic forecasts, the commissions redrafted the texts. Starting with innumerable amendments, P. Haubtmann entirely reshaped the schema on the "Church in the modern world." Once back from Bombay, the pope named new cardinals, and these reinforced the majority; following the foundation of the Secretariat for non-Christian religions (1964), he founded the Secretariat for non-believers; he encouraged the dialogue of charity with the Orthodox (Orthodoxy*).

e) *Fourth Session (14 September–8 December 1965)*. Following the study of the declaration on religious freedom, redrafted by the American J.C. Murray, Mgr G.M. Garonne was entrusted with the schema on the Church in the world. On 28 October three decrees were promulgated (on the training of priests, on the renewal of religious life, and on the pastoral duties of bishops), as well as two declarations (on Christian education and on the relations of the Church with the non-Christian religions); the passage regarding the Jews raised some difficulties to the very end. On 18 November the council adopted the decree on the apostolate of lay people and the dogmatic constitution on revelation, revised by Father Betti and amended at the pope's suggestion. There were still four documents, which were promulgated on 7 December: the decrees on the ministry* and the life of priests (the pope excluded the topic of celibacy from the council's agenda); the missionary activity of the Church, with its doctrinal and ecumenical complements; the declaration on religious freedom; and the pastoral constitution on the Church in the modern world. The latter text, the longest, in keeping with the pastoral orientation desired by John XXIII, completed the work of the council.

On 4 December a farewell ceremony at the church of Saint-Paul-Without-The-Walls saw the bringing together, for the first time, of a pope with non-Catholic observers. On 6 December Paul VI announced the reform of the Holy Office, renamed the Congregation for the Doctrine of the Faith. The following day the lifting of the reciprocal anathemas of 1054 was published, in Constantinople and in Rome. During the solemn closing session, on 8 December, in the presence of 81 governmental delegations and of nine international organizations, the council addressed specific messages to rulers, men of science and intellectuals, artists, women*, workers, poor and sick people, and the young. One day earlier, Paul VI had insisted on the religious worth of the council: it meant that the Church had meditated on its mystery and it expressed its sympathy for contemporary man, whom it wanted to serve.

3. Coherence and Implementation of the 16 Documents

a) The Texts: Their Character and Their Authority. Three types of documents were promulgated: four *constitutions,* among which two were dogmatic (*Lumen gentium* and *Dei Verbum*), one pastoral (*Gaudium et spes*), and one that was both doctrinal and practical, on the liturgy (*Sacrosanctum concilium,* which allowed the vernacular to be used in the liturgy instead of Latin); nine enforcement *decrees;* and three *declarations (Gravissimum educationis, Nostra aetate, Dignitatis humanae).* Vatican II broke new ground with these declarations, which have the authority of official teaching by the Church on a point of doctrine. Unlike all the councils since Nicaea*, Vatican II did not pronounce any anathema, but it denounced some errors. It did not formulate any formal dogmas*, but its decisive affirmations on the sacramental character

of the episcopate and on the collegiality of bishops (*LG* III) are close to dogmatic formulas. Two constitutions, on the Church and on Revelation, have a "dogmatic" character. The qualifier "pastoral," which was given to the constitution on "the Church in the modern world," represents another innovation: the problems of the world are approached in the light of Catholic doctrine, in a language that is accessible to contemporary people.

b) The Church, "entirely from Christ, in Christ, and for Christ, entirely from men, among men, and for men" (Paul VI, 14 September 1964). The mystery* of the Church, in the biblical and patristic sense of the word *(the eternal secret of God manifested and realized by Christ in history),* is at the heart of the work accomplished by Vatican II. The constitution *Lumen gentium* is "the backbone" of the texts, since the decrees each refer to one or more of its chapters: *Ad gentes* (missionary activity) in chapters I and II; *Orientalium Ecclesiarum* (the Eastern Catholic churches) and *Unitatis redintegratio* (ecumenism) in chapter II; *Christus Dominus* (the pastoral responsibilities of bishops), *Presbyterorum ordinis* (the ministry and life of priests), and *Optatam totius* (the training of priests) in chapter III; *Apostolicam actuositatem* (the apostolate of lay people) in chapter IV; and finally *Perfectae caritatis* (renewal and adaptability of the religious life), in chapter VI.

The Church, which has no end in its own self, enjoys a double relation with Christ and with human beings, as illustrated in the links between the four constitutions. Those that deal with revelation and with the liturgy affirm that the Church receives everything from Christ, "mediator and fulfillment of all revelation," and that Christ is at the heart of its prayer and its worship, as the sole high priest. The constitution on "the Church in the modern world" underscores its will to serve humankind: no human being is excluded from the relationship that the Church wishes to establish with all due respect for the freedom of every person.

c) Aspects of the Implementation. The reforms affecting the government of the Church (regarding the Curia, Holy Office, secretariats that had become advisory commissions, and bishops' synods) had started even before the closing of the council, and they came in rapid succession. The liturgical reform emphasized the place of the Bible* in the life and worship of the church, and it stressed the communal dimension of the Eucharist* and of the other sacraments*. New modalities were sought for mission, which was to be inseparable from dialogue with other religions: the exhortation of *Evangelii nuntiandi* (1975) was a decisive step. Ecumenical relations were numerous, in spite of some incidents and sometimes even backward steps. The ecumenical directorate of 1993 acknowledged what had been achieved, and the encyclical *Ut unum sint* (25 May 1995) called for a deeper engagement, and proposed a dialogue on exercising primacy. The first meeting with the representatives of other religions, who had come to pray for peace, was held in Assisi in October 1986. In 1993 Pope John Paul II paid a visit to the synagogue of Rome, and the Holy See recognized the State of Israel; these were important steps in the evolution of the church's relations with Judaism*. Finally, the same pope's numerous apostolic journeys were a way of defending everywhere the rights of human beings, the right to life, and to religious freedom.

Despite the traditionalist schism and protests regarding the slow pace of the expected reforms, the bishops' synod of 1985, which had been convoked to mark the 20th anniversary of the council, confirmed the orientations being taken by insisting on the *ecclesiology** of *communion**. Hailed by all as an event that marked the end of the Constantinian era and of the Counter-Reformation, Vatican II opened up new avenues for the thought and life of the Catholic Church, which became engaged from that time onward in a necessary dialogue with all human beings, believers and non-believers. Vatican II was a decisive step in the march toward the third millennium.

● *Acta et documenta concilio œcumeniceo Vaticano II apparando: Series I antepraeparatoria* (1960–61), 4 vols.; *Series*

II praeparatoria (1965–89), 3 vols.; *Acta synodalia sacrosancti concilii oecumenici Vaticani II* (1970–89), 4 vols.; *Sacrosanctum Oecumenicum Concilium Vaticanum II: Constitutiones, decreta, declarationes* (1966), Vatican City.

Decrees
COD 817–1135 (*DCO* II/2, 1661–2300).
X. Ochoa (1967), *Index verborum cum documentis Concilii Vaticani secundi*, Rome.

♦ **Commentaries**
Y. Congar (Ed.) (1965–70), *Vatican II* (UnSa, 16 vol., from issue 51 to 76), Paris.
LThK2 (1966–68), vols. 12–14, *Das zweite vatikanische Konzil.*

Works
R. Laurentin (1962–65), *L'enjeu du Concile,* 4 vols., Paris.
A. Wenger (1963–66), *Vatican II,* 4 vols., Paris.
G. Caprile (1965–68), *Il concilio Vaticano II,* 5 vols., Rome.
R. Laurentin (1966), *Bilan du Concile,* Paris.
R. Rouquette (1968), *La fin d'une chrétienté,* 2 vols., Paris.
R. Aubert (Ed.), 1975, *Nouvelle histoire de l'Église,* no 5: *L'Église dans le monde moderne,* Paris.
P. Levillain (1975), *La mécanique politique de Vatican II,* Paris.
G. Defois (Ed.) (1983–86), *L'héritage du Concile,* 13 vols., Paris.
R. Latourelle (Ed.), 1988, *Vatican II: bilan et perspectives vingt-cinq ans après (1962–1987),* 3 vols., Montréal-Paris.
G. Alberigo (Ed.) (1997–), *Histoire du concile Vatican II,* Paris.

CLAUDE BRESSOLETTE

See also **Collegiality; Council; Church; Exegesis; Gospel; Freedom, Religious; Liturgy; Ministry; Mission; Ecumenicism**

Vengeance of God

In modern languages, the word *vengeance* means an act opposed to justice* and pity, an act that consists of instinctively responding to a wrong with immoderate and cruel actions. Attributed to barbaric states of society*, vengeance is unanimously condemned by present-day law. Some passages in the Bible, therefore (especially in the Old Testament), raise a problem. These passages prescribe vengeance legally (Ex 21:20–21 and Nm 31:2), invoke it in prayer* (Jer 11:20 and 20:10–12), and attribute it to God* (Lev 26:25; Dt 32:43; and Sir 48:7), who is described as an

Avenger (Na 1:2; Ps 94:1 and 99:8). Vengeance's kinship with anger (Lev 19:18; Ez 25:14–17; Mi 5:14, and so on) and certain of its particularly violent manifestations (Dt 32:41–42; Is 34:6–7, and 63:3–4; and Jer 46:10) make the notion of vengeance even more unacceptable. This explains the interpreter's need to elucidate its meaning.

The first question to clear up is the accuracy of our translations. Modern-language Bibles translate the verbal and nominal expressions from the root of the Hebrew *nqm* (used in one-fifth of the passages) as "to avenge [oneself]" and "vengeance." Only in certain specific cases is an analogous meaning given to the root *g'l* (Is 59:17 and 63:4), especially in the syntagm *go'él ha-dâm,* usually translated as "avenger of blood" (Nm 35:19–27; Dt 19:6; Jos 20:5–9; and 2 Sm 14:11).

In reality, the root *nqm* expresses only the act of compensating, of responding to the wrong suffered by inflicting a punishment. The parallel terminology belonging to the field of retribution, such as *shlm* (Dt 32:35–41 and Is 34:8), *gml* (Is 59:17–18; Joel 4:4; and Ps 103:10), *shwv [hi]* (Is 66:15; Jl 4:7; and Ps 79:10–11) brings out that fact clearly. Likewise, the terms *ekdikeô, ekdikèsis,* used for preference in the Septuagint, or else the *vindicatio* ("vindication") of the Vulgate, do not necessarily have a negative connotation, for they refer, in fact, to the rendering of justice or the request for it, as in the English term "to claim compensation."

Therefore, it is sometimes possible to translate *nqm* as "to avenge [oneself]" (Jgs 15:7 and Ps 44:17), but in numerous cases it is necessary to emphasize the meaning of "right the legal wrong" (Dietrich), by choosing therefore equivalences such as "to punish" (the guilty), "to compensate" or to "indemnify" (the victim), "to remedy" (a wrong), "to get satisfaction," etc. This method of translation seems especially necessary when the subject of the verb *nqm* is God, a model of justice (Dt 32:35–36 and 32:41–42; 1 Sm 24:13, Is 59:17 and so on).

However, the problem of the legitimacy of vindictive retaliation, condemned by legally advanced societies, still remains. We know that the Scriptures* condemn arbitrary and excessive vengeance—such as Lamech's, avenging 77 times (Gn 4:23–24). Improperly called the law of the talion or of retaliation, the law, in fact, prescribes that public authorities should inflict on the guilty party a punishment "in proportion" to the crime committed (Ex 21:23–24 and parallels). However, "vindication," which consists of meting out a fair legal punishment for the crime, is not always possible; it often happens that the victims do not get satisfaction from the competent authorities and that they are consequently tempted to seek their own justice by answering like with like, with the risk of choosing the way of hatred and unjustified violence.

Then the thought occurs that the just man does well to renounce vengeance, leaving it up to God the "king, judge, and warrior" (Peels 1995) to take charge of imposing the law that has been flouted (Gn 50:19; Lev 19:18; 1 Sm 24:13–14; Ps 37:1–11; Prv 3:31–35; Sir 28:1 and so on). The "day of divine vengeance" (Is 34:8, 61:2, and 63:4; Jer 46:10; and Hos 9:7) thus alludes to the Lord's eschatological judgment, feared by the wicked but awaited by the victims as a day of reparation and salvation* (Is 35:4, 59:17, and 61:2; 1 Thes 4:6; 2 Thes 1:5–10; Heb 10:30; and Rev 6:10 and 19:2).

The Scriptures thus promise man the justice that provides for the rigorous punishment of the guilty and, on the other hand, refuses to answer violence with violence (Sir 28:2–8). The latter attitude, which suggests the possibility of pardon, is fully realized in the New Testament teachings (Mt 5:38–42; Rom 12:17–21; 1 Thes 5:15; 1 Pt 3:9 and so on). The perfect model of such an action against the guilty is God himself, whose immense patience is recognized (Wis 12:19; Mt 5:43–48). It is the sign of God's goodness and an opportunity for sinners to repent (Wis 11:23, 12:2, and 12:8–10; Lk 13:6–9; Rom 2:4, 3:5–6, and 9:22–23; 1 Pt 3:20; and 2 Pt 3:9 and 3:15), until, at the end of time, he will bring about the just restoration of rights abused (Lk 18:7–8; Rom 12:19; 2 Thes 1:8; and Heb 10:30).

● E. Merz (1916), *Die Blutrache bei den Israeliten, BWAT* 20.

P. Ducrot (1926), "De la vendetta à la loi du talion," *RHPhR* 6, 350–65.

H. A. Brongers (1963), "Die Rache- und Fluchpsalmen im Alten Testament," in coll., *Studies on Psalms,* OTS 13, 21–42.

P. Rémy (1967), "Peine de mort et vengeance dans la Bible," *ScEc* 19, 323–50.

E. Mendenhall (1973), "The Vengeance of Yahweh," in *The Tenth Generation: The Origins of the Biblical Tradition,* Baltimore, 69–104.

W. Dietrich (1976), "Rache: Erwägungen zu einen alttestamentlichen Thema," *EvTh* 36, 450–72.

G. Cardascia (1979), "La place du talion dans l'histoire du droit pénal à la lumière des droits du Proche-Orient ancien," in *Mélanges offerts à J. Dauvilliez,* Toulouse, 169–83.

P.-E. Dion (1980), "Tu feras disparaître le mal du milieu de toi," *RB* 87, 321–49.

R. Gelio (1981), "Sangue e vendetta," *Atti della settimana Sangue e antropologia biblica 1980,* Rome, 515–28.

E. Lipinski (1986), "Na'qam," *ThWAT* 5, 602–12.

H. G. L. Peels (1995), *The Vengeance of God: The Meaning of the Root NQM and the Function of the NQM-Texts in the Context of Divine Revelation in the Old Testament,* OTS 31, Leyden, 1995.

F. Stolz (1997), "Rache," *TRE* 28, 82–88.

PIETRO BOVATI

See also **Apocalyptic Literature; Eschatology; Judgment; Justice; Law and Legislation; Punishment; Violence; War; Wrath of God**

Veracity

The concept of veracity has been the source of much hesitation, and it might even be doubted whether it really is a philosophically univocal concept: veracity can be considered to be both a pure and simple conformity to truth* as well as an intention of truth, the "good faith" to which it is sometimes reduced. "This word [veracity] designates, most of the time, the good faith of the person who is speaking" (Lalande, *Vocabulaire...*). This ambiguity can be partially overcome through lexical distinctions, for example between *verum* and *verax* in Latin, between *truthfulness* and *veracity* in English, and between *véridicité, vérisimilitude,* and *véracité* in French.

The meaning of "veracity" as pure and simple "good faith" can be found in Kant*, for example: "Veracity in declarations is also called loyalty, and, if these declarations are also promises, uprightness and general good faith" (*Doctrine of Virtue,* §9, III). We would undoubtedly use the notion of sincerity more readily than that of veracity where promises are concerned: the theory of acts of language has taught us that a promise is either sincere or insincere, a threat is either serious or feigned, and a declaration is either veracious or mendacious. Moreover, in the more precise definition of veracity that Kant gives a little further on, he limits veracity to declarations: "Because he is a moral being *(homo noumenon),* man cannot make use of himself, as a physical being *(homo phaenomenon),* as if he were a simple tool (word machine) not connected to an internal purpose (the communication of thought); on the contrary, he is subject to the condition of agreeing with himself in the declaration *(declaratio)* of his thoughts and is obligated to himself to seek veracity." (ibid.). Veracity, then, plays a double role: to use contemporary language, it represents both a condition of success, of *felicity* in acts of language (such as assertions and promises); and a transcendental basis for communication, which leaves open the possibility of a reinterpretation of veracity in an "ethic of communication" (K.O. Apel).

For Descartes*, however, veracity is invested with a very different role than that of a moral regulation of exchanges of language, for divine veracity is at the basis of truth. It is in fact because God* cannot and does not want to deceive me that I can be certain of the reality of matter *(6th Meditation).* Divine veracity can then be invoked to revoke any possible doubt, as in the case of the atheist mathematician who, if he is unsure of God, will never know of a "true science" ("and since one supposes that the mathematician is an atheist, he cannot be certain not to be deceived by the things which seem perfectly obvious to him," *Réponses aux secondes objections,* A-T IX, 111). This veracity is a consequence of God's perfection; supremely perfect, God cannot know how to deceive: "For as God is the sovereign Being*, he must of necessity also be the sovereign good* and the sovereign truth, and consequently he abhors that anything should emanate from him which might tend towards falseness...and since we have within a real faculty enabling us to know the truth and distinguish it from what is false...if this faculty did not tend toward the truth, at least when we use it in a proper manner...it would not be without reason that God, who gave us that faculty, could be considered to be a deceiver." (ibid. 113). Thus this perfection is a consequence both of God's divinity and of his kindness toward us. God is veracious because he is good.

Veracity, if it is a result of the goodness of God and constitutes therefore more of a restraint upon malice, of a "good deed," than a standard of exactness, can henceforth be understood, no longer from the angle of ethics of communication (Kant) or as an ultimate guarantee that the sensible will not deceive us (Descartes), but within the dimension of ethics* *simpliciter.* Moreover, for Thomas* Aquinas, truth is a virtue*; not a theological virtue, or even—as one might expect—an intellectual virtue, but a moral virtue (*ST* IIa IIae, q. 109, 1 ad 3). In this respect, truth and veracity are the same: "One might imply by truth that which causes us to speak truly, that which, in consequence, makes man truthful. This truth or veracity *[veracitas]* must be a virtue, for to speak the truth is a good action, and moreover, virtue is that which confers goodness upon those who possess it, and which makes their acts good" (ibid.). Truth is a "part of justice*" where veracity's role is that of a condition for an equitable life in community: "As man is a social animal, one man naturally owes to another that which is essential to the preservation of human society. Humans could not live together if they did not believe in each other, in a reciprocal exchange of truth. That is why the object of the virtue of truth is a thing which is, in a certain fashion, due" (ibid.). The "virtue of truth" extends far beyond Kantian "good faith," and divine veracity is simply its fulfillment: by being veracious, God exercises his justice* (which allows him to punish us if we deliberately choose to lie). Thomas Aquinas pointed out two obstacles to truth, two types or systems of stabilized discourse that, while they do not adopt the perverse form of lying, are nevertheless diminishments of virtue: conceit and irony (*ST* IIa IIae, q. 112–13) Conceit is opposed "by excess" to the virtue of veracity, and irony opposes it "by default," and we can therefore conclude that veracity as a condition and practice of the virtue of truth is linked to moderation. La Bruyère translates *eironeia* as "dissimulation," the word corresponding to *cavillatio* (pleasantries or mockery); Thomas would simply use the Ciceronian derivative, *ironia*.

But is there not a risk of confusing moral truth and veracity? Leibniz*, in particular, was aware of this difficulty and in an attempt to preclude it proposed the following convention, which simply makes the equivalence presented by Aquinas more explicit: "Moral truth is called veracity by some and metaphysical truth is vulgarly perceived by metaphysicians as an attribute of being, but it is a perfectly useless attribute.... We should remain content with seeking truth in the correspondence of the propositions in one's mind with the things they are concerned with" (*New Essays* IV, 5, §11). The aim in this case was to avoid a confusion between veracity, identified with moral truth, and truth, understood as the semantic predicate of correspondence, limited to a propositional level. However, the expression "moral truth" remains ambiguous. Does it mean truth as a moral virtue, in the Thomist sense, or rather, truth in the moral domain? It would seem that veracity was more often identified with the moral aspect of truth (*see* "'Veracity' Has Always Had a Moral Significance," Lalande's *Vocabulaire*).

Taken in this sense, Leibniz's cautiousness sanctions a modern divorce of veracity and truth. But insofar as theology* cannot be indifferent to the nature of human veracity, or endorse a pure and simple naturalist statement of fact that would reduce veracity to the status of a guarantee of a well-regulated communication, it cannot be content with ratifying this divorce. It is because veracity is a debt of truth that lies are more than a ruse of communication.

● M. Eck (1965), *Mensonge et vérité,* Tournai.
R. L. Martin (Ed.) (1970), *The Paradox of the Liar,* New Haven.
G. Durandin (1972), *Les fondements du mensonge,* Paris.
S. Bok (1978), *Lying: Moral Choice in Public and Private Life,* Hassocks, Sussex.
R. L. Martin (1984), *Recent Essays on Truth and the Liar Paradox,* Oxford.
P. Zagorin (1990), *Ways of Lying,* Cambridge, MA.
D. Nyberg (1993), *The Varnished Truth,* Chicago.
J. A. Barnes (1994), *A Pack of Lies: Towards a Sociology of Lying,* Cambridge.
J. Laurent (1994), *Du mensonge,* Paris.
J.-L. Marion (1996), *Questions cartésiennes II,* Paris.

FRÉDÉRIC NEF

See also **Truth; Virtues**

Vestige (Vestigium). *See* **Trace (Vestige)**

Vetus Latina. *See* **Translations of the Bible, Ancient**

Vienne, Council of

1311–1312

The council that assembled in Vienne (on the Rhône in south-central France), the 15th ecumenical council of the Catholic church, had been requested for several years by Philip IV (the Fair), king of France; he had wished, first of all, to put Pope Boniface VIII on trial, and he also wanted to get rid of the Knights Templars, whose territory he wished to absorb himself. The Council was the consequence of a new balance of power between the French monarch and the papacy, following the violent conflicts that had opposed Philip the Fair and Boniface VIII. The new pope, Clement V (the former archbishop of Bordeaux, Bertrand de Got, elected to the papal throne in 1305), wished to reconcile with the French monarchy.

The papal bull convening the ecclesiastics to the Council was issued in August 1308, following negotiations with the king, and one year after the arrest of the Templars, who had been forced to confess. The Council's official goal was the resolution of the Templar question; but the recapture of the Holy Land and the reform of the Church* were also mentioned in the bull of convocation. Under pressure from Philip the Fair, the pope began making a selection among the convened prelates; a new distinction was introduced between bishops invited by name to take part in the Council's debates (they were mainly French) and the others, who had to be "represented". According to E. Müller, only 170 prelates took part in the Council, which opened on 16 October 1311. Most of the work was accomplished not in the plenary sessions (reduced to three), but through special commissions whose conclusions were submitted to the pope, who heard them in consistory.

The most important committee was in charge of examining the Templar question; it had at its disposal the acts of episcopal and pontifical commissions from preceding years (1308–11). According to the majority of committee members, it was not possible to condemn the Templars before hearing their defenders. While the work of the Council progressed, however, the fate of the Templars was actually settled by Clement V, through secret negotiations with the advisers to the king of France. On 3 April 1312, in the presence of Philip the Fair, who had come to Vienne with his sons, his brothers, his court and an army, the pope pronounced, with the Council's approval, the dissolution of the order, not by judicial sentence (following a regular procedure and condemnation), but in virtue of his apostolic authority*. As for the Templars' assets, they were transferred a few weeks later to the knights of the Order of the Hospital (bull of 2 May 1312), whose reform was forthcoming.

On 3 April, Clement V announced also the organization of a crusade, to be financed by the collection of a 10 percent tax that Philip the Fair had pledged to support. The Council's work on the crusade had been prepared by the drafting of several reports. According to the *Liber de acquisitione Terrae Sanctae* by Raymond Lulle, who was present at the Council, they first had to disarm the infidels by using force; once rendered powerless, the infidels would then be converted through rational theological discussion. With this type of tactic, it was obvious that knowledge of the Oriental languages was necessary, so the Council decided to put in place the teaching of Hebrew, Arabic, and Syriac within the Curia Romana, as well as in the Universities of Paris, Oxford, Bologna, and Salamanca.

The Council of Vienne was also induced to take a position on the controversies that were tearing the Franciscans apart regarding the evolution of their order. Since 1309, Clement V had had several reports prepared on the observance of the rule within the order, on the persecutions inflicted upon the spirituals by the superiors of the community, and on the doctrinal orthodoxy of Pierre de Jean Olivi (or Olieu), the leader of the Provençal spirituals (*see* Bonaventure*). Two commissions were created in Vienne: the first, made up of 14 members who were not part of the order, was entrusted with examining the question of poverty (the *usus pauper*); the second one, made up of seven members, had to give a verdict on Olivi's writings.

The conclusions of the first commission were favorable for the spirituals: its report presents, in fact, certain analogies with some of the writings of the spiritual Ubertin de Casale. On 5 May 1312, the pope declared that the inquiry conducted by the Council's commission had shown that the spirituals' lifestyle was licit and respectable, and the following day, he promulgated the constitution *Exiui de paradiso;* it defined the appropriate manner for the observance of the rule and declared the vow of poverty to be an essential element in Franciscan life. This constitution (which is sometimes omitted in the collections of decrees originating from the Council of Vienne) did nothing, however, to resolve the internal problems of the Franciscan order.

The report of the commission charged with the examination of Olivi's doctrine is lost, but the conclusions expressed by four commission members on five incriminated propositions have been found: the censors expressed the opinion that it was possible to give these propositions an orthodox explanation. Promulgated on 6 May, the constitution *Fidei catholicae* condemns nonetheless three theses that had been attributed to Olivi, though without naming their author. The first point discussed concerns the exegesis* of the spear attack on Christ* while he was on the cross: according to the constitution, it was *after* Christ's death that his side was pierced by a soldier's spear. The second point discussed is at the source of the Council's definition on the union of soul* and body: according to the constitution, "whosoever dares henceforth declare, defend or assert with obstinacy that the rational and intellectual soul is not in itself and essentially the shape of the body must be considered a heretic." Finally, as a third point, the constitution states as "more probable" the theological teaching according to which children, as well as adults, receive divine grace* at the time of baptism*.

As far as the reform of the Church was concerned, a commission presided over by the pope was entrusted with the task of examining the reports and the petitions that had been requested at the time the Council was convened. In their reports, Guillaume Le Maire, bishop of Angers (1291–1317), and Guillaume Durant (or Durand), bishop of Mende (1296–1330), criticized the Curia's takeover of benefices, which restricted the bishop's role in his diocese. Thus, it was important to reform the Church "in its leader and its members" (according to G. Durand's *De modo generalis concilii celebrandi*). The question of the exemption of religious orders, in particular the mendicants, was also the object of a vast episcopal offensive in which Gilles de Rome, archbishop of Bourges, notably took part. Furthermore, the prelates complained about the intrusion of lay* people in the affairs of the Church and their encroachment on ecclesiastical jurisdiction*.

Finally, at the request of the German bishops, the Council of Vienne gave its verdict on the fate of the Beguines* and the Beghards. A first decree *(Cum de quibusdam mulieribus)*, essentially of a disciplinary nature, condemned the Beguines' lifestyle; it ruled that they could not be considered "nuns" because "they did not take a vow of obedience, did not renounce their assets and did not follow any approved rule"; it also denounced those among them who, "pushed by some

folly of the mind, debate and hold forth ideas on the Holy Trinity* and on the divine essence," spreading, "on the subject of the articles of faith* and on the sacraments* of the Church, opinions that are contrary to the Catholic faith." The same decree authorizes, however, the lifestyle of "the pious women who live honestly in their hospices, whether or not they have taken the vow of chastity" and who wish to "do penance* and serve God* in a spirit of humility." A second decree *(Ad nostrum)*, exclusively dogmatic in nature, condemns eight errors attributed to the Beghards and the Beguines, which are placed in the same category as the "heresy* of the Free Spirit," and which were in reality taken from the condemned theses of the Beguine Marguerite Porète (†1310). The proposition according to which "man may already obtain, in this life, the final beatitude*, as he will obtain it in the hereafter *[in vita beata],* depending on his degree of perfection" was particularly denounced.

As S. Kuttner has written (1964), the promulgation of the decrees at the Council represented only one step in the process of the "fabrication" of conciliar law (canon* law). The wording of the decrees was reread, amended, and corrected before what the pope considered to be the legislative work of the Council was ready to be disseminated. A postconciliar commission was therefore entrusted with the task of revising and finalizing the decrees, particularly because Clement V wanted to include, as part of the council's juridical corpus, texts that had not been completed before its closure. Thus, it was not until March 1314 that the pope approved the body of (revised and completed) decrees. They were supposed to form the seventh book of the Decretals, following the *Sexte* of Boniface VIII. The death of Clement V, on 20 April 1314, further delayed the project. His successor, John XXII, made a few more corrections to the decrees, before sending the collection of "Clementines" to the universities on 25 October 1317.

● Acts: Mansi 25, 367–426.
Decrees: *COD* 333–401 *(DCO* II/1, 691–830).
♦ F. Ehrlé (1886, 1887), "Zur Vorgeschichte des Concils von Vienne," *ALKGMA* 2, 353–416; 3, 1–195.
F. Ehrlé (1888), "Ein Bruchstück der Acten des Concils von Vienne," ibid., 4, 361–470.
G. Lizerand (1910), *Clément V et Philippe le Bel*, Paris.
C.J. Hefele, H. Leclercq (1915), *Histoire des conciles* 6, 643–719.
E. Müller (1934), *Das Konzil von Vienne, 1311–1312: Seine Quellen und Geschichte*, Münster.
S. Kuttner (1964), "The Date of the Constitution *Saepe*, the Vatican Manuscripts and the Roman Edition of the Clementines," *Mélanges Eugène Tisserant* 4, Vatican City, 427–52.
J. Lecler (1964), *Vienne, HCO*, vol. 8.
T. Schneider (1973), *Die Einheit des Menschen: die anthropologische Formel* anima forma corporis...*Ein Beitrag zur Vorgeschichte des Konzils von Vienne*, Münster, 1973.

J. Tarrant (1974), "The Clementine Decrees on the Beguines: Conciliar and Papal Versions," *AHP* 12, 300–308.

J. Avril, "Les conceptions ecclésiologiques de Guillaume le Maire, évêque d'Angers (1291–1317)," *La littérature angevine médiévale,* Angers, 1981, 111–34.

P. Giannoni (1992), "La definizione del Concilio di Vienne sull'anima," *Vivens Homo* 3, 101–18.

C. Trottmann (1995), *La Vision béatifique: Des disputes scolastiques à sa définition par Benoît XII,* Rome, 607–8.

MICHEL LAUWERS

See also **Beguines; Ecclesiastical Discipline; Life, Spiritual**

Vincent of Lérins. *See* Dogma

Violence

A. Biblical Theology

a) Extension. Violence—*Châmâs* in Hebrew (the word appears 60 times in the Old Testament), *bia* or *hubris* in Greek—not only kills, it is also an outrage against dignity and truth*. It is coupled with sexual abuse (Gn 19:5, 9; Jgs 19), but even more often with falsehood (Ps 5:10, 10:7, 27:12; Is 53:9; Sir 28:18; *see* Ex 21:12ff.). The devil is "a murderer from the beginning" and "the father of lies" (Jn 8:44). The law is one (Jas 2:10f.) and essential violence is the absence of law, the anomie that destroyed the creation when "the earth was filled with violence" (Gn 6:11). Violence is most often discerned through its effects (*see* Hebrew *shâchat* [225 times]: to corrupt, mislead). The triangle of blood, sex, and words is the true site of violence (Ez 16, 23:37ff.); Wisdom 14:23–27 reveals idolatry* as its source (*see* Decalogue*). The idol, a substitute for death*, wants blood ("Moloch": Lv 18:21, 20:2–5). Under the name of "the Beast," it is the unnamable that overwhelms human beings and exacts adoration. The Beast brought the "woman drunk with the blood of the saints, the blood of the martyrs of Jesus" (Rev. 17:6); it will devour her (17:16). Violence destroys itself.

b) Law, Prophets, Other Writings. The Yahwist establishes the genealogy of violence. It multiplies, from Cain seven times avenged (Gn 4:15) to his descendent

Lamech, 70 times avenged. Then comes the cosmic unleashing (Gn 6). The "sacerdotal" Torah stresses the symbol of blood. Man, created in the image of God*, is given power over the animals*. Since his nourishment is exclusively vegetarian (Gn 1:29f.), this power is exclusively of gentleness. Genesis 9 demonstrates it *a contrario:* God gives mankind, through Noah, a regime of non-gentleness: man will be the "terror" of animals, will eat their flesh, but not their blood. This rite commemorates the original status that is contradicted by the new status. It is commemorative, and also anticipatory.

In the prophets* the child king will reconcile the animals with each other (Is 11). Disarmament and the covenant* with the animal world coincide (Hos 2:20). Thus oriented, mankind can both understand itself as overcome by violence and understand violence as overcome by something more fundamental. This clarifies the aporia of sacrifice*, a violent act demanded by the law, often rejected by the prophets. The biblical God takes upon himself a provisional or "economic" violence.

He orders the extermination of enemies in the war of conquest (Jos 6:21, 8:2, 8:23–39, 9:24, 10:22–26), because their way of life will contaminate his people* (Ex 23:33; *see* Gn 15:16; Dt 20:16f.). Elijah slaughters the prophets of Baal (1 Kgs 18:20–40; *see* 2 Kgs 1). Children insult Elisha; he curses them and they are killed by bears (2 Kgs 2:24). The history of Israel* is not limited to these extremes, no matter how often they appear. The biography of David is arranged according to an unstable division between retaliation and clemency, the latter based sometimes on calculation and sometimes on a true sense of God (1 Sm 24:20, 25:33; 2 Sm 16:12; but 1 Kgs 2).

The supplicant victim of violence—whether speaking individually or collectively—expresses himself in violent terms. He asks that his enemies be humiliated (Ps 6:11, 31:18f., 40:15, 71:13), chastised (Ps 17, 28:4f., 35:4–8, 55:16–24, 58:7–11, 63:10ff., 69:23–29, 125:5, 139:19–22, 140:10ff., 143:12 and so on), or he cries out for vengeance (Ps 109:18ff., 137, 149:7 and so on). He asks that the king crush or enslave enemy nations (Ps 2:8f., 21, 45:6, 110:1, 118:10ff.); that God terrify or destroy them (Ps 9:21, 10:15f., 79:6, 83:10–19, 97:3). The principal lesson is that the supplicant, overwhelmed by violence, will not be liberated by his own force alone.

c) Conversion of Violence. It is precisely at the site of violence that its opposite springs up. In a state of peril Israel hears itself told not to make a move: God alone will vanquish (Ex 14:13f.; 2 Chr 20:15–20; Is 7:4, 7: 9, 8:6f.). Expressions of patience, or even non-resistance (Ps 37), mingle with the violent supplications. Of course when man renounces the use of his sword he counts on God's sword (Ps 44:4). Other notions are asserted: let evil* destroy itself (Ps 7:16, 9:16, 34:22, 37:14f., 57:7, 140:10). Or again: the earth itself vomited up the incestuous, the infanticides, the idol-worshippers of Canaan (Lv 18:25, 18:28). In Wisdom (5:20, 16:17, 16:24) the theme is extended to the entire cosmos and all of history, to shed light on the last stage.

d) New Testament. The New Testament shows with the cross of Jesus* the paroxysm of violence and of its opposite. This opposite is the other violence, that of the Spirit of God. It marks Jesus' hyperbolic precepts of perfect justice* (Mk 9:42–49; Mt 5:29f.), of non-resistance against the wicked (Mt 5:39), of the necessary ruptures (Mk 8:34f.; Mt 8:21f.; Lk 9:61). The invisible "strong man" is to be mercilessly crushed (Mk 3:27; Lk 11:22). Jesus brings "the sword" (Mt 10:34). Whereas in Matthew 11:12 the violence is that of the enemies of the Kingdom, in Luke 16:16 it is rather the force that brings down the ancient barriers (Schrenk 1933).

For Luke, those close to Jesus await liberation and a new royalty for Israel (Lk 1:68, 1:71, 1:74, 24:21, Acts 1:6). James and John count on compulsion from heaven, as in the days of Elijah (Lk 9:54), an idea rejected by Jesus. Despite the confrontations (*see* Mt 12:30, 12:34f.; 23; Lk 11:44), the narrators are careful not to attribute any provocation to Jesus. Driving the merchants from the temple* (Mk 11:15ff.; with a whip: Jn 2:15) is a symbolic gesture, not an action with a concrete aim (*see* Mk 11:12ff., 11:20–24). In the Passion*, the Jesus/Barabbas (zealot) alternative clearly opposes the solution of violence to that of Jesus. When the time came, Jesus gave himself up to death without resisting (Mt 26:53; Jn 18:36), but without persuading his disciples to join him (*see* the swords of Lk 22:36ff., 22:49ff.). He acquiesced entirely in that obedience, interpreted by the entire New Testament as the fulfillment of the Scriptures*.

The victory of the violence of love dissipates the counterfeits of gentleness, which are a trap for Christians. This is why the Pauline* vocabulary retains the violent terms of the Old Testament literally: the cross is the victory over the enemy that is death (1 Cor 15:25ff.; *see* Ps 110:1); it kills hatred (Eph 2:16), Jesus takes prisoner the images of death (Eph 4:8 citing Ps 68:19; *see* Col 2:15), he will destroy them (1 Cor 15:26), the apocalyptic animals of Daniel 7 will be under the feet of the Son* of man (ibid., Ps 8:6f.), death will be swallowed up (1 Cor 15:54f.; see Hos 13:14; Is 25:8 LXX; Ex 15:4 LXX). This style is related to an apocalyptic* idiom (2 Thes 2:8), in which all the Old Testament images are carried to an extreme: the "Word* of God" makes war in "a robe dipped in blood" (Rev 19:13; *see* 14:20): it is "the time... for destroying the destroyers of the earth" (Rev 11:18).

● G. Schrenk (1933), "Biazomai, Biastès," *ThWNT* 1, 608–13.

A. Trocmé (1961), *Jésus et la révolution non violente*, Geneva.

M. Hengel (1970), *War Jesus revolutionär?*, Stuttgart.

R. Girard (1978), *Des choses cachées depuis la fondation du monde*, vol. II: *L'Écriture judéo-chrétienne*, Paris.

J. Pons (1981), *L'oppression dans l'Ancien Testament*, Paris.

N. Lohfink (1983), "Die Schichten des Pentateuchs und der Krieg," in *Gewalt und Gewaltlosigkeit im Alten Testament*, Freiburg-Basel-Vienna, 15–110.

P. Beauchamp (1987), "Création et fondation de la loi en Gn 1, 1–24," in *La création dans l'Orient ancien, Congrès ACFEB*, Paris, 139–82.

G. Barbaglio (1991), *Dio violente? Lettura delle Scritture ebraiche e cristiane*, Assisi.

P. Beauchamp. D. Vasse (1991), *La violence dans la Bible*, CEv 76.

PAUL BEAUCHAMP

See also **Animals; Decalogue; Legitimate Defense; Ethics, Sexual; Evil; Hell; Scapegoat; Vengeance of God; War**

B. Moral Theology

Violence means the use of illegitimate physical force to inflict an illegitimate physical wrong; it is thus distinguished from legitimate force and all rightful punishment. It may also imply a psychological wrong (such as sexual harassment, mental cruelty) and a non-physical use of force (such as economic repression). Violence may be directed against an individual or a community (such as apartheid). In the 20th century any discussion of violence must finally also deal with the reality of the excess of evil such as was manifested by the Holocaust.

Violence can be understood in the following ways: 1) physical aggression of an individual (murder, rape); 2) acts without physical reality producing a psychological and spiritual wrong; 3) social violence (slavery, racism, sexism); 4) genocide; 5) all use of instruments of mass destruction. In any one of these forms of violence it is the same negation of man by man that is expressed, amid a reality whose only characteristic is hardness. As Levinas writes of war*: "Trial by force is the test of the real. But violence does not consist so much in injuring and annihilating persons as in interrupting their continuity, making them play roles in which they no longer recognize themselves, making them betray not only commitments but their own substance, making them carry out actions that will destroy every possibility of action" *(Totality and Infinity).*

The Christian moral tradition* prohibits on principle all violence. The most ancient texts warn against abortion* and infanticide (e.g. *Didache* 2). In the patristic period a unanimous opposition to suicide gradually developed: prohibitions already formulated by Plato (*Laws* IX, 872 *Sq*) and Aristotle (*Nicomachean Ethics* III, 11; V, 15) were definitively expressed by Augustine*: "he who kills himself is a murderer" (*City of God* I, XVII; *see* Landsberg 1951). As for war and military service, the consensus evolved from condemnation to limited permission (but here the motives are religious rather than moral); and yet does the prohibition against killing weigh strictly on the Christian soldier? (Tertullian*, *Cor.* 11; Arnobius, *Adv. nat.* 1, 6). The social legislation of Constantine (280?–337) and his successors reflected the Christian concern with protecting women, children, and slaves from all domestic violence (Cochrane 1940, 1944).

Christian exhortations against violence appeal to the teachings of Jesus* and find a pledge in his sacrifice*, interpreted as the repudiation of all violence: this is the argument used by Thomas* Aquinas to prohibit all

clergymen from bearing arms (*ST* IIa IIae, q. 40, a. 2). In the final analysis such appeals are based on the doctrine of *imago Dei* and the insistent affirmation in the Old Testament that all life belongs to God*. Along with the Bible*, Christian thought recognizes the complete vulnerability of human beings. Man is placed in the hands of man. Violence is therefore inevitable. The human society in which violence is transmitted is nonetheless itself a created good* redeemed in Christ*: "The life of the saints is social," says Augustine (*City of God* XIX, V). And more fundamental than violence is the double sin* that makes it possible: the refusal of the individual to live according to the mode of availability and the desire to take advantage of the availability of others in order to do them wrong. What the Christian moral tradition condemns is not wrath, because that is only an emotion, but the disposition to wrath. Because it is an outrage against the human community, wrath is counted among the seven "deadly" sins (Gregory the Great, *Magna moralia* 31, 45; Thomas Aquinas, *ST* Ia IIae, q. 84, a 4).

Contemporary theological thinking on violence is concentrated in several areas. 1) An awareness that sexual crimes have more to do with wrath than desire has made it possible to study the relations between "sexualized violence" and the systemic violence practiced against women and minorities. 2) The fact of the Holocaust, which arose in a nominally Christian culture, has reinforced the challenges already brought to an officially non-violent Christianity (Nietzsche). Furthermore, by forcing a deeper consideration of the essential or inessential status of violence in Christianity, these challenges have given rise to renewed analyses of the theory of redemption (R. Girard), as well as numerous reconstructions of the relations of Jesus* and his "movement" to politics (Yoder, Schuessler-Fiorenza). 3) Theological study is inevitably subject to the influence of the increasingly common thesis that all order is equivalent to violence (Derrida), or inextricably linked to it. Thus, Arendt (1963) observes that political liberty requires violence to establish itself, while Levinas asserts (1984) that ethics* emerges when I realize that the *Da* of my *Dasein* is but a violent usurpation of the place of my fellow human being. Even if these viewpoints echo Christian themes, they leave a crucial theological question unanswered: is it possible to conceive of a restoration of a true (therefore non-violent) order that saves human beings from violence, or is salvation* only thinkable in terms of a flight from the net of an order that must remain intrinsically violent? Weil has said that the fundamental human choice is between violence and the dialogue of those who live in community (*Logique de la philosophie,* Paris, 2nd Ed. 1974). The contribution of Christianity to this debate lies perhaps in the rediscovery and articulation of a concept of power that brings into play order and charity in total compatibility. And since the churches* do not possess order without having to possess a right (even if it is a "right of grace*," H. Dombois), the question of a strict repudiation of all violence in ecclesial use of power and force cannot fail to be urgently significant amid the everyday concerns of Christian life.

● C.N. Cochrane (1940), *Christianity and Classical Culture,* Oxford (Revised Ed. 1944).

P.L. Landsberg (1951), *Essai sur l'expérience de la mort,* Paris (2nd Ed. 1993).
H. Arendt (1963), *On Revolution,* Harmondsworth, 59–114.
J. Derrida (1967), "Violence et métaphysique," in *L'écriture et la différence,* Paris, 117–228.
J.H. Yoder (1972), *The Politics of Jesus,* Grand Rapids.
R. Girard (1978), *Des choses cachées depuis la fondation du monde,* Paris.
S. Hauerwas (1983), *The Peaceable Kingdom,* Notre Dame, IN.
E. Schuessler-Fiorenza (1983), *In Memory of Her: A Feminist Theological Reconstruction of Christian Origins,* New York.
E. Levinas (1984), *Justifications de l'éthique,* Brussels.
J.G. Williams (1991), *The Bible, Violence and the Sacred,* San Francisco.
G. Pontara (1996), "Violence," *DEPhM,* 1,597–1,601.

Thomas E. Breidenthal

See also **Death; Peace; War**

Virgin Birth. *See* **Mary**

Virtues

Virtue is an admirable or praiseworthy trait of character*. Different societies identify certain virtues as being especially important or desirable, and link particular configurations of virtues and vices to specific social roles. These traditions provide the starting point for much of the systematic moral reflection.

1. Virtues in Antiquity

For Plato and Aristotle, the question was what counts as true virtue. According to Plato, virtue is essentially insight into what is truly good (*Meno* 81a–e; *Laws* 643b–44c). This knowledge enables the individual who possesses it to act appropriately, because through it he is able to bring the different components of his soul* into a proper relationship. Because the virtues are forms of knowledge, they are essentially one (*Phaedo* 67c–70a); subsequently, this was known as the unity of the virtues.

Aristotle grounds his account of the virtues in a philosophical view of human flourishing, in terms of which he systematized popular accounts of the virtues and developed criteria for distinguishing true virtues from their similitudes. Virtue should be distinguished from both passions* and faculties; virtue is a hexis—that is to say, an enduring state of character—which consistently produces certain kinds of action, characterized by the right mean: a virtue is a "midpoint." This does not refer to an intermediate state between extremes of feeling, but an appropriate balance among competing claims, as determined by practical wisdom*, or prudence* (*NE* 2, 1106b 35–07a 25). All the virtues are connected, because they reflect the judgments of practical wisdom, but they are nonetheless distinct qualities (*NE* 6, 1144b 30–45a 6). Thus, Aristotle defends the connection of the virtues, but not their unity in Plato's sense.

Although the theories of virtue offered by the Stoics differ in some respects, they generally agree that the basis of virtue lies in the intention* to act in accordance with reason*. They have been criticized for promoting detachment and a lack of feeling as ideals of virtue. However, closer examination suggests that they reject, not emotion as such, but excessive or inappropriate passions that are contrary to reason.

2. The Christian Conception of Virtue

a) The New Testament. The earliest Christian writings contain very little systematic reflection on the virtues, but they do reflect the influence of the popular ideals of the time. In particular, the so-called "housetable codes," or lists of the virtues appropriate to the different members of a household (Eph 5:21, 6:9, and parallels) were probably influenced by Stoic models. However, as a result of the primacy of love in the New Testament, faith*, hope*, and love*, which Paul makes into the ideals of the Christian life (1 Cor 13:13), were considered to be of much greater importance. Subsequently, these three virtues were identified as the paradigmatic theological virtues, which are bestowed by God*, in contrast to the classical cardinal virtues, namely prudence, justice*, fortitude, and temperance, which are the highest humanly attainable virtues.

b) The Fathers and the Early Middle Ages. Considered in terms of long-term influence, the most important Christian theory of the virtues in antiquity, at least for the Latin West, was that of Augustine*, whose account combines Stoic and Neoplatonic elements with the Christian tradition of the theological virtues. Like Plato and the Stoics, Augustine argues that the virtues are all fundamentally expressions of one quality, but in his view that quality is charity (*De moribus ecclesiae catholicae*, BAug 1, 15, 25). As such, true virtue can be bestowed only by God. What characterizes charity is the ability to place all human affections in their right order, loving God above all and loving creatures only insofar as they can be referred to God. Thus, even though the seeming virtues of non-Christians are genuinely praiseworthy and beneficial to society, they are not true virtues, because they are directed toward the wrong ends (*Civ. Dei* BAug 33, 12, 14).

However, Augustine's account was perhaps less influential in the short term than the lists of vices and virtues developed by Cassian (c. 360–435) and Gregory* the Great. Cassian wrote primarily for monks (*see* monasticism*), whereas Gregory was more concerned with the laity*, but for both of them the most important task facing the Christian is to extirpate his sins*. To aid the penitent, the abbot or pastor needs some practical knowledge of the qualities that correct the vices. Thus, throughout the Middle Ages, there were at least two ways of organizing the virtues: by classifying them into cardinal virtues and theological virtues, or by contrasting them with the seven deadly sins. This helps to account for the fact that little systematic attention was given to the virtues until the 12th century. Nonetheless, pastors and preachers continued to refer to virtues and vices, together with such related topics as the gifts of the Holy* Spirit and the Beatitudes*. As a result, by the time Scholasticism* emerged, there was a considerable tradition that invited reflection and analysis.

c) Thomas Aquinas. It is often assumed that Thomas* Aquinas's analysis of virtue follows Aristotle's in every respect, except where he adds distinctively theological claims. This assumption is increasingly criticized today, for the structure of Aquinas's treatise on the virtues (*ST* Ia IIae, q. 49–67) is very different from Aristotle's. Furthermore, Aquinas takes Augustine's definition of virtue, rather than Aristotle's, to be paradigmatic, and develops his own account in the context of a Neoplatonic conception of the good*, as mediated through Augustine, Pseudo-Dionysius*, and a number of other patristic sources. At the same time, Aquinas's account, like Aristotle's, is developed within the framework of a carefully elaborated psychology that draws heavily on Aristotelian elements.

Aquinas follows Aristotle in holding that the virtues are semi-permanent dispositions of the intellect, will, and passions, which incline a person to act in some way (Ia IIae, q. 55, a. 1). In other words, a virtue is a *habitus*. However, it is misleading to translate this as "habit," since it should not be understood as a tendency to act in a stereotypical and unreflective way. These dispositions are necessary for a rational creature to be capable of action; for example, one's linguistic capacities must be qualified by proficiency in a language if one is to be able to speak (Ia IIae, q. 49, a. 4). So understood, the virtues include intellectual as well as practical capabilities (Ia IIae, q. 56, a. 3; q. 57, a. 1; q. 58, a. 3). Such virtues are morally neutral, although they are good in the sense of being perfections of the agent. However, those virtues that shape the passions and the will—and the intellect insofar as it is practically oriented—are necessarily moral (Ia IIae, q. 58, a. 1). Because these faculties are distinct, each has its distinctive virtue. Prudence enables the agent to choose in accordance with the good; justice orients the will toward the common good; and temperance and fortitude shape the passions in such a way that the agent desires what is truly in accordance with the good, and is prepared to resist obstacles to attaining it (Ia IIae, q. 59, a. 2; q. 60, a. 3–5). In this way, Aquinas incorporates the traditional schema of the four cardinal virtues into his moral psychology.

Despite his very broad definition of virtue, Aquinas insists that only moral virtue, in its perfect form, can lead to actions that are good without qualification (Ia IIae, q. 65, a. 1). Not only will acts of perfect virtue be good in every respect, they will also be done for the right reasons, that is, out of accurate knowledge of, and abiding desire for, the true human good. Thus, Aquinas takes Augustine's definition of virtue, rather than Aristotle's, to be paradigmatic: "Virtue is a good quality of the mind, by which we live righteously, of which no one can make bad use, and which God brings about in us without us" (Ia IIae, q. 55, a. 4).

The last clause, Aquinas adds, applies only to the "infused" virtues, which God bestows on us without action on our part (see Ia IIae, q. 63, a. 2). These virtues have union with God as their direct or indirect aim, in contrast to the "acquired" virtues, which are directed toward the attainment of the human good as discerned by reason. As such, the infused virtues include not only the theological virtues, but also forms of the cardinal virtues, which are specifically different from their acquired counterparts because they are directed toward a different end (Ia IIae, q. 63, a. 3, 4). No one can attain salvation* without the infused virtues, both theological and cardinal, but those virtues that are acquired by human effort, and that aim toward human well-being, are genuinely good, albeit in a limited way (Ia IIae, q. 62, a. 1, 2).

3. Modern and Contemporary Theology

a) Vicissitudes of the Notion of Virtue. Philosophers and theologians continued to discuss virtue until practically the end of the 18th century (*see* Jeremy Taylor 1613–67, *Holy Living,* in *Whole Works* IV, London 1822, or Jonathan Edwards*, *Charity and its Fruits,* in *Works* VIII, New Haven 1989). After this period, however, Kantianism and utilitarianism* came to dominate moral philosophy*, and interest in the idea of virtue faded, whether because the ideal of individual autonomy rendered it incomprehensible, or because the traditional discourse on the virtues seemed too simple to modern minds.

Then things began to change. Elizabeth Anscombe, for example, argues (1958) that, since the idea of a moral law* makes no sense, now that most educated persons have rejected the idea of a divine legislator, we should revive moral philosophy on the basis of an Aristotelian account of the virtues. Alasdair MacIntyre argues (1981) that contemporary morality is made up

merely of fragmentary survivals from earlier traditions, and for that reason it is impossible to define the principles of any ethics*. In MacIntyre's view, coherence in moral discourse requires the context of a particular tradition*, which is given concrete content by the virtues that it commends and the vices that it rejects *(After Virtue).* P. Foot and P. Geach have also helped to introduce the virtues onto the agenda of contemporary moral philosophy.

There has since been continual discussion of virtue and related topics, including character*, judgment, and the moral significance of the emotions. There have been many lively critiques of the moral ideas of industrial societies. Other advocates of the ethics of virtue have preferred to criticize the incoherence of moral theories, rather than attack the difficulties inherent in the general concept of morality. According to these "antitheorists," the modern conception of moral theory can offer us nothing, and should be abandoned in favor of the notion of virtue and related concepts. For some of them, reflection on the virtues offers a way to acknowledge the irreducible pluralism of contemporary moral values. Others seek within the ethics of virtue a means to escape from modern procedural ethics, often by making themselves the defenders of an Aristotelian conception of prudential judgment.

Christian ethics has also been renewed by a return to the idea of virtue. Protestants, whose conceptions generally owe a great deal to MacIntyre, focus in particular on the virtues that are distinctive to the Christian community, as that is shaped by the fundamental narratives* of Scripture*. Within Catholicism*, the Thomist revival of the first half of the 20th century has permitted a new understanding of Aquinas's moral theology and his treatment of the theological virtues. This work has been one of the sources for the contemporary renewal of Catholic moral theology.

b) Current Issues. Questions of meaning are at the forefront today. What do we mean by "virtue," and how is the concept of virtue related to such notions as habit and disposition? It does not seem that specific virtues are tied to particular kinds of action (in such a way that there are determinate acts that are always associated with, or are always contrary to, specific virtues). Yet, if that is so, the way in which specific virtues are conceptualized is not clear.

One of the main issues concerns the role of moral rules in virtue. No one is willing to reduce virtue to obedience to rules, but there is considerable debate over how their relationship is to be understood. For some, such rules are at best rough guidelines that can and should be supplanted by prudential judgment as soon as one has sufficient practical wisdom. Others are willing to allow an independent place for obedience to rules in the moral life, although such obedience is linked to specific virtues such as justice or conscientiousness. For still others, moral rules foster practices that themselves foster the virtues. This issue has been of special interest in moral theology, since it may be thought that the ethics of virtue might offer a way out of the debate between traditionalists and advocates of proportionalism* over the force of moral norms.

● M. Scheler (1915), "Zur Rehabilitierung der Tügend," in *Vom Umsturz der Werte*, GW 3, Berne, 1950, 16–31.
V. Jankélévitch (1949), *Traité des vertus*, Paris.
J. Pieper (1949a), *Traktat über die Klugheit*, Munich.
J. Pieper (1949b), *Zucht und Maß*, Munich.
J. Pieper (1954), *Über die Gerechtigkeit*, Munich.
G. E. M. Anscombe (1958), "Modern Moral Philosophy," in *Collected Philosophical Papers* 3, Oxford, 1981, 26–42.
J. Pieper (1959), *Vom Sinn der Tapferkeit*, Munich (Trans. as *The Four Cardinal Virtues*, Notre Dame, IN, 1965).
S. Hauerwas (1974), *Vision and Virtues*, Notre Dame, IN.

P. T. Geach (1977), *The Virtues*, Cambridge.
P. Foot (1978), *Virtues and Vices and Other Essays in Moral Philosophy*, Oxford.
A. MacIntyre (1981), *After Virtue*, London.
G. Meilander (1984), *The Theory and Practice of Virtue*, Notre Dame, IN.
B. Häring (1986), *Timely and Untimely Virtues*, Slough.
M. Colish (1990), *The Stoic Tradition from Antiquity to the Early Middle Ages*, Leyden.
J. B. Schneewind (1990), "The misfortunes of virtue," *Ethics* 101, 42–63.
R. Cessario (1991), *The Moral Virtues and Theological Ethics*, Notre Dame, IN.
G. S. Harak (1993), *Virtuous Passions*, Mahwah, NJ.
Konrad Stock (1995), *Grundlegung der protestantischen Tugendlehre*, Gütersloh.
N. J. H. Dent (1996), "Vertu," *DEPhM*, 1,571–78.

JEAN PORTER

See also **Aristotelianism, Christian; Character; Ethics; Kant, Immanuel; Platonism, Christian; Stoicism, Christian; Thomism**

Vision, Beatific

The Beatific Vision *(visio beatifica)* refers to the act of understanding by which the blessed will know God* clearly and directly "face to face" (1 Cor 13:12). Since this expression seems to neglect the realism of the resurrection* and the cosmic aspect of eschatology*, its scriptural roots must be remembered before its theological elaborations are shown, and before asking how the vision of God "as he is" (1 Jn 3:2) harmonizes with his radical invisibility (1 Tm 6:16), for, "God, no one has ever seen him" (1 Jn 4:12; *see* Ex 33:20–23).

1. Biblical Foundations

a) In *Paul*, the term "knowledge" *(gnôsis)* plays a major role in the account of eschatological hope*: "We see at present in a mirror, like an enigma, but then it will be face to face *[tode de prosôpon pros prosôpon]*. At present my knowledge is limited, then I shall know as I am known *[tode de epignôsomai katôs epegnôsthen]*" (1 Cor 13:12). Paul extends his thought on a vision of God, described in the tradition of Israel* as a

vision "face to face" (Gn 32:24–30; Ex 33:11, 34:29; Dt 34:10; Ps 23:4; Mt 18:10, Rev 22:4).

Faith* in the resurrection had become spiritualized since the intertestamentary period, when the vision of God came to be understood as the essential element of happiness. Job 19:25ff. is translated by the Vulgate: "For I know that my Redeemer lives and at the last he will stand upon the Earth. And after my skin has thus been destroyed, yet in my flesh I shall see God, whom I shall see for myself and my eyes shall behold and not another." Similarly, Hosea 6:3 is understood in this sense by the Septuagint, which translates: "On the third day, we shall rise again, we shall live before him and we shall know the Lord."

b) For John the evangelist, knowledge is an essential element in the realization of the promised happiness. In the priestly prayer, Jesus says to his Father: "Life eternal is that they know you, the only true God, and the one you sent, Jesus Christ" (Jn 17:3); this knowledge will be fulfilled in the vision of God: "At the time of the [eschatological] display, we shall be like him [God], because we shall see him as he is *[katôs estin]*" (1 Jn 3:2).

c) The intellectual aspect is present in the symbol of light, associated with the light of life, to tell about the new existence of the children of God, to the point that this light can encompass the whole eschatology. Judgment is the throwing of light on what was hidden; the reward is a flowering in the light of good*; condemnation is the manifestation of evil*. The image can also serve to tell about purification. Thus, Eastern theology* (which does not mention purgatory*) explains through the symbolism of light all that has been said about what lies beyond death*, without needing to specify places in order to evoke the state of those souls which are on the way toward the Beatific Vision (see Congar 1951).

2. Patristic Developments

a) Heirs to the disagreement between the hope of the vision of God and the affirmation of the invisibility and incomprehensibility of God, the first Fathers* stressed the mediation of the Word* made flesh (Clement of Rome [c. 90], *1st Epistle* 59, 2; 36, 2; *2nd Epistle,* 6, 6). Refuting the Gnostic temptation, Irenaeus* of Lyons (c. 130–202) favored the term "vision" to tell of the Christian condition (*Adversus Haereses* IV, 20, 7) and stressed both the Trinitarian aspect of the present Christian life and its flowering in eschatology (ibid., V, 8, 1). Clement of Alexandria (150–211; *see* School of Alexandria*) insisted on the value of a "gnose" [knowledge] which ends with the contemplation* of God beyond the current vicissitudes (*Stromata* 6:12; 7:10). According to Origen* (185–255), eternal life is a knowledge *(gnosis)* that is realized through the soul*'s close bond with God (Commentary on John 1, XVI, §92; *De Principiis* II, XI, 3 and 7).

b) In the circle of influence of Neoplatonism, the Cappadocians emphasized the contemplative aspect of union with God. Gregory* of Nyssa (c. 331–94) showed the way to knowledge of God *(theognôsia)* by which, like Moses on the mountain *(De Vita Moysis),* the believer arrived at the summit of contemplation. What cannot be acquired except in a limited and fragmentary way will be acquired definitively in eternal life, when nothing will be able to separate the soul from God. For the Cappadocians, contemplation is tied to Trinitarian theology, with varying degrees of emphasis; Gregory of Nyssa favored contact with the *Logos*, while Basil* of Caesarea (330–79) emphasized the role of the Holy* Spirit (*De Spiritu Sancto* IX, 22).

c) In the West, Ambrose of Milan (339–98) transmitted the Eastern doctrine. Augustine (354–430) favored desire and the emotional aspect of charity (*Confessions, X*). Desire is assuaged by the possession of God known and loved, and happiness lies in the joy that springs from the truth* (see *Confessions* x, XXXIII, 33–34). The climate of the possession of the truth remains affected by the primacy of love* (*see* "the ecstasy of Ostia," *Confessions,* IX, X, 24).

d) Opposing Eunomius, who claimed that God was knowable through natural reason* in the same way as he knows himself, and in order to protect the notion of God's transcendence, Theodoretus of Cyrus (393–466) and John Chrysostom* (344–407), the latter in his *De Incomprehensibili,* distinguish between the vision of glory and the vision of the essence of God.

This distinction would give rise to Hesychasm*, developed in monastic circles and founded on the works circulated under the name of Symeon the New Theologian (949–1022) concerning the Light of Mount Tabor. To protect the contemplative Hesychastic tradition, Gregory* Palamas (1296–1359) would develop a patristic distinction between the inaccessible divine essence and the energy to be found in the radiation of his glory, a doctrine which has become traditional in the East but has been rejected in the West. It has analogies with the Talmudic distinction between *shekînâh* and *kabâd,* God's majesty and his dazzling presence.

3. Theological Questions and Scholastic Solutions

Faithful to its patristic sources, Scholastic theology favored the vision of God in its meaning of eternal happiness.

a) Acknowledging that vision is first of all a sensory act in life, Thomas* Aquinas (1225–74) agreed that by extension the term meant all knowledge. Knowledge through vision is superior to any other, because it is a direct contact with the object. It puts into the shade conceptual or symbolic mediations and the processes of abstraction or reason. The immediacy of vision presumes that one recognizes the presence of God, who no longer lets himself be known in an indirect but in a direct way (Saint Thomas 1a, q. 12; *CG* III, 50–63).

The notion of vision is extended to its strongest meaning. It is a question of a clear and manifest knowledge of God, in the sense that the manifestation of God neither dazzles nor blinds. Such a vision is therefore proper to the blessed—which excludes all reality in the present time. Mystical experience is not identical to vision. This attitude gives priority to knowledge and therefore the act of intelligence, which has priority over the other component elements of beatitude*: love, union, and joy. For this reason, there is a difference between the theology of Thomas Aquinas and that of Bonaventure (1218–74), which remains very close to Augustine's formulation.

b) The theology of the Beatific Vision is based on three questions.

1) Can the human soul attain to the vision of God? For one thing, "no one has ever seen God" (Jn 18), invisible by nature, "inhabitant of an inaccessible light" (1 Tm 6:16); for another, the human mind can only attain God through the mediation of reason, that is, through analogy* (Wis 13:1; Rom 1:21). Since God infinitely surpasses all creaturely conditions of being and functioning, he could not be accurately represented in a human mind by an intelligible form corresponding to his own conditions of being and functioning. Therefore the affirmation of the Beatific Vision is indissolubly linked to the theology of grace* or of divinization or deification, that is, to the transformation of the capacity to know and to love by means of participation in the divine nature (*hina genesthe theias koinônoi phuseôs,* 2 Pt 1:4).

Is such a transformation possible without the destruction of human nature? Theology answers affirmatively because the human mind is open to the infinite. The human mind is capable of acceding to the whole being, to *being* in its full scope. This ability makes it capable of receiving something more than what is naturally possible. Scholastic theology specified this point by using the idea of obediential power, a power of being passive when faced with an initiative that comes from elsewhere. Scholastic theology distinguishes between the proper object and the appropriate object of human intelligence. The proper object is the essence of beings reached through abstraction, and the appropriate object, the being of existents. This distinction makes it possible to acknowledge the natural desire to see God (*ST* 1a IIae, q. 3, a 2).

2) The second question is how the Beatific Vision is brought about. By essence, God is inaccessible; since he is by nature invisible, he cannot be grasped in a sensory way. Therefore, God gives himself in a new way, which is neither a theophany* nor an incarnation*, but a heightening of the intelligence. The vision is created outside of the senses and the imagination through an act of an intelligence raised so as to participate in the divine life (Thomas Aquinas, *In Sent.,* IV, d. 49,

q. 2, a.1; Debated question, *de Veritate,* q. 8, q.1; *CG* III, 51; *ST* Ia, q. 12, a. 5 and 9). This elevation of the intelligence is made possible by a gift of God, which theology has synthesized around the notion of the light of glory *(lumen gloriae).* God is presented as light; he is the subsisting truth, sovereignly intelligible in itself. The light of glory represents a participation in the uncreated light, which raises the intelligence as far as the divine light and prepares it for the Beatific Vision.

The existence of this created light is founded on the Scriptures, in Psalm 35: "In thy light we shall see the light" (v. 10). This line, which was given a Trinitarian interpretation by the Fathers (Basil of Caesarea, *De Spiritu Sancto* XVIII, 47), was given a psychological interpretation by Thomas Aquinas and his commentators: it signified the elevation of an intelligence that was rendered capable of seeing God. In human knowledge there are mediations—indispensable images. Now, there is no image capable of suitably representing the essence of God, for every image is finite and limited. But here the divine essence plays the role of noetic mediations. In the light, which is God himself, the blessed see the essence of God; through God's mediation the vision of God himself is possible.

Because of this light, human intelligence is capable of seeing God. The light of glory raises the intelligence from the natural to the supernatural level; it disposes the intelligence toward union with God and it cooperates in the act of vision. This gift verifies what is said about grace in general, a vital act of the elevated human mind. It is not inert passivity but an act in which the natural intelligence is perfected. In fact it receives an extra force and virtue, a special union with the uncreated light and the fulfillment of faith. This question concerns the supernatural* (Lubac* 1946).

3) The third question is about the object of vision. Is God seen in a comprehensive way? Is there not only a real grasp of the truth but also a global and total penetration? On this point, Latin theology diverges from Eastern theology, which distinguishes between the glory of God and his nature (Gregory* of Nazianzus, John Chrysostom, and Theodoretus of Cyrus), a tradition developed in Orthodox mysticism* (*see* Meyendorff 1959).

Western theologians have rejected that distinction between God's glory and his nature, such as it was introduced by Almaric de Bene. For Scholastic theology, the Beatific Vision gives knowledge of God's nature or essence. Thus, God is seen completely, but not totally *(totus Deus sed non totaliter);* a distinction is made between vision and understanding. God is seen in all that he is; it is therefore a true knowledge of God. But God is not encountered in a way that exhausts all possible knowledge. God is not seen to the extent that he is visible; but it really is him who is seen. God is known as infinite* being, but knowledge of him remains human, characterized by the finite; it is not infinite.

The interpretation of the medieval doctrine gave rise to controversies based on the theses of Baius (1513–89), according to whom the desire to see God might have been natural and effective for man before the original fall. Thomas Aquinas's commentators (Bañez [1528–1604] and John of Saint-Thomas [1589–1644]) restrict themselves to speaking about obediential power and, following Cajetan (1468–1534), maintain a strict separation between the natural and the supernatural order. This interpretation has been criticized by the moderns (see Lubac 1946, 1965; Laporta 1965).

4. Beatitude and Life Eternal

The theology of Gregory* Palamas, founded on the question of the light of Tabor, opens out onto questions of the supernatural, of divinization through grace, and of glory. For Palamas the divine energy is uncreated; through this energy all Christians become participants in the divine nature. For that to happen, an elevation of the natural faculties is required. This elevation is itself an uncreated divine operation, and therefore divinization produces nothing created in the deified soul. The Western theology of grace as entitative *habitus* is unknown in the East, where the balance between the affirmation of the reality of the vision and its beatifying nature is not organized in the same way.

These controversies led the Roman Magisterium* to intervene in the matter of the Beatific Vision. The Council of Vienne* (1331) condemned the doctrine of the Beghards (and Beguines), who asserted that here below the just could already attain final beatitude and know God (DS 474–75). Pope Benedict XII (1334–42) condemned the position attributed to the Armenians, who separated God's essence from his manifestation. In addition, in the Constitution *Benedictus Deus* (23 January 1336), Benedict XII corrected the preaching of his predecessor; he specified that the blessed enjoy the vision of God from the moment of their death, a doctrine adopted at the Council of Florence (*DS* 693).

Although the Magisterium's definitions free us from certain equivocal statements, linked to Millenarianism* and the vagueness of the theology of purgatory, they raise fundamental anthropological questions—

particularly the fact that the vision has absolutely no need of the body's participation. This spiritualistic conception is in disagreement with biblical anthropology*. In effect, Scholastic theology does not mention the corporeal and emotional aspects of beatitude except as the effects of the vision of God in the transfigured affectivity and corporeality at the time of the Last Judgment; and this does not respect the dynamism of the biblical texts, in which the human person cannot not be reduced to its intellectual dimension. For that reason, the notion of the intuitive or beatific Vision, being too reliant on a spiritualistic anthropology, is not at the forefront of revisions of Christian eschatology in 20th-century works which base themselves on a better knowledge of the Scriptures (O. Cullmann) and on the central place of faith in the resurrection (Rahner, Pannenberg, Moltmann, Kasper, Martelet, Moingt).

The theological idea of vision might be renewed under the influence of modern philosophical debates about intuition, providing an opportunity to stress the mind's transcendence in relation to cognitive processes identified with the exercise of reason (H. Bergson, J. Maritain). The aesthetic aspects of revelation are better served by such an approach (H. U. von Balthasar*).

The phenomenological study of vision (M. Merleau-Ponty) plays a role in theology, for it stresses the importance of alterity (P. Ricoeur, E. Levinas); it makes it possible to give Christian mysticism a non-fusional aspect that respects human freedom, and to augment the distinction between God and the one who contemplates him. Similarly, the rise of psychoanalysis and the importance of the theme of desire renew the debate about the desire to see God (D. Vasse 1969).

Vatican* II's revisions have given a new sense to the communal dimension of beatitude: "Receive the [dead] in your kingdom where we hope to be fulfilled by your glory, all together and for ever, when you will wipe away every tear from our eyes; when we see you, you our God, such as you are, we shall be like you eternally, and without end we shall sing your praises, through Christ our Lord" (Eucharistic Prayer no. 3).

Such a wording links up again with the concern to inscribe the vision of God in the life of the Trinity, a concern previously expressed by the Fathers (see Irenaeus of Lyons, *Adversus Haereses* v, 8, 1) and explored by the mystics (in the Rhineland*-Flemish tradition in particular).

● A. Michel (1923), "Intuitive (vision)," *DThC* 7, 2351–94.
H. de Lubac (1946), *Surnaturel,* Paris.
G. Bardy (1948), "Béatitude," *Cath* 1, 1342–55.
J. Dupont (1949), *Gnosis: la connaissance religieuse dans les épîtres de saint Paul,* Paris-Louvain.
Y. Congar (1951), "Le purgatoire," in Coll., *Le mystère de la mort et sa célébration,* LO 12, 279–336.

C. H. Dodd (1953), *The Interpretation of the Fourth Gospel*, Cambridge.

J. Daniélou (1954), *Platonisme et théologie mystique*, Paris.

O. Cullmann (1956), *Immortalité de l'âme ou résurrection des morts? Le témoignage du Nouveau Testament*, Neuchâtel.

J. Meyendorff (1959), *Saint Grégoire Palamas et la mystique orthodoxe*, Paris.

Vl. Lossky (1962), *Vision de Dieu*, Paris.

J. Laporta (1965), *La destinée de la nature humaine selon Thomas d'Aquin*, Paris.

H. de Lubac (1965), *Augustinisme et théologie moderne*, Paris.

D. Vasse (1969), *Le temps du désir*, Paris.

Ton H. C. van Eilk (1974), *La résurrection des morts chez les Pères apostoliques*, ThH 25.

G. Martelet (1975), *L'au-delà retrouvé*, Paris (2nd Ed. 1995).

Ch. Trottmann (1995), *La vision béatifique: Des disputes scolastiques à sa définition par Benoît XII*, Rome.

JEAN-MICHEL MALDAMÉ

See also **Beatitude; Eschatology; Eternity of God; Life, Eternal; Resurrection of the Dead**

Vitoria. *See* Thomism

Voluntarism

1. Definition

"Voluntarism" made its appearance in the historiography of the Latin Middle Ages at the end of the nineteenth century, as an antonym of "intellectualism." It is a concept made up by commentators, however, and does not appear in texts. It is used to designate different theses that draw from a common inspiration: the affirmation of the primacy of will over the intellect.

2. Timeframe

The most propitious time for the application of the concept was the Latin Scholasticism* of the 13th and 14th centuries. The polemics that sprang up at the end of the 13th century, especially those opposing Franciscans and Dominicans, clearly presented the alternative, which had been latent, of the primacy of the intellect or the will. The Franciscan thought (Bonaventure*, Duns* Scotus) was then mainly voluntarist, in opposition to the intellectualism of the Dominicans (Albert* the Great, Thomas* Aquinas, Thomism*, naturalism*). This voluntarism continued in the nominalist trend of the 14th century, notably with the Franciscans William of Ockham and Gabriel Biel (nominalism*). These controversies arose in a climate of opposition to Aquinas's thought, which was evidenced by the condemnations of 1277, in Paris as well as in Oxford. It was also made clear in the "Correctorium Fratris Thomae" by the Franciscan William de la Mare, a work that the general chapter of Minors imposed in 1282 as a necessary supplement to all readings of the *Summa Theologica* in the Franciscan Order. In fact, this correctorium opposed Thomas Aquinas's intellectualist theses. Also witness to the opposition of the two orders on this subject was the dispute that opposed—directly or indirectly—Meister Eckhart and Gonzales of Spain around 1302 (*Quaestio Magistri Gonsalvi continens rationes magistri Echardi utrum laus Dei in patria sit nobilior eius dilectione in via?*).

3. The Spirit of Medieval Voluntarism

Thomas Aquinas was the preferred target of voluntarism, but it is more the influence of Greco-Arabic peripatetism on Latin Christian thought—particularly strong in the 13th century—that was attacked through his intellectualism. Voluntarism established itself especially in reaction to the theological adaptation of Aristotle's *Nicomachean Ethics*, carried out during the 13th century. This adaptation took two forms. Either

Aristotle's theoretic happiness was assimilated with the supernatural beatitude* of Christians and placed outside the reach of man's natural faculties (such as, at the faculty of arts, of pseudo-Peckham's and Arnoul of Provence's commentary of *The Nicomachean Ethics*). Or, Aristotelian happiness and Christian beatitude, while remaining distinct, were thought of on the same model; both mostly concerning the intellect, and both essentially consisting in the knowledge of God*. Philosophical happiness, however, was nothing but an imperfect beatitude: the difference resided in the obtaining (grace* is necessary for beatitude) and in the type of knowledge of God that was reached ("in a mirror" or "face to face"). This perspective, that of Thomas Aquinas, of Boethius of Dacia, and of Masters of Arts such as Gilles of Orleans and Peter of Auvergne, was linked to the declaration of the will's inferiority to the intellect. The supreme perfection of man must principally concern his most noble faculty.

Voluntarism denounced the risks of such an alliance with heathen thought (philosophy*). The first risk was that of naturalism, since this alliance encouraged conceiving beatitude on the model of philosophical happiness, naturally accessible to man. On the other hand, voluntarism denounced the renewal of heathen thought in questions that brought into play that which is the most characteristic of Christian faith: beatitude and liberty*. Divine liberty, which is expressed in creation* and grace, and human liberty, which opposes ancient determinism, were threatened by intellectualism.

4. Theological Stakes

The affirmation of the primacy of the will over the intellect particularly referred to two questions: the foundation of creatures' liberty, and the nature of the beatifying process.

a) Liberty. With regard to the foundation of the liberty of creatures, voluntarism generally admitted that knowledge was a condition for acts of will, since one wouldn't desire what is not known; but it reacted against all intellectual interpretations of this dependence by stating that the intellect was not the determining cause of the specificity of the will's act. If intellect enlightened will and allowed it to determine its act, it was in the manner of a servant and not of a master. Will itself exercised the choice that decided its object (at least where completed things were concerned), and it was completely free to follow, or not, the intellect's judgment. In other words, the representation of a finished thing as a good* is not restricting for the will, and free will was based on will's indetermination, and not on judgment's. Thus, voluntarism tried to preserve the conception of will as a self-determining faculty, at

least when it came to choosing the means. In extreme forms (John Duns Scotus, *Opus Oxoniense* IV, d. 49, q. 9 and 10; and Ockham, *Quaestiones in librum quartum Sententiarum,* q. 16), voluntarism even admits that will is not determined to an end, that it can turn away from beatitude, conceived as well *in particulari* as *in universali,* and that it remains free to turn away from it up to the vision of God. The intention that inspired this theory on will is clear: it was about subtracting will from the determinism that characterizes nature.

This voluntarist concept of liberty was supported by Alexander of Hales, John of La Rochelle, Albert the Great, Bonaventure, Matthew of Aquasparta, Henry the Great, Peter John Olivi, Giles of Rome, John Duns Scotus, William of Ockham, and Gabriel Biel. It had roots in Anselm* of Canterbury (who already saw will as an *instrumentum seipsum movens—see De conceptione virginali et pecatto,* c. 4), Bernard* of Clairvaux, Hugh of Saint Victor, and Philippe le Chancelier, all of whom confirmed the independence of the will from reason* and based human liberty on this independence.

b) The Nature of the Beatifying Process. In discussing this question, diverse arguments helped establish the primacy of will over intellect. Will could be thought of as superior to the intellect, as a *power:* 1) In so much as it was a self-determining power and that it escaped natural determinism, which still somewhat subjected the intellect to its regard—which is what made the nobility of the will and based its claim of being the subject of the process through which superior creatures meet God. Also, voluntarism often relied on a comparison of "acts." 2) Respective to both will and intellect, but also in the prospect of union with God. The question then is to know which act would best unite us with its object, and whether one can think that love* transcends the limits of knowledge. Voluntarism states that the voluntary act unites us more perfectly and more immediately with God than the act of "intellection," because will is drawn toward its object as it is and not toward an object known by a finite intellect: in other words, the will's act of love goes beyond the act of "intellection" because the latter reflects more the limitations of the knowing subject than the perfection of its object—a fault that does not affect the act of will because it is linked to the object in its actual reality. Thus, voluntarism rejects the unlimited confidence that intellectualism gives to intellection.

Among the sources of the voluntarist concept of love must be mentioned Bernard of Clairvaux, to whom the formula *ubi deficit intellectus ibi proficit affectus* is attributed; William of Saint Thierry, who proclaimed the superiority of love in accessing God (since only love allows us to know God intimately); and Hugh of Saint Victor. For the beginning of the 13th century, Thomas Gallus (Thomas of Vercelli) must be named. Both relied on the writings of Pseudo-Dionysius* (for example *De divines nominibus,* c. 4).

3) The discrimination of faculties was also done from the point of view of the *habitus*: since charity is the highest form of theological *habitus,* according to Paul (1 Cor 13:13), the faculty that brought it is also the noblest, and therefore it is responsible for the superior creatures' highest operations. 4) At other times, it was from the point of view of the object that discrimination was done: either because God is desired as a good, or because good, an object of will, is seen as nobler than the real object of intellect, following a concept that can be traced back to Plotinus, for whom Good was above being and intelligence (*see* Christian Platonism*). All these reasons led to situating the beatifying act in will and not in intellection.

During the 13th and 14th centuries, the most famous supporters of this voluntarist concept of beatitude were Alexander of Hales, Matthew of Aquasparta, Richard of Middleton (Mediavilla), Henry of Gand, Giles of Rome, John Duns Scotus, William of Ockham, and Gabriel Biel. Bonaventure's case is delicate: to the extent that his mysticism* claimed the primacy of love over knowledge (*Itinerarium mentis ad Deum,* c. VII), his theory of beatitude showed a concern for considering them equal (in *IV Sent.*, d. 49, p. I, q. 5).

5. The Voluntarist Theory Applied to God

Applied to God, the notion of voluntarism principally serves to analyze the question of divine liberty. Here also, there is the concern of taking will away from any form of predetermination. In this case, however, one would not define voluntarism by the primacy of will over the intellect because the indetermination of divine will does not depend on a distinction between intellect and will in God. Quite the contrary: the voluntarist concept of the divine developed in a privileged manner among authors who rejected all distinction, including that of reason, between divine attributes*, which is perfectly clear among the nominalists of the 14th and 15th centuries and in Descartes*. The question in any case is not about the relation between will and the intellect in God, but on the relation between God and good: is the good imposed on divine will and intellect, or is it God who decides? One can measure, in such a case, what inadequacies the mention of voluntarism may have.

The most widespread expression of the idea of voluntarism applied to God consists of stating that divine action *ad extra* is not normalized by terms that would preexist divine choice: good and evil do not impose

upon divine action, but result from it. It is not because one thing is just and good that God wants it; on the contrary, it is because God wants it that the thing is good and just. Therefore, divine will is the source and the measure of good and evil, and there is no objective morality in contingent things. This is the most widespread figure of voluntarism as applied to God. In a way, the origin of this concept of values goes back to Abelard*, who had already stated, concerning the punishment inflicted on children who had died without baptism*, that it was not unjust in that it was wanted by God. The source of discrimination between good and evil is divine will, which is for us the norm of justice* (in *epist. Ad Rom.,* L. II, c. V). It remains that this statement belongs to a conception of divine action that subjects it to the principle of the better, and whose viewpoint consequently opposes voluntarism. Instead, one should search out the origin of voluntarism applied to God in John Duns Scotus, for whom the good in the domain of contingent things was also as contingent as the things themselves and came under divine will. (God, however, cannot not want his own necessary and perpetual goodness.) This form of voluntarism developed next with the nominalism of the 14th and 15th centuries, in solidarity with the negation of all distinction other than the real: the lack of distinction between divine intelligence and divine will guaranteed that will was not subjected to any rule external to itself. For William of Ockham, Gabriel Biel, and John Gerson, this independence resided in the fact that divine will was not determined with the just and good; on the contrary, it is what God wants that defines the just and the good, divine will having no other rule but itself. William of Ockham stretched this thesis up to its extreme consequences when he claimed that, *de potentia absoluta,* God could have commanded man to hate him, which would have made this act a right act, even meritory (in *I Sent.,* d. 17, q. 3, a. 5). The theory reappeared with Descartes, who stated that good was as such because God wanted it.

The same inspiration is at the heart of a concept of omnipotence according to which divine thought and action are not subjected to a possible that would precede them, nor even to the principle of contradiction. Far from bowing to an intelligible object and to principles of intelligibility, divine omnipotence* is their source. This conception, much less widespread than the previous concept of voluntarism and still more improperly called "voluntarism," blossomed in the Cartesian theory of the creation of eternal truths, but it was already furtively supported at the beginning of the 13th century by the Dominican Hugh of Saint Cher.

●Abelard, *In epistolam ad Romanos,* l. II, c. V, PL 178, 869.
Anselm, *De libertate arbitrii,* Schmitt I, 201–26; *De conceptu virginali et originali peccato,* Schmitt II, 135–73; *De con-*

cordia praescientiae et praedestinationis et gratiae Dei cum libero arbitrio, Schmitt II, 243–88.

Bernard de Clairvaux, *De gratia et libero arbitrio,* c. II, 3–4, and *De diligendo Deo,* PL 182, 1003–4 and 974–1000.

Bonaventure, *Sent.* II, d. 25; d. 23, a. 2; IV, d. 49, *Opera omnia,* vol. 2 and 4, Quaracchi, 1882–1902; *Itinerarium mentis in Deum,* c. VII, trans. H. Duméry, Paris, 1967, 100–7.

Descartes, *Lettres à Mersenne de 1630: Réponses aux sixièmes objections; Lettre à Mesland du 2 mai 1644,* A-T, I, 135–54; VII, 431–33; and IV, 110–20.

Duns Scotus, *Sent.* II, d. 25; *Sent.* IV, d. 49, particularly q. 4, q. *ex latere* (*post.* q. 4), q. 9, q. 10, *Opera omnia,* Ed. Wadding, vol. 13 and 21, Paris, 1893, 1894 (Repr. Hildesheim 1968).

Gabriel Biel, *Collectorium circa quatuor libros Sententiarum,* New York, 1977–84.

Jean Gerson, *Contra vanam curiositatem, De vita spirituali animae, De consolatione theologiae,* in *OC,* Paris, 1960–73.

Gilles de Rome, *Quodlibeta* I, q. 19; III, q. 15–16; IV, q. 21, Frankfurt, 1966; *Sent.* III, d. 14, a. 3; IV, d. 49, Rome, 1623.

P. Glorieux, *Les premières polémiques thomistes: I. Le correctorium corruptorii "quare,"* Kain, 1927; *II. Le correctorium corruptorii "sciendum",* Paris, 1956.

William of Ockham, *Opera theologica,* vols. I-VII, esp. *In I Sent.,* d. 1, q. 1, q. 4, q. 6; *In III Sent.,* q. 12, q. 20; *In IV Sent.,* q. 16, New York, 1967–86.

William of Saint-Thierry, *De contemplando Deo,* c. VIII, and *De natura et dignitate amoris,* c. VIII, PL 184, 375–377 and 393–395; *Speculum fidei, Expositio super Cantica canticorum,* PL 180, 390–94 and 473–546.

Henri de Gand, *Quodlibeta,* Louvain, 1979–, esp. I, q. 14, 15, 16, 20; IX, q. 5–7; X, q. 9, 10, 13, 14, 15; XI, q. 6; XII, q. 26; *Summa quaestionum ordinarium,* New York, 1953 (2nd Ed.), esp. art. 49.

Hugh of Saint-Victor, *Summa sententiarum* III, 8, PL 176, 101–2; *Commentaria in hierarchiam caelestiam dionysii areopagitae* VI, PL 175, 1038 D.

Matthieu d'Aquasparta, *Quaestiones disputatae selectae,* esp. *De cognitione,* q. 9, 1903.

Peter John Olivi, *Quaestiones in secundum librum Sententiarum,* Quaracchi, 1922–26, q. 57–59.

E. Randi, *"Potentia Dei conditionata*: una questione di Ugo di Saint-Cher sull'omnipotenza divina, *In I Sent.,* d. 42, q. 1", *RSF* 39 (1984), 521–36.

Thomas of Verceil, *Extractio des Noms divins,* c. 7, in *Dionysiaca* I, Bruges, 1937, p. 206–7 and 225–26; *Commentaire du "Cantique des Cantiques,"* Paris, 1967.

♦ P. Minges (1905), "Ist Duns Skotus indeterminist?," *BG-PhMA* 5.

É. Gilson (1934), *La théologie mystique de saint Bernard,* Paris, (5th Ed. 1986), esp. Appendix V: "Notes sur Guillaume de Saint-Thierry."

J. Rohmer (1939), *La finalité morale chez les théologiens de saint Augustin à Duns Scot,* Paris.

O. Lottin (1942), *Psychologie et morale aux XIIe et XIIIe siècles,* Louvain.

J. Déchanet (1945), "*Amor ipse est intellectus:* La doctrine de l'amour-intellection chez Guillaume de Saint-Thierry", *RMAL* 1, 349–74.

A. Michel (1950), "Volontarisme," *DThC* 15/2, 3,309–22.

É. Gilson (1952), *Jean Duns Scot, introduction à ses positions fondamentales,* Paris.

F. A. Prezioso (1964), *L'evoluzione del volontarismo da Duns Scoto a Guglielmo Alnwick,* Naples.

R. Prentice (1968), "The Voluntarism of Duns Scotus, as Seen in his Comparison of the Intellect and the Will," *FrSA* 6, 63–103.

R. Macken (1975), "La volonté humaine, faculté plus élevée que l'intelligence, selon Henri de Gand," *RThAM* 42, 5–51.

R. Hissette (1977), *Enquête sur les 219 articles condamnés à Paris le 7 mars 1277,* Louvain-Paris.

J.-L. Marion (1981), *Sur la théologie blanche de Descartes,* Paris.

E. zum Brunn, Z. Kaluza, A. de Libera (1984), *Maître Eckhart à Paris: Une critique médiévale de l'ontothéologie,* studies, texts and trans., Paris.

O. Boulnois (Ed.) (1994), *La puissance et son ombre: De Pierre Lombard à Luther,* Paris.

O. Boulnois (1995), "La base et le sommet: la noblesse de la volonté selon Duns Scot," in B.C. Bazan (Ed.), *Les philosophies morales et politiques au Moyen Age,* New York-Ottawa-Toronto, 1,183–98.

F.-X. Putallaz (1995), *Insolente liberté: Controverses et condamnations au XIIIe siècle,* Fribourg-Paris.

C. Trottmann (1995), *La vision béatifique: des disputes scolastiques à sa définition par Benoît XII,* Rome.

F.-X. Putallaz (1996), *Figure Francescane alla fine del XIII secolo,* Milan.

LAURENCE RENAULT

See also **Love; Charity; Intellectualism; Liberty**

Vulgate. *See* **Translations of the Bible, Ancient**

Waldensians

The Waldensian movement appeared toward the end of the 12th century. From the outset, it claimed the freedom to live Christianity according to the model of the primitive Church* and dismissed the mores of the Catholic Church of the time. Its followers were for the most part members of the laity*. They asserted the necessity of living frugally like Christ* and the apostles*, hence the attribution to them of the name the *poor of Christ;* they were also called the *poor of Lyon* because of the geographical origin of the movement. As for the term Waldensian (in Latin *valdenses*—the word is not found in any document originating from within the community), historians have proposed two hypotheses to explain its meaning and origin. According to one, the name comes from its founder, the Lyon native Valdesius (whose name is recorded in his profession of faith* of the diocesan synod* of Lyon of 1180), or Vaudès (Gonnet 1980), or Valdès (Thouzellier 1982); the name Valdo is merely an Italian version of Vaudès or Valdès. The first name Pierre, with which it is associated from the second half of the 14th century onward (recorded in an exchange of letters between the Waldensians of Lombardy and those of Austria), reflects the intent to make a historical connection between the Waldensian movement and the apostolic age; further, the Waldensians are said from the outset to have claimed their apostolic succession*, basing it on Scripture*. All of this constitutes a Waldensian myth* that no longer has currency. The second hypothesis is based on toponymy: the adjective *valdensis* is said to mean inhabitant of the "vaudes," which designates a certain configuration of the landscape (*see* Bosio 1995).

If we follow the first hypothesis, which is the one that has most stimulated the imagination in the past, we are also forced to accept the "history" and its *topoi,* namely, that Valdesius or Vaudès was a rich merchant who one day decided to change his life. Among the numerous versions of his conversion* story, two particularly attractive ones converge on one point: poverty.

The first version relates that Vaudès was converted after hearing the legend of Saint Alexis sung by a troubadour. According to the *Golden Legend,* Alexis, son of a rich and noble Roman prefect of the fourth century, decided on his wedding night to give up the comfort of married life and to flee to Asia Minor, where he distributed all his wealth; poor with the poor, he in turn asked for charity. He later returned unwillingly to the house of his father, who did not recognize him; he thus continued to receive charity in his own home. The second version has it that Vaudès, a rich merchant with two daughters, fearing for his eternal salvation* because of his great wealth, decided to consult a theologian, who reminded him of the parable of the rich man (Luke 18:18–30). Following literally the advice given by Jesus* to distribute his wealth to the poor, Vaudès left his possessions to his wife, placed his daughters in the abbey of Fontevrault, and left his home; thereafter, "naked as the naked Christ," he set about preaching repentance, drawing after him a group of the poor of Lyon, or Waldensians. Here legend ends and history begins.

A delegation of Waldensians, probably headed by Vaudès himself, went to Rome in 1179 to ask Pope Alexander III to approve the movement. The welcome was fraternal and positive, but the following year in Lyon Vaudès had to subscribe to a profession of faith as proof of his orthodoxy. And as he did not comply with the prescriptions of canon* law prohibiting the laity from preaching without authorization, Vaudès was excommunicated by the archbishop of Lyon and banished with his disciples. The Waldensians were subsequently condemned by the Council of Verona (1184), which excommunicated them and declared them schismatics, and then by the Fourth Lateran* Council in 1215 (Gonnet, *EFV* I, 50–53 and 158–60).

These events were at the origin of the Waldensian diaspora, to which were joined a few years later the poor of Lombardy, who shared the same convictions. This diaspora, starting out from the Lyon region and from Lombardy, spread throughout continental Europe, from the Mediterranean to the Baltic and from the Alps to the Danube. "This prodigious extension of the Waldensian movement toward the east constitutes one of the major events of the thirteenth century" (Audisio). A. Molnar points out that in Bohemia from the late-14th to the early-16th century, the Hussites (*see* Hus) shared on may points—poverty, proclamation of the word of God, rejection of oath taking and of the death penalty—the world-view of the Waldensians; the Czech historian even goes so far as to speak of a "Waldensian-Hussite international," which Audisio disputes, calling it "more a project than a reality."

In France, the Waldensians reached the south, as well as Alsace and Lorraine; in Italy, they turned toward the center (Umbria, the Abruzzi) and toward the south (Calabria and Puglia), where they established agricultural settlements that survived into the middle of the 16th century despite the persecution they suffered under the Inquisition.

This expansion in space and over time led to a large variety of sociological and doctrinal characteristics from one group to another. The Waldensian movement was in fact characterized by the dynamics of the different groups that made it up, who were united by a deep desire to restore the Church to the purity of its origins. Because of all this diversity, some historians now prefer to speak of Waldensian movements in the plural, in order to show the plurality of the theological and ideological positions running through them (Merlo).

The Waldensians practiced a religious propaganda that was transmitted from person to person, in cities and in the countryside, always clandestinely because of the Inquisition. The itinerant preachers, who were called *barba* ("uncle" in Piedmontese) in the 15th and 16th centuries, were generally merchants, artisans, or peasants. Among them at the beginning were also women*, a few defrocked priests*, and a few monks. Their culture was essentially biblical. Preaching* was done in the language of the audience rather than in Latin; the ministry* of the word was carried out on the basis of translations of the Scriptures, such as the "Bibles*" of Vaudès of Lyon or the Waldensians of Metz, or the German translation of the Tepl codex.

From the point of view of "ecclesiastical organization," the Waldensian groups met once a year in general "chapters" in the various countries in which they were located. On this occasion, they would take up collections designed to ensure the subsistence of preachers and of the poor.

In the beginning, there were no notable distinctions among the members of the Waldensian brotherhood, defined in 1218 as *societas* rather than *congregatio;* later, a first division separated ministers and simple believers, then the ministers themselves were divided into bishops, elders, and deacons*: a rudimentary hierarchy of *primi inter pares* analogous to what is set out in the epistles of Paul, with at its head a *mayoralis* to whom all owed obedience.

Doctrinally, the poor of Lyon were placed in the same category as the heretics of the Middle Ages, and this was true from the time they were banished from their city of origin; this is evidenced by the general excommunication of 1215 pronounced by Lateran IV, including within a single anathema all those who, although having different faces, were linked by their tails (*see* the foxes of Jgs 15:4) because of their common aversion to "holy orthodoxy and the Catholic faith."

"Excommunicamus…et anathematizamus omnem haeresim, extollentem se adversus hanc sanctam orthodoxam et catholicam fidem…condemnantes haereticos universos, quibuscumque nominibus censeantur, facies quidem diversas habentes, sed caudas ad invicem colligatas, quia de vanitate conveniunt in id ipsum" (G. Gonnet, *EFV* I, 161): "We excommunicate…and anathematize every heresy* that rises up against this holy, orthodox, and Catholic faith, condemning all heretics, whatever name they are given, who have different faces, but tails linked to one another, for their vanity comes together in this very way."

Despite changes and adaptations, the inevitable syncretism with other heretical credos, and the numerous attempts at concealment or Nicodemism, the unchanging bases of Waldensianism stood firm on three pillars: poverty, preaching, and the Gospels. Of these "three piers" (Audisio), it was preaching that brought about the break with Rome, since the ministry of the word, for the Catholic church, could be exercised only by the clergy.

While three fundamental elements characterized the Waldensian movement at the beginning, four major attitudes ran through it throughout the late Middle Ages. In summary, they were: 1) the rejection of the hierarchical structure of the official church and its salvific power; 2) the devaluation of sacraments* celebrated by unworthy priests (Donatism*); 3) hostility toward cemeteries, buildings for worship, and even chasubles, incense, holy water, images*, and the sound of bells, as symbols of the official church; 4) the rejection of any practice or ceremony without justification in the Scriptures, particularly in the New Testament (the center of which was represented by the Sermon on the Mount), such as holidays in honor of saints or of the Virgin, processions, fasting, adoration of the cross and its symbolic representation, indulgences*, prayers for the dead, and the existence of purgatory*; more concretely, the rejection of lying, oath taking, and any act of violence*, including the death penalty. (On confession and the Eucharist*, *see* Audisio 1989.) In political and social terms, all these rejections led to the wholesale rejection of the *Constantinian status* of the church. The hostility of the Waldensians toward every form of religious or civil compromise led to their being outlawed from society until the years 1530–60. The signal of change came from the synod of Chanforan (a Piedmont village), where the leaders of the movement decided to become a church on the model of the Reformed churches. Between the formal adhesion to the Reformation (Chanforan) and the implementation of these decisions, thirty years went by, in the course of which the Waldensians changed radically. Indeed, they abandoned evangelical poverty, they accepted oath taking, they authorized private property for ministers, and they rejected confession and their other pious practices. At Chanforan, the Waldensian movement died (Audisio); the *Valdese* church, which took its place, no longer had anything in common with what Waldensianism had been: "With Chanforan in 1532 in principle, and in practice around 1560, Waldensianism died out. Practically everything that made up the religious characteristics of this dissident movement—and that defined its specificity in Europe, with respect to both the Roman Church and the Churches of the Reformation—disappeared. I repeat, religiously speaking, being a Waldensian and being Reformed is contradictory. One could only be one or the other. From this point of view, Waldensianism was drowned in the Reformation. It is appropriate to speak of death" (Audisio).

These remarks seem categorical, but Audisio ("practically everything") nevertheless leaves a gap through which one might slip in an attempt to show that being Waldensian and Reformed is not as contradictory as he claims, at least on two important points: the *sola scriptura* (the insistence that Scripture is the sole source of authority for Christian doctrine) and the assertion that Christ is the only bishop* of the Church.

Whereas Waldensian historiography from the 13th to the 15th century is essentially based on documents coming from the Inquisition, from controversy, and from chronicles, there was a flowering of confessional historiographies starting in the 16th, and particularly in the 17th century: Protestant (Miolo and Lentolo along with two anonymous writers, Perrin, Gilles, Morland, and Léger) and Catholic (Rorengo, Belvedere, and Charvaz). On both sides, the historiography took the form of apologetics.

All those who had in one way or another opposed the prerogatives of Rome before the Protestant Reformation, in the dogmatic and ecclesiastical realm or simply in matters of morals and politics, were considered as martyrs of the true faith, as *testes veritatis* (Crespin) or as *reclamatores* (Flacius Illyricus). The 18th century produced only the *Histoire des Vaudois* of Jacques Brez (1796), written along Voltairean lines with the aim of condemning all forms of religious intolerance. It was not until the late-19th century that the first scientific study of *Histoire vaudoise* appeared, in which history triumphs over mythology (Emilio Comba).

The colloquia of Aix-en-Provence (1988) and Torre Pellice (1992) illustrate the tendencies of 20th-century Waldensian historiography, situated between two extreme approaches: the first, ultra-apologetic, is represented by Giorgio Tourn, who has attempted to rehabilitate the legends about the existence of Waldensians before Vaudès himself, placing them in a schema in which the "theology* of history" is to be understood in the sense of a "theology realized in history"; the second is the approach of Gabriel Audisio, which can only be defined as nonconformist, going so far as to doubt the legitimacy of the term Waldensian, and for whom the synod of Chanforan represents the death of Waldensianism. From the religious point of view, according to him, no continuity is possible between Waldensianism before and after Chanforan. As a consequence, the *Valdese* church, which claims to be its legitimate descendant, is, in his view, anything but its heir.

● B. Gui (1926–27), *Manuel de l'inquisiteur,* 2 vols., Paris.
G. Gonnet (1958), *EFV (Critical Collection of Sources on Waldensians in the Middle Ages),* 1, Torre Pellice.
A. Patschovsky and K.-V. Selge (1973), *Quellen zur Geschichte des Waldenser,* TKTG 18.
A. Patschovsky and K.-V. Selge (1979), *Quellen zur bömischen Inquisition im 14. Jahrhundert,* Weimar.

G. Audisio (1989), *Les "Vaudois": Naissance, vie et mort d'une dissidence (XIIe–XVIe s.),* Turin (manuscript sources).

♦ G. Amati (1865), "Processus contra valdenses in Lombardia superiori, anno 1387," *ASI* 37 and 39.

P.-F. Fournier (1942), "Les Vaudois en Auvergne vers la fin du XVe siècle d'après les interrogatoires de deux barbes," *BHSA* 49–63.

A. Molnar (1964), "Les Vaudois en Bohême avant la révolution hussite," *BSSV* 116, 3–17.

C. Thouzellier (1966), *Catharisme et valdéisme en Languedoc à la fin du XIIe et au début du XIIIe siècle,* Paris.

C. Thouzellier (1967), *Vaudois languedociens et Pauvres catholiques, CFan* 2.

G. Gonnet, A. Armand-Hugon (1967), *Le confessioni di fede valdesi prima della Riforma,* Turin.

K.-V. Selge (1967 *a*), *Die ersten Waldenser,* 2 vols., Berlin.

K-V. Selge (1967 *b*), "Caractéristiques du premier mouvement v. et crises au cours de son expansion," *CFan* 2, *V. languedociens et Pauvres catholiques,* 110–42.

K.-V. Selge (1967 *c*), "Discussions sur l'apostolicité entre vaudois, catholiques et cathares," ibid., 143–62.

K.-V. Selge (1968), "Die Erforschung der mittelalterlichen Waldensergeschichte," *ThRNF* 33, 281–343.

C. Thouzellier (1969), *Hérésie et hérétiques,* Rome.

K.-V. Selge (1974), "La figura e l'opera di Valdez," *BSSV* 136, 4–25.

A. Armand-Hugon (1974), *Storia dei Valdesi,* vol. 2. *Dal sinodo di Chanforan al 1848,* Turin.

G. Gonnet and A. Molnar (1974), *Les Vaudois au Moyen Age,* Turin.

D. Kurze (1975), *Quellen zur Ketzergeschichte Brandeburgs und Pommerns,* Berlin.

G. Audisio (1979), *Le barbe et l'inquisiteur: Procès du barbe vaudois Pierre Griot par l'inquisiteur Jean de Roma,* Aix-en-Provence.

G. Gonnet (1980), "Pierre Valdo ou Vaudès de Lyon?" *BSHPF* 135, 247–50.

M. Schneider (1981), *Europäisches Waldensertum im 13. und 14. Jahrhundert,* Berlin and New York.

R. Cegna (1982), *Fede ed Etica valdese nel quattrocento,* Turin.

P. Biller (1982), "*Curate infirmos:* The Medieval Waldensian Practice of Medecine", *SCH(L)* 19, 55–77.

C. Thouzellier (1982), "Considérations sur les origines du valdéisme," *I Valdesi e l'Europa,* Torre Pellice, 3–25.

G.G. Merlo (1982), "Sul valdismo 'colto' tra il XIII e il XIV secolo", ibid., 67–98.

G. Audisio (1984), *Les Vaudois du Lubéron: Une minorité en Provence (1460–1560),* Mérindol.

G.G. Merlo (1984), *Valdesi e valdismi medievali,* Turin.

E. Cameron (1984), *The Reformation of the Heretics: The Waldenses of the Alps 1480–1580,* Oxford.

P. Biller (1985 *a*), "Medieval Waldensian Abhorrence of Killing, Pre-c. 1400," *SCH(L)* 22, 215–18; (1985 *b*), "Multum ieiunantes et se castigantes: medieval waldensian asceticism," ibid., 22, 219 *Sq.*

J. Gilmont (1987), "La publication de la Bible d'Olivétan, traducteur de la Bible," in G. Casalis and B. Roussel (Ed.), *Colloque de Noyon,* Paris.

G. Gonnet (1989), *Il grano e le zizzanie: Tra eresia e riforma (secoli XII–XVI),* Soveria Mannelli.

G.G. Merlo (1989), *Eretici ed eresie medievali,* Bologna.

G. Audisio (1990) (Ed.), *Les Vaudois des origines à leur fin (XIIe-XVIe siècles): Actes du Colloque international d'Aix-en-Provence, avril 1988,* Turin.

G.G. Merlo (1991), *Identità valdese nella storia e nella storiografia: Studi e discussioni,* Turin.

P. Paravy (1993), *De la chrétienté romaine à la Réforme en Dauphiné,* Rome.

E. Bosio (1995), "Origine e significato del nome 'Valdese'," *BSSV* 175, 3–33.

G. Audisio (1998), *Les Vaudois: Histoire d'une dissidence, XIIe–XVIe siècle,* Paris.

G. Gonnet and A. Armand-Hugon (1953), *Bibliografia valdese,* Torre Pellice.

FRANCO GIACONE

See also **Beguines; Catharism; Heresy; Hus Jan; Protestantism**

War

A. Biblical Materials

1. The Conduct of War in the Ancient Middle East

In Mesopotamia (*Gilgamesh* I ii 7–17) as in Palestine, the earliest armies originated from militias composed of the property-owning members of the village, tribe, or other form of community. In societies that did not yet possess state structures, the challenge was to bring such small contingents together in times of danger so that they would be capable of forming a force adequate for waging war (Jgs 5:14–18; 1 Sm 11; Am 5:3). Once states had been formed, permanent corps attached to the "king's household" appeared alongside the militias. Such corps could be formed from vassals, mercenaries, or slaves (1 Sm 8:11f.; Dt 17:16). David started out as the "captain" of a band of outlaws (1 Sm 22:2;

see also Jgs 11:3 on Jephthah), but once he had become king in Jerusalem* he had a guard made up of foreigners, "the Cherethites and the Pelethites" (2 Sm 8:18 and 20:23). These professional soldiers were generally better equipped and more effective than the militiamen were. After his flight across the Jordan, David and his "servants" defeated the "men of Israel" (*'am yisra'el*) commanded by Absalom (2 Sm 18:7). In the narratives* on the premonarchical period, we frequently find militias attempting to compensate for their operational inferiority by means of ruses (Jos 7ff.; Jgs 1:24ff., 7, and 9:43ff.).

Groups of soldiers were organized along administrative lines rather than on a tactical basis, with divisions into units of 10, 50, and so on. A commander could deploy his troops on the terrain before a battle, but once the attack had been launched there was no way in which he could make any further intervention. The soldiers' action consisted in throwing themselves into the mêlée while making as much noise as possible, in the hope that the enemy would take fright and flee (*see* Jgs 7:16ff.). When this did not happen, each side regarded itself as victorious (e.g., at the battle of Qarqar, between Salmanasar III and the Syrian alliance, in 853 B.C.). Not many soldiers died in battle: there were fewer than 100 fatalities in the battles of Thutmose III. Hot pursuit of a defeated army could end in a massacre, but everyone knew that a runaway who got rid of his equipment could run faster than a fully armed soldier. From the time of the Hyksos up to that of the Persians, chariots were used mainly to instill terror in the enemy's footsoldiers (*see* Ex 14:7; Jgs 1:19, 4:3, 5:22); they had limited effectiveness in battle, particularly on uneven or waterlogged terrain (Ex 14:25 and 15:21; Jgs 5:20f.). Away from the battlefield, the chariot was no more than a symbol of prestige (2 Sm 15:1). In general, wars broke out only in good weather (2 Sm 11:1), when the rains had made the terrain practicable and the first harvests made it possible to feed the troops.

2. The Theology of War

a) Was Israel Unique? In 1951, G. von Rad suggested that an institution that he called "holy war" (an expression that does not appear in the Bible) lay behind the biblical texts. He believed that this was a unique type of warfare, specific to ancient Israel. This suggestion has been subjected to far-reaching reconsideration in recent years. On the one hand, much has been made of the fact that the texts are *literary* reworkings, often undertaken at a later date, of archaic practices, some real, some imaginary. On the other hand, and even more importantly, we can now take account of the fact that all the elements that von Rad took to be characteristic of the "war of YHWH"—rituals of convocation, rules of purity*, consultation of a divine oracle, the symbolic presence of God* inside a palladium of war (the Ark), God's intervention in combat, divine terror paralyzing the enemy, the offering of spoils to God after a victory, and so on—were by no means specific to Israel, but can also be found in other war narratives from the ancient Middle East, notably those of the Assyrians (*see* Weippert).

b) Content. The underlying conception is always the same. Only the gods who established the order of the world are capable of preserving and modifying it. The king is charged with executing the divine will by protecting order against chaos. His mission is therefore to combat anything that poses a threat, internal or external, to the creation*, whether it be human enemies or wild animals: thus, both war and hunting become royal obligations (but also prerogatives) *par excellence*. Hence, it is natural for gods to intervene in war (Ex 14:14; Jgs 5:4ff.) and for a king and his soldiers to obey the requirements of ritual (Jos 7; 1 Sm 13–15; 2 Sm 2:1 and 11:11). Victory in turn is always attributed to the divinity. Only the divinity, who accompanies his or her protégé, the king, onto the battlefield, is capable of unleashing the panic that scatters the enemy, as witness the way in which Rameses III's victories, whether over foreign armies or over bands of wild animals, are represented on the walls of the temple of Medinet Habu. All these features are especially clear from the second half of the second millennium B.C.: the iconography of Syria and Palestine shows that this was a period of increasing "militarization" of the pantheon (Keel and Uehlinger 1992).

Israel too developed in this context: the Israelites' self-definition as *'am YHWH* should be understood, not as "people of YHWH," but, first and foremost, as "militia of YHWH" (Jgs 5:2), women, children, and the old being excluded from it (Lohfink 1971). Israel, in this sense, was understood to be an army in the service of YHWH; J. Wellhausen was quite right to say that for Israel the military camp was "the cradle of the nation" (1894). YHWH's primary function was to wage "YHWH's wars," a function dreaded even by his enemies (Jgs 5; 1 Kgs 20:23).

c) Rereadings and Reinterpretations. After the fall of the northern kingdom to the Assyrians in 720 B.C., neither Israelites nor Judeans were in any position to wage war any longer. They compensated for what could have appeared to be YHWH's defeat on the battlefield with intensive literary activity, producing narratives in which the very birth of Israel was described as the victory of a warrior god over a powerful enemy (Ex 14). In this literature, now known as "Deuteronomist," the existence of Israel in the land is attributed to a founding act of violence*, which, however, is historically fictitious: the conquest of Canaan under Joshua's command. The writers of these texts emphasize the radical character of this conquest (Jos 11:16–20) and YHWH's nature as a warrior; they even exaggerate the latter, somewhat paradoxically, since they were writing at a time when Israel no longer had either a state or an army. In this warlike utopia, God's actions are so powerful and so decisive that they come to be sufficient in themselves, so that human actors are reduced to passivity (Ex 14:13f.; Jos 10:10; Jgs 4:15; 1 Sm 7:10). From this there followed what may be called the "pacifism" of the "holy war" in Israel.

d) Oppositions. The Deuteronomist theology* was originally formulated in response to the Assyrian invasion, but, from the outset, its radical emphasis on YHWH the warrior aroused some opposing voices. In the tradition of the classic prophets*, there are several passages in which excessive violence (Is 7:9b; Hos 1:4) or the illusory character of military power (Is 31:1; Hos 1:7) are denounced, and hope is expressed for the disappearance of war (Is 2:4 and 11:6–9; Hos 2:20; Mi 4:1–4; compare Jl 4:10). In Amos's oracles against the nations (Am 1:3–2:3), one can even discern the beginnings of the idea of "war crimes." In the context of war, which itself seems to be attributed to fate, the prophet denounces precisely those acts that, no longer being explicable by strategic necessities, arise from gratuitous cruelty: the putting to death of entire populations (1:3), large-scale deportation (1:6), the disemboweling of pregnant women (1:13), and the profanation of corpses (2:1). The latter two crimes symbolize attacks on life beyond the limits of a human lifetime (Amsler 1981). The Deuteronomist legislation on war (Dt 20) contains not only prescriptions directly inspired by the brutality of the Assyrians (20:10–18), but additions aimed at humanizing war (20:19f.) or making it impossible to wage war in practice (20: 5–9).

The theological current that was at the greatest distance from the Deuteronomist perspective was the "priestly" theology. Its version of the birth of Israel does not present the departure from Egypt as a battle, nor does it conceive the entry into Canaan as a war of conquest. Indeed, in the priestly version violence is part of the corruption of the creation (Gn 6:9–13). Accordingly, in the covenant* concluded with Noah—that is, with the whole of humanity—God himself renounces war, in order to inaugurate a world based on justice and no longer on violence. He provides a sign of this intention by suspending a bow (the quintessential weapon of divine war) in the clouds. Visible to every human being, the rainbow is to serve as a permanent reminder that God has put away his weapon and that they too are invited to conceive their lives without recourse to war (Gn 9:12–17; *see* Zenger and Batto). As for the writer of the Chronicles, with his particular interest in the Temple, he introduces into the ancient narrative a new view that is resolutely opposed to war: God did not permit David to build the Temple because he had shed blood in battle (1 Chr 22:8).

3. The New Testament

The New Testament texts, pervaded as they are by the expectation of an imminent eschatological dénouement, display a correspondingly lesser interest in the state and its institutions: as a result, war is not among their concerns. Luke's Gospel*, the only one to make any allusion to war, seems to regard it as no more than a distant phenomenon (Lk 14:31) that has little impact on the conditions of Christians' lives, even in the case of Christian soldiers (Lk 3:14). The warrior heritage of the Old Testament tradition appears, if at all, only in Jesus' saying, "I have not come to bring peace, but a sword" (Mt 10:34). The Pauline* corpus contains metaphors drawn from war and from sporting combat alike, but they have more to do with Paul's polemical style of rhetoric than with any expression of opinion on war (Merkelbach 1975). Large-scale scenes of war are staged in Revelation, but the focus of the text is on the sacrificial Lamb (Rev 5:6; and *see* 12:11).

● J. Wellhausen (1894), *Israelitische und jüdische Geschichte,* Berlin.

G. von Rad (1951), *Der Heilige Krieg im alten Israel,* Göttingen (5th Ed. 1959).

R. de Vaux (1960), *Les Institutions de l'Ancien Testament,* II, Paris.

N. Lohfink (1971), "Beobachtungen zur Geschichte des Ausdrucks ᶜ*am yhwh,*" in H.-W. Wolff (Ed.), *Probleme biblischer Theologie. Festschrift von Rad,* Munich, 275–305.

F. Stolz (1972), *Jahwes und Israels Kriege. Kriegstheorien und Kriegserfahrungen im Glauben des alten Israels,* AThANT 60.

M. Weippert (1972), "'Heiliger Krieg' in Israel und Assyrien," *ZAW* 84, 460–93.

R. Merkelbach, H.C. Youtie (1975), "Der griechische Wortschatz und die Christen," *ZPE* 18, 101–54.

S. Amsler (1981), "Amos et les droits de l'homme," in P. Grelot (Ed.), *De la Torah au Messie: Mélanges H. Cazelles,* Paris, 181–87.

A. de Pury (1981), "La guerre sainte israélite, réalité historique ou fiction littéraire?" *ETR* 56, 5–38 (on history of research).

N. Lohfink (1983), "Die Schichten des Pentateuch und der Krieg," in N. Lohfink (Ed.), *Gewalt und Gewaltlosigkeit im Alten Testament,* QD 134, 51–110.

E. Zenger (1983), *Gottes Bogen in den Wolken,* SBS 112

R.M. Good (1985), "The Just War in Ancient Israel," *JBL* 104, 385–400.

B. F. Batto (1987), "The Covenant of Peace: A Neglected Ancient Near Eastern Motif," *CBQ* 49, 187–211.

S. M. Kang (1989), *Divine War in the Old Testament and in the Ancient Near East*, BZAW 177.

A. Van der Lingen (1990), *Les Guerres de Yahvé*, LeDiv 139.

P. Beauchamp and D. Vasse (1991), *La violence dans la Bible*, CEv 76.

O. Keel and C. Uehlinger (1992), *Göttinnen, Götter und Gottessymbole*, QD 134 (2nd Ed. 1993).

W. Klassen (1992), "War in the NT," *AncBD* 6, 867–75.

J. Keegan (1993), *History of Warfare*, New York.

S. Niditch, *War in the Hebrew Bible: A Study of the Ethics of Violence*, New York and Oxford.

R. P. Knierim (1994), "On the Subject of War in Old Testament and Biblical Theology," *HBT* 6, 1–19.

E. Otto (1994), "Das Kriegslager—die Wiege der altisraelitischen JHWH-Religion?" in H. M. Niemann (Ed.), *Nachdenken über Israel, Bibel und Theologie. Festschrift für Klaus-Dietrich Schunck*, Frankfurt, 357–73.

T. R. Hobbs (1995), "*BTB* Readers Guide: Aspects of Warfare in the First Testament World," *BTB* 25, 79–90.

ALBERT DE PURY

See also **Animals; Apocalyptic Literature; City; Creation; Decalogue; Israel; Peace; People; Priesthood; Violence**

B. Moral Theology

There have been three positions on the subject of war in the history of Christianity: pacifism (there can be no true Christian justification of war); the theory of just war (there are criteria for the moral justification of war); and realism (no limit can be placed on war beyond reason of state). The theory of just war, which holds that it may be a duty to defend political order (city*) and justice* by war, has contributed to the formation of the international law* of war.

a) Patristic Era. The church* did not face the question of participation in war until the fourth century. Before then, Christians had largely stood apart from social responsibility. There is clear evidence, however, that Christians served in the Roman army from before 200, although bishops* and theologians appealed to the faithful to avoid military service and bloodshed (e.g., Athenagoras in the second century, Clement of Alexandria [c. 150–c. 215], Tertullian*, Origen*, Lactantius [c. 240–c. 320]). Pacifists appealed to love of enemies (Mt 5:44) and the concern to avoid bloodshed.

Augustine*, like Ambrose*, held that one should not defend himself against violence on his own account, but that one may have a duty to defend the innocent. This is why, according to Augustine, the wise man may wage a just war (*De Civitate Dei* XIX, 7). Augustine's arguments for the tragic necessity of warfare rested on the conviction that injustice is worse than death (*Contra Faustum Manichaeum* XXII, 74). The foundations of the idea of just war are all to be found in Augustine's writings (*see*, e.g., *Ep.* 47, 189). The soldier may rightly obey the commands of public authority* to fight in a just cause, the evils of war being limited to those that are necessary to remedy injustice.

b) Middle Ages and the 16th century. Thomas* Aquinas gives three criteria of just war: 1) the authority of the sovereign that decides upon it; 2) the existence of a just cause (some wrong is to be put right); and 3) the existence of a right intention* that aims to promote the good* and avoid evil* (*ST* IIa IIae, q. 40). There are classes of people that are not to be involved in fighting, including priests* and members of religious orders.

Aquinas's successors developed these ideas with the aid of arguments drawn from natural law, *ius gentium* (the law of nations), and the gospel, and articulated a theological and legal casuistry* of war. Their theories defined who legitimately had authority to wage "private wars" as well as those decided upon by the state (*see* church* and state); what the nature of the just cause was; and what just means could be used in war: thus, they recommended the humane treatment of women, children, and prisoners.

This tradition culminated in the work of Vitoria (c. 1483–1546) and Suarez*. Vitoria criticized certain aspects of the Spanish wars of conquest in South America, arguing strongly against some of the justifications offered by the conquistadors, and condemning their lack of humanity. Controversially, he thought it possible that both sides in a conflict could rightly consider themselves to be defending a just cause (*De iure belli* 2, 4). Suarez combined thorough analysis with a keen awareness of practical realities. A just cause is, in principle, "a grave injustice that cannot be avenged or repaired in any other way," yet Suarez adds that an apparently slight matter may be serious since it may lead to greater harm (*De bello*, diss. XIII, 4 in *De fide, spe et caritate*).

Grotius (1583–1645) stood in the same tradition of synthesis of theology and law. Since war is analogous to judicial proceedings, those who undertake war are subject to legal restraints. The only legitimate cause is injury received; the grounds for a war must therefore be either legitimate* defense, or recovery of property, or punishment of wrong (*De iure belli ac pacis* II, I, 2). Grotius distinguishes (ibid., III, 8, 6–12) between conduct actually permitted by international law, and the requirements of moderation laid down by natural law* and the gospel (for instance, in sparing captives—*temperamenta belli*, that which makes war more temperate). Grotius consistently rejects the view that war lies outside the constraint of law, as merely a matter of reason of state. His new synthesis of natural law with *ius gentium*, which he interpreted as the customary law of nations, did much to provide foundations for international law.

The use of force has rarely been held to be a legitimate means of promoting the Christian faith*, despite the Crusades. Claims of a holy war have recurred from time to time, justified perhaps by invoking the Old Testament or the will of God*, for example in Innocent III's view that the pope may authorize war to punish sins* and overcome heresy*, or the view of John Knox (c. 1514–72) that there is a religious duty of revolution to oppose idolatry*. The main theorists of just war never accepted such views, but they never wholly repudiated the use of force when justice requires it. For Vitoria, for instance, it is legitimate to wage war in order to ensure unhindered passage for missionaries (*De Indis* 3, 2).

c) 17th–19th Centuries. The pleas of Grotius for the legal restraint of war largely fell on deaf ears in the international community. Shifts in the political and philosophical climate meant that the just-war tradition fell into disuse from the 17th to the 19th centuries. A divinely given framework for political morality was replaced by a construction of social morality beginning from individual rights. An important implication was the increased role of legitimate defense as a justification for war. When self-defense, based on the individual right of self-preservation, became the foundational element of justice, it led eventually to the concept of total war, because the right to self-preservation can effectively legitimize any action to that end. Another rationale for total war suggests that the more horrible war can be made, the more human beings will be discouraged from undertaking it—an idea that later became important for deterrence theories (*see* Tolstoy, *War and Peace* III, 2, 25).

d) 20th Century. The law of war had to wait until the Hague Conventions (1899, 1907) for systematic codi-

fication. These conventions eschewed the problem of just cause, concentrating on restraints on the conduct of war. The effect of these conventions was somewhat undermined by technological developments, especially in aviation, that transformed the conditions of war in the 20th century. Attempts to renew them in the Geneva Conventions of 1949 concentrated on the humanitarian aspect of law—that is, on the treatment of prisoners of war, the wounded, and civilians—rather than on the conduct of war. The traditional concerns of *ius in bello* were not brought up to date in international law until the Geneva Protocols of 1977. Meanwhile, the United Nations Charter (1945) had modified the law of just cause to restrict independent states to any but defensive resorts to war.

The revival of the theory of just war began significantly only with World War II. Until then, the churches' reactions were divided between pacifism and realism. The just-war tradition survived mainly as a more-or-less conventional list of seven criteria of justice. Five of these concern just recourse to war (*ius ad bellum*): war may be waged only by legitimate authority; there must be just cause to go to war; there should be right intention (such as to restore peace); war must be the last resort; and there must be a reasonable prospect of success. The other two criteria concern the just conduct of war (*ius in bello*): there should not be any direct attack on those not materially assisting the fighting (the principle of discrimination); and the costs of war should be in proportion to the benefits expected from it (the principle of proportion).

The aerial bombardment of cities raised sharp doubts about the concept of total, unlimited war (Ford 1944). Further pressing questions were raised by nuclear arms and deterrence; the weakness of the just-war tradition, combined with war-weariness, led many to espouse one form or other of pacifism. In relating just-war criteria to modern war, the principle of discrimination most evidently required clarification. According to P. Ramsey (1913–88) (1968), the principle requires not that noncombatants should be completely immune from any danger, but that they should not be directly attacked (the principle of double-effect intention allowing that civilians may suffer unintended hurt). Further, in relation to aerial bombing, it is not necessary to distinguish precisely between combatants and noncombatants, since one can distinguish attacks on civilian populations generally from those on armed forces. Ramsey holds that this principle of discrimination is morally exceptionless. On the realist side, W. O'Brien (1981) and R. Harries (1986) interpret the principle with greater flexibility, as an aspect of the principle of proportion. The debate is complex, for example in handling the awkward question of the moral relationship between the use of nuclear weapons and nuclear deterrence. Those who have most strongly insisted on the primacy of discrimination (W. Stein 1961, J. Finnis, G. Grisez 1987) have tended toward "nuclear pacifism" (no nuclear weapons should ever be used), a view often hard to distinguish from pure pacifism (e.g., J. Yoder 1984). Many others have striven to reconcile the tradition with the complexities of deterrence theory and the concern for international security (e.g., J. Hehir 1976, D. Hollenbach 1983, F. Böckle 1984). Vatican* II, and the US Catholic bishops (1983), both allow nuclear deterrence a provisional legitimacy, as an interim arrangement. The realists stress the gains of deterrence, while others emphasize the urgency of disarmament. Others again point out that it is the hope of total security that has fueled strategies of deterrence, and that more limited political hopes need to accompany more limited possibilities for war (Ramsey; O. O'Donovan 1989).

The contemporary renewal of the idea of just war has concerned more than nuclear deterrence. In the case of international law itself, there has been strong moral pressure to limit the means of war, and this has had some effect on armaments policies. Relationships between international authority and individual states also call attention to questions of just authority and the right of intervention (as in the Gulf War, 1991). With the collapse of the Soviet empire and the fading of the Cold War, questions of national self-determination claim greater attention. The morality of insurgency and counter-insurgency warfare raises acute questions, which should be addressed from both *ius ad bellum* and *ius in bello* perspectives.

The just-war tradition has lost none of its relevance, provided that one accepts its central contention, and believes that it is possible to impose moral and legal limits on justified war. Maritain (1882–1973) observed that morality is the claim of reason to direct life (cited in Ramsey 1968). War is in its own way a rational activity, and is therefore potentially subject to the claims of natural law and the gospel—or so the tradition has claimed.

- P. T. Forsyth (1916), *The Christian Ethic of War*, London.
J. C. Ford (1944), "The Morality of Obliteration Bombing," *TS* 5/3, 261–273, 308–9 (Repr. in Miller 1992, 138–77).
J. C. Murray (1959), "Remarks on the Moral Problem of War," *TS* 20, 40–61 (Repr. in Miller, 1992, 247–71).
P. Ramsey (1961), *War and the Christian Conscience*, Durham, NC.
W. Stein (1961), *Nuclear Weapons and Christian Conscience*, London.
R. H. Bainton (1961), *Christian Attitudes Toward War and Peace*, London.
John XXIII (1963), *Pacem in terris*, AAS 55, 257–304.
J.-M. Hornus (1963), *Évangile et labarum*, Geneva.
Vatican II (1965), *GS*.
P. Ramsey (1968), *The Just War: Force and Political Responsibility*, New York.
S. D. Bayley (1972), *Prohibitions and Restraints in War*, Oxford.
J. Ellul (1972), *Contre les violents*, Paris.
R. Aron (1976), *Penser la guerre: Clausewitz*, Paris.
J. Hehir and R. Gessert (1976), *The New Nuclear Debate*, New York.
W. O'Brien (1981), *The Conduct of Just and Limited War*, New York.
United States Conference of Catholic Bishops (1983), *The Challenge of Peace*, New York.
D. Hollenbach (1983), *Nuclear Ethics: A Christian Moral Argument*, New York.
J. H. Yoder (1984), *When War is Unjust: Being Honest in Just-War Thinking*, Minneapolis.
F. Böckle and G. Krell (Ed.) (1984), *Politik und Ethik der Abschreckung*, Mainz.
R. Harries (1986), *Christianity and War in a Nuclear Age*, Oxford.
J. Finnis, J. Boyle, G. Grisez (1987), *Nuclear Deterrence, Morality and Realism*, Oxford.
J. Helgeland (1987), *Christians and the Military: The Early Experience*, London.
O. O'Donovan (1989), *Peace and Certainty*, Oxford.
R. B. Miller (Ed.) (1992), *War in the Twentieth Century*, Louisville.
C. W. Morris (1996), "Guerre et paix," *DEPhM*, 617–625.

DAVID ATTWOOD

See also **Authority; Law and Christianity; Peace; Revolution; Violence**

Wesley, John. *See* Methodism

Wholly Other

The idea of God* as "wholly other," *das Ganz Andere,* appeared in 1917 in *The Idea of the Holy,* a book by the neo-Kantian philosopher R. Otto. It was adopted and abundantly orchestrated in the "crisis theology" of the young Karl Barth* and his friends. Its distant origins lie in ancient assertions of the transcendence of God, or of the One, as the other (*thatéron* in Plotinus), or the entirely other (*aliud valde* in Augustine*). Its immediate origin, with respect to "dialectical" theologies, is the "infinite qualitative difference" that separates God from man in Kierkegaard*. Nicholas* of Cusa provided in advance a significant nuance by also using, with reference to God, the concept of "non-other" *(non aliud).* The idea of God as being "always greater" (Rahner*), or of the dissimilarity always being greater than any resemblance (Przywara, re-reading Lateran* IV on analogy*), is sometimes close to the concept of God as "wholly other."

JEAN-YVES LACOSTE

See also **Analogy**

William of Auxerre. *See* Scholasticism

William of Champeaux. *See* **Saint-Victor, School of**

William of Conches. *See* **Chartres, School of**

William of Ockham. *See* Nominalism

William of Saint Thierry. *See* **Bernard of Clairvaux**

Wisdom

A. Biblical Theology

In the Bible*, "wisdom" is the practical capacity to use methods, in trade (Ez 28:4f.), handicrafts (Sir 38:31), navigation (Ez 27:8f.), the art and profession of the scribe (Prv 22:29; Ps 45:2; Sir 38:24), and strategy (2 Sm 16:23), as well as in politics and other domains. Wisdom serves to resolve everyday problems in order to achieve one's purpose in life. It is neutral: the term is applied to the competence of the craftsman whether he makes idols (Is 40:20; Jer 10:9) or accessories for the cult* of YHWH (Ex 28:3, 31:3, and 31:6; 1 Kgs 7:14), and it is even used to describe criminal scheming (Ex 1:10; *see* Acts 7:19 and 2 Sm 13:3) or the plan of salvation* (Rom 11:33). Since law* was seen as being both the medium that encompasses all the domains of life and the method that leads human beings to God*, there was increasingly a tendency in Israel* to identify the law of Moses with wisdom (Dt 4:6; Sir 24:23; Bar 4:1). Biblical wisdom is exemplary in its sobriety and has little to do with the unfathomable. Nevertheless, the people of Israel, who had at least as much wisdom as any other people, could not help but wonder what relationship could bring together God and the sum of his manifestations. Their God, who was more and more firmly recognized as unique (monotheism*), had always spoken and acted as if he was very intimate with this world*, yet remained other than this world. In uniting this sum of manifestations under the name "wisdom," a number of texts animate the concept, giving it the vivid characteristics of a being born from God (Prv 8:22–31; Sir 24; Bar 3:9–4:4; Wis 6:12–8:21). These texts were to catch the attention of those who wrote the New Testament.

1. Old Testament

a) Vocabulary. The Hebrew terminology is fairly diverse: *chakam,* "the wise one" (which appears 138 times), is endowed with "wisdom," *chokemah* (153 times) or *tevounah* (42 times); *binah* (36 times), "penetration" or "discernment"; or *da'at,* "knowledge" (with God as object in Is 11:9; Hos 4:1 and 4:6; Wis 2:13 and so on). *Sakal* and other related forms, such as *sakal (hi),* which appear 58 times and have a less certain meaning (Gn 3:6; Is 52:13; Dn 11:33, 12:10), evoke light, expansion, and success. Wisdom functions through advice or plan (*'eçah;* 88 times), or through calculation (*machashavah);* is transmitted through education (*mousar;* 50 times), and is related to secrets (*sod;* 21 times) and mystery* (Aramaic *raz,* as in Dn 9:9).

b) Location and Transmission of Wisdom. Wisdom is especially associated with the family home and the entourage of chiefs, as well as with the king's court, his army, and his advisers. Some women* are presented as exemplars of wisdom within the political order (1 Sm 25:33; 2 Sm 14:2) or the economy (Prv 31:10–31). God possesses his own wisdom, and applies its technical genius in the work of creation* and of salvation. However, for a long time the domain of wisdom remained separate from that of religion, and wisdom is explicitly acknowledged as existing outside Israel (Jer 49:7; Is 19:11; Ez 28:3; Ob 8; Dn 2:18 and so on; and *see* universalism*). Yet, after all was said and done, the Torah was a written text, and the priesthood could not exercise any of its function without wisdom. The importance of the scribes within the social fabric increased continuously, and it was through them that human beings were made aware of the Law and the Prophets*; hence their link with wisdom. The main product of the scribes was the Bible itself, and it was they who frequently remodeled the text.

c) Literary Genres. The forms specifically associated with wisdom and practiced in the schools include proverbs, enigmas, parables*, macarisms ("Happy is he who..."), numbered lists, and alphabetical poems. Other forms, such as satire, or songs for funerals, weddings, or grape harvests, were brought by the scribes from folk sources into literature, and were used by the major prophets under the monarchy. In the Law and the Prophets, God speaks to humanity, but in these texts human beings speak on their own behalf; hence the difference in tone, for example in those psalms* that are typical of "wisdom literature" (such as Ps 1, 34, 73). The wise man does not decree law, but records observations on the good life, on the principle that doing good* makes for happiness. He also celebrates the good life, as, for example, in the Song of Songs, in which God, without being named, is praised in his double aspect as masculine and feminine (couple*). The wise were concerned with life and means of protecting life: a long time was to pass before their reflections on death* became prominent.

d) Mutations. Wisdom was praised for being unchanging, and yet it had a history. The monarchy was a time of crisis for wisdom. The king was the living symbol of wisdom, and several books were conventionally attributed to Solomon, but he was also the symbol of the dangers of wisdom. Withdrawal and reliance on adequate means took the place of the achievement of liberty*, and Israel was absorbed into the nations (giving rise to paganism*), instead of opening up to them. The sources diverge in two contradictory directions. The narrative of Adam and Eve's sin (Gn 3) can be interpreted as describing the king being tempted (temptation*) to use knowledge in order to efface the difference between good and evil*: the king's human wisdom is set up as a rival to God's wisdom. The Book of Proverbs reminds its readers of the revelations imparted to Israel simply by using the name YHWH (56 times in Prv 10:1–22:29) and is "universalistic" to the point of closing following the Egyptian narrative of the wisdom of Amenemope (Prv 22:17–23:14). Deuteronomy is the first text in which the law of Moses is identified with wisdom. It follows that wisdom becomes a central "character" in a narrative that, rather than being limited to phases in the creation of the world (Prv 8:22–31), pervades the whole of history, whether undramatically (Sir 24 and 44–50) or with its own tragedies (Bar 3:9–4:4; Wis 10 and so on). The literary genre of ironic wisdom, which was widely known outside Israel as well, reveals wisdom being defeated: in Job's case, traditional wisdom (*see* H. Rowley, *BJRL* 41, pp. 167–207), and, in the case of Ecclesiastes, any kind of wisdom at all.

These aporias prefigure apocalyptic* literature, which is the most paradoxical category among biblical texts since it combines two domains that were originally completely separate, wisdom and revelation*. This is both a scholarly and anthologizing genre, and many of its enigmas cannot be deciphered without help from the interpreting angel*. The secrets plumbed by this new wisdom are inaccessible, and yet they are communicated; they range from the beginning to the end of history, and back again. The central mystery is the suffering of the just, whether taken as individuals or as a group. It is possible to reconstruct some of the stages in this mutation. Ironic wisdom (Prv 30:2ff.) had already led the wise close to the dying (Job; Ecclesiastes); the poems of the Servant are saturated with the vocabulary of wisdom; the apocalyptic genre was already well-developed when, during the reign of Augustus, the martyrdom* of the just man, victim of his own faithfulness to God and God's law, is described in the Book of the Wisdom of Solomon as "the end of the wise" (Wis 4:17). Here we see the return of the ancient hope of the wise. The conclusion of the same book presents the departure out of Egypt as a "mobilized" renewal of the creation (Wis 5:17–23, 16:17b, 19:6) in order to raise the bodies (*see* soul*-heart-body) of the just from death (*see* resurrection* of the dead). This is an encyclopedic (Wis 7:16–21), eloquent, thoughtful wisdom that welcomes the impossible.

e) Is Wisdom a Living Being (Hypostasis)? The primary mode of transmission of wisdom was the tradition passed on from earlier generations: it seemed natural that wisdom would induce its disciples to turn to their ancestors and instructors, and to earlier ancestors and instructors, and so on back to the primordial origin of all truth*. Through poetic means, Proverbs 8:22–31 and, later, Wisdom 7:25 suggest that Wisdom emanates eternally from God, but is not merged with the world. Its opposite, Folly, is also personified, but the symmetry is not exploited, while reflection on Wisdom goes further, as Wisdom accompanies human beings, or the people, up to the end. Wisdom has spoken, taking itself as the subject of its own discourse, and for this purpose it borrows forms from mythology, such as the lists of virtues or "self-preachings" of the goddess Isis (*see* A.J. Festugière, *HThR*, 42, pp. 209–34). Following the translation into Greek of Ecclesiasticus and, even more importantly, the Wisdom of Solomon, the opportunity arose for Hellenism to insert the rudiments of philosophy into the biblical tradition: thought became less naïve, but was no less audacious. Wisdom, an entity distinct from God, and as intimate with human beings as with God, is never addressed as a divinity or as a mediator that can intercede for human beings. Instead, it is sought from God as his supreme gift, and it sums up in itself all the other entities through which

God manifests himself: Name, Presence, Glory*, Cloud, Angel of YHWH, Spirit (Wis 7:22–25a), Holy* Spirit (Wis 9:17), Word* (Wis 9:1). Christian biblical theology, immobilized by a legitimate fear of projecting the revelation of the New Testament onto the Old Testament, and distrustful of ideas expressed in poetic forms, has often responded nervously to the audacity of such texts. Nevertheless, it has not been able to ignore this way of handling the problem of monotheism*, these poetic traces of an inquiry into the nature of God. To do so would be to ignore the effects that this approach has had upon several traditions that cannot be reduced to the New Testament alone (*see* G. W. McRae 1970), as well as to project onto the Old Testament the image of a stiff and conceptually impoverished monotheism, on the pretext of maintaining the difference between the two.

Within Judaism*, there have been debates on, for example, the *shekînah* or "habitation" of God upon Earth or in a chosen place. This notion has been maintained within monotheism without, however, being reduced to functioning merely as literary ornament (Urbach 1979).

2. New Testament

a) Vocabulary. The terminology of wisdom (*sophia*, "wisdom," 51 times; *phronimos*, "sensible," 14 times; and related terms) is more diverse than that of its opposites. Syntagms include: "wisdom of God" (Lk 11:49; Rom 11:33; 1 Cor 1:21, 1:25, 2:7; Eph 3:10); "foolishness of God" (1 Cor 1:25); and "Christ Jesus, whom God made our wisdom" (1 Cor 1:30).

b) Jesus. The Gospels* take to an extreme the proximity of God, the possibility of joining with him in the most common forms of life, indeed everything that was to be expressed in later times in the word "incarnation*." In this way, it takes on the heritage of biblical wisdom, as may be verified on a number of levels. Wisdom is attributed to Jesus* as a characteristic (Mt 13:54; Mk 6:2; Lk 2:40 and 2:52; *see* Mt 12:42). Above all, wisdom permeates the language of the gospels, and is expressed in maxims (e.g., Mt 5:13a, 5:14f., 5: 18, 20:6, 22:21; Lk 15:27; Jn 8:7; Mk 4:25), many of them preserved in the form of proverbial phrases (paremic), such as "salt of the earth," "light of the world," "eleventh hour," "render to Caesar," "killed the fattened calf," "the first to throw the stone," "the wheat from the chaff," or "not an iota" (N. Gueunier, *CILL* 1991, 17/4). These phrases have not yet disappeared from our language.

In itself, this style is evidence that close attention is being paid to contemporary life; and this is confirmed by the general tone of the teaching. The Gospels contain references to domestic, agricultural and military experience (Lk 14:28–32); above all, and to a greater extent than in any other biblical texts, there are references to the handling of money (nine different monetary denominations are mentioned). This is a revealing trait: the purpose is less to evoke simple moderation than to recommend shrewdness, from the praise for the foresight or calculation of the architect (Mt 7:24), the householder (Mt 24:43), the organizer of the wedding feast (Jn 2:10), the guest (Lk 14:7–11 and 21:9), the judge (Lk 18:4), and the litigant (Mt 5:25f.), to the praise of the steward who does well to be dishonest (Lk 16:1–12). The same trait is confirmed, most notably, in the parables*, which subject their listeners to radical tests, overturning the usual notion of wisdom with an effect already observed in the Old Testament. Daniel praised God for giving wisdom to the wise; Jesus praises him for hiding it from them and revealing it to the simple (Dn 2:22f.; Mt 11:25; *see* Lk 10:21f.). In Mark's Gospel in particular, parables contain secrets that challenge the intellect and cause the appearance of resistance in the heart (Mk 4:12), since they are concerned with the "secret of the kingdom" (Mk 4:11). This phrase, along with the enigmatic character of the parables, brings a genre that originated in wisdom literature closer to the apocalyptic. Jesus "teaches" (Mk 9:31) his disciples that his crucifixion and resurrection* are necessary; according to Luke, it is foolishness (Lk 24:25) as much as hardheartedness that causes this truth not to be understood.

In the synoptic gospels, wisdom structures the events of salvation (Mt 11:19; Lk 7:35 and 11:49; *see* Mt 23:34f.), but Jesus's filiation* is still not assimilated to that of wisdom, which precedes history. This assimilation is prefigured nonetheless. The Gospels come closest to wisdom literature when Jesus gives himself as the source of truth*, a source that itself issues from the Father* in the beginning. Such language is not to be found anywhere in the Old Testament except in precisely those passages where Wisdom is taken to be a living entity. Such precedents can be recognized in Jesus' use of the word "I" and in his command, "Come to me" (Mt 11:28; *see* Lk 6:47 and Prv 9:5; Sir 24:19; Is 55:1ff.).

The apostolic writings frequently recommend that the disciples speak and act wisely (Rom 16:19; 1 Cor 6:5; Col 4:5 and so on), as Jesus did (Mt 10:16). James's epistle in particular has all the flavor and meets any definition of a piece of wisdom literature.

c) Pauline Theology. In the Pauline* corpus, theology is rooted in the scandal* of a form of wisdom that defeats the wise and is opposed to any known wisdom (the same scandal as that of the parables, according to

Mk 4): this wisdom is therefore "foolishness" (1 Cor 1:17–2:14, 3:18f., 4:10). However, revelation makes it possible to recognize it as wisdom (1 Cor 2:6f.), linking it to the notion of mystery*. It is "foolish" (Gal 3:1 and 3:3) to turn away from it. Romans mounts a confrontation between the two failed forms of wisdom that preceded the Gospel: the interaction of the idolatrous pagans (1:22) with those who "call yourself a Jew" but have transgressed God's law and have not transmitted his light (2:17–21), forms a plot in which sin (2:24, 11:22) is intermingled with salvation (11:30ff.). Paul sees God working through this plot with the greatest skill, detecting both a mystery that "I want you to understand" (11:25) and the unfathomable wisdom (see 11:33f.) of "the only wise God" (16:27).

The early Pauline writings mention only in passing the place of Christ* in that which founds and precedes history (1 Cor 8:4ff.; 1 Cor 10:1–4 has a precedent in Philo's *Legum Allegoriae* ["Of the Laws of Allegory"] II, 86: wisdom and "rock" according to Ex 17:5f.; see senses of Scripture*). The Christology of Colossians 1:15–20 draws on ancient poems about preexisting Wisdom, principally Proverbs 8:22–31. Ephesians 1:8f., 1:12, and 3:10 present Christ and the church in the eternal perspective of a single act of God; hence the use of the vocabulary of wisdom (1:8, 1:17, 3:10). One polemical function of this vocabulary is to oppose Christ to the Torah as the seat of wisdom (Col 2:8, 2:16–23). The author of the preamble to Hebrews (1:1–4) cannot have been unaware of Wisdom 7:21 and 9:9.

d) Johannine Theology. In the prologue to John's Gospel (1:1–18), the theme of wisdom acquires an unequalled breadth (Word*), incorporating its dramatic aspect. The fourth gospel highlights and accentuates the emphatic use of "I" (Jn 5:40, 6:37, 7:37). John 6:57—"whoever feeds on me"—has a precedent in Sirach 24:21: "they that eat me."

• C. M. W. Grimm (1860), *Das Buch der Weisheit*, Leipzig.
H. Ringgren (1947), *Word and Wisdom: Studies in the Hypostatisation of Divine Qualities and Functions in the Ancient Near East*, Lund.
W. G. Lambert (1960), *Babylonian Wisdom Literature*, Oxford.
P. Beauchamp (1964), "Le salut corporel des justes et la conclusion du livre de la Sagesse," *Bib* 45, 491–526.
H. Conzelmann (1965), "Paulus und die Weisheit," *NTS* 12, 231–44.
A. Feuillet (1966), *Le Christ Sagesse de Dieu d'après les Épîtres pauliniennes*, EtB.
Ch. Kayatz (1966), *Studien zu Proverbien 1–9*, WMANT 22.
P.-É. Bonnard (1966), *La Sagesse en personne annoncée et venue*, LeDiv 44.
F. Christ (1970), *Jesus Sophia: Die Sophia-Christologie bei den Synoptikern*, Zurich.
G. W. McRae (1970), "The Jewish Background of the Gnostic Sophia Myth," *NT* 12, 86–101.
G. von Rad (1970), *Weisheit in Israel*, Neukirchen-Vluyn.
P. W. Skehan (1971), *Studies in Israelite Poetry and Wisdom*, *CBQ* Monograph Series I.
P. Beauchamp (1976), *L'un et l'autre Testament: Essai de lecture*, 106–35; 219–28.
M. Gilbert (Ed.) (1979), *La Sagesse de l'Ancien Testament*, BEThL 51.
E. E. Urbach (1979), *The Sages: Their Concepts and Beliefs*, Jerusalem.
Ch. Larcher (1983–85), *Le livre de la Sagesse ou la Sagesse de Salomon*, EtB.NS no 1, vols. 1–3.
A. Vanel (1986), "Sagesse (Courant de)," *DBS* 11, 4–58.
M. Gilbert (1986), "Sagesse de Salomon (ou Livre de la Sagesse)," ibid. 58–119.
H. D. Preuss (1987), *Einführung in die alttestamentliche Weisheitsliteratur*, Stuttgart.
H. von Lips (1990), *Weisheitliche Traditionen im Neuen Testament*, WMANT 64.
P. Beauchamp (1992), *Le Récit, la lettre et le corps: Essais bibliques*, 2nd Ed., Paris, 129–54.
J.-N. Aletti (1993), *Saint Paul: Épître aux Colossiens*, EtB.NS 20.
M. Gilbert (1995), "Qu'en est-il de la Sagesse?" in J. Trublet (Ed.), *La Sagesse biblique: De l'Ancien au Nouveau Testament*, ACFEB Meeting, 1993, LeDiv 160, 19–60.
J. Vilchez-Lindez (1995), "Panorama des recherches actuelles sur la Sagesse dans l'AT," ibid., 129–38.

PAUL BEAUCHAMP

See also **Apocalyptic Literature; Book; City; Filiation; Idolatry; Incarnation; Knowledge of God; Law and Christianity; Monotheism; Mystery; Paganism; Parable; Person; Reason; Revelation; Universalism; Word**

B. Moral and Systematic Theology

Three factors conspired to ensure that in early Christianity wisdom was both a fully theological notion and a convenient term to designate virtue or the sum of all the virtues*. 1) It was possible to speak christologically of wisdom, within the framework of a theory of the divine wisdom, on the basis of the New Testament exegesis of such texts as Proverbs 8. The apologists* who elaborated the identification of Christ with the

Word* of God (Justin, Theophilus, Athenagoras) found support for their approach in the hypostatization of Wisdom. This combination of titles still prevailed as a commonplace at the height of the Arian controversy (Arianism*). However, when the Logos tradition extended itself into a fully Trinitarian conception (Trinity*) of the divine work of creation*, Wisdom was sometimes differentiated from the Word and treated as a name of the Holy* Spirit (as in the writings of Theophilus of Antioch and Irenaeus*). 2) The sociological assimilation of Christians to disciples of a philosophical school allowed them to conceive their doctrine as a form of wisdom which, following a common definition, they understood as "knowledge of what truly is" (Justin). The religious tone adopted in some philosophic schools reinforced the association: the notion that wisdom is God-given was by no means unique to Christianity. A more differentiated account of the relation between wisdom and philosophy* was given in the school of Alexandria*: following a Stoic* definition adopted before him by Philo, Clement affirms that philosophy is the love of wisdom, and wisdom the knowledge of things divine and human, together with their causes. Wisdom is therefore the queen of philosophy, as philosophy is the queen of the propaedeutic studies. Moral philosophy is the point of contact between prophetic wisdom and the pagan traditions of philosophy; but pagans are closed to prophetic inspiration by their self-love (*Strom.* 1, 5; 6, 7). 3) The polemical engagement with Gnosis* required a definition of intellectual perfection that rescued it from the sectarian claims of certain groups of initiates and integrated it (*see* Jas 3:17) into the life of the Christian community.

Clement of Alexandria was especially responsible for developing the ideal of a Christian knowledge*— "gnosis" in its positive sense—that embraces wisdom on the moral as well the theological level. According to classical definitions, wisdom has to do with first causes and intellectual essences; it includes knowledge of God and of human nature; it presupposes rectitude of soul*, rectitude of reason*, and purity of life (*Strom.* 2, 5; 6, 7). Moreover, it is achieved only by divine grace* illuminating the mind. Above all, it is taught by the incarnation* and by the witness of the prophets*. Hence, wisdom represents a specific category under which the notion of Christian maturity is explored. It has a common boundary with faith*, and it is by faith that one accedes to the status of disciple and is led through wisdom toward perfection. On the other hand, it has a common boundary with gnosis, which is perfection itself: knowledge is intuitive and immediate, while wisdom is discursive and exploratory; it is the harmonious totality of experience, while wisdom is dialectical and progressive (*Strom.* 7, 10). More generally, "wisdom" can also be used as a generic term under which any aspect of intellectual virtue can be discussed; it can even be used for purely practical arts (*Strom.* 2, 5; 6, 17).

The polemic context of early Christian theology did not allow the Pauline* critique of worldly wisdom (1 Cor 1–2) to be forgotten; and it retained its topicality for a long time, since it was still being exploited in the later patristic era, in the sharp polemic between Christians and pagans over educational ideals. Thus, Gregory* of Nazianzus distinguishes between false wisdom—rhetorical training for public life—and true wisdom, represented by the peaceful and holy life of a Christian bishop (*Or.* 16, 2; 25, 2). The route of true wisdom lies through the counsel of the Delphic oracle: "Know thyself" (*Or.* 32, 21). For John Chrysostom*, rhetoricians and writers are the objects of Paul's criticisms, together with the "education given without" and its "sophisms" (*Hom.* in 1 Cor 7:1; in 2 Cor 3:1). Augustine* (*Trin.* 10–13) undertakes an extended attempt to map the ascent of the soul, assigning the crowning place to wisdom. Again, the Delphic maxim is the point of departure. Heeding the invitation to "know ourselves" allows us to pass from *notitia,* an uncertain and, so to speak, impressionistic knowledge of appearances, to a reflective and self-critical *cogitatio.* This then allows us to make a further distinction between an active activity and a contemplative activity of human reason. On the one hand, there is *scientia,* which has to do with the organization of the material world; on the other there is *sapientia,* which is concerned with eternal things. However, the active element and the contemplative element are not distinguished in Augustine's mind in the same way as practical and intellectual activity are. *Scientia* is also intellectual, since it is engaged in our knowledge of the history of salvation*; *sapientia* is also practical, because it is inseparable from love* of God and neighbor. Knowledge and will, as images of the second and third persons of the Trinity*, are absolutely consubstantial and coeternal; *scientia* does not imply any preeminence of love, nor *sapientia* any preeminence of knowledge.

In eastern Christian theology, the transition from the "practical" to the "theoretical" life also plays a large role in the ascent of the soul, but the unity of the two levels is secured by positing a third form of life, the "mystical" life (mysticism*), which achieves the dialectical unity of the two preceding it. Thus, there is an emphasis on the unity of the intellectual and the affective, which is achieved in the "core" of the soul. In the writings of Maximus* the Confessor, wisdom, the sum of the intellectual virtues, is united with "victory," the sum of the practical virtues, to radiate "glory" (*Qu. ad*

Thal. 54). In the traditional list of virtues, as handed down from Evagrius, love is the highest of the practical virtues; gnosis, "theology," and "blessedness" come after it, and represent the mystical stage beyond it. For Maximus, even this hierarchy is unsatisfying: he puts love at the head of his list, but defines it in terms of its relation to knowledge: "the person who loves God values gnosis of God more than anything" (*Cap. car.* 1, 4). Elsewhere in his writings, under the influence of Isaiah 11:2 (read backwards, as often in the tradition), the stages of ascent take a more intellectual turn, and wisdom becomes the last stage, "the clear contemplation of universal truth" (*Qu. ad Thal.* 54).

In medieval Latin theology, the privileges accorded to the will presented new problems. If moral significance attaches uniquely to the affective or voluntative aspects of the soul's activity, how is the unity of the practical and the theoretical to be conceived? The quite different results to which this approach could lead may be seen by comparing the respective positions of Bonaventure* and Thomas* Aquinas. For Bonaventure, who bears witness to the revival of Pseudo-Dionysius*, wisdom is attained in an ascending series of transformations: it is successively "uniform," "multiform," "omniform," and, finally, "nulliform," this last stage representing the point at which the intellect is superseded by the affections in a mystical contact with God (*Itin.* 7; *Hex.* 2, 8). By contrast, in the writings of Aquinas the sharp distinction of the faculties of the soul into *intellectus* and *appetitus* allows him to consider the intellectual virtues as half-virtues (with the exception of *prudentia,* which bridges the divide between the moral element and the intellectual element). While these virtues imply the capacity to function, they do not ensure the "use" of this capacity, because they do not perfect the will (*ST* Ia IIae, q. 57, a. 1). Among the intellectual virtues, *sapientia, scientia,* and *intellectus* (the list is from Aristotle, but happily overlaps with Is 11:2) form a class apart: intellect is immediate, wisdom and science are discursive; wisdom consists in understanding the whole, science in understanding specific spheres of knowledge; the "sciences" are therefore plural, while wisdom is one.

Yet, having thus divided the sphere of the intellect from the sphere of moral virtue, Aquinas reunites them again. The intellectual virtues have, as it were, a second life in the existence of the believer: he or she has been touched by grace, and they appear henceforth (under the tutelage of Is 11:2) as "gifts of the Spirit." Intellect is the gift by which one apprehends the truth about the end of man. It is accompanied by wisdom, the gift by which one knows that the end is to be clung to. This time, wisdom is distinguished from science in the Augustinian manner, as the knowledge of eternal realities, as distinct from knowledge of temporal things (*ST* IIa IIae, q. 8, a. 6). As the gift of intellect corresponds to theological faith, so the gift of wisdom corresponds to the theological virtue of love, or charity (q. 45). In this setting, Aquinas restores what he seemed to have lost in his earlier analyses: the coinherence of the intellectual and the affective. Accordingly, wisdom implies a "sympathy or co-natuarality with divine things" that has its cause in the will.

By establishing a sharp contrast between a purely moral will and a wholly dispassionate intellect, medieval theology indisputably played a leading part as one of the causes of the collapse of wisdom and the loss of its status as a central moral category in the early modern period. In this context, moreover, the Pauline critique of wisdom exercised a certain subversive attraction. Skeptical humanism (Erasmus*, Charron, Montaigne; see Christian skepticism*) found in it a good reason to distrust not only formal systems of learning, such as Scholasticism*, but the very idea that wisdom could represent a pinnacle of any kind. The only true wisdom was the distrust of pretended wisdom, and it was to be acquired, not through a long process of maturing, but in a moment of disenchantment that involved something of a return to simple piety. This doubtful attitude to wisdom is not entirely absent from the theology of the Reformers; yet it would be wrong to see it as one of the strong points of their theory of the knowledge of God. Following the example of Luther* in his commentary on Romans 11:33 (*WA* 56), the Reformers could easily adopt the familiar approaches of the church Fathers* and of Scholasticism in order to discuss wisdom. However, using alternative categories meant that it was not often necessary to do so. As for the casuistry* that motivated the clearest efforts that the Catholic Reformers made on moral questions, in order to face up to the self-understanding of modern humanity, it is at least certain that it was incapable of restoring life or giving life to a doctrine of the virtues and therefore to a Christian doctrine of wisdom.

The definitive ousting of wisdom can be attributed to the influence of the Enlightenment. Henceforth, a more egalitarian and less moral ideal of reason took its place as a personal ideal, while the progress of human beings toward their true humanity, which the idea of wisdom had served to formulate, was reduced to an "education" relegated to childhood, where it became an undertaking for the art of tutors and schoolteachers.

● Augustine, *De trinitate* (CSEL 50 and 50A; BAug 15 and 16).
Bonaventure, *Opera omnia,* vol. 5, Quaracchi, 1891, *Collationes in Hexaemeron* (Trans. M. Ozilou, 1991).
Bonaventure, *Itinerarium mentis in Deum* (Trans. H. Duméry, 1960).
Clement of Alexandria, *Stromata* (SC 30, 38, 278 and 279).

John Chrysostom, *Homiliae XLIV in Epistolam primam ad Corinthios* (PG 61, 9–382).

John Chrysostom, *Homiliae XXX in Epistolam secundam ad Corinthios* (PG 61, 381–610).

Luther, *Vorlesung über den Römerbrief* (WA 56).

Maximus the Confessor, *Capita de caritate* (PG 90, 959–1080), *Quaestiones ad Thalassium* (CChr.SG 7).

Thomas Aquinas, *ST* Ia IIae, q. 57, a. 2; q. 66, a. 5; IIa IIae, q. 8, a. 6; q. 9, a. 2; q. 45.

♦ E.F. Rice (1958), *The Renaissance Idea of Wisdom,* Cambridge, MA.

J. Boisset (1959), *Sagesse et sainteté dans la pensée de Jean Calvin,* Paris.

J. Ratzinger (1959), *Die Geschichtstheologie des heiligen Bonaventura,* Munich.

J.D. Collins (1962), *The Lure of Wisdom,* Milwaukee.

K. Conley (1963), *The Theology of Wisdom,* Dubuque, IA.

L. Thunberg (1965), *Microcosm and Mediator: the Theological Anthropology of Maximus the Confessor,* Chicago (2nd Ed. 1995).

O. O'Donovan (1981), *The Problem of Self-Love in S. Augustine,* New Haven.

OLIVER O'DONOVAN

See also **Anthropology; Character; Intellectualism; Prudence; Soul-Heart-Body; Virtues; Voluntarism**

Wittgenstein, Ludwig Josef Johann

1889–1951

Ludwig Wittgenstein was born in Vienna to a family of Jewish descent that had converted to Christianity. Although his father was Protestant, he was raised in his mother's Catholic faith. If any religion was practiced at the Wittgenstein's home, however, it was that of art, and the book of choice was Schopenhauer's *The World as Will and Idea.*

Before going to Cambridge to study logic with Bertrand Russell, who early on saw in him a worthy successor "apt to make the next decisive step in philosophy," Wittgenstein studied science and technology in Vienna and in England. In 1914, he voluntarily enlisted in the Austro-Hungarian army, where he would receive several medals and become an artillery lieutenant. In 1918 he began writing the only work published during his lifetime, the *Tractatus Logico-philosophicus.* The work knew a growing influence in Austria, with the members of the Circle of Vienna, and then in Britain, even as Wittgenstein considered his work done and retired from philosophical study. After the war, he renounced his personal fortune and became successively a teacher, a gardener at the Convent of Hütteldorf, and the architect of his sister's famous Viennese home, before returning to philosophy after the appeal from his English friends (notably F. P. Ramsey) and becoming a fellow at Trinity College and a professor at Cambridge University. There, interspersed with solitary visits to Ireland and Norway, he led the life of a nonconformist academic, fascinating most of those who talked to him, publishing near to nothing, but profoundly influencing 20th-century philosophy with his teaching (often gathered by his students) and the texts he left after his death.

In 1914, Wittgenstein discovered the summary of the Gospel written by Tolstoy. From then on, the soldiers called him "the one who reads the Gospels*." The notebooks he filled during the war reveal a constant religious torment, and the renunciation of his paternal inheritance could have been decided under the influence of Matthew 19:23f. and Luke 14:13. His "Conference on Ethics," held in 1929–30 (pub. 1966), contains a formula that echoes Psalm 23: "I fear no evil," an experience that seemed fundamentally religious to him. Much indicates that Wittgenstein, as he told one of his friends, without being a religious man, couldn't help but see all problems from a religious point of view. (For a more precise listing of testimonies about Wittgenstein's religious preoccupations, *see* Malcolm 1994.) There are two periods in Wittgenstein's philosophy: the period of the *Tractatus* and the period that would lead to his writing the *Philosophical Investigations.*

a) The Tractatus Logico-Philosophicus. The *Tractatus* differentiates that which can be said, by way of propositions that are pictures of facts (the natural sciences* being the most elaborate form), and that which can only be shown. How the world is, can be said; that the world be, on the other hand, can be shown, but not said. That there is a world is not a fact in the world; it cannot be represented by facts, images, or statements, that is what facts show. The factuality of a fact is not in itself a fact. It is a formal characteristic of a fact. The shape of all facts is the limit of the world of facts and does not enter the realm of the expressable. This is what Wittgenstein calls the "mysticism*," *das Mystische (Tractatus,* 6.44, 6.45, 6.522). And, as stated in the last and most famous of the *Tractatus* propositions, "whereof one cannot speak, thereof one must be silent."

According to Wittgenstein himself, the *Tractatus* contains two parts: there is that which is said and that which is silent. The second part was the most, if not the only, important one for him. In fact, and herein lies the *Tractatus*'s paradox, Wittgenstein speaks well, even if little, about God*, of the inexpressible, of mysticism: only to exclude them from the expressible. They constitute the limit of the world, that is to say its general form, the possibility of the domain that is the world. To be the form of a domain is also to be its meaning; meaning and essence are identical. Since Wittgenstein identifies God and the meaning of the world, one can say: the meaning of the world = the form of the world = God. It is not a question of negative* theology, the apophatic conception of an inexpressible God, whose negative formulas would be the least-bad approximation. On the contrary, God is the world to be as it is, which cannot be said, but which is shown in the world as it is. God is higher up and does not reveal himself in the world (6.432).

The representation above corresponds to the first reading that can be done about the meaning of the world in the *Tractatus:* that which is reached by understanding logic as the reflected picture of the world, as transcendental (6.13). The second is an ethical reading (worth), also transcendental (6.421). Neither logic nor ethics* deal with the world; they are the transcendental conditions of the world. They provide two possible methods of projection for finding meaning to the world. For logic, the meaning of the world is its form, God. For ethics, it is the willing subject. But nothing can be said of will (6.423) because the subject as will is not a fact. In other words, the ethical attitude situates me outside of the world, outside of facts. In the ethical attitude, the world becomes another world: "The world of a happy man is a different one from that of an unhappy man" (6.43).

How can the statism of the logical entry in the *Tractatus* be reconciled with what an ethical entry says, from will, which seems to suppose the possibility of radical change? Seemingly, Wittgenstein meant that by recognizing his absolute dependence on facts, their own factuality, man becomes independent from destiny, freeing himself from time* and from the fear of death*. It is as he noted in his *Notebooks*—at a time when his life was constantly in danger—"to do God's will." (8.7.1916) Good will desires nothing and simply gives its assent to whatever happens. This means seeing the world *sub specie aeterni* (6.45) or, which is the same, living in the present (6.4311).

b) Philosophical Researches. In the 1930s, Wittgenstein started to reconsider his thoughts on the *Tractatus,* especially on the pictorial theory of linguistic signification that he had supported. The result is often referred to as Wittgenstein's "second philosophy." It led to the *Philosophical Investigations.* His reexamination of the *Tractatus* also bore on the few remarks that dealt with religious attitude. In this second phase, Wittgenstein came to think that language could not be separated from the notion of usage. Philosophy's task is then the patient description of "language games." These belong to the field of human activities from which they cannot be abstracted. These activities make up forms of life and culture. In *Lectures and Conversations,* the place occupied by the notions of sin*, redemption, judgment*, and grace* in the way a human community lives, as well as in their irreducibility to theoretical explanations and scientific predictions, becomes the main theme.

The resurrection is an example. "You may be surprised that no one said, facing those who believe in resurrection, 'After all, it is possible.' Evidently, in this case, the role of the belief is more of the following type: Imagine that a certain image is said to have the role to remind me constantly of my duties, or that I don't stop thinking about it. There would be an enormous difference between the people for whom this image would constantly be in the foreground, and others who would make absolutely no use of it." (*Lectures and Conversations,* 111). The resurrection is not a hypothesis that scientific control could make more or less credible, and it is not the subject of historical enquiry. To believe in the resurrection, is to do certain things not done by those who do not believe in it, it is to have an attitude comprehensible only if one adopts this belief. The resurrection is not a factual possibility. In no way does this signify that the belief is nothing, that it is not necessary for a believer to state the truth of these religious beliefs. Contrary to what is sometimes hinted, Wittgenstein in no way adopts the modernist affirmation by which faith would subsist even if all the historic events it calls upon in the creed were fictional. Faith consists precisely in not holding the historical events it calls upon as possibly being fictional. Religious beliefs are not the psychological crutches of a generous moral attitude, and of an attitude that could even be adopted without religious beliefs. To believe in the last judgment, for example, makes one's ethical attitude completely different from what it would be if one did not have that belief.

For Wittgenstein, religious beliefs are inseparable from the sense given to the concepts used to express them, and these concepts cannot be detached from the attitudes we adopt, nor indeed from what these attitudes consist of. This means that a religious attitude does not consist of referring to something in the world, God, to organize one's life. If it were the case, religious beliefs could be true or false, and could be epistemologically justified. Since it is not the case, the true rationality of religious belief cannot be shown without stating that the apologetic is derisory (*Lectures and Conversations,* p. 114), whether it is positive (God exists) or negative (God does not exist). Not only are religious beliefs immunized against any rational criticism seeking to destroy them, they also render vain any attempt at rational justification; their rationality resides in the fact that they permeate all of the believer's actions and decisions, and not in what they would have that would be founded or "foundational."

The philosophical problem of religion is not about knowing whether the word "God" has a sense. Nor is it about knowing whether religious beliefs are confused or systematically superstitious. Looking into such problems means having already missed what constitutes religious belief, its belonging to a practice. Wittgenstein said of the Scottish ethnologist James Frazer, "What narrowness of spiritual life in Frazer! Hence: how impossible for him to comprehend a life different from the English life of his time" (*Remarks on the Golden Bough;* see Winch, 1958). To judge the outside of the forms of life, of human phenomena, like those studied by Frazer, from conceptions considered superior, amounts to missing what makes them practices inside which people think, feel, and decide. The forms of life are made of linguistic practices, of implicit presumptions, of behaviors felt to be appropriate, of "instinctive" reactions. A religion examined from the outside is unintelligible, because a human phenomenon does not depend on validity criteria that are exterior to it or that could be abstracted from it. A man struggles not to die in the fire without having to make an induction that will lead him to decide to flee; to believe that he will die and to fight to the death are but one and the same thing. Believing in God and, in some circumstances, to behave in a certain way, or to abstain from doing certain things, are not two different things. Thus there is something primitive in the religious attitude, in the sense that the explanation stops when witnessing the role this attitude plays in the forms of life, without giving it an external justification.

This concept of religiosity has at times been mistaken for a form of fideism*. Wittgenstein does not promote, however, the opposition of faith and of reason*, let alone the humiliation of reason by faith. Religion does not need to be founded on or against theoretic evidence, since it constitutes a practice. This thesis, which can be called "Religious Wittgensteinism," found its main proponent in D. Z. Phillips (also in Kerr 1986), who opposed it to any "evidentialism" (looking for a rational justification of faith), as well as to any "realistic" conception of faith (according to which religious belief would correspond to a real object, such as the belief in the reality of miracles*). Religious Wittgensteinism is in fact a relatively original theological path between rationalism* and fideism. On this path, religious beliefs need not correspond to facts. Still, they should not be considered mythical simply because they are not scientifically founded, nor should they be considered nonrational or intrinsically irrational (to believe because it is absurd). It would be meaningless to ask a believer if he thinks his beliefs are true; better to ask him (if not to witness) what role they play in his life. A person who believes that life continues after death does not act as one who thinks life stops at death. The prayer for healing a sick child, for example, is not an attempt to influence divine will; it is the manifestation of the resolution to resist despair and bitterness; or a proof of trust in God during hardship, in spite of human vulnerability (Phillips 1965), a trust which is understood as a gift from God. What is meant by "king," "castle," or "knight" in a game of chess, as well as the effective practice of chess, does not correspond to anything that would exist outside the game itself; religious practices need not correspond to realities for which they would bear witness. The meaning of religious terms (faith, sin, resurrection, love* of one's neighbor and so on) is not to be sought outside religion.

Nothing indicates that Wittgenstein thought that a form of life that includes the defense of theological and metaphysical doctrines, such as theism, was in itself intrinsically absurd, but he seems to have thought not only that religion does not consist in stating doctrines and defending them argumentatively, calling forth the evidence of an independent reality, but also that such considerations are not at all necessary. To this religious Wittgensteinism, one could object that believing in the existence of God can hardly be reduced to an existential engagement in the shape of a communal practice impossible to consider from the outside and which becomes meaningful only inside its own (religious) concepts. Because "if Christ has not been raised, then our preaching is in vain and your faith is in vain" (1 Cor 15:14).

How could faith do without a significantly vigorous form of religious realism? How could it only be the social coordination of a practice without losing its sacred character and being reduced to a human phenomenon like any other, such as artistic practice, or even the practice of the game of chess? Such questions, however, should not divert from a serious examination of Wittgenstein's position toward faith and religion, because it is not without advantages: to do away with skepticism toward faith, it does not need to reestablish theoretical religious truths, but simply to acknowledge the forms of life that are guided by faith.

- *Werkausgabe,* Frankfurt 1989, 8 vols. (contains the originals of most of the texts written in German, and the German translations of the *Blue Book,* of the *Brown Book,* and of the *Lectures.*
- *Wiener Ausgabe,* Ed. M. Nedo, Vienna 1994–, 15 vols. in the press, a diplomatic edition of *Nachlaß* for the years 1931–36, with more to come.
- C. Diamond (1975), *Wittgenstein's Lectures on the Foundation of Mathematics, Cambridge 1939,* Chicago.
- D. Lee (1980), *Wittgenstein's Lectures, Cambridge 1930–1932,* Oxford.
- A. Ambrose (1989), *Wittgenstein's Lectures, Cambridge 1932–1935,* Oxford.
- L. Wittgenstein (1958 posth.), *The Blue and Brown Books,* Oxford.
- L. Wittgenstein, *Lectures and Conversations on Aesthetics, Psychology and Religious Belief,* Berkeley.
- L. Wittgenstein (1993) *Philosophical Occasions, 1912–1951,* Indianapolis (precious collection of texts that are difficult to obtain elsewhere).
- L. Wittgenstein (1995), *Cambridge Letters: Correspondence with Russell, Keynes, Moore, Ramsey, and Sraffa,* Oxford.
- ♦ P. Winch (1958), *The Idea of a Social Science,* London.
- D. Z. Phillips (1965), *The Concept of Prayer,* Oxford.
- R. H. Bell (1968), "Theology as Grammar," thesis, Yale University, New Haven.
- R. Rhees (1970), *Discussions of Wittgenstein,* Bristol (2nd Ed. 1996).
- P. J. Sherry (1971), "Truth and the 'Religious Language Game'," thesis, Cambridge University.
- A. Janik and S. Toulmin (1973), *Wittgenstein's Vienna.*
- H. Frei (1974), *The Eclipse of Biblical Narrative,* New Haven and London.
- A. Keightley (1976), *Wittgenstein, Grammar and God,* London.
- P. Holmer (1978), *The Grammar of Faith,* New York.
- J. Lindbeck (1984), *The Nature of Doctrine,* Philadelphia.
- F. Kerr (1986) *Theology After Wittgenstein,* Oxford.
- D. Z. Phillips (1988), *Faith After Foundationalism,* London.
- D. Z. Phillips (1993) *Wittgenstein and Religion,* New York.
- N. Malcolm (1994), *Wittegenstein: A Religious Point of View?,* edited with a response by P. Winch, London.
- N. Malcolm (1995), *Wittgensteinian Themes, Essays 1978–1989,* Ithaca.

ROGER POUIVET

See also **Existence of God, Proofs of; Fideism; Language, Theological; Religion, Philosophy of**

Woman

A. In the Bible

Until recent times the question of the role of women in biblical tradition was ignored or reduced to a few negative or idealizing clichés, but it is now enjoying an unprecedented level of interest.

a) Minor Status. The most direct evidence in the Old Testament reveals a status accorded to women that is typical of a patriarchal society*. Dependent on male power (father* or husband), women were legally and socially speaking minors in a society that practiced polygamy and allowed them to be repudiated without compensation (Dt 24:1). Only motherhood brought them any social standing. Their economic situation was likewise precarious. As widows they did not in-herit their husbands' estates (Nm 27:8ff.): hence the law of levirate (the deceased's brother was obliged to marry his widow if she had no sons: Dt 25:5–10), and the oft-repeated exhortations to assist widows, in the same way as orphans and foreigners (*see* especially Dt and the prophets*: Is 1:17, 23; Jer 7:6; Ez 22:7 and so on). Nonetheless, the role of the feminine in the Bible* goes beyond these circumstances.

b) The Symbolism of Origin. Looming over all the female figures of biblical history*, the first three chapters of Genesis have had a powerful effect upon the representations of woman and the feminine in cultures influenced by the Bible. The resources of modern exegesis* give access to the subtleties of a highly elaborate symbolic text, and also make it easier to identify improper interpretations that exploit these texts for misogynistic purposes.

So it may be noted that the book* of Genesis contains a specific narrative* of the creation* of woman (Gn 2:18–25) which supplements the first chapter's declaration of the simultaneous involvement of the masculine and feminine in the identity of a humanity made in God*'s image (Gn 1:27). The creation of woman finds its place and its necessity in Adam*'s experience of solitude (Gn 2:18). Woman is declared to be man's "counterpart" *(kenègedô)* and his "helper" (v. 18b: *'ézèr*), necessary not in the first instance in order to perpetuate humanity, but in order that man's life should be ontologically viable. Coming after man in the narrative sequence, woman is here defined in terms of her "being for the other," which is not unreminiscent of the being of God himself—a frequently overlooked subtlety of the text, as is that of the narrative of transgression in chapter 3. The episode of the serpent has been stubbornly interpreted as confirming the image of woman as a dangerous temptress, responsible for man's misfortune. In fact, however, what is portrayed here is above all a maternal figure, in keeping with the text's etiological viewpoint. While dealing with the evil* that strikes all generations, the narrative actually foregrounds the female element of the couple* because it is more directly concerned with the transmission of life and its inheritance. At the very heart of the Bible (Sir 25:24) there is adduced an interpretation of this narrative which takes it as the basis for a negative vision of woman. This interpretation is questioned, however, not only by the letter of the text, but by the end of the speech to the serpent (Gn 3:15), which outlines the prospect of a story of combat, and bears a promise*. Woman will share in this through her descendants' mysterious victory over the descendants of the serpent. Revelation 12 confirms this prospect with its reference to "a woman clothed with the sun, with the moon under her feet, and on her head a crown of twelve stars" (v.1; *see* Is 7:11) in the person of a woman victoriously confronting the "ancient serpent, who is called the Devil and Satan" (v. 9).

Finally, it should be observed that the final structure of the first pages of Genesis prefaces the more concentrated narrative of chapters 2 and 3 with an opening chapter that evokes the relationship between man and woman in decidedly calm and optimistic terms (Gn 1:1–2, 4a).

c) The Women of the Bible. The text of the Bible preserves the memory of women who, in spite of unfavorable legal and social conditions, played a major part in the history of Israel*, saving the people from mortal dangers. The books of Judith and Esther and the story of Susanna attest to the recognition accorded, at a late period, to exceptional women. But the feminine is encountered elsewhere, too, in the course of biblical history. Right from the time of the patriarchal narratives, matriarchs have a decisive if unofficial role in the sequence of events (e.g. Rebecca, Gn 27:1–29). Bathsheba, at the time of the kingdom, obtains Solomon's promotion (1 Kgs 1:11–40). While foreign women (e.g. Jezebel, 1 Kgs 21:25) are made the object of warnings or, after the exile, are to be repudiated (Ezr 10:2; Neh 13:23, 26), some are presented in a remarkably positive light, for example Rahab (Jos 2:1–21, 6:22–25), Ruth (book of Ruth), and the Queen of Sheba (1 Kgs 10:1–13). Even if political activity was in the hands of men, even if—unlike in neighboring religions—women had no function in the ritual worship of Israel (only the role of prophetess is attested), biblical tradition thus marks out another register of history, guided by God and specifically incorporating feminine roles.

d) Other Representations of the Feminine. Besides the female figures who punctuate its story, the Old Testament contains, in two separate movements, two other essential representations of the feminine. The first is linked to the covenant*, which presents God's love* and faithfulness in terms of a relationship of marriage in which the people receives a feminine identity. This imagery is used negatively to express the infidelity of Israel. It becomes resolutely positive in the prophetic texts that refer to the new covenant and the sacred figure of Zion, the New Jerusalem*, adorned with justice* (Is 62:1ff.). The Song of Songs, which proclaims the pure song of human love, giving full weight to the feminine voice of the beloved, was seen by a long interpretative tradition as a prophecy and expression of the perfection of Israel, the beloved bride of God.

Biblical meditation on wisdom* also favors the feminine on an unprecedented scale. At the margins of the wisdom texts that display a popular and traditional misogyny (Prv 21:19; Sir 25:23), a personification of Wisdom takes shape from the time of the return from exile—a mysterious female being, present at the creation of the world (Prv 8:22–31), guardian of God's secrets (Jb 28:1–28), and one who gives order to the world (Wis 7:21 and Prv 8:30 [LXX]). The depiction of the "excellent wife" in Proverbs 31 may in this context be accompanied by a symbolic resonance. Whatever external models (the figure of the Egyptian goddess Maat, for example) may be influential here, this is a powerful and daring figure, which made its presence felt in Israel's thinking over the last centuries before the Christian era.

e) "Jesus born of a woman" Reference to the feminine is instantly engraved at the heart of the New Testament since Jesus* is confessed the Son of God, "born of woman" (Gal 4:4). With the female figure of Mary*, humanity is directly involved in the event of salvation*: she represents an essential aspect of the Incarnation, which the Old Testament prophetic tradition illuminates in retrospect. John 19:26f., which describes Mary at the foot of the cross welcoming John as a son, has been read as symbolic of the spiritual motherhood that she receives: becoming the mother of those who are begotten in Christ's Passion*—in other words of the Church*—she appears as the new Eve.

This symbolic and theological prominence of woman seems to have been echoed in the daily life of the first generations of Christians. New Testament texts attest to the place of women in Jesus' entourage, and their elevation in Christian circles: in particular Luke 8:2f.; Luke 10:38–42 (the episode of Martha and Mary); Luke 23:27ff. (the occasion of the Passion); and equally John 12:3ff. (the anointing at Bethany) and Matthew 27:19 (the episode of Pilate's wife). It is notable that Jesus pays very close attention to the condition of women. He highlights the hypocrisy of a legislation that condemns women to stoning while shutting its eyes to the sins* of the men (Jn 8:1–11). He welcomes prostitutes in the same way as the righteous (Mt 21:31f.). Women are the first witnesses of the Resurrection* (Mt 28:1–9 and par.; Jn 20:11–18). Others are involved in the beginnings of evangelization (Acts 12:12, 16:11–15, 18:2 and v. 18, corroborated by Rom 16:3; 1 Cor 16:19; and 2 Tm 4:19). Nevertheless, their role does not supplant that of the men who surround Jesus and who are appointed as apostles* of the Gospel*.

Unquestionably, the texts present a specifically feminine register. This may be defined negatively with reference to the restrictions that still characterize the condition of women in the New Testament, as asserted in some Pauline texts (1 Cor 7:1ff., which warns against the constraints of marriage*; 1 Cor 14:34, which insists that women should be silent in assemblies; Col 3:18, which reiterates the instruction that women should be submissive). However, the feminine can also be viewed in a positive light through other Pauline texts, which either propose a fundamental equality between men and women (1 Cor 11:12, "as woman was made from man, so man is now born of woman"), or lay the foundations of an ecclesiology* in which, alongside a masculine apostleship in the service of the Church, the feminine vocation of all in the Church is affirmed. The femininity of the Church, of which 2 Cor 11:2 and Rev 22:17 speak, is no longer limited to one gender: rather it denotes the character of the relationship which humanity as a whole receives as a vocation for its life in relation to God.

● J.-J. von Allmen (1951), *Maris et femmes d'après saint Paul,* CT 29.

R. de Vaux (1958), *Les Institutions de l'Ancien Testament,* vol. I, 37–92, Paris.

A. Marx (1969–71), "Les racines du célibat essénien," *RdQ* 7, 323–42.

A. Jaubert (1972), "Le voile des femmes," *NTS* 18, 419–30.

F. Quéré (1982), *Les Femmes dans l'Évangile,* Paris.

G. Dautzenberg et al. (Eds.) (1983), *Die Frau im Urchristentum,* QD 95.

J.-L. Ska (1984), "'Je vais lui faire un allié qui soit son homologue' (Gn 2:18): A propos du terme *'ézèr*—'aide'," *Bib.* 65, 233–38.

C. Camp (1985), *Wisdom and the Feminine in the Book of Proverbs,* Sheffield.

L. Aynard (1989), *La Bible au féminin,* Paris.

P. Beauchamp (1990), *L'un et l'autre Testament,* 2: *Accomplir les Écritures,* Paris, 115–195.

A.-M. Pelletier (1991), "Le signe de la femme," *NRTh* 113, 665–89; (1993), "Il n'y a plus l'homme et la femme," *Com(F)* 18/2, 25–35.

W. Schrage, *Der erste Brief an die Korinther,* vol. 2: *1 Kor 6, 2–11, 16,* EKK VII/2, Neukirchen and Vluyn.

ANNE-MARIE PELLETIER

See also **Adam; Anthropology; Church; Couple; Ethics, Sexual; Family; Marriage; Mary; Ministry**

B. In the Church

Christian anthropology* emphasizes the common humanity and dignity of men and women by virtue of their creation in the image of God* (Gn 1:27), their salvation* by Christ* (*anthrôpos* rather than *anèr* according to the Nicene-Constantinopolitan creed) and their calling to live in mutual love* (*agape*). Innovative as they were, however, these perceptions did not abolish androcentrism, either among the societies in which Christianity arose, or in those which it has encountered up until the present day. This system of values and representations, according to which women are far more dependent upon men than men are on women, did not lose its credibility until the 20th century—and even then only in Western societies, in which women have from that time enjoyed "natural" and (at least in legal terms) unrestricted access to the whole public sphere. In contrast, the Christian tradition's pronouncements on the respective roles of men and women are inseparable from a social outlook in which women have only an exceptional and limited access to the public sphere.

a) Women in New Testament Communities. According to the testimonies of the very first Christian communities, women enjoyed the gifts of the Holy* Spirit just like men—a sign of the fulfillment of the covenant* (Acts 2:16–18, cit. Jl 3:1–5)—and prophesied (Acts 21:8–9; 1 Cor 11:5). The baptismal confession of faith* of Gal 3:28 establishes parity between men and women, at least in eschatological terms. Women were very active in the missions to the pagan Christians (in Rom 16, for example, Paul mentions nine women as against nineteen men among his collaborators). Was there, then, an "initial community of equals," which little by little succumbed to a "repatriarchalization of the Church*" (Schüssler Fiorenza 1983)?

In reality, what Paul imperiously proposed at the very outset was an androcentric interpretation of Genesis. In 1 Cor 11 (which has been dated as early as the year 52) we read that "the head of a wife is her husband" (1 Cor 11:3), which is clarified in vv. 7b–9: "man . . . is the image and glory of God, but woman is the glory of man. For man was not made from woman, but woman from man. Neither was man created for woman, but woman for man." This symbolic scheme would facilitate the gradual adoption by Christian churches—domestic churches—of the Judeo-Hellenistic *ethos* which set down the duties of the inhabitants of a household in a threefold code: the wife should submit to her husband, the children to their parents, and the slaves to their masters. Christianized by reference to the Lord, this code was presented more and more as the norm (Col 3:18–4, 1; Eph 5:21–6, 9; 1 Pt 2:18–3, 7; Ti 2:3–10); and in its ultimate form, androcentrism would be founded on the Old Testament, without reference to any prescription of the Lord's: "Let a woman learn quietly with all submissiveness. I [Paul] do not permit a woman to teach or to exercise authority over a man; rather, she is to remain quiet. For Adam was formed first, then Eve; and Adam was not deceived, but the woman was deceived and became a transgres-

sor. Yet she will be saved through childbearing—if they continue in faith and love and holiness, with self-control" (1 Tm 2:11–15).

The most plausible explanation for the reception of these rules seems to be that there was a need to reassure potential pagan converts as to the consequences of the conversion of slaves and women, while a further desire for respectability saw women consigned to silence in assemblies. Apologetic and missionary motives thus played their part in the exclusion of women from any ministry of the Word* and from authority* (Nuremberg 1988), and it was moreover for similar reasons that this exclusion was questioned in the 20th century.

b) The subordination of women to men excluded them from public ministry, with the exception of the diaconate. 1 Tm 2:12's prohibition on women preaching (echoed by 1 Cor 14:34, perhaps an interpolated verse) and holding authority over men is the best-documented source for their exclusion from the priesthood and the episcopacy. However the diaconate—which in Antiquity involved neither ministry of the Word, nor sacramental ministry, nor jurisdiction*—was open to them, especially in the East (Gryson 1972; Martimort 1982). Within the Church before the division of Eastern from Western, there is no trace of any controversy over women's access to the responsibilities of community government (no more than in ancient Judaism*). The possibility seems never to have been envisaged, and it appears that only the Montanists (according to Epiphanius) practiced it: Epiphanius counters them by referring to 1 Tm (*Adv. Haer.* 49, 3; GCS 31, 243–444).

On the other hand, exegetical commentaries and liturgical and canonical documents take issue with women's desire to teach or to baptize. Origen* calls the prophecy of the Montanist women unseemly (*Fragmenta ex commentariis in epistulam I ad Corinthios* 74; *JThS* 10, 1909, 41–42). The *Didascalia Apostolurum* (Syria, third century) forbids widows to preach for the same reason (the heathens would mock them), but adds that they should not baptize because there is no evidence that Christ entrusted this responsibility to women (ed. Funk, 190, 8–17). The *Apostolic Constitutions* forbade women to preach (III, 6, 1–2, SC 329, 132) or to baptize (III, 9; SC 329, 142–144); but recognizing that "the Lord prescribed or conveyed nothing to us," they refer the matter "to the order of nature and propriety." The *Ecclesiastical Canons of the Holy Apostles* (Egypt, fourth century) are the only source, and in a rather unclear text, to attribute to the Lord the exclusion of women from the ministry of the Eucharist* (24, 1–28, 1; ed. Schermann 31, 10–33, 6).

It is noteworthy that Epiphanius takes up an argument which is also to be found in the *Didascalia* and the *Apostolic Constitutions:* if Mary*, the most perfect of women, was not a priest*, then the role cannot be suitable for any woman (*Adv. Haer.* 79, 3, 1–2; GCS 31–3, 477–478). This argument is taken up again by Innocent III (decr. *Nova Quaedam* 1210), and John Paul II (*Sacerdotalis Ordinatio* 3) repeats the judgment. John Chrysostom*, however, only considers public teaching to be forbidden to women (in Ti 4; PG 62, 683).

In the West, according to Ambrosiaster, the basis of the exclusion is to be found in the subjection of women to men (in 1 Cor 14:34–35; CSEL 81–82, 163, 3–164, 7; in 1 Tm. 2:11–14; CSEL 81–83, 263, 18–264, 8). For Jerome it is a question of conforming to the natural order (in Ep. 1 Cor 25; PL 30, 762). According to Pelagius, Paul does not allow a woman to teach "in public, since it is in private that she should instruct a son or a brother" (in 1 Tm 2:12; PLS 1, 1349).

The Latin Middle Ages approached the question in academic terms. For Thomas* Aquinas, women cannot validly be ordained because they have no *eminentia gradus:* they are in a state of subjection by nature, which is not the case for male slaves (in *IV Sent.*, dist. 25, q. 2, a. 1 resp. and a. 2 resp.). According to Bonaventure* (in *IV Sent.*, dist. 25, a. 2, q. 1, concl.), the Mediator appeared in the male gender and so only men may naturally represent him. Duns* Scotus, on the other hand (in *IV Sent.*, d.25, q. 2), considers that beyond the Church and St Paul there must be a decision on the Lord's part, or else the exclusion of women would be immoral.

The Reformation continued to exclude women from public ministry, in fidelity to 1 Timothy. According to Luther*, "the Holy Spirit has excluded women, children, and the incapable [1 Cor 14]: women must not teach the people. In short, what is needed is a capable and carefully chosen man.... To women it is said 'You must be submissive to men,' and the gospel does not abolish this natural order, but rather confirms it as the divine order and the order of the Creation." (*WA* 50, 633, 11–24). Calvin*, too, excludes women in the name of orderliness: "Responsibility for teaching or preaching is a distinction of the Church, and is therefore contrary to subjection. For how improper it would be if she [woman] who is subject to one member were to have distinction and authority over the whole body.... Preaching and teaching are not fitting occupations for a woman" (*Comm. Nouveau Testament*, Paris, 1854, on 1 Cor 14:34).

c) In the age of early and medieval Christianity, the destiny of women was family and private life; nonetheless, their status as virgins allowed some nuns to play a public role. Patristic and medieval commentaries on Genesis provide the key to the specific status of women: created after Adam, from him and for him (as an aid to procreation*), Eve was subordinate to him—though inasmuch as she received her soul* directly from God, she was his equal (Børresen 1968).

It should be pointed out, however, that this equality was subject to certain reservations. For Clement of Alexandria (*Strom.* II, XIX, 102, 6 [SC 38, 113]), certainly, and perhaps also for Augustine* (*De Gen. ad Litt.* III, 22; CSEL 28, 1, 88–90), woman was a complete image of God in his spiritual essence; but Ambrose*, Ambrosiaster, and their medieval commentators—heirs to the spiritual exegesis* of Philo, for whom Adam represented the *noûs* and Eve the *sensus* (*Op.* 66, 134–35 [*Works* 1, 186, 230–32]; 165 [ibid., 1, 252] and *Quaest. in Gn.* 1, 33; 37–38; 43; 45–47 [ibid., 34 a, 100; 104; 108–112])—remained cautious (Børresen 1985; Dassmann 1995), as did Thomas Aquinas (*ST* Ia, q. 93, a. 4, ad 1: "As regards certain secondary characteristics, the image of God is to be found in man in a way which is not evident in woman").

This equality has been a historical factor in the emancipation of women (the freedom to marry and to choose a husband; the prohibition of polygamy, of repudiation, and then of divorce); but in terms of the same anthropology it went hand in hand with a subordination from which only virgins, whose life was directly turned toward God, were exempt. In practice the only Christian women to play a public role were nuns, or those equivalent to them.

Some abbesses are recorded as having jurisdiction over the clergy by virtue of the right of feudal patronage (for example at Conversano, Las Huelgas, Quedlinburg, and Fontevrault, where the abbess was also in charge of the adjoining male monastery). Beyond this canonical oddity, the number of female mystics who have had a profound influence on the life of the Church is impressive: Hildegard of Bingen, Julian of Norwich, Julienne of Mont-Cornillon, Bridget of Sweden, Catherine of Siena, Teresa of Ávila, and Theresa of Lisieux—the last three were proclaimed Doctors of the Church, Catherine and Teresa by Paul VI in 1970 and Theresa of Lisieux by John Paul II in 1997—as well as many founders of congregations.

Despite the exceptional development of the cult of Mary, the mother of God, in the Catholic and Orthodox churches, ordinary women remained in the background, sometimes tragically so (as with the persecution of witches), but generally in anonymity: among the saints canonized by popes from the 10th to the 19th century inclusive, only 16 percent were women, including hardly more than ten mothers, most of these of royal origin (P. Delooz [1969], *Sociology and Canonizations,* The Hague, 270).

d) Contemporary Issues. At the end of the beginning of the 21st century, androcentrism has lost much of its credibility. We owe this to the feminist movements, but even more so to the introduction of universal education for girls on the same basis as boys, and the progress of medicine (the victory over infant mortality and death in childbirth; effective contraception; unparalleled longevity), which has left women free to take salaried work in a postindustrial society. The new social and financial condition of women has brought about a partnership with men that goes to the heart of the family unit, altering the condition of men at the same time; this equality between men and women is now enshrined in legislation.

The positive aspects of this historical evolution, hailed as a "sign of the times" by John XXIII (*PC* 41), have influenced Christian institutions and theology*. On a legal level, the *CIC* (1983) makes lay* men and women equal in almost every respect (only the posts of reader and acolyte are reserved for men); and on a theological level, John Paul II rejected androcentrism in *Mulieris Dignitatem* (1988). In this context the most important task for Christian anthropology is not to develop a discourse on woman, but to offer at one and the same time considered images of masculinity and femininity, of fatherhood and motherhood, and constantly to reinforce men's and women's capacity for alliance in Christ in the face of natural limits and of sin*.

In this new social context all the Protestant churches of Europe, reinterpreting the principle of *Scriptura sola,* decided in the course of the second half of the 20th century to call women to the priesthood (Reformed Church of France, 1965; Church of England, 1994). The Orthodox Church refuses to take this step—insofar as the question is put to it, which is very little.

Modern popes (Paul VI [1976], *Inter Insigniores, AAS* 69, 1977, 98–116; John Paul II [1994], *Ordinatio Sacerdotalis, AAS* 86, 1994, 545–548) have held the question to be a non-negotiable doctrine. According to John Paul II the non-ordination of women as priests and bishops "is part of the deposit of faith" (*AAS* 87, 1995, 1114), since the ordination of women has never been practiced—anywhere or by anybody—within the Catholic church, from its inception to the present day; though the Congregation for the Doctrine of the Faith has specified further that this is "in the present instance an act of the ordinary pontifical magisterium*, not in itself infallible" (*DC* 92, 1995, 1081; see Torrell 1997).

The adoption of inclusive language (i.e. systematically including masculine and feminine forms) in the liturgy*, the translation of the Bible, and the designation of God have become controversial subjects within English-speaking Christianity. The Catholic church regards such language as desirable in the liturgy when the congregation are referring to themselves, but refuses to employ it in the translation of the Bible: to do so would erode its historicity, which is precisely what prevents all its expressions from being considered as archetypes (as in the mythical narratives*).

● G. von Le Fort (1934), *Die ewige Frau,* Munich.

E. K. Børresen (1968), *Subordination et équivalence: Nature et rôle de la femme d'après Augustin et Thomas d'Aquin,* Paris and Oslo.

R. Gryson (1972), *Le ministère des femmes dans l'Église ancienne,* Gembloux.

I. Raming (1973), *Der Ausschluß der Frau vom priesterlichen Amt. Gottgewollte Tradition oder Diskriminierung? Eine rechtshistorische-dogmatische Untersuchung der Grundlagen von Kanon 968, §1 des Codex Iuris Canonici,* Köln and Vienna.

H. U. von Balthasar (1978), *Theodramatik* II/2, Einsiedeln, 260–330.

K. Thraede (1980), "Zum Hintergrund der 'Haustafeln' des NT," *JAC.E* 8, 359–68.

A.-G. Martimort (1982), *Les diaconesses: Essai historique,* Rome.

G. Dautzenberg et al. (Ed.) (1983), *Die Frau im Urchristentum,* QD 95.

E. Schlüssler Fiorenza (1983), *In Memory of Her,* New York.

Th. Hopko (Ed.) (1983), *Women and the Priesthood,* Crestwood.

I. Ludolphy et al. (1983), "Frau V–VIII," *TRE* 11, 436–69.

E. K. Børresen (1985), "*Imago Dei,* privilège masculin? Interprétation augustinienne et pseudo-augustinienne de Gn 1, 27 and 1 Co 11, 7," *Aug.* 25, 213–34.

P. Fiedler (1986), "Haustafel," *RAC* 13, 1063–73.

R. Nürnberg (1988), "*Non decet neque necessarium est, ut mulieres doceant:* Überlegungen zu einer neuen Forschungsrichtung," *JAC* 31, 57–73.

H. Legrand (1990), "*Traditio perpetuo servata?* La non-ordination des femmes: tradition ou simple fait historique?" in P. De Clerck and E. Palazzo (Ed.), *Rituels* (Mél. Gy), Paris, 393–416.

E. A. Johnson (1992), *She Who Is: The Mystery of God in Feminist Theological Discourse,* New York.

E. Dassmann (1995), "*Als Mann und Frau erschuf er sie.* Gn 1, 27 c im Verständnis der Kirchenväter," *JAC.E* 22, 45–60.

B. Heller et al. (1995), "Frau," *LThK*3 4, 63–72 (bibl.).

P. Coté, J. Zylberberg (1996), "Théologie et théalogie: les légitimations religieuses du fait féminin en Amérique du Nord," *ASSR* 41, no 95, 95–114.

J.-P. Torrell (1997), "Note sur l'herméneutique des documents du magistère: A propos de l'autorité d'*Ordinatio sacerdotalis,*" *FZPhTh* 44, 176–94.

HERVÉ LEGRAND

C. Feminist Theology

1. Origins

Feminist theology arose in the 19th century at the same time as women's struggles to improve their legal, social, and economic conditions. Toward the end of the century, the woman suffragist Elizabeth Cady Stanton, an American Presbyterian by then aged over eighty, assembled a team of collaborators to produce a commentary on everything relating to women in the Bible*. The result of this endeavor was *The Woman's Bible* (1895 and 1898), a bestseller which is still in print. Her celebrated speech at the women's convention at Seneca Falls (19 July 1848) and the declaration of principles adopted on that occasion were the direct ancestors of 20th-century work in feminist biblical criticism—hence the title of the recent *Women's Bible Commentary,* recalling her initiative. Feminist biblical commentary aims to show the limits and the richness of the canonical books. In themselves and in terms of the use to which they are put, these texts may have the effect of persuading women of their inferiority, particularly from the standpoint of their supposed incapacity to represent God* or Christ*. They therefore bear a share of responsibility for the perpetuation of androcentrism; but if carefully read they also offer the means to transform the present situation and make the future better. Feminist theology makes a special study of the feminine images that Scripture employs to express God, and seeks to apply them to the divine Sophia/wisdom* in order to overcome the traditional reluctance to associate the feminine with the divine.

2. Reactions to Vatican II

a) Mary Daly. Mary Daly acted as a catalyst to the reactions aroused by Vatican* II, and thus played a defining role in the development of feminist theology in the 20th century. The conciliar documents barely mention women, except in the message of 8 December 1965 (a model example of the traditional view of their role). In reaction Daly published *The Church and the Second Sex* (1968), whose title echoes the work by Simone de Beauvoir (1908–1986; *Le deuxième sexe,* 1949). Daly was to abandon Christianity with the publication of *Beyond God the Father* (1973), but not before she had drawn attention to the obstacle that Christianity's essential symbolism represents for feminists, as a result of the image it offers them of themselves, and its assumptions about their relationship with God. "If God is male, then the male is God." Daly cast light on the prejudices (theoretical and practical) engendered by traditional ideas of feminine "nature," showing how little importance she accorded to the past. She ended by viewing the women's movement as a community in "exodus," gathering together women whose sense of transcendence sought expression in ways other than those possible within Christian institutions.

b) Biblical Theology. Phyllis Trible (1978) compared Genesis 2–3 to the *Song of Songs,* and traced the evolution of the metaphor of the "bowels of compassion" as applied to the God in whose image men and women were created (Adam*). She also attacked (1984) the misogyny of the Bible, and of Church tradition and customs.

Elisabeth Schüssler Fiorenza's book *In Memory of Her* was a landmark in feminist theology. Its central idea is that women in the Church can draw on Jesus* and the practices of the early Church to conceptualize their own history in terms of its present-day openness to feminist transformation. The section on "the God/Sophia of Jesus and women" was developed further in *Jesus, Miriam's Child, Sophia's Prophet.* Her work is marked by a hope that one day authority* in the Church will no longer be the preserve of men. The two studies of the Bible published under her direction (1993, 1994) go much further than Cady Stanton's program. Laying bare the diversity of the biblical texts' ethnic and cultural sources, they insist on the need to go beyond the boundaries of the canon* in order to reconnect tradition with lived experience. These works also testify to the importance of Jewish and Islamic feminism and their efforts to achieve the ultimate goal of feminist theology: a theology* that excludes nobody. E. Schüssler Fiorenza's theory of the "equality of disciples" is, however, contested by other writers (e.g. Migliorno Miller 1995), who emphasize the importance of gender difference for an understanding of the Christian revelation as "nuptial mystery."

c) Theology and Ethics. The work of Rosemary Radford Ruether, almost contemporary with that of Daly and Schüssler Fiorenza, is constructed around the question of whether a male savior can save women. In her view, Jesus's kenosis* brings about an iconoclastic reversal of all religious status, and the Christian community continues in this direction, so that we encounter Christ "in the form of our sister," as for example did those who were present at the martyrdom* of Blandina. She has also launched the "women's Church" movement, on the model of the base communities of liberation* theology (itself hardly feminist until very recently). This movement has impelled women to take an interest in the liturgy* and spirituality. Recently, Radford Ruether and Sallie McFague have studied creation*, redemption, and the sacraments*, while others have addressed almost all the key points of theology, including moral theology. Much remains to be done, however.

3. The Maturity of Feminist Theology

A hundred years after Cady Stanton, feminist theology is adult, and is engaged in a lively debate as to the respective importance that should be accorded to reason* and experience, as well as the traditions of the churches. Liberation theology has begun to take an interest in women (the great majority of the poor are women with children) and will perhaps help to clarify the meaning of the doctrines and symbols associated with Mary*, the mother of Jesus. Orthodoxy* has also made a contribution to feminist theology, particularly thanks to the work of E. Behr-Siegel (1907–) on female ministry.

One may be struck by the variety of these investigations, which strive to renew theology. Feminist theology is well aware that the triune God transcends any sexual existence and remains in the last analysis mysterious to us, but it aspires to find a theological language that does not favor either sex. It also aims to renew the various theological disciplines so that the Church may become an institution in which men and women can be reconciled to each other and be mutually enriched by their differences.

● K. E. Børresen (1968), *Subordination et équivalence*, Paris.
M. Daly (1968, new ed. 1985), *The Church and the Second Sex*, Boston.
M. Daly (1973), *Beyond God the Father*, Boston.
P. Trible (1978), *God and the Rhetoric of Sexuality*, Philadelphia.
C. Walker Bynum (1982), *Jesus as Mother: Studies in the Spirituality of the High Middle Ages*, London.
E. A. Clark (1983), *Women in the Early Church* (*Message of the Fathers of the Church* 13), Wilmington.
R. Radford Ruether (1983), *Sexism and God-Talk*, London.
E. Schüssler Fiorenza (1983), *In Memory of Her*, London.
P. Trible (1984), *Texts of Terror*, Philadelphia.
J. Dempsey Douglass (1985), *Women, Freedom and Calvin*, Philadelphia.
R. Radford Ruether (1985) (Ed.), *Women-Church*, San Francisco.
E. Behr-Siegel (1987), *Le ministère de la femme dans l'Église*, Paris.

M. Dion (1987), "Mary Daly, théologienne et philosophe féministe," *ETR* 62/4, 515–34.
C. Walker Bynum (1987), *Holy Feast and Holy Fast: The Religious Significance of Food to Mediaeval Women*, London.
M. Dumais, M. A. Roy (1989) (Eds.), *Souffles de femme*, Montreal.
I. Gebara and M. C. Bingemer (1989), *Mary, Mother of God, Mother of the Poor*, London.
J. Grant (1989), *White Women's Christ and Black Women's Jesus*, Atlanta.
M. Grey (1989), *Redeeming the Dream*, London.
T. Berger, A. Gerhards (1990) (Eds.), *Liturgie und Frauenfrage*, St. Ottilien.
A. Loades (1990) (Ed.), *Feminist Theology: A Reader*, London.
E. A. Johnson (1992), *She Who Is*, New York.
C. A. Newson, S. H. Ringe (1992) (Ed.), *The Women's Bible Commentary*, London.
T. Berger (1993), *Liturgie und Frauenseele*, Stuttgart.
J. C. Exum (1993), *Fragmented Women*, Sheffield.
C. W. M. Kim, S. M. St. Ville, S. M. Simonattis (1993) (Ed.), *Transfigurations: Theology and the French Feminists*, Minneapolis.
G. Lloyd (1993), *The Man of Reason*, London.
S. McFague (1993), *The Body of God*, London.
R. Radford Ruether (1993), *Gaia and God*, London.
E. Schüssler Fiorenza (1993) (Ed.), *Searching the Scriptures: A Feminist Introduction*, London.
C. Mowry LaCugna (Ed.) (1993), *Freeing Theology*, San Francisco.
L. K. Daly (1994) (Ed.), *Feminist Theological Ethics: A Reader*, Louisville.
U. King (1994) (Ed.), *Feminist Theology from the Third World: A Reader*, London.
K. M. Sands (1994), *Escape from Paradise*, Minneapolis.
E. Schüssler Fiorenza (1994) (Ed.), *Searching the Scriptures: A Feminist Commentary*, London.
G. Cloke (1995), *"This Female Man of God": Women and Spiritual Power in the Patristic Age*, A.D. 350–450, London.
E. Graham (1995), *Making the Difference: Gender, Personhood and Theology*, London.
G. Jantzen (1995), *Power, Gender and Christian Mysticism*, Cambridge.
M. Miller Migliorino (1995), *Sexuality and Authority in the Catholic Church*, London.
E. Moltmann-Wendel (1995) (Ed.), *Die Weiblichkeit des Heiligen Geistes*, Gütersloh.
E. Schüssler Fiorenza (1995), *Jesus: Miriam's Child, Sophia's Prophet*, London.
A. West (1995), *Deadly Innocence: Feminism and the Mythology of Sin*, London.
S. F. Parsons (1996), *Feminism and Christian Ethics*, Cambridge.
E. Schüssler Fiorenza and M. Shawn Copeland (1996) (Ed.), *Les théologies féministes dans un contexte mondial*, Conc(F) no 263.

ANN LOADES

See also **Exegesis; Inculturation; Language, Theological; Liberation Theology; Mary**

Word

A. Biblical Theology

"Word," Greek *logos,* as applied to Christ without complement, appears in the Bible* only in the prologue to John's Gospel, in John's First Epistle (1:1 "the word of life"), and in Revelation (19:13 "The Word of God"). There is thus a clear contrast between the later development of this theme and its comparative rarity in the scriptures.

a) Origin of the Prologue.   Opinions have varied. The prologue (Jn 1: 1–14) may have had its origin in Gnostic movements (gnosis*), although they probably postdate it. It may represent an older and perhaps pre-Christian hymn to the Logos, which was modified before being affixed to John's Gospel. There have been diverse reconstitutions of this hymn (Bultmann*, Haenchen, Käsemann, Schnackenburg, Lund, Boismard, and Brown). Again, the prologue may be a reinterpretation of Genesis 1 (Borgen) in the context of wisdom* literature, composed either in a Judeo-Hellenistic milieu (Philo) or in a Palestinian one. The prologue may have been added at a late stage in the redaction of the Johannine* corpus, in the late first century and probably at Ephesus.

b) Biblical Reinterpretations.   Several targums (ancient translations of the Bible), principally the Palestinian targum of the Pentateuch (MS Neofiti 1, ed. Diez Macho, 1968–79), attest the diffusion of the theme of the Word* (Aramaic: *memra*) at the beginning of the Christian era. The form of words in Genesis 1, "God said," was thus transposed into the nominative ("the word of the Lord") and became a grammatical subject, not only of verbs concerned with speaking ("to say," "to call," "to bless"), but also of verbs to do with actions ("to create," "to complete," "to separate"). As in the poem known as the "poem of four nights" (targum of Ex 12:42), the personified Word* of God presides at the judgment* and fulfillment of history, alongside the royal Messiah and the mosaic Prophet*.

The *Demonstration of Apostolic Preaching* by Irenaeus*, a later text that retains traces of Judeo-Christian traditions*, accords the divine Word the status of a son of God (filiation*) already in existence at the time of the creation* (§43). The Neofiti manuscript targum of Genesis 1:1 itself appears to have been influenced by speculations about the "beginning," understood as a "principle" or "first-born." These titles, which may have been inspired by Proverbs 8:22, are also found in Colossians 1:15 and Revelation 3:14, where they are applied to the person of Christ. Bultmann (1967) has demonstrated the influence of the wisdom tradition over John's prologue, not only through the personification of Wisdom (Prv 8–9; Jb 28; Sir 24; Wis 7–9), but also through the narrative of the vicissitudes related to the reception of Wisdom (Bar 3:9–4:4; 4 Ezr 5:9; 2 Bar 48:36).

c) Interpretation of the Prologue.   John's prologue christianizes the divine Word by linking it to the concrete person of Jesus*. This entry into history is expressed in a narrative mode and functions as a prelude to the whole of the Gospel account. There is an obvious allusion to Genesis 1: the Word is presented as an actor in every creative labor, without any exception and without any dualism; the separation of light from darkness is recounted in the spirit of Genesis 1:4. In verse 1, the relationship of the Word to God is characterized in terms of "proximity to" (*pros* + accusative, to be translated literally as "near to" or "turned toward"), as well as in an affirmation of divine identity ("the Word was God," John 1:1) that was to become the basis for later developments of the doctrine of the Trinity*. By contrast, both pagan humanity ("the world") and the people of Israel* refuse to welcome the Word.

It is in this context that the Word becomes "flesh" by fully assuming the destiny of a specific human being, Jesus of Nazareth. Some scholars (Lagrange, Loisy, Hoskyns) consider that the whole of the prologue is to be applied to the historical Christ; others (Dodd, Feuillet, Léon-Dufour) take the view that, while the author's intention is to designate Christ, verses 1–11 evoke the Word as preceding its entry into history. In that case, the two references to the Baptist in verses 6ff. and 15—which are often interpreted as additions, on the hypothesis of the primitive hymn—are taken to indicate the historical grounding of the event.

As a result of this humanization, those who adhere to

the incarnate Word accede to the condition of children of God (1:12f.); although a minority view, supported by Boismard, is that this identification applies to Christ himself, with reference to the immaculate conception. Those who adhere to the Word receive the revelation* of glory (the Son's relationship to the Father*). Strictly speaking, then, the incarnation* of the Word amounts to a manifestation of the invisible God (1:18).

● R. Bultmann (1923), "Der religionsgeschichtliche Hintergrund des Prologs zum Johannes Evangelium," in *Eucharisterion H. Gunkel*, Göttingen, Repr. in E. Dinkler (Ed.) *Exegetica* (1967), Tübingen.

R. E. Brown (1966), *The Gospel According to John*, New York, vol. 1, 1–37.
A. Feuillet (1968), *Le Prologue du IVe Évangile*, Paris.
M. Gourgues (1982), *"Pour que vous croyiez…": Pistes d'exploration de l'Évangile de Jean*, 105–8, Paris.
X. Léon-Dufour (1988), *Lecture de l'Évangile selon Jean*, vol. 1, 35–149, Paris.
C. A. Evans (1993), *Word and Glory: On the Exegetical and Theological Background of John's Prologue*, Sheffield.

YVES-MARIE BLANCHARD

See also **Christ/Christology; Creation; Incarnation; Johannine Theology; Trinity; Wisdom; Word of God**

B. Historical and Systematic Theology

a) Contemporary Views. The term *logos* in Greek covers both written and spoken word; in theology*, it covers both Scripture* and the second person of the Trinity*. The same is true in German *(Wort)* and English ("Word"), but this is not the case in French *(Verbe)*. For Luther*, Christ* is the "meaning" of scripture. For Emil Brunner (1889–1966), *Wort* is the proper translation of *Logos,* since it expresses the act of God* in his self-revelation, and not merely an abstract truth. Karl Barth*'s hostility to natural* theology and mysticism* led him to argue that encounter with Scripture is the only means of knowing Christ as Word* of God, while only Christ will enable us to comprehend the word of Scripture. Dietrich Bonhoeffer* (1933) writes that Christ as Logos is the truth* of God, distinct from the word of man, truth presented to us *in* and *as* the word of proclamation.

In modern Catholic thought the notion of Christ as archetype (another sense of *logos*) is more prominent. Taking a strongly Platonic view, Hans Urs von Balthasar* (1959) sees him as the realm of ideas and values translated into history*. Karl Rahner* maintains that the perfection of God entails constant self-expression, which is consummated only in the incarnate Christ. Neither identifies knowledge of Christ entirely with the hearing of scripture, but E. Schillebeeckx seems to approach the Protestant notion with his argument that theology is the critical hermeneutic* of a continuing dialogue between man and God.

b) Pagan Usage. In Greek, *logos* implies both spoken word and the principle of reason*. Heraclitus (sixth century B.C.) conflates both senses with his demand that we listen to the *logos* in order to understand the world (Fr. B1 Diels-Kranz). Claiming Heraclitus as a precursor, the Stoics conceived the *Logos* as a demiurgic principle by which God produces from himself the ingredients of the cosmos* (Diogenes Laertius VII, 134–36). Human beings have their own *logoi,* and the intellect of each human being is a seed of the divine *logos*. The thought in the mind (*logos endiathetos*) is contrasted with the uttered word *(logos prophorikos)* in both God and humanity (Sextus Empiricus, *Adv. Mathematicos* VIII, 275).

Plato does not use the word *logos* in a sense relevant to Christian theology, but in *Timaeus* (28) he speaks of the Demiurge and his eternal paradigm, and the word *eidos* is used for the archetypes of particular species. The *logos* as written word is an object of suspicion, since such words are imperfect images of reality and writing fixes thought (*Phaedrus* 274 c–277 a). It was the desire for divine authentication of human concepts that led such later Platonists as Alcinous (second century A.D.?) to equate the ideal archetypes with the thoughts of God (*Didascalia* 9). Through their own *logoi*, human beings participate in divinity (*Timaeus* 90).

The Neoplatonists posited *logos* as the means by which forms inhere in concrete subjects. Some of them, such as Proclus, followed Plato's *Cratylus* in the search for a "natural" expression of the divine through words or images. Plotinus (204/205–70) weds Platonic and Stoic beliefs. The universe is pervaded by a providential *logos,* the eternal radiation of the Intellect and World-Soul (*Enneads* III, 2.16). Individual *logoi* are particular and temporal manifestations of that Soul

(III, 3.1), and dictate both physical growth and moral choice. Being the definitions *(horismoi)* of their subjects (II, 7.3), they combine their ingredients, although they do not create them. Individual *logoi* are like seeds, and the *logos* of the universe is a principle of order and of law reigning over it (IV, 4.39). This *Logos* is related to Soul as energy is to its source (VI. 7.5.); it can even be called the eternal offspring *(gennema)* of the Intellect. Soul may be called the *logos* of Intellect, but *logos* is not a name for any of the "three hypostases."

c) Later Judaism. In rabbinic thought, *dabar* ("the word") is not personified, although Wisdom* is identified with the Torah (Sir 24:18). In the targums, *memrah* can signify God's order or divine revelation*, as well as those anthropomorphic manifestations of God that are distinct from his true essence. Notwithstanding Philo, there may be no Platonic influence on the rabbinic and cabalistic reification of the written word.

d) Patristic. In the second century, Christ is the "Word who proceeds from silence" for Ignatius of Antioch (*Magnesians* 8), while in *De Pascha,* by Melito of Sardis, he is the *logos* that fulfills the Law. Consubstantiality with the Father* does not imply coeternity. Theophilus of Antioch (*Ad Autolycus* II, 22) and Clement of Alexandria (*Stromateis* V, 3, 16) follow the Stoics and Philo in distinguishing the eternal reason of God from his Word brought forth for creation. Tertullian* (*Adv. Praxean* 5–7) renders the Greek *logos endiathetos* by the Latin *ratio* ("reason") and *logos prophorikos* by *sermo* ("word").

Irenaeus* affirms the eternity of the Logos against the Gnostic myth of a fall of Wisdom (*Adv. Haer.* II, 28, 6). Justin assimilates the Logos to the revelatory and creative "second God" of middle Platonism (*1 Apol.* 22, 60), but the primacy of Scripture over reason is affirmed in the *Dialogue with Trypho* (3–8); and even the *"Logos spermatikos"* of *2 Apol.* (13, 3–5), which teaches pagans, works chiefly through the dissemination of the prophetic word (*1 Apol.* 44). Appearances of "the Lord" in the Old Testament are preliminary manifestations of the embodied Logos.

Origen* was the first to affirm the eternity of the Logos, on the grounds that God must always have a world. The eternal world consists of forms and species created in the Word (*De Princ.* I, 4, 5), who remains, however, subordinate to the Father (e.g., *Comm. John* II, 2). The Logos reveals the character of God to the *logikoi* ("rational beings"—*Comm. John* I, 16 and I, 24). The latter partake of him by nature (*De Princ.* I, 3, 6), but are not strictly consubstantial with him. Origen emphasizes the procession of the Word (*Comm. John* I,

25), the source and substance of scriptural revelation (*Philokalia* 5, 4). In the incarnation*, the Logos transmutes human nature into his own (*De Princ.* II, 6, 4), and he brings about the same effect in us by his teaching (*Contra Celsum* IV, 15).

Jesus*' teaching office is stressed in the treatise *De Incarnatione* by Athanasius*, but it is his role as the creator of humanity that makes redemption possible. In relation to man, therefore, the Logos is archetypal; in relation to the Father, he is consubstantial*. He is not, as Arius held, a creature of the Father's will, but that will itself (*Contra Arianos* II, 9). He is the Wisdom of God, as Proverbs 8:22 implies, but this is not a created wisdom (II, 16 *Sq*). As the image of God (Col. 1:15), he is all that the Father is (III, 5). The Word is defined as Wisdom, Truth, and source of all other essences (*De sententia Dionysii* 25).

Gregory* of Nyssa resists any notion that the Logos is more intelligible than the Father; he maintains that the nature of all three persons of the Trinity is equally inscrutable (e.g., *Contra Eunomium, Ad Ablabium*). He rejects Platonic forms, but says that creation has its own *logos* (*Contra Eunomium* 937 *a*); thus, the incarnation of the eternal Word reveals and perfects the *logos* of man.

For Cyril* of Alexandria (*On the Creed* 13), *logos* can describe the incarnate Word and emphasizes the initiative of God. For the heretics Arius and Apollinarius, the *logos* replaced the human intellect of Christ.

e) Later Developments. Augustine* defines *verbum* in *De Trinitate* (I, 9, 10) as *notitia cum amore,* knowledge accompanied by love*. In contrast to Athanasius, he correlates the Son* with understanding and the Spirit with will or love. Nevertheless, he observes (*De Trin.* VII, 2–3) that Christ is called *Verbum* only "relatively," not in himself, and that wisdom belongs equally to all three divine persons. According to *Hom. John I,* the failure to see the world as the creation of God's word explains the errors of pagans, especially their inability to recognize the fulfillment of the revealed word of Scripture in the cross (*see* scripture*, fulfillment of). The translation of *logos* as *verbum,* not *sermo,* stresses his timelessness rather than his historical activity, but in *De Trin.* (XV, 11, 20) the *logos prophorikos* is the incarnate Christ.

John the Scot Eriugena (ninth century) follows Origen in his *Periphuseon* by maintaining that a realm of eternal forms subsists in the Word. Anselm* may have Augustine in mind when he argues that God's eternal self-conception necessarily entails an eternal self-expression (*Monologium* 32). As an image of the Father, the Word is inexpressibly distinguished from him (38–39); in relation to creation, "spoken" by the

Word, he is the *principalis essentia,* the fundamental essence (33). Christ's role as creative Word enables Augustine (*De Vera Religione,* 36), Anselm (*De Veritate*), and Thomas* Aquinas (*Quaest Disp.* 1256–57) to say that truth is that which God ordains. Aquinas quotes John Damascene (*De Fide Orthodoxa* I, 13) to support the view that the word is the inner concept (*interior mentis conceptus, ST* Ia, q. 34, a. 1; see Ia, q. 27, a. 1–2), but, against Anselm, he refuses to equate the speech *(dicere)* characteristic of the second person with timeless understanding *(intelligere).* As with Augustine, the term "Word" denotes the person (i.e. relation) not the essence (described by *Filius*); other terms (such as "image") are of equal validity (e.g., Ia, q. 34, a. 1–2; q. 35).

f) Perspectives. The extensive theological vocabulary that allows us to ground the word of God in the very being of God also allows us to accede to the inherent possibility of what Christianity calls revelation. To speak of the word is to speak of liberty*: the human being who wishes to be "within the hearing of the Word" (Rahner) perhaps hears only God's silence. To speak of the word is also to speak of an event, and of a doubling: initially, the minor details of Middle-Eastern history, in which the "word of God" has ceased to be a matter of anthropomorphism* because God, the Word, has taken on the appearance and the voice of a human being; and then, in the contemporaneity granted by faith (Kierkegaard*), the events of the word that the "new hermeneutic" (E.

Fuchs, G. Ebeling) has instructed us to think and live. Perhaps there is more: if the word of God is given and perpetually restated in the Scriptures, read with faith and commented upon with authority, the word of human beings may itself become the vehicle of the Word of God. The whole Christology of the Word calls for a theology of the human word.

● G.F. Moore (1922), "Intermediaries in Jewish Theology," *HThR* 15, 41–86.
E. Brunner (1927), *Der Mittler,* Zurich.
K. Barth (1932 and 1939), *Die Lehre vom Worte Gottes, KD* I/1, I/2 (*Dogmatique,* Geneva, 1953–55).
D. Bonhoeffer (1933), *Christologie, GS* 3, Munich, 1966, 166–244.
H. Willms (1935), *EIKON I: Philon von Alexandrie,* Münster.
H.A. Wolfson (1956), *The Philosophy of the Church Fathers* I, Cambridge, MA.
R. Holte (1958), "Spermatikos logos," *SST* 12, 110–68.
H.U. von Balthasar (1959), *Theologie der Geschichte,* Basel.
J. Daniélou (1961), *Message évangélique et culture hellénistique,* Tournai, 317–54.
J.M. Rist (1967), *Plotinus: The Road to Reality,* Cambridge.
W. Rordorf (1979), "Christus als Nomos und Logos," in A.M. Ritter (Ed.), *Kerygma und Logos,* (festschrift for C. Andresen), 424–434, Göttingen.
M. Hirschle (1979), *Sprachphilosophie und Namenmagie im Neuplatonismus,* Meisenheim.
A. Grillmeier (1979, 1986), *Jesus der Christus im Glauben der Kirche, I, II/1,* Freiburg-Basel-Vienna.

MARK J. EDWARDS

See also **Christ/Christology; Father; God; Jesus, Historical.**

Word of God

A. Biblical Theology

The word of God* is inscribed, according to diverse modalities, in a history. Taking the measure of that history, the author of the Epistle to the Hebrews (1:1f.) declares: "Long ago, at many times and in many ways, God spoke to our fathers by the prophets, but in these last days he has spoken to us by his Son, whom he appointed the heir of all things, through whom also he created the world." This word resounds from the beginning to the end, relayed by envoys who can be designated generally as prophets. Here we will confine

ourselves to occurrences of the theme through the two biblical Testaments.

I. Old Testament

1. The Expression "Word of God": Usage and Variants

a) Prophetic Books. Though the prophets mentioned in Hebrews are not the only ones who spoke, they are the ones who testified directly that God is the source of their word. The formulas encountered in the prophetic books bear witness. For example, the audience may be addressed by "hear the word of the Lord" (*devar YHWH:* e.g. in Am 3:1, 4:1, 5:1, 7:16). The words of the prophets may be punctuated by "the word of the Lord" at the beginning or the end (e.g. 162 times in the book of Jeremiah). Overflowing the limits of particular oracles, the formula "the word of the Lord that came to [a particular prophet]" may cover the whole of a prophetic book (Hos 1:1; Jl 1:1; Mi 1:1; Zep 1:1; *see* Jer 1:2f). In the book of Ezekiel the general formula of Ezekiel 1:3 is relayed by the frequent affirmation that "the word of the Lord came to me" (48 times). Thus it is no surprise to encounter 240 times the expression "word of the Lord" in the Old Testament, designating either a particular word or the whole of a prophet's activity. Outside the religious context the envoy introduces his message with the words "thus said" followed by the name of the one who sends him (Gn 32:4ff.; Jgs 11:15; 2 Kgs 18:29): similarly, the phrase "thus said the Lord" introduces many prophetic oracles (with the verb *'amar:* 13 times in Amos, 128 times in Jeremiah, and 124 times in Ezekiel). When God speaks in the first person his word may be punctuated by a simple "…said the Lord" (Hg 1:8; Mal 1:2, 2:16, 3:13). In this case the prophet is completely effaced before God.

b) The Law. Prophetic formulas are rare in the Torah (*see* Gn 15:1). In Exodus 9:20f., "the word of YHWH" is none other than the word spoken by God to Moses, who is to transmit it to the Pharaoh (Ex 9:13–19). The pharaoh's attendants react to this word either by obeying it or disdaining it. In Nm 15:31 "the word of YHWH" is a way of designating the commandments (*see* Dt 5:5). From this perspective the expression "the words of YHWH" in Exodus 24:3 designates the Decalogue*. Outside of these few texts, anonymous narrators have God intervene as the one who addresses himself directly: to man and woman* (Gn 2–3), to Noah, the patriarchs, or Moses and Aaron, and especially Moses, who is God's interlocutor at the time of the Exodus from Egypt, the crossing of the desert, and the conclusion of the covenant*.

c) Writings. In the rest of the Bible* God speaks less directly. The Book of Proverbs collects mainly the words of sages, while often referring to YHWH. This divine name does not figure in Ecclesiastes nor in the Song of Songs.

Though it is true that the different parts of the Old Testaments are unevenly qualified as "the word of YHWH," Jews and Christians consider the book as a whole to be the word of God.

2. Bearers of the Word

As we have seen, those who transmit the word of God are the prophets. Next to the prophet who knows himself to be God's envoy should be placed the priest whom people consult and who transmits YHWH's reply (e.g. in 1 Sm 14:17ff.; 14:36f.; 22:11–17). And then come the sages (even if they may sometimes repudiate the phrase "the word of YHWH": Jer 8:9). According to the division of functions articulated in Jeremiah 18:18, instruction is entrusted to the priest, counsel to the sage, and the word to the prophet (*see* Ez 7:26): these distinctions should not be made too rigidly, because these are really three types of word, each referring itself to God. And in fact the word of God is placed in parallel with instruction in the Book of Isaiah (1:10, 2:3; *see* Mi 4:2). The word is not limited to the oracle: it is expressed by all those who, guided by the Spirit of God, have written anonymously according to the norms of their times.

3. Attributes of the Word

The word of God is at once single and diverse, even contrasting. Through the prophet, God expresses himself differently according to the times, circumstances, and phases of history. The prophets employ various literary forms—promises*, reproaches, accusations, announcements of chastisement, calls for conversion*—and distinct literary genres correspond to the diversity of functions in the community. The word of God transmitted by the prophet is above all an event that asks to be received by listeners; it is not imposed by constraint. The word of the prophet can be refused, in which case it is the word of God that is refused. Ezekiel had been so informed: "The house of Israel* will not be willing to listen to you, for they are not willing to listen to me" (Ez 3:7). Even though it comes up against human liberty*, the word of God is efficacious. The prophet Elijah confesses: "I have done all these things at your word" (1 Kgs 18:36). This effectiveness of the divine word is proclaimed by Isaiah 55:11: "So shall my word be that goes out from my mouth; it shall not return to me empty, but it shall accomplish that which I purpose, and shall succeed in the thing for which I sent it." In this text the word of YHWH acquires a sort of autonomy so as to give an enhanced sense of his intervention in history, while nevertheless maintaining the divine transcendence. It is presented as a power that nothing can resist. Already the Deuteronomist reading of the history of Israel makes of the word of God a power working in the heart of events. A late text of Deuteronomy proposed a unification of the multiple laws under the name of "the Word" (Dt 30:11–14). In the same spirit Psalm 119 reiterates the formula "your word," a word that is the object of desire and hope. It is notable that this autonomy of the Word is personified, as with Wisdom*, whose discourse is addressed to all so that everyone might find life (Prv 1–9). When speaking of the creation* of the world by God, Genesis 1 is satisfied with ten occurrences of "God said," to signify the omnipotence* of the divine word, for which saying is doing. The word becomes a substantive in Sirach 42:15 ("through your words") and Wisdom 9:1f. ("through your word," "through your wisdom"). The expression "word of God" may also belong to the theme of the fulfillment of the oracles and promises in the Torah (Nm 11:23, 23:19), as well as those in Deuteronomist history (Jos 4:10, 21:45, 23:14; 1 Kgs 8:24; 2 Kgs 24:2) and the prophetic books (Jer 17, 15:33, 14). The divine word is revealed there in all its power, giving life or causing death.

Thus, the word of God has numerous aspects. It can illuminate the present moment, reinterpret the past, and announce the future. It covers what theology* calls revelation*.

II. New Testament

The expression "word of God" is rare in the Gospels*, more frequent in the Acts of the Apostles, Paul's epistles, and the rest of the New Testament, but the Christian message is also designated as the "word of the Lord" or "the word of Christ*," and more rarely as the "word of Jesus*."

1. Scripture and Word of God

Scripture is recognized as the word of God, but not in the sense of an immediate equivalence. In an episode of debate with the Pharisees (Mt 15:1–9; Mk 7:1–13) Jesus brings into opposition the commandment of the Decalogue* concerning the honor due to parents (Ex 20:12; Dt 5:16) and an interpretive tradition that turns away from obedience to it. In such a case Scripture is no longer the word of God—it is not truly recognized as the word of God unless the divine will it expresses is respected. In John 10:35 the context is again controversial. Jesus is there seen opposing Scripture, designated as "your law," and the word of God it contains but the understanding of which escapes those being addressed. Similarly in John 5:37ff., Jesus says to those who "search the Scriptures": "You do not have his [God's] word abiding in you, for you do not believe the one whom he has sent." The reading of the Scriptures should lead to acceptance of the one who realizes God's plan; it is only on this condition that they are the word of God.

In Luke 5:1 the multitude listens to the "word of God," of which Jesus makes himself the preacher: the

occasion is unique in the Gospels. Here the expression may designate the Scripture that Jesus interprets, and from which he read in the synagogue of Nazareth (Lk 4:16–30). It is also possible that Jesus is being presented here as the model of the Christian preacher.

2. Word of God and Christian Message

In the Acts of the Apostles the "word of God" (the phrase appears 11 times) takes on a specifically Christian content because the apostles, filled with the Holy* Spirit (Acts 4:31), speak this word with assurance, a word that includes the testimony of Jesus's resurrection* (Acts 4:33). Like the word of the Old Testament this word is endowed with its own energy: "the word of God continued to increase" (Acts 6:7, 12:24, 19:20), just like the word of the Lord in Acts 13:49.

Devoted to the service of the word of God (Acts 6:2; *see* Lk 1:2), the disciples must announce it (Acts 13:5, 17:13), teach it (18:11), so that it will be heard (13:7, 13:44) and received (8:14, 11:1). The same applies to the word of the Lord (13:44, 13:49, 15:35, 16:32, 19:10). However, the principal content of the "word of God" is God's plan, known from the Scriptures, where the death* and resurrection of Jesus come to be inscribed. The expression already had this Christian meaning in the Gospel of Luke (Lk 8:21, 11:28).

In Paul, as in Luke, the "word of God" designates the Christian message and underscores its divine origin. 1 Thes 2:13 is the best example: "And we also thank God constantly for this, that when you received the word of God, which you heard from us, you accepted it not as the word of men but as what it really is, the word of God, which is at work in you believers." In the manner of the prophets, Paul is the preacher of this word that comes from God (Gal 1:15, *see* Jer 1:5; Is 49:1). What Paul preaches is the work of salvation* realized by God in Jesus Christ, which he calls the kerygma (Rom 16:25; 1 Cor 1:21, 2:4, 15:14) or the gospel.

With regard to Israel (Rom 9:6), Paul asks himself whether the word of God failed. The numerous citations from the Old Testament in Rom 9:7–17 show that he refers back to Scripture, but more generally to the salvific will of God and the fulfillment of the promises. Nevertheless, the apostle knows that the word of God is realized in time and that it must first be announced (Phil 1:14; Col 1:25) without being falsified (2 Cor 2:17), because the word comes from God and must keep all its paschal force.

In Paul the word of God is relayed by "the word of the Lord" (1 Thes 1:8), which has its own autonomous energy that follows its course (2 Thes 3:1) even when Paul is in chains, because "the word of God is not bound" (2 Tm 2:9).

3. From the Word of Jesus to the Logos

According to the Fourth Gospel Jesus reveals himself as a prophet (Jn 4:19, 9:17) through his words and acts, even as the Prophet (Jn 1:21; 6:14; 7:40). However, from John 3:31ff. the role of Jesus is distinguished from that of John the Baptist by a clear opposition between the terrestrial origin of the latter and the celestial origin of the former: "He who comes from heaven is above all . . . he whom God has sent utters the words of God" (v. 31, 34). The mission of Jesus finds here its best definition; it is not that of a simple messenger, but reveals Jesus' intimacy with God.

To perceive all the dimensions of Jesus' mission is to have some understanding of its divine condition. As Jesus says: "For I have not spoken on my own authority, but the Father who sent me has himself given me a commandment—what to say and what to speak" (Jn 12:49, see 14:10). The verb "to speak" (lalein, which appears 59 time in John), also known to other evangelists, particularly Luke, conveys the status of Jesus as the word of the Father. "The Father loves the Son and has given all things into his hand" (Jn 3:35).

Totally submissive to the Father, Jesus speaks of his own word in the first person and, through expressions such as "whoever hears my word" (Jn 5:24, 8:43, see 18:37; "listens to my voice") or "keeps my word" (8:51–52, 14:23, 15:20, see 1 Jn 2:5), with the frequent parallel "keep my commandments" (Jn 14:15, 15:10), he invites his listeners to adopt an attitude of faith* and obedience. In this, the word of Jesus effects a judgment* and has eschatological bearing, because keeping the word has a close relation with eternal life* (Jn 8:51). The most solemn affirmations of Jesus, in particular those that begin with "I am," reveal a connection with eternal life by way of a symbolism rooted in the Old Testament. By his testimony relayed from the Father, Jesus reveals that God is truthful (Jn 3:33) because the promises of God are fulfilled in him.

From this identification of Jesus and the Word, as well as the bond between Jesus and the Father, the Fourth Gospel confesses Jesus as the Logos, the Word* made flesh (Jn 1).

Conclusion

The word of God, designated and transmitted by Scripture, overflows it. The expression may refer to the public reading of the Bible within the liturgy* (1 Tm 4:5); it may also evoke the creative word of God (in 2 Pt 3:5; see Gn 1). More often it encompasses God's plan for Israel and humankind, within which is inserted the testimony of Jesus Christ rendered to the end times (Rev 1:2, 9, 6:9, 20:4). The word of God is alive and permanent (1 Pt 1:23), so as to be "the message of this salvation" (Acts 13:26), "the word of his grace" (Acts 14:3; 20:32), "the word of life" (Phil 2:16), and especially "the message of reconciliation" (2 Cor 5:19).

● H. Ringgren (1947), Word and Wisdom, Lund.
A. Robert (1957), "Logos, II. La p. divine dans l'Ancien Testament," DBS 5, 442–65.
Coll. (1961), La parole de Dieu en Jésus-Christ, CAR 15, 11–119.
P. Grelot (1962), Sens chrétien de l'Ancien Testament: Esquisse d'un traité dogmatique, Tournai, 126–34.
L. Bouyer (1974), Le Fils Éternel: Théologie de la parole de Dieu et christologie, Paris.
W. H. Schmidt (1977), "dabhar," ThWAT 2, 101–33.
R. E. Brown (1981), "'And the Lord said': Biblical Reflections on Scripture as the Word of God," TS 42, 3–19.

JACQUES BRIEND

See also **Anthropomorphism; Book; Creation; Gospels; History; Holy Scripture; Jesus, Historical; Judgment; Law and Christianity; Preaching; Prophet; Scripture, Fulfillment of; Revelation; Wisdom; Word**

B. Systematic Theology

The notion of word of God* is central to Christian faith*. By his word God called into existence that which was not, and by his word he will bring the dead back to life (see Rom 4:17). By his word, made flesh in Jesus Christ, he came into the world of human beings. From beginning to end, Holy* Scripture, the Bible*, attests to this vivifying presence of the word of God. This is why what it proclaims is quickly applied to Scripture itself: it becomes the word of God. The written word (verbum scriptum) that must be read according to the incarnate Word (verbum incarnatum) of which it speaks to us and wishes, through it, constantly to re-emerge as preached word (verbum praedicatum).

This is the central task of hermeneutics*: to assume the interpretation of Scripture as the word of God in its movement from incarnation* to preaching.*

1. Developments in the Early and Medieval Church

The formation of the biblical canon*, which occurred in the first centuries of the Christian era, placed theology* in a hermeneutic context: it is in interpreting Scripture that I reach the word of God. The church Fathers, commenting on the biblical texts, gradually established an interpretive tradition that would be followed by succeeding generations. The tradition, which laid down the rule of the faith*, became the standard for interpretation of Scripture. Transforming a Pauline* passage ("The letter kills, but the Spirit gives life," 2 Cor 3:6) into a rule of interpretation, ancient hermeneutics established a distinction between the literal and the spiritual sense. On this basis, extending certain ancient lines of thought, medieval commentators progressively developed their theory of the four senses of Scripture* (a literal sense and three different spiritual senses).

Down through the centuries, institutional regulation of relations between Scripture and tradition was reinforced, and the ecclesial ministry*, inscribed in the apostolic* succession, then became the guarantee of the veracity* of the word of God. This institutionalized hermeneutic was clearly established at the Council of Trent* by a Catholicism* that wanted to set itself at a critical distance from the Protestant principle of *sola scriptura*. The hermeneutic function of the Roman magisterium*, specifically as a magisterium of teaching, was progressively reinforced in modern times.

2. Word of God and Holy Scripture in the Protestant Reformation

Opposed to the idea of a tradition that would be a path of access to Scripture, the Reformation distinguished itself by posing its principle of *sola scriptura:* "Scripture alone." How should this emphasis be understood?

a) The Gospel, an Oral Word. If Holy Scripture has a particular status, it is not so much as a sort of formal authority: it is first a question of its being entirely inhabited by the dynamics of the word of God. This word, before its conservation in writing, was an oral word, a word proclaimed aloud *(viva vox)*. It is the gospel, the good tidings that give life. Or, to express it in the more classical terms of the Reformation, it is the word that justifies, that declares just, and that makes just solely by the force of this "performative" declaration. This word is therefore eminently creative: because it created all things at the beginning, it is the word that creates faith in those who receive it, helps them understand and receive the Word; and it creates the Church (of which Luther* can say that it is the creature of the word of God, *creatura verbi*). This is why the word of God must constantly be proclaimed in the Church, which is the major task of the minister in his preaching. In this face-to-face encounter of the Church and the word of God, this remains the first and

active principle; and it stands as the reason why neither the Church nor its minister can intervene as guarantee of the veracity of the word of God *sola scriptura*.

b) Distinguishing Scripture and Gospel. In its first sense, the gospel is indeed "the Scripture that vivifies." By becoming Scripture, it becomes letter. But it is never frozen in this letter, and this is why the gospel is never identified with Scripture. Scripture contains it, but it seeks constantly to burst forth from it in a living word, as at the beginning. This is what gives Scripture its clarity and allows it to interpret itself *(scriptura sui ipsius interpres)*. The Spirit contains the key to its own interpretation: it is clear in the extent to which, from being the letter that kills, it becomes the Spirit that vivifies. Luther expressed this in speaking of a Scripture criss-crossed by the incessant movement from law to gospel.

c) A Christological Criterion. For critical evaluation of the evangelical authority* of Holy Scripture, Luther was able to isolate a christological principle from his hermeneutic reflections: the true word of God is "that which puts Christ* forward" ("was Christum treibet," *WA.* DB 7, 384), even if it is a text by Judas, Anne, Pilate, or Herod. (This is the principle that led Luther to express reservations on the true meaning of the Epistle of James and Revelation.) The message of Christ, whose death* and resurrection* justify human beings and make them live, is like the "sunlit center" of Scripture (the tradition speaks of a "canon* within the canon"). If adversaries oppose Scripture to Christ, then Christ must be opposed to Scripture (*WA* 39/1, 47, thesis 49).

3. Theology of the Word in the 20th Century

a) Modern Developments. A toughening of the scriptuary principle occurred within 16th- and 17th-century Protestant orthodoxy: the word of God is identified then with Scripture in its literal given, which at the same time takes on a value of sacred authority, demanding a sacred hermeneutic. It is this sacralization that modern historico-critical exegesis* combated when it claimed (in the principle of Semler) a free critical reading of biblical texts. But such a reading carried to an extreme can end up making the Bible just one document among others of human religious culture, as shown by certain results of 19th-century liberal theology.

b) The Word of God in Dialectical Theology. Under the effect of the crisis of World War I, which marked the end of the liberal ideal and its illusions, dialectical theologians reaffirmed the true theological dimension of the word of God: in crisis the judgment* of God rings out and, through it, gives us the gift of his grace*. And the word of God manifests the "infinite qualitative difference" (Kierkegaard*) that separates the Altogether Other from human beings, and it invites the latter to come out of themselves and open themselves to a salvation* that remains *extra nos*.

c) Hermeneutic Reprise.   Whereas this rediscovery of the theology of the Word led Barth* to an antihermeneutic attitude, it is the great merit of the school of Bultmann* to have operated a systematic reprise on the level of hermeneutics. This allows it to make a coherent articulation of a theology of the Word and historico-critical exegesis. This connection operates by way of an existential interpretation inspired by Heidegger*: through a methodical reading of interpellations that the kerygma addresses to readers and that must be released from its mythological hobbles (which puts the program of demythologization in the service of a theology of the Word). In the work of G. Ebeling, this hermeneutic of the word of God opened onto the field of Church history* and dogmatics*.

4. Current Debates

The understanding of the word of God has been and remains the subject of ecumenical debates in which the Protestant tradition must be situated in relation to various modes of questioning. With Catholic and Orthodox partners there is discussion of the relations between Church and tradition (notably renewed by the constitution *Dei Verbum* of Vatican* II). The challenge here is to ask if a traditional instance can pronounce itself on the value of Scripture as word of God or if the question plays out in a hermeneutic circle at the very interior of Scripture ("Scripture, interpreter of itself").

The fundamentalism* characteristic of certain trends within Protestantism* provokes other debates. Toughening the Protestant *sola scriptura* in a literalist manner, it identifies the word of God with the letter of Scripture (verbal inspiration, in the manner of Protestant orthodoxy), thereby giving Scripture a status of infallibility*. Protestant hermeneutics counters such a position with the distinction between Scripture and gospel developed above, to avoid a legalist fixation of the word of God and to maintain the free play of the "conflict of interpretations" (P. Ricoeur).

Marked for a long time by the monopoly of the historico-critical method, the interpretation of Scripture is today open to a plurality of methods. Some of them—for example the pragmatics of communication, narratology, or the theory of the act of reading—help in grasping the dialectical connection between the word of God and Scripture, and in maintaining in the face of doctrinaire hardening a space of liberty* indispensable to a vital interpellation of the reader: "You are the man!" (2 Sm 12:7).

● K. Barth (1924), "Das Wort Gottes als Aufgabe der Theologie," in J. Moltmann (Ed.), *Anfänge der dialektischen Theologie* I, Munich, 1962, 197–218.
E. Brunner (1931), *The Word and the World,* London.
K. Barth (1932), *KD* I/1 (*Dogmatique,* Geneva, I/1*, 1953, 45–276).
G. Ebeling (1960), "Wort Gottes und Hermeneutik," in *Wort und Glaube I,* 3rd Ed., Tübingen, 1967, 319–48.
G. Ebeling (1969), "Gott und Wort," ibid. II, 396–432.
F. Hesse et al. (1961), "Schriftauslegung," *RGG*3 5, 1513–37.
W. Zimmerli et al. (1962), "Wort Gottes," *RGG*3 6, 1809–21.
W. Mostert (1979), "Scriptura sacra sui ipsius interpres," *LuJ* 46, 60–96.
M. Lienhard (1989), *L'Évangile et l'Église chez Luther,* Paris.
G. Ebeling (1994), "L'herméneutique entre la puissance de la parole de Dieu et sa perte de puissance dans les Temps modernes," *RThPh* 126, 39–56.
P. Bühler, C. Karakash (Ed.) (1995), *Quand interpréter c'est changer: Pragmatique et lectures de la Parole,* Geneva.
P. Gisel, J. Zumstein (1995), "Bible," in P. Gisel (Ed.), *Encyclopédie du protestantisme,* Paris and Geneva, 115–37.

PIERRE BÜHLER

See also **Bible; Canon of Scriptures; Exegesis; Gospels; Hermeneutics; Holy Scripture; Preaching; Scripture, Senses of**

Work

A. Historical Theology

---

a) *Christian Origins.* The earliest Christian theology*
did not see work, or at least manual work, as a subject
for theology. Those Christians who had come from Judaism* certainly shared Israel*'s respect for the working aspect of existence. Those who had come from
among the Gentiles belonged above all to the urban
middle class, and thus to a stratum of the population
with little tendency toward an aristocratic disdain for
negotium. In either case, there is no clear suggestion that
the fervor of their eschatological expectations led them
to attitudes critical of the practical necessities of life,
among which work occupies a key place. Paul expected
Christ*'s imminent return, yet he worked with his hands
and urged the idle people of Thessalonica to work.

Is there not a connection, however, between the two
problems specifically treated in 2 Thessalonians—erroneous eschatological speculation (2:1–12) and the idleness of the *ataktoi* (3:6–12)? Such has been the
contention. "This issue [of the end of the world] haunted
people's imaginations and excited them greatly. Some
took advantage of these imminent prophecies* to give
up work. On the basis that the world was about to end, it
was considered pointless to go on busying oneself about
other things" (C. Toussaint in *DB* 5, 1928, 2186). However, recent research has more than anything emphasized the lack of a convincing connection (for example
B. Rigaux, G. C. Holland [*The Tradition that you received from us...,* Tübingen, 1988], W. Trilling [EKK
XIV] and F.B. Hughes [JSNTSS 30, Sheffield, 1989]),
and there has been a demand for a sociology of the earliest Christian communities to shed some light on the
facts mentioned by Paul (R. Russell, *NTS* 34 [1988]):
"some Christians of this city aim to justify a form of
economic parasitism in religious terms" (Salamito
1996).The eschatological argument has recently been
revived by M. J. J. Menken (*NTS* 38 [1992]).

Certain professions (actor, soldier, schoolteacher)
were forbidden to Christians by reason of their connections with the religious, cultural, and political life of a
pagan Empire, but work itself was an unquestioned
backdrop. Disciples of a master whom the Gospel text
presents without embarrassment—albeit without the
slightest emphasis—as the son of a carpenter, guardians
of a Gospel which was initially transmitted via the Em-

pire's commercial communications network, the first
Christians certainly did not set about theorizing their
work. What they thus left unconsidered, however, was
nothing of which they would have been afraid or
ashamed. Within the conscious and unconscious fabric
of their experience, work could meet only with approval. The church Fathers* echoed those communities
that were opposed to idleness (*Didasc.* 13; Tertullian*,
Idol. 5, 12; Ambrose*, *Cain.* II, 2, 8) and which honored manual work (1 *Clem.* 49, 5; Minucius Felix, *Oct.*
8; Origen*, *Cont. Cels.* III, 55, VI, 36; survey in
Salamito 1996). The Christian work ethic, moreover,
was to pervade people's mentalities to the point where
the priest's *opus animarum,* his pastoral work, was
sometimes not readily recognized as work: so Caesar-
ius of Arles had to ask his priests not to spend more
than two or three hours a day cultivating the soil, so as
to be able to cultivate the souls who were entrusted to
them (*Sermo* 1, 7, CChr.SL 103).

The Christian ethos of work also had a political
complexion. In practice, only landowners could take
part in the political life of the Roman Empire, and it
was upon those who did not run the city that the necessity of working fell. The Christian approach to work,
however, was associated with a different approach to
participation. Whatever their position within relationships of production, all had an equal place in the
Church; thus the life of the Church was at odds with
the public life of the Empire.

b) *Prayer and Work.* With this subject as with others,
history has the official christianization of the Empire
and a related phenomenon, monasticism*, to thank for
the appearance of a problem. A substitute for martyrdom* in an age when all persecution had ceased,
monasticism took the form of a breaking off and a
withdrawal: a monk was somebody who broke with
the "world" or the "age" to attend to the task of a radical conversion*; somebody who symbolically poured
out his blood in ascetic* practices so as to receive the
Holy* Spirit (*Apophteg.*, Longinus 5). However, while
the monk did not wish to exist in the desert except face
to face with God* (and perhaps also in a brotherly
community rich in eschatological meaning), his life as

an anchorite could not be understood as *otium,* and the contemplation which he aimed to attain was no mere Christian repetition of the philosophical *theôria.* The monk actually worked with his hands, as much to earn his keep as to avoid distraction. The work he undertook, moreover, was the simplest and most humble possible (basket-weaving). Most important, the time he spent at this work was not taken at the expense of prayer, but was stipulated for him: the dual command of the Rule of St Benedict, "pray and work," *ora et labora,* did not sanction the existence of two distinct spheres of experience, but called for the conception of a single unified activity in which the work of the body served the "work" of the soul*, and in which the monotony of manual labor without intrinsic interest made it possible, not to turn work into a prayer, but simply to pray while working. It was thus possible to say that the true *ergon* was the spiritual and ascetic exercise, and that by comparison, manual work merely fulfilled the role of a *parergon* or incidental (*Apophteg.,* Theodore of Phermia 10).

Messalianism* and the "perfect ones" spoken of in the *Book of Degrees* (ed. M. Kmosko, PS 3) nonetheless prove that a monasticism did exist in which work was perceived as inimical to the perfect life, in other words as an obstacle to the constant prayer called for by Paul (1 Thes 5:17). This tendency was refuted by Epiphanius in his *Panarion,* by Augustine*'s *De opere monachorum,* and by monastic texts of Egyptian origin which in particular extol the value of work in the struggle against temptations, especially acedia (*see* Guillaumont 1979).

c) Action and Contemplation. The Christian Middle Ages made no more of a theme of work than Antiquity had done. Work continued to have a theological meaning in medieval monasticism: the labor of the sinful man, weighed down beneath the curse pronounced in Gn 3:17ff., work was above all a process of penitence—and it was as a supreme penitent that the monk labored. Nonetheless monastic work tended to disappear after Benedict of Aniane's reforms (817), and the monk appeared increasingly and exclusively as the man of "God's work," the *opus Dei.* Henceforth the life referred to as "contemplative" was to be distinguished not from the life of labor, but quite simply from the sphere of activity as a whole. In a society* that organized and viewed itself in terms of the three functions fulfilled by men of prayer *(oratores),* warriors *(bellatores),* and workers *(laboratores),* the active life was defined negatively, even when placed under the patronage of the Gospels. Whatever order it belonged to, action was less perfect than contemplation*: this was a widespread opinion, formulated by

Thomas* Aquinas (*ST* IIa IIae, q. 179–182). A life truly worthy of being lived could certainly be lived amid the activities of the world—but it would owe nothing to secular work; it would owe its dignity to an exercise of the virtues* in which, moreover, it is still easy to see a process of negation of the world. The development of Third Orders from the thirteenth century onwards furthermore expressed very clearly a sufficiently strict identification between the contemplative life and the religious life that the lay person could only be fully Christian by participating to some extent in institutional religious life.

d) Trades and the Reformation. While criticism of the monastic institution is not at the center of Luther*'s theology (nor that of other Reformers), it is nonetheless a good indication of one of its main directions. Although the monastic experience is criticized, in practice this is because it appears to represent the triumph of a logic of works and merits: considered as a human project, asceticism actually betrays a lack of faith. Since "the first and highest of all noble and good works is faith in Christ" (*WA* 6, 204), it is to the world (and a world thereby relieved of most of its negative connotations) that the believer is referred as offering the only possible context for an authentically Christian life. Henceforth there can be no tension between "action" and "contemplation." The service of God and the service of one's neighbor can be fully accomplished in the world. And as the life lived in the world generally involves the practice of a trade, *Beruf,* it requires little stretching of the word to interpret it as a vocation—*Berufung.* Station in life, work or trade, secular realities become fully part of the Christian experience; work ceases to have the minimal sense accorded it in the Middle Ages (necessary *ad otium tollendum…ad corpus domandum…ad quaerendum victum,* Thomas Aquinas, *Quaest. quodlib.* VII, q. 7, a. 1 [17]) and acquires a properly liturgical dimension. Whatever his trade, the believer works before God, and his work partakes of a logic of worship that does away with the distinction between the active and the contemplative life. The main referents of this theory remained unchanged right up until 20th-century Protestantism, whether work or trade was spoken of in the context of a doctrine of the created order (Barth*, E. Brunner) or of a theory of divine mandates (Bonhoeffer*).

Finally, it may be suggested that recent Catholicism has witnessed the development of related themes in the work of J. Escrivá de Balaguer (1902–75), the founder of *Opus Dei* and instigator of a spirituality of work with strong soteriological overtones, whose goal was the "theological assumption of secular activity" (survey in J.-L. Illanes, *La santificación del trabajo*).

e) Industrial Work and the Ontology of Work. Between Lutheranism* and Neoprotestantism there had however appeared a new form of organization of work—industrial, mechanized and capitalist; and it was this that had the effect of turning work into a major theoretical subject. According to Marx*, in his *1844 Manuscripts,* work was a two-edged reality. By working on that which is other than himself, by humanizing nature, on the one hand man creates himself (a point that Marx owed to Hegel*)—his work is the physical locus of his coming into being. On the other hand, in terms of the capitalist organization of production, work is treated as goods are treated—work can be bought, the worker is reduced to the status of workforce, quantifiable and marketable. In this way the locus of humanization becomes simultaneously that of alienation. Because work is not external to the history of the self, the self becomes separated from itself once work (of the wage-earner, and most obviously of the laborer) is bought and sold. And because capitalist society exists by reducing work to a workforce, it takes the shape of the most violent of all societies—one that ensures its own well-being by making the worker into his own Other.

Can the ontogenic aspect of work be dissociated from the alienating dialectics analyzed by Marx? All the contemporary theologies that have taken up work as a theme have assumed this dissociation to be possible. The working man, of whom it has been recognized since the dawn of the modern period that he may at times lay claim to the title of "creator," may also appear as creator of himself without the vocabulary's being intended to provoke: it is thus possible to speak of "man, a collaborator in creation and demiurge of his own evolution in the discovery, exploitation and spiritualization of nature" (Chenu 1955). The idea of work in an initially postlapsarian sense thus gives way to the (equally Biblical—Gn 2:15) idea that human toil has a prelapsarian significance. Of course work may be unnatural, and cause the worker hardship. Nonetheless, the "theology of work" claims to appeal to the original meaning of the created realities: and if man was created specifically in the image of a creator God, then it may be said that man "participates through his work in the Creator's undertaking, and in a sense continues, as far as he is capable, to develop and complete it" (John Paul II 1981, no. 25).

The euphoria of this conclusion nonetheless calls for qualification—which circumstances have already provided by making the axioms used problematic. The theology of work was actually set out as a theology of the product, of manual work understood as an activity of production—as something more than mere labor, indeed practically sharing in the privileges of the artist. The worker thus entered the discussion as somebody who *made* things; and the church projected onto his handiwork a light that emanated from the origin of everything, from the God whom Biblical anthropomorphism* does not hesitate to describe as the author of the greatest works. However, the "gospel of work" (Doncœur 1940, see John Paul II 1981, no. 26) gives rise to some difficulties when non-work is no longer a matter of idleness but of unemployment; when the multiplicity of jobs seems hard to subsume within a single concept of work; when most jobs have no sense of handiwork or making, and bring no humanizing action to bear on nature; and when it appear that man is less God's collaborator in a work of creation than a disturbing creature who is forever erasing the traces of his creation from the world. It is still allowable—and necessary, indeed—to maintain a moral discourse on the work that occupies our lives, for there can be no theory of work that does not invoke a theory of justice; and in the "social doctrine" that Catholicism* has developed since 1891 in the face of the "new realities" of the industrial world, what has been constructed is not a theological ontology of making, but a new face of moral theology. It is still allowable and necessary, moreover, to distinguish and prescribe the conditions for a non-alienating relationship between the worker and his work. But in the meaningful totality of human experience, how much of ourselves is brought into play by our work? Here the text of the Bible holds the elements of an answer.

● P. Doncœur (1940), *L'évangile du travail,* Paris.

F. Battaglia (1951), *Filosofia del lavoro,* Bologna.

A. Richardson (1952), *The Biblical Doctrine of Work,* London.

M.-D. Chenu (1955), *Pour une théologie du travail,* Paris (see also "Trente ans après," *LV[L]* XXV [124], 72–77).

H. Rondet (1955), "Éléments pour une théologie du travail," *NRTh* 77, 27–48, 123–43.

H. Arendt (1958), *The Human Condition,* Chicago and London.

R. C. Kwant (1960), *Philosophy of Labor,* Pittsburgh.

H. Dörries (1966), "Mönchtum und Arbeit," in *Wort und Stunde,* Göttingen, 277–301.

Y. Simon (1971), *Work, Society and Culture,* New York.

H. D. Preuß et al. (1978), "Arbeit," *TRE* 3, 613–69.

A. Guillaumont (1979), "Le travail manuel dans le monachisme ancien," in *Aux origines du monachisme chrétien,* SpOr 30, 117–26.

Jean-Paul II (1981), *Laborem exercens,* Vatican City.

G. Baum (1982), *The Priority of Labour,* Mahwah.

R. Kramer (1982), *Arbeit: theologische, wirtschaftliche und soziale Aspekte,* Göttingen.

W. Pannenberg (1983), *Anthropologie in theologischer Perspektive,* Göttingen, 404–15.

L. Schottroff (Ed.) (1983), *Mitarbeiter der Schöpfung,* Munich.

S. Felici (Ed.) (1986), *Spiritualità del lavoro nella catechesi die Padri del III-IV secolo,* Rome.

W. Korff (1986/1987), "Wandlungen im Verständnis der Arbeit aus der Sicht der katholischen Soziallehre," *JCSW* 11–34.

W. Krämer (1991), "Arbeit/Freizeit," *NHThG* 1, 51–65.

M. Volf (1991), *Work in the Spirit,* Oxford.

C. H. Grenholm (1993), *Protestant Work Ethics,* Uppsala.

P. Marshall (1996), *A Kind of Life Imposed on Man: Vocation and Social Order from Tyndale to Locke,* Toronto.
J.-M. Salamito (1996), "De l'éloge des mains au respect des tra-vailleurs: Idées gréco-romaines et christianisme antique," in *La main,* Orléans, 51–75.

JEAN-YVES LACOSTE

B. Biblical Theology

a) Old Testament.   According to the "Yahwist" narrative of the beginnings of human history (Gn 2:4 *b*–3, 24), the first man was a farmer (Gn 2:5, 2:15). Work is not presented as a punishment, since Adam* is placed in Eden "to work it and keep it" (Gn 2:15), before he has sinned. The text reconciles several versions of the origins. Nothing clear appears by way of an original "work," which was reduced to gathering because "there was no man to work the ground" (Gn 2:5; compare Dt 11:10). This feature is intentional: man was certainly not created idle.

After his sin, man's punishment was to be unable to survive except by struggling every day with a "cursed" (Gn 3:17) soil, with no relief until death. Here, fundamentally, we have a work without achievement. This theme is developed when Ecclesiastes exposes the fact that human effort turns endlessly around in the same circle, and is "vain." The oppressiveness of the task is not man's only reason to complain: there is also the question of its meaning (Jb 7:1–11). Besides work on the land, Job, written at a late period, gives a vivid description of work beneath the earth: prospecting, mining, the trade in precious stones—all tasks that remain worthless for the man who wishes to obtain wisdom* (Jb 28).

The "priestly" Gn 1:1–2, 4 *a,* compiled later, tells the story of the creation* of the cosmos*. The command addressed to the first couple*, "have dominion over" the earth (Gn 1:28), has been taken in the sense of a power given to man over nature, as though nature could be subjugated without a thought for the danger of a relationship of domination arising between men. The text however rules out the image of a direct dominion over nature. It restricts nature to "the earth" (extended by Wis 10:2, "master of all," [Gr. *apantôn*]). Above all, it inserts the totality of living creatures between the human and the earth: it is these in the first place that man will "dominate" (1:26, 1:28), and only on these terms will he "subjugate" the earth. The sense of the power given to mankind over the animal kingdom is therefore the key to a correct interpretation.

Kbsh (to subjugate) is used for the conquest of a territory (Jos 18:1; 2 Sm 8:11; 1 Chr 22:18) or the enslaving of its inhabitants, actions which normally went hand in hand. In the case of Genesis 1, dominion over the original occupant (the animal*), which alone ensures the "subjugation" of the earth, raises in anticipation the question of the relationship of domination between the human occupants of the same territory, once they have multiplied. It must therefore exclude any violence*, since man born of God does not spill blood (*see* Gn 1:29; 9:5f.).

The implication of "subjugate" is thus essentially political. It does not follow that the dimension of work should be kept at arm's length because the culmination of this narrative of the creation is the Sabbath*. It must be recognized though that the key aspect of God*'s operation does not require him to rest: tradition* has rightly recognized that he created by the word.

However, Genesis 1 also keeps a place for the divine "making" (1:7, 1:16, 1:25f., 2:2), because the tradition that preceded this text had used images of artistic skill or human (even military) strength to describe the creation, especially of man (Jb 10:8ff.; Ps 139:13; Is 64:7; Jer 18:6). God was seen as "resting" (Ex 20:11); he even "rested and was refreshed" (Ex 31:17). Moreover, the construction of the Temple* and the fashioning of cult objects were described at length as a "work" or piece of workmanship (Ex 31, 35–36; 1 Kgs 6) and even attributed to a man "filled with the Spirit of God with skill, with intelligence, with knowledge, and with all craftsmanship" (Ex 35:31). It is in this light that Genesis 1 interprets the "task" of the world's creation.

At the same time, this is above all a piece of work. Any piece of work worthy of the name must have a plan and thus a conclusion: so God "finished his work" (Gn 2:2f.). For the divine workman the Sabbath is a time of reward and satisfaction more than of rest: "And God saw everything that he had made, and behold, it was very good" (Gn 1:31; in Is 41:7, the maker of idols uses the same terms!). In the view of the (priestly) author, the Sabbath was no doubt instituted primarily so that man could echo the Creator's "very good" with his praise*—it was first and foremost a liturgical time.

In an indirect but significant way the commandment*

of the Sabbath indicates the place of work in the Biblical world: "Six days you shall labor, and do all your work" (Ex 20:9f.). Addressed to hunter-gatherers, this precept would be meaningless. Indeed, it would have had little meaning in a purely agrarian society, since it presupposes first of all a relationship with a "work" in which it may itself become an occasion for idolatry*, and then a situation in which man is no longer capable of conquering the earth without "subjugating" his fellow men, rather than the animals alone. The idolatrous tendencies of work (the thing made inciting man to "submit" to it) are suggested in the Ten Commandments (Decalogue*) of Ex 20:1–21. God's creative act is given here as the motivation for the Sabbath, which is a time to worship the God who made the world and mankind (20:4, 20:11)—whereas the idolater worships what he has made himself, and enslaves himself to it by way of an image. The description of idols as man's "handiwork" is common (e.g. Dt 4:28; 27:15; Jer 1:16; Wis 13:10; for God's "handiwork", see for example Ps 8:4, 8:7; 19:2 and so on). The most detailed descriptions of a process of manufacture are to be read in some of deutero-Isaiah's diatribes against idolaters: the fervor of their worship of the idol is proportionate to the efforts of strength and intelligence that it has demanded (Is 40:19f.; 41:6f.; 44:9–20; Wis 13:10–19; 15:7–13). These texts skillfully intertwine three themes: divine handiwork, the making of idols, and purely useful work (Bar 6:58) with which the worker is right to be satisfied. The disparagement of work is alien to the Bible*. While the art of making an object derives from a wisdom given by God, making an object into an idol so as to enslave oneself to it is the result of madness. The Ten Commandments of Deuteronomy (5:12–15) specifies the direct recipient of this law of the Sabbath: the master (along with his wife—the latter goes without saying), whose unquestioned power appears in Proverbs 31:15, 31:27. To do their work, such a couple have sons and daughters, servants (or slaves), animals, and also "the sojourner who is within your gates"(Dt 5:14). It is written that all these will rest "as well as you." Considered from this economic (Gr. *oikos*) and "political" (Gr. *polis*) point of view the Sabbath is, even more than a memory of the Creation, an explicit reenactment of Israel*'s exodus out of the "house of slavery" (Dt 5:6).

The Sabbath was developed into the "sabbatical" year, a time of rest for the earth (Ex 23:10f; Lv 25:2–7), of the remission of debts (Dt 15:1–6), and of liberation for Hebrew slaves (Ex 21:2–6).

The recollection of Egypt was fixed for ever in the people's memory as a perversion of the first task given by the Creator: man took the place of the animals and was treated worse than them by his fellow man. The foundations of a theology of liberation* were no doubt laid. At the same time, two characteristics of the original vocation (multiplying, and subduing the earth: Gn 1:28) came into conflict. The confrontation between the status of "slave" and that of "son" was the impulse of the drama (Ex 4:22f), and remained so for a long time: Pharaoh resolved to lose his son in order to keep his slaves. So the alliance between work and life was broken, and the son was the victim.

b) New Testament. The Gospels* continue with the themes that the Old Testament had highlighted. Jesus' speeches reveal a great familiarity with the world of work, and more specifically with the social relationships within which work takes place. The vocabulary of apostolic activity ("laborer," "reaper," "fisherman," "wages" and so on) consistently expresses a fundamental relationship between the mission that Christ gave to those whom he charged with the Gospel, and that which the world at large understands by "work." Time after time, the parables* represent various types of service: bailiffs, stewards, serving-men, maidservants and laborers, not to forget the unemployed (Mt 20:1–7). One of the dominant motifs is administration on behalf of another person who is absent. The rich man who talks only to himself about the accumulation of his wealth is something of an exception (Lk 12:16–21). Of course, since these are parables, all these activities are mentioned only so as to signify something else—in particular the fact that God has gone away, leaving man, his steward, free (Lk 12:42, 16:1–8). But the fact that such keen attention is paid to what remains a parable, a moral fable, reveals a dual movement: on the one hand, the reality of what "work" means is in no way played down, since it is or has been fully experienced; and on the other hand the reality is genuinely transcended, since it is considered so freely.

Above all, money is omnipresent, as witness the number of denominations of currency referred to by Jesus, and their range of uses, both legitimate (wages, alms, taxes, deposits, inheritances, investments, loans, debts, fines and so on) and iniquitous (bribes, embezzlement, blood money). "You cannot serve God and money" (Mt 6:24): these words denote the empty space left by the idols of earlier times, which since Jesus' time has been occupied specifically by "Mammon," in other words, "Money." Once deposed from its enslaving royalty, however, money is not anathematized but rather neutralized: it would be a pity not to know how to use it for the benefit of those who need it most (Lk 16:9ff.; *see* 19:23, 20:24). Jesus' irony and detachment on this subject speak volumes about true liberation. However, the decisive meeting, for Jesus, takes place in the sacred domain, in the Temple, on the Sabbath day. Commerce is also a form of work.

Whether or not it is carried out inside the temple, it is hard to see how animal sacrifice could go on without money and without middlemen: but Jesus, in a symbolic gesture, drives them out.

The Sabbath, for its part, is the occasion for severe confrontations. It presents the theme of work and life: Jesus says that his Father "does greater works than these" because he "raises the dead and gives them life" and, like a true Father, "shows" his son what he is doing (Jn 5:20). Life for Jesus is beyond the opposition of work and rest: the essential is there. This leads him to an irrepressible questioning of the Sabbath law, intended and perceived beyond any casuistry. The Sermon on the Mount (Mt 5–7), which is based on a reworking of the Ten Commandments, advocates (without offering an opinion on the Sabbath) a mode of life exemplified by the birds, which "neither sow nor reap nor gather into barns" (Mt 6:26), and the lilies of the field, which "neither toil nor spin" (Mt 6:28). This is not a matter of the imposition of a new law, but the inauguration of a new basis for any activity: "Is not life more than food, and the body more than clothing?" (Mt 6:25). Daily activity joins the liturgical service, in not being defined by its product: "on the Sabbath the priests in the temple profane the Sabbath and are guiltless" (Mt 12:5; *see* Jn 7:22f.). This new order is neither a state of being, nor strictly speaking a goal to be attained, but a beginning set forth.

● O.H. Pesch (1967), *Theologie der Rechtfertigung bei Martin Luther und Thomas von Aquin: Versuch eines systematisch-theologischen Dialogs,* Mainz.

Y. Congar and V. Vajta (1970), "Mérite," *in* Y. Congar (Ed.), *Vocabulaire œcuménique,* Paris, 233–52.

O.H. Pesch and A. Peters (1981), *Einführung in die Lehre von Gnade und Rechtfertigung,* Darmstadt.

A. Birmelé (1986), *Le salut en Jésus-Christ dans les dialogues œcuméniques,* Paris.

K. Lehmann and W. Pannenberg (Ed.) (1986), *Lehrverurteilungen-Kirchentrennend?,* Freiburg-Göttingen (*Les anathèmes du XVIe siècle sont-ils encore actuels?,* 1989).

B. Sesboüé (1988, 1991), *Jésus-Christ l'unique médiateur,* 2 vols., Paris.

B. Sesboüé (1990), *Pour une théologie œcuménique,* Paris.

ANDRÉ BIRMELÉ

See also **Augustine of Hippo; Grace; Justification; Luther, Martin; Pelagianism; Salvation; Scholasticism; Thomism**

Works

a) The Old Testament praises the great works of God* (Ps 8:4–7; 104:24–31 and so on) Sometimes it evokes the creative work of the artisan (Is 44:13; Jer 19:11; 2 Kgs 19:18; 2 Chr 34:25) but it rarely uses "works" to refer to human actions that either please or displease God (Jb 34:11; Eccl 12:14). In the New Testament, "works" *(ergon)* designate either the salvific action of Jesus Christ (Acts 13:41; 1 Cor 15:58; Phil 1:6) or the ethical acts of the baptized. The works are evoked positively as corresponding to the requirements of faith* (Mt 5:16; Acts 9: 36; Eph 2:10; 1 Pt 2:12), themselves God's work in the life of the disciple (2 Cor 9:8; Phil 1:6; Col 3:16s). They glorify God (Mt 5:16; 1 Pt 2:12) and will be decisive when the judgment comes (Rom 2:6; 2 Cor 5:10; Mt 25:31–46). By insisting on justification through faith (Rom 3:28) and by rejecting salvation through works (Rom 3:20, 11:6; Gal 2:16) the apostle Paul denied even the salvific value of the works. Works are the consequences and not the preconditions of salvation. Thus, man could not claim his works to appear as just before God. But the life of the justified necessarily bears fruit; it is rich in works of love* (Rom 7:4; 2 Cor 9:10; Gal 5:6).

b) The question about works would become one of the major controversies at the heart of the Western Churches. It would be absent from Eastern churches, which offered a more inclusive, more cosmic, and less personal vision of grace* (*theôsis,* see Orthodoxy*, modern and contemporary). It has been decisive since the time of Augustine* (354–430), who averred, against Pelagianism*, that the good works of the believer are not of human origin but are the fruits of the sole grace of God. Against the objections that came from the position that would be known as "semi-

Pelagian," he stated that the loving act of God only elicited faith. Given the original sin* and the corruption of human nature, faith could not be the result of good human works. The first condemnation of Pelagianism by the synod* of Carthage (418) was confirmed by the second synod of Orange (529). Not only is it stated that man could not carry out his own salvation by his works, but also that the original sin forbade human will and reason to create faith. Without going back to Augustinian options with regards to predestination*, the synod of Orange insisted on the works of the Holy* Spirit, who prepares for justification and precedes all human initiative (*DH* 371–397).

c) During the Reformation, these stakes would hold a particular place. The question of works appeared on several levels:

1) A first controversy bears on the salvation through works, which Reformers denounced in the Church practices of the time. This alternative was proposed by diverse theologies* (such as Gabriel Biel) and common in popular piety (as evidenced in the sale of indulgences* to be freed from purgatory*). The official teaching of the Catholic church as confirmed by the Council of Trent*, however, never stated that the human being could save himself without having recourse in the grace of God (*DH* 1551 *Sq*). Luther* rejected the idea of *fides capite formata* (faith completed by works of love) as a reason for salvation. This formulation was ambiguous because it implied that faith would obtain its salvific character only through works. It also called for a distinction between intelligence (reason) and will (source of the works of love) that seemed dictated by the Aristotelian influence. In this light, it was inconceivable that salvation would happen only through faith, which was nothing but reason supporting truth*. It had to be completed by love. Luther, who was of the Augustinian school, had a global understanding of faith. It is trust in God and personal relationship with God. These two different understandings of faith would lead to a serious misunderstanding that would take centuries to be clarified, yet the intention of the one or other was to insist on salvation, the gift from the grace of God. The Council of Trent's condemnation, which would blame the Reformers for not having stated the necessity of good works as a necessary consequence of faith, stemmed from the same misunderstanding (*DH* 1570), the Reformers always having insisted on the necessity of works, consequences

of faith, and on their inclusion in faith itself (*see CA*, art. 4).

2) A second debate bears on man's ability to prepare himself for faith through his works. Various Scholastic trends taught that grace was a quality whose human nature* was covered in accordance with its creation* and that, in spite of sin, reason and human will were able to do good works, preparing the justifying grace. Faced with what it saw as a resurgence of Pelagianism, and cautious to avoid any justification through works, the Reformers insisted on the character always external to grace, which could not be understood as human *habitus*. Only works carried out by the Holy Spirit in the believer could be called good, whether they preceded or followed justification. The Council of Trent would condemn this option (*DH* 1554 *Sq*).

3) The third dispute relates to the meritorious character of the works of the justified. Scholasticism had distinguished between *de condigno* merits (direct relation between action and reward) and *de congruo* merits (relation of convenience). For Thomas* Aquinas, only Christ* can deserve *de condigno* the grace of man, the *de congruo* merit depending only on the will of God who can access the believer's prayer. Late Scholasticism, however, stated that the good works of the non-justified represented a *de congruo* merit for justification, the works of the justified being a *de condigno* merit for eternal life* (Franciscan school and nominalism*). The Reformation radically rejected this understanding in the name of salvation through faith alone (*see CA*, art. 4). The Council of Trent confirmed that the believer earned an "increase of grace" through his good works (*DH* 1582).

d) These different approaches to the value of works would be central to controversies between the Western churches for centuries. A significant degree of consensus has only appeared in the past fifty years. All agree to say that works are only the consequence, but the necessary consequence, of the justification of the believer whom the Holy Spirit arouses to faith and who could not deserve the grace granted. Good works are born from the new relationship that unites God and man. A dispute remains among Christian families as to the manner and meaning of man's cooperation in his salvation, but this question is no longer seen as separating churches. For the most part, this progress is the result of bringing together anthropological and philosophical visions: today, a more relational understanding of faith, of grace, and of works replaces the more sapient and ontological (O. H. Pesch) alternatives of Scholasticism.

- O. H. Pesch (1967), *Theologie der Rechtfertigung bei Martin Luther und Thomas von Aquin: Versuch eines systematisch-theologischen Dialogs*, Mainz.
- Y. Congar and V. Vajta (1970), "Mérite," in Y. Congar (Ed.), *Vocabulaire œcuménique*, Paris, 233–52.
- O. H. Pesch and A. Peters (1981), *Einführung in die Lehre von Gnade und Rechtfertigung*, Darmstadt.
- A. Birmelé (1986), *Le salut en Jésus-Christ dans les dialogues œcuméniques*, Paris.

K. Lehmann and W. Pannenberg (Ed.) (1986), *Lehrverurteilungen-Kirchentrennend?*, Freiburg-Göttingen.
B. Sesboüé (1988, 1991), *Jésus-Christ l'unique médiateur*, 2 vols., Paris.
B. Sesboüé (1990), *Pour une théologie œcuménique*, Paris.

ANDRÉ BIRMELÉ

See also **Augustine; Grace; Justification; Luther, Martin; Pelagianism; Salvation; Scholasticism; Thomism**

World

A. Biblical Theology

The terms in biblical Greek which may be translated by "world" are *kosmos* (world), *oikoumenè* (terrestrial universe) and *aiôn* (age), along with the Hebrew *tévél* and (post-Biblical in this sense) *'ôlâm*. In the Christian vocabulary, "world" may either denote simply the totality of created things, or this totality insofar as it is under the influence of evil* or unable to attain God* of its own accord. Nor is this complexity always absent from biblical usage. The first sense is dealt with in the entry "Cosmos*" in this encyclopedia. Here we are concerned with the second, which can already be glimpsed in the later periods of Jewish literature—without forgetting that the same instance can carry a number of meanings.

I. Origins of the Theme in the New Testament

1. The Book of Wisdom

According to Wisdom, the world, in its origins completely good, is subject in its entirety to the attacks of evil. Moreover, the author insists on the link between the world and the theme of salvation* (Wis 6:24), which was to be widely taken up by the first Christian theology*, that of Paul and of John. The main characters in the history of salvation are linked to the world: Adam is "the father of the world" (Wis 10:1); Noah's ark "bears the hope of the world" (Wis 14:6); the long-skirted robe of Aaron, priest and intercessor, is "decorated with the whole world" (Wis 18:24). Ever since "the entry into the world" of Satan (2:24) or of idols

(14:14), the world has been mysteriously linked with sin*. It was along these lines that the Pauline* (Rom) and Johannine* (Jn 8; Rev 12) traditions would present the world as the plaything of hostile forces, inasmuch as human beings fall into the clutches of the "ruler of this world" (Jn 12:31).

2. Apocalyptic Literature

Apocalyptic* literature distinguishes above all between "this world" and "the world to come": "The Most High has made the present world for many, but the future world for few... Such is also the rule of the present world: many are created, but few are saved." (4 Ezr 8:1, 8: 3) "As for the righteous... this world is for them a struggle and a labor with many troubles, but the world which is coming is a crown with great glory" (2 Ba 15:7f.) The expression "to leave the world" may mean quite simply "to die" (*Test. of Abraham* 8:11). But the world which is being left may take on a negative connotation: the moment arrives for Abraham when "he must leave behind this world of vanity, when he must leave his body" (*Test. of Abraham* 1:7). In the course of his heavenly journey, the patriarch sees "all that was in the world: what was good and what was bad" (10:3).

In the *Test. of Moses* 1:10–14, "The Lord of the World created the world for his people*; but he did not wish to reveal this purpose of creation* from the beginning of the world." For the apocalyptic authors, the time of the end of the world is the time of its judgment* (4 Ezr 9:2), accompanied by disasters (4 Ezr 9:1–13). This is the point of separation between this world and the world to come, the latter being synonymous with heavenly bliss (1QHVIII, 26).

II. New Testament Theological Perspectives

Kosmos assumes a particular importance in the writings of St Paul, though more than a third of the instances of this word in the New Testament (186) are from the Fourth Gospel* alone.

1. Pauline Writings

a) The Foolish Wisdom of the World. 1 Corinthians contrasts the wisdom* of the world, which it calls "folly" (1 Cor 1:20, 3:19), with God's wisdom, and the "spirit of the world" with the Holy* Spirit that comes from God (1 Cor 2:12). The formula *kata sarka* (according to the flesh*) corresponds to this same viewpoint. Taking his inspiration from Is 19:11ff. and 29:14, Paul denounces a world whose wisdom is ignorant of God, and proclaims salvation for those who believe (1 Cor 1:21; *see* Jn 1:10–13). In 1 Cor 1–4 he sets out the elements of a train of thought that both he and his disciples were to pursue (Pauline* theology). In 2:6–15 he is already adapting these elements to Christian anthropology, distinguishing the psychological from the spiritual man.

In order to do this he opposes "the wisdom of this world" to that of God (2:7). It should, however, be noted that "world" here translates the Greek *aiôn*, in other words, the age, or the present world. The Christian's status in the new creation *(kainè ktisis)* implies a fundamental turning aside from "this world" so as to free oneself from its influence, since "the god of this world" is called Satan (2 Cor 4:4; *see also* Jn 12:31). The closing exhortation of the Epistle to the Romans opens with a strong injunction: "Do not be conformed to this world *[aiôn]*, but be transformed by the renewal of your mind" (Rom 12:2).

2 Corinthians uses antithesis, in the style of Stoic rhetoric, to express the brevity of time, since "the present form of this world is passing away" (1 Cor 7:31; *see* 1 Jn 2:17). As a newly created being, a Christian should not concern himself with the matters of "this world," but with that of the Lord (7:32ff.). The tone is already set in the First Epistle to the Corinthians: the world is called to judgment and condemnation (11:32). Admittedly the Apostle turns his readers' attention to eschatology* and to the world to come; but his thinking leads him above all to a theology of the cross, the instrument of "God...reconciling the world to himself" (2 Cor 5:19).

b) The World Crucified, and Salvation Through the Cross. The most emphatic expression of the world's salvation through the cross comes in the Epistle to the Galatians: subservience to "the elementary principles of the world" (Gal 4:3), liberation through the Spirit, the eschatological mission of the believer-apostle in the face of the world: "the cross of our Lord Jesus Christ, by which the world has been crucified to me, and I to the world" (Gal 6:14). The Epistle to the Romans systematizes this train of thought even further (Rom 5:10). Paul reinterprets the Wisdom texts concerning the entry of sin into the world (Wis 2:24, 14:14—*see above*) and adapts them to Christian theology: "Just as sin came into the world through one man, and so death spread to all men because all sinned" (Rom 5:12), an uncompleted sentence whose development appears in 5:15–20, the first outline of Christian thinking on original sin*.

The *stoikheia tou kosmou* ("elementary principles of the world," Gal 4:3, 4:9; Col 2:8, 2:20) are the forces by which the worldly sphere is made opaque to God's revelation* and action. They are invisible, and yet of the world; though they are obstacles to salvation, they are not wholly identified with evil, nor with sin. They belong to an intermediate, angelic sphere that is separate from that of the devil.

2. The Johannine Literature

a) The Fourth Gospel. John presents the world in a negative and in a positive manner: the world has refused God's word* (1:10), and is henceforth synonymous with sin (1:29). The coming of the "light of the world" is by way of a judgment (9:5, 9:39). This judgment takes effect at the moment of the crucifixion, or, to use the Johannine* term, at the "hour" of the revelation of the Son* of Man, which is the hour of the world's condemnation, and that of its prince (12:31, 14:30, 16:11). Jesus* appears as the light of the world (Jn 8:12 and so on): the imagery of light is employed only in chapters 1–12, which correspond to his earthly ministry*. Christ offers himself in order to rescue the world from darkness (1:5); he designates himself as the bearer of this missionary intention—he, the Son sent into the world by God who "so loved the world, that he gave his only Son...for God did not send his son into the world to condemn the world, but in order that the world might be saved through him" (Jn 3:16–17). Everything is summarized in the speech on the bread of life: he has come to give his flesh "for the life of the world" (Jn 6:51).

Christ's victory over the world is won. If, in spite of this, Christ urges his followers not to let themselves be imprisoned by the world (Jn 13–17), it is because the liberty* of the believer's response has lost none of its value. The salvation of the cross is a gift to be received, freely, in the face of the world. John contains no apocalypse like those of the synoptic Gospels (Mk 13 par.), although, in a way, the Evangelist gathers a number of parallel themes into the farewell speeches (Jn 13–17): the disciples will incur the hatred of the world, and will have to carry on the struggle in this world, since they are sent forth to do so (Jn 17).

b) The First Epistle of St John. 1 John reflects the same viewpoint as chapters 13–17 of the Gospel: it is good to be hated by the world (1 Jn 3:13), which is synonymous with sin (2:16–17). But, as in the Gospel, the call to be suspicious of the world (2:15) goes hand in hand with the declaration of salvation for the sins of the whole world (1 Jn 2:2). Confronted with the false prophets*, referred to as the Antichrist (2:18; 4:3), Christ alone receives the title of "Savior of the world" (4:14, *see* Jn 4:42). The author of the Epistle is aware that his community is threatened. After the warnings in an apocalyptic vein comes the appeal to be in this world (4:17) as conquerors of the world (5:4), in other words as believers (5:5) who remain actively vigilant—since "the whole world lies in the power of the evil one" (1 Jn 5:19). This conclusion to the Epistle is of a piece with its beginning, where Christ appears as the Paraclete, for the forgiveness of the whole world's sins (2:2). The originality of John's eschatology is expressed in the interval between the two, experienced in danger.

c) The Johannine Tradition and Gnosticism. The Johannine tradition provided Gnosticism (gnosis*) with a good deal of material, as can be seen for example in the *Apocryphon of John* (Tardieu 1984), in the *Hypostasis of the Archons* and in the *Untitled Text* (Ed. B. Barc, Laval [Quebec], 1980), which also draw on the Wisdom and apocalyptic traditions mentioned above. Studies of the successive layers of these writings (coll. "BCNH") shed light on the history of the reception of the Johannine corpus (Kuntzmann and Dubois 1986). Gnosticism is distinguishable from the canonical Christian tradition by its focus on a higher spiritual world which it reserves for an elite. The influence of this topic of reflection on the world would also be very pronounced in hermetic literature (A.-J. Festugière 1954).

● H. Sasse (1938), "Kosmos," *ThWNT* 3, 867–96.
A.-J. Festugière (1954), *La révélation d'Hermès Trismégiste,* vol. 4: *Le Dieu inconnu et la gnose,* Paris, (New Ed. 1990), 1st part, 2nd section, p. 54–77, and 2nd part, 1st section, p. 141–99.
O. Böcher (1965), *Der johanneische Dualismus im Zusammenhang des nachbiblischen Judentums,* Gütersloh.
A. Vögtle (1970), *Das Neue Testament und die Zukunft des Kosmos,* Düsseldorf.
R.E. Brown (1979), *The Community of the Beloved Disciple,* London.
H. Balz (1981), "Kosmos," *EWNT* 2, 765–73.
M. Tardieu (Ed.) (1984), *Écrits gnostiques: Codex de Berlin,* Paris.
R. Kuntzmann and J.-D. Dubois (1986), *Nag Hammadi, Évangile selon Thomas: Textes gnostiques aux origines du christianisme,* CEv.S 58, 66–69.

MICHÈLE MORGEN

See also **Angels; Apocalyptic Literature; Cosmos; Creation; Eschatology; Flesh; Gnosis; Johannine Theology; Judgment; Pauline Theology; Sin**

B. Historical Theology

Theology can endow the "world" with two distinct conceptual connotations. As the totality of beings and things, the world must first of all acknowledge the goodness of its creation*. But if it is to be understood, directly or symbolically, as the place of human life, its conceptualization must incorporate the sinful and uncreated dimension of that life.

a) The World: Between Cosmology and Anthropology. The Pauline* and Johannine* theologies had already given a negative emphasis to the concept of *kosmos* (cosmos*); and the idea of a fundamental break with the sinful world, and of an individual mode of behavior that would enact Christ*'s disciples' independence of the world (Jn 15:19), were commonplaces among the first Christians. So for Ignatius of Antioch there was an incompatibility between "speaking of Jesus Christ and desiring the world" (Rom. 7:1, SC 10, 134–135); and Polycarp called on his readers to "cut out the desires of the world" (*Phil.* 5, 3, SC 10, 210–211). The theme of *contempt for the world* was made much of by Tertullian* ("*sæculi totius contemptus,*" *De spectaculis* 29, 2, SC 332, 308) and later writers, who urged their readers to "pass through the world without sharing its corruption" (Cyprian*, *De habitu virginum* 22, CSEL, 3, 203). Drawing partly on Platonic (*Phaedo* 67 *c* and *Theaetetus,* 176 *a-b*) and Plotinian (*Enn.* I, 6, 5–8; VI, 9, 11) themes, Origen* wrote: "[Let us strive] to avoid being men, and [let us] zealously [seek] to become gods, since while we are men we are liars" (*Comm. in Jo.* XX, 29, 266, SC 290, 286–287). To accept martyrdom* was thus to free oneself from the world (Tertullian, *De testimonio Animæ* 4, CChr.SL 1, 178–80).

This conception of the relationship between human beings and the world was particularly marked within monasticism*: the anchorite (from the Greek *anakhôreô,* "to separate or withdraw oneself"), indeed, was one who attempted to detach himself from the world in the most visible way possible: his hermitage purported to be outside the world.

The distance between the monk's ascetic experience and the life of the world was expressed in a number of ways by the church Fathers*: in their view, monks led the life of angels*, and were true *liturges* (Is 6:1–3—*see* Origen, *Peri Archôn* I, 8, 1, SC 252, 220–221) who achieved the ideal of continual contemplation* (Basil* of Caesarea, *Hom. in Ps.* 1, 1, PG 29, 213; Evagrius, *On Prayer,* 113, PG 79, 1192 d). John Chrysostom* emphasized that their lives, like that of Adam before the Fall, evaded the sinful world: "The occupation of monk was Adam's occupation in the beginning before he had sinned, when, clothed in glory, he talked familiarly with God" (*In Matth.*, Hom. 68, 3, PG 57, 643–44). For some Fathers, the existence of monks had a precedent, too, in the displacement to which Abraham was summoned (Gn 12:7; Heb 11:8–13), or even in the wandering life of Christ: both were examples of the "way of life of the traveler, easy to lead and easy to leave" (Clement of Alexandria, *Pedagogue* I, 12, 98, SC 70, 287), of the stranger who merely passes through a world of which he is unaware or to which he does not want to belong. Finally, others made monastic life equivalent to martyrdom: "The patience and strict faithfulness with which monks persevere in the profession which they have embraced once and for all, never indulging their will, daily crucifies them in the world and makes them living martyrs" (John Cassian, *Conf.* 18, 7, SC 64, 20–21). So, one way or another, the Fathers indicate that the monk is the exception to the world and its sin*, which are identified with the flesh*, sexuality, wealth, and so on. However, it is noteworthy that this conception of the world is not based on an ontology or cosmology identifying the world with evil*: in its created reality, the world is actually a good thing. Rather, the Fathers employ an anthropology* of man's corrupt desire to emphasize the negative dimension of worldly, secular existence.

This vision of the relationship with the world is thus notably different from the conceptions peculiar to Gnosticism. Christian orthodoxy and the Gnostics agree in asserting man's superiority over the world and in emphasizing that man, while he is in the world, is not "of" the world. The distinctive feature of Gnosticism, however, is that it sees man's presence in the world as one of pure alienation, and the world merely as the kingdom of evil; for Christianity, in contrast, the world is only *this* world as a result of sin—it is specifically by man that the world is engendered as such (Jonas 1960).

Augustine*'s approach is based on this refusal of Gnostic dualism as well as on the desire to point out what, *in human beings,* constitutes the origin of the world. Referring to John 1:10, Augustine recognizes that there are two meanings to the concept of "world": on the one hand there is the world created by God, and on the other there is the world engendered by human sin (*En. Ps.* 141, 15, CChr.SL 40, 2055–2056). The *City of God* (XIV, 28) thus emphasizes that "two loves have made two cities: self-love to the point of contempt for God has made the earthly city, and the love of God to the point of contempt for the self has made the heavenly city." But these two cities do not represent two opposed worlds. The search for peace* is in fact common to them both (*City of God* XIX, 12); and moreover, as the basis of the distinction between the two cities already suggests (it is the object of love that differentiates them), the purpose assigned by human beings to their use of the world either closes the world in upon itself or, on the contrary, turns it toward God's delight: "The use of the resources necessary for this mortal life is common to two kinds of men, and to two kinds of houses. But the end of that use is peculiar to each, and quite different" (*City of God* XIX, 14–17). Thus, this distinction between *uti* and *frui* does not prescribe flight from the world, but rather a particular use of the world; referring to Ambrose*'s *De fuga sæculi* I, 1 (PL 14, 569), Augustine writes that "it is not with the body, but with the heart, that one must flee the world" (*De dono perseverantiæ* 8, 20, BAug. 24, 639; *see* soul*-heart-body).

Despite the subtlety of Augustine's analysis, throughout the Middle Ages theological thinking about the relations of Christians with the world continued to be governed by suspicion. Treatises on contempt for the world continued to be produced (Roger of Caen, who died in 1090, wrote a *Carmen de contemptu mundi,* PL 158, 705–708), and the new medieval religious orders still tended to identify life outside the world with monastic life. Several practices bear witness to this identification: laypeople* tried to have themselves buried in a monastery, to be entered in the necrology, or even to take the monastic habit on their deathbeds *(professio ad succurendum)*.

b) Theological Redefinitions of the Concept of World. In this context the Reformation marks a notable break. Luther* takes as a starting point the Augustinian theology of history, which urges against the separation of two cities that cannot be separated: "The two cities, in this life, are entangled and intermingled, until the time when they will be separated by the last judgment" (*City of God,* I, 35; *see also Ep. 138, Ad Marcellinum* II, 9–15, PL 33, 528–32). Referring moreover to certain Old Testament (for example Sir 11:20–21) or New Testament (1 Cor 7:17) texts, Luther promotes the fulfillment of the Christian vocation in the task, job, or profession that providence assigns to each person in the world. So his translation of the Bible* uses the same word *(Beruf)* to render on the one hand the idea of a vocation or divine calling (in Greek *klèsis, see* 1 Cor 1:26, Eph 1:18 and so on) and on the other hand the idea of a task or work* (the Septuagint, e.g. in Sir 11:20–21, uses the Greek *ponos* and *ergon*). As articles 26 and 27 of the Augsburg Confession (1530) point out, the Christian should not pass by the demands of the life of this world, but rather take them on. From the Protestant standpoint, any flight from the world, for example into monastic life, constituted a breach of the duty to love one's neighbor, and moreover implied that salvation* could be gained through works. Daily activity, in its most secular aspects, was thereby endowed with a religious dimension. A number of initiatives emphasized this new way of envisaging the links between the Christian and the world: the ministries* of the church were desanctified and seen in functional terms, the Bible was translated into the vernacular, and popular music* found its way into the liturgy*.

With Calvin* the break begun by Luther took a more specific turn: because his thought was centered not on the idea of providence* but on that of predestination*, Calvin linked the certainty of salvation to the accomplishment of a temperate and methodically organized life. Later Calvinism*, being especially puritanical, would go beyond the spirit and the letter of his theology, making it every Christian's duty to ensure his own state of grace by the methodical control of his existence and the rationalization of the link, often based on self-interest, that connected him to the world. From this standpoint, ascetic Protestantism* carried "traditional asceticism into worldly life itself" (Weber 1956).

Post-Tridentine Catholicism*, for its part, tended to maintain the same negative discourse with regard to the world, which continued to be, if not identified with sin, at least regarded as that which led to sin. So, in the 17th century, Pascal* emphasized the fact that the Church and the world represent two contrary powers, and deplored the gradual erosion of the "essential distinction" between the two (*Comparaison des chrétiens des premiers temps avec ceux d'aujourd'hui,* Ed. Lafuma, 360–62, and *Prière pour demander à Dieu le bon usage des maladies,* 362–65): the Church, by reason of its sheer conspicuousness, must therefore aim to escape the world and its powers. This would remain the church's position until the advent of Vatican* II. The ecclesiology of Cardinal Journet, however, taking up Augustine's analysis, emphasized that the boundary between Church and world is internal to every person and that the two do not constitute two distinct realities between which Christianity is torn: "The Church is not without sinners, but it is without sin.... Its boundaries cross our hearts, there to separate light from darkness" (1941–69, II, 1103; *see also* III, 78–93).

c) The 20th Century and the Theology of the World. It was not until the mid-20th century that there developed a genuine theological consideration of the world understood as a reality endowed with an autonomy which was not contrary to faith*. Partly under the influence of Barth*, and later within Catholicism in the wake of the Second Vatican Council, theologians such as D. Bonhoeffer*, F. Gogarten, and J.-B. Metz attempted to construct a theology of the world. In *Zur Theologie der Welt* (1968), Metz suggests that "in the very movement of growing worldliness which began with modern times, there is an authentically Christian impulse at work": contemporary atheism* and the very process of secularization* are implicit in faith itself, and above all in the event of the Incarnation*. These phenomena bear witness to the "many-sided truth of the event of Christ, by virtue of which, through God's incarnation, the flesh is at last seen fully as 'flesh,' as earth, as the finite world, while God at last appears fully as God in his supreme transcendence of the world" (ibid.)—so God's divinity appears more clearly as the world becomes more worldly.

The 20th century also saw the beginning of a philosophical definition of the world. In the work of Heidegger* the world is not conceived as an object located outside man and from which man is able to cut himself off; neither is it a vessel containing the totality of existing things, among which man must be counted (*see Sein und Zeit,* §12). Rather, the world is that which makes it possible to define man's being as being-in-the-world *(In-der-Welt-sein);* it thus appears as the transcendental structure that defines man's being, the originating condition by means of which man may be what he is: "*That toward which* human reality [*Dasein*] as such transcends, we call the world, and we define the transcendence as *being-in-the-world*" *(Von Wesen der Grundes).* It seems, however, that the existential analytics offered by *Sein und Zeit* is such that, in the "world" so conceived and described, man need not concern himself with God. Theological thought has therefore tried to take Heidegger's definition of the world seriously, but only in order to consider its limitations in an attempt to grasp what in the Christian experience of the world might subvert its logic (Brague 1984; Lacoste 1994).

● M. Weber (1922), *Gesammelte Aufsätze zur Religionssoziologie,* 2nd Ed., Tübingen, 3 vols., reprint 1988.
M. Heidegger (1929), "Von Wesen des Grundes," in *Wegmarken, GA* 9, 123–75.
C. Journet (1941–69), *L'Église du Verbe incarné,* Paris, 3 vols.

F. Gogarten (1956), *Der Mensch zwischen Gott und Welt,* Stuttgart.
H. Jonas (1960), "Gnosis und moderner Nihilismus," *KuD* 6, 78–93.
Z. Alszeghy (1964), "Fuite du m.," *DSp* 5, 1575–1605.
J. B. Metz (1968), *Zur Theologie der Welt,* Stuttgart.
P. Miquel (1980), "Monachisme," *DSp* 10, 1547–57.
E. Pousset (1980), "M.," *DSp* 10, 1633–46.
M. Heidegger (1983), *Die Grundbeggriffe der Metaphysik, GA* 29/30, Frankfurt.
R. Brague (1984), "Vers un concept de l'être-au-m.: la presse *(thlipsis),*" in P. A. Simon (Ed.), *Pela Filosopha: Homenagem ao Prof. T. M. Padilla,* Rio de Janeiro, 229–41.
J.-Y. Lacoste (1994), *Expérience et Absolu,* Paris.
R. Brague (1999), *La sagesse du monde,* Paris.

THIERRY BEDOUELLE

See also **Asceticism; Church; Monasticism; Secularization**

World Council of Churches

"The World Council of Churches (WCC) is a brotherhood of churches that confess the Lord Jesus Christ* as God and Savior in accordance with the Scriptures*, and that strive to answer together to their common vocation for the glory of the one God, Father*, Son, and Holy* Spirit" (*Constitution* of WCC, article 1).

Delegates of 145 churches founded this federation in Amsterdam in 1948. By 1995, it included 321 church members (more than 400 million Christians), bringing together the great majority of confessional families, including, since 1961, the Orthodox Churches. While maintaining close ties with the WCC, some Christian churches have not joined it, including a few major Baptist churches (e.g., the Southern Baptist Convention of the United States) and, notably, the Roman Catholic church and the Eastern churches, which depend on the primate of Rome.

1.

As early as the end of the 19th century, the Churches planned to have a common body to coordinate their efforts. The missions scattered throughout several countries had triggered this need within the Western Protestant churches, generally organized into national Churches. In 1910, in Edinburgh, one of the first international missionary conferences attracted 1,200 delegates. The call for inter-church cooperation grew and soon went beyond the sole Protestant context. Thus, the synod* of the Orthodox Church of Constantinople (the Ecumenical patriarchate), in 1920, wanted to see the formation of a worldwide alliance of churches. At this time, two movements emerged, and their union led to the 1948 WCC.

a) The first of these precursor movements, Faith and Order, attempted to go beyond the doctrinal conflict and institutional questions that separated the different Christian families. Coming from the commitment of laity* in Anglican (Episcopalian) churches of the United States, this movement proposed, as early as 1910, that there be a worldwide gathering. The war of 1914–18 delayed this plan, which would not materialize until 1927, when the Lausanne congregation convened. Ecclesiological questions (such as those on the Church, the sacraments*, and the ministry*) and ethical questions were pivotal. Delegates from all the Christian churches, except for the Roman Catholic church, called for a unity* of all churches at this time. The themes were touched on again during various regional meetings that aimed to prepare a new international conference in Edinburgh in 1937. The new political situation in Europe made Christian witnessing in society a new major concern.

b)   The second early movement, Life and Work, focused from the start on questions of peace, justice, and social ethics. A first meeting in Uppsala in 1917 attracted only delegates from countries not engaged in World War I. It was only in 1925, at the Stockholm conference, under the decisive influence of the Lutheran Archbishop of Uppsala, Nathan Söderblom, that the idea of an international council was raised again, thus sowing the seed of a common service of churches in the world. Its slogan, "doctrine divides but service unites," remained topical until this organization assembled again in 1937 at Oxford. At that time, the necessary affiliation between more ethical challenges and traditional doctrinal questions (such as ecclesiology* and creeds*) was understood. At the same time, priority was given to urgent problems, such as the relationship between churches on the one hand, and states and nations on the other (see church* and state).

c)   The war of 1939–45 was decisive in bringing together the two movements, which federated in 1948, becoming a unique organization, the WCC. At the heart of this common structure, Faith and Order bore the responsibility of doctrinal dialogue between churches, a trickier task than first thought. It was only in 1981 that it produced its first major text of consensus, a report on Baptism, Eucharist*, and Ministry (BEM). In 1991 common commentary was added regarding the confession of faith of Nicaea-Constantinople of 381. Although it had not been affiliated with the WCC, in 1968, after Vatican* II, the Catholic church became a member of the Faith and Order Commission and actively participated in developing united texts on this multilateral dialogue. The goals of the Life and Work Commission were taken up by all the sections of the WCC, structured accordingly; the plan to fight racism (particularly the opposition to apartheid in South Africa) and the commitment to justice, peace, and saving creation (at the Seoul Gathering in 1990) are solid examples.

d)   The general assembly in New Delhi in 1961 was important and inaugurated a new phase in the life of the WCC. The Orthodox churches decided to join the organization. The Catholic church, for the first time, was represented by observers. Furthermore, the International Council of Missions, which helped organize the Edinburgh meeting in 1910, merged with the WCC. In 1971 the World Council of Education did the same. It was also at this first general assembly in Asia that the "young churches," the churches of the developing world now independent after many years of submission to Western missions, emerged. The influence of these Churches grew, and today they form the majority of the WCC. Having become more representa-

tive, the WCC henceforth became an important catalyst in integrating and coordinating all the ecumenical efforts of Churches, of their service for and witness to humanity. National church conferences continued in the same vein in various countries, and continental conferences in Africa, Asia, Latin America, and Europe were established. A mixed work party reunited the WCC and the Vatican authorities on a regular basis and joined the regular meetings of worldwide confessional families.

2.

According to the constitution of the WCC, the organization's goal is to implement the visible unity of churches, to facilitate their common testimony everywhere, to support them in their mission* and evangelization work, to come to the help of all those in need, to break down the barriers between people, and to promote the advent of a single human family living in justice and in peace.

a)   The evolution of the programs set forth by the WCC reflects its history. At first, the stress was on Western Protestantism*—that is, on ideas that especially involved bearing witness to Christ throughout the world. The integration of the Orthodox and the growing participation of the Catholics would lead to a shift toward questions that were more ecclesiological (including questions on the church and ministries) and more pneumatological (relating to the Holy* Spirit, sanctification and so on). The inclusion of Asian, African, and Latin American Churches fundamentally modified traditional objectives. Questions of justice*, of education, of dialogue with other religions, and of development, liberation, and church cooperation became more important. These changes did bring about conflict, because priorities were contested.

After the general assembly in Vancouver (1983), special emphasis was placed on the "council process." In comparison to the biblical notion of alliance, agreement between Christian groups of diverse origin allows for better common commitment to a specific cause (Seoul Gathering, 1990). The current subdivision of WCC activity into four units illustrates its many concerns. The first is Unity and Revival, dealing with doctrinal questions, the visible unity of churches, cult* and spirituality, and theological training. The second unit is Mission Churches, concerned with mission and evangelization, Gospel and culture, dialogue with other religions, education, family life, and health. The third is Justice, Peace, and Creation, involved in the fight against racism and issues of exclusion, violence*, and socioeconomic, ecological, and political challenges. The remaining unit is Sharing and Service, which deals with cooperation and sharing, solidarity with outsiders, the roles of women and youth, refugee services, and the development of inter-church structures.

These different focuses are filled with the conviction that the unity of the Church is inextricably linked to the unity and revival of all of humanity. From this perspective, the WCC works closely with several international organizations, such as UNESCO.

b)   The life of the WCC is structured by the general assemblies, at which time the delegates of the church members decide upon the fundamental orientations of the movement. Assemblies were held in Amsterdam in 1948, Evanston in 1954, New Delhi in 1961, Uppsala in 1968, Nairobi in 1975, Vancouver in 1983, Canberra in 1991, and Harare in 1998. A central committee made of approximately 150 members is elected by these assemblies and meets annually. Moreover, several meetings are organized by the work parties, and decentralized council boards allow for widespread participation in the life of the WCC. A general secretariat based in Geneva coordinates the body, manages finances, and acts as a press-relations department.

c)   It should be noted that the WCC is a federation of churches and not one church. Its authority is limited and its decisions do not apply automatically to member churches. For a community, joining the WCC does not involve adapting its individual ecclesiology, as was made clear in the Toronto declaration of 1950. The WCC thus unites Churches that are separate and do not necessarily live in full church communion*, but rather have their own traditions regarding the celebration of the Word*, sacraments, and recognition of ministries. An instrument servicing a plurality of churches, the WCC hopes to be able to transform itself progressively into a council community. Although far from reaching this goal, the WCC has come a long way over the years.

● L. Vischer (1968), *Foi et Constitution 1910–1963,* Geneva.
B. Chenu (1972), *La signification ecclésiologique du COE (1945–1963),* Paris.
M. Henriet (1976), *Briser les barrières: Rapport officiel de l'assemblée du COE à Nairobi (1975),* Paris.
Coll. (1979), *Le COE: Pourquoi?,* Geneva.
Baptême, eucharistie, ministère (1982), French text by Max Thurian, Taizé.
W. A. Visser't Hooft (1982), *The Genesis and Formation of the World Council of Churches,* Geneva.
J.-M. Chappuis and R. Beaupère (1984), *Rassemblés pour la vie: Rapport officiel de l'assemblée du COE, Vancouver 1983,* Paris.
M. Van Elderen (1988), *Ainsi dressons des signes…Les quarante premières années du COE,* Geneva.
Th. Best (Ed.) (1990), *De Vancouver à Canberra (1983–1990),* Geneva.
K. Blaser (1990), *Une Église des confessions,* Geneva.
M. Westphal (Ed.) (1991), *Signes de l'Esprit: Rapport officiel, Septième assemblée Canberra,* Geneva.
N. Lossky et al. (Eds.) (1991), *Dictionary of the Ecumenical Movement,* Geneva.
M. Van Elderen (1992), *Le COE: aujourd'hui et demain,* Geneva.
R. Frieling (1992), *Der Weg des ökumenischen Gedankens,* Göttingen.
Foi et Constitution (1993), *Confesser la foi commune,* Paris.

ANDRÉ BIRMELÉ

See also **Family, Confessional; Ecumenicism; Protestantism; Unity of the Church**

Wrath of God

Biblical writings, notably the prophetic* and wisdom books, are strongly marked by manifestations of wrath.

The vocabulary is rich in terms that signify "wrath," ranging from annoyance to indignation, rage, fury. *'Ap* is the most common; other terms, such as *chémâ, chârôn, qèçèp, 'everâh, za'am,* and *ka'as,* with their corresponding verbal roots, are also found (Bovati 1986). The Septuagint limits itself to *thumos* and *orgè* (with their derivatives), without making a distinction between the sentiment and its manifestation. The New Testament adopts basically the same approach. Paul particularly uses *orgè* for the wrath of God* (with the redundant *thumos* in Rom 2:8).

It is particularly in the wisdom texts that human wrath figures. This wrath is almost always evaluated negatively, as a lack of wisdom* with destructive effects (Jb 5:2; Prv 14:17, 27:4, 29:22; Eccl 7:9; Mt

5:22). Thus, we find exhortations to bridle wrath: "Refrain from anger, and forsake wrath" (Ps 37:8, *see* Prv 14:29, 15:18, 16:32, 29:11; Eph 4:26; Col 3:8; Jas 1:19f.). However, in both the Old and the New Testament it is the wrath of God that is highlighted, to the point of appearing as one of the primary manifestations of the biblical God (Na 1:2; Ps 7:2).

Wrath is expressed in the flared "nostrils" of God (Ez 38:18; Ps 18:8f.); he is seen getting annoyed, becoming heated, inwardly burning (2 Kgs 22:13, 22:17; Is 30:27; Hos 8:5; Ps 89:47; Est 1:2). "Fire" (Na 1:6; Jer 4:4, 21:12; Ez 25:14, 35:11, Lam 2:4) and "furnace" (Ez 22:2ff.; Ps 21:10) are common metaphors of his wrath.

The Jew Philo and the first Christian theologians had already inquired not only into this anthropomorphism*, which they saw as incompatible with divine impassibility, but also into the nature of such an irrational, violent affect.

YHWH is defined as being by nature "slow to anger" (Ex 34:6; Nm 14:18; Jon 4:2 and so on). His wrath then signifies that the offense is overwhelming, that a situation is absolutely unacceptable to him. This presupposes that the relation to God is subject to a law of truth; lying, abusing trust, exploiting patience are the things that provoke legitimate wrath. It appears that God is bound to demonstrate that he does not connive with evil* and that his will is to eliminate it (Ex 32:9f.; Dt 32:19; Mi 7:9 and so on). Jesus* displays wrath on numerous occasions (Mt 17:17; Mk 3:5; Jn 2:15ff.).

The aim of wrath is to put an end to that which is unbearable. Vengeance, because it confines people within themselves, is condemned (Gn 49:6f.; Am 1:11). Wrath leaves the sphere of psychology to enter the sphere of law (Bovati 1986). Metaphorically it then designates the punitive procedure (2 Sm 12:5; Ez 20:33) which, by chastising the guilty, tears the victims out of their grasp (Ex 15:6f.; Ps 7:11f.).

The wrath of the Lord is exercised with moderation and for a short time (Is 54:7f.; Hos 11:8f.; Wis 11:23, 12:2, 12:8). As it is often said, repentance and penitential prayer (penitence*) can appease it (Ex 32:11; 2 Kgs 13:4; Jer 26:19): then God "relents" from his anger and shows mercy* (Ex 32:12; Mi 7:18f.; Ps 78:38).

Prophetic and apocalyptic* literature presents human history, as a whole, as a history of sin* punishable by the wrath of God, that is, his judgment*. In particular, the group against whom God's wrath is intended broadens to include the whole of humankind (Is 26:20f., 30:27f., 34:2; Jer 25:15–29; Ez 36:5f.; Am 1:3–2, 16 and so on). The destruction is cosmic (Is 13:10, 30:30; Jer 30:23f.; Jl 2:10; Am 5:8f.; Na 1:2–8) and eschatological (with the motif of the *dies irae:* Is 13:9; Ez 7:19, 22, 24; Zep 1:14–18; Dn 8:19, 11:36; *see* "the cup of his wrath," Is 51:17, 51:22; Jer 25:15).

It is precisely the latter aspects that the New Testament authors adopted: 1) in the Gospels* (Mt 3:7, 18:34, 22:7; Lk 21:22f.; Jn 3:36); 2) in Paul (Rom 1:18; 2:5, 2:8; 5:9; 1 Cor 5:5; Eph 2:3, 5:6; 1 Thes 1:10, 2:16, 5:9f.); 3) in the Apocalypse (Rev 2:21, 6:15f., 14:10, 15:1, 16:1–21, 19:15 and so on). "The wrath of God is revealed from heaven" (Rom 1:18); it is "the wrath to come" (1 Thes 1:10): here it is a matter of a reality of law, a verdict bearing on the totality of history and whose effect is, by contrast, to exalt the announcement of the pardon and gratuitous salvation* that Christ* realizes and grants to all who believe in him (Rom 2:16f., 3:21–26). "God has not destined us for wrath" (1 Thes 5:9).

- R. V. Tasker (1951), *The Biblical Doctrine of the Wrath of God,* London.
- H. Ringgren (1963), "Einige Schilderungen des göttlichen Zornes," in *Tradition und Situation: Studien zur Alttestamentlichen Prophetie—Festschrift Weiser,* Göttingen, 107–13.
- H. A. Brongers (1969), "Der Zornesbecher," *OTS* 15, 177–92.
- C. Westermann (1981), "Boten des Zorns: Der Begriff des Zornes Gottes in der Prophetie," *Die Botschaft und die Boten, Festschrift Wolff,* Neukirchen, 147–56.
- R. Schwager (1983), "Der Zorn Gottes: Zur Problematik der Allegorie," *ZThK* 105, 406–14.
- P. Bovati (1986), *Ristabilire la Giustizia: Procedure, vocabulario, orientamenti,* Rome.
- M. Girard (1987), "La violence de Dieu dans la Bible juive: approche symbolique et interprétation théologique," *ScEs* 39, 145–70.
- H. Spieckermann (1989), "*Dies irae*: der alttestamentliche Befund und seine Vorgeschichte," *VT* 39, 194–208.
- V. Morla Asensio (1991), "Aspectos forenses de la terminología de la cólera en el Antiguo Testamento," *III Simposio Biblico-espanol (I Luso-Espanhol),* Valencia and Lisbon, 241–56.
- G. A. Herion and S. H. Travis (1992), "Wrath of God," AncBD6, 989–98.

PIETRO BOVATI

See also **Anthropomorphism; Apocalyptic Literature; Jealousy, Divine; Ethics; Expiation; Hell; Judgment; Justice; Punishment; Vengeance of God; War**

Wyclif, John. *See* Hus, Jan

YHWH. *See* **Name**

Z

Zoroaster

Zoroaster was the great religious prophet whose teaching was promulgated in the late-seventh and early-sixth centuries before the Christian era among the loose federation of Iranian tribes centered in Chorasmia, principally in the extensive territory of Iranian Khorasan, western Afghanistan, Turkmenistan, Uzbekistan, and Tajikistan. He is of immense importance in the history of Western theology, both because the three great Middle Eastern religions to have dominated the history of the West—Judaism, Christianity, and Islam—derived much from his religious system, and also because the study of that system does not, as we might have hoped, furnish evidence of some primitive religion linking the Semite theism of Western cultures with the speculative mystical systems of the Indo-Iranian-Aryan social, national, and religious families of India.

"Zoroaster" is a Greek rendition of the Old Iranian "Zarathustra," which contains the root for "camel." We first hear about the prophet in a fragment of Xanthus and in Plato's *Alcibiades*. He is also mentioned by Plutarch, Diogenes Laërtius, and a number of their contemporaries, but has historically been seriously misrepresented, his monotheism presented by the Magi of the Levant as a rigid dualism of rival and coeternal principles. He has been "travestied as a magician, astrologer, and quack...by Nietzsche himself...as a witch-doctor...or a political intriguer" (R. C. Zaehner). The ruling house under which Zoroaster found protection was eventually conquered by Cyrus the Persian in 550 B.C.

Zoroastrianism survived under the subsequent Persian Achaemenian dynasty, but its priesthood was taken over by the Median priestly caste called the Magi. These held a religious monopoly in Media, the northwestern portion of the Iranian plateau overlooking the Tigris and Euphrates basins (the Assyria and Babylonia of the ancients, today's Iraq). When the Medes swooped on to the Mesopotamian plain to destroy the Assyrians, they released Israel from servitude to return to the Holy Land, but not before the fruitful encounter took place between Israel and the monotheistic Zoroastrianism of the Medes. Isaiah was to salute Cyrus, Israel's liberator, as the Lord's anointed, and R. Zaehner, the authority on Zoroastrianism, regards it as certain that the Zoroastrian doctrine of eternal rewards and punishments exercised a direct influence on post-exilic Judaism. It appears in Daniel, and replaces the insubstantial doctrine of *sheol,* that "shadowy and depersonalized existence" common to all. Zaehner points to the belief in the resurrection of the body common to Israel and Zoroastrianism, itself a corollary of the view held by both that body and soul are ultimately inseparable aspects of a single personality.

Zoroastrianism eventually became the religion of the Achaemenian kings, whose dynasty lasted until its overthrow by Alexander the Great in 330 B.C. The prophet's teaching was diffused in various corrupt versions until its purity was reestablished in A.D. 226, when Ardashir overthrew the last of the Achaemenids and made Zoroastrianism the national religion of the Sassanian empire. It was to diminish in importance after the Muslim conquest of the Persian empire in 652, although it is not yet totally extinct in Gujarati-speaking India, where its followers are known as Parsis.

Only a portion of the sacred Zoroastrian text, the Avesta, survives, but more about Zoroastrian belief and practice can be deduced from inscriptions and from the ninth-century Pahlavi liturgical books, which appear to reproduce an authentic original no longer understood by the copyists. As far as can be ascertained with reasonable probability, Zoroaster preached a new religion of "truth" opposed to the established followers of "the lie" in the nation of King Vishtaspa, the head of the Chorasmian confederation. This opposition appears to have been founded on confrontations between the agricultural and cattle-breeding followers of truth and the predatory nomadic tribes, followers of the lie. Each person must ultimately choose between the traditional but false nomadic religion and the new pastoral religion of truth. Zoroaster begins to elevate opposed ethical principles into a cosmic clash between good and evil, and advances the status of the good spirit into

the monotheistic creator and preserver of everything that exists, both spiritual and material, including the spirit which chose to be evil.

The supreme God thinks his creation into existence through his Holy Spirit who, with the Good Mind and Truth, is an aspect of his own essence. Wholeness and immortality are also inseparable from his essence, but they are the reward of those who do his will in Right-Mindedness, an entity common to God and humans. God alone stands beyond the reach of evil. The same word is used for prosperity on earth and for posthumous felicity. At the center of the Zoroastrian cult is fire, the symbol of truth and at the same time destroyer of darkness.

Into the primitive monotheism of Zoroaster grew a slow repaganization, readmitting some of the old traditional gods and veering toward a pantheism in which nature is penetrated by the divine. Finally, in its Sassanian resurgence, Zoroastrianism becomes a dualist orthodoxy in which the Wise Lord is matched by a co-eternal Destructive spirit.

● R.C. Zaehner (1955) *Zurvan: a Zoroastrian Dilemma*, Oxford.
R. C. Zaehner (1961) *The Dawn and Twilight of Zoroastrianism*, London.

ANTHONY LEVI

Zwingli, Huldrych

1484–1531

Huldrych Zwingli was born at Wildhaus in the Toggenburg, in the Swiss canton of Saint Gall, into a prominent family whose concerns shaped his understanding of the political and social problems of the Swiss confederation of his time. These problems principally included the tensions between the Holy Roman Empire, to which the cantons belonged, and their own sovereignty; the disparities between the cities and rural areas; the conflict between allegiance to foreign lords and local interests (as in the tradition of mercenaries); and the social troubles that resulted from these problems. As for religion, Zwingli very quickly became caught up in the turmoil of humanist dissent on the one hand, and on the other, the latent conflicts over authority between local magistrates and episcopal governments.

Zwingli received his primary education from an uncle, a priest, who prepared him for entry into the Latin school in Basel. He studied at the universities of Vienna and Basel from 1498 to 1506; while he was in Basel he joined a circle of humanists and came into contact with Erasmus*, who was to have a decisive influence on him. In 1506 Zwingli was awarded the degree of master of arts, ordained as a priest by the bishop of Constance, and appointed to a parish in the canton of Glarus, where he remained for the following ten years. From 1516–18 he was a preacher at the celebrated abbey of Einsiedeln, but in the meantime he had also been appointed as a chaplain to the Swiss mercenaries serving the Papal States. In that capacity he took part in the Italian Wars and witnessed the mercenaries' famous defeat in the Battle of Marignano in 1515. The dreadful experiences of these mercenaries had a profound impact on Zwingli. From this time onward he changed his views, called for the Swiss confederation to become neutral, and opposed both the Francophile policy of his city and the hiring of Swiss mercenaries by the French King Francis I. War for Swiss freedoms was acceptable to Zwingli, but war for money was not, and he was convinced that the moral degradation of his country was largely due to this type of policy.

Continuing his training, Zwingli committed himself to the theological tradition of the *via antiqua,* with its Aristotelian and Thomist presuppositions. His encounter with Erasmus's ideas, notably through his reading of that great humanist master's edition of the Greek New Testament in 1516, led him to make his own theology absolutely biblical*, even "biblicist." The influence of both the *via antiqua* and Erasmus remained as an underpinning to all Zwingli's later opinions, causing him to avoid adopting the theology of Luther*, and indeed to oppose it. As a result he acquired a distinctive status among the Protestant reformers.

In 1518 Zwingli was appointed *Leutpriester* ("people's priest") in the *Grossmünster* (Great Minster, or Cathedral) in Zurich, where he was required to take on the important position of preacher. This position helped to give his reform, which started in Zurich, then spread to other German-speaking regions and other parts of Switzerland, its typically "Zwinglian" style, with its emphasis on sermons, and on the training of Christians through meditation and systematic listening to scriptural texts. This orientation toward preaching* at the expense of sacramental practice became characteristic of the reform of worship in Zurich, and distinguished it from Luther's reform in Wittenberg. At a later stage Zwingli himself was fond of emphasizing his independence from his fellow reformer. If he found confirmation in Luther's writings for his own reforming breakthroughs, notably on the question of justification* by faith*, his pastoral experiences in Zurich pushed his activities in a different direction. Zwingli's reformation unfolded in its own way, marked by a form of humanism that was less optimistic than that of Erasmus, as well as by a theology centered on pneumatology rather than Christology*. It was this centrality of the Holy* Spirit in Zwingli's theology that led him, from 1522 onward, to declare explicitly that Scripture*, under the inspiration of the Spirit, is the only basis for Christian doctrine and life.

In this way Zwingli put down markers for his break, not only with traditional theology and ecclesiology*, but also with the other tendencies, such as Anabaptism,

that were developing within the Reformation. The conflict with the established church* broke out in the spring of 1522 when traditionalist and reformist preachers hurled abuse at each other over the fact that some of Zwingli's friends had eaten sausages during Lent. This provocative act was stigmatized by the bishop, but Zwingli referred it to the civil authorities. In the controversy that followed Zwingli skillfully played off the civil authorities against the episcopal government, and thus opened the way for collaboration between the secular power and church leaders that was to be inevitable in those cities and regions that embarked upon the Reformation. Indeed, Zwingli's reform thus became more closely linked to a secular power than any other, and more dependent upon it. The magistrates of Zurich took Zwingli's side, organized debates, acted as judges, and established scriptural norms as authoritative guides in implementing reforms.

Zwingli then extended the influence of the Zurich reform to other German-speaking territories. Bern, Basel, Saint Gall, Mulhouse, Strasbourg, and several other cities adopted his theology, while Zwingli himself expressed his ideas in several texts written in 1524 and 1525, including his magnum opus, the *Commentary on True and False Religion* (written in Latin). He reorganized the churches that had accepted his reform, and endowed them with "reformed" synods*, constitutions that had no precedent, matrimonial courts, and new liturgies*. Worship in these churches was centered on the sermon, and the Lord's Supper was celebrated only four times each year.

Conflicts erupted not only with those cantons that remained loyal to the traditional faith, but also with the Lutheran and "radical" tendencies within the Reformation. The first Anabaptist* martyrs were drowned in Zurich in January 1527, and at Marburg in 1529 Zwingli broke irrevocably with Luther over the question of the real presence in the Eucharist*, completing the rupture within the Protestant Reformers' camp. Zwingli's reform continued to spread, notably in the French-speaking parts of Switzerland, where it merged with the Calvinist Reformation led by Guillaume Farel during the 1530s.

Zwingli's work was left unfinished. Having been drawn into the political and military conflicts that arose from the first religious struggles within the Swiss confederation, he was killed on the battlefield at Kappel in 1531. Thanks largely to his successor Heinrich Bullinger, Zwingli's work of reform was consolidated and widened in Zurich and elsewhere, right up to 1549, which was the year the *Consensus Tigurinus* sealed the fusion with the Calvinist reform, creating a single Zwinglian-Calvinist or "Reformed" Protestantism* in opposition to the Lutheran movement. Certain features of the Zwinglian reform were to have a decisive effect on the whole of Protestantism in later years, including its emphasis on sermons, its marginalization of the communion service, its concept of pastoral ministry*, its distrust of sacred art, and its attitude to the role of civil authorities in religious affairs.

- The complete works of Zwingli are being published in the *Corpus Reformatorum* series, vol. 88ff.: *Huldreich Zwinglis Sämtliche Werke* (1905–), Berlin.

Works:
Der Hirt (1523); *Eine christliche Anleitung an die Seelsorger* (1523); *Von göttlicher und menschlicher Gerechtigkeit* (1523); *Eine göttliche Vermahnung an die ältesten Eidgenossen zu Schwyz* (1522); *Eine treue und ernstliche Vermahnung an die frommen Eidgenossen* (1524); *Erste Predigt in Bern* (1528); *Expositio christianae fidei* (1539); *Huld. Z. quo pacto ingenuii adolescentes formandi sint praeceptiones pauculae* (1523).
♦ Up until 1971, the bibliography is listed and annotated in U. Gäbler (1975), *Huldrych Z. Forschungsbericht und annotierte Bibliographie 1897–1971,* Zurich.
J. Courvoisier (1947), *Zwingli,* Geneva.

G. H. Williams (1962), *The Radical Reformation,* Philadelphia.
J. Courvoisier (1965), *Zwigli, théologien réformé,* Neuchâtel.
G. Locher (1979), *Die Zwinglische Reformation im Rahmen der europäischen Kirchengeschichte,* Göttingen and Zurich.
W. J. Neuser (1983), "Zwingli und der Zwinglianismus," *HDThG,* 167–238.
U. Gäbler (1983), *Huldrych Zwingli: Eine Einführung in sein Leben und sein Werk,* Munich.
P. Blickle et al. (Ed.) (1985), *Zwingli und Europa,* Zurich.
W. P. Stephens (1986), *The Theology of Huldrych Zwingli,* Oxford.
J. V. Pollet (1988), *Huldrych Zwingli et le Zwinglianisme: Essai de synthèse historique et théologique mis à jour d'après les recherches récentes,* Paris.
H. Oberman et al. (1991–92), *Reformiertes Erbe: Festschrift für Gottfried Locher zu seinem 80. Geburtstag,* 2 vols., *Zwingliana,* 1991/2 and 1992/2, Zurich.
M. Baumgartner (1993), *Die Täufer und Zwingli Eine Dokumentation,* Zurich.
M. Lienhard (1994), "L'action et la doctrine de Huldrych Zwingli," *Histoire du Christianisme,* vol. 8: *De la Réforme à la Réformation (1450–1530),* Paris, 771–86.

GOTTFRIED HAMMANN

See also **Anabaptists; Calvin, John; Calvinism; Erasmus, Desiderius; Humanism, Christian; Luther, Martin; Lutheranism; Protestantism.**

WOLVERHAMPTON LIBRARIES

Contributors

Jean-Noël ALETTI, Pontifical Biblical Institute, Rome: *Mystery; Pauline Theology*

Ysabel de ANDIA, CNRS, Paris: *Attributes, Divine; Dionysius the Pseudo-Aeropagite; Negative Theology; Simplicity, Divine*

Jean-Robert ARMOGATHE, École pratique des Hautes Études, Paris: *Bellarmine, Robert; Leibniz, Gottfried Wilhem; Quietism*

David ATTWOOD, Trinity College, Bristol: *Legitimate Defense; War*

Gennaro AULETTA, Doctor of Philosophy, Rome: *Providence*

Joseph AUNEAU, École supérieure de théologie catholique, Issy-les-Moulineaux: *Blessing; Holiness; Temple*

Peter BAELZ, Oxford University: *Ethics*

Michael BANNER, University of London: *Ethics, Sexual; Relativism*

Edmond BARBOTIN, Université de Strasbourg: *Experience*

Richard BAUCKAM, University of St. Andrews: *Ecology*

Oswald BAYER, University of Tübingen: *Law* (with **Axel WIEMER**)

Paul BEAUCHAMP, Institut supérieur de théologie et de philosophie de la Compagnie de Jésus, Paris: *Biblical Theology; Creation; God; Hell; Holy Spirit; Miracle; Scripture, Fulfillment of; Scripture, Senses of; Soul-Heart-Body; Violence; Wisdom; Work*

Pierre-Marie BEAUDE, Université de Metz: *Myth*

David W. BEBBINGTON, University of Stirling: *Baptists*

Jürgen BECKER, University of Kiel: *Resurrection of Christ*

Guy BEDOUELLE, University of Fribourg-Misericorde: *Erasmus, Desiderius; Humanism, Christian; Lateran V, Council; Trent, Council of*

Thierry BEDOUELLE, agrégé de l'Université, Vire: *Secularization; World*

John BEHR, St Vladimir's Theological Seminary, Crestwood, NY: *Adam; Anthropology*

Wolfgang BEINERT, University of Ratisbonne: *Council; Government, Church; Hierarchy; Structures, Ecclesial; Synod*

Olivier de BERRANGER, Bishop of Saint-Denis: *Lubac, Henri Sonier de*

Nigel BIGGAR, Oriel College, Oxford: *Casuistry; Obligation*

André BIRMELÉ, Université de Strasbourg: *Ecclesiology; Ecumenism; Family, Confessional; Protestantism; Unity of the Church; World Council of Churches; Works*

Yves-Marie BLANCHARD, Institut catholique de Paris: *Johannine Theology; Lamb of God/Paschal Lamb; Word*

Neal BLOUGH, Centre mennonite d'études et de rencontre, Saint-Maurice: *Anabaptists*

François BOESPFLUG, Université de Strasbourg: *Images; Nicaea I, Council of*

Hubert BOST, Institut protestant de théologie, Montpellier: *History of the Church; Tradition*

Jacques-Guy BOUGEROL, 1909–1997: *Bonaventure*

Olivier BOULNOIS, École pratique des Hautes Études, Paris: *Analogy; Duns Scotus, John; God; Nature; Omnipotence, Divine; Realism; Supernatural*

Dominique BOUREL, CNRS, Jérusalem: *Pietism*

Daniel BOURGEOIS, Fraternité Saint-Jean-de-Malte, Aix-en-Provence: *Lay/Laity*

Henri BOURGEOIS, Université catholique de Lyon: *Purgatory*

Pietro BOVATI, Pontifical Biblical Institute, Rome: *Jealousy, Divine; Judgment; Vengeance of God; Wrath of God*

Rémi BRAGUE, Université de Paris I: *Aristotelianism, Christian; Judaism*

René BRAUN, Université de Nice: *Docetism; Gnosis; Marcionism; Tertullian*

John BRECK, St Vladimir's Theological Seminary, Crestwood, NY: *Imitation of Christ*

Thomas E. BREIDENTHAL, General Theological Seminary, New York: *Passions; Violence*

Claude BRESSOLETTE, Institut catholique de Paris: *Liberalism* (with **Jean-Yves LACOSTE**), *modernism; traditionalism; Vatican I, Council of; Vatican II, Council of*

Jacques BRIEND, Institut catholique de Paris: *Decalogue; Passover; Scapegoat; Word of God*

Emilio BRITO, Université catholique de Louvain: *Dogmatic Theology; Hegel, Georg Wilhem Friedrich; Hegelianism; Kenosis; Schleiermacher, Daniel*

Lynne M. BROUGHTON, Doctor of Philosophy, Cambridge: *Architecture*

Jean-Louis BRUGUÈS, Institut catholique de Toulouse: *Death*

Pierre BÜHLER, Université de Neuchâtel: *Creeds; Preaching; Word of God*

Heinz BÜRKLE, University of Munich: *Religions, Theology of*

James T. BURTCHAELL, University of Notre Dame, Ind.: *Abortion; Precepts*

Raniero CANTALAMESSA, Doctor of Theology, Rome: *Passover*

Vincent CARRAUD, Université de Caen: *Descartes, René; Heart of Christ; Knowledge, Divine; Nothingness; Pascal, Blaise; Skepticism, Christian*

Maurice CARREZ, Faculté de théologie protestante, Paris: *Eucharist; Jerusalem; Ministry; Son of Man*

Dominique CERBELAUD, Université catholique de Lyon: *Mercy; Millenarianism*

Louis-Marie CHAUVET, Institut catholique de Paris: *Penance; Sacrament*

Carlo CICONETTI, couvent San Martino, Rome: Carmel (avec Stéphane-Marie **MORGAIN**)

Gérard CLAUDEL, Université de Metz: *Peter*

Richard J. CLIFFORD, Weston School of Theology, Cambridge, Mass.: *Bible* (with **Daniel J. HARRINGTON**)

Jean-François COLLANGE, Université de Strasbourg: *Barth, Karl; Bultmann, Rudolf; Tillich, Paul*

Matthieu COLLIN, Abbaye de la Pierre-qui-Vire: *Law*

John J. COLLINS, University of Chicago: *Apocalyptic Literature; Parousia*

Patrick COLLINSON, University of Cambridge: *Puritanism*

Jean-François COLOSIMO, Institut de théologie orthodoxe Saint-Serge, Paris: *Gregory Palamas; Hesychasm*

Jean COMBY, Université catholique de Lyon: *Lyons I, Council of; Lyons II, Council of*

Marie-Hélène CONGOURDEAU, CNRS, Paris: *Constantinople IV, Council of*

Michel CORBIN, Institut catholique de Paris: *Trinity*

Antoine CÔTÉ, University of Ottawa: *infinite*

Henri CROUZEL, Gregorian University of Rome and Institut catholique de Toulouse: *Modalism; Subordinationism*

Elian CUVILLIER, Institut protestant de théologie, Montpellier: *Filiation*

Brian E. DALEY, University of Notre Dame, Ind.: *Anhypostasy; Constantinople II, Council of; Idioms, Communication of*

Irénée-Henri DALMAIS, Institut catholique de Paris: *Maximus the Confessor*

André DARTIGUES, Institut catholique de Toulouse: *Resurrection of the Dead*

Paul DE CLERCK, Institut catholique de Paris: *Baptism; Confirmation; Holy Oils; Initiation, Christian; Laying on of Hands*

Jean DELORME, Université catholique de Lyon: *Narrative*

Nicolas DERREY, Séminaire interdiocésain, Reims: *Mystery*

Placide DESEILLE, Institut de théologie orthodoxe Saint-Serge, Paris: *Temptation; Soul-Heart-Body*

Andreas DETTWILER, University of Zurich: *Holy Spirit* (with **Jean ZUMSTEIN**)

Patrick DONDELINGER, Doctor of Theology, Paris: *Exorcism*

Joseph DORÉ, Institut catholique de Paris: *Christ's Consciousness; Passion*

Étienne DUCORNET, Doctor of Theology, Paris: *Rites, Chinese*

Bernard DUPUY, Centre Istina, Paris: *Solovyov, Vladimir*

Christian DUQUOC, Université catholique de Lyon: *Resurrection of Christ*

Georges Mathieu de DURAND, 1923–1997: *Fathers of the Church*

Xavier DURAND, Centre culture chrétienne, Limoges: *City; People of God*

Stefanus DU TOIT, Doctor of Philosophy, Coetzenburg, South Africa: *Race*

Mark J. EDWARDS, Oxford University: *Monotheism; Word*

Gillian R. EVANS, University of Cambridge: *Boethius; Gregory the Great*

Eva-Maria FABER, Université de Fribourg-en-Brisgau: *Grace*

Antoine FAIVRE, École pratique des Hautes Études, Paris: *Theosophy*

Jacques FANTINO, Université de Metz: *Circumincession; Irenaeus of Lyons; Judeo-Christianity*

Michel FÉDOU, Institut supérieur de théologie et de philosophie de la Compagnie de Jésus, Paris: *Chalcedon, Council of; Monophysitism*

Irène FERNANDEZ, Doctor of letters, Paris:

Beauty; Cosmos (with **Jean-Yves LACOSTE**);
Creation; Eternity of God; Justice, Divine

Gianfranco FIORAVANTI, University of Pisa: *Naturalism*

Rino FISICHELLA, Gregorian University of Rome: *Balthasar, Hans Urs von*

Claude FLIPO, directeur de *Christus,* Paris: *Spirituality, Ignatian*

Camille FOCANT, Université catholique de Louvain: *Holy Scripture*

Vittorio FUSCO, Bishop of Nardò-Gallipoli: *Choice; Hardening; Israel*

Jacques GAGEY, Université de Paris VII: *Freud, Sigmund*

Pierre GAUTHIER, Université de Strasbourg: *Newman, John Henry*

Claude GEFFRÉ, École biblique et archéologique française, Jerusalem: *Life, Eternal; Natural Theology; Truths, Hierarchy of*

Franco GIACONE, University La Sapienza, Rome: *Waldensians*

Pierre GIBERT, Université catholique de Lyon: *Literary Genres in Scripture; Promise*

Maurice GILBERT, Facultés universitaires Notre-Dame de la Paix, Namur: *Canon of Scriptures; Idolatry; Resurrection of the Dead; Sheol*

Paul GILBERT, Gregorian University of Rome: *Ontologism*

Marie-Christine GILLET-CHALLIOL, Doctor of Philosophy, Paris: *Schelling, Friedrich Wilhelm*

Michel GITTON, Doctor of History of Religions, Paris: *Hellenization of Christianity*

André GOUNELLE, Institut protestant de théologie, Montpellier: *Process Theology*

Jérôme de GRAMONT, Doctor of Philosophy, Alençon, *Anthropology; Nietzsche, Friedrich Wilhelm* (with **Ulrich WILLERS**)

Christian GRAPPE, Université de Strasbourg: *Sacrifice* (with **Alfred MARX**)

Jacques M. GRES-GAYER, Catholic University of America, Washington, D.C.: *Gallicanism; Jansenism; Ultramontanism*

Gisbert GRESHAKE, Université de Fribourg-en-Brisgau: *Eschatology*

Jean-Noël GUINOT, CNRS, Lyon: *Antioch, School of*

Pierre-Marie GY, Institut catholique de Paris: *Agape; Anointing of the Sick; Blessing; Cleric; Cult of Saints; Diaconesses; Epiclesis; Eucharist; Liturgical Year; Liturgy; Mass, Sacrifice of the; Relics; Sunday; Validity*

Gottfried HAMMANN, Université de Neuchâtel: *Bucer, Martin; Zwingli, Huldrych*

Jean-Yves HAMELINE, Institut catholique de Paris: *Cult; Music*

Yves-Jean HARDER, Université de Paris IV: *Atheism; God; Love*

John E. HARE, Calvin College, Mich.: *Ethics, Autonomy of*

Daniel J. HARRINGTON, Weston School of Theology, Cambridge, Mass.: *Bible* (with **Richard J. CLIFFORD**)

Anthony E. HARVEY, Abbey of Westminster: *Exegesis*

Noëlle HAUSMAN, Institut d'études théologiques, Bruxelles: *Religious Life*

Leonhard HELL, Université de Fribourg-en-Brisgau: *Catholicism; Positive Theology*

Philippe HENNE, Université catholique de Lille: *Apostolic Fathers*

Alasdair I. C. HERON, University of Erlangen: *calvin, John; Calvinism*

Richard HIGGINSON, Ridley Hall, Cambridge: *Market Economics, Morality of*

George HOBSON, Doctor of Philosophy, Paris: *Pentecostalism*

Marten J. F. M. HOENEN, Université catholique de Nimègue: *Nominalism*

Peter HÜNERMANN, University of Tübingen: *Judgment; Kingdom of God*

Max HUOT de LONGCHAMP, Centre Saint-Jean-de-la-Croix, Mers-sur-Indre: *Childhood, Spiritual; John of the Cross; Mysticism; Spirituality, Salesian*

Ruedi IMBACH, Université de Fribourg-Miséricorde: *Dante* (with **Silvia MASPOLI**)

Werner JEANROND, University of Lund, Sweden: *Character*

Brian JOHNSTONE, Academia Alfonsiana, Rome: *Proportionalism; Scandal/Skandalon; Utilitarianism*

Jean JOLIVET, École pratique des Hautes Études, Paris: *Chartres, School of; Saint-Victor, School of*

Maurice JOURJON, Université catholique de Lyon: *Mary* (with **Bernard MEUNIER**)

Éric JUNOD, Université de Lausanne: *Apocrypha; Origen*

Zénon KALUZA, CNRS, Paris: *Conciliarism; Constance, Council of; Hus, Jan*

Charles KANNENGIESSER, University of Notre Dame, Ind.: *Arianism; Athanasius of Alexandria; Consubstantial; Nicaea I, Council of*

Shinji KAYAMA, Exeter College, Oxford: *Peace*

Walter KERN, University of Innsbruck: *Heresy; Fundamental Theology*

Fergus KERR, University of Edinburgh: *Language, Theology*

Ulrich KÜHN, University of Leipzig: *Church*

Jean-Yves LACOSTE, College of Blandings: *Antinomy; Antinomianism; Atheism; Beatitude; Bérulle,*

Pierre de (with **Stéphane**-Marie **MORGAIN**)*; Charisma; Consubstantiation; Cosmos* (with **Irène** FERNANDEZ)*; Credibility; Diphysitism; Evil; Faith* (with **Nicolas LOSSKY**)*; Febronianism; Fundamental Choice; God; Heidegger, Martin; Hermeneutics; History; Hope; Inerrancy; Integrism; Knowledge, Divine; Knowledge of God; Liberalism* (with **Claude BRESSOLETTE**)*; Literature; Lutheranism* (with **Harding MEYER**)*; Miracle; Orthodoxy; Paganism; Philosophy; Proexistence; Providence; Rationalism; Realism; Reason; Revelation; Situation, Ethics; Sophiology; Soul-Heart-Body; Synergy; Theological Schools; Theologoumen; Theology; Time; Truth; Wholly Other; Work*

Ghislain LAFONT, Gregorian University of Rome: *Adoptionism*

Jacqueline LAGRÉE, Université de Rennes: *Deism/Theism; Pantheism; Stoicism, Christian*

Matthew LAMB, Boston College, Boston, Mass.: *Lonergan, Bernard John*

Gilles LANGEVIN, Université Laval, Québec: *Cyril of Alexandria; Ephesus, Council of; Hypostatic Union; Nestorianism*

Nicholas LASH, University of Cambridge: *Marx, Karl*

Michel LAUWERS, Université de Nice: *Beguines; Devotio Moderna; Vienna, Council of*

Marc LECLERC, Gregorian University of Rome: *Blondel, Maurice; Evolution; Monogenesis/ Polygenesis*

Hervé LEGRAND, Institut catholique de Paris: *Bishop; Collegiality; Deacon; Ministry; Ordination/Order; Pope; Presbyter/Priest; Priesthood; Regional Church; Woman*

François-Marie LÉTHEL, Teresianum, Rome: *Constantinople III, Council of; Monothelism/ Monoenergism*

Anthony LEVI, Chipping Norton, Oxfordshire, *Crusades; Enlightenment; Gratian; Manning, Henry Edward; Mendicant Religious Orders; Moses; Nationalism; Neoplatonism; Pagans; Renaissance; Thomas à Kempis*

Alain de LIBERA, École pratique des Hautes Études, Paris: *Albert the Great; Rhineland-Flemish Mysticism; Scholasticism*

Fritz LIENHARD, Université de Strasbourg: *Mission/Evangelization*

Marc LIENHARD, Université de Strasbourg: *Luther, Martin*

Ann LOADES, University of Durham: *Woman*

Norbert LOHFINK, Hochschule Sankt Georgen, Frankfurt am Main: *Covenant*

Jean LONGÈRE, Institut de recherche et d'histoire des textes, Paris: *Lateran I, Council; Lateran II, Council; Lateran III, Council; Lateran IV, Council*

Nicolas LOSSKY, Institut de théologie orthodoxe Saint-Serge, Paris and Université de Paris-Nanterre: *Faith* (with **Jean-Yves LACOSTE**)*; Orthodoxy; Orthodoxy, Modern and Contemporary; Patriarchate*

Andrew LOUTH, University of Durham: *Asceticism; Life, Spiritual; Martyrdom; Prayer; Spiritual Theology*

José LOZA VERA, École biblique et archéologique française, Jerusalem: *Theophany*

Scott MacDONALD, University of Iowa: *Good*

Goulven MADEC, CNRS, Paris: *Augustinianism*

Jean-Michel MALDAMÉ, Institut catholique de Toulouse: *Vision, Beatific*

Pierre MARAVAL, Université de Strasbourg: *Apollinarianism; Messalianism; Pilgrimage*

Alain MARCHADOUR, Institut catholique de Toulouse: *Book*

Massimo MARCOCCHI, University of the Sacred Heart, Milan: *Alphonsus Liguori*

Daniel MARGUERAT, Université de Lausanne: *Jesus, Historical*

Gustave MARTELET, Institut supérieur de théologie et de philosophie de la Compagnie de Jésus, Paris: *Hell; Predestination*

François MARTY, Institut supérieur de théologie et de philosophie de la Compagnie de Jésus, Paris: *Anthropomorphism; Kant, Immanuel*

Martin E. MARTY, University of Chicago: *Fundamentalism*

Alfred MARX, Université de Strasbourg: *Sacrifice* (with **Christian GRAPPE**)

Silvia MASPOLI, Université de Fribourg-Miséricorde: *Dante* (with **Ruedi IMBACH**)

Taddée MATURA, Couvent des franciscains, Avignon: *Spirituality, Franciscan*

Paul McPARTLAN, Heythrop College, London: *Holiness; Person*

Bernard MEUNIER, Université catholique de Lyon: *Basel-Ferrara-Florence, Council of; Mary* (with **Maurice JOURJON**)

Constant MEWS, Monach University, Clayton, Victoria (Australia): *Abelard, Peter*

Harding MEYER, Centre d'études œcuméniques, Strasbourg: *Lutheranism* (with **Jean-Yves LACOSTE**)

Cyrille MICHON, Université de Paris IV: *Loci Theologici* (with **Gilbert NARCISSE**)*; Omnipresence, Divine*

Dietmar MIETH, University of Tübingen: *Narrative Theology*

John MILBANK, University of Cambridge: *Im-*

mutability/Impassibility; Liberation Theology; Political Theology; Postmodernism

Roland MINNERATH, Université de Strasbourg: *Church and State*

Burkhard MOJSISCH, University of Bochum: *Nicholas of Cusa*

Stéphane-Marie MORGAIN, Teresianum, Rome: *Bérulle, Pierre de* (with **Jean-Yves LACOSTE**); *Carmel* (with **Carlo CICONETTI**)

Michèle MORGEN, Université de Strasbourg: *Flesh; World*

Robert MURRAY, Heythrop College, London: *Adam; Animals; Cosmos*

Gilbert NARCISSE, Couvent des dominicains, Bordeaux: *Doctor of the Church* (with **Galahad THREEPWOOD**); *Loci Theologici* (with **Cyrille MICHON**); *Sensus Fidei*

Frédéric NEF, Université de Rennes: *Beatitude; Contemplation; Truth*

Karl Heinz NEUFELD, University of Innsbruck: *Descent into Hell; Fideism; Rahner, Karl; Tradition*

Bruno NEVEU, École pratique des Hautes Études, Paris: *Notes, Theological*

Philippe NOUZILLE, Abbaye de Ligugé: *Bernard of Clairvaux*

Joan L. O'DONOVAN, Doctor of Philosophy, Oxford: *Authority; Property; Society*

Oliver O'DONOVAN, University of Oxford: *Epieikeia; Evil; Liberty; Punishment; Revolution; Wisdom*

Paul OLIVIER, agrégé de l'Université, Nice: *Existence of God, Proofs of*

Jean-Pierre OSIER, agrégé de l'Université, Paris: *Unitarianism*

Annette PALES-GOBILLIARD, École pratique des Hautes Études, Paris: *Catharism* (with **Galahad THREEPWOOD**)

George PATTISON, King's College, Cambridge: *Kierkegaard, Soren Aabye*

Keith PAVLISCHEK, Crossroads, Wynnewood, Penn.: *Freedom, Religious*

Anne-Marie PELLETIER, Université de Marne-la-Vallée: *Couple; Woman*

Romano PENNA, Pontificia Università Lateranense, Rome: *Salvation*

Éfoé-Julien PÉNOUKOU, Grand séminaire de Dogbo, Benin: *Inculturation*

Michel-Yves PERRIN, Centre Lenain-de-Tillemont, Paris: *Hilary of Poitiers; Rome*

Charles PERROT, Institut catholique de Paris: *Gospels*

Stephen PISANO, Pontifical Biblical Institute, Rome: *Translations of the Bible, Ancient*

Jean PORTER, University of Notre Dame, Ind.: *Justice; Virtues*

Gian-Luca POTESTA, University of the Sacred Heart, Milan: *Millenarianism*

Bernard POTTIER, Institut d'études théologiques, Bruxelles: *Creeds*

Roger POUIVET, Université de Rennes: *Wittgenstein, Ludwig Josef*

John C. PUDDEFOOT, Eton College: *Sciences of Nature*

Albert de PURY, Université de Genève: *War*

Bernard RENAUD, Université de Strasbourg: *Messianism/Messiah; Servant of YHWH*

Laurence RENAULT, agrégée de l'Université, Paris: *Bañezianism-Molinism-Baianism; Intellectualism; Suarez, Francisco; Voluntarism*

Jürgen ROLOFF, University of Erlangen: *Apostle*

Michael ROOT, Centre d'études œcuméniques, Strasbourg: *Intercommunion; Reception; Priesthood; Apostolic Succession*

Risto SAARINEN, University of Helsinki and Centre d'études œcuméniques, Strasbourg: *Authority; Indefectibility of the Church; Infallibility; Magisterium; Schism*

Jean-Marie SALAMITO, Université de Strasbourg: *Ambrose of Milan; Cyprian of Carthage; Chrysostom, John*

Jean-Pierre SCHALLER, Doctor of Theology, Doctor of Letters, Basel and Paris: *Spiritual Direction*

Ernst-Albert SCHARFFENORTH, University of Heidelberg: *Bonhoeffer, Dietrich*

Adrian SCHENKER, Université de Fribourg-Miséricorde: *Expiation; Purity/Impurity*

Jacques SCHLOSSER, Université de Strasbourg: *Kingdom of God*

Heinrich SCHMIDINGER, University of Salzbourg: *Tübingen, Schools of*

Werner H. SCHMIDT, University of Bonn: *Monotheism*

Raymund SCHWAGER, University of Innsbruck: *Salvation*

Philibert SECRETAN, Université de Fribourg-Miséricorde: *Agnosticism*

Laurent SENTIS, Séminaire du diocèse de Toulon: *Sin, Original; Traducianism*

Bernard SESBOÜÉ, Institut supérieur de théologie et de philosophie de la Compagnie de Jésus, Paris: *Appropriation; Basil (The Great) of Caesarea; Christ/Christology; Constantinople I, Council of; Indulgences; Solidarity*

José Luis SICRE, Theological Faculty of Granada: *Prophet and Prophecy*

Gérard SIEGWALT, Université de Strasbourg: *Local Church; Pastor*

Yves SIMOENS, Institut supérieur de théologie et de philosophie de la Compagnie de Jésus, Paris: *Father; Glory of God; Priesthood*

Robert SONG, St John's College, Durham: *Democracy*

Lisa SOWLE CAHILL, Boston College, Boston, Mass.: *Family; Procreation*

Jörg SPLETT, Hochschule Sankt Georgen, Frankfurt am Main: *Religion, Philosophy of*

Christopher STEAD, University of Cambridge: *Platonism, Christian*

Claude TASSIN, Institut catholique de Paris: *Intertestament; Paganism; Universalism*

Michael THEOBALD, University of Tübingen: *Truth*

Wolfgang THÖNISSEN, Université de Fribourg-en-Brisgau *Liberty*

Galahad THREEPWOOD, MA, London: *Catharism* (with **Annette PALES-GOBILLIARD**); *Congregationalism; Doctor of The Church* (with **Gilbert NARCISSE**); *Limbo; Sabbath*

Jean-Marie R. TILLARD, Dominican Convent, Ottawa: *Communion*

Jean-Pierre TORRELL, Université de Fribourg-Miséricorde: *Thomas Aquinas; Thomism*

Yves TOURENNE, Institut supérieur de théologie et de philosophie de la Compagnie de Jésus, Paris: *Rahner, Karl*

Cécile TURIOT, Institut catholique de Paris: *Healing*

Patrick VALDRINI, Institut catholique de Paris: *Canon Law; Ecclesiastical Discipline; Jurisdiction*

Pierre VALLIN, Institut supérieur de théologie et de philosophie de la Compagnie de Jésus, Paris: *Marriage*

Albert VANHOYE, Pontifical Biblical Institute, Rome: *Faith; Passion*

Marie-Anne VANNIER, Université de Strasbourg: *Augustine of Hippo; Donatism; Manicheanism; Pelagianism; Trace (Vestige)*

Allen VERHEY, Hope College, Holland, Mich.: *Ethics, Medical*

Jacques VERMEYLEN, Centre d'études théologiques et pastorales, Bruxelles: *Name*

Miklos VETÖ, Université de Poitiers: Edwards

Françoise VINEL, Doctor of Greek Studies, Strasbourg: *Alexandria, School of; Gregory of Nazianzus; Gregory of Nyssa; Montanism; Nicaea II, Council of* (with **François BOESPFLUG**); *Novatianism*

Coloman VIOLA, CNRS, Paris: *Anselm of Canterbury; Aseitas; Tritheism*

Adalbert de VOGÜÉ, Abbaye de la Pierre-qui-Vire: *Monasticism*

Geoffrey WAINWRIGHT, Duke University: *Methodism*

Peter WALTER, Université de Fribourg-en-Brisgau: *Dogma; Scheeben, Matthias Joseph*

Bernd WANNENWETSCH, University of Erlangen: *Marriage*

Édouard-Henri WÉBER, CNRS, Paris: *Angels; Deity; Demons*

John WEBSTER, Christ Church, Oxford: *Conscience*

André WÉNIN, Université catholique de Louvain: *Conversion; Fear of God; Sabbath; Soul-Heart-Body; Temptation*

Daniel WESTBERG, Université de Terre-Neuve: *Action; Intention; Prudence*

Lionel WICKHAM, University of Cambridge: *Catechesis*

Axel WIEMER, University of Tübingen: *Law* (with **Oswald BAYER**)

Ulrich WILLERS, Catholic University of Eichstatt: *Nietzsche, Friedrich Wilhelm* (with **Jérôme** de **GRAMONT**)

Rowan WILLIAMS, Bishop of Monmouth: *Justification; Sin*

John WITTE, Emory Law School, Atlanta: *Law and Legislation*

Joseph WOLINSKI, Institut catholique de Paris: *God; Holy Spirit; Trinity*

J. Robert WRIGHT, General Theological Seminary, New York: *Anglicanism*

Nicole ZEEGERS-VANDER VORST, Université catholique de Louvain: *Apologists*

Jean ZUMSTEIN, University of Zurich: *Holy Spirit* (with **Andreas DETTWILER**); *Parable; Protocatholicism*

Index

Index

Index

Elijah
  YHWH, opposition to, 749
Elipandus of Toledo, 14
Elizabeth I, 35, 36–37, 1507
Elizabethan Settlement and Puritanism, 1324
Élizade, Michel de
  on credibility, 388
Elohist (E) source of Bible, 204
Emanation, 1613
Emet
  on truth, 1633
Emotions
  heart as seat of, 1496, 1513
  See also Passions
Empirical tradition, 780
Empty grave, concept of, 1374
Enchiridion Militis Christiani (Erasmus), 485
Encratism
  Marcionism and, 984, 985
  Montanism and, 1069
Encyclopedia of the Philosophical Sciences
  (Hegel), 671, 672
Encyclopédie (Diderot), 477
Encyclicals. *See specific titles*
End of time. *See* Eschatology
Enemy
  love for one's, 951
Enhypostasy. *See* Anhypostasy
Enlightenment, **477–479**
  atheism and, 107–108
  Augustinianism and, 124
  autonomy of ethics, 501–502
  Christology and, 292
  creation, 382
  dogma and, 449–450
  dogmatic theology and, 453
  eschatology and, 488–489
  ethics and, 497–498
  faith and, 558
  God and, 620–621
  hermeneutics and, 689
  history of the Church and, 710
  judgment and, 836
  law and legislation, 899–900
  Lutheranism, effect on, 968–969
  marriage and, 991
  miracle, theory of, in, 1042–1043
  myth and, 1089
  philosophy and, 1238–1239
  racism and, 1334
  reason and, 1350–1351
  resurrection of the dead and, 1381
  revelation and, 1386–1388
  school of Tübingen and, 1643
  theology of history and, 706
  theology of religions and, 1364
  unity of the Church and, 1653
  wisdom and, 1708
Enneads (Plotinus), 1114
Enoch, Book of, 64, 65–66, 1176
  See also Apocalyptic literature
Ephesians, Letter to
  on omnipresence of God, 1153
  on praise of God, 1264
  providence in, 1308

wisdom in, 1706
Ephesus, Council of, 273, **479–481**
  Christology and, 290
  condemnation of Pelagianism by, 1216
  Cyril of Alexandria and, 406
  hypostatic union and, 745
  on incarnation, 764
  on Mary, Mother of Jesus, 1002–1003,
    1005
  on Messalianism, 1022
  on resurrection, 1373
Ephraem Syrus, 10
Epiclesis, **481–482**
  on ordination, 1159
Epicureans
  on deism and theism, 424
Epieikeia, **482–483**
Epilog (Balthasar), 140
Epiphanius
  on women's role, 1715–1716
  on work, 1730
Episcopalians
  Unitarianism and, 1652
Episcopate. *See* Bishops
Epistemology
  philosophy of science and, 1455
Epistle. *See specific name of writer or recipi-*
    ents (e.g., Ephesians, Letter to)
Epistle of Barnabas. *See* Apostolic Fathers
Epistle to Diognetus. *See* Apostolic Fathers
Equiprobabilism, 21, 263
  See also Alphonsus Liguori
Equivocity. *See* Analogy
Erasmus, Desiderius, **484–485**
  canon of scriptures and, 254
  on Christ's consciousness, 296
  on Cicero, 1180
  on liberty, 741, 918
  Luther's opposition to, 962
  on peace, 1213
  on pilgrimages, 1246
  Renaissance and, 1368–1369
  on vernacular scriptural teaching, 1369
  Zwingli and, 1748–1749
Erastianism, **486–487**
Erastus, Thomas, 486
  See also Erastianism
Eriugena, John the Scot. *See* John the Scot
  Eriugena
Eros. *See* Love
Escclesiam suam, encyclical
  Vatican II and, 1669
Eschatological manifestation, 1565
Eschatology, **487–492**
  apologists and, 75
  asceticism and, 96
  Beatific Vision and, 1684–1687
  beatitude and, 168, 172–173
  Bultmann on, 238
  death and, 415–420
  discourse in Gospels on, 640
  fulfillment of the Scriptures and,
    1456–1457
  hell and, 683
  Holy Spirit and, 727

messianism and, 1024–1025
  parables and, 1184
  passion of Christ and, 1193–1194
  Pauline theology on, 1206–1207
  Pentecostalism and, 1223
  Rahner on, 1340
  sabbath and, 1406
  sacrament and, 1408–1409
  sacrifice and, 1417
  salvation and, 1422, 1424
  soul-heart-body and, 1501
  theology of history and, 707–708
  vengeance of God and, 1672–1673
  See also Apocalyptic literature; Judgment
Esoterism. *See* Theosophy
E source of Bible, 204
Essai due le panthéisme des sociétés
    modernes (Maret), 1182
Essence
  mysticism of, 1396–1397
  of religion, 1361
  See also Being; Deity; Nature
Esther, Book of
  role of women in, 1713
Estheticism
  Balthasar as esthete, 140
  Bernard de Clairvaux and, 199
Esthetics
  beauty and, 175, 176
Eternal life. *See* Life, eternal
Eternity of God, **493–494**
Eternity of the World, The (Aquinas), 1573
Ethica Nicomachea, 276, 482
Ethics, **495–499**
  Ambrose of Milan on social morality, 24
  Barth on, 161
  beatitude and, 170–171
  Bonhoeffer on, 231–232
  Bultmann on, 238
  character and, 275–276
  Church and, 309–310
  Duns Scotus on, 461–462
  God of ethics, 621
  Grotius on, 1506
  Holy Spirit and, 727
  infinity and, 780–781
  love and, 949, 953–954
  Pauline theology on, 1208–1209
  scandal and, 1435
  Schleiermacher on, 1446
  Schleiermacher on culture and, 1447
  situation ethics, 1482–1483
  Suarez on, 1529
  Ultramontanism and, 1649
  unity of the Church and, 1654
  veracity and, 1674
  violence and, 1680
  virtues and, 1682–1684
  William of Ockham on, 1136
  See also Ethics, autonomy of; Ethics, medi-
    cal; Ethics, sexual
Ethics (Bonhoeffer), 232
Ethics (Spinoza), 102
Ethics, autonomy of, **499–502**
Ethics, medical, **503–505**

Index

Index